written and researched by

**Greg Ward**

www.roughguides.com

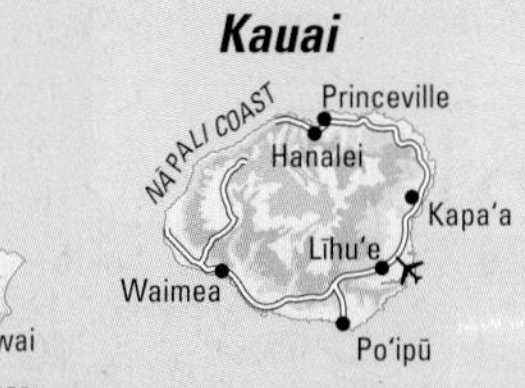


Niihau

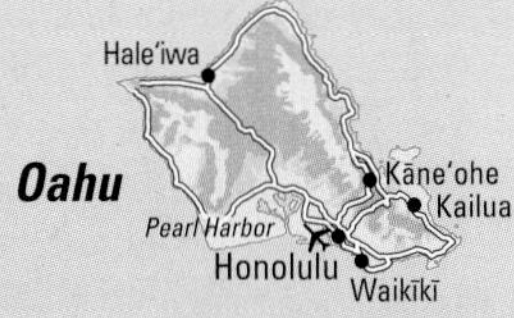


40°N
USA
NORTH PACIFIC OCEAN
MEXICO
TROPIC OF CANCER
20°N
Hawaiian Islands
Micronesia
Christmas I.
0°
EQUATOR
Polynesia
Melanesia
Marquesas Islands
Samoa Islands
Fiji Islands
Cook Islands
Tahiti
Society Islands
Mangareva
20°S
TROPIC OF CAPRICORN
Tonga Islands
Tubuai Islands
Easter I.
SOUTH PACIFIC OCEAN
0 Miles 1500
New Zealand
160°E
180°
160°W
140°W

N

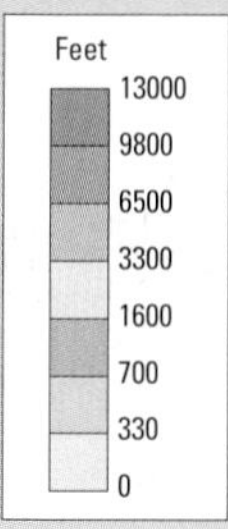
Feet
13000
9800
6500
3300
1600
700
330
0

Molokai
Kalaupapa Peninsula
Kaluako'i
Halāwa Valley
Maunaloa
Kaunakakai
Kapalua
Kā'anapali
Kahului
Maui
Lana'i City
Lahaina
Wailuku
Wailua
Lanai
Hāna
Kīhei
Manēle Bay
Wailea
Mākena
HALEAKALĀ NATIONAL PARK
Kahoolawe

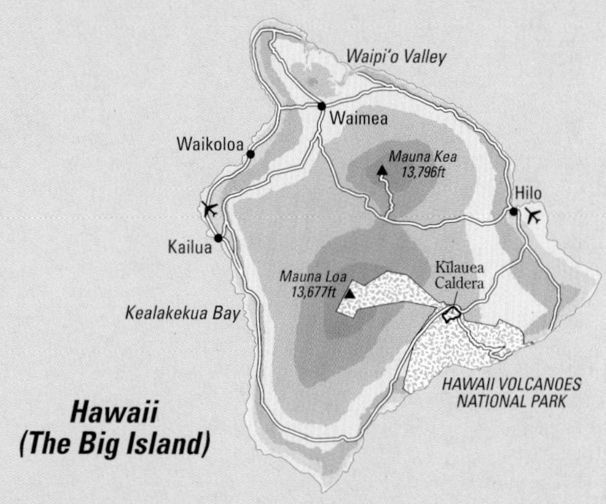
Waipi'o Valley
Waimea
Waikoloa
Mauna Kea 13,796ft
Hilo
Kailua
Kīlauea Caldera
Mauna Loa 13,677ft
Kealakekua Bay
HAWAII VOLCANOES NATIONAL PARK
Hawaii (The Big Island)
0 Miles 40

## Introduction to

# Hawaii

**The islands of Hawaii poke from the Pacific more than two thousand miles off the west coast of America. In total, there are well over a hundred of them, the weather-beaten summits of a chain of submarine volcanoes that stretches almost to Japan. Most, however, are no more than tiny atolls. Only the seven largest, lying south of the Tropic of Cancer at the southeast end of the archipelago, are inhabited, and only six welcome visitors. Those are Oahu (the site of the state capital Honolulu and its resort annex of Waikīkī), Hawaii itself (more commonly known as the Big Island in a vain attempt to avoid confusion), Maui, Lanai, Molokai and Kauai.**

All the islands share a similar topography, having been formed in the same way and exposed to the same winds and rains. Each is much wetter on its north and east – **windward** – coasts, which are characterized by stupendous sea cliffs, verdant stream-cut valleys and dense tropical vegetation. The south and west – **leeward** or "Kona" – coasts are much drier, often virtually barren, and make ideal locations for big resorts.

With its majestic volcanoes and palm-fringed beaches, Hawaii holds some of the most superb scenery on earth. Firmly established among the world's greatest vacation playgrounds, it combines top-quality hotels and restaurants with almost unlimited opportunities not only for sheer self-indulgence, but also for activities such as surfing, diving, golf and hiking. Visiting Hawaii does not, however, have to be expensive; budget facilities

## Fact file

- Hawaii's first human settlers, Polynesian voyagers, arrived less than two thousand years ago. The first European sailor known to have reached the islands was England's Captain Cook, in 1778. Hawaii remained an independent kingdom until 1898, when it became a territory of the United States. It was admitted as the fiftieth US state in 1959.
- The combined land area of all the Hawaiian islands is 6470 square miles; the Big Island alone accounts for 4028 square miles. The state's population is 1.21 million, of whom just under 900,000 live on Oahu. The Big Island has a population of 150,000, Maui 120,000, and Kauai almost 60,000. Lesser Molokai has around 7000, Lanai not even 3000, and Niihau is home to a mere 250 citizens.
- Some 80,000 of Hawaii's citizens consider themselves to be "Native Hawaiians," while 503,000 are of Asian descent, 294,00 say they are "White," and 22,000 that they are "Black." Over half of all marriages are classified as inter-racial, so such statistics grow ever more meaningless; 21.4 percent of the population regard themselves as combining two or more races, as opposed to 2.4 percent in the US as a whole.
- Seven million tourists visit Hawaii each year, around two million of whom are Japanese. By far the most popular destination is Oahu, with 4.8 million visitors a year. Maui comes second, welcoming 2.2 million, while 1.3 million spend time on the Big Island, and one million on Kauai. Fewer than 100,000 visit either Molokai or Lanai; Nihau is barred to outsiders altogether.
- Mauna Kea on the Big Island is the highest mountain in the Pacific, at 13,796 feet. Mount Wai'ale'ale on Kauai is the wettest place on earth, receiving an average of 440 inches of rain per year.

on all the islands are listed throughout this book, together with advice on making the most of your money.

Despite the crowds, the islands have not been ruined by tourism. Resort development is concentrated into surprisingly small regions – Waikīkī is the classic example, holding half the state's hotel rooms in just two square miles – and it's always possible to venture off into pristine wilderness, or to camp on the seashore or mountainside.

# Where to go

The key decision in any Hawaiian itinerary is whether to go to **Oahu**, and specifically **Waikīkī**, which holds virtually all its accommodation. If you enjoy cities, and prefer nightlife and crowds to deserted beaches – or simply if you don't want to drive – then it's worth staying for three or four days in Waikīkī. Otherwise, unless you're a **surfer** heading for the legendary North Shore, you may end up regretting any time you choose to spend on Oahu.

Each of the other islands – referred to as the **Neighbor Islands** – has its own

**Despite the crowds, the islands have not been ruined by tourism. Resort development is concentrated into surprisingly small regions.**

strengths and weaknesses. Maui, Kauai and the Big Island all offer accommodation for every budget, and all cost the same to reach from Oahu, as well as being accessible by direct flights from the US West Coast. The best for **beaches** is probably Maui, followed by Kauai and then the Big Island; for **scenery**, and also **hiking**, Kauai beats the Big Island, with Maui well behind. The Big Island boasts the awesome spectacle of the world's most active **volcano** – Kīlauea, which has been erupting ever since 1983 – although slumbering Haleakalā on Maui is also impressive.

Among more specialized interests, Maui offers the best conditions for

## Surfing

As ancient rock carvings and the eyewitness accounts of explorers prove, **surfing** was the most popular activity in pre-contact Hawaii. When the surf was up, entire communities would spend whole days in the ocean. Christian missionaries attempted to stamp the pastime out, as a fruitless and immoral waste of time, but it was revived in the 1880s during the reign of King David Kalākaua, aka the "Merrie Monarch."

Surfing first came to global prominence in the early twentieth century, when champion Olympic swimmer Duke Kahanamoku toured Australia and North America with his sixteen-foot board. Developments in board technology during the 1960s and 1970s, together with the surfing boom in California, led to a massive influx of tourists to the sport's spiritual home in Hawaii. Oahu's North Shore (see p.134) is the Mecca for most surfing pilgrims, regularly hosting world championship events, but Maui and Kauai also boast legendary surfing breaks.

## Hawaiian language

Almost everyone in Hawaii speaks English, and as a rule the **Hawaiian language** is only encountered in the few words – such as aloha or "love", the all-purpose island greeting, and mahalo, meaning "thank you" – that have passed into general local usage. A glossary of Hawaiian words appears on p.545.

The **Hawaiian alphabet** consists of just twelve letters, together with two punctuation marks, the macron and the glottal stop. Strictly speaking, the word Hawaii should be written **Hawai'i**, with the glottal stop to show that the two "i"s are pronounced separately; the correct forms for the other islands are O'ahu, Lāna'i, Moloka'i, Kaua'i, Ni'ihau and Maui. Convention has it however that words in common English usage are written without their Hawaiian punctuation. Thus, although this book uses Hawaiian place names wherever possible, all the island names appear in their familiar English form.

**windsurfing** and **whale watching**; Maui and the Big Island are equally well-equipped for **diving**, **snorkeling** and **golf**; and the Big Island has great deep-sea **fishing**, as well as being the best suited for a **touring** vacation. The appeal of the lesser islands rests largely on their sense of seclusion; **Molokai** is a down-home, inexpensive and very traditional Hawaiian island, while **Lanai** has become a haven for the mega-rich.

**Kīlauea has been in constant eruption ever since 1983.**

Visitors in search of the **ancient Hawaii** may be disappointed by the few vestiges that remain. The Hawaiians themselves destroyed many of their *heiaus* (temples) following the collapse of the traditional religion, and traces of the pre-contact way of life tend to survive

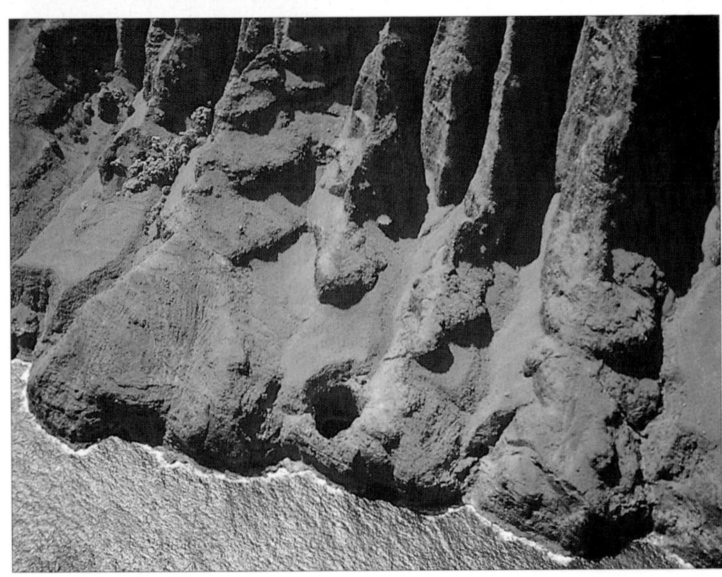

## Food and ritual

Only men were allowed to cook or prepare food in ancient Hawaii. Women were forbidden to eat pork, bananas or coconuts, as well as several kinds of fish, or to use the same utensils or even eat at the same table as the men.

These days, although Hawaii boasts many fabulous restaurants, there's no such thing as an authentic "Hawaiian" restaurant. The closest you can come to eating traditional foods is at a ***lū'au***, a "feast" staged for tourists where you should be able to sample *poi*, a purple-gray paste made from the root of the *taro* plant (and described by one of Captain Cook's crew as "a disagreeable mess"); *kālua* pork, an entire pig wrapped in leaves and baked in an underground oven; *poke*, marinated raw fish, shellfish or octopus; and *lomi-lomi*, made with raw salmon. You're unlikely, however, to be given another historically authentic specialty: boiled hairless dogs. See "Food and drink," p.29, for more.

only in out-of-the-way places (notably on the Big Island). Otherwise, what is presented as "historic" usually post-dates the missionary impact. The former plantation villages often have an appealing air of the nineteenth-century West about them, with their false-front stores and wooden boardwalks, but of the larger towns only Honolulu, Lahaina on Maui, and Kailua on the Big Island offer much sense of history.

If you have **one week** or less, it makes sense to concentrate on just one island. Five days on either Kauai or the Big Island, combined with two days in Waikīkī, makes a good introduction to the state, while if you fly direct to Maui you can explore that island in depth and still have time to cross over to Molokai or Lanai. With **two weeks**, you could spend four or five days each on three of the major islands – though it would be easy to fill a week or more on the Big Island – and it's

**Hawaiians destroyed many of their temples following the collapse of the traditional religion . . . traces of the pre-contact way of life tend to survive only in out-of-the-way places.**

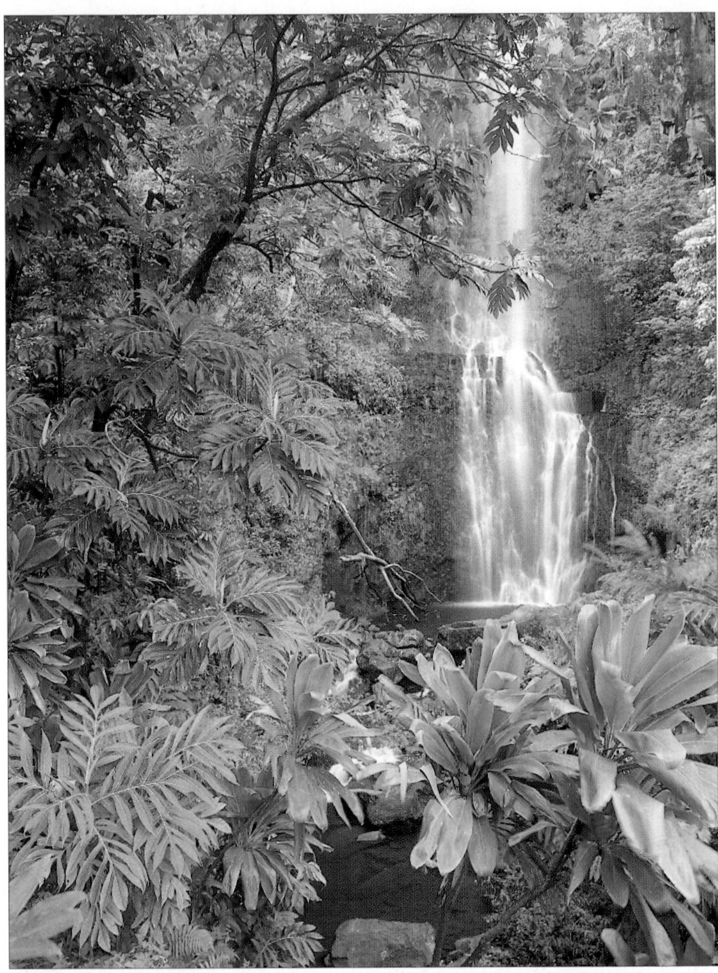

worth considering a couple of days on Molokai as well. Any more than two weeks, and you can consider seeing all the major islands.

# When to go

Although Hawaii's **high season** for tourism is mid-December to March, when typical room rates for mid-range hotels rise by perhaps $25 per night, its **climate** remains pretty constant year-round.

Specific information for each island appears in the chapter introductions throughout this book. In general, despite the power of the tropical sun, Hawaii is not prone to extremes. **Temperatures** in all the major coastal resorts vary between a daily maximum of around 80°F (27°C) from January to March up to perhaps 87°F (30°C) from July to October. **Rainfall** is heaviest from December to March, but while the mountaintops are among the wettest places on earth, you'd have to be very unlucky to get enough rain in any of the resort areas to spoil your vacation.

**You'd have to be very unlucky to get enough rain in any of the resort areas to spoil your vacation.**

The one seasonal variation that does affect tourists is in the state of the **ocean**. Along protected stretches of the shoreline, you can expect to be able to swim all year round in beautiful seas where the water temperature stays between 75°F and 82°F (24–28°C). From October to April, however, high surf can render unsheltered beaches dangerous in the extreme, and some beaches even lose their sand altogether. Conditions on specific beaches are indicated throughout this book; see also the section on Ocean Safety on p.36.

## Flora and fauna

While Hawaii does face serious environmental problems, as detailed on p.524, it remains so staggeringly beautiful thanks in large part to the diversity of its flora and fauna.

When the islands first emerged from the Pacific as outcrops of barren lava, a new species – perhaps a windblown bird, or a floating seed or insect – managed to find them but once every 100,000 years. Each evolved at breakneck speed, to produce such unique variations as the spectacular silversword plant (p.336), or the fifty distinct honey-creepers, ranging from the scarlet *'i'iwi* to the tiny yellow *'anianiau*, that were descended from a single finch. Then came the first Polynesian voyagers, carrying coconut palms and bananas, pigs and dogs. The Europeans in turn brought horses and cattle, as well as pests like the mosquito and the mongoose, and the process continues to this day, as "stowaway" species arrive clinging to tourist jets.

For most of the year, the trade winds blow in from the northeast, though they're occasionally replaced by humid "Kona winds" from the south. Despite the much-publicized onslaught of Hurricane Iniki on Kauai in September 1992, hurricanes are very rare. However *tsunamis* (often erroneously called tidal waves) do hit from time to time, generally as a result of earthquakes or landslides caused by volcanic eruptions.

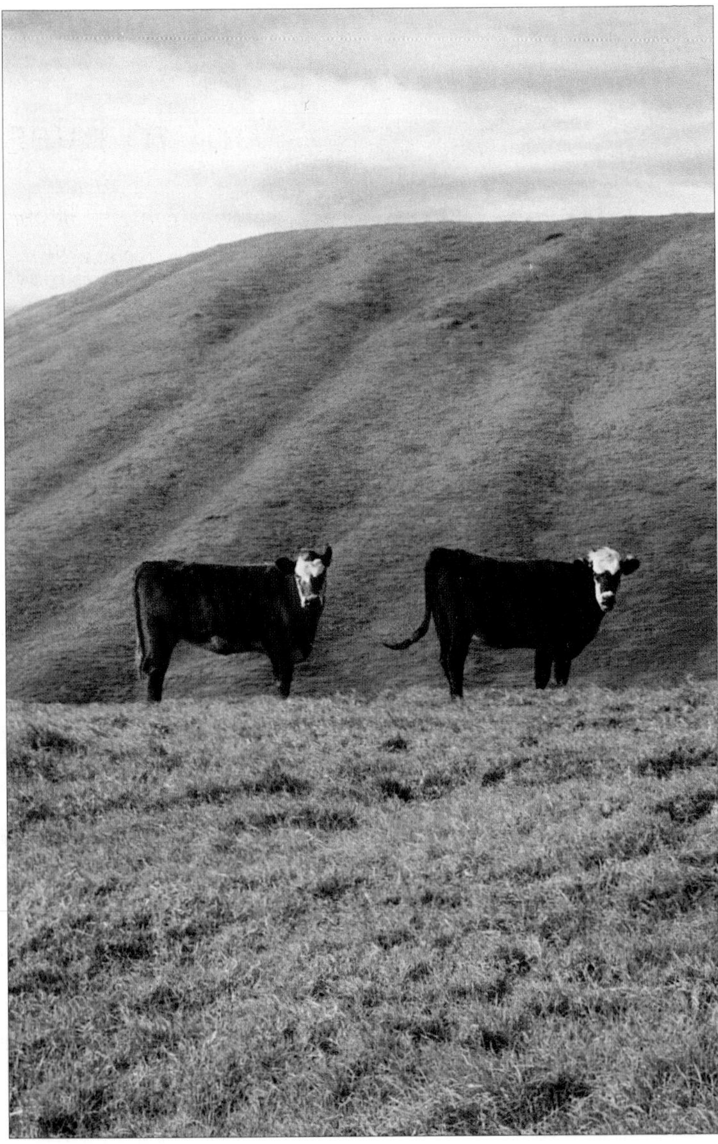

# things not to miss

*It's not possible to see everything that Hawaii has to offer in one trip – and we don't suggest you try. What follows is a selective taste of the highlights on the islands: outstanding beaches, spectacular tropical wonders, exciting outdoor activities – even good places to enjoy a cocktail. Arranged in five color-coded categories, you can browse through to find the very best things to see, do and experience. All highlights have a page reference to take you straight into the guide, where you can find out more.*

**01** **Haleakalā Crater** Page **328** • Every day, legions of visitors drive through the darkness to catch the unforgettable moment when the sun's first rays strike the multi-colored crater of Haleakalā, at the core of eastern Maui.

**02 Pāpōhaku Beach** Page **407** • Molokai's windswept western shore is seldom safe for swimming, but it's great for long solitary strolls – and sunset views all the way to Waikīkī.

**03 Mauna Kea** Page **227** • Even Hawaii sees a little snow sometimes – at least if you drive to the summit of the Pacific's highest mountain, on the Big Island; it's a surreal landscape made even more so by the presence of many powerful telescopes used for astronomical observations

**04 Hālawa Valley** Page **389** • This lush valley at Molokai's eastern tip, home to some of Hawaii's first-ever settlers, makes a fitting reward at the end of the slow but spectacular drive out from Kaunakakai.

**05 Hiking in Hawaii Volcanoes National Park**

Page **242** • As you venture along the well-marked trails of the Big Island's most visited tourist attraction, a single step can take you from dense rainforest to a stark volcanic moonscape.

**06 Kehena Beach**

Page **233** • A pristine, palm-fringed black-sand beach created by lava from nearby Kīlauea, Kehena is a favorite with the back-to-nature inhabitants of the Big Island's "alternative" Puna district.

**07 The Kīlauea eruption** Page **249** • Kīlauea volcano on the Big Island, whose name means "much spewing", has been in a constant state of eruption since 1983; see it from a helicopter or even, when conditions are right, on foot.

**08 Big Beach** Page **320** • Beyond its resorts and high-rise hotels, Maui still holds ravishing unspoiled beaches, where you may well find the sands undisturbed by a single footprint.

**09 Kalaupapa Peninsula** Page **398** • Pilgrims flock to take the legendary Molokai Mule Ride down to Father Damien's celebrated leper colony, located on an all-but-inaccessible promontory at the foot of the world's tallest sea cliffs.

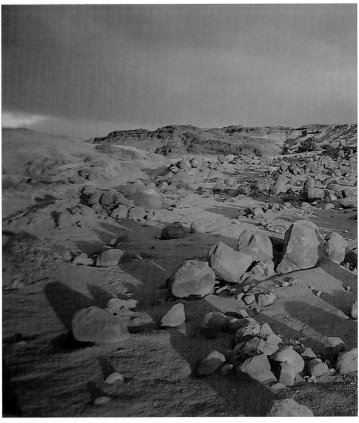

**10** **Garden of the Gods** Page **373** • These eerie rock formations, located down a dirt road in central Lanai, make a superb spot to catch a radiant sunset.

**12** **Lāna'i City** Page **361** • Lanai's only town, all but unchanged despite the passing of the plantation era, has a friendly village atmosphere that just invites you to while away a lazy day.

**11** **Snorkeling in Molokini Crater** Page **310** • Though the ocean has all but submerged this long-extinct crater off the Maui coast, a slender crescent wall survives to shelter the boat-loads of snorkelers and divers who come to ogle its colorful fish population.

ACTIVITIES | CONSUME | EVENTS | NATURE | SIGHTS

**13 Mānele Bay Hotel** Page **367** • Even if you can't afford the room rates on the former pineapple island of Lanai, you can always pamper yourself with poolside cocktails at this lavish beachfront hotel.

**14 Swimming with dolphins** Page **183** • The Disneyesque *Hilton Waikoloa Village* hotel, on the Big Island, is wildly popular with families – and especially with those who get to swim with its resident dolphins.

**15 Hawaiian Monarchy** Page **78** • Discover the pride and the passion that still surrounds the tragic saga of Hawaii's royal family, as witnessed by the statues and museums of Honolulu, and especially 'Iolani Palace.

**16 Unique wildlife** Page **524** • From silversword plants to the rarest 'ō'ō 'ā'ā honey-creeper, you'll never cease to be awed by the islands' tropical flora and fauna.

**17 Kona Coffee** Page **169** • Be sure not to leave the Big Island without sampling some strong, flavorful Kona coffee, a gourmet specialty grown on the slopes above Kealakekua Bay.

**18 Helicopter trips** Page **422** • Taking a helicopter tour of Kauai is the perfect, albeit expensive, way to get a bird's-eye view of the island's spectacular scenery – its hidden waterfalls, tall sea cliffs, and remotest valleys.

**19 Secret Beach** Page **449** • Hidden away on Kauai's north shore, Secret Beach may be the finest – and most enticingly named – strand on an island that's bursting with delightful sands.

**20** **Hanauma Bay** Page **115** • Just a short bus ride out from Waikīkī, lagoon-like Hanauma Bay formed when a crater wall collapsed, to create Oahu's best-loved snorkeling destination.

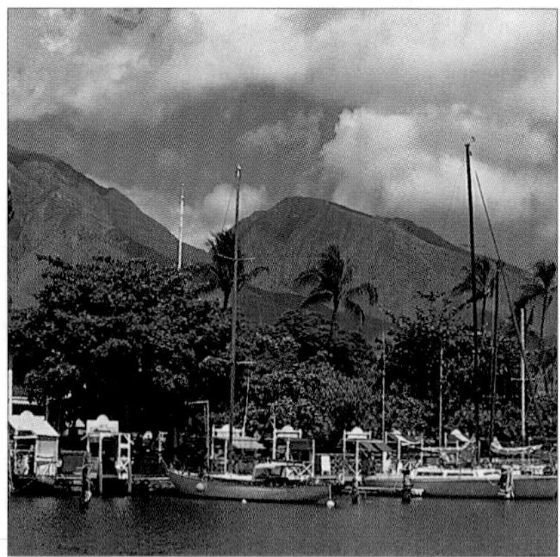

**21** **Lahaina** Page **276** • Seen at its best from just off the west Maui shoreline, laid-back Lahaina has lost none of its charm in making the transition from whaling port to vacation resort.

**22** **Whale migrations** Page **272** • Cavorting humpback whales, who spend each winter calving in the warm Hawaiian waters, are frequently visible off the beaches of west Maui.

**23 Merrie Monarch Festival** Page **212** • *Hula* shows and festivals take place on all the islands throughout the year, but this Big Island event is the highlight of the annual calendar.

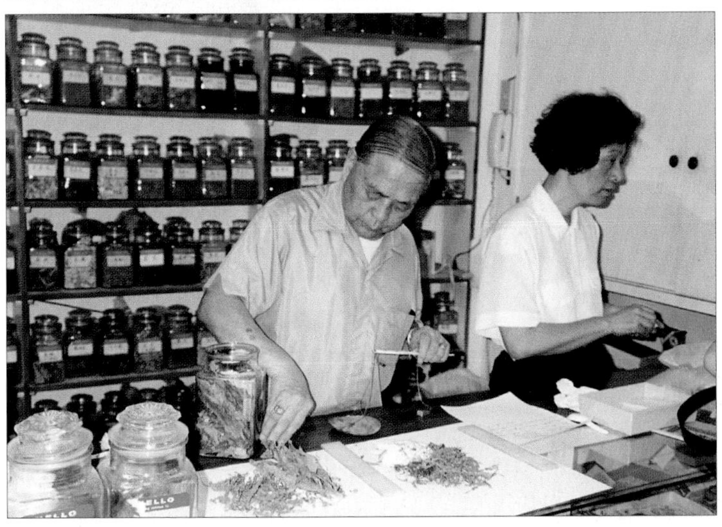

**24 Chinatown** Page **83** • Honolulu's most atmospheric quarter makes a welcome change from Waikīkī; join the locals in exploring the open-air markets, shopping for herbs and other delicacies, or simply hanging out and "talking story."

**25 Surfing** Page **35** • This traditional Polynesian sport may have spread all over the globe, but for locals and tourists alike, Hawaii's thunderous waves still represent the ultimate challenge.

**26 Princeville, Kauai** Page **452** • Kauai's stunning Nā Pali cliffs can be experienced along grueling hiking trails, or simply admired from afar as you enjoy a cocktail in the exclusive Princeville resort.

**27 Nighttime in Waikīkī**

Page **101** • Though it might sound cheesy or kitsch, few can resist the romance of an evening spent taking in the restaurants and entertainment of Oahu's premier resort, rounded off with a moonlit stroll.

**28 Kōke'e State Park** Page **496** • Perched above the dazzling rainbow-hued gorge of Waimea Canyon, this lushly vegetated state park offers breathtaking views of the remote valleys along Kauai's North Shore.

## 29 Punchbowl Crater

Page **89** • This natural volcanic amphitheater, towering above downtown Honolulu, makes an utterly appropriate setting for the National Memorial Cemetery of the Pacific.

## 30 Wai'ānapanapa State Park

Page **345** • Not far from the time-forgotten village of Hāna, this ravishing black-sand beach offers the best camping along the Maui coast.

## 31 Akaka Falls

Page **217** • Mighty Akaka Falls is simply the largest of countless waterfalls that cascade down the richly-vegetated flanks of the Big Island's Hāmākua Coast.

**32** **Oahu's Circle-Island Drive** Page **120** • To get away from the bustle on Oahu, drive the full length of the gorgeous Windward Shore, pausing at the many remote beaches along the way.

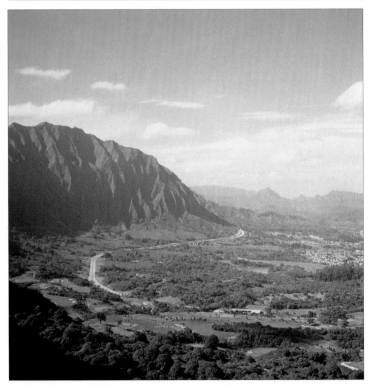

**33** **Nu'uanu Pali** Page **95** • Just minutes from central Honolulu, this spectacular state park provides visitors with their first heart-stopping glimpse of the stupendous scenery of windward Oahu.

# contents

# using the Rough Guide

We've tried to make this Rough Guide a good read and easy to use. The book is divided into five main sections, and you should be able to find whatever you want in one of them.

## front section

The front colour section offers a quick tour of Hawaii. The **introduction** aims to give you a feel for the place, with suggestions on where to go. We also tell you what the weather is like and include a basic state fact file. Next, our author rounds up his favourite aspects of Hawaii in the **things not to miss** section – whether it's a great beach, amazing hike or a special hotel. Right after this comes the Rough Guide's full **contents** list.

## basics

You've decided to go and the basics section covers all the **pre-departure** nitty-gritty to help you plan your trip. This is where to find out which airlines fly to your destination, what paperwork you'll need, what to do about money and insurance, about internet access, food, security, public transport, car rental – in fact just about every piece of **general practical information** you might need.

## guide

This is the heart of the Rough Guide, divided into user-friendly chapters, each of which covers a specific island. Every chapter starts with a list of **highlights** and an **introduction** that helps you to decide where to go, depending on your time and budget. Likewise, introductions to the various towns and regions within each chapter should help you plan your itinerary. We start most town accounts with information on arrival and accommodation, followed by a tour of the sights, and finally reviews of places to eat and drink, and details of nightlife. Longer accounts also have a directory of practical listings.

## contexts

Read Contexts to get a deeper understanding of how Hawaii ticks. We include a brief **history**, articles about **environmental issues**, **indigenous music** and **ancient culture and society**, together with a detailed further reading section that reviews dozens of **books** relating to the state.

## index + small print

Apart from a **full index**, which includes maps as well as places, this section covers publishing information, credits and acknowledgements, and also has our contact details in case you want to send in updates and corrections to the book – or suggestions as to how we might improve it.

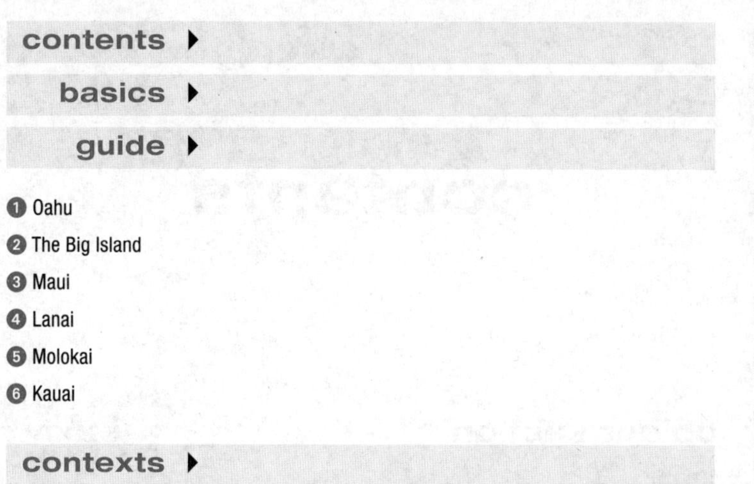




## chapter map of **Hawaii**

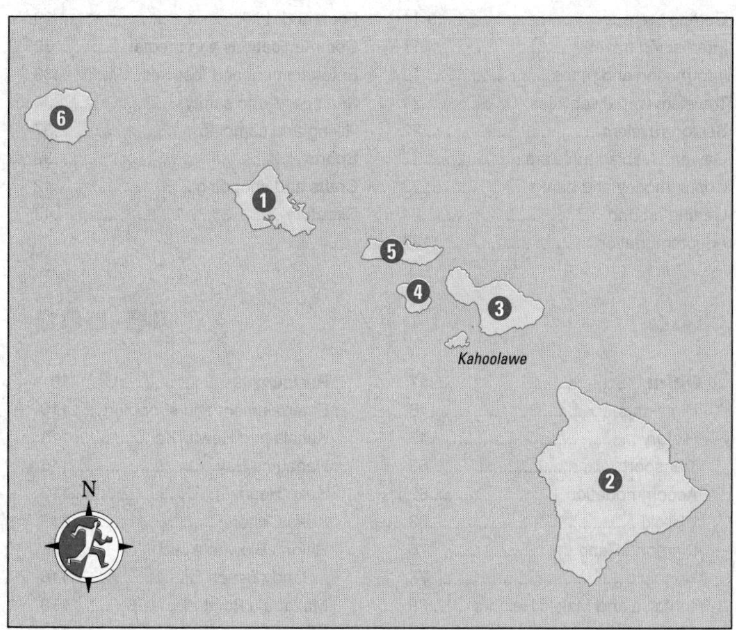

# contents

## colour section i–xxiv



## basics 9–44



## guide 45–502

## contexts 503–546



## index + small print 547–559

# map symbols

## symbols

maps are listed in the full index using coloured text

Highway
Road
One-way street
Track
Trail
Railway
River
Airport
Hotel/Restaurant
Campsite
Church
Buddhist temple
Chinese temple
Ancient site
Museum
Battleground
Public gardens
Peak
Viewpoint
Lighthouse
Waterfall
Marshland
Shipwreck
Tourist office
Post office
General point of interest
Building
Church
Park
National park
Lava flow

# basics

# basics

# Getting there



**You'll almost certainly have to fly to get to any of the Hawaiian islands (unless you're heading out on a luxury cruise) – and more likely than not pass through Honolulu, regardless of whether you plan on spending any measurable time in Oahu. Though the winter is peak season in Hawaii, fares to get there are typically highest from around June to August, and again around Christmas and New Year's. Note that flying on weekdays might save you a bit of money on your flight.**

The simplest way to save money on a trip to Hawaii, however, is to buy a **package** deal including both flight and accommodation (and possibly car rental as well). Even if you normally prefer to travel independently, you'll get a much better deal on room rates if you book ahead as part of a package. Most of the operators listed on p.13 can tailor an itinerary to meet your specific needs and are able to reserve accommodation in more than one hotel or on more than one island.

If all you want to buy is the flight itself, you can normally cut costs by going through a **specialist flight agent** – either by phone or on the web (see p.13). At a very rough estimate, given plenty of notice, you should be able to save around forty percent on the regular fares, bringing a round-trip from New York to Honolulu down from $1050 to $650, or the cost of a round-trip flight from the West Coast down to more like $350 instead of $550. You should be able to save similar percentages coming from Britain or Australasia. Remember that you don't have to reserve onward flights to the other islands at the same time.

## From North America

Almost all **flights** to Hawaii from the US mainland and Canada land at the state capital, **Honolulu**, on the island of Oahu. Virtually every large US airline flies to Honolulu, with United being the major player; Hawaiian Airlines also runs its own services to and from the western states. The only other airports that receive nonstop flights from the continental US are Kahului on **Maui** (served by Hawaiian, United, Delta and American from LA; by United and American from San Francisco; and by Hawaiian from Seattle); Kona/Keahole on the **Big Island** (United from LA and San Francisco, and Aloha from San Francisco only); and Līhu'e on **Kauai** (United only, from LA and San Francisco).

So long as you arrive in Honolulu by about 7pm, you should be able to connect with an onward flight to any of the other islands. Although this might be on the same airline, or even the same aircraft, in most cases it will be with one of the two main inter-island carriers – Aloha Airlines and Hawaiian Airlines. For more details, see "Inter-island travel" on p.17.

### Booking flights online

Many airlines and discount travel websites offer you the opportunity to book your tickets online, cutting out the costs of agents and middle-men. Some auction sites offer you the chance to name your own price, while other sites might specialize in last-minute booking deals. We've listed websites where applicable with all airlines and tour operators in Basics, as well as given addresses for those travel agents that operate solely through online booking. Obviously if you don't feel fully comfortable using your credit card online, or buying a ticket without talking to someone in person, you may want to think twice before using such a service.

As for the **journey time**, crossing the Pacific from the West Coast to Honolulu takes roughly five and a half hours. For a note on time differences, see p.43.

## Flights from the US West Coast

Round-trip fares **from the West Coast to Honolulu** tend to be from $350 to $550. **Los Angeles** is generally the cheapest departure point and is served by six carriers: Hawaiian, United, American, Continental, Northwest and Delta.

Hawaiian Airlines flies from six mainland US cities to Honolulu. Daily flights leave from **Las Vegas** at 10.10am; from **Los Angeles** at 8.55am, 12.30pm and 5.25pm; from **Portland** at 9.10am; from **San Diego** at 9.15am; from **San Francisco** at 8.40am and 10.15am; and from **Seattle** at 8.50am (with an additional later flight five days a week).

United flies to Honolulu from **San Francisco** at 9.05am, 1.40pm, 4.30pm and 7.25pm daily, and from **Los Angeles** daily at 8am, 1.45pm, 5.20pm and 7.15pm.

Of the **other operators** who fly to Honolulu from the West Coast, Delta offers four daily flights from LA and one daily from San Francisco; American has two daily flights from LA, one from San Francisco, and one from San Jose; Northwest has two daily services from LA and two from Seattle; and Continental flies once a day from LA.

### To the Neighbor Islands

The number of nonstop flights to Kahului airport on **Maui** has increased greatly in recent years. Most come from **Los Angeles**; Hawaiian Airlines flies the route four times daily, United and American twice, and Delta once. Daily service from **San Francisco** is provided by United (twice daily) and American (once), while Hawaiian flies once a day from Seattle. During peak season, Midwest-based charter airline American Trans Air offers regular flights to Kahului from both San Francisco and Los Angeles.

In addition, United operates two daily services from Los Angeles, and one from San Francisco to Kona on the **Big Island**, and flies once daily from each of those cities to Līhu'e on **Kauai**. Aloha also flies to Kona once daily from the Bay Area's Oakland airport.

## Flights from the rest of the US

There are no scheduled nonstop flights from the **East Coast** to Hawaii (although charter service American Trans Air has in recent years offered once-weekly nonstop flights in high season between New York's JFK airport and Honolulu). Most visitors fly via California, though American flies direct to Honolulu **from Chicago** and **Dallas,** as do Northwest **from Minneapolis**, Continental **from Houston**, Delta **from Atlanta**, and TWA **from St Louis**; all flights take 8–10 hours. Round-trip fares from East Coast cities generally range from $750 to $1050.

## Flights from Canada

Getting to Hawaii from any **Canadian** city apart from Vancouver will almost certainly require you to change planes on the US mainland. United offers routings from **Toronto** via San Francisco for around CDN$1250, and from **Vancouver** for CDN$700–850. Better from Vancouver is Northwest, with fares starting at CDN$650, via Seattle. If you're flying from either **Toronto** or **Montréal**, you can go via Chicago or Dallas with American (CDN$1300); via Detroit or Minneapolis on Northwest (CDN$1250); or via Atlanta on Delta (CDN$1350).

Air Canada flies daily to Honolulu from **Toronto** (CDN$1200) via **Vancouver** (CDN$700). Canadian has daily nonstop flights to Honolulu from **Vancouver**, with fares around CDN$700, and flights three times weekly (Tues, Wed & Fri) from **Toronto** starting around CDN$1000. Through trips from **Montréal**, via Vancouver, start at around CDN$1050.

Note that Canadians flying to Hawaii on vacation should carry valid passports, but do not need visas.

## Airlines

**Air Canada** ⓣ1-888/247-2262, ⓦwww.aircanada.ca

**Aloha** ⓣ1-800/367-5250, ⓦwww.alohaairlines.com

**American** ⓣ1-800/433-7300, ⓦwww.aa.com

**American Trans Air** ⓣ1-800/435-9282, ⓦwww.ata.com

**Canadian** ⓣ1-888/247-2262, ⓦwww.aircanada.ca

**Continental** ⓣ1-800/523-3273, ⓦwww.continental.com
**Delta** ⓣ1-800/221-1212, ⓦwww.delta.com
**Hawaiian** ⓣ1-800/367-5320, ⓦwww.hawaiianair.com
**Northwest** ⓣ1-800/225-2525, ⓦwww.nwa.com
**TWA** ⓣ1-800/221-2000, ⓦwww.twa.com
**United** ⓣ1-800/241-6522, ⓦwww.ual.com

## Flight agents

**Airhitch** ⓣ1-800/326-2009, ⓦwww.airhitch.org
**Cheap Tickets** ⓣ1-888/922-8849, ⓦwww.cheaptickets.com
**Council Travel** ⓣ1-800/226-8624, ⓦwww.counciltravel.com
**Expedia** ⓦwww.expedia.com
**High Adventure Travel** ⓦwww.airtreks.com
**Hotwire** ⓦwww.hotwire.com
**Orbitz** ⓦwww.orbitz.com
**Priceline** ⓦwww.priceline.com
**Qixo** ⓦwww.qixo.com
**STA Travel** ⓣ1-800/777-0112, ⓦwww.sta-travel.com
**TicketPlanet** ⓦwww.ticketplanet.com
**Travelocity** ⓦwww.travelocity.com
**Travelscape** ⓦwww.travelscape.com

## Tour operators

**American Airlines Vacations**; ⓣ1-800/321-2121, ⓦwww.aa.com. Independent package tours to Hawaii, taking care of your flight, accommodation and car rental.
**Backroads**, Berkeley CA; ⓣ510/527-1555 or 1-800/462-2848, ⓦwww.backroads.com. Biking tours of the Big Island, with stays in top-quality accommodation, priced at $2300 for six nights, not including air fares.
**Continental Airlines Vacations**; ⓣ1-800/634-5555, ⓦwww.coolvacations.com. Individually tailored Hawaiian vacations, with flights, accommodation and car rental.
**Crane Tours**, Chatsworth CA; ⓣ818/773-4601 or 1-800/653-2545. Guided, week-long backpacking expeditions on Kauai, Maui and the Big Island, for $750–1000 excluding flights.
**Delta Vacations**; ⓣ1-800/654-6559, ⓦwww.deltavacations.com. Good-value Hawaiian package vacations with all combinations of flights, accommodation and car rental. A five-night stay in Waikīkī from New York ranges from $699 to $1159.
**Earthwatch**, Watertown MA; ⓣ617/926-8200, ⓦwww.earthwatch.org. Organization that recruits paying volunteer field researchers to assist scientists. The Honolulu-based Humpbacks of Hawaii program focuses on whales (twelve days in winter; $1995), while the Threatened Reefs program features scuba dives in Maui (twelve days May–Oct; $1895–1995). Prices do not include flights.
**Globus and Cosmos**, Littleton CO; ⓣ1-800/221-0090, ⓦwww.globusandcosmos.com. Independent and escorted tours in multi-island permutations; thirteen days on Oahu, Maui, Kauai and the Big Island, or fourteen days focusing on the national parks of Maui and the Big Island. Land-only rates start around $750, but they can also arrange air fare and the like for you.
**New England Hiking Holidays**, North Conway NH; ⓣ603/356-9696 or 1-800/869-0949. Guided seven-day springtime hiking tours of the Big Island, for $1695, excluding air fare.
**Pacific Quest**, Hale'iwa HI; 1-800/776-2518. Adventurous ecotourism: guided hiking, swimming and camping vacations, with a multi-island tour for $2000, excluding air fare.
**Pleasant Hawaiian Holidays**, Westlake Village CA; ⓣ1-800/7HAWAII, ⓦwww.2hawaii.com. The leading supplier of independent packages, combining flights, car rental, accommodation, etc, on any island. Eight days on Maui, Oahu or both from LA can cost under $800.
**Questers Worldwide Nature Tours**, New York NY; ⓣ212/251-0444 or 1-800/468-8668, ⓦwww.questers.com. Two-week nature tours; Volcanoes National Park and Kona coast on the Big Island, or bird watching on Maui, Kauai and Molokai, for $4000, excluding air fare.
**Sierra Club**, San Francisco CA; 415/977-5522, ⓦwww.sierraclub.org. Guided wilderness travel trips to all the islands, from around $1000 per week, excluding air fare. The Big Island tour concentrates on hiking and backpacking.
**Tauck Tours**, Westport CT; ⓣ203/226-6911 or 1-800/788-7885, ⓦwww.tauck.com. Fully escorted tours, staying at the very top hotels. Eight days on Oahu, Maui and Kauai starting at $2490, and thirteen days including the Big Island starting at $3680; both excluding air fare.
**TWA Getaway Vacations**; ⓣ1-800/GETAWAY, ⓦwww.twa.com. All permutations of islands and accommodation.
**United Vacations**; ⓣ1-800/328-6877, ⓦwww.unitedvacations.com. Custom-made individual vacations, combining islands and hotels to your specifications, but requiring a two-night stay on one island.
**Windsurfari**, Kahului HI; ⓣ808/871-7766 or 1-800/736-MAUI, ⓦwindsurfari.com. Windsurfing and custom vacation packages on Maui, including

condo, car and equipment rental – but not flights – from $500 per week.

**World of Vacations**, Etobicoke, Ontario; ⓣ416/620-8050, ⓦwww.macktravel.ca. Customized independent packages to all islands with flights and accommodation included.

## Cruises

No scheduled American **ships** travel between the US mainland and Hawaii. That means it's only possible to sail to Honolulu on a luxury **cruise**, most of which start in Canada or Mexico. Look for information about upcoming cruises, and possibly bargain rates, on websites such as ⓦwww.bestcruises.com and ⓦwww.consolidatedcruises.com. For details of the weekly **inter-island cruises** aboard the *Independence* and the *Patriot*, see p.18.

## Insurance

Your existing insurance may offer full coverage when you're away from home. Some homeowners' policies are valid on vacation, and credit cards such as American Express often include medical or other insurance. Most Canadians are covered for medical mishaps overseas by their health plans.

If you're not already covered, either contact a specialist travel insurance company, or consider Rough Guides' own travel insurance, customized for our readers and available for anyone, of any nationality, traveling anywhere in the world.

There are two main plans: Essential, for basic, no-frills coverage, and Premier, which offers more generous benefits. You can also take out annual multi-trip insurance, which covers you for any number of trips (maximum 60 days each) throughout the year. If you intend to be away for the whole year, the Adventurer policy will cover you for 365 days. Each plan can be supplemented with a "Hazardous Activities Premium" if you plan to indulge in sports considered dangerous, such as scuba diving.

For a policy quote, call the Rough Guide Insurance Line: ⓣ1-866/220 5588 (US toll-free), ⓣ0800 015 0906 (UK), or, if you're calling from elsewhere, ⓣ44 1243/621 046. Alternatively, get an online quote at ⓦwww.roughguides.com/insurance.

## From Australia and New Zealand

There's no shortage of flights from Australia and New Zealand to **Honolulu**, and very little price difference between airlines. Five airlines operate daily services, with journey times of around nine hours.

**From Australia**, most flights to Honolulu are out of **Sydney**, with daily nonstop service on Qantas, American Airlines and Air Canada for around AUS$1500 in low season or AUS$1750 in high season. For around the same price, United flies via Auckland.

**From New Zealand**, the best deals to Honolulu are those out of Auckland offered by the United/Air New Zealand partnership; flights cost from NZ$1599 in low season and up to NZ$1899 in high season, whether you fly nonstop, or via Fiji, Tonga or Papeete. Air Canada also flies nonstop from Auckland, while Qantas can take you from Auckland to Honolulu via either Sydney or Western Samoa.

### Airlines

**Air New Zealand** ⓣ13/2476 (Aus), ⓣ0800 737 000 (NZ), ⓦwww.airnz.com
**Air Pacific** ⓣ1-800/230 150 (Aus), ⓣ09/379 2404 (NZ), ⓦwww.airpacific.com
**Cathay Pacific** ⓣ13/1747 (Aus), ⓣ09/379 0861 (NZ), ⓦwww.cathaypacific.com
**Qantas** ⓣ13/1313 (Aus), ⓣ0800/808 767 (NZ), ⓦwww.qantas.com.au
**Singapore** ⓣ13/1011 (Aus), ⓣ0800/808 909 (NZ), ⓦwww.singaporeair.com

### Flight agents

**Anywhere Travel**, Sydney ⓣ02/9663 0411, ⓔanywhere@ozemail.com.au
**Budget Travel**, Auckland ⓣ09/366 0061
**Destinations Unlimited**, Auckland ⓣ09/373 4033
**Flight Centre** ⓣ02/9235 3522 (Sydney), ⓣ09/ 358 4310 (Auckland), ⓦwww.flightcentre.com.au
**Northern Gateway**, Darwin ⓣ08/8941 1394, ⓔoztravel@norgate.com.au
**STA Travel** ⓣ1-300/360 960 (Aus), ⓣ09/366 6673 (NZ), ⓦwww.statravel.com.au

### Tour operators

**Creative Tours**, Sydney; ⓣ02/386 2111, ⓦwww.creativeholidays.com.au. Car rental, accommodation and inter-island travel packages.

**Hawaiian Island Golf Tours**, Sydney; ⓣ02/968 1778. The name says it all; tailor-made golfing itineraries on the Big Island, Maui or Kauai.
**Hawaii Unlimited**; ⓣ03/9650 5333, ⓔcitytravel@hotmail.com. Tours and packages to Hawaii.
**Padi Travel Network**, Sydney; ⓣ02/9417 2800 or 1-800/678100, ⓦwww.padi.com.au. Tailored dive packages to Hawaii's prime dive sites.
**Pro Dive Travel**, Sydney; ⓣ02/264 9499. Tailor-made dive packages to the Big Island and Maui, primarily for qualified divers.
**The Surf Travel Co**, Sydney; ⓣ02/9299 8000, ⓦwww.surftravel.com.au. Surf tours to Oahu's North Shore; accommodation ranges from hostels to *Hiltons*.
**Sydney International Travel Centre**, Sydney; ⓣ02/9299 8000 or 1-800/251 911, ⓦwww.sydtrav.com.au. Specialists in all types of holidays in Hawaii and the US.
**Wiltrans/Maupintour**, 10/189 Kent St, Sydney; ⓣ02/9255 0899. Five-star all-inclusive escorted Hawaiian sightseeing holidays.

### Entry requirements

Under the visa waiver scheme, Australian and New Zealand passport holders who stay less than ninety days in the US **do not require visas**, so long as they have an onward or return ticket.

For longer stays, a 12-month US tourist or business visa costs AUS$85.50/NZ$108. You'll need an application form – available from the US visa information service (ⓣ1-902/262 682) – one signed passport photo and your passport. For details, contact the US Embassy (Aus: 21 Moonah Place, Canberra ⓣ02/6214 5600; NZ: 29 Fitzherbert Terrace, Thorndon, Wellington). In both countries, you can apply and pay for US visas at all post offices.

There's an **Australian Consulate** in Honolulu at 1000 Bishop St (ⓣ545-5423), but New Zealand has no official representative in Hawaii.

### Insurance

**Travel insurance**, including medical cover, is essential in view of the high costs of health care in the US. For details of Rough Guides' own policies, see p.14.

## From Britain and Ireland

Much the quickest and cheapest route from the UK or Ireland to Hawaii is to fly via the mainland United States or Canada, so your options are more or less the same as they are for North Americans. Fly to one of the mainland US cities mentioned on pp.12 and change there for your onward trip.

With a ten-hour flight across the Atlantic to the West Coast, and a five-hour flight over the Pacific, that makes for a very long journey. On the other hand, it is however possible to get to any of the major islands on the same day you set off, thanks to the ten- or eleven-hour time difference (see p.43). In any case, it's the journey home that's the really exhausting leg – if you fly direct, you're likely to arrive home on the second morning after you leave, having "lost" two nights' sleep.

Four airlines can get you all the way **from London** to Honolulu in a single day: United via Los Angeles and San Francisco (taking the 9am flight to San Francisco enables you to touch down in Honolulu at 3.55pm); Delta via Atlanta; Air Canada via Toronto; and British Airways, in conjunction with Air New Zealand, via Vancouver. If you're heading for Maui, United can get you there in a single day via LA or San Francisco, and they can do the same for the Big Island via LA only.

**From Ireland**, Delta provides same-day connections between Dublin and Honolulu, Maui or the Big Island via Atlanta and Los Angeles, and also from Shannon via New York and Los Angeles. Aer Lingus and American also offer daily services to Los Angeles, where you can join other carriers for the onward leg to Hawaii.

A typical return ticket from London to Honolulu through the operators and specialists listed below costs around £450 from January to March, and up to as much as £800 in July and August. For an extra £100 or so, most airlines can book you right through to any of the other Hawaiian islands, on Hawaiian or Aloha.

Also listed are a number of specialists who can tailor **package deals** to suit your needs; if you want to stay in one of the larger hotels, they should be able to get you considerable savings on the hotels' quoted rates.

### Airlines

**Aer Lingus** ⓣ020/8899 4747, ⓣ01/705 3333 (Dublin), ⓦwww.aerlingus.ie
**Air Canada** ⓣ08700/524 7226, ⓦwww.aircanada.ca

**Air New Zealand** ⓣ 020/8741 2299, ⓦ www.airnz.co.uk
**American** ⓣ 0845/778 9789, ⓦ www.aa.com
**British Airways** ⓣ 0845/773 3377, ⓦ www.britishairways.com
**Continental** ⓣ 0800/776464, ⓦ www.flycontinental.com
**Delta** ⓣ 0800/414767, ⓣ 1800/414 767 (Dublin), ⓦ www.delta.com
**Hawaiian** ⓣ 01753/664406, ⓦ www.hawaiianair.com
**KLM/Northwest** ⓣ 08705/074 074, ⓦ www.klmuk.com
**United** ⓣ 0845/844 4777, ⓦ www.ual.com
**Virgin Atlantic** ⓣ 01293/747747, ⓦ www.virgin-atlantic.com

## Flight agents

**1stnetflights** ⓦ www.1stnetflights.com
**a2btravel** ⓦ www.a2btravel.com
**The Airline Network** ⓦ www.netflights.com
**Bridge The World** ⓣ 020/7911 0900, ⓦ www.bridgetheworld.com
**Ebookers** ⓦ www.ebookers.com
**Flynow** ⓦ flynow.com
**Seaforths Travel** ⓦ www.telme.com
**STA Travel** ⓣ 0870/1606070, ⓦ www.statravel.co.uk
**Trailfinders** ⓣ 020/7628 7628, ⓦ www.trailfinders.com
**Travel Bag** ⓣ 0870/9001350, ⓦ www.travelbag.co.uk
**USIT Campus** ⓣ 0870/240 1010, ⓦ www.usitcampus.co.uk
**USIT Now** Dublin ⓣ 01/602 1777, ⓦ www.usitnow.ie

## Tour operators

**Bon Voyage**, Southampton; ⓣ 0800/316 3012, ⓦ www.bon-voyage.co.uk. One of the best-informed and most helpful operators in the business. Flights only or complete packages to all the main islands. A week in Waikīkī, for example, starts at under £1000, including flight.
**Destination Pacific**, London; ⓣ 020/7400 7003. Full itineraries that can take in the mainland US or the South Pacific as well as Hawaii. A week at the *Hilton Waikoloa* on the Big Island, including car and air fare from London, starts around £1100.
**The Hawaiian Dream**, London; ⓣ 020/8552 1201. Package trips and cruises in Hawaii and the South Pacific. A week in Waikīkī costs around £700; two weeks at the plush *Four Seasons* on Maui is more like £2000.
**Hawaiian Travel Center**, London; ⓣ 020/7706 4142. Hawaiian holidays tailor-made by expert enthusiasts who can provide anything from flights only to all-inclusive packages such as a week on Kauai or Molokai in spring for under £1000, two weeks in a top-quality Maui hotel in summer for around £1200, and eighteen-day winter tours of all four major islands for around £2000. Also car rental, West Coast stopovers, and Hawaiian weddings.
**Page & Moy**, Leicester; ⓣ 0870/010 625, ⓦ www.page-moy.co.uk. Package deals to all the islands. Fifteen nights in Waikīkī can cost as little as £799, and they can arrange good deals at the luxury resorts on Kauai, Maui and the Big Island. Also wedding specials, and two-week combined packages with San Francisco and Las Vegas.
**United Vacations**; ⓣ 0845/844 4777, ⓦ www.unitedvacations.com. Good-value personalized packages, arranged with United. A week in Waikīkī can work out at under £800, while the *Hilton* on the Big Island costs around £1500 for a week, including air fares and car rental.

## Entry requirements

Passport-holders from **Britain, Ireland** and most European countries do not require visas for trips to the United States of less than ninety days. Instead you simply fill in the **visa waiver form** handed out on incoming planes. Immigration control takes place at your point of arrival on US soil, which, if you're flying from Britain, will not be in Hawaii. For further details, contact the **US embassy** in Britain (24 Grosvenor Square, London W1A 1AE; ⓣ 020/7499 9000; premium-rate visa hotline ⓣ 0906/820 0290) or Ireland (42 Elgin Rd, Ballsbridge, Dublin; ⓣ 01/668 8777).

There is no British or Irish **consulate** in Hawaii.

## Insurance

**Travel insurance**, including medical cover, is essential in view of the high costs of health care in the US. For details of Rough Guides' own policies, see p.14.

# Inter-island travel



**Virtually all travel between the Hawaiian islands is done by air; in fact, the route between Honolulu and Kahului on Maui ranks as the busiest domestic route in the entire United States, with more than three million passengers each year. Honolulu is the main hub; apart from very short hops, it's unusual to be able to fly between two of the outer islands without a stop on Oahu.**

## Flights

The two major **airlines**, Hawaiian and Aloha, both connect Honolulu at least ten times daily with the airports at Kona and Hilo on the **Big Island**, Kahului on **Maui**, and Līhu'e on **Kauai**, and with the islands of **Molokai** and **Lanai** slightly less frequently. With so many services, it's rarely difficult to make an onward connection at Honolulu for a flight to another island. Hawaiian and Aloha also operate a handful of nonstop services each day between Maui and both Kauai and the Big Island.

Aloha's affiliate, Island Air, serves lesser routes between the islands, flying from Honolulu to Molokai, Lanai, and the quieter airport of Kapalua on Maui. It also offers nonstop flights to Lanai from Maui, the Big Island and Molokai.

Don't expect to be able to fly late in the evening; the last scheduled flights on all the airlines usually depart at around 8pm.

### Discount travel agents in Hawaii

**Cheap Tickets Inc**

ⓦ www.cheaptickets.com

| | |
|---|---|
| US | ⓣ 1-888/922-8849 |
| Oahu | ⓣ 947-3717 |
| Maui | ⓣ 242-8094 |

**Cut-rate Tickets**

ⓦ www.cutratetickets.com

| | |
|---|---|
| US | ⓣ 1-800/297-5093 |
| Kailua | ⓣ 326-2300 |
| Hilo | ⓣ 969-1944 |
| Kahului | ⓣ 871-7300 |
| Lahaina | ⓣ 661-5800 |

## Fares and discounts

Both Hawaiian and Aloha have standard one-way **fares** on all inter-island routes of around $85, although Hawaiian sells cut-price seats on early-morning and late-evening flights daily for more like $50. Both airlines offer all sorts of **discount packages**. The most common deal is a "book" of six coupons valid for any inter-island flight; these cost around $380 on Hawaiian or Aloha, and $420 on Aloha affiliate Island Air. Hawaiian's Hawaiian Inter-Island Pass allows unlimited travel for five days ($321), one week ($345), ten days ($409), or two weeks ($469), while Aloha's similar Visitor Seven-Day Island Pass costs $321.

Many **discount travel agents** in Hawaii sell airline coupons over the counter, offering individual tickets rather than entire "books" for around $65. Remember also that virtually all the resorts, hotels, B&B agencies and even hostels in Hawaii can arrange discounts on inter-island flights.

## Inter-island airlines

A number of small-scale airlines also operate in Hawaii. **Pacific Wings** (ⓣ 887-2104 or 1-888/575-4546, ⓦ www.pacificwings.com) offers daily flights from **Honolulu** and Kahului on **Maui** to both **Molokai** and the tiny commuter airport at Waimea on the **Big Island**. In fact, **Molokai** is a particular target for minor airlines, with other players including Molokai Air Shuttle and Paragon Air; for full details, see p.380.

## Inter-island packages

Waikīkī travel agents such as Magnum Tickets & Tours, 2134 Kalākaua Ave (ⓣ 923-

## Inter-Island Carriers

| | Aloha | Island | Hawaiian |
|---|---|---|---|
| website | ⓦwww.alohaair.com | | ⓦwww.hawaiianair.com |
| US & Can | ⓣ1-800/367-5250 | ⓣ1-800/323-3345 | ⓣ1-800/367-5320 |
| Oahu | ⓣ484-1111 | ⓣ484-2222 | ⓣ1-800/882-8811 |
| Big Island | ⓣ935-5771 | ⓣ1-800/652-6541 | ⓣ1-800/882-8811 |
| Kauai | ⓣ245-3691 | ⓣ1-800/652-6541 | ⓣ1-800/882-8811 |
| Lanai | | ⓣ1-800/652-6541 | ⓣ1-800/882-8811 |
| Maui | ⓣ244-9071 | ⓣ1-800/652-6541 | ⓣ1-800/882-8811 |
| Molokai | | ⓣ1-800/652-6541 | ⓣ1-800/882-8811 |

7825), and Aloha Express, 2464 Kalākaua Ave (ⓣ924-4030), offer inexpensive **package tours** to the other islands. Available at extremely short notice, these are designed to suit short-stay visitors keen to see more of Hawaii than just Oahu. All-inclusive flight, accommodation and rental-car deals cost around $100 per person for one night, $130 for two nights, and $30 for each additional night. Fly-drive deals typically start at around $40 per person one-way.

## Ferries and cruises

Only two scheduled **ferry services** operate in the state of Hawaii, both from Lahaina on **Maui**. Expeditions (ⓣ661-3756 or 1-800/695-2524) runs five boats each day to Mānele Bay on **Lanai**, while the *Molokai Princess* (ⓣ667-6165 or 1-800/275-6969, ⓦwww.mauiprincess.com) makes one round-trip each day between Lahaina and Kaunakakai on Molokai. For details of both, see p.279.

In addition, weekly **luxury cruises** between the islands, on board the *Independence* and the *Patriot*, are operated by American Hawaii Cruises (2 North Riverside Plaza, Chicago IL 60606; ⓣ312/466-6000 or 1-800/513-5022, ⓦwww.cruisehawaii.com) and United States Lines respectively (same address; ⓣ312/466-6000 or 1-877/330-6871, ⓦwww.unitedstateslines.com). Both run round-trips from Honolulu that call at Maui, Kailua and Hilo on the Big Island, and Kauai. Add-on stays on any island can be arranged before or after your cruise, at rates similar to those offered by other agents, but you can't interrupt the cruise itself to stay at any of the ports en route. Quoted fares per person start at as little as $559 on the *Independence* and $809 on the *Patriot*, and range up to over $3000 for an ocean-view suite; they do not include off-ship excursions. You may be able to secure better prices, and also find occasional cruises offered by other companies, on the websites mentioned on p.13.

# Information and maps



**A vast quantity of written information is available about Hawaii. Tourism is big business on all the islands, and plenty of people and organizations are eager to tell you all about what's on offer.**

Foremost among these is the **Hawaii Visitors Bureau**, which has offices (known as chapters) on every island, as well as representatives all around the world. Contact the nearest office – listed in the box below – or simply call in when you arrive in Hawaii, and you'll be deluged with all sorts of handouts and brochures. The most useful is the free annual *Connections Hawaii*, which has detailed listings for accommodation, restaurants, car rental, activities and tour operators. You can also get free copies of the glossy *Islands of Aloha* travel guide, which will whet your appetite with color photos and is packed with listings but devoid of anything approaching critical reviews. The main drawback with the **HVB** (as it's usually abbreviated) is that it's a member-driven organization, which means that hotels, restaurants and other operators pay to join and to have their activities publicized. If you can't find something in an HVB publication, that doesn't mean that it doesn't exist or isn't any good: the chances are the relevant business is not an HVB member.

Racks of leaflets, brochures and magazines – a good source of free offers and discount coupons – are prominently displayed in all the major hotels, malls and airports. In heavily touristed areas such as Waikīkī, Kīhei and Lahaina on Maui, Kapa'a on Kauai, and Kailua on the Big Island, you'll also find plenty of **activities centers**. Masquerading as information kiosks, these are primarily concerned with persuading you to buy tickets for some specific activity such as a cruise, horse ride, island tour or whatever; the worst are often fronts for time-share companies as well.

An ever-increasing amount of information is also available on the **Internet**. Web addresses for hotels, activity operators and other businesses are listed throughout this book, as well as on the official HVB site, ⓦwww.gohawaii.com. You can also find copious links and listings on sites such as: Aloha from Hawaii (ⓦwww.aloha-hawaii); ⓦwww.e-hawaii.com; ⓦwww.maui.net; and ⓦwww.hawaiian.net (which focuses on Kauai, and features a "Virtual Taro Patch" at ⓦwww.hawaiian.net/~cbokauai/ahupuaa.html). The most useful sites for current news and listings are run by the two daily Honolulu newspapers, the *Star Bulletin* (ⓦwww.starbulletin.com) and the *Advertiser* (ⓦwww.honoluluadvertiser.com), and also the weekly *Honolulu Weekly* (ⓦwww.honoluluweekly.com).

## Hawaii Visitors Bureau Offices

### In Hawaii

**Main Office**, Waikīkī Business Plaza, Suite 801, 2270 Kalākaua Ave, Honolulu, HI 96815; ⓣ923-1811, ⓕ924-0290, ⓦwww.gohawaii.com.

**Big Island Visitors Bureau**, 250 Keawe St, Hilo, HI 96720; ⓣ961-5797, ⓕ961-2126; *and* 250 Waikoloa Beach Drive, Suite B-15, Waikoloa HI 96748; ⓣ886-1655, ⓕ886-1652, ⓦwww.bigisland.org.

**Kauai Visitors Bureau**, 4334 Rice St, Suite 101, Līhu'e, HI 96766; ⓣ1-800/262-1400 or 245-3971, ⓕ246-9235, ⓦwww.kauaivisitorsbureau.org.

**Destination Lanai**, PO Box 700, Lānai City, HI 96763; ⓣ565-7600, ⓕ565-9316, ⓦwww.visitmaui.com.

**Maui Visitors Bureau**,1727 Wili Pā Loop, Wailuku, HI 96793; ⓣ244-3530 or 1-800/525-MAUI, ⓕ244-1337, ⓦwww.visitmaui.com.

**Molokai Visitors Association**, PO Box 960, Kaunakakai, HI 96748; ⓣ553-3876, 1-800/800-6367 (US & Can), 1-800/553-0404 (HI), ⓕ553-5288, ⓦwww.molokai-hawaii.com.

**Oahu Visitors Bureau**, 733 Bishop St, Suite 1872, Honolulu, HI 96813; ⓣ1-877/525-OAHU or 524-0722, ⓕ521-1620, ⓦwww.visit-oahu.com.

### Elsewhere

**Australia** ⓣ02/9955 2619, ⓕ02/9955 2171
**Canada** ⓣ604/669-6691, ⓕ604/683-9114
**New Zealand** ⓣ09/379 3708, ⓕ09/309 0725
**United Kingdom** ⓣ020/8941-4009, ⓕ020/941-4011

## Maps

The best general-purpose **maps** of the individual islands – there's one each for the Big Island, Maui and Kauai, while Molokai and Lanai are combined on a single sheet – are published by the University of Hawaii, at either $2.95 or $3.95. The cartographer for all those maps, James A Bier, has recently gone into business on his own behalf, so his single-sheet map of Oahu is now no longer available. Instead he publishes three separate sheets: Honolulu and Oahu South Shore ($4.50), Central Oahu and the Windward Coast ($4.50), and North Shore and Leeward Coast ($2.95). Quite possibly future editions of his other maps will also be self-published rather than bearing the University of Hawaii name. In any case, they're sure still to be widely available at island bookstores.

Plenty of free maps are also distributed on the islands themselves, most issued as advertising ventures – you'll almost certainly get a booklet of maps from your rental car agency, for example. These can be useful for pinpointing specific hotels and restaurants, but only the James Bier maps are at all reliable for minor roads.

If you need detailed **hiking maps**, call in at the state parks office in Honolulu or on each specific island, as detailed in the text of this book; their free map of Kauai, for example, is excellent. You could also buy the **topographical maps** produced by the United States Geological Survey (PO Box 25286, Denver Federal Center, Denver, CO 80225), which are widely sold at specialist bookstores in Hawaii.

### Map Outlets

#### Australia and New Zealand

**Mapland**, 372 Little Bourke St, Melbourne; ⓣ03/9670 4383, ⓦwww.mapland.com.au.
**Perth Map Centre**, 1/884 Hay St, Perth WA 6000; ⓣ08/9322 5733, ⓦwww.perthmap.com.au.
**Specialty Maps**, 46 Albert St, City, Auckland; ⓣ09/307 2217, ⓦwww.ubd-online.co.nz/maps.
**The Map Shop**, 6 Peel St, Adelaide; ⓣ08/8231 2033, ⓦwww.mapshop.net.au.

#### US and Canada

**Adventurous Traveler Bookstore**, PO Box 64769, Burlington, VT; ⓣ1-800/282-3963, ⓦwww.AdventurousTraveler.com.
**Book Passage**, 51 Tamal Vista Blvd, Corte Madera, CA; ⓣ415/927-0960, ⓦwww.bookpassage.com.
**The Complete Traveler Bookstore**, 199 Madison Ave, New York, NY 10016; ⓣ212/685-9007.
**Distant Lands**, 56 S Raymond Ave, Pasadena, CA 91105; ⓣ626/449-3220, ⓦwww.distantlands.com.
**GORP Adventure Library** ⓣ1-800 754 8229, ⓦwww2.gorp.com/advenlib/.
**Map Link**, 30 S La Petera Lane, Unit #5, Santa Barbara, CA 93117; ⓣ805/692-6777, ⓦwww.maplink.com.
**Phileas Fogg's Books & Maps**, Stanford Shopping Center, Palo Alto, CA; ⓣ1-800/533-3644, ⓦwww.foggs.com.
**Rand McNally** has 24 stores across the US; ⓣ1-800/333-0136 (ext 2111), ⓦwww.randmcnally.com.
**Sierra Club Bookstore**, 6014 College Ave, Oakland, CA 94618; ⓣ510/658-7470.
**Travel Books & Language Center**, 4437 Wisconsin Ave, Washington, DC; ⓣ1-800/220-2665, ⓦwww.bookweb.org/bookstore/travelbks.
**Ulysses Travel Bookshop**, 4176 St-Denis, Montréal; ⓣ514/843-9882, ⓦwww.ulysses.ca.
**World Wide Books and Maps**, 1247 Granville St, Vancouver; ⓣ604/687-3320, ⓦwww.worldofmaps.com.

#### UK and Ireland

**Blackwell's Map and Travel Shop**, 53 Broad St, Oxford; ⓣ01865/792 792, ⓦwww.bookshop.blackwell.co.uk.
**Daunt Books**, 83 Marylebone High St, London W1; ⓣ020/7224 2295.
**Easons Bookshop**, 40 O'Connell St, Dublin; ⓣ01/873 3811, ⓦwww.eason.ie.
**John Smith and Sons**, 57–61 St Vincent St, Glasgow; ⓣ0141/552 3377, ⓦwww.johnsmith.co.uk.
**Stanfords**, 12–14 Long Acre, London WC2; ⓣ020/7836 1321, ⓦwww.stanfords.co.uk.
**The Travel Bookshop**, 13–15 Blenheim Crescent, London W11; ⓣ020/7229 5260, ⓦwww.thetravelbookshop.co.uk.

# Travelers with disabilities



**Hawaii is among the best-equipped vacation destinations in the world when it comes to meeting the needs of travelers with disabilities, with most of its hotels scrupulously providing wheelchair ramps and other facilities. Oahu has been ranked as the most accessible place in the United States by the Society for the Advancement of Travel for the Handicapped. This nonprofit travel industry group includes tour operators, travel agents, managers of hotels and airlines as well as people with disabilities, and given time will pass on all queries to the relevant members; the head office is at 347 Fifth Ave, Suite 610, New York NY 10016 (Ⓣ212/447-7284, Ⓦwww.sath.org).**

The **State of Hawaii Disability and Communication Access Board** produces the *Aloha Guide to Accessibility in the State of Hawaii*, which details facilities for travelers with disabilities on each of the islands. It's available in full on their website, or you can ask for a printed copy to be mailed to you; contact their head office at 919 Ala Moana Blvd, Honolulu HI 96814 (Ⓣ586-8121, Ⓕ586-8129, Ⓦwww.state.hi.us/health/dcab/). You can also obtain copies from the Hawaii Center for Independent Living, Suite 102, 414 Kauwili St, Honolulu HI 96817 (Ⓣ522-5400, Ⓦwww.hawaii.gov/health/cpd_indx.htm). For more general information, Access–Able (Ⓦwww.access–able.com) is a wide-ranging online resource for travelers with disabilities.

**Rental cars** with hand controls are available from Avis and Hertz outlets; arrangements should be made at least a month in advance. Accessible Vans of Hawaii, 186 Mehani Circle, Kīhei HI96753 (Ⓣ879-5521, Ⓦwww.accessiblevans.com), rents out wheelchair-accessible vans on Oahu, Maui, Kauai and the Big Island, and also runs island tours and shuttle services. On Oahu, transportation for travelers with disabilities, including sightseeing tours and trips to special events, is available through Handi-Cabs of the Pacific, PO Box 22428, Honolulu HI 96823 (Ⓣ524-3866), while C R Newton, 1575 S Beretania St (Ⓣ949-8389, Ⓦwww.crnewton.com), rents wheelchairs, scooters and crutches. Most TheBus vehicles are adapted to suit passengers with physical disabilities.

Guide dogs for the blind are exempt from Hawaii's otherwise strict **quarantine** regulations; full details can be obtained from the Animal Quarantine Facility (Ⓣ483-7171, Ⓦwww.hawaii.gov).

# Senior travelers

**Hawaii is a popular destination for senior travelers; most attractions offer reduced rates for seniors and many hotels have special deals on rooms in quiet periods. For discounts on accommodation and vehicle rental, US residents aged 50 or over should consider joining the American Association of Retired Persons, 601 E St NW, Washington DC 20049 (ⓣ202/434-2277 or 1-800/424-3410, ⓦwww.aarp.com). The Golden Age passport, which entitles holders to free admission to US National Parks, is detailed on p.38.**

The University of Hawaii at Hilo on the Big Island runs Elderhostel programs each summer on all the Hawaiian islands. Participating senior citizens take courses in various aspects of Hawaiian culture and history, with fees covering board, lodging and tuition. For details contact the Program Director, UH Hilo Conference Center, 200 W Kawili St, Hilo HI 96720 (ⓣ974-7555, ⓦconference.uhh.hawaii.edu/elderhostel.html). Elderhostel's national headquarters is at 11 Ave de Fayette, Boston MA 02111 (ⓣ978/323-4141 or 1-877/426-8056, ⓦwww.elderhostel.org).

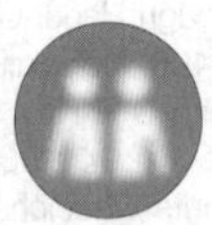

# Gay and lesbian travelers

**The greatest concentration of gay and lesbian activism in Hawaii is in Honolulu, though the state as a whole is liberal on social issues. It's one of 25 states to allow consensual "sodomy," with no criminal laws against private sex acts and a guarantee of privacy in the constitution. Hawaii hit the national headlines in May 1993 when a decision of its Supreme Court was seen as clearing the way for the legalization of same-sex marriages, and a 1997 state law granted equal rights to same-gender couples and their families in most areas of the law. "Gay marriage" as such, however, is not yet on the statute book.**

Full listings for **Honolulu**'s gay and lesbian scene appear on p.110. Gay-friendly **accommodation** can be found on all the islands, including the *Waikīkī Beachside Hotel & Hostel* in Waikīkī (ⓣ923-9566; see p.63); the *Wailana Inn* (ⓣ874-3131; see p.315) on **Maui**; *Mahina Kai* (ⓣ822-9451; see p.447) on **Kauai**; and *Kalani Oceanside Eco-Resort* (ⓣ965-7828; see p.233) and *Hale Ohia* (ⓣ967-7986; see p.253) on the **Big Island**.

The best-known gay **beaches** are Queen's Surf and Diamond Head on Oahu, Donkey Beach on Kauai, Honokōhau Beach on the Big Island, and the Little Beach at Mākena on Maui.

Among the state's gay **organizations** are the Gay & Lesbian Community Center (ⓣ951-7000) and Honolulu Gay Support Group (ⓣ532-9000) on Oahu; Gay Lesbian 'Ohana Maui on Maui (ⓣ224-4566); and

Lambda Aloha on Kauai (ⓣ823-MAHU).

Pacific Ocean Holidays, PO Box 88245, Honolulu HI 96830-8245 (ⓣ923-2400 or 1-800/735-6600, ⓕ923-2499, ⓦwww.gayhawaii.com/vacation/index.html), organizes all-inclusive **package vacations** in Hawaii for gay and lesbian travelers. It also publishes the thrice-yearly *Pocket Guide to Hawaii*, a useful booklet of gay listings throughout the state (available free in Hawaii, or by mail for $5 per issue, one year's subscription $12). Other useful sources of **information** include Matthew Link's *Rainbow Handbook* (ⓦwww.rainbowhandbook.com), a self-published guidebook to all the Hawaiian islands available from local bookstores for $15, and various websites such as ⓦgayhawaii.com.

# Costs, money and banks

**Although it's possible to have an inexpensive vacation in Hawaii, there's no getting away from the fact that prices on the islands are consistently higher than in the rest of the United States. With 85 percent of the state's food and 92 percent of its fuel having to be shipped in, the cost of living is reckoned to be around forty percent above the US average. Locals call it the "Paradise Tax," saying it's the price you pay for living in paradise.**

## Daily costs

How much you spend each day is, of course, up to you, but it's hard to get any sort of breakfast for under $6, a cheap lunch can easily come to $12, and an evening meal in a restaurant, with drinks, is likely to be $25–30, even if you're trying to economize. Buying groceries and cooking for yourself can obviously cut costs, but wherever you shop prices will probably be more than you're used to. All the major islands have at least one hostel, charging around $16–20 for a dorm bed, but otherwise even the cheapest hotels and B&Bs tend to charge well over $60 a night for a double room, and a rental car with gas won't cost less than $25 a day. It's easy to spend $75 per person per day before you've even done anything: pay for a snorkel cruise, let alone a helicopter ride, and you've cleared $100.

Throughout this book, you'll find detailed price information for lodging and eating on all the islands. Unless otherwise indicated, hotel price symbols (explained on p.27) refer to the price of a double room for most of the year, exclusive of taxes, while restaurant prices are for food only and don't include drinks or service.

A state **sales tax** of 4 percent is currently imposed on all transactions, and is almost never included in the prices displayed in stores or on menus. Hotels impose an additional 7.25 percent tax, adding a total of 11.25 percent to accommodation bills.

## Money and banks

US dollar **travelers' checks** are the best way to carry significant quantities of money, for both American and foreign visitors, as they offer the security of knowing that lost or stolen checks will be replaced. Foreign currency, whether cash or travelers' checks, can be hard to exchange, so foreign travelers should change some of their money into dollars at home. However, Hawaii is absolutely bursting with **automatic teller machine (ATMs)**, which accept most cards issued by domestic and foreign banks. Call your bank before you leave home to make sure that your card will work in Hawaii.

For many services, it's taken for granted that you'll be paying with a **credit card**.

Hotels and car rental companies routinely require an imprint of your card whether or not you intend to use it to pay.

The two major **banks** in Hawaii are the Bank of Hawaii and the First Hawaiian Bank. Both have branches on all the islands, and even the smallest town tends to hold one or the other. Usual opening hours are from 8.30am until 3.30pm Monday through Thursday, and until 6pm on Friday; some branches also open on Saturdays. The Bank of Hawaii belongs to the Plus network of **ATMs**, and the First Hawaiian Bank to the Plus and Cirrus networks, so if you have a cash withdrawal card the chances are you'll be able to use it. Every sizeable shopping mall holds a large array of ATMs; to find the location of the nearest one, call Plus at ⓣ1-800/843-7587, or Cirrus at ⓣ1-800/424-7787.

### Lost Credit Cards and Travelers' Checks – Emergency Numbers

**American Express** checks ⓣ1-800/221-7282
**American Express** cards ⓣ1-800/528-4800
**Diners Club** ⓣ1-800/234-6377
**Mastercard** ⓣ1-800/826-2181
**Thomas Cook** ⓣ1-800/223-9920
**Visa** checks ⓣ1-800/227-6811
**Visa** cards ⓣ1-800/336-8472

# Getting around

**The only way to explore the Hawaiian islands at all thoroughly is to drive. For those planning a completely Waikīkī-centered vacation, Oahu has a reasonable public transport system; everywhere else, if you're not on a package tour, you'll be floundering from the moment you touch down at the airport.**

## Renting a car

The demand for **rental cars** in Hawaii is great – in addition to the millions of tourists, there are all the locals who can't take their cars with them when they travel from island to island – but there's such a plentiful supply that competition among the rental companies is fierce. The average Honolulu rate of $41 per day ranks as the lowest of all the hundred largest cities in the US.

As you'll see from the chart opposite, the **national rental chains** are represented on all the major islands, and every airport in the state has at least one outlet. Call their toll-free numbers for reservations, as most individual offices cannot even advise on rates or availability. With so much competition between the various outlets, and so many short-lived special offers, it's hard to quote specific prices, but a target rate for the cheapest economy car with unlimited mileage should be something around $35 per day or $175 per week. Alamo can usually be relied upon for budget rates. Avis and Hertz allow drivers to pay the weekly rate even when driving different cars on different islands; all the rest charge separately for each vehicle. At present, no companies will rent cars to anyone under 21, and drivers ages 21–24 often have to supply additional guarantees or simply pay extra.

Before you commit yourself to a rate, check whether your **airline** – or your **hotel**, **B&B** or **hostel** – can offer a discount on car rental. Some hotels even supply free cars for guests who stay for a week or longer. In **Waikīkī** in particular, you can save money if you shop around. Budget, for example, offers $75 three-day rentals on compact cars, and throws in a slew of free and discount coupons for island attractions, while

## Car Rental Chains

| | Alamo | Avis | Budget | Dollar | Hertz | National |
|---|---|---|---|---|---|---|
| **OAHU** | | | | | | |
| Honolulu Airport | ✔ | ✔ | ✔ | ✔ | ✔ | ✔ |
| Waikīkī | ✔ | ✔ | ✔ | ✔ | ✔ | ✔ |
| **BIG ISLAND** | | | | | | |
| Hilo Airport | ✔ | ✔ | ✔ | ✔ | ✔ | ✔ |
| Kona Airport | ✔ | ✔ | ✔ | ✔ | ✔ | ✔ |
| Waikoloa Resort | | | ✔ | | | |
| Mauna Lani Resort | | | ✔ | | ✔ | |
| **MAUI** | | | | | | |
| Kahului Airport | ✔ | ✔ | ✔ | ✔ | ✔ | ✔ |
| Kā'anapali/Kapalua | ✔ | ✔ | ✔ | ✔ | ✔ | ✔ |
| Hāna | | | | ✔ | | |
| Kīhei/Wailea | | ✔ | ✔ | | | |
| **KAUAI** | | | | | | |
| Līhu'e Airport | ✔ | ✔ | ✔ | ✔ | ✔ | ✔ |
| Po'ipū | | ✔ | | | | |
| **MOLOKAI** | | | ✔ | ✔ | | |
| **LANAI** | | | | ✔ | | |

| | US/Canada | Hawaii | Britain | Australia | Web (Ⓦwww.) |
|---|---|---|---|---|---|
| Alamo | 1-800/327-9633 | As US | 0870/606 0100 | | alamo.com |
| Avis | 1-800/331-1212 | 1-800/831-8000 | 020/8848 8733 | 1-800/225 533 | avis.com |
| Budget | 1-800/527-0700 | As US | 0800/181181 | 1-300/362 848 | drivebudget.com |
| Dollar | 1-800/800-4000 | 1-800/367-7006 | 01895/233300 | 1-800/358 008 | dollar.com |
| Hertz | 1-800/654-3001<br>1-800/263-0600(Can) | As US | 0181/679 1799 | 13/3039 | hertz.com |
| National | 1-800/227-7368 | As US | 0870/536 5365 | | nationalcar.com |

**Discount car rental websites**

Ⓦwww.expedia.com (US) Ⓦwww.travelocity.com (US) Ⓦwww.travelnow.com (US)
Ⓦwww.expedia.co.uk (UK) Ⓦwww.travelocity.co.uk (UK)

agencies such as Magnum, 2134 Kalākaua Ave (Ⓣ923-7825), and VIP Car Rental, 234 Beach Walk (Ⓣ922-4605), offer advantageous rates.

When you rent, you'll probably be pressured to pay around $12 extra per day for **Collision Damage Waiver** (CDW), a form of insurance that absolves you of liability for any damage to your vehicle. Controversially, Hawaii is a "no-fault state," meaning that drivers are always held responsible for whatever befalls their own vehicle, so CDW cover is more important here than elsewhere. American car owners should call their insurance companies to check if they're covered by policies they already hold; some credit card companies also provide card holders with car-rental insurance coverage. Whether or not you choose to buy CDW is a purely personal decision; some people regard it as little short of extortion; others feel it gives them peace of mind.

## Driving in Hawaii

On the whole, **driving** in Hawaii is both easy and enjoyable. Most of the islands effectively have just one main road, so there's little risk of getting lost, and with such small distances to cover no one seems to be in too much of a hurry. The main problem is learning not to dawdle too much while you admire the scenery.

However, there are a few provisos. **Honolulu** is a large and confusing city, with major rush-hour traffic congestion, a short-

## Flight-Seeing Tours

Over the last couple of decades, helicopter flight-seeing tours have been one of the few booming sectors of the Hawaiian economy. On most of the islands, you can circle the entire island in a relatively short flight and feel that you've glimpsed wonders you would otherwise never have seen.

However, the industry ran into difficulty in the 1990s, after fifteen accidental deaths in three years. Most of those involved plunges over the enormous Nā Pali cliffs of Kauai, while on the Big Island there was a much-publicized incident in which a camera crew crash-landed as they filmed Kīlauea and were trapped for two days in the erupting crater. As a result, restrictions were hastily imposed, requiring all single-engine aircraft, including helicopters, to maintain a minimum altitude of at least 500 feet. Helicopter rides these days are now more sedate affairs, not the roller-coaster rides they used to be, and they no longer swoop down to hover over single spots. However, fixed-wing, twin-engine aircraft can still fly low; as they're cheaper than helicopters, they make a good-value alternative to a chopper flight.

Operators on each island are listed in the relevant chapter introductions.

age of parking spaces, and a good bus system. There's no real need to drive while you're there, and renting a car at the airport after a tiring flight can be a recipe for disaster. Elsewhere, the **coastal highways** can be slow and tortuous, and often narrow to a single lane to cross tiny bridges. Bear in mind, too, that it's dark by 7pm, and stretches of road between towns are not lit, so **driving at night** is no fun.

Apart from the obvious fact that in Hawaii, as in the rest of the US, you drive on the right, the one rule of the road that can trouble foreign visitors is that, unless specifically prohibited, drivers are allowed, after a careful pause, **to turn right on a red light**.

Typical **gas** prices are around thirty percent above the US average, so you can easily pay $2.20 per gallon. Keep a closer eye on your fuel gauge than usual; sightseeing expeditions can carry you 25 miles into the wilderness on dead-end roads, which makes for a fifty-mile round-trip before you see another gas station.

### Cycling

As detailed throughout this book, **bikes** are available for rent on all the Hawaiian islands, usually for in-town use rather than long-distance explorations. There's also a craze for **"downhill cycling adventures,"** in which groups of tourists are taken by van to some appropriately lofty spot and then allowed to freewheel back to base. The most famous of these is the daily dawn descent from the top of Haleakalā on Maui, from which you can ride forty miles without pedalling once (see p.329). Note that cycles are not allowed on hiking trails in national or state parks.

Some of the companies listed on p.13 organize guided **cycle-touring** vacations, but few visitors bring their own bikes and tour the islands themselves. There's no compelling reason why not; the Big Island in particular would make an excellent destination for a camping trip by bike, while over the last decade Maui has added cycle lanes to all its main highways.

"Getting around" sections for each island, with full details of public transport and island tours, appear in the introductions to each chapter.

### Public transport

While Oahu can boast an excellent network of **buses** – detailed on p.53 – **public transport** on the other islands is minimal in the extreme. Kauai and the Big Island both have much more restricted bus systems, Maui and Lanai have a few very localized shuttle services, and Molokai has nothing at all. To get to or from the airport, you can always call a taxi or minivan service, but that's no way to go sightseeing.

The only **railroads** still operating in Hawaii are the "Sugar Cane Train," which offers daily musical excursions between Lahaina and Kā'anapali on Maui (see p.279), and a short stretch in southwest Oahu, where the Hawaii Railway Society runs Sunday afternoon jaunts (see p.142).

# Accommodation

**Prospective visitors who think of Hawaii as an expensive destination won't be reassured to know that the average cost of a single night's accommodation is around $155. That figure, however, is boosted by the three- or four-hundred-dollar rates for the lavish resorts at the top end of the spectrum. On all the islands, you can reasonably expect to find a good standard of hotel, condo or B&B for under $100 per night: Molokai is the cheapest, followed in ascending order by Oahu, the Big Island, Kauai, Maui and Lanai. Overall occupancy rates tend to hover between seventy and eighty percent, so at most times of the year it's possible to book a room at short notice.**

All these prices, along with the prices indicated throughout this book, are based on the hotel's own **rack rates** – the rate you'll be offered if you simply walk through the door and ask for a room for the night. While there's little room for bargaining in the smaller inns or B&Bs, in the larger hotels it's very possible to cut costs by buying a **package deal** through one of the operators or airlines listed in the "Getting there" sections of this book. Ask your local travel agent or even inquire directly from the hotel, which should be able to offer you an all-inclusive deal. If you're happy to stay in local inns and hostels, then you can of course budget for lower room rates – and it's worth considering the possibility of **camping** (see p.37 for further details).

Detailed advice on where to stay on each individual island, with specific recommendations, appears at the start of the relevant chapter. With the exception of the Big Island, it's relatively easy to explore each island from a single base. Few people tour from place to place on any one island, staying in a different town each night, and hotels much prefer guests to make reservations well in advance.

## Resorts

If you haven't visited a major tropical vacation destination before, you may not be familiar with the concept of a **resort** in the sense of an individual property run (most often) by a major chain such as *Hyatt*

### Accommodation Price Codes

Throughout this book, accommodation prices have been graded with the symbols below, covering the full spectrum of available rooms in each establishment and ranging upwards from the quoted nightly rate for the least expensive double room for most of the year, not including state taxes of 11.25 percent.

Hostels, in which dorm beds (rather than double rooms) are usually available for $15-20, have been coded with symbol ❶. Both hostels and budget hotels usually keep the same rates throughout the year, but in more expensive properties, rooms normally priced above $70 tend to rise by an average of $15–30 in the peak seasons – from Christmas to Easter and June to August. However, it's possible to obtain much better rates for top-range accommodation by booking your room as part of an all-inclusive package. Detailed lists of tour operators appear on p.13 (US/Can), p.14 (Aus/NZ) and p.16 (UK).

❶ up to $40
❷ $40–70
❸ $70–100
❹ $100–150
❺ $150–200
❻ $200–250
❼ $250–300
❽ $300–400
❾ over $400

*Regency* or *Sheraton*. These gigantic, sprawling enclaves, each holding hundreds or even thousands of rooms, are more than just hotels. Often located far from any town, they are equipped with their own restaurants, stores, swimming pools, beaches, golf courses, tennis courts, walking trails and anything else you can think of, all designed to ensure that guests never feel the need to leave the property. Such luxury doesn't come cheap – typical ocean-view rooms are likely to cost over $300 a night, and suites can go for $2000 or more – and since the resorts are located purely for sun rather than culture or even scenery, they often hold little to remind you that you're in Hawaii at all.

This kind of development was pioneered on Maui and the Big Island during the 1960s, when entrepreneurs realized that the islands' bleak and inhospitable leeward coasts were dry and hot enough to make it worth constructing brand-new oases from scratch. Where beaches didn't exist they were sculpted into the coastline; coconut palms were flown in and replanted; and turf was laid on top of the lava to build championship-quality golf courses.

Waikoloa, Mauna Lani and Mauna Kea on the Big Island, and the larger conglomerations of Kā'anapali, Kapalua and Wailea on Maui, have been joined by the *Ihilani Resort* and *Turtle Bay Hilton* at opposite corners of Oahu, the *Lodge at Kō'ele* and *Manele Bay Hotel* on Lanai, and the *Kauai Marriott* and the new town of Princeville on Kauai.

## Hotels, motels and condos

In addition to the paramount example of **Waikīkī** on Oahu, large clusters of conventional **hotels** have grown up in areas such as **Kīhei** on Maui, **Kailua** on the Big Island, and **Po'ipū** on Kauai. While these may look far less opulent and distinctive than the resorts described above – and barely distinguishable from each other – the standard of the rooms is dependably high. You can be sure of the amenities that American travelers take for granted, certainly including an en-suite bathroom and, as a rule, a balcony of some description as well (which is universally known as a ***lānai***). Room rates vary from perhaps $250 per night at the top of the spectrum down to a little below $100. Virtually every hotel has at least one **restaurant**, where charges can be billed to your room account; hotel restaurants are usually open to nonresidents as well.

The distinction between a hotel room and a **condominium** apartment is not always clear, as the same building may hold some private condo apartments and others rented by the night to short-term guests. The difference lies in the types of facilities each offers. An individual condo unit is likely to be more comfortable and better equipped than a typical hotel room, often with a kitchenette, but on the other hand, a condominium building may not have a lobby area, daily housekeeping service, restaurants or other hotel amenities.

**Motels** on the usual American model are very rare, and representatives of the major national motel chains all but nonexistent. Certain older towns – often those that declined rather than grew in the last century – do, however, retain basic hotels that were originally built to accommodate migrant agricultural laborers. In most cases these are minimally equipped flophouses, which may charge as little as $20 per night, though those that haven't shut down altogether have tended to upgrade over time.

## Bed and breakfasts

The definition of **bed and breakfast** accommodation stretches from a simple room or two in a private home, through self-contained, self-catering cottages, to luxurious fifteen-room inns; surprisingly, not all include breakfast. In principle, however, the standards are very high. The cheapest rooms, perhaps sharing a bathroom with one other guest room, start at around $50 per night, while for more like $90 per night you can expect your own well-furnished apartment, with all facilities. The owners are often friendly and full of advice on making the most of your vacation, though it's unusual to find a B&B run by anyone other than relatively recent immigrants from the mainland.

Most small-scale B&Bs are located away from the busier tourist areas, in the more scenic, but perhaps slightly wetter or cooler parts of the islands where people actually choose to live. Thus there are particular concentrations in the upcountry meadowlands of Maui and the Big Island, across the mountains from Honolulu on Oahu's windward coast, and a couple of miles back from the ocean on the east coast of Kauai. If you plan

## Hostels

Each of the four largest islands has at least one budget hostel, where you can get a bed in a dormitory for under $20 per night or a very basic private double room for $30–40. Few of these are affiliated to international hosteling organizations, and some only admit non-US citizens. As a rule, they're strongly geared towards young surfers.



to spend a night or two at Hawaii Volcanoes National Park on the Big Island, there's little alternative to the wide assortment of B&Bs in the nearby village of Volcano.

For a strong and reliable selection of top-quality B&Bs on all the islands, and an especially wide range on the Big Island, you can't do better than to contact **Hawaii's Best Bed & Breakfasts** agency, PO Box 563, Kamuela HI 96743 (Ⓣ885-4550 or 1-800/262-9912, Ⓕ885-0559, Ⓦwww bestbnb.com).

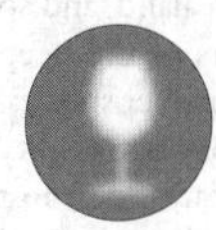

# Food and drink

**If you imagine that eating in Hawaii will consist of an endless feast of fresh fruit and fish, you'll be disappointed to find that the islands are not bountiful Gardens of Eden: the state produces less than twenty percent of the food it consumes. Year by year less of its land is devoted to agriculture, with the main crops in any case being sugar and pineapples. Polynesian cuisine can mean little more than putting a pineapple ring on top of a burger, and amazingly, more than half of all the Spam eaten in the United States is consumed in Hawaii.**

However, there are two strong factors working in your favor. First of all, there's the state's **ethnic diversity**. Immigrants from all over the world have brought their own national dishes and recipes here, which you can sample in restaurants all over the state. In some cases, traditions have mingled to create intriguing new cuisines. Second, the presence of thousands of **tourists**, many prepared to pay top rates for good food, means that the islands have some truly superb restaurants, run by internationally renowned chefs.

## Local restaurants

While the national fast-food chains are well represented in Hawaii, locally owned budget restaurants, diners and takeout stands throughout the state serve a hybrid cuisine that draws on the traditions of the US mainland along with Japan, China, Korea and the Philippines; the resultant mixture has a slight but definite Hawaiian twist. In fact, **"local"** food has a distinct meaning in Hawaii and specifically applies to this multicultural melange.

**Breakfast** tends to be the standard combination of eggs, meat, pancakes, muffins or toast. At midday, the usual dish is the **plate lunch**, a tray holding meat and rice as well as potato or macaroni salad and costing something between $6 and $9. **Bento** is the Japanese equivalent, with mixed meats and rice; in Filipino diners, you'll be offered **adobo**, which is pork or chicken stewed with garlic and vinegar and served in a similar way. Korean barbecue, **kal bi** – prepared with sesame – is especially tasty, with the word "barbecue" indicating that the meat or fish has been marinated rather than necessarily cooked on an open grill. One simple but filling recipe – thought to be of Chinese origin – is **saimin** (pronounced *sy-min* not *say-min*), a bowl of clear soup filled with noodles and other mixed ingredients that has become something of a Hawaiian state dish. The carbohydrate-packed ***loco moco*** is a fried egg served on a hamburger with gravy and rice, while the favorite local dessert is **shave ice**, slushy scrapings of ice flavored with rainbow-colored syrups. Finally, a **malasada** is a sweet Portuguese doughnut, best eaten hot and fresh.

Food in general is often referred to as ***kaukau***, and it's also worth knowing that **pūpūs** (pronounced *poo-poos*) is a general term for little snacks, the kind of finger food that is given away at early evening Happy Hours.

## Fine dining

A captive clientele of affluent tourists enables the more exclusive resort regions of Hawaii

### Hawaiian Fish

Although the ancient Hawaiians were expert offshore fishermen, as well as being highly sophisticated fish farmers, with intricate networks of fish ponds laced around the coastline, the great majority of the fish eaten in Hawaii nowadays is imported. Local fishing is not done on a large enough scale to meet the demand, and in any case many of the species that tourists expect to find on menus thrive in much cooler waters. Thus salmon and crab come from Alaska, mussels from New Zealand, and so on, although Maine lobsters are now being farmed in the cold waters of the deep ocean off Honokōhau, and aquafarms on several islands are raising freshwater species.

However, if you feel like being adventurous, you should get plenty of opportunity to try some of the Pacific species caught nearby; the list below translates the most common Hawaiian names. If it still leaves you in the dark, personal recommendations include *opah*, which is chewy and salty like swordfish; the chunky *'ōpakapaka*, which because of its red color (associated with happiness) is often served on special occasions; the succulent white *ono* (which means "delicious" in Hawaiian); and the dark *'ahi*, the most popular choice for sashimi.

| | |
|---|---|
| *'ahi* | yellow-fin tuna |
| *aku* | skipjack tuna |
| *a'u* | swordfish or marlin |
| *'ehu* | red snapper |
| *hāpu'upu'u* | sea bass |
| *hebi* | spear fish |
| *kākū* | barracuda |
| *kalekale* | pink snapper |
| *kāmano* | salmon |
| *kūmū* | red goat fish |
| *lehi* | yellow snapper |
| *mahimahi* | dorado or dolphin fish |
| *mano* | shark |
| *moi* | thread fish |
| *onaga* | red snapper |
| *ono* | mackerel/tuna-like fish |
| *'ōpae* | shrimp |
| *opah* | moonfish |
| *'ōpakapaka* | pink snapper |
| *pāpio* | pompano |
| *uhu* | parrot fish |
| *uku* | gray snapper |
| *ulua* | jack fish |
| *weke* | goat fish |

to hold some of the world's most lavish and inventive **restaurants**. These are the places where something approaching a distinctive Hawaiian cuisine is being created, known variously as **Pacific Rim**, **Euro-Asian** or **Hawaii Regional**. In its ideal form it combines foods and techniques from all the countries and ethnic groups that have figured in Hawaiian history, using the freshest ingredients possible. The top chefs – such as Jean-Marie Josselin, whose **Pacific Café** can be found on Kauai and Maui, and Roy Yamaguchi, who runs **Roy's** restaurants on all four major islands – seek to preserve natural flavors by such methods as flash-frying meat and fish like the Chinese, baking it whole like the Hawaiians, or even serving it raw like the Japanese. The effect is enhanced by the delicate addition of Thai herbs and spices, and by the sheer inventiveness of modern Californian cooking.

Throughout the islands, you'll also find plenty of conventional **American** shrimp and steak specialists, as well as high-class **Italian**, **Thai** and **Chinese** places. Many restaurants offer all-you-can-eat **buffets** one or more nights of the week; they all sacrifice quality for quantity, so you might as well go for the cheaper ones. Lastly, to cater for that much-prized customer, the Japanese big spender, many of the larger hotels have authentic and very good **Japanese** restaurants, which tend to specialize in discreet sushi and sashimi dining rather than the flamboyant *teppanyaki* style, where knife-juggling chefs cook at your table.

## Local ingredients

As well as the many kinds of **fish** listed in the box opposite, widely used **local ingredients** include **ginger** and **macadamia nuts** (large, creamy, and somewhat bland white nuts said to contain a hundred calories per nut, even when they aren't coated with chocolate). Bright red **'ōhelo berries**, which taste like cranberries, were once sacred to the volcano goddess Pele and to eat one was punishable by death; now they're served up in gourmet restaurants. **Avocados** are widely grown and are even richer than you may be used to, as are fruits such as **guava** (an imported pest that's a staple for hikers, as it grows wild along most wilderness trails), **papaya** and **mango**. Watch out also for the small yellow **apple bananas**, with their distinct savory tang and, of course, the ever-present **coconut**.

## Drink

The usual range of **wines** (mostly Californian, though both Maui and the Big Island have their own tiny wineries) and **beers** (mainly imported either from the mainland or Mexico) are sold at Hawaiian restaurants and bars, but at some point every visitor seems to insist on getting wiped out by a tropical **cocktail** or two. Among the most popular are the **Mai Tai**, which should contain at least two kinds of rum, together with orange Curaçao and lemon juice; the **Blue Hawaii**, in which vodka is colored with blue Curaçao; and the **Planter's Punch**, made with light rum, grenadine, bitters and lemon juice.

Tap **water** in Hawaii is safe to drink, though it's a scarce enough resource in places that some restaurants will only bring it to your table on request. If you're hiking, however, make sure you take enough water with you. Never drink untreated stream water: see p.38.

Mention should also be made of Hawaii's most famous gourmet product, **Kona coffee**. Deliciously rich local coffees are available in small cafés and espresso bars throughout the state, although the Kona name can only be used for coffees grown on the southwestern slopes of the Big Island. For more details, see p.169.

# Communications and media

**Telephone connections on and between the Hawaiian islands and across the Pacific to the mainland US are generally efficient and reliable. The snail-like pace of mail service to and from the islands means that fax and email are probably the best options for written communications.**

## Phones and the mail

The **telephone area code** for the entire state of Hawaii is ⓣ 808. Calls within any one island count as local; you don't need to dial the area code and it costs a flat-rate 25¢ on pay phones. To call another island, prefix ⓣ 1-808 before the number; charges vary according to the time of day and distance involved. The cheapest long-distance rates apply between 11pm and 8am from Monday to Thursday and between 5pm Friday and 8am Monday; an intermediate rate applies between 5pm and 11pm from Monday to Thursday.

Hotels impose huge surcharges, so it's best to use a **phone card** for long-distance calls. In preference to the ones issued by the major phone companies, you'll find it simpler and cheaper to choose from the various **pre-paid** cards sold in almost all groceries and general stores.

There are **post offices** in all the main towns, generally open between 8.30am and 4pm on weekdays and for an hour or two on Saturday mornings. **Mail service** is extremely slow as all mail between Hawaii and the rest of the world, and even between Hawaiian islands other than Oahu, is routed via Honolulu. From anywhere except Honolulu, allow a week for your letter to reach destinations in the US and as much as two weeks or more for the rest of the world. From Honolulu itself, reckon on four days to the mainland US and eight days to anywhere else in the world.

### Telephone

To make an **international call** to Hawaii, dial your country's international access code, then 1 for the US, then 808 for Hawaii.

To place a call from Hawaii to the rest of the world, dial ⓣ 011 then the relevant country code as follows:

| | | | |
|---|---|---|---|
| Britain | 44 | Australia | 61 |
| Ireland | 353 | New Zealand | 64 |
| Canada | 1 | | |

## Newspapers, magazines, radio and TV

In addition to Hawaii's two statewide daily **newspapers**, the *Honolulu Advertiser* and *Honolulu Star-Bulletin*, each island has at least one regular newspaper of its own. In addition, you're certain to come across glossy **free magazines** aimed at tourists, such as the *This Week* and *Gold* chains (*Oahu This Week, Big Island Gold*, etc), which are widely available all over the islands. The copy – predominantly advertising – may barely change from week to week, but they're filled with useful discount offers and coupons.

The average rental-car **radio** will pick up perhaps half-a-dozen homegrown stations on each island, plus another half-dozen Honolulu stations. Wherever you are, you'll probably be able to pick up Hawaii Public Radio on 90.7FM, and CNN on 650AM, and if you can't live without Rush and G Gordon Liddy, you'll find them somewhere too. In the backwoods, however, huge volcanoes tend to block the reception, so the station selection can drop to next to nothing.

All the principal US **TV** networks are also available, along with some very low-key local **cable TV** stations. In almost every hotel, at least one channel plays an endless loop of tourist information about whichever island you're on, consisting mainly of promotional clips on tourist activities.

# Entertainment and festivals



**If you consider wild nightlife essential to the success of your Hawaiian vacation, head straight for the bright lights and glitter of Waikīkī. Everywhere else on the islands, with the possible exception of Lahaina on Maui, any attempt to do some serious clubbing is likely to prove a severe disappointment. That's not to say there's nothing going on at all, but Hawaii is a rural state, and away from Honolulu there's nothing larger than a small country town. On Maui they call 10pm "Maui midnight" because everyone has gone to bed; Kauai and the Big Island are even sleepier.**

Full entertainment listings for Honolulu and Waikīkī appear on p.110 onwards. Otherwise most of the nightlife and entertainment in Hawaii is arranged by the major **hotels** – almost all put on some form of entertainment for their guests, and many feature live musicians every night. The music as often as not consists of anodyne medleys of 1950s Hawaiian hits with a cocktail-jazz tinge, but the setting is usually romantic enough for that not to matter. **Restaurants** and **cafés** also use live music to attract diners, whether in the form of full-fledged bands or simple acoustic strummers.

Unless you coincide with one of the major annual festivals, you're unlikely to see an authentic *hula* performance, though all the main islands have several weekly commercial ***lū'aus*** or "traditional feasts", which can be fun if you're in the right mood. Big-name touring musicians tend to perform in Honolulu, and with luck on Maui as well, while the other islands have to settle for regular concert appearances by the stars of the Hawaiian music scene. For more about *hula* and Hawaiian music, see p.535.

## Holidays and Festivals

### Public holidays

As well as observing the national public holidays, Hawaii also has a number of its own:

**Jan 1** New Year's Day
**3rd Mon in Jan** Dr Martin Luther King Jr's Birthday
**3rd Mon in Feb** Presidents' Day
**March 26** Prince Kūhiō Day
**Easter Monday**
**May 1** Lei Day
**Last Mon in May** Memorial Day
**June 11** Kamehameha Day
**July 4** Independence Day
**3rd Fri in Aug** Admission Day
**1st Mon in Sept** Labor Day
**2nd Mon in Oct** Columbus Day
**Nov 11** Veterans' Day
**4th Thurs in Nov** Thanksgiving
**Dec 25** Christmas Day

### Annual festivals and events

**Jan** Maui Pro Surf Meet; surfing competition, Honolua Bay and Ho'okipa Beach (Maui)
**Feb** Mardi Gras, Hilo (Big Island)
**early March** Whale Fest Week; whale-related events, Lahaina and Kā'anapali (Maui)
**March 17** St Patrick's Day Parade, Waikīkī (Oahu)
**March 26** Prince Kūhiō Day; statewide celebrations
**early April** Maui O'Neill Pro Board; windsurfing competition, Ho'okipa (Maui)
**April** Merrie Monarch Festival, Hilo (Big Island)
**April** Hawaiian Professional Championship Rodeo, Waimānolo (Oahu)
**May 1** Lei Day; statewide celebrations
**3rd Sat in May** Molokai Ka Hula Piko; *hula* festival, Pāpōhaku Beach Park (Molokai)
**late May** Da Kine Classic; windsurfing competition, Kanahā Beach (Maui)
**late May** Bankoh Ho'omana'o; outrigger canoe race, Kā'anapali (Maui) to Waikīkī (Oahu)
**late May/early June** State Fair, Aloha Stadium, Honolulu (Oahu)
**June 11** Kamehameha Day; statewide celebrations

**June** Bankoh Kiho'alu, slack-key guitar festival, Maui Arts and Cultural Center (Maui)
**July 4** Parker Ranch Rodeo, Waimea (Big Island)
**July 4** Makawao Rodeo, Makawao (Maui)
**early July** Quicksilver Cup; windsurfing competition, Kanahā Beach Park (Maui)
**mid-July** Slack Key Festival, Hilo (Big Island)
**mid-July** Hawaii International Jazz Festival, Honolulu (Oahu)
**mid-Aug** Hawaiian International Billfish Tournament, Kailua (Big Island)
**early Sept** Queen Lili'uokalani Long-Distance Canoe Races, Kailua (Big Island)
**late Sept** Run to the Sun: foot race, Pā'ia to Haleakalā (Maui)
**late Sept** Molokai Music Festival; day-long music, crafts and food fair, Meyer Sugar Mill (Molokai)
**Sept/Oct** Aloha Festival; consecutive week-long festivals on each island
**First Sat in Oct** Molokai Mule Run, Kaunakakai (Molokai)
**early Oct** Ironman Triathlon World Championship, Kailua (Big Island)
**Oct** Hāmākua Music Festival, Honoka'a (Big Island)
**late Oct** Mokihana Festival; week-long *hula*, music and crafts festival (Kauai)
**Oct 31** Halloween parade, Lahaina (Maui) and Waikīkī (Oahu)
**early Nov** World Invitation *Hula* Festival, Honolulu (Oahu)
**early Nov** Aloha Classic; windsurfing competition, Ho'okipa (Maui)
**mid-Nov** PGA Grand Slam; golf tournament, Po'ipū (Kauai)
**mid-Nov** Triple Crown of Surfing, Hawaiian Pro, Ali'i Beach Park, Hale'iwa (Oahu)
**Nov** Hawaii International Film Festival, Honolulu (Oahu)
**late Nov/early Dec** Triple Crown of Surfing, World Cup, Sunset Beach (Oahu)
**early Dec** Triple Crown of Surfing, Pipe Masters, Banzai Pipeline (Oahu)
**2nd Sun in Dec** Honolulu Marathon (Oahu)
**Dec 25** Aloha Bowl Football Classic, Aloha Stadium, Honolulu (Oahu).

Note that the exact dates of surfing contests, and in some cases the venues as well, depend on the state of the waves. A more detailed selection of festivals and events on each island appears in the relevant chapter introduction.

# Sea sports and safety

**Hawaii's vast tourism industry is rooted in the picture-book appeal of its endless palm-fringed sandy beaches and crystal-clear fish-filled turquoise ocean. The opportunities for sea sports in the islands are almost infinite, ranging from swimming through snorkeling, scuba diving, fishing and whale watching, to Hawaii's greatest gift to the world, the noble art of surfing. It's all too easy, however, to forget that Hawaiian beaches can be deadly as well as beautiful, and you need to know exactly what you're doing before you enter the water. As well as the general ocean safety advice below, safety tips for specific beaches are given throughout this book.**

No one owns any stretch of beach in Hawaii. Every beach in the state – defined as the area below the vegetation line – is regarded as **public property**. That doesn't mean that you're entitled to stroll across any intervening land between the ocean and the nearest highway; always use the clearly signposted "**public right of way**" footpaths. Whatever impression the large oceanfront hotels may attempt to convey, they can't stop from you using "their" beaches; they can only restrict, but not refuse to supply, parking places for nonguests.

What constitutes the **best beach** in Hawaii is a matter of personal taste, but there are candidates on each of the major islands. For sheer looks, head for **Mākena Beach** on Maui, **Sunset Beach** on Oahu, **Kē'ē Beach** on Kauai, **Kehena Beach** on the Big Island, or **Pāpōhaku Beach** on Molokai. If you want to swim in safety as well, then try **Hāpuna Beach** on the Big Island, **'Anini** on Kauai, **Kailua** on Oahu, or the **Kama'ole** beaches on Maui. And for glamour, of course, there's no beating **Waikīkī**.

## Ocean fun

With average water temperatures of between 75°F and 82°F (24–28°C), the sea in Hawaii is all but irresistible, and most visitors are tempted to try at least one or two of the state's wide range of **ocean sports**.

### Snorkeling

Probably the easiest activity for beginners is **snorkeling**. Equipped with mask, snorkel and fins, you can while away hours and days having face-to-face encounters with the rainbow-colored populations of Hawaii's reefs and lava pools. Well-known sites include **Hanauma Bay** in southeast Oahu, **Kealakekua Bay** on the Big Island, and the islet of **Molokini** off Maui.

You can **rent** snorkel equipment on all the islands, at rates ranging upwards from $2.50 per day/$14 per week. One reliable source is Snorkel Bob's, whose outlets on each island are listed at the start of the relevant chapter.

### Scuba

**Scuba diving** is both expensive and demanding, but with endless networks of submarine lava tubes to explore, and the chance to get that bit closer to some amazing marine life forms, Hawaii is a great diving destination. The Big Island and Maui are the most popular of the islands, but experts rate Lanai even higher, and Kauai is also acquiring a reputation; you'll find a detailed overview, plus lists of diving-boat operators, in the introduction to each chapter of this book. Note that for medical reasons you shouldn't dive within 24 hours of flying or even ascending significantly above sea level, for example towards the summits of Haleakalā on Maui or Mauna Kea on the Big Island.

For a taste of what it's all about, you might like to try **snuba**, which is basically snorkeling from a boat equipped with a longer breathing tube. Many snorkel cruises offer snuba for an extra charge.

### Surfing

The place that invented **surfing** – long before the foreigners came – remains its greatest arena. A recurring theme in ancient legends has young men frittering away endless days in the waves rather than facing up to their duties (see p.518); now young people from all over the world flock to Hawaii to do just that. The sport was popularized early in the twentieth century by champion Olympic swimmer **Duke Kahanamoku**, the original Waikīkī Beach Boy. He toured the world with his sixteen-foot board, demonstrating his skills to admiring crowds and was responsible for introducing surfing to Australia.

Waikīkī lost its best surf breaks when it was re-landscaped at the start of the tourist boom, but with advances in techniques and technology, surfing has never been more popular. Oahu's fabled **North Shore** is a mecca for surf-bums, who ride the waves around Waimea Bay and hang out in the coffee bars of Hale'iwa. Favored spots elsewhere include **Hanalei Bay** on Kauai and **Mā'alaea Bay** on Maui, but surfing at such legendary sites is for experts only. However much you've surfed at home, you need to be very sure you're up to it before you have a go in Hawaii, so start by sampling the conditions at the lesser surf-spots to be found on all the islands. Be warned that surfing is forbidden at some of Hawaii's most popular beaches, to prevent collisions with ordinary bathers.

Inexpensive **surfing lessons** for beginners are on offer in most tourist areas, costing perhaps $20 per hour and coming with a guarantee that you'll ride a wave on your own before it's over. They're great fun, and they really work. An equally exhilarating way to get a taste for the surf is to start out by using a smaller **boogie board**, which you lie on.

### Windsurfing

Since Robbie Naish of Kailua won the first world championships in the 1970s, at the age of 13, Hawaii has also been recognized as the spiritual home of **windsurfing**. This time it's **Maui** that's the prime goal for enthusiasts from around the world, and once again many of them find that Hawaiian waters present challenges on a vastly different scale to what they're used to at home. If you find an oceanfront parking lot on Maui filled with shiny rental cars and bursting with tanned tourists sporting Lycra clothing and expensive equipment, the chances are you're at a beginners' beach. Salt-caked local rustbuckets and cut-off denims are the markers of demanding beaches like **Ho'okipa Beach Park**, the venue for windsurfing's World Cup.

### Fishing

Big-game **fishing**, for marlin especially, is a major attraction for many visitors to Hawaii. On the Kona coast of the **Big Island**, Kailua plays host each August to the prestigious Hawaiian International Billfish Tournament, while fishing charter vessels are available year-round at Honokōhau Harbor, a few miles north. A smaller selection of boats leave from Lahaina and Mā'alaea harbors on **Maui**.

Details on fishing regulations, and thirty-day licenses for freshwater fishing ($4), can be obtained from the Department of Land and Natural Resources, 1151 Punchbowl St, Room 311, Honolulu HI 96813 (☎587-0077).

### Whale watching

A large proportion of the North Pacific's three thousand **humpback whales** winter in Hawaiian waters, between late November and early April. They're especially fond of the shallow channels between Maui, Molokai and Lanai, and are often clearly visible from the coastal highways. In season, **whale-watching** boats set off from all the major islands, and most operators are confident enough to guarantee sightings.

## Ocean safety

It's essential whenever you're in or near the ocean to be aware of **safety issues**. Hawaii is the remotest archipelago on earth, which means that waves have two thousand miles of the misnamed Pacific Ocean to build up their strength before they come crashing into the islands. People born in Hawaii are brought up with a healthy respect for the sea and learn to watch out for all sorts of signs before they swim. You'll be told to throw sticks into the waves to see how they move, or to look for disturbances in the surf that indicate powerful currents, Unless you have local expertise, however, you're better off sticking to the official beach parks and most popular spots, especially those that are shielded by offshore reefs. Not all beaches have lifeguards and warning flags, and unattended beaches are not necessarily safe. Look for other bathers, but whatever your experience elsewhere, don't assume you'll be able to cope with the same conditions as the local kids. Always ask for advice and above all follow the cardinal rule – **Never turn your back on the water**.

The beaches that experience the most accidents and **drownings** are those where waves of four feet or more break directly onto the shore. This varies according to the season, so beaches that are idyllic in summer can be storm-tossed death traps between October and April. If you get caught in a rip current or undertow and find yourself being dragged out to sea, stay calm and remember that the vast majority of such currents disappear within a hundred yards of the shore. Never exhaust yourself by trying to swim against them, but simply allow yourself to be carried out until the force weakens, and then swim first to one side and then back to the shore.

**Sea creatures** to avoid include *wana* (black spiky **sea urchins)**, Portuguese men-of-war **jellyfish**, and **coral** in general, which can give painful, infected cuts. **Shark attacks** are much rarer than popular imagination suggests; in 2000, 79 occurred worldwide, of which ten were fatal. Two of the nonlethal attacks were in Hawaii, both off Maui. Those that do happen are usually due to "misunderstandings," such as surfers idling on their boards who look a bit too much like turtles from below.

## Sun safety

Only expose yourself to the harsh **tropical sun** in moderation; a mere fifteen to thirty minutes is the safe recommendation for the first day. The sun is strongest between 10am and 3pm, and keep in mind that even on overcast days human skin still absorbs harmful UV rays. Use plenty of **sunscreen** – doctors recommend Sun Protection Factor (SPF) 30 for Hawaii – and reapply after

### Emergency Numbers

| | |
|---|---|
| Police, Fire and Ambulance | ☎911 |
| Ocean Search and Rescue | ☎1-800/552-6458 |

swimming. Note, however, that some marine life sanctuaries forbid the use of sunscreen by bathers, which should be enough to discourage you from swimming altogether. Drink lots of (non-alcoholic) liquids as well, to stave off dehydration.



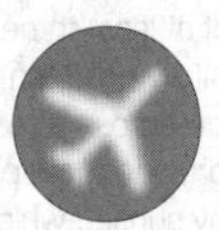

# Hiking and camping

**Hawaii is one of the most exciting hiking destinations imaginable. Well-maintained trails guide walkers through scenery that ranges from dense tropical rainforest to remote deserts and active volcanoes. It's essential, however, to remember that Hawaii is more than a vacation playground, and you may find yourself in some pretty uncompromising wilderness.**

But **camping** in Hawaii need not be a battle with the elements. All the islands hold lovely oceanfront campgrounds where you don't have to do anything more than drive in and pitch your tent; some offer cabins for rent so you needn't even do that.

## Camping

Advice on the best **campgrounds** on each island, and how to obtain permits to stay at them, is given in the introduction to each chapter of this book. The majority of campgrounds are in the various public **parks** scattered across each island. There's a complicated hierarchy of county, state and national parks, each with different authorities, so it's not always obvious whom to contact for permission to camp in a particular spot. However, one thing you cannot do is just set up your tent on some unoccupied piece of land; only camp at designated sites.

On a camping (as opposed to backpacking) vacation, your best bet is to spend most of your time at the **County Beach Parks** ranged along the shoreline of each island. The most appealing of these are on the **Big Island** – where Spencer Beach Park and Punalu'u are especially attractive – and along the north shore of **Kauai**, but Maui and Oahu also have their moments.

County authorities are engaged in a constant struggle to prevent semi-permanent encampments of homeless local people developing at certain sites, so precise regulations on maximum lengths of stay, and even whether a particular park is open at all, tend to change at a moment's notice. On Oahu, for example, all public campgrounds are closed on Wednesday and Thursday nights.

Many of the campgrounds in Hawaii's **state** and **national parks** are in remote spots that can only be reached on foot, but they tend to be set amid utterly sublime scenery. Among the best are the backcountry sites along the **Kalalau Trail** on Kauai's Nā Pali coast, and the national park campgrounds in **Hawaii Volcanoes** park on the Big Island, and atop **Haleakalā** on Maui, both of which also offer rudimentary cabins for rent.

For a full list of state parks and their facilities, contact the Department of Land and Natural Resources, Division of State Parks, 1151 Punchbowl St, Honolulu HI 96813 (Ⓣ587-0300, Ⓦwww.hawaii.gov/dlnr).

## Hiking

All the best **hiking trails** in Hawaii are described in detail in the relevant chapters of this book. Every island has at least one inspiring trail, but the two best destinations for hikers have to be **Kauai** and the **Big Island**.

Kauai has the dual attractions of the spectacular Nā Pali coast, where the **Kalalau Trail** clings to the cliffs through eleven miles of magnificent unspoiled valleys, and Kōke'e State Park high above, where the **Alaka'i**

**Swamp Trail** and the **Awa'awapuhi Trail** trek through the rainforest for amazing overviews of similar rugged scenery.

On the Big Island, it would be easy to spend a week day-hiking trails such as the **Halemaumau** and **Kīlauea Iki** trails in Volcanoes National Park, without the thrill of being inside an active volcano wearing off, and there's potential for countless longer backpacking expeditions.

Maui can offer the **Sliding Sands Trail** through the heart of Haleakalā, and mountain hikes like the **Waihe'e Ridge Trail**, while on Molokai you can clamber through the verdant **Hālawa Valley** to reach a pair of superb waterfalls. Even Honolulu itself has the lovely rainforest trails through **Makiki** and **Mānoa** valleys.

As a rule, all trails remain passable all year, but you can expect conditions to be much muddier between November and April.

## Equipment and safety

All the Hawaiian islands are basically large piles of rough lava, and any **footwear** except sturdy boots is likely to be torn to shreds. Other equipment should include rain gear, a flashlight, insect repellent, sunscreen and sunglasses, some attention-seeking device such as a whistle or a piece of brightly colored clothing, and a basic first aid kit. If you're backpacking, of course, you'll need a waterproof tent and sleeping bag as well. Take things slowly if you're heading up the volcanoes on Maui or the Big Island, as there's a real risk of altitude sickness; if you feel symptoms such as a heavy pulse, shortness of breath, headache and nausea, come back down again. Warm clothing is also essential, with night temperatures low enough to cause hypothermia.

Other safety advice worth bearing in mind: do not hike alone (groups of at least three are preferable), be wary of following even dry streambeds and never wade across streams that are more than waist-high, and allow plenty of time to finish any trail by sunset, which is never later than 7pm and usually much earlier. On typical Hawaiian trails you shouldn't reckon on walking more than 1.5 miles per hour. Most hiking deaths occur when hikers are stranded on cliffs or ledges and then panic; certain trails, as indicated throughout this book, but especially on Kauai, have some really hair-raising spots that you should avoid if you're prone to vertigo.

Carry plenty of **water** when you hike, and drink it as you need it. Trying to conserve water supplies is a false economy, as it takes more water to recover from dehydration than it does to prevent it. Never drink untreated water; **leptospirosis**, a bacterial disease carried by rats and mice in particular, can be contracted through drinking stream water (filtering alone will not purify it) or even from wading through fresh water if you have any cuts or abrasions. Symptoms range from diarrhea, fever and chills through to kidney or heart failure, and appear in anything from two to twenty days. In case of infection, seek treatment immediately; for more information, call the Hawaii Department of Health on Oahu (Ⓣ586-4586, Ⓦwww.state.hi.us/health).

## National Parks Admissions

Hawaii has two full-fledged national parks, Healeakalā on Maui (p.328) and Hawaii Volcanoes on the Big Island (p.234).

They charge for admission, but the park system's national passes, which give free access into all national parks, can be obtained at both. The Golden Eagle pass, which covers almost all public lands in the US, is available to anyone, US citizen or otherwise, for $65 and is valid for one year. The $50 National Parks pass, which provides admission to all national parks and monuments, will suffice for visitors to Hawaii. Both the Golden Access passport, free to US citizens or residents with disabilities, and the Golden Age passport, available to US citizens or residents aged over 62 for a $10 one-time fee, offer unlimited admission for life to all national parks in the US.

# Sports

**Competitive sports are not very much in evidence in Hawaii although local schools and the University of Hawaii boast enthusiastically supported football, basketball and baseball teams. A number of showpiece events take place each year, however, with the highlights of the calendar being December's Honolulu Marathon and the women's and men's outrigger canoe races from Molokai to Oahu in September and October. The big surfing and windsurfing championships take place on Oahu and Maui respectively between October and December, while mid-October sees the Ironman Triathlon on the Big Island. Its superhuman participants race to complete a 2.4-mile ocean swim across Kailua Bay, a 112-mile cycle ride and a full 26-mile marathon – all on the same day.**

As for **participant sports**, many of the most popular activities are ocean-related (see pp.34–37). Most of the larger hotels have **tennis courts** for their guests, and there are public courts on all the islands.

## Golf

A complete list of **golf courses** in Hawaii appears overleaf. The spectacular ocean-front courses at the major **resorts**, designed to tournament specifications, have the highest reputations, but they also have the highest **green fees** – all are well over $100, and the reductions for hotel guests are not all that significant. Rates at **municipal** courses, by contrast, can start as low as $10, while typical **public** courses charge $50–60 per round, with reduced rates early in the morning and last thing at night. Stand-By Golf (Ⓣ1-888/645-2265) is a company that specializes in finding discounted and short-notice golfing opportunities on all the Hawaiian islands.

Golf in Hawaii is not necessarily all that relaxing. Honolulu's public courses are said to be the busiest in the world, using sophisticated computer systems to schedule tee-off times to the minute from dawn until dusk.

The annual ***Hawaii Golf Guide***, published by the Aloha Section PGA (770 Kapi'olani Blvd, Suite 715, Honolulu HI 96813; Ⓣ593-2230), carries complete listings and details of all Hawaii's golf courses.

## Rodeo

Hawaii's tradition of cattle ranching, and the legendary skills of its *paniolo* cowboys – see p.195 – are reflected in several large **rodeos** each summer. The Hawaiian Professional Championship Rodeo takes place at **Waimānolo** on Oahu in April, while **Makawao** on Maui is the scene of the Coors Rodeo on the first weekend in July. The largest ranch in the state, the Big Island's Parker Ranch, celebrates July 4 with a rodeo at **Waimea**. The Molokai Ranch also stages regular events at Maunaloa on **Molokai**.

## Golf Courses in Hawaii

| | Area | Holes | Kind | Fee | Phone |
|---|---|---|---|---|---|
| **Big Island** | | | | | |
| Big Island Country Club | Waikoloa | 18 | Semi-private | $125 | ☎ 325-5044 |
| Hāmākua Country Club | Honoka'a | 9 | Public | $15 | ☎ 775-7244 |
| Hāpuna Golf Course | Kohala | 18 | Resort | $185 | ☎ 880-3000 |
| Hilo Municipal Golf Course | Hilo | 18 | Municipal | $25 | ☎ 959-9601 |
| Kona Country Club | | | | | |
| Ali'i Course | Kailua | 18 | Semi-private | $175 | ☎ 322-2595 |
| Ocean Course | Kailua | 18 | Semi-private | $175 | ☎ 322-2595 |
| Makalei Hawaii Country Club | Kona | 18 | Semi-private | $110 | ☎ 325-6625 |
| Mauna Kea Beach Golf Club | Kohala | 18 | Resort | $195 | ☎ 882-5400 |
| Mauna Lani Resort | | | | | |
| Francis H I'i Brown: North | Kohala | 18 | Resort | $185 | ☎ 885-6655 |
| Francis H I'i Brown: South | Kohala | 18 | Resort | $185 | ☎ 885-6655 |
| Naniloa Country Club | Hilo | 9 | Semi-private | $45 | ☎ 935-3000 |
| Sea Mountain Golf Course | Punalu'u | 18 | Resort | $40 | ☎ 928-6222 |
| Volcano Golf & Country Club | Volcano | 18 | Public | $62 | ☎ 967-7331 |
| Waikoloa Golf Club | | | | | |
| Beach Course | Waikoloa | 18 | Resort | $195 | ☎ 885-6060 |
| Kings' Course | Waikoloa | 18 | Resort | $195 | ☎ 886-7888 |
| Waikoloa Village Golf Club | Waikoloa | 18 | Semi-private | $95 | ☎ 883-9621 |
| Waimea Country Club | Waimea | 18 | Semi-private | $85 | ☎ 885-8777 |
| **Kauai** | | | | | |
| Grove Farm Golf Course | Līhu'e | 9 | Public | $65 | ☎ 245-8756 |
| Kauai Lagoons Resort | | | | | |
| Kiele Course | Līhu'e | 18 | Resort | $170 | ☎ 241-6000 |
| Lagoon Course | Līhu'e | 18 | Resort | $100 | ☎ 241-6000 |
| Kiahuna Golf Club | Po'ipū | 18 | Resort | $75 | ☎ 742-9595 |
| Kukiolono Golf Course | Po'ipū | 9 | Public | $9 | ☎ 332-9151 |
| Po'ipū Bay Resort Golf Course | Po'ipū | 18 | Resort | $170 | ☎ 742-8711 |
| Princeville Golf Club | | | | | |
| Makai Course | Princeville | 27 | Resort | $120 | ☎ 826-3580 |
| Prince Course | Princeville | 18 | Resort | $175 | ☎ 826-5000 |
| Wailua Golf Course | Wailua | 18 | Municipal | $25 | ☎ 241-6666 |
| **Lanai** | | | | | |
| Cavendish Municipal Golf Course | Lanai City | 9 | Municipal | free | No phone |
| The Challenge at Mānele | Mānele Bay | 18 | Resort | $200 | ☎ 565-2222 |
| The Experience at Kō'ele | Lanai City | 18 | Resort | $200 | ☎ 565-4653 |
| **Maui** | | | | | |
| Dunes at Maui Lani | Kahului | 18 | Public | $85 | ☎ 873-0422 |
| Elleair Golf Course | Kīhei | 18 | Public | $75 | ☎ 874-0777 |
| Grand Waikapū Country Club | Waikapū | 18 | Private | $200 | ☎ 244-7888 |
| Kā'anapali Golf Course | | | | | |
| North Course | Kā'anapali | 18 | Resort | $150 | ☎ 661-3691 |
| South Course | Kā'anapali | 18 | Resort | $142 | ☎ 661-3691 |

| | | | | | |
|---|---|---|---|---|---|
| Kapalua Golf Club | | | | | |
| Bay Course | Kapalua | 18 | Resort | $180 | Ⓣ 669-8820 |
| Plantation Course | Kapalua | 18 | Resort | $220 | Ⓣ 669-8877 |
| Village Course | Kapalua | 18 | Resort | $180 | Ⓣ 669-8835 |
| Mākena Golf Club | | | | | |
| North Course | Mākena | 18 | Resort | $110 | Ⓣ 879-3344 |
| South Course | Mākena | 18 | Resort | $110 | Ⓣ 879-3344 |
| Maui Country Club | Pā'ia | 9 | Private | $65 | Ⓣ 877-7893 |
| Pukalani Country Club | Upcountry | 18 | Public | $55 | Ⓣ 572-1314 |
| Sandalwood Golf Course | Waikapū | 18 | Public | $75 | Ⓣ 242-4653 |
| Wai'ehu Municipal Golf Course | Wailuku | 18 | Municipal | $26 | Ⓣ 243-7400 |
| Wailea Golf Club | | | | | |
| Blue Course | Wailea | 18 | Resort | $140 | Ⓣ 875-7450 |
| Emerald Course | Wailea | 18 | Resort | $160 | Ⓣ 875-7450 |
| Gold Course | Wailea | 18 | Resort | $150 | Ⓣ 875-7450 |
| **Molokai** | | | | | |
| Ironwood Hills Golf Club | Kualapu'u | 9 | Private | $20 | Ⓣ 567-6000 |
| Kualako'i Golf Course | Kualako'i | 18 | Resort | $85 | Ⓣ 552-2555 |
| **Oahu** | | | | | |
| Ala Wai Golf Course | Honolulu | 18 | Municipal | $42 | Ⓣ 733-7387 |
| Bayview Golf Links | Kāne'ohe | 18 | Public | $45 | Ⓣ 247-0451 |
| Coral Creek Golf Course | 'Ewa Beach | 18 | Semi-private | $125 | Ⓣ 441-4653 |
| 'Ewa Beach Golf Club | 'Ewa Beach | 18 | Semi-private | $80 | Ⓣ 689-8317 |
| Hawaii Country Club | Wahiawā | 18 | Public | $45 | Ⓣ 621-5654 |
| Hawaii Kai Golf Course | | | | | |
| Championship Course | Hawaii Kai | 18 | Public | $90 | Ⓣ 395-2358 |
| Executive Course | Hawaii Kai | 18 | Public | $29 | Ⓣ 395-2358 |
| Hawaii Prince Golf Club | 'Ewa Beach | 27 | Public | $135 | Ⓣ 944-4567 |
| Honolulu Country Club | Honolulu | 18 | Private | $55 | Ⓣ 833-4541 |
| Kahuku Golf Course | North Shore | 9 | Municipal | $20 | Ⓣ 293-5842 |
| Kapolei Golf Course | Ko 'Olina | 18 | Semi-private | $70 | Ⓣ 674-2227 |
| Ko 'Olina Golf Club | Ko 'Olina | 18 | Resort | $145 | Ⓣ 676-5300 |
| Ko'olau Golf Course | Kāne'ohe | 18 | Public | $125 | Ⓣ 236-4653 |
| Luana Hills Country Club | Kailua | 18 | Semi-private | $95 | Ⓣ 262-2139 |
| Mākaha Resort Golf Club | Mākaha | 18 | Resort | $100 | Ⓣ 695-9544 |
| Mākaha Valley Country Club | Mākaha | 18 | Public | $55 | Ⓣ 695-9578 |
| Mililani Golf Club | Mililani | 18 | Public | $89 | Ⓣ 623-2222 |
| Moanalua Golf Club | Honolulu | 9 | Semi-private | $20 | Ⓣ 839-2411 |
| Olomana Golf Links | Waimanālo | 18 | Public | $65 | Ⓣ 259-7926 |
| Pali Golf Course | Kāne'ohe | 18 | Municipal | $42 | Ⓣ 266-7612 |
| Pearl Country Club | 'Aiea | 18 | Semi-private | $65 | Ⓣ 487-3802 |
| Ted Makalena Golf Course | Waipahu | 18 | Municipal | $42 | Ⓣ 675-6052 |
| Turtle Bay Hilton & Country Club | | | | | |
| The Links at Kuilima | Kahuku | 18 | Resort | $135 | Ⓣ 293-8574 |
| Turtle Bay Country Club | Kahuku | 9 | Resort | $90 | Ⓣ 293-8574 |
| Waikele Golf Club | Waipahu | 18 | Semi-private | $107 | Ⓣ 676-9000 |
| West Loch Golf Course | 'Ewa Beach | 18 | Municipal | $42 | Ⓣ 296-2000 |

# Crafts and shopping

**All the stories of Japanese tourists who come to Hawaii specifically to shop apply only to Honolulu, where malls like the Ala Moana Center hold outlets of all the big names in world fashion. Many residents of the other islands think nothing of flying to Honolulu for a day's shopping, and if you don't spend much time on Oahu you may come home from your vacation with fewer gifts and souvenirs than you expected. The prints, posters and T-shirts piled high along the sidewalks of Waikīkī and other major tourist areas are all well and good if you think that whales are interplanetary voyagers from another dimension, or that a gecko on a surfboard is real neat, but stores and galleries selling high-quality indigenous arts and crafts are few and far between. For more on shops and malls in Honolulu and Waikīkī, see pp.113.**

## Hawaiian crafts and produce

Some of the most attractive products of Hawaii are just too ephemeral to take home. That goes for virtually all the orchids and tropical flowers on sale everywhere, and unfortunately it's also true of ***leis***.

*Leis* (pronounced *lays*) are flamboyant decorative garlands, usually composed of flowers such as the fragrant *melia* (the plumeria or frangipani) or the bright-red *lehua* blossom (from the *'ō'hia* tree), but sometimes also made from feathers, shells, seeds or nuts. They're worn by both men and women, above all on celebrations or gala occasions – election-winning politicians are absolutely deluged in them, as are the statues of Kamehameha the Great and Queen Lili'uokalani in Honolulu on state holidays. The days are gone when every arriving tourist was festooned with a *lei*, but you'll probably be way-*leied* at a *lū'au* or some such occasion, while if you're around for Lei Day (May 1), everyone's at it. If you want to buy one, most towns have a store or two with a supply of flower *leis* kept in refrigerated cabinets, but Chinatown in Honolulu is the acknowledged center of the art.

Colorful Hawaiian **clothing**, such as aloha shirts and the cover-all "Mother-Hubbard"-style *mu'umu'u* dress, is on sale everywhere, though classic designs are surprisingly rare and you tend to see the same stylized prints over and over again. Otherwise, the main **local crafts** to look out for are *lau hala* **weaving**, in which mats, hats, baskets and the like are created by plaiting the large leaves (*lau*) of the spindly-legged pandanus (*hala*) tree, and **wood turning**, with fine bowls made from native dark woods such as *koa*.

# Directory



**AREA CODE** The telephone area code for the whole state of Hawaii is ⓣ808.

**CLIMATE** For an overview of the climate in Hawaii, see the *Introduction*.

**ELECTRICITY** Hawaii's electricity supply, like that on the US mainland, uses 100 volts AC. Plugs are standard American two-pins.

**HUNTING** Unless you can produce a photo ID and a Hunter Safety card issued in another state, if you want to hunt in the Hawaiian islands you must first pass a free two-day hunter education course. A one-year non-resident Hawaii State Hunter's License costs $95. For details, contact the Department of Land and Natural Resources (ⓣ587-0300, ⓦwww.hawaii.gov/dlnr).

**INOCULATIONS** No inoculations or vaccinations are required by law in order to enter Hawaii, though some authorities suggest a polio vaccination.

**QUARANTINE** Very stringent restrictions apply to the importation of all plants and animals into Hawaii, mainly as a protection for the state's many endangered indigenous species. Cats and dogs have to stay in quarantine for 120 days; if you were hoping to bring an alligator or a hamster, forget it. For full regulations on animals, call ⓣ483-7151; for the rules regarding plants, call ⓣ586-0844; or access ⓦwww.hawaiiag.org.

**RESTROOMS** Doors in some public restrooms are labeled in Hawaiian: *Kāne* for Men, *Wahine* for Women.

**TIME** Unlike most of the United States, Hawaii does not observe Daylight Saving Time. Therefore, from 2am on the last Sunday in April until 2am on the last Sunday in October, the time difference between Hawaii and the US West Coast is three hours, not the usual two; the time difference between Hawaii and the mountain region is four hours, not three; and the islands are six hours earlier than the East Coast, not five. Hawaiian time is from ten to eleven hours behind the UK. In fact it's behind just about everywhere else; although New Zealand and Australia might seem to be two and four hours respectively behind Honolulu time, they're on the other side of the International Date Line, so are actually almost a full day ahead.

**TIPPING** Wait staff in restaurants expect tips of fifteen percent, in bars a little less. Hotel porters and bellhops should receive around $1 per piece of luggage, and housekeeping staff $1 per night.

**WEDDINGS** To get married in Hawaii, you need a valid state license, obtainable from either the Department of Health, Marriage License Office, 1250 Punchbowl St, Honolulu HI 96813 (Mon–Fri 8am–4pm; ⓣ586-4545, ⓦwww.hawaii.gov), or agents on the other islands (hotels have details). Licenses cost $50 and are valid for thirty days; there's no waiting period. You also have to show proof of rubella immunization or screening, which can be arranged through the Department of Health. Weddings are very big business here; most major resorts offer their own marriage planners, and the Hawaii Visitors Bureau keeps full lists of organizers. Specialists include Aloha Wedding Planners (ⓣ1-800/288-8309, ⓦwww.alohaweddingplanners.com) and Traditional Hawaiian Weddings (ⓣ1-800/884-9505) on Oahu; A Beautiful Hawaii Wedding (ⓣ661-6655, ⓦwww.oldlahaina.com) and Marry Me Maui (ⓣ1-800/745-0344, ⓦwww.marrymemaui .com) on Maui; Wedding in Paradise (ⓣ1-800/733-7431, ⓦwww.paradiseservices.com) and Coconut Coast Weddings (ⓣ1-800/585-5595, ⓦwww.kauaiwedding.com) on Kauai; and Paradise Weddings Hawaii (ⓣ883/9067, ⓦplanet-hawaii.com/weddings/) and Aloha Weddings in Paradise (ⓣ776-1420, ⓦwww.alohaweddingsinparadise.com) on the Big Island.

# guide

# guide

# 1

# Oahu

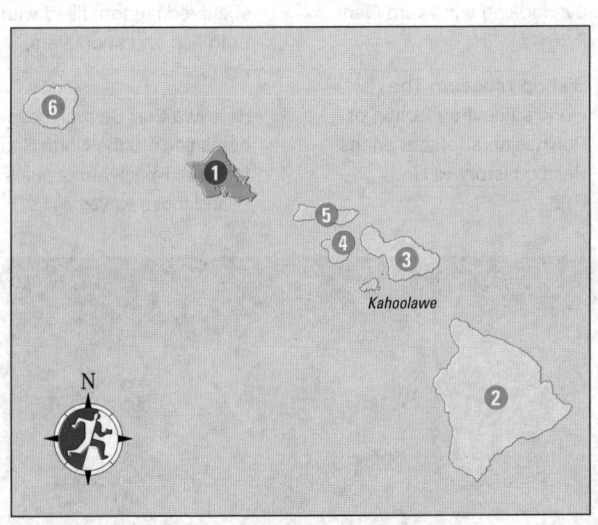

# CHAPTER 1 Highlights

* **Waikīkī Beach** Learn to surf, or just sip a cocktail, on Hawaii's most famous beach. P.69
* **Diamond Head** Hiking to the top of this Oahu landmark enables you to look down on all Waikīkī. P.76
* **Nu'uanu Pali State Park** Site of an ancient battle, now a breathtaking viewpoint overlooking windward Oahu. P.95
* **Bishop Museum** The world's finest collection of Polynesian artefacts brings Pacific history to life. P.96
* **Pearl Harbor** The *USS Arizona* still lies beneath the waters of Pearl Harbor, where it settled in December 1941. P.97
* **Ala Moana Center** Every visitor to Honolulu spends at least half a day in this vast, cosmopolitan shopping mall. P.114
* **Hanauma Bay** Gorgeous sheltered lagoon, filled with both fish and snorkelers. P.115
* **Hale'iwa** Surf Central; beach bums flock to the North Shore for its laid-back atmosphere . . . and those waves. P.134

# Oahu

Around eighty percent of the population of Hawaii – almost 900,000 people – live on the island of **OAHU**. More than half of them are packed into the city of **Honolulu**, which remains the economic powerhouse of the whole archipelago. They're here because the jobs and the tourists are here; ninety percent of visitors to Hawaii spend at least one night on Oahu.

With virtually every hotel room on the island located in the tower-block enclave of **Waikīkī**, just east of downtown Honolulu, Oahu offers less scope for a personal, individual travel experience than anywhere else in the state. **Surfers**, of course, flock to the fabled **North Shore**, but almost everyone else ends up in Waikīkī, where even the most determined hedonist can find the hectic resort lifestyle palls after a few days.

That said, Oahu does have its strong points. Honolulu is a remarkably attractive city, ringed by eroded volcanoes and reaching back into a succession of gorgeous valleys, while as a major world crossroads it has a broad ethnic mix. There are great beaches scattered all over the island – not just in Waikīkī – and plantation towns, ancient ruins and luscious scenery await more adventurous explorers.

Tourist organizations like to claim that Oahu means "the gathering place." Both the translation, and the common suggestion that in order to see Hawaii, you must first see Oahu, are spurious. Don't feel that Oahu is a place to be avoided at all costs, but if you spend more than a couple of days in Waikīkī at the start of your Hawaiian vacation, you may end up looking back on them as wasted time.

## A brief history of Oahu

Before the coming of the foreigners, Oahu was probably the least significant of the four major Hawaiian islands. Nonetheless, it was among the very first places in the state to attract Polynesian settlers. Traces of occupation dating back to around 200 AD have been found at Kahana Valley and Bellows Field. The windward valleys of the east coast are thought to have held sizeable agricultural populations, while the sheltered coastline of Pearl Harbor supported an intricate network of fishponds. Not until the eighteenth century, however, did any individual chief become powerful enough to subdue the whole island, and by that time the rulers of Maui and Hawaii (the Big Island) were capable of launching successful invasions.

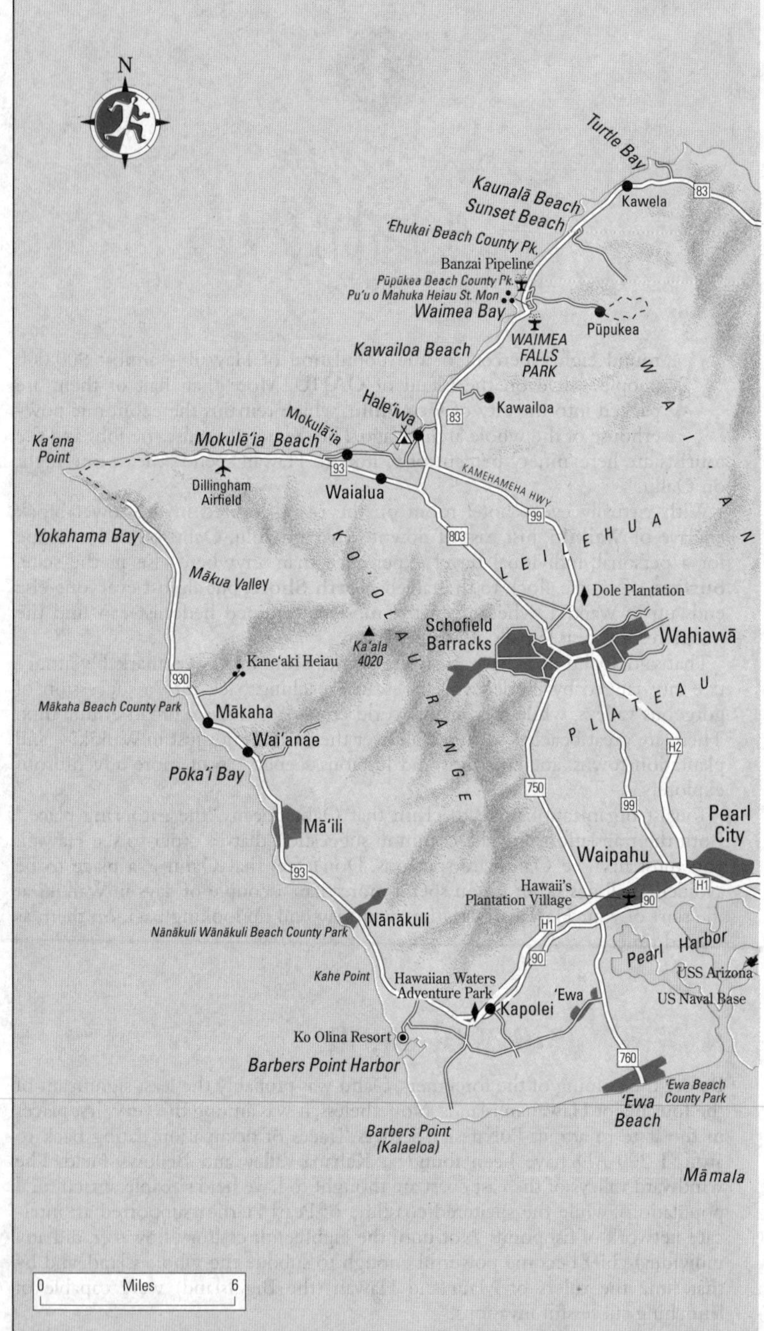
N
Turtle Bay
Kaunalā Beach
Sunset Beach
Kawela
83
'Ehukai Beach County Pk.
Banzai Pipeline
Pūpūkea Beach County Pk.
Pu'u o Mahuka Heiau St. Mon
Waimea Bay
Pūpukea
WAIMEA FALLS PARK
Kawailoa Beach
Kawailoa
Hale'iwa
Mokulā'ia
Ka'ena Point
Mokulē'ia Beach
Dillingham Airfield
Waialua
93
KAMEHAMEHA HWY
99
803
Yokahama Bay
KO'OLAU RANGE
LEILEHUA
WAIANAE
Mākua Valley
Dole Plantation
Schofield Barracks
Wahiawā
Ka'ala 4020
Kane'aki Heiau
930
PLATEAU
Mākaha Beach County Park
Mākaha
Wai'anae
Pōka'i Bay
H2
750
99
Mā'ili
Pearl City
Waipahu
93
H1
Hawaii's Plantation Village
90
Nānākuli
Nānākuli Wānākuli Beach County Park
H1
Pearl Harbor
90
USS Arizona
Kahe Point
Hawaiian Waters Adventure Park
Kapolei
'Ewa
US Naval Base
Ko Olina Resort
Barbers Point Harbor
760
'Ewa Beach County Park
'Ewa Beach
Barbers Point (Kalaeloa)
Māmala
0 Miles 6

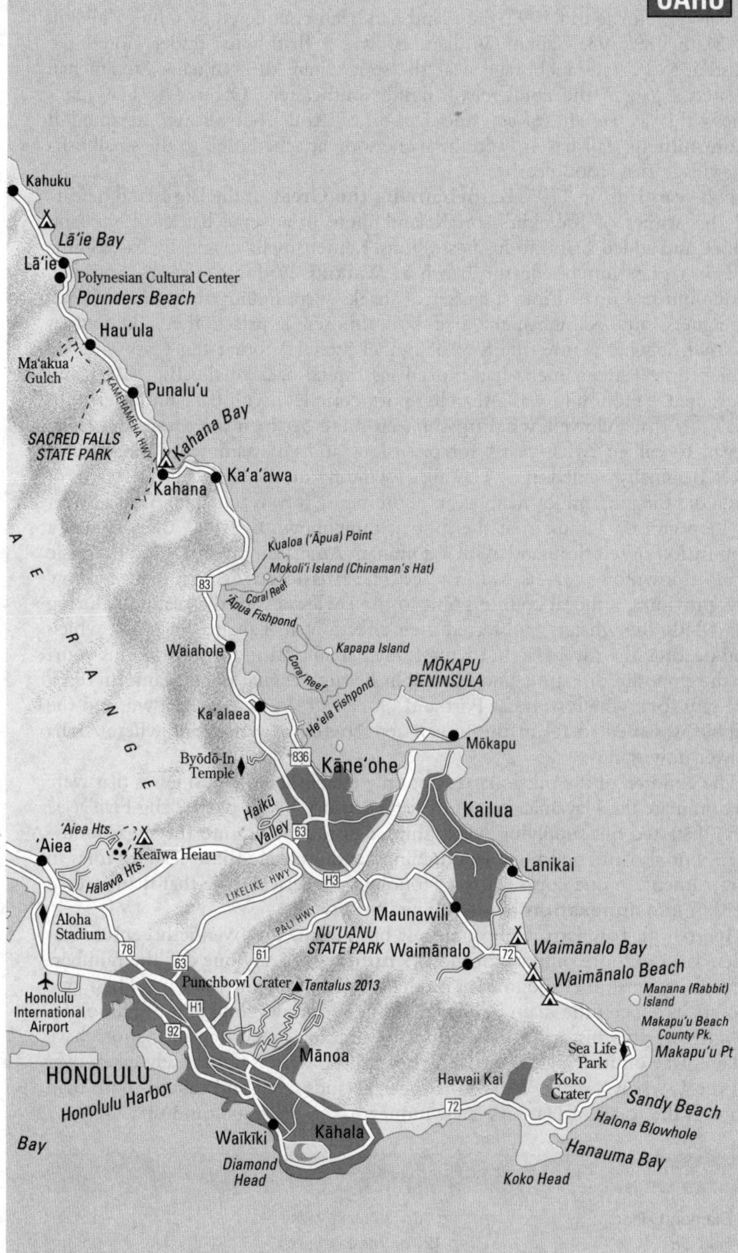
OAHU
Kahuku
Lā'ie Bay
Lā'ie
Polynesian Cultural Center
Pounders Beach
Hau'ula
Ma'akua Gulch
Punalu'u
KAMEHAMEHA HWY
Kahana Bay
SACRED FALLS STATE PARK
Kahana
Ka'a'awa
Kualoa ('Āpua) Point
Mokoli'i Island (Chinaman's Hat)
83
Coral Reef
'Āpua Fishpond
Waiahole
Kapapa Island
Coral Reef
MŌKAPU PENINSULA
Ka'alaea
He'ela Fishpond
Mōkapu
Byōdō-In Temple
836
Kāne'ohe
Haikū Valley
Kailua
'Aiea Hts.
'Aiea
Keaīwa Heiau
Hālawa Hts.
63
Lanikai
LIKELIKE HWY
H3
Aloha Stadium
PALI HWY
Maunawili
NU'UANU STATE PARK
Waimānalo
Waimānalo Bay
78
63
61
72
Waimānalo Beach
Honolulu International Airport
Punchbowl Crater
Tantalus 2013
Manana (Rabbit) Island
H1
Makapu'u Beach County Pk.
92
Sea Life Park
Makapu'u Pt
Mānoa
HONOLULU
Hawaii Kai
Koko Crater
Honolulu Harbor
72
Sandy Beach
Halona Blowhole
Waīkīki
Kāhala
Bay
Hanauma Bay
Diamond Head
Koko Head
K O ' O L A U R A N G E

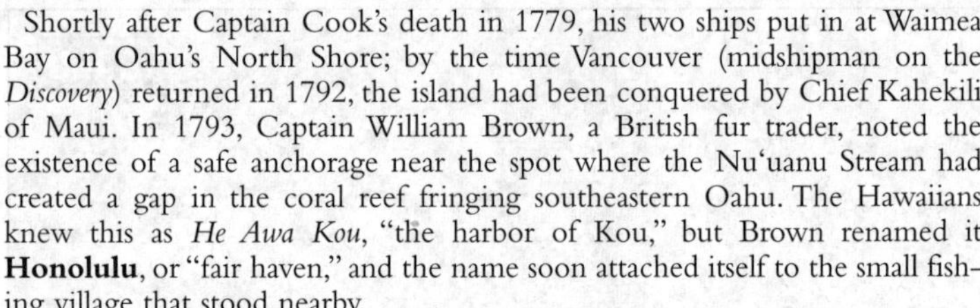

Shortly after Captain Cook's death in 1779, his two ships put in at Waimea Bay on Oahu's North Shore; by the time Vancouver (midshipman on the *Discovery*) returned in 1792, the island had been conquered by Chief Kahekili of Maui. In 1793, Captain William Brown, a British fur trader, noted the existence of a safe anchorage near the spot where the Nu'uanu Stream had created a gap in the coral reef fringing southeastern Oahu. The Hawaiians knew this as *He Awa Kou*, "the harbor of Kou," but Brown renamed it **Honolulu**, or "fair haven," and the name soon attached itself to the small fishing village that stood nearby.

Two years later, in 1795, **Kamehameha the Great** of the Big Island defeated the armies of Kahekili's son Kalanikūpule in an epic battle at Nu'uanu Valley, and added Oahu to his possessions. Kamehameha originally based himself in a grass hut beside the beach at **Waikīkī**. Within ten years, however, Honolulu had turned into a cluster of shacks surrounding the homes of sixty foreigners, and Kamehameha had built himself a palace there, known as *Halehui*, at what is now the foot of Bethel Street. Another ten years on – by which time Kamehameha had moved his capital back to the Big Island, and then died – Honolulu was a thriving port, complete with bars and taverns. In the years that followed, **whaling** ships en route between the Arctic and Japan began to call in twice-yearly for provisions and entertainment. The whalers were originally hauled in by Hawaiians standing on the reef; later on, teams of oxen did the job, and for many years an immense rope reached up Alakea Street to loop around a capstan at the foot of Punchbowl. By 1830, the city had a population of ten thousand, with a dominant American presence, and the basic grid of downtown streets was in place. The **missionaries** were here by now too, providing a moral counterpoint to the lawlessness of the seamen. During the 1840s, the whalers transferred their affections to Lahaina on Maui, which had become the royal seat, but King Kamehameha III in turn moved his court in the opposite direction, and Honolulu became capital once again. In 1857, the city **fort**, which stood at Fort and Queen streets, was torn down, and the rubble was used to fill in the fifteen-acre stretch of waterfront where Aloha Tower now stands.

The children of the missionaries not only established the businesses that were to dominate the Hawaiian economy for a century – four of the "Big Five" (see p.513) started out supplying whale ships, before moving into the sugar industry – but also amassed huge landholdings, and gravitated into leading roles in government. In due course, it was Honolulu's American elite that maneuvered Hawaii into **annexation** by the United States.

Apart from **tourism**, Oahu's biggest business in the twentieth century has been as an offshore outpost for the **US military**; on any one day, the numbers of military personnel and tourists on the island are roughly the same. These two factors have been the main influences in the recent development of Honolulu. While the city's historic core remains recognizable, great transformations have taken place on its fringes. **Pearl Harbor**, to the west, is completely taken over by the US Navy, while Waikīkī has been relandscaped and rebuilt more than once as the focus of Hawaii's latest moneymaker, the tourist industry.

## Oahu Favorites: Hikes

| | | | |
|---|---|---|---|
| Diamond Head | p.76 | Makiki Valley | p.90 |
| Hau'ula | p.127 | Mānoa Falls | p.93 |
| Kahana Valley | p.126 | | |

# Around the island

Roughly speaking, Oahu is shaped like a butterfly, with its wings formed by the volcanoes of the **Waianae Range** in the west and the wetter, mostly higher **Ko'olau Range** in the east. In between lies the narrow, flat **Leilehua Plateau**, with the triple lagoon of **Pearl Harbor** at its southern end. The symmetrical outline is only spoiled where the southeast coastline thrusts further into the ocean, thanks to the later eruptions that produced craters such as **Punchbowl**, **Diamond Head** and **Koko Head**.

With all its suburbs and satellite communities, **Honolulu** stretches along a substantial proportion of the southern coast, squeezed between the mountains and the sea. The golden beaches of Waikīkī are what draw in the tourists, but the city can also boast world-class museums, a historic downtown area, and some surprisingly rural hiking trails.

Just across the Ko'olaus, the green cliffs of the **windward coast** are magnificent, lined with safe, secluded beaches and indented with remote time-forgotten valleys. Towns such as **Kailua**, **Kāne'ohe** and **Lā'ie** may be far from exciting, but you're unlikely to tire of the sheer beauty of the shoreline drive – so long as you time your forays to miss the peak-hour traffic jams.

Mere mortals can only marvel at the winter waves that make the **North Shore** the world's premier **surfing** destination; for anyone other than experts, entering the water at that time is almost suicidal. However, **Waimea**, **Sunset** and **'Ehukai** beaches are compelling spectacles, little **Hale'iwa** makes a refreshing contrast to Waikīkī, and in summer you may manage to find a safe spot somewhere along the North Shore for a swim.

Although the **west** or **leeward coast** of Oahu also holds some fine beaches – including the prime surf spot of **Mākaha** – it remains very much off the beaten track. There's just one route in and out of this side of the island, and the locals are happy to keep it that way.

### Oahu Favorites: Beaches

**Swimming beaches**

| | | | |
|---|---|---|---|
| Kailua Beach Park | p.122 | Waikīkī Beach | p.69 |
| Mālaekahana Bay | p.129 | Waimānolo Beach | p.119 |
| Sandy Beach | p.118 | | |

**Snorkel Spots**

| | | | |
|---|---|---|---|
| Hanauma Bay | p.115 | Shark's Cove | p.138 |
| Sans Souci Beach | p.72 | Waimea Bay Beach Park | p.137 |

**Surf Sites**

| | | | |
|---|---|---|---|
| 'Ehukai Beach Park | p.140 | Pūpūkea Beach Park | p.138 |
| Mākaha Beach | p.143 | Sunset Beach | p.140 |

# Getting around Oahu

Oahu is blessed with an exemplary network of public **buses**, officially named **TheBus.** Radiating out from downtown Honolulu and the Ala Moana Shopping Center, it covers the whole of Oahu (contact ⓣ848-5555 or

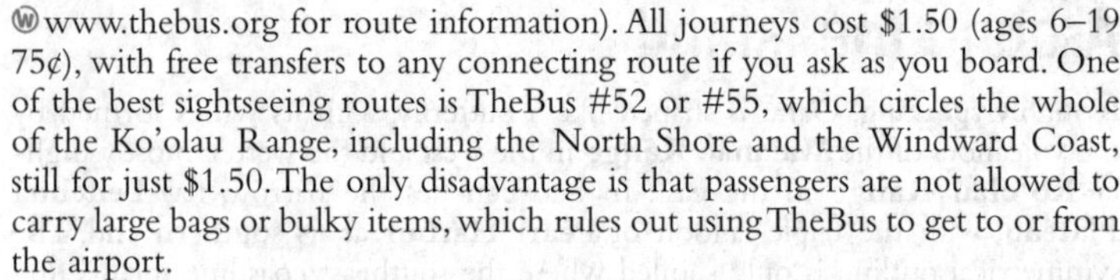
Ⓦ www.thebus.org for route information). All journeys cost $1.50 (ages 6–19 75¢), with free transfers to any connecting route if you ask as you board. One of the best sightseeing routes is TheBus #52 or #55, which circles the whole of the Ko'olau Range, including the North Shore and the Windward Coast, still for just $1.50. The only disadvantage is that passengers are not allowed to carry large bags or bulky items, which rules out using TheBus to get to or from the airport.

For full details of transportation between Waikīkī and the airport, see p.58. Services in Honolulu and Waikīkī are summarized on p.59, together with companies offering **island tours**.

If you want to explore Oahu at your own pace, you'd do best to rent a **car** through one of the agencies listed on p.24. However, with limited parking and heavy traffic, a car is a liability in Waikīkī itself, so think carefully before renting one for your entire stay.

# Where to Stay

The overwhelming majority of visitors to Oahu stay in **Waikīkī**, a couple of miles east of central Honolulu. The rest of the island holds very few alternatives; the only hotels are the *Hilton* and *Ihilani* resorts, at the far northeast and southwest corners respectively, while the bargain *Backpackers Vacation Inn*, on the North Shore, caters to the surf crowd. Other than a few tiny B&Bs at Kailua and Kāne'ohe on the windward coast, that's about it.

According to official figures, the average room in Waikīkī costs almost $130. There's a heavy premium for oceanfront accommodation, however, and away from the beach – bearing in mind that nowhere in Waikīkī is more than a few minutes' walk from the sea – it's easy enough to find something for half that. The sheer quantity of rooms ensures that you're unlikely to find yourself stranded if you arrive without a reservation, and there are several hostels available for budget travelers.

You can **camp** in county parks on Oahu for free, and in state parks for $5 per night, with a permit from the relevant office. However, few sites are worth recommending, and none of those is especially convenient to Honolulu. Furthermore, all county and state campgrounds are closed on both Wednesday and Thursday nights, and you can't stay at any one site for more than five days in one month. The best options among the state parks are those at Keaīwa Heiau (see p.132), Mālaekahana Bay (p.129), Waimānolo Bay (p.119), and Kahana Valley (p.126); appealing county parks include Bellows Field Beach (p.120), and Kaiaka Bay Beach Park, a mile out of Hale'iwa near the mouth of Kaiaka Bay (p.135). The **state parks office** accepts postal applications seven

## Accommodation Price Codes

All the accommodation options listed here have been graded with the symbols below, which refer to the quoted rates for a double room in high season (December to March), not including state taxes of 10.17 percent. For a full explanation, see p.27.

| | | |
|---|---|---|
| ❶ up to $40 | ❹ $100–150 | ❼ $250–300 |
| ❷ $40–70 | ❺ $150–200 | ❽ $300–400 |
| ❸ $70–100 | ❻ $200–250 | ❾ over $400 |

to thirty days in advance; it's located in Room 310, 1151 Punchbowl St, Honolulu HI 96813 (Mon–Fri 8.30am–3.30pm; ⓣ587-0300). **County** permits can be obtained, in person only, from 650 S King St (Mon–Fri 7.45am–4pm; ⓣ523-4525) or from the subsidiary "City Hall" in the Ala Moana Center (Mon–Fri 9am–4pm, Sat 8am–4pm; ⓣ973-2600).



# When to go

Of all major US cities, Honolulu is said to have both the *lowest* average annual maximum temperature and the *highest* minimum, at 85°F and 60°F respectively. Neither fluctuates more than a few degrees between summer and winter. Waikīkī remains a balmy tropical year-round resort, and the only seasonal

### Oahu Festivals and Events

| | |
|---|---|
| **Early Jan** | Morey Bodyboards World Championships, Banzai Pipeline |
| **Jan/Feb** | Narcissus Festival and Chinese New Year, Chinatown |
| **Feb** | Buffalo's Big Board Surfing Classic, Mākaha Beach |
| **3rd Mon in Feb** | Presidents Day; Great Aloha Run, from Aloha Tower to Aloha Stadium. |
| **March 17** | St Patrick's Day Parade, Waikīkī |
| **Easter Sunday** | Easter Sunrise Service at dawn, Punchbowl, Honolulu |
| **April** | Hawaiian Professional Championship Rodeo, Waimānolo |
| **May 1** | *Lei* Day; public holiday, statewide celebrations |
| **May 2** | *Lei* ceremony at Royal Mausoleum, Honolulu |
| **late May** | Molokai–Oahu kayak race ends at Hawaii Kai |
| **late May** | Maui–Oahu Bankoh Ho'omana'o canoe race ends at Waikīkī Beach |
| **late May/early June** | State Fair, Aloha Stadium, Honolulu |
| **June 11** | Kamehameha Day; public holiday, statewide celebrations, Honolulu to Waikīkī parade |
| **late June** | King Kamehameha *Hula* Festival, Blaisdell Center, Honolulu |
| **early July** | Na Wahine O Hawaii; Hawaiian women performers, Ala Moana Park |
| **mid-July** | Hawaii International Jazz Festival, Honolulu |
| **3rd Sat in July** | Prince Lot *Hula* Festival, Moanalua Gardens, Honolulu |
| **mid-Aug** | Floating Lantern Ceremony, Waikīkī |
| **mid-Sept** | Aloha Festival, island-wide |
| **late Sept** | Molokai–Oahu women's outrigger canoe race ends at Waikīkī |
| **early Oct** | Molokai–Oahu men's outrigger canoe race ends at Waikīkī |
| **Oct 31** | Halloween parade, Waikīkī |
| **early Nov** | World Invitation *Hula* Festival, Honolulu |
| **Nov** | Hawaii International Film Festival, Honolulu |
| **mid-Nov** | Triple Crown of Surfing; Hawaiian Pro, Ali'i Beach Park, Hale'iwa |
| **late Nov/early Dec** | Triple Crown of Surfing; World Cup, Sunset Beach |
| **early Dec** | Triple Crown of Surfing; Pipe Masters, Banzai Pipeline |
| **2nd Sun in Dec** | Honolulu Marathon |
| **Dec 25** | Christmas Day; Aloha Bowl Football Classic, Aloha Stadium, Honolulu |
| **Dec 31** | First Night Festival, downtown Honolulu |

*Note that the exact dates of surfing contests, and in some cases the venues as well, depend on the state of the waves.*

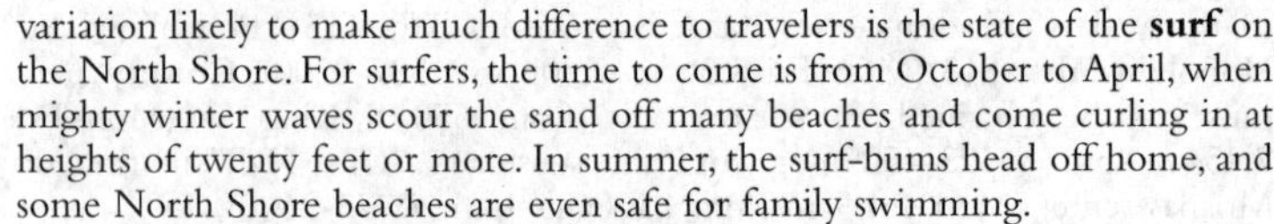

variation likely to make much difference to travelers is the state of the **surf** on the North Shore. For surfers, the time to come is from October to April, when mighty winter waves scour the sand off many beaches and come curling in at heights of twenty feet or more. In summer, the surf-bums head off home, and some North Shore beaches are even safe for family swimming.

As for room rates, peak season in Waikīkī runs from December to March, and many mid-range hotels lower their prices by ten or twenty dollars during the rest of the year. Waikīkī is pretty crowded all year, though, and coming in summer will not yield significant savings.

# Honolulu and Waikīkī

Stretching for around a dozen miles along the southern coast of Oahu, and home to more than 400,000 people, **HONOLULU** is by far Hawaii's largest city. As the site of the islands' major **airport** and of the legendary beaches and skyscrapers of **WAIKĪKĪ**, it also provides most visitors with their first taste of Hawaii. Many, unfortunately, leave without ever realizing quite how out of keeping it is with the rest of the state.

Honolulu only came into being after the arrival of the foreigners; from the early days of sandalwood and whaling, through the rise of King Sugar and the development of Pearl Harbor, to its modern incarnation as a tourist dreamland, the fortunes of the city have depended on the ever-increasing integration of Hawaii into the global economy. Benefits of this process include an exhilarating energy and dynamism, and the cosmopolitan air that comes from being a major world crossroads. Among drawbacks are the fact that there's little genuinely Hawaiian about Honolulu, and the rampant over-development of Waikīkī.

The **setting** is beautiful, right on the Pacific Ocean and backed by the dramatic *pali* (cliffs) of the Ko'olau mountains. **Downtown Honolulu**, centered around a group of administrative buildings that date from the final days of the Hawaiian monarchy, nestles at the foot of the extinct **Punchbowl** volcano, now a military cemetery. It's a manageable size, and a lot quieter than its glamourous image might suggest. Immediately to the west is livelier **Chinatown**, while the **airport** lies four or five miles further west again, just before the sheltered inlet of **Pearl Harbor**.

The distinct district of **Waikīkī** is about three miles east of downtown, conspicuous not only for its towering hotels but also for the furrowed brow of another extinct volcano, **Diamond Head**. Although Waikīkī is a small suburb, and one that most Honolulu residents rarely visit, for package tourists it's the tail that wags the dog. They spend their days on Waikīkī's beaches, and their nights in its hotels, restaurants and bars; apart from the odd expedition to the nearby **Ala Moana** shopping mall, the rest of Honolulu might just as well not exist.

The sun-and-fun appeal of Waikīkī may wear off after a few days, but it can still make an excellent base for a longer stay on Oahu. Downtown Honolulu is easily accessible, and holds top-quality museums like the **Bishop Museum**

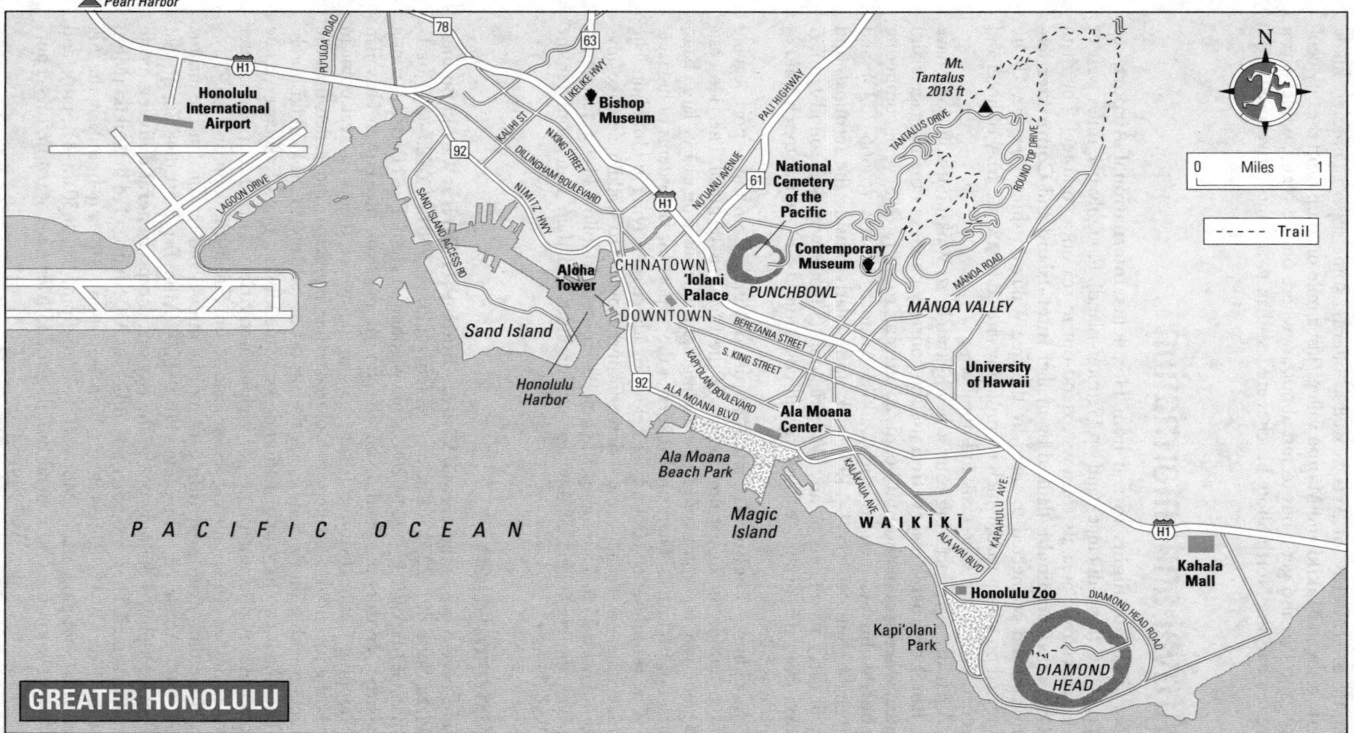
GREATER HONOLULU
Pearl Harbor
Honolulu International Airport
PU'ULOA ROAD
LAGOON DRIVE
H1
78
63
92
61
LIKELIKE HWY
Bishop Museum
KALIHI ST
N.KING STREET
DILLINGHAM BOULEVARD
NIMITZ HWY
SAND ISLAND ACCESS RD
Sand Island
Honolulu Harbor
Aloha Tower
CHINATOWN
DOWNTOWN
'Iolani Palace
NU'UANU AVENUE
PALI HIGHWAY
National Cemetery of the Pacific
PUNCHBOWL
Contemporary Museum
Mt. Tantalus 2013 ft
TANTALUS DRIVE
ROUND TOP DRIVE
MĀNOA ROAD
MĀNOA VALLEY
BERETANIA STREET
S. KING STREET
KAPI'OLANI BOULEVARD
ALA MOANA BLVD
Ala Moana Center
University of Hawaii
Ala Moana Beach Park
Magic Island
KALĀKAUA AVE
WAIKĪKĪ
ALA WAI BLVD
KAPAHULU AVE.
Honolulu Zoo
Kapi'olani Park
DIAMOND HEAD ROAD
DIAMOND HEAD
Kahala Mall
PACIFIC OCEAN
N
0 Miles 1
Trail

and the **Academy of Arts** as well as offering some superb rainforest hikes, especially in **Makiki** and **Mānoa** valleys, just a mile or so up from the city center. You can also get a bus to just about anywhere on the island, while, if you rent a **car**, the North Shore beaches are less than two hours' drive away.



## Arrival and information

For details of **flights** to and from Honolulu's **International Airport**, see pp.11–15 (long-distance), and pp.17 (inter-island). Roughly five miles west of the downtown area, its runways extend out to sea on a coral reef. The main **Overseas Terminal** is flanked by smaller **Inter-Island** and **Commuter** terminals, and connected to them by the free Wikiwiki shuttle service. All are located on a loop road, which is constantly circled by a wide array of hotel and rental-car pickup vans, taxis and minibuses.

Virtually every arriving tourist heads straight to Waikīkī; if you don't have a **hotel or hostel reservation** use the courtesy phones in the baggage claim area, where you'll also find boards advertising room rates. Several competing **shuttle buses**, such as the Waikīkī Airport Express (ⓣ566-7333) and Reliable Shuttle (ⓣ591-1493), pick up regularly outside the terminals and will carry passengers to any Waikīkī hotel ($8 one-way, $13 round-trip). A **taxi** from the airport to Waikīkī will cost around $20, and a stretch limo as little as $25.

In addition, **TheBus** #19 and #20 run to Waikīkī from the airport, leaving from outside the Departures lounge of the Overseas Terminal. The ride costs $1 one way, but you have to be traveling light: TheBus won't carry large bags, cases or backpacks. There are **lockers** at the airport for large items of luggage.

**Car rental** outlets abound; see below for advice on driving in Honolulu. The nine-mile – not at all scenic – **drive** from the airport to Waikīkī can take anything from 25 to 75 minutes; the quickest route is to follow H-1 as far as possible, running inland of downtown Honolulu, and then watch out for the Waikīkī exit.

### Information

The head office of the **Hawaii Visitors Bureau (HVB)** is at Waikīkī Business Plaza, Suite 801, 2270 Kalākaua Ave, Honolulu, HI 96815 (ⓣ923-1811 or 1-800/GO HAWAII, ⓕ924-0290, ⓦwww.gohawaii.com). The HVB also runs a **visitor center** in Waikīkī, on the fourth floor of the Royal Hawaiian Shopping Center (Mon–Fri 8am–4.30pm). However, there's no real point in visiting it: it holds a smaller stock of free listings magazines and leaflets than the racks in either the Arrivals hall at the airport or virtually all the Waikīkī hotels. The hotels also have information desks, while kiosks around Kalākaua Avenue offer greatly discounted rates for various "**activities**" – island tours, helicopter rides, dinner cruises, surfing lessons, and so on. Full listings appear on p.71.

Honolulu's main **post office**, facing the inter-island terminal at the airport at 3600 Aolele St, Honolulu, HI 96820 (Mon–Fri 7.30am–8.30pm, Sat 8am–2.30pm), is the only one in the city that accepts **general delivery** (poste restante) mail. There are other post offices at 330 Saratoga Rd in Waikīkī (Mon, Tues, Thurs & Fri 8am–4.30pm, Wed 8am–6pm, Sat 9am–noon); at the Ala Moana shopping mall (Mon–Fri 8.30am–5pm, Sat 8.30am–4.15pm); and downtown in the Old Federal Building at 335 Merchant St (Mon, Tues, Thurs & Fri 8am–4.30pm, Wed 8am–6pm).

## Getting around

While renting a car enables you to explore Oahu in much greater depth, **driving** in Honolulu is not a pleasant experience. The **traffic** on major roads, such as H-1 along the northern flanks of the city, and Likelike Highway and the Pali Highway across the mountains, can be horrendous, and **parking** is always a problem. You may find it easier to travel by **bus**, thanks to the exemplary TheBus network.

### Buses

A network of over sixty **bus** routes, officially named TheBus and centered on downtown Honolulu and the Ala Moana shopping mall, covers the whole of Oahu (ⓣ848-5555; ⓦwww.thebus.org). All journeys cost $1.50 (ages 6–19 75¢), with free transfers on to any connecting route if you ask as you board. The **Oahu Discovery Passport**, available from ABC stores in Waikīkī, offers four days' unlimited travel on TheBus for $15; monthly passes are also available. The most popular routes with Waikīkī-based tourists are **#2** to downtown, **#8** to Ala Moana, **#19** and **#20** to the airport, **#20** to Pearl Harbor, **#22** to Hanauma Bay, and the bargain "**Circle Island**" buses that take four hours to tour Oahu, still for just $1: **#52** (clockwise) and **#55** (counterclockwise).

Rival companies operate a number of alternative bus services from Waikīkī. The open-sided and overpriced **Waikīkī Trolley** (ⓣ596-2199) tours a circuit of Honolulu's main attractions at half-hour intervals, with the first departure from Waikīkī's Royal Hawaiian Shopping Center at 8am daily, and the last at 4.30pm, for a daily rate of $18 ($8 for under-12s). The similar **Rainbow Trolley** (daily 8.30am–11pm; ⓣ539-9495) makes elaborate loops between the main Waikīkī hotels and Honolulu's Aloha Tower Marketplace, charging adults $10 per day, while the **Aloha Tower Express** (daily 9am–9pm; ⓣ566-2337) runs direct from Waikīkī to the Aloha Tower Marketplace, for a much more reasonable $1 one-way fare.

### Car and bike rental

All the major **car rental** chains have outlets at the airport, and many have offices in Waikīkī as well. Reservations can be made using the national toll-free numbers listed on p.25, but check first to see if you can get a better room-and-car deal through your hotel.

Waikīkī hotels charge around $6–12 per night for **parking**, and there are meters on the back streets of Waikīkī, near the Ala Wai Canal. Downtown, the largest metered parking lot is on the edge of Chinatown at Smith and Beretania streets.

Lots of Waikīkī-based companies rent out **mopeds** and **bicycles**, including Aloha Funway (ⓣ942-9696), which has seven locations; Island Scooters (ⓣ924-6743), which has six; and Adventure Rentals, which adjoins the *Island Hostel* at 1946 Ala Moana Blvd (ⓣ944-3131). Typical rates for bikes are $15 per day (8am–6pm) or $20 for 24 hours; mopeds cost a couple of dollars extra.

### Taxis and limousines

Honolulu **taxi** firms include Charley's (ⓣ531-2333), Sida's (ⓣ836-0011) and TheCab (ⓣ422-2222). Alternatively, you could rent a **limousine** with tinted windows – for $45 per hour, or $30 for a one-way airport ride – from Continental (ⓣ226-4466). Accessible Vans of Hawaii (ⓣ879-5521, ⓦwww.accessiblevans.com) provides transportation for **disabled visitors**.

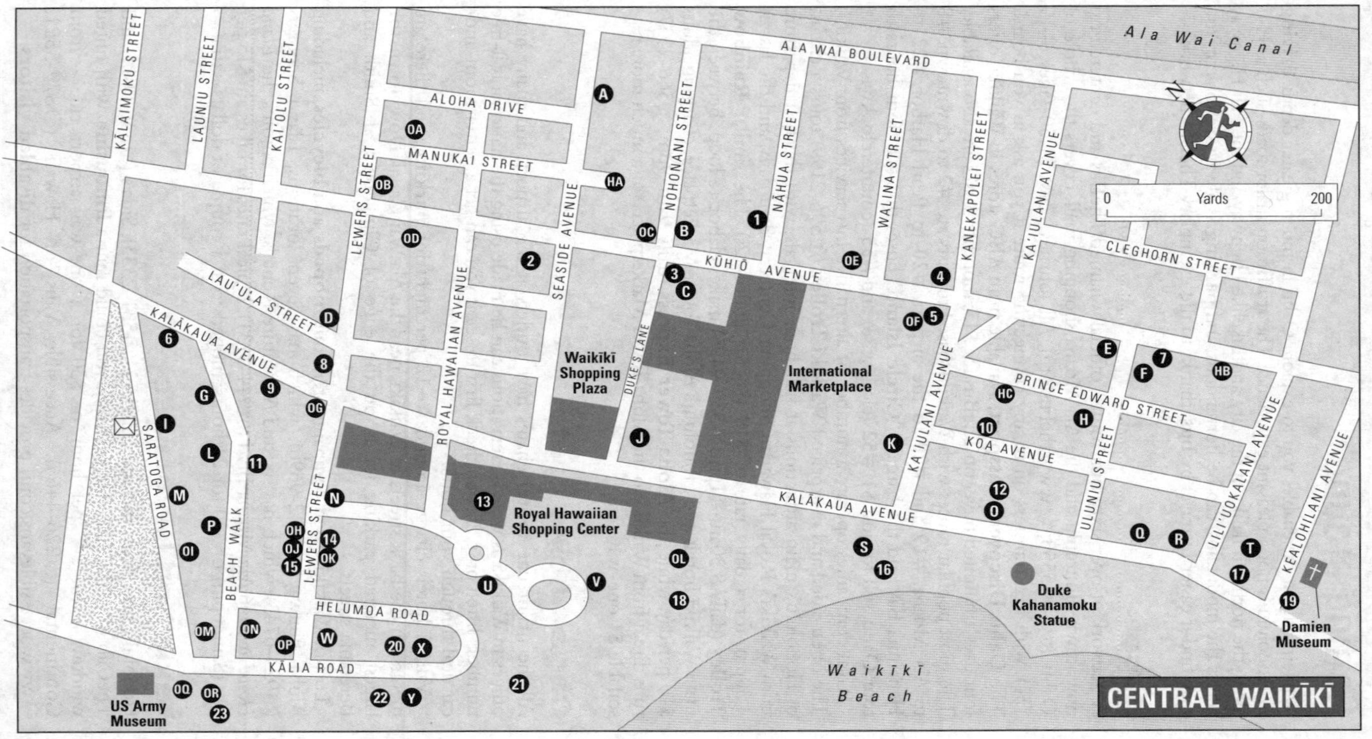
CENTRAL WAIKĪKĪ
Ala Wai Canal
ALA WAI BOULEVARD
N
0 Yards 200
ALOHA DRIVE
MANUKAI STREET
KĀLAIMOKU STREET
LAUNIU STREET
KAI'OLU STREET
LEWERS STREET
ROYAL HAWAIIAN AVENUE
SEASIDE AVENUE
NOHONANI STREET
NĀHUA STREET
WALINA STREET
KANEKAPOLEI STREET
KA'IULANI AVENUE
CLEGHORN STREET
KŪHIŌ AVENUE
LAU'ULA STREET
KALĀKAUA AVENUE
DUKE'S LANE
PRINCE EDWARD STREET
KOA AVENUE
ULUNIU STREET
LILI'UOKALANI AVENUE
KEALOHILANI AVENUE
SARATOGA ROAD
BEACH WALK
HELUMOA ROAD
KĀLIA ROAD
Waikīkī Shopping Plaza
International Marketplace
Royal Hawaiian Shopping Center
Duke Kahanamoku Statue
Damien Museum
US Army Museum
Waikīkī Beach

## Central Waikīkī

**Hotels**

| Hotel | Key |
|---|---|
| Aloha Punawai | I |
| Aston Coral Reef Hotel | C |
| Aston Waikīkī Beachside Hotel | Q |
| Aston Waikīkī Circle Hotel | R |
| The Breakers | L |
| Halekūlani | Y |
| Hale Pua Nui | P |
| Hawaiiana Hotel | G |
| Hyatt Regency Waikīkī | O |
| Ilima Hotel | B |
| Imperial of Waikīkī | W |
| Island Colony | A |
| Kai Aloha | M |
| Pacific Beach Hotel | T |
| Pacific Monarch | E |
| Royal Grove | F |
| The Royal Hawaiian | V |
| Sheraton Moana Surfrider | S |
| Sheraton Princess Ka'iulani | K |
| Sheraton Waikīkī Hotel | U |
| Waikīkī Beachcomber | J |
| Waikīkī Joy | D |
| Waikīkī Parc | X |
| Waikīkī Prince | H |
| Waikīkī Royal Suites | N |

**Outrigger Hotels**

| Hotel | Key |
|---|---|
| East | OF |
| Islander Waikīkī | OG |
| Reef on the Beach | OR |
| Waikīkī on the Beach | OL |
| Waikīkī Shore | OQ |

**Ohana Hotels**

| Hotel | Key |
|---|---|
| Surf | OC |
| Waikīkī Coral Seas | OJ |
| Waikīkī Edgewater | ON |
| Waikīkī Malia | OD |
| Waikīkī Reef Lanai | OI |
| Waikīkī Reef Towers | OK |
| Waikīkī Royal Islander | OM |
| Waikīkī Surf | OB |
| Waikīkī Surf East | OA |
| Waikīkī Tower | OP |
| Waikīkī Village | OH |
| Waikīkī West | OE |

**Hostels**

| Hostel | Key |
|---|---|
| Banana Bungalow | HB |
| Hawaiian Hostel | HA |
| Hostelling International Waikīkī | HC |

**Restaurants**

| Restaurant | No. |
|---|---|
| Arancino | 11 |
| Banyan Veranda | 16 |
| Cheeseburger in Paradise | 19 |
| China Garden | 3 |
| Ciao Mein | 12 |
| The Colony | 12 |
| Duke's Canoe Club | 18 |
| Hanohano Room | 21 |
| House Without a Key | 22 |
| Kacho | 20 |
| Keo's in Waikīkī | 5 |
| La Cucaracha | 1 |
| Lewers Street Fish Company | 14 |
| Matteo's | 2 |
| Moose McGillycuddy's | 8 |
| Oceanarium | 17 |
| Parc Café | 20 |
| Perry's Smorgy | 4 |
| Perry's Smorgy | 15 |
| Planet Hollywood | 9 |
| Restaurant Suntory | 13 |
| Ruffage Natural Foods | 7 |
| Shore Bird Beach Broiler | 23 |
| Tanaka of Tokyo | 10 |
| Texas Rock'n'Roll Sushi Bar | 12 |
| Tokyo Noodle House | 6 |

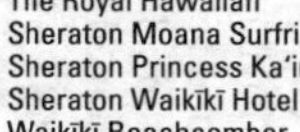
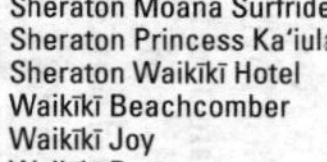
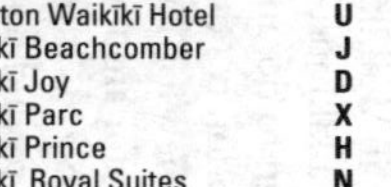


## Waikīkī

**Hotels**

| Hotel | Key |
|---|---|
| Ala Moana Hotel | AA |
| Hawaiian Waikīkī Beach Hotel | DD |
| Hilton Hawaiian Village | EE |
| New Otani Kaimana Beach Hotel | FF |
| Queen Kapi'olani | CC |
| Waikīkī Gateway Hotel | BB |
| W Honolulu | FF |

**Ohana Hotels**

| Hotel | Key |
|---|---|
| Ala Moana Towers | OT |
| Maile Sky Court | OS |
| Waikīkī Hobron | OU |

**Hostels**

| Hostel | Key |
|---|---|
| Central Branch YMCA | HD |
| Island Hostel | HE |
| Polynesian Hostel Beach Club | HF |
| Waikīkī Beachside Hostel | HF |

**Restaurants**

| Restaurant | No. |
|---|---|
| Bali by the Sea | 31 |
| Diamond Head Grill | 32 |
| Eggs'n'Things | 26 |
| Ezogiku | 30 |
| Genki Sushi | 24 |
| Golden Dragon | 31 |
| Hard Rock Café | 25 |
| Hau Tree Lanai | 32 |
| Hawaiian Seafood Paradise | 29 |
| Leonard's Bakery | 24 |
| Nick's Fishmarket | 27 |
| Sam Choy's Diamond Head | 24 |
| Singha Thai Cuisine | 28 |
| Todai Seafood Buffet | 28 |

## Bus tours

Countless operators in Waikīkī, such as Polynesian Adventure Tours (Ⓣ833-3000, Ⓦwww.polyad.com), E Noa Tours (Ⓣ591-2561, Ⓦwww.enoa.com), and Roberts (Ⓣ539-9400, Ⓦwww.roberts-hawaii.com), advertise bus tours of Honolulu and Oahu. The standard choice is between a half-day city tour, including Pearl Harbor, for around $14–20, and a full-day island tour starting at around $24. Hawaii Film and Celebrity Tours (Ⓣ926-3456, Ⓦwww.hawaiifilmtours.com) runs daily five-hour $45 narrated bus tours of Oahu movie locations, visiting sites familiar from the likes of *Pearl Harbor*, *Blue Hawaii* and, of course, *Hawaii Five-O*.

## Walking tours

Both Waikīkī and downtown Honolulu are compact enough to explore on foot on your own, but you can get a great sense of their histories and hidden byways by joining an expert-led **walking tour**.

Honolulu Time Walks runs a regular program of entertaining and informative tours on subjects such as Haunted Honolulu, Old Waikīkī, Mark Twain's Honolulu, and Scandals and Sinners ($7–8; Ⓣ943-0371). Similar tours, on topics including Hawaiian royalty, plantation life, and the history of Chinatown, are conducted by Kapi'olani Community College ($5–10; reserve on Ⓣ734-9245). The American Legion organizes one-hour walking tours of the National Cemetery of the Pacific in Punchbowl Crater (adults $15, under-10s free; includes Waikīkī hotel pick-up; Ⓣ946-6383).

For more energetic hiking, the Hawaii chapter of the Sierra Club sponsors treks and similar activities on weekends (Ⓣ538-6616, Ⓦwww.hi.sierraclub.org), while the Hawaii Nature Center arranges hikes most weekends (Ⓣ955-0100). Likehike (Ⓣ455-8193, http://gayhawaii.com/likehike/index .html) is a gay **hiking** club that runs group hikes on alternate Sundays. On Saturdays, the Clean Air Team (Ⓣ948-3299) runs a **Diamond Head walk**, meeting at 9am in front of the Honolulu Zoo; adults pay $5, kids go free.

# Accommodation

Virtually all the **accommodation** available in the city of Honolulu is confined to **Waikīkī**, which holds an extraordinary concentration of hotels in all price ranges. Unless you're happy to spend hundreds of dollars per night for world-class luxury, however, Waikīkī rooms are far from exciting. Most are in anonymous tower blocks, charging at least $100 for a standard en suite double room, with another $50 for an ocean view, and $50 more again if they're right on the seafront. Few have any sort of personal touch, and there are no local B&Bs. Assuming that you're committed to staying in Waikīkī in the first place – and you shouldn't feel that you *have* to come to Waikīkī just because you're coming to Hawaii – think carefully about what you plan to do, and how much you want to spend. The very cheapest accommodation option is a dorm bed in a hostel, but as long as you don't mind missing out on a sea view, or having to walk a few minutes to the beach, you can find adequate rooms for around $50 a night. To get your first-choice hotel in peak season, always **reserve** well in advance. However, with so many rooms available it's usually possible to find something at short notice.

Except for the very top-of-the-line properties, there's little point choosing a hotel with a **swimming pool** – most are squeezed onto rooftop terraces, overlooked by thousands of rooms in the surrounding high-rises and attracting all the dirt and fumes of the city.

There are no **campgrounds** in Waikīkī, and camping at Honolulu's only site, in Sand Island State Park (see p.88), is not recommended.

All of the hotels in Waikīkī have the zip code HI 96815. Also note that although Waikīkī is part of Honolulu, any hotel or restaurant said to be in "Honolulu" in this chapter is not in Waikīkī.

### Waikīkī hostels

**Banana Bungalow Waikīkī Beach Hostel**, 2463 Kūhiō Ave; ⓣ924-5074 or 1-888/2-HOSTEL, ⓕ924-4119, ⓦwww.bananabungalow.com. Part hostel, part bargain-rate hotel, this central tower block is an invaluable resource for budget travelers. All its sixty or so rooms have en-suite bathrooms, balconies, phones and TVs; roughly half are six- to eight-bed dorms priced at $18 per person, the rest are $55 private doubles. There's cheap internet access downstairs, free airport pickup, and island tours run several days per week; parking costs $7 per night. ❶–❷.

**Hale Aloha Hostel (Hostelling International Waikīkī)**, 2417 Prince Edward St; ⓣ926-8313, ⓕ922-3798. Official but informal youth hostel in the heart of Waikīkī, in a turquoise four-story building a couple of minutes from the beach. Dorm beds in four-person rooms are $17 ($19 for non-members), while double rooms cost $42–48; guests share a kitchen and patio. Office open 7am–3am; no curfew. Reservations recommended, especially the four double rooms. ❶–❷.

**Hawaiian Hostel**, 419 E Seaside Ave; ⓣ924-3303, toll-free 1-866/924-3303, ⓕ923-2111, ⓦwww.hawaiianhostel.com. Basic, independent hostel, for travelers with passports and onward flight tickets only (US citizens included). Tucked back from the street around a courtyard, it's a few blocks from the beach in a quiet area of central Waikīkī. A bed in a six-person dorm costs $17, in a two-person dorm it's $20, and a private double is $52; discounts for stays of three or more days, seventh night free. No curfew, free breakfasts, $5 dinners, free airport shuttle, and internet access. ❶–❷.

**Island Hostel**, Hawaiian Colony Building, 1946 Ala Moana Blvd; ⓣ & ⓕ924-8748. Independent, good-value hostel, a little way back from the *Hilton Hawaiian Village*, in western Waikīkī. Not quite in the thick of things, but a good base. Beds in four-person dorms $17 per night or $105 per week, doubles with kitchenette and TV $50 per night. No curfew. ❶–❷.

**Polynesian Hostel Beach Club**, 2584 Lemon Rd; ⓣ922-1340 or 1-877/504-2924, ⓕ923-4146, ⓦwww.hostelhawaii.com. Former motel converted into clean, private, air-conditioned hostel, a block from the sea at the Diamond Head end of Waikīkī. All rooms have en-suite bathrooms; some hold four bunk beds priced at $15 for one or $26 for two, while others serve as private doubles ($39) and studios ($51). Cash only. Van tours of the island are offered, and meals are served in the communal area some nights. Free snorkels, boogie boards and internet access. ❶–❷.

**Waikīkī Beachside Hotel & Hostel**, 2556 Lemon Rd; ⓣ923-9566, ⓕ923-7525, ⓦwww.hokondo.com. Motel near the park in eastern Waikīkī that has been rather perfunctorily rejigged as a private hostel; it looks a lot smarter from the outside than it does once you go in. It offers dorm beds ($17.50) and double rooms ($70), some of which are two-room suites capable of sleeping four guests, which isn't a bad deal if you're traveling as a group. An additional night's rent is taken as a deposit. ❶–❷.

### Waikīkī hotels: budget

**Aloha Punawai**, 305 Saratoga Rd; ⓣ & ⓕ923-5211, ⓦwww.alternative-hawaii.com/alohapunawai/. Miniature hotel, opposite the post office, whose well-priced studios and apartments – with and without air-conditioning – are furnished in a crisp, vaguely Japanese style. All units have kitchens, bathrooms, balconies and TV. Small discounts for weekly stays. ❸.

**The Breakers**, 250 Beach Walk; ⓣ923-3181 or 1-800/426-0494, ⓕ923-7174, ⓦwww.breakers-hawaii.com. Small, intimate hotel on the western edge of central Waikīkī, offering two-person studio apartments and four-person garden suites; all have kitchenettes and TV, and there's a bar and grill beside the flower-surrounded pool. ❸–❹.

**Hale Pua Nui**, 228 Beach Walk; ⓣ923-9693, ⓕ923-9678. Small, unprepossessing but clean motel-like hotel, among the cheapest deals in central Waikīkī. The studio apartments are far from fancy, but all have two twin beds, kitchenettes, cable TV and free local calls. Reserve well ahead. ❷.

**Hawaiian Waikīkī Beach Hotel**, 2570 Kalākaua Ave; ⓣ922-2511 or 1-800/877-7666, ⓕ923-3656, ⓦwww.hawaiianWaikikibeach.com. A 25-story behemoth at the Diamond Head end of Waikīkī, notable for its above-average nightly entertainment. Rooms further back from the ocean – especially in the separate Mauka Tower – are a much better value than those overlooking the beach. ❸–❺.

## Outrigger and Ohana Hotels

Until 1999, the family-oriented **Outrigger** chain ran twenty hotels in Waikīkī, with a total of more than 7500 rooms. To convey the differences among its various properties, the Outrigger company has now divided them into two separate categories. The five most luxurious kept the Outrigger brand name, while the rest have become **Ohana** (which means "family") hotels. By Waikīkī standards, all remain competitively priced. Even the fanciest of the Outriggers, the oceanfront *Reef on the Beach*, is less opulent than places like the *Hyatt Regency* or the *Hilton Hawaiian Village*, and costs significantly less per night. The Ohana properties all charge between $110 and $140 per night for a clean, well-maintained room with standard upmarket hotel furnishings, and offer discounted "Simple Saver" rates in low season (April–June and Sept to mid-Dec).

A high proportion of Outrigger and Ohana guests are on all-inclusive vacation packages. If you contact either chain directly – reservations are handled centrally, at the numbers below – be aware that both offer one free night to guests who stay six nights or more, and a plethora of room-and-car deals. Standard room rates, however, remain constant year-round; where the price codes below indicate ranges, these refer to the rate for a standard double room with and without ocean views.

**Outrigger Hotels:**

| | |
|---|---|
| *East*, 150 Ka'iulani Ave | 5 |
| *Islander Waikīkī*, 270 Lewers St | 5 |
| *Reef on the Beach*, 2169 Kālia Rd | 6–8 |
| *Waikīkī on the Beach*, 2335 Kalākaua Ave | 6–8 |
| *Waikīkī Shore*, 2161 Kālia Rd | 6 |
| Outrigger Reservations | W www.outrigger.com |
| US & Canada | T 1-800/688-7444 |
| Australia | T 0011-800/688-74443 |
| New Zealand | T 00-800/688-74443 |
| UK | T 1-800/688-74443 |
| Ireland | T 001-800/688-74443 |

**Ohana Hotels:**

| | |
|---|---|
| *Ala Moana Towers*, 1700 Ala Moana Blvd | 4 |
| *Maile Sky Court*, 2058 Kūhiō Ave | 4 |
| *Surf*, 2280 Kūhiō Ave | 4 |
| *Waikīkī Coral Seas*, 250 Lewers St | 4 |
| *Waikīkī Edgewater*, 2168 Kālia Rd | 4 |
| *Waikīkī Hobron*, 343 Hobron Lane | 4 |
| *Waikīkī Malia*, 2211 Kūhiō Ave | 4 |
| *Waikīkī Reef Lanai*, 225 Saratoga Rd | 4 |
| *Waikīkī Reef Towers*, 227 Lewers St | 4 |
| *Waikīkī Royal Islander*, 2164 Kālia Rd | 4 |
| *Waikīkī Surf East*, 422 Royal Hawaiian Ave | 4 |
| *Waikīkī Surf*, 2200 Kūhiō Ave | 4 |
| *Waikīkī Tower*, 200 Lewers St | 4 |
| *Waikīkī Village*, 240 Lewers St | 4 |
| *Waikīkī West*, 2330 Kūhiō Ave | 4 |
| Ohana Reservations | W www.ohanahotels.com |
| US & Canada | T 1-800/462-6262 |
| Worldwide | T 303/369-7777(US) |

**Hawaiiana Hotel**, 260 Beach Walk; ⓣ 923-3811, 1-800/628-3098 (HI) or 1-800/367-5122 (US & Can), ⓕ 926-5728, ⓦ www.hawaiianahotelatWaikiki.com. Pleasant low-rise family motel close to the heart of Waikīkī. Rooms – all with kitchenettes, but equipped to varying degrees of luxury – are arranged around two pools. ❸–❺.

**Kai Aloha**, 235 Saratoga Rd; ⓣ 923-6723, ⓕ 922-7592 ⓔ kaialoha@gte.net. Tiny, very central hotel. *Lānai* studios plus apartments that sleep up to four, all with kitchenettes, bathrooms, TV and air-conditioning. ❸.

**Royal Grove**, 151 Uluniu Ave; ⓣ 923-7691, ⓕ 922-7508, ⓦ www.royalgrovehotel.com. Small-scale, family-run hotel with a personal touch in central Waikīkī. The facilities improve the more you're prepared to pay, but even the most basic rooms, which lack air-conditioning, are of a reliable standard. There's also a courtyard pool, making the *Royal Grove* one of Waikīkī's best bets for budget travelers. Special weekly rates apply April–Nov only. ❷.

**Waikīkī Gateway Hotel**, 2070 Kalākaua Ave; ⓣ 955-3741 or 1-800/247-1903, ⓕ 923-2541, ⓦ www.waikiki-gateway-hotel.com. High-rise hotel on the western side of central Waikīkī, budget-oriented by local standards. Free continental breakfast on 16th-floor *lānai*. The highly rated lobby restaurant, *Nick's Fishmarket*, is reviewed on p.106. ❸.

**Waikīkī Prince**, 2431 Prince Edward St; ⓣ 922-1544, ⓕ 924-3712. Slightly drab but perfectly adequate and very central budget hotel. All rooms offer air-conditioning, en-suite baths and basic cooking facilities, but no phones; the "very small" and "small" categories are even cheaper than "economy" units. Office open 9am–6pm only; seventh night free April–Nov. ❷.

## Waikīkī hotels: mid-range

**Aston Coral Reef Hotel**, 2299 Kūhiō Ave; ⓣ 922-1262, 1-800/321-2588 (HI) or 1-800/922-7866 (US & Can), ⓕ 922-8785, ⓦ www.aston-hotels.com. Relatively inexpensive but still classy hotel, a couple of blocks back from the beach near the International Marketplace. The extra-large rooms sleep three or four people, while room rates drop by $25 April–June and Sept–Christmas. ❺.

**Aston Pacific Monarch**, 2427 Kūhiō Ave; ⓣ 923-9805, 1-800/321-2588 (HI) or 1-800/922-7866 (US & Can), ⓕ 924-3220, ⓦ www.aston-hotels.com. Tall condo building in the heart of Waikīkī, holding small studios with kitchenettes, plus larger four-person suites with full kitchens and balconies. ❹–❺.

**Aston Waikīkī Beachside Hotel**, 2452 Kalākaua Ave; ⓣ 931-2100, 1-800/321-2588 (HI) or 1-800/922-7866 (US & Can), ⓕ 931-2129, ⓦ www.aston-hotels.com. An elegant oceanfront option, with a marble lobby, and paneled chinoiserie in the bathrooms. Though it styles itself as "the only luxury boutique hotel in Waikīkī," the cheapest rooms are worth avoiding: glibly promoted as "inside cabins," they have no windows. There's no restaurant, but a continental breakfast is included, and guests can charge meals at the *Hyatt Regency* to their accounts. Standard ❻, partial ocean view ❼, deluxe ❽.

**Aston Waikīkī Circle Hotel**, 2464 Kalākaua Ave; ⓣ 923-1571, 1-800/321-2588 (HI) or 1-800/922-7866 (US & Can), ⓕ 926-8024, ⓦ www.aston-hotels.com. Bright and cheery tower, dwarfed by its surroundings but one of the cheapest options along the oceanfront. Each of its thirteen circular floors is divided into eight identical rooms, with prices varying according to how much sea you can see. The hotel is the base for Aloha Express Tours; see p.71. City view ❹, ocean view ❺.

**Ilima Hotel**, 445 Nohonani St; ⓣ 923-1877 or 1-800/367-5172 (US & Can), ⓕ 924-8371, ⓦ www.ilima.com. Good-value small hotel, near the canal on the *mauka* side of central Waikīkī and catering to a mainly local clientele. Spacious condo units, each offering two double beds, its own kitchen, and free local calls. ❹.

**Imperial of Waikīkī**, 205 Lewers St; ⓣ 923-1827 or 1-800/347-2582 (US & Can), ⓕ 923-7848, ⓦ www.imperialofwaikiki.com. Studio rooms and one- or two-bedroom balcony suites in a tower block set slightly back from the beach, just south of Kalākaua Avenue. A bit hemmed in by the oceanfront giants, but not bad for groups traveling together. The best views are from the terrace around the 27th-floor pool. ❹.

**Island Colony – A Marc Suite**, 445 Seaside Ave; ⓣ 923-2345; reserve through *Marc Resorts*, ⓣ 922-9700 or 1-800/535-0085 (US & Can), ⓕ 922-2421 or 1-800/633-5085 (US & Can), ⓦ www.marcresorts.com. Anonymous-looking high-rise at the quieter inland side of Waikīkī, still within five minutes' walk of the beach. Despite the name, it holds conventional hotel rooms as well as more luxurious suites; all are furnished to a high standard and have their own balconies. Hotel rooms ❹, studios ❺, suites ❻.

**New Otani Kaimana Beach Hotel**, 2863 Kalākaua Ave; ⓣ 923-1555 or 1-800/421-8795, ⓕ 922-9404, ⓦ www.kaimana.com. Intimate, Japanese-owned, Japanese-toned hotel on quiet and secluded Sans Souci Beach (see p.72), half a mile east of the bustle of central Waikīkī and boasting lovely backdrops of Diamond Head. The *Hau Tree Lanai* restaurant is reviewed on p.106. ❹.

**Pacific Beach Hotel**, 2490 Kalākaua Ave; ⓣ922-1233, 923-4511 or 1-800/367-6060, ⓕ922-8061, ⓦwww.pacificbeachhotel.com. The *Pacific Beach* boasts 830 rooms in two separate towers, at the Diamond Head end of Kalākaua Avenue. The high central tower contains the Oceanarium – a three-story fish tank that's the focus for diners in the *Neptune* and *Oceanarium* (see p.104) restaurants. ❻–❼.

**Queen Kapi'olani**, 150 Kapahulu Ave; ⓣ922-1941,1-800/533-6970 or 1-800/367-5004 (US & Can), ⓕ922-2694, ⓦwww.castle-group.com. One of Waikīkī's older high-rises, overlooking Kapi'olani Park and Diamond Head at the east end of town. Recently spruced up, it's relatively good value, so long as you don't get one of the handful of undersized rooms. ❹–❺.

**Sheraton Princess Ka'iulani**, 120 Ka'iulani Ave; ⓣ922-5811 or 1-800/782-9488, ⓕ931-4577, ⓦwww.sheraton-hawaii.com. Tower-block hotel, not quite on the seafront but big enough to command wide views of ocean and mountains. A spacious and attractive garden surrounds the tiny street-level pool. Standard ❻, ocean view ❼.

**Waikīkī Beachcomber**, 2300 Kalākaua Ave; ⓣ922-4646 or 1-800/622-4646 (US & Can), ⓕ923-4889, ⓦwww.waikikibeachcomber.com. A gleaming and centrally located white tower block, just "297 steps" from the beach. The 500 rooms are all but identical, with private balconies and above-average comforts – though all have showers not baths. Ask about special room/car deals. ❻.

**Waikīkī Joy**, 320 Lewers St; ⓣ923-2300, 1-800/321-2588 (HI) or 1-800/922-7866 (US & Can), ⓕ924-4010, ⓦwww.aston-hotels.com. Friendly, small-scale hotel. Marble decor throughout, from the airy garden lobby through the well-appointed rooms – all of which contain Jacuzzis. ❹–❺.

**Waikīkī Parc**, 2233 Helumoa Rd; ⓣ921-7272 or 1-800/422-0450, ⓕ923-1336, ⓦwww.waikikiparc.com. Modern high-rise set slightly back from the beach, operated by the same management as the *Halekulani* opposite, and offering a taste of the same luxury at more affordable prices. Conventional top-of-the-line rooms, plus two good restaurants: *Kacho* and the *Parc Café* (see p.106). Standard ❺, ocean view ❻.

**Waikīkī Royal Suites**, 255 Beach Walk; ⓣ926-5641; reserve through Marc Resorts, ⓣ 922-9700 or 1-800/535-0085 (US & Can); ⓕ922-2421 or 1-800/633-5085 (US & Can), ⓦwww.marcresorts.com. Plush all-suite property in the heart of Waikīkī. The building itself is not all that large, which gives it a friendly atmosphere, but each individual suite, complete with living room and *lānai*, offers extensive living space for families. ❻.

## Waikīkī hotels: expensive

**Halekūlani**, 2199 Kālia Rd; ⓣ923-2311 or 1-800/367-2343, ⓕ926-8004, ⓦwww.halekulani.com. Stunning oceanfront hotel, arranged around an exquisite courtyard and pool in a prime location for views along the beach to Diamond Head, but aloof from the Waikīkī bustle. Probably the most luxurious option in the area, and home to the highly rated *La Mer* restaurant. The open-air *House Without a Key* bar (see p.111) is perfect for sunset cocktails. Garden view ❽, ocean view ❾.

**Hilton Hawaiian Village**, 2005 Kālia Rd; ⓣ949-4321 or 1-800/221-2424, ⓕ947-7898, ⓦwww.hiltonhawaiianvillage.com. The biggest hotel in Hawaii, with more than 2500 rooms and counting, the *Hilton* is a scaled-down version of all of Waikīkī, holding almost a hundred of the exact same stores and restaurants you'd find out on the streets. The center of Waikīkī is a 15min walk away, and with a good pool, a great stretch of beach (see p.70), and even its own flamingo-filled lagoon, there's little incentive to leave the hotel precincts – which is, of course, the point. If you like this kind of self-contained resort, however, there are better ones on the other islands. Garden view ❻, ocean view ❽.

**Hyatt Regency Waikīkī**, 2424 Kalākaua Ave; ⓣ923-1234 or 1-800/233-1234, ⓕ923-7839, ⓦwww.hyatt.com. Very lavish, very central property, across the road from the heart of Waikīkī Beach, and consisting of two enormous towers engulfing a central atrium equipped with cascading waterfalls and tropical vegetation. Also holds a sixty-store shopping mall, a third-story open-air pool, a nightclub, 1230 "oversized" rooms, a spa, and six restaurants, of which three, *Ciao Mein*, *The Colony* and *The Texas Rock'n'Roll Sushi Bar*, are reviewed on pp.105–106. ❼–❾.

**The Royal Hawaiian**, 2490 Kalākaua Ave; ⓣ922-7311 or 1-800/782-9488, ⓕ931-7840, ⓦwww.sheraton-hawaii.com. The 1920s "Pink Palace" (see p.75), now owned by Sheraton, remains one of Waikīkī's best-loved landmarks. The original building still commands a great expanse of beach, and looks over the terrace gardens to the sea, but is now flanked by a less atmospheric tower block holding the most expensive suites. ❽–❾.

**Sheraton Moana Surfrider**, 2365 Kalākaua Ave; ⓣ922-3111 or 1-800/782-9488, ⓕ923-0308, ⓦwww.sheraton-hawaii.com. Waikīkī's oldest hotel, built at the end of the nineteenth century (see p.73). Despite extensive restoration, the "Colonial" architectural style of the original building – now the focus of the Banyan wing – remains intact, though these days it's flanked by two huge towers. The main lobby, with its wooden walls, plush settees and old-time atmosphere, is a delight. City view ❼, ocean view ❾.

**Sheraton Waikīkī Hotel**, 2255 Kalākaua Ave; Ⓣ 922-4422 or 1-800/782-9488, Ⓕ 923-8785, Ⓦ www.sheraton-hawaii.com. Ultra-modern, 1715-room skyscraper on Waikīkī Beach, with beachside gardens and pool. The rooms are deluxe, but can't compete with the thrill of the high-speed, glass-sided, ocean-view elevators. The separate *Sheraton Manor* wing offers much cheaper and smaller rooms with poor views. *Sheraton Manor* ❺; *Sheraton Waikīkī* city view ❼, ocean view ❾.

**W Honolulu**, 2885 Kalākaua Ave; Ⓣ 922-1700 or 1-877/W-HOTELS, Ⓕ 923-2249, Ⓦ www.whotels.com. Intimate, very chic little fifty-unit oceanfront hotel, just over half a mile east of Waikīkī, and part of an exclusive international chain. All rooms have balconies, CD players and cordless phones, and the *Diamond Head Grill* restaurant (see p.105) is downstairs. Rooms ❽, suites ❾.

## Honolulu YMCAS and hostels

**Central Branch YMCA**, 401 Atkinson Drive, Honolulu HI 96814; Ⓣ 941-3344, Ⓕ 941-8821. Set in attractive grounds opposite the Ala Moana shopping mall, only just outside Waikīkī, with an on-site swimming pool and a beach nearby. Accommodations include plain rooms with shared bath for men only, at $30 single or $41 double, plus some nicer en-suite doubles available to women too, at $38 single, $53 double. All guests must reserve at least two weeks in advance, and have a definite check-out date; no walk-ins are accepted. ❷.

**Fernhurst YWCA**, 1566 Wilder Ave, Honolulu HI 96822; Ⓣ 941-2231, Ⓕ 949-0266, Ⓔ fernywca@get.net. Women-only lodging, not far west of the University and quite a way from the ocean, that's intended primarily for locals in need. Double rooms share a bathroom with one other room, and cost $25 per person; some can be rented by single travelers for $30. Rates include simple buffet breakfasts and dinners served Mon–Sat; a $30 membership is compulsory. ❶–❷.

**Honolulu International AYH Hostel (Hostelling International Honolulu)**, 2323-A Seaview Ave, Honolulu HI 96822; Ⓣ 946-0591, Ⓕ 946-5904. Youth hostel in college residence, a couple of miles from Waikīkī, across from the University of Hawaii in Mānoa. There's no direct bus from the airport: change at Ala Moana to TheBus #6 or #18; get off at Metcalfe Street/University Avenue, one block south of the hostel. Office hours 8am–noon and 4pm–midnight; no curfew. Dorm beds are $13.50 for AYH/IYHA members, $16.50 for nonmembers, and there's a three-night maximum stay for non-members. ❶.

**Nu'uanu YMCA**, 1441 Pali Hwy, Honolulu HI 96813; Ⓣ 536-3556, Ⓕ 533-1286. Basic single rooms, sharing bath, for men only at $30 per night. The well-equipped new building is just up from downtown and easily accessible by bus. ❷.

## Honolulu hotels and B&Bs

**Ala Moana Hotel**, 410 Atkinson Drive, Honolulu HI 96814; Ⓣ 955-4811, 1-800/446-8990 (HI) or 1-800/367-6025 (US & Can), Ⓕ 944-2974, Ⓦ www.alamoanahotel.com. Thousand-room tower block right alongside the Ala Moana Center, just down the road from the Convention Center, and five minutes' walk from Waikīkī. Though it's targeted primarily at business visitors and shopaholics, it offers the lively *Rumours* nightclub and some good restaurants, and there's an excellent beach close at hand (see p.88). ❺.

### Airport accommodation

If you find yourself stuck at Honolulu Airport and desperate for sleep, the ideal solution is right there in the main lobby. The **Honolulu Airport Mini Hotel** (Ⓣ 836-3044, Ⓕ 834-8985; ❷) – also known as *Sleep & Shower* – offers tiny but clean private rooms, for single occupancy only, at $30 for eight hours or $17.50 for two hours, including shower.

Nearby on N Nimitz Highway, and served by complementary shuttle buses, there's a *Best Western Plaza* (3253 N Nimitz Hwy; Ⓣ 836-3636 or 1-800/800-4683, Ⓕ 833-2349; ❹) and a *Holiday Inn* (3401 N Nimitz Hwy; Ⓣ 836-0661 or 1-800/800-3477, Ⓕ 833-1738; ❺).

**Aston at the Executive Center Hotel**, 1088 Bishop St, Honolulu HI 96813; ⓣ539-3000, 1-800/321-2588 (HI) or 1-800/922-7866 (US & Can), ⓕ523-1088, ⓦwww.aston-hotels.com. All-suite downtown hotel, enjoying great harbor views from the top of a 40-story skyscraper. Geared to business travelers, but with prices that compare well with similar standard Waikīkī hotels. ❺.

**Mānoa Valley Inn**, 2001 Vancouver Drive, Honolulu HI 96822; ⓣ947-6019, ⓕ946-6168, ⓦwww.aloha.net/~wery/. One of Honolulu's most relaxing options: a plush, antique-filled B&B inn, near the University in lush Mānoa Valley. Waikīkī feels a lot farther away than the mile it really is. Eight rooms, some sharing bathrooms and some en-suite. Sit in one of the wicker chairs on the back porch and linger over breakfast. ❹–❺.

**Pagoda Hotel**, 1525 Rycroft St, Honolulu HI 96814; ⓣ923-4511 or 1-800/367-6060, ⓕ922-8061, ⓦwww.pagodahotel.com. Roughly halfway between downtown Honolulu and Waikīkī, within easy walking distance of Ala Moana mall. The *Pagoda* has conventional, comfortable hotel rooms and one- and two-bedroom suites, plus two pools and three restaurants. ❺.

# Waikīkī

On any one day, half of all the tourists in the state of Hawaii are crammed into the tiny, surreal enclave of **WAIKĪKĪ**, three miles east of downtown Honolulu. Effectively, it's an island in its own right, a two-mile-long, quarter-mile-wide strip sealed off from the rest of the city by the Ala Wai Canal and almost completely surrounded by water. Its incredible high-rise profusion of skyscrapers, jostling for position along the shoreline, hold enough hotel rooms to accommodate more than 100,000 guests, restaurants by the hundred, and stores providing anything the visitor could possibly want.

Long before Kamehameha the Great built a thatched hut here at the start of the nineteenth century, Waikīkī – the name means "spouting water" – was a favored residence of the chiefs of Oahu. They coveted not only its waterfront

## Street names of Waikīkī

Waikīkī's unfamiliar street names may seem easier to remember if you know the stories that lie behind them:

**Helumoa Road**: Literally, "chicken scratch"; the road crosses the site of a *heiau* used for human sacrifices, which was frequented by chickens that scratched for maggots amid the corpses.

**Ka'iulani Avenue**: The young Princess Victoria Ka'iulani (1875–99) was immortalized in a poem by Robert Louis Stevenson.

**Kālaimoku Street**: Kamehameha the Great's Prime Minister, Kālaimoku, who died in 1827, also called himself "William Pitt" in honor of his British equivalent.

**Kalākaua Avenue**: Originally named Waikīkī Road, it was renamed in honor of the "Merrie Monarch" (1836–91; see p.514) in 1905.

**Kūhiō Avenue**: Prince Jonah Kūhiō Kalaniana'ole (1871–1922), or "Prince Cupid," bequeathed much of the eastern end of Waikīkī to the city after his death.

**Lili'uokalani Avenue**: Queen Lili'uokalani was the last monarch to rule over Hawaii (1838–1917; see p.514).

**Nāhua Street**: Chiefess Nāhua once owned an oceanfront estate in Waikīkī.

**'Olohana Street**: The captured English sailor, John Young (1745–1835; see p.287), was known as Olohana to the Hawaiians after his naval cry of "All hands on deck."

**Tusitala Street**: Named after author Robert Louis Stevenson, whose Hawaiian name was taken from the Samoan word for "story-teller."

**Uluniu Avenue**: Literally, "coconut grove," it marks the site of a cottage owned by King David Kalākaua.

coconut groves and well-stocked fishponds, but also the mosquito-free swamps and wetlands that lay immediately behind them – prime *taro*-growing land at a time when such land was a rare and valuable resource. By the end of the century, however, with Hawaii annexed by the United States, it was considered all but useless. Waikīkī's value lay instead in its being the best beach within easy reach of Honolulu. When the *Moana* hotel went up in 1901, signaling the start of the tourist boom, a handful of inns were already dotted among the luxurious homes of elite missionary and merchant families.

However, Waikīkī only began to regain a significant population during the 1920s, when a vast program of land reclamation was instigated. The Ala Wai Canal was dug to divert the mountain streams into flowing around the edge of Waikīkī, and the central area was filled in with chunks of coral sawn from the reef that then ran the full length of the shoreline. Since then, Waikīkī has mushroomed beyond belief. By looking beyond the tower blocks, to Diamond Head or the mysterious valleys that recede into the mountains, you can remind yourself that you're on a Pacific island, but there's precious little of the real Hawaii left in Waikīkī.

As long as you're prepared to enter into the spirit of rampant commercialism, it's possible to have a great time in Waikīkī. You could, just about, survive with little money, buying snacks from the omnipresent ABC convenience stores, but there would be no point – there's very little to see, and the only alternative to surfing and sunbathing is to shop until you drop.

## Waikīkī Beach

Viewed objectively, **Waikīkī Beach** would rank pretty low down any list of Hawaii's best beaches. Even in other parts of Oahu, it's not hard to find a stretch of deserted, palm-fringed, tropical shoreline, whereas at Waikīkī you can hardly see the sand for the sunbathers, and the traffic on Kalākaua Avenue outroars the surf. Somehow, however, that barely seems to matter. Waikīkī Beach may be crowded, but it's crowded with enthusiastic holiday-makers, wringing every last minute's pleasure they can from being on one of the most famous beaches in the world. Incidentally, whatever it may look like, no hotel ever owns the beach adjacent to it; public access is guaranteed on every single beach in Hawaii.

Simply glance towards the ocean, and you'll be caught up in the ever-changing action. At the edge of the water, family groups splash and thrash while oblivious honeymoon couples gaze hand-in-hand at the horizon; beyond them, circling surfers await the next wave, now and then parting abruptly to allow outrigger canoes to glide through; further still, pleasure yachts and parasailers race back and forth; and, out in the deep-water channel, cruise liners, merchant ships, aircraft carriers and oil tankers make their stately way towards the docks of Honolulu and Pearl Harbor.

Meanwhile, the beach itself plays host to a constant parade of characters; undiscovered starlets in impenetrable sunshades sashay around in the latest swimsuits; local beach boys busy themselves making new friends and renting out the occasional surfboard; over-excited children dart between the sedate seniors with their fancy deckchairs and bulging coolers; and determined European backpackers pick their way through the throng on their dogged search for the perfect plot of sand. On the sidewalk behind, jet-lagged new arrivals wonder how they'll ever get through the crush to dabble their toes in the Pacific for the first time.

Waikīkī's natural setting is just as beguiling as its melee of activity. Off to the east, the sharp profile of Diamond Head spears the ocean, while straight back inland the lush green Ko'olau mountains soar between the skyscrapers. In the early evening especially, as the orange sun sinks far out to sea and the silhouettes of the palm trees grow ever starker, the overall effect is magical.



Few visitors, however, realize that Waikīkī Beach is almost entirely **artificial**. The landscaping that created Waikīkī changed the ocean currents so that its natural beaches were swept away; ever since, the hotels have had a considerable stake in importing sand. So much was shipped in – much of it from Pāpōhaku Beach, on Molokai (see p.407) – that the contours of the sea bottom have been permanently altered. As a result, the **surfing** conditions at what is generally acknowledged to be the birthplace of the modern sport are no longer all that spectacular – which is why the experts head straight up to Oahu's North Shore.

## Exploring Waikīkī Beach

Although Waikīkī Beach officially stretches the full length of the Waikīkī shoreline, from the Ala Wai Harbor in the west to within a couple of hundred yards of Diamond Head, each of its many distinct sections has its own name. The **center** of the beach – the segment that everyone still calls Waikīkī Beach – is the point near Duke Kahanamoku's statue (see p.73) where the buildings on the ocean side of Kalākaua Avenue come to a halt, and the sidewalk turns into a beachfront promenade. Swimmers here enjoy the best conditions of the entire seafront, with softly shelving sands, and waters that are generally calm.

To the **west**, central Waikīkī Beach merges into **Royal-Moana Beach**, fronting the *Royal Hawaiian* and *Sheraton Moana* hotels. It can sometimes be a struggle to walk along this narrow, busy strip because of the crowds it draws, but the swimming is, again, excellent. It's also the best spot for **novice surfers**: head slightly to the right as you enter the water to reach the easy break known as Canoes' Surf (so called because these gentle waves were all the heavy old *koa* canoes could ride). The waves are slightly stronger further left, at the Queen's Surf break.

West of the *Royal Hawaiian*, a raised walkway curves in front of the *Sheraton Waikīkī*, where the sea comes right over the sand. After a tiny little "pocket beach," where the only shade to be found is beneath some very low branches, a long walkway squeezes between the waves and the grand *Halekūlani Hotel*. At the far end comes a slightly larger stretch of beach, extending from the *Halekūlani* as far as the groin in front of the *Outrigger Reef on the Beach*. This is generally known as **Halekūlani Beach**, or, in memory of a small inn that previously stood here, **Gray's Beach**. There's still plenty of sand on the seabed, so it's another popular swimming spot.

Beyond Gray's Beach, the sands grow broader as you pass in front of the military base. The walking can be a bit slow on **Fort DeRussy Beach** itself, but it's backed by some pleasant lawns and an open pavilion naturally sheltered by interlaced trees. As the ocean floor at this point is sharp and rocky, few people swim here. The westernmost section of the Waikīkī shorefront, **Kahanamoku Beach**, flanks the *Hilton Hawaiian Village* (reviewed on p.66). Duke Kahanamoku's grandfather was granted most of the twenty-acre plot on which the *Hilton* now stands in the Great Mahele of 1848. Thanks to its carefully sculpted shelf of sand, the beach where Duke was raised is ideal for family bathing, but it somehow lacks the concentrated glamour or excitement of central Waikīkī.

## Watersports and Cruises

The listings below provide a sample of **water-based activities** on offer in Waikīkī. **Activities desks** in the hotels, and **"activity centers"** elsewhere, sell tickets for water-borne pursuits of all kinds. If you're prepared to shop around, you'll find rates much lower than those quoted by the operators; look for discount coupons in free magazines, and handbills distributed on street corners. Aim to pay perhaps $25 per person for a basic cruise (including a buffet dinner), up to $60 for a cruise on a submarine or with a better standard of food.

Note also that activity centers offer discounts on **airport shuttles, land-based tours** (see p.62), **excursions** to the *lū'aus* (p.103), and on **air tickets** and packages to the other Hawaiian islands.

For details about watersports on the North Shore, see p.136.

### Activity Centers

**Aloha Express**, *Waikīkī Circle Hotel*, 2464 Kalākaua Ave; ⓣ924-4030.
**Magnum Tickets & Tours**, 2134 Kalākaua Ave; ⓣ923-7825.
**Pacific Monarch Travel**, 2426 Kūhīo Ave; ⓣ924-7717.
**Polynesian Express**, Kūhīo Mall, 2301 Kūhīo Ave #222; ⓣ922-5577 or 1-800/903-9970.
**Tours 4 Less**, 159 Ka'iulani Ave; ⓣ923-2211.

### Dinner and Sightseeing Cruises

**Ali'i Kai Catamaran** (ⓣ539-9400 or 1-800/831-5541). Giant catamaran offering kitsch sunset cruises along Waikīkī Beach.
**Dream Cruises** (ⓣ592-2000 or 1-800/400-7300, ⓦwww.dream-cruises.com). Lunch and sunset cruises on Oahu's south and north shores, including snorkeling, and whale-watching in winter.
**Navatek I** (ⓣ973-1311, ⓦwww.go-atlantis.com). Giant catamaran, based at Pier 6 in Honolulu, providing lunchtime and sunset buffet cruises, complete with Elvis impersonator.
**Paradise Cruise** (ⓣ983-7827). Sightseeing, snorkeling, dinner and whale-watching cruises, starting alongside Aloha Tower.

### Submarines

**Atlantis Submarines** (ⓣ973-9811 or 1-800/548-6262, ⓦwww.go-atlantis.com). 45-min dives to the seabed off the *Hilton Hawaiian Village*, where you cruise past two sunken airplanes before circling a full-size shipwreck.
**Voyager Submarines** (ⓣ539-9400 or 1-800/831-5541, ⓦwww.robertshawaii.com). The "yellow submarine" descends to the atmospheric shipwreck of the *Sea Tiger*, off Kewalo Basin.

### Diving

A typical rate for a two-tank scuba-diving trip is $90. Operators include the **Aloha Dive Shop** at Koko Marina, not far from Hanauma Bay (ⓣ395-5922); **Surf'n'Sea** in Hale'iwa (ⓣ637-9887 or 1-800/899-SURF, ⓦwww.surfnsea.com); Ed Masucci's **Taking The Plunge** (ⓣ922-2600, ⓦwww.takemediving.com); and **Ocean Concepts** (ⓣ677-7975 or 1-800/808-3483, ⓦwww.oceanconcepts.com). An unusual variation is offered by **Bob's Hawaii Adventure** at Koko Marina (ⓣ943-8628); no diving experience is required to take a half-hour ride along the ocean floor on an **underwater moped**, for $110.

### Other Watersports

Concession stands near the Duke Kahanamoku statue in central Waikīkī rent out surfboards for around $10 per hour and offer **surfing lessons** for beginners that cost more like $40 per hour, including board rental. **Kayaks** for inshore expeditions can readily be rented, also for about $10 per hour, from Prime Time Sports (ⓣ949-8952). For around $50, you can also **waterski** in Koko Marina with Suyderhoud's Waterski Center (ⓣ395-3773), or try **parasailing** with Aloha Parasail (ⓣ521-2446) or Hawaiian Parasail (ⓣ591-1280).

Large segments of the long beach that runs **east** of central Waikīkī did not even exist until well after World War II. Previously there were only sporadic patches of sand, and several structures stood *makai* (on the ocean side) of Kalākaua Avenue as recently as 1970. Now, however, Kūhiō Beach is one of Waikīkī's busiest areas. The protective walls and breakwaters that jut out into the ocean here shelter two separate lagoons in which swimming is both safe and comfortable. The easternmost of these walls, the **Kapahulu Groin**, projects from the end of Kapahulu Avenue, following the line of the vanished Ku'ekaunahi Stream. Standing well above the waterline, it makes a good vantage point for photos of the Waikīkī panorama. On the other hand, the long, seaweed-covered **Slippery Wall**, parallel to the beach roughly fifty yards out, is washed over by every wave in turn. Daredevil locals boogie-board just outside the wall, but the currents are so strong that you should only join them if you really know what you're doing.

East of the Kapahulu Groin, at the end of the built-up section of Waikīkī, comes a gap in the beach where the sand all but disappears and the waters are not suitable for bathing. Beyond that, to either side of the Waikīkī Aquarium, **Kapi'olani Park Beach** is the favorite beach of many local families and fitness freaks, and is also known for having a strong gay presence. Its lawns offer plenty of free shade and make a perfect picnic spot. Waikīkī's only substantial stretch of reasonably unspoiled coral reef runs a short distance offshore, shielding a pleasant, gentle swimming area. The most used segment of the beach, nearest to Waikīkī, is **Queen's Surf Beach Park** – confusingly named after a long-gone restaurant that was itself named after the Queen's Surf surf break, way away to the west.

Not far past the Aquarium (see p.76) stands the solemn concrete facade of the decaying **War Memorial Natatorium**. This curious combination of World War I memorial and swimming pool, with seating for 2500 spectators, was opened with a 100-meter swim by Duke Kahanamoku (see opposite) in August 1927. During its inaugural championships, Johnny "Tarzan" Weissmuller set world records in the 100-, 400- and 800-meter races. Ironically, the Natatorium has never really recovered from being used for training by the US Navy during World War II, and for many years it was in a very sorry state indeed. Bit by bit, it's now being restored, in face of vociferous opposition from those who argue that the last thing this relatively quiet section of Waikīkī needs is a major tourist attraction.

East of the Natatorium, palm-fringed **Sans Souci Beach** commemorates one of Waikīkī's earliest guesthouses, built in 1884 and twice stayed in by Robert Louis Stevenson. In addition to being sheltered enough for young children, the beach also offers decent snorkeling. That's unusual for Waikīkī, where most of the reef has been suffocated by dumped sand. The *New Otani Kaimana Beach* hotel (see p.65), now occupying the site of the *Sans Souci*, marks the return of buildings to the shoreline and is as far as most visitors would consider strolling along Waikīkī Beach. However, beyond it lies the Outrigger Canoe Club Beach, which was leased in 1908 by the Outrigger Canoe Club on the condition that its waters be set aside for surfing, canoeing and ocean sports. The club headquarters was later replaced by the first of the Outrigger chain of hotels, but the ocean remains the preserve of surfers and snorkelers.

As Kalākaua Avenue heads out of Waikīkī beyond the Outrigger Canoe Club Beach, curving away from the shoreline to join Diamond Head Road and skirt the base of the volcano, it passes a little scrap of sandy beach known as **Kaluahole Beach** or **Diamond Head Beach**. Though too small for anyone to wants to spend much time on the beach itself, it does offer some quite good swimming, and makes a good launching-point for windsurfers.

The coast immediately to the east, on the other hand, officially **Diamond Head Beach Park**, is much too rocky and exposed for ordinary swimmers. It's noteworthy as the site of the 55-foot **Diamond Head Lighthouse**, built in 1899 and still in use. A short distance further on, the highway, by now raised well above sea level, rounds the point of Diamond Head; the island of Molokai to the east is visible across the water on clear days. As a rule, only keen surfers pick their way down to the shoreline from the three roadside lookouts that constitute **Kuilei Cliffs Beach Park**.

Opposite the intersection where Diamond Head Road loops back inland and Kāhala Avenue continues beside the ocean, **Ka'alāwai Beach**, at the end of short Kulumanu Place, is a narrow patch of white sand popular with snorkelers and surfers. It is brought to a halt by Black Point, where lava flowing from Diamond Head into the sea created Oahu's southernmost point.

## Waikīkī on foot

Most of the **walking** you do in Waikīkī is likely to be by necessity rather than choice; it offers little in the way of conventional sightseeing. Its roads may once have been picturesque lanes that meandered between the coconut groves and *taro* fields, but they're now lined by dull concrete malls and hotels, and a building erected before 1970 is a rare sight. In addition, the daytime **heat** can make walking more than a few blocks uncomfortable.

However, vestiges of the old Waikīkī are still scattered here and there, as pointed out by the helpful surfboard-shaped placards of the waterfront **Waikīkī Historical Trail**. There are also a couple of museums illustrating aspects of Hawaiian history, and the lawns of Kapi'olani Park to the east make a welcome break from the bustle of the resort area. It may come as a surprise that for some people Waikīkī still counts as home; you may well see groups of seniors practicing their ukuleles or playing chess in the oceanfront pavilions.

### West from the Duke Kahanamoku statue

The logical place to start a walking tour is in the middle, on seafront **Kalākaua Avenue**. The central stretch of Waikīkī Beach here is marked by a statue of **Duke Kahanamoku** (1890–1968), which is always wreathed in *leis.* The archetypal "Beach Boy," Duke represented the US in three Olympics, winning swimming golds in both 1912 and 1920. His subsequent exposition tours popularized the Hawaiian art of surfing all over the world, and as Sheriff of Honolulu he continued to welcome celebrity visitors to Hawaii until his death in 1969. Sadly, Duke's back is to the ocean, a pose he seldom adopted in life; otherwise he'd be gazing at the spot where in 1917 he rode a single 35-foot wave a record total of one and a quarter miles.

Slightly west of the statue, alongside a small police station in a railed enclosure, stand four large boulders known as the **sacred stones of Ulukou**. These are said to embody the healing and spiritual powers of four magician-priests from Tahiti, who set them in place before returning to their homeland in the fourteenth century.

Still further west, the wedge of the **Sheraton Moana Surfrider** forces Kalākaua Avenue away from the ocean. Though not Waikīkī's first hotel, the *Moana* is the oldest left standing, and since 1983 it has been transformed back to a close approximation of its original 1901 appearance. Like all Waikīkī hotels, the *Moana* is happy to allow nonguests in for a peek; the luxurious

63

settees of its long Beaux Arts lobby make an ideal spot to catch up with the newspapers.

Follow Kalākaua Avenue west from here, and you'll come to the **Royal Hawaiian Shopping Center**, Waikīkī's most upmarket mall (though not a patch on Honolulu's Ala Moana Center; see p.114), and across from that the tackier open-air **International Marketplace**, which has a bargain food court (see p.102). Once the site of an ancient *heiau*, and later of the ten-thousand-strong royal Helumoa coconut grove – of which a few palms still survive – the beachfront here is today dominated by the **Royal Hawaiian Hotel**, also known as the "Pink Palace." Its Spanish-Moorish architecture was all the rage when it opened in 1927, with a room rate of $14 per night, but its grandeur is now somewhat swamped by a towering new wing.

On the map, the military base of **Fort DeRussy**, beyond, looks like a welcome expanse of green at the western edge of the main built-up area of Waikīkī. In fact, it's largely taken up by parking lots and tennis courts, and is not a place to stroll for pleasure. At its oceanfront side, however, the **US Army Museum** (Tues–Sun 10am–4.30pm; free) is located in a low concrete structure which, as **Battery Randolph**, housed massive artillery pieces that were directed by observers stationed atop Diamond Head during World War II. Displays here trace the history of warfare in Hawaii back to the time of Kamehameha the Great, with the bulk of the collection consisting of the various guns and cannons that have been used to defend Honolulu since the US Army first arrived, four days after annexation in 1898. One photo shows a young, giggling Shirley Temple perched astride a gun barrel during the 1930s, but the mood swiftly changes with a detailed chronicling of the pivotal role played by the state during the Pacific campaign against Japan.

## East from the Duke Kahanamoku statue

The first thing you come to as you head **east** from the Duke Kahanamoku statue is a magnificent, well-groomed Indian Banyan tree, supported by two "trunks" that on close inspection turn out to be tangled masses of aerial roots. This area has been attractively landscaped in the last few years, and kitted out with appealing little lagoons and waterfalls' as well as shaded pavilions and lots of open-air benches. Across the street, the central atrium of the *Hyatt Regency Waikīkī* hotel holds a much larger waterfall, surrounded by palm trees.

**Father Damien**, the nineteenth-century Belgian priest who ranks with Hawaii's greatest heroes, is commemorated in the simple **Damien Museum** at 130 Ohua Ave (Mon–Fri 9am–3pm; free; ⓣ923-2690), one block east of the *Pacific Beach Hotel*. This unobtrusive shrine sits beneath a schoolroom behind the angular modern Catholic church of **St Augustine**. Damien's life and work is evoked by an assortment of mundane trivia, such as receipts for cases of soda and barrels of flour, and his prayerbooks and vestments. Although he established churches all over Hawaii, Damien's fame derives principally from his final sojourn in the leper colony at **Kalaupapa** on Molokai. He eventually succumbed to the disease himself on April 15, 1889, at the age of 49; harrowing deathbed photos show the ravages it inflicted upon him. For a full account of Father Damien's life, see p.400.

### Kapi'olani Park

Beyond the eastern limit of central Waikīkī, as defined by Kapuhulu Avenue, lies Hawaii's first-ever public park, **Kapi'olani Park**, which was established in 1877. Locals flock to this much-needed breathing space from dawn onwards, with joggers pounding the footpaths, and practitioners of t'ai chi weaving slow-motion spells beneath the trees. Tourists pour in from 9am on Tuesdays, Wednesdays and Thursdays, for the free **Pleasant Hawaiian Hula Show**, which starts at 10am. This kitsch relic of bygone days culminates with grass-skirted *hula* "maidens" (some of whom have participated since it began in 1937) holding up letters to spell out A-L-O-H-A H-A-W-A-I-I. The adjoining **Waikīkī Shell** nearby hosts large concerts, especially in summer, while the Royal Hawaiian Band performs on the park's **bandstand** on Sundays at 2pm.



### Honolulu Zoo

**Honolulu Zoo** occupies a verdant wedge on the fringes of Kapi'olani Park (daily 8.30am–5.30pm, last admission 4.30pm; adults $6, ages 6–12 $1). With its main entrance barely a minute's walk from the bustle of Waikīkī, its luxuriant tropical undergrowth and blossoming trees, set against the backdrop of Diamond Head, are as much of an attraction as the animals, which range from wallowing hippos and gray kangaroos to some unfortunate monkeys trapped on tiny islands in a crocodile-infested lagoon. The zoo's pride and joy, the African Savanna exhibit, was designed to re-create the swamps and grasslands of Africa. This it manages to do reasonably successfully. In this world of reddish mud live "black" rhinos, which are, in fact, the color of their surroundings.

### Waikīkī Aquarium

A few minutes' walk further east, along the Kapi'olani Park waterfront, stands the slick, but disappointingly small, **Waikīkī Aquarium** (daily 9am–5pm; adults $7, seniors and students $5, ages 13–17 $3.50, under-12s free). Windows in its indoor galleries offer views into the turquoise world of Hawaiian reef fish, among them the lurid red frogfish – an ugly brute that squats splay-footed on the rock waiting to eat unwary passers-by – and a teeming mass of small sharks. One whole tank is devoted to Hanauma Bay (see p.115). Outside, the mocked-up "edge of the reef," complete with artificial tidepools, feels a bit pointless with the real thing just a few feet away. Nearby is a long tank of Hawaiian monk seals, dog-like not only in appearance but also in their willingness to perform tawdry tricks for snacks. As well as a description of traditional fish farming, there's a display of the modern equivalent, in which *mahimahi* fish grow from transparent eggs to glistening six-footers in what appear to be lava lamps.

# Diamond Head

The craggy 762-foot pinnacle of **Diamond Head**, immediately southeast along the coast from Waikīkī, is Honolulu's most famous landmark. It's among the youngest of the chain of volcanic cones – others include Punchbowl (see p.89) and Koko Head (p.117) – that stretch across southeast Oahu. All were created by brief, spectacular blasts of the Ko'olau vent, which reawakened a few hundred thousand years ago after slumbering for more than two million years. The most recent of the series date back less than ten thousand years, so geologists consider further eruptions possible. Diamond Head itself was formed in a matter of a few days or even hours: the reason its southwestern side is so much higher than the others is that the trade winds were blowing from the northeast at the time.

Ancient Hawaiians knew Diamond Head as either Lei'ahi ("wreath of fire," a reference to beacons lit on the summit to guide canoes) or Lae'ahi ("brow of the yellow-fin tuna"). They built several *heiaus* in and around it, slid down its walls to Waikīkī on *hōlua* land-sleds as sport, and threw convicted criminals from the rim. Its modern name derives from the mistake of a party of English sailors early in the nineteenth century, who stumbled across what they thought were diamonds on its slopes and rushed back to town with their pockets bulging with glittering but worthless calcite crystals.

For most of this century, Diamond Head was sealed off by the US military, who based long-range artillery here during World War I, and after Pearl Harbor used the bunkers to triangulate and aim the guns of Waikīkī's Fort DeRussy. Only in the 1960s was it reopened as the **Diamond Head State Monument** public park.

Access to the crater is via a short road tunnel that drills through the surrounding walls from its *mauka* side. The entrance is around two miles by road from Waikīkī; it's not a particularly pleasant walk, so most people either drive or take the bus. Buses #22 and #58 from Waikīkī climb up Monsarrat Avenue past the zoo to join Diamond Head Road, and stop not far from the tunnel; if you're driving, you can also follow the shoreline highway below the mountain and climb the same road from the bottom.

As the floor of the crater stands well above sea level – it's gradually filling in as the walls erode – Diamond Head is not quite so dramatic from the inside. In fact, the lawns of the crater interior are oddly bland, almost suburban. Often parched, but a vivid green after rain, they're still dotted with little-used military installations, some of which remain restricted. There have been suggestions that these should be replaced by tennis and golf facilities, but the prevailing wisdom is to allow the place to return to nature in due course. For details of guided Diamond Head hikes, see p.62.

## The hike to the rim

The reason most people come to Diamond Head is to **hike** the hot half-hour trail up to the rim, for a superb panorama of the whole southern coast of Oahu. It's a more demanding climb than you may be led to expect, so be sure to wear suitable footwear and bring a flashlight.

Rangers stationed alongside the parking lot collect $1 from each hiker; the paved trail is open daily from 6am until 6pm. Having first climbed slowly away from the crater floor, it meanders up the inside walls. Many of the holes visible but out of reach on the hillside are ancient burial caves. Before long, you're obliged to enter the vast network of military bunkers and passageways that riddle the crater. Immediately after passing through the first long, dark tunnel – watch out for the bolts poking from the ceiling – a tall, narrow flight of yellow-painted stairs leads up between two high walls to the right. It's also possible to head left here to join a path along the outside – a reasonably safe option as long as you follow the contours, and bear in mind that several people have fallen while attempting to scramble straight up.

If you continue up the steps instead, you soon come to another tunnel, then climb a dark spiral staircase through four or so cramped tiers of fortifications, equipped with eye-slit windows and camouflaged from above. Beyond that, a final outdoor staircase leads to the summit, where you get your first sweeping views of Waikīkī and Honolulu. In theory an official geodetic plate marks the highest point, but however often it's replaced it soon gets stolen again.

On days when a *kona* (southwest) wind is blowing, planes landing at Honolulu Airport approach from the east, passing low enough over Diamond Head for you to see the passengers inside.

Taxis wait in the parking lot back on the crater floor, ready to ferry weary hikers who can't face the walk back to Waikīkī.



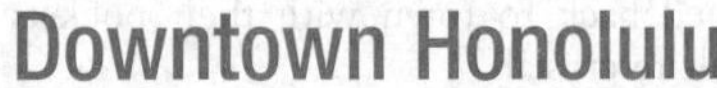

# Downtown Honolulu



**Downtown Honolulu**, the administrative heart of first the kingdom, and now the state, of Hawaii, stands a few blocks west of the original city center. Most of the compact grid of streets where the port grew up is now taken up by Chinatown, while downtown is generally considered to focus on the cluster of buildings that surround **'Iolani Palace**, home to Hawaii's last monarchs. This is certainly a presentable district, with several well-preserved historic buildings, but it's not a very lively one. At lunchtime on weekdays office workers scurry through the streets, but the rest of the time the contrast with the frenzy of Waikīkī is striking. With few shops, bars or restaurants to lure outsiders, the whole place is usually empty by 8pm.

## 'Iolani Palace

**'Iolani Palace** was the official home of the last two monarchs of Hawaii. It was built for **King David Kalākaua** in 1882, near the site of a previous palace that had been destroyed by termites, and he lived here until his death in 1891. For his sister and successor, **Queen Lili'uokalani**, it was first a palace, and then, after her overthrow in 1893 (see p.514), a prison. Until 1968, by which time the termites had pretty much eaten up this palace too, it was the Hawaiian state capitol building. Since the completion of the new Capitol in 1969, it has been preserved as a museum, open for guided **tours** only (by reservation, ⓣ 522-0832; Tues–Sat every 15min 9am–2.15pm; adults $15, ages 5-12 $5, under-5s not admitted).

Although the palace has become a symbol for the sovereignty movement (see p.515) and is occasionally the scene of large pro-independence demonstrations, the tours are firmly apolitical. Guides revel in the lost romance of the Hawaiian monarchy without quite acknowledging that it was illegally overthrown by the United States. The fact that visitors have to shuffle around in cotton bootees to protect the hardwood floors adds to the air of unreality.

Apart from its *koa*-wood floors and staircase, the palace contains little that is distinctively Hawaiian. In the largest of its **downstairs** rooms, the **Throne Room**, Kalākaua held formal balls to celebrate his coronation and fiftieth birthday, and Lili'uokalani was tried for treason for allegedly supporting moves for her own restoration. The *kapu* stick that separates the thrones of Kalākaua and his wife Kapi'olani was made from a narwhal tusk given to Kalākaua by a sea captain. Other reception rooms lead off from the grand central hall, with all available wall space taken up by formal portraits of Hawaiian and other monarchs. Though the plush **upstairs** bedrooms feel similarly stately and impersonal, there's one touching exhibit — the glass case in the front room containing a quilt made by Queen Lili'uokalani during her eight months under house arrest.

A grass-covered mound in the garden marks the original resting place of King Kamehameha II and Queen Kamamalu. Their remains, brought here by George Byron (the cousin of the poet) after they died of measles in England in 1824, were later moved to the royal mausoleum in Nu'uanu (see p.94).

The palace's **ticket office** is housed in the castellated 'Iolani Barracks on the west side of the grounds, an odd structure that predates the palace by about

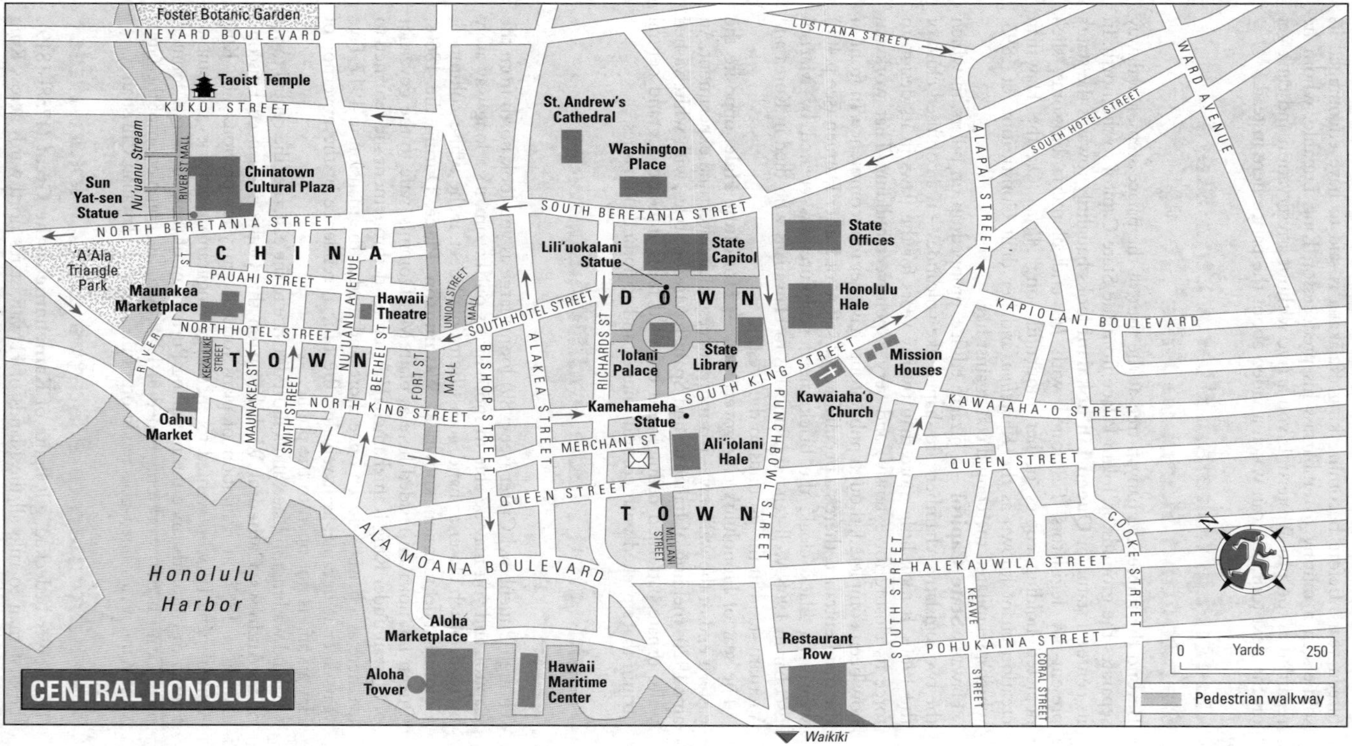

## CENTRAL HONOLULU

Foster Botanic Garden
VINEYARD BOULEVARD
Taoist Temple
KUKUI STREET
Nu'uanu Stream
RIVER ST MALL
Chinatown Cultural Plaza
Sun Yat-sen Statue
NORTH BERETANIA STREET
'A'Ala Triangle Park
CHINA
TOWN
ST
PAUAHI STREET
Maunakea Marketplace
NORTH HOTEL STREET
KEKAULIKE STREET
RIVER
MAUNAKEA ST
SMITH STREET
NU'UANU AVENUE
BETHEL ST
FORT ST
MALL
UNION STREET
MALL
Hawaii Theatre
NORTH KING STREET
Oahu Market
Airport
Honolulu Harbor
Aloha Marketplace
Aloha Tower
Hawaii Maritime Center
ALA MOANA BOULEVARD
BISHOP STREET
ALAKEA STREET
SOUTH HOTEL STREET
St. Andrew's Cathedral
Washington Place
SOUTH BERETANIA STREET
Lili'uokalani Statue
State Capitol
DOWN
TOWN
RICHARDS ST
'Iolani Palace
State Library
Kamehameha Statue
MERCHANT ST
Ali'iolani Hale
QUEEN STREET
MILILANI STREET
PUNCHBOWL STREET
SOUTH KING STREET
State Offices
Honolulu Hale
Kawaiaha'o Church
Mission Houses
LUSITANA STREET
ALAPAI STREET
KAPIOLANI BOULEVARD
KAWAIAHA'O STREET
WARD AVENUE
SOUTH HOTEL STREET
COOKE STREET
HALEKAUWILA STREET
SOUTH STREET
KEAWE STREET
CORAL STREET
POHUKAINA STREET
Restaurant Row
Waikīkī
N
0 Yards 250
Pedestrian walkway

fifteen years. Before becoming king, Kalākaua is said to have encouraged its soldiers in a mutiny to embarrass his predecessor, King Lunalilo, whom he regarded as too pro-Western. If you arrive without a reservation and can't get on the next tour, you can watch a video about the palace here instead.



## Queen Lili'uokalani Statue, the State Capitol and Honolulu Hale

Beyond the impressive banyan tree at the foot of the palace steps, a walkway separates the grounds of 'Iolani Palace from the State Capitol to the north. In its center, a statue of **Queen Lili'uokalani** looks haughtily towards the state's present-day legislators. Festooned with *leis* and plumeria blossoms, she's depicted holding copies of her mournful song *Aloha 'Oe*, the Hawaiian creation chant known as the *Kumulipo*, and her draft Constitution of 1893, which precipitated the coup d'état against her.

Hawaii's **State Capitol** – a bizarre edifice, propped up on pillars, in which the two legislative chambers are shaped like volcanoes – is a confused child of the 1960s. It took little more than twenty years for the flaws in its design to force its closure for extensive and very expensive rebuilding. That work has now been completed, though public tours have yet to recommence. In front of the main entrance, there's a peculiar cubic statue of Father Damien (see p.400) wearing a black cloak; the black metal sculpture was created by Marisol Escobar in 1968. Well-tended memorials to Hawaiians who died in Korea and Vietnam stand in the grounds to the west.

The seat of Honolulu's city government – **Honolulu Hale**, opposite the eastern end of the walkway – is a more successful architectural experiment. An airy 1920s melding of Italianate and Spanish Mission styles, with whitewashed walls, ornate patterned ceilings, and red-tiled roofs, it boasts a grand central atrium that's packed with colorful murals and sculptural flourishes.

## Washington Place and St Andrews Cathedral

Though Punchbowl Crater (see p.89) looms large as you look north from the Capitol, and you may be able to spot visitors on the rim, it's a long way away by road. Much closer at hand, across Beretania Street, is the white-columned, Colonial-style mansion known as **Washington Place**. During the 1860s, Queen Lili'uokalani resided here as plain Mrs Dominis, wife to the governor of Hawaii under King Kamehameha V. After her dethronement she returned to live here as a private citizen once more, and died at the mansion in 1917. Five years later it became, as it remains, the official residence of the governor of Hawaii and is not open to the public.

Behind Washington Place, and a short distance to the east, rises the central tower of **St Andrews Cathedral**. Work began on this Gothic-influenced Episcopal church in 1867, in realization of plans formed ten years previously by King Kamehameha IV, who wanted to encourage Anglican missionaries to come to Hawaii to counterbalance the prevailing Puritanism of their American counterparts. Construction work only ended in 1958, with the completion of the Great West Window, a stained-glass rendition of the story of Hawaiian Christianity.

## The Kamehameha Statue and Ali'iolani Hale



The flower-bedecked, gilt figure of **Kamehameha the Great** (1758–1819), the first man to rule all the islands of Hawaii, stares northwards across King

Street towards 'Iolani Palace from outside Ali'iolani Hale. Kamehameha is depicted wearing the *'ahu'ula* (royal cloak), *malo* (loincloth), *kā'ei* (sash), and *mahiole* (feather helmet), and clutching a spear. The work of Thomas R Gould, an American sculptor based in Florence, the statue was commissioned by the Hawaiian legislature in 1878 to celebrate the centenary of the arrival of Captain Cook. On its way to Hawaii, however, it was lost in a shipwreck, so a second copy was cast and dispatched. That arrived in 1880 and was unveiled by King Kalākaua at his coronation in 1883; surplus insurance money from the lost statue paid for the sequence of four panels depicting scenes from Kamehameha's life around its base. Meanwhile, the original statue was found floating off the Falkland Islands, was purchased by a whaling captain in Port Stanley, and also turned up in Hawaii. It was packed off to Kamehameha's birthplace on the Big Island. Ceremonies are held at the Honolulu statue on June 11 each year to mark Kamehameha Day, a state holiday.

Erected in 1874, **Ali'iolani Hale** – "House of the Heavenly King" in Hawaiian – was Hawaii's first library and national museum; it was also the first building taken over by the conspirators who overthrew the monarchy in 1893. Throughout its history, however, its main function has been as the home of the state's Supreme Court. The first floor houses the fascinating **Judiciary History Center** (Mon–Fri 10am–4pm; free). This outlines the history of Hawaiian law from the days of the ancient *kapu* onwards and chronicles the role played by the Supreme Court in replacing the tradition under which all land was held in common with the concept of private ownership. There's also a scale model of Honolulu in 1850, watched over by the now-vanished fort and with thatched huts still dotted among its Victorian mansions.

## Kawaiaha'o Church

Although **Kawaiaha'o Church**, just east of 'Iolani Palace near the junction of Punchbowl and King streets, was erected less than twenty years after the first Christian missionaries came to Hawaii (see p.509), it was the fifth church to stand on this site. According to its Protestant minister, Rev Hiram Bingham, each of the four predecessors was a thatched "cage in a haymow." This one, by contrast, was built with thousand-pound chunks of living coral, hacked from the reef. It's not especially huge, but the columned portico is grand enough, topped by a four-square clock-tower.

Inside, broad balconies run down both sides of the nave, lined with royal portraits. Below, plaques on the walls honor early figures of Hawaiian Christianity, such as Henry 'Opukaha'ia (see p.509). The plushest pews – at the back of the church, upholstered in velvet and marked off by *kahili* standards – were reserved for royalty.

In the gardens on the *mauka* side of the church, a fountain commemorates the site of a spring formerly known as *Ka wai a Ha'o*, "the water of Ha'o." A rare treasure in this barren region, it was reserved for *ali'i nui*, or high chiefs, such as chiefess Ha'o.

The small mausoleum in the grounds fronting the church holds the remains of **King Lunalilo**, who ruled for less than two years after his election in 1872. Feeling slighted that his mother's body had not been removed from the churchyard to the royal mausoleum (see p.94), he chose to be buried here instead. The rest of the graves in the **cemetery** around the back serve as a brief history of Hawaii's nineteenth-century missionary elite, with an abundance of Castles and Cookes, Alexanders and Baldwins, and the only president of the Republic, Sanford B. Dole.

## The Mission Houses

Hawaii's first Christian missionaries are recalled by the partly reconstructed **Mission Houses** behind Kawaiaha'o Church. Standing cheek by jowl at 553 S King St (Tues–Sat 9am–4pm; adults $6, under-19s $3; ⓣ531-0481), these three nineteenth-century buildings commemorate the pioneers of the Sandwich Islands Mission, who arrived from Boston in 1820.

The oldest edifice, the two-story **Frame House**, was shipped in whole from New England in 1821. Reluctant to let outsiders build permanent structures, the king only allowed it to go up with the words "when you go away, take everything with you." Local fears that its cellar held weapons for use in a planned takeover of the islands were allayed when Kamehameha's principal adviser, Kalanimoku, built a house with a larger cellar across the street. The house, whose tiny windows were entirely unsuited to the heat of Honolulu, was home to four missionary families. A kitchen had to be added because cooking outdoors attracted too much attention from the islanders, as it was *kapu* for women to prepare food.

One of the missionaries' first acts, in 1823, was to set up the **Print House**, which produced the first Hawaiian-language Bible – *Ka Palapala Hemolele*. The current building – not the original, but its 1841 replacement – holds a replica of its imported Ramage printing press, whose limitations were among the reasons why to this day the Hawaiian alphabet only has twelve letters.

The largest of the three buildings, the **Chamberlain House**, started life in 1831 as the mission storehouse. As the missionary families became increasingly embroiled in the economy of the islands, that role turned it into the commercial headquarters of Castle and Cooke, one of the original "Big Five" (see p.513).

## Honolulu Academy of Arts

Honolulu residents take great pride in the stunning fine art on display at the **Academy of Arts**, 900 S Beretania St (Tues–Sat 10am–4.30pm, Sun 1–5pm; tours Tues–Sat 11am, Sun 1.15pm; free first Wed of month, otherwise $7, under-13s free; ⓣ532-8700). Few tourists find their way here – half a mile east of the Capitol – but two or three hours wandering the galleries of this elegant former private home, with its open courtyards and fountains, is time well spent.

The bulk of the Academy's superb collection of **paintings** adorns the galleries that surround the **Mediterranean Court**, to the right of the entrance. Highlights include Van Gogh's *Wheat Field*, Gauguin's *Two Nudes on a Tahitian Beach* and one of Monet's *Water Lilies*. Other pieces date from the Italian Renaissance, with two separate *Apostles* by Carlo Crivelli, as well as engravings by Rembrandt and Dürer; more recent canvases include lesser works by Picasso, Léger, Braque, Matisse and Tanguy.

A separate gallery has been set aside to house fascinating **depictions of Hawaii** by visiting artists. Most of these works, including an 1838 pencil sketch of Waikīkī, have more historic value than artistic merit. The much-reproduced portrait of *Kamehameha in Red Vest*, painted by the Russian Louis Choris in 1816, shows the redoubtable monarch in his later years, and there are several dramatic renditions of the changing face of the volcano at Kīlauea. John Webber, who accompanied Cook to Hawaii in 1779, contributes a pen and watercolor sketch of the village of "Kowrooa" (Ka'awaloa), nestling beneath the palms of Kealakekua Bay, where Cook died.

The Academy's **Modern and Contemporary** collection ranges from a Francis Bacon triptych and a Nam June Paik video installation to Yan

Pei-Ming's 1997 portrait of the singer Israel Kamakawiwo'ole (see p.536) in slathered black and grey oils. Tucked away in a side corridor are Georgia O'Keeffe's vivid, stylized studies of Maui's 'Iao Valley and Hāna coast.

To the left of the entrance is the **Asian Court**, whose centerpiece is a collection of 2000 pieces of ancient **Chinese** art, a 1993 bequest. Among these magnificent artifacts are beautiful ceramics, four-thousand-year-old jade blades, green Zhou bronzes, and a column from a two-thousand-year-old Han tomb that looks like an Easter Island statue. There then follows a cornucopia of works from all over the world: Buddhist and Shinto deities, plus miniature *netsuke* (buckles) from Japan; Tibetan *thangkas* (religious images); Indian carvings ranging from Rajasthani sandstone screens to a stone Chola statue of Krishna; Mayan effigies and Indonesian stick figures; Melanesian masks incorporating such elements as boars' tusks and cobwebs; and pottery from the pueblos of Arizona and New Mexico. There are also a few ancient Hawaiian artifacts, though better ones are on display at the Bishop Museum (see p.96).

The Academy's appealing **courtyard café** serves lunch (Tues–Sat 11.30am–2pm; reservations ⓣ532-8734) and tea (Tues–Sun 2–4pm).

# Chinatown

Barely five minutes' walk west of 'Iolani Palace, a pair of matching stone dragons flank either side of Hotel Street, marking the transition between downtown Honolulu and the oldest part of the city, **Chinatown**. For well over a century, this was renowned as the city's red-light district. Though most of the pool halls, massage parlors and tawdry bars that formerly lined the narrow streets leading down to the Nu'uanu Stream have now gone, the fading green clapboard storefronts and bustling market ambience still make **Chinatown** seem like another world. Cosmopolitan, atmospheric and historic in equal proportions, it's the one local neighborhood that's genuinely fun to explore on your own. It's also changing fast, blending futuristic elements in with its relics of the past to create a hybrid of old and new, East and West.

To join an organized **walking tour** of Chinatown, call either the Chinese Chamber of Commerce (Tues 9.30am; $5; ⓣ533-3181) or the Hawaii Heritage Center (Fri 9.30am; $5; ⓣ521-2749).

Of the district's two main axes, N Hotel and Maunakea streets, **Hotel Street** best lives up to the area's lowlife reputation, with drunken sailors lurching to and from the *Club Hubba Hubba Topless-Bottomless* and assorted sawdust-floored bars. At the intersection with Maunakea Street stands the ornate facade of **Wo Fat's** – at a hundred years old, Chinatown's longest-standing restaurant. Its main rival as the leading local landmark is the Art Deco **Hawaii Theatre**, further east at 1130 Bethel St, which reopened after extensive restoration in 1996. Guided tours of the theater ($5) take place on the first Monday of each month, at 10am and 2pm, but a far better way to appreciate the gorgeous interior is by attending one of its varied program of (mostly one-off) performances; contact ⓣ528-0506 or ⓦwww.hawaiitheatre.com for current schedules.

Many of Chinatown's old walled courtyards have been converted into open malls, but the businesses within remain much the same. Apothecaries and herbalists weigh out dried leaves in front of endless arrays of bottles, shelves and wooden cabinets, while groups of deft-fingered women gather around tables to thread *leis*. Every hole-in-the-wall store holds a fridge bursting with colorful blooms, while appetizing food smells waft from backstreet bakeries.

If you get hungry, call in at *Char Hung Sut*, on N Pauahi at Smith (Mon & Wed–Sat 5.30am–2pm, Sun 5.30am–1pm) for freshly made *dim sum*, or browse through the Oriental food specialities at **Oahu Market**, on N King and Kekaulike. This traditional market was scheduled for demolition in 1988, but the traders banded together to buy it. The fastest-selling item seems to be *ahi* (yellow-fin tuna), used for making *sashimi* or *poke*, but this is also the place to go if you're looking for a pig's snout or a salmon's head.



## The Chinese in Hawaii

Strangely enough, there was a Hawaiian in China before there were any **Chinese** in Hawaii – Kai'ana, a chief from Kauai, was briefly abandoned in Canton in 1787 by a British fur-trader he had thought was taking him to Europe. Within three years, however, Chinese seamen were starting to jump ship to seek their fortunes in the land they knew as Tan Hueng Shan, the Sandalwood Mountains. Trading vessels regularly crossed the Pacific between China and Hawaii, and Cantonese merchants and entrepreneurs became a familiar sight in Honolulu. Even the granite that paved the streets of what became Chinatown was brought over from China as ballast in ships.

Some of Hawaii's earliest Chinese settlers were **sugar boilers**, and the islands' first sugar mill was set up by a Chinese immigrant on Lanai in 1802. American capital proved itself more than a match for any individual Chinese endeavor, however, and the Chinese only began to arrive in Hawaii in sizeable numbers when the sugar plantations started to import laborers in 1852. Workers were usually indentured for five years, so by 1857 Chinese laborers were leaving the plantations and using their small savings to finance their own businesses. At first, the majority were on Kauai, where they began to turn neglected Hawaiian farmlands in places such as Hanalei Valley (see p.457) into rice paddies, even using water buffalo shipped over from China.

In time, however, the Chinese settled increasingly in Honolulu, where "friendly societies" would help new arrivals find their feet. Inevitably, many of these were renegades and outlaws, ranging from gang members to political dissidents. Sun Yat-sen, for example, who became the first President of the Republic of China when the Manchu Dynasty was overthrown in 1911, was educated at 'Iolani School.

By the 1860s there were more Chinese than white residents in Hawaii. With the native Hawaiian population shrinking, the pro-American establishment in Honolulu felt threatened. In response, they maneuvered to ensure that white residents could vote for the national legislature while Asians could not. They also induced the plantations to switch their recruiting policies and focus on other parts of the globe.

At the end of the nineteenth century, Chinatown was at its zenith. Its crowded lanes held more than seven thousand people, including Japanese and Hawaiians as well as Chinese. When bubonic plague was detected in December 1899, however, city authorities decided to prevent its spread by systematic burning. The first few controlled burns were effective, but on January 20, 1900, a small fire started at Beretania and Nu'uanu rapidly turned into a major conflagration. The flames destroyed Kaumakapili Church as well as a 38-acre swathe that reached to within a few yards of the waterfront. Police cordons prevented the quarantined residents from leaving during the fire, while any already outside were unable to return to salvage possessions. White-owned newspapers were soon rhapsodizing about the opportunity to expand downtown Honolulu, convincing the Chinese community, which never received adequate compensation, that the destruction was at the very least welcome and at worst deliberate.

Nonetheless, Chinatown was rebuilt, and it remains Honolulu's liveliest, most characterful district, albeit now much more commercial than residential. Most local Chinese, like the rest of the city's inhabitants, live in outlying suburbs.

The best selection of fast food in Chinatown is at the newer **Maunakea Marketplace**, a couple of blocks north and entered off either Hotel or Maunakea streets. Once you enter the main building, beneath the watchful gaze of the statue of Confucius in its central plaza, the temperature is likely to be sweltering, but the choice of cuisines is amazing, and at the lowest prices in Honolulu.

Chinatown is bordered to the west by **Nu'uanu Stream**, flowing down to Honolulu Harbor. **River Street**, which runs alongside, becomes an attractive, restaurant-filled pedestrian mall between Beretania and Kukui streets. At the port end stands a *lei*-swaddled statue of **Sun Yat-sen**, while over Kukui Street at the opposite end is the tiny Lum Hai So Tong **Taoist temple**. Most of the interior of the block next to the mall is occupied by the **Chinatown Cultural Plaza**, filled with slightly tacky souvenir stores and conventional businesses that cater to the Chinese community.

### Foster Botanic Garden

At the top end of River Street, and entered via a short driveway that leads off N Vineyard Boulevard beside the Kuan Yin **Buddhist temple**, is the twenty-acre **Foster Botanic Garden** (daily 9am–4pm; adults $5, under-13s $1; guided tours, no extra charge, Mon–Fri 1pm). Established in the middle of the nineteenth century as a sanctuary for Hawaiian plants and a testing ground for foreign imports, it has become one of Honolulu's best-loved city parks. Different sections cover spices and herbs, flowering orchids and tropical trees from around the world. As well as sausage trees from Mozambique, the latter collection includes a *bo* (or *peepal*) tree supposedly descended from the *bo* tree at Bodh Gaya in north India where the Buddha achieved enlightenment.

## Waterfront Honolulu

It's all too easy to lose sight of the fact that central Honolulu stands just a few yards up from the turquoise waters of the Pacific, clean enough here to support conspicuous populations of bright tropical fish. Sadly, pedestrians exploring Chinatown or downtown have to brave the fearsome traffic of **Nimitz Highway** in order to reach the ocean. That effort is rewarded by a short but enjoyable stroll along the segment of the waterfront that stretches for a couple of hundred yards east of the venerable **Aloha Tower**. Until 1857, this area was covered by the waves; then the city **fort**, which had previously stood at Fort and Queen streets, was torn down, and the rubble used to fill in a fifteen-acre expanse of the sea floor. Now, in addition to watching the comings and goings of **Honolulu Harbor**, you can join a sunset dinner cruise or similar expedition from the piers nearby or learn something of the port's history in the **Hawaii Maritime Center**.

Long and surprisingly quiet **beaches** fringe the shoreline a little further to the east, especially in the vicinity of **Ala Moana**, which is home to the city's largest beach park as well as a huge shopping mall.

### Aloha Tower

The **Aloha Tower**, on Pier 9 of Honolulu Harbor, was built in 1926 to serve as a control center for the port's traffic and a landmark for arriving cruise passengers. At 184ft high, it was then the tallest building in Honolulu; with its four

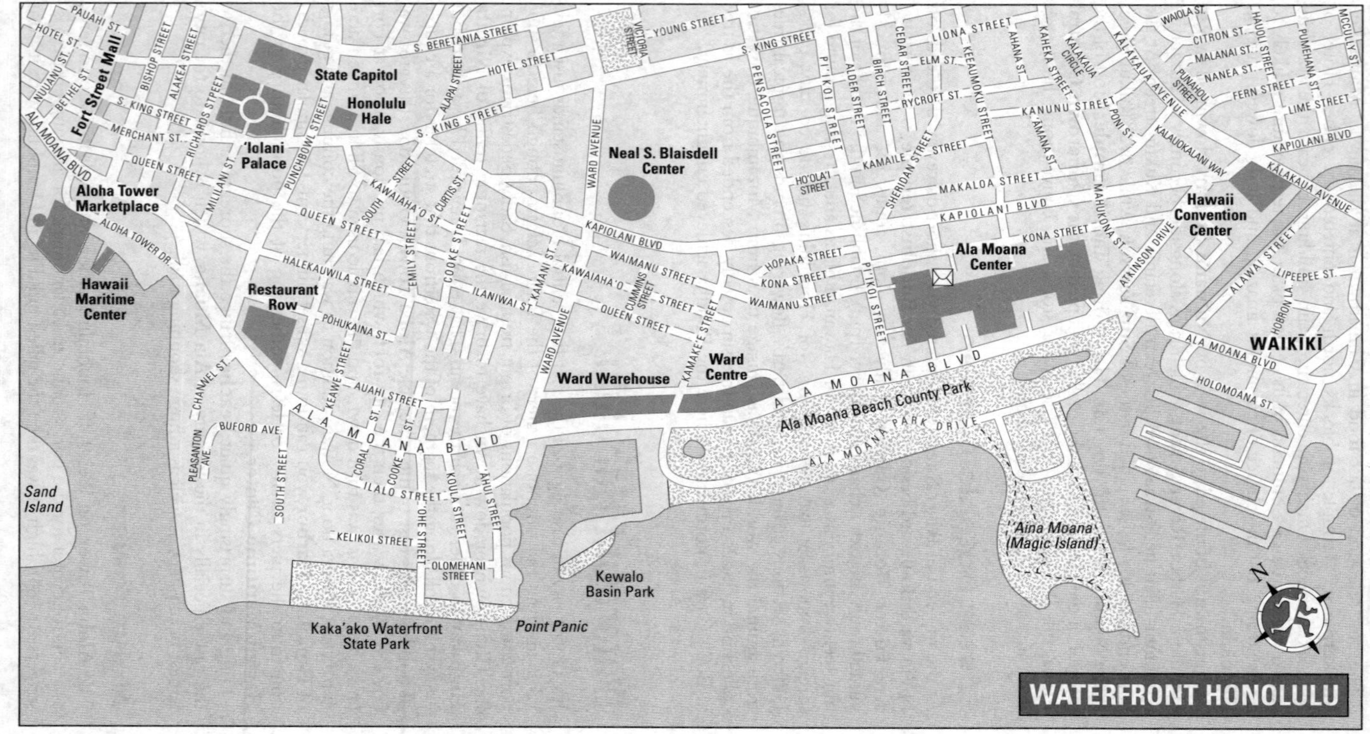
WATERFRONT HONOLULU
N
WAIKĪKĪ
Hawaii Convention Center
Ala Moana Center
Ala Moana Beach County Park
'Aina Moana (Magic Island)
Ward Centre
Ward Warehouse
Neal S. Blaisdell Center
Kewalo Basin Park
Point Panic
Kaka'ako Waterfront State Park
State Capitol
Honolulu Hale
'Iolani Palace
Restaurant Row
Aloha Tower Marketplace
Hawaii Maritime Center
Fort Street Mall
Sand Island
MCCULLY ST.
PUMEHANA ST.
HAUOLI STREET
CITRON ST.
MALANAI ST.
NANEA ST.
FERN STREET
LIME STREET
KAPIOLANI BLVD
KALAKAUA AVENUE
ALAWAI STREET
LIPEEPEE ST.
HOBRON LA.
ALA MOANA BLVD
HOLOMOANA ST.
WAIOLA ST.
PUNAHOU STREET
KALAUOKALANI WAY
ATKINSON DRIVE
PONI ST.
KALAKAUA CIRCLE
MAHUKONA ST.
KAHEKA STREET
KANUNU STREET
'AMANA ST.
KONA STREET
AHANA ST.
MAKALOA STREET
LIONA STREET
KEEAUMOKU STREET
ELM ST.
RYCROFT ST.
KAMAILE STREET
SHERIDAN STREET
CEDAR STREET
BIRCH STREET
PI'IKOI STREET
ALDER STREET
HO'OLA'I STREET
HOPAKA STREET
WAIMANU STREET
ALA MOANA PARK DRIVE
PENSACOLA STREET
S. KING STREET
YOUNG STREET
VICTORIA STREET
KAMAKE'E STREET
CUMMINS STREET
QUEEN STREET
KAWAIAHA'O STREET
WARD AVENUE
KAMANI ST.
ILANIWAI ST.
HOTEL STREET
S. BERETANIA STREET
ALAPAI STREET
CURTIS ST.
COOKE STREET
'AHUI STREET
KOULA STREET
OLOMEHANI STREET
'OHE STREET
EMILY STREET
AUAHI STREET
ILALO STREET
KELIKOI STREET
SOUTH STREET
CORAL ST.
HALEKAUWILA STREET
PŌHUKAINA ST.
KEAWE STREET
PUNCHBOWL STREET
BUFORD AVE.
MILILANI ST.
CHANNEL ST.
PLEASANTON AVE.
RICHARDS STREET
ALAKEA STREET
BISHOP STREET
MERCHANT ST.
ALOHA TOWER DR.
PAUAHI ST.
BETHEL ST.
NUUANU ST.
HOTEL ST.

giant clock-faces, each surmounted by the word "ALOHA," it was also the most photographed. Seventy years of skyscraper construction have made it seem progressively smaller and smaller, but the tower returned to prominence in the late 1990s as the centerpiece of the **Aloha Tower Marketplace** shopping mall.

The stores and restaurants tend to be expensive and predictable (see p.114), and with much fewer parking spaces available here than at the major malls, they're heavily dependent on day-trippers from Waikīkī as opposed to local residents. As for the tower itself, it feels a little stranded and incongruous; as the placard at its base puts it, "Aloha Tower now stands alone for the first time in its history." However, with the mall walkways ending right at the dockside, and several restaurants and bars offering large open-air terraces, this is an unexpectedly enjoyable place to get a sense of the ongoing life of the port. Cargo vessels from all over the world tie up alongside, and there's always something going on out in the water.

Taking a free trip up to the tenth-floor **Observation Deck** of the Aloha Tower is also worthwhile (April–Sept daily 9am–7.30pm, Oct–March daily 9am–7pm). Balconies on each of its four sides, originally used as lookouts by harbor pilots, offer views that are just short of ugly – freeways, airport runways and grimy harbor installations – but provide an excellent orientation to the city. As you look towards Diamond Head, which may well be obscured by haze, the twin pink-trimmed "stereo speakers" of the Waterfront Towers condominiums loom above the black glass of Restaurant Row (see p.109); meanwhile, Pearl Harbor sprawls to the west, and the green mountains soar inland.

## Hawaii Maritime Center

A short walk east of the Aloha Marketplace, the **Hawaii Maritime Center**, at Pier 7 (daily 8.30am–5pm; adults $7.50, under-18s $4.50; ⓣ536-6373), illustrates Hawaii's seafaring past in riveting detail.

You may prefer to explore the modern museum building – known as the King Kalākaua Boathouse – at your own pace, rather than following the audio-cassette tour, but in any case, begin on the second floor. Displays here trace the voyages of **Captain Cook**, who sailed the world in small flat-bottomed boats originally designed for trips along the English coast and named "Whitby Cats" after his home port. A crude copper plaque left by an English ship at the site of Cook's death – and seen there by Mark Twain in 1866, as noted in his book, *Roughing It* – stands alongside a cannonball found nearby.

The **whaling** industry is then recalled by exhibits such as huge iron try-pots, scrimshaw carved by nineteenth-century seamen on ivory smoothed with sharkskin "sandpaper," and a large painting of whalers at anchor at Lahaina. In the center of the gallery hangs the skeleton of a humpback whale beached on Kahoolawe in 1986.

Posters, timetables, menus and reconstructed interiors cover the growth of **tourism** and the heyday of cruise ships and passenger ferries – Hawaii's last inter-island steamer, the *Humu'ula*, ceased regular runs in 1952. Having examined plans and photos showing the development of Honolulu Harbor, you can see the whole thing yourself by climbing the 81 steps up the museum's observation tower.

On the first floor, the emphasis is on the **Polynesians**. A full-sized, double-hulled canoe has been cut in half and framed in cross section behind clear plastic to show the equipment and cargo carried by the first voyagers. There's also a wall of huge historic **surfboards** – and some smaller *pāipus*, the ancient equivalent of today's boogie boards – together with a brief history of the sport. Its modern popularity stems from the international successes of Olympic champion Duke Kahanamoku during the early 1900s, who features prominently in photos of Waikīkī's first surfing clubs.

For many, however, the **chief attractions** of the Maritime Center are the two distinguished vessels moored on the adjacent dock. The **Falls of Clyde**, floating to the right of the entrance, is the only four-masted, full-rigged sailing ship left in the world. Built of wrought iron in Glasgow in 1876, it's also the world's only sail-powered oil tanker; after years of ferrying sugar and passengers between California and Hawaii, it was converted to carry petroleum in 1907.

When it's not sailing to Tahiti, New Zealand or the far reaches of the South Pacific, the replica Polynesian canoe **Hōkūle'a** is moored at the end of the pier. Its voyages have inspired a huge revival of interest in traditional methods of navigation – for a full account, see p.521 – and parties of eager schoolchildren flock here for close-up inspections. During its frequent absences, visitors have to content themselves with "navigating" an enjoyable computer simulation of the *Hōkūle'a*.

## The Western Waterfront: Sand Island

Honolulu Harbor, which is inaccessible to casual viewing west of the Aloha Tower, is a relatively narrow deep-water channel shielded from the open ocean by the bulk of **Sand Island**. The seaward side of the island is a state park, where the plentiful supply of restrooms, showers and pavilions does little to alleviate the impression of being trapped in an industrial wasteland. There's a certain amount of sandy beach, and locals come to hang out and fish, but it's hard to see why any tourist would drive five miles to get here. If you insist on doing so, follow Nimitz Highway almost as far as the airport, and then loop back along Sand Island Access Road.

## East to Waikīkī: Ala Moana

East of Aloha Tower and the Maritime Center, **Ala Moana Boulevard** runs along the shoreline towards Waikīkī. Along the way it passes a few more of Honolulu's main **shopping malls** – the Ward Warehouse, the Ward Centre, and the pick of the bunch, the Ala Moana Center. Year after year, the stores here seem to increase both in quality and quantity, and for an ever-greater proportion of visitors to Waikīkī, the Ala Moana district constitutes their only foray into Honolulu proper. For more details on Honolulu shopping, see p.113 onwards.

The first spot where you can enter the ocean in this stretch is the unenticingly but appropriately-named **Point Panic**, in **Kaka'ako Waterfront State Park**. Serious board- and body-surfers swear by its powerful waves, but a lack of sand, an abundance of sharks, and the fact that the surf hammers straight into a stone wall combine to ensure that few visitors are tempted to join them.

Next up, across from the Ward Warehouse, **Kewalo Basin Park** occupies the thin oceanfront groin that shelters the Kewalo Basin harbor, used by several small-boat operators. Though the setting is attractive enough, the park's role as a hangout for local transients makes it a bit of a no-go area for outsiders.

Though tourists tend not to realize it, the long green lawns across Ala Moana Boulevard from the malls flank a superb **beach** – the long white-sand strand preserved as the **Ala Moana Beach County Park**. This is where Honolulu city-dwellers come, in preference to Waikīkī, to enjoy excellent facilities and, especially during working hours, a relative absence of crowds. Like most of the beaches in Waikīkī, it's artificial, having been constructed during the 1930s on the site of a garbage dump; the name "Ala Moana," meaning "path to the sea," is a postwar coinage. Inshore swimming is generally safe and good, and there's some potential for snorkeling around the reef; just watch out for the steep drop-off, only a few yards out at low tide, that marks the former course of a boat channel.

At its eastern end, Ala Moana Beach curves out and around a long promontory. Known as **Magic Island** or **'Aina Moana**, this too is artificial. It was one of the most ambitious elements of the state's plans to expand tourism in the early 1960s, the idea being to reclaim an "island" of shallow coral reef, connect it to the mainland, and build luxury hotels on it. The hotels never materialized, so the vast sums of money involved have instead resulted in the creation of a tranquil park that's ideal for sunset strolls. It takes five minutes to walk from the parking lot to the lovely little crescent lagoon at its tip, which is just far enough to ensure that it feels like a haven of peace away from the city. Joggers, ta'i-chi practitioners and picnickers enjoy the roomy lawns, while surfers and swimmers congregate around the gently sloping beach.



# Tantalus and Makiki Heights

If constant glimpses of the mountains that soar inland of downtown Honolulu entice you into exploring, there's no better choice of route than **Tantalus** and **Round Top** drives. They're actually a single eight-mile road that climbs up one flanking ridge of **Makiki Valley** and then wriggles back down the other, changing its name from Tantalus Drive in the west to Round Top Drive in the east. Along the way you'll get plenty of views of Honolulu and Waikīkī, but the real attraction is the dense rainforest that cloaks the hillside, with greenery often meeting overhead to turn the road into a tunnel. It's a slow drive, which in places narrows to just a single lane of traffic, but a spellbinding one.

To join Tantalus Drive from downtown, follow signs for the **Punchbowl cemetery** until you reach the right turn onto Pūowaina Drive, and head straight on instead. Coming from Waikīkī, take Makiki Street up from Wilder Avenue, which runs parallel to and just north of H-1 west of the University. It's also possible to skip the bulk of the circuit by taking **Makiki Heights Drive**, which holds the stimulating **Contemporary Museum** as well as trailheads for some superb mountain **hikes**.

## Punchbowl: National Memorial Cemetery

The extinct volcanic caldera known as Punchbowl, perched above downtown Honolulu, makes an evocative setting for the **National Memorial Cemetery of the Pacific** (March–Sept daily 8am–6.30pm, Oct–Feb daily 8am–5.30pm). To ancient Hawaiians, this was Pūowaina, the hill of human sacrifices; somewhere within its high encircling walls stood a sacrificial temple. It's now possible to drive right into the crater – having first spiralled around the base of the cone to meet up with Pūowaina Drive from the back – and park in one of the many small bays dotted around the perimeter road.

Beneath the lawns that carpet the bowl-shaped interior, far removed from the noise of the city, well over 25,000 victims of US Pacific wars, including Vietnam, now lie buried. Famous names include the Hawaiian astronaut Ellison Onizuka, killed when the *Challenger* shuttle exploded, but no graves are singled out for special attention. Instead, each gravestone, marked perhaps with a bouquet of ginger and heliconia, is recessed into the grass, with space left for their families or still-living veterans to join those laid to rest.

At the opposite end to the entrance rises the imposing marble staircase of the **Honolulu Memorial**, where ten "Courts of the Missing" commemorate a further 28,778 service personnel listed as missing in action. It culminates in a thirty-foot marble relief of the prow of a naval ship, bearing the words sent by President Lincoln to Mrs Bixby, whose five sons were killed in the Civil War: "The solemn pride that must be yours to have laid so costly a sacrifice upon the altar of freedom." As with all such US memorials, a "graphic record" of the conflicts is provided, so incongruous colored maps of the war in the Pacific cover the walls to either side.

Only when you climb the footpath to the top of the crater rim and find yourself looking straight down Punchbowl Street to the Capitol do you appreciate how close this all is to downtown Honolulu. During World War II, before the creation of the cemetery, this ridge held heavy artillery trained out to sea.

## Contemporary Museum

At 2411 Makiki Heights Drive, a short distance east of that road's intersection with Mott-Smith Drive, a grand 1920s country estate houses the lovely **Contemporary Museum** (Tues–Sat 10am–4pm, Sun noon–4pm; $5, free on the first Thurs of every month, under-13s free; ⓣ526-1322). Tastefully landscaped with ornamental Oriental gardens that offer a superb overview of Honolulu – and are packed with playful sculptures – the museum hosts changing exhibitions of up-to-the-minute fine art. Few last more than eight weeks, but each is installed with lavish attention to detail, and the effect is consistently magnificent. A separate pavilion houses a permanent display of the sets created by David Hockney for the Metropolitan Opera's production of Ravel's *L'Enfant et les Sortilèges*; a recording of the work plays constantly. Excellent lunches, with daily specials priced at $10–12, are available at the on-site *Contemporary Café* (Tues–Sat 11am–3pm, Sun noon–3pm; ⓣ523-3362), and there's also a very good gift store.

## Makiki Valley trails

Honolulu's finest **hiking trails** wind their way across and around the slopes of **Makiki Valley**. The network is most easily accessed via a short spur road that leads inland from a hairpin bend in Makiki Heights Drive, roughly half a mile east of the Contemporary Museum, or half a mile west of the intersection with Makiki Street. Follow the dead-end road to park just beyond the ramshackle green trailers of the **Hawaii Nature Center**, a volunteer educational group that works mainly with schoolchildren and organizes guided hikes, open to all, on weekends (call ⓣ955-0100 for details). If you haven't already picked up trail maps from the state office downtown (see p.55), they may have some at the center.

The best loop trip from this point begins by following the **Maunalaha Trail**, which starts across the Kanealole Stream beyond the center's restrooms. From the banana grove here, you swiftly switchback on to the ridge for a long straight climb, often stepping from one exposed tree root to the next. Despite being in the shade most of the way, it's a grueling haul. Looking back through the deep green woods, you'll glimpse the towers of downtown Honolulu and then of Waikīkī. At first you can see the valleys to either side of the ridge, but before long only Mānoa Valley to the east is visible. After roughly three-quarters of a mile, you come to a **four-way intersection** at the top of the hill.

Continuing straight ahead from here for around three miles connects you, via the Moleka and Mānoa Cliff trails, to the Nu'uanu Valley Lookout, described on p.92; turn left and you're on the Makiki Valley Trail, detailed below. Turning right onto the **'Ualaka'a Trail**, however, adds an enjoyable if muddy half-mile to the loop trip. Plunging into the forest, the level path soon passes some extraordinary banyans, perched on the steep slopes with their many trunks, which have engulfed older trees. Having rounded the ridge, where a magnificent avenue of Cook pines marches along the crest in parallel rows, an armspan apart, you curve back to cross Round Top Drive twice. In between the two crossings, take the short spur trail that leads left and up to the highest point on the hike. A clearing here perfectly frames Diamond Head against the ocean, with Waikīkī to the right of Diamond Head and the gleaming silver dome of the sports stadium at the University of Hawaii straight below. Once you rejoin the main trail on the far side of Round Top Drive – it starts fifty yards to the right – a brief woodland walk returns you to the four-way junction.

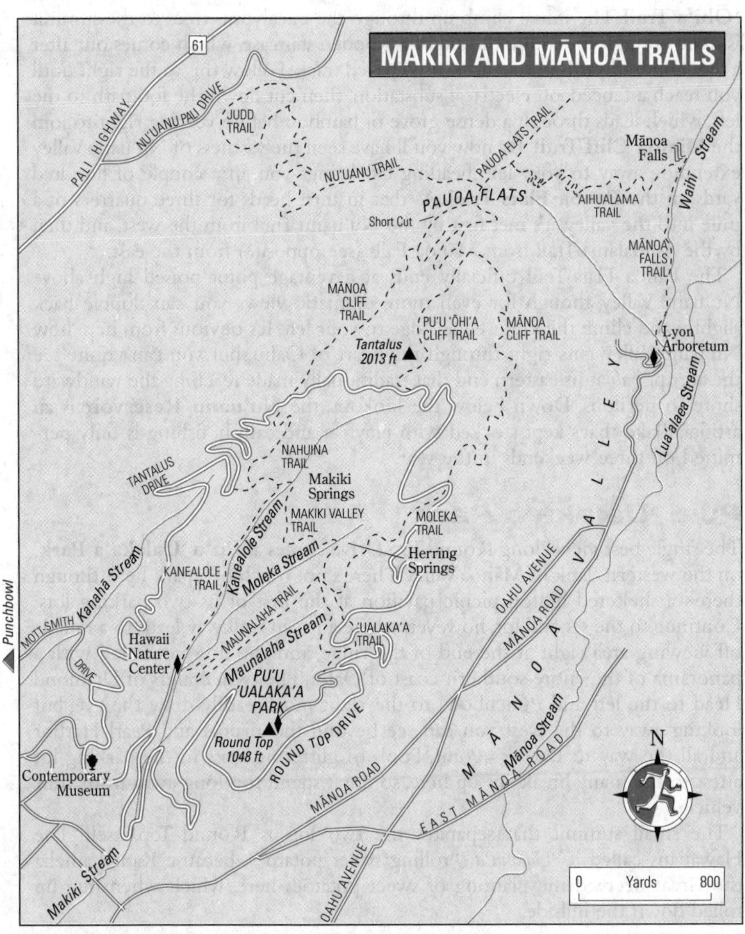

The next stretch, on the **Makiki Valley Trail**, is the most gorgeous of the lot. A gentle descent angled along the steep valley wall, it heads inland to cross Moleka Stream at Herring Springs, amid a profusion of tiny bright flowers. Climbing away again you're treated to further ravishing views of the high valley, bursting with bright gingers and fruit trees. Birds are audible all around, and dangling lianas festoon the path. Take **Kanealole Trail**, which cuts away to the left shortly before this trail meets Tantalus Drive, and you'll drop back down through endless guava trees to your starting point at the Nature Center.

In total, the loop hike detailed here is three miles with the extra 'Ualaka'a segment, or 2.5 miles without it.

## Tantalus trails

Tantalus Drive is at its highest just below the 2013-foot pinnacle of **Tantalus** itself, near the point, halfway between the two intersections with Makiki Heights Drive, where it changes its name to Round Top Drive. Two roadside parking lots here stand close to the trailhead for the three-quarter-mile **Pu'u 'Ōhi'a Trail**. The initial climb up through the eucalyptus trees to the summit is steep enough to require the aid of a wooden staircase, which comes out after a few hundred yards onto a little-used paved track. Follow this to the right until you reach a fenced-off electrical substation, then cut down the footpath to the left, which leads through a dense grove of bamboo before veering right to join the **Mānoa Cliff Trail**. By now you'll have seen the vastness of Nu'uanu Valley extending away to your left; heading left brings you, in a couple of hundred yards, to the **Pauoa Flats Trail**. As that in turn heads for three quarters of a mile into the valley, it's met first by the Nu'uanu Trail from the west, and then by the Aihualama Trail from Mānoa Falls (see opposite) from the east.

The Pauoa Flats Trail officially ends at a vantage point poised high above Nu'uanu Valley, though for even more dramatic views you can double back slightly and climb the knife-edge ridge to your left. It's obvious from here how Nu'uanu Valley cuts right through the heart of Oahu, but you can't quite see the abrupt *pali* at its eastern end that traditionally made reaching the windward shore so perilous. Down below the lookout, the **Nu'uanu Reservoir** is an artificial lake that's kept stocked with crayfish and catfish; fishing is only permitted on three weekends in the year.

## Pu'u 'Ualaka'a Park

The single best view along Round Top Drive comes at **Pu'u 'Ualaka'a Park**, on the western flank of Mānoa Valley. There's not much of a park here, though there's a sheltered hilltop picnic pavilion at the first of its two parking lots. Continue to the second lot, however, where a paved walkway leads to a railed-off viewing area right at the end of the ridge, and you'll be rewarded with a panorama of the entire southern coast of Oahu. The twin craters of Diamond Head to the left and Punchbowl to the right most readily draw the eye, but looking away to the west you can see beyond the airport and Pearl Harbor and all the way to Barber's Point. Pools of glittering glass in the parking lot attest to the many break-ins up here, so don't spend too long away from your vehicle.

The small summit that separates the two lots is Round Top itself. The Hawaiians called it *'Ualaka'a* ("rolling sweet potato"), because Kamehameha the Great decreed the planting of sweet potatoes here, which when dug up rolled down the hillside.

# Mānoa Valley

**Mānoa Valley** may lie just a couple of miles from Waikīkī – directly inland, to the north – but it's light-years away from the commercial hustle of the city. Behind the **University of Hawaii** – a mecca for students from around the Pacific, but of no great appeal for casual visitors – lies a quiet residential suburb that peters out as it narrows into the mountains, to culminate in a spectacular tropical **waterfall**.

## University of Hawaii

The main campus of the **University of Hawaii** sprawls along University Avenue in Mānoa, bounded on its southern side by H-1, Honolulu's major east-west freeway. The University has recently undergone massive budget cuts and has found itself forced to choose between providing a full spectrum of courses or concentrating on its specialities of geology, marine studies, astronomy and other Pacific-related fields. As only a tiny proportion of students live on campus, there are fewer stores, restaurants and clubs in the vicinity than you might expect. The **Campus Center**, set a little way back from University Avenue, is the place to head for general information and orientation. **Hemenway Hall** alongside holds the inexpensive *Mānoa Garden* café, as well as a movie theater, and its noticeboards carry details of short-term courses open to visitors.

## Lyon Arboretum and Mānoa Falls

To drive to the uppermost reaches of Mānoa Valley, continue along University Avenue beyond the campus, cross E Mānoa Road onto Oahu Avenue, and then turn right onto Mānoa Road itself. Immediately you'll see the silver stream of Mānoa Falls amid the trees at the head of the valley. Mānoa Road comes to a halt just beyond the **Lyon Arboretum**, which belongs to the University and preserves Hawaiian and imported trees in a reasonable approximation of their native environment (Mon–Sat 9am–3pm; $1 donation). Several short trails crisscross beneath the canopy.

Parking at the end of the road should be no problem, though, as ever, it's unwise to leave valuables in your car. The half-hour trail to **Mānoa Falls** follows straight on ahead; be sure not to set off without mosquito repellent. Having passed over a footbridge and through a soggy meadow, the trail soon starts to climb beside one of the two main tributaries of Mānoa Stream. After scrambling from root to protruding root, over intertwined banyans and bamboos, you come out at the soaring high falls, where the flat, mossy cliff face is at enough of an angle that the water flows rather than falls into the small pool at its base.

Many hikers cool off in the pool before attempting the more demanding **Aihualama Trail**, which switchbacks away west of the falls. After something over a mile, it comes out on top of the ridge, amid a thick cluster of bamboo, to connect with the Makiki network of trails half a mile short of the Nu'uanu Lookout (see opposite).

# Pali Highway

Until 1997, only the **Pali Highway** and **Likelike Highway** negotiated the Ko'olau Mountains to connect Honolulu with windward Oahu; they have now, at last, been joined by the **H-3** freeway. Thirty-seven long years in the making, thanks to an interminable series of disputes over its environmental and archeological impact, H-3 was originally intended for military use, as a direct link between Pearl Harbor and the Marine Corps base at Kāne'ohe. In the last four decades, however, windward communities such as **Kailua** and **Kāne'ohe** (see p.122 and p.123) have become home to an ever-higher proportion of Honolulu's workforce, and H-3 has considerably eased the strain for local commuters.

The opening of H-3 has little significance for tourists, on the other hand, as the Pali and Likelike highways hold far more potential for sightseeing. Both can still get hideously congested at peak times, but the Pali Highway in particular is an exhilarating drive, whether you head straight for the clifftop **Nu'uanu Pali Lookout**, or call in at the various **royal sites** on the way up.



## Royal Mausoleum

The Gothic-influenced **Royal Mausoleum** is located very near the top of Nu'uanu Avenue, shortly before it joins the Pali Highway. It would be very easy to miss – there's no sign, so watch out on the right as soon as you've passed the Japanese cemetery – and frankly it's not worth losing any sleep over if you do.

The drab, gray mausoleum itself, built in 1865 to replace the overcrowded Kamehameha family tomb at 'Iolani Palace, stands at the end of a short oval driveway ringed with lumpy palm trees. It's now simply a chapel, as the bodies it held for its first forty years or so were later moved to various sarcophagi dotted around the lawns. Kamehameha the Great was buried in secret on the Big Island (see p.161), but most of his closest family, as Christians, now lie here. His widow Ka'ahumanu, along with Kamehameha II to V, are in the pink granite tomb to the left, while members of the separate Kalākaua dynasty were reinterred in the gilded vault beneath the central black column. Incidentally, this spot is said to be the precise site where the Nu'uanu Valley battle began in 1795.

## Queen Emma Summer Palace

A couple of miles up the Pali Highway, just over half a mile after its intersection with Nu'uanu Avenue, a former royal retreat stands on the brow of a small hill to the right of the road. The **Queen Emma Summer Palace** made a welcome escape from the heat of Honolulu for the former Emma Rooke, who married King Kamehameha IV in 1856, was queen consort until 1863, and lived here until her death in 1885. It's now run as a somewhat cloying shrine to Emma by the Daughters of Hawaii, a group composed of descendants of missionary families (daily 9am–4pm; adults $5, under-12s $1; ⓣ 595-3167).

Behind its entrance stairway, framed with six Doric pillars, the single-story white frame house is surprisingly small. Guided tours proceed at a snail's pace through rooms lined with royal souvenirs; only the splendidly grumpy Princess Ruth relieves the monotony of the official portraits. Among touching memorabilia of the young Prince Albert Edward – Queen Emma's only child, who died at the age of four – are his beautiful *koa*-wood crib, carved to resemble a canoe rocked by the waves, and a fireman's outfit he once wore in a parade. Gifts from Queen Victoria – after whose husband the boy was named – make up a large proportion of the items on display. Both Victoria and Emma were widowed – Emma was only 27 when her husband died a year after their son – and the two women continued to exchange presents for the rest of their lives.

## Nu'uanu Pali State Park

Half a mile up the Pali Highway beyond Queen Emma's palace, an inconspicuous right turn leads onto **Nu'uanu Pali Drive**. Other than having to drive slower, you lose nothing by taking this detour into succulent rainforest, which curves back to meet the highway two miles up. There are no specific stops en route, but the density of the overhanging tropical canopy, lit with flashes of color, is irresistible.

Back on the highway, it's now just a mile until the next right turn – confusingly, it too is Nu'uanu Pali Drive – which leads in a few hundred yards to **Nu'uanu Pali State Park** (daily 4am–8pm; free). Miss this, and you'll miss a staggering overview of the cliffs of windward Oahu; the highway goes into a tunnel at this point, and emerges much lower down the hillside. At the edge of a small parking lot – which is the most notorious spot in the state for **car break-ins**, so leave no valuables in your vehicle – the railed viewing area of the **Nu'uanu Pali Lookout** turns out to be perched near the top of a magnificent pleated curtain of green velvet, plunging more than a thousand feet. Straight ahead lie the sprawling coastal communities of **Kailua** and **Kāne'ohe**, separated by the Mōkapu Peninsula, but your eye is likely to be drawn to the north, where the mighty *pali* seems to stretch away forever, with a waterfall in every fold.

It was over this fearsome drop that the defeated warriors of Oahu were driven in 1795 (see box below); placards at the overlook explain the course of the battle and point out assorted landmarks. Notches higher up the ridge are said to have been cut to provide fortified positions for the defenders, an estimated four hundred of whose skulls were found down below when the Pali Highway was built a century later. The stairs that lead down to the right enable you to join the highway's original route (abandoned when it was upgraded to take automobiles) as it edges its way above the precipice. It's blocked off about a mile along, but walking to the end makes a good, if windy, mountain hike.

### The Battle of Nu'uanu Valley

For early foreign visitors, the ride to the top of Nu'uanu Pali was an essential part of a Hawaiian itinerary. As their horses struggled up, native guides would recount tales of the epic **Battle of Nu'uanu Valley** in 1795, in which Kamehameha the Great (from the Big Island) defeated Kalanikūpule and conquered the island of Oahu.

No two versions completely agree, but according to James Macrae, who accompanied Lord Byron to Hawaii in 1825 (soon enough after the battle to meet some of the participants), Kamehameha's army landed at Honolulu to find Kalanikūpule waiting for them in Nu'uanu Valley. Kamehameha sent men along the tops of the ridges to either side, and advanced towards Kalanikūpule in the center himself. By this time, his entourage included Europeans and, crucially, a few European guns. Isaac Davis, who five years previously had been the sole survivor of a Hawaiian raid on a small boat at Kawaihae on the Big Island (see p.287), positioned himself at the front of the attack.

Before the usual ritual of challenges and counter-challenges could even begin, Davis killed Kalanikūpule's leading general with a single lucky shot. The soldiers of Oahu turned and ran, pursued all the way to the head of the valley. When they reached the top, where the thousand-foot Nu'uanu Pali precipice drops away on the far side, they had no choice. To a man, they hurtled to their deaths.

If you're heading across the island, you would naturally expect to turn right as you leave the parking lot. In fact, you have to drive back down to rejoin the highway where you left it. To the right, Nu'uanu Pali Drive crosses over the tunnel and meets the highway's other carriageway on the far side, to drop back into Honolulu.



# Likelike Highway

You're most likely to use the Pali Highway (see p.93) to get to windward Oahu from Honolulu, but the **Likelike Highway** provides a less spectacular alternative. Starting roughly two miles to the west, it runs through residential Kalihi Valley and then passes through its own tunnel to emerge just above Kāne'ohe. There's no great reason to cross the island this way – the traffic is unlikely to be any easier – but you'll have to drive a short stretch of Likelike Highway to visit Honolulu's best museum, the **Bishop Museum**.

## Bishop Museum

The best museum of **Hawaiian history**, **anthropology** and **natural history** – and the world's finest collection of the arts of the Pacific – is located in an otherwise obscure district of Honolulu, two miles northwest of downtown. To reach the **Bishop Museum**, at 1525 Bernice St, catch TheBus #2 from Waikīkī or drive to the foot of Likelike Highway and follow the signs from the first exit on the right (daily 9am–5pm; adults $14.95, ages 4–12 and seniors $11.95; prices include the planetarium; ⓣ 847-3511, ⓦ www.bishop.hawaii.org).

The Bishop Museum was founded in 1889 by Charles Reed Bishop to preserve the heirlooms left by his wife, Princess Bernice Pauahi, the last direct descendant of Kamehameha the Great. Spread across three principal buildings on a 12-acre hillside estate, it sets out to demonstrate the reality of Polynesian culture, as opposed to the fakery of Waikīkī.

The first section you come to, beyond the ticket hall – Hawaii's only **planetarium** – has a practical relevance to the current "Hawaiian Renaissance." Master navigator Nainoa Thompson of the *Hokule'a* studied the virtual sky here to reinvent traditional Polynesian navigational techniques, as used in the voyages described on p.521 onwards. Shows take place daily at 11am and 2pm, plus Friday and Saturday at 7pm; admission to those alone costs $4.50. An attendant stationed in the adjoining **observatory** helps visitors to make their own observations.

The huge main building of the museum houses the bulk of its historic displays. To the right of the entrance, the **Hawaiian Hall** consists of a large ground-level room overlooked by two tiers of wood-paneled balconies. Suspended in the central well is the skeleton of a sperm whale, half clad in papier-maché skin. Among the priceless ancient artifacts down below are carved stone and wooden images of gods, including what may be at least one of the legendary "poisonwood gods" from Molokai (see p.404), and Kamehameha the Great's own personal image of the war god Kūkā'ilimoku, found in a cave in Kona on the Big Island. You'll also see *koa* platters and calabashes, and multicolored feather *leis* and capes.

A scale model of the Big Island's Waha'ula *heiau*, built in 1903 using stones from the site, now serves as a valuable record of an important piece of Hawaiian history. The original – thought to have been founded thirty generations ago by the warrior-priest Pā'ao from Tahiti – was recently overrun by lava from

Kīlauea. Nearby stands a sharkskin drum that was once used to announce human sacrifices in a similar *luakini* temple on the seaward slopes of Diamond Head – the only such drum known to have survived the overthrow of the *kapu* system. There's also a full-sized *hale,* or traditional hut, brought here from Hāʻena on Kauai. Standing as usual on a platform of smooth stones, it's windowless, and thatched with *pili* grass.

On the lower of the Hawaiian Hall's balconies you'll find weapons, including swords embedded with sharks' teeth, plus exhibitions on the nineteenth-century distribution of land known as the Great Mahele (see p.512), whaling, and the creation and dyeing of *tapa* (the bark-cloth also known as *kapa*). The higher balcony is devoted to the contributions of Hawaii's immigrants, with costumes and artifacts from such countries as Germany, Spain, Portugal, the Philippines, Japan, Korea and China.

The **Polynesian Hall**, above the entrance in the same building, emphasizes the full diversity of Polynesia. After the breaking of the *kapu* (see p.520), the Hawaiians themselves set about destroying the relics of their ancient religion; most other Polynesian cultures have preserved far more of their heritage. Stunning exhibits here include woven-grass masks and dance costumes from Vanikoro, modeled skulls and figures from Vanuato, stark white and red sorcery charms from Papua New Guinea, and stick charts used by Pacific navigators. The Maoris of New Zealand are represented by the facade of a storehouse, carved in high relief with human figures and inlaid with abalone-shell eyes.

On the top floor, the **Hall of Hawaiian Natural History** explains the origin of the Hawaiian islands with a large-scale relief model of the entire chain, then covers the development of life here, from the first chance arrivals to recently introduced pests. The new **Castle Building** next door houses top-quality temporary exhibitions.

The Bishop Museum holds an excellent bookstore as well as *Woody's Snack Bar* (daily 9am–4pm). On the first Sunday of every month, known as **Family Sunday**, Hawaii residents are allowed in free and the lawns play host to food stalls, *hula* performances and all sorts of other activities.

# Pearl Harbor

Ancient Hawaiians knew the vast inlet of **Pearl Harbor**, reaching deep into the heart of Oahu, as *Wai Momi*, "water of pearl," on account of its pearl-bearing oysters. Their canoes had no need of deep-water anchorages, but Westerners came to realize that dredging its entrance would turn it into the finest harbor in the Pacific. Such was its strategic potential that the desire to control Pearl Harbor played a large and explicit role in the eventual annexation of Hawaii by the United States. The US first received permission to develop installations here in 1887, in return for granting Hawaiian sugar duty-free access to US markets, and construction of the naval base commenced in 1908.

To this day, the 12,600-acre Pearl Harbor Naval Complex is the headquarters from which the US Pacific Fleet patrols 102 million square miles of ocean. The entire fleet consists of 265 ships, 1900 aircraft and 268,000 personnel, while Pearl Harbor itself is the home port for twenty surface vessels and twenty nuclear submarines.

Except for the offshore **Arizona Memorial**, commemorating the surprise **Japanese attack** with which Pearl Harbor remains synonymous, almost the whole area is off-limits to civilians.

## The Attack on Pearl Harbor

As the winter of 1941 approached, with German soldiers occupying most of Europe and moving into Soviet Russia, and Japanese forces advancing through Southeast Asia, the United States remained outside the global conflict. However, negotiations to halt Japanese progress had stalled, and on November 27 the US government sent secret "war warnings" to its military units throughout the world. The version received by the commanding general in Hawaii read: "Japanese future action unpredictable but hostile action possible at any moment. If hostilities cannot, repeat cannot, be avoided the United States desires that Japan commit the first overt act."

A few days earlier, a Japanese attack fleet, with six aircraft carriers among its 33 vessels, had sailed from northern Japan. By maintaining strict radio silence, it dodged American surveillance. The conventional wisdom was that it must be heading towards the Philippines, site of the furthest-flung US base in the Pacific, and a detachment of B-17 "Flying Fortress" aircraft was sent from Hawaii to bolster the islands' defenses. In fact, however, Hawaii itself, where Pearl Harbor had since the previous spring been the headquarters of the US Pacific Fleet, was the target. The Japanese fleet sailed there along an icy, rarely used northerly course, keeping well clear of usual shipping lanes. The Japanese did not expect to achieve complete surprise and were prepared to engage the US fleet in battle if they met them on the open sea; but reconnaissance flights from Pearl Harbor only covered the likeliest angle of attack, from the southwest, and the Japanese approach was not detected. By the early morning of December 7, the fleet was in position 230 miles northwest of Oahu.

The first wave of the attack, consisting of 183 aircraft, was launched at 6am. As the planes passed over the western Wai'anae mountains, they were picked up by radar screens at a nearby tracking station. When the operators called Honolulu with the news that a large group of aircraft had been spotted, they were told "Well, don't worry about it," in the belief that these were replacement B-17s arriving from the mainland. Meanwhile, the cloud cover had lifted to give the attackers a perfect view of Pearl Harbor, where seven of the US fleet's nine battleships lay at anchor along "Battleship Row." At 7.53am, Commander Mitsuo Fuchida sent the codeword "*Tora! Tora! Tora!*" (Tiger! Tiger! Tiger!) to his flagship, the *Akagai*, signalling that a surprise attack was under way.

Within two hours the US Navy lost eighteen warships – eight battleships, three light cruisers, three destroyers and four auxiliary craft – and 87 planes. Simultaneous attacks on other bases on Oahu destroyed 77 Air Force planes and damaged 128 more. Following recent warnings, the planes were parked wingtip-to-wingtip on the airfields. This was supposed to make them easier to protect against sabotage by Japanese agents among the *nisei* (Hawaiian residents of Japanese ancestry); instead it left them utterly exposed to aerial attack. During the onslaught, the expected squadron of B-17s arrived from California; unarmed, several were shot down.

In total, 2403 US military personnel were killed, and 1178 wounded. The Japanese lost 29 aircraft, plus five midget submarines that had sneaked into Pearl Harbor

## Arizona Memorial

Almost half the victims of the December 1941 Japanese attack on Pearl Harbor were aboard the battleship **USS Arizona**. Hit by an armor-piercing shell that detonated its magazine and lifted its bow twenty feet out of the water, it sank within nine minutes. Of its crew of 1514 – who had earned the right to sleep in late that Sunday morning by coming second in a military band competition – 1177 were killed.

during the previous night in the hope of torpedoing damaged ships. Ten hours later, Japanese aircraft did indeed attack Clark Airfield in the Philippines, and there too they destroyed large numbers of aircraft on the ground. The next day, declaring the United States to be at war with Japan, President Franklin D. Roosevelt condemned the "dastardly" Pearl Harbor attack as "a day that will live in infamy."

The official postwar inquiry into "the greatest military and naval disaster in our nation's history" set out to explain why the attack was possible, let alone successful. Considering why the fleet was based in Hawaii in the first place, instead of the relative safety of the US West Coast, it was told that, despite its weakness at the time, that would have signaled a lack of US will to resist Japanese expansion in the Pacific. As to whether the fleet's vulnerability had invited the attack, Japanese plans were drawn up expecting a much larger fleet at Pearl Harbor, and they were disappointed to find that both US aircraft carriers were out of port. The fact that the Japanese withdrew from Hawaii almost immediately, instead of following up their initial success by destroying port installations such as the vast oil tanks, and thereby crippling US Navy operations for years – or even by invading the islands – suggests that if anything they overestimated US defenses.

No hard evidence has been produced to support revisionist assertions that Roosevelt knew the attack was coming, but allowed it to happen because he wanted an excuse to join the war, or that the British knew, and they deliberately failed to warn the Americans for the same reason. It makes no sense, if Roosevelt did know, that he didn't at least alert US defenses a few hours in advance, when an unprovoked Japanese attack was demonstrably imminent.

Mistakes were certainly made. Among the most glaring was the fact that Navy authorities were never told of intercepted messages from Tokyo in which the Japanese consulate in Honolulu was asked to divide the moorings in Pearl Harbor into five separate areas and specify which ships were anchored in each section. The best explanation can probably be found in a pair of statements by the two leading protagonists. The overall Japanese commander, reporting to his superiors a fortnight later, wrote that "good luck, together with negligence on the part of the arrogant enemy, enabled us to launch a successful surprise attack." Admiral Husband E. Kimmel, in charge of the US Pacific Fleet, was asked informally why he had left the ships exposed in Pearl Harbor, and replied, "I never thought those little yellow sons-of-bitches could pull off such an attack, so far from Japan." Although Kimmel was stripped of his rank in the immediate aftermath, he was posthumously promoted back to admiral by both Senate and Congress in 1999, but that still-controversial move has yet to be ratified by the president.

In the long run, the Japanese decision to provoke the US into all-out war in the Pacific was to prove suicidal. What's more, most of the vessels damaged and even sunk at Pearl Harbor eventually returned to active service. Only the *Arizona* and the *Utah* could not be salvaged, while the *Oklahoma* sank once again, 500 miles off the Big Island. By contrast, just two of the Japanese ships that were involved in the attack survived the war; four of the anti-aircraft carriers were sunk during the Battle of Midway. In 1945, the *West Virginia*, risen from the waters of Pearl Harbor, was in Tokyo Bay to witness the Japanese surrender.

The *Arizona* still lies submerged where it came to rest, out in the waters of the harbor along "Battleship Row," next to Ford Island. Its wreck is spanned (though not touched) by the curving white **Arizona Memorial**, maintained by the National Park Service in honor of all the victims of the attack; small boats ferry a stream of visitors out from the mainland.

The **visitor center** for the memorial is located six miles west of Honolulu, just over a mile after Kamehameha Highway cuts off to the left of H-1 (center open daily 7.30am–5pm; tours 8am–3pm; free; ⓣ422-0561). It takes up to an hour to drive across town from Waikīkī. TheBus #20 runs direct from Waikīkī, as do overpriced commercial tours ($20). On arrival, pick up a numbered ticket for the free memorial tour; in peak season, it can be two or three hours before you're called to board the ferry. Many people try to beat the crowds by arriving early, but if anything your chances of a short wait may be better in the afternoon.

Perhaps because so many of the 1.5 million annual visitors are Japanese, the displays in the visitor center are surprisingly even-handed, calling the attack "a daring gamble" by Admiral Yamamoto to knock out the US fleet and give the Japanese time to conquer Southeast Asia. The center has long been scheduled to hold a new **museum**, designed to trace the events leading up to the attack, the bombing itself, and the course of the war in the Pacific. Only a few exhibits were in place as this book went to press, however, including models of both the *Arizona* and the Japanese flagship, the *IMS Akagi*; an actual aerial torpedo; and some personal items salvaged from the wreck.

Until the museum is completed, the best place to get a sense of what happened is in the waterfront **garden** outside. From here, you see the low and undramatic mountain ridges that ring Pearl Harbor, together with the gap down the center of the island through which the first planes arrived. Captioned photographs clearly illustrate the disposition of the ships moored along "Battleship Row" on the fateful morning, as well as their eventual fate. Survivors of the attack are often on hand to tell their stories.

When your number finally comes up, you're first shown a twenty-minute film that pays tribute to "one of the most brilliantly planned and executed attacks in naval history." A pained female voice narrates the course of the attack, over footage of Japanese planes taking off from their aircraft carriers.

Crisp-uniformed Navy personnel then usher you onto open-sided boats, which they steer for ten minutes across a tiny fraction of the naval base. At the memorial, whose white marble walls are inscribed with the names of the dead, you disembark for the twenty minutes until the next boat arrives. The outline of the *Arizona* is still discernible in the clear blue waters, and here and there rusty metal spurs poke from the water. All those who died when the *Arizona* went down remain entombed in the wreckage, occasionally joined by veteran survivors who choose to be buried here.

## USS Bowfin Submarine Museum and Park

Located alongside the *Arizona* visitor center, the **USS Bowfin Submarine Museum and Park** serves as an alternative distraction if you have a couple of hours to wait before your ferry (daily 8am–5pm; sub and museum, adults $8, under-13s $3; combined with *Missouri* admission, adults $18, ages 4–12 $9; museum only, adults $4, under-13s $2). Its main focus, the claustrophobic *Bowfin* itself, is a still-floating, 83-man submarine that survived World War II unscathed, having sunk 44 enemy vessels. Once you've explored it on a self-guided audio tour – complete with a first-person account of one of the *Bowfin*'s most hair-raising missions, narrated by the captain in charge — you can learn more about the whole story of twentieth-century submarines in the adjoining museum.

The park outside, to which access is free, holds various missiles and torpedoes, including the Japanese naval equivalent of a *kamikaze* airplane, a *kaiten*. Such manned, single-seater torpedoes were designed for suicide attacks on larger ships; only one, piloted by its inventor, ever succeeded in sinking a US Navy ship.

## USS Missouri

Since 1998, the decommissioned battleship **USS Missouri**, also known as the "Mighty Mo", has been permanently moored close to the USS Arizona Memorial. The last battleship to be constructed by the United States, she was christened in January 1944. After service in the Pacific and Korean wars, she was decommissioned in 1955 and remained mothballed until being refitted in 1986. Operation Desert Storm saw the *Missouri* firing Tomahawk missiles against Iraq, but she was finally retired once more in 1992, as the last operational battleship in the world. Should the need arise, she's still capable of being recommissioned in 45–90 days.

Several different US locations competed for the honor of providing a final berth for the *Missouri*. Pearl Harbor won, on the basis that the place where World War II began for the United States should also hold the spot where it ended; the Japanese surrender of September 2, 1945, was signed on the deck of the *Missouri*, then moored in Tokyo Bay. In addition to being a monument in her own right, part of the battleship's new role is as a recruiting tool for the US Navy; it's even possible to arrange kids' sleepover parties on board.

Since the battleship is located alongside Ford Island, which is officially part of the naval base, visitors can only reach it by shuttle bus. These depart from the USS Bowfin visitor center, which is also where you purchase tickets (daily 9am–5pm; adults $14, ages 4–12 $7; guided tours $6 extra per person. ⓣ973-2494, ⓦwww.ussmissouri.com).

Having crossed the harbor via one of only six retracting bridges in the world, you're deposited at the entrance gate. Depending on whether you've paid extra to join one of the regular hour-long guided tours – which you might as well, given that you're interested enough to have made it this far – you're then shepherded either towards your personal guide or simply left to climb up to the deck.

The overwhelming first impression for all visitors is the *Missouri*'s sheer size; at 887 feet long, she's the length of three football fields. Next you're likely to focus on her colossal twin gun turrets, each of which is equipped with three guns. By contrast, once you go below decks, the crew's quarters are cramped in the extreme, bringing home the full claustrophobic reality of her long and dangerous missions. The principal highlights are the dimly lit Combat Engagement Center, set up as it was during the Gulf War but now looking very antiquated; the surrender site, on the deck nearby; and the spot where a *kamikaze* fighter careered into the side of the ship, as captured in a dramatic photo. Thus far, however, the *Missouri*'s four engine rooms are not open to the public.

# Restaurants

With most of its 100,000 daily visitors eating out at least once a day, **Waikīkī** supports an incredible number and variety of **restaurants**. In the rest of **Honolulu**, you'll find somewhere to eat pretty much anywhere you go – the shopping malls are packed with identikit places – but only the restaurants of **Chinatown** merit a special trip from Waikīkī.

## Waikīkī

Almost all of Waikīkī's hotels have an on-site American restaurant, and usually one or two other more specialized options as well. As you'd expect, the standards in the major hotels are very high, but out on the streets the emphasis is

**Honolulu and Waikīkī Favorites**

| | | | |
|---|---|---|---|
| Breakfast | *Shore Bird Beach Broiler* | Waikīkī | p.103 |
| Buffet | *Todai Seafood Buffet* | Waikīkī | p.105 |
| Chinese | *Indigo* | Honolulu | p.109 |
| Fast food | International Marketplace | Waikīkī | p.102 |
| | Maunakea Marketplace | Honolulu | p.85 |
| Gourmet | *Alan Wong's* | Honolulu | p.109 |
| Greek | *Olive Tree Cafe* | Honolulu | p.108 |
| Italian | *Arancino* | Waikīkī | p.103 |
| Japanese | *L'Uraku* | Honolulu | p.109 |
| Korean | *Yakiniku Canellia* | Honolulu | p.108 |
| Local | *Kaka'ako Kitchen* | Honolulu | p.107 |
| Pacific Rim | *Bali By The Sea* | Waikīkī | p.105 |
| | *Sansei* | Honolulu | p.109 |
| Pizza | *California Pizza Kitchen* | Honolulu | p.108 |
| Seafood | *Sam Choy's Breakfast, Lunch & Crab* | Honolulu | p.109 |
| Steak | *The Colony* | Waikīkī | p.106 |
| Thai | *Singha Thai Cuisine* | Waikīkī | p.105 |
| Vietnamese | *Maxime* | Honolulu | p.107 |

on keeping the price low, rather than the quality high. Many of the better restaurants don't bother to open for lunch, but takeouts, fast-food chains and snack bars are everywhere you turn; the largest concentrations are along **Kūhiō Avenue** and, with more of a Japanese emphasis, on **Kalākaua Avenue** west of Lewers Street. The easiest **fast-food** option must be the International Food Court, in the International Marketplace on Kalākaua. Takeout counters with self-explanatory names – *Joe's Hamburger Grill*, *Yummy Korean B-B-Q*, *Bautista's Filipino Kitchen*, etc. – surround a sheltered area of tables, and there's often free musical entertainment of some kind. There's a similar, smaller food court beneath the Waikīkī Shopping Plaza at 2250 Kalākaua Ave, while *Starbucks* coffee outlets are located in the **Waikīkī Trade Center** at Kūhiō and Seaside, and the Discovery Bay Center at 1778 Ala Moana Blvd.

If you want to cook for yourself, try the Food Pantry, a good-value 24-hour **supermarket** at the northwest corner of Kūhiō Avenue and Walina Street. Wholefood enthusiasts will probably prefer *Down to Earth Natural Foods*, a mile or so out of Waikīkī near the University, at 2525 S King St (☎947-7678).

## Inexpensive

**China Garden**, *Aston Coral Reef Hotel*, 2299 Kūhiō Ave; ☎923-8383. Inexpensive Chinese restaurant serving $6 lunch specials and $9 one-plate dinners with rice and soup. Entrees cost $9–14; set meals for two or more are $14–18 per person. Daily 11am–10pm.

**La Cucaracha**, 2310 Kūhiō Ave; ☎922-2288. Budget Mexican food, served from early afternoon until late in a party atmosphere. Standard Mexican favorites like enchiladas and chimichangas are around $10; fancier seafood combos cost $20 or so. Daily 2pm–midnight.

**Eggs'n'Things**, 1911B Kalākaua Ave; ☎949-0820. All-night diner drawing a big breakfast crowd for its bargain omelets, waffles and crepes. The Early Riser (before 9am) and Late Riser (1–2pm) specials give you three pancakes or two eggs for just $3. Daily 11pm–2pm.

**Ezogiku**, 2546 Lemon St; ☎923-2013. Plain and very inexpensive Japanese diner, with three branches in Waikīkī – the others are at 2420 Koa Ave and 2146 Kalākaua Ave. Ramen soups plus rice and curry dishes, all at $6–7, to eat in or take out. Daily 7–10am & 11am–11pm.

**Hawaii Seafood Paradise**, 1830 Ala Moana Blvd; ☎946-4514. Almost three restaurants in one, not far from the *Hilton* at the Ala Moana end of Waikīkī. At breakfast, the food is American and very inexpensive. Chinese-style lunch specials cost around $7, and only in the evening is it really a "seafood paradise," with high-quality Chinese and

Thai entrees such as crispy oysters and steamed catfish generally priced at $10–15. Daily 6.30am–3am.

**Leonard's Bakery**, 933 Kapahulu Ave; ⓣ737-5591. Long-standing Portuguese bakery on the northeastern fringes of Waikīkī, renowned for its delicious desserts and *malasadas*. Most of the pastries cost under $1. Sun–Thurs 6am–9pm, Fri & Sat 6am–10pm.

**Moose McGillycuddy's**, 310 Lewers St; ⓣ923-0751. Nightclub and drinking venue, with booths in the bar downstairs, and a dining room on the second floor. Among the breakfast options are a $2 special that includes two eggs and bacon. Later on you can get burgers and sandwiches for $6–9, snacks like quesadillas, wings or nachos for $5–8, or full dinners of fajitas, pasta, steak or chicken for $10–15. Youth Hostel Association members receive a fifteen percent discount on all entrees. Mon, Tues & Sun 7.30am–2am, Wed–Sat 7.30am–4am.

**Perry's Smorgy**, 2380 Kūhiō Ave; ⓣ926-0184. Bland all-you-can-eat buffets, served indoors or in a nice little garden. The food is filling, but the place is always crowded, and hardly anything actually tastes that great. The $5.25 breakfast includes ham, beef, sausages, pancakes, pastries and juices; the $6.25 lunch consists of *mahimahi*, Southern fried chicken, garlic bread, rice, baked macaroni and desserts; and the $9.25 dinner features beef, shrimp, ribs, turkey and teriyaki chicken. Note that there's another *Perry's* at the *Ohana Coral Seas*, 250 Lewers St (ⓣ922-8814), but it's indoor-only and less appealing. Daily 7–11am, 11.30am–2.30pm & 5–9pm.

**Ruffage Natural Foods**, 2443 Kūhiō Ave; ⓣ922-2042. Tiny wholefood grocery with a takeout counter and patio seating. Avocado and bean-sprout sandwiches, plus salads and vegetables with pasta or tofu all cost under $7, and they do great real-fruit smoothies. The front part of the shop becomes an inexpensive sushi bar from 6pm onwards. Mon–Sat 9am–7pm. Closed Sun.

**Shore Bird Beach Broiler**, *Outrigger Reef on the Beach*, 2169 Kālia Rd; ⓣ922-2887. Open-air hotel restaurant on the oceanfront serving an $8 breakfast buffet, and dinner with an open salad bar for $13–19, depending on your choice of entree. There's a communal grill on which guests cook their own meat or fish. Excellent value, especially if you use the $1-off coupons in the free magazines. Daily 7–11am & 4.30–10pm.

**Tokyo Noodle House**, 2113 Kalākaua Ave; ⓣ922-3479. Clean, glass-fronted Japanese eatery offering large, tasty servings of ramen noodle soups, fried noodles and rice dishes, all priced at $6–7. Cash only. Daily 11am–2am.

## Moderate

**Arancino**, 255 Beach Walk; ⓣ923-5557. Surprisingly authentic Italian trattoria – albeit decorated an unlikely lurid orange – in central Waikīkī. The basic dinner menu of pasta dishes and pizza ($8–12) is supplemented by tasty specials such as a steamed clams appetizer ($7.50), and *spaghetti alla pescatore* ($14.50), with all kinds of fish swimming in olive oil and garlic. There's always plenty of Chianti to go around. Daily 11.30am–2.30pm & 5–10pm.

**Banyan Veranda**, *Sheraton Moana Surfrider*, 2365 Kalākaua Ave; ⓣ922-3111. Poolside hotel café on Waikīkī Beach. A full $19 breakfast buffet is available daily except Sunday, when the lavish brunch costs $35. Instead of lunch, they perform the time-honored ritual of serving tea every afternoon: $18 buys a plate of scones and pastries and a pot of tea to be enjoyed as you listen to a Hawaiian guitarist. The nightly sunset buffet costs $27 and includes dim sum and sushi as well as the usual meat and fish entrees; your meal is accompanied by Hawaiian music from 5.30 to

### Lū'aus

If you insist on going to a *lū'au* – supposedly, a traditional Hawaiian feast – while you're in Waikīkī, go to the *Royal Hawaiian Hotel* on Monday at 6pm (ⓣ923-7194). Their *lū'au* costs around $80, but the food's not bad, the Waikīkī Beach setting is romantic, and you can get there and back easily.

The two biggest *lū'aus* on Oahu, which you'll see advertised everywhere, are *Germaine's* (nightly; ⓣ1-800/367-5655 or 949-6626, ⓦwww.germainesluau.com) and *Paradise Cove* (nightly; ⓣ973-5828). What the ads don't tell you is that they are both thirty miles from Waikīkī, in the far southwestern corner of the island. The price – reckon on $40 from an activity center – includes an hour-long bus trip each way (singalongs compulsory), and your reward at the end is the chance to spend hours looking at tacky overpriced souvenirs, eating indifferent food, drinking weak cocktails and watching third-rate entertainment.

7.30pm, followed by a pianist from 7.30 to 10.30pm. Mon–Sat 7–11am, 1–4.30pm & 5.30–10pm; Sun 9am–1pm, 3–5pm & 5.30–10pm.

**Cheeseburger in Paradise**, 2500 Kalākaua Ave; ☎ 923-3731. The Waikīkī outlet of this successful Maui burger joint occupies a prime position facing the ocean and shares its twin's retro 1950s South Seas/beachcomber style. The food, however, is uninspired – the $7 cheeseburgers are adequate, the $7–11 salads less so – and the service perfunctory. Daily 8am–midnight.

**Duke's Canoe Club**, *Outrigger Waikīkī on the Beach*, 2335 Kalākaua Ave; ☎ 922-2268. Open-air beachfront restaurant/bar named after legendary surfer Duke Kahanamoku, and boasting a great view of the waves. The good-value buffet breakfasts (until 11am) are available with hot items ($10) or just cold ($8); the fairly basic lunch buffets are $10. At night, there's a full (if unimaginative) dinner menu, with a $10 salad bar and chicken, beef and fish entrees at around $20. The bar stays open until after midnight and features live music. Daily 7am–1am.

**Genki Sushi**, 900 Kapahulu Ave; ☎ 735-8889. Weekdays-only conveyor-belt sushi bar, a mile or so northeast of Waikīkī. Each plate is color-coded according to price, with two pieces of sushi starting at just $1.20, so grab whatever you fancy from the very broad range as it drifts by. Other Honolulu locations of this popular chain offer drive-through sushi. Mon–Thurs 11am–3pm & 5–9pm, Fri 11am–3pm & 5–10pm. Closed Sat & Sun.

**Golden Dragon**, *Hilton Hawaiian Village*, 2005 Kālia Rd; ☎ 946-5336. The classiest Chinese restaurant in Waikīkī, with garden seating overlooking a lagoon, and a tasteful indoor dining room. The food is good, too, and the prices surprisingly low. Entrees such as crispy lemon chicken, roast duck, and noodles with fish or chicken cost under $15, while set menus start at $29.50 per person. Tues–Sun 6–9.30pm. Closed Mon.

**Hard Rock Café**, 1837 Kapi'olani Blvd; ☎ 955-7383. Just across the Ala Wai Canal from Waikīkī, this is one of the earliest *Hard Rock Cafés*, here since 1971, and is usually jammed with memorabilia-hungry tourists. The food – ribs, burgers and so on – is predictable but not at all bad, and most menu items cost under $10. The drinking and the music get progressively heavier as the night wears on. Mon–Thurs & Sun 11.30am–11pm, Fri & Sat 11.30am–11.30pm.

**House Without a Key**, *Halekūlani*, 2199 Kālia Rd; ☎ 923-2311. Waikīkī's classiest venue for an open-air sunset cocktail (see p.111) is open all day, every day, and serves good, relatively simple food at prices well below what you might imagine. True, the ample breakfast buffet costs $20, but a Greek salad with shrimp at lunchtime is just $7, and dinner entrees like roasted half chicken and lump-crab-crusted *mahimahi* are less than $20. Daily 7.30am–10pm.

**Keo's in Waikīkī**, 2028 Kūhiō Ave; ☎ 951-9355. Although *Keo's* has only recently moved to central Waikīkī, it has long proclaimed itself to be Hawaii's best Thai restaurant. Its walls are festooned with photos of celebrities enticed by trademark dishes such as the "Evil Jungle Prince" curries, made with basil, coconut milk and red chili. The increasing worldwide familiarity of Thai cooking means that *Keo's* is no longer a novelty, and its menu may seem unexceptional, but the food tastes as good as ever, and with all entrees under $15, the prices are reasonable. Breakfast is both American and Asian; lunch and dinner are entirely Thai. There are several other *Keo's* branches in Honolulu, including *Keoni by Keo's* at 150 Ka'iulani Ave in Waikīkī, and one at the Ward Centre (see p.114). Daily 7.30am–2pm & 5–10.30pm.

**Lewers Street Fish Company**, 247 Lewers St; ☎ 971-1000. Basement fish restaurant below the *Ohana Reef Towers*, where they make their own pasta (the linguini is good) and serve it with grilled or sauteed island fish. Steaks are available as well. Most of the menu has a strong Italian twist, with dishes typically priced at $17–20, but there's also *mahimahi* fish'n'chips for $8. Selected specials cost $6 between 5pm and 6pm. Daily 5–10pm.

**Oceanarium**, *Pacific Beach Hotel*, 2490 Kalākaua Ave; ☎ 922-6111. Minimally furnished restaurant with a big gimmick, which is more fun for kids than for adults – one wall of the dining room is a gigantic aquarium, so as you eat your meal you can watch (and be watched by) 400 live fish, plus the occasional scuba diver. The day starts with a continental breakfast (6–11am) for $7.50 or a $9.50 buffet. Lunchtime noodles, burgers, salads or sandwiches all cost under $10, while the dinner menu features seafood pancakes for $24 or prime rib for $18.50, as well as surf'n'turf combos. Daily 6am–2pm & 5–10pm.

**Peacock Room & Garden Lanai**, Third Floor, *Queen Kapi'olani Hotel*, 150 Kapahulu Ave; ☎ 931-4451. Buffet-style restaurant in an old-fashioned Waikīkī hotel. The $11 breakfast buffet features fruit, eggs, meat and so on. Lunch and dinner both feature the same types of food: Mon–Wed it's Hawaiian à la carte; Thursday features a Japanese buffet; and Fri–Sun there's a Hawaiian buffet. The Japanese lunch buffet is $13, the Hawaiian one, $11. Dinner buffets cost $17, or $8 if you just choose from the salad bar. Daily 6.30–10am, 11am–2pm & 5.30–9pm.

**Planet Hollywood**, 2155 Kalākaua Ave; ⓣ 924-7877. Frenetic theme restaurant enlivened by faux zebra-skin and neon trimmings and cases of movie memorabilia (Hawaii-related where possible, so there's an abundance of discarded *Waterworld* costumes), but with very little substance – the food, be it $10 burgers and pizzas or $15 chicken or pork chops, is glossy but mediocre. You may have to wait as much as an hour for a table – kill time by looking at Michael J Fox's high school yearbook, and reading house instructions on how to go about tipping. Daily 11am–2am.

**Restaurant Suntory**, Third Floor, Royal Hawaiian Shopping Center, Orchid Court, 2233 Kalākaua Ave; ⓣ 922-5511. The teppanyaki menu, cooked at your table in this viewless Japanese restaurant, features squid or steak for around $16, and shrimp or scallop for more like $20, as well as mixed sashimi for $27; there's also a full sushi bar. Weekday lunches with sushi and steak cost $10, but set dinners range from $55 to $100. Mon–Fri 11.30am–1.30pm & 5.30–9.30pm, Sat & Sun 5.30–9.30pm.

**Singha Thai Cuisine**, 1910 Ala Moana Blvd; ⓣ 941-2898. Bright, modern, dinner-only place that serves delicious Thai food with a definite Hawaiian tinge. All sorts of fresh fish and scallop dishes, plus curries, pad thai, and hot and sour tom yum soups; vegetables are organic, and salads available fat-free. Typical entrees cost $15–20, while set menus start at $35 per person. Thai dancers perform nightly 7–9pm. Mon–Fri 4–11pm.

**Tanaka of Tokyo**, Third Floor, King's Village, 131 Ka'iulani Ave; ⓣ 922-4233. Large, open Japanese place, serving teppanyaki cuisine sizzled at your table by chefs-cum-jugglers. You'll be squashed up with a bunch of strangers, but the food is good – and the experience is fun. A full steak meal comes to around $25, scallops and shrimps about the same, and there's a salmon special for $19. Mon–Fri 11.30am–2pm & 5.30–10pm, Sat & Sun 5.30–10pm.

**Texas Rock'n'Roll Sushi Bar**, *Hyatt Regency Hotel*, 2424 Kalākaua Ave; ⓣ 923-7655. A high-concept, postmodern restaurant/bar on the ground floor of the giant *Hyatt Regency*, the *Rock'n'Roll Sushi Bar* is part Hawaiian *paniolo* cowboy, part Japanese, and part *Hard Rock Café*. They've largely given up their previous mix'n'match approach, so they no longer serve seaweed-wrapped beef sushi, for example; instead you can get conventional sushi specialties for around $8, and straightforward barbecue beef, ribs and chicken for $17–20. It all tastes surprisingly good, with full meals featuring both cuisines at $21–31. (Before dining at any of the *Hyatt Regency* restaurants, pick up a free coupon book in the hotel lobby, for a 10–15 percent discount on your check.) Full restaurant menu daily 6–10pm, sushi daily 6–11.30pm.

**Todai Seafood Buffet**, 1910 Ala Moana Blvd; ⓣ 947-1000. Stylish-looking outlet of an upmarket Japanese chain, in western Waikīkī, with huge curved windows outside and a 160-ft buffet bar inside. Lunch costs $15 and dinner $26, but the range and quality of the food makes it a real bargain; there's plenty of sushi, shrimp, crab and lobster, as well as chicken and pork. Sun–Thurs 11am–2.30pm & 5–9pm, Fri & Sat 11am–2.30pm & 5–10pm.

## Expensive

**Bali By The Sea**, *Hilton Hawaiian Village*, 2005 Kālia Rd; ⓣ 941-2254. Highly refined gourmet restaurant, with the tables arrayed along a curving window that offers irresistible views of the full length of Waikīkī. Very tasteful modern Hawaiian cuisine, with appetizers such as seared *ahi* or the succulent Island Bouillabaisse at $9–12, and entrees like rack of lamb, roasted duck breast or *opakapaka* with kaffir lime more like $30. The wine list is enormous, with bottles from $22 up to $4000, and the desserts do as claimed make a "Grand Finale"; one is a chocolate Diamond Head overflowing with dry ice. Though the atmosphere is formal, formal dress is not required. Mon–Sat 6–9pm.

**Ciao Mein**, *Hyatt Regency Waikīkī*, 2424 Kalākaua Ave; ⓣ 923-2426. Huge restaurant, serving an odd but successful mixture of Chinese and Italian cuisine. Not all dishes actually combine the two, though "Collision Cuisine" specials at around $16 include "Hot Bean Salmon *alla Siciliana*" and Chinese roast duck *cannelloni*. In general, the Italian dishes are more sophisticated and less expensive. There's an excellent focaccia appetizer for under $7, and most pasta entrees cost $15. Chinese entrees include sizzling Mongolian beef ($17), honey walnut shrimp ($23) and steamed fish ($27), and there are vegetarian options, too. Set meals cost from $29 per person. Daily 6–10pm.

**Diamond Head Grill**, *W Honolulu*, 2885 Kalākaua Ave; ⓣ 922-3734. Ultramodern, over-chic hotel restaurant, kitted out with lots of gleaming metal and specializing in Pacific Rim cuisine. The food is fussy, perhaps, but very good, with appetizers like ginger-glazed macadamia nut oysters baked with spinach ($10), and entrees such as juicy lemongrass and Asian pesto-scented rotisserie chicken ($22). However, little about the ambience is at all

Hawaiian – when there's not smooth Latin or jazz playing live, it's Elton John on the stereo – and despite the name, the only views you get at dinnertime are of the long curving bar. Breakfast is rather more ordinary hotel food, while a limited bistro menu is served 10–11.30pm. Mon–Fri 7–10.30am & 6–11.30pm, Sat & Sun 7–11.30am & 6–11.30pm.

**Hanohano Room**, *Sheraton Waikīkī Hotel*, 2255 Kalākaua Ave; ⓣ922-4422. Glamourous restaurant, stacked thirty stories above Waikīkī, with nightly dancing to "contemporary jazz." Fixed-price menus with a contemporary Pacific Rim tinge range from $53 to $75; à la carte dishes average $32, whether you go for one of the rich array of meats with sauces, or for the broiled fresh fish. Mon–Fri 6.30–10.30am & 6–10pm, Sat 6–10pm, Sun 8am–1pm & 6–10pm.

**Hau Tree Lanai**, *New Otani Kaimana Beach Hotel*, 2863 Kalākaua Ave; ⓣ921-7066. Intimate oceanfront restaurant, set beneath the shade of a magnificent spreading *hau* tree beside Sans Souci Beach, and perfect for romantic sunsets. Cuisine is mostly continental/American, but with added Pacific Rim touches: choose from top-quality breakfasts (go for the $13 eggs Benedict), lunches ranging from sandwiches to crab-cake burgers or chicken curry for under $15, or dinner entrees like beef Madagascar or pan-roasted seafood risotto at $25–35. Mon–Sat 7–11am, 11.30am–4pm & 5.30–9pm, Sun 7–11am, noon–4pm & 5.30–9pm.

**Kacho**, *Waikīkī Parc*, 2233 Helumoa Rd; ⓣ921-7272 ext 6045. Superb Japanese restaurant, with typically understated decor. The menu emphasizes Kyoto cuisine, with lots of raw and pickled fish; look for crab *sunomono* (in vinegar), and the delicious, cod-like butterfish. A basic salmon dinner costs $21, a bento box or sushi assortment more like $30–40, and the full chef's dinner is $65 per person. Daily 6–10am, 11.30am–2pm & 5.30–10pm.

**Matteo's**, *Marine Surf Hotel*, 364 Seaside Ave; ⓣ922-5551. Dinner-only Italian restaurant, with added flavor drawn from modern Southwest (chili, sundried tomato) and Hawaiian cuisines. Quite pricey and formal, but the food is well above average. Appetizers (around $10) are predominantly seafood; the highlight is the spicy clams. A $10 Early Bird Special is served nightly 5.30–6.30pm, but otherwise entrees start at $18 for ravioli, and range through grilled fish and meats up to a $33 rack of Molokai lamb. Daily 5.30–11pm.

**Nick's Fishmarket**, *Waikīkī Gateway Hotel*, 2070 Kalākaua Ave; ⓣ955-6333. Waikīkī's top fish restaurant, with dark leatherette seating, glittering glass and mirrors, and a formal atmosphere. The cooking is not especially innovative and the sauces are rich, but the preparation is meticulous and the range of choices amazing. Appetizers, generally priced $10–13, include sauteed crab and steamed mussels. A typical main dish like Hawaiian swordfish costs around $30, a mixed seafood grill $35, and lobsters up to $50. The same menu is served until midnight nightly in the less formal adjoining café, which also has live music. Mon–Thurs & Sun 5.30–10pm, Fri & Sat 5.30–11pm.

**Parc Café**, *Waikīkī Parc*, 2233 Helumoa Rd; ⓣ931-6643. Upmarket hotel restaurant boasting the best buffets in Waikīkī. Breakfast costs $13, while the lunchtime choice is either Hawaiian *lū'au* food (Wed & Fri; $17), a pan-Asian spread (Mon, Tues, Thurs & Sat; $16), or Sunday's sushi brunch ($26). Depending on the day, the dinner buffet features prime rib alone (Mon, Tues &Thurs; $19), Hawaiian food once again (Wed; $19), or prime rib plus high-quality Japanese, Hawaiian and American seafood (Fri, Sat & Sun; $27). À la carte entrees are also available. Mon–Sat 5.30–10.30am, 11.30am–2pm & 5.30–9.30pm Sun 11am–2pm & 5.30–9.30pm.

**Sam Choy's Diamond Head**, 449 Kapahulu Ave; ⓣ732-8645. Very popular, dinner-only "New Hawaiian" restaurant, a mile or so northeast of Waikīkī. TV chef Sam Choy has a reputation for feeding his customers to the bursting point, and the portions of the $20–30 entrees such as seafood *laulau* (steamed in *ti* leaves) and veal *ossobucco* are truly enormous in addition to being deliciously flavored with local herbs and spices. The $25 Sunday brunch buffet features Choy's trademark fried *poke* (diced fish). Mon–Thurs 5.30–9.30pm, Fri & Sat 5–10pm, Sun 9.30am–2pm & 5–10pm.

**The Colony**, *Hyatt Regency Waikīkī*, 2424 Kalākaua Ave; ⓣ923-1234 ext 6510. Appetizers at this, the most traditional of the *Hyatt's* restaurants, include a three-onion soup for $5. Steaks, which cost from $19, are available in all sorts of combinations (steak with lobster is $55), and you can also get a delicious fresh catch for $22, or a "Hukilau" of steamed seafood for two or more diners at $28 per person. Daily 6–10pm.

## Honolulu

No single district of **Honolulu** can quite match Waikīkī for its sheer concentration and range of eating options. Although **downtown** is all but deserted at night, nearby **Chinatown** abounds in inexpensive Chinese and Vietnamese places, and the malls along the **waterfront** – especially Aloha Tower Marketplace, Restaurant Row, and the Ward Center – hold an abundance of delectable alternatives. Many of Honolulu's finest restaurants are also tucked away in tourist-free zones, for example around the University or in more upscale residential areas.

## Inexpensive

**Cafe Laniakea**, YWCA, 1040 Richards St; ⓣ524-8789. Lunch-only downtown cafeteria, very close to 'Iolani Palace, and run by a non-profit adult training organization. Lots of inexpensive vegetarian dishes, such as a $1.25 mini *manapua* and a $7 plate lunch with *taro* and sweet potato salad and pesto pasta, plus meat sandwiches and burgers. On Sundays, the mood changes for a jazz brunch, with à la carte New Orleans specialties like gumbo and softshell crab at $9–13. Mon–Sat 10.30am–2.30pm, Sun 8.30am–2pm.

**Café Peninsula**, 1147 Bethel St; ⓣ533-2233. Oddly groovy Chinatown coffee shop, near the Hawaii Theater, with sprawling rattan armchairs and a hip soundtrack. It serves simple plate lunches such as spam and egg ($5), and *saimin* ($3.50), as well as sandwiches, croissants and espressos. Mon–Fri 6.30am–5.30pm.

**Coffee Cove Online**, 2600 S King St; ⓣ955-2683. Grungy espresso bar at King and University that offers pastries and cereal for breakfast, simple snacks and sandwiches ($4–6) later on, and internet access at $7 per hour. Mon–Fri 7.30am–11pm, Sat & Sun 10am–11pm.

**Coffeeline Campus Coffeehouse**, 1820 University Ave; ⓣ947-1615. Inconspicuous student café, upstairs in the Atherton YMCA volunteer center at Seaview Ave, across from the University of Hawaii campus, and handy to the *Honolulu International Hostel* (see p.67). It's basically a takeout counter with terrace seating, and serves a small selection of snacks along with espresso coffees. There's a ten percent discount on food for Youth Hostel Association members. Mon–Fri 7am–4pm, Sat 7am–noon.

**Down to Earth**, 2525 S King St; ⓣ947-7678. Long-standing wholefood store near the University. It offers a full vegetarian menu of deli dishes, baked pies and pastas – some with tofu, some with cheese – plus a varied salad bar at $5 per pound and a hot bar at $6 per pound. Daily 7.30am–10pm.

**Honolulu Coffee Co**, 741 Bishop St; ⓣ533-1500. Busy, large downtown coffee bar, at the south end of Bishop Street near the Aloha Tower, with seating indoors and out. Open weekdays only, it serves espressos and smoothies plus gourmet salads and sandwiches for $6–7, and daily specials such as $9.50 crab cakes. Mon–Fri 6am–5pm.

**Kaka'ako Kitchen**, Ward Center, 1200 Ala Moana Blvd; ⓣ596-7488. Mall diner, with easy off-street parking on the Auahi Street side, that dishes up Hawaiian-style fast food. The presentation is no-frills – after ordering at the counter, you eat your selections with plastic cutlery from styrofoam boxes at plain indoor and outdoor tables – but the food is of a uniformly high-quality. Pretty much everything, from the hamburger stew to the signature dish chicken linguine, costs $6–9, and there's a rotation of daily $7.25 specials like meat loaf or pot roast. Credit cards accepted for checks of $50 and over only. Mon–Fri 7–10am & 10.30am–9pm, Sat 7–11am & 11.30am–9pm, Sun 7–11am & 11.30am–5pm.

**Legend Seafood Restaurant**, 100 N Beretania St; ⓣ532-1868. Chinatown seafood specialist in a modern building whose big plate-glass windows look out over the Nu'uanu Stream. The lunchtime dim sum trolleys are piled with individual portions at $2–3; full Chinese meals, with entrees including whole lobster or crab at $8–16, are served at both lunch and dinner. Mon–Fri 10.30am–2pm & 5.30–10pm, Sat & Sun 8am–2pm & 5.30–10pm.

**Legend Vegetarian Restaurant**, 100 N Beretania St; ⓣ532-8218. Bright, clean Chinese vegetarian restaurant in the heart of Chinatown, looking out across the Nu'uanu Stream. The menu features faux beef balls, cuttlefish, pork ribs and tenderloin – all the dishes are actually tofu or other organic, vegetarian ingredients shaped and flavored to resemble the specified meats and fishes. There's also a wide selection of vegetarian dim sum, plus conventional vegetable dishes. Entrees are priced well under $10; set meals for four or more work out at under $10 per person. No alcohol is served. Daily except Wed 10.30am–2pm & 5.30–9pm.

**Maxime**, 1134 Maunakea St; ⓣ545-4188. This bright, clean, Chinatown restaurant is the best place to sample Vietnamese *pho* (noodle soup). Some is served with tripe, but *pho tai*, with thin slices of beef, is a reliable option ($6.25). There are also lots of other noodle dishes for around $7, plus Vietnamese crepes, seafood specials and even a catfish sour soup at $9. Wash it all down with *chanh muoi* (sweet and sour lemon juice), for $1.75. Daily 10am–9pm.

**Mei Sum**, 65 N Pauahi St at Smith; ⓣ531-3268. Plain but appealing traditional dim sum restaurant, serving a wide assortment of lunchtime snacks at $2–3 each. Tasty options include seafood or mushroom chicken dumplings, turnip cake, and *char siu* buns. Noodle, rice and wonton entrees, featuring chicken, prawns, scallops or calamari, are served later in the day for $7–10 per plate. A full dinner for four is just $32. Daily 7am–9pm; dim sum until 3pm only.

## Moderate

**California Pizza Kitchen**, Ala Moana Center; ⓣ941-7715. Postmodern pizzeria on a bright deck on the top floor of the Ala Moana mall. One-person pizzas ($10) – including such unusual varieties as goat's cheese and bacon, and Peking duck and wonton – are served in a high-tech, new-Asia sort of atmosphere. They also have pasta with ginger and black-bean sauce ($12), and focaccia sandwiches ($7–8). Sun–Thurs 11am–10pm, Fri & Sat 11am–1am.

**Gordon Biersch Brewery Restaurant**, Aloha Tower Marketplace, 101 Ala Moana Blvd; ⓣ599-4877. This restaurant with a built-in brewery is one of Aloha Tower's more stylish options. Seating is either outdoors on a large dockside terrace, or indoors, near a long bar that's brimming with beers from around the globe. For lunch ($10–11) try a pizza, hummus salad, a burger or grill item, or the cashew chicken stir-fry. The dinner menu offers the same pizzas and salads, plus Hawaiian regional dishes such as peppered *ahi* ($19) and kaffir lime grilled chicken ($15), and Japanese, Thai and even Tahitian specialties. Live music Wed-Sat evenings. Mon–Thurs 10.30am–10pm, Fri–Sun 10.30am–11pm; bar open until midnight Mon–Wed & Sun, 1am Thurs–Sat.

**La Mariana Sailing Club**, 50 Sand Island Access Rd; ⓣ848-2800. An atmospheric oceanside restaurant – technically a yacht club – on a *very* obscure stretch of Honolulu's industrial waterfront, *La Mariana* is bursting with *tiki* images and South Seas decor rescued from the ever-dwindling 1950s-style bars and clubs of Waikīkī. The decor is great, and the food's pretty good too. There are hearty appetizers like *taco poke* (marinated octopus) for $9, full dinners such as seafood brochette or *ahi* Cajun for well under $20, and a good-value $14 buffet brunch on Sundays. However, the real reason to come is for the impromptu semi-professional performances of Hawaiian music on Friday and Saturday evenings, from 9pm until late; for more details, see p.111. Daily 11.30am–11.30pm.

**Ocean Club**, Restaurant Row, 500 Ala Moana Blvd; ⓣ526-9888. Big, loud, and very glitzy bar that's a major hangout for downtown's after-work crowd and won't admit anyone under 23 years old or wearing a T-shirt. The extensive menu of excellent finger-food (all seafood) is served at roughly half-price before 8pm, with teriyaki steak at $8, coconut shrimp, crab dip or sashimi for under $4, *poke* for $3, and a *kalua* pig wrap just $2.50. Tues–Fri 4.30pm–3am, Sat 6pm–3am. Closed Sun & Mon.

**Olive Tree Café**, 4614 Kilauea Ave; ⓣ737-0303. Simple but tasteful Greek deli, adjoining but not technically within Kahala Mall, with some outdoor seating. The value is unbeatable, and the food is great, ranging from refreshing tomato and feta cheese salads to a lovely *ceviche* of New Zealand mussels ($5), to *souvlaki* skewers of chicken ($7) or fish ($9). Mon–Fri 5–10pm, Sat & Sun 11am–10pm.

**OnJin**, 401 Kamake'e St; ⓣ589-1666. Bright, smart little café, one block inland from the Ward Center, offering quality cooking at very reasonable rates. At lunchtime, when orders are taken at the counter, pretty much everything costs $6–7 – and that includes the crispy snapper in lemon *beurre blanc*, and the daily specials like Thursday's roast leg of lamb, as well as wraps, burgers, and sandwiches. The service is more formal in the evening, and the prices are significantly higher, with entrees such as half a duck in Grand Marnier for $17.50, and bouillabaisse for $22. Mon 11am–2pm, Tues–Thurs 11am–2pm & 5–9pm, Fri 11am–2pm & 5–10pm, Sat 5–10pm. Closed Sun.

**Yakiniku Canellia**, 2494 S Beretania St; ⓣ1-800/331-9698. Korean buffet restaurant about a mile north of Waikīkī, just south of the University, with very simple decor; the few English speakers who venture in have to fend for themselves. Whether at lunch ($10) or dinner ($16), the food is a treat; you select slices of marinated beef, chicken or pork from refrigerated cabinets and grill them yourself at the gas-fired burners set into each table. There are also lots of vegetables, which you can cook or not as you choose, as well as a wide assortment of interesting salads, including octopus, pickles and delicious tiny dried fish. Daily 11am–10pm.

## Expensive

**Chai's Island Bistro**, Aloha Tower Marketplace, 101 Ala Moana Blvd; ⓣ585-0011. Very busy, very smart place, half indoors and half out at the inland side of the Aloha Tower Marketplace, so there are no ocean views. Though it's owned by the same chef as Waikīkī's Singha Thai (see p.105), the food is not so much Thai as pan-Asian, and it's every bit as exquisite as the decor. For dinner, the prices are extremely high, but that's largely because *Chai's* books the absolute crème de la crème of Hawaiian musicians to perform live, currently including Hapa on Thursdays and Fridays, and the Makaha Sons on Mondays. Miss the show, scheduled for 7–8.30pm, and you'll be paying well over the norm for delicious entrees like Chinese-style steamed *onaga* ($37) or grilled Mongolian lamb chops ($38). Lunchtime prices are half that, except for Sunday's $35 buffet brunch. Note that at the time this book went to press, ongoing problems concerning the immigration status of the Thai owner, Chai himself, were threatening his restaurant's continued existence. Mon–Fri 11am–10pm, Sat 4–10pm, Sun 10am–10pm.

**Duc's Bistro**, 1188 Maunakea St; ⓣ531-6325. Sophisticated Asian-influenced French restaurant in Chinatown, which hosts live jazz in the evenings. Dinner appetizers ($7–8) include gravlax, escargots, and crab cakes; a basic lemongrass chicken entree costs $14, fancier options like duck breast in Grand Marnier or flambéed steak are $20–25. Portions and prices are significantly smaller at lunchtime. Mon–Fri 11.30am–2pm & 5.30–10pm, Sat 5.30–10pm, closed Sun.

**Indigo**, 1120 Nu'uanu Ave; ⓣ521-2900. Chinatown's classiest option serves delicious nouvelle Chinese-Californian crossover food. In addition to the bargain $13 lunch buffet, dim sum ranges from *taro* dumplings and goat's cheese wontons for around $6, to mussels in black bean and cilantro oil for $10. Dinner entrees, under $20, include duck confit, *miso*-grilled salmon, cacao bean curried shrimp, and grilled lamb. Tues–Fri 11.30am–2pm & 6–9.30pm, Sat 6–9.30pm, closed Sun & Mon.

**Sam Choy's Breakfast, Lunch and Crab**, 580 N Nimitz Hwy; ⓣ545-7979. A mile or two west of downtown, and sandwiched so tightly between the west- and east-bound sides of Nimitz Highway that it only offers valet parking, this updated version of a local Hawaiian diner looks unenticing from the outside. It's a different story inside, however, where you'll find a full-sized *sampan* fishing boat, the gleaming *Big Aloha* microbrewery, and mosaic floors, plus crowds of diners seated at the many tables or along the stainless-steel counter facing the vast open-plan kitchen. Plate lunches, at around $10, come very big indeed – the fried *poke* is a must – and there's a $13 brunch on Sundays (9am–noon). Evening entrees, at $17–27, include fresh fish, paella, crabs' legs and roasted or steamed whole crabs. The desserts are enormous, and beer is half-price daily 3–6pm. Restaurant Mon-Sat 6.30am–10pm, Sun 9am–10pm, brewery daily 10.30am until late.

**Sansei**, Restaurant Row, 500 Ala Moana Blvd; ⓣ536-6286. The Restaurant Row setting may not be particularly attractive, but whether you go for the full Pacific Rim menu or stick to the sushi bar, the food is excellent and very well priced. Sushi starts at $4 (a fruity mango crab salad roll is $8), while entrees like grilled *opah* on succulent chanterelle mushrooms, Japanese jerk chicken, or Peking duck breast are mostly around $20. The adjoining karaoke bar gets going when the restaurant closes, and serves a limited half-price menu. Restaurant daily 5–10pm; karaoke with food service daily 10pm–1am.

**L'Uraku**, 1341 Kapi'olani Blvd; ⓣ955-0552. Quirky, hip Japanese restaurant – the name means "happiness" – on a busy street a block inland from the Ala Moana mall. The interior is festooned with crudely hand-painted umbrellas that trace the saga of artist Kiyoshi's lost Somalian cat. Most of the menu is solidly Japanese, with lots of soy marinades and stir-fried bok choy, but there's a strong Italian flavor as well, including a daily pasta special. Appetizers range from a single baked oyster ($2.50) up to a bento box filled with goodies ($13), and for once the entrees ($18–25), including steamed fish and garlic steak, are just as good as the starters. A dinner "tasting" menu is $34 ($47 with wine), while at lunchtime on weekends they offer a bargain $15 set meal. Daily 11am–2pm & 5.30–10pm.

**Alan Wong's**, 1857 S King St; ⓣ949-2526. Though expensive and hard to find – it's tucked away on the fifth floor in a nondescript area southwest of the University – *Alan Wong's* has nonetheless rapidly become Honolulu's most fashionable gourmet rendezvous, thanks to its superb food. Besides changing daily specials, appetizers always include the signature "*Da Bag*," a giant foil bag holding clams steamed with *kalua* pig, shiitake mushrooms and spinach ($11.50), and salads such as marinated eggplant with Maui onions and seared *ahi* ($6). Typical entrees ($25–35) include ginger-crusted *onaga* (snapper), and a spicy Hawaiian reinterpretation of paella. There's a five-course tasting menu each night ($65). Valet parking only. Daily 5–10pm.

# Entertainment and nightlife

Most of Honolulu's **nightlife** is concentrated in Waikīkī, where fun-seeking tourists set the tone. On the whole, however, entertainment tends to be bland. Hawaii is usually bypassed by touring mainstream musicians, so if you enjoy **live music** you'll probably have to settle for little-known local performers (even rising stars of contemporary Hawaiian music try to keep their credibility by not playing in Waikīkī too often). As for **bars**, Chinatown has the most raucous in town, but they're way too hair-raising for most tastes.

Various magazines and papers will keep you abreast of what's going on; the best are the free *Honolulu Weekly* newspaper (Ⓦ www.honoluluweekly.com), and the *TGIF* section of Friday's *Honolulu Advertiser* (Ⓦ www.honoluluadvertiser.com). See p.55 for a list of annual festivals and events on Oahu.

## Hawaiian entertainment

The popular image of Hawaiian tourism may still revolve around lilting ukuleles and swaying grass skirts, but it's surprisingly difficult to find good **Hawaiian entertainment** in Waikīkī or Honolulu, and genuine *hula* performances are

### Gay Honolulu

While Honolulu's gay scene still has plenty to offer visitors, its long-standing epicenter has suffered a major blow. Until 1998, a single block of **Kūhīo Avenue** in central Waikīkī housed virtually all Oahu's best-known gay businesses, including the legendary *Hula's Bar and Lei Stand*. That entire block has now been bulldozed, and developers have set about constructing a major shopping complex on the site. Only *Hula's* has found a permanent new home; see below. For gay travelers, an evening at *Hula's* is the obvious first step. Step two would be to join one of the two weekly **catamaran cruises**; *Hula's* organizes one on Saturdays at 3pm ($10), *Angles* (see below) another on Sunday mornings at 11am (also $10).

For general information on gay life in Honolulu, contact the Gay & Lesbian Community Center, 2424 S Beretania St, Honolulu (Ⓣ 951-7000). *Pacific Ocean Holidays* (PO Box 88245, Honolulu HI 96830-8245; Ⓣ 923-2400 or 1-800/735-6600; Ⓦ www.gayhawaii.com/vacation/index.html) organizes all-inclusive **package vacations** in Hawaii for gay and lesbian travelers, and publishes the thrice-yearly *Pocket Guide to Hawaii*. Taking The Plunge (Ⓣ 922-2600; Ⓦ www.takemediving.com) is a highly recommended gay-friendly **scuba diving** company, while a gay **hiking** club, Likehike (Ⓣ 455-8193; http://gayhawaii.com/likehike/index.html), organizes different group hikes on alternate Sundays at 9am.

#### Gay Bars and Clubs

**Angles Waikīkī**, 2256 Kūhīo Ave, Waikīkī; Ⓣ 926-9766 or 923-1130. Dance club with lively bar and street-view patio, plus bar games including pool and darts. Daily 10am–2am.

**Fusion**, 2260 Kūhīo Ave, Waikīkī; Ⓣ 924-2422. Wild, split-level nightclub, with male strippers, female impersonators and special drink discounts. Mon–Thurs 9pm–4am, Fri & Sat 8pm–4am, Sun 10pm–4am.

**Hula's Bar and Lei Stand**, *Waikīkī Grand Hotel*, 134 Kapahulu Ave, Waikīkī; Ⓣ 923-0669. Waikīkī's most popular and long-standing gay club now occupies a suite of ocean-view rooms on the second floor of the *Waikīkī Grand*, across from the Honolulu Zoo. In addition to a state-of-the-art dance bar equipped with giant video screens, there's a more casual lounge area. Daily 10am–2am.

**In-Between**, 2155 Lau'ula St, Waikīkī; Ⓣ 926-7060. Local gay bar in the heart of Waikīkī, open Mon–Sat 4pm–2am, Sun 2pm–2am.

rare. By far the best idea is to look out for events that are arranged for Hawaiian, rather than tourist, audiences, such as the frequent one-off performances and benefit concerts at downtown's beautiful Hawaii Theater (see p.83). Otherwise, settle for evoking bygone days with a sunset cocktail at one of Waikīkī's grander hotels, most of which feature accomplished Hawaiian musicians most evenings.

A number of regular **free shows** also take place each week, most of greater appeal to older travelers. In addition to the **Pleasant Hawaiian Hula Show** at the Waikīkī Shell (see p.76), there are Polynesian-themed performances in Waikīkī at the Royal Hawaiian Shopping Center (Tues & Thurs 6.30pm) and the DFS Galleria at Royal Hawaiian and Kalākaua avenues (daily 7pm), and in Honolulu at the Aloha Tower Marketplace (Mon & Wed–Fri 11.30am). In addition, the **Royal Hawaiian Band** gives free hour-long performances on Fridays at noon on the lawns of 'Iolani Palace downtown.

For more on *hula* and Hawaiian music, and recommendations on specific musicians to watch out for, see p.535.

**Banyan Court**, *Sheraton Moana Surfrider*, 2365 Kalākaua Ave, Waikīkī; ☎922-3111. Open-air beach bar that was home to the nationally syndicated *Hawaii Calls* radio show from the 1930s to the 1970s. Steel guitar and *hula* dancers nightly 5.30–7.30pm, followed by a pianist 7.30–10.30pm. No cover but a one-drink minimum.

**Chai's Island Bistro**, Aloha Tower Marketplace, 101 Ala Moana Blvd; ☎585-0011. Sumptuous and very expensive Thai restaurant, currently under a cloud due to its owner's legal battle to remain in Hawaii, with a policy of booking the very finest Hawaiian musicians to perform for diners nightly 7–8.30pm. For a full review, see p.109.

**Duke's Canoe Club**, *Outrigger Waikīkī on the Beach*, 2335 Kalākaua Ave, Waikīkī; ☎923-0711. Smooth Hawaiian sounds wash over this ocean-front cocktail bar nightly from 4–6pm and 10pm–midnight. On weekends, the afternoon show is usually a big-name "Concert on the Beach." No cover charge.

**House Without a Key**, *Halekūlani*, 2199 Kalia Rd, Waikīkī; ☎923-2311. This romantic beach bar was named after a Charlie Chan mystery that was written by Earl Derr Biggers after a stay at the hotel. The name of both book and bar alludes to the fact that no one in Honolulu used to lock their doors; in fact the *House Without A Key* barely has walls, let alone a door. Old-time Hawaiian classics performed nightly 5–8.30pm, with *hula* dancing by a former Miss Hawaii. No cover.

**La Mariana Sailing Club**, 50 Sand Island Access Rd; ☎848-2800. Waterfront restaurant – the food is reviewed on p.108 – with a wonderful 1950s feel, hidden away amid the docks of Honolulu. Pianist Ron Miyashiro and a group of semi-professional singers gather each Fri & Sat, from 9pm onwards, to work their way through a nostalgic set of classic Hawaiian songs. Daily 11am–11pm.

**Lobby Bar**, *Hawaiian Regent Hotel*, 2552 Kalākaua Ave, Waikīkī; ☎922-2611. A consistently good roster of Hawaiian musicians perform at this cocktail bar Mon–Wed, Fri & Sat from 7pm, and Sun from 8pm. The highlight comes on Thursdays, however, when the magnificent falsetto singer Auntie Genoa Keawe appears 5.30–7pm. No cover.

**Pier Bar**, Aloha Tower Marketplace; ☎536-2166. Open-air bar whose waterfront stage features live nightly performances by top Hawaiian musicians until late, plus regular lunchtime and sunset entertainment. No cover.

## Bars, live music and dancing

There's rarely a clear distinction between **bars**, **live music venues** and **nightclubs** in Honolulu, and many restaurants get in on the act as well. While there's plenty of live music around – especially in Waikīkī – the overall standard tends to be disappointing. In addition, few Waikīkī clubs get to build a regular clientele, so the atmosphere is unpredictable. The biggest touring acts tend to appear at Pearl Harbor's Aloha Stadium (☎545-4000); watch for announcements in the local press.

If you're especially keen to find live **jazz**, your best bet is in restaurants such as the *Diamond Head Grill* in Waikīkī's *W Hotel* (see p.103), *Duc's Bistro* in

Chinatown (see p.109), and *Cafe Laniakea* in Honolulu's downtown *YWCA* (see p.107), which hosts a Sunday jazz brunch.

There's a cover charge at the venues listed below unless otherwise noted.

**Anna Banannas**, 2440 S Beretania St, Honolulu; ⓣ 946-5190. A University district bar with reasonable prices, live R&B and reggae most nights, and a hectic weekend atmosphere. Daily 9pm–2am.

**The Blue Room**, 327 Keawe St; ⓣ 585-5995. Major student hangout near the Ward Center. Between the two diminutive dance floors, the music runs the gamut: hip-hop, drum and bass, trance, reggae and just plain "alternative." Tues–Sat 10 pm until late.

**The Cellar**, 205 Lewers St, Waikīkī; ⓣ 923-9952. Basement joint in central Waikīkī that calls itself "Waikīkī's coolest Top 40 Dance Club" and attracts a predominantly tourist crowd. Daily except Mon 9pm–4am.

**Lewers Lounge**, Halekūlani, 2199 Kalia Rd, Waikīkī; ⓣ 923-2311. Sophisticated nightspot that looks more like an English drawing room than a Waikīkī bar. Live jazz nightly 9pm–12.30am, at its best Tues–Sat, when Bruce Hamada performs.

**Nashville Waikīkī**, 2330 Kūhiō Ave, Waikīkī; ⓣ 926-7911. If you're hankering to hoedown in Hawaii, this country music club below the *Outrigger West* has plenty of room to show off your rhinestones. Check ahead, though; it also hosts hip-hop and DJ nights. There are pool tables and darts, too. Daily 4pm–4am.

**Ocean Club**, Restaurant Row, 500 Ala Moana Blvd, Honolulu; ⓣ 526-9888. Flamboyant, frenetic downtown bar-cum-restaurant, which serves inexpensive food in the early evening (see p.108) and turns into a wild dance club as the night wears on. Over-22s only; no T-shirts. Open until at least 2am Tues–Sat.

**Rolando's Salsa Club**, Kahala Mall; ⓣ 677-3642. Long a fixture of Honolulu's nightlife scene, Rolando Sanchez and his Salsa Hawaii Band now have their own place to do their Latin thing. They perform Thurs–Sat nights and also tend to join the Sunday night Latin jazz jam. On other nights the dance music is provided by DJs instead. Mon & Tues 9pm–midnight, Wed 9.30pm–midnight, Thurs–Sat 10pm–1am, Sun 9–11pm.

**Rose and Crown**, King's Village, 2400 Koa Ave, Waikīkī. Not a bad approximation of an English pub; the beer pumps are fake, but it's appropriately dark and gloomy even at noon. From 11am until 7.30pm a draught Bud or Miller costs $1.50, and there's a Happy Hour 4.30–7.30pm. No cover. Daily 11.30am–2am.

**Rumours**, *Ala Moana Hotel*, 410 Atkinson Drive, Honolulu; ⓣ 955-4811. Mainstream disco in business hotel behind the Ala Moana mall, extremely popular with the after-work local crowd. Friday's '70s night is a fixture on many calendars. Daily 5pm onwards.

**Sand Island Restaurant and Bar**, 197 Sand Island Access Rd, Honolulu; ⓣ 847-5001. Honolulu's one real blues venue, en route to Sand Island, in an area where you're unlikely to see any tourists. Gigs are usually scheduled for Wed–Sat, starting at 9pm.

**Warriors Lounge**, *Hale Koa Hotel*, 2055 Kalia Rd, Waikīkī; ⓣ 955-0555. Only military personnel can stay at this seafront hotel, but the no-cover dance floor is open to all, and features a changing program of country, Latin, big band, and contemporary Hawaiian music, plus karaoke most nights. Daily 5pm–midnight.

**Wave Waikiki**, 1877 Kalakua Ave, Waikīkī; ⓣ 941-0424. In so far as Waikīkī has an alternative rock scene, this is it. Large venue, with a bar upstairs and dance floor down below, and DJs rather than live bands most nights. No cover before 10pm. Open nightly 9pm–4am.

**World Café**, Nimitz Business Center, 1130 N Nimitz Highway, Honolulu; ⓣ 599-4450. Three-level club not far west of Chinatown that boasts Hawaii's largest dance floor and offers differing themed dance nights as well as live big-name

## Honolulu Movie Theaters

The best spot to catch a new **movie** in Honolulu is on one of the nine screens at Restaurant Row, near downtown (ⓣ 526-4171). Less mainstream offerings are shown at the Academy of Arts (900 S Beretania St; ⓣ 532-8768) and the Movie Museum (3566 Harding Ave; ⓣ 735-8771). The only choice in Waikīkī lies between the two screens of the Waikīkī Theaters (Seaside at Kalākaua Ave; ⓣ 971-5133). The giant-screen **Imax Theater** in Waikīkī, 325 Seaside Ave (ⓣ 923-4629), has hourly showings of films such as *Cyberworld*, *Extreme* and *Hidden Hawaii* (daily 11am–9pm, adults $7.50 one show, $12 two, $15 three; under-12s $5/$8/$10). They also put on laser shows and rock-concert films.

acts. Hip-hop, house and trance music predominates. As one of the few local clubs to admit under-21s, it tends to be crammed with hyped-up youngsters. Daily 9pm until late.

## Shows and spectaculars

The days when every major Waikīkī hotel put on its own Las Vegas-style, big-budget show seem to be over. Some people choose to see that as the loss of something authentically Hawaiian, but it has more to do with the nationwide decline of an audience for middle-of-the-road pap entertainment. Nonetheless, there are still a few nightly shows on offer. For most of the shows below, specific prices are not listed because you can get much better deals by buying **reduced-price tickets** through "activity centers" (see p.88). Expect to pay \$20–25 if it's possible to book for the show alone (and bear in mind you'll be expected to drink once you're there), or more like \$50 if you eat as well.

**Creation – A Polynesian Odyssey**, Ainahau Showroom, *Sheraton Princess Ka'iulani*, 120 Ka'iulani Ave, Waikīkī HI 96815; ⓣ 931-4660. Lavish Polynesian revue, complete with fire-dancing, *hula*, and a buffet dinner, and aimed at tempting the middle-of-the-road customers who might otherwise head for the Polynesian Cultural Center or the big commercial *lū'aus*. Hotel guests get a discount for the early-evening performance. Daily 5.15pm & 8pm.

**Legends in Concert**, Aloha Showroom, Royal Hawaiian Shopping Center, Waikīkī; ⓣ 971-1400. An enjoyable tribute show of quick-fire impersonations, though your tastes have to stretch pretty wide to want to see Elvis, Prince, Jackie Wilson, Michael Jackson, Judy Garland and Dolly Parton (to name but a few) on the same bill. You can get the general idea from free "taster" shows on the mall's open-air stage, at odd times throughout the day. Two shows nightly at 6.30pm & 9pm; dinner served at 5pm.

**Society of Seven**, *Outrigger* Main Show Room, 2335 Kalākaua Ave, Waikīkī; ⓣ 922-6408. *Very* long-standing song-and-dance ensemble, which performs Broadway musical routines and pop hits with amazing energy. Mon 8.30pm, Tues–Sat 6.30pm & 8.30pm.

# Shopping

Virtually all the shops in both Honolulu and Waikīkī are in purpose-built **malls**, so shopping in the city is easy, if not all that exciting. For many years, Honolulu's **Ala Moana Center** held undisputed sway as the city's premier

### Bookstores and Music Stores

**Bookstores**

Barnes & Noble, Kahala Mall (ⓣ 737-3323).
Best Sellers, 1001 Bishop St (ⓣ 528-2378) and *Hilton Hawaiian Village* (ⓣ 953-2378).
Bishop Museum, 1525 Bernice St (ⓣ 848-4158).
Borders Books & Music, Ward Center (ⓣ 591-8995).
Rainbow Books & Records, 1010 University Ave at King St (ⓣ 955-7994).
Rand McNally, Ala Moana Center (ⓣ 944-6699).
Waldenbooks, Waikīkī Shopping Plaza (ⓣ 922-4154), Waikīkī Trade Center (ⓣ 924-8330), Kahala Mall (ⓣ 737-9550), and several other Honolulu locations.

**Music Stores**

Barnes & Noble, as above.
Borders Books & Music, as above.
Hungry Ear Records & Tapes, 1518E Makaloa St (ⓣ 944-5044).
Rainbow Books & Records, as above.
Tower Records, 611 Ke'eaumoku Ave (ⓣ 941-7774), Kahala Mall (ⓣ 737-5088), and two other outlying Honolulu locations.

mall for serious shoppers, but it has been so successful in attracting big spenders that new rivals now seem to be springing up all the time. Even Waikīkī is starting to move away from its traditional emphasis on souvenirs and beach accessories.



## Waikīkī shopping



If you want to buy a T-shirt, a beach mat, or a monkey carved out of a coconut, Waikīkī is still definitely the place for you. Kalākaua and Kūhiō avenues especially are lined with cut-price souvenir stores; there are 37 shops in the ABC chain alone, all open daily from 7am to midnight and selling basic groceries along with postcards, sun lotions and other tourist essentials.

Waikīkī's largest malls, the monolithic **Royal Hawaiian Shopping Center** and the five-floor **Waikīkī Shopping Plaza**, across the street at 2250 Kalākaua Ave, are aseptic, upmarket enclaves, packed with designer-clothing shops, jewelry stores and sunglasses emporiums. The trend these days is for the major hotels to build their own upscale shopping malls; the two largest, the *Hyatt Regency* and, especially, the *Hilton Hawaiian Village*, now hold conglomerations of stores to rival any in Honolulu.

For the moment, the venerable 1950s-style open-air **International Marketplace**, 2330 Kalākaua Ave, still survives. With its simple wooden stalls scattered among the trees, it has a lot more atmosphere, though it has to be admitted that the "crafts" on sale tend to be made-in-Taiwan, while the "psychic readers" are as a rule devoid of paranormal powers.

It's harder than you'd expect to find that quintessential emblem of old Hawaii, the authentic **aloha shirt**; try Bailey's, 517 Kapahulu Ave (Ⓣ734-7628).

## Honolulu shopping

The **Ala Moana Center** (Mon–Sat 9.30am–9pm, Sun 10am–7pm; Ⓦwww.alamoana.com), a mile west of Waikīkī, has since 1959 been Hawaii's main shopping destination; neighbor-island residents fly to Honolulu specifically in order to shop here. One of the largest open-air malls in the world, it holds several major department stores, including Sears, JC Penney, Neiman Marcus, and Hawaii's own Liberty House. (The direct descendant of a ships' chandlery store that opened downtown in 1849, Liberty House has hit financial trouble of late, amid accusations of neglecting its traditional customers in pursuit of the elusive yen.) Be sure to explore the Japanese Shirokiya, which has a fabulous upstairs food hall, piled high with sushi and *poi*, and also stocks a great array of bargain electronic goodies.

Stretching along and back from Ala Moana Boulevard from a couple of blocks west of the Ala Moana Center, the various **Ward** malls – the Center, Warehouse, Farmers Market and Village Shops – have been greatly spruced up in the last few years. Anchored by a giant Borders, the **Ward Center** (Mon–Sat 10am–9pm, Sun 10am–5pm) in particular has become a serious rival to the Ala Moana Center, with a more intimate atmosphere and a much better selection of bars and restaurants. Its finest stores include the Kamehameha Garment Company, for aloha-wear, and Handblock, selling household linens. Among highlights in the longer-established **Ward Warehouse** (Mon–Sat 10am–9pm, Sun 10am–5pm) alongside are the Nohea Gallery, which sells contemporary artwork from paintings and ceramics to woodcarvings, and distinctive clothing boutiques such as Aloha Tower Traders and Mamo Howell.

Downtown's **Aloha Tower Marketplace** (Mon–Thurs & Sun 9am–9pm, Fri & Sat 9am–10pm; see p.85) has yet to lure significant numbers of tourists away from Ala Moana, but the dockside setting makes it a fun place to wander around. Most of the stores are one-of-a-kind rather than chain outlets, and souvenir possibilities range from the fake vomit at Monty's World of Magic and the grunting "Mr Bacon" pigs at Magnet Five-O to the beautiful and very expensive *koa*-wood furniture and aloha-wear at Martin & MacArthur.

Only a couple of miles from Waikīkī, *mauka* of Diamond Head, the **Kahala Mall**, 4211 Waialae Ave (Mon–Sat 10am–9pm, Sun 10am–5pm), is almost as chic as – and far less frenzied than – Ala Moana. As well as Liberty House, Longs Drugs, Banana Republic, an eight-screen movie theater, and a fine assortment of restaurants, it holds a large Tower Records and an excellent Barnes & Noble bookstore.

Finally, the **Aloha Flea Market**, held at the Aloha Stadium in Pearl Harbor on Wednesday, Saturday and Sunday mornings, provides an entertaining opportunity to look for (mostly secondhand) bargains. The Aloha Flea Market Shuttle Bus (Ⓣ 955-4050) runs there from Waikīkī, charging $7 round-trip, including admission.



# Southeast Oahu

The high crest of the Ko'olau Mountain Range curves away to the east beyond Honolulu, providing Oahu with its elongated **southeastern promontory**. The built-up coastal strip is squeezed ever more tightly between the hills and the ocean, but not until you reach **Koko Head**, eight miles out from Waikīkī and eleven from downtown, do you really feel you've left the city behind. Thereafter, however, the shoreline is so magnificent – punctuated by towering volcanoes, sheltered lagoons and great beaches – that there have been serious proposals to designate the entire area as a state park devoted to eco-tourism, under the Hawaiian name of **Ka Iwi**.

## Kāhala and Hawaii Kai

H-1 ends at the Kahala Mall, just beyond Diamond Head (see p.76), to become Hwy-72, or **Kalaniana'ole Highway**. Both **Kāhala** itself, and **Hawaii Kai** further along, are upmarket residential communities that have little to attract visitors, and no desire to encourage them. Hawaii Kai spreads back inland to either side of the large Kuapā Pond, an ancient fishpond that has been remodeled to create the Koko Marina; the one reason to stop is to eat at the dinner-only gourmet restaurant *Roy's* (6600 Kalaniana'ole Highway; Ⓣ 396-7697), the first incarnation of the well-known island chain. None of the beaches along this stretch merits even a pause.

## Hanauma Bay

Beautiful **Hanauma Bay** is barely half a mile beyond Hawaii Kai, just across the volcanic ridge of Koko Head. So curved as to be almost round, the bay was created when part of yet another volcano – southeast Oahu is one long chain of minor volcanic cones – collapsed to let in the sea.

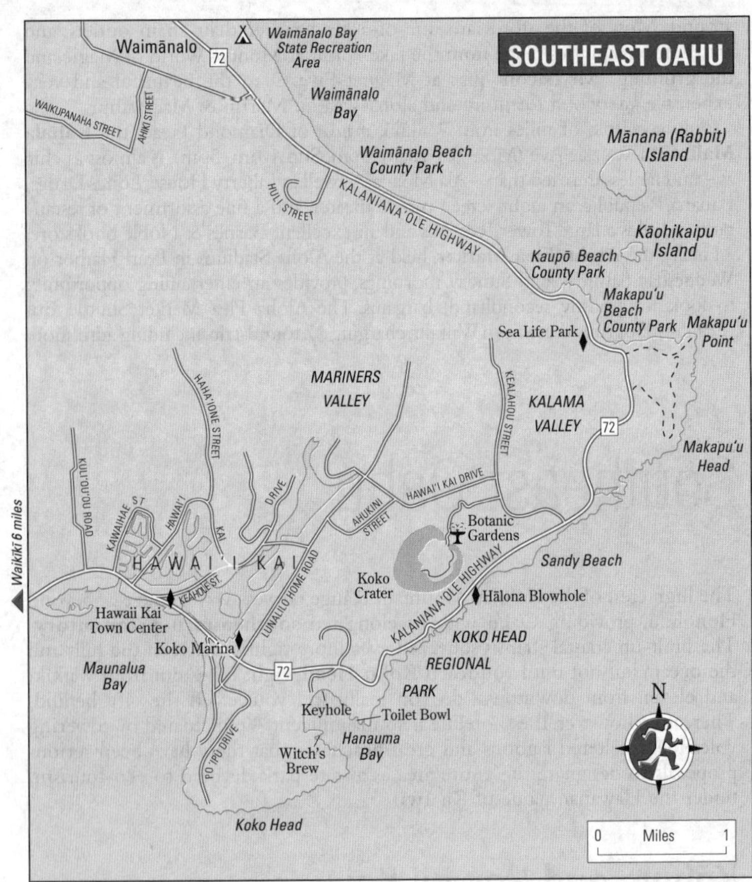


This spellbinding spot, where a thin strip of palms and sand nestles beneath a green cliff, has long been famous as Oahu's best place to **snorkel**. Unfortunately, however, the sheer quantity of Waikīkī-based beach-lovers who come here poses a constant threat to the fragile underwater environment. Since the 1960s, Hanauma Bay has been a Marine Life Conservation District, and organized tour parties are now banned, but all the inshore coral reef has nonetheless died. Though the sea still holds enough brightly colored fish to satisfy visitors, they're sustained these days by handouts of fish food; the minute coral creatures that should underpin the food chain have gone.

## Visiting Hanauma Bay

As this book went to press, Hanauma Bay was open to visitors daily except Tuesday between 7am and 6pm; admission was $3 for adults, free for under-13s, with parking an additional $1. However, as part of a controversial scheme to restrict the number of visitors to Hanauma Bay, a large new visitor center should have opened on the hilltop above Hanauma by the time you read this, adjoining the parking lot just off the highway and alongside the stop used by

TheBus #22, the regular "Beach Bus" from Waikīkī. The plan is that first-time visitors will be required to watch a video about Hanauma and marine conservation in general. For the moment, a rundown pavilion down on the beach serves as the place both to buy snacks and rent snorkel equipment, at around $6 per day (you'll be asked to leave some form of deposit; rental car keys, but not hotel keys, are acceptable). In the long run, however, all facilities will probably re-locate up to the visitor center.

The beach is five minutes' walk from the visitor center, down a gently winding road used only by a regular open-sided "trolly" (75¢). As you walk down, the ridge rises like a rich green curtain ahead of you, but the vegetation on the more exposed northeast side of the bay, off to your left, is generally dry and faded. From here you can see patches of reef in the turquoise water, standing out against the sandy seabed, and swarms of fish are clearly visible. The largest gap in the reef, at the parking lot end of the bay, is known as the **Keyhole**.

Even if the crowds spoil the romance a little, it's worth spending a few hours at Hanauma Bay whether or not you go in the water. The crisp green lawns along the foot of the *pali*, dotted with banyan trees, are ideal for picnics. At either end of the beach you can walk along the rocky ledge that rings the old crater walls, just above sea level, though there is a real risk of being swept off by the waves. Just before the open ocean, at the far northeastern limit of the bay, the indelicately named **Toilet Bowl** is a natural hole in the lava that repeatedly fills with gushing sea water and then gurgles dry. On the western limit of the bay, there's the similar **Witch's Brew**, which fills and empties like a whirlpool. You may see people jumping into these pools, but that doesn't mean it's safe to do so.

Snorkeling at Hanauma is a bit like snorkeling in an aquarium. You'll see a lot of fish, but it can all feel rather tame and predictable. The shallowness of the water near the shore can make it hard to stay off the reef, but it's essential that you try — walking on a coral reef not only kills the reef, but can easily cause cuts that take weeks to heal. Reasonably skilled swimmers who want to see living coral, and bigger fish, can swim out to the deeper waters beyond the inner reef. However, the currents through a couple of gaps in the reef can be very strong, while the one that sweeps across the mouth of the bay is known as the "Molokai Express" because it's capable of carrying you all the way to Oahu's easterly neighbor.

## Koko Head

A dirt road leads away immediately right after the highway turnoff for Hanauma Bay – before the parking lot – to climb straight along the bare ridge above the beach. Whether it's open to hikers seems to vary, but take it if you can – there are great views from the 642-foot summit of **Koko Head**, roughly a fifteen-minute walk away. From there you can see back to the similar peak of Diamond Head above Waikīkī and also walk down a footpath around the lesser of its two craters to peek into the southern end of Hanauma Bay.

## Koko Crater

Koko Head Regional Park, which covers Koko Head and Hanauma Bay, extends another couple of miles northeast to take in **Koko Crater**. The youngest – and thus the largest and most completely formed – of southeastern

Oahu's volcanic cones, this is considerably higher than Koko Head and makes a very impressive spectacle. Like its neighbor, it is topped by a double crater. The road up its far side – reached direct from Hawaii Kai, or by doubling back further along the coastal highway – comes to a dead end at Koko Crater Stables. Alongside you'll find the barely developed **Botanic Garden** (daily 9am–4pm; free), where a twenty-minute stroll is rewarded by a grove of sweet-smelling, heavy-blossomed plumeria trees. It's no longer possible to walk up to or around the crater rim, however.



## Hālona Blowhole and Sandy Beach

A couple of miles beyond Hanauma Bay, where Kalaniana'ole Highway is hard-pressed to squeeze in between Koko Crater and the ocean, a roadside parking lot enables round-island drivers – and a *lot* of tour buses – to stop off for a look at the **Hālona Blowhole**. All this coastline consists of layer upon layer of flat lava, each sheet set slightly back from the one below to form a stairway that climbs up from the sea. Here, the waves have carved out a cave below the visible top layer and, as each new wave rushes in, it's forced out through a small hole to create a waterspout that can reach up to fifty feet high. The hole itself does not go straight down, but is stepped; if you fall in – and people do – it's almost impossible to get out.

Little **Hālona Cove**, to the right of the Blowhole overlook and sheltered by tall stratified cliffs, holds enough sand to make a welcome private beach, if you're lucky enough to have it to yourself. Only swimming within the cove itself is at all safe, and even then only in summer.

Avoiding the crowds is not at all the point at **Sandy Beach**, half a mile further on as the shoreline flattens out between Koko Crater and Makapu'u Head. Kids from both sides of Oahu meet up here most weekends for what's said to be the best **body-surfing** and **boogie-boarding** in Hawaii. This is also one of the few places on the island where the waves remain high enough in summer to tempt pro surfers. Tourists who try to join in soon find that riding surf of this size takes a lot of skill and experience; Sandy Beach is notorious for serious injuries. If you just want to watch, settle down in the broad sands that lie southwest of the central lava spit; swimming is never safe at Sandy Beach, but beyond the spit it's all but suicidal.

## Makapu'u Point

The rising bulk of Oahu's easternmost point, **Makapu'u Head**, pushes Hwy-72 away from the coastline as it swings round to run back up the island's windward flank. Shortly before it finishes climbing up the last low incline of the Ko'olau Ridge, there's just about room to park beside the road at **Makapu'u State Wayside**.

A dirt road here snakes off to the right, soon curving south towards the hillock of Pu'u O Kīpahulu. An hour-long hike (there and back) wends around the hill and back north along the line of the coastal cliffs to **Makapu'u Point**. From the railed-off viewing platform at the end, you can look straight down the cliffs to the Makapu'u lighthouse down below, out to Molokai on the horizon, back to Koko Head and up along the spine of eastern Oahu.

Rounding Makapu'u Point on the highway – especially if you manage to stop at the small official **lookout** at the top – is an equally memorable experience. The coastal *pali* suddenly soars away to your left, while straight out to sea a couple of tiny islands stand out in misty silhouette. The larger of the two, Mānana, is also known as **Rabbit Island**; it was named not for its slight resemblance to a bunny but for its population of wild rabbits, introduced for no particular reason in the nineteenth century. They share their home only with seabirds – both Mānana and its neighbor, Kāohikaipu, or Turtle Island, are bird sanctuaries, and off-limits to humans.



## Makapu'u Beach County Park

Few drivers who miss the lookout can resist stopping to drink in the views as they descend from Makapu'u Point. The first proper parking lot, however, is down below, at **Makapu'u Beach County Park**. In summer, this is a broad and attractive strip of sand; in winter, pounded by heavy surf, it's a rocky stretch. Swimming is rarely safe even at the best of times – ask the lifeguards if you're in doubt. Like Sandy Beach (see opposite), however, it's a greatly loved **body-surfing** and **boogie-boarding** site, and with the same propensity to lure unwary tourists into the water, it boasts a similarly dismal record of fatalities.

## Sea Life Park

Immediately opposite the Makapu'u Beach parking lot stands the entrance to the expensive **Sea Life Park**, which tends to hold greater appeal for children than for their parents (Mon–Thurs & Sat 9.30am–5pm, Fri 9.30am–10pm; adults $24, ages 4–12 $12; ⓣ259-7933). It has recently been reported to be in economic difficulty, and it's conceivable it may have closed down by the time you read this. For the moment, along with the predictable dolphin and porpoise shows, which feature human co-stars dressed up as pirates and princesses, there's a giant Reef Tank, a penguin enclosure, and a hospital for injured monk seals. The park also raises rare green sea turtles for release into the ocean and has even bred a **wholphin** – half-whale, half-dolphin. With a couple of snack bars, where live entertainment is provided by unidentifiable costumed characters who have yet to secure their own TV series, plus a bar run by the *Gordon Biersch Brewery*, it's all too possible to find yourself spending an entire day here. Call ⓣ259-7933 for details on free shuttle buses to the park from Waikīkī.

# Waimānalo

**WAIMĀNALO**, four miles on from Makapu'u, holds one of the highest proportions of native Hawaiians of any town on Oahu and has become a stronghold of supporters of the movement for Hawaiian sovereignty (see p.515). The main drag, lined with fast-food joints, is far from picturesque, but as long as you take care not to intrude, you can get a real glimpse of old-time Hawaii by exploring the backroads. The small family-run farms and nurseries along Waikupanaha Street, which runs inland along the base of the *pali*, are particularly rural and verdant.

The most compelling reason to come to Waimānalo, however, is its **beach**. At over three miles long, it's the longest stretch of sand on Oahu, and the setting, with high promontories to either end and a green cradle of cliffs behind, is superb. The most accessible place to park, and also the safest swimming spot, is **Waimānalo Beach County Park** at its southern end, but wherever you start you're likely to feel tempted to stroll a long way along the seemingly endless sands.

About a mile further north, where the fir trees backing the beach grow thicker again beyond a residential district, you come to **Waimānalo Bay State Recreation Area**. The waves here are a little rougher than those at the county park, but it feels even more secluded, and you can **camp** for up to five days with a permit from the state parks office in Honolulu ($5; closed Wed & Thurs; see p.55).

Further on still, and reached by a separate road off the highway, lies **Bellows Field Beach Park**. Access to this pristine spot, ideal for lazy swimmers and novice body-surfers, is controlled by the adjoining Air Force base; the public is only allowed in between noon on Friday and 8am on Monday. This time it's the county parks office (see p.55) that runs the **campground**, also open weekends only.

# Windward Oahu

Less than ten miles separates downtown Honolulu from Oahu's spectacular **windward coast**. Climb inland along either the **Pali Highway** (see p.93) or **Likelike Highway** (see p.96), and at the knife-edge crest of the Ko'olau Mountains you're confronted by amazing views of the serrated *pali* that sweeps from northwest to southeast. As often as not, the abrupt transition from west to east is marked by the arrival of **rain** – it has, after all, been raining on this side of the island for several million years, cutting away at the cliffs to create a long, sheer wall.

The mountain highways drop down to the twin residential communities of **Kailua** and **Kāne'ohe**, both large towns by Hawaiian standards but of minimal appeal to visitors. Staying in one of the handful of local B&Bs makes an appealing alternative to Waikīkī, but if you're on a day's driving tour of Oahu you'd probably do better to avoid Kailua and Kāne'ohe altogether, and head straight off north on **Hwy-83**. This clings to the coastline all the way up to Oahu's northernmost tip, sandwiched between a tempting fringe of golden sand and a ravishing belt of well-watered farmland and tree-covered slopes. On most Hawaiian islands, the windward shore is too exposed to be safe for swimming, but here a protective coral reef makes bathing possible at a long succession of narrow, little-used **beaches**. All are open to the public, but use proper paths to reach them.

Oahu is also exceptional among the Hawaiian islands in having a chain of picturesque little **islets** just offshore; you're unlikely to set foot on any of them, but they provide a lovely backdrop.

Though driving through such luscious scenery is a real joy, there are few specific reasons to stop. The **Byōdō-In Temple** provides a great photo opportunity, while further north the **Polynesian Cultural Center** attracts a million visitors each year; otherwise you might want to spend an hour or two hiking in the backcountry, somewhere like **Kahana Valley** or **Hau'ula**.

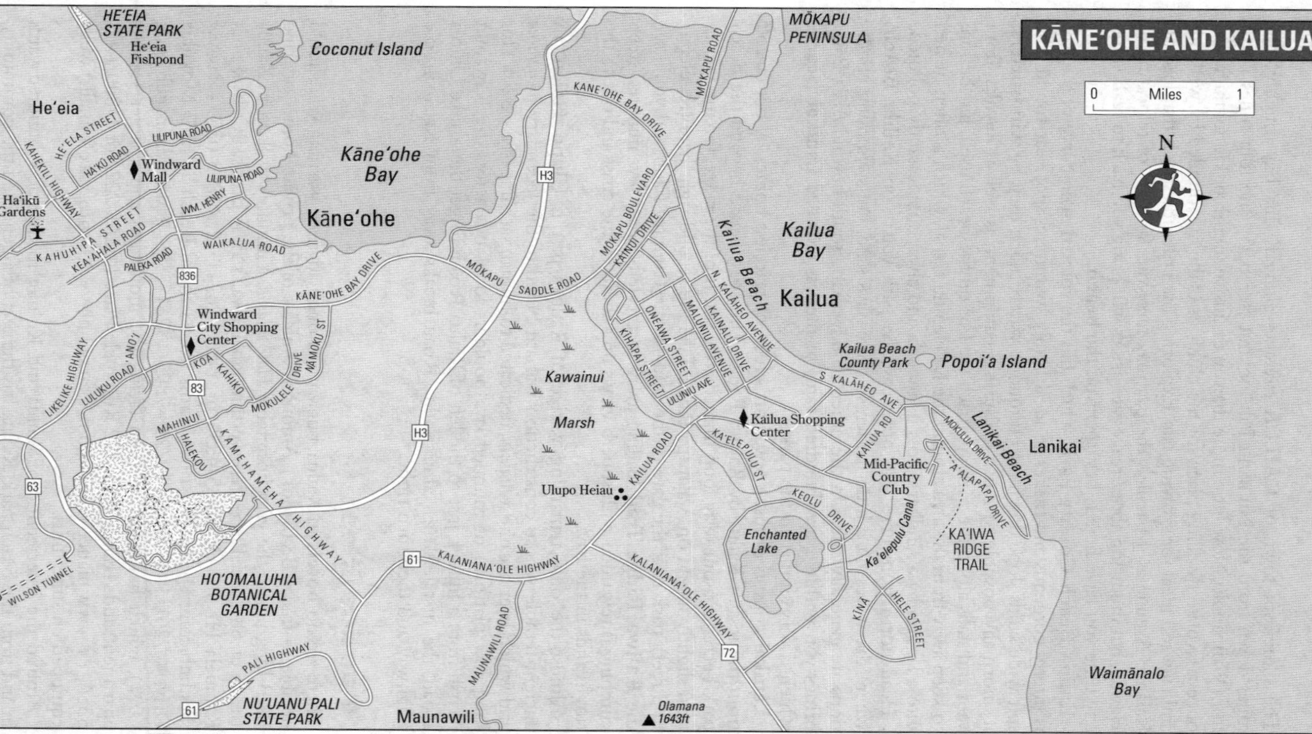
KĀNE'OHE AND KAILUA
0 Miles 1
N
HE'EIA STATE PARK
He'eia Fishpond
Coconut Island
He'eia
Byōdō-In Temple
Ha'ikū Gardens
HE'ELA STREET
HA'KŪ ROAD
LILIPUNA ROAD
Windward Mall
KAHEKILI HIGHWAY
WM. HENRY
KAHUHIPA STREET
KEA'AHALA ROAD
WAIKALUA ROAD
PALEKA ROAD
836
Kāne'ohe Bay
Kāne'ohe
KĀNE'OHE BAY DRIVE
Windward City Shopping Center
KOA
KAHIKO
MOKULELE DRIVE
NĀMOKU ST
83
LIKELIKE HIGHWAY
LULUKU ROAD
'ANO'I
MAHINUI
HALEKOU
KAMEHAMEHA HIGHWAY
63
Honolulu
WILSON TUNNEL
HO'OMALUHIA BOTANICAL GARDEN
PALI HIGHWAY
61
NU'UANU PALI STATE PARK
Maunawili
MAUNAWILI ROAD
H3
MŌKAPU SADDLE ROAD
MŌKAPU BOULEVARD
KAINUI DRIVE
MŌKAPU ROAD
MŌKAPU PENINSULA
Kawainui Marsh
Ulupo Heiau
KAILUA ROAD
KALANIANA'OLE HIGHWAY
Olamana 1643ft
72
Waimānalo
Kailua Bay
Kailua Beach
Kailua
N. KALĀHEO AVENUE
KAINALU DRIVE
MALUNIU AVENUE
ONEAWA STREET
KĪHĀPAI STREET
ULUNIU AVE.
Kailua Shopping Center
KA'ELEPULU ST
KEOLU DRIVE
Enchanted Lake
KĪNĀ
HELE STREET
Ka'elepulu Canal
Mid-Pacific Country Club
KAILUA RD
S. KALĀHEO AVE
Kailua Beach County Park
Popoi'a Island
MOKULUA DRIVE
'A'ALAPAPA DRIVE
KA'IWA RIDGE TRAIL
Lanikai Beach
Lanikai
Waimānalo Bay

# Kailua

The shorefront town of **KAILUA** stretches along Kailua Bay roughly four miles down from the Nu'uanu Pali lookout (see p.95), and four miles north from Waimānolo. Now little more than an exclusive suburb of Honolulu, it was once a favorite dwelling place for the chiefs of Oahu, surrounded by wetlands and rich soil ideal for growing *taro*. Exploring the little side streets that lead off Kalāheo Avenue as it parallels the bay may fuel your fantasies of relocating to Hawaii, but inquiring about real estate prices will bring you back to reality, and any time you have here is best spent on the **beach**.

**Kailua Beach County Park**, which fills the colossal main curve of the bay, is utterly gorgeous and makes an ideal family swimming spot year-round. The soft wide sands slope down into turquoise waters much used by **windsurfers**; it's normally possible to rent windsurfing equipment, as well as **kayaks**, from vans and stalls along the park approach road or on the beach itself. Just be sure to keep away from the area around the Ka'elepulu Canal, which is often turned into a lagoon by a sandbar across its mouth, and always unpleasantly polluted.

Head north from here, and once past the park you're on **Kailua Beach**, where the waves hit a little harder, so there's less sand, but swimming conditions are generally safe. On the other hand, walking south beyond Alāla Point brings you within a few hundred yards to the less crowded **Lanikai Beach**, which is very similar to the park.

**Lanikai** consists of just a few short streets of priceless homes, all but cut off from the rest of Kailua by Ka'iwa Ridge. The coastal road beyond the beach park becomes a one-way loop immediately south of the ridge, forcing you to turn slightly inland on A'alapapa Road. Take the second right here (Ka'elepulu Street), park near the gate of the Mid-Pacific Country Club, and you'll see the **Ka'iwa Ridge Trail** leading away to the left. Just a few minutes' steep climbing is rewarded with superb views up and down the coast and out to the tiny islands in the bay.

Almost the only remaining vestige of Kailua's past is **Ulupo Heiau**, an ancient temple whose construction was attributed to the legendary *menehune* and which later became a *luakini*, dedicated to human sacrifice (see p.520). This long, low platform of rounded lava boulders looks out across the Kawainui Marsh from a hillock just to the left of Kailua Road. To get there, take Uluo'a Road, the first left turn after Kailua Road breaks away from Kalaniana'ole Highway, and then turn right.

## Practicalities

There are no **hotels** in Kailua, but with enough advance warning you should be able to find a B&B room. Among the nicest of the private homes offering B&B lodging are the very hospitable *Hale Makai*, a minute's walk from Kailua Beach at 68 Laiki Place (reserve through Hawaii's Best B&Bs, PO Box 563, Kamuela HI 96743; ⓣ885-4550 or 1-800/262-9912, ⓕ885-0559, ⓦwww.bestbnb.com; ❸); *Lanikai B&B*, across from Lanikai Beach at 1277 Mokulua Drive (ⓣ261-1059 or 1-800/258-7895, ⓕ261-7355, ⓦwww.lanikaibb.com; ❸/❹), which has a studio room facing the mountains and a larger seaview apartment; and *Akamai B&B*, 172 Ku'umele Place (ⓣ261-2227 or 1-800/642-5366, ⓦwww.planet-hawaii.com/akamaibnb; ❸), with two small, well-equipped en suite units.

Around the intersection of Kailua and Ku'ulei roads, a few hundred yards inland from the beach park, Kailua has the feel of a genuine little community, holding assorted neighborhood stores as well as the **Kailua Shopping Center** mall at 572 Kailua Road. *Morning Brew* here (Mon–Thurs 6am–9pm, Fri 6am–10pm, Sat 6.45am–10pm, Sun 6.45am–8pm; ⓣ262-7770) is a nice local coffee bar that's bravely clinging on despite the arrival of *Starbuck's* opposite. A couple of doors along, *Otaru* (Mon–Fri 11am–2pm & 5–9.30pm, Sat & Sun 5–9.30pm; ⓣ263-4482) calls itself a Pacific Rim restaurant, but most of the menu is straightforward, good-value Japanese, with sushi rolls starting at $4 and combos at $14. *Assaggio*, tucked away on a quiet side street a block north, at 354 Uluniu Ave, is a wildly popular upmarket Italian restaurant (Mon–Thurs 11.30am–2.30pm & 5–9.30pm, Fri & Sat 11.30am–2.30pm & 5–10pm, Sun 5–9.30pm; ⓣ261-2772).

## The Mōkapu Peninsula

Kailua's northern limit is defined by Oneawa Ridge, stretching towards the ocean and culminating in the **Mōkapu Peninsula**. More of an island than a peninsula, joined to the rest of Oahu by two slender causeways, Mōkapu is entirely taken up by a Marine base, and no public access is permitted. It was to connect the base with Pearl Harbor that H-3, the new trans-Ko'olau highway, was originally commissioned. Archeologists have found the extensive sand dunes along Mōkapu's northern shore to be the richest ancient burial site in all Hawaii.

## Kāne'ohe

Slightly smaller than Kailua, and boasting a far less robust economy, as well as considerably fewer amenities for visitors, **KĀNE'OHE** is seldom seen as an exciting destination in its own right. That's largely because none of its silty beaches are suitable for swimming. However, seven-mile **Kāne'ohe Bay**, reaching northwards from the Mōkapu Peninsula, is the largest bay in Hawaii and, once you're outside the main built-up strip, one of the most beautiful. If you want to join the local pleasure-boaters out on the calm waters of the bay, take a one-hour **cruise** from He'eia Kea Pier on the glass-bottomed *Coral Queen* (Mon–Sat 10am, 11am, noon & 1.30pm; adults $8, under-13s $4; ⓣ235-2888).

**He'eia State Park**, on the headland immediately before the pier, is a landscaped area set aside largely for its views of the adjoining **He'eia Fishpond**. Ancient Hawaiians built the low curving stone walls that enclose this saltwater lagoon; it's now once more being used to raise mullet. What little you see from the park probably won't hold your attention long, however. Tiny **Coconut Island**, out to sea, is used for marine research by the University of Hawaii, but is better known from the credits sequence of *Gilligan's Island*.

Inland, Kāne'ohe holds several attractive public **gardens**. One of the quietest and most relaxing of these is the nature reserve of **Ho'omaluhia Botanical Garden** (daily 9am–4pm; free), at the top of Luluku Road, which loops back into the hills off Kamehameha Highway between Pali and Likelike highways. Take any of the pleasant short trails away from the visitor center, and you'll soon be out in the wilderness. If you'd prefer a more commercial display of flowers, fruits and orchids, head instead for **Senator Fong's Plantation**, near Kahalu'u in northern Kāne'ohe (daily 9am–4pm; adults $10, children $6), where trams whisk visitors along the paved walkways. The smaller, free **Ha'ikū Gardens**, just off Hwy-83 at the entrance to glorious **Ha'ikū Valley**, is a nice little lily pond that serves mainly to lure diners into the on-site *Hale'iwa Joe's* restaurant (Ⓣ247-6671; for a review of the branch in Hale'iwa, see p.136).

## Byōdō-In Temple

A clearly marked side road *mauka* of Hwy-83 (Kahekili Highway) just beyond central Kāne'ohe leads to the interdenominational cemetery known as the **Valley of the Temples** (daily 8.30am–4.30pm; adults $2, under-12s $1). Several religions have chapels and monuments here, but the one that draws in casual visitors is the Japanese Buddhist **Byōdō-In Temple**, built in the 1960s to celebrate a hundred years of Japanese immigration to Hawaii. This unexpected replica of a 900-year-old temple at Uji in Japan looks absolutely stunning, its red pagodas standing out from the trees at the base of the awesome *pali*.

Having parked outside the temple gates, you cross an arching footbridge to stroll through the peaceful gardens. A fishpond here is so full of orange, gold and mottled carp that they squeeze each other out of the water in their frenzy for fish food. Before you reach the main pavilion, you're encouraged to use a suspended battering ram to ring a three-ton brass bell; you'll probably have heard it echoing through the valley as you arrive. Once inside (with your shoes left at the threshold), you're confronted by a nine-foot meditating Buddha made of gilded, lacquered wood.

## Practicalities

Like Kailua, Kāne'ohe has a number of small-scale private **B&Bs**. Both the *Kane'ohe Bay B&B*, 45-302 Pu'uloko Place (reserve through Hawaii's Best B&Bs, PO Box 563, Kamuela HI 96743; Ⓣ885-4550 or 1-800/262-9912, Ⓕ885-0559, Ⓦwww.bestbnb.com; ❹) and *Hula Kai Hale*, 44-002 Hulakai Place (Ⓣ235-6754; ❸) overlook Kāne'ohe Bay, with en-suite facilities and swimming pools. *Hula Kai Hale* has two guest rooms to the *Kane'ohe Bay*'s one, but the setting of the latter is quite superb, and the hosts are absolute local experts.

None of the main-road **eating** options is especially appetizing. *Chao Phya Thai*, in the Windward City mall where Likelike and Kamehameha highways meet (Mon–Sat 11am–2pm & 5–9pm, Sun 5–9pm; Ⓣ253-3355), sells tasty Thai food at bargain prices. Otherwise take your pick from burgers, *saimin* or Korean fast food as you head north.

# Kualoa Point and Mokoli'i

At **Ka'alaea**, a mile north of the Byōdō-In Temple, Kahekili Highway joins Kamehameha Highway on its way up from He'eia State Park, and the two then run on together as Kamehameha Highway. The tumbling waterfalls at the heads of Waihe'e and Waiāhole valleys, visible as you look inland, are superb, but the next point worthy of a halt is at the northern tip of Kāne'ohe Bay.

From the crisp green lawns of **Kualoa Point**, out on the headland, you can look through a gap-toothed straggle of windswept coconut palms to conical **Mokoli'i Island**. To ancient Hawaiians, this picturesque little outcrop was the tail of a dragon killed by Pele's sister Hi'iaka as she made her way to Kauai (see p.464); its more banal modern nickname is "Chinaman's Hat." At low tide, you can wade out to it along the reef – the water should never rise more than waist high, and reef shoes are an absolute must – to find a tiny hidden beach on its northern side. Otherwise, content yourself with a swim from the thin shelf of sand at Kualoa Park.

### Kualoa Ranch

Roughly 200 yards north of Kualoa Park, a driveway *mauka* of the highway (left if you're heading north) leads into the expansive grounds of **Kualoa Ranch**. Until recently a conventional cattle ranch, this now plays host to flocks of Japanese tourists instead. Individual travelers are welcome to sign up for any of the wide range of activities on offer, which include horse riding, bicycling, helicopter rides, parasailing and snorkeling, as well as a controversial "Haunted House" in a natural cave at the foot of the *pali*, but the place is dominated by large groups of honeymooners. For full details, including rates and schedules for specific activities, contact Ⓣ 237-7321 or Ⓦ www.kualoa.com. By way of example, a "Three Activity Adventure Tour," including round-trip transportation from Waikīkī, costs $99.

### Ka'a'awa

Several more good beaches lie immediately north of Kāne'ohe Bay. There's no danger of failing to spot them; in places the highway runs within a dozen feet of the ocean. So long as the surf isn't obviously high, it's generally safe to park by the road at any of the consecutive **Kanenelu**, **Kalae'ō'io**, and **Ka'a'awa** beaches, and head straight into the water. Only **Swanzy Beach County Park**, a little further along, really demands caution, on account of its unpredictable currents. It became a beach park thanks to a rich Kailua resident of the 1920s, who donated this land to the state on condition that they didn't create any other public parks nearer her home.

## Kahana Valley

The whole of the deeply indented **Kahana Valley**, tucked in behind a high serrated *pali* immediately around the corner from the Crouching Lion, is a state park. The basic economic unit of ancient Hawaii was the *ahupua'a*, a wedge of land reaching from the high mountains down to a stretch of coastline; Kahana is now the only *ahupua'a* to be entirely owned by the state. Still farmed by native Hawaiian families, it aims to be a "living park," though what that means has never quite been settled. In theory, the residents educate visitors in Hawaiian traditions, but while traditional crops are still grown, they don't dress up or pretend to *be* ancient Hawaiians. There's a friendly, helpful **visitor center** (Mon–Fri 7.30am–4pm; Ⓣ 237-7766) a little way back from the highway as it curves around Kahana Bay, but most people who call in have come simply to **hike**. Be sure to bring waterproof clothing if you plan to join them; upper Kahana Valley receives 300 inches of rain per year.

### Kahana trails

The easiest of Kahana Valley's attractive **trails** starts by following the dirt road that heads to the right in front of the visitor center. After passing a few houses, it heads out into a lush meadow scattered with fruit trees, and then veers left at a far-from-obvious junction to climb into the woods. It soon reaches a clearing where you can gaze across the valley to the high walls on the far side, and watch as it recedes away inland. Not far beyond, a few weather-worn stones mark the site of the **Kapa'ele'ele Ko'a** fishing shrine. As usual at such places, signs warn you not to "move, remove or wrap rocks" – a reference to the common but largely bogus practice of tying a small stone in a *ti* leaf as an offering. A steep climb then leads up to **Keaniani Kilo**, a *kilo* being a vantage point from which keen-eyed Hawaiians would watch for schools of fish (usually *akule*, or big-eyed scad), and signal canoes waiting below to set off in pursuit. There's nothing here now, and young trees have partially obscured the beach, but it's a lovely spot. The trail drops down to the highway, and you can make your way back along the beach.

To take the **Nakoa Trail**, which heads for the back of the valley, you should once again leave your car at the visitor center. Assuming that it hasn't been raining (in which case the valley streams will be too high to cross; check at the visitor center), you keep walking along the main valley road for a mile or so before a gate bars the way. The trail then rambles its way up and around the valley walls for roughly four miles, with some great views and plenty of mosquitoes to keep you company. For a shorter adventure, simply head left at the very start and you'll soon come to an idyllic little swimming hole in **Kahana Stream**.

### Kahana Bay

The beach at **Kahana Bay**, straight across from the park entrance, hangs onto an ample spread of fine sand all year round, and is very safe for swimming. It's possible to **camp** in the woods that line its central section; $5 permits are issued by the park visitor center, or the state parks office in Honolulu (see p.55).

## Hau'ula and Punalu'u

Beyond Kahana, the highway continues to cling to every curve of the coastline, and traffic tends to move slowly. Island maps show **HAU'ULA** and **PUNALU'U** as being distinct towns, but on the ground it's hard to tell where one ends and the next begins. Both are quiet little local communities that barely reach a hundred yards back from the shore.

Of the half-dozen named beaches in this stretch, **Punalu'u Beach Park**, the furthest south, is the best for swimming, so long as you keep away from the mouth of Wai'ono Stream. The strip of sand is so thin at this point that the coconut palms rooted in the lawns behind it manage to curve out over the waves. **Hau'ula Beach Park**, a few miles along, is equally sheltered, but only snorkelers derive much pleasure from swimming out over the rocks.

Nestling beneath the palm trees at a curve in the road roughly a mile south of Punalu'u Beach Park, and marked by a vintage delivery truck parked permanently outside, *Ahi's* (Mon–Sat 11am–9pm; ⓣ293-5650) is a single-story local **restaurant** that specializes in delicious shrimp dishes.

### Sacred Falls State Park

A very inconspicuous parking lot, mauka of the highway a mile past Punalu'u, is the trailhead for Sacred Falls. Two miles up from here – half through flat and featureless fields, and half hacking through the undergrowth beside Kalanui Stream – the Kaliuwa'a Falls plummet eighty feet from a green crevice in the hillside.

Although this area remains a state park, it has been closed to the public since the disaster of May 1999, when a sudden landslide killed eight hikers immediately below the falls. That was merely the most recent of several such landslides, and there was also a notorious incident when a tourist group was held up at gunpoint. The park is not expected to reopen in the near future.

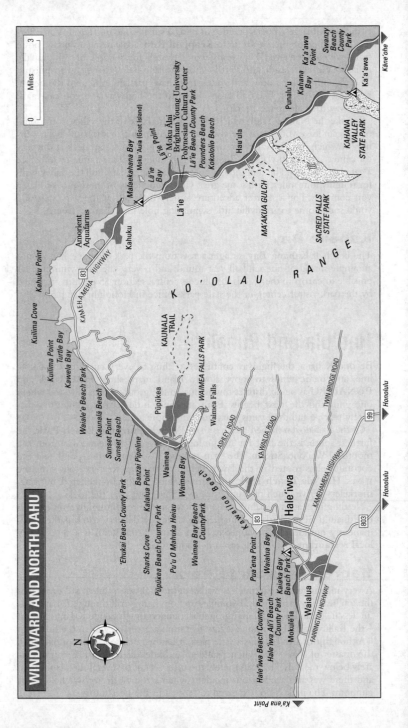

## WINDWARD AND NORTH OAHU

0 Miles 3

N

Kuilima Cove
Kahuku Point
Kuilima Point
Turtle Bay
Kawela Bay
Waiale'e Beach Park
Kaunalā Beach
Sunset Point
Sunset Beach
'Ehukai Beach County Park
Banzai Pipeline
Sharks Cove
Kalalua Point
Pūpūkea Beach County Park
Pūpūkea
Waimea
Pu'u O Mahuka Heiau
Waimea Bay
Waimea Bay Beach CountyPark
WAIMEA FALLS PARK
Waimea Falls
KAUNALA TRAIL
Kawailoa Beach
ASHLEY ROAD
KAWAILOA ROAD
TWIN BRIDGE ROAD
KAMEHAMEHA HIGHWAY
FARRINGTON HIGHWAY
83
99
803
Pua'ena Point
Hale'iwa Beach County Park
Waialua Bay
Hale'iwa Ali'i Beach County Park
Kaiaka Bay Beach Park
Hale'iwa
Mokulē'ia
Waialua
Ka'ena Point
Honolulu
Honolulu
KAMEHAMEHA HIGHWAY
Amorient Aquafarms
Kahuku
Malaekahana Bay
Moku 'Auia (Goat Island)
Lā'ie Bay
Lā'ie Point
Moku Ālai
Lā'ie
Brigham Young University
Polynesian Cultural Center
Lā'ie Beach County Park
Pounders Beach
Kokololio Beach
KO'OLAU RANGE
Hau'ula
MA'AKUA GULCH
SACRED FALLS STATE PARK
Punalu'u
Kahana Bay
Ka'a'awa Point
Swanzy Beach County Park
KAHANA VALLEY STATE PARK
Ka'a'awa
Kāne'ohe

## Hau'ula trails

Three exhilarating but muddy trails enable hikers to explore **Ma'akua Gulch**, behind central Hau'ula. To reach them, park at the *mauka* end of Hau'ula Homestead Road, which starts opposite the northern limit of Hau'ula Beach Park. Having walked a hundred yards up the track (officially Ma'akua Road) from here, you'll see a small driveway on the left, with a mailbox-style check-in station where you should write down your details before you set off.

The best short hike is the **Hau'ula Loop Trail**, which branches off to the right from just beyond the entrance gate. In something under two hours, with a few stretches of steep climbing, it carries you up and over the high ridge to the north, through sweet-smelling forests of ironwood and pine. As well as views across the ocean, you get amazing panoramas of neighboring Kaipapa'u Valley, reaching far inland and looking as though no human has ever entered it.

The similar but more overgrown **Ma'akua Ridge Trail** twists its own circuit around the southern wall of the gulch, while the **Ma'akua Gulch Trail** follows the central stream back towards the mountains. As the gulch narrows, you're forced to hike more and more in the streambed itself, making this a very dangerous route after rain. Otherwise, it's a good opportunity to see the luscious blossoms for which Hau'ula – meaning "red *hau* trees" – is named.

# Lā'ie

The neat, even prim air of the town of **LĀ'IE**, three miles on from Hau'ula, is explained once you realize that it was founded by Mormons in 1864, and remains dominated by the Latter-Day Saints to this day. This was the second major Mormon settlement in Hawaii; the first, on Lanai, was abandoned when church elders discovered that its President, William Gibson, had registered all its lands in his own name. Gibson went on to be Prime Minister of Hawaii, while his congregation moved to Oahu. Lā'ie now holds an imposing **Mormon Temple**, built in 1919 as the first such temple outside the continental United States (a visitor center, rather than the temple itself, is open daily 9am–9pm), and a branch of the Mormon-run **Brigham Young University**, but is best known to visitors for a less obviously Mormon enterprise, the **Polynesian Cultural Center**.

Mormon colleges tend not to spawn lively alternative scenes, and Lā'ie is no exception. Local students do at least get to body-surf the heavy waves at **Pounders Beach** at the south end of town, but if you lack their know-how don't be tempted to join in. **Kokololio Beach** just south of that is an attractive curve of sand where swimming is only safe in summer, while **Lā'ie Beach** in the center of town is prone to strong currents. The two-part **Mālaekahana Bay State Recreation Area** further north provides the best local recreational swimming, and also makes an excellent place to camp (pick up a free state permit in Honolulu; see p.56). At low tide, it's possible to wade out from here to **Goat Island**, a bird sanctuary where the Mormons once kept their goats, which has a beautiful protected beach on its north shore.

## The Polynesian Cultural Center

An incredible one million paying customers each year head to Lā'ie for the **Polynesian Cultural Center** (Mon–Sat 12.30–9pm; adults $27, ages 5–11 $16; Ⓣ 293-3333, Ⓦ www.polynesia.com). Part entertainment (with joke-telling

guides and displays of fire-walking) and part educational (with step-by-step demonstrations of traditional crafts), it's a haphazard mixture of real and bogus Polynesia. Kids tend to love it, while adults think of it either as uproarious kitsch or insulting, according to the mood they're in.

Daytime visits consist of touring seven themed "villages" – by tram, on foot or in a canoe – to learn about seven Polynesian groups. Unless you time your visit to each village to coincide with the daily schedule of presentations, there's very little to see, so if you're going to come at all be prepared to spend at least half a day in total. In addition to Hawaii, Tahiti and the Marquesas, the further-flung cultures of Fiji, Tonga, Samoa and the Maori are represented. Most of the staff are students from the adjoining University, who don't necessarily come from the relevant parts of the Pacific – some of the milder-mannered Mormons have a hard time looking suitably ferocious when they're pretending to be Maori warriors, for example. It's also worth bearing in mind that the information they give you is laced with Mormon theology; thus the Polynesians are said to be descended from one of the lost tribes of Israel, who migrated from Central America under the leadership of a certain Hagoth. Come in the evening, pay extra – the full "Ambassador Package" works out at $95 for adults, $63 for children – and you can eat bad *lū'au* food and watch a banal program of amateurish song-and-dance routines.

### Practicalities

A clean, modern **motel** – anonymous and well away from the ocean, but quite good value – is located less than a hundred yards north of the Polynesian Cultural Center. Each room at the *Best Inn – Hukilau Resort*, 55-109 Laniloa St, Lā'ie, HI 96762 (Ⓣ293-9282 or 1-800/526-4562, Ⓕ293-8115, Ⓦwww.hawaiibestinn.com; ❸), has its own *lānai* overlooking the swimming pool. It shares its driveway with the oddest *McDonalds* you ever saw, converted from a leftover section of the Polynesian Cultural Center and still featuring an entrance carved to resemble a South Seas longhouse. There are several predictable **fast-food** places in and around the Lā'ie Shopping Center, but nothing any more distinctive.

## Kahuku

**KAHUKU**, a couple of miles on from Lā'ie, may look run-down by comparison, but is considerably more atmospheric. Though the plantation it served went out of business in 1971, the rusting hulk of the **Kahuku Sugar Mill** still overshadows this small town. Assorted outbuildings now house a half-hearted shopping mall. Unidentified lumps of machinery are dotted around the courtyard, painted in peeling pastel blues and yellows. Most of the old mill workings remain in place; some parts have been color-coded according to their former function, as you'll see while exploring inside on the metal walkways. The *Country Kitchen* (Mon–Sat 9am–5pm; Ⓣ293-2110), outside, serves up shrimp and barbecue, and you can also pick up freshly cooked shrimp from a couple of white trucks stationed permanently beside the highway; of the two, *Giovanni's*, to the south, serves the spicier food.

Behind the sugar mill are a few dirt lanes holding tin-roofed plantation homes. The long **beach** beyond is not suitable for swimming, but stretches a full five miles up to Turtle Bay if you fancy a solitary, bracing hike.

Beyond Kahuku, the highway veers away from the shore to run alongside the **Amorient Aquafarms**. Fresh shrimp from this series of ponds can be bought from trucks and vans stationed along the highway nearby. The Walsh Farms complex of small, brightly painted shacks at the far end sells fresh fruit, shrimp, and an entertaining mixture of antiques and junk.

## Turtle Bay

Just before Kamehameha Highway rejoins the ocean on the North Shore, an obvious spur road leads *makai* past some expensive condos and private homes to end at **Turtle Bay**. Photogenic beaches lie to either side of **Kuilima Point** here – long, wave-raked Turtle Bay to the west, and the sheltered artificial lagoon of Kuilima Cove to the east – but you'd only choose to come here if you were staying at the luxury **hotel** on the point itself.

The thousand-acre *Turtle Bay Hilton Golf and Tennis Resort*, 57-091 Kamehameha Hwy, PO Box 187, Kahuku HI 96731 (Ⓣ293-8811 or 1-800/221-2424, Ⓕ293-9147, Ⓦwww.turtlebayresort.hilton.com; ocean view ❻, oceanfront ❼), holds almost five hundred ocean-view rooms, as well as two golf courses, ten tennis courts and three restaurants. Handily positioned for the North Shore, but priced far beyond the pockets of the surfing crowd, it feels oddly out of place in this remote corner, and apart from children enthralled by the nearby beaches, most guests seem to end up wondering what they're doing here.

The *Palm Terrace* restaurant (Mon–Thurs & Sun 7am–10pm, Fri & Sat 7am–11pm) is busy at lunchtime with island bus tours, but its breakfast, lunch and dinner buffets are equally poor whatever time you come. The *Cove* (Tues–Sat 6–9pm) is much better, though entrees such as *kiawe*-smoked rack of lamb and fresh Maine lobster cost $25 each. Accessed via the same impressive indoor labyrinth of artificial waterfalls and sharing the same great views, the *Sea Tide Room* hosts a good Sunday brunch (10am–2pm; $27).

The *Turtle Bay Hilton* marks the spot where TheBus #55 from the south becomes #52 as it heads west, and vice versa.

# Central Oahu

Thanks to the island's butterfly-like shape, much the quickest route from Honolulu to the North Shore lies across the flat agricultural heartland of **central Oahu**. Cradled between the mountains, the **Leilehua Plateau** was created when lava flowing from the Ko'olau eruptions lapped against the older Wai'anae Range. Sugar cane and pineapples raised in its rich volcanic soil were the foundation of the Hawaiian economy until less than fifty years ago. As commercial farming has dwindled, however, the area has acquired a neglected and dejected atmosphere. More people than ever live in towns such as **Waipahu** and **Wahiawa** – many of them personnel from the military bases tucked into the hillsides – but there's very little here to interest tourists. If you plan to drive around Oahu in a single day, you'd do better to press straight on to Hale'iwa (see p.134).

# 'Aiea and Pearl City

Whichever road you follow, you have to drive a long way **west of Honolulu** before reaching open countryside. H-1, the main "interstate," curves past the airport and Pearl Harbor, while Hwy-78 sticks closer to the Ko'olau foothills, but they eventually crisscross each other to run through the nondescript communities of **'AIEA** and **PEARL CITY**. Restaurants where commuters can grab a quick meal loom on all sides, but neither town has a center worth stopping for.

## Keaīwa Heiau State Park

Only hilltop **Keaīwa Heiau State Park**, in suburban **'Aiea Heights** above 'Aiea proper, merits a detour from the highway, and even that appeals more to local residents than to outsiders. The road up heads right from the second stoplight after the 'Aiea Stadium turnoff on Hwy-78, and then twists for almost three miles through a sleepy residential area.

**Keaīwa Heiau**, whose ruined walls are on the left as soon as you enter the park, was a center where healers known as *kahuna lapa'au* once practiced herbal medicine, using plants cultivated in the surrounding gardens. The most famous of those healers was Keaīwa – "the mysterious" – himself. Lots of *ti* plants, together with a few larger *kukui* trees, still grow within the otherwise well-maintained precinct, which also holds a little shrine and a central ring of stones that encloses a small lawn. This layout is largely conjectural, however, as the *heiau* was severely damaged during the sugar-plantation era.

There are no views from the *heiau*, but a mile-long **loop road** circles the ridge that lies beyond, where the ironwood forest is punctuated with meadows and picnic areas looking out over Pearl Harbor. Halfway around, you'll come to the trailhead for the **'Aiea Loop Trail**, a five-mile circuit through the woods, offering views of the interior valleys as well as Honolulu. The highlight is the wreckage of a World War II cargo plane that crashed into a remote gully.

**Camping** at the park's cool, secluded campground (closed Wed and Thurs) costs $5, with a state permit.

# Waipahu

Just beyond Pearl City, both H-2 and Kamehameha Highway branch away to head north across the central plateau. Only a mile or so west, however, the small town of **WAIPAHU** holds one of Hawaii's best historical **museums**, an evocative memorial to the early days of immigration. It's also home to the unexpectedly upmarket **Waikele Center** shopping mall, with a giant Borders bookstore and lots of discount "factory outlets."

## Hawaii's Plantation Village

A mile south of H-1 on Waipahu Street in Waipahu, just below the sugar mill to which it owes its existence, stands **Hawaii's Plantation Village** (Mon–Fri 8am–3pm, Sat 10am–3pm; guided tours only, hourly until 3pm; adults $7, seniors $4, under-13s $3; ⓣ667-0110). It's a loving, nonprofit re-creation of the living conditions of the almost 400,000 agricultural laborers who migrated to

Hawaii between 1852 and 1946, and were largely responsible for spawning the ethnic blend of the modern state.

Enthusiastic local guides lead visitors around a small museum and then through a "time tunnel" onto the former plantation estate. Simple houses – some of which have always stood on this site, others brought in from elsewhere – contain personal possessions, illustrating both how much the migrants brought with them, and how much the different groups shared with each other in creating a common Hawaiian identity. Cumulatively, the minor domestic details – pots, pans, buckets, family photographs, even the tiny boxing gloves used to train Filipino fighting cocks – make you feel the occupants have merely stepped out for a minute. The most moving artifacts in the museum are the *bangos*, the numbered metal badges which helped the *lunas* (whip-cracking Caucasian plantation supervisors) to distinguish each anonymous worker from the next. Goods could be obtained in the company store by showing your *bango*, with the cost deducted from your next pay packet.



# Wahiawā

All routes across central Oahu – whether you take H-2 or Kamehameha Highway from Pearl City, or the more scenic **Kunia Road** that leads up through the fields from Waipahu – have to pass through the large town of **WAHIAWĀ** in the heart of the island. The main drag holds the dismal array of bars, fast-food outlets and gun stores that you'd expect to find this close to the **Schofield Barracks**, Oahu's largest military base (which by all accounts is actually very pretty, if you can get through the gates).

A couple of mildly diverting sites lie just outside the town. The **Wahiawā Botanical Gardens** (daily 9am–4pm; free), a mile east, is a reasonably attractive enclave of tropical trees and flowers, welcome if you live here but nothing special by Hawaiian standards. To the north, on Whitmore Avenue off Kamehameha Highway, what look like faintly marked reddish-brown lava boulders beneath a cluster of palm trees in a pineapple field constitute an archeological site known as **Kukaniloko**, or more colloquially as the **Birthing Stones**. Tradition had it that any chief hoping to rule Oahu should be born here; the equivalent site on Kauai is described on p.437.

## Dole Plantation

The single-story modern building of the **Dole Plantation** stands to the east of Kamehameha Highway roughly a mile north of Wahiawā (daily 9am–6pm; free). Though the large number of cars and tour buses parked outside might lead you to expect something more interesting, the plantation is basically a large covered mall-cum-marketplace, which sells the usual assortment of tacky souvenirs and craft items, as well as fresh pineapples and pineapple products such as juices and frozen "whips."

The gardens alongside the mall hold what the *Guinness Book of Records* considers to be the world's largest **maze** (daily 9am–5.30pm; $4.50), composed of Hawaiian plants. The aim here is not to reach the center, let alone escape; instead you're expected to traipse around in the hot sun to find six separate color-coded "stations." If you'd rather do that than head for the beach, go right ahead.

# The North Shore



Although the **surfing beaches** of Oahu's **North Shore** are famous the world over, the area as a whole is barely equipped for tourists. **Waimea**, **Sunset** and **'Ehukai** beach parks are all laid-back roadside stretches of sand, where you can usually find a quiet spot to yourself. In summer, the tame waves may leave you wondering what all the fuss is about; see them at full tilt in the winter, between October and April, and you'll have no doubts.

If you plan to do some surfing – and this is no place for casual amateurs – then you'd do best to base yourself in **Pūpūkea** (see p.138). Otherwise, you can see all there is to see in an easy day-trip from Waikīkī, with a pause to shop and snack in **Hale'iwa**.

## Hale'iwa

The main town on the North Shore stands at the point where Kamehameha Highway reaches the ocean, 24 miles north of Honolulu. For most visitors, **HALE'IWA** (pronounced "*ha-lay-eve-a*") comes as a pleasant surprise. It's one of the very few communities on Oahu whose roots have not been obscured by a century of rebuilding and development, despite the fact that tourists have been coming here ever since the opening of a direct train line from Honolulu in 1899.

Since the 1960s, the town has become a mecca for **surfers** from all over the world. Many of the originals, lured here from California by the cult movie *Endless Summer*, seem to have remained not only in Hawaii, but also in the 1960s. The town these days is bursting with half-hippy businesses such as surf shops, tie-dye stores, wholefood restaurants and galleries of ethnic knickknacks. Add those to a scattering of upfront tourist traps, and local stores and diners, and you've got an intriguing, energetic blend that entices many travelers to stay for months.

That said, there's precious little to see in Hale'iwa. Its main street, **Kamehameha Avenue**, runs for a mile from the Paukauila Stream to the Anahulu River, well back from the ocean, passing a cluster of gas stations and then a succession of low-rise malls. In the largest of these, the **North Shore Marketplace**, Strong Current is the most interesting of the **surf shops**, for devotees and idle browsers alike. As well as selling nine-foot boards for anything from $700 up to $2500 (no rentals), it holds a small section set aside as the **Hale'iwa Surf Museum**, crammed with historic boards, books, memorabilia and videos. Another nearby building, still within the North Shore Marketplace, also calls itself a **Surf Museum** (open "most of the time"; free), this time with slightly more justification. It traces the history of Hawaiian surfboards from the hollow wooden boards of the 1930s through early fiberglass models from the 1950s, and holds shrines to Duke Kahanamoku in particular, and the 1960s in general.

Only as you approach the river do you finally come to the heart of Hale'iwa, a short stretch of old-fashioned boardwalk lined with false-front wooden buildings. One of these houses, Matsumoto's, a Japanese grocery store also selling T-shirts and memorabilia, has become so renowned for its **shave ice** that it's now an all-but-obligatory stop on round-island tours. Shave ice is the Hawaiian equivalent of a sno-cone, a mush of ice saturated with sickly sweet syrup.

Beyond that, the narrow Rainbow Bridge crosses Anahulu River, with great views upstream towards the green slopes of the Anahulu Valley. The small bay

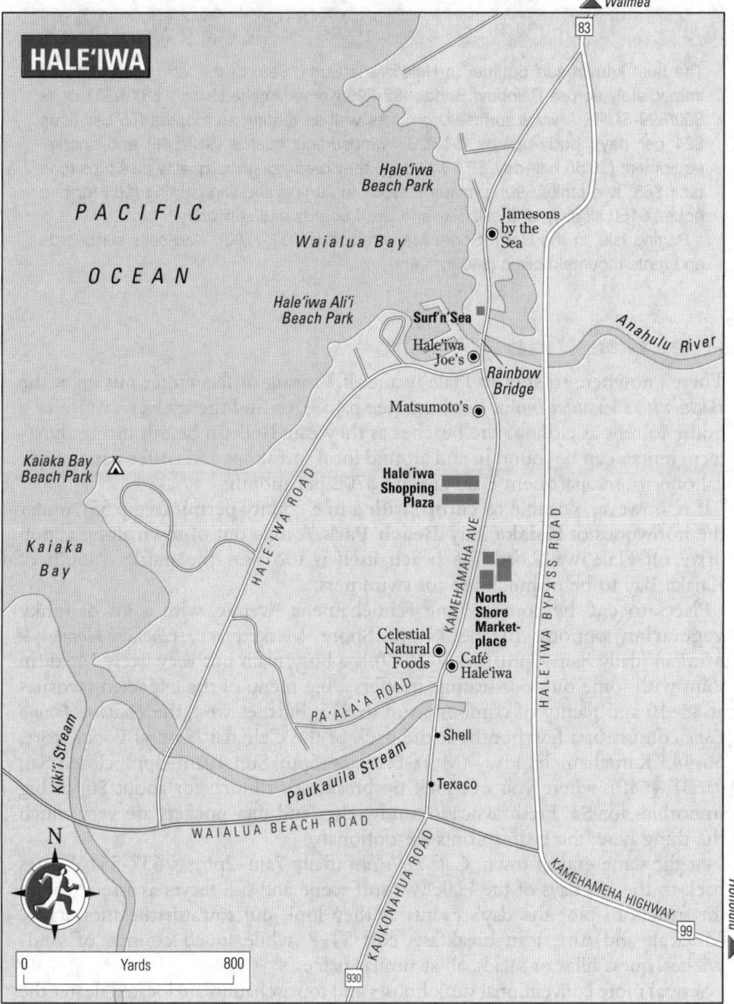


at the rivermouth is **Waialua Bay**, with Hale'iwa Harbor sheltered by a breakwater on its southwestern side. Southwest of the harbor, **Hale'iwa Ali'i Beach Park** is a favorite place for local kids to learn to surf – there are even **free surfing lessons** on weekend mornings in winter – but inexperienced outsiders who have a go are taking their lives in their hands. That was the excuse for making this the fictional location of TV's *Baywatch Hawaii*, a short-lived, state-subsidized experiment in relocating the Californian show to Hawaii that cost Hawaiian taxpayers dearly.

Just to reach the waves at Hale'iwa Ali'i, you have to pick your way across a tricky shallow coral reef; once you're out there, you're at the mercy of strong crosscurrents. Swimming at **Hale'iwa Beach Park**, on the northeast shore of the bay, is much safer.

## Hale'iwa Equipment Rental

The best known surf outfitter in Hale'iwa is Surf'n'Sea, to the left of the highway immediately across Rainbow Bridge (62-595 Kamehameha Hwy; ⓣ 637-9887 or 1-800/899-SURF, ⓦ www.surfnsea.com). As well as renting surfboards ($5 per hour, $24 per day), body-boards ($4/$20), windsurfing boards ($12/$45) and snorkel equipment ($6.50 half-day, $9.50 all day), they organize good-quality dive trips (one tank $65, two tanks $90), provide lessons in surfing and windsurfing ($65 for two hours, $150 all day), and sell new and used boards and souvenirs.

Raging Isle, in the North Shore Marketplace (ⓣ 637-7700), also sells surfboards and rents mountain bikes ($40 for 24hr).



## Practicalities

There's nowhere to **stay** in Hale'iwa itself. Visiting surfers either put up at the *Backpacker's Vacation Inn* in Pūpūkea (see p.139), or find themselves a room or a home to rent as close to the beaches as they can. Bulletin boards listing short-term rentals can be found in and around local surf shops and coffee bars; a typical one-room apartment costs around $700 per month.

It is, however, possible to **camp**, with a free county permit (see p.55), under the ironwoods of **Kaiaka Bay Beach Park**. A mile out of town along a loop drive off Hale'iwa Road, the beach itself is too near the murky mouth of Kaiaka Bay to be of much use for swimmers.

Places to **eat**, by contrast, line Kamehameha Avenue, with a lot of funky **vegetarian** options. In the North Shore Marketplace, *Cholo's Homestyle Mexican* (daily 8am–9pm; ⓣ 637-3059) is a busy, plain but very lively Mexican joint with some outdoor seating; it offers a big menu of the expected favorites at $8–10 and plenty of combos at up to $15. Further west, the *Paradise Found Café* consists of a few booths at the back of the Celestial Natural Foods store, 66-443 Kamehameha Hwy (Mon–Fri 9am–5pm, Sun 10am–5pm, closed Sat; ⓣ 637-4640), where you can pick up breakfast or lunch for about $6, or big smoothies for $3. Fresh avocado sandwiches and pita pockets are very much the thing here; the bean sprouts are optional.

At the same end of town, *Café Hale'iwa* (daily 7am–2pm; ⓣ 637-5516) dates back to the old days of the Hale'iwa surf scene and still serves as a rendezvous for surfers to plot the day's events as they look out towards the mountains. Mexican and American breakfasts cost $4–8, while lunch consists of sandwiches, quesadillas or salads, all at similar prices.

Several more conventional steak houses and tourist haunts are located nearer the harbor. The pick of the bunch is *Hale'iwa Joe's*, at the mouth of the Anahulu River (Mon–Thurs & Sun 11.30am–9.30pm, Fri & Sat 11.30am–10.30pm; ⓣ 637-4336), which has an outdoor terrace. At lunchtime, sandwiches or salads cost around $10, and most of the items on the dinner menu are also available; in the evening, sushi or *poke* appetizers cost around $7, while a New York steak is $20. Just across the river, the similarly priced *Jamesons by the Sea*, 62-540 Kamehameha Hwy (daily 11am–9pm; ⓣ 637-4336), is famous for its sunset views.

# Kawailoa



Despite appearances, Hale'iwa was not so much a plantation town as a fishing and farming community. Around the turn of the century, indentured plantation laborers gravitated to the shoreline as their contracts with the Waialua Sugar Company expired. So long as they worked for the plantation, however, they lived in the hilltop settlement of **KAWAILOA**, a mile east of Hale'iwa. Frozen in time by the decline in the sugar industry, Kawailoa is still up there, a few red-dirt streets of simple timber-frame homes surrounded by ever-encroaching tropical gardens.



# Waimea Bay

Long **Kawailoa Beach** stretches for almost five miles northeast of Hale'iwa, interrupted repeatedly by rocky reefs and swept by fierce currents. Driving along the highway, however, virtually the first glimpse you get of the ocean is as you crest a small promontory to look down on **Waimea Bay**.

## Death in Waimea Valley

In 1779, shortly after Captain Cook's death at Kealakekua Bay on the Big Island (see p.171), one of his ships, the *Resolution*, put in at Waimea to collect water for the long voyage north. **Waimea Bay**, the first spot on Oahu to be visited by foreigners, was described by the new Captain Clerke as "by far the most beautifull Country we have yet seen among the Isles . . . bounteously cloath'd with Verdure, on which were situate many large Villages and extensive plantations."

Thirteen years later, on May 12, 1792, one of Clerke's crew returned to Waimea. **Lieutenant Richard Hergest**, in command of the *Daedalus*, had become separated from the rest of an expedition led by Captain George Vancouver. By this time, Kamehameha the Great's access to European weapons was enabling him to defeat all his rivals. However, when locals eager to barter for arms came aboard the *Daedalus*, Hergest refused to trade and threw their leader overboard, leaving him to swim ashore ignominiously.

Hergest then took a party ashore, landing in Waimea Bay just west of the river mouth. As his men filled their casks, he set off to explore inland. Accompanying him were a young astronomer, **William Gooch** – who just a week earlier had stayed as an overnight guest in Kamehameha's hut in Kealakekua – and a Portuguese sailor named Manuel. A mile or so up the valley – a site now located between the aviaries of Waimea Falls Park – the unarmed men were alarmed to see a group of Hawaiians rushing down the slopes towards them from the Pu'u o Mahuka *Heiau* (see p.139). Each was a fearsome **pahupu** or "cut-in-two" warrior, having tattooed half his body – either top to bottom, or his entire head – completely black. Hergest, Gooch and Manuel were swiftly cut down, and their corpses taken as sacrificial offerings to another *heiau* at Mokulē'ia, to be baked and stripped of their flesh.

Waimea was then under the control of warrior priests who lived at the Pu'u o Mahuka *heiau*. Their leader, **Koi**, had been stationed here by Chief Kahekili of Maui to guard the traditionally rebellious north coast of Oahu; he was probably the man whom Hergest pushed into the ocean, and it was probably he who took his revenge. Nonetheless, when Vancouver called into Waikīkī the next year and demanded that the culprits be handed over for trial, he was presented with three men picked virtually at random. Although no one seriously believed they were guilty, they were summarily executed as an example of British justice. In 1799, the tattooed Koi was pointed out to another visiting captain at Waikīkī, who shot and wounded him in his canoe, and then hanged him.

This story is told in full in *The Death of William Gooch*; see Books, p.539.

Waimea Bay is the most famous **surfing** spot in the world, thanks to what are generally believed to be the biggest rideable waves on the planet. During the summer, it's often calm as a lake, but in winter the break off its craggy headlands can remain over twenty feet high for days at a time. Anywhere else, even the waves right on the beach would count as monsters, and lethal rip currents tear along the shoreline. While entering the ocean at Waimea in winter is extremely dangerous for anyone other than expert surfers, the beautiful sands of **Waimea Bay Beach County Park** are usually crowded with swimmers, snorkelers and boogie-boarders in summer, and with awestruck spectators in winter.

Until a huge flood in 1894, Waimea River flowed freely into the sea, and the valley behind was densely populated. Most of its farms and homes were destroyed, however, and the mouth of the river is now blocked by a sandbar that forms part of the beach park.

## Waimea Valley and Adventure Park

All of Waimea Valley inland of the highway bridge is now occupied by the commercially-run **Waimea Valley and Adventure Park** (daily 10am–5.30pm; adults $24, ages 4–12 $12; ⓣ638-8511). In theory, the intention of this tame exploitation of the island's most beautiful valley is to introduce Hawaii and its natural history to first-time visitors; it's considerably higher-minded than the Polynesian Cultural Center (see p.129), for example. However, the park has been in financial crisis for several years, amid allegations that its previously sensitive attempts to preserve and cultivate rare Hawaiian plant species have been all but abandoned. It may well have closed down altogether by the time you read this, though the city of Honolulu has been trying to put together a rescue package to keep it open in some form.

Assuming it's still possible to enter the valley, its most prominent historical relic is the restored *Hale O Lono* or "House of Lono," an ancient *heiau* whose three stone terraces rise next to the main gate; in fact you could take a look without entering the park. If you pay to go in, once past the entrance complex of gift stores and snack bars you can wander along stream-side walkways that lead past botanical gardens, aviaries and the fenced-off ruins of further *heiaus* and ancient burial sites. Almost a mile up from the gates, beyond a *hula* demonstration area and a mock-Hawaiian village of thatched huts, the path reaches the double **Waimea Falls** at the head of the valley. Cliff divers regularly leap sixty feet into the pool below.

## Pūpūkea

Immediately beyond Waimea Bay, Kamehameha Highway starts to cruise beside a succession of magnificent surfing beaches. Driving here demands patience; at the best of times, vehicles pull off without warning, while during major competitions traffic slows to a virtual standstill.

**Pūpūkea Beach County Park**, which, like Hanauma Bay (see p.115), is a Marine Life Conservation District, stretches for well over a mile from the mouth of Waimea Bay. At its western end, the Three Tables surf break is named after three flat-topped chunks of reef, where plenty of unwary swimmers have come to grief, while **Shark's Cove** to the east, riddled with submarine caves, is a popular site for snorkelers and scuba divers in summer.

Bumper stickers all over Oahu carry the slogan "Save the North Shore," a reference to the planned Lihi Lani real-estate development on the cliffs above **PŪPŪKEA**. For the moment, Pūpūkea is a low-key community composed largely of international surf-bums, with a few stores and no restaurants. It offers by far the best **accommodation** along the North Shore, however. The *Backpacker's Vacation Inn*, 59-788 Kamehameha Hwy, Hale'iwa HI 96712 (Ⓣ638-7838 or 1-888/628-8882 in HI only, Ⓕ638-7515, Ⓦwww.backpackers-hawaii.com; ❶–❸), was founded by Mark Foo, a daredevil Hawaiian surfer who died surfing in California in 1994. Its rambling main building, *mauka* of the highway, has dorm beds for $18 per night in high season, and simple private double rooms sharing kitchen and bath for $60. Across the street, in low oceanfront buildings, dorm beds cost $21 a night, and good-value studio apartments with great views start at $95. The *Plantation Village*, a hundred yards down the road, across from the sea and run by the same management, consists of nine restored plantation cabins, with dorm beds, private rooms, and larger cabins at similar rates. All rates are discounted for stays of a week or longer, and drop by fifteen percent between April and November. Communal buffet dinners on Tuesday, Wednesday, Friday and Sunday cost $6, and there's a free daily bus to Honolulu Airport. They also provide free snorkeling equipment and boogie boards, offer net access at $7 per hour, and arrange island tours, plus scuba diving in summer.

## Pu'u O Mahuka Heiau State Monument

For a superb view of Waimea Valley and the bay, head up to the **Pu'u O Mahuka Heiau**, perched on the eastern bluff above the mouth of the river. As Oahu's largest temple of human sacrifice, this was once home to a terrifying brotherhood of *pahupu* warrior-priests (see p.137). To reach it, turn off the coastal highway at the Foodland supermarket, a few hundred yards beyond the bay. Having climbed the hill on twisting Pūpūkea Road, turn right onto a narrow level track that skirts the cliff edge for just under a mile.

The parking lot at the end of the track is alongside the higher of the temple's two tiers. The meadow that from here appears to lie just beyond the *heiau* is in fact on the far side of the deep cleft of Waimea Valley. **Trails** lead around and partly through the old stone walls, within which it's easy to make out the outlines of several subsidiary structures; most were originally paved with water-worn stones carried up from Waimea Bay. The main "altar" at the *mauka* end is usually covered with wrapped offerings and probably bears little resemblance to its original configuration. From the little loop path around the java plum trees nearby, you can see right along the North Shore to Ka'ena Point in the western distance.

## Kaunala trail

Beyond the *heiau* turnoff, Pūpūkea Road heads inland for another two miles, to end at the gates of a Boy Scout Camp. From here, the five-mile **Kaunala Trail**, open to the public on weekends only, runs along the thickly wooded crest of a high mountain ridge. As well as views of the deep and inaccessible gorges to either side, if the clouds clear you'll eventually get to see Oahu's highest peak, 4020-ft **Mount Ka'ala**, far across the central plains.

# Sunset Beach

With its wide shelf of yellow sand, lined by palm trees, **Sunset Beach**, to the northeast of Pūpūkea, is perhaps the most picture-perfect beach on Oahu.

Only occasional gaps between the oceanfront homes allow access, but once you get there you're free to wander for two blissful miles of paradise-island coastline. Unless you come on a calm and current-free summer's day (ask the lifeguards), it's essential to stay well away from the water; the "Sunset Rip" has been known to drag even beachcombers out to sea.



In winter, when the waves are stupendous, Sunset Beach fills with photographers in search of the definitive surfing shot, while reckless pro surfers perform magazine-cover stunts out on the water. Each of the breaks here has its own name, the most famous being the **Banzai Pipeline**, where the goal is to let yourself be fired like a bullet through the tubular break and yet manage to avoid being slammed down onto the shallow, razor-sharp reef at the end. To watch the action, walk a few hundred yards west (left) from **'Ehukai Beach County Park**, where a small patch of lawn separates the beach from the road.

**Sunset Beach**, a mile past 'Ehukai, was where North Shore surfing first took off, following advances in surfboard technology in the early 1950s, and remains the venue for many contests. The break known as **Backyards** is renowned as being especially lethal, though it's a popular playground for windsurfers. **Kaunala Beach** beyond that, the home of the **Velzyland** break, is the last major surf spot before the highway curves away towards Turtle Bay (see p.131) and the Windward Coast. Velzyland offers reliable rather than colossal waves, but riding them with any degree of safety requires immense precision.

## Practicalities

No formal overnight accommodation is available beyond the *Backpacker's Vacation Inn* (see p.139). As for eating, fruit stands and snack bars are normally scattered along the *mauka* side of Kamehameha Highway from Pūpūkea onwards, though few seem to survive more than a season or two. Look out for the giant totem pole dedicated to Maui Pōhaku Loa, six miles north of Hale'iwa between Sunset and 'Ehukai beaches, however, and alongside it you'll find *Taste of Paradise* (Mon–Fri 11am–6pm, Sat & Sun 11am–8pm; ⓣ348-5886). This quintessential North Shore hangout is not so much a restaurant as a greenhouse-like awning with a van parked at the far end. In addition to cheap fruit smoothies, they sell sandwiches, burgers and kebabs for $4–7, shrimp plates for around $10, and a tiger shrimp and *ahi* combo for $12.50.

# West from Hale'iwa: Waialua and Mokulē'ia

The coast of northern Oahu to the **west of Hale'iwa** lacks suitable surfing beaches, and is so rarely visited that most people don't really count it as part of the North Shore at all.

The area's principal landmark is the **Waialua Sugar Mill**, gently rusting away at the foot of the Wai'anae mountains since the closure of the local sugar company in 1996. A moderately interesting driving tour leads down the backroads of the village of **Waialua** and along oceanfront Crozier Drive to even smaller **Mokulē'ia**, but while that gives you attractive views of Hale'iwa in the distance, you might as well go straight to Hale'iwa itself.

# Ka'ena Point

The westernmost promontory of Oahu, **Ka'ena Point**, is only accessible on foot or mountain bike; it's not possible to drive all the way around from the North Shore to the Leeward Shore. As Farrington Highway runs west of Waialua and Mokulē'ia, the landscape grows progressively drier, and the road eventually grinds to a halt a couple of miles beyond Dillingham Airfield, where Skysurfing Glider Rides offers glider flights (from $35 per person; daily 10am–5.30pm; ⓣ256-0438).

On the far side of the gate, you can follow either a bumpy, dusty dirt road beside the steadily dwindling Wai'anae Ridge, or a sandy track that straggles up and down across the coastal rocks. The only sign of life is likely to be the odd local fisherman, perched on the spits of black lava reaching into the foaming ocean.

After roughly an hour of hot hiking, the ridge vanishes altogether, and you squeeze between boulders to enter the **Ka'ena Point Natural Area Reserve**. This largely flat and extremely windswept expanse of gentle sand dunes, knitted together with creeping ivy-like *naupaka*, is used as a nesting site in winter by Laysan **albatrosses**. At the very tip, down below a rudimentary lighthouse – a slender white pole topped by flashing beacons – tiny little beaches cut into the headland. Winter waves here can reach more than fifty feet high, the highest recorded anywhere in the world. That's way beyond the abilities of any surfer, though humpback whales often come in close to the shore.

From Ka'ena Point, you can see the mountains curving away down the leeward coast, as well as the white "golfball" of a military early-warning system up on the hills. Just out to sea is a rock known as **Pōhaku O Kaua'i** ("the rock of Kauai"); in Hawaiian legend, this is a piece of Kauai, which became stuck to Oahu when the demi-god Maui attempted to haul all the islands together.

If you'd prefer to try the slightly longer hike to Ka'ena Point from the end of the road on the western coast, see p.144.

# The Leeward Coast

The **west** or **leeward coast** of Oahu, cut off from the rest of the island behind the Wai'anae mountains, is only accessible via the **Farrington Highway** that skirts the southern end of the ridge. Customarily dismissed as "arid," it may not be covered by tropical vegetation, but the **scenery** is still spectacular. As elsewhere on Oahu, the mountains are pierced by high green valleys – almost all of them inaccessible to casual visitors – while fine beaches such as Mākaha Beach Park line the shore.

However, the traditionally minded inhabitants of towns such as **Nānākuli** are not disposed to welcome the encroachment of hotels and golf courses, and visitors tend to be treated with a degree of suspicion. The further north you go, the stronger the military presence becomes, with soldiers in camouflage lurking in the hillsides. Farrington Highway once ran all the way around Ka'ena Point, at the northwest corner of the island – which explains why the road has the same name on both coasts – but it's no longer possible to drive right up to the point.

# The southwest corner

The strip development that characterizes both sides of Hwy-1 from Honolulu to Waipahu finally comes to an end as you enter the southwest corner of Oahu. Long-cherished plans by the state authorities to turn this region into a major tourism and residential center seem finally to be approaching fruition, however, as the former plantation settlement of **'Ewa** becomes ever more overshadowed by the burgeoning modern community of **Kapolei**.

## 'Ewa

A couple of miles south of Farrington Highway along Fort Weaver Road, **'EWA** is a picturesque little hamlet of wooden sugar-plantation homes arranged around a well-kept village green. Other than snapping a few photos along the back lanes, the only reason to come here is to take a **train excursion** with the Hawaii Railway Society, based just west of town along Renton Road. Their souvenir store and museum is open all week (Mon–Sat 9am–3pm, Sun 10am–3pm; free), but only on Sunday afternoons (at 12.30pm and 2.30pm) does the restored *Waialua* #6 locomotive set out on its ninety-minute round-trip journey (adults $8, seniors and under-13s $5; ⓣ681-5461) to the Ko Olina Resort (see below). On the second Sunday of each month, by reservation only, you can have a private narrated tour in the comfort of a restored luxury parlor car ($15).

**'Ewa Beach Park**, three miles south of the village, is an attractive oceanfront park popular with sailors from the nearby base. It has plenty of sand, and views across to Diamond Head, but the water tends to be too murky for swimming, and there's an awful lot of seaweed around.

## Kapolei

Until very recently, the name **KAPOLEI** did not appear on even the most detailed maps of Oahu. Now, however, it's the island's fastest-growing town, stretching alongside H-1 as it approaches its end in the southwest corner of the island. Homes, movie theaters and shopping malls have sprung up at an astonishing rate, but the new town has so far made only one bid to attract tourists, in the shape of the **Hawaiian Waters Adventure Park**, at 400 Farrington Hwy (hours vary; adults $30, ages 4–11 $20; ⓣ674-9283; ⓦwww.hawaiianwaters.com). Hawaii's first water park follows the model of its predecessors in California, Florida and elsewhere, with lots of swirling plastic tubes for visitors to raft or simply slide down, children's play areas, and an exhilarating wave pool. It's all great fun, though with so many wonderful beaches on the island to compete with, it hasn't yet succeeded in attracting great numbers of visitors. In principle, it's open daily from 10.30am until dusk, but it often seems to close its gates as early as 4pm; call ahead before you make the drive.

## Ko Olina Resort

A great deal of money was poured during the 1980s into landscaping the new **Ko Olina Resort**, just north of **Barbers Point** at the southwest tip of the island. Four successive artificial lagoons were blasted into the coastline, each a perfect semicircle and equipped with its own crescent of white sand. Work also began on creating a marina for luxury yachts at the Barbers Point Harbor. However, of the projected residential estates, condo buildings, shopping centers and hotels, only the *Ihilani Resort* has so far materialized. Its one neighbor, the relentlessly tacky *Paradise Cove lū'au* site (see p.103), is something of a poor relation.

The **Marriott Ihilani Resort and Spa** (92-1001 Olani St, Kapolei HI 96707-2203; Ⓣ679-0079 or 1-800/626-4446, Ⓕ679-0080, Ⓦwww.ihilani.com; ⑧–⑨) opened in 1993 as Oahu's closest approximation to the resort hotels of the outer islands. It's an absolute idyll if you can afford it; its fifteen stories of state-of-the-art rooms are equipped with every high-tech device imaginable, from computerized lighting and air-con systems to CD players and giant-screen TVs. The adjoining spa boasts thalassotherapy and sauna facilities, plus rooftop tennis courts and a top-quality golf course. The in-house restaurants are excellent – a meal at the least expensive, the poolside *Naupaka*, will set you back at least $50, though its delicate Pacific Rim fish dishes are well worth trying; alternatives include the formal *Azul* grill.

# Nānākuli

Farrington Highway reaches the Wai'anae coast at **Kahe Point Beach Park**, near the section known as "Tracks" because of the adjacent railroad tracks. As well as being a small but pretty strip of sand, this is Oahu's most popular year-round **surfing** site. The waves offshore remain high (but not overpoweringly so) even in summer, and break much closer to the shore than usual. Since the bay itself is relatively sheltered, swimming usually only becomes dangerous in the depths of winter.

A couple of miles further on, **NĀNĀKULI** is the southernmost of a string of small coastal towns. According to local legends, its name means either "look at knee" or "pretend to be deaf" – neither of which seems to make much sense. The population is largely Hawaiian, and there's little attempt to cater to outsiders. **Nānākuli Beach Park**, which runs alongside the highway all through town, is another good summer swimming beach, while **Zablan Beach** at its southern end is much used by scuba divers. The beach immediately north of Nānākuli is called **Ulehawa** or "filthy penis," after a particularly unsavory ancient chief.

# Wai'anae

**WAI'ANAE**, five miles up the coast, centers on curving **Pōka'ī Bay**. Thanks to the breakwaters constructed to protect the boat harbor at its northern end, the main sandy beach here is the only one on the Leeward Coast where swimming can be guaranteed safe all year round. An irresistible backdrop is provided by the high-walled amphitheater valley behind.

Beyond a flourishing coconut grove at the tip of the flat spit of land that marks the southern end of Pōka'ī Bay stand the ruined walls of **Kū'īlioloa Heiau**. Unusual in being virtually surrounded by water, this three-tiered structure is said to mark the place where the first coconut tree to be brought from Tahiti was planted in Hawaiian soil. Kamehameha offered sacrifices here before launching his first invasion attempt against Kauai (see p.415).

# Mākaha

**MĀKAHA**, or "savage," the last of the leeward towns, was once the hideout of a dreaded band of outlaws. Now famous for the savagery of its **waves**, it began to attract surfers in the early 1950s. Before World War II, virtually all Oahu surfing was concentrated in Waikīkī. When changes in the ocean conditions there, and the development of new techniques and equipment led surfers to start looking elsewhere, Mākaha was the first place they hit on. The waves at its northern end are said to be the largest consistently reliable surf in Hawaii, and several major surfing contests are still held at **Mākaha Beach Park** each year. In summer, when sand piles up in mighty drifts, it's often possible to swim here in safety, and Mākaha retains enough sand to remain a beautiful crescent beach even in winter. You'll probably notice what look like hotels along the oceanfront nearby, but they're all long-term rental condos intended for local families.

A couple of miles back from the ocean in Mākaha Valley, beyond the defunct *Sheraton Mākaha Resort*, a private driveway leads to **Kāne'āki Heiau**. The most thoroughly restored ancient temple in Hawaii, it was excavated by Bishop Museum archeologists in 1970 and can now be visited with permission from the security guards at the gate (Tues–Sun 10am–2pm; free); you'll have to leave a drivers' license or passport as surety. Its principal platform of weathered, lichen-covered stones is topped once more by authentic thatched structures such as the *anu'u* ("oracle tower"), as well as carved images of the gods. The *heiau* originated as an agricultural temple to the god Lono in the fifteenth century. Two hundred years later, it was converted into a *luakini*, where human sacrifices were dedicated to the god Kū – a typical progression indicating that the valley had come to support a large enough population to have its own paramount chief.

## The road to Ka'ena Point

Beyond Mākaha, the highway traces a long, slow curve up the coast to Yokohama Bay. Barely populated, and splendidly bleak, this region attracts very few visitors other than a handful of daredevil surfers prepared to risk its sharks, currents and mighty waves.

Looking inland, the rolling green slopes of **Mākua Valley** also conceal dangerous secrets. Used by the Air Force for bombing practice during and after World War II, the valley is still barred to the public owing to unexploded ordnance. Gaping **Kāneana Cave** to the south is too vandalized to be worth investigating.

Not even the sturdiest four-wheel-drive vehicle could negotiate the dirt road that continues from the end of the highway. In any case, the dunes beyond were designated as the **Ka'ena Point Natural Area Reserve** to help repair damage done by military jeeps and motorbikes. However, an exposed one-hour hike along the route of the old railroad tracks will bring you to the very tip of the island. The walk is substantially similar to the corresponding trail along the North Shore, described on p.141.

# 2

# The Big Island

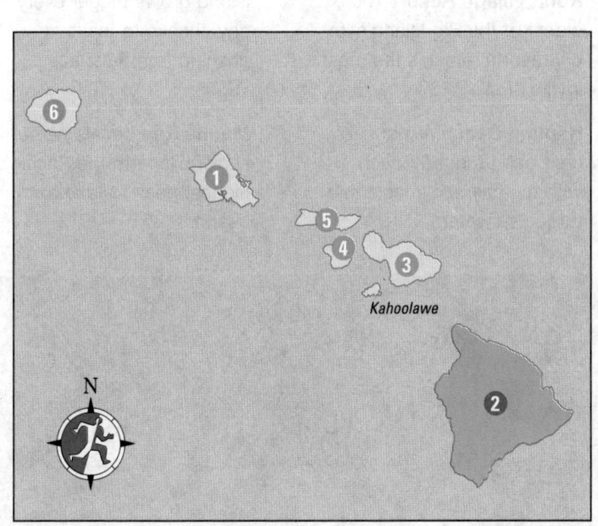

CHAPTER 2

# Highlights

* **The Coffee Shack** Simple roadside café, serving up fresh Kona coffee to go with its stupendous ocean views. P.170

* **Pu‘uhonua O Hōnaunau** Atmospheric "place of refuge" that conjures up vivid images of life in ancient Hawaii. P.174

* **Kona Village Resort** The oldest of the Big Island's luxury resorts remains the most idyllic of all. P.180

* **Hāpuna Beach** A magnificent palm-fringed beach with the calmest imaginable turquoise waters. P.187

* **Hwy-250** The drive along the pastoral flanks of Kohala Mountain is among the most beautiful in all Hawaii. P.198

* **Kehena Beach** Wild parrots and naturists share the pleasures of this little-known black-sand beach. P.233

* **Kīlauea Eruption** The Big Island grows bigger every day, thanks to the lava gushing from Kīlauea. P.249

* **Mauna Kea** Locals gather snowballs from the Pacific's highest peak to take to the beach. P.251

# 2

# The Big Island



All the Hawaiian islands were formed by volcanic action, but only on the **Big Island of Hawaii** are those volcanoes still active. Visitors flock to watch the fiery eruptions that continue to shape the youngest land on earth. Such sheer rawness might make the island seem an unlikely tourist destination, but it also offers everything you could want from a tropical vacation – dependable sunshine, sandy beaches, warm turquoise fish-filled waters, swaying coconut palms and pristine rainforest.

Though tourism is crucial to its economy, the Big Island lags well behind Oahu and Maui in terms of annual visitors. It has nothing to match the Waikīkī skyscrapers, or the large-scale strip development of the west Maui shoreline. In the 1960s the island was expected to emerge as the first serious rival to Oahu. Large sums were spent on building a highway system to cope with the anticipated influx, and luxury resorts shot up on bare lava, while more reasonably priced hotels appeared in the Kailua area. As things turned out, however, it was Maui that mushroomed, to become plagued by traffic problems and overcrowding, while the Big Island remains remarkably stress-free.

The Big Island is not the cheapest destination in Hawaii – though it does have a few budget inns and hostels – and it can't compete with Honolulu for frenzied shopping or wild nightlife. The entire island has the population of a medium-sized town, with 145,000 people spread across its four thousand square miles; it has its fair share of restaurants, bars and so on, but basically it's a rural community. There's plenty of opportunity to be active – hiking in the state and national parks, deep-sea fishing off the Kona coast, golfing in the Kohala resorts or snorkeling in Kealakekua Bay – but most visitors are content to while away their days meandering between beach and brunch.

As befits the birthplace of King Kamehameha, the first man to rule all the Hawaiian islands, the Big Island maintains strong links with its Polynesian past. Only just over two centuries have passed since the isolation of its original inhabitants came to an end, and their *heiaus*, petroglyphs and abandoned villages are scattered throughout the island. Otherwise, though many of its smaller towns have an appealing air of the nineteenth-century West about them, with their false-front stores and wooden boardwalks, few historical attractions are likely to lure you away from the beaches. Any time you can spare to go sightseeing is better spent exploring the waterfalls, valleys and especially the volcanoes, that were so entwined with the lives of the ancient Hawaiians.

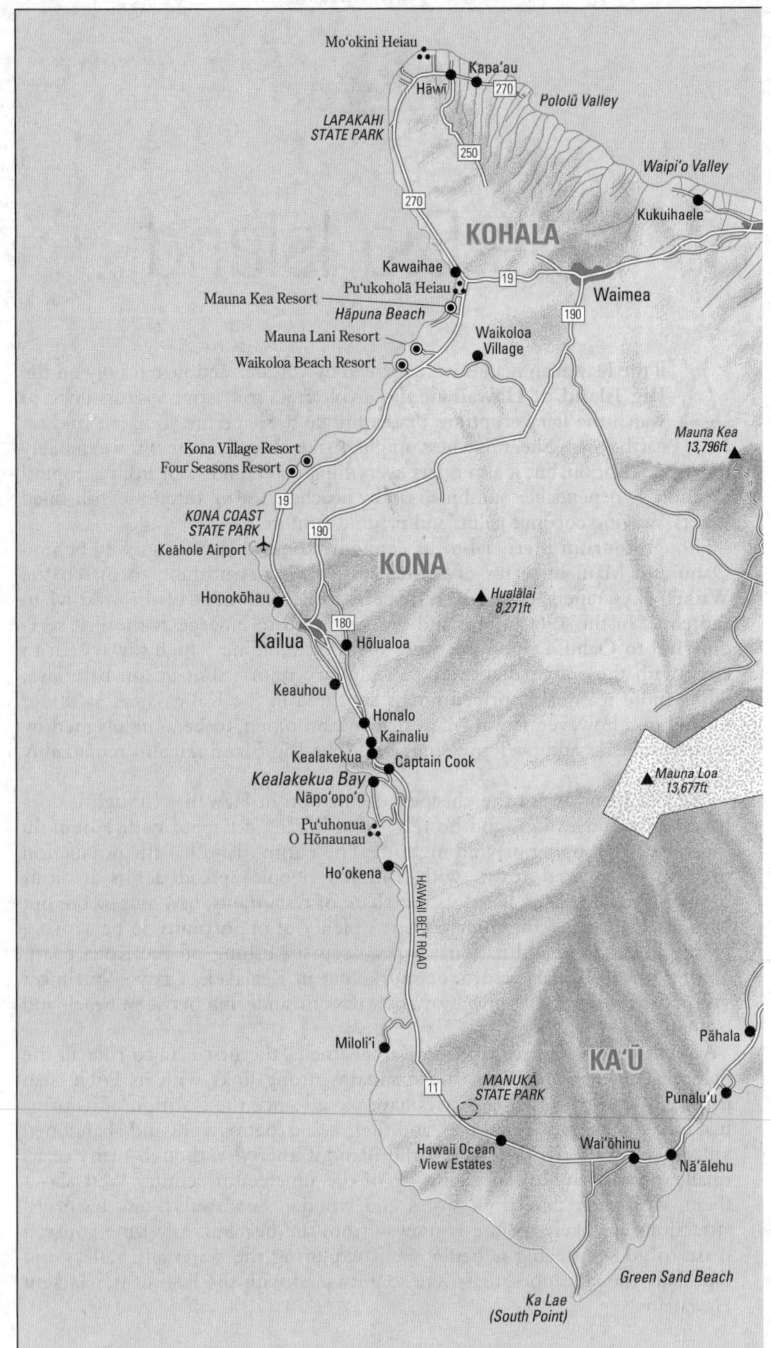
Mo'okini Heiau
Kapa'au
Hāwī
270
Pololū Valley
LAPAKAHI
STATE PARK
250
Waipi'o Valley
270
Kukuihaele
KOHALA
Kawaihae
Pu'ukoholā Heiau
19
Mauna Kea Resort
Waimea
Hāpuna Beach
190
Mauna Lani Resort
Waikoloa
Village
Waikoloa Beach Resort
Mauna Kea
13,796ft
Kona Village Resort
Four Seasons Resort
19
KONA COAST
STATE PARK
190
Keāhole Airport
KONA
Hualālai
8,271ft
Honokōhau
180
Kailua
Hōlualoa
Keauhou
Honalo
Kainaliu
Kealakekua
Captain Cook
Mauna Loa
13,677ft
Kealakekua Bay
Nāpo'opo'o
Pu'uhonua
O Hōnaunau
Ho'okena
HAWAII BELT ROAD
Pāhala
Miloli'i
KA'Ū
11
MANUKĀ
STATE PARK
Punalu'u
Hawaii Ocean
View Estates
Wai'ōhinu
Nā'ālehu
Green Sand Beach
Ka Lae
(South Point)

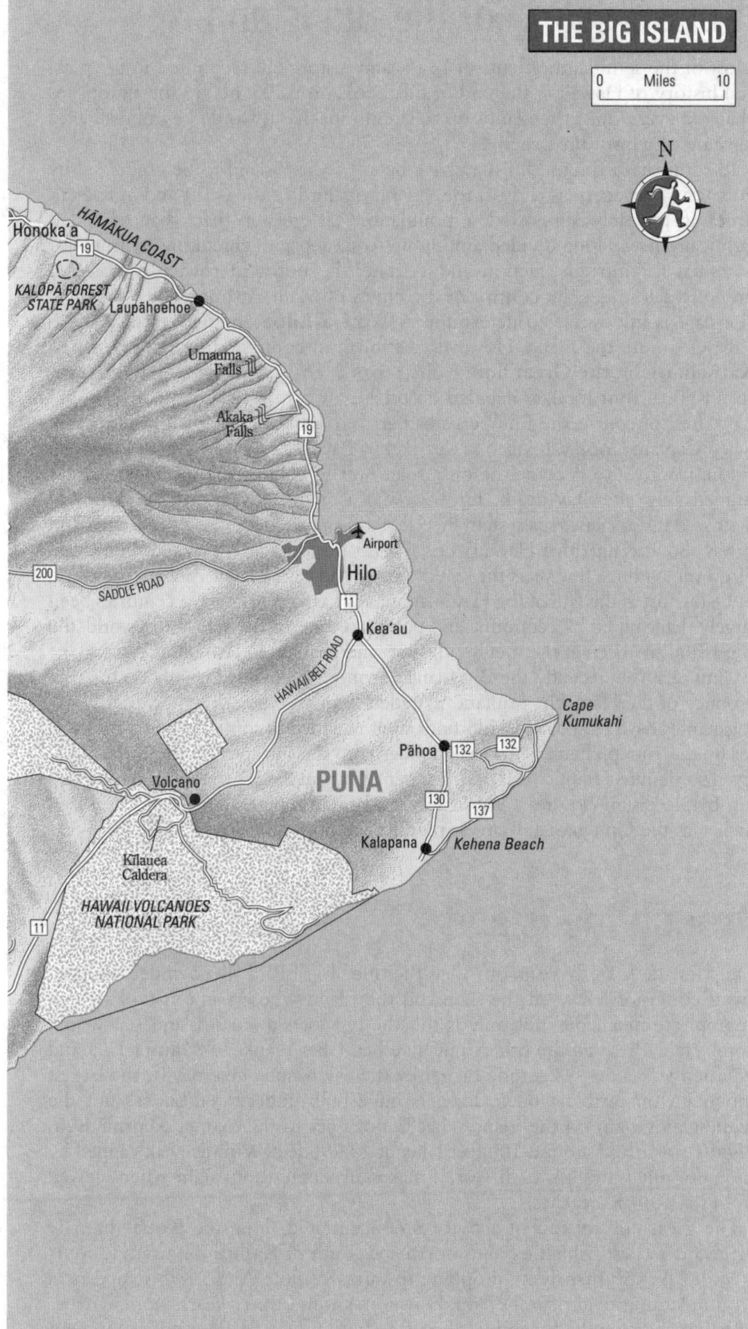
THE BIG ISLAND
0 Miles 10
N
HĀMĀKUA COAST
Honoka'a
19
KALŌPĀ FOREST STATE PARK
Laupāhoehoe
Umauma Falls
Akaka Falls
19
Airport
200
SADDLE ROAD
Hilo
11
Kea'au
HAWAII BELT ROAD
Cape Kumukahi
Pāhoa
132
132
Volcano
PUNA
130
137
Kalapana
Kehena Beach
Kīlauea Caldera
HAWAII VOLCANOES NATIONAL PARK
11

# A brief history of the Big Island

Most of the seminal moments of Big Island history are recounted in the general history of Hawaii at the end of this book, on p.505; before the Europeans changed everything, the island was so significant that it would be impossible to separate one from the other.

To summarize things, this may have been the first island to be colonized by Polynesian voyagers, as early as the second or third century AD, and in ancient times it probably supported a population far greater than that of today. Politically, it was long divided among up to six separate chiefdoms, with major potential for intrigue, faction and warfare; the north in particular was also prone to fall under the control of the chiefs of Maui. At one stage – the precise date is impossible to determine – **'Umi-a-Liloa** emerged from Waipi'o Valley to unite the island. However, factionalism continued until 1791, when **Kamehameha the Great** from Kohala won a ten-year civil war with his great rival Keōua from Ka'ū, as detailed on p.190.

By then, of course, the Europeans had arrived. Kamehameha had been present when Captain Cook was killed at Kealakekua Bay (see p.171), and with European aid he went on to become the only ruler ever to conquer all the other islands. Immediately after his death, his widow, Ka'ahumanu, and his son Liholiho destroyed the ancient *kapu* system by celebrating a banquet together at Kailua, and it was also at Kailua that Hawaii's first Christian missionaries reached the islands. However, within a few years the seat of power had passed irreversibly to the island of Oahu. Just as the fate of the Hawaiian islands has for the last two centuries been largely determined by economic and political events in the rest of the world, the Big Island has been at the mercy of events and changes in Honolulu.

Until relatively recently, the Big Island's economy depended largely on the rich produce of the Hāmākua plantations, traded through Hilo. Now, however, all the sugar mills have closed, and Hilo finds itself regarded as something of a backwater by the entrepreneurs who have flooded into the sun spots of the Kona coast. Even so, despite a frantic rush of investment, tourism has yet to replace all the jobs lost by plantation closures. Otherwise, the island occupies a couple of specialized niches, as the United States' largest producer of both ginger and coffee.

# Around the island

Only for the last fifty years or so has the title "Big Island" been widely used, to avoid confusion between the state and the island whose name it took. It's an appropriate nickname: not only is this the biggest Hawaiian island – it would comfortably hold all the others put together – but thanks to **Mauna Loa** and **Kīlauea** volcanoes, it's getting bigger by the day. Mauna Loa may be the largest mountain on earth if you include its huge bulk underwater, but it's not the highest mountain on the island. That honor goes to the extinct **Mauna Kea**, slightly north and around 100 feet taller at 13,796 feet. With its peak capped by snow for a few months each year, it makes an incongruous sight when viewed from the Kohala beaches.

The great bulk of tourist activity is concentrated along the **Kona** (literally "leeward") coast, which extends north and south of **Kailua** for around seventy miles. As you first fly in, dropping towards Keāhole Airport, this appears as an unrelenting field of black lava. However, around thirty years ago its virtues of being consistently dry and hot began to be appreciated. Resort development

### Big Island Favorites: Hikes



took off, and this became one of Hawaii's prime tourist destinations. Although the five-mile stretch from Kailua to Keauhou has acquired a succession of hotels and condos, Kailua itself remains recognizable as the sleepy little town where Kamehameha the Great had his palace. To the **south**, reached by a gorgeous road through lush coffee groves, lies **Kealakekua Bay**, where Captain Cook met his end, with the nearby **Pu'uhonua O Hōnaunau**, or "Place of Refuge," bearing witness to a vanished Hawaiian way of life and death.

The **northernmost** spur of the Big Island is its oldest segment, named after the first of its five volcanoes to appear above the ocean – the long-extinct **Kohala Mountain**. The Big Island's largest **coral reefs** – albeit small by most standards – lie just offshore, and its only sizeable **white-sand beaches** have been washed into nearby sheltered coves. Although the landscape gets more dramatic the further north you go, facilities for tourists are almost entirely restricted to **South Kohala**. This region, too, consists of barren lava flats, but lavish resorts such as the Disney-esque *Hilton Waikoloa Village* are now tucked into inlets all along the coastline.

Continuing around the island, beyond the upland cattle country of **Waimea** – home to the Parker Ranch and generations of lasso-toting *paniolo* cowboys – you reach the magnificent **Hāmākua Coast**, to be confronted by archetypal South Seas scenery. Even before the emergence of commercial agriculture, these rain-drenched slopes formed the fertile heartland of Hawaii: broad, green **Waipi'o Valley** was capable of feeding the entire island. After a century of growing sugar, however, the small towns here are reeling from the closure of the plantations. So is the Big Island's only city, its capital **Hilo**, where attempts to attract tourists have always been thwarted by the rainfall. Nonetheless it's an attractively low-key community, renowned for spectacular flowers and orchids.

Finally, the **south** of the island is dominated by the exhilarating wilderness of **Hawaii Volcanoes National Park**. Apart from the steaming craters and cinder cones of Mauna Loa and Kīlauea, its terrain ranges from arctic tundra and sulphurous desert to lowland rainforest and remote Pacific beaches. This is one of the world's most exciting hiking destinations, with scores of trails running through still-active craters. Here and there along the shore the volcanoes have deposited beaches of jet-black sand, while near **South Point** – the southernmost point of the United States – you can hike to a remote beach composed of green(-ish) sand. Otherwise, the southern coastline is now sparsely populated, and few visitors bother to leave the highway in the time-forgotten regions of **Puna** and **Ka'ū**.

# Getting to the Big Island

In the absence of any **boat** services to the Big Island, the only way to get there is to **fly**. The island has two main airports. Keāhole Airport is on the west coast, seven miles north of Kailua, and is universally referred to as **Kona Airport** (see p.156); **General Lyman Field** is on the outskirts of **Hilo** (see p.205), on the east coast. Most tourists arrive at Kona, but Hilo is kept busy with local

## Big Island Favorites: Beaches

| | | | |
|---|---|---|---|
| Green Sand Beach | p.258 | Punalu'u Beach | p.255 |
| Hāpuna Beach | p.187 | Spencer Beach Park | p.189 |
| Kona Coast State Park | p.179 | | |

**Snorkel and Dive Spots**

| | | | |
|---|---|---|---|
| Kahalu'u Beach | p.164 | Kealakekua Bay | p.173 |
| Kauna'oa Beach | p.189 | Pu'uhonua O Hōnaunau | p.175 |

travelers, and the two airports receive similar numbers of flights each day. A total of four scheduled **nonstop flights** come straight to the Big Island from the US mainland – United offers two daily flights from Los Angeles and one from San Francisco, while Aloha flies from San Francisco four times weekly. Full details of flights to and from the state of Hawaii are given on p.12 onwards.

Between them, the two major airlines, Hawaiian and Aloha, fly both to **Kona** and to **Hilo** around thirty times daily from **Honolulu**; nearly all those flights connect with service to and from **Kauai.** They also run around four daily flights from Kahului on **Maui** to each airport. Hawaiian operates one daily flight each from both **Molokai** and **Lanai** to both Kona, and Hilo. For more details, see p.17.

Finally, it's also possible to fly direct to **Waimea** from Honolulu on tiny Pacific Wings (Ⓣ887-2104 or 1-888/575-4546, Ⓦwww.pacificwings.com).

# Getting around the Big Island

The only practicable way to explore the Big Island is to **drive**. All the major automobile rental chains are represented at both main airports; the relevant phone numbers are listed on p.25.

In a sense, there's just one main road, the **Hawaii Belt Road**, which circles the entire island. However, traffic problems are all but nonexistent, and if you have to, you can get from anywhere on the island to anywhere else pretty quickly. It's possible to sleep in Kailua and catch a plane out from Hilo the next day, and a nightly exodus of cars drive the hundred-plus miles from the volcanoes back to Kona. Unlike all the other islands, however, the Big Island is too big to make it worth attempting a complete one-day circuit, while visiting the volcanoes as a day-trip from Kona won't give you enough time at the park.

You should also keep a close eye on your fuel gauge. **Gas stations** are common around Kailua and Hilo, but in several regions, including the National Park, you can drive up to fifty miles without seeing one.

## Big Island Favorites: Eating

These restaurants are in ascending order of price, not quality.

| | | | |
|---|---|---|---|
| *The Coffee Shack*, Captain Cook | p.170 | *Kīlauea Lodge*, Volcano | p.253 |
| *Bamboo Restaurant and Bar*, Hāwī | p.200 | *Merriman's*, Waimea | p.196 |
| *Maha's*, Waimea | p.196 | *Roy's*, Waikoloa | p.185 |
| *The Seaside Restaurant*, Hilo | p.213 | *Hale Moana, Kona Village Resort* | p.181 |
| *Cassandra's Greek Taverna*, Kailua | p.165 | *Coast Grille, Hapuna Beach Prince* | p.187 |

The national chains forbid drivers to take their vehicles onto lesser roads such as **South Point Road** (see p.257) or the high-altitude **Saddle Road** (see p.226). The only legal way to explore those areas is in a **four-wheel-drive vehicle**, which can be rented from Harper Car & Truck Rentals (Ⓣ 1-800/852-9993, 329-6688 in Kona, 969-1478 in Hilo, Ⓦ www.harpershawaii.com) at $60–90 per day. This also enables you to drive to the summit of Mauna Kea, but you still can't go off-road along the dirt track to Green Sand Beach (see p.258), or down the surfaced but incredibly steep road into Waipi'o Valley (see p.222).

As for **public transport**, the Hele On Bus Company (Ⓣ 961-8744) runs **buses** between Hilo and Kailua (Mon–Sat, 1 daily; full timetable on p.205), and between Hilo and the volcanoes (Mon–Fri, 1 daily; see p.237). There are also minimal local services in Kailua and Hilo, and resort shuttle buses between Kailua, Waikoloa and the Kohala resorts, as detailed on p.158 and p.184.

Details on seeing the island by air are on p.156; for boat tours see p.173 and p.179; and for getting around by motorbike or bicycle, see p.158. Otherwise, the only alternatives to driving are the round-island **minibus tours** run by companies such as Roberts Hawaii (Ⓣ 329-1688, Ⓦ www.roberts-hawaii.com).

# Where to stay

**Where you stay** depends on what sort of vacation you're planning. If most of your time will be spent on the beach, the prime areas are the **Kona** and **Kohala coasts**, filled with upscale **hotels**, **condos** and self-contained **resorts**. Many of the cheapest options on this side of the island are in **Kailua**, though that town too has its share of luxury properties. Elsewhere, **Hilo** offers large hotels as well as smaller, more characterful inns, while both the **National Park** area and **Waimea** have some medium-scale lodges and an abundance of **B&Bs** in private homes.

Official statistics show the **average cost** of Big Island accommodation to be around $185 per night. That alarming figure, however, is boosted by the rates at the mega-resorts of Kohala; the average cost for the Kailua area is a more reasonable $120 per night, and Hilo's average is considerably less. At most times of the year it's possible to book a room at short notice.

Bear in mind when you book that it's barely possible to see the entire island from a single base. Even if you plan to concentrate on the Kona or Kohala coasts, reckon on spending at least a night or two in the National Park area, or possibly in Hilo. It may even be worth simply forgoing a pre-paid Kona-side room for one night, to give yourself time at the volcanoes.

## Accommodation Price Codes

All the accommodation options listed here have been graded with the symbols below, which refer to the quoted rates for a double room in high season (December to March), not including state taxes of 10.17 percent. For a full explanation, see p.27.

| | | |
|---|---|---|
| ❶ up to $40 | ❹ $100–150 | ❼ $250–300 |
| ❷ $40–70 | ❺ $150–200 | ❽ $300–400 |
| ❸ $70–100 | ❻ $200–250 | ❾ over $400 |

**Big Island Favorites: Accommodation**

| | | | |
|---|---|---|---|
| *Pineapple Park*, Kealakekua (❶/❷) | p.176 | *Waimea Gardens Cottage*, Waimea (❹) | p.194 |
| *Arnott's Lodge*, Hilo (❶/❷) | p.206 | *Shipman House B&B Inn*, Hilo (❺) | p.207 |
| *Manago Hotel*, Captain Cook (❶/❷) | p.176 | *Hilton Waikoloa Village* (❻–❼) | p.183 |
| *Kona Tiki Hotel*, Kailua (❷) | p.159 | *Hapuna Beach Prince* (❽–❾) | p.187 |
| *Dolphin Bay Hotel*, Hilo (❷–❸) | p.206 | *Kona Village Resort* (❾) | p.180 |



# When to go

Throughout the year, sea-level thermometers rarely drop below the low seventies Fahrenheit (around 22°C) in the daytime, or reach above the low eighties (around 28°C); at night the temperature seldom falls below the low sixties. Average daily temperatures in Hilo range from 71°F in February to 76°F in August, while Kailua fluctuates between 72°F and 77°F. Waimea has similar daily maximums, but drops to the low fifties (around 11°C) at night. The highest temperature recorded in the state was 100°F (38°C), at Pāhala, while the summit of Mauna Kea ranges from 31°F up to 43°F.

In principle the rainiest months are from December to February, but where you are on the island makes far more difference than what time of year it is. Hilo is the wettest city in the US, with an annual rainfall of 128 inches, while the Kona coast, and especially the Kohala resort area, receive very little rain at any time. Kawaihae in Kohala gets a mere ten inches each year.

As usual in Hawaii, the state of the **ocean** varies with the seasons. It's possible to swim all year round in more sheltered areas, but the high surf between October and April makes certain beaches (indicated throughout this chapter) extremely dangerous.

Mention should also be made of a unique Big Island phenomenon. While the summits of Mauna Loa and Mauna Kea are renowned for having the clearest air on earth, down below, when the tradewinds drop, the island is prone to a choking haze of sulphurous volcanic emissions known as "**vog.**" The pollution on such days hits levels worse than those in Los Angeles or London; the only spot on the island that is consistently downwind of Kīlauea, the Ka'ū Desert, is a lifeless wasteland.

**Big Island Favorites: Camping**

| | | | |
|---|---|---|---|
| Halapē, Volcanoes National Park | p.250 | Namakani Paio, Volcanoes National Park | p.241 |
| Hāpuna Beach, Kohala | p.187 | Punalu'u County Beach Park, Ka'ū | p.255 |
| Kalōpā State Park, Hāmākua | p.219 | Spencer County Beach Park, Kohala | p.189 |
| Kulanaokuaiki, Volcanoes National Park | p.247 | Waipi'o Valley, Hāmākua | p.225 |

For state park camping permits, contact the Division of State Parks, 75 Aupuni St, Hilo HI 96720 (rates vary; ⓣ974-6200). County park permits, at $3 per day, are administered by the Department of Parks and Recreation, 25 Aupuni St, Hilo HI 96720 (Mon–Fri 7.45am–4.30pm; ⓣ961-8311, ⓦwww.hawaii-county.com), which has subsidiary offices at Hale Halawai on Ali'i Drive in Kailua (same hours), Yano Hall in Captain Cook (Mon–Fri noon–2pm), and Waimea Community Center in Waimea (Mon–Fri 8.30–10.30am).

## Big Island Festivals and Events

By far the most important of the Big Island's annual festivals is Hilo's **Merrie Monarch Festival**, a *hula* showcase for which tickets sell out almost immediately. For more details, see p.212.

| | |
|---|---|
| **Feb** | Mardi Gras, Hilo |
| **Feb** | Waimea Cherry Blossom Festival, Waimea |
| **Feb** | Tahiti Fête of Hilo |
| **March** | Kona Brewers Festival, Kailua |
| **March 26** | Prince Kūhiō Day (public holiday) |
| **April** | Merrie Monarch Festival, Hilo |
| **May 1** | Lei Day (public holiday) |
| **June 11** | Kamehameha Day (public holiday); Floral Parade in Kailua, also ceremonies at Kapa'au |
| **mid-June** | Waiki'i Music Festival, Waiki'i Ranch, Saddle Road |
| **Late June** | Pu'uhonua O Hōnaunau Cultural Festival |
| **Late June** | Kona Marathon, Kailua |
| **July 4** | Parker Ranch Rodeo, Waimea |
| **mid-July** | Kīlauea Cultural Festival, Volcano |
| **mid-July** | Slack Key Festival, Hilo |
| **late July** | Kīlauea Volcano Wilderness Runs, Volcano |
| **Aug–Oct** | International Festival of the Pacific, Hilo |
| **mid-Aug** | Hawaiian International Billfish Tournament, Kailua |
| **3rd Fri in Aug** | Admissions Day (public holiday) |
| **early Sept** | Queen Lili'uokalani Long-Distance Canoe Races, Kailua |
| **early Sept** | Parker Ranch Round-Up Rodeo, Waimea |
| **Sept** | Aloha Week Festival, island-wide |
| **early Oct** | Ironman Triathlon World Championship, Kailua |
| **Oct** | Hāmākua Music Festival, Honoka'a |
| **Nov** | Taro Festival, Honoka'a |
| **Nov** | Kona Coffee Cultural Festival, South Kona |
| **Nov** | Hawaii International Film Festival, island-wide |
| **mid-Nov** | King Kalākaua Hula Festival, Kona |
| **Dec** | Christmas Parade, Waimea |

# Nightlife and entertainment

Most of what limited **nightlife** the Big Island has to offer is arranged by the major hotels – almost all put on some form of entertainment for their guests, and many feature live musicians every night. In a typical week, the biggest events are the various **lū'aus** listed on p.166, but visiting artists from the other islands or the mainland also make regular concert appearances. Nearly all such activity happens in the prime tourist areas of Kona and Kohala, but the biggest venue for Hawaiian performers with strong local followings is the *Crown Room* at Hilo's *Hawaii Naniloa Hotel* (see p.206).

## Big Island Flight-Seeing

Unlike the other Hawaiian islands, the Big Island is too large to see in a single air tour, but it has the incomparable attraction of the unpredictable Kīlauea eruption. If it's the volcano you want to see, opt for a flight from Hilo or Volcano; many of the cheaper ones on the Kona side go up the Kohala coast and miss Kīlauea.

**Prices** generally start at around $100–120 for a 45-minute flight, and can reach up to over $300 for a full circle-island flight with a good long stare at the eruption. It is, however, well worth shopping around for **discounts** and two-for-one deals; the Activity Connection (Ⓣ329-1038, Ⓦwww.beachactivityguide.com) can usually offer up to fifteen percent off the standard rates.

For more about flight-seeing tours in general, see p.26.

**Helicopters**

| | Number | Web (Ⓦwww.) | Departs |
|---|---|---|---|
| Blue Hawaiian | Ⓣ961-5600 | bluehawaiian.com | Hilo, Waikoloa |
| Safari | Ⓣ969-1259 | safariair.com | Hilo, Kona |
| Sunshine | Ⓣ882-1223 | sunshinehelicopters.com | Hilo, Hapuna |
| Tropical | Ⓣ961-6810 | tropicalhelicopters.com | Hilo, Kona |
| Volcano | Ⓣ967-7578 | | Volcano |

**Fixed-wing**

| | Number | Web (Ⓦwww.) or email (Ⓔ) | Departs |
|---|---|---|---|
| Big Island Air | Ⓣ329-4868 | bigisle@ilhawaii.net | Kona |
| Island Hoppers | Ⓣ969-2000 | above@aloha.net | Hilo, Kona |
| Mokulele | Ⓣ326-7070 | mokulele.com | Kona |

# Kailua

Considering that **KAILUA** is the oldest Western-style community on the Big Island – Hawaii's first Christian missionaries arrived here from New England in 1820 – and was before that a favorite home of Kamehameha I, it took a surprisingly long time to grow to its present size. Before the 1980s spurt that made Kailua the Big Island's busiest tourist area, things had stood still for over a century, a fact that has left the town with an oddly dual personality. While the harbor area continues to center around the simple palace and church, built in the 1830s, it's increasingly surrounded by modern malls. The high-rise hotels conspicuous to either side of the center form just a small part of the ribbon of beachfront properties that accommodate several thousand visitors per day. That said, Kailua's heyday as a resort seems already to be over, as the great majority of new investment in hotels is now taking place further up the coast. While the town continues to expand, it is doing so primarily as a residential, rather than a tourist, area.

Kailua is still a very long way from the overkill of Waikīkī, however. When Mark Twain called it "the sleepiest, quietest, Sundayest looking place you can imagine" he meant to be pejorative, but if you've come to relax you'll probably find its low-key pleasures appealing. At least one of the local beaches is bound to suit you, and there are plenty of alternative activities. In particular, sitting on the *lānai* of one of the many waterfront cafés and bars, for a blast of Kona coffee in the morning or for a cocktail at sunset, is enough to make anyone feel that all's right with the world.

Many new arrivals assume that Kailua, not Hilo, is the island's capital. Infuriated residents of Hilo console themselves with the thought that hardly anyone seems to get the name of their rival right. Officially, it's called Kailua, hyphenated by the post office to "Kailua-Kona" to distinguish it from the Kailuas on Oahu and Maui. Most tourists, however, have only heard of Kona and not of Kailua. Compound that with the fact that most of the businesses and other facilities that people generally refer to as being "in Kona" are in fact in Kailua, and you have a recipe for confusion.

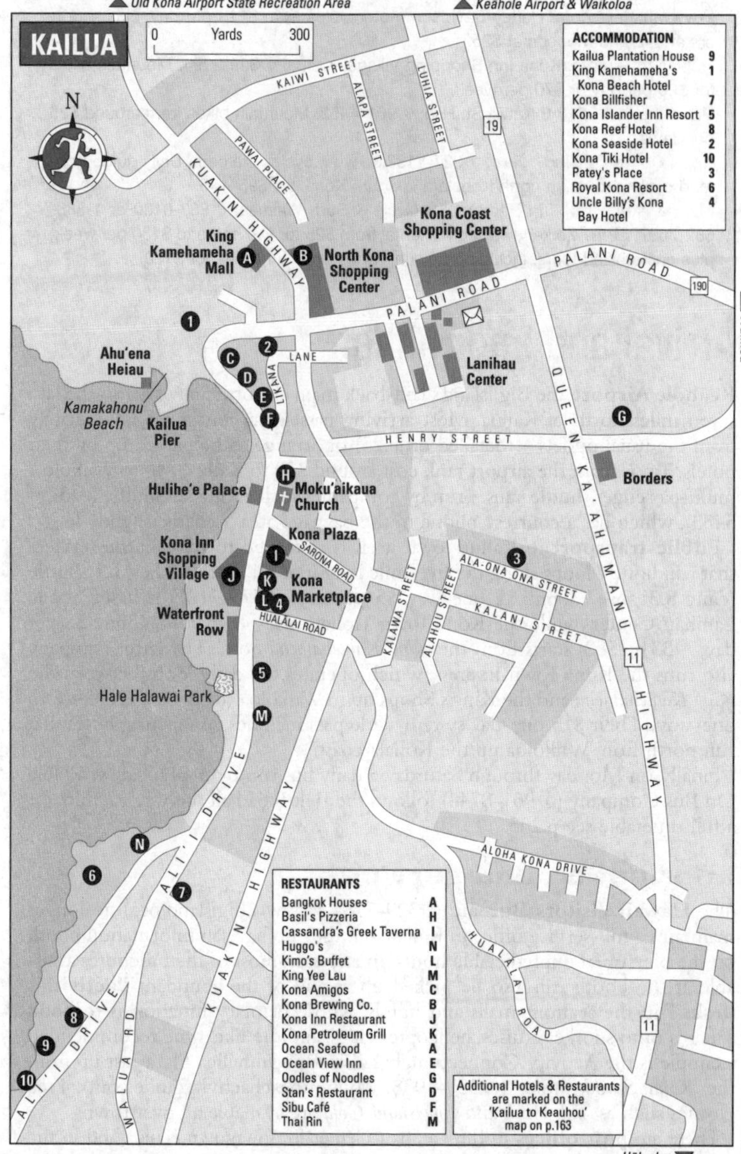

## Bike and Motorbike Rental and Tours

For general advice on **cycling** in Hawaii, see p.26. The nonprofit Big Island Mountain Bike Association (PO Box 6819, Hilo HI 96720-8934; ⓣ961-4452, ⓦwww.interpac.net/~mtbike) can suggest specific routes.

**Chris' Adventures**, PO Box 869, Kula HI 9679; ⓣ326-4600. Mountain-bike tours, some also involving hiking, from $60 for half a day.

**DJ's Rentals**, 75-5663A Palani Rd, Kailua-Kona; ⓣ329-1700 or 1-800/993-4647, ⓦwww.harleys.com. Harley-Davidson motorcycles from $119 per day, plus scooters at $45 and mopeds at $25.

**Hawaiian Pedals**, Kona Inn Shopping Village, Kailua; ⓣ329-2294. Mountain bikes for $20 per day or $70 per week.

**Hilo Bike Hub**, 318 E Kawili St, Hilo; ⓣ961-4452. Mountain bikes from around $25 per day.

**Kona Coast Cycling Tours**, ⓣ327-1133, ⓦwww.cyclekona.com. Daily guided on-road cycling tours, in north Kohala and south Kona, for $95–145.

**Mauna Kea Mountain Bikes**, C&S Cycle & Surf, Waimea; ⓣ883-0130 or 1-888-682-8687, ⓦwww.bikehawaii.com. Rental from $25 for five hours to $130 per week, plus customized tours, including downhill rides on Mauna Kea for $120.

# Arrival and information

**Keāhole Airport**, the Big Island's laid-back main airport, sprawls across the lava seven miles north of Kailua. Most arriving passengers rent a car immediately from the usual outlets – (detailed on p.25) or arrange to be picked up by their hotels. **Taxis** from the airport rank cost around $20 to Kailua, $40 to Waikoloa; multi-passenger shuttle vans – run by companies such as Speedi Shuttle (ⓣ329-5433), which has a courtesy phone in the baggage area – charge slightly less.

**Public transport** in Kailua town itself is restricted to two shuttle services that run hourly loops along the five-mile length of Ali'i Drive. The Ali'i Shuttle (daily 8.30am–7.30pm; $2 one-way, $5 per day; ⓣ775-7121) is based at the Lanihau Center, while the Kona Town Trolley (daily 8.45am–8.45pm; $5 per day; ⓣ331-1582) starts from the *King Kamehameha* hotel. The latter company also runs the Kona Town Express, which operates ten daily loops between the *King Kamehameha* and the King's Shops up in Waikoloa (daily 8am–9.30pm; $5 one-way). Their $15 one-day system-wide pass includes connecting buses that run north from Waikoloa up the Kohala coast.

Finally, on Monday through Saturday, a daily bus run by the Hilo-based Hele On Bus Company (ⓣ961-8744) follows the Belt Road all the way to Hilo; for a full timetable see p.205.

## Information and services

The **Hawaii Visitors Bureau** (ⓣ329-7787, ⓦwww.bigisland.org) no longer maintains a full-service office in Kailua, but they do have an information booth on the pier, open unpredictable hours. In any case, most of the brochures available at the booth can also be picked up at any of the abundant **"activities desks"** in the seafront malls and hotels, whose primary function is to book tourists onto snorkel cruises, helicopter rides, and the like. One recommended example is the Activity Connection, based in Bougainvillea Plaza just up from the *Kona Seaside* hotel (ⓣ329-1038, ⓦwww.beachactivityguide.com). Free glossies such as *This Week* and *Big Island Gold* are available all over town.

There are **post offices** in the Lanihau Center in downtown Kailua and in the

Keauhou Shopping Village, five miles south at the far end of Ali'i Drive. If you need **money**, the branches of the Bank of Hawaii, First Hawaiian Bank, and American Savings Bank in the Lanihau Center hold virtually every ATM under the sun.

Snorkel Bob has an outlet of his inimitable **snorkeling equipment** rental service (daily 8am–5pm; ⓣ329-0770, ⓦsnorkelbob.com) opposite *Huggo's*, near the *Royal Kona Resort*.

## Accommodation

Well over half of all the Big Island's **hotel** and **condo** rooms are concentrated in or near Kailua, the vast majority of them along the roughly five-mile oceanfront stretch of Ali'i Drive. However, in terms of quality, the area is falling way behind the resorts to the north. A steady decline in investment has seen standards drop alarmingly, and certain well-known properties, such as the *Kona Surf Resort*, have closed down altogether. That said, there are still some attractive and good-value places to be found, and if you prefer to spend your vacation in a real town rather than a self-contained resort, Kailua is still the best option on the island.

Ali'i Drive also holds a handful of **B&Bs**, though visitors in search of a traditional B&B experience tend to prefer to drive the three miles up from the ocean to the idyllic seclusion of the "coffee town" of **Hōlualoa**. B&Bs there, along with a wide range of inexpensive, small-scale alternatives to Kailua's hotels, are listed under "South Kona Accommodation" on p.175.

If you plan to spend your entire vacation in Kailua, remember that you can get far better rates by booking an all-inclusive package before you leave home.

**Aston Keauhou Beach Resort**, 78-6740 Ali'i Drive, Kailua-Kona HI 96740; ⓣ322-3441 or 1-877/532-8468, or through Aston 1-800/922-7866 (US & Can), 1-800/321-2558 (HI); ⓕ322-6586, ⓦwww.aston-hotels.com. Seven-story hotel jutting into the sea on a black-lava promontory at the southern end of Kahalu'u Beach Park, five miles south of central Kailua. All rooms have been renovated to a high standard of comfort. Facilities include tennis courts and a pool; trails around the grounds lead past ruined temples and petroglyphs, as well as the site of the twice-weekly lū'au (Sun & Thurs 5.30pm; $68. The open-air Verandah Bar is a good spot for an evening drink and live Hawaiian music. Garden view ❺, ocean view ❻.

**Aston Royal Sea Cliff Resort**, 75-6040 Ali'i Drive, Kailua-Kona HI 96740; ⓣ329-8021, or through Aston 1-800/922-7866 (US & Can), 1-800/321-2558 (HI), ⓕ326-1887, ⓦwww.aston-hotels.com. White multilevel complex of luxurious one- and two-bedroom condos, dropping down to the coast a mile south of central Kailua, and laid out around a lush courtyard garden to maximize ocean views. You can't swim in the sea here, but it has fresh- and saltwater pools, plus a sauna and Jacuzzi. Garden view ❺, ocean view ❻.

**Kailua Plantation House**, 75-5948 Ali'i Drive, Kailua-Kona HI 96740; ⓣ329-3727, ⓕ326-7323, ⓦwww.tales.com/KPH. Dramatic oceanfront mansion, a mile south of central Kailua, now run as an upmarket B&B. All five luxury suites have their own spacious *lānais*, and they share use of a pool, Jacuzzi and living area. ❺–❻.

**King Kamehameha's Kona Beach Hotel**, 75-5660 Palani Rd, Kailua-Kona HI 96740; ⓣ329-2911, 1-800/367-6060, ⓕ329-4602, ⓦwww.konabeachhotel.com. Long-established family-oriented hotel, centered around picturesque Kamakahonu Beach (see p.163), with a pool, a small shopping mall and an unexceptional restaurant. Kayaks, pedaloes and other watersports equipment are available for rent. The lobby hosts Hawaiian music performances and crafts displays, while the gardens make an attractive *lū'au* setting (Tues–Fri & Sun 5.30–8.45pm; $55). Standard ❹, oceanfront ❺.

**Kona Billfisher**, 75-5841 Ali'i Drive, Kailua-Kona HI 96740; ⓣ329-3333 or 1-800/622-5348 (US & Can), ⓕ326-4137, ⓦwww.konahawaii.com. Well-maintained, good-value condos in a complex of coffee-colored three-story units that sprawls up the hillside across from the *Royal Kona Resort*, a short walk south of central Kailua. Each unit has a kitchen and balcony. ❸.

**Kona Islander Inn Resort**, 75-5776 Kuakini Hwy, Kailua-Kona HI 96740; ⓣ329-3333 or 1-800/622-5348, ⓕ326-4137, ⓦwww.konahawaii.com. These centrally located 1960s condos, just behind the

Coconut Grove Marketplace, may not seem the height of style from the outside, but they're perfectly adequate and offer some of the coast's best rates. Prices rise significantly from mid December through March. The front desk is also a reservations office for several other local condo resorts. ❷.

**Kona Reef**, 75-5888 Ali'i Drive, Kailua-Kona HI 96740; ⓣ 329-2959 or through Castle Resorts 1-800/367-5004 (US & Can) or 1-880/272-5275 (HI), ⓕ 329-2762, ⓦ www.castle-group.com. Attractive modern condo development, on the southern edge of Kailua, with several levels of very comfortable, blue-roofed, one-, two- and three-bed units dropping down to the ocean. No on-site beach, but a good pool. ❺.

**Kona Seaside Hotel**, 75-5646 Palani Rd, Kailua-Kona HI 96740; ⓣ 329-2455 or 1-800/560-5558, reservations 922-1228, ⓕ 922-0052, ⓦ www.sand-seaside.com. The 223-room property sprawls across central Kailua, just up from Ali'i Drive. Several three-story wings of small, good-value air-con rooms cluster around a central pool, while a newer six-floor building overlooks another, smaller, pool. Reservations for this Hawaiian-owned chain are handled in Honolulu. ❹.

**Kona Tiki Hotel**, 75-5968 Ali'i Drive, Kailua-Kona HI 96740; ⓣ 329-1425, ⓕ 327-9402. This three-story, motel-style property, inches from the ocean a mile from central Kailua, is an absolute gem for budget travelers. The winter season is often completely booked up three years in advance. All rooms have private oceanfront balconies, some also have kitchenettes, and rates even include breakfast beside the tiny pool. No TVs, phones or credit cards; three-night minimum stay. ❷.

**Patey's Place**, 75-195 Ala-Ona Ona St, Kailua-Kona HI 96740; ⓣ 326-7018, ⓕ 326-7640, ⓔ ipatey@gte.net, ⓦ www.hawaiian-hostels.com. Chaotic, ramshackle and unappealing hostel that's nonetheless popular with backpackers and surfers. It's a few hundred yards *mauka* of the town center, reached by taking Kalani Street up from Kuakini Highway at *McDonald's*, and then the second turning on the left. Minimally furnished, thin-walled doubles for $41.50, or four-bed dorms for $17.50 a bed, plus a communal kitchen and TV room, but no restaurant. As well as the odd $5 barbecue, it offers a $10 airport shuttle service, bikes at $15 per day, and its own cheap island tours. It can also arrange discounts on car rental and air fares. ❶–❷.

**Royal Kona Resort**, 75-5852 Ali'i Drive, Kailua-Kona HI 96740; ⓣ 329-3111, 1-800/919-8333 (US & Can), ⓕ 329-7230, ⓦ www.royalkona.com. The gleaming white pyramids of the *Royal Kona Resort* (originally the *Kona Hilton*), where almost all of the 452 rooms have their own *lānais*, dominate the headland at the southern end of central Kailua. The standard rooms are nothing special, but ones in the more expensive categories are very nice. Its main restaurant, *Tropics Café*, has beautiful views and serves good-value buffets of above-average Asian and Pacific food, while the "Drums of Polynesia" *lū'au* (Mon, Fri & Sat 5.30pm; $55), open to nonresidents, is one of the best in town. Garden view ❹, ocean view ❺.

**Uncle Billy's Kona Bay Hotel**, 75-5739 Ali'i Drive, Kailua-Kona HI 96740; ⓣ 329-6488, 1-800/367-5102 (US & Can), 1-800/442-5841 (HI), ⓕ 935-7903, ⓦ www.unclebilly.com. Friendly central hotel, run by the same family as the *Hilo Bay* (see p.207). Far from fancy, occasionally noisy, but reasonably comfortable rooms, all with air-con and private bath, are arranged in a crescent around a small pool and *Kimo's* restaurant (see p.165). ❸.

# The Town

Central Kailua still retains something of the feel of a seaside village. Every visitor should set aside an hour or two to take a leisurely oceanfront stroll along the old Seawall, whose scenic route runs for a few hundred yards around the bay from the **Ahu'ena Heiau**, jutting into the ocean in front of the *King Kamehameha* hotel, to the **Hulihe'e Palace** and **Moku'aikaua Church**.

At its heart is the jetty of **Kailua Pier**, a small expanse of asphalt popular with anglers, courting couples and surf-bums alike. Until as recently as the 1960s there were still cattle pens here, but these days most commercial boats leave from the marina at Honokōhau Harbor, three miles north (see p.173), and the mood tends to be slightly aimless. At least the time-honored tradition of fishermen displaying their catches in the early evening persists, with the biggest fish of all weighing in during August's International Billfish Tournament. More gleaming flesh is on show in mid-October each year, when the pier is the starting-point of the 2.4-mile swimming leg of the **Ironman Triathlon**, which also requires its participants to cycle 112 miles and run a marathon on the same day.

The resort area stretches away to the south, while up from the seafront ever-increasing numbers of **shopping malls** seem to appear each year, catering more to the needs of local residents, and less to those of tourists, the higher you climb from the shoreline. For everyday shopping and services, locals tend to head for Costco or Kmart, on the northeastern edge of town, or the **Lanihau Center** near the main stoplights on the highway.



## Ahu'ena Heiau

The **Ahu'ena Heiau** guards the mouth of Kailua Bay in a too-good-to-be-true setting beside a sandy little beach, in front of the *King Kamehameha* hotel. Kamehameha the Great held sway from this ancient temple, dedicated to Lono, between his return from Honolulu in 1812 and his death here on May 8, 1819. Soon afterwards, his son Liholiho, spurred on by Kamehameha's principal queen, Ka'ahumanu, broke the ancient *kapu* system by hosting a banquet here, and thereby inadvertently cleared the way for the missionaries.

Thanks to detailed drawings made in 1816, archeologists have been able to restore the *heiau* to its original appearance, but it still possesses great spiritual significance, and all access to the platform is forbidden. You can get a close-up view by walking to the end of the King Kamehameha beach – officially Kamakahonu Beach (see p.163) – or by swimming out a short way. The *heiau* itself is small, but follows the conventional Hawaiian template, consisting as it does of three distinct structures set on a *paepae* (platform) of black volcanic rock. The largest hut is the *hale mana* ("house of spiritual power") a place of prayer and council. The smaller *hale pahu* ("house of the drum") alongside is thatched with *hala* leaves, while the ramshackle, tapering structure nearby is the *anu'u*, or "oracle tower," used by the priests to intercede with the gods. In addition, half a dozen *ki'i akua*, carved wooden images symbolizing different gods, stand on the platform; the tallest, a god of healing known as Kōleamoku, has a golden plover on his head.

After his death, Kamehameha's bones were prepared for burial on a similar rock platform adjacent to the *heiau*, then interred in a location that remains a secret to this day. The platform still exists, though the *hale pōhaku* that stood upon it, in which the ceremonies took place, has long since disappeared.

## Hulihe'e Palace

Though the four-square, two-story **Hulihe'e Palace** (Mon–Fri 9am–4pm, Sat & Sun 10am–4pm; $5; ⓣ 329-1877), facing out to sea from the center of Kailua, was built in 1838 for Governor John Adams Kuakini, it soon passed into the hands of the Hawaiian royal family. It was constructed using lava rock, coral and native hardwoods, but you wouldn't know that from a glance at its coffee-colored modern exterior. Visiting this mildly quaint Victorian private residence is not very enthralling, nor is its limited charm enhanced by the ponderous reverence of the staff. The interior is notable mainly for its massive *koa*-wood furnishings, made to fit the considerable girth of such dignitaries as the four-hundred-pound Princess Ruth, and its countless fading photographs of the bewhiskered King David Kalākaua and his stately relatives.

The room immediately to the left of the entrance holds a small but interesting collection of Hawaiiana, including bone fishhooks and stone adzes and hammers. Alongside a small feather cape, King Kalākaua's desk and guitar, and several bowls made from *koa* wood, there's a narrow replica *hōlua* sled, of the kind once raced by the *ali'i* down artificial slides of grass-covered rock. On display in the master bedroom upstairs are a mighty four-poster bed, a beautiful inlaid table and a colossal and highly ornate wardrobe, all fashioned from dark hardwood.

Pleasant *lānais* run the full length of the ocean side of both the first and second floors. Visitors are free to wander into the well-maintained gardens, which play host to free *hula* performances on the fourth Sunday of each month (except June & Dec).

## Moku'aikaua Church

The original **Moku'aikaua Church**, directly opposite the palace, was the first church to be built on the Hawaiian islands. It was constructed in 1820 for the use of Reverend Asa Thurston, one of the first two Christian missionaries despatched to Hawaii from New England (see p.509), who had arrived in Kailua Bay on April 4 that year. At that time it closely resembled a *heiau*, being just a thatched hut perched on a stone platform. The current building was erected immediately before Hulihe'e Palace by the same craftsmen, using the same methods, and incorporates large chunks of lava into a design clearly related to the clapboard churches of New England. Open daily from dawn to dusk, it's free to visitors, and particularly welcomes worshippers to its Congregational services (Sun 8am & 10.30am).

The church itself is not of great interest, though part of it has been set aside as a museum of the early days of Hawaiian Christianity. Displays include a large model of the ship *Thaddeus*, Hawaii's equivalent of the *Mayflower*, and an exhibition on traditional Polynesian navigational techniques featuring, among other things, a fascinating Micronesian "stick chart," in which an intricate latticework of pandanus (*hala*) twigs and cowrie shells depicts ocean currents, swells and islands. Such charts were committed to memory rather than carried on board, and served to guide canoes across thousands of miles of the open Pacific.

A bizarre "sausage tree" grows in the grounds of the church. A native of Mozambique, it is named after the pendulous, elongated and foul-smelling fruit that dangles on long cords from its branches. One of only two on Hawaii, it was planted here on a whim in the 1920s.

## South along Ali'i Drive

Heading south from both the church and palace, **Ali'i Drive** is at first fringed with modern malls housing T-shirt stores, boutiques and restaurants. Beyond Kailua proper, it stretches five miles along a rugged coastline scattered with tiny lava beaches and lined all the way with hotels and condos. The only thing you could call a "sight" along here is the tiny, blue, and highly photogenic **St Peter's Church**, built in 1880. It takes perhaps a minute to admire its waterfront setting, on a tiny patch of lawn at the north end of Kahalu'u Bay, and to glance in through the open door at the etched glass window above the altar.

# Beaches

Considering its reputation as a resort, central Kailua is surprisingly short of **beaches**. There are enough patches of sand along Ali'i Drive to satisfy those who like the convenience of being able to walk to and from their hotels; but most visitors tend to drive north when they fancy a swim. The Big Island's best beaches – such as the Kona Coast State Park (p.179), Hāpuna Beach (p.187), and Spencer Beach Park (p.189) – start ten miles or more up the coast, but a good nearby alternative is the Old Kona Airport park, just a few minutes from town.

**Camping** is not permitted on any of the beaches covered in this section.

## Old Kona Airport State Recreation Area

When Keāhole Airport opened in 1970, the lands of its predecessor on the northern outskirts of Kailua, which had become too small to meet the requirements of the tourist trade, were set aside for public use as the **Old Kona Airport State Recreation Area**. Though it's not all that attractive, it's now Kailua's most extensive and popular beach. Driving in along the long former runways, which run par-

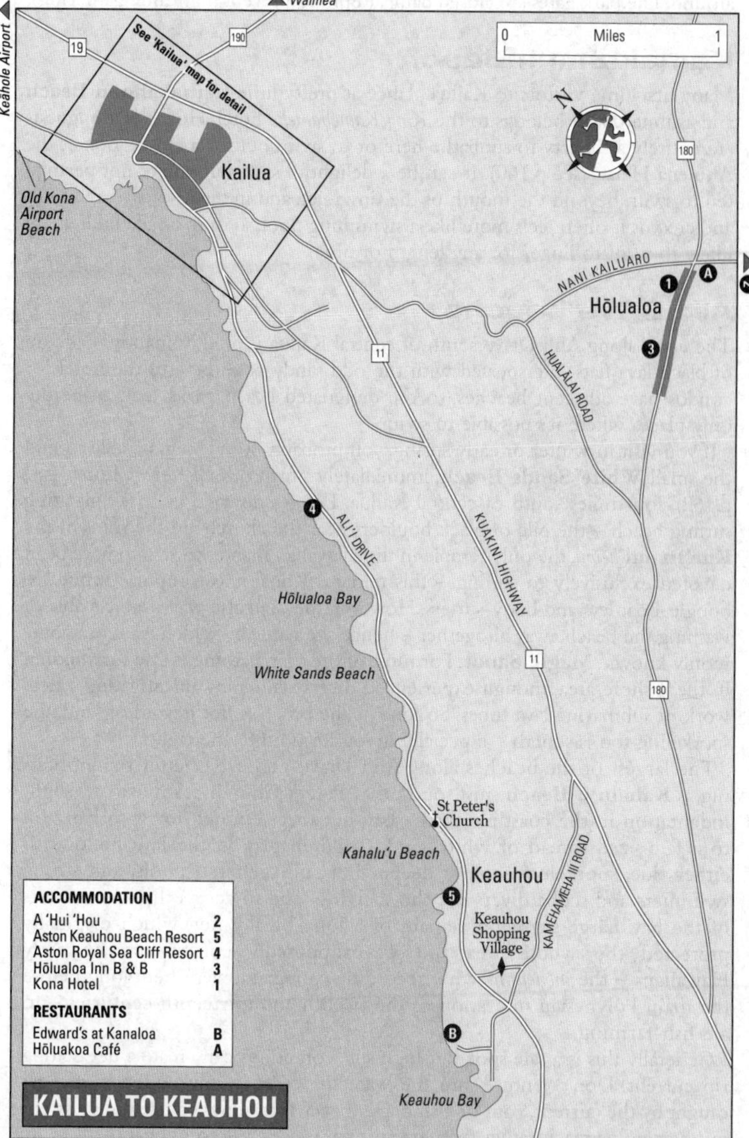

allel to the sea, is either hair-raising or fun depending on your state of mind, as no one ever seems sure which, if any, of the plentiful road markings to follow.

A strip of coarse, whitish sand lies beyond the fringe of low palm trees, while the shoreline itself consists almost entirely of flat, smooth *pāhoehoe* lava, indented with calm shallow pools that are ideal for children to splash in. Sheltered pavilions and barbecue facilities are scattered all the way along, and despite the lack of food and drink outlets, there always seems to be plenty of people around. The park gates are closed daily at 8pm to prevent nighttime gatherings.



## Kamakahonu Beach

Many first-time visitors to Kailua glance at pretty little **Kamakahonu Beach** and assume that it belongs to the *King Kamehameha* hotel. However, nonguests are entirely at liberty to sunbathe here or to swim out for a closer look at the Ahu'ena Heiau (see p.160). It can be a delightful spot, but you're not permitted to swim beyond the mouth of the tiny inlet, and in terms of size, calmness and crowds it often feels more like a swimming pool, so only small children are likely to want to linger for any length of time.

## Ali'i Drive beaches

The coast along Ali'i Drive south of central Kailua is predominantly made up of black lava flats interspersed with the odd sandy cove. Few of the hotels or condos have adjacent beaches, so the designated beach parks tend to be the only places where it's possible to swim.

If you visit in winter or early spring, you probably won't even be able to find the small **White Sands Beach**, immediately north of St Peter's Church (see p.162), four miles south of central Kailua. Long renowned as an exhilarating surfing beach – the pile of black boulders near the church are the ruins of the **Kue'manu** *heiau*, the only temple in the Hawaiian islands known to have been devoted exclusively to surfing – this remains Kona's most popular venue for boogie-boarders and body-surfers. However, the dramatic waves are capable of washing the beach away altogether – hence the name by which it's more commonly known, **Magic Sands**. For most of the year, bathing is safe for children in the inshore area, though experienced divers will enjoy investigating a network of submarine lava tubes. So long as the beach is not devoid of sand, the snorkeling too is superb – especially if you head off to the right.

The largest of the beaches along Ali'i Drive, and even better for snorkeling, is **Kahalu'u Beach**, just south of St Peter's Church. It's more of a slight indentation in the coastline than a bay, but that's enough for it to hang on to a fair-sized spread of white sand. Children play in the lava hollows to either side, snorkelers explore deeper but still sheltered pools, and strong swimmers and scuba divers use the shelving sand to access the open waters of the bay. Large segments remain of a long breakwater, which originally protected the whole area and was supposedly constructed by early Hawaiians – the *menehune* who, according to legend, were here long before the main Polynesian migration of the twelfth and thirteenth centuries – to aid fish-farming.

Generally this is a safe spot, but high surf conditions can create a devastating rip current. Don't venture into the water if you're in any doubt; if you get caught by the current, your best strategy, as ever, is to allow yourself to be swept out beyond its reach rather than exhaust yourself trying to fight it.

# Restaurants

Though Kailua is filled with **places to eat**, it's surprisingly short of anything that could be considered fine dining. Each of its many malls has at least a couple of restaurants, while those that stand more than a block or so up from the ocean, such as the Lanihau Center, also house outlets of every imaginable fast-food chain. Asian cuisines, especially Thai, are strongly represented, and there are plenty of raucous, heavy-drinking, pseudo-Mexican options.

Most of the restaurants along Ali'i Drive tend to be pricier, but offer views of the bay and serve slightly better-quality food. Even along the waterfront, however, there are still some determinedly old-fashioned, inexpensive diners.

## Inexpensive

**Kimo's Buffet Restaurant**, *Kona Bay Hotel*, 75-5739 Ali'i Drive; ⓣ329-1393. The palm-fringed and vaguely Polynesian open-air terrace beside the hotel pool hosts plain but good value all-you-can-eat buffets, costing $7 Mon–Fri, $8 Sat & Sun for breakfast and $11 or $12 for dinner. Daily 7–10am & 5.30–9pm.

**King Yee Lau**, Ali'i Sunset Plaza, 75-5799 Ali'i Drive; ⓣ329-7100. Large Chinese restaurant at the rear of a modern plaza. Most entrees (such as lemon chicken, beef in oyster sauce, and mussels in black bean sauce) cost around $8. You can also get fresh lobster and crab, and budget lunch buffets. Mon–Sat 11am–2pm & 5–9pm, Sun 5–9pm.

**Kona Brewing Co**, North Kona Shopping Center, 75-5744 Ali'i Drive; ⓣ329-2739. Large brewpub in an unexciting mall behind the *King Kamehameha*, with lots of indoor and outdoor seating but no views. As well as home-brewed beers like Longboard Lager and even a Kona Coffee Stout, they sell inventive salads and sandwiches in both half and full sizes for $5–10, and inexpensive pizzas made to your specifications. Food service stops an hour before closing time. Mon–Thurs 11am–10pm, Fri & Sat 11am–11pm, Sun 4–10pm.

**Ocean Seafood**, King Kamehameha Mall, 75-5626 Kuakini Hwy; ⓣ329-3055. Indoor Chinese dining in a small mall, one block back from the sea, behind the *King Kamehameha*. There are no views, and the food is served at plain glass-topped tables, but it's tasty and inexpensive: weekday plate lunches such as ribs or barbecue pork cost $6.50, while set dinners start around $12, with sizzling platters for a little less. Lots of shrimp and scallop entrees, plus a small vegetarian selection. Mon–Fri 10.30am–9pm, Sat & Sun 11am–9pm.

**Ocean View Inn**, 75-5683 Ali'i Drive; ⓣ329-9998. Old-style Hawaiian diner, facing the jetty near Hulihe'e Palace, with drab fittings but magnificent views. Crowds flock for $8–11 dinner plates such as roast pork or roast beef, plus breakfasts and lunches, good-value sandwiches and all-day cocktails; there's also a large and even cheaper Chinese menu. Tues–Sun 6.30am–2.45pm & 5.15–9pm.

**Sibu Café**, Banyan Court Mall, 75-5695 W Ali'i Drive; ⓣ329-1112. Popular, informal Indonesian restaurant, with no views but some atmospheric outdoor seating. Tasty $11–14 entrees include a great shrimp *sate*, cooked in coconut milk. Daily 11.30am–3pm & 5–9pm.

**Stan's Restaurant**, 75-5685 Ali'i Drive; ⓣ329-4500. Open-sided dining area, facing the sea in the center of Kailua's most attractive stretch. Full breakfasts, including $6 Royal Hawaiian Hotcakes with banana, pineapple, papaya and coconut syrup, as well as an extensive dinner menu featuring "Granny's 50-Year Fish Recipe" for $8.50, and stuffed *mahimahi* at $11. Daily 7–9.30am & 6–8pm.

## Moderate

**Bangkok Houses**, King Kamehameha Mall, 75-5626 Kuakini Hwy; ⓣ329-7764. Light, airy Thai restaurant where lunch features $5.50 specials, plus slightly pricier fish and meat salads. The dinner menu includes an $8 appetizer of New Zealand mussels, and plenty of Thai curries, among them a delicious mixed seafood curry for $15. Mon–Sat 11am–9pm, Sun 5–9pm.

**Basil's Pizzeria**, 75-5707 Ali'i Drive; ⓣ326-7836. Unadventurous Italian eatery, immediately north of Moku'aikaua Church. Seated near the door you can enjoy sea views; further back there's little to do but get stuck into either the individual pizzas for $6–11, a variety of pasta entrees, or tasty Italian daily specials. Daily 11am–10pm.

**Cassandra's Greek Taverna**, Kona Plaza, 75-5719 Ali'i Drive; ⓣ334-1066. Friendly European taverna that's a very welcome addition to Kailua's dining scene. There's plenty of outdoor seating, but no views. At lunchtime a Greek salad costs $8, while in the evening appetizers such as *taramasalata* or *dolmades* run to $5–8, a substantial *moussaka* is $15, and sensational *uvetsi* dishes, of shrimps or scallops baked with feta cheese, are $19. Mon–Fri 11.30am–10pm, Sat & Sun 4.30–10pm.

**Kona Amigos**, 75-5669 Ali'i Drive; ⓣ326-2840. Mexican restaurant-cum-bar that sprawls along a large open-air deck across from the *King Kamehameha*. A vast list of cocktails, plus the usual array of enchiladas, burritos and fajitas priced at around $11–15 for a full meal. Daily 11am–10pm.

**Kona Inn Restaurant**, Kona Inn Shopping Village, 75-5744 Ali'i Drive; ⓣ329-4455. Conventional waterfront fish place. The *Café Grill*, on an open-air *lānai* by the sea, sells bar snacks, salads and sandwiches; there's a plusher and more formal dining room inside. Clam chowder and sashimi feature among the dinner appetizers, while entrees – mostly seafood, but including steaks – cost around $20. *Café Grill* daily 11.30am–10pm, dinner daily 5.30–9.30pm.

**Kona Petroleum Grill**, 75-5725 Ali'i Drive; ⓣ326-1311. Diner with a very central location, spread across a second-floor terrace opposite the *Kona Inn*, and filled with 1950s antiques – gas pumps, vintage signs and the like – to create a fun road-food theme. Lunchtime burgers and sandwiches for up to $10, with $1 draft beer and free pool tables, and rib and steak dinners for just under $20. Sun–Thurs 11.30am–10pm, Fri & Sat 11.30am–11pm.

**Thai Rin**, Ali'i Sunset Plaza, 75-5799 Ali'i Drive; ⓣ329-2929. Smart, somewhat minimalist Thai restaurant, facing the sea in front of a modern mall, south of central Kailua towards *Huggo's*. Weekday lunch specials go for $7–8; for dinner, try *satay* or *poocha* (crab and pork patties) to start, for $7–8, followed by either *tom yum* soup or one of the many Thai curries ($9–12). Mon–Fri & Sun 11am–2.30pm & 5–9pm, Sat 5–9pm.

### Expensive

**Edward's at Kanaloa**, Kanaloa at Kona, 78-261 Manukai St; ⓣ322-1003. Hard to find but attractive and romantic restaurant, squeezed between the ocean and the pool in a luxury condo complex at the (very) quiet southern end of Keauhou. The menu is hard to categorize but generally Mediterranean, with a tendency toward rich sauces. Appetizers such as escargots, stuffed mussels and the shrimp with couscous are either side of $10, while entrees, including fresh fish cooked to your specifications and rack of lamb, hover around $25. By Kailua standards it's very good, if not quite up to the level of the Kohala resorts. Daily 8am–2pm & 5–9pm.

**Huggo's**, 75-5828 Kahakai St; ⓣ329-1493. Large wooden oceanfront *lānai*, where lunch includes salads, burgers and sandwiches, for $8–14. The dinner menu features a range of Pacific Rim cuisines, including fish stuffed with prawns, grilled lamb chops, and island-raised lobster, typically priced at $25–35. Prices owe as much to the location as to the food, so come while there's light to enjoy the views. There's often live evening entertainment, usually a local easy-listening band. Mon–Fri 11.30am–2.30pm & 5.30–10pm, bar open until 12.30am; Sat & Sun 5.30–10pm.

**Kona Beach Restaurant**, *King Kamehameha's Kona Beach Hotel*, 75-5660 Palani Rd; ⓣ329-2911. Completely enclosed, not very atmospheric dining room, with a $10 breakfast buffet every morning. Most full dinners, such as steaks or prime rib, cost around $15, though there's a $25 seafood and rib buffet on Friday and Saturday nights, and a $14 Hawaiian one on Monday nights. Sunday's $26 champagne brunch buffet, served 9am–1pm, is the best meal of the week. Mon–Sat 6–10.30am & 5.30–9pm, Sun 6am–1pm & 5.30–9pm.

**Oodles of Noodles**, Crossroads Shopping Center, 75-1027 Henry St; ⓣ329-2222. Extremely successful gourmet noodle joint, making the most of its dull mall setting adjoining Safeway, just off Hwy-19 a mile up from the ocean. The food is excellent, combining both Asian and Italian flavors; fettucine dishes range

## Big Island Lū'aus

There are currently seven regular *lu'aus* on the Big Island, all based at major Kona-side hotels. The *Kona Village Resort*'s *lu'au* wins hands down for atmosphere, due in part to its remote location.

**Drums of Polynesia**, *Royal Kona Resort* ⓣ329-3111; Mon, Fri & Sat 5.30pm; $55.

**Island Breeze**, *King Kamehameha's Kona Beach Hotel* ⓣ326-4969; Tues–Fri & Sun 5.30pm; $55.

**Kona Village Lu'au**, *Kona Village Resort* ⓣ325-5555; Fri 5pm; $72.

**Legends of the Pacific**, *Hilton Waikoloa Village* ⓣ885-1234; Fri 5.30pm; $55.

**Mauna Kea Lu'au**, *Mauna Kea Beach Hotel* ⓣ882-7222; Tues 6pm; $70.

**Royal Lu'au**, *Outrigger Waikoloa Beach* ⓣ886-6789; Wed & Sun 6pm; $64.

**Traditions at Kahalu'u**, *Aston Keauhou Beach Resort* ⓣ322-3441; Thurs & Sun 5.30pm; $68.

## Shopping

Generally speaking there's little difference among Kailua's various malls, though as a rule those closer to the sea tend to be more firmly geared towards tourists, with the predictable array of T-shirts, sun hats, postcards and sundry souvenirs on sale, and the odd ABC convenience store thrown in. For everyday shopping and services, locals tend to head for Costco or Kmart, on the northeastern edge of town, or the **Lanihau Center** near the main stoplights on the highway. The **Crossroads Center**, well above town on the main Kuakini Highway, boasts a large Borders bookstore and an even bigger Safeway.

The two-part **Kona Marketplace**, near Moku'aikaua church, immediately south, has a two-screen movie theater, plus assorted galleries, trinket shops, and jewelry stores, while **Kona Plaza**, hidden behind the northern section of the Marketplace, is home to the Middle Earth Bookshoppe, with its copious selection of Hawaiiana. The largest and most tourist-oriented seafront mall, the **Kona Inn Shopping Village** across Ali'i Drive, holds several clothing stores such as the excellent Hula Heaven.

Perched above the sea at the far southern end of Ali'i Drive, the modern **Keauhou Shopping Village** centers on KTA and Longs Drug superstores. It also houses a post office, a *Bad Ass* coffee bar, and a few unexciting fast-food places.

$10–15, while the wok-seared *ahi* (tuna) casserole costs $16. The lunch menu is shorter, with prices $2–4 cheaper. Mon–Fri 11.30am–9pm,Sat & Sun noon–9pm.

**Sam Choy's**, Kaloko Light Industrial Park, 73-5576 Kauhola St; ⓣ326-1545. Living proof that if your restaurant is good enough, decor and even location don't matter. Celebrity Hawaiian chef Sam Choy's original outlet is tucked away amid a maze of warehouses *mauka* of Hwy-19, three miles north of Kailua, and has basic canteen furnishings, but the crowds still flock for his extra-large portions of local favorites. Lunch is a ludicrously good value, with steak, *poke* or noodles for well under $10, while dinner entrees that rival the finest Pacific Rim cuisine cost up to $30. Mon 6am–2pm, Tues–Sat 6am–2pm & 5–9pm, Sun 7am–2pm.

# South Kona

South of Kailua and Keauhou, the Belt Road, as **Hwy-11**, sets off on its loop around the island by rising away from the sea to run through attractive verdant uplands. Trees laden with avocados, mangos, oranges and guavas stand out from the general greenery, and the route is characterized by the blossom of coffee bushes and the occasional aroma of the mills.

**Kealakekua Bay**, along the south Kona coast, is where Captain Cook chose to anchor, as it was then both the best harbor and the main population center on the island. Within a century, however, the seafront slopes were largely abandoned, and these days even the area higher up is inhabited only by a sparse scattering of old-time farmers and New Age newcomers. Most tourists scurry through, put off perhaps by the lack of beaches and the ramshackle look of the small towns that sprawl along the highway. However, many of these hold one or two welcoming local cafés or intriguing stores, and it's certainly worth dropping down to visit the restored **Pu'uhonua O Hōnaunau**, or "Place of Refuge."

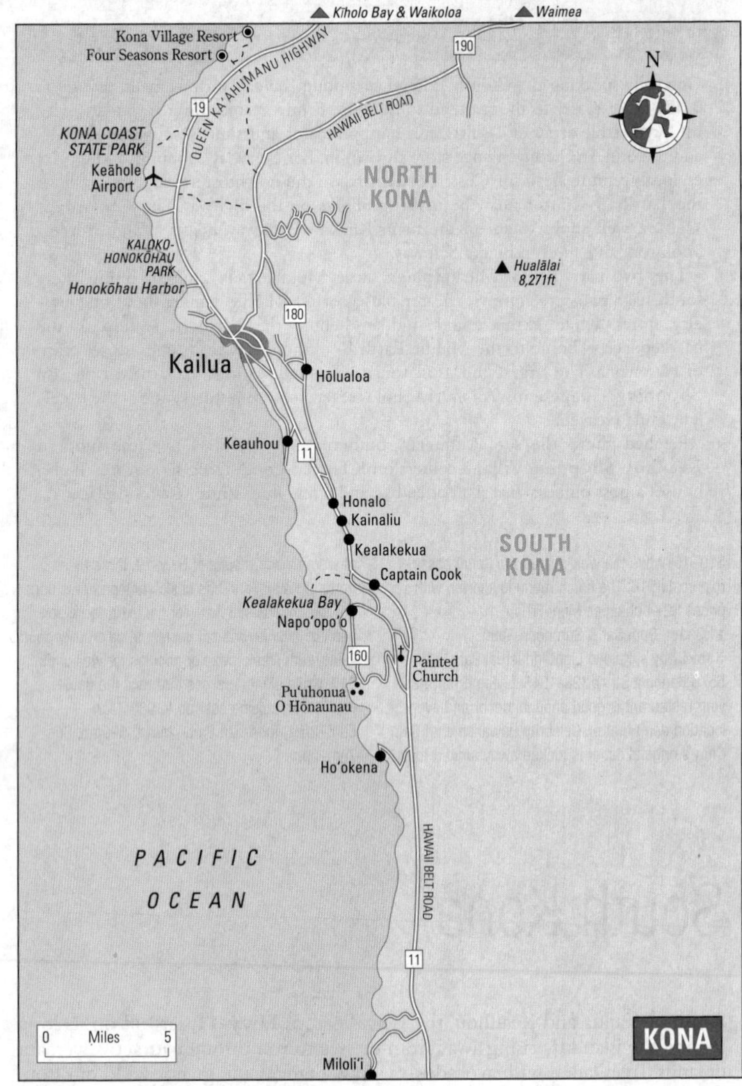




# Hōlualoa

**HŌLUALOA**, the first and nicest of the coffee-growing towns, stands well above the Belt Road, scarcely three miles out of Kailua, and feels a long way removed from the hurly-burly below. This sleepy village consists of a single quiet road (Hwy-180) that meanders across the flanks of Hualālai, 1400 feet up from the ocean, and is lined on either side with small galleries and workshops, as well as orchards brimming with tropical blooms.

The production of **art** in Hōlualoa remains essentially a cottage industry, though more galleries open each year and several now also display pieces by mainland artists. Prices are seldom low, but half a day can enjoyably be spent admiring the paintings and ceramics of the Hōlualoa Gallery, the fine art and sculpture in Studio Seven, and the general creative free-for-all that is the Coffee Mill Workshop, also known as the Kona Arts Center. Most galleries and workshops are closed on Saturday afternoons and Sundays; some take Mondays off as well.

The friendly German-owned *Hōluakoa Café* (Mon–Sat 6.30am–3pm; ⓣ322-2233), at the top end of the village, serves **coffees and snacks** in a pleasant garden. On Thursday evenings it also opens from 7pm until 10pm for live music. **B&Bs** in Hōlualoa are reviewed on p.176.

# Along Hwy-11: the coffee towns

In theory there are four separate towns within the first four miles south of the junction of Hwy-180 and Hwy-11, though where one ends and the next begins is far from obvious. Any points of interest can be easily spotted as you drive through, be they wayside coffee stalls, antiquated general stores, local diners or simply junkyards.

If you want to sample the atmosphere, the best stop comes just south of tiny Honalo, in the shape of **KAINALIU**'s friendly *Aloha Café* (Sun–Wed 8am–3pm, Thurs–Sat 8am–3pm & 5–9pm; ⓣ322-3383). Housed in the lobby of the 1930s Aloha Theater – still an active community theater, with performances by local

## Kona Coffee

Succulent, strong-smelling **Kona coffee** has been grown on the Kona coast since the first seedlings arrived from Brazil in 1828. Strictly speaking, the Kona name only applies to beans grown between 800ft and 2000ft up the western slopes of Hualālai and Mauna Loa. This narrow strip, extending from Hōlualoa to Hōnaunau, offers perfect greenhouse conditions: bright sunny mornings, humid rainy afternoons, and consistently mild nights.

Though Kona boasts an enviable reputation, and demand always outstrips supply, large corporations tend to leave the labor-intensive processes of planting and tending the coffee bushes and harvesting the ripe red "cherry" from the tangled branches to small-scale family concerns. Only 1300 acres are now under cultivation in Kona, although the predominantly Japanese farmers have been joined by an influx of back-to-the-land *haoles*.

Independent farmers have long campaigned to restrict the label "Kona" to coffee consisting of one hundred percent pure Kona beans. Hawaiian state law, which allows any coffee containing at least ten percent Kona-grown beans to be sold as Kona coffee, has had the unfortunate effect of encouraging Californian bulk buyers to use a smattering of Kona beans to improve lesser coffees and then to sell them at inflated prices. In a locally notorious case, the Berkeley-based owner of the Kona Kai brand was recently convicted of a multimillion dollar fraud that involved passing off Costa Rican coffee as true Kona.

Coffee **prices** in the area range from around $15 per pound for the lowest ("prime") grade up to as much as $30 for a pound of the gourmets' favorite, Peaberry, while roadside outlets serve fresh Kona coffee in whatever form may take your fancy. Visitors are welcome at working coffee farms such as the **Bay View Farm**, half a mile north of the Painted Church (daily 9am–5pm; free; ⓣ328-9658), and **Greenwell Farms**, just off the highway in Kealekekua (Mon–Sat 8am–4pm; free; ⓣ323-2862). In addition, the **Kona Historical Society** offers regular tours of the old Uchida coffee farm, restored to illustrate agricultural life during the 1920s and 1930s (Tues & Thurs 8.30am & 11am, Fri 10am; $30; ⓣ323-2006, ⓦwww.konahistorical.org).

groups and visiting musicians, and occasional movie shows – this all-day town forum serves coffees, snacks, pastries and a limited dinner menu.

To the south of Kainaliu, set back from the highway in a former general store in **KEALAKEKUA**, is the **Kona Historical Society Museum** (Mon–Fri 9am–3pm; $2; ⓣ323-3222). This low-key assortment of photographs and heirlooms documents Kona's history from the perspective of its immigrant farmers and also offers tours of a restored old coffee farm nearby (see p.169). A little further on, across from the *Pineapple Park* **hostel** (see p.176), *Billy Bob's Restaurant* (Mon–Fri 11am–2.30pm & 5–9pm, Sat & Sun 5–9pm; ⓣ323-3371) is a cheap and cheerful barbecue joint, which has sadly changed its name from the more colorful *Billy Bob's Park'n'Pork*. Also in Kealakekua, you can stop for an espresso and sandwich at the *Kona Mountain Cafe* (Mon–Sat 6.30am–6pm, Sun 8am–1pm; ⓣ323-2700), which may look unimpressive from the front but has a terrace with a panoramic view around the back.

Immediately beyond Kealekekua, a minor road branches off the highway to lead down to Nāpo'opo'o Beach (see p.172), at the southern end of Kealakekua Bay. Stay on the main road, however, and you soon find yourself in the small community of **CAPTAIN COOK**, which is most noteworthy as the site of the venerable *Manago* hotel and restaurant, reviewed on p.176.

South of Captain Cook's minimal "downtown," *makai* of the highway near mile marker 108, the *Coffee Shack* (daily 7am–3.30pm; ⓣ328-9555) is the quintessential South Kona café, serving wonderfully fresh coffee on a terrace perched above gorgeous gardens and enjoying staggering views all the way down to Kealakekua Bay. Their smoothies are sensational too, as are the colossal $7–9 sandwiches made with fresh-baked breads.

## Kealakekua Bay

**KEALAKEKUA BAY** may be familiar because of Captain Cook's fatal encounter with the rulers of old Hawaii – as well as the *Little Grass Shack* of the song – but it's a surprisingly inaccessible spot. Very few visitors make it as far as the actual site of Cook's death, on the north shore of the bay, and most of those who see the obelisk to the navigator's memory do so from the south side, across a mile of shark-infested sea. **Nāpo'opo'o Beach** is the only point that can be reached by car; to see the bay otherwise, you either have to undertake a strenuous hike or come by boat.

The name Kealakekua, which means "pathway of the god," refers to the five-hundred-foot cliff that backs the sheltered crescent bay. It was said that this *pali*, which slopes down from north to south, was used as a slide by the god Lono when he needed to leave his mountain home in a hurry. When Cook was here, around 80,000 Hawaiians are thought to have lived on the coastal lava plain that extends to the north and south. Though the mummified bodies of their

### Kealakekua on Horseback

Four-wheel-drive vehicles are out of the question on the narrow track down to Kealakekua Bay, and the only alternative to walking is to go on **horseback**. Individual or group trips can be arranged, with advance notice, through King's Trail Rides O Kona, based at mile marker 111 in Kealakekua (PO Box 1366, Kealakekua HI 96750; ⓣ323-2388, ⓦwww.konacowboy.com). The cost for the enjoyable half-day round-trip is around $95 per person.

## The Death of Captain Cook

When **Captain James Cook** sailed into Kealakekua Bay on January 17, 1779, he was on his second visit to the Hawaiian islands, on his way home after a year spent searching in vain for the fabled Northwest Passage. His ship, the *Resolution*, had circled the Big Island for seven weeks, trading with canoes that came alongside but not allowing anyone ashore. Finally Cook anchored in this sheltered bay, where a vast crowd of Hawaiians had gathered to greet him. For three weeks, he was feasted by Chief Kalaniopu'u and his priests, attending temple ceremonies and replenishing his supplies.

The departure of the *Resolution*, amid declarations of friendship, might have been the end of things, had it not been forced to return just a week later, following a violent storm. This time the islanders were not so hospitable, and far from keen to part with further scarce resources. On February 14, Cook led a landing party of nine men in a bid to kidnap Kalaniopu'u and force the islanders to return a stolen small boat. In an undignified scuffle, surrounded by thousands of warriors, including the future Kamehameha the Great, Cook was **stabbed** and died at the water's edge. His body was treated as befits a dead chief: the skull and leg bones were kept, and the rest cremated (though supposedly his heart was eaten by children who mistook it for a dog's).

The **interpretation** of Cook's death has always been surrounded by controversy. It became widely believed by Europeans that the Hawaiians had taken Cook to be the great god Lono. The legend goes that, by chance, Cook had arrived at the temple of Lono at the height of the Makahiki festival, a major annual celebration in honor of Lono. The billowing sails of the *Resolution* were taken to be Lono's emblems, while the ship itself was believed to be the floating island of tall trees on which he was expected to voyage around Hawaii.

Some argue, however, that this story is based in part on a *European* view of Cook and of primitive people in general, rather than on Polynesian perceptions of the man. The European mentality of the time assumed that a noble figure of the Enlightenment such as Cook must appear god-like to the superstitious "natives." His voyage was perceived by the British as bringing civilization and order to heathen lands, while Cook saw himself as a stern father forever having to chastise the islanders who were his "insolent" children. His last recorded words are "I am afraid that these people will oblige me to use some violent measures; for they must not be left to imagine that they have gained an advantage over us." Cook would have been shocked had he realized that the Hawaiians surmised that "Brittanee" must be suffering from a severe famine, judging by the hunger of its sailors.

Cook may have wanted to be seen as the representative of a superior civilization and creed, but to Pacific islanders his superiority was largely a matter of **firepower**. A common theme in European contacts with the peoples of Polynesia is the attempt to draw well-armed foreigners into local military conflicts. Ironically, in 1777 Cook had sailed away from Tonga, having named it one of "the Friendly Islands," without ever knowing that in doing so he had narrowly avoided a plot to kill him and seize his ships. It's impossible now to say whether the elaborate ceremonies at Hikiau Heiau in Kealakekua Bay (see p.173), during which Cook was obliged to prostrate himself before an image of the god Kū, were designed to recognize him as Lono, or simply an attempt to incorporate him into the *kapu* system (see p.520) as a man of equal ranking with the high chiefs.

The major anomaly in the Cook-as-Lono legend is quite why the Hawaiians would have killed this "god." Some say it was a ritual sacrifice, while others argue that the man who struck the final blow had only just arrived from upcountry, and "didn't know" that Cook was a "god." The usual explanation, that it was simply an accident, serves both to perpetuate the idea of Hawaiians as "innocent" savages, and to absolve Cook himself of any responsibility for his fate. Though the British version of the dismantling of Hikiau Heiau has the priests eager to cooperate in return for iron trinkets, other sources, including Hawaiian tradition, have Cook's peremptory behavior seen as outrageous, sacrilegious enough to merit his death. That suggests that while Cook might have appeared a valuable potential ally to the chiefs, the priests and commoners viewed him as a blasphemer, and when he antagonized the chiefs by seizing Kalaniopu'u, deference gave way to defiance.

chiefs, and possibly that of Cook as well, remain entombed in lava-tunnel "caves" high on the cliff face, all that remains below are overgrown walls and ruined *heiaus*.

Plans have been put forward to restore the area around Cook's monument as a state park, with a visitor center atop the cliffs, but at present only the waters of the bay itself are formally protected. As a Marine Life Conservation District, it offers some of the best snorkeling on the island.



## Walking to the bay

Walking down to the site where Cook was killed – or, more accurately, walking back up again – is a serious undertaking, though well worth it for keen hikers. With no facilities at the bottom, not even water, you have to carry everything you need; allow a total walking time of at least four hours for the round-trip.

The unmarked trail starts a hundred yards down Nāpo'opo'o Road, which leaves Hwy-11 a quarter-mile before Captain Cook. Take a dirt road that drops to the right, and keep going straight when that road veers off to the right within a couple of hundred yards. A rutted track, fringed with bright purple and red flowers, continues down for about a mile through open pastureland and avocado orchards. Eventually the vegetation thins out, and you find yourself on very exposed black lava fields, picking your way over jagged rocks. Avoid climbing this stretch in the midday sun.

From this high vantage point you can discern the worn path of the old King's Trail that once encircled the entire island, paved with river-rounded boulders. The trail then drops abruptly down to the foot of the hill, before pushing its way into a tangle of scrubby undergrowth at the bottom. Soon you can make out the ruined black walls of the long-vanished Hawaiian village of **KA'AWALOA**, half submerged by twisted pandanus trees. Somewhere here stood the house of the high chief Kalaniopu'u, whose attempted kidnapping by Captain Cook precipitated the final drama of Cook's life (see p.171).

The trail reaches the sea at the precise spot where Cook died; a bronze **plaque** reposes in a rocky pool under a couple of inches of water. Fifty yards away to the left, on what is legally a small patch of England, stands a white marble **obelisk**, 27 feet high, that was raised to Cook's memory in 1884. Visiting ships traditionally set their own small plaques in the cement at its base – a tradition that continues to this day. An equally well-established tradition is for such plaques to be prised away by souvenir hunters, so the most interesting ones, together with all earlier memorials, have long since disappeared; some recent, boring ones remain.

Snorkelers from the cruise boats will ensure that you don't have the place to yourself, although they're not allowed to leave the water. Kayakers, however, tend to use the surround of the monument as a convenient place to haul in their vessels. As there's no proper beach, it's also the easiest launching-point if you want to snorkel yourself.

## Nāpo'opo'o Beach County Park

To drive to the south shore of Kealakekua Bay, follow the road down from just before Captain Cook as it twists for four miles around the great *pali*. It reaches sea level at the small, usually crowded, parking lot of **NĀPO'OPO'O BEACH COUNTY PARK**, and then continues a few yards north to dead-end at the "beach" itself. Not that there's much of one; Nāpo'opo'o used to be a reasonably pleasant beach, but all its sand has progressively been whipped away – a process completed by Hurricane Iniki in 1992 – and it now consists of a jumble of black lava boulders.

## Kealakekua Snorkel Cruises

The whole of Kealakekua Bay is an **underwater state park**. Much of it is very deep, as the sheer *pali* simply drops beneath the surface of the ocean. The shallowest and most sheltered spot is in the immediate area of Captain Cook's monument, where the reef provides perfect conditions for snorkelers. Swarms of yellow butterfly fish and tangs, plus parrotfish, triggerfish and hundreds of other species can always be found circling near the edge.

For centuries, this area has been a favorite haunt of **"spinner" porpoises**. Marine biologists have yet to explain why, but the porpoises gather here in schools of up to a hundred individuals to while away the afternoons by arching in and out of the water. Mark Twain described them as "like so many well-submerged wheels," but they do vary their routines by rotating on their own axes and even flipping the occasional somersault. At the end of the day, they head out once more to the open sea, to feed on the deep-water fish that come to the surface at night.

**Snorkel cruises** are extremely popular, so the number of vessels allowed into the bay each day is strictly limited. If possible, choose a boat that starts from Keauhou, as this gives you more time at Kealakekua. Bear in mind that passengers are forbidden to set foot ashore, so snorkeling has to be your priority. The following operators are recommended:

**Fair Wind** (ⓣ322-2788 or 1-800/677-9461, ⓦwww.fairwind.com). A large catamaran sails from Keauhou Pier at 9am ($85; 4hr 30min) and 1.30pm ($50; 3hr 30min) and also offers snuba and scuba. The raft *Orca* leaves Kailua Pier at 8.15am ($69; 4hr) and 12.45pm ($50; 3hr).

**Sea Quest** (ⓣ329-7238). Shadeless, bouncy six-person Zodiac rafts leave from Keauhou at 8am ($69; 4hr) and 1pm ($52; 3hr).

The **snorkeling** at Napo'opo'o remains as good as ever, however – once you've eased across the rocks at the water's edge. Fish congregate in greater numbers on the far side, near the conspicuous obelisk, but you may be swimming with the sharks for a mile to get there. Most visitors make the crossing by **kayak** instead. There aren't any rental outlets down here, but there are plenty in Kailua and on the upper highway around Kealakekua town. It's only legal to launch kayaks into the water from the ramp beside the jetty at the parking lot.

Stone steps beside the end of the road climb the stout black-lava tiers of **Hikiau Heiau**, the temple where Captain Cook was formally received in January 1779. During a baffling ceremony that lasted several hours, he was fed putrefied pig, had his face smeared with chewed coconut and was draped with red *tapa* cloth. Shortly afterwards, it was also the site of the first Christian service on the islands – the funeral of William Whatman, an elderly member of Cook's crew who died of a stroke. Visitors are not allowed onto the temple platform, and in any case nothing remains of its former structures. In fact, Cook may well have precipitated his death by dismantling the wooden palings that surrounded it for use as firewood. It is possible to clamber your way around the perimeter, to get a sense of its scale and atmosphere.

# Pu'uhonua O Hōnaunau National Historical Park

A featureless one-lane road runs south from Nāpo'opo'o for four miles, across the scrubby coastal flatlands, before meeting another road down from the main highway. The two converge at the entrance to the single most evocative historical site in all the Hawaiian islands, **PU'UHONUA O HŌNAUNAU** (daily 7.30am–5.30pm; $2 per person; Ⓣ 328-2288, Ⓦ www.nps.gov/puho; US National Park passes are sold and valid).

This small peninsula of jagged black lava, jutting out into the Pacific, holds the preserved and restored remains of a royal palace, complete with fishpond, beach and private canoe landing, plus three heiaus, guarded by carved effigies of gods. However, it is most famous for the **pu'uhonua** sanctuary that lies firmly protected behind the mortarless masonry of its sixteenth-century Great Wall.

## Visiting the park

Visits to the Pu'uhonua O Hōnaunau start at the small information desk at the far end of the parking lot. A schedule of daily talks by rangers is posted here, while immediately to the right is a sequence of large 3-D tiled murals, illustrating themes explained by brief taped messages.

Next you descend along paved walkways through the black lava field, into a grove of rustling giant palms. A couple of typical structures have been erected here on individual lava platforms – a small tent-like shelter for storage, and a larger house, as used by the *ali'i* (chiefs). To one side is a small but perfect sandy beach that once served as the royal canoe landing. Picnicking, sunbathing and smoking are all forbidden here, but swimming and snorkeling are permitted.

### Cities of Refuge

*Pu'uhonuas* used to be promoted to tourists under the name of **"Cities of Refuge"** because of their alleged parallels with the cities mentioned in the Bible. That term is now discouraged, as these were not cities but sacred precincts, and unlike the Jewish model, they served not to protect the innocent but to absolve the guilty. The idea was that any condemned criminal who succeeded in reaching a *pu'uhonua* would undergo a ritual lasting a few hours – at the very most, overnight – and then be free to leave. As *pu'uhonuas* always stood near strongly guarded royal enclaves, however, the condemned had first to run a gauntlet of armed warriors by land, or dodge canoeists and sharks by sea.

The survival of the fittest was a fundamental principle of ancient Hawaiian law, in which might was generally considered to be right. The laws were determined by gods, not men, and concerned not with acts such as theft and murder but with infractions of the intricate system of *kapu* – for which the penalty was always death. *Pu'uhonuas* provided a sort of safety valve to spare prime citizens from summary execution. They served other purposes as well. In times of war, noncombatants, loaded with provisions, could go to the nearest one to sit out the conflict, while defeated armies might flee to a *pu'uhonua* to avoid death on the battlefield. Each island had at least one, and the Big Island is thought to have had six. Other sites included Waipi'o Valley and Coconut Island in Hilo. In addition, certain high chiefs, such as Kamehameha's wife Queen Ka'ahumanu, were considered to be living, breathing *pu'uhonuas*.

Away to the left is the King's Fishpond, as placid as a hotel swimming pool. Various lava boulders nearby were hollowed out by early Hawaiians to serve as bowls or salt pans; one was leveled to create a playing surface for *kōnane*, a game in which black and white pebbles were used as counters.

A simple A-frame thatched structure serves as a carving shed, and usually holds one or two idols on which work is still in progress. Master craftsmen also fashion outrigger canoes here, from mighty trunks of beautiful dark *koa* wood.

Beyond the royal area, the L-shaped **Great Wall** – 10 feet high and up to 17 feet wide – runs across the tip of the promontory, sealing off the sanctuary itself. Its northern end is guarded by the **Hale O Keawe Heiau**, once used to house the bones of powerful chiefs, possibly including those of Captain Cook. When dismantled and stripped by Lord George Byron in July 1825, this was the last *heiau* in the islands to remain in perfect condition. Now, like the houses, it has been reconstructed. All the fearsome wooden idols that surround it are modern reproductions, but they're still eerie in their original setting.

Few buildings now stand beyond the wall. Apart from a couple of bare *heiau* platforms, there's just a scattering of trees on the rippling *pāhoehoe* lava that runs into the ocean. One large gray stone, supposedly the favorite spot of the chief Keōua, is surrounded by six holes that may have held the wooden poles of a canopy. Black crabs scuttle across the waterfront rocks, and countless pools are alive with tiny, multicolored fish.

You can't linger on the beach in the main part of the park, but stretches of **public beach** lie both north and south. The northern section, within sight of the sanctuary, is a renowned **snorkeling** spot, while a short walk or drive south from the parking lot brings you to the more attractive southern section. Even here there's very little sand along the shoreline, which consists of a broad expanse of black lava, but the shady grove beneath the coconut palms makes a great spot for a picnic. Visitors who come for the beach alone are not obliged to pay the *pu'uhonua* admission fee.

In ancient times, the coastal flatlands to the south were densely populated, and traces remain everywhere of house-sites and other structures. Schemes are afoot to expand the existing park to incorporate trails through the most rewarding archeological areas.

## St Benedict's Painted Church

When you visit the *pu'uhonua*, be sure also to make the slight detour north from Hwy-160, the spur road to Hwy-11, to see **St Benedict's Painted Church**. This small wooden church, an intriguing hybrid of medieval Europe and Hawaii, was decorated between 1899 and 1904 by a Belgian priest, Father John Velge, with brightly colored Biblical and allegorical scenes. Columns with Hawaiian texts erupt into palm leaves on a vaulted ceiling depicting a tropical sky, and the walls behind the altar are painted with a trompe l'oeil Gothic cathedral modeled on that in Burgos, Spain. Orchids and *leis* festoon the altar and statuary within, while purple bougainvilleas fill the lush tropical gardens outside. The spectacular views down the hillside at sunset look out over the flat expanse of trees that line the coast between Hōnaunau and Nāpo'opo'o.

# South Kona accommodation

Low-key **accommodation** options are scattered throughout the various "coffee towns," ranging from simple traditional village **hotels** to luxurious purpose-built **B&Bs**. Not all are conspicuous from the main road; several of the most distinctive properties are hidden away from view on the lush South Kona slopes.

## B&Bs

**A 'Hui 'Hou**, PO Box 349, Hōlualoa HI 96725; ⓣ 324-0510 or 1-800/396-5369 (US & Can), ⓦ www.bbonline.com. Multilevel B&B set in a sprawling modern house on a three-acre coffee plantation a mile above Hōlualoa and a total of four miles from Kailua. Three guest rooms and two luxury suites share a common dining area, a huge verandah, and a hot tub. Rooms ❸, suites ❺.

**Dragonfly Ranch**, PO Box 675, Hōnaunau HI 96726; ⓣ 328-2159 or 1-800/487-2159 (US & Can), ⓕ 328-9570, ⓦ www.dragonflyranch.com. Tropical retreat, just below the Painted Church, geared to New Age travelers. A bit too "back to nature" for some tastes, it offers Hawaiian massage, aromatherapy, and other treatments. One of the two rooms in the main house has a bathroom, the other just a shower, and there are three separate suites with stereos, TVs and outdoor showers. Rooms ❸, suites ❺.

**Hale Aloha Guest Ranch**, 84-4780 Mamalahoa Hwy, Captain Cook HI 96704; ⓣ & ⓕ 328-8955 or 1-800/897-3188 (US & Can), ⓦ www.halealoha.com. Comfortable guest rooms, not all en suite, on a German-owned farm a mile up from the highway. There are tremendous views, and rates include fresh fruits and coffee, plus a complimentary Hawaiian massage. ❸–❹.

**Hōlualoa Inn B&B**, PO Box 222, Hōlualoa HI 96725; ⓣ 324-1121 or 1-800/392-1812 (US & Can), ⓕ 322-2472, ⓦ www.konaweb.com/HINN. Exquisite B&B, just below the main road through Hōlualoa, three miles and 1400 feet up the hill from Kailua. Six tasteful en-suite guest rooms arranged around a Japanese-style open-plan living room, plus a pool, Jacuzzi, and homegrown coffee. A crow's-nest seating area on top of the small central wooden tower looks down on the rest of Kona, enjoying incredible views. Reservations essential, two-night minimum stay, no children under 13. ❺.

**Kalahiki Cottage**, reserve through Hawaii's Best Bed & Breakfasts, PO Box 563, Kamuela HI 96743; ⓣ 885-4550 or 1-800/262-9912 (US & Can), ⓕ 885-0559, ⓦ www.bestbnb.com. Secluded and colorful cattle ranch, south of Hōnaunau, has a superb one-bedroom cottage as well as space for additional guests in the main house. The grounds feature a large swimming pool. ❺.

**Rainbow Plantation**, PO Box 122, Captain Cook HI 96704; ⓣ 323-2393 or 1-800/494-2829 (US & Can), ⓕ 323-9445, ⓦ www.wwte.com/hawaii/rainbow. Appealing en-suite B&B accommodation on a working coffee plantation, off Hwy-11 a quarter of a mile north of the top of Nāpo'opo'o Road. There are two guest rooms, a separate cottage, and even a converted fishing boat. ❸.

## Hotels and Hostels

**Kona Hotel**, 76-5908 Māmalahoa Hwy, Hōlualoa HI 96725; ⓣ 324-1156. Extremely basic, very old-fashioned (and very pink) family-run hotel in the attractive village of Hōlualoa, three miles up-slope from Kailua. Offers the plainest of double rooms for under $30 a night. ❶.

**Manago Hotel**, PO Box 145, Captain Cook HI 96704; ⓣ 323-2642, ⓕ 323-3451, ⓦ www.managohotel.com. Century-old wooden hotel in the center of Captain Cook, offering some of the best-value, most "Hawaiian" lodging on the island. Cheaper rooms, in the main building, share bathrooms and have minimal facilities, but those in the newer three-story wing at the back, where the rates rise floor by floor, enjoy magnificent ocean views. Each of the faintly musty conventional suites has a small *lānai*, a strong hot shower and a period-piece radio, but no phone; there's also one special deluxe Japanese room, costing $62 per night. The *Manago*'s paneled dining room (daily except Mon 7–9am, 11am–2pm & 5–7.30pm) is cooled by whirring fans and breezes wafting up from the bay; full breakfasts cost $5, while later in the day a couple of lightly breaded pork chops go for $8. ❶/❷.

**Pineapple Park**, Hwy-11, Kealekekua; mailing address PO Box 639, Kurtistown HI 96760; ⓣ 323-2224 or 1-877/865-2266 (US), ⓦ www.pineapple-park.com. Clean, appealing budget hostel-cum-hotel, attached to a fruit stand on Hwy-11 in Kealekekua, halfway between mileposts 110 and 111. A bunk in one of the downstairs dorms costs just $17, while top-of-the-range en-suite rooms go for $65 per night. The nicer private rooms have far-reaching views. Airport pickup costs $15 per group. The same owners run another budget hotel/hostel near Hawaii Volcanoes National Park; see p.206. Dorms ❶, rooms ❷.

## Ho'okena Beach County Park

Continue south along Hwy-11, for just under three miles from the Hwy-160 turnoff, and another small road leads to the sea at **HO'OKENA BEACH COUNTY PARK**. The vegetation thins out as you drop the two miles down the hillside, but the park itself is pleasant enough. It consists of a genuine, if grayish, sandy beach, pressed against a small *pali*, and shaded with coconut palms and other trees. Getting in and out of the water across the sharp lava can be a bit grueling, but the **snorkeling** is once again excellent.

This sheltered, south-facing bay was once a regular port of call for inter-island steamers, but it now houses very few buildings, although it does have toilets and a picnic area. It also allows **camping**; permission, as usual, must be obtained from the Department of Parks and Recreation in Hilo (☎961-8311) at a cost of $3 per day. *Neoki's Corner,* at the foot of the road, sells soft drinks and has public showers.

## Miloli'i

The last point in South Kona at which access to the sea is practical is another twelve miles beyond Ho'okena, where a very tortuous five-mile single-lane road winds down the steep, exposed ridge of Mauna Loa. Having reached the sea at **Ho'opuloa** – no more than a few houses on bare rock – the road follows the coastline south, to drop to the small bay of **MILOLI'I**. The tiny stretches of beach here are mere indentations in the black lava along the shore, filled with a random scattering of white coral and black lava pebbles, and backed by groves of coconut palms. The thick tongue of the most recent lava flow (in 1926) can be seen spilling over the sparse slopes above; it obliterated Ho'opuloa, and disputes over the allocation of land to rehouse the victims lasted for well over fifty years thereafter.

At the south end of the cove there's another county **beach park**, with a thatched picnic shelter and a restroom, near an especially sheltered pond that's a favorite with children. Camping is once again permitted, but this is too public a spot for that to hold much appeal, and most visitors content themselves with snorkeling around the rocks. A short way back from the sea, the Miloli'i Grocery Store sells snacks and sodas. The road ends next to the pastel-yellow, red-roofed **Hau'oli Kamana'o Church**.

# North Kona

Until the 1970s, it was barely possible to travel overland along the coast **north of Kailua** – and few people had any reason to do so. Then **Queen Ka'ahumanu Highway**, Hwy-19, was laid across the lava, serving the new airport and granting access to previously remote beaches. Many of these were swiftly engulfed by plush resorts – especially in the South Kohala district (see p.181) – but, with the road running on average a mile in from the ocean, the beaches remain occasional, distant bursts of greenery in an otherwise desolate landscape.

Despite the huge sums spent on all this construction, Big Island tourism is not on the scale that was originally envisaged. As a result, the highway system is unusual for Hawaii in that it's more than adequate to handle the volume of traffic. The one potential hazard for drivers is posed by the unpredictable "Kona Nightingales" (scrawny descendants of the donkeys that once hauled loads to and from the shoreline), which roam wild across the barren slopes.





## Honokōhau Harbor

A couple of miles north of Kailua, a short avenue leads down to narrow **HONOKŌHAU HARBOR**, which provides safe moorings for the town's pleasure boats and thereby leaves the jetty in Kailua free from congestion. This is a functional rather than a decorative place, and the only reason for coming here is to take one of the many boat trips which leave from the far end of the quay. The most appealing spot to sit and watch the proceedings is the open-air deck of the *Harbor House* (Mon–Sat 11am–7pm, Sun 11am–5.30pm; ⓣ326-4166), a bar in the central Kona Marina complex that also offers a menu of reasonably priced snacks and sandwiches. To its left is a line of fishing charter vessels, together with an information kiosk on what they offer, the Charter Desk (ⓣ329-5735, ⓦwww.charterdesk.com).

If you have an hour or two to kill before or after an excursion, a small, secluded and sandy beach, ideal for snorkelers, can be reached by hiking south for ten minutes across the lava, while a five-minute walk around to the north of the harbor brings you out at the southern access to the Kaloko-Honokōhau National Historic Park.

## Kaloko-Honokōhau National Historic Park

The **KALOKO-HONOKŌHAU NATIONAL HISTORIC PARK**, north of the harbor and south of the airport (daily 8am–3.30pm; free; ⓣ329-6681), was established in 1978 to preserve one of the state's last surviving natural wetlands. Despite being administered by the National Park Service, it remains almost entirely undeveloped, and the goals of re-creating ancient techniques of aquaculture and farming, protecting endangered Hawaiian water birds, and returning the area to its pre-contact appearance seem as distant as ever. The few visitors the park attracts are usually – like the birds – here to fish, and it tends to disappoint anyone other than naturalists.

Even the entrance is almost impossible to find, via a scarcely discernible driveway *makai* of the highway, opposite Kaloko Industrial Park between mileposts 96 and 97. The bumpy lava track down, which is just barely passable in ordinary rental cars, ends after 0.7 miles beside the tranquil Kaloko Fishpond, sealed off from the ocean by a massive stone wall that has been extensively restored and rebuilt by the park authorities. The wetlands stretch away from the seafront picnic area, while a coastal footpath leads south to Honokōhau Harbor via the 'Aimakapa Fishpond.

Scattered across the mostly trackless expanse of the park are several *heiaus* as well as a *hōlua* ("land-surfing") slide and fields of petroglyphs. Descendants of Kamehameha the Great took pains to reserve this area for themselves, which suggests that one of its countless caves may still hold his bones.

## Boat Trips on the Kona and Kohala Coasts

Most Kona and Kohala coast boat trips depart from Honokōhau Harbor. Precise arrangements vary from day to day; contact the companies below for details. Activities desks in Kailua can usually offer discounted rates.

### Dive Boats

One-dive cruises tend to cost $60–80, two-dive trips more like $85–100, with a $20–30 surcharge for unqualified divers, and equipmental rental costing $5 per item. Most operators offer two-day certification courses for around $300.

| | | |
|---|---|---|
| **Big Island Divers** | ⓣ329-6068 | ⓦwww.bigislanddivers.com |
| **Eco Adventures** | ⓣ1-800/949-3483 | ⓦwww.ecodive.com |
| **Jack's Diving Locker** | ⓣ329-7585 | ⓦwww.divejdl.com |
| **Kona Coast Divers** | ⓣ329-8802 | ⓦwww.konacoastdivers.com |
| **Rainbow Diver** | ⓣ325-1687 | ⓦwww.rainbowdiver.com |
| **Red Sail Sports** | ⓣ885-2876 | ⓦwww.redsail.com |
| **Torpedo Tours** | ⓣ938-0405 | ⓦwww.torpedotours.com |

### Snorkel Cruises

Typical morning or afternoon snorkel cruises cost $45–70. The prime destination is Kealakekua Bay; for more details, see p.173.

| | | |
|---|---|---|
| **Body Glove** | ⓣ326-7122 | ⓦwww.snorkelkona.com |
| **Captain Zodiac** | ⓣ329-3199 | ⓦwww.captainzodiac.com |
| **Dolphin Discoveries** | ⓣ322-8000 | ⓦwww.dolphindiscoveries.com |
| **Fair Wind** | ⓣ322-2788 | ⓦwww.fairwind.com |
| **Kamanu** | ⓣ329-2021 | ⓦwww.kamanu.com |
| **Rainbow Diver** | ⓣ325-1687 | ⓦwww.rainbowdiver.com |
| **Red Sail Sports** | ⓣ885-2876 | ⓦwww.redsail.com |
| **Sea Quest** | ⓣ329-7238 | ⓦwww.seaquesthawaii.com |

### Sightseeing Cruises

**Atlantis Submarines** (ⓣ329-6626, ⓦwww.go-atlantis.com; $79 for 1hr trip). Cramped but fascinating ocean-floor cruises, with foolhardy divers trying to entice sharks alongside. Hourly from Kailua Pier.

**Dan McSweeney's Whale Watch** (ⓣ322-0028; $55 for a morning's excursion). Departs 9am daily from Honokōhau. From December to March there's an excellent chance of sneaking up on some humpback whales.

**Lilikoi** (ⓣ936-1470, ⓦwww.dolphinshawaii.com; $45 for half-day trip). Seasonal whale-watching trips from Honokōhau Harbor.

### Deep-Sea Fishing

Fishing trips cost from $75 per person for a half-day to $400-plus for a whole boat for a whole day. For a broad selection of charter vessels, contact the Charter Desk (ⓣ329-5735, ⓦwww.charterdesk.com) or Charter Services Hawaii (ⓣ334-1881).

# Kona Coast State Park

One of the Big Island's least-known but most beautiful beaches, designated as the **KONA COAST STATE PARK** and also known as **Kekaha Kai State Park**, lies a couple of miles north of Keāhole Airport (daily except Wed, 9am–8pm; free). Once again, you need to keep your eyes peeled to spot the driveway, and then be prepared to bump your vehicle for 1.5 miles over rippling *pāhoehoe* lava, on a virtually unsurfaced track.

At the bottom of the track, there's a parking lot; from its *mauka* end take the obvious path that sets off northwards across 200 yards of bare lava towards a dense grove of coconut palms. When you come to a single portable toilet, you can either cut in through the trees to reach the beach directly, or follow the path round until it emerges in the middle of a perfect horseshoe-shaped bay. All around you is an exquisite beach of coarse golden sand, lightly flecked with specks of black lava – what the locals call "salt and pepper" sand. Each of the headlands jutting to either side is a spur of rougher *'a'ā* lava, topped with its own clump of palms. Immediately behind the beach is the looming bulk of Hualālai, and at this point Mauna Kea becomes visible far inland, as does Haleakalā across the sea on Maui. The calm waters of the bay provide sheltered swimming, local surfers ride the tumbling waves offshore, and divers delve into submarine caves and tunnels.

Kona Coast State Park has **no food and drink** facilities for visitors.

# Ka'ūpūlehu

The area known as **KA'ŪPŪLEHU**, five miles north of the airport, consists of a forbidding expanse of rough, jet-black lava that was deposited by an eruption of the Hualālai volcano in 1801. Its utter inaccessibility led it to be chosen as the site of the *Kona Village Resort* in 1961 – at first, in the absence of a road, all guests and employees alike had to be flown in – though with the recent completion of the *Four Seasons Resort* it now feels significantly less secluded.

## Four Seasons Resort Hualālai

The Big Island's newest resort, the sprawling *Four Seasons Resort* at Hualālai (PO Box 1269, Kailua-Kona HI 96745; Ⓣ325-8000 or 1-888/340-5662 in US & Can, Ⓕ325-8100, Ⓦwww.fourseasons.com; ⑨), was finally completed in 1996, after being delayed for several years by the discovery that its original site lay above an ancient Hawaiian burial ground. Plans for a conventional high-rise hotel were at that point abandoned in favor of a complex of smaller units, known as "bungalows" despite being two stories high. On first impression, they're not wildly prepossessing, but the individual rooms inside justify the minimum $450-per-night rate. Each holds a four-poster bed plus a bath and shower, and many have an additional outdoor, lava-lined shower. Set on an exposed headland, the *Four Seasons* stands a bit too close to the ocean for comfort, and unlike the neighboring *Kona Village Resort* it lacks a proper beach – although high surf can unceremoniously dump sand into its three swimming pools. The real architectural success of the *Four Seasons* is its gorgeous *Pahui'a* restaurant, comprising several interlinked wooden pavilions laid open by sliding panels to the ocean. Sea breezes waft in, and spotlights play on the surf, while the food itself is excellent, with a wide range of Asian and American dishes. Appetizers such as a sashimi and *tako poke* combo cost $17, meat and fish entrees average around $30.

## Kona Village Resort

If you cherish a fantasy of staying in a paradise where every whim is anticipated – and you have unlimited funds – you could do no better than to stay at the oldest of the Big Island's luxury resorts, the *Kona Village Resort* (PO Box 1299,

Kailua-Kona HI 96745; Ⓣ325-5555 or 1-800/367-5290 in US & Can, Ⓕ325-5124, Ⓦwww.konavillage.com; ⑨). Supposedly it's a re-creation of the Polynesian past, but its main appeal lies in the very fact that it bears so little relation to reality of any kind. Set in the black Kona desertscape, the resort consists of 125 thatched South Pacific-style *hales*, or huts, most of which are surrounded by bright flowers. The huts have no phones, TVs or radios, but each has a private *lānai*, a hammock and an alarm clock that wakes you by grinding fresh coffee beans. Beach gear, such as masks, fins and even kayaks, is provided free for guests, and scuba equipment and instruction are also available for a fee. The daily rates of $450 to $795 for two include all meals at the *Hale Moana* and *Hale Samoa* restaurants; for nonresidents, a five-course dinner at the *Hale Moana* costs $62 and consists of a seafood appetizer, soup, salad and fresh fish prepared to your exact specifications. Most outsiders visit on *lū'au* night – Friday – when $72 buys an atmospheric beachside feast plus Polynesian entertainment; advance reservations are essential. The resort sits on sandy Ka'ūpūlehu beach, which is superb for snorkeling; stately turtles cruise by and manta rays billow in at night. Anyone can visit this isolated beach, though the resort's security guards do their best to discourage nonresidents. There's also a self-guided petroglyph trail on the property.

## Kīholo Bay

As Hwy-19 crests a small hill a short way south of mile marker 82, an overlook offers a tantalizing glimpse of the turquoise waters of **KĪHOLO BAY**. This crescent lagoon, dotted with black-lava islands, is in part artificial, having been re-shaped by ancient Hawaiians to serve as a fishpond. Most of their work was destroyed by the 1801 eruption of Hualālai, and that lava flow unfortunately makes access difficult to this day. The only way to reach the bay is via a 1.5-mile hike on a rough path that leaves the highway a mile further on. If you do make the effort, it's a fabulous place for a swim, though there's no beach to speak of.

# The South Kohala Coast

Though the whole of the western seaboard of the Big Island tends to be referred to as the Kona coast, the most famous of its resorts are in fact situated in the district of **South Kohala**, which starts roughly 25 miles north of Kailua. Overlooked by the volcanoes of Mauna Kea, Hualālai and Kohala – and on clear days by Mauna Loa, to the south, and even Haleakalā on Maui – this region was all but inaccessible by land until the 1960s. The only visitors to the inlets along the shore were local fishermen and the occasional intrepid hiker or surfer. The Hawaiian villages that had once flourished here were long gone and only wealthy landowners maintained a few private enclaves.

In the forty years since Laurance Rockefeller realized the potential that lay in South Kohala's status as the sunniest area in all Hawaii, the landscape has undergone an amazing transformation. Holes large enough to hold giant hotels

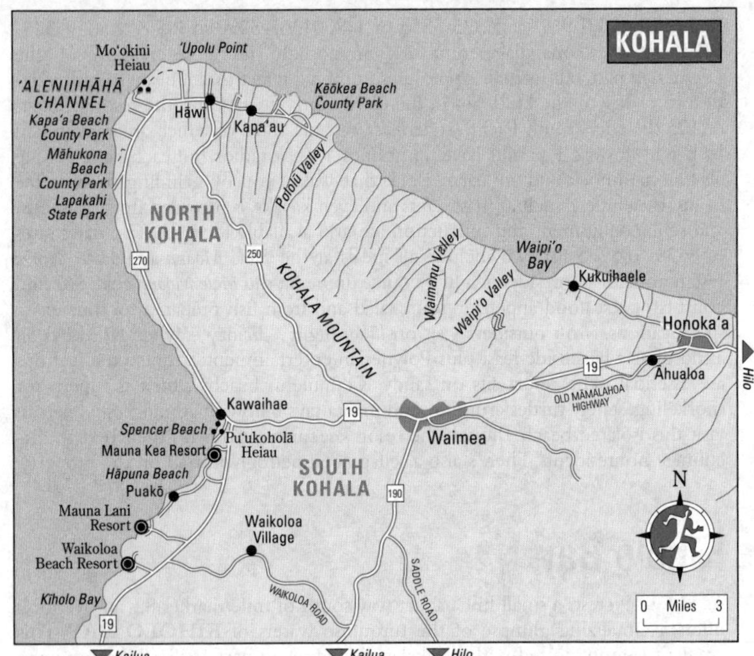




have been blasted into the rock, and turf laid on top of the lava to create lawns and golf courses. **Queen Ka'ahumanu Highway** (Hwy-19) pushed its way across the bare lava slopes, and multi-property resorts appeared in quick succession at **Waikoloa** and then **Mauna Lani**, a couple of miles further north.

Most of South Kohala's **beaches** were probably destroyed by lava early in the 1800s – so the *Hilton*, for example, had to build its own beach from scratch – but as you head north towards Kawaihae you come to some of the finest expanses of sand on the island. These were prime targets for the developers: the first of the luxury hotels was the *Mauna Kea Beach Hotel*, which went up at Kauna'oa in the 1960s, while what may well be the last was the *Hapuna Beach Prince Hotel*, erected on beautiful Hāpuna Beach in 1994, despite strong local opposition.

Since it's illegal for anyone to deny access to the Hawaiian shoreline, local people, and visitors not staying at the Kohala resorts, are entitled to use all the beaches along the coast. Some hotels make things difficult by restricting the number of parking permits they issue to nonguests – as few as ten per day – but so long as you can get to the sea, you're entitled to stay there.

For **information** on South Kohala as a whole, with a special emphasis on accommodations, contact the Kohala Coast Resort Association, 69-275 Waikoloa Beach Drive, Kohala Coast (Ⓣ 1-800/318-3637, Ⓦ www.kkra.org).

## Waikoloa

For the ancient Hawaiians, the fundamental division of land was the *ahupua'a*, a wedge-shaped "slice of cake" reaching from the top of the mountain down to a stretch of the sea. The name "Waikoloa" referred to such a division, which is why modern visitors are often confused as to where exactly **WAIKOLOA** is.

The community called Waikoloa, generally referred to as **Waikoloa Village**, lies six miles *mauka* of Queen Ka'ahumanu Highway, halfway up to the Belt Road, while the **Waikoloa Beach Resort** – reached by a mile-long approach road that leaves the highway a little way south of mile marker 76, 25 miles north of Kailua – is, unsurprisingly, down by the sea. It holds little other than the *Hilton* and *Outrigger Waikoloa Beach* hotels and the King's Shops mall.

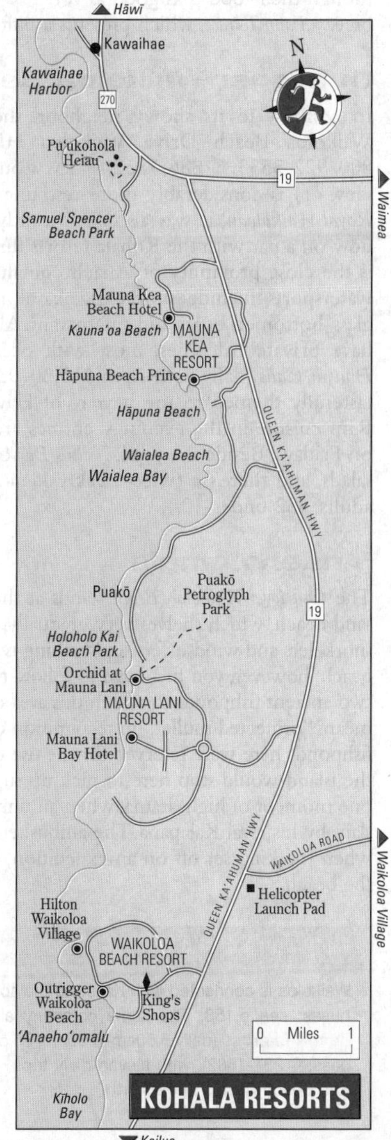


## Hilton Waikoloa Village

The 1240-room *Hilton Waikoloa Village* (425 Waikoloa Beach Drive, Waikoloa HI 96738; ⓣ886-1234 or 1-800/221-2424, ⓕ886-2900, ⓦwww.HiltonWaikoloaVillage.com; garden view ❺, ocean view ❼) is almost a miniature city. Guests travel between its three seven-story towers on a light railway system, a mile-long network of walkways, or in boats along the canals. It boasts a four-acre artificial lagoon complete with waterfalls, and a beach of imported sand lined by coconut palms, some of which were flown here by helicopter from Kalapana on the south coast, just before it was engulfed by lava (see p.232). This synthetic tropical paradise cost a fortune to build, but opened (as the *Hyatt Regency*) in 1988, just in time to be hit by the Gulf War economic downturn. Hilton bought out the original developers in 1993, for a rumored 25¢ on the dollar, and it's now the most popular of the Kohala resorts. If you book through a package-tour operator, it can also work out to be one of the cheapest. However, it can feel a bit like staying in a theme park, and thus appeals most to families with young children, and those who are quite happy to see nothing of the rest of the island. One of the resort's highlights is its "swim with a dolphin" program; although an hour in the lagoon with your favorite sea mammal can cost as much as $150, the experience is so much in demand that a lottery is held to decide which guests can take part. You can also take a free guided tour through the network of underground tunnels, used by staff to ensure unobtrusiveness. Surprisingly, neither of the more formal of the *Hilton*'s seven restaurants – the north Italian *Donatoni's,* and the Japanese sushi and teppanyaki specialists *Imari*, both of which serve dinner only – offer sea views, though their food is as good as you'd expect. The best casual alternative is the breezy *Palm Terrace*, which presents a different $32 dinner buffet every night.



## Outrigger Waikoloa Beach

In contrast to its showy neighbor, the *Outrigger Waikoloa Beach* (69-275 Waikoloa Beach Drive, Waikoloa HI 96738-5711; Ⓣ886-6789 or 1-800/922-5533, Ⓕ886-7852, Ⓦwww.outrigger.com; garden view ❼, ocean view ❽) is considerably more restrained and elegant. Until recently, as the *Royal Waikoloan*, it was also significantly cheaper, but in style and price it's now on a par with the Kohala resorts further north. The main attraction here is the close proximity of 'Anaeho'omalu beach (see below), where available watersports include snorkeling, kayaking, scuba diving and excursions in glass-bottomed boats and catamarans. All the 500-plus well-equipped rooms have private balconies, most with ocean views. The principal restaurant, *Hawaii Calls* (daily 6am–2pm & 5.30–9.30pm), overlooks a carp pond and is tastefully themed to the heyday of Hawaiian tourism. It offers fine Pacific Rim cuisine in the evenings; entrees are $25–30, with a $35 seafood buffet on Fridays. Beside the pool, *Nalu's Bar & Grill* serves alfresco sandwiches and salads, and there's a twice-weekly *lū'au*, open to all (Wed & Sun 6pm; $64 adults, $32 under-12s).

## 'Anaeho'omalu

The *Outrigger Waikoloa Beach* stands at the northern end of a sheltered white-sand beach, which shelves very gradually out to sea. This is a favorite spot with snorkelers and windsurfers, and bathing is generally considered safe. To reach the beach, however, you first have to follow the landscaped walkways that skirt the two ancient fishponds to which this area owes its name. **'ANAEHO'OMALU** means "protected mullet," in recognition of the fact that the mullet raised in the fishponds here were reserved for the use of chiefs alone – *ali'i* voyaging around the island would stop here to pick up supplies. The beach itself also witnessed one moment of high drama, when an unpopular king of Hawaii, Kamaiole, was slain by his rival Kalapana. The ambushers took advantage of the tradition that when the king set off on an expedition, his canoe was always the last to leave the beach.

### Waikoloa Shuttle Buses

Waikoloa is connected with Kailua to the south by the **Kona Town Express** shuttle buses; see p.158. The same company also runs the **Kohala Coast–Waikoloa Resort Express** (daily 6.50am–9.50pm, $5 one-way, $15 for a one-day system-wide pass; Ⓣ331-1582), with eleven daily trips between the King's Shops and Mauna Kea Beach Resort to the north.

### The King's Shops

As a shopping destination, the 40-store **King's Shops mall** (daily 9.30am–9.30pm), sited at the point where the approach road splits off to the different hotels, can't begin to compete with Kailua – let alone Honolulu. It is an attractive little spot, however, arrayed along one side of an artificial lagoon, and its open courtyard features interesting plaques explaining Big Island geology and history.

Though it also holds several upscale clothing stores, Chinese and Japanese restaurants, and a small food court with good juice and coffee bars, the mall is best known as the home of the Big Island's only outlet of *Roy's* gourmet **restaurant** chain (daily 11.30am–2pm & 5.30–9.30pm; ⓣ885-4321). Flamboyant Pacific Rim dinners – best enjoyed in the moonlight on the lakeside terrace – feature dim-sum-style appetizers priced individually at $7–9, and entrees such as potato-spinach-crusted swordfish and candied macadamia nut rack of lamb at $23–29. The shorter and simpler lunch menu offers great value, with gourmet sandwiches and salads for around $10, and Roy's signature baby-back ribs for even less.

### Waikoloa Village

Most visitors to the Waikoloa resorts never head the eight miles up to **WAIKOLOA VILLAGE** itself. Should you want to do so, take the road that leaves Queen Ka'ahumanu Highway a short distance north of the resort turnoff, halfway to Mauna Lani. A small lot at this otherwise desolate intersection is the base for **helicopter** trips (see p.156) run for resort guests by Kenai Helicopters (ⓣ885-5833) and Blue Hawaiian (ⓣ961-5600), among others.

There's nothing to the village apart from a supermarket, a gas station, a golf course, and the **Waikoloa Highlands Village** mall, which features a couple of snack places.

## Mauna Lani Resort

A mile or so north of the Waikoloa Village turnoff, another approach road *makai* of Queen Ka'ahumanu Highway heads through lurid green lawns down to the plush **Mauna Lani Resort**. Two major resorts face the sea here in splendid isolation, sharing the use of two golf courses. The name *Mauna Lani*, a modern coinage, means "mountains reaching heaven," and refers to the misty volcanoes that loom in the distance to the north, south and east.

### Mauna Lani Bay Hotel

With its central building thrusting like an arrow into the Pacific, and an oceanfront golf course to either side, the gleaming white *Mauna Lani Bay* (68-1400 Mauna Lani Drive, Kohala Coast HI 96743; ⓣ885-6622 or 1-800/367-2323, ⓕ885-6183, ⓦwww.maunalani.com; garden view ❽, ocean view ❾) is a classic, unabashed resort hotel. Lavish rooms are accessed via a waterfall- and lagoon-filled central atrium, and offer extensive ocean views. (Another perk: the fifth night of your stay is free.) Traces of ancient occupation are everywhere on the extensive grounds, though the Kalāhuipua'a Trail, which leads back from the beach and the shoreline fishponds, soon turns into a grueling two-mile walk across craggy *'a'ā* lava. The *Bay Terrace* commands ocean views from its indoor and outdoor dining room; appetizers range $7–16, entrees, like the seafood Thai curry or Kona-coffee-marinated lamb chops, are more like $30. The flamboyant open-air Polynesian-style *Canoe House*, close to the sea and surrounded by fishponds, serves some of Hawaii's finest but most expensive Pacific Rim cuisine, while the *Gallery* (Tues–Sat), beside the golf course, is similarly superb.



## The Orchid at Mauna Lani

What was, until 1995, the *Ritz-Carlton Mauna Lani* is now the *Orchid at Mauni Lani* (1 North Kanikū Drive, Kohala Coast HI 96743; ⓣ885-2000, 1-800/845-9905 in US & Can or 0800/973119 in UK, ⓕ885-5778, ⓦwww.orchid-maunalani.com; ⑨). Under its new owners, Sheraton, it has shaken off some of the stuffiness of the *Ritz-Carlton* image, while remaining the most sophisticated and elegant of the Kohala giants. All 539 rooms in this spacious complex of six-story buildings have en-suite bathrooms with "twin marble vanities," and enjoy extensive views either over the sea or up to the volcanoes across one of the two golf courses in the area. As well as a lovely seafront swimming pool and Jacuzzi, there's an open-air "spa without walls." Both the principal restaurants, the *Orchid Court* and the *Grill*, serve fine Pacific Rim dinners nightly, with a full meal at either costing around $50; the *Orchid Court* also offers buffet breakfasts and lighter lunches.



## Puakō

An impressive array of ancient **petroglyphs** is located between the *Ritz-Carlton* and the small community of **PUAKŌ**. The Malama Trail to **Puakō Petroglyph Park** heads inland from the *mauka* end of the Holoholo Kai Beach Park parking lot; there's no drinking water along the mile-long trail which, though not difficult, crosses rough terrain.

For the first 150 yards, the trail is paved, crossing open lava to some replica petroglyphs set up so visitors can take rubbings. From these, you plunge into a tinderbox-dry *kiawe* forest. Five hundred yards in, a few petroglyphs can be discerned on nearby rocks. Many visitors turn back here under the impression that they've seen all there is to see, but you should continue another 250 yards and cross an unpaved track. A short way beyond this track, a fenced-off viewing area brings you to a halt in front of a slightly sloping expanse of flat, reddish rock. This is covered with simple stick figures, most a couple of feet tall, still lying where they were left to bake centuries ago. Laboriously etched into bare *pāhoehoe* lava, the petroglyphs range from matchstick warriors to abstract symbols and simple indentations where the umbilical cords of newborn babies were buried. They're easiest to see early in the morning or late in the evening, when the sun creates shadows.

**Holoholo Kai Beach Park** is a mixture of black lava and white coral, not especially good for swimming. Puakō itself is beyond it to the north, but there's no through road from here. It's more of an exclusive residential area than a town, and all you'll see if you turn on to Puakō Beach Drive from Hwy-19, three miles down the road, is a long succession of private villas.

# Waialea, Hāpuna and Kauna'oa beaches



The best of the natural white-sand beaches of South Kohala are along the coast just south of Kawaihae Harbor. Such beaches are formed from the skeletal remains of tiny coral-reef creatures, which explains why they're found in the most sheltered areas of the oldest part of the island. They're now at the foot of Mauna Kea rather than Kohala Mountain, because lava from Mauna Kea has progressively swamped its venerable neighbor.

Of the three best-known beaches, separated by short stretches of *kiawe* forest, only the southernmost one, **Waialea**, remains in anything approaching a pristine state. Comparatively small, and sheltered by jutting headlands, it's a perfect base for recreational sailing, while the gentle slope into the sea makes it popular with family groups. The magnificence of both **Hāpuna**, and **Kauna'oa** to the north, has been impaired by the addition of mighty resort hotels.

## Hāpuna Beach

With its gentle turquoise waters, swaying palm groves, and above all its broad expanse of pristine white sand, **HĀPUNA BEACH** has often been called the most beautiful beach in the United States. Though in summer it's the widest beach on the Big Island, capable of accommodating large crowds of day-trippers, it always seems to retain an intimate feel, thanks in part to the promontory of black lava that splits it down the middle. However, its northern end is dominated by the giant *Hapuna Beach Prince Hotel*, which opened in 1994 despite bitter opposition from campaigners who treasured Hāpuna's status as an unspoiled state recreation area. Although the hotel is forbidden to leave unoccupied furniture on the beach, to serve food or alcohol there, or to discourage public access to any area below the tree line, hotel guests inevitably dominate the sands north of the promontory.

Nonetheless, Hāpuna Beach remains a delightful public park, well equipped with washrooms and pavilions. *Three Dog Cafe*, a kiosk adjoining the parking lot, sells snacks and rents beach equipment. In deference to the safety of bodysurfers, who consider this the best spot on the island, surfboards are forbidden. There's always the chance of unruly weather between October and March, so look for the warning flags that fly outside the hotel before you enter the water.

Six simple A-frame **shelters**, set well back from the beach itself, above the parking lot, and capable of holding up to four people, can be rented for $20 per night through the state parks office in Hilo (Ⓣ974-6200). Tent camping is not permitted.

### Hapuna Beach Prince Hotel

Standing roughly six miles north of Mauna Lani, the luxurious *Hapuna Beach Prince Hotel* (62-100 Kauna'oa Drive, Kohala Coast HI 96743; Ⓣ880-1111 or 1-800/882-6060, Ⓕ880-3026, Ⓦwww.hapunabeachprincehotel; limited view ❽, ocean view ❾) has since 1994 occupied the northern flanks of Hāpuna Beach. Despite being molded to the contours of the hillside, it's inevitably somewhat intrusive. The prospect from the inside looking out is superb: the hotel's giant central lobby is open to cooling sea breezes, while the turquoise pool is set flush with a broad patio, complete with whirlpool spa. Few resorts in the world can offer the same combination of opulent accommodation and idyllic situation. Of its two dinner-only gourmet restaurants, the circular *Coast Grille* occupies by far the better location; it specializes in adventurous Pacific Rim fish dishes, such as *opah* in a ginger and pistachio crust, at around $30 per entree. At the elegant but viewless Japanese *Hakone* (closed Mon & Tues), you can get a full sashimi or chicken dinner for $30–$40 or enjoy a copious buffet for $52.

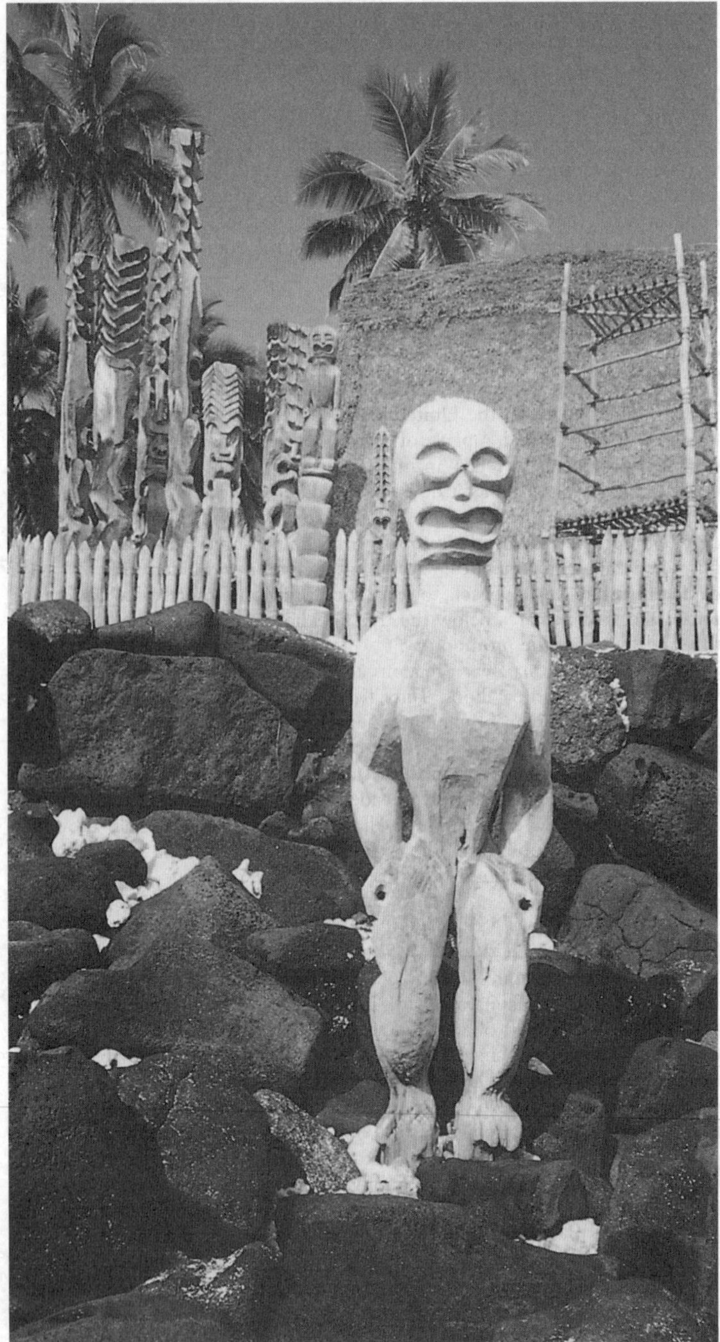

## Kauna'oa Beach

A mile north of Hāpuna Beach, barely a hundred yards beyond the turn for the *Hapuna Beach Prince*, and a mile south of the point where Hwy-19 meets Hwy-270, a separate approach road cuts down to reach the ocean at Kauna'oa Beach. Like its neighbors, this offers superb conditions for much of the year, but is exposed to very strong winds and high surf in winter, when much of the sand is washed away and swimming becomes very hazardous. The construction here of the *Mauna Kea Beach Hotel*, which opened for business in 1965 as the first of the Kohala resorts, was almost as controversial as the more recent development on Hāpuna Beach. However, although local Hawaiians fought and won an eight-year legal battle to have their rights of access respected, Kauna'oa Beach is barely used these days by anyone other than guests at the hotel.

### Mauna Kea Beach Hotel

Although it has undergone an extensive overhaul, and its guest rooms are kitted out to the highest of standards, for all its landscaping and lagoons the *Mauna Kea Beach Hotel* (62-100 Mauna Kea Beach Drive, Kohala Coast HI 96743; Ⓣ882-7222 or 1-800/882-6060, Ⓕ882-5748, Ⓦwww.maunakeabeachhotel.com; ⑨) still looks its age. The property's one great strength is its fabulous setting: effectively if not legally, Kauna'oa Beach serves as the *Mauna Kea*'s own exquisite private beach. The dinner-only *Batik* restaurant (closed Tues & Sat), unique on the Big Island in requiring male diners to wear jackets, serves a hybrid Mediterranean-Hawaiian cuisine; appetizers are $15–20 and entrees $30–50. The *Pavilion* prepares breakfast buffets and conventional American dinners, while the lovely outdoor *Terrace* is a great spot for a buffet lunch. The weekly *lū'au* (Tues 6pm; $70) takes place well away from the ocean, but there is a $70 Saturday-night clambake at the *Hau Tree* beachfront bar.

# Kawaihae

For the ancient Hawaiians, the natural harbor at **KAWAIHAE**, a couple of miles north of Hāpuna Beach, was one of the most important landing points along the coast of the Big Island. Over the last fifty years, massive earthmoving projects have destroyed any beauty that it once possessed, but in terms of population it remains no more than a tiny settlement.

## Samuel M Spencer Beach County Park

The last significant beach along the Kohala coast, **'Ohai'ula Beach**, is one of the few still geared towards low-tech, low-budget family fun. Better known as the **SPENCER BEACH PARK**, it offers the best oceanfront **campground** on the island, as well as full day-use facilities, but it can get very crowded, and with the access road extending along its full length it's seldom peaceful either. No cabins are available: campers are expected to bring their own tents or trailers and to obtain permits in advance from the Hawaii County Parks office in Hilo (Ⓣ961-8311).

The beach itself, sheltered by a long reef, is popular with recreational swimmers as well as more serious snorkelers and scuba divers; it takes a major storm to render bathing unsafe.

## Pu'ukoholā Heiau National Historic Site

The single most dramatic and imposing Hawaiian temple still standing on any of the islands is **PU'UKOHOLĀ HEIAU** (daily except holidays

7.30am–4pm; free; ⓣ882-7218, ⓦwww.nps.gov/puhe). Its construction between 1790 and 1791 by the future Kamehameha I is one of the greatest – and most horrific – epics of Big Island history.

The story of this *luakini*, a "war temple" fed by human sacrifice, began in 1782, when the young warrior Kamehameha seized control of the northwest segment of the Big Island. Over the years that followed, he conquered Maui, Lanai and Molokai, but failed to defeat his rivals on the rest of his home island of Hawaii. Eventually he heard that his cousin Keōua wanted to expand out from Ka'ū, in the southwest of the Big Island, so Kamehameha sent his aunt to consult the prophet Kapoukahi of Kauai, who suggested that building a *luakini* at Pu'ukoholā and dedicating it to his personal war god Kūkā'ilimoku would guarantee success in the coming conflict.

Kapoukahi himself came to the Big Island to oversee the construction of the new temple, on the site of a ruined *heiau* erected two centuries before by the legendary Lonoikamakahiki. The process was accompanied throughout by precise, exacting ritual: in the words of an old Hawaiian proverb, "the work of the *luakini* is like hauling *ohia* timber, of all labor the most arduous." First of all, the entire island had to be purified, by means of clearing the circle road and erecting altars at regular intervals.

For Kamehameha's rivals, the start of work was a clear announcement of impending war. They set out to sabotage the project, knowing that its completion would give Kamehameha irresistible *mana*, or spiritual power. Not only Keōua, but also the defeated chiefs of Maui, Lanai and Molokai, and even the rulers of Kauai and Oahu, joined forces to attack, but Kamehameha managed to hold them all off and pressed on with construction.

When the *heiau* was completed, in the summer of 1791, the prophet ordained a great feast, involving the sacrifice of 400 pigs, 400 bushels of bananas, 400 coconuts, 400 red fish, 400 pieces of *oloa* cloth and plenty of human beings, preferably themselves possessing considerable *mana*. Kamehameha therefore invited Keōua to attend the dedication, and make peace. Like a figure from Greek tragedy, Keōua accepted the invitation.

The moment Keōua stepped ashore on the beach, he was slain with a spear thrust by Kamehameha's trusted warrior Ke'eaumoku (the father of Ka'ahumanu). All his companions were also killed before Kamehameha, who later insisted that he had not sanctioned the slaughter, called a halt upon recognizing the commander of the second canoe as his own son Kaoleioku. Keōua's body was the main sacrifice offered, together with those of ten of his associates (the war god, who did not like blood on his altar, preferred his victims to have been killed elsewhere).

As sole ruler of the Big Island, Kamehameha went on to reconquer first Maui, Lanai and Molokai, then Oahu, all of which had been recaptured by their original rulers during the building of the temple. Finally he exacted tribute from Kauai, whereupon the whole archipelago took on the name of Kamehameha's native island, and thus became known as Hawaii.

The altar and idols at Pu'ukoholā were destroyed in 1819 on the orders of Kamehameha's successor Liholiho, shortly after the breaking of the ancient *kapu* system (see p.509).

### Visiting Pu'ukoholā Heiau

The parking lot for the heiau stands just off Hwy-19, at the start of the approach road to Spencer Beach Park and next to a small visitor center. The temple's three colossal tiers of black stone are not immediately visible from here, so follow the signed trail for a couple of hundred yards down towards the sea.

As the path rounds "the hill of the whale" after which the heiau was named, the vast platform of the temple – 224 feet long by 100 feet wide – looms above you, commanding a long stretch of coastline. Disappointingly, this is as close as you'll get; access is forbidden, in part because this remains a sacred site, but also because recent earthquake damage has rendered it unstable. No traces survive of the thatched houses and other structures that originally stood upon it.

A little further towards the sea stands the subsidiary **Mailekini Heiau**, narrower but longer, and much older than the main temple. It, too, is inaccessible to visitors. Both heiaus loom large above Pelekane Beach, which you are free to walk along, although nowadays it's not all that spectacular. In Kamehameha's era the beach was far longer, and there was a royal compound in the palm grove just back from the sea. The land that now lies immediately to the north is infill created during the construction of Kawaihae Harbor, when the beach itself was largely obliterated.

Breeding sharks still circle the **Haleokapuni Heiau**, dedicated to the shark deities, which lies beneath the waves around 100 feet out. The voracious beasts would devour offerings beneath the watchful gaze of the king, who would stand beside the stone Leaning Post that's still visible – though now in a sorry state – above the shore. Swimming is neither permitted nor particularly desirable: if the sharks aren't enough to put you off, the water is also clogged with gritty silt, which has completely obscured, and probably damaged, the underwater heiau.

## Kawaihae Harbor and Shopping Center

Despite remaining without a wharf until 1937, **KAWAIHAE HARBOR** has long been the most important anchorage on the leeward coast of Hawaii. It was always the major port for the cattle of the Parker Ranch (see p.195); in the old days, intrepid cowboys would swim both cows and horses from the beach out to sea, then lasso them in the water and lash a dozen of them to the outside of flimsy whaleboats, which in turn rowed them to larger vessels anchored offshore.

The bay was finally dredged by the military during the 1950s. Casualties of the process included an assortment of delightful, grassy islands, each of which held a thatched shack or two, and most of the Big Island's best coral reef. Nevertheless, the port remains relatively low-key, poorly protected from occasional violent storms, and with few services nearby. Its biggest flurry of activity for many years came with the much-troubled filming of the Kevin Costner blockbuster *Waterworld* in 1994–95, during which the movie's centerpiece, a floating "slave colony," sank at least once to the bottom of the harbor.

Kawaihae's only shops and restaurants are to be found in the **Kawaihae Shopping Center**, at the junction of Hwy-19 and Hwy-270. This small, two-story mall is more upmarket than the location might suggest. As well as a few clothes stores and the Harbor Gallery of fine arts, there's a *Café Pesto* (Mon–Thurs & Sun 11am–9pm, Fri & Sat 11am–10pm; ⓣ882-1071), serving the same menu of delicious calzones and pizzas as the branch in Hilo (see p.213). Upstairs and around the back, you'll find a Mexican bar/restaurant and the very "local" Akizuki's Takeout (Mon–Sat 6am–3pm; ⓣ882-7776), which in addition to cooked breakfasts and plate lunches sells coffees and smoothies.

# Waimea and the Kohala uplands





The only town of any significant size in Kohala, **Waimea**, is poised between north and south, a dozen miles up from the sea on the cool green plains between Kohala Mountain and Mauna Kea. For many of the visitors who climb inland from Kawaihae on Hwy-19, the interior of Hawaii comes as a surprise. These rolling uplands are cowboy country, still roamed on horseback by the *paniolos* of the United States' largest private cattle ranch, the **Parker Ranch**. Only when you look closely at the occasional rounded hills that dot the landscape do you spot signs of their volcanic origin; many are eroded cinder cones, topped by smoothed-over craters. The fact that temperatures are distinctly cooler here than by the sea is one reason why locals are moving to Waimea in ever-increasing numbers; visiting sun-worshippers tend not to be quite so keen.

## Waimea

Kohala's largest community, **WAIMEA**, is no longer the company town it used to be; the Parker Ranch now employs just one hundred of its eight thousand inhabitants. While still proud of its cowboy past – memorabilia of the much-mythologized *paniolos* (see p.195) is prominent everywhere – Waimea has become more of a sophisticated country resort and is now home to a diverse community that includes international astronomers from the Mauna Kea observatories and successful entrepreneurs from the mainland. Poised halfway between the contrasting Kohala and Hamākua coasts, Waimea has "wet" and "dry" sides of its own; it's the drier Kohala side, not surprisingly, where real estate is at a premium.

There's not all that much to Waimea as a destination; most visitors simply while away an afternoon or so enjoying its dramatic setting between the volcanoes. What town there is consists of a series of low-slung shopping malls lining Hwy-19 to either side of the central intersection, where it makes a sharp turn towards Honoka'a and Hilo. The most interesting gift and souvenir shopping is to be had at little **Parker Square**, on the west side of town, which holds several intriguing specialty stores. The much larger **Parker Ranch Shopping Center** is home to the local post office and the visitor center for the ranch itself (see p.194); as this book went to press, it was being greatly expanded, with the promise of a new bookstore and a "national brand coffeehouse." Head a quarter-mile east from here to see an appealing little cluster of clapboard **churches**, set well back from the road.

To avoid confusion with other Waimeas on Kauai and Oahu, the post office calls the Big Island's Waimea "Kamuela." Neither older nor more authentic, this name is simply a nineteenth-century corruption of "Samuel," one of the many scions of the house of Parker.

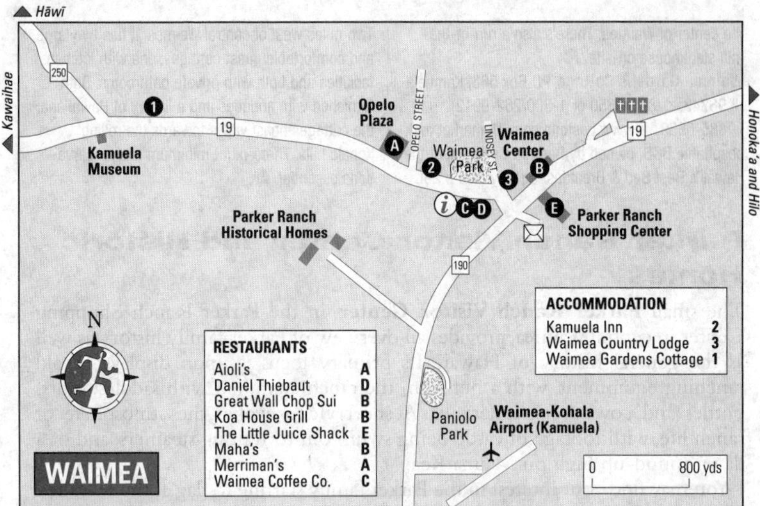


## Arrival and information

Waimea does have its own tiny **airport**, in the rolling ranchlands just south of town, but it sees very little use. The only airline offering scheduled service is Pacific Wings (Ⓣ887-2104 or 1-888/575-4546, Ⓦwww.pacificwings.com), which operates daily flights to Honolulu (Mon–Sat 8am, Sun 3.10pm) and Kahului on Maui (daily 6.10pm). The standard one-way fare of $93 is reduced to $49 for Hawaii residents.

The town has also recently acquired a helpful **visitor center**, behind the High Country Traders building and alongside Parker Square on Hwy-19, on the Kawaihae side of town (Mon–Sat 9.30am–4.30pm; Ⓣ885-6707, Ⓦwww.NorthHawaii.net). As well as brochures and maps, it holds current menus for all the local restaurants.

## Accommodation

Few visitors spend the night in Waimea, although it's one of the most pleasant towns on the island; the chief drawback is that the nights are significantly colder here than down by the ocean. For Hawaiians, that's a plus point, and the attractive local B&Bs are often booked well in advance.

**Kamuela Inn**, PO Box 1994, Kamuela HI 96743; Ⓣ885-4243 or 1-800/555-8968, Ⓕ885-8857, Ⓦwww.hawaii-bnb.com/kamuela.html. Former motel, set back from the road a half-mile west of the central intersection, within easy walking distance of several restaurants. Refurbished and given an extra wing, it now holds rooms of varying but generally high quality, all with private baths, and some "penthouse suites" with kitchenettes as well. Rates include basic continental breakfast. Rooms ❷, suites ❸.

**Tina's Country Cottage**, reserve through Hawaii's Best Bed & Breakfast, PO Box 563, Kamuela HI 96743; Ⓣ885-4550 or 1-800/262-9912, Ⓕ885-0559, Ⓦwww.bestbnb.com. Two-bedroom, two-bathroom cottage, with kitchen, wood-burning stove and spacious gardens, overlooking the Parker Ranch. Two-night minimum stay; reservations essential. ❹.

**Waimea Country Lodge**, 65-1210 Lindsey Rd, Kamuela HI 96743; Ⓣ885-4100; or reserve through Castle Resorts, Ⓣ1-800/367-5004 (US & Can) or Ⓣ1-800/272-5275 (HI), Ⓕ885-6711, Ⓦwww.castle-group.com. Simple and predictable motel units backing on to the Kohala slopes, at the start of the road to Kawaihae from the junction in the center of Waimea. There's also a run-of-the-mill steakhouse on-site. ❸.

**Waimea Gardens Cottage**, PO Box 563, Kamuela HI 96743; Ⓣ885-4550 or 1-800/262-9912; Ⓕ885-0559, Ⓦwww.bestbnb.com. Upmarket and hospitable B&B, owned by Barbara Campbell of the Hawaii's Best Bed & Breakfast agency (see p.29). Two miles west of central Waimea, it has two large and comfortable guest cottages, one with kitchen facilities and both with private bathrooms. Both furnished with antiques and a library of Hawaiiana, the cottages boast views towards the rolling Kohala hills. Three-night minimum stay; reservations essential. ❹.



## Parker Ranch Visitor Center and Historic Homes

The small **Parker Ranch Visitor Center**, in the Parker Ranch Shopping Center in central Waimea, provides an overview of Parker family history as well as the general history of Hawaii. Its primary focus is upon displays of old ranching equipment, with a hut from the ranch crammed with saddles, spurs, bottles and cowboy paraphernalia. A short video evokes the atmosphere of ranch life, with footage of cattle being swum out to waiting steamers, and of a dawn round-up high on Mauna Kea.

You may find your interest in the Parker family starting to flag at the so-called **Historic Homes**, half a mile out of Waimea towards Kailua, on Hwy-190. Construction of the stately **Pu'u'ōpelu** started in 1863, but it was completely remodeled in 1969 and now lacks any apparent connection with things Hawaiian. Its pastel yellow rooms are filled instead with minor European paintings, while through the air waft the melodious tones of its last owner, Richard Smart, in recordings he made as a Broadway musical star.

The **Mana House** alongside looks like an ordinary white clapboard house, but the interior gleams with dark, heavy *koa* wood, which groans under your every step. These timbers were the only components robust enough to be moved in 1970, when it was decided to reconstruct the house here, twelve miles from the site where it originally went up during the 1840s. The walls of the tiny building are packed with family documents and fading photographs.

Five hundred yards beyond the Historic Homes towards Kailua, and six miles before the Saddle Road turnoff, **Paniolo Park** is the home each July 4 of the **Parker Ranch Rodeo** (for information, contact Ⓣ885-7655 or Ⓦwww.parkerranch.com).

## Kamuela Museum

For sheer entertainment value, the best museum on the island is the **Kamuela Museum,** two miles west of the central Waimea intersection, almost directly opposite the junction of highways 250 and 19 (daily 8am–5pm; $5 adults, $2 under-12s; Ⓣ885-4724). Its most memorable specimen is its owner and curator, Albert Solomon, who was in charge of the Honolulu police force motor-

### Parker Ranch practicalities

Visitor Center daily except hols 9am–5pm, last entry 4pm, $6, under-12s $4.50.
Historic Homes daily except hols 10am–5pm, last entry 4pm, $8.50/$6.
Combined ticket, sold 9am–3pm only, $12/$9.50.
Wagon Tours, hourly Tues–Sat 10am–2pm, $15/$12.
Parker Ranch Experience, including wagon tour and lunch at Koa House Grill, $42/$35.
For more information, contact Ⓣ885-7655 or Ⓦwww.parkerranch.com.

## The Parker Ranch

At its largest, in the nineteenth century, the **Parker Ranch** spread across more than half a million acres of the Big Island. It still covers more than ten percent of the island, currently holding around sixty thousand cattle on over 200,000 acres. The bulk of the land is divided into three huge parcels: one takes up most of North Kohala, one curves around the higher Hāmakua reaches of Mauna Kea, and the largest runs for forty miles up the western slopes of Mauna Kea from the ocean at Kawaihae.

It all dates back to **John Palmer Parker**, a ship's clerk from Massachusetts, who jumped ship in Kawaihae Harbor in 1809 and soon came to the attention of King Kamehameha, who gave him the job of maintaining the fishponds at Hōnaunau (see p.174).

In February 1793, Captain George Vancouver of the *Discovery* had presented Kamehameha with six cows and a bull and suggested that a *kapu* be placed on the cattle to allow a population to grow. By 1815, wild cattle had become a serious problem, destroying crops and terrorizing villages, and wild mustangs too were roaming unmolested. Kamehameha gave Parker permission to shoot the cattle, and from a base near Pololū he set out to impose discipline on the unruly beasts. With the decline of the sandalwood trade, the supply of fresh beef and hides to visiting whalers became crucial to the Hawaiian economy. Parker managed the business for the King, and by taking his pay in live animals built up his own herds. Marrying Kamehameha's granddaughter **Kipikane**, he soon integrated into local society and was one of only two foreigners present at the famous banquet in 1819 when Liholiho broke the age-old *kapu* on men and women dining together (see p.509). He moved to the village of Waimea in 1835, established his homestead at Mana, and built a separate house for his son, John Palmer Parker II.

The ponchos, bandanas and rawhide lassos of the Mexican, Native American and Spanish *vaqueros* who were brought to work on the ranch were adopted by the Hawaiian cowboys they recruited and trained. They called themselves **paniolos** (from *Españoles*, or Spaniards).

Like many outsiders, Parker seized his opportunity in the Great Mahele of 1847, when private land ownership was first allowed (see p.512). He was granted two acres, and his wife, Kipikane, received 640 more. Soon he was in a position to buy another thousand acres and to lease the entire *ahupua'a* (see p.517) of Waikoloa.

After the ranch was divided among Parker's immediate heirs, and the high-living **Samuel Parker** then frittered much of it away, the property was reunified under Thelma Parker in 1906. Attempts to diversify into sugar production and beekeeping came to nothing, but the cattle ranch went from strength to strength for the rest of the twentieth century. When the last Parker to control the operation, the sixth-generation **Richard Smart**, died in November 1992, he chose to leave just one percent of his holdings to his family. The ranch now belongs to a charitable trust, with assorted schools and health-care facilities in the Waimea area among the beneficiaries of its profits.

cycle escort team when Franklin Roosevelt came to Hawaii in 1934 – and can show you the great man's slippers to prove it. If you have an hour or two to spare, both he and his wife, Harriet, can tell some great tales; she is a direct Parker descendant, and their family anecdotes cover the entire period since Americans first arrived in Hawaii. However, as both are nonagenarians, and they've been attempting to sell the museum, which is also their home, for several years, it's possible that they will be no longer be here by the time you visit.

The museum spreads through several rooms of the Solomons' bungalow. Each of the dozens of display cases contains an unpredictable mixture of items and hand-written labels, which categorize the objects from "unique" (the rope used to haul the Apollo 11 astronauts out of the Pacific), through "quite rare" (a desiccated Hawaiian bat suspended by its feet), down to simply "old" (a motley assortment of toothpick holders, Japanese noodle-cutting machines, accordions, "historic reptile dung," chicken spectacles and can openers). An intriguing collection of Chinese and Japanese porcelain, costumes and weaponry culminates with a gun retrieved from the wreckage of a *kamikaze* plane that attacked the USS *West Virginia* in April 1945.

Most visitors are especially drawn to the unusual and extensive range of ancient **Hawaiian artifacts**, among them sinister-looking idols of wood and stone, rows of daggers, "death cups" used in magic rituals, and lava knuckle dusters worn by fistfighters. Laid out for your inspection are all the daily implements of a world without metal, including wooden hooks that were baited with human flesh and used to catch sharks, fish hooks made from human bone, *poi* pounders and *tapa* beaters, and colorful feather *leis* and helmets.



## Restaurants

As one of the Big Island's most exclusive residential areas, Waimea has finally acquired the **restaurants** to befit its status. In addition, a few old-style cowboy places are still piling up meaty mountains of ribs, while the Waimea Center mall, down the road towards Hilo, is the place to head for **fast food**, with McDonalds, TCBY and Subway outlets.

**Aioli's**, Opelo Plaza, 65-1227A Opelo Rd; ⓣ885-6325. French bakery-cum-deli-cum-bistro, tucked away in an unexciting mall. Fresh breads and great sandwiches for lunch; dinner offerings include ratatouille crepes for $14, and rack of lamb with Asian mustard for $15. Tues 11am–4pm, Wed & Thurs 11am–8pm, Fri & Sat 11am–9pm, Sun 8am–2pm.

**Great Wall Chop Sui**, Waimea Center; ⓣ885-7252. Extensive and inexpensive Chinese menu in an unatmospheric mall. *Chop sui*, noodles and seafood for as little as $6, plus cheap buffets for both lunch ($8) and dinner ($10). Mon, Tues, Thurs & Fri 11am–8.30pm, Sat & Sun 9am–8.30pm, closed Wed.

**Daniel Thiebaut**, 65-1259 Kawaihae Rd; ⓣ887-1200. Classy Mediterranean/Pacific restaurant in the attractive timber-framed "Historic Yellow Building," a short way up from Parker Square, specializing in Asian-style searing and spicing but rich European sauces. Appetizers like Hilo sweetcorn crab cakes or chicken wontons cost around $8; entrees such as wok-fried scallops, and five-spice-dusted duck breast are $20–25. There are also plenty of vegetarian entrees, and a changing daily three-course prix fixe menu for $33. Daily 5.30–9.30pm.

**Koa House Grill**, Hwy-19 at Waimea Center; ⓣ885-2088. This large modern highway diner is the best of the chicken-and-ribs cowboy places in Waimea, with a menu that strays into Pacific Rim territory as well with seared *ahi* and Thai curries. Lunch will run around $10; dinner entrees range from $15 to $25. Mon–Sat 11.30am–10pm, Sun 11am–2pm.

**Maha's**, Waimea Center; ⓣ885-0693. Friendly, pretty, antique-furnished café in an unlikely 1852 clapboard house at the front of an otherwise modern mall. Breakfast features granola for $4 or eggs for $5; lunchtime offerings ($6–11) include top-quality fish or chicken sandwiches plus smoked *ahi* tortillas or fresh *ahi* salads. Daily except Tues 8am–4.30pm.

**Merrimans**, Opelo Plaza, 65-1227A Opelo Rd; ⓣ885-6822. Gourmet restaurant with an emphasis on organic produce. Lunches are simple, with a $12 grilled shrimp on linguini the most expensive dish. Dinner entrees, priced at $20–30, tend to be much richer, but the signature wok-charred *ahi* is irresistible. Mon–Fri 11.30am–1.30pm & 5.30–9pm, Sat & Sun 5.30–9pm.

**The Little Juice Shack**, Parker Ranch Center; ⓣ885-1686. Clean, busy deli next to the Parker Ranch visitor center, which serves $3–4 juices and smoothies, $5 salads and sandwiches, and daily lunch specials such as Thai curry. Mon–Fri 7am–4pm, Sat 9am–4pm.

**Waimea Coffee Co**, Parker Square; ⓣ885-4472. Lively vegetarian café where the fresh coffee is complemented by an array of very inexpensive soups, salads and sandwiches, all priced at well under $5. Mon–Fri 7am–5pm, Sat 8am–4pm.

# Onwards from Waimea

Whichever direction you head from Waimea, there's spellbinding scenery just a few miles down the road. Heading east towards Hilo on Hwy-19 brings you to Honoka'a in less than twenty minutes, with Waipi'o Valley not far beyond (see p.222). From an intersection just six miles south of Waimea, the **Saddle Road** starts its dramatic climb across the heart of the island between Mauna Kea and Mauna Loa – a journey covered in detail on p.226. The most attractive drive of all is **Hwy-250** along Kohala Mountain to Hāwi. However, the transition from the dry to the wet side of the Big Island can be experienced at its most marked if you make a slight detour off Hwy-19 three miles east of Waimea and follow the atmospheric and little-used **Old Māmalahoa Highway**.

## Old Māmalahoa Highway

Once part of Kamehameha's round-island trail, the **Old Māmalahoa Highway** was known to the ancient Hawaiians as "mudlane" and was notorious as a site where *'oi'o*, or processions of the souls of the dead, might be encountered at night as they headed for the underworld said to lie below Waipi'o Valley. Now it's a minor road, somewhat slow and sinuous, but not difficult, even for cyclists.

The road heads first through treeless volcanic uplands where the rolling meadows, misty when they're not windswept, are grazed by horse and cattle. After about eight miles, you abruptly plunge into a magnificent avenue of stately old ironwoods. Thereafter, the vegetation is tropical and colorful, and homes with glorious gardens dot the hillside. Soon after passing through the residential community of **Āhualoa**, you rejoin the Belt Road near Honoka'a.

# North Kohala

The district of **North Kohala**, which officially starts four miles or so north of Kawaihae, to all intents and purposes comprises the low-rise flanks of Kohala Mountain itself. Spreading across both sides of the mountain, it's a microcosm of the whole island, with its dry leeward side separated by rolling uplands from the precipitous wet valleys of the eastern coastline. The road that curves around the north comes to an end at **Pololū Valley**, the last of a chain of valleys that begins with Waipi'o (see p.222). Like Waipi'o, Pololū was home to generations of ancient *taro* farmers; in fact, two centuries ago this region was the original powerbase of Kamehameha the Great, and several sites associated with Hawaii's first monarch can still be seen. The traditional Hawaiian way of life came to an end in 1906, when the waters from Pololū were diverted for irrigation. However, the last of the sugar plantations closed down in 1975, and these days the area is relatively unpopulated, scattered with tiny and characterful communities that are attempting to diversify into coffee and macadamia nut production.

Though North Kohala holds some of the most beautiful of all the Big Island's scenery, few visitors take the time to explore it. Its major drawback is that access to the sea is restricted on both the leeward side, which is almost entirely devoid of beaches, and the rugged windward coast. While almost no overnight accommodation is available, several local businesses are encouraging day-trippers to take adventure expeditions up into the hills, and there are at least several appealing little restaurants and snack bars.

## Across the mountain: Hwy-250



With a maximum elevation of 5408 feet, Kohala Mountain is considerably lower than its younger Big Island rivals. Its summit is always green, never covered by snow, and its smooth velvet knobs betray few traces of their violent volcanic past. This landscape might not conform with what's usually thought of as Hawaiian, but the varying views of it obtained from a trip along **Hwy-250** are among the most sublime in the entire state.

For the first four miles or so out of Waimea, as the highway climbs the west flank of Kohala Mountain, a panorama of the Kohala coast gradually unfolds. At first the rolling lava landscape is covered with wiry green turf. Then scattered trees start to appear, together with clumps of flat-bladed cactus, often growing straight out of bare outcrops of chunky black lava. Higher still you enter proper ranching country; for a while the road becomes an avenue lined with two rows of splendid ironwood trees, between which you catch glimpses of undulating pastureland grazed by sleek horses. At various points along the way, vivid green turf-covered cinder cones bulge from the meadows, speckled with black and brown cattle.

Unfortunately, you never get the chance to turn off the road and explore the magnificent scenery higher up the mountain. As well as large landholdings of the Parker Ranch, concentrated as the northern end, there are several other private estates and even one or two old-style cattle-ranching communities hidden away along the northern half. The top of the mountain is a surreal landscape of eroded hillocks, which across the watershed become so thickly forested as to be almost impenetrable. Rudimentary trails lead down to valleys such as Waipi'o, and the rough terrain is still cut through in places by irrigation channels such as the famous **Kohala Ditch**, constructed in the early 1900s to service the sugar industry.

### Kohala Mountain adventures

The only way to experience the unique backcountry of Kohala Mountain is on a guided **adventure tour**.

**Flumin' Da Ditch** (daily 8.15am & 12.15pm; adults $85, ages 5–18 $65; ⓣ889-6922 or 1-877/449-6922, ⓦwww.flumindaditch.com) drives groups from the town of Hāwī up to a remote spot in the hills. There you're loaded into five-person kayaks and paddled on an extraordinary 3.5-mile ride along the narrow irrigation channel known as the Kohala Ditch. The trip involves plunging through the mountains along thousand-foot dank tunnels and crossing deep gorges on wooden flumes. Once you're in the ditch, there are no long-distance views, but you do see rainforest waterfalls close-up. All in all, it's a great, if very wet, wilderness trip.

As HMV Tours, the same company also runs daily 4WD **jeep tours** into the hills, as does ATV Outfitters (closed Sun; ⓣ889-6000) from its base in Kapa'au; prices range from $90 upwards. Kohala Eco Adventure in Hāwī (ⓣ327-1133) specializes in guided **mountain bike tours** in the region starting at $89.

Finally, you can also see the mountain on **horseback**. Kohala Na'alapa Trail Rides (ⓣ889-0022) sets off daily into the uplands from the ironwoods of Kohala Ranch (2hr 30min ride at 9am, $75 per person; 1hr 30min ride at 1.30pm, $55). Paniolo Riding Adventures (ⓣ889-5354), based at Ponoholo Ranch, offers slightly more expensive rides.

## Along the coast: Hwy-270

The only alternative to Hwy-250 if you want to see North Kohala is the coastal **Hwy-270**, which heads north from Kawaihae Harbor. Most visitors drive a circular route that takes in both; the shoreline road is not as immediately attractive, but it does offer a handful of interesting historic sites, the occasional beach park and, in winter, the possibility of spotting humpback whales in the waters of the ʻAlenuihāhā Channel.

For its first dozen miles Hwy-270 has no access to the ocean; if you want to snorkel in the bays at the foot of the low cliffs, join a boat excursion with Red Sail Sports (Ⓣ885-2876, Ⓦwww.redsail.com).

### Lapakahi State Historical Park

Fourteen miles north of Kawaihae, the first turning *makai* of the highway leads a short way down to **LAPAKAHI STATE HISTORICAL PARK** (daily 8am–4pm; free). The ancient village of Koaiʻe here is thought to have been inhabited for more than five hundred years until it was abandoned during the nineteenth century.

A hot, exposed, but fascinating one-mile-long trail leads through what appears to have been a sizeable subsistence-level community of ordinary Hawaiians. They probably chose this site because of its white coral beach and lack of cliffs, which made it the safest year-round canoe landing for many miles. Sustaining a population on such barren land must always have been hard, and the struggle seems to have been defeated in the end by a combination of a drop in the water table and the economic changes taking place in the islands as a whole.

You pass the villagers' dwelling places – not necessarily roofed, their low walls served primarily as windbreaks – as well as assorted traces of their day-to-day life. Most of these are simply hollowed-out rocks; some were used to hold lamps, others served as salt pans of varying depths, and there's even a little indented stone, holding scattered black and white pebbles, used to play the game *kōnane*. Beside a fish shrine, where offerings would have been left to ensure a successful catch, a carved decoy rests on a open net; the shy *ahu* fish was captured when it attempted to make friends with its wooden counterpart.

The **beach** at Lapakahi is composed of medium-sized boulders rather than fine sand. This is a marine conservation area and the water is very clear, with parrotfish and darting yellow shapes visible in its turquoise depths. Visitors are only allowed to swim or snorkel north of the ancient village and even there the use of sunscreen and towels is forbidden. From the bluff near the end of the trail, you can see Maui's towering Haleakalā volcano.

### Moʻokini Heiau and the Kamehameha Birthplace

At the island's northernmost tip, beyond the nondescript Māhunukona and Kapaʻa beach parks (both of which are seldom suitable for casual swimming), a long, straight road drops down to the perimeter fence of **ʻUpolu**'s barely used military airport. From there, an unpaved road winds west along the coastline, degenerating occasionally into pools of mud. Though quite rutted, in dry conditions it poses few problems for ordinary rental cars. There are no trees along this exposed and windy stretch, where the rolling meadows halt a few feet up from the black lava shoreline.

One of Hawaii's remotest but most significant ancient temples, **MO'OKINI HEIAU**, is roughly two miles from the airport. It's accessible from a rudimentary parking lot, via a footpath up a small bluff. Though the gate is usually locked, visitors can go through the gap in the low walls. The *heiau*, in the center of a large green lawn, is a ruined but impressive pile of lichen-covered rocks; you can enter the structure and discern the traces of separate rooms, as well as a boulder on which victims were prepared for sacrifice.

Two conflicting legends make the temple's origins obscure. Its current guardians state that it was built between sunset and sunrise on a single night in 480 AD by Kuamo'o Mo'okini, using water-worn basalt stones passed from hand to hand along a fourteen-mile human chain from Pololū Valley. Alternative sources suggest it was created by the Tahitian warrior-priest Pa'ao seven centuries later, as a temple to Kū, the god of battle. The most likely explanation, though, is that Pa'ao simply rededicated an existing temple to Kū; it may even have been the site where the practice of human sacrifice was first introduced to Hawaii. The Kahuna Nui, the hereditary priesthood of Kū, has maintained an unbroken descent; the traditional *kapu* barring female priests has long since been broken, however, and the current Kahuna Nui, Leimomi Mo'okini Lum, is the seventh woman to hold the position.

A few hundred yards further along, the **KAMEHAMEHA AKAHI AINA HANAU** is a low, double-walled enclosure that slopes down a little closer to the sea. Kamehameha the Great is said to have been born here in 1758 – the date is known thanks to the appearance of Halley's Comet – at a time when his parents were in the retinue of King Alapa'i, who was preparing to invade Maui. Whisked away in secret and brought up in Waipi'o Valley, he returned to live in Kohala in 1782 (see opposite). The entrance to the large compound is from the south, *mauka* side; you can't go into the central enclosure, which amounts to little more than a patch of scrubby soil scattered with a few boulders. One rock marks the precise birthsite; visitors still leave offerings to Hawaii's greatest ruler on the walls nearby.

## Hāwī

More than 25 years after the closure of its *raison d'être* – the Kohala Sugar Company mill – the tiny town of **HĀWĪ**, a mile beyond the 'Upolu turnoff, is hanging on as one of the nicest little communities in Hawaii. It is an attractive place, with its all-purpose stores and new galleries and snack outlets still connected by creaking boardwalks, and every yard bursting with bright flowers.

Once you've filled up with gas at the intersection of highways 250 and 270, there's nothing to see or do in Hāwī beyond strolling across the village green and along the hundred yards of its main street. However, the spacious *Bamboo Restaurant and Bar* (Tues–Sat 11.30am–2.30pm & 6–8.30pm, Sun 11am–2pm; ⓣ889-5555) is perhaps the Big Island's nicest **restaurant**, serving "island-style" cuisine in a dining room furnished with bamboo and rattan furniture and festooned with tropical plants. A lunchtime salad, burger or plate of stir-fried noodles costs $5–8, while dinner entrees ($14–22) include fish cooked to your specification in a range of styles such as "Hawaii Thai," as well as chicken, beef and lamb from local farms. There's live Hawaiian music on weekend evenings, and the attached store-cum-gallery sells attractive *koa*-wood gifts and other crafts. If you're just after a light snack, the *Kohala Coffee Mill* (ⓣ889-5577), across the street, has fresh Kona coffee plus burgers, bagels and ice cream.

# Kapa'au

The main feature in the even smaller hamlet of **KAPA'AU**, a couple of miles east of Hāwī on Hwy-270, is its **statue** of King Kamehameha. The original of the one facing 'Iolani Palace in Honolulu (see p.80), it was commissioned from an American sculptor in Florence for the coronation of King Kalākaua in 1883, lost at sea, and then miraculously recovered after the insurance money had paid for a replacement. Kamehameha had established his headquarters in **Hālawa** in 1782, in order to prepare for the imminent contest over the right to succeed the aging King Kalaniopu'u. All traces of Hālawa were ploughed over to plant cane many years ago, but it was very close to where modern Kapa'au now stands, and so this sleepy town seemed a reasonable alternative location for the surplus statue.

Immediately behind the statue, the former courthouse now serves as the **Kohala Information Center** (Mon–Fri 10am–4pm). Staffed by local senior citizens, it holds a few rudimentary exhibitions, but it's basically a place to hang out and talk story. *Jen's Kohala Café*, opposite (daily 10am–6pm; Ⓣ889-0099), serves sandwiches, salads, wraps, smoothies, and all sorts of ice cream. In the restored Nanbu Hotel building, just up the street, the smart little *Nanbu Courtyard* (Mon–Fri 6.30am–4pm, Sat & Sun 8am–4pm) sells **espresso coffees** and lunchtime deli sandwiches, while the well-stocked and very welcoming *Kohala Book Shop* (Tues–Sat 11am–5pm; Ⓣ889-6400) claims to be the largest used bookstore in Hawaii.

Not far east of town, a narrow road *mauka* of the highway leads through some verdant countryside to the picturesque **Kalāhikiola Church**, built in 1855.

## Kēōkea Beach County Park

The road on from Kapa'au runs past the site of Hālawa; a huge wayside boulder at this tight curve is known as **Kamehameha Rock**, as the future king is said to have demonstrated his right to rule by having sufficient *mana*, or spiritual power, to raise it above his head.

Immediately beyond, a lane leads, via a Japanese cemetery dotted with small black steles, down to **KĒŌKEA BEACH COUNTY PARK**. In the center of a rocky bay, a small stream flows into the ocean, and the surrounding hillsides have been pounded to pieces by high surf. An open-sided lookout shelter, exposed to the winds on a small hillock, makes a nice picnic spot, but there is no beach.

A short way along the side road to the beach, *Kohala's Guest House* (PO Box 172, Hāwī HI 96719; Ⓣ889-5606, Ⓕ889-5572, home1.gte.net/svendsen/index.htm; ❷) is the best accommodation option in North Kohala, doubling as both a **B&B** for short visits and a longer-term vacation rental. Each of the two separate houses has three guest rooms, and there's also a separate studio with kitchenette. The rooms are clean, fresh and comfortable, the rates are excellent, fruit trees fill the yard, and owner Nani Svendsen delights in sharing her extensive knowledge of North Kohala with her guests.

# Pololū Valley

As Hwy-270 reaches its dead end at a tiny parking lot, you get a view over one final meadow to the open cliff face that abuts the sea. Stretching away into the distance, it's punctuated by a succession of valleys, only accessible to visitors on foot and each therefore progressively less frequented and wilder than the last. The last of these, not visible from here, is Waipi'o (see p.222); the first, spread out beneath you, is **POLOLŪ VALLEY**.

If not quite on the scale of Waipi'o, Pololū was also once heavily planted by *taro* farmers. Regular *tsunamis* did little to encourage a stable population, however, and the death knell came when completion of the Kohala Ditch in 1906 drained the valley's previously plentiful water supply off for use on the nearby sugar plantations.

Pololū Valley remains a magnificent spectacle, and nowhere more so than from the initial overlook. If you take the time to explore it close up you may well find the hike down less strenuous, and more private, than its better-known equivalent further east. The pedestrian-only trail from the end of the parking lot takes twenty minutes without ever being steep, but when it's wet – which is almost always – it's an absolute quagmire of gloopy brown mud. Conditions are at their worst at the very start of the trail, which drops immediately into dense, head-high grasses. From there you wind down the hillside among ironwood, guava and *hala* trees. Occasionally the trees yield to stretches of loose lava pebbles, which come as a welcome relief from the prevailing mud, and offer glimpses of the shore below.

Once on the valley floor, the trail remains thoroughly squelchy as it approaches the broad river-cum-lake that meanders across the terrain, surrounded by marshy reeds. Hikers who try to head inland are swiftly confronted by "Private Property" signs warning you to go no farther.

Though Pololū's **beach**, like the one at Waipi'o, is commonly referred to as being black sand, it's basically gray grit, littered with decaying detergent bottles and pulverized flotsam. More welcome touches of color are added by the yellow and purple blooms that back the black lava rocks. In winter, the shore is prone to strong winds and heavy surf; there's no question of swimming even at the best of times. Take care, too, as you wade across the shallow but fast-flowing stream to reach the longer segment of the beach; high water is capable of carrying hikers out to the sharks offshore. On the far side of the stream, the beach is lined by gentle woodlands of pine-needle-covered hillocks, grazed by mules and horses.

### Onwards from Pololū

A conspicuous but virtually impossible-to-follow trail switchbacks eastwards from Pololū over to the next valley, **Honokāne Nui**, and on to **Honokāne Iki** beyond that. The track doesn't go all the way through to Waipi'o, so at some point the few suicidal hikers who attempt it have to double back. As a rule the path follows the contours of the hillsides and doesn't drop back down to the sea each time, but it's in roughly the same bedraggled condition as the trail down to Pololū and is certainly no easier. Only experienced wilderness backpackers should even consider an expedition into this remote and uninhabited terrain.

## Hilo

Until recently, windward Hawaii's major city, **HILO**, was the economic and political powerhouse of the island. It's still the capital, and home to 45,000 people, but as the sugar mills close and the significance of Kona-side tourism increases, it now feels more like a rather traditional small town. As a place to visit, it's relaxed and attractive, spread over a surprisingly large area but with an appealingly old-fashioned downtown district where you can stroll between friendly cafés, street markets and historic sites.

In the early 1970s, Hilo made a bid to become a major tourist center, but mass tourism has never taken off here; quite simply, it rains too much. Hilo averages 130 inches of rainfall annually, with fewer than ninety rain-free days per year. Most mornings, however, start out clear and radiant; the rain falls in the afternoon or at night, and America's wettest city blazes with wild orchids and tropical plants.

As well as having the only **airport** along the Hāmākua coast, Hilo holds all its **hotels**. There are no sizeable sandy beaches, and tourists who come here are drawn largely by the beauty of the nearby coast. The fifty-mile excursion up to Waipi'o Valley is irresistible, but nearer at hand you can enjoy the delightful Pepe'ekeo Scenic Drive, or the mighty Akaka and Rainbow falls.

Hilo stands where the Wailuku and Wailoa rivers empty into an enormous curving bay, named "Hilo" by ancient Hawaiians in honor of the first crescent of the new moon. In 1796, Kamehameha the Great chose the best natural harbor on the island to build his *peleleu,* a fleet of eight hundred war canoes for his campaigns against the other Hawaiian islands. Characterized by his enemies as "monstrosities," these hybrid Western-influenced vessels carried mighty armies of warriors; some say they were never destroyed and still lie hidden in caves along the Kona coast.

The port prospered in the nineteenth century, when a strong missionary influence enabled it to present itself as a clean-living alternative to dissolute Honolulu. In the words of the evangelist Titus Coan in 1848:

> **No man staggers, no man fights, none are noisy and boisterous. We have nothing here to inflame the blood, nothing to madden the brain. Our verdant landscapes, our peaceful streets, our pure cold water, and the absence of those inebriating vials of wrath which consume all good, induce wise commanders to visit this port in order to refresh and give liberty to their crews.**

Hilo became the center of the Big Island's burgeoning sugar industry, shipping out raw cane and serving as the arrival point for immigrants from around the world, and in the process acquired an unusually radical labor force. From the 1930s onwards, local workers spearheaded successive campaigns against the "Big Five" companies that had long dominated the Hawaiian economy (see p.513). Fifty people were injured in the "Hilo Massacre" of August 1, 1938, when strikers were attacked by armed police, and strikes in 1946 and 1949 helped to end the long-term Republican domination of state politics.

The innermost segment of the bay, encompassing both port and town, is protected by a long breakwater. In principle, this is a very calm stretch of water, but its funnel shape means that during great storms it can channel huge waves directly into the center of town. Cataclysmic *tsunamis* killed 96 people in April 1946, and an additional 61 in May 1960. Lava flows have also repeatedly threatened to engulf Hilo; in 1881 Princess Ruth Ke'elikōlani summoned up all her spiritual power (see p.244) to halt one on the edge of town, while in 1984 another flow stopped eight miles short.

## Arrival and information

Compact and walkable, downtown Hilo focuses on the junction of seafront Kamehameha Avenue, and Waianuenue Avenue, which heads towards the

# HILO

| ACCOMMODATION | |
|---|---|
| Arnott's Lodge | 1 |
| Dolphin Bay Hotel | 2 |
| Hawaii Naniloa Hotel | 6 |
| Hilo Hawaiian Hotel | 4 |
| Hilo Seaside Hotel | 7 |
| Shipman House B&B | 8 |
| Uncle Billy's Hilo Bay Hotel | 5 |
| Wild Ginger Inn | 3 |

| RESTAURANTS | |
|---|---|
| Harrington's | B |
| Ken's House of Pancakes | C |
| Nihon Cultural Center | D |
| The Seaside Restaurant | A |

For downtown restaurants, see 'Downtown Hilo' map

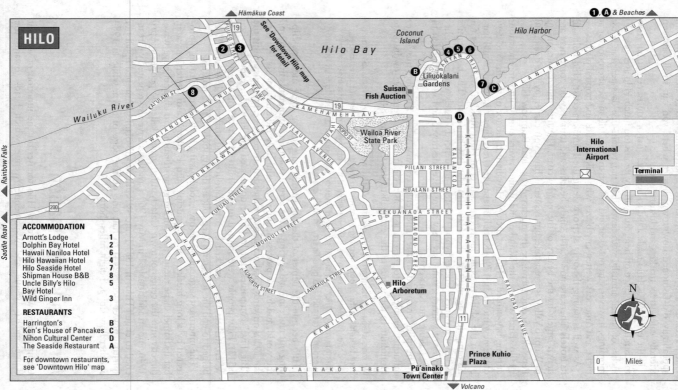

### Hilo–Kona bus timetable

| | From Hilo | To Hilo |
|---|---|---|
| HILO Prince Kūhiō Plaza | 1.10pm | 10.05am |
| HILO Mooheau Bus Terminal | 1.30pm | 9.45am |
| Pepe'ekeo | 1.45pm | 9.30am |
| Honomu | 1.50pm | 9.25am |
| Laupāhoehoe | 2.10pm | 8.55am |
| Honoka'a *Dairy Queen* | 2.40pm | 8.30am |
| Waimea Parker Ranch | 3.20pm | 8.05am |
| Waikoloa | 3.45pm | 7.25am |
| KAILUA Lanihau Center | 4.25pm | 6.45am |
| Keauhou *Kona Surf* | 4.50pm | 6.25am |
| Kainaliu | 5.05pm | 6.15am |
| Captain Cook | 5.15pm | 6.00am |
| Hōnaunau | 5.20pm | 5.55am |
| Keālia | 5.30pm | 5.45am |

Mon–Sat only; fares 75¢–$6. Call ⓣ961-8744 for more details.

Saddle Road across the island. However, the urban area extends for several miles, and the **airport** at General Lyman Field (ⓣ935-4782), on the eastern outskirts, is well beyond walking distance. If you're not renting a car at the airport, you'll need to take an $8 taxi ride into town.

Limited **bus** service is offered by the HeleOn Bus Company (ⓣ961-8744). Its base, **Mooheau Bus Terminal**, is an open-air bayfront pavilion on Kamehameha Avenue, between the two highways. In addition to city routes, scheduled for commuters and of little use to visitors, there are a few longer-distance services. On weekdays only, the "9 Pāhoa" leaves Hilo at 2.40pm and 4.45pm to reach Pāhoa, twenty miles southeast of Hilo, at 3.45pm and 5.40pm respectively; the "7 Downtown Hilo" leaves Pāhoa at 6.05am and arrives in Hilo at 7.35am. Several daily buses also run from Hilo to Honoka'a and Waimea, but almost all are extremely early in the morning. The bus to **Hawaii Volcanoes National Park** and Ocean View, which leaves Mooheau Bus Terminal at 2.40pm on Monday through Friday only, is detailed on p.237.

Details of helicopter and fixed-wing **flight-seeing** operators based at General Lyman Field appear on p.156; Big Island boat trips are restricted to the Kona side of the island.

# Information and services

The **Hawaii Visitors Bureau** is at 250 Keawe St, one block up from the bayfront in the center of downtown (Mon–Fri 8am–4.30pm; ⓣ961-5797, ⓕ961-2126, ⓦwww.bigisland.org). Its helpful staff can advise on accommodation and tours, and have piles of brochures for you to take away.

Hilo's main **post office** (Mon–Fri 8.15am–4.45pm, Sat 8.30am–12.30pm) is on the approach road to the airport, but there's another one downtown in the Federal Building on Waianuenue Ave (Mon–Fri 8am–4pm). **Banks** are dotted all over town and in the malls, with the most central branch of the Bank of Hawaii based at 117 Keawe St.

# Accommodation

Although downtown Hilo is extremely short of **hotels**, several options line the oceanfront crescent of **Banyan Drive**, a mile or so southeast. Sadly, most of these have become rather rundown in recent years, but the state has stepped in to provide incentives for regeneration, and the situation should improve within the lifetime of this book. In addition, there are also a number of B&Bs in the vicinity, while a couple of welcoming and inexpensive inns can be found north of the Wailuku River, a short walk from downtown.

Room rates are lower on this side of the island, in part because hotel owners assume that you'll be out exploring the volcanoes or the Hāmākua Coast during the day. If that *is* what you're going to be doing, there's no great reason to spend more than a couple of nights in Hilo; if you plan to spend most of your time on the beach, then it's probably the wrong side of the island for you altogether.

**Arnott's Lodge**, 98 Apapane Rd, Hilo HI 96720; ⓣ969-7097, ⓕ961-9638, ⓦwww.arnottslodge.com. Laid-back but safe and clean budget accommodation in a two-story, motel-style lodge just off the road to Onekahakaha beach, a couple of miles southeast of downtown. The downstairs dorm rooms have twelve beds for $17 each, while the second floor is divided into two-bedroom units; a private double is $47, or $57 en suite. You can also camp in the grounds for $9. There's a tree house and bar, but no food except a twice-weekly barbecue. The management provides free airport pickup, a $2 shuttle service into Hilo, and assorted van day-trips; excursions to South Point, North Kohala, and Volcanoes National Park cost $43 each; a trip to the summit of Mauna Kea is $48. ❶/❷.

**Dolphin Bay Hotel**, 333 Iliahi St, Hilo HI 96720; ⓣ935-1466, ⓕ935-1523, ⓦwww.dolphinbayhilo.com. Very nice, very friendly little hotel within walking distance of downtown across the Wailuku River. Spotlessly clean studios and one- and two-bedroom suites are fully equipped with TV, bathroom and kitchen. No pool or restaurant, but free papayas and bananas dangle everywhere, and the owner is a mine of useful advice. ❷–❸.

**Hale Kai Bjornen**, 111 Honoli'i Pali, Hilo HI 96720; ⓣ935-6330, ⓕ935-8439, ⓦwww.interpac.net/~halekai. Small, comfortable B&B, perched above the ocean a couple of miles north of downtown. Each of the three rooms in the main building (two-day minimum stay) has its own bath and shares a living room; the adjacent guest cottage (five-day minimum) has a living room and kitchenette. All share use of pool and Jacuzzi. No credit cards; reservations essential. ❸–❹.

**Hawaii Naniloa Hotel**, 93 Banyan Drive, Hilo HI 96720; ⓣ969-3333, 1-800/367-5360 (US & Can), 1-800/442-5845 (HI), ⓕ969-6622, ⓦwww.naniloa.com. Hilo's principal high-rise hotel, built in the 1970s, is seriously showing its age. The rooms are thin-walled, overpriced, and long overdue for refurbishment; the pool is good, though. Restaurants include the formal *Sandalwood*, and the *Ting Hao*, while the *Crown Room* features local musicians. Rooms ❹, suites ❺–❻.

**Hilo Hawaiian Hotel**, 71 Banyan Drive, Hilo HI 96720; ⓣ935-9361; or reserve through Castle Resorts ⓣ1-800/367-5004 (US & Can) or ⓣ1-800/272-5275 (HI), ⓕ961-9642, ⓦwww.castle-group.com. Upmarket, luxury hotel, in a superb setting; the only Banyan Drive property still maintaining the highest standards. The long white crescent directly faces Coconut Island, out in the bay, but there's no beach. All rooms fall within price code ❹, but those with the best ocean view cost $30 extra. The *Queen's Court* restaurant is reviewed on p.213. ❹.

**Hilo Seaside Hotel**, 126 Banyan Drive, Hilo HI 96720; ⓣ935-0821 or 1-800/560-5557, ⓕ922-0052, ⓦwww.sand-seaside.com. Simple, not particularly well-priced rooms in low motel-style units near Kamehameha Avenue. Part of a small Hawaiian-owned chain, the hotel has a tiny pool, and offers discounts for seniors and on car rental. ❹.

**Holmes' Sweet Home**, 107 Koula St, Hilo HI 96720; ⓣ961-9089, ⓕ934-0711, ⓦwww.stayhawaii.com/holmes.html. Two comfortable en-suite B&B rooms in welcoming private home, a mile off the Saddle Road three miles up from downtown Hilo, with extensive views. ❷/❸.

**Pineapple Park**, PO Box 639, Kurtistown HI 96760, Hilo HI 96720; ⓣ323-2224 or 1-877/865-2266 (US), ⓦwww.pineapple-park.com. Large, modern budget hostel, 15 miles out of town in a remote area south of Hwy-11, halfway between Hilo and Volcano. For the moment, it no longer boasts the nighttime views of the erupting volcano that accounted for its location, but if you have your own transport it's not a bad option. Bunks in its 18-person dorms cost $17 each, and it also offers comfortable en-suite private rooms and fully equipped two-bedroom bungalows. Dorms ❶, rooms ❷, bungalows ❹.

**Shipman House B&B Inn**, 131 Kaiʻulani St, Hilo HI 96720; Ⓣ & Ⓕ934-8002 or 1-800/627-8447, Ⓦwww.hilo-hawaii.com. Magnificent, turreted Victorian mansion, which once hosted author Jack London and Hawaiian royalty, has been converted by descendants of its original owners into a plush B&B. There are three grand antiques-furnished en-suite rooms in the main house, which has a lovely *lānai*, and two more in a guest cottage. Rates include breakfast and afternoon tea. ❺.

**Uncle Billy's Hilo Bay Hotel**, 87 Banyan Drive, Hilo HI 96720; Ⓣ961-5818, 1-800/367-5102 (US & Can),1-800/442-5841 (HI), Ⓕ935-7903, Ⓦwww.unclebilly.com. The oldest of the Banyan Drive hotels, run by Uncle Billy and his family. The thatched chandeliers in the lobby set the tone: everything is relentlessly, but enjoyably, Polynesian. Two wings of basic rooms, not particularly well priced considering their fading charms, spread to either side of a tropical garden that's filled at sunset with birdsong. There's a small pool and a free nightly *hula* show (see p.213). Very popular with visitors from the other Hawaiian islands, it also offers car-rental discounts. ❹.

**Wild Ginger Inn**, 100 Puʻuʻeo St, Hilo HI 96720; Ⓣ935-5556 or 1-800/882-1887 (US & Can), Ⓦwww.wildgingerinn.com. Pink-painted, somewhat spruced-up inn in a quiet residential area just across the Wailuku River from downtown. While second-best to the nearby *Dolphin Bay*, it remains an invaluable resource for budget travelers. About thirty basic but adequate en-suite rooms arranged around attractive gardens, plus a few slightly more secluded "deluxe" rooms with TVs. Rates include a simple breakfast buffet. ❷.

# The City

There is a simple and tragic reason why **downtown Hilo** seems so low-key, with its modest streets and wooden stores: all the buildings that stood on the *makai* side of Kamehameha Avenue were destroyed by the *tsunamis* of 1946 and 1960. Furthermore, the large gap between downtown and Banyan Drive, now occupied by the Wailoa River State Park, is there because the city was literally cut in two by the inundation of 1946. After the waters returned in 1960, all hope was abandoned of rebuilding the "little Tokyo" of Japanese-owned family stores, which lined Kamehameha Avenue all the way to the Wailoa River. Instead, the destroyed area was cleared as a "buffer zone," creating a new administrative complex above the high-water mark.

Little in central Hilo today bears witness to its long history, but it's a pleasant place to amble around. That's especially so on Wednesdays and Saturdays, when a colorful **open-air market** takes place on Mamo Street, across the highway from the open ocean. As you wander past stalls selling orchids, tropical fruits and coffee fresh from the farm, it's hard to believe you're still in the USA.

## The Pacific Tsunami Museum

Downtown Hilo's latest attraction is the high-tech **Pacific Tsunami Museum**, housed in a former bank at the corner of Kamehameha Ave and Kalākaua St (Mon–Sat 10am–4pm; adults $5, under-18s $2; Ⓣ935-0926, Ⓦwww.tsunami.org). Although its primary emphasis is on the causes and effects of the two lethal *tsunamis* of the last century, and of similar and potential events throughout the Pacific, it also documents the entire history of Hilo. A scale model, complete with a running train, shows how the city looked before the 1946 disaster; contemporary footage and personal letters bring home the full impact of the tragedy. The section devoted to the wave of 1960, which hit just 53 days after the official reopening of Hwy-19, is even more poignant. It was caused by an earthquake off Chile, so locals had several hours' warning that it was on its way. Amazingly enough, many flocked down to the seafront to watch it come in; photos show them waiting excitedly for the cataclysm that was about to engulf them. A total of 61 people were killed.

## The Lyman Museum and Mission House

The two-part **Lyman Museum**, at 276 Haili St, a few blocks up from the ocean, is downtown Hilo's principal historic site and offers an interesting introduction to the Big Island (Mon–Sat 9am–4.30pm; adults $7, children 6–18 $3; ⓣ 935-5021). Its main focus is the original **Mission House** of Calvinist missionaries David and Sarah Lyman, built in 1839. Guided tours of the oldest surviving wooden house on the island start at regular intervals from the adjacent museum.

The Lymans waited until they felt Christianity was firmly established in Hilo before constructing this, the finest home in the city, fit to welcome Hawaiian royalty and foreign dignitaries alike. It had neither kitchen – for fear of fire – nor bathroom, but stood three storys high, with a towering thatched roof, a roomy *lānai* running around the first two levels, and a spacious attic. Most of the furniture is made of dark *koa* wood, as are the floors, whose broad planks are up to nineteen inches wide.

The modern museum alongside traces the history of Hawaii from its earliest settlers, with a map of the Pacific to show the routes they followed, as well as a relief model of the Big Island, complete with black lava flows. A thatched hut holds the basic utensils of the ancient Hawaiians, with stone tools and fish hooks, rounded calabashes of *kou* and *koa* wood, and ornaments of dogs' and whales' teeth and even human bone (believed to transmit the spiritual power of the original owner to the wearer).

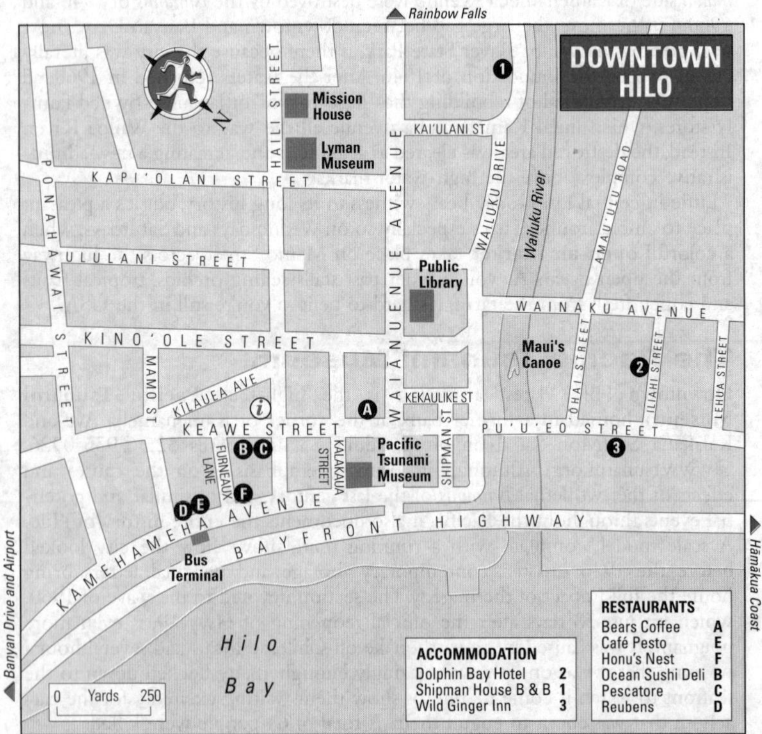

After a history of the missions comes a fascinating section on Hilo's different ethnic groups. The Japanese are represented by an ornate wooden "wishing chair," the Chinese by a resplendent red and gilt Taoist shrine rescued from a temple destroyed by the *tsunami* of 1960, and the Portuguese by the little four-string *braginha* guitar that was to become the ukulele.

Most of the space upstairs is occupied by the **Earth Heritage Gallery**, focusing on the geology and astronomy of the island. A model of the summit of Mauna Kea shows the various international observatories – computer-literate visitors can tap into their latest discoveries – while a brief account of Polynesian techniques of stellar navigation mentions that the Ahua'umi Heiau on Mauna Kea, now badly damaged, was probably the first observatory to be built up there. A huge sonar map of the entire archipelago shows how alarmingly prone Hawaii is to massive landslides, and pinpoints the fiery submarine volcano of Lō'ihi thrusting its way to the surface just off the southeast coast of the Big Island. Another collection contains corals, shells – including those of some unique indigenous land snails – a few stuffed birds and fossils, and colorful minerals from around the world, some of which glow in the dark. The small **Shipman Gallery of Chinese Art**, also upstairs, consists mostly of delicately painted but uninspiring porcelain.

## Wailuku River and Rainbow Falls

The **Wailuku River**, which defines the western limit of downtown Hilo, is at eighteen miles the longest river in the Hawaiian archipelago. Now safely channeled and crossed by three road bridges, it once had a fearsome reputation; *wailuku* means "destroying water," as it was considered extremely dangerous during periods of high rain.

A large rocky outcrop in the river bed, visible upstream from the bridge that connects Puueo and Keawe streets, is known as **Maui's Canoe**. In legend, it was abandoned by the mighty warrior after he'd raced it back from Haleakalā on his namesake island (with just two paddle strokes). Maui was hurrying to rescue his mother, Hina, who lived in a cave further up the river and had become trapped by rising waters engineered by a dragon.

Maui's route is now followed by Waianuenue ("rainbow seen in the water") Avenue, and the site of Hina's cave, two miles out from downtown, is known as **Rainbow Falls**. Sightseers drive out to admire this broad waterfall from a safe distance; short trails lead to different viewpoints, but don't let you anywhere near the actual water. From the fenced-off viewing area to the right of the parapet wall of the parking lot, you can see the falls square-on as they shoot over a thick shelf of hard rock. In the pool down below, the water has progressively scooped out the hollow that was supposedly home to Maui's mother. Climb a small but often very muddy and slippery staircase off to the left to draw level with the streambed at the top of the falls, with the summit of Mauna Kea looming high in the distance.

Just over a mile on up the road, the **Boiling Pots** are a succession of churning, foaming pools in the river as it drops towards the ocean, with another, smaller, set of falls. A treacherous ungraded path to the right of the viewing area allows you to approach the maelstrom, but you'd be crazy to swim.

## Wailoa River State Park

**Wailoa River State Park**, created in the aftermath of the 1960 *tsunami* in what had been downtown Hilo, is a tranquil – if marshy – landscaped park of lawns, coconut palms and dazzling orange-blossomed *lehua* trees. It's a little hard to find your way in: turn down Pauahi Street, which runs between Kilauea and Kamehameha avenues, and then take curving Piopio Street halfway along.

Paved footpaths cross the river and clear-watered lagoons on double or even triple-humped footbridges, with one pair leading to and from a tiny island, and another one connecting with Kamehameha Avenue and the seafront. A moving memorial, dedicated to all victims of Big Island *tsunamis*, consists of two low, black-lava ridges that shield a central tiled design.



## Banyan Drive

Green, semi-rural **Banyan Drive**, a mile east of downtown Hilo and not far from the airport, has become the prime hotel district for the city since being spared by the *tsunamis*. Though the hotels themselves are deteriorating – see p.206 – it's an attractive area, graced by curving rows of the eponymous giant drooping banyan trees. Incredibly, these magnificent specimens are barely seventy years old, having been planted in the 1930s by the celebrities after whom they're named – Franklin Roosevelt, Babe Ruth and King George V among others.

The best place for a stroll among the trees is **Liliuokalani Gardens**, an ornamental Japanese park built to honor Japanese migrants to Hawaii. A slender footbridge stretches out to **Coconut Island**, now just a green speck on the

### Hilo's Gardens

Hilo is renowned for its **tropical gardens**, which include commercial orchid farms, public parks and scientific research facilities. The best combination of a wide range of plants in a scenic setting is the **Hawaii Tropical Botanical Garden** (see p.215). However, within the city confines there are several alternatives, of which the following are just a selection:

**Hilo Arboretum**
Kilauea Ave and Kawili St; Mon–Fri 8am–3pm; admission free.
Almost twenty acres of woodlands, just over a mile from downtown. This is one of Hilo's most peaceful spots, since it's primarily a research establishment, intended to include specimens of all trees that currently grow anywhere in Hawaii. Trails are virtually nonexistent, but the overgrown lawns present no challenge to walkers.

**Hilo Tropical Gardens and Gallery**
1477 Kalaniana'ole Ave; daily 8.30am–5pm; adults $6, children 13–18 $3, under-12s free; ⓣ935-4957.
Two acres of colorful gardens laid out among tidepools just south of Onekahakaha Beach Park, on the *makai* side of the highway. In addition to the abundance of orchids and heliconia, there's a gift store and free coffee.

**Nani Mau Gardens**
421 Makakila St; daily 8am–5pm; adults $10, children 6–18 $6; ⓣ959-3541, ⓦwww.nanimau.com.
Formal commercial gardens, between the three- and four-mile markers on Hwy-11, which can be explored on foot or, for $5 extra, on a narrated tram tour. There's also a butterfly house, costing another $3. Its main business, however, is as a stop for tour parties; there's a copious $14.50 lunch buffet (10.30am–1.30pm), while Sunday's spread, served in the gardens from 10am to 1pm, is more of a brunch.

edge of the bay but once, as Mokuola ("healing island"), the site of a *pu'uhonua* or "place of refuge," like that at Hōnaunau (see p.174). There was also a *luakini*, where human offerings were killed by having a huge stone dropped on their chests while lying bound to a rock. When the temple was dismantled during the 1870s, its stones were used to build a quarantine hospital, but that was in turn destroyed almost immediately by a *tsunami*.

A small covered market area next to the quayside on Lihiwai Street, just off Kamehameha Avenue, is the site (daily except Sun) of the **Suisan Fish Auction**. You have to arrive at around 7am to be sure of seeing anything; a nearby coffee stall will help wake you up. *Suisan* is a large operation, and fishing vessels from all over the island come here to sell their catch. Most of the trays are packed with glistening tuna, but you can also see red snapper, parrotfish, squid, ripped-up multicolored reef fish speared by scuba divers, and the occasional unfortunate shark. Though it's a hectic and lively spectacle, there's no dramatic shouting: buyers simply inspect the shiny rows of fish and write down their bids.



## Panaewa Rainforest Zoo

The little-known **Panaewa Rainforest Zoo** (Mon–Fri 9am–4pm, Sat 11am–2pm; free; ⓣ 959-7224) holds a relatively small menagerie of animals, few of them all that unusual. The main pleasure of stopping here en route to the volcanoes is the chance to roam beneath the zoo's canopy of tropical vegetation. Coming south from Hilo on Hwy-11, turn right just after mile marker 4, along the signed turning a short way beyond Stainback Highway.

On weekdays you may find that you're the rarest species of all, and that the animals will go out of their way to have a closer look at you. Walkways through the dense, steamy undergrowth lead past various enclaves holding a pigmy hippo (with giant-sized teeth), a Shetland pony, an ominously rotund American alligator, iguanas from South America, giant land turtles from the Seychelles, and wide-eyed lemurs and bushy-tailed colobuses from Madagascar. Several impressive peacocks wander the grounds at will, displaying their plumage to all and sundry, while rare Hawaiian owls and hawks are confined in rusty cages. The largest, lushest enclosure holds Bengal tigers, though the vegetation is so thick that you may well not spot any unless you're prepared for a long wait by their watering hole.

# Beaches

If you're not bothered by sharks or pollution, you could in theory swim out among the canoes and fishing boats from the **Hilo Bayfront Park**, across the highway from downtown Hilo. It's said that this was one of the finest black-sand beaches in all the islands, before the construction of the breakwater in 1908 and the dredging of the harbor in 1913. Now it's a pleasant place for a picnic, but the only spot nearby where you might be tempted to swim is at Coconut Island, off Banyan Drive (see opposite).

All Hilo's **beach parks** lie southeast of downtown, facing Mauna Kea across the bay and reached by following Kalaniana'ole Avenue beyond Banyan Drive. As few have any sand – they consist of shallow pools in the black lava at the ocean margin, usually backed by small grass clearings ringed with coconut palms – they attract local families rather than tourists, and so are only crowded on weekends. You'll notice, incidentally, that Kalaniana'ole Avenue is lined with blue signs indicating the "Evacuation Route" in the event of a *tsunami*; not surprisingly, the idea is to get away from the sea as fast as possible.

## The Merrie Monarch Festival

Since 1963, the city of Hilo has celebrated the week-long **Merrie Monarch** *hula* festival during the third week of April. The festival's centerpiece is a royal parade down the main street in honor of the "Merrie Monarch" himself, King David Kalākaua. He was largely responsible for the revival of *hula* following decades of missionary disapproval, when, at the time of his coronation in February 1883, he staged a performance of women dancers and male drummers on the lawns of Honolulu's 'Iolani Palace.

Performers from around thirty different *hula hālua* (schools) – of which eighteen tend to be female and twelve male, and not all are necessarily from Hawaii – compete for awards in both *kahiko* (ancient) and *'auana* (modern) styles of *hula*. Official events take place in the evenings at the six-thousand-seat **Kanaka'ole Stadium**, named after Auntie Edith Kanaka'ole, one of the Big Island's best-loved twentieth-century *kumu hulas* (*hula* teachers). In addition, informal demonstrations and associated events are held during the daytime in the *Hilo Hawaiian* and *Hawaii Naniloa* hotels.

Full schedules are available from the Merrie Monarch office at the *Hawaii Naniloa Hotel*, 93 Banyan Drive, Hilo HI 96720 (☎935-9168). Tickets go on sale each year on January 1 but sell out almost immediately.

Probably the best spot for family groups is **Onekahakaha Beach Park**, a mile and a half down Kalaniana'ole Avenue. Here a solid breakwater of boulders has created a safe, calm lagoon for swimming, while the spacious lawns alongside are good for picnics. The open ocean beyond the breakwater can, however, be extremely dangerous, while fifty yards or so back from the sea the park acquires from time to time a sizeable population of homeless people. That's the main reason why none of Hilo's beach parks currently allows **camping**.

**Leleiwi Beach Park**, a couple of miles further along, is a little more exposed, with no sandy beach and some dangerous currents. Away from the open sea, the lagoon is so supremely still and tranquil as to appeal primarily to anglers, who stand in quiet contemplation almost entirely undisturbed by bathers.

Just beyond Leleiwi, and four miles from downtown, Kalaniana'ole Avenue comes to a dead end at **Richardson Ocean Park**, where a tiny black-sand beach among the coconut groves is very popular with young children. Some venture out to play in the surf as it sweeps into the bay, beyond the snorkelers exploring the rock pools. Behind the sea wall there's a larger "beach" area – more of a sandpit, really – while the adjacent gardens are laid out around some ancient fishponds, with a few explanatory labels.

# Restaurants

Hilo offers an unusually varied assortment of **restaurants**, most of which are aimed more at locals than at visitors, and thus tend to have more at stake in satisfying their customers than some of the fly-by-night Kona-side joints. **Downtown** is at its busiest during the working week, however, and you may be surprised at how **quiet** things are on weekends. If you're looking for crowds, you're probably better off spending the evening along **Banyan Drive**.

As for **fast food**, a wide selection of outlets can be found at malls such as the Prince Kūhiō Plaza (KFC, Pizza Ala Slice, Woolworth and half a dozen others) and the Puainako Town Center (McDonald's, Pizza Hut, Taco Bell, Subway); both KFC and McDonald's have downtown restaurants as well.

**Bears Coffee**, 110 Keawe St; ⓣ935-0708. Hilo's coolest breakfast hangout, one block from the ocean downtown. All kinds of coffees are available, plus bakery goodies, freshly squeezed juices and a menu of specials such as souffléed eggs on muffin with spinach for around $3. Lunch consists of $5 sandwiches, salads and some Mexican specialties. Mon–Sat 7am–5pm, Sun 8am–noon.

**Café Pesto**, S Hata Building, 130 Kamehameha Ave; ⓣ969-6640. Large, light and modern, Pacific-influenced Italian restaurant at the southern end of downtown Hilo. For a substantial snack, the $8–10 lunchtime sandwiches, such as the Japanese eggplant *Sandalwood* and the shrimp *Miloli'i*, are excellent values. There's a wide selection of pizzas and calzones, with tasty, inventive fillings such as lime-marinated fish, and eggplant and artichokes. The dinner menu also features fresh fish, and a risotto with lobster, shrimp and scallops for $25. There's another *Café Pesto* at Kawaihae Harbor; see p.191. Mon–Thurs & Sun 11am–9pm, Fri & Sat 11am–10pm.

**Harringtons'**, 135 Kalaniana'ole Ave; ⓣ961-4966. Popular, informal restaurant, a mile out of downtown, looking out over Reeds Bay from a low timber building *makai* of Kalaniana'ole Avenue. Lunchtime salads and sandwiches cost under $10. Dinner appetizers include steamed clams and *escargots* at around $9, and an inexpensive seafood chowder, while among the entrees are steaks and excellent seafood dishes for $16–20. There's live Hawaiian music on Fridays and Saturdays. Mon–Fri 11am–2pm & 5.30–9.30pm, Sat & Sun 5.30–9.30pm.

**Honu's Nest**, 270 Kamehameha Ave; ⓣ935-9321. Very central Japanese diner, with just a handful of tables set out in front of the service counter. An ample bowl of noodle soup costs $6, tempura chicken or shrimp are $10, and a substantial portion of *ahi* (tuna) sashimi goes for $10.50. Mon–Sat 10am–4pm.

**Ken's House of Pancakes**, 1730 Kamehameha Ave; ⓣ935-8711. A much-loved Hilo landmark, near the intersection of Kamehameha Avenue and Banyan Drive; open 24 hours for snacks, sandwiches and pancakes galore.

**Nihon Cultural Center**, 123 Lihiwai St; ⓣ969-1133. Just off Banyan Drive, this Japanese restaurant has exquisite fresh fish and magnificent views. Lunch specials cost under $10. Reservations are required for dinner, when full meals starting at $15 are served until 9pm; the sushi bar remains open later. Mon–Sat 11am–1.30pm & 5–10pm.

**Ocean Sushi Deli**, 239 Keawe St; ⓣ961-6625. Simple Japanese cafeteria, serving good and inexpensive sushi (from $2 for 2 pieces) and bento meals to the downtown crowd. All-you-can-eat sushi costs $16 at lunchtime, $20 in the evening. Mon–Sat 10am–12.30pm & 4.30–9pm.

**Pescatore**, 235 Keawe St; ⓣ969-9090. Formal Italian dining in a pastel-yellow building opposite the HVB. Lunchtime pasta specials cost $7–10, while pricier meat and pasta entrees, such as the anchovy-rich *pasta puttanesca* ($16), are served for dinner. Try the delicious $25 *cioppino classico*, a stew of lobster, mussels, scallops and clams, with garlic bread. Sun–Thurs 11am–2pm & 5.30–9pm, Fri & Sat 11am–2pm & 5.30–10pm.

**Queen's Court**, *Hilo Hawaiian Hotel*, 71 Banyan Drive; ⓣ935-9361. With its panoramic views, this huge dining room makes a perfect setting for top-quality buffets. In addition to breakfast and lunch spreads, it offers dinner buffets at $24–27: *paniolo* (barbecue) on Monday and Thursday, Italian on Tuesday, Chinese on Wednesday, seafood on Friday, and seafood and Hawaiian *lū'au* dishes on Saturday and Sunday; Sunday also sees a very reasonable $23.50 champagne brunch. Mon–Sat 6.30–9.30am, 11.15am–1.15pm & 5.30–9pm, Sun 6.30–9am, 10.30am–1.30pm & 5.30–9pm.

**Reubens**, 336 Kamehameha Ave; ⓣ961-2552. Mexican restaurant just south of *Café Pesto*, serving a predictable menu of flautas and chile rellenos beneath a ceiling festooned with Mexican flags. Entrees cost $8–12 at night, more like $5 for lunch. Mon–Fri 11am–9pm, Sat noon–9pm.

**The Seaside Restaurant**, 1790 Kalaniana'ole Ave; ⓣ935-8825. The full name of this lively family restaurant continues "and Aqua Farm," which has to be a good sign. Located just over two miles out of town, beyond Onekahaka Beach, it's almost entirely surrounded by water, with its thirty-acre fishponds full of trout, mullet and catfish. The dining room decor is pretty minimal, although there are a few outdoor tables. But the fish is great. Unless you want a steak with your mullet, or you opt for the more expensive imported specials, you'd be hard-pressed to spend $20 on a full fish supper. Daily except Mon–Fri 5–8.30pm.

**Uncle Billy's**, *Hilo Bay Hotel*, 87 Banyan Drive; ⓣ935-0861. Themed Polynesian restaurant, where most of the menu consists of steak and breaded fish entrees for $11–20; the $20 seafood platter is excellent. Free nightly Hawaiian music and *hula* dancing, often presided over by beaming Uncle Billy himself, and featuring members of his extensive family. Mon–Sat 7–10am & 5.30–9pm, Sun 7–11.30am & 5.30–9pm.

## Shopping

Although **downtown Hilo** is an enjoyable district to walk around, few of its stores are worth going out of your way for. Those that there are are mainly concentrated along sea-facing Kamehameha Avenue, with assorted outlets selling clothes, T-shirts, souvenirs and fairly undistinguished "crafts." The best times for a stroll are Wednesday and Saturday mornings, to coincide with the **market** on Mamo Street (see p.207).

Most locals do their shopping at the various **malls**, of which **Prince Kūhiō Plaza** (Mon–Fri 10am–9pm, Sat 9.30am–7pm, Sun 10am–6pm), just south of the airport on Hwy-11, is the most extensive. As well as Sears, Liberty House, J.C. Penney and Woolworth department stores, it has its own movie theater (☎959-4955), two bookstores, and a music store. The **Waiakea Center**, across the street, holds a large Borders bookstore (☎933-1410). **Banyan Drive** has a very limited selection of convenience stores.

# The Hāmākua coast

The **Hāmākua coast** extends for fifty ravishing and colorful miles north and west from Hilo up to Waipi'o Valley. This spectacular landscape has been carved by the torrents of rain unleashed when the trade winds hit Mauna Kea after crossing two thousand miles of open ocean. Countless streams and waterfalls cascade down the cliffs and gullies, nourishing jungle-like vegetation filled with multicolored blossoms and iridescent orchids. Hāmākua farms once fueled the economy of the Big Island. Now agribusiness has all but pulled out – the last sugar mill closed in 1994 – and no one knows quite what might take its place.

For most of this stretch of shoreline, the Belt Road (Hwy-19) follows the original route of the sugar-company railroad, which carried local produce to ships waiting in Hilo and other smaller harbors. Barely rising or falling, the highway clings to the hillsides, crossing a succession of ravines on slender bridges. Damage to these bridges in the 1946 *tsunami* put the railroad out of business, but they were sufficiently repaired to be able to carry the road instead.

The drive is neither difficult nor particularly tortuous, but it's so beautiful that you may find it impossible to exceed the posted minimum speed of 40mph. Each little bridge offers its own glimpse of the verdant scenery – sometimes close to the ocean but high above it, sometimes winding further in to follow the contours of the gorges and passing babbling streams and waterfalls.

At first, the fields are crammed into narrow, stream-carved "gulches," and there are few places to stop and enjoy the views. The two most popular off-road sightseeing spots are the **Hawaii Tropical Botanical Garden**, just a few miles north of Hilo, and the impressive **Akaka Falls**, another ten miles on, where a short loop trail through the rainforest offers a rare view of the interior. Otherwise, if you just want to pause and take a few photos along the way, look out for the bridge just north of mile marker 18 (and south of Nīnole), from which you can watch the Waihaumalo River crash into the sea amid dramatic orange-blossomed trees and giant fanning palms, and the deeply indented Maulua Gorge at mile marker 22.

Further north, beyond **Laupāhoehoe**, the land spreads out, allowing room for larger plantations. The Belt Road veers inland towards Waimea just before the old-fashioned sugar town of **Honoka'a**, but keeping on another eight miles on dead-end Hwy-240 brings you out at one of the most unforgettable viewpoints on all the islands – the **Waipi'o Valley overlook**.





# Pepe'ekeo Scenic Drive

**PEPE'EKEO SCENIC DRIVE**, a small side road that drops towards the sea four miles north of Hilo, then curves for four miles before rejoining Hwy-19 at Pepe'ekeo, makes a worthwhile detour from the Belt Road. Until the highway came through, this was part of the Old Māmalahoa Highway that once encircled the island (see p.197). That explains why the trouble was taken to plant its most impressive stretch, a superb avenue of overhanging Alexandra palms imported from Queensland, Australia. They make their appearance just beyond a delightful gorge that bursts with African tulip trees.

Close to the north end of the road, *What's Shakin* (daily 10am–5pm; Ⓣ964-3080) serves the best **smoothies** on the island – succulent $4 concoctions of fresh tropical fruits – plus sandwiches for around $7, and has a nice verandah overlooking its own orchards.

Few visitors make it to the end of the Scenic Drive without indulging in a daydream or two about the various real-estate parcels on sale on its *makai* side. Rest assured, even if you could afford the asking price for a piece of land, the restrictions on development would ensure that you couldn't do much with it once you'd bought it.

## Hawaii Tropical Botanical Garden

Occupying almost the entirety of **Onomea Bay** – one of the lushest, prettiest bays of the Hāmākua coast – is the Big Island's premier showcase for tropical trees, orchids and flowering plants, the **Hawaii Tropical Botanical Garden** (daily 9am–5pm; adults $15, under-17s $5; Ⓣ964-5233, Ⓦwww.hawaiigarden.com or Ⓦwww.htbg.com). The collection includes specimens from Brazil, Malaysia, Madagascar and Guatemala, alongside endemic Hawaiian species, and is garnished with flamingos and macaws. Though a major stop on the tour-bus circuit, with crowds and prices to match, it still comes closer than anywhere on the island to matching the popular conception of what a tropical rainforest should look like.

From the garden headquarters, halfway along the Scenic Drive, a signposted self-guided trail drops around 500 feet to the ocean. Insect repellent, drinking water and umbrellas are available at the start, and it takes roughly an hour to complete its full length.

Striking features during the descent include views of a tall waterfall, on the innermost wall of the valley, visible at the upper end of the "palm jungle" of Alexandra palms. A little lower, a huge Cook pine is surrounded by spectacular heliconia and vast spreading "travelers' trees," said always to hold a little water at the base of their leaves. Most of the plants are labeled, and there's a heady succession of gingers, bromeliads, dramatic orange and yellow heliconia, coconut palms with their writhing worm-like roots, and *hala*, or pandanus

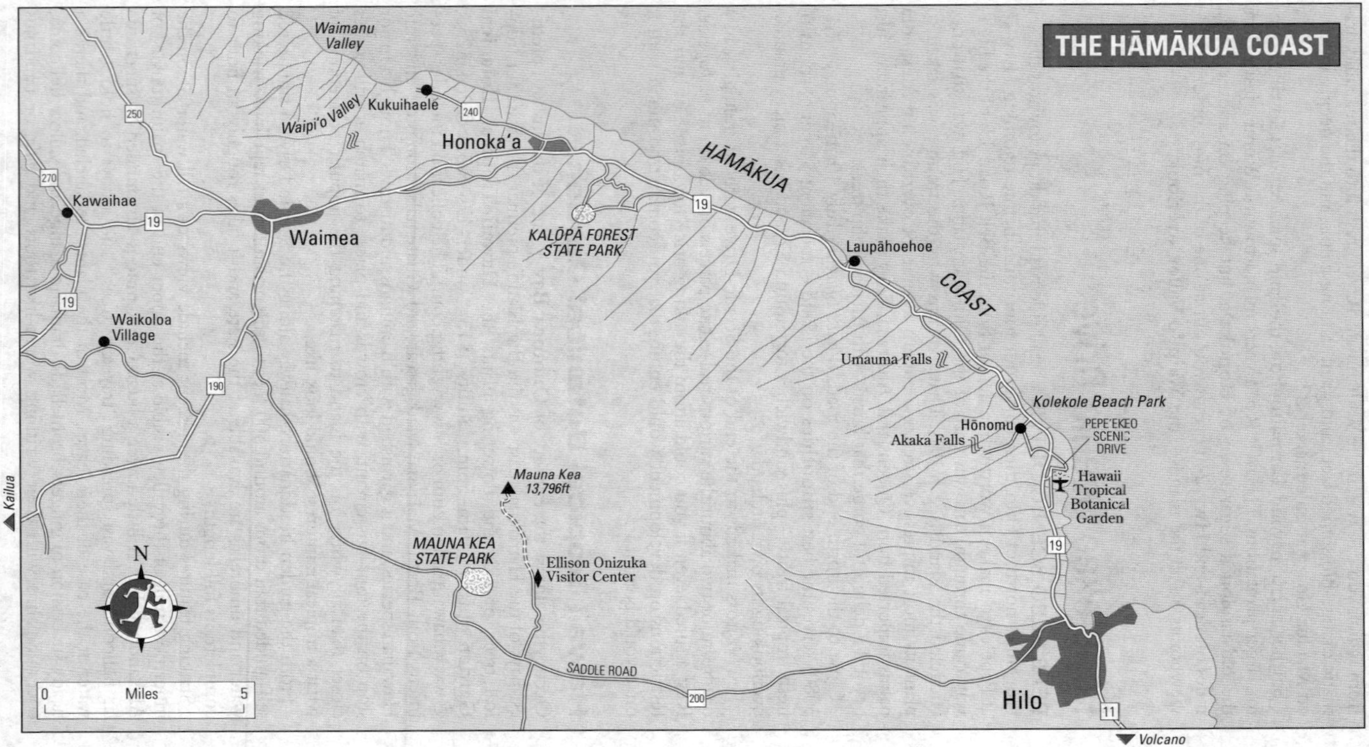

## THE HĀMĀKUA COAST

Waimanu Valley
Waipi'o Valley
Kukuihaele
240
Honoka'a
HĀMĀKUA
COAST
250
270
Kawaihae
19
Waimea
KALŌPĀ FOREST STATE PARK
Laupāhoehoe
Waikoloa Village
190
Umauma Falls
Kolekole Beach Park
Hōnomu
Akaka Falls
PEPE'EKEO SCENIC DRIVE
Hawaii Tropical Botanical Garden
Mauna Kea 13,796ft
Kailua
N
MAUNA KEA STATE PARK
Ellison Onizuka Visitor Center
SADDLE ROAD
200
Hilo
11
Volcano
0 Miles 5

trees, whose roots serve as stilts that seem to lift the trunk off the ground. Perhaps the most prominent of all is the red-leafed *obake*, which with its lurid white or yellow "prong" is something of an island trademark.

At three little inlets in Onomea Bay you can enjoy fine views of the verdant shoreline; the largest, Turtle Bay, has a small black-sand beach, but at none of them are visitors allowed to leave the paths and approach the water.

# Akaka Falls

Three or four miles up Mauna Kea from the Belt Road, and fifteen miles out of Hilo, **Akaka Falls** is one of the Big Island's most photogenic sights. Though not the highest waterfall on the island, its setting is unrivaled – a sheer drop through a chasm overrun by tropical vegetation and orchids. An easy and enjoyable mile-long trail leads visitors through a dense "jungle" and past other falls, culminating at a viewpoint looking upstream to Akaka itself. You don't get close to the riverbed, let alone the falls, so the only dangers to contend with are the steamy heat and persistent mosquitoes.

The trail starts from a parking lot that's reached by following a straightforward series of signs off the highway, through Hōnomu (see below) and up Hwy-220 via a small belt of meadowland. A narrow staircase leads down from the edge of the parking lot, plunging you into dense tropical foliage, with thickets of bamboo soaring from the gorge below to meet high above your head. Few of the plants lining the route are native to Hawaii, and the whole forest is a battleground of yellow, purple and pink blossoms. Among the most lurid are the fiery "lobster-claw" heliconia and birds of paradise, bedecked in either orange and blue, or white.

Shortly after you cross a narrow stream, the canopy opens up and you reach an overlook facing **Kapuna Falls**. Mighty trees stand alongside the path, festooned with thick green mosses, fern and creepers, with all kinds of parasitic plants erupting from their branches and trunks. To the left, a vast banyan drips with tendrils.

Across the next bluff, you get your first view of Akaka Falls itself, foaming through a narrow channel to plunge around 450 feet down a mossy cliff face and disappear in a cloud of spray into the pool below. After leaving the viewing area, you recross the stream at a higher point, where a small waterfall bubbles beneath another overhanging bamboo grove.

## Hōnomu

Were it not for the steady flow of visitors to Akaka Falls, tiny **HŌNOMU**, on the *mauka* side of Hwy-19, a mile or so south of Kolekole Beach Park, would probably have been swallowed up by the rainforest by now. As it is, the village consists of a row of little timber-framed galleries and crafts stores, a couple of which sell sodas, juices and snacks as well as run-of-the-mill souvenirs. To sample the flavor of the place, the best stop is Ishigo's General Store, an authentic plantation store that has been run by the same family since 1910.

# Kolekole Beach Park

Having cascaded over Akaka Falls, Kolekole stream reaches the ocean a mile or so north of Hōnomu, at the only sizeable seafront park between Hilo and

Laupāhoehoe. Look out for a small turning on the left of the highway, just before a tall, narrow bridge.

The road down to **Kolekole Beach Park**, lush even by Hāmākua standards, doubles back to end at the foot of the bridge struts, far below the highway. On both sides, the gorge is thick green, half-swallowing the rusting tin-roofed pavilions of the park. There's no beach, however, and while local youths thrill to ride the breakers back into the mouth of the river, lesser mortals should be wary of submitting themselves to the high surf that lies just a few yards beyond the rounded black boulders of the shoreline.



## Umauma Falls

Heading inland from Hwy-19 along any of the little access roads around milepost 16, roughly two miles north of Kolekole, enables you to join the minor road, parallel to the main highway, that leads to **Umauma Falls**. These previously little-known falls have become more prominent on tourist itineraries since 1995, when the surrounding land was opened to the public as the **World Botanic Gardens** (Mon–Sat 9am–5.30pm; $7; ⓣ963-5427).

So far, the gardens themselves are small and unexciting, but visitors who drop in at their roadside headquarters and pay the high admission fee are furnished with directions for reaching an overlook beside the Umauma Stream that commands a superb prospect of the tripled-tiered falls themselves. They're not nearly as dramatic as Akaka Falls, but that doesn't make them bad; if paying $7 to admire an attractive waterfall seems worth it to you, go right ahead. The whole experience may become a better value for the money if the owners' ambitious schemes to develop the gardens ever come to fruition; plans include the construction of a chocolate factory.

## Laupāhoehoe

For most of the Hāmākua coast, the shoreline cliffs are too abrupt to leave room for settlements by the sea. Hence the significance of **LAUPĀHOEHOE**, twelve miles up the coast from Kolekole, where a flow of lava extruding into the ocean has created a flat, fertile promontory (*lau* means leaf, and *pāhoehoe* is smooth lava).

As the best canoe landing between Hilo and Waipi'o, Laupāhoehoe has long been home to a small community; the location has its perils, however. On April 1, 1946, a ferocious *tsunami* destroyed the school at the tip of the headland, killing 24 teachers and children; rescue attempts were delayed as all boats and canoes in the vicinity were wrecked by waves up to thirty feet high.

As the approach road to Laupāhoehoe rounds the first tight corner on its way to the sea, you're confronted by a stunning view of the green coastal cliffs stretching away to the south. After rain, countless small waterfalls cascade from crevices in the rock.

The narrow road winds down past the **Jodo Mission**, a temple built by Japanese immigrants in 1899, and arrives at a flat spit of land at the bottom of the cliffs. Most of the space here is taken up by a large lawn, fringed with tall coconut palms that have an alarming tendency to shed their fruit in high winds. A number of seafront parking lots are squeezed in before the forbidding black-lava coastline and its pounding surf, in which swimming is definitely not advisable. To the right is the small boat-launching ramp of Laupāhoehoe Harbor, so dangerous that it's usually sealed off from public access, while round to the left an open-sided beach pavilion tends to be the preserve of locals around sunset.

Until the *tsunami* of 1946, the main coastal road passed through Laupāhoehoe at sea level. Part of the village had already relocated higher up the hillside in 1913, however, when the sugar company **railroad** reached this far up the Hāmākua coast. Both the lower road and the railroad were destroyed by the *tsunami* – the railroad lost not only much of its track and its trestle bridges, but also the actual engines. The whole community, including a new school built to replace the one lost in the storm, subsequently shifted to the top of the cliffs.

Since the last of the local sugar mills closed, Laupāhoehoe has been facing an uncertain future. A fair few people still live along the various backroads in the district, but there's no town for visitors to explore, and no accommodation is currently available. The one concession to tourism is the little **Laupāhoehoe Train Museum**, housed in the former ticket agent's home alongside the highway (Mon–Fri 9am–4.30pm, Sat & Sun 10am–2pm; donations). Enthusiastic volunteers explain the history of the railroad, aided by a plethora of photos and artifacts, and can tell you how far they've got with their schemes to restore some of the rusted-up old machinery.

## Kalōpā Forest State Park

A final opportunity to investigate the upland slopes of Mauna Kea comes a couple of miles south of Honoka'a and a mile *mauka* of Hwy-19, in the Kalōpā Forest State Park.

Though the reserve covers 615 acres, the only readily accessible part is the **Native Forest Nature Trail**, a loop of less than a mile that starts from the State Park parking lot and winds through variegated woodlands. Most of what you see is planted rather than natural, but it still provides an interesting introduction to the native flora of the island. By the end of the trail you should be able to spot the difference between the *'ōhi'a* and *kopiko* trees, be familiar with ferns such as the *hāpu'u* and the *nianī'au*, and be appalled by the evil ways of the aggressive strawberry guava plant. The *'io* (Hawaiian hawk) and the tiny but melodious *'elepaio* make their nests in this area, though it may turn out that you see no creatures larger than voracious mosquitoes.

The park has a small, tent-only **campground**, charging $5 per night, as well as four eight-bunk cabins, each equipped with bath, bed linen and blankets, and sharing the use of a central kitchen and communal area. The cabins are let for up to five nights, at $55 per night. Reserve on the spot by finding the caretaker before 4pm, or call the state parks office in Hilo (Ⓣ974-6200).

## Honoka'a

The largest and most characterful of the Hāmākua towns is rough-and-tumble **HONOKA'A**, forty miles north of Hilo where the Belt Road curves west to run across the island to Waimea (see p.192). Consisting largely of a row of quaint timber-framed stores set on the wooden boardwalks of Mamane Street, it stands a couple of miles back from the ocean and is surrounded by rolling meadows.

Just over two thousand people live in Honoka'a, whose economy depended on a mill belonging to the Hāmākua Sugar Company from 1873 until it finally shut down in 1994. Still, this is one of several Big Island communities to have been spruced up and revitalized by federal funding, and its historic downtown district makes it an appealing port of call.

The most conspicuous landmark along Mamane Street is the Art Deco **Honoka'a People's Theater**, built as a movie theater in 1930 by the Tanimoto family (who were also responsible for the Aloha Theater in Kainaliu; see p.169). Restored and repainted over the last decade, it is now in use once again for occasional movie performances and musical evenings, and each October hosts the Hāmākua Music Festival, featuring Hawaiian bands and singers.

If you're lucky enough to find it open – afternoons are a better bet than mornings, but that's as far as regular hours go – a visit to octagenarian James Rice's **Hawaiian Shop,** also on Mamane Street, is the most memorable experience Honoka'a has to offer. At first glance it looks like a typical junk shop, but many of the artifacts piled high on all sides are anthropological museum pieces. The place heaves with Buddhas, bottles, Aladdin's lamps, stuffed hog's heads, carved-lava Hawaiian deities and swathed mummies, but most importantly with idols, fertility symbols and masks from Papua New Guinea. The town's handful of other antique and junk stores, a couple of hundred yards up the road to Hilo, pall by comparison.

A steep road drops straight down towards the sea from the center of Honoka'a. As yet, despite the closure of the sugar mill that blocks the way, you can't get right to the ocean. However, the **Macadamia Nut Factory** (daily 9am–6pm; free; ⓣ775-7201), very near the bottom, is, for no very good reason, a stop on many bus tours of the Big Island. It basically consists of a gift shop selling cookies, coffees and the oleaginous nuts themselves. A window runs along the interior wall, enabling you to see into the factory and affording an insight into the zany world of mac-nut preparation.

## Practicalities

The only **accommodation** in central Honoka'a is the *Hotel Honoka'a Club*, on Mamane Street at the Hilo end of town (PO Box 247, Honoka'a HI 96727; ⓣ & ⓕ775-0678 or 1-800/808-0678; ❶–❷). A rambling, thin-walled and quite spartan old wooden structure, it offers a wide range of rooms, including appealing antique-furnished en-suite ones on the upper floor with sweeping ocean views, and much more basic alternatives downstairs, some of which serve as $15-per-bed hostel-style dorms.

Two miles out of Honoka'a towards Waipi'o, the *Waipi'o Wayside B&B* (PO Box 840, Honoka'a HI 96727; ⓣ775-0275 or 1-800/833-8849, ⓦwww.waipiowayside.com; ❸–❹) has five themed en-suite rooms in an attractive old plantation house. In Pa'auilo, six miles southeast, *Suds' Acres* is an appealing and more economical rural B&B, with two en-suite rooms in the main house, plus a two-bedroom guest cottage (PO Box 277, Pa'auilo HI 96776; ⓣ & ⓕ776-1611 or 1-800/735-3262; ❸).

The best place to **eat** in Honoka'a is *Jolene's Kau Kau Korner* (Mon–Wed & Fri 10.30am–8pm, Thurs & Sat 10.30am–3pm; ⓣ775-9498), next to the Lehua–Mamane intersection in the center of town. A lunchtime burger or stir-fry in this clean, attractive Hawaiian-style diner will set you back $4–8; more substantial dinner entrees, such as the tasty seafood platter of breaded fish, cost $12–17. If you're looking for something a little lighter, the main alternatives are the *Mamane Street Bakery Café* next door (Mon 6.30am–5.30pm, Tues, Wed & Sat 6.30am–5pm,

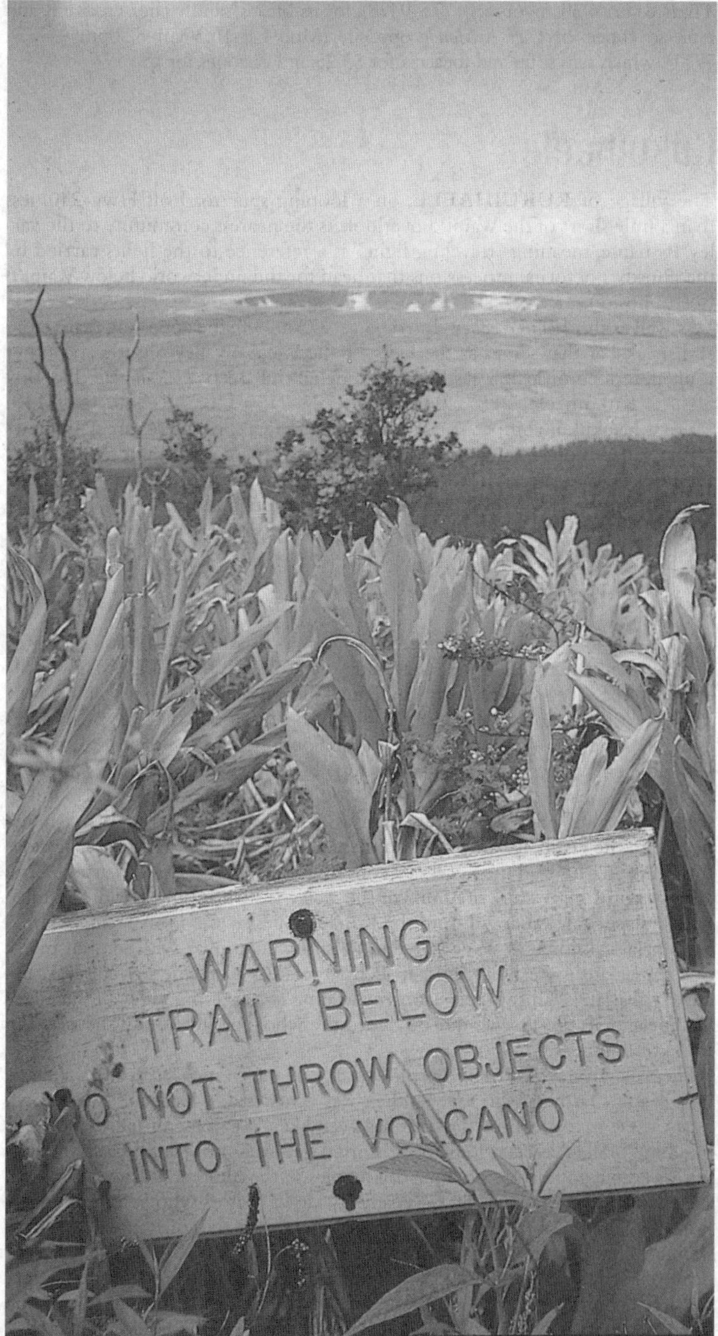
WARNING
TRAIL BELOW
O NOT THROW OBJECTS
INTO THE VOLCANO

Thurs & Fri 6.30am–6pm; ⓣ 775-9478), for its breads, sandwiches, croissants and espresso coffee, or *Café Il Mondo* opposite (Mon–Sat 10.30am–8.30pm; ⓣ 775-7711), which sells soup and focaccia for $3.25 and calzones for $8.

## Kukuihaele



The village of **KUKUIHAELE**, on a looping spur road off Hwy-240, less than a mile short of the Waipi'o overlook, is the nearest community to the valley. Its name, meaning "traveling light," is a reference to the lights carried by the ghostly nocturnal processions that head for the underworld below Waipi'o (see opposite).

As well as the *Waipi'o Valley Art Works* (ⓣ 775-0958), the appealing crafts store and snack bar that serves as the base for the Waipi'o Valley Shuttle and other tours described on p.225, it's home to a delightful **B&B**, *Hale Kukui* (PO Box 5044, Kukuihaele HI 96727; ⓣ 775-7130 or 1-800/444-7130, ⓦ www.halekukui.com; ❸/❹). Set in lush gardens above the ocean, with views of the valley mouth, the guest cottage here stands a couple hundred yards off the loop road as you head towards Waipi'o. Accommodation is in a one-bedroom studio or a two-room unit; credit cards are not accepted.

## Waipi'o Valley

Beyond Honoka'a, Mamane Street continues north as Hwy-240, and comes to an abrupt end after nine miles at the edge of **WAIPI'O VALLEY**. The southernmost of a succession of deeply indented, sheer-walled valleys stretching away up the coast to Pololū (see p.202), Waipi'o is the only one accessible by road. It's as close as the Big Island gets to the classic South Seas image of an isolated and self-sufficient valley, sparkling with waterfalls, dense with fruit trees, and laced by footpaths leading down to the sea. More dramatic examples of this kind of scenery abound on older islands such as Kauai, but as the Big Island is the newest in the chain, it's only here on the flanks of Kohala – its oldest volcano – that rainwater has had the necessary eons to gouge out such spectacular chasms.

Between its high walls, the floor of the valley is surprisingly broad, and filled with rich silt carried down from the Kohala slopes by the meandering Waipi'o Stream (also known as Wailoa Stream). Visitors unfamiliar with Hawaii might not appreciate quite how unusual such large areas of prime agricultural land are in the islands. This was probably the leading *taro*-farming valley of the entire archipelago; its produce alone could feed the whole population of the island in times of famine.

The valley is now far more overgrown than it was in its heyday, and inhabited by just a few farmers who squelch their way across paddy-like *taro* fields (known as *lo'i*, these have a consistency that has been likened to a "semi-jelled chocolate pudding"). They've been joined by assorted get-away-from-it-all *haoles*, including a sizeable population of latter-day hippies in the remoter reaches.

Only a small proportion of the steady trickle of visitors who admire the view from the Waipi'o overlook make their way down into the valley itself. It's a very strenuous hike, so most people join a motorized or horseback tour (see p.225 for details). Facilities at the bottom are minimal; there's nowhere to eat and a very restricted choice of accommodation. However, it's a magical, irresistible spot, and one that deserves to figure on even the most breakneck Big Island itinerary.

## The history of Waipi'o

*Wai* being Hawaiian for "water," and *pi'o* meaning "a loop, bow or thing bent on itself," Waipi'o Valley was named "curving water" to describe the sinuous course of the Waipi'o Stream across its floor. This beautiful and enormously productive location occupies a crucial place in Big Island history and retains a great cultural significance.

The Hawaiian word for "law," *kanawai*, literally means "the equal sharing of water," and the system to which it refers is said to have been instigated in Waipi'o at some indeterminate time by **'Umi-a-Liloa**. The first ruler to unite the entire Big Island, as a *taro* farmer he was responsible for the development of the valley's highly complex network of irrigation channels. Many remain in use to this day. 'Umi also had his nastier side, as one of the first major practitioners of large-scale human sacrifice. Victims, such as his rival high chief and half-brother Hakua-a-Liloa, were baked in an *imu* pit and their remains placed on the altar of Waipio's Moa'ula Heiau.

Both 'Umi and Hakua were the sons of the previous chief, Liloa. 'Umi, the product of a secret liaison, was raised in obscurity near Laupāhoehoe. As an adult, he revealed himself to his father in Waipi'o by swimming across the stream and climbing the walls of his stockade – an offense that would have been punishable by death had he not been able to prove his birthright.

Another Waipi'o legend states that a pit at the mouth of the valley (now ploughed over) marked the entrance to the underworld known as Kapaaheo, the Hawaiian equivalent of ancient Greece's Hades. This insubstantial and barren wasteland was said to be populated by famished ghosts gnawing on lizards and butterflies; dead souls could occasionally be seen making their way to it at night, in stately processions along the Old Māmalahoa Highway (see p.197).

Waipi'o was also the boyhood home of **Kamehameha the Great**, another future chief brought up in secrecy for his own safety. It was here that chief Kalaniopu'u granted Kamehameha custody of the war god Kūkā'ilimoku in 1780, thereby sanctioning his ambitions to become ruler. Eleven years later, his warriors fought Kahekili of Maui just offshore in the inconclusive but bloody "Battle of the Red-Mouthed Gun," in which, for the first time, Hawaiian fleets were equipped with cannons, operated by foreign gunners.

All sorts of estimates have been made of the population of Waipi'o in different eras. In Kamehameha's day, there may have been as many as 7500 inhabitants; within a century that was down to more like 2000, but you may still meet people brought up in the valley who can point out overgrown spots where Catholic, Protestant and Congregational churches, and a Chinese temple, were thriving as recently as the 1930s.

However, large-scale settlement of Waipi'o came to an end after the *tsunami* of April 1, 1946, which scoured the valley from end to end. No one died, but few felt much inclination to rebuild their devastated homes. The busiest Waipi'o has been since then was during the 1960s, when it was used by the Peace Corps to train volunteers heading to work in Asia.

These days, sixty percent of the land is owned by one landlord – the Bishop Estate – which leases it to private farmers. So far, all threats to "develop" Waipi'o have come to nothing – tourists, and golfers in particular, don't like the rain. The latest scheme is for a complex of tree houses to be erected near the valley rim; just possibly, they'll be in place by the time of your visit.

## Exploring the Valley

If you just want to say you've seen Waipi'o, the view from the overlook is more comprehensive than any you get down below. Assuming that you've driven here, you must in any case leave your vehicle at the top. A few yards down from the parking lot, a pavilion stands in a small grassy area on the very lip of the cliff, about 900 feet above the sea. Off to your left is the green floor of Waipi'o, with terraced fields but barely a building in sight as it reaches back towards misty Kohala Mountain. As you look straight up the coast, across the beach at the mouth of the valley, you should be able to make out three distinct headlands. The first is etched with the zigzagging trail that climbs up towards Waimanu Valley (see opposite). The second is Laupāhoehoe Iki, while Kauhola, beyond that, is up in North Kohala, near the town of Kapa'au on the road route to Pololū (see p.201). Unless you are the hardiest of hikers or kayakers, or take a flight-seeing tour, you'll never see the hidden valleys that lie in between. On clear days, Maui is visible in the far distance.

A rough paved track heads down the side of the *pali* from the parking lot, but don't try to drive it yourself. Without four-wheel-drive it's suicidal – as the rusting relics in the undergrowth at the foot of the slope attest – and even if you do have 4WD you need to know exactly what you're doing.

That leaves you with the choice of either taking a tour – see opposite – or **walking** down. It takes about fifteen minutes to reach the floor, but be warned: the 25 percent gradient makes the return trip heavy going.

One thing the tour operators don't mention is that they're not allowed to take visitors to the seashore. On foot, however, you're free to make your own way there. As soon as you come to the yellow warning sign at the bottom of the slope, double back onto what swiftly becomes a muddy lane. Don't stray off this path; the *taro* fields to either side are strictly private.

It takes about a five-minute walk, through a fine avenue of ironwood trees, to reach the flat **beach** of gray sand, fronted by small black lava boulders. You may have heard stories about the black-sand beaches of Hawaii, but whatever people say, this isn't one of them. The sand here is simply silt washed down the mountainside, whereas a true black-sand beach is absolutely jet black and composed of tiny glass-like fragments of freshly spewn lava. The wide mouth of Waipi'o Stream cuts the beach in two; usually it's not too difficult to wade across, but you shouldn't attempt it if the water is any deeper than your thighs. Neither should you drink it, as it's liable to carry diseases from wild animals in the hills. Leptospirosis in particular is a major problem here, so don't let the water come into contact with the smallest open wound (see p.38). Surfers and boogie-boarders while away days on end playing in the white breakers, but it's no place for a casual dip.

If, instead of heading for the beach, you keep going at the foot of the slope, towards the back of Waipi'o, you soon come within sight of the 1200-foot **Hi'ilawe waterfall**, with the parallel but slimmer **Nani** cascade plummeting to its left. Both feed Waipi'o Stream as it emerges into the heart of the valley. The waterfall is further away than it looks; walking to its base takes an hour and a half and involves scrambling up a channel of giant boulders. This spot was once the site of Nāpo'opo'o, Waipio's main village, which was said to have had several thousand inhabitants.

A disused, century-old trail runs on a ledge behind and halfway up Hi'ilawe, following the line of the aqueducts and tunnels that formerly carried water to the sugar farms. The square building to the left of the falls, conspicuous for its mirrored paneling, is also empty. It was built as a restaurant in the 1960s, but local protests at the developers' ever more grandiose plans, which included installing a cable-car ride to the top of the falls, led to the project being abandoned.

## Waipi'o tours

An ever-increasing range of **organized tours** around the floor of Waipi'o Valley (available in horse-drawn wagons, on horseback and in 4WD vans), which drive visitors down the access road, offer a chance to learn more about the valley from local people. Many of the guides were born in Waipi'o and are eager to share stories of the old days. However, regulations as to what each operator is allowed to do tend to change from year to year. The beach is off-limits and the waterfalls are too remote, so most tours consist of anecdotal rambles through the *taro* fields and along the riverbank.

The Waipi'o Valley Shuttle, which runs ninety-minute **van trips** from the overlook, is based at the *Waipi'o Valley Art Works* (see p.222) in Kukuihaele, a mile from the end of the road. They prefer that you call ahead to reserve a trip, but there's often a driver hanging around the overlook itself waiting to fill up his vehicle (Mon–Sat, departures usually at 9am, 11am, 1pm & 3pm; $40 per person; ⓣ775-7121).

The Last Chance Store, also in Kukuihaele, is the headquarters for Waipi'o Valley Wagon Tours, which takes groups of up to twelve people on two-hour **covered-wagon excursions** (Mon–Sat, up to four tours daily, usually at 9.30am, 11.30am, 1.30pm & 3.30pm; $40 per person; ⓣ775-9518), and for Waipi'o on Horseback (daily 9.30am & 1.30pm; ⓣ775-7291), which runs **horseback expeditions** costing around $75 for a couple of hours. Waipi'o Na'alapa Trail Rides (Mon–Sat 9.30am & 1pm; ⓣ775-0419) offers similar excursions at similar prices.

In addition, various tours explore the backcountry close to and along the upper rim of Waipi'o without making the descent into the valley itself. Waipi'o Ridge Stables (ⓣ775-1007, ⓦwww.topofwaipio.com) offer both **horse** rides ($75 for 2hr 30min, $145 for 5hr) and, as Waipi'o Rim Adventures (same number and website), **off-road vehicle** tours, either in individual all-terrain buggies ($85 for 2hr) or in 4WD jeeps ($85 for 3hr). Hawaiian Walkways organizes none-too-strenuous guided **hikes** ($85 for 4–5hr; ⓣ775-0372 or 1-800/457-7759, ⓦwww.hawaiianwalkways.com).

## Accommodation

Waipi'o Valley has neither restaurant nor café, nor does it any longer hold hotels or hostels of any kind. However, permission for up to four nights' free tent **camping** in the woodlands just inland from Waipi'o Beach, on the near side of the stream, is granted by the Bishop Estate, whose office is in the Keauhou Shopping Center near Kailua (78-6831 Alii Drive, Kailua-Kona HI 96740; ⓣ322-5300).

## Hiking beyond Waipi'o

The moment you arrive at Waipi'o overlook and look across to the trail that climbs the far wall of the valley, you'll probably start wondering what lies **beyond Waipi'o**. Very few people ever find out – it's one of the most difficult hikes in all Hawaii, way beyond what it's possible to achieve in a single day. In addition, the trail only continues as far as **Waimanu Valley**, eleven miles away. The four more valleys before Pololū (see p.202) are inaccessible from this side; a trail from Pololū in theory gets to two of them, but that too is an extremely demanding undertaking.

Because it involves wading through at least two deep and fast-flowing streams, the trail to Waimanu is only passable between May and October. Only consider setting off from Waipi'o if you're equipped with a camping permit (see below) and everything necessary for a backcountry expedition – most notably a rainproof tent and clothing, and some kind of water purification system.

Start by heading slightly inland from the far end of Waipi'o beach, and you'll soon pick up the uphill path. For most of the way, it passes through thick woodlands, so there are virtually no views of either sea or valley. The trail doesn't drop to sea level again until Waimanu, but climbs up and down through what feels like an endless succession of gullies.

Waimanu itself is a sort of miniature Waipi'o, with even more waterfalls. It, too, was once densely populated by *taro*-farmers and only abandoned after the *tsunami* of 1946. The beach itself is made up of large boulders, which means that not only is it not safe for swimming, you can hardly even walk along it.

The main **campground** is on the far side of Waimanu stream. **Camping** is free, but limited to nine sites, and you can stay a maximum of six nights. Obtain a permit from the Department of Forestry in Hilo (1643 Kilauea Ave, Hilo HI 96720; ⓣ933-4221).

Local experts say that the easiest way to get to Waimanu and beyond is not by hiking at all, but by **kayak**. Naturally, only experienced kayakers should attempt such an expedition.



# The Saddle Road

From a glance at the map, the **SADDLE ROAD** looks the quickest route from one side of the Big Island to the other. What no map can convey, however, is quite how high and remote it is, involving a long slow haul to an altitude of well over 6000 feet in order to cross the "saddle" of land that lies between **Mauna Kea** to the north and **Mauna Loa** to the south. The fifty-mile stretch from Hilo to the point where it rejoins the Belt Road – six miles south of Waimea, and more than thirty northeast of Kailua – is one of the bleakest stretches of road imaginable, utterly unlike anything you'd expect to encounter in the middle of the Pacific Ocean.

Even if the Saddle Road is not much use as a short cut, it is an enjoyable adventure in its own right. Despite the elevation, it passes a long way below the summits of the two mountains, so you probably won't see the snowcaps, but there's some memorable scenery en route. The trouble is, all the car-rental chains **forbid** drivers to take their vehicles along the Saddle Road, on pain of forfeiting your insurance cover and all rights to emergency rescue. The only way around this is to rent a four-wheel-drive vehicle (see p.153).

The rental-car ban was originally imposed because the road was poorly surfaced, and narrowed in several sections to a single lane. These days, the surface is always reasonable, and even at its narrowest cars traveling in opposite directions can pass each other comfortably. Certain dangers remain, however: the road was built to serve the military bases in the high stretches and still sees a lot of uncompromising military traffic, and also the weather is often atrocious, so visibility can be very bad. Above all, there are no facilities of any kind for the entire 85 miles from Hilo to Kailua, so if you do get stuck or break down, rescuing you is a difficult and expensive job. If you choose to risk it, take it slowly and be sure to allow time to complete your journey in daylight.

**Leaving Hilo**, along first Waianuenue Avenue and then Kaūmana Drive, the Saddle Road seems to go on climbing forever, straight from the ocean. Beyond the suburbs with their tropical gardens, it heads up into the clouds, winding through a moist and misty heathland of spindly trees, then undulating across bare lava fields, until with any luck it emerges into the sun, on what feels like a wide grassy plain between Mauna Loa and Mauna Kea.

Gradually the road then curves to the north, circling Mauna Kea and bringing Hualālai into view. Various plans have been put forward over the years to cut a more direct course down to Kailua, saving perhaps twenty miles on the total distance; so far the presence of environmentally or archeologically important sites has prevented them from materializing. In 1997, however, federal money was earmarked to upgrade the Saddle Road in its entirety, and it seems likely that it will in time finally become serviceable as the fastest cross-island route.

## Mauna Kea

For the moment, **MAUNA KEA** is, at 13,796 feet, the highest mountain in the entire Pacific, let alone in Hawaii. Being extinct, however, and therefore already eroding away, it's steadily losing ground to still-active Mauna Loa, 25 miles southwest. Nonetheless its height and isolation make Mauna Kea one of the very best sites for **astronomical observatories** on earth. Its summit is an otherworldly place, not just because of the surreal ring of high-tech telescopes trained out into the universe, but because it's so devoid of life, its naked hillocks composed of multicolored minerals. A spur road ascends to the summit from the Saddle Road, though its last nine miles are restricted to four-wheel-drive vehicles only, and the observatories are seldom open to casual visitors.

The ancient Hawaiians named Mauna Kea the "white mountain," as it is capped by snow for over half the year. That didn't deter them from climbing right to the top, however. Like Mauna Loa, Mauna Kea is a shield volcano (see p.237), so most of its slope is very gentle. It differs from its neighbor in having been here during the last Ice Age, making it the only spot in the central Pacific to have been covered by **glaciers**. The ice had the effect of chilling its molten lava to create the best basalt in the islands. Incredibly, there's an ancient **adze quarry** 12,400 feet up the mountain. Dating as far back as 1100 AD, it was probably the major source of the stone used for all the islanders' basic tools.

### Ellison Onizuka Visitor Center

The turnoff to the summit of Mauna Kea comes at mile marker 28 on the Saddle Road. At first the road passes through grazing land, covered with wiry grass but devoid of trees. Most of this land is open cattle range – a broad swathe of this flank of Mauna Kea, just like the northern side, belongs to the Parker Ranch (see p.195). The road surface is good for the nine miles to the **Ellison Onizuka Visitor Center**, a small facility that houses displays about the observatories and also has its own much more basic telescope, used for the daily after-dark **stargazing** sessions (center open Mon–Fri 9am–noon & 1–5pm, Sat & Sun 9am–6pm; stargazing daily 6–10pm; free; Ⓣ961-2180, Ⓦwww.ifa.hawaii.edu/info/vis). On the first Saturday of each month, an astronomer gives a talk about some aspect of the observatories' work, while the third Saturday sees a Hawaiian cultural program.

Whether or not you plan to continue on to the summit, the eerie views here, at 9000 feet, make it worth coming this far. Bizarre reddish cinder cones and other volcanic protrusions float in and out of the mists that swathe the grasslands; in the afternoon, the clouds usually obscure Hilo and the coast altogether. In any case, to help prevent **altitude sickness** and related problems, you should remain for at least an hour at this level before going any higher. It's also important to drink as much water as possible – and not to come this high within 24 hours of **scuba diving**.

## The Road to the Summit

The road on from the Visitor Center is kept in reasonably good condition – the astronomers who work at the top have to commute this way – but it's only safe to attempt it in a **four-wheel-drive** vehicle. In anything else, you'd quickly burn out your brakes coming down. The surface is unpaved for the first five miles, largely to deter visitors; for its final four miles the road is paved once more, in order to avoid churning up dust that might interfere with the telescopes.

Locals delight in driving to the top of Mauna Kea to fill their pickup trucks with snow. Most tourists, however, are keen to see the inside of the observatories. If that's your goal, the best day to come is either Saturday or Sunday, when staff at the visitor center coordinate **free summit tours**. Participants are required to bring their own 4WD vehicles. If you don't have one, you could try to hitch a ride, but you can't arrange it in advance and it's a big favor to ask, as you'll be dependent on your new friend for several hours. The tour parties assemble at 1pm to watch a very dated video presentation about the observatories, and then set off in convoy at around 2pm.

In addition, three operators run **guided tours** to the summit of Mauna Kea, with pickups at either Kona coast or Waimea hotels: Paradise Safaris ($144; Ⓣ322-2366), Hawaiian Eyes ($99; Ⓣ937-2530), and the more perfunctory Waipi'o Valley Shuttle ($85; Ⓣ775-7121). Alternatively, if you're feeling energetic, you can **hike** up. This involves a grueling haul up six miles of exposed road, with an elevation increase of 4000 feet, before you're rewarded with your first glimpse of the summit.

**Weather** conditions at and near the summit can be absolutely atrocious. Wind speeds of over 170 mph have been measured (at which point the anemometer snapped), twelve feet of snow has fallen in a single night, and visibility is always liable to drop to zero. It's essential to bring very warm, windproof clothing, sunscreen, and sunglasses.

### The observatories

When you finally reach the top of Mauna Kea, it's far from obvious which of the many rusty red and gold cinder cones in the vicinity is the actual summit. In fact, out of deference to Hawaiian sensibilities, all the gleaming golf-ball-shaped **observatories** are clustered on slightly lesser eminences; the highest mound of all is topped only by a small Hawaiian shrine.

Mauna Kea was first opened up to astronomical use in the 1960s and now holds a total of thirteen observatories. Each is leased to a different academic institution or consortium, but the entire site remains under the auspices of the University of Hawaii. No further telescopes will be built, though existing ones can be replaced as they become outdated.

The most technologically advanced facilities are the two identical domes of the **Keck** observatories, which function in tandem, and the giant **Subaru Observatory**, which boasts the world's largest glass mirror, at 8.3 meters (about 27ft 5inches) across. (The latter is not sponsored by the car company – Subaru is also the Japanese name for the Pleiades, or "Seven Sisters" stars.)

Some observatories, such as the Keck pair, are remote-controled by technicians in Waimea and Hilo, while others require human operators to be on hand. Working at this altitude brings unique problems; however often you come here, the thin air is liable to render you light-headed, and greatly affects your ability to concentrate. As a result, the weekend guided tours (see above) tend to be rather surreal, with guides and visitors alike unable to string coherent thoughts together. Those tours take you into three or four different observatories; if you arrive alone, the original Keck installation, Keck I, is the only one with a visitor gallery (Mon–Fri 10am–4pm; free).

Don't expect to able to peer through the eyepieces of the telescopes; all information is digitally processed and can only be seen on computer screens. Astronomers from all over the world, including amateur hobbyists, can however submit proposals to use the telescopes for their pet projects, at typical fees of around $1 per second.

### The summit of Mauna Kea

The summit of Mauna Kea, the cinder cone officially known as **Pu'u Wēkiu**, stands off to the right of the observatory access road. It can only be reached via a short, steep hike up the crumbling slope. Alongside the geodesic plate at the top you'll find a simple cairn of rocks, erected as a Hawaiian shrine. The view, of course, is awesome, with assorted natural cones and craters nearby, and the mighty shapes of Mauna Loa and Haleakalā on the horizon.

If there's any snow on the ground, you may well find yourself sharing this magnificent spot with groups of teenagers, rendered imbecilic by the altitude, who come up here to **snowboard** down the rough surrounding slopes.

Mauna Kea holds one last surprise. Reached by a ten-minute hiking trail that leaves the main road at a hairpin bend just below the summit, **Lake Wai'au** is a permanent lake set in a cinder cone 13,020 feet above sea level. Some visitors swim in its icy waters, which are replenished by thawing permafrost. It makes more sense to wander over to the brass plaque by the shore, which marks where the ashes of Ikua Purdy, the 1908 World Rodeo champion, were scattered. He and his fellow Parker Ranch cowboys (see p.195) would come all the way up here when roping wild horses.

## Mauna Kea State Park

Once past the summit approach road, the Saddle Road starts to head slightly north, and views begin to open up of the whole Kona coast. Very near mile marker 35, a short, but very tiring two-mile hike in **MAUNA KEA STATE PARK** can bring you to superb views of the island's three largest volcanoes.

From the parking lot, head past the wooden cabins – available for rent through the state parks office in Hilo ($45 per night; ⓣ974-6200) – and follow a jeep track towards Mauna Kea. Having made your way as far as three pale-blue water towers, continue along the track until just before you reach an older and rustier tower. So far the trail has all been flat, but now a footpath leads straight up a small-looking mound to the right. The next few hundred yards are chest-thumpingly steep. Climbing across a loose surface of powdery brown dust, you pass a wide range of brittle high-altitude plants, including desiccated shrubs and a few native silverswords. Though far below the top of Mauna Kea, the crest of the mound makes a perfect vantage point for views of the entire slope of Mauna Loa across the saddle, Hualālai away to the west, and the sprawling army camp below.



# Puna

With the compelling attractions of Hawaii Volcanoes National Park just further on, few tourists bother to leave the highway as they pass through the district of **PUNA**, which takes up the southeastern corner of the Big Island. The county government too seems to see it as a land apart, a quirky enclave that

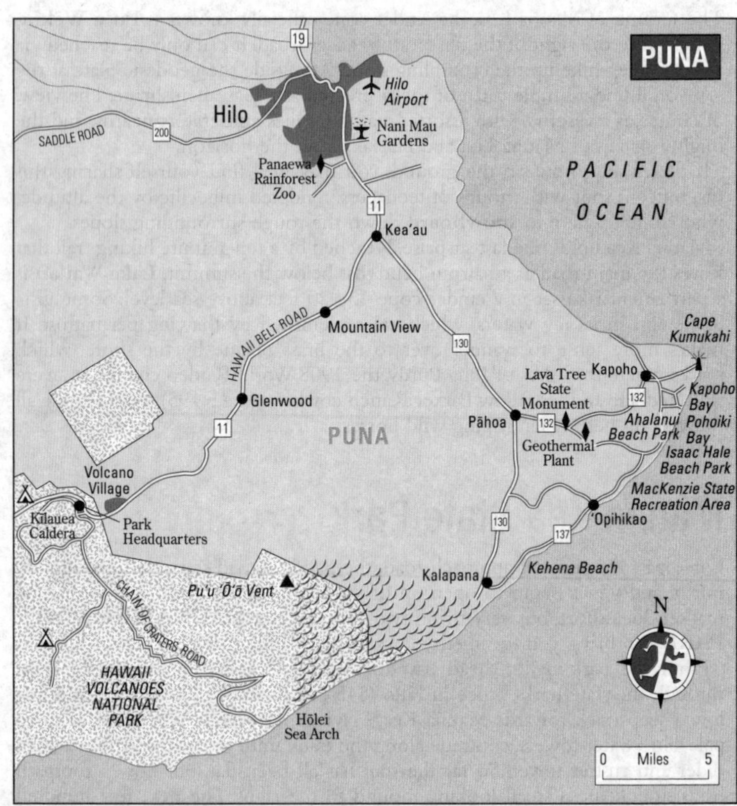

doesn't quite fit in with the rest of the island. In the 1960s and 1970s, large portions of the region were re-zoned for residential development, but it still lacks the infrastructure that you – and the twenty thousand people who live here – would expect. The volcanoes haven't helped matters either, incinerating newly built homes and cutting the coastal road to leave poor, traffic-ridden **Kea'au** as the only point of access to the whole region.

Although the eleven-mile stretch of oceanfront highway that has so far survived the volcanoes makes an attractive drive, there's no great reason to spend more than a couple of hours in Puna. Stop for lunch in the self-consciously outlaw town of **Pāhoa**, dominated by latter-day hippies and back-to-the-landers, but don't expect to swim from any of Puna's photogenic but dangerous beaches. Incidentally, Puna has long had the reputation of being the Big Island's main center for the cultivation of *pakololo* ("crazy weed"), also known as **marijuana,** but police crackdowns have put an end to most large-scale activity.

# Kea'au

The town of **KEA'AU** lies just south of Hwy-11 as it climbs towards the volcanoes, little more than three miles beyond Hilo's city limits. As a dormitory for Hilo's workers, and the gateway to Puna, it's choked morning and evening by huge traffic jams.

Kea'au consists of little more than the large parking lot for the **Kea'au Shopping Center**. This low-key wooden shopping mall holds the Sure-Save supermarket and its funkier rival, Kea'au Natural Foods, as well as a laundromat, a raucous sports bar and a couple of small Asian fast-food diners.

# Pāhoa

With its false-front stores and rudimentary timber boardwalks, tiny **PĀHOA**, a dozen miles southwest of Kea'au, is a distinctive blend of Wild West cowboy town and Shangri-la. Life here moves so slowly that it hasn't quite kept up with the rest of America; the streets seem to be filled with refugees from the 1960s – even if most of them were born a decade or two later – watched by occasional equally incongruous groups of *aloha*-shirted tourists.

The only building of any size in Pāhoa is the venerable **Akebono Theater**, founded in 1917, where the parking lot is the scene of a lively Sunday morning flea market. Fifty yards away on the boardwalk, the Hawaiian Hemp Co serves as headquarters for a campaign to legalize marijuana, and sells hemp (*cannabis sativa*) products of all kinds, including textiles from China and paintings.

## Practicalities

Although Pāhoa no longer offers any **accommodation** for visitors, it holds several reasonable **restaurants**, plus an ever-changing cast of coffeehouse hangouts filled with barefoot, tie-dyed locals. At the bottom end of the village, beyond the boardwalk and boasting a spacious wooden *lānai*, the *Godmother* (daily 7.30am–9pm; ⓣ965-0055) is the most upmarket option. It specializes in Italian cuisine, with pasta entrees costing around $8 at lunchtime and up to $16 at dinner. More adventurous alternatives include *Sawasdee* , a small Thai diner on the boardwalk (daily except Wed noon–8.30pm; ⓣ965-

8186). They offer the same delicious menu at both lunch and dinner, with *tom yum* soup ($7–11) in vegetarian or seafood versions, and red, green and yellow curries for around $9.

## Lava Tree State Monument

Set back in the rainforest just off Hwy-132, almost three miles out of Pāhoa, **LAVA TREE STATE MONUMENT** (daily dawn–dusk; free) preserves the petrified record of a double catastrophe that took place two centuries ago. First a fast-flowing lava stream destroyed the underbrush and lapped against the *ʻōhia* trees of the forest, clinging to their trunks and cooling as it met resistance. Then an earthquake opened fissures in the ground into which the liquid rock quickly drained. They left the landscape scattered with upright columns of lava, hollow inside where the trees themselves had burned away.

It takes around half an hour to walk the level, paved trail that loops around the finest specimens, which look like black termite mounds or gnarled old candles. While this landscape may be unusual and striking, if your time is limited it's best to push on to the main attractions of the National Park.

## The Puna Coast

Hwy-130 continues for just under ten miles from Pāhoa before its luck finally runs out a few hundred yards up from the sea. Halfway down from Pahoa, the "scenic point" to the left of the road at mile marker 15 marks the start of a short trail to a cluster of natural **steam vents**. Locals climb into these small cones to use them as steam baths, but you'd be crazy to follow suit; see p.240 for a salutary warning.

A thick layer of shiny black lava, unceremoniously dumped by Kilauea in 1988, brings the highway to a halt close to mile marker 21. Some trees are still visible beyond, and new plant growth is starting to appear, but barely a trace survives of the extensive Royal Gardens residential area that once stood here.

Almost all the village of **Kalapana**, down below, has also been destroyed, though the timber-framed **Star of the Sea church** was hauled a few miles up the slopes to safety and now serves as a makeshift community center. Fortunately, however, it's still possible to join up with the coast road, Hwy-137, at this point, allowing you to complete an enjoyable loop drive back to Pahoa that takes you about as far off the usual tourist track as you can hope to get on the Big Island.

Hwy-137 reaches the ocean slightly to the east of the former site of Kaimū black-sand beach, which until it was obliterated in 1990 was one of the most photographed spots on the island. Only the adjacent restaurant, now closed, was spared by the lava, but some of the coconut palms from the beach were rescued and airlifted to the *Hilton Waikoloa* hotel in Kohala (see p.183).

It is in theory possible to walk out across the lava field from beside the abandoned restaurant. At those times when the active flow from Kīlauea is entering the ocean, the plume of steam where it hits the water is often just visible from this end, as it is from the bottom of Chain of Craters Road (see p.249). However, only owners of the few Royal Grove homes that still survive – now without road access – are allowed to set out into the wilderness. Unless you know exactly where you're going, which in this ever-changing topography is all but impossible, you could easily get yourself into very serious danger.

Driving east along Hwy-137 takes you through a landscape that varies from one minute to the next, depending on the age of the lava flow you're crossing. In places the undergrowth thins out to bare black rock, but most of the route is dripping with tropical vegetation. From time to time you get glimpses of the ocean and successive palm-bedecked headlands, but only rarely is it possible to get down to the seashore.

The best spot to do so is **Kehena Beach**, close to the 19-mile marker, where a cluster of parked cars usually betrays the presence of a small path down the cliffs. At the bottom you'll find an absolutely stupendous little **black-sand beach**, backed by coconut palms that are home to a colony of wild parrots, and forever battered by spectacular crashing surf. Boogie-boarding and body-surfing can only be recommended if you know exactly what you're doing – locals do both naked – but from the jet-black shoreline it's often possible to watch dolphins at play in the water.

A mile beyond Kehena, as the road approaches the tiny community of **'OPIHIKAO**, it burrows its way beneath a dense canopy of trees outside the *Kalani Honua Culture Center and Retreat* (PO Box 4500, Pahoa HI 96778; Ⓣ965-7828 or 1-800/800-6886, Ⓦwww.kalani.com; ❷–❻). Part New Age teaching center, with courses in yoga, massage and the like, and part B&B, the *Kalani Honua* offers an idyllic situation for long-stay visitors. It holds three lodges, ten cottages and three tree houses, and provides guest rooms with and without en-suite facilities, plus camping at $30 per site or $20 per person. There's also a small evening-only café.

Another three miles on, **Mackenzie State Recreation Area** is a large-level picnic ground in a grove of ironwood on the oceanfront cliffs, where the earth underfoot is crisp with shed needles. Access to the seashore here is all but impossible: high surf scoops inexorably at the shallow cliff faces, hollowing them out to the extent that even walking to the edge is foolhardy. This tranquil forest glade is popular with locals, though tourists may feel it's not quite "Hawaiian" enough to be worth a stop.

Two miles further on, **Isaac Hale Beach Park**, just north of the junction with a minor road from Pāhoa, finally lets you get down to the sea. Set in **Pohoiki Bay**, with a small beach of black and white pebbles, overhanging green vegetation and high surf, the park is popular with surfers, anglers and picnickers, though it's not a place for family bathing or for anyone inexperienced in the ways of the rough Hawaiian seas. A small boat ramp, protected by an army-built breakwater, is used by local vessels; surfers occasionally hitch rides out into the breakers. Not far from Pohoiki Bay, the *Pamalu Hawaiian Country House* (PO Box 4023, Pāhoa HI 96778; Ⓣ965-0830, Ⓕ965-6198; 3-night minimum stay; ❹/❺) is a gay-friendly B&B. The five-acre property offers four en-suite guest rooms and has its own swimming pool.

A mile past Isaac Hale park, **Ahalanui Beach Park** is a much safer proposition for families. On paper, it sounds virtually irresistible – it's a sheltered oceanfront lagoon, filled with water that's naturally heated by volcanic action to 90°F, and surrounded by coconut palms. In reality, it feels more like an open-air swimming pool, having been shaped into a neat rectangle and surrounded by walls of cemented black lava boulders, complete with several small staircases into the water and attendant lifeguards. At weekends, it gets very crowded with local families.

As a paved road, Hwy-137 comes to an end four miles on from Pohoiki Bay, where it meets Hwy-132 from Pāhoa. To reach this spot, you pass over the site of Kapoho, yet another town swallowed up by the lava, this time in January 1960. A dirt road east from the intersection leads in just over a mile to the rudimentary lighthouse at Cape Kumukahi, which is not open to visitors. Much of the land in this area is entirely new, though at the edge of the vegetated zone you may spot an old Japanese cemetery and a *heiau* platform.



# Hawaii Volcanoes National Park

**HAWAII VOLCANOES NATIONAL PARK** may well be the most dynamic, unpredictable place you'll ever visit, and it's one where normal rules just don't seem to apply. What you see, and how long it takes to see it, is beyond all human control. The raw power of an active volcano is not something that can be tamed and labeled to suit those who like their scenery to stay still and their sightseeing to run to schedule. **Kīlauea**, at the heart of the park, is often called the "drive-in volcano"; it's said to be the only volcano in the world where news of a fresh eruption brings people flocking *towards* the lava flows. Only very rarely does the lava claim lives, but much of the excitement of coming here stems from the ever-present whiff of danger.

The park entrance is roughly a hundred miles southeast of Kona, thirty miles southwest of Hilo, and ten miles (as the crow flies) from the ocean. Driving from the west of the island takes at least two hours, with the last thirty miles or so spent ascending through barren lava landscape similar to that in the Kona airport region. The road from Hilo, on the other hand, climbs more steeply through thick, wet rainforest.

You arrive at the park headquarters, beside the caldera (summit crater) of Kīlauea, with no real sense of being on top of a mountain. That's because Kīlauea, at only four thousand feet high, is a mere pimple on the flanks of **Mauna Loa**, which, despite its deceptively gentle incline, stands almost ten thousand feet taller. Furthermore, for all its trails and overlooks, the crater area is a long way from the park's most compelling attraction. Somewhere down the side of the mountain, molten lava is bursting out of the ground and cascading down to the sea – assuming that the eruption that has been going nonstop ever since 1983 has not died down by the time you visit.

### Park information

The park is open 24 hours daily, 365 days a year; $10 per vehicle, $5 for cyclists, motorcyclists and hikers (valid for seven consecutive days). An annual Hawaii Volcanoes Pass costs $20, and system-wide national parks passes are both sold and valid; eruption information ⓣ985-6000; visitor center ⓣ967-7311, ⓦwww.nps.gov/havo.

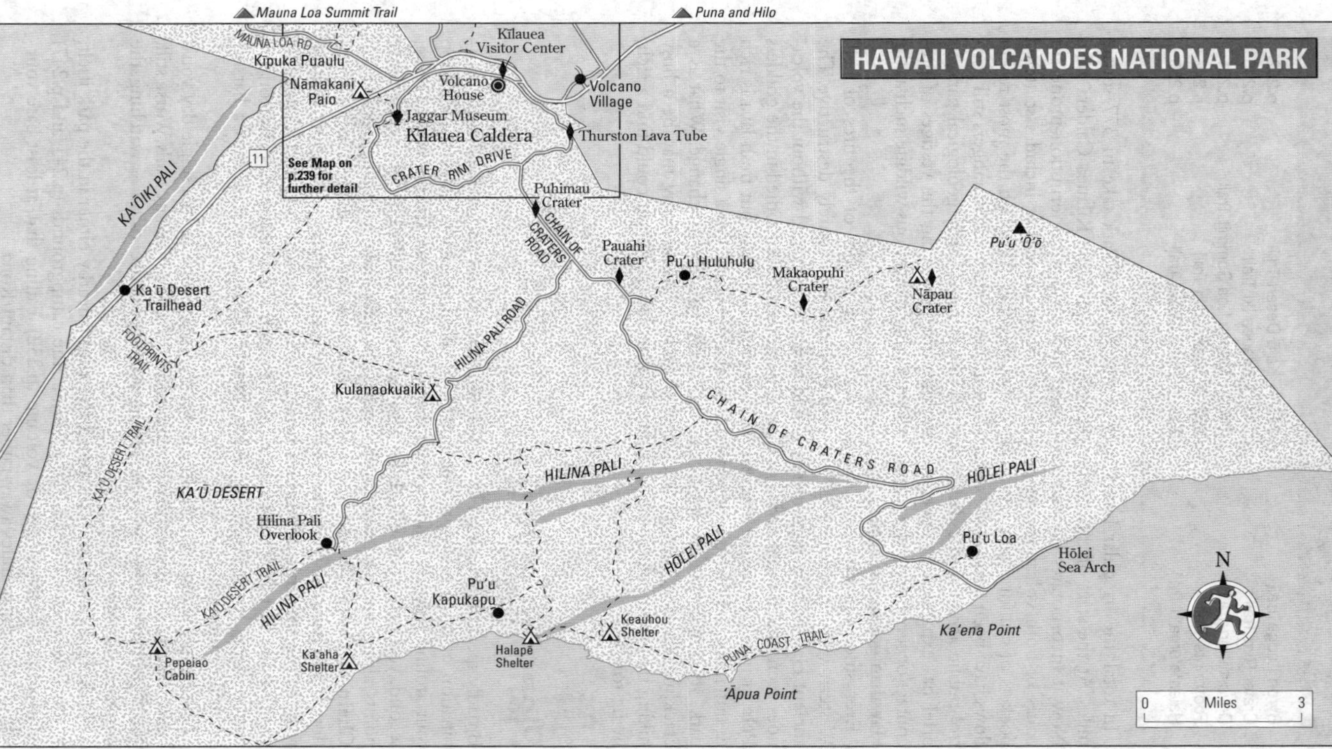
HAWAII VOLCANOES NATIONAL PARK
Mauna Loa Summit Trail
Puna and Hilo
Ka'ū and Kailua
MAUNA LOA RD
Kīpuka Puaulu
Nāmakani Paio
Kīlauea Visitor Center
Volcano House
Volcano Village
Jaggar Museum
Kīlauea Caldera
Thurston Lava Tube
CRATER RIM DRIVE
See Map on p.239 for further detail
11
KA'ŌIKI PALI
Puhimau Crater
CHAIN OF CRATERS ROAD
Pauahi Crater
Pu'u Huluhulu
Makaopuhi Crater
Nāpau Crater
Pu'u 'Ō'ō
Ka'ū Desert Trailhead
FOOTPRINTS TRAIL
HILINA PALI ROAD
Kulanaokuaiki
KA'Ū DESERT TRAIL
KA'Ū DESERT
HILINA PALI
HŌLEI PALI
Hilina Pali Overlook
Pu'u Kapukapu
Pu'u Loa
Hōlei Sea Arch
Keauhou Shelter
Halapē Shelter
Ka'aha Shelter
Pepeiao Cabin
PUNA COAST TRAIL
Ka'ena Point
'Āpua Point
N
0 Miles 3

## Hikes in the Park

| | | | |
|---|---|---|---|
| Byron Ledge Trail | p.245 | Ka'ū Desert Trail | p.252 |
| Crater Rim Trail | p.243 | Kīlauea Iki Trail | p.245 |
| Devastation Trail | p.246 | Mauna Loa Summit Trail | p.251 |
| Footprints Trail | p.252 | Mauna Ulu Trail | p.247 |
| Halema'uma'u Trail | p.243 | Puna Coast Trail | p.250 |



In total, the irregular boundaries of the National Park take in 377 square miles. At the start of this century, it only occupied the Kīlauea Caldera area. Now it incorporates the summit craters and most of the eruption-prone rift zones of both volcanoes, an area that is largely desert but includes scattered pockets of rainforest and even one or two beaches. Although the most recent flows have been beyond the official boundaries of the park, its rangers still control public access to the danger spots. From being a solely geological park, its brief has expanded to cover responsibility for preserving the vestiges of precontact occupation in the region and protecting indigenous wildlife such as the Hawaiian goose, the *nēnē*.

Ever since the early missionaries, with their images of the fires of hell, Western visitors have tended to see the volcanoes as purely destructive. The ancient Hawaiians, whose islands would never have existed without the volcanoes, were much more aware of their generative role, embodied in the goddess **Pele**. It may take longer to create than it does to destroy, but fresh lava is rich in nutrients, and life soon regenerates on the new land. On a single visit to the park, it's impossible to appreciate the sheer rapidity of change. What is a crackling, flaming, unstoppable river of molten lava one day may be a busy hiking trail the next. Come back twenty years later, and you could find a rich, living forest.

# Planning a visit

Broadly speaking, visiting Hawaii Volcanoes National Park involves some combination of three principal elements. First of all, there's the eleven-mile loop tour around Kīlauea Caldera from the visitor center, on **Crater Rim Drive**; second, you may choose to **hike** into or near the caldera, from one or more points along the way; and finally comes the fifty-mile round-trip down the **Chain of Craters Road** to the ocean, ending at the site of the current eruption. If you have the time, two additional areas are open to exploration. Getting right to the **summit of Mauna Loa** involves a four-day hike, but it's possible to drive the first 3000 feet of the route to gain a different perspective on the region. Away to the west, the **Ka'ū desert** offers more trails into a harshly beautiful moonscape.

Few people allow enough time to see the park properly. In a single day you'd be hard pushed to drive the two main roads, let alone hike any trails. Worse still, you'll probably miss the most spectacular experience of all – watching the eruption after dark.

Much the best option is to **spend the night** nearby, either in the park itself, at the *Volcano House* hotel (see p.238), at the campgrounds (p.241 and p.247) or in a B&B in the village of Volcano (p.252). Failing that, at least base yourself in Hilo, thirty miles away, rather than distant Kona.

## The Shield Volcanoes of Hawaii

According to the classic popular image, a volcano is a cone-shaped mountain, with a neat round crater at the top that's filled with bubbling lava and spouts columns of liquid fire.

Hawaiian volcanoes aren't like that. Although you may be lured to the park by photos of pillars of incandescent lava, you're unlikely to see any such thing. These are **shield volcanoes**, which grow slowly and steadily rather than violently, adding layer upon layer as lava seeps out of fissures and vents all along the "**rift zones**" that cover their sides. The result is a long, low profile, supposedly resembling a warrior's shield laid on the ground.

Mauna Loa and Kīlauea are simply the latest in the series of volcanoes responsible for creating the entire Hawaiian chain. Like all the rest, they are fueled by a "**hot spot**" in the earth's crust, way below the sea floor, which has been channeling magma upwards for seventy million years. As the continental plates drift northwest, at around three inches per year, that magma has found its way to the surface in one volcano after another. Each island in turn has clawed its way up from the depths, emerged above the waves, and then ceased to grow as its volcanoes became ever farther removed from the life-giving source. In time, erosion by rain and sea wears away the rock, sculpting the fabulous formations seen at their most dramatic on Kauai, and eventually the ocean washes over it once more, perhaps leaving a ring of coral – an **atoll** – to bear witness. Though Kauai is the oldest Hawaiian island of any size, the oldest of all are by now 3500 miles away, mere specks in the Emperor chain, off the coast of Japan.

Look at the gentle slope of **Mauna Loa**, project that gradient down through almost 20,000 feet of ocean, and you'll see why its Hawaiian name, "long mountain," is so appropriate. It's the most massive single object on earth; its summit is, at 13,677 feet, very slightly lower than Mauna Kea, but its volume of 10,000 cubic miles makes it a hundred times larger than Washington's Mount Rainier. It took two million years for Mauna Loa to swell from the bed of the Pacific into the air, and for another million years it has continued to climb. In the last 150 years, the world's highest active volcano has erupted every three or four years – in a single hour in 1984, it let forth enough lava to pave a highway from Honolulu to New York. Geologists predict that every spot on its surface will receive at least one more coating of fresh lava before the fires die down.

Only around once a century does Mauna Loa erupt simultaneously with **Kīlauea**, however. Of late the younger upstart – its name means "much spewing" – has been grabbing the attention, having been in a record-breaking continuous state of eruption since 1983. Although fed by a separate conduit from the fires below, Kīlauea emerged as a lump on the side of Mauna Loa, so you can hardly tell it's a separate mountain. Its lava tends to flow consistently in the same direction, down towards the ocean. Since 1983, it has added well over 500 acres of new land to a nine-mile stretch of the Puna coastline.

Meanwhile the next volcano is on its way. Scientists are monitoring the submarine "seamount" of **Lō'ihi**, twenty miles southeast of the Ka'ū coast. Were you to stay around for three thousand years, you might see it poke its head out for the first time. One day it may seem no more than a blemish on the vast bulk of Mauna Loa – or it may be destined to overrun its older sisters altogether.

Although the best way to explore the park is in your own vehicle, you can at least get there by **public bus** from Hilo. On Monday through Friday only, the Hele On Bus Company (☎935-8241) runs a service that leaves Hilo's Mooheau Bus Terminal at 2.40pm and calls at both Volcano village and the park visitor center around an hour later. The return ride is in the morning, leaving the visitor center at 8.10am. Buses continue beyond the park as far as

Ocean View (see p.258), but not all the way to Kailua. Alternatively, you could opt for an organized **bus tour** (some are listed on p.153), but generally these are not a good idea. They'll show you Kīlauea Caldera from above, but are unlikely to give you the flexibility to approach the eruption.

Inevitably, what you do will depend on conditions on the day you arrive. The active lava flow might be right there at the end of the road, it might be an hour's hike away, it might be somewhere else entirely or it might have stopped altogether. If it *is* flowing, then seeing it should be your top priority; why linger over photos in a museum when you can see the real thing?



## Crater Rim Drive and the park headquarters

The **park entrance** is just off Hwy-11, the Belt Road, about a mile west of the village of **Volcano** (see p.252). If you're coming from the Kona side you can visit the park without ever passing through Volcano, though as it holds the only gas station for miles, you may well have to anyway. From the **Visitor Center**, on the right within a few yards of the main gate, **Crater Rim Drive** takes eleven miles to loop around the summit crater ("caldera") of Kīlauea – for safety reasons, not always in sight of the edge.

Looking from a distance like a large oval of predominantly gray lava, roughly three miles long by two miles wide, **Kīlauea Caldera** is ringed on two sides by a steep *pali*, around 400 feet high. On those sides, and in places down below the wall as well, patches of rainforest have escaped the fires; off to the south and east, however, the cliff dwindles to almost nothing, and strong-smelling sulphur drifts across the plains to ensure that nothing living can find a foothold. It's possible to walk right to the edge of the main center of activity within the caldera, **Halema'uma'u Crater**, either from a parking lot on Crater Rim Drive or all the way across from *Volcano House*.

### Kīlauea Visitor Center

Though **KĪLAUEA VISITOR CENTER** does not overlook the crater of Kīlauea, call in as soon as you arrive, to pick up the latest information on the eruption and advice on hiking trails (daily 7.45am–5pm; ⓣ967-7311, ⓦwww.nps.gov/havo). The center has a bookstore and a small museum, and provides lots of excellent free literature. Every hour on the hour, from 9am to 4pm, it also shows a ten-minute video that's packed with eruption footage. Frequent lectures explain aspects of local geology, botany and environmental issues; at 7pm on most Tuesdays, the center reopens for a series of talks called "After Dark in the Park." Note that if you plan to camp in the backcountry, you must register here.

Just beyond the visitor center, set a little way back from the road, the **Volcano Art Center** (daily 9am–5pm; ⓣ967-7565), is a nonprofit gallery and crafts store that sells the work of local artists. Prices are slightly higher than elsewhere, but the standard of the artwork tends to be *much* higher.

### Volcano House

Pride of place on the lip of Kīlauea Caldera belongs to the **Volcano House** hotel (PO Box 53, Hawaii Volcanoes National Park, HI 96718; ⓣ967-7321,

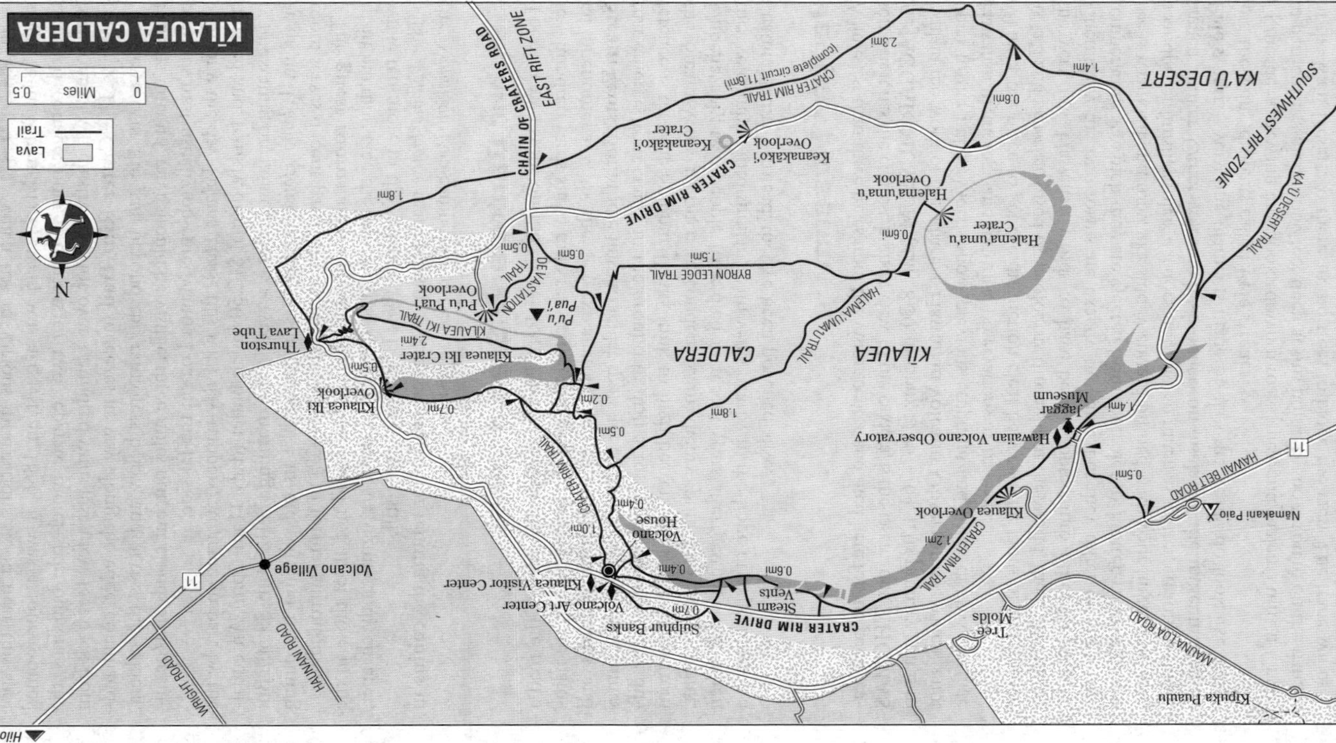
KĪLAUEA CALDERA
Lava
Trail
0 Miles 0.5
N
Hilo
Kailua
WRIGHT ROAD
HAUNANI ROAD
11
Volcano Village
Sulphur Banks
Volcano Art Center
Kīlauea Visitor Center
Volcano House
CRATER RIM TRAIL
CRATER RIM DRIVE
Steam Vents
Kīlauea Iki Overlook
Thurston Lava Tube
Kīlauea Iki Crater
KILAUEA IKI TRAIL
Pu'u Pua'i Overlook
Pu'u Pua'i
DEVASTATION TRAIL
CHAIN OF CRATERS ROAD
EAST RIFT ZONE
CALDERA
KĪLAUEA
BYRON LEDGE TRAIL
HALEMA'UMA'U TRAIL
Keanakāko'i Crater
Keanakāko'i Overlook
CRATER RIM TRAIL (complete circuit 11.6mi)
Halema'uma'u Overlook
Halema'uma'u Crater
Hawaiian Volcano Observatory
Jaggar Museum
Kīlauea Overlook
Tree Molds
Kīpuka Puaulu
MAUNA LOA ROAD
HAWAII BELT ROAD
Nāmakani Paio
KA'Ū DESERT
SOUTHWEST RIFT ZONE
KA'Ū DESERT TRAIL
0.7mi
0.4mi
0.4mi
1.0mi
0.6mi
1.2mi
1.4mi
0.5mi
0.5mi
0.2mi
0.7mi
0.5mi
2.4mi
1.8mi
1.8mi
0.5mi
0.6mi
1.5mi
0.6mi
0.6mi
2.3mi
1.4mi

Ⓕ 967-8429; ❸–❺), which has in various incarnations stood near this spot since 1846. When Mark Twain was a guest, in 1866, it was a four-roomed thatched cottage; now it consists of two separate motel-style buildings, the main one of which stretches for over a hundred yards just a few feet back from the abyss. The **Crater Rim Trail** squeezes its way along the edge, commanding views over the *pali*, beyond the rainforest below and across the caldera. Halema'uma'u Crater should be visible, three miles out, but clouds and/or sulphurous mist usually obscure Mauna Loa on the far side.

During the day, *Volcano House* fills with day-trippers, attracted in part by the hurried and, frankly, dismal $12.50 lunch buffet (daily 11am–2pm). An equally unexciting breakfast buffet is served in the morning (7–10.30am; $9.50). But at night, *Volcano House* reverts to something like its old self, and the dining room serves decent pasta and meat entrees ($14–22) in formal surroundings.

The **guest rooms** are simple and slightly faded, and not all of those in the main building face the volcano; the twelve that don't are significantly cheaper, while ten more in the separate *Ohia Wing* are cheaper still.

The *Volcano House* management is also responsible for renting the **cabins** in the *Nāmakani Paio* campground (see opposite).

## Sulphur Banks and Steam Vents

The first two stops on the Crater Rim Drive, on opposite sides of the road a few hundred yards and a mile respectively beyond the visitor center, are natural phenomena with the self-explanatory names of **Sulphur Banks** and **Steam Vents**. Both these unspectacular spots are characterized by white fumes that emerge from cracks in the ground to drift across open meadows; the difference is that the Sulphur Banks stink to high heaven, while the vapor from the Steam Vents is, once it condenses, in theory pure enough to drink. Unbelievably, two people have died in recent years after getting stuck when they've climbed into similar steam vents nearby in the hope of experiencing a "natural sauna"; instead, they've been poached alive.

## Jaggar Museum

A little less than three miles from the visitor center, and sited here for the good reason that it has the clearest, highest view of the caldera, is the fascinating **THOMAS A. JAGGAR MUSEUM** (daily 8.30am–5pm; Ⓣ 967-7643). Its primary aim is to explain the work of the adjacent **Hawaiian Volcano Observatory**, which is not open to the public. Videos show previous eruptions and panel displays illustrate Hawaiian mythology and historical observations by travelers.

This is the place to get the distinction clear between the kinds of lava known as *'a'ā* and *pāhoehoe* (used by geologists throughout the world, these are among the very few Hawaiian words to have been adopted into other languages). Chemically the two forms are exactly the same, but they differ owing to the temperature at which they are ejected from the volcano. Hotter, runnier *pāhoehoe* is wrinkled and ropy, like sludgy custard pushed with your finger, but with a sandpaper finish; cooler *'a'ā* does not flow so much as spatter, creating a sharp, jagged clinker. Other volcanic by-products on display in the museum include **Pele's hair** – very fine filaments made of glass that really do look like hair – and the shiny droplets called **Pele's tears.**

Outside, a viewing area looks down into Kīlauea, and Halema'uma'u Crater in particular, which is 360 feet deep at this point. By now you're on the fringes of the Ka'ū Desert, so there are no trees to block the view. The trade winds

## Controlling The Flow

When ancient Hawaiians found their homes threatened by approaching lava, they usually attempted to propitiate Pele with offerings (see p.244), but if in the end they had to move away they were not greatly inconvenienced. Unlike their modern counterparts, they did not own the land on which they lived, and could simply rebuild elsewhere. They could also load their possessions into canoes and paddle out of harm's way.

A full-scale emergency in Puna today would be very different, with hundreds of vehicles attempting to flee along the one road out, which might be rendered impassable at any moment. What's more, anyone unfortunate enough to lose a home may face economic ruin.

That sort of scenario loomed in the mind of Thomas Jaggar when he founded the **Hawaiian Volcano Observatory** in 1911. Its Latin motto, *ne plus haustae aut obratae urbes*, means "no more swallowed up or buried cities," and one of its main goals was to understand the behavior of the volcanoes enough to control them.

In both 1935 and 1942, when Hilo appeared to be under threat from eruptions of Mauna Loa, attempts were made to **bomb** the lava flow. Angled walls have also been constructed at strategic points on the slopes, in the hope of channeling the stream away from specific targets. A military installation high on Mauna Loa seems to have been spared as a result, though a similar scheme in the Kapoho district (see p.234) could not prevent the town's destruction.

These days the emphasis is much more on prediction than containment; the emergency services are briefed to stop fires but not to try to divert the flow. Only partly is that out of respect for Pele – more important is the fear of **litigation**. Directing lava away from one site might have the effect of "aiming" it at another; aggrieved homeowners who lost their property could then blame – and sue – the authorities responsible.

have for millennia blown the noxious emissions from the crater southwest, so despite receiving large quantities of rainfall the land supports no growth.

## Nāmakani Paio

A ten-minute walk from the Jaggar Museum parking lot, away from the caldera, brings you to the only **campground** in the main area of the park, **NĀMAKANI PAIO**. It's actually just across the Belt Road, so if you're driving to it you don't enter the park proper. The pleasant wooded sites are **free** and available on a first-come, first-served basis for maximum stays of seven nights (in any one year).

Basic **cabins**, sharing use of the campground's restrooms and showers, can be rented for $40 per night through *Volcano House* (see opposite; ⓣ967-7321; ❷). Each holds one double bed and two bunk beds, and has a picnic table and barbecue area. Bed linen is provided, but there's no heating, so bring a sleeping bag or extra blanket as it can be very cold at night.

## Halema'uma'u Crater

Kīlauea may be extremely active, but currently it's unusual for eruptions to take place up here at the summit. Since 1980, it's happened only twice, both times for less than a day. Such eruptions can create smaller craters within the caldera; the most conspicuous of these, **HALEMA'UMA'U CRATER**, is just over a mile from the museum.

Although you can see the crater from the roadside parking lot, you'll get a better idea of it by walking a couple of hundred yards across the caldera floor. The trail is clearly marked and there's a handrail, but with gusts of white mist spouting from crevices in the rock you feel as if you're taking your life in your hands.

As you look from the rim into a steaming abyss heavy with the stench of white and yellow sulphur, it's easy to see where sections of the wall have collapsed, as well as the yawning cracks where they will do so in future. In the 1830s, Halema'uma'u was described as a dome rising out of the lava field; when Mark Twain saw it in 1866 it was a "heaving sea of molten fire," with walls a thousand feet high. Since a huge explosion in 1924, however, it's been shallower and quieter, and it's now a circular depression that drops about 400 feet below the rest of the caldera. If this walk whets your appetite, you might be tempted to brave the entire three-mile length of the **Halema'uma'u Trail**, right across the caldera from *Volcano House* (see opposite).

## Keanakāko'i and Pu'u Pua'i

From time to time, the route of the Crater Rim Drive has had to be redrawn, as fresh lava paves over the road and a new layer of tarmac is in turn laid down on top of the lava. The stretch immediately to the east of Halema'uma'u was cut in two in 1982 and now passes in between the sites of two recent eruptions.

Until it was filled almost to the brim by new outpourings, **KEANAKĀKO'I CRATER**, south of the road, was the site of an ancient adze quarry, a source of the hard stone used by Hawaiians to make tools and weapons. **PU'U PUA'I**, farther along, is a bare rust-colored cinder cone thrown up in 1959 and accessible along the Devastation Trail (see 246).

## Thurston Lava Tube

Once past the Chain of Craters turnoff (see p.246), Crater Rim Drive plunges back into dense rainforest. This much less intimidating landscape is the location of the only short walk attempted by most tour groups, into the **THURSTON LAVA TUBE**.

As soon as you cross the road from the parking lot, a mile or so short of the visitor center, you're faced by a large natural basin bursting with huge *'ōhi'a* trees. Beneath it is the tube itself, created when the surface of a lava stream hardened on exposure to the air and the lava below was able to keep flowing with only a slight loss of temperature. When the lava eventually drained away, it left behind a damp, empty tunnel, an artificially lit portion of which is now open to the public. If you've ever descended into a subway system, the basic concept and appearance will be familiar.

It takes less than ten minutes to walk to and through the tube, which is remarkable only for the smoothness of its walls and its conveniently flat natural floor. Occasionally roots from the gigantic ferns that grow up above have worked their way through cracks in the rock to dangle from the ceiling. Back outside, the native red-billed *'i'iwi* bird can always be heard, if not seen.

# Hiking in Kīlauea Caldera

Laying a road across the unstable surface of the caldera itself would be ludicrous even by the standards of this topsy-turvy park, so the only way to experience the crater floor is by **hiking**.

The only safe trails are those maintained by the park service and shown on their free handouts; venturing off these would be suicidal. To embark on even the most popular trails requires an act of faith verging on the superstitious: they're no more than ill-defined footpaths across the bare, steaming lava, guided only by makeshift rock cairns known as *ahus*. Frequent cracks reveal a crust that is on average around four inches thick – though considering the many such layers of lava piled up beneath you, that's not as alarming as it may sound. Geologists estimate that the molten lava here is two miles down.

The caldera is not for agoraphobics; you can't assume that anyone will be on the same trail as you. Only two people in two centuries have been killed by eruptions, both photographers in search of the perfect shot. However, more mundane accidents happen frequently, and trying to hike at night is a very bad idea.

The longest trail in the caldera area, the 11.6-mile **CRATER RIM TRAIL**, is not described in detail here because it so closely parallels the Crater Rim Drive, though it generally runs nearer the edge than the road. It is an exciting, dramatic walk, and a level and easy one too, but it shows you very little that you can't see from a car. All the trails in this section start from or cross the Crater Rim Trail, however, so you're likely to walk at least a short section of it. Note that there's no need to register for any of the caldera hikes. You must do so, however, if you're heading into the backcountry (see p.238).

## The Halema'uma'u and Byron Ledge trails

Two separate hiking trails – the **Halema'uma'u** and the **Byron Ledge** – cross the main floor of Kīlauea Caldera. However, as they meet each other twice, it makes sense to combine the two into one single round-trip, of roughly seven miles and around four hours.

The obvious place to start is along the Crater Rim Trail from *Volcano House*. Heading northwest (away from the park entrance), the path drops slightly for a hundred yards, until a signpost points to the left down the **HALEMA'UMA'U TRAIL**. From there, a clear, easy walkway descends through thick **rainforest**, with the bright orange heliconia growing to either side interspersed with delicate white-blossomed shrubs and green *hāpu'u* ferns. Except when the odd helicopter passes overhead, the only sounds are the chatter of the tiny bright birds that flit through the canopy, and the steady drip of rain falling from the highest branches. Soon a sheer wall of rock to your left marks the abrupt fault line of the outermost crater rim. Less than half a mile down, from a small rain shelter, views open out across a small gorge filled with gently stirring jungle.

Not far beyond are the massive rock slides left by an earthquake in November 1983; the giant cubic boulders that tumbled down the cliff face now reach to the very edge of the path. Thereafter the vegetation thins out, and shortly after the first intersection with the Byron Ledge Trail, which you can ignore at this point, you come to the edge of the vast black expanse of the **crater floor**. The trail from here on is nowhere near as distinct as you might expect. At first the passage worn by the feet of previous hikers is clear enough, but before long you're gingerly picking your way from cairn to crude cairn, the schoolyard game of not treading on the cracks taking on a real urgency when you think of the lake of molten lava somewhere beneath your feet. The state of the trail depends on the age of the flow at each precise spot. Different vintages overlap in absurd profusion, and from time to time the path becomes a jumble of torn, cracked and uplifted slabs of rock.

## Pele: The Volcano Goddess

Every visitor to Hawaii Volcanoes National Park soon hears the name of **Pele**, the "volcano goddess" of the ancient Hawaiians. The daughter of Haumea the Earth Mother and Wākea the Sky Father, she is said to have first set foot in the Hawaiian chain on Kauai. Pursued by her vengeful older sister, the goddess of the sea, she traveled from island to island and finally made her home in the pit of Kīlauea. As well as manifesting herself as molten lava, she appeared sometimes as a young woman, sometimes as an elderly crone. Small acts of charity to her human forms could spare the giver a terrible fate when she returned as fire.

Imbued as they are with poetry, legend, history and symbolism, it's impossible now to appreciate all that the tales of Pele meant to those who once recounted them by the distant glow of Kīlauea. Certainly these were a people who studied the volcanoes carefully; specific places appear in the chants describing Pele's progress through the archipelago in the exact order of age agreed by modern experts. However, the destructive power of the volcanoes was just one small aspect of the goddess; she was also associated with the *hula*, with fertility, and with creation in general.

Talk of Hawaiian religion as a single system of belief ignores the fact that different groups once worshipped different gods. The god Kū, to whom human sacrifices were made in the *luakinis* (see p.520), was probably the chosen deity of the warrior elite; Pele may have been far more central to the lives of most of the islanders. She seems to have been a Polynesian deity whose worship became prominent in Hawaii around the thirteenth century. That may be because, together with Kū, she was brought to the islands by the wave of migrants who arrived at that time from Tahiti, or it may be that that was when Kīlauea entered the period of high activity that still continues today.

The earliest Christian missionaries to the Big Island were disconcerted to find that even after the *kapu* was broken and the old ways supposedly abandoned, belief in Pele endured. They made great play of an incident in 1824, when Queen Kapi'olani, a recent convert to Christianity, defied the goddess by descending into the caldera (probably on what's now known as the Byron Ledge), reading aloud from her Bible, eating the *kapu* red *'ōhelo* berries and throwing their stones into the pit. Less fuss was made in 1881, when an eight-month flow from Mauna Loa had reached within a mile of central Hilo, Christian prayers had elicited no response, and Princess Ruth Ke'elikōlani was called in from Oahu to help. Under the gaze of journalists and missionaries, she chanted to Pele at the edge of the molten rock and offered her red silk handkerchiefs and brandy. By the next morning, the flow had ceased. Well into the twentieth century, inhabitants of Puna and Ka'ū brought up in the old traditions would state that their families were directly descended from Pele and that, in a sense, each individual *was* Pele.

For at least half an hour you cross a plain where tiny ferns have taken root in every fissure, creating a green latticework of fault lines. Here and there *'ōhelo* bushes bearing the dew-glistening red berries sacred to Pele have established themselves. Then the ground begins to rise again, the cairns become harder to pick out against the general chaos, and wisps of sulphurous steam gust across the path with ever-greater regularity.

In due course you're confronted by what appears to be a low ridge of sharp, rough hills, with no indication of what lies behind. A single clear footpath leads up to a gap; through that gap, a similar landscape opens up once again. If you don't know what a **spatter cone** is yet, turn around; on this side the walls of most of the castellated hillocks are hollow, exposing fiery red interiors. They were created by the eruption of April 1982, when hikers in this lonely spot had to be evacuated immediately before a nineteen-hour onslaught.

This spot is clearly marked as the intersection of the Halema'uma'u and Byron Ledge trails, which head on together for a couple of hundred yards to the very lip of **Halema'uma'u Crater**. At this point you'll probably encounter other sightseers who have got here the easy way, via the short trail from the Crater Rim Drive; that walk, and the actual crater, are described on p.242. If you can arrange to be picked up at the parking lot, you can end your hike here. Alternatively, double back and take your choice as to your return route.

If you decide to head back along the **BYRON LEDGE TRAIL**, you'll find it considerably easier to follow, with a shorter distance across the crater floor; the walk to the edge of the crater from the junction of the two trails takes around half an hour. This trail is more even underfoot, although once or twice it requires you to step across narrow (roughly nine inches) but alarmingly dark cracks in the ground, including one with a small tree in it.

The ascent to **Byron Ledge** (named after the cousin of the poet who came here in 1825) is quite precipitous. The surface of the path is unstable gravel, of the same sharp shards of black glass as a new "black-sand" beach, and occasionally the scree slope plunges away below your feet. It can be very vertiginous; from this close, the black crater floor is so huge and featureless that the brain can't really take it in. The rainforest at the top is gloomier and less lush than on the Halema'uma'u Trail.

At one point along the ledge, you pass a spur trail that leads within minutes to the Kīlauea Iki Trail (see below). Sticking to the Byron Ledge Trail involves dropping right back down to cross a small segment of the caldera floor, in order to rejoin the Halema'uma'u Trail back to *Volcano House*.

## The Kīlauea Iki Trail

Just east of Kīlauea Caldera proper, but still within the Crater Rim Drive, the subsidiary crater of **KĪLAUEA IKI** ("little Kīlauea") took on its current shape during a gigantic eruption in 1959. Prodigious quantities of lava, shooting 1900 feet high, raised the crater floor by around 350 feet; some of it is still thought to be red-hot, a few hundred feet below the surface. Though Kīlauea Iki may not have quite the same sense of scale as the main caldera, it offers in some ways an even more spectacular assortment of terrain, which can be explored along the two-hour, four-mile **KĪLAUEA IKI TRAIL**.

The trail is most easily done as an anticlockwise hike from the **Thurston Lava Tube** (see p.242), a mile south of the visitor center. Start by following the Crater Rim Trail for about a mile, as it circles close to the lip of the gulf. At a three-way junction with the spur to Byron Ledge (see above), signs point left to the Kīlauea Iki Trail proper. Now the rainforest becomes especially dense, with ultra-dark, oily green leaves, startled wild game birds running along the path ahead, and songbirds overhead.

Soon you glimpse the far wall of Kīlauea Iki, tinged with pastel greens and yellows against the general darkness. Views of the crater floor thus far have made it appear smooth, but after a half-mile or so the path drops abruptly down to reach a primeval mess of jagged *'a'ā* lava. Follow the line of cairns for a few hundred yards before arriving at the vent where the 1959 eruption took place. This sudden, gaping maw in the hillside, filled like an hourglass with fine reddish-orange sand, is seen across an open scar in the lava; a barrier makes it clear that you should approach no closer.

The trail then descends slightly to a more even, but no less alarming, expanse of undulating *pāhoehoe*, punctuated by white- and yellow-stained cracks that ooze stinking plumes of white vapor. You have to step across the odd fissure and, once again, it takes an act of faith to follow the scattered cairns that mark the way. Eventually, however, you pass through a final chaos of rocks into the dripping, dank bosom of the rainforest. The path then zigzags back up to the rim; the gradient is never steep, but it's a fair walk and can get pretty muddy.



### Devastation Trail

Much of the lighter debris from the 1959 Kīlauea Iki eruption (see above) was blown clear of the crater itself, then carried by the wind to pile up as a **cinder cone** near its southwestern edge. This is **Pu'u Pua'i**, which can be reached along the half-mile **DEVASTATION TRAIL** between two parking lots on Crater Rim Drive.

If you set out from the Devastation parking area, opposite the top of Chain of Craters Road, you start by following the old route of Crater Rim Drive, which was severed at this point by the eruption. A paved pathway snakes through low, light-pink undergrowth – a favorite haunt of the park's population of *nēnē* geese. Most of what you see is new growth, though a few older trees survived partial submersion in ash by developing "aerial roots" some way up their trunks. Pu'u Puai itself is just a heap of reddish ash, while the land around it is barren, scattered with bleached branches.

## Chain of Craters Road

**CHAIN OF CRATERS ROAD** winds down to the ocean from the south side of Crater Rim Drive, sweeping around successive cones and vents in an empty landscape where only the occasional dead white tree trunk or flowering shrub pokes up. From high on the hillside, the lava flows look like streams of black tarmac, joining in an ever-widening highway down to the Pacific. Long **hiking trails** and the minor **Hilina Pali Road** lead to sites of geological and historic interest all the way down, but the real reason to head this way is to see what may be at the end – the ongoing **eruption of Kīlauea**.

Chain of Craters Road used to run all the way to Puna, then loop back up to the highway. The scale of the damage since 1983 has been too great to repair, however, so now it's a dead end, and getting shorter year by year. One by one, the landmarks along its seafront stretch – such as **Waha'ula Heiau**, another temple believed by some to have been where human sacrifice was introduced to Hawaii, and the gorgeous black-sand beach at **Kamoamoa**, whose short existence lasted only from 1988 until 1992 – have been destroyed, and before long the road may not follow the shoreline at all.

Check current conditions at the visitor center when you arrive and make sure you have enough gas. The end of the road is a fifty-mile round-trip from the park entrance, and there are no facilities of any kind along the way.

### Hilina Pali Road

Four miles down Chain of Craters Road, a sign to the right points out **HILINA PALI ROAD**. This crosses the bleak Ka'ū Desert for nine miles, to reach an overlook above the main 1200-foot drop of **Hilina Pali**. *Pali* is the Hawaiian word for cliff; you may be used to hearing it applied to the lush razorback hills of the Hāmākua coast, but Hilina is much starker and rawer than that, being the huge wall left behind when a piece of the island dropped into the sea. The views are immense, but desolate in the extreme. Infrequent clusters of battered palms in the distance show the locations of former coastal villages; the hillock of Pu'u Kapukapu, near the shore to the southeast, however, obscures the most popular of the park's backcountry campgrounds, at Halapē.

Halfway along the road, **Kulanaokuaiki** is one of the park's two fully-equipped, drive-in **campgrounds**. Smaller and somewhat more basic than Nāmakani Paio (see p.241), it's free, and available on a first-come, first-served basis for up to seven nights in any one year. It opened in 1999 as a replacement for the nearby Kīpuka Nēnē campground, which has closed permanently in order to allow its resident population of *nēnē* geese to breed in peace.

All **hiking** in this area involves extended periods of walking across barren, exposed and baking-hot lava flats. If you want to get to the shoreline, it makes more sense to hike the **Puna Coast Trail** (see p.250), than to climb up and down the *pali* as well. However, gluttons for punishment have a choice of two trails to the sea. Both the **Hilina Pali** and **Ka'aha** trails start by zigzagging down the cliff along the same poorly maintained footpath; the Ka'aha leads for just under four miles to **Ka'aha Shelter** (see p.251), while the Hilina Pali covers the eight miles to the **Halapē Shelter**, joining the **Halapē Trail** from Kīpuka Nēnē. In addition, you can even walk to the Hilina Pali overlook from the Jaggar Museum, along the eighteen-mile **Ka'ū Desert Trail** (the "Footprints" section of which is detailed on p.252).

## Mauna Ulu Trail and Pu'u Huluhulu

Another three miles along Chain of Craters Road beyond the Hilina Pali turnoff, a small approach road on the left leads to the **MAUNA ULU TRAIL**. A couple of miles along, this becomes the **Nāpau Trail**, then runs for ten miles to the open **Pu'u 'Ō'ō** vent, far out along Kīlauea's East Rift Zone – the culprit responsible for most of the lava flows since 1983. At present, it's illegal to continue along the trail any further than the basic **campground** at Nāpau Crater, three miles short of the end. If you plan to spend the night here, you must register at the visitor center; see p.238.

Most hikers content themselves with the three-mile round-trip to **Pu'u Huluhulu**, an ancient cinder cone that has somehow escaped inundation for several millennia. It owes its name (*huluhulu* means "very hairy") to the dense coating of unspoilt, old-growth rainforest that surrounds it as a result. Following the footpath to the top of this small mound enables you to peer into its inaccessible hollow interior, circled by craggy red rocks and filled with primeval-looking green ferns and darting birds. The sensation of being in a real-life "Lost World" is enhanced by the wasteland visible all around. With luck, you should be able to see the smoldering cone of Pu'u 'Ō'ō away to the east, while views to the south are dominated by the miniature shield volcano of **Mauna Ulu**, created between 1971 and 1974 and already home to native trees and shrubs like the *'ōhi'a* and *'ōhelo*.

## Pu'u Loa petroglyphs

Ten miles beyond Mauna Ulu, and just after its descent of the 1000-foot Hōlei Pali, Chain of Craters Road passes within a mile of the most extensive field of **petroglyphs** – ancient rock carvings – on the island.

The level trail east to **PU'U LOA** ends at a circular raised boardwalk. Most of the petroglyphs visible from here are no more than crude holes in the lava, and only inspire any wonder if you're aware that each was probably carved to hold the umbilical cord of a newborn infant. *Pu'u loa* means "long hill," and by

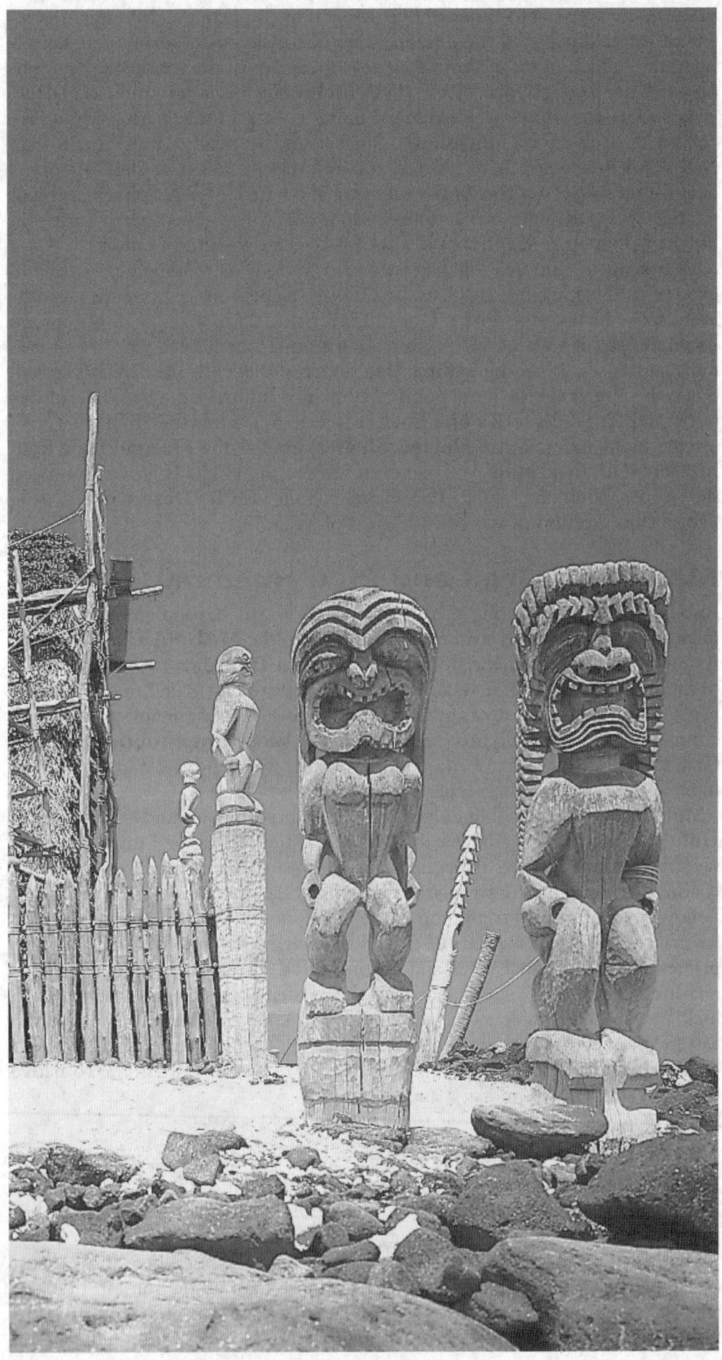

extension "long life," so this was considered a lucky spot for the traditional ceremony. The purpose of the boardwalk is not to display the most elaborate petroglyphs, but to discourage you from exploring further, for fear that you might damage such irreplaceable works of art as the images of pre-contact **surfers**, said to lie somewhere in the area.

## Hōlei Sea Arch

Chain of Craters Road comes to an end just beyond mile marker 20, with the small parking lot near **HŌLEI SEA ARCH** used as a turn-around point for all vehicles. Less than two miles survive of the road's previous eleven-mile shoreline route to Kalapana, and soon it may not reach the coast at all.

Until recently, few visitors bothered to pause at the sea arch; now it's the only named feature left in what was once a very scenic area. From the parking lot, cross a few yards of sparsely grassed lava and you'll see a chunky pillar of basalt blocks to your right, tenuously connected to the rest of the island by the top slab. The thudding of the waves against the cliffs makes the ground reverberate beneath your feet – clear evidence of the fragility of this coastline, most of which is too dangerous to approach.

## Approaching the eruption

It's impossible to do more than generalize as to what might lie beyond the end of Chain of Craters Road. Assuming that the eruption is still continuing, somewhere high on the hillside one or more fissures in the earth will be spilling out large quantities of molten lava, which then sets off towards the ocean. En route it may or may not have to pour over fault scarps (cliffs formed by minor earthquakes), and its surface may or may not harden to create an underground stream. You can only view the lava itself if the nearest active flow has reached a point you can walk to from the road; if it is flowing directly into the ocean, which is easy to spot because the contact produces great plumes of steam; or if it is crossing or flowing along the road itself.

Find out if any of these scenarios apply by calling the park's **Volcano Update line** (Ⓣ 985-6000); its website (Ⓦ www.nps.gov/havo) also carries up-to-date information. The Kīlauea visitor center (Ⓣ 967-7311) can offer more detailed advice and implores all visitors to view a three-minute safety video. During the 1990s, five visitors died in separate incidents, including two fatalities at the eruption site, and many more had to be rescued after becoming stranded out on the lava at night. The most dangerous situation occurs when lava flows directly into the **ocean**, when there's a risk of inhaling toxic fumes that contain not only acids but even tiny particles of glass. In addition, new land is extremely unstable; it may be no more than a thin layer of solidified lava resting on seawater – a "bench" – and thus liable to collapse at any moment. Swirling mists can make it hard to keep your bearings and can also mean that only occasionally do you see the actual lava. According to rangers, most problems arise when walkers attempt to approach the operation from the east, from the foot of Hwy-130, as described on p.232.

The park service maintains a wooden information shack (on wheels, for obvious reasons) at the end of the road, where they hand out alarming leaflets explaining that new lava is unstable and may collapse at any time, and that it's best to avoid clouds of hydrochloric acid. When safety permits, rangers lead **guided hikes** to the site of the eruption. A daily schedule is posted at the visitor center; as a rule they start in the early afternoon, in order to get back to the road before nightfall.

Walking across flaky, crumbling, new lava is an extraordinary experience. Every surface is like sandpaper, a fall can shred your skin and, even far from the apparent center of activity, the ground can be too hot to touch. Heavy rain dries off without penetrating your clothing. The sight of liquid rock oozing towards you, swirling with phlegmy gobbets and destroying all it touches; the crackle as it crunches across previous layers of lava; the sudden flash as a dried-out tree bursts into flame: all leave you with a disconcerting sense of the land itself as a living, moving organism.





**After dark**, the orange glow of the eruption becomes even more apparent. Pinpoint incandescent lights become visible all across the slopes and leave the mountain looking like the proverbial city on a hill. Without official sanction or approval, and heedless of the immense risks, many visitors stay out all night to marvel at the glowing rivers of molten rock. If you try it, be sure to carry a flashlight for the walk back across the lava.

Finally, it's only fair to warn you that when current activity is occurring several miles beyond the end of the road, as it has for much of the last three or four years, you may well feel a profound sense of **anticlimax** at the little you see. Children in particular, excited by photographs of lava fountains, are liable to be very disappointed by the reality. On the other hand, they may see something that one day they will tell their own kids about.

## Puna Coast Trail

Although it's roughly a mile up from the sea, the Pu'u Loa parking lot (see p.247) is also the point at which the **PUNA COAST TRAIL** sets off west, away from the eruption area, towards the coastal campgrounds at **Keauhou** and **Halapē.**

Also known as the **Puna Ka'ū Trail**, this long and very challenging hike is only worth attempting if you have several days to spare. It's possible to get to 'Āpua Point and back in a single day, but that's a thirteen-mile round-trip that still stops a long way short of the more interesting spots along the trail. If you plan to camp out, you must register at the visitor center in Kīlauea, as this area is prone to landslides and *tsunamis*. Collected rainwater is available at the shelters, but carry plenty more yourself. All three shelters consist of three-walled shelters, so you'll need a tent as well.

From Chain of Craters Road, the trail makes its way across a patchwork of lava flows, the new ones glistening in the sun and crunchy underfoot, the older ones worn and smooth. Roughly four miles along, you reach the low seafront cliffs, which you follow for a couple more miles to **'Āpua Point**. From a distance it's a welcome flash of green against the relentless grays and blacks of the lava; when you arrive it turns out to have just a few coconut palms emerging from a tangled carpet of the ivy-like native *naupaka* shrub.

With no water, shelter or other facilities at 'Āpua, you either have to turn back to the road, or continue along the coast. Heading west, you're faced by the massive fault scarp of Hilina Pali looming ever larger inland. As well as releasing cascades of rock and even lava towards the ocean, landslides like those that created the *pali* also produce *tsunamis* that flood the coastal plains, so little is left standing along this stretch of the shoreline. Both the **Keauhou** and **Halapē** campgrounds, three and five miles respectively from 'Āpua, remain visibly scarred by the battering they received in November 1975 (when two campers lost their lives at Halapē). However, the park service has been replanting coconut palms to restore their lost beauty, and Halapē still has the feel of a little oasis beside the sea. Unfortunately, so many campers trek out to its white-sand beach that the cabins at both campsites are infested with ants and cockroaches. Snorkeling in the tidal pools is excellent, but the open sea can be very dangerous. In theory these are nesting grounds for sea turtles, though the regulations against disturbing them seem to be a case of too little, too late and hardly any seem to land here any more.

To get to the final oceanfront campground, at **Ka'aha**, requires a very difficult six-mile hike from Halapē, up and along the top of a lesser *pali*. You can also climb down, with equal effort, from Hilina Pali Road (see p.247). Either way, it too is riddled with insects and even more dangerous for swimming.

# Mauna Loa

If you're interested in seeing a bit more of **MAUNA LOA**, as opposed to Kīlauea, leave the caldera area by the main entrance and head west for a couple of miles. The third turning on the right, **Mauna Loa Road**, winds up towards the summit from there, although it stops a long way short and only very rarely allows you views either up the mountain or down towards Kīlauea and the sea.

## Kīpuka Puaulu

Most visitors take the drive of less than a mile up Mauna Loa Road to see the enchanting little forest sanctuary of **KĪPUKA PUAULU**. Known as the "bird park," this enclave is an utter contrast to the raw landscape elsewhere in the National Park. A *kīpuka* is a patch of land that has by chance been left untouched by lava, and thus forms a sort of natural island. Kīpuka Puaulu's well-preserved rainforest serves as a sanctuary for rare native birds such as the *'elepaio* flycatcher and the *'amakahi* honey-creeper.

A woodland stroll around the two-mile loop path takes you past some huge old *koa* trees and through sun-dappled clearings, with birds audible on all sides. However, unless you have a lot of patience – and binoculars – you may not manage to see more than the odd flash of color. Your best bet is to walk slowly and quietly and hope to surprise a group on the ground.

A covered picnic area makes this a popular lunchtime halt for park visitors.

## The Mauna Loa Summit Trail

Beyond Kīpuka Puaulu, Mauna Loa Road climbs through thick woodland virtually all the way to the end, fourteen miles up, crossing just one stray lava flow. Its width varies between one and two lanes, but it's driveable if not exactly conducive to a quick journey. The surrounding tree-cover gradually changes from tropical to high-altitude before the road finally stops in a small clearing, 6662 feet up.

The parking lot here is the trailhead for the **MAUNA LOA SUMMIT TRAIL**. As the very explicit signs in the small pavilion explain, this is no trail to attempt on a whim. The summit is a gradual but exhausting 19 miles further on across bleak, barren lava, with a round-trip usually taking four days. There's no shelter along the way except for two crude cabins – check with the Park Service, with whom you must register anyway, to see whether they are stocked with water. Hypothermia is a very real threat, as the higher slopes are prone to abominable weather conditions. If you make it to the top, you're confronted by the **Moku'āweoweo Caldera**, similar to Kīlauea's, which last erupted in 1984.

# The Ka'ū Desert

All the land in the National Park that lies to the south and west of Kīlauea Caldera is officially known as the **KA'Ū DESERT**. By the conventional definition of a desert, it should therefore receive no rain: in fact it receives almost as much as the rainforest to the east, but here it falls as a natural acid rain, laden with chemicals from Kīlauea. Only a few desiccated plants ever managed to adapt to this uncompromising landscape, and most of those have in the last century been eaten away by ravenous wild goats.

Walking the eighteen-mile **Ka'ū Desert Trail** can bring you into close contact with this region if you so desire; there's one overnight shelter, the three-bed **Pepeiao Cabin**, about nine miles along the trail's great curve from the Jaggar Museum down to Hilina Pali Road. From the cabin you can choose instead to hike another six miles down to **Ka'aha Point** and connect with the Puna Coast Trail (see p.250).

## The Footprints Trail

Ten miles west of the park entrance on the Belt Road, an inconspicuous roadside halt marks the start of the **FOOTPRINTS TRAIL**, which leads due south for just under a mile across rough *'a'ā* lava. A small shelter at what might seem like a random spot covers a bunch of depressions in the rock, which popular legend says are human footprints. Whether or not you agree, the factual basis for the story is bizarre.

In 1790, Keōua, a rival of Kamehameha, was returning to his own kingdom of Ka'ū after two major battles in Puna. As his armies, complete with attendant women and children, traversed this stretch of desert, he divided them into three groups. The first group got safely across; then Kīlauea erupted, and the third group found the members of the second strewn across the pathway. All were dead, poisoned by a cloud of gas from the volcano. Supposedly, their footprints in the falling ash solidified and can still be seen, alternately protected and exposed as sand blows across the desert.

Keōua himself, incidentally, met a no less dramatic end: see p.190.

# Volcano village

Unless you stay in *Volcano House* (p.238) or the park-service campgrounds (p.241 and 247), the village of **VOLCANO** offers the only **accommodation** in the vicinity of the park. Though it's just a mile or so east of the park entrance, towards Hilo, it would be easy to drive straight past it without realizing it's there. The main street runs parallel to the highway, on the *mauka* (uphill) side, but it's well hidden by a roadside fringe of trees. Along it you'll find nothing much of interest other than a small post office, a couple of general stores and the only gas station for miles.

## Accommodation

The strange thing about staying in Volcano is that there's nothing to suggest you're anywhere near an active volcano – only *Volcano House* in the park can offer crater views. Instead, the village's crop of small-scale **bed and breakfast** places are tucked away in odd little corners of a dense rainforest. Be warned, incidentally, that it rains a *lot* in Volcano.

**Carson's Volcano Cottage**, 505 Sixth St, Volcano HI 96785; Ⓣ967-7683 or 1-800/845-5282 (US), Ⓕ967-8094, Ⓦwww.carsonscottage.com. A friendly, romantic little place, south of the highway, with three en-suite guest rooms and three private garden cottages, plus an open-air Jacuzzi. They also offer three separate rental cottages. ❸/❹.

**The Chalet Kilauea Collection**, PO Box 998, Volcano HI 96785; Ⓣ967-7786 or 1-800/937-7786 (US), Ⓕ987-8660, Ⓦwww.volcano-hawaii.com. This assortment of B&Bs and vacation rentals, all under the same management, offers accommodation for all budgets. The owners' original property, now known as the *Inn at Volcano* (❹–❽), is a very plush, lavishly furnished B&B, set well north of the highway on Wright Road, with themed individual rooms in the main house and separate cottages, including a "tree house," on the grounds. Their cheapest alternative is the simple *Volcano B&B* (❷), where six rooms share bathrooms and use of a common lounge, while the luxurious *Castle Suites at Mauna Loa* (❺–❻), five miles west near the golf course, offers very quiet, secluded en-suite lodgings. ❷–❽.

**Hale Ohia**, PO Box 758, Volcano HI 96785; Ⓣ967-7986 or 1-800/455-3803, Ⓕ967-8610, Ⓦwww.haleohia.com. Very attractive and tastefully furnished accommodation, ranging from studio apartments in a lovely converted water tank (really) to a three-bedroom cottage. The buildings are scattered across the ravishing rainforest gardens of a former plantation estate, south of the highway across from the village. ❸–❺.

**Holo Holo Inn**, 19-4036 Kalani Honua Rd, Volcano HI 96785; Ⓣ967-7950, Ⓕ967-8025, Ⓦwww.enable.org/holoholo/. Volcano's cheapest option, this HI-AYH-affiliated hostel consists of a rambling rainforest home, half a mile up from the highway, that offers beds in rudimentary but adequate dorm rooms for $17, and private doubles for $40. ❶/❷.

**Kilauea Lodge**, PO Box 116, Volcano HI 96785; Ⓣ967-7366, Ⓕ967-7367, Ⓦwww.kilauealodge.com. Imposing former YMCA on the main street, now converted into an upmarket B&B, with some of its twelve en-suite bedrooms in secluded chalets and cottages dotted across the grounds. The central lodge building holds a good restaurant (see below). ❹.

**My Island**, PO Box 100, Volcano HI 96785; Ⓣ967-7216, Ⓕ967-7719, Ⓦwww.myislandinnhawaii.com. Several different grades of accommodation in individual buildings set amid dense tropical vegetation. The friendly owner lives in the central lodge; guests can use his library and a communal TV lounge. ❷–❹.

**Volcano Rainforest Retreat**, reserved through Hawaii's Best Bed & Breakfast. PO Box 563, Kamuela HI 96743; Ⓣ885-4550 or 1-800/262-9912, Ⓕ885-0559, Ⓦwww.bestbnb.com. Two striking, recently built en-suite B&B units set in a beautiful garden – a cottage with kitchen and living room, and a much smaller, hexagonal studio. ❹/❺.

## Restaurants

Although *Volcano House* (see p.238) holds the only **restaurant** within the National Park itself, Volcano village offers a good range of nearby alternatives. In addition to the upmarket restaurants listed below, it also has a couple of funky local **cafés** – the *Steam Vent* (daily 6.30am–4pm) behind *Surt's*, and the *Lava Rock Café* (Mon & Tues 7.30am–6pm, Wed–Sat 7.30am–9pm, Sun 7.30am–4pm) at the Aloha gas station – both of which serve inexpensive snacks, plate lunches and espresso coffees.

**Kilauea Lodge**, Volcano Village; Ⓣ967-7366. Large inn dining room, with rich wooden furnishings and a blazing log fire. A full range of strong-flavored European-style meat and game entrees for $20–25, including *hasenpfeffer*, a braised rabbit dish not found on many Big Island menus, plus house specialities such as *Seafood Mauna Kea* (seafood and mushrooms on pasta). Nonresidents should reserve well in advance. Daily 5.30–9pm.

**Surt's**, Volcano Village; Ⓣ985-6711. Friendly fine-dining restaurant, furnished in appealingly local style, with a menu of Asian-cum-European dishes. The daily fish specials, many in fiery Thai sauces and priced at $20 or more, are consistently excellent, while the less expensive salads and meat entrees are reliably good. Lunch offerings range from sandwiches for $6–7 to Thai curries for $10 to pasta dishes for $11–15. Daily noon–9.30pm.

**Thai Thai**, Volcano Village; Ⓣ967-7969. Unassuming but high-quality dinner-only Thai place on the main village road. Almost all the entrees, which include salads as well as green and yellow curries and pad thai noodles, cost well under $15. Daily 5–9pm.

**Volcano Golf & Country Club**, Hwy-11; Ⓣ967-7331. Up a side road two miles west of the park entrance, this daytime-only golf course restaurant serves a conventional but adequate menu of steaks, fish and salad at around $10 per entree. Its large picture windows look out across unlikely, but boring, meadows. Mon–Fri 8am–3pm, Sat & Sun 6.30am–4pm.



# Ka'ū



The district of **KA'Ū** occupies the southern tip of the Big Island, which is also the southernmost point of the United States. Stretching for roughly fifty miles along the southern side of the immense west flank of the "long mountain," Mauna Loa, it ranges from the bleak Ka'u Desert area, now included in Volcanoes National Park, across fertile, well-watered hillsides, to the windswept promontory of **South Point** itself. Situated downwind of the acrid volcanic fumes emitted by both Mauna Loa and Kilauea, it's far from being the most enticing area of the island. Nonetheless, it may well have been home to the first Polynesian settlers, and remains one of the last bastions in the state of anything approaching the traditional Hawaiian way of life.

Ka'ū was a separate kingdom right up to the moment of European contact. Its last independent ruler was Kamehameha the Great's arch-rival, **Keoua**, some of whose warriors met a bizarre end in the Ka'ū Desert (see p.252) and who was himself killed during the dedication of Pu'ukoholā Heiau (see p.190).

The population today is very sparse, and it's likely to get sparser now that the sugar mill at **Pahala**, the last working mill on the island, has closed. All the towns in the area are absolutely tiny; on the map the grid of streets at **Hawaiian Ocean View Estates** (usually abbreviated to either Ocean View or H.O.V.E.) may look impressive, but this thirty-year-old residential development remains barely occupied, thanks to a lack of employment in the region.

In recent years, the state government has repeatedly come up with schemes to revitalize the local economy. After environmental campaigners managed to thwart proposals to develop a vast new luxury resort below Ocean View, the state vigorously promoted a plan to build a commercial **spaceport** at Pālima Point, just three miles outside the National Park, to launch satellites and the Space Shuttle. That would supposedly have created ten thousand jobs, but the concept of positioning such a facility on the *tsunami*-battered slopes of an active volcano attracted so much derision that it now seems to have been quietly abandoned. The spaceport was due to be named after the late *Challenger* astronaut and local hero Ellison Onizuka, who came from Ka'ū, until enterprising journalists uncovered remarks he made before his death opposing the plan. The most recent project being considered by the authorities in Honolulu – the construction of a maximum-security prison in Ka'ū – has been revived several times in the past few years, though there's still no definite decision as to whether it will ever happen.

Although it has a handful of accommodation options, few people spend more than a day at most exploring Ka'ū. Access to the sea is limited, as the highway curves around the ridge of Mauna Loa roughly ten miles up from the shoreline. The two most obvious stops are **South Point**, to admire the crashing waves and perhaps hike to **Green Sand Beach**, and **Punalu'u**, which since the demise of Kalapana boasts the island's finest **black-sand beach**.

As you pass through Ka'ū, look out for the strange, eroded cinder cones that dot the landscape. Some of these craters are so steep-sided as to have been forever inaccessible to man or beast, and paleobotanists are intrigued by the pre-contact vegetation that is thought to survive within.

Huge **Kahuku Ranch**, which stretches inland from the Belt Road near South Point Road almost to the summit of Mauna Loa, is currently being considered for incorporation into Hawaii Volcanoes National Park, which may have the effect of opening this entire region up to hiking and backcountry exploration.

# Pāhala and Wood Valley

As the vegetation reasserts itself after the bleak Ka'ū Desert, 23 miles west of the National Park entrance, little **PĀHALA** stands just *mauka* of the highway. Apart from its tall-chimneyed sugar mill, a gas station and a small shopping mall, there's nothing to catch the eye here, but a drive back up into the hills to the northwest takes you through some appealing agricultural scenery.

Just when you think the road is about to peter out altogether, it enters a grove of huge eucalyptus trees and you're confronted with one of the Big Island's least likely buildings: on top of a hill, and announced by streamers of colored prayer flags, stands a brightly painted **Tibetan temple**. Originally built by Japanese sugar laborers, the **Wood Valley temple** (or Nechung Dryung Ling) was rededicated by the Dalai Lama in 1980 and now serves as a retreat for Tibetan Buddhists from around the world (PO Box 250, Pāhala HI 96777; ⓣ928-8539, ⓦwww.planet-hawaii.com/nechung; ❶–❷). Priority is given to religious groups, but when there's room, travellers can stay in the simple dormitory accommodation or private rooms at the temple.

# Punalu'u

Five miles beyond Pāhala, at the point where the highway drops back down to sea level, **PUNALU'U** has been flattened by *tsunamis* so often that it's given up trying to be a town any more. A single road loops from the highway to the ocean and back, running briefly along what is now the largest **black-sand beach** on the island.

Black sand is a finite resource, as it's only created by molten lava exploding on contact with the sea, and at any one spot that happens very rarely. Even those beaches not destroyed by new lava usually erode away within a few years. Each time the coastline of Punalu'u Bay gets redrawn, however, its black sand washes in again, piling up to create a new beach. At the moment it's irresistible, a crescent of jet-black crystals surrounding a turquoise bay and framed by a fine stand of coconut palms.

On the north side of the bay, you can make out the remains of an old concrete **pier**. Until a century ago tourists used to disembark from their ships at Punalu'u for the ride up to the volcanoes by horse; later it became the terminus of a short railroad from Pahala and was used for shipping sugar. In 1942, by which time it had fallen into disuse, the military destroyed it as a potential landing site for Japanese invaders.

Swimming in these rough waters is out of the question, but many people come to Punalu'u to **camp**. Hawksbill turtles drag themselves ashore on the main beach at night, so camping on the sand is forbidden, but there's a pleasant, if incredibly windy, campground tucked into the rolling meadows of Punalu'u Beach Park, immediately to the south. Permits can be obtained from the Depart of Parks and Recreation in Hilo ($3 per day; Ⓣ961-8341).

The dilapidated complex of pseudo-Polynesian buildings behind the palms in the center of the beach, facing the sea across its own private lagoon, holds a restaurant that has been closed since the early 1990s downturn in tourism.

The only **accommodation** nearby is in the *SeaMountain at Punalu'u* condo complex, a few hundred yards from the beach on the southern segment of the loop road (PO Box 70, Pāhala HI 96777; Ⓣ928-8301 or 1-800/488-8301, Ⓕ928-8008, Ⓦwww.seamtnhawaii.com; ❸–❺). It's an incredibly remote and often very windy place to stay, but most of its studios and one- and two-bedroom apartments, arrayed along what looks like a typical suburban residential street, are well equipped and comfortable. A two-night minimum stay is required. Alongside it, but a separate entity, is the *SeaMountain* **golf course** (Ⓣ928-6222), where the $40 green fees are among the lowest on the island. The name "Sea Mountain," incidentally, refers to the underwater volcano of Lō'ihi, here just 20 miles offshore (see p.237).

# Nā'ālehu

You can't miss **NĀ'ĀLEHU** as you drive through Ka'ū. Eight miles south of Punalu'u, it lines each side of the highway for around half a mile, without stretching very far away from the central ribbon. Although it bills itself as "America's southernmost town," Na'alehu offers little to induce drivers to stop. **Whittington Beach Park**, a couple of miles outside it to the north, is not so much a beach as a picnic ground, and the only reason to call in at Na'alehu is for a quick lunch.

The town has a handful of **snack places**, which change names with monotonous regularity. The longest survivor, the *Na'alehu Fruit Stand* (Ⓣ929-9099), is a general store that sells sandwiches and drinks as well as lots of fresh island fruit. There's also an espresso café and a Japanese takeout counter.

# Wai'ohinu

Having climbed away from the sea for two miles west of Nā'ālehu, the highway makes a sweeping curve around the small settlement of **WAI'OHINU**. This held a dozen houses when Mark Twain passed through in 1866, and boasts barely more than that today. Twain planted a monkey-pod tree here, but even that has now been dead for forty years. Alongside what may or may not be its descendant, a few hundred yards east of the center, *Mark Twain Square* is a gift shop that also sells sandwiches, cakes and coffee (Ⓣ929-7550). Nearby, the basic but appealing *Shirikawa Motel* (PO Box 467, Nā'ālehu HI 96772; Ⓣ929-7462; ❶) is gradually being overwhelmed by trees, while just around the highway bend you pass a pretty chapel, the white-and-green clapboard 1841 **Kauahā'ao Church**.

Half a mile south of the church, *Macadamia Meadows* (94-6263 Kamaoa Rd; reserve through Hawaii's Best Bed & Breakfast, PO Box 563, Kamuela HI 96743; Ⓣ885-4550 or 1-800/262-9912, Ⓕ885-0559, Ⓦwww.bestbnb.com; ❸) is a large modern home that offers four comfortable, spacious B&B rooms. Guests have use of the on-site pool and tennis courts.

# South Point Road

As you circle the southern extremity of the Big Island on the Belt Road, you're too far up from the ocean to see where the island comes to an end. It is possible, however, to drive right down to the tip along the eleven-mile **SOUTH POINT ROAD**, which leaves the highway six miles west of Wai'ohinu.

Car rental agencies forbid drivers from heading to South Point because vehicle damage is more likely on poor road surfaces and providing emergency recovery is inconvenient. Like the similarly proscribed Saddle Road (see p.226), however, it's not a difficult or dangerous drive. Most of the way it's a single-lane paved road, with enough room to either side for vehicles to pass comfortably.

The road heads almost exactly due south, passing at first through green cattle-ranching country. As it starts to drop, the landscape takes on a weather-beaten look, with pale grass billowing and the trees bent double by the trade winds. It comes as no surprise to encounter the giant propellers of the **Kamoa wind farm**, though you're unlikely to see many of them turning: the winds have proven too gusty and violent for the farm to be a commercial success.

## Ka Lae

After ten miles, the road forks 100 yards beyond a sign announcing the **KA LAE NATIONAL HISTORIC LANDMARK DISTRICT**. The right fork ends a mile later at a red-gravel parking lot perched above a thirty-foot cliff. Local people fish over the edge, and ladders drop down the cliff face to boats bobbing at a small mooring below.

Walk a couple of minutes south and you come to **Ka Lae**, or **South Point**, where you can reflect that everyone in the United States is to the north of you, and in much less danger of being blown to Antarctica. The earliest colonizers of Hawaii battled against the winds to reach this spot long before the Pilgrims crossed the Atlantic, and in doing so travelled a far greater distance from their homes in the distant South Seas. Abundant bone fishhooks found in the area are among the oldest artifacts unearthed in Hawaii, dating as far back as the third century AD. At the newly restored **Kalalea Heiau**, at the very tip, offerings wrapped in *ti* leaves are still left by native Hawaiians. Beyond that is a ledge of black lava, steadily pounded by high surf.

The deep waters offshore were renowned not only for holding vast quantities of fish, but also because they're prey to such fierce currents that it can take days on end for human- or sail-powered boats to negotiate the cape. An old legend tells of a king of Ka'ū who became deeply unpopular after stealing fish from fishermen and forcing his people to build heavy-walled fishponds for his benefit. He was finally abandoned by his warriors after he plundered a fleet of canoes near Ka Lae and stole so much fish that his own canoe began to founder. The currents swept him away to a lonely death.

Among the rocks at the headland, you can still see holes drilled for use as **canoe moorings**. In ancient times, fishermen would tie their canoes to these loops by long cords so that they could fish in the turbulent waters without having to fight the sea. Looking inland, you can follow the grey outline of Mauna Loa in the distance; on a cloudless day, you might even make out its snow-capped peak. Nearer at hand, across a foam-flecked sea to the northwest, is the stark shoreline cinder cone of **Pu'u Waimanalo**.

## Green Sand Beach

**GREEN SAND BEACH**, a couple of miles northeast of Ka Lae, doesn't live up to its name. It is a beach, and it is greenish in a rusty-olive sort of way, but if you're expecting a dazzling stretch of green sand backed by a coconut grove you'll be disappointed. The only reason to venture here is if you feel like a bracing, four-mile hike along the oceanfront, with a mild natural curiosity at the end. Without great expectations, and on a rain-free day, it's worth the effort.

If you want to try it, go back to the junction on South Point Road a mile short of Ka Lae, and drive down the left fork as far as you can go, which is a turn-around point just beyond some military housing. If conditions are dry enough, you might continue down to the boat landing below on any of the many rutted mud tracks that criss-cross each other down the slope. However, you'd have to have a very high-clearance four-wheel-drive vehicle to follow the two-mile track from there to the beach.

Apart from one or two heavily-rutted sections, the walk itself is very easy, although on the way out you can expect to be pushing into a stiff tradewinds breeze. For most of the route you cross rolling, pastel-green meadows – an oddly pastoral landscape considering the mighty surf pummeling at the lava rocks alongside.

Your destination comes in sight after just over a mile – the crumbling **Pu'u O Mahana** cinder cone that forms the only significant bump on the line of the coast. As you approach you can see that half the cone has eroded away, and the resultant loose powder has slipped down the cliffs to form a long sloping beach. You can see all there is to see from up above, but with care it's possible to scramble down to the seashore and examine handfuls of the "green sand." Close inspection reveals shiny green-tinged crystals of various sizes – this is in fact a mineral called **olivine**, which once formed part of a lava flow. Green Sand Beach is, however, much too exposed for swimming – or even walking too close to the sea.

## Hawaiian Ocean View Estates

West of South Point Road, you can't get down to the sea again in the twelve miles before the Belt Road reaches South Kona. The road does, however, run past a few isolated buildings and communities where you can get a snack or fill up with gas.

For the views from its blue *lānai*, it's fun to stop for a meal or drink at the *South Point Bar & Restaurant*, raised above the highway at the 76-mile marker (Mon–Sat noon–8pm, Sun 8am–8pm; ☎929-9343). They try out a different menu every month, but don't bank on anything more exotic than burgers, grilled chicken and steak. They occasionally offer live entertainment as well.

A little further on, you enter the residential zone of **HAWAIIAN OCEAN VIEW ESTATES**, also known as "Ocean View" or "H.O.V.E.," an area designated for development during the 1960s. Intricate grids of roads were planned, and some sites were sold that were no more than patches of bare lava. Only a tiny proportion of the lots have been built on and many of the roads still don't exist. Unless the plans to develop a mega-resort at Pohue Bay, a currently inaccessible white-sand beach directly below Ocean View, ever get off the drawing board, there's little prospect of the area acquiring a substantial population.

The center of Ocean View consists of two small malls: one has a Texaco gas station and the *Ohia Cafe* espresso bar, while the other is home to the friendly, clean little *Desert Rose* (daily 7am–7pm; ☎939-ROSE), which serves simple breakfasts and lunchtime sandwiches and salads. Just off the highway a couple of hundred yards north, the takeout counter at *Mr Bell's* (daily 7am–9pm; ⓣ929-9291) offers breakfast for $5, and basic plate lunches taken on a shady *lānai*.

Convenient places to **stay** nearby include the four-roomed *Bougainvillea B&B* (PO Box 6045, Ocean View HI 96737; ⓣ929-7089 or 1-800/688-1763; ❷) and the three-roomed *South Point B&B*, *mauka* of the highway on Ocean View's eastern fringes (92-1408 Donola Drive, Donola HI 96704; ⓣ929-7466; ❷).



## Manukā State Park

Ka'ū comes to an end half a dozen miles west of Ocean View, as you finally cross the long ridge of Mauna Loa. The former royal lands on the border with Kona, once the *ahupua'a* of **MANUKA**, remain set aside to this day as the **Manuka Natural Area Reserve** – at 25,000 acres, the largest natural reserve in the state.

Only a small segment of the reserve is open to the public – **Manuka State Park**, three miles west of Ocean View on the *mauka* side of the highway. From its leafy roadside parking lot, equipped with a picnic pavilion, restrooms, benches and rolling lawns, the one-hour, two-mile **Manuka Nature Trail** leads into peaceful woodlands. Almost all the terrain is *'a'a* lava, and although there's no great climb, the path can be very rough underfoot. Humans aren't the only ones who find it hard to cross lava flows, so pigs and exotic plants alike are relatively scarce, and the area remains a haven for native plants. One of the main features of long-established native species tends to be that they've lost unnecessary defences against predators; thus you'll see a mint with no smell and a nettle with no sting. The trail's only dramatic feature is a collapsed lava pit, whose sides are too steep to permit access to wild pigs (see p.526), and which gathers enough moisture to feed plants such as the *'ie 'ie* vine, which normally only grows in much wetter areas.

Free maps, available at the trailhead, explain how the vegetation varies with the age of the lava flow. Some of the ground is new and barren, and some is around two thousand years old, but those areas that date back four thousand years have managed to develop a thick coating of topsoil.

About eight miles beyond Manuka, as the road heads due north towards Kailua, you come to the turnoff down to **Miloli'i Beach** – see p.177.

# 3

# Maui

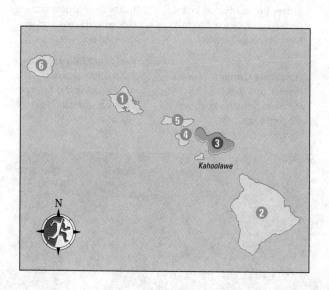

# CHAPTER 3 Highlights

* **Sunset in Lahaina** Best admired from the West Maui seafront, the sun sets nightly behind the russet island of Lanai. P.276

* **The Feast at Lele** A sumptuous banquet of Polynesian specialties to beat any *lū'au* in the state. P.285

* **Molokini snorkel cruises** A daily flotilla of small boats ferries snorkelers out to this tiny submerged crater. P.310

* **Haleakalā Crater** An eerie moonscape that feels far removed from the bustle of modern Maui. P.328

* **Downhill biking** Free-wheeling down the forty-mile Haleakalā Crater Road offers amazing views at every turn. P.329

* **Ho'okipa Beach Park** The world's premier windsurfing destination hosts the sport's top competitive events. P.338

* **The Road to Hāna** Legendary day-trip drive that twists its way past dozens of hidden waterfalls and verdant valleys. P.339

* **Red Sand Beach** Maui's most unusual beach, reached by a short but perilous trail from the town of Hāna. P.349

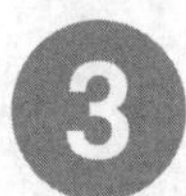

# Maui



Widely trumpeted, not least by its own inhabitants, as the world's most glamorous vacation destination, the island of **Maui** has long proclaimed its charms with the slogan *Maui Nō Ka 'Oi* – "Maui is the Best." In fact, it's the second largest, second youngest of the Hawaiian chain, and ranks a distant second to Oahu in terms of annual visitors. Even the state itself is called "Hawaii" rather than "Maui," because just when Maui seemed set to conquer all its neighbors, it was itself overrun by warriors from the island of Hawaii.

Maui does, however, have a lot to boast about, not least the sheer variety of its landscapes. The windward flanks of its two mountains are ravishingly beautiful, with the east-coast **road to Hāna** winding through fifty miles of quintessentially tropical scenery, while cool, green **Upcountry Maui** is an unexpected pastoral idyll, and the volcanic desert on top of **Haleakalā** offers an unforgettable spectacle at sunrise. The drier, less photogenic western coastlines of the island hold some of Hawaii's most popular **beaches**; resorts like Kā'anapali and Kīhei may not be attractive in their own right, but they perfectly meet the needs of tourists who come specifically for sun, sand and swimming. In West Maui, you can walk the streets of old **Lahaina**, once the capital of Hawaii and rendezvous for the wild-living Pacific whaling fleet, while atmospheric smaller towns elsewhere, such as **Makawao** and **Hāna**, evoke the island's plantation and ranching heritage.

In addition, Maui entices a younger, more dynamic crowd than Waikīkī by offering Hawaii's most exhilarating range of vacation **activities**, including windsurfing, diving, sailing, snorkeling, cycling, hiking and horse riding.

## A brief history of Maui

Ancient Maui was not the fertile island it is today; both the central isthmus and the upcountry slopes were arid wastelands, and the population was crowded into scattered coastal valleys. For its first thousand years of human occupation, the island consisted of several independent regions, each constantly at war with the rest. Both the two main centers were in **West Maui** – one was the northwestern shoreline, the other was the region of **Nā Wai 'Ēha**, which stretched northwards from 'Īao Valley – while remote **Hāna** on the east coast was a lesser chiefdom, prone to fall under the control of Big Island invaders.

The first chief to rule over all of Maui was **Pi'ilani**, who is thought to have reigned during the fifteenth or sixteenth centuries. He conquered all the way

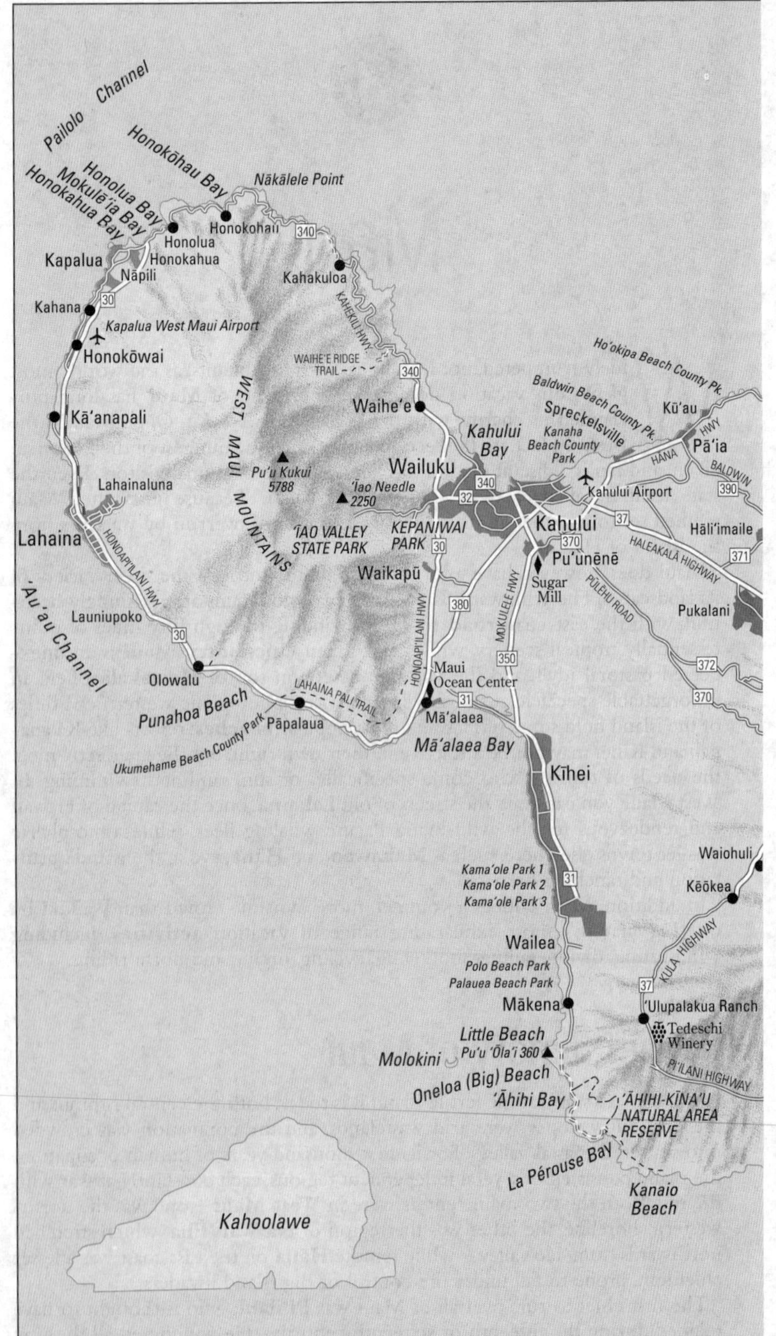

Pailolo Channel
Honokōhau Bay
Honolua Bay
Mokulē'ia Bay
Honokahua Bay
Nākālele Point
Honokohau
Honolua
Honokahua
Kapalua
Nāpili
Kahakuloa
Kahana
Kapalua West Maui Airport
Honokōwai
KAHEKILI HWY
WAIHE'E RIDGE TRAIL
Waihe'e
WEST MAUI MOUNTAINS
Kā'anapali
Pu'u Kukui 5788
'Iao Needle 2250
Lahainaluna
Lahaina
HONOAPI'ILANI HWY
'ĪAO VALLEY STATE PARK
KEPANIWAI PARK
Wailuku
Kahului Bay
Kahului
Kahului Airport
Ho'okipa Beach County Pk.
Baldwin Beach County Pk.
Spreckelsville
Kanaha Beach County Park
Kū'au
Pā'ia
HANA HWY
BALDWIN
Hāli'imaile
HALEAKALĀ HIGHWAY
Pu'unēnē
Sugar Mill
PŪLEHU ROAD
MOKULELE HWY
Pukalani
Waikapū
'Au'au Channel
Launiupoko
Olowalu
Maui Ocean Center
Mā'alaea
LAHAINA PALI TRAIL
Punahoa Beach
Pāpalaua
Ukumehame Beach County Park
Mā'alaea Bay
Kīhei
Kama'ole Park 1
Kama'ole Park 2
Kama'ole Park 3
Waiohuli
Kēōkea
KULA HIGHWAY
Wailea
Polo Beach Park
Palauea Beach Park
Mākena
'Ulupalakua Ranch
Tedeschi Winery
Little Beach
Pu'u 'Ōla'i 360
Molokini
Oneloa (Big) Beach
'Āhihi Bay
PI'ILANI HIGHWAY
'ĀHIHI-KĪNA'U NATURAL AREA RESERVE
La Pérouse Bay
Kanaio Beach
Kahoolawe
30
340
32
37
370
371
380
350
31
390
372

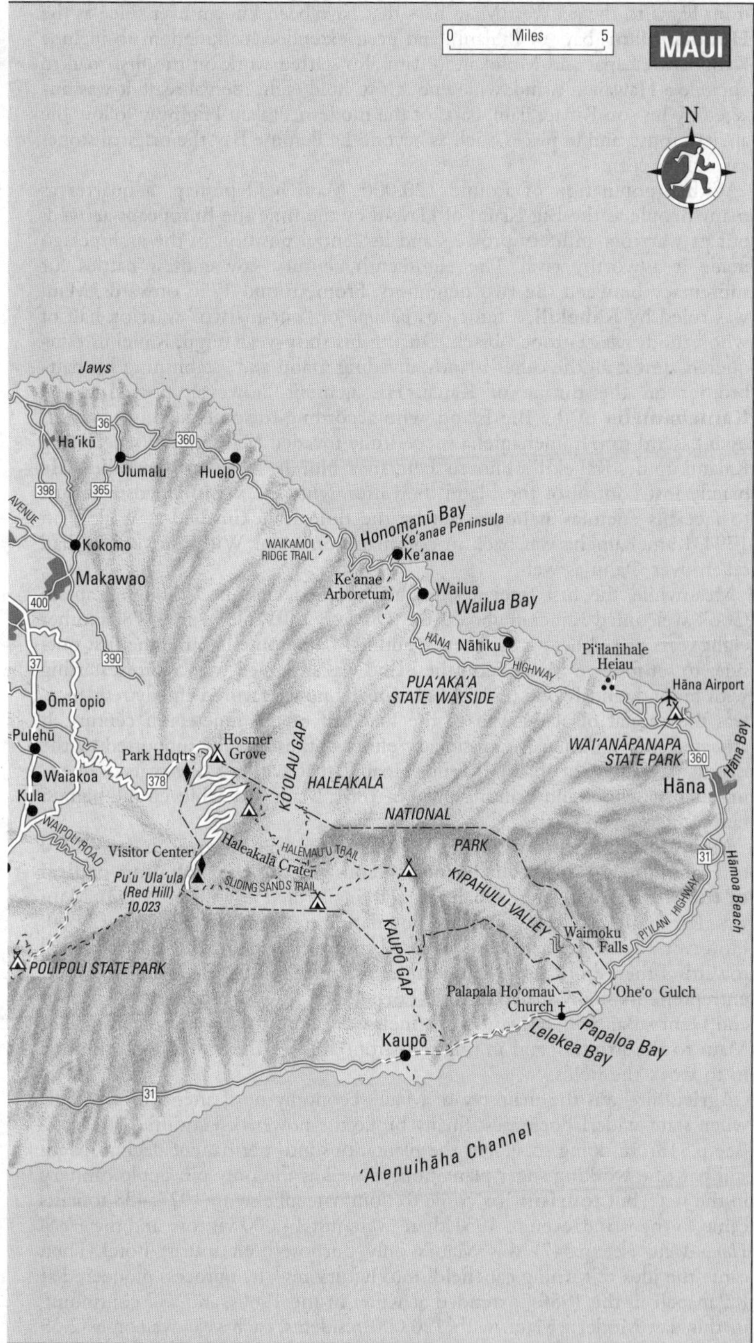

0 Miles 5
MAUI
N
Jaws
Ha'ikū
Ulumalu
Huelo
36
360
398
365
AVENUE
Kokomo
Makawao
400
37
390
Ōma'opio
Pulehū
Waiakoa
Kula
WAIPOLI ROAD
Honomanū Bay
Ke'anae Peninsula
Ke'anae
WAIKAMOI RIDGE TRAIL
Ke'anae Arboretum
Wailua
Wailua Bay
HĀNA HIGHWAY
Nāhiku
Pi'ilanihale Heiau
Hāna Airport
PUA'AKA'A STATE WAYSIDE
WAI'ANĀPANAPA STATE PARK
Hāna
Hāna Bay
Hosmer Grove
Park Hdqtrs
378
KO'OLAU GAP
HALEAKALĀ NATIONAL PARK
Visitor Center
Haleakalā Crater
HALEMAU'U TRAIL
SLIDING SANDS TRAIL
Pu'u 'Ula'ula (Red Hill) 10,023
KIPAHULU VALLEY
KAUPŌ GAP
Waimoku Falls
PI'ILANI HIGHWAY
Hāmoa Beach
POLIPOLI STATE PARK
Palapala Ho'omau Church
'Ohe'o Gulch
Papaloa Bay
Lelekea Bay
Kaupō
31
'Alenuihāha Channel

from Hāna to the six West Maui bays that have been known ever since as the **Honoapi'ilani** (bays of Pi'ilani), and even extended his kingdom to include Kahoolawe, Lanai and Molokai. Pi'ilani also started work on the first road to encircle a Hawaiian island; wide enough to hold eight men abreast, it was finished by his son Kihapi'ilani. Parts of the modern Pi'ilani Highway follow the ancient route, and in places, such as beyond La Pérouse Bay, the original stones can still be seen.

With a population of around 120,000, Maui held perhaps a quarter as many people as the Big Island of Hawaii by the time the Europeans arrived, but its warriors' military prowess and its central position in the archipelago made it a worthy rival. The eighteenth century saw endless battles for supremacy between the two neighbors. From around 1736 onwards, Maui was ruled by **Kahekili**, a ferocious *pahupu* or "cut-in-two" warrior, half of whose body was tattooed black. During his sixty-year reign, Kahekili conquered almost all the other islands, invading Oahu and establishing his half-brother on the throne of Kauai. His nemesis, however, proved to be **Kamehameha** of the Big Island, who according to some accounts was his own bastard son. Kamehameha successfully invaded Maui in 1790, defeating Kalanikūpule, Kahekili's chosen heir, in a bloody battle at 'Īao Valley. He briefly lost control of the island thereafter, when he was obliged to return to face his enemies at home, but by the time Kahekili died at Waikīkī in 1794, Kamehameha was back in command on Maui. Within a year, he had taken over Oahu as well.

Meanwhile, the first foreign ships had reached Hawaii. Although Captain Cook welcomed Kahekili aboard the *Discovery* off Wailuku in 1778, another eight years passed before the French admiral La Pérouse became the first outsider to set foot on Maui. Soon the island was swamped with visitors, starting with fur and sandalwood traders. **Lahaina**, by now a favored chiefly residence, was the capital of all Hawaii in the first half of the nineteenth century. It attracted such an intensive missionary effort, enthusiastically supported by the island's devoutly Christian Governor Hoapili, that, within a few years of opening its first school and printing press in 1831, Maui had achieved the highest rate of literacy on earth.

After Hoapili died in the early 1840s, and the seat of government shifted to Honolulu, Lahaina spent twenty raucous years as the "**whaling capital of the world**." When the whaling trade finally died down (see p.513), Maui was left high and dry, with its population reduced to a mere 12,000. However, the lands that had been used to grow food for the sailors turned towards other crops, especially **sugar**. Thanks to the frenzied efforts of entrepreneurs such as the German-born Claus Spreckels, Samuel Alexander and Henry Baldwin, irrigation channels were built to carry water from East Maui to the isthmus, and immigrants from all over the world were shipped in to work the fields.

Agriculture was the mainstay of Maui's economy until after World War II, when state-wide labor unrest finally broke the power of Hawaii's "Big Five" (see p.513). In doing so, it sent the plantations into permanent decline. Maui still has one working sugar plantation, as well as the only pineapple cannery in the state, but **tourism** has come to dominate all else. In 1927, 428 tourists came to the island; even in 1951 there were just 14,000 visitors, and the *Hotel Hāna-Maui* (see p.347) was Maui's only purpose-built tourist hotel. Then came the idea of turning canefields into luxury resorts, a process pioneered at Kā'anapali in the 1950s, extended at Kīhei in the 1960s, and still continuing to this day. Modern Maui, with 120,000 residents, each year welcomes 2.35

million tourists, who stay for an average of 6.7 days (longer than on any other island). On a typical day, 44,000 visitors are present, spending an average of $171 each.

## Around the island

The island of Maui is what's known as a "volcanic doublet," consisting of two originally separate but now overlapping volcanoes. The older of the two, known to geologists as *Mauna Kahalawai,* has eroded to become a serrated ridge that's usually referred to as the **West Maui Mountains**; it's now dwarfed by the younger **Haleakalā** to the southeast. Haleakalā itself is not what it was: around 400,000 years ago it stood several thousand feet taller and dominated the landmass of *Maui Nui*, which took in what are now Kahoolawe, Molokai and Lanai. Although the ocean has flowed in to create four distinct islands, the channels between them are the shallowest, and the calmest, in the state of Hawaii. That's one reason why the **western coastlines** of both parts of Maui are its most popular tourist playgrounds, with safe, sandy beaches and good sailing conditions.

Once you've tired of the rather sterile atmosphere of resorts such as **Lahaina** and **Kā'anapali** in West Maui, or **Kīhei** in South Maui, there's plenty to explore elsewhere on the island. The central isthmus, or "neck," between the volcanoes can be so flat you fear the waves will wash right over it. It holds **Kahului**, the main commercial center, and the faded but somehow appealing older town of **Wailuku**, standing guard over the once-sacred **'Īao Valley**.

To the east, **Upcountry Maui**, on the lower slopes of Haleakalā, is a delight, its meadows and flower farms offering a pastoral escape from the bustle below. Higher up, beyond the clouds, you can look out across the many-hued volcanic wasteland of the vast **Haleakalā Crater** or dwindle into cosmic insignificance by hiking down into it.

Tortuous, demanding roads wind right around the **windward coasts** of both halves of the island. The better known of the two, the **road to Hāna** in the east, does not quite merit its legendary status, but its countless waterfalls and ravines make for a wonderful day-trip, culminating at lush **'Ohe'o Gulch**. West Maui's equivalent, **Kahekili Highway**, enables visitors to explore the remote Waihe'e Valley and offers a glimpse of how Maui must have looked before the tourists arrived.

### Maui Favorites: Beaches

**Swimming beaches**

| | | | |
|---|---|---|---|
| Kā'anapali Beach | p.288 | Polo Beach | p.318 |
| Kapalua Beach | p.292 | Wai'ānapanapa Beach | p.345 |
| Oneloa (Big) Beach | p.320 | | |

**Snorkel Spots**

| | | | |
|---|---|---|---|
| Honolua Bay | p.294 | La Pérouse Bay | p.321 |
| Kā'anapali Beach | p.288 | Molokini | p.310 |

**Surfing and Windsurfing**

| | | | |
|---|---|---|---|
| Honolua Bay | p.294 | Kanahā Beach | p.300 |
| Honomanū Bay | p.341 | Mā'alaea Bay | p.309 |
| Ho'okipa Beach | p.338 | | |

# Getting to Maui

Of the three airports on Maui, **Kahului** (see p.299) is by far the largest and is the only one capable of handling trans-Pacific flights. For full details of flights to and from the state of Hawaii, and contact numbers for the airlines mentioned below, see p.11 onwards.

In fact, the route between Honolulu and Kahului ranks as the busiest domestic route in the entire United States, with over three million passengers each year. Both of the two major local airlines, Hawaiian and Aloha, fly this way about twice an hour, all day every day. In addition, Hawaiian operates two daily nonstop flights between Kahului and both Hilo and Kona on the Big Island, as well as one to Kauai, while Aloha serves the same Big Island cities and has two nonstop flights each day to and from Kauai. Aloha's affiliate, Island Air, also connects Kahului with Molokai three times daily. In addition, Pacific Wings (Ⓣ248-7700 or 1-888/575-4546, Ⓦwww.pacificwings.com) operates one or two scheduled flights each day between Molokai and Kahului, while Paragon Air (Ⓣ1-800/428-1231), an on-demand charter service, connects Molokai with any airport on Maui.

**Kapalua** in West Maui – see p.292 – receives around eight Island Air flights from Honolulu each day. Scheduled flights to and from **Hāna**, the third, tiny airport, are currently only available on Pacific Wings (see above), which operates three or four daily round-trip flights between Kahului and Hāna, and also one or two nonstop flights between Honolulu and Hāna.

The only **ferries** to Maui connect Lahaina with Lanai and Molokai; see p.279.

# Getting around Maui

Maui has less of a **public transport** system than any of the other major Hawaiian islands. However, as detailed on p.299, the Maui Airporter Shuttle (Ⓣ877-7308 or 1-800/259-2627) and TransHawaiian (Ⓣ877-0380 or 1-800/231-6984) run regular scheduled **buses** from the airport at Kahului to Kā'anapali by way of Lahaina, for $13 one way or $19 round-trip, while Speedishuttle (Ⓣ875-8070) and Airport Shuttle (Ⓣ661-6667) run shuttle vans on demand to all destinations, charging around $20 to Kīhei, $32 to Lahaina, and $45 to Nāpili. Additional scheduled shuttle buses run between Lahaina and Kā'anapali; see p.279 for details.

All the national **rental-car** chains are represented at Kahului Airport and at or near Kapalua Airport; in addition, Avis has branches in Kihei, Wailea and Kapalua; Budget has an office in Wailea; and Dollar is in Hāna. Local alternatives include Wheels R Us, which rents cars, motorcycles and mopeds, and accepts drivers under age 25, at two locations: 741 Wainee St in Lahaina (Ⓣ667-7751), and 75 Kaahumanu Ave, Kahului (Ⓣ871-6858).

### Maui Favorites: Hikes

| | | | |
|---|---|---|---|
| Halemau'u Trail | p.335 | Sliding Sands Trail | p.334 |
| Kaupō Trail | p.337 | 'Ula'ino Road | p.344 |
| Pīpīwai Trail | p.351 | Waihe'e Ridge Trail | p.296 |
| Pu'u 'Ōla'i | p.321 | Waikamoi Nature Trail | p.340 |

In the absence of adequate roads to cope with its volume of tourists, the **traffic** on Maui is consistently bad. The worst area is the narrow **Honoapi'ilani Highway** around West Maui, where the universal habit of suddenly stopping to watch whales in the ocean doesn't help. At least the snail's pace along the **Haleakalā** and **Hāna** highways is owing to the natural obstacles en route, and gives you a chance to appreciate the scenery. The rental companies forbid their clients to use certain roads altogether, notably the **Kahekili Highway** in West Maui, and the remote **Pi'ilani Highway** along the southern coast of East Maui.

The most popular **bus tours** on the island run around East Maui to Hāna (typically they cost around $70 per person from South Maui and $85 from West Maui), and up the volcano to Haleakalā Crater ($30–40). Operators include Akina Aloha Tours (ⓣ879-2828), Polynesian Adventure Tours (ⓣ877-4242), Ekahi Tours (ⓣ877-9775) and Ali'i Coach Service (ⓣ871-2544).

Among companies renting out **mountain bikes**, typically at $20–25 per day or up to $100 per week, are South Maui Bicycles, 1993 S Kīhei Rd, Kīhei (ⓣ874-0068); West Maui Cycles, 840 Wainee St, Lahaina (ⓣ661-9005); and Island Biker, 415 Dairy Rd, Kahului (ⓣ877-7744). Chris' Bike Adventures (ⓣ871-2453) can arrange customized **bike tours** of Maui to your specifications. A full list of operators running **downhill bike rides** on Haleakalā appears on p.329.

Finally, Pacific Wings **flies** between Kahului and Hāna; see p.346.

## Flight-seeing Tours

All the **helicopter** companies listed below run tours from Kahului Airport; none currently operates from Kapalua. Maui is large enough for a full round-island flight to take more than an hour and cost around $200; if you'd prefer a shorter flight, try a 20- or 30-minute loop over West Maui. For discounted rates, buy tickets through an activities operator such as Tom Barefoot's, as detailed on p.271. Target prices: $75 for a 20-minute jaunt, $150 to fly over Haleakalā and Hāna, and more than $200 to fly over to Molokai or Lanai as well. Visibility is almost always best in the early morning.

It's also possible to take **airplane** or "fixed-wing" tours. Volcano Air Tours (ⓣ877-5500, ⓦwww.volcanoairtours.com) flies across to the active volcano on the Big Island from Kapalua or Kahului for around $250. Pacific Wings (ⓣ873-0877, ⓦwww.pacificwings.com) runs a full-day tour to Hāna from Kahului on Tuesdays only, featuring two 15min flights and a ground tour by coach, for $190. The company has a similar day-long tour to Kalaupapa on Molokai on Wednesdays for $210, and even offers a private 4hr **flying lesson**, touching down at Lanai, for $322.

### Helicopter tour operators

| | | |
|---|---|---|
| **Air Maui** | ⓣ877-7005 | ⓦwww.airmaui.com |
| **Alexair Helicopters** | ⓣ871-0792 or 1-888/418-8458 | ⓦwww.helitour.com |
| **Blue Hawaiian Helicopters** | ⓣ871-8844 or 1-800/745-2583 | ⓦwww.bluehawaiian.com |
| **Hawaii Helicopters** | ⓣ877-3900 or 1-800/994-9099 | ⓦwww.hawaii-helicopters.com |
| **MauiScape** | ⓣ877-7272 | |
| **Sunshine Helicopters** | ⓣ871-0722 or 1-800/469-3000 | ⓦwww.sunshinehelicopters.com |

## Horse Riding

**Adventures on Horseback** ⓣ 242-7445 or 572-6211, ⓦ www.mauihorses.com. 6hr expeditions to swim in Ha'iku Falls, including picnic, for $185.
**Ironwood Ranch** ⓣ 669-4991. Riding excursions up to the forest above Kapalua, at $78 for 1hr 30min or $104 for 2hr.
**Mākena Stables** ⓣ 879-0244, ⓦ www.makenastables.com. Mon–Sat 2–3hr morning or evening rides from 'Āhihi Bay along coastline to La Pérouse, or 5hr 30min trips up to Tedeschi Winery, with tour; $110–175. No credit cards.
**Mendes Ranch** ⓣ 871-5222. Mon–Sat half-day tours of cattle ranch in East Maui's Waihe'e Valley, with barbecue lunch; $130 per person or $219 with a 30min helicopter flight. Shorter 2hr tours cost $85.
**'Ohē'o Stables** ⓣ 667-2222. 3hr rides from Kīpahulu, up to 'Ohē'o Gulch waterfalls; 10.30am $119, 11.30am (with lunch) $139.
**Pony Express Tours** ⓣ 667-2200, ⓦ www.ponyexpresstours.com. Mon–Fri 1hr ($55), 2hr ($85), and 2hr 30min (with picnic; $95) tours of Haleakalā Ranch, Maui's largest cattle ranch. Mon–Sat 5hr 30min descent to Ka Moa O Pele junction in Haleakalā Crater ($145) or 8hr trip to Kapalaoa Cabin ($180), both with picnic lunch.
**Thompson Ranch** ⓣ 878-1910. Half-day, full-day and overnight rides through Haleakalā Crater; $120 and up.

# Where to stay

Maui is an extreme example of the typical Hawaiian pattern, in that most of the accommodation for tourists is situated in the drier and less scenic parts of the island. The majority of its hotels and condos are located either along the leeward coast of **West Maui**, in the highly developed strip that runs from Lahaina up to Kapalua, or on the southwest shores of **East Maui**, between Kīhei and Mākena. If beaches or golf are your main priority, that's fine; most of Maui's historic sites and most attractive landscapes, however, are a long way away.

Travelers looking for a paradise-island hideaway would do better to consider one of the many plush little **B&Bs** tucked away in the meadows of Upcountry Maui and the rainforests around Hāna in the east. (Don't expect to spot any as you drive around; county regulations forbid B&Bs to display signs.) If you're not planning to rent a car, **Lahaina** is the only place where you can stay in a real town with sightseeing, beaches and restaurants within easy walking distance. For **budget travelers**, the cheapest options of all are in faded downtown Wailuku.

## Maui Favorites: Accommodation


| | |
|---|---|
| *Banana Bungalow*, Wailuku (1) | p.304 |
| *Wailana Inn*, Kīhei (3) | p.315 |
| *Old Lahaina House*, Lahaina (3) | p.280 |
| *Silver Cloud Guest Ranch*, Kula (3–5) | p.326 |
| *The Mauian*, Napili (4/5) | p.293 |
| *Best Western Pioneer Inn*, Lahaina (4) | p.280 |
| *Hotel Hāna-Maui*, Hāna (6) | p.347 |
| *Hāmoa Bay Bungalow*, Hāna (6) | p.347 |
| *Embassy Vacation Resort*, Honokōwai (8) | p.292 |
| *Kea Lani Hotel*, Wailea (8/9) | p.317 |

## Accommodation Price Codes

All the accommodation options listed here have been graded with the symbols below, which refer to the quoted rates for a double room in high season (December to March), not including state taxes of 10.17 percent. For a full explanation, see p.27.

| | | |
|---|---|---|
| ❶ up to $40 | ❹ $100–150 | ❼ $250–300 |
| ❷ $40–70 | ❺ $150–200 | ❽ $300–400 |
| ❸ $70–100 | ❻ $200–250 | ❾ over $400 |



Opportunities to **camp** on Maui are very limited, with the best sites in **Haleakalā National Park**, up near the crater (see p.332), and also at Kīpahulu on the southeast shore (see p.351). Cabins and tent camping are also available at Maui's two **state parks**, Polipoli (see p.326) and the much nicer Wai'ānapanapa (see p.345); $5 permits are issued, by mail or in person, by the Department of Land and Natural Resources, 54 S High St, Wailuku, HI 96793 (Mon–Fri 8am–noon & 1–4pm; ⓣ984-8109). At the time this book went to press, no **county parks** were currently open to campers; for the latest information, contact the Department of Parks and Recreation, 1580 Ka'ahumanu Ave, Wailuku, HI 96793 (Mon–Fri 8am–4pm; ⓣ270-7389).

# When to go

Maui basks in the usual balmy Hawaiian **climate**, with temperatures along the coast rarely reaching lower than the mid-seventies Fahrenheit or higher than the mid-eighties. The busiest tourist season, between December and February, coincides with the "rainiest" time of year, but the main leeward tourist areas seldom receive more than the occasional light shower even then.

Unless you have specialized interests, there's no overriding reason to visit the island at one time rather than another. To avoid the crowds, and take advantage of lower room rates, come between March and June or from September through November. The best **swimming** conditions are between April and September, but the peak **surfing** season arrives with the higher winter waves, from November through March – which is also the time when there's every chance you'll see humpback whales. The **flowering trees** along the Hāna Highway reach their peak in June, while July and August are the best months to see the extraordinary blossoming **silversword** plants of Haleakalā.

# Watersports and other activities

From the moment you arrive on Maui, handouts and free magazines will bombard you with details of the island's vast range of tours and activities.

**Activities operators** in all the tourist areas, especially along Front Street in Lahaina, offer **cut-price deals** well below the advertised rates. Tom Barefoot's Cashback Tours – at 834 Front St, Lahaina (ⓣ661-8889 or 1-888/222-3601, ⓦwww.tombarefoot.com) and Dolphin Plaza, 2395 S Kīhei Rd, Kīhei (ⓣ879-4100) – and The Activity Connection (ⓣ661-1038, ⓦwww.beachactivityguide.com) are among the few that don't also try to sell time-shares. Both run websites that detail every imaginable island activity, along with the latest prices.

In addition to those activities detailed below, you'll find lists of Molokini **snorkel cruises** on p.310; downhill **bike rides** on p.329; **helicopter tours** on p.269; and **horse riding** on p.270. Maui golf courses are listed on p.40.

## Diving

Maui and its immediate neighbors offer probably the best **scuba diving** in the Hawaiian islands. The most popular spots are in the vicinity of **Molokini Crater**, off South Maui. Learners and inexperienced divers start by exploring the sheltered, shallow "Inside Crater" area, and eventually progress to the "Back Wall," with its huge drop-offs. There's also good **shore diving** at Black Rock in Kā'anapali and in La Pérouse Bay, while the most spectacular dives of all lie off southern Lanai, within easy reach of a day's boat-trip from Maui.

A huge number of companies arrange **diving excursions** in the waters off Maui and Lanai, with the largest operator being **Maui Dive Shop**; full listings appear on below. Prices generally start at around $70 for a one-tank trip, $90 for two tanks. Equipment rental costs an additional $20–25. Almost all offer multi-day packages for beginners, leading to PADI certification; a typical price would be $220–250 for three days, and $300 for four. Note that many of the Molokini snorkel cruises listed on p.310 actually offer diving as well as snorkeling.

### Ocean Activities

**Dive Operators**

| | | | |
|---|---|---|---|
| Divers Locker | Kīhei | ⓣ 280-3483 | ⓦ www.diverslocker.com |
| Ed Robinson's Dive Tours | Kīhei | ⓣ 879-3584 | ⓦ www.mauiscuba.com |
| Extended Horizons | Lahaina | ⓣ 667-0611 | ⓦ www.scubadivemaui.com |
| Lahaina Divers | Lahaina | ⓣ 667-7496 | ⓦ www.lahainadivers.com |
| Maui Diamond | Mā'alaea | ⓣ 879-9119 | ⓦ www.mauiscubatours.com |
| Maui Dive Shop | All over | ⓣ 879-3388 | ⓦ www.mauidiveshop.com |
| Maui Diving | Lahaina | ⓣ 667-0633 | ⓦ www.mauidiving.com |
| Maui Sun Divers | Kīhei | ⓣ 879-3337 | ⓦ http://mauisundivers.com |
| Mike Severn's | Kīhei | ⓣ 879-6596 | ⓦ http://severns.maui.his.us |
| Trilogy | Lahaina | ⓣ 661-4743 | ⓦ www.sailtrilogy.com |

**Boat Tours**

**Atlantis Submarines** ⓣ 667-2224 or 1-800/548-6262, ⓦ www.atlantisadventures.com. One-hour underwater excursions off Lahaina ($79).

**Club Lanai** ⓣ 871-1144, ⓦ www.clublanai.com. Full-day catamaran snorkeling trips from Lahaina to Lanai, with a stop at Mānele Bay ($69), or 2hr sunset dinner cruises ($75). Tues–Sat only.

**Maui Princess** ⓣ 661-8397, ⓦ www.whalewatchmaui.com or ⓦ www.mauiprincess.com. Dinner ($75) and whale-watching ($30) cruises from Lahaina, plus one-day excursions to Molokai (from $79; see p.279).

**Navatek II** ⓣ 873-3475. Full-day snorkel cruises around Lanai, with breakfast and lunch, for $120, and 2hr sunset cruises for $87; departs from Mā'alaea.

**Pacific Whale Foundation** ⓣ 879-8811, ⓦ www.pacificwhale.org. Nonprofit organization offers 2–3hr whale-watching cruises from Lahaina or Mā'alea (Nov–April; $21–25), plus snorkeling and dolphin-watching tours to Molokini ($49) or Lanai ($79).

**Reefdancer** ⓣ 667-2133. Sixty- or ninety-minute cruises ($33/$45) in a semi-submersible from Lahaina; passengers view the reef from an underwater cabin.

**Sea View** ⓣ 661-5550. Lahaina-based semi-submersible offers 2hr cruise for $45; passengers also have the chance to snorkel.

**Trilogy Ocean Sports** ⓣ 661-4743 or 1-888/628-4800, ⓦ www.sailtrilogy.com. Day-long sailing trips from Lahaina to Lanai, including snorkeling, beach barbecue and

Be sure not to dive within 24 hours of flying or ascending to any significant altitude. The summit of Haleakalā is certainly out of bounds, while you should ask your dive operator for advice before even driving into the Upcountry.

## Parasailing

**Parasailing**, which is a bit like waterskiing, except you suddenly find yourself several hundred feet up in the air, has become very popular in the waters just off Kā'anapali and Lahaina in West Maui. To avoid disturbing humpback whales during their winter migrations, however, it's only permitted between mid-May and mid-December. Expect to pay $40–50 for a fifteen-minute ride with operators such as Parasail Kā'anapali (Ⓣ669-6555), UFO Parasail (Ⓣ661-7836) and West Maui Parasail (Ⓣ661-4060).

## Surfing

**Surf** aficionados rate several Maui sites as equal to anything on Oahu's fabled North Shore, with **Honolua Bay** on the northern tip of West Maui, and **Jaws** off Ha'iku in the east, as the greatest of all. You need to be a real expert to join

Lanai van tour ($160). They also offer diving and snorkeling at Molokini and off Lanai.

Also see the list of Molokini snorkel cruises on p.310.

### Kayak Tours

**Rainbow Kayak Tours** Ⓣ1-800-923-4004, Ⓦwww.travelhawaii.com/rainbow.htm. 3hr ($52) and 5hr 30min ($80) kayak tours from bases in Lahaina and Kīhei.

**South Pacific Kayaks**, Rainbow Mall, 2439 S Kīhei Rd (Ⓣ875-4848, Ⓦwww.mauikayak.com). 2hr 30min whale-watching (in season) or 3hr guided excursions at Mākena or Lahaina for $59; 6hr trip around La Pérouse for $89.

### Equipment Rental

**Auntie Snorkel**, 2439 S Kīhei Rd, Kīhei (Ⓣ879-6263). Snorkels and kayaks.

**Boss Frog's Dive Shop**, 2395 S Kīhei Rd, Kīhei (Ⓣ875-4477); 150 Lahainaluna Rd, Lahaina (Ⓣ661-3333); 4310 Lower Honoapi'ilani Rd, Kahana (Ⓣ669-6700); and Nāpili Plaza, Nāpili (Ⓣ669-4949). Activity center that also rents out scuba, snorkeling and surf gear.

**Maui Dive Shop**, 1455 S Kīhei Rd, Kīhei (Ⓣ879-3388); Honokowai Marketplace, 3350 Lower Honoapi'ilani Rd (Ⓣ661-6166); and five other Maui locations. Dive specialists who rent scuba and snorkeling equipment.

**Maui Ocean Activities**, Whalers Village, Kā'anapali (Ⓣ667-2001). Kayaks, windsurfing equipment, and two-person "Seacycles."

**Rental Warehouse**, Azeka Place II, 1279 S Kīhei Rd, Kīhei (Ⓣ875-4050), and 602 Front St, Lahaina (Ⓣ661-1970). Pretty much anything, from golf clubs and snorkel gear up to a Harley Davidson.

**Snorkel Bob's**, 2411 S Kīhei Rd, Kīhei (Ⓣ879-7449); 1217 Front St, Lahaina (Ⓣ661-4421); and *Nāpili Village Hotel*, Nāpili (Ⓣ669-9603). Snorkel gear, which can be returned on any island.

**South Pacific Kayaks**, Rainbow Mall, 2439 S Kīhei Rd (Ⓣ875-4848, Ⓦwww.mauikayak.com). Kayaks, surfboards, snorkels, boogie boards, beach chairs and the like.

**West Maui Cycles**, 840 Wainee St, Lahaina (Ⓣ661-9005). Snorkels, mountain bikes, boogie boards and surfboards.

the locals who surf at these kind of places, however – beginners would do better to start out at spots such as Lahaina and Kāʻanapali beaches. The peak **season** is between November and March.

Companies that offer **surfing lessons** in the Lahaina area include the Goofy Foot Surf School (Ⓣ244-9283) and Soul Surfing Maui (Ⓣ870-7873). South Maui instructors include Hawaiian Style Surf School (Ⓣ874-0110) and Maui Waveriders (Ⓣ875-4761).



## Windsurfing

Maui is renowned as the world's most sublime **windsurfing** destination. Legendary **Hoʻokipa Beach Park**, just east of Paʻia on the central isthmus, is a mecca for devotees and plays host to major championships throughout most of the year.

Strong winds rather than high surf are of most importance to windsurfers, so the peak season is the summer. Between December and February the winds tend to drop for days on end, but even then conditions are usually good enough somewhere on the island; **Maʻalaea Bay** on the south shore of the isthmus is the likeliest spot.

The best place to **learn** to windsurf is Kanahā Beach near Kahului, a few miles west of Hoʻokipa. Expect to pay around $65 for a three-hour lesson, including equipment rental, with a company such as Action Sports Maui (Ⓣ871-5857, Ⓦwww.actionsportsmaui.com), Alan Cadiz's HST Windsurfing School (Ⓣ871-5423, Ⓦwww.hstwindsurfing.com), Hawaiian Island Surf & Sport (Ⓣ871-4981), or Maui Ocean Activities (Ⓣ667-2001).

Maui Windsurfing Vacations specializes in putting together all-inclusive packages for windsurfers (Ⓣ871-7766 or 1-800/736-6284, Ⓦwww.maui.net/~mwvg).

# Nightlife and entertainment

Although it can't compete with the big-city atmosphere of Honolulu, and island residents jokingly refer to the hour of 10pm as "Maui midnight," by Hawaiian standards Maui offers visitors a reasonably lively **nightlife**.

### Maui Favorites: Eating

These are not so much the ten best restaurants on Maui as ten very good places to eat, drawn from all price categories and arranged in ascending order of price.

| | |
|---|---|
| *Auntie Jane's Kau Kau Wagon*, Kaupō | p.353 |
| *Java Jazz*, Honokōwai | p.294 |
| *Sunrise Café*, Lahaina | p.285 |
| *Kaka'ako Kitchen*, Kahului | p.303 |
| *Pacific 'O*, Lahaina | p.285 |
| *Sansei Seafood Restaurant*, Kapalua | p.294 |
| *Roy's Kahana Bar & Grill*, Kahana | p.294 |
| *Merriman's Bamboo Bistro*, Mā 'alaea | p.310 |
| *Pacific Café Maui*, Kīhei | p.316 |
| *The Feast at Lele*, Lahaina | p.285 |

## Maui Festivals and Events

| | |
|---|---|
| **Jan 1** | New Year's Day (public holiday) |
| **Jan** | Maui Pro Surf Meet; surfing competition, Honolua Bay and Ho'okipa Beach |
| **3rd Mon in Jan** | Dr Martin Luther King Jr's Birthday (public holiday) |
| **3rd week in Jan** | Hula Bowl Football All-Star Classic; college football tournament, War Memorial Stadium. |
| **3rd Mon in Feb** | Presidents Day (public holiday) |
| **early March** | Whale Fest Week; whale-related events, Lahaina and Kā'anapali |
| **early March** | Hawaii Pro Am Windsurfing Tournament, Ho'okipa Beach |
| **mid-March** | Maui Marathon, Kahului to Kā'anapali |
| **March 26** | Prince Kūhiō Day (public holiday) |
| **March/April** | East Maui Taro Festival, Hāna |
| **early April** | Maui O'Neill Pro Board; windsurfing contest, Ho'okipa Beach |
| **Easter Monday** | Public holiday |
| **late April** | David Malo Day, Lahainaluna High School, Lahaina |
| **late April** | Maui County Agricultural Trade Show, Ulupalakua Ranch |
| **May 1** | Lei Day (public holiday) |
| **late May** | Da Kine Classic; windsurfing competition, Kanahā Beach |
| **late May** | Bankoh Ho'omana'o Challenge; outrigger canoe race, Kā'anapali to Waikīkī |
| **last Mon in May** | Memorial Day (public holiday); In Celebration of Canoes, Lahaina |
| **June 11** | Kamehameha Day (public holiday) |
| **June** | Bankoh Kiho'alu; slack-key guitar festival, Maui Arts & Cultural Center |
| **end June** | Art Night; music and arts festival, Lahaina |
| **July 4** | Independence Day (public holiday); Makawao Rodeo, Makawao |
| **early July** | Quicksilver Cup; windsurfing competition, Kanahā Beach |
| **early Aug** | Hawaii State Championships; windsurfing competition, Kanahā Beach |
| **3rd Fri in Aug** | Admission Day (public holiday) |
| **1st Mon in Sept** | Labor Day (public holiday) |
| **mid-Sept** | A Taste of Lahaina; food festival, Lahaina |
| **late Sept** | Run to the Sun; foot race, Pā'ia to Haleakalā |
| **Sept/Oct** | Aloha Festival; consecutive week-long festivals on each island |
| **2nd Mon in Oct** | Columbus Day (public holiday) |
| **early Oct** | Maui County Fair, Wailuku |
| **Oct 31** | Halloween Mardi Gras of the Pacific, Lahaina |
| **early Nov** | Aloha Classic World Wavesailing Championships; windsurfing competition, Ho'okipa |
| **Nov 11** | Veterans' Day (public holiday) |
| **4th Thurs in Nov** | Thanksgiving Day (public holiday) |
| **Dec 25** | Christmas Day (public holiday) |
| **Dec 31** | First Night arts festival, Maui Arts & Cultural Center |

Note that the exact dates of surfing contests, and in some cases the venues as well, depend on the state of the waves.

As ever, most of the activity is confined to the tourist ghettoes, and the resort hotels in particular, but if you enjoy wandering the streets from bar to bar the oceanfront at **Lahaina** provides almost the same buzz as Waikīkī. The south coast, from **Kīhei** on down, is too spread out to have the same intensity, but it's always party time somewhere along the strip. *Maui Brews*, in the Lahaina Center, and *Hapa's Brew Haus* in Kīhei, are the likeliest venues to catch

## Maui Lū'aus

The *lū'aus* listed below charge anything from $60 to $90 per adult, and $28–60 per child; you can buy discounted tickets (perhaps $10 off the usual price) from activities operators all over the island. While The Feast at Lele offers the best food (see p.285), the Old Lahaina Lū'au is generally considered to be the best value of them all.

**Beachcombers Lu'au**, *Royal Lahaina Resort*, Kā'anapali ⓣ661-9119. Daily 5pm. $89.

**Drums of the Pacific**, *Hyatt Regency Maui*, Kā'anapali ⓣ667-4420. Daily 5pm. $75.

**The Feast at Lele**, 505 Front St, Lahaina ⓣ667-5353. Tues, Wed, Fri & Sat 5.30pm. $89.

**Marriott Lu'au**, *Maui Marriott*, Kā'anapali ⓣ661-5828. Daily 5pm. $75.

**Old Lahaina Lu'au**, Lahaina Cannery Mall, Lahaina ⓣ667-1998. Daily 5.30pm. $69.

**Royal Lahaina Lu'au**, *Royal Lahaina Resort*, Kā'anapali ⓣ661-9119. Daily 4.45pm. $67.

**Wailea Sunset Lu'au**, *Renaissance Wailea Beach Resort*, Wailea ⓣ879-4900. Tues, Thurs & Sat 5.30pm. $68.

**Wailea's Finest Lu'au**, *Outrigger Wailea Resort*, Wailea ⓣ879-1922. Mon, Tues, Thurs & Fri 5pm. $62.

contemporary Hawaiian music, while the *Tsunami* at the *Grand Wailea* resort in Wailea is renowned as Maui's glitziest nightclub.

Away from the resorts, the local community of rock exiles and ex-Californians makes *Casanova's* in upcountry **Makawao** an amazingly happening venue for such a tiny town, while the Maui Arts and Cultural Center by the harbor in **Kahului** attracts big-name touring bands.

# Lahaina

Seen from a short distance offshore, **LAHAINA** is one of the prettiest towns in all Hawaii, still recognizable as the peaceful, tropical village it used to be. Its main oceanfront street is lined with timber-frame buildings; a tall-masted sailing ship bobs in the harbor; coconut palms sway to either side of the central banyan tree; surfers swirl into the thin fringe of beach to the south; and the mountains of West Maui dominate the skyline, ringed as often as not by beautiful rainbows. Up close, however, many of Lahaina's decrepit-looking structures turn out to be mere fakes, housing T-shirt stores and tacky themed restaurants, and the crowds and congestion along **Front Street** can seem all too reminiscent of Waikīkī.

Even so, Lahaina makes an attractive base, sandwiched in a long thin strip between the ever-fascinating ocean and equally spellbinding hills. Early evening is especially unforgettable, with the sun casting a rich glow on the mountains as it sets behind the island of Lanai. Lahaina is lively and by Maui standards inexpensive, with a huge range of activities and little rainfall, but above all it's the only town on Maui to offer lodging, sightseeing, nightlife and an abundance of restaurants within easy walking distance of each other.

Although there's little left to show for it nowadays – you can easily see all the town has to offer in a couple of hours – Lahaina boasts a colorful past. By the time the first foreigners came to Hawaii, it was already the residence of the high *ali'i* of Maui. **Kamehameha the Great** sealed his conquest of Maui by sacking the town in 1795, then returned in 1802 and spent a year preparing for what was to be an unsuccessful invasion of Kauai (see p.415). His successors, Kamehameha II and III, made Lahaina their **capital** between the 1820s and 1840s, ruling from the island of **Moku'ula**, in a lake in what is now Malu 'ulu o Lele Park, south of downtown.

When **whaling** ships started to put in during the 1820s, seeking to recuperate from their grueling Pacific peregrinations, fierce struggles between the sailors and Lahaina's Christian **missionaries** became commonplace. Whaling

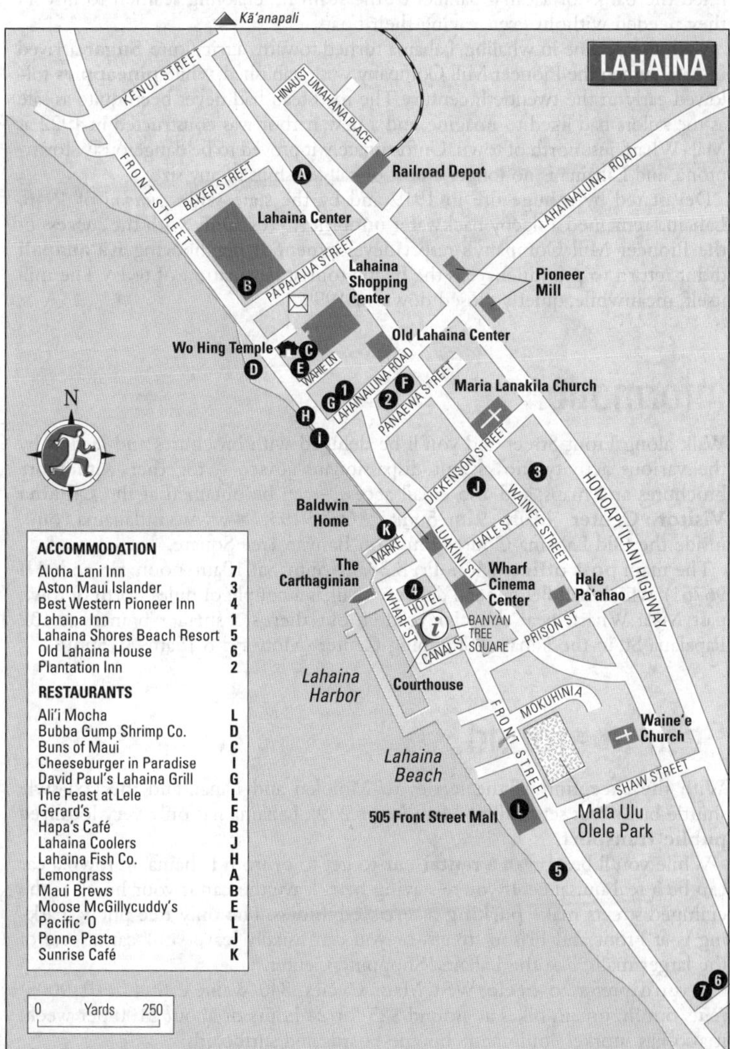

crews, incensed by missionary attempts to control drinking and prostitution, repeatedly attacked the home of Rev William Richards, but in due course chose to head instead for the fleshpots of Honolulu. In the 1840s, however, following the death of Maui's devout Governor Hoapili, the whalemen returned en masse to Lahaina. For the next two decades, it was a lawless and rip-roaring frontier town, described by another missionary as "one of the breathing holes of Hell."

Surprisingly, Lahaina has never been a true deep-water port. Its prosperity was based on its calm, shallow roadstead, sheltered by the islands of Molokai and Lanai. For the most part, sailing ships simply anchored anything from a couple of hundred yards to three miles offshore, and sent their crews ashore by rowboat. During the nineteenth century, in fact, a long covered marketplace lined the banks of a canal parallel to the seafront, enabling seamen to buy all they needed without ever leaving their boats.

With the decline in whaling, Lahaina turned towards agriculture. **Sugar** arrived in 1862, when the Pioneer Mill Company was established, while **pineapples** followed early in the twentieth century. The roadstead had never been quite as safe as the sailors had liked to imagine, and a new harbor was constructed in 1922 at Māla Wharf, just north of town. Unfortunately it proved to be dangerously storm-prone, and Lahaina is no longer a port of call for ships of any size.

Devastated by a huge fire in 1919 and by the state-wide *tsunami* of 1946, Lahaina remained a sleepy backwater until the 1970s. Only with the success of the Pioneer Mill Company's resort development at neighboring **Kā'anapali** did it return to prominence, as the hectic tourist destination of today. The mill itself, meanwhile, quietly closed down in 1999.

## Information

Walk along Front Street and you'll be deluged with brochures and leaflets by the various activity kiosks, but dispassionate advice – together with more brochures and maps, and also email access – can be obtained at the **Lahaina Visitor Center** (daily 9am–5pm; ⓣ667-9193, ⓦwww.visitlahaina.com), inside the Old Lahaina Court House on Banyan Tree Square.

The main **post office** (Mon–Fri 8.30am–5pm, Sat 10am–noon; zip code HI 96761), which handles general delivery mail, is a couple of miles north of town past Māla Wharf, near the civic center, but there's a smaller branch at 132 Papalaua St, in the Lahaina Shopping Center (Mon–Fri 8.15am–4.15pm).

## Getting around

With the exception of the ferries to Molokai and Lanai, and the taxi-style shuttle buses that serve all of Maui (see p.299), Lahaina has only very localized **public transport**.

While you'll be glad of a **rental car** to get to or from Lahaina, in town a car can be a real nuisance. If you're staying here, leave the car at your hotel, as the cramped streets make **parking** a terrible business. The only free public parking is at Front and Prison streets, or you can usually leave your car at one of the larger malls, like the Lahaina Shopping Center.

If you'd prefer to **cycle**, West Maui Cycles, 840 Waine'e St (ⓣ661-9005) rents out mountain bikes at around $25 for 24 hours or about $100 per week; it also has snorkel equipment, boogie boards and surfboards.

## Buses

The West Maui Shopping Express (Ⓣ877-7308) operates two **bus** routes in the Lahaina area, both connecting the Wharf Cinema Center with the Whaler's Village mall in **Kā'anapali** and both charging a flat one-way fare of $1. One runs thirteen times daily and stops at all the major hotels in Kā'anapali. The first departure from the Wharf Cinema Center is at 10.10am and the last at 10.10pm; the first bus of the day from Kā'anapali on this route leaves Whaler's Village at 9.55am, the last at 9.55pm. The other route connects the two malls with the Lahaina and Pu'ukoli'i train stations (see below), with seven trips each day. Buses leave the Wharf Cinema Center between 9.25am and 4.30pm; buses from Kā'anapali operate between 8.45am and 4.10pm.

## The Sugar Cane Train

The **Sugar Cane Train** (adults $11.50 one-way, $15.75 round-trip; under-13s $6.75/$8.75; Ⓣ667-6851 or, in the US only, 1-800/499-2307) is a restored locomotive (complete with "singing conductor") which runs six-mile, half-hour excursions through the cane fields along the tracks of the old Lahaina & Kā'anapali Railroad. It travels from Lahaina to Kā'anapali and then half a mile beyond to turn around at Pu'ukoli'i. For anyone other than a small child, it's not an exciting trip. The first departure from Lahaina is at 9.45am daily and the last at 4.50pm; from Kā'anapali, the first is at 9.05am daily, the last at 4.10pm. Free shuttle buses connect the Lahaina and Kā'anapali stations with the Wharf Cinema Center and the Whaler's Village, respectively.

## Ferries

In addition to its many excursion vessels, Lahaina Harbor is home to the only scheduled **inter-island ferry services** in Hawaii. *Expeditions* (Ⓣ661-3756 or, off Maui, 1-800/695-2624) sails from in front of the *Pioneer Inn* to Mānele Bay on **Lanai** daily at 6.45am, 9.15am, 12.45pm, 3.15pm and 5.45pm. Departures from Lanai are at 8am, 10.30am, 2pm, 4.30pm and 6.45pm; the adult fare is $25 each way, while under-12s go for $20. The trip takes approximately 50 minutes.

It's also possible to make a 1hr 15min ferry crossing between Maui and Molokai on the *Molokai Princess* (adults $40 one-way, children $20; Ⓣ667-6165 or 1-800/275-6969, Ⓦwww.mauiprincess.com). On Monday through Saturday, the boat brings commuters over from Molokai to their jobs on Maui, leaving Kaunakakai Harbor at 6am and setting off on the return trip from Lahaina at 5.15pm. On Sundays, it runs day-trips in the other direction, leaving Lahaina at 7.30am and Kaunakakai at 3.30pm. The *Molokai Princess* also offers commercial sightseeing cruises.

# Accommodation

In terms of **accommodation**, Lahaina has nothing to rival the opulence of Kā'anapali and Kapalua, further up the coast. However, the *Pioneer Inn* harks back romantically to the old days of Hawaiian tourism, and there are also a couple of classy B&B inns, plus a few central but quiet hotel-cum-condos.

**Aloha Lani Inn**, 13 Kaua'ula Rd, Lahaina HI 96761; Ⓣ 661-8040, Ⓕ 661-8045, Ⓦ www.maui.net/~tony. Two small, simple rooms in a welcoming private house, a stone's throw from the beach, roughly half a mile south of central Lahaina. Guests share a bathroom plus use of the kitchen (no breakfast is served); laundry facilities are available. The resident owner can advise on activities. Two-night minimum stay. ❸.

**Aston Maui Islander**, 660 Waine'e St, Lahaina HI 96761; Ⓣ 667-9766, 1-800/922-7866 (US & Can) or 1-800/321-2558 (HI), Ⓕ 661-3733, Ⓦ www.aston-hotels.com. Low-key but attractively refurbished and good-value complex a couple of blocks from the sea in central Lahaina. Options range from hotel rooms to two-bedroom condos; the buildings are connected by a rambling system of walkways through colorful gardens. Free use of a swimming pool and tennis courts is included. Rooms ❹, suites ❺.

**Best Western Pioneer Inn**, 658 Wharf St, Lahaina HI 96761; Ⓣ 661-3636 or 1-800/457-5457, Ⓕ 667-5708, Ⓦ www.pioneerinnmaui.com. Historic, highly atmospheric wooden hotel on the seafront in the very center of Lahaina (described on opposite). The tastefully furnished rooms, all with private bath and air-conditioning, open onto a lovely *lānai* overlooking Banyan Tree Square, and there are also some luxurious two-bedroom suites. Rooms ❹, suites ❺.

**Lahaina Inn**, 127 Lahainaluna Rd, Lahaina HI 96761; Ⓣ 661-0577 or 1-800/669-3444, Ⓕ 667-9480, Ⓦ www.lahainainn.com. Luxurious, antique-furnished re-creation of how a century-old inn ought to look, set slightly back from Front Street above the *Lahaina Grill* (see p.285). Twelve air-con rooms of varying sizes, equipped with private baths and phones, but no TV. Two-night minimum Friday and Saturday. No children under 15. ❹–❺.

**Lahaina Shores Beach Resort**, 475 Front St, Lahaina HI 96761; Ⓣ 661-3339 or 1-800/642-6284 (US & Can), Ⓕ 667-1145, Ⓦ www.lahaina-shores.com. Large, light-filled, shorefront hotel building, facing a pretty little beach a few hundred yards south of central Lahaina, next door to the 505 Front Street mall. Two-, three- and four-person rooms and suites, all with kitchens and *lānais*; an ocean view costs around $30 more than a mountain view. Rooms ❺, suites ❼.

**Old Lahaina House**, PO Box 10355, Lahaina HI 96761; Ⓣ 667-4663 or 1-800/847-0761, Ⓕ 667-5615, Ⓦ www.oldlahaina.com. Good-quality B&B accommodation in friendly private home complete with pool, a few hundred yards south of downtown Lahaina. There's one guest room in the house and four more in a separate garden wing; all are en-suite, with refrigerators, TVs, and air-conditioning. Rates include breakfast on the *lānai*. ❸.

**Plantation Inn**, 174 Lahainaluna Rd, Lahaina HI 96761; Ⓣ 667-9225 or 1-800/433-6815, Ⓕ 667-9293; Ⓦ www.theplantationinn.com. Luxury B&B hotel, not far back from the sea and styled to resemble a Southern plantation home, with columns and verandahs. All rooms have bathrooms and *lānais*; some also have kitchenettes, and there's a twelve-foot-deep pool. Guests get a discount at the downstairs restaurant, *Gerard's* (see p.285). Rooms ❹–❺, suites ❻.

# Downtown Lahaina

Almost all the activity of modern Lahaina is concentrated along **Front Street**, where a few historic buildings, such as the Baldwin Home and Wo Hing Temple, hang on amid an awful lot of shopping malls, souvenir stores and fast-food outlets. The very heart of town is **Banyan Tree Square**, an attractive public space kept too busy for comfort by coachloads of tourists.

For respite, locals and visitors alike gravitate towards the **waterfront**. The views are superb, whether you look straight across to the island of Lanai, where you'll probably be able to make out the crest of Norfolk pines along its topmost ridge, or north towards Molokai, where the west-end mountain of Mauna Loa is visible on a clear day. Closer at hand, fishermen angle for sand fish in the inshore waters, boats and yachts bob beyond the placid roll of white surf fifty yards out, and parasailers peer down upon all this activity from on high.

If you're looking for **shops**, the two largest malls are the modern **Lahaina Shopping Center**, three blocks north of downtown and still a long way short of filling up – despite the recent addition of a reproduction Hawaiian village, the **Hale Kahiko**, which stages *hula* shows and is open for explanatory tours (daily 11am–4pm) – and the **Lahaina Cannery**, a long walk further north near Māla Wharf.

## Banyan Tree Square

A magnificent banyan tree, planted on April 24, 1873, almost completely fills **Banyan Tree Square**. It consists of at least twenty major trunks, plus any number of intertwined tendrils pushing back down into the ground. A phenomenal number of chirruping birds congregate in the branches, while portrait artists tout for customers in the shade below.

Here and there on the surrounding lawns, a few outlines mark the former extent of **Lahaina Fort**, started by Governor Hoapili in 1832. Its walls once held as many as 47 cannons, salvaged from assorted shipwrecks throughout Hawaii; a drum was beaten on its ramparts at nightfall as a signal for all foreign seamen to return to their ships. The fort was demolished in 1854, but one small corner has been reconstructed, at the southwest end of the square.

The **Court House**, on the harbor side of Banyan Tree Square, was constructed in 1859, after a storm had destroyed most of Lahaina's previous official buildings. It now holds the small local visitor center (see p.278), as well as the Banyan Tree Gallery, which hosts interesting, free **art exhibitions** (daily 9am–5pm).

Across Canal Street from the Court House, the **Pioneer Inn** has, since 1901, been the main social center of Lahaina. Its original owner was a Canadian "Mountie." Having pursued a criminal all the way to Maui, he decided to stay on and go into the hotel business, catering to passengers on the Inter-Island Steamship line. It makes an atmospheric spot to stop in for a beer, though it's hardly very peaceful.

## The Brick Palace and the Hauola Stone

Lahaina Public Library, immediately north of the *Pioneer Inn*, stands on the site of the former **royal *taro* patch**, personally tended by the first three Kamehamehas. A line of bricks set into the grass on its seaward side traces the foundations of the **Brick Palace**, the first Western-style building in Hawaii. Two stories high and measuring 20ft by 40ft, it was built for Kamehameha the Great in 1798 by an English convict who had managed to escape from Australia; the palace survived until the 1860s.

Poking out from the waves beyond the seawall to the north, the approximately chair-shaped **Hauola Stone** was a "healing rock" where Hawaiian women would give birth. In thanks for a trouble-free labor, the umbilical cord (*piko*) of the infant would be left under the rock.

## The Carthaginian

The square-rigged sailing brig *Carthaginian* may look like a superb relic of Lahaina's whaling days, gently swaying at its permanent moorings in front of the *Pioneer Inn*, but in fact it's a rather pointless fake (daily 10am–5pm, last admission 4pm; $3 per person, $5 per couple or family). Even the original *Carthaginian*, which was moored here until it sank in 1972, was only a replica of a nineteenth-century whaling vessel, refitted for use in the movie version of James Michener's *Hawaii*. This one started life in 1920 as a two-masted German schooner, then plied the Baltic for several decades as a diesel-powered cement carrier, and only took on its present shape after being brought from Europe in 1973 to replace the previous version.

Paying the steep admission charge entitles you to cross the gangplank and descend into its interior. As a whaling museum, it's not a patch on the free displays at Ka'anapali (see p.290): half the space within is taken up by a plain nineteenth-century whaleboat from Alaska, and half by benches facing a TV screen showing endless video commercials for local whale-watching trips. The highlight is the chance to pick up a phone and hear recorded whale songs "for education or entertainment."

## Lahaina Harbor

Alongside the *Carthaginian*, a simple and modern white structure has replaced what was the oldest **Pacific Lighthouse**, built to serve the whaling fleet in 1840. Shielded by a breakwater of boulders, **Lahaina Harbor** now serves as a pleasure-boat marina, which is ever less able to cope with the scale of West Maui's tourist activity. The harbor wall holds kiosks for most local **boat operators**, but it's not much of an area to stroll around. You can, in any case, usually get better prices from the activity centers along Front Street.

## Lahaina Beach

Immediately south of the marina, **Lahaina Beach**, with its shallow water, sandy bottom and gentle breaks, is where companies such as the Goofy Foot Surf School (☎244-9283) and Soul Surfing Maui (☎870-7873) teach their clients the rudiments of **surfing**, and beginners and old-timers alike swoop back and forth – the latter with rather more panache. The beach itself is too narrow for long days of family fun, but it's fine for a stroll.

## Baldwin Home

The **Baldwin Home**, on Front Street just north of Banyan Tree Square, is the oldest surviving building in Lahaina. Dating from the days when this was Hawaii's royal capital, it was built as the Maui base of the Sandwich Islands Mission and is now a reasonably interesting museum of missionary and local history (daily 10am–4.15pm; $3 per person, $5 per couple or family; ☎661-3262). The price of admission includes a brief narrated tour, after which visitors are free to take a closer look around.

Although its 24-inch-thick walls of plastered lava and coral were constructed in 1834 by Reverend Ephraim Spaulding, the house bears the name of Reverend Dwight Baldwin, who took it over when Spaulding fell sick three years later. Baldwin remained as pastor of Lahaina's Waine'e Church until 1871, and much of his original furniture is still in place. Oddly frivolous touches among the chairs, quilts and gifts to and from whaling captains include an inlaid *koa* gaming table, and a table-top croquet set. On one wall hangs a "Native Doctor's License" from 1865, with a scale of charges ranging from $50 down to $10, according to whether the patient had a "Very great sickness," "Less than that," "A Good Deal Less," a "Small sickness" or a "Very Small."

The **Masters' Reading Room**, next door to the Baldwin Home and of similar vintage, is the headquarters of the Lahaina Restoration Foundation, which manages most of Lahaina's historic sites. It's not open to the public.

## Wo Hing Temple

The distinguished-looking building with an unmistakably Oriental facade, a short walk north of downtown Lahaina on Front Street, is now known as the **Wo Hing Temple** (Mon–Fri 10am–4.30pm; free). It was built in 1912 as the meeting place for the Wo Hing Society, a mutual-aid organization established in China during the seventeenth century. Until the 1970s it housed elderly members of the society, but it's now an interesting little museum devoted to the subject of Chinese immigration to Hawaii, with a small Taoist altar on its second story.

Amid the faded signs and battered pots and pans in the decrepit adjacent **cookhouse**, there are continuous showings of scratchy film footage shot by Thomas Edison in Hawaii in 1898.

## Hale Pa'ahao

At the corner of Prison and Waine'e streets, the plain one-story **Hale Pa'ahao** replaced the Fort as Lahaina's prison during the 1850s; in fact, as the Fort came down, the prison went up, using the same stones. Now a public hall, it's usually left open, and you're free to wander into the former cells, which hold a few exhibits about the days when they were filled to bursting with drunken sailors.

## Waine'e Church

The first church on Maui, built in 1828 after five years of open-air services, was **Waine'e Church**, one block back from the sea. Twice destroyed by hurricanes, and burned down in 1894 in protests against the overthrow of the Hawaiian monarchy, this less-than-enthralling edifice has been known as Waiola Church since it was last rebuilt in 1953.

Tombs in the sun-scorched graveyard alongside, however, include some of the greatest names in early Hawaiian history. A simple monument commemorates the last king of Kauai, **Kaumuali'i**, who was buried here in 1825 after being kidnapped by Liholiho and forced to live in exile (see p.415). Nearby are **Queen Keopuolani**, one of the many wives of Kamehameha the Great, who was of such distinguished *ali'i* blood that her husband could only enter her presence naked on all fours; the governor of Maui, **Hoapili Kāne**, who died in 1840; and his widow and successor **Hoapili Wahine**, who passed away two years later.

## Lahainaluna

High above Lahaina town, reached by a winding two-mile climb up Lahainaluna Road past the Pioneer Sugar Mill, **Lahainaluna Seminary** was founded by American missionaries in 1831. Its goal was to teach Hawaiians to read and write, in the hope of producing future teachers and ministers. In 1850, however, the seminary passed into government control, and it eventually became Hawaii's most prestigious public **high school**. Although not originally on US soil, it's regarded as being the first American educational institution west of the Rockies, and in the Gold Rush years many Californians sent their children here rather than risk the long journey East.

Visitors are welcome to take a quick look around the high school grounds; pause to identify yourself at the gate first. The only building you can enter is the seminary's small printing house, **Hale Pa'i** (Mon–Fri 10am–3pm; free). Dating from 1837, it holds some of Hawaii's first printed books, as well as a replica of the press that produced them.

Among Lahainaluna Seminary's earliest pupils were Hawaii's most famous native historians, **Samuel Kamakau** and **David Malo**. Malo had been brought up at the court of Kamehameha the Great on the Big Island and was 38 when he first came here. Although he became a Christian, and was a minister at the old village of Kalepolepo in what's now Kīhei, he was also a passionate defender of the rights of the Hawaiian people. At the time of the Great

## Warren and Annabelle's Magic Show

Apart from eating and drinking, Lahaina is very short on evening entertainment. Well worth recommending, therefore, is **Warren and Annabelle's Magic Show**, presented in a purpose-built theater in the oceanfront Lahaina Center (Mon–Sat 5.30pm; adults only, $36; 900 Front St; ⓣ667-6244, ⓦwww.warrenandannabelles.com). The whole experience has been very thoughtfully designed. Each group of guests has to solve a puzzle to gain admission to the pre-show bar, where cocktails and a substantial selection of appetizers and desserts are served while an invisible pianist (the ghostly "Annabelle") plays show tunes. The whole audience then moves to the intimate showroom, where they're treated to a wonderful display of sleight-of-hand magic by Warren Gibson, originally from South Carolina. Gibson works very hard to keep his audience entertained – he manages to know almost everyone by name after the first few minutes – and many of his tricks are truly mind-boggling. It's a shame that the show bears no relevance to Hawaii whatsoever, but for a fun night out it's unbeatable.



Mahele – the disastrous 1848 land division that made the American takeover of Hawaii possible (see *Contexts*, p.512) – Malo was regarded as the firebrand behind native Hawaiian resistance. Before he died in 1853, he asked to be buried "beyond the rising tide of the foreign invasion." His gravesite is above Lahainaluna at **Pu'u Pa'upa'u**; it is marked with a huge letter "L" (for Lahainaluna) etched into the hillside and visible from all over Lahaina.

# Restaurants

Literally dozens of places to **eat** line the waterfront in Lahaina, with sophisticated gourmet **restaurants** mingling with national and local chain outlets and takeout places. Not all are good by any means, but you should find something to suit you within a few minutes' wandering.

For a quick snack, the best local **fast-food court** is in the Lahaina Cannery mall, a mile north of downtown. There's also a *Starbucks* next to the Foodland supermarket in the Old Lahaina Center.

Note that full listings of all Maui's lū'aus appear on p.276.

### Inexpensive

**Ali'i Mocha**, 505 Front St; ⓣ661-7800. Small café in oceanfront mall, with indoor and outdoor seating, offering espresso coffees and smoothies, bagels and pastries, and internet access. Daily 6am–11pm.

**Buns of Maui**, 878 Front St; ⓣ661-4877. Appealing little bakery, tucked away just behind Front Street, that serves fresh pastries and muffins along with its coffees in the morning, and graduates to sandwiches later on. Mon–Sat 6am–6pm.

**Cheeseburger in Paradise**, 811 Front St; ⓣ661-4855. Busy, crowded seafront restaurant, perched on stilts above the water, with great views and seafaring bric-a-brac. Very much what the name suggests, though in addition to meaty $7–8 cheeseburgers they have fish sandwiches and spinach-nut-burgers at similar prices. There's live music nightly. Daily 8am–midnight.

**Hapa's Café**, Lahaina Center, 900 Front St; ⓣ661-8988. Owned by popular Hawaiian musicians, this late-night smoothie and espresso bar also sells sandwiches and snacks. Sun–Tues 8am–7pm, Wed–Sat 8am–2am.

**Moose McGillycuddy's**, 844 Front St; ⓣ667-7758. Hectic restaurant-cum-nightclub that starts the day with very cheap breakfasts (twenty different omelets at $4–5, plus $2 specials); follows up with standard lunches and dinners of burgers, sandwiches, pastas and steak; and tops things off with live music and/or dancing nightly 9.30pm–2am ($2 cover charge). Restaurant open daily 7.30am–10pm.

**Penne Pasta**, 180 Dickenson St; ⓣ661-6633. Cheerful Italian café, with sidewalk and indoor seating, serving straightforward but tasty pastas, salads and pizzas for under $10. The flatbread topped with olives, capers, basil, oregano and roasted peppers is particularly good. Mon–Fri 11am–9pm, Sat & Sun 5–9pm.

**Sunrise Café**, 693A Front St at Market St; ⓣ661-8558. Small, laid-back and very central café, with outdoor seating beside its own tiny patch of beach. Coffees, smoothies and full cooked breakfasts from dawn onwards, plus $6–9 salads, sandwiches and plate lunches later on. Daily 6am–6pm.

## Moderate

**Bubba Gump Shrimp Co**, 889 Front St; ⓣ661-3111. Lahaina didn't exactly need another themed diner, but at least this outlet of a burgeoning national chain, styled to resemble a tumbledown shrimp shack (as in the movie *Forrest Gump*), serves reasonably tasty food in an attractive waterfront setting. Shrimp entrees, priced at $13–18, are prepared in every imaginable way, from steamed-in-beer or flash-fried with ginger and garlic to New Orleans blackened. You can also get $4 smoothies and $8–9 sandwiches, and there's live music nightly. Daily 11am–10.30pm.

**Lahaina Coolers**, 180 Dickenson St; ⓣ661-7082. Central bistro restaurant serving eggy breakfasts, then an extensive menu of salads, pastas, pizzas, tortillas, steaks and fresh Hawaiian fish, priced at $10–16, for lunch and dinner. A couple of blocks from the sea, but it's open and breezy, with a pleasant atmosphere. Daily 8am–2am.

**Lahaina Fish Co**, 831 Front St; ⓣ661-3472. High-quality seafood restaurant, poised on a beautiful *lānai* that juts out over the ocean. Hawaiian fish entrees ($20–24) are available broiled, grilled or blackened Cajun-style, while a raw bar serves clams and oysters on the half-shell for around $10 and fresh sashimi for $13. Devout carnivores can stick to chicken or ribs. Daily 11am–midnight.

**Lemongrass**, 930 Waine'e St; ⓣ667-6888. Bright little Vietnamese/Thai restaurant, behind the Lahaina Center. In addition to soups and noodle dishes such as beef *phó* ($7) and pad thai with shrimp or chicken (under $10), they serve a full menu of meat and seafood entrees, including plenty of curries, almost all under $12. Daily 10am–9pm.

**Maui Brews**, Lahaina Center, 900 Front St; ⓣ667-7794. Busy, loud and popular bistro-cum-nightclub, serving snacks and sandwiches plus a full menu of pasta, meat and seafood entrees at well under $20. It's not a brewpub, but there is a copious selection of beers. Restaurant daily 11.30am–10pm, nightclub 9pm until late.

## Expensive

**David Paul's Lahaina Grill**, *Lahaina Inn*, 127 Lahainaluna Rd; ⓣ667-5117. Upmarket restaurant serving some of Maui's finest Pacific Rim cuisine, set a few yards back from Front Street in northern downtown Lahaina. The setting is slightly cramped and unatmospheric, but the food is great. Of the appetizers, the terrine of salmon and scallop is superb, and the deep-fried oysters succulent; entrees include rack of lamb flavored with coffee ($38), *kālua* duck ($29), and various fish dishes; the fruity desserts are wonderful. A five-course tasting menu costs $67. Daily 6–10pm.

**The Feast at Lele**, 505 Front St; ⓣ667-5353. An inspired cross between a *lū'au* and a gourmet restaurant, which, for once, lavishes as much care on the food as on the entertainment. Chef James McDonald, of nearby restaurants *'Io* and *Pacific 'O*, prepares a feast of Polynesian specialties, including *kālua* pork from Hawaii, *fafa* (steamed chicken) and *e'iota* (marinated raw fish) from Tahiti, and grilled fish in banana leaves from Samoa. Each of the five courses consists of at least two dishes – it really is a colossal amount of food, but it's both excellent and unusual. The beachfront setting is also superb and very romantic, with individual white-clothed tables set out facing the ocean at sunset, and dance, music, and *hula* performances between the bursts of gluttony. The one drawback is the cost, though at least the $89 adult charge includes unlimited cocktails and other beverages; for children, it's $59. Reservations are essential. April–Sept Tues–Sat 6pm, Oct–March Tues–Sat 5.30pm; schedules may vary.

**Gerard's**, *Plantation Inn*, 174 Lahainaluna Rd; ⓣ661-8939. Adding a Hawaiian twist to traditional French cuisine results in a menu of $10–25 appetizers such as snails with wild mushrooms or foie gras with truffles, and entrees like stuffed quails, veal sweetbreads, and roasted *opakapaka* priced at up to $40. Desserts include profiteroles and other classic patisserie. Nightly 6–9.30pm.

**Pacific 'O**, 505 Front St; ⓣ667-4341. Really nice oceanfront mall restaurant, serving Pacific Rim cuisine on a beach-level terrace with indoor dining above. Typical, relatively simple lunch specials for $10–15 include satay, shrimp pasta and chicken sandwiches. In the evening, try $9–12 appetizers such as fish tartare with raw *'ahi*, or shrimp won tons in Hawaiian salsa, and $20 entrees like fish tempura or fish grilled in a banana leaf. The Shrimp Nui is amazing; *nui* means "big," and for $28 you get four lobster-sized shrimp in a sumptuous lemongrass pesto broth. The delicious chocolate desserts are similarly huge. Sun–Thurs 11am–4pm & 5.30–10pm, Fri & Sat 11am–4pm & 5.30–10.30pm; live jazz Fri & Sat from 9pm.

# West Maui

Over the eons, the older of Maui's two volcanoes has eroded away to create a long, curving ridge, whose serrated peaks are known collectively as the **West Maui Mountains**. The highest point – Pu'u Kukui, barely six miles inland from Lahaina – is deluged by around 400 inches of rain per year and is almost always obscured by clouds. However, the leeward (western) slopes are consistently dry, and for eight miles north of Lahaina the sun-baked beaches are lined by a seamless succession of hotels and condos, in purpose-built resorts such as **Kā'anapali**, **Honokōwai** and **Kapalua**.

No road crosses the mountains; parts of the all-but-impenetrable wilderness of the interior have never been explored. The main road to Lahaina from central Maui – **Honoapi'ilani Highway**, named after the six northwestern bays conquered by the great Maui chief Pi'ilani – is forced to loop laboriously around the southern end of West Maui. Thanks to a sensible policy of only allowing development on its *makai* (oceanward) side, it's an attractive drive, with the inland hills and valleys largely untouched except by drifting rainbows; it's also a very slow one.

At the northern end of West Maui, beyond Kapalua, the weather becomes progressively wetter; the coast is more indented with bays; and driving conditions grow increasingly difficult. Honoapi'ilani Highway eventually gives up altogether around Nākālele Point. Sinuous, undulating **Kahekili Highway** beyond narrows to a single lane for several miles, and rental-car companies forbid their clients to use it. Nonetheless, it is possible to complete a full circuit of West Maui, and the extravagant beauty of the windward coast – best seen from hiking trails in and above **Waihe'e Valley**, easily accessible from Wailuku – should not be missed.

## South of Lahaina

Few people live along the parched coastline to the **south of Lahaina**, though ditches in the hillside still irrigate extensive green cane fields. There are no significant settlements, but the only road, Honoapi'ilani Highway, is prone to hideous traffic congestion, especially as it narrows to climb around McGregor Point in the far south and head back to **Mā'alaea** (see p.309).

### Launiupoko State Wayside Park

While always scenic enough, the beaches that lie immediately south of Lahaina are not nearly as appealing as those to the north, consisting as a rule of narrow strips of sand deposited atop sharp black rocks. The first one you come to, **Puamana Beach County Park**, offers no visitor facilities, but **Launiupoko State Wayside Park**, three miles out, makes an attractive picnic spot. Coconut palms lean out from the shoreline, while larger trees shade the tables on the lawn; the only snag is that it's very much in earshot of the highway. From the center of the park, boulder walls curve out to enclose a shallow artificial pool, suitable for small children, with two narrow outlets to the sea. South of that is a small beach of gritty sand, while to the north the lava rocks create a sea wall, alive with scuttling black crabs. The offshore waters here are a good spot for beginners to practice their surfing skills – thus the parking lot normally holds plenty of gleaming rental cars, but few local rustbuckets. Launiupoko has showers and rest rooms, but camping is forbidden.

## The Olowalu Massacre

Olowalu was the site of the worst **massacre** in Hawaiian history, perpetrated by **Captain Simon Metcalfe** of the American merchant ship *Eleanora* in 1790. After Hawaiians had killed a member of his crew as they stole one of the ship's boats off East Maui, Metcalfe set fire to the nearest village and then sailed for Olowalu, which he was told was the home of the chief culprit. Offering to continue trading, he lured more than two hundred canoes out to the *Eleanora*, many of them filled with children coming to see the strange ship. Metcalfe placed a *kapu* on the port side of the vessel, so all the canoes flocked to starboard and then, without warning, bombarded them with his seven cannons. More than a hundred Hawaiians died.

Ironically, Captain Metcalfe's 18-year-old son, **Thomas**, was to pay for his father's sins. Metcalfe had previously antagonized a Big Island chief, Kame'eiamoku, who vowed to kill the next white man he met. Ignorant of events at Olowalu, Thomas Metcalfe landed his tiny six-man schooner *Fair American* at Kawaihae on the Big Island a few days later and was killed when it was stormed and captured by Kame'eiamoku and his men. Of its crew, only **Isaac Davis** was spared, for putting up such valiant resistance.

In due course, the *Eleanora* arrived at Kawaihae in search of the younger Metcalfe, and first mate **John Young** was sent ashore to investigate. Kamehameha the Great himself prevented Young from rejoining his vessel with the news of the killings, whereupon Captain Metcalfe concluded that his envoy had been killed and sailed away. Metcalfe himself was killed soon afterwards and never learned of the death of his son; both Davis and Young, however, remained on the islands for the rest of their lives, taking Hawaiian names and becoming valued advisors to the king. They were responsible for teaching the Hawaiians to fight with muskets and cannon – the royal arsenal began with two guns seized from the *Fair American* – and personally directed Kamehameha's armies at battles such as 'Īao Valley on Maui (see p.307) and Nu'uanu Pali on Oahu (see p.95).

# Olowalu

There's little more to **OLOWALU**, six miles south of Lahaina, than a tiny row of stores *mauka* of the highway. The most noteworthy of these is *Chez Paul* (☎661-3843), an incongruous and very expensive French bistro set behind a pretty little brick wall. It's open for dinner only, nightly except Sunday, with two seatings, at 6.30pm and 8.30pm. Most of the appetizers cost at least $10, though there's caviar for $65, while entrees such as seafood bouillabaisse or Tahitian duck are well over $30.

Although there's no public access to the ocean on the promontory across the road, where all the land belongs to the Pioneer Mill Company, a short hike towards the mountains leads you to a cluster of ancient **petroglyphs**. Start by heading round to the left behind the stores and then continue inland, following not the dirt road facing you, but the one that starts immediately left of the nearby water tower. After about ten minutes' walk through the cane fields, you'll notice that the nearest side of the cinder cone straight ahead of you has sheared off to create a flat wall of red rock. Fresh-painted red railings a few feet up the rock mark the site of the petroglyphs, but the stairs and walkways that once enabled visitors to climb up to them have largely vanished. So too have many of the petroglyphs, and others have been vandalized. However, you should still spot several wedge-shaped human figures etched into the rock, together with a sailing canoe or two, characterized by their "crab-claw" sails. Looking back, you'll also get good views across to Lanai.

## Ukemehame and Pāpalaua

South of Olowalu, the cane fields come to an end, and Hwy-30 skirts the shoreline only a few feet above sea level. It's possible to park just about anywhere, and in whale-watching season that's exactly what people do – often with very little warning.

**Ukemehame Beach County Park**, three miles along, consists of a very small area of lawn between the highway and the ocean, with picnic tables and a couple of portable rest rooms, fringed by a small strip of sand. Lots of trees have been planted, but they remain very short so far. By now, the mountains begin to rise only just inland of the road and are much drier and barer than further north.

**Pāpalaua State Wayside**, which leads on south from Ukemehame, is a long dirt strip used as a parking lot, separated from the sand by a thin line of scrubby trees. Local surfers and snorkelers set up tents among the trees, but there are virtually no facilities. Immediately beyond Pāpalaua, the highway starts its climb over (and through) the headland of **Papawai Point**, where a roadside lookout is one of Maui's best **whale-watching** sites. From there it's less than two miles to Mā'alaea (see p.309) and the isthmus.

## The Lahaina Pali Trail

Until the hard labor of convicts constructed the first road around the southern coast of West Maui, in 1900, the only way to reach Lahaina via dry land was to follow the centuries-old *alaloa*, or "long road," across the mountains. A five-mile stretch of this has recently been re-opened as the **Lahaina Pali Trail**. It's a grueling hike, climbing 1600 feet above sea level and, being situated at the dry, exposed southern tip of the island, it's also a very hot one. Don't expect to penetrate into the mysterious green heart of the interior; for that, the Waihe'e Ridge Trail (see p.296) is a better bet. Your rewards instead will be the sight of some ravishing upland meadows, carpeted with magnificent purple, yellow and red flowers, and long-range views out to the islands of Lanai and Kahoolawe and down across the isthmus.

Both ends of the trail are a long way from the nearest town, so you'll need a car to reach either trailhead and, unless you can arrange to be picked up at the far end, hiking its full length necessitates a ten-mile round trip. The path leaves Honoapi'ilani Highway from a parking lot near the 11-mile marker at Ukemehame and rejoins it five miles south of Wailuku, immediately south of the white bridge that lies between its intersections with highways 31 (to Kīhei) and 380 (to Kahului). Whichever end you start – the eastern slope is the steeper – you'll have at least a mile of stiff climbing before the trail levels out, still far below the top of the mountains. As it then meanders through successive gulches to cross Kealaloloa Ridge, almost the only – very welcome – shade is provided by the occasional native dryland sandalwood tree.

# North from Lahaina: Kā'anapali

When American Factors (Amfac), the owners of the Pioneer Sugar Mill, decided in 1957 to transform the oceanfront cane fields of **KĀ'ANAPALI** into a luxury tourist resort, they established a pattern that has been repeated throughout Hawaii ever since. There had never been a town at Kā'anapali, just a small plantation wharf served by a short railroad from the sugar mill at Lahaina. What Kā'anapali did have, however, was a superb white-sand **beach** – far better than anything at Lahaina – backed by a tract of land that was ripe for development and more than twice the size of Waikīkī.

## Kā'anapali Shuttle Buses

The **West Maui Shopping Express** runs between Kā'anapali and Lahaina; see p.279 for details. The same company also offers bus service between Whaler's Village Kā'anapali and Kapalua to the north, making eleven trips each day between 9am and 8.20pm; the flat fare is $2. The free **Ka'anapali Trolley** circles the Kā'anapali resort area several times daily (9am–11pm; ⓣ667-0648), calling at the golf course as well as all the hotels.

Kā'anapali's first hotel opened in 1963 and has been followed by half a dozen similar giants, whose four thousand rooms now welcome half a million visitors each year. It took a good twenty years before the resort began to feel at all lived in, however, and there's still nothing else here apart from the central, anodyne **Whaler's Village** mall. Kā'anapali is a pretty enough place, with its two rolling **golf courses** and sunset views of the island of Lanai filling the western horizon, but it's only worth staying here if you know you're happy with the same bland lifestyle you could find at a hundred tropical resorts around the world.

As for **Kā'anapali Beach**, it's divided into two separate long strands by the forbidding, 300-foot cinder cone of Pu'u Keka'a, known as the **Black Rock**. The sand shelves away abruptly from both sections, so swimmers soon find themselves in deep water, but bathing is usually safe outside periods of high winter surf. The rugged lava coastline around the Black Rock itself is one of the best **snorkeling** spots on Maui.

Nonguests of Kā'anapali's hotels are free to use the main beach, but there are also a couple of **public beach parks** just around the headland to the south. Both **Hanaka'ō'ō** and **Wahikuli** are right alongside Hwy-30; swimming is generally safer at Wahikuli, but the facilities and general ambience are more appealing at Hanaka'ō'ō.

## Accommodation

Kā'anapali is very far from being a budget destination, but its consistently lavish **hotels** do at least compete in offering cut-price deals on rental cars or longer stays, and all feature activity programs for kids. For the latest offers, and general information on Kā'anapali, call the Kā'anapali Beach Resort Association on ⓣ661-3271 or 1-800/245-9229 (US & Can).

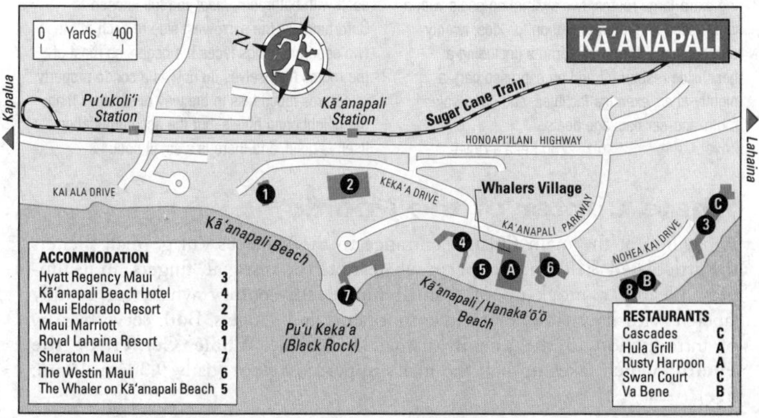

**Hyatt Regency Maui**, 200 Nohea Kai Drive, Lahaina HI 96761; Ⓣ 661-1234 or 1-800/554-9288, Ⓕ 667-4498, Ⓦ www.maui.hyatt.com. Possibly Kā'anapali's grandest hotel, approached via an avenue lined with flaming torches at the south end of the resort. The lobby has colossal chandeliers; the atrium is filled with coconut palms and holds a pool filled with live penguins; the gardens are opulent; there's a full-service spa; and the vast labyrinth of swimming pools includes a swinging rope bridge and bar. The main tower has ten stories, and there are subsidiary wings to either side, with a total of 815 luxurious rooms and five restaurants. Rack-rate guests get the fifth night free, except in high season. Mountain view ❽, ocean view ❾.

**Kā'anapali Beach Hotel**, 2525 Kā'anapali Parkway, Lahaina HI 96761; Ⓣ 661-0011 or 1-800/262-8450 (US & Can), Ⓕ 667-5978, Ⓦ www.kbhmaui. com. The least expensive beachfront option in Kā'anapali, this low-rise property, arrayed around spacious lawns, is poised between Whaler's Village and the Black Rock and enjoys a fine stretch of beach plus a whale-shaped swimming pool. All its large, well-equipped rooms have balconies or patios, though some offer shower rather than bath. Garden view ❺, ocean view ❻.

**Maui Eldorado Resort**, 2661 Keka'a Drive; Ⓣ 661-0021 or 1-800/688-7444 (US & Can), Ⓕ 667-7039, Ⓦ www.outrigger.com. Condo property consisting of several low buildings ranged up the hillside, well back from the shoreline; shuttle buses run to the resort's own reserved beach area. All units offer air-conditioning, *lānai*, washer/dryer, and a kitchenette if not a full kitchen. Garden view ❺, ocean view ❻.

**Maui Marriott**, 100 Nohea Kai Drive, Lahaina HI 96761; Ⓣ 667-1200, 1-800/228-9200 (US & Can) or 1-800/763-1333 (HI), Ⓕ 667-8192, Ⓦ www.marriott.com. Imposing, luxurious resort hotel at the south end of Kā'anapali Beach, offering extra-large rooms, two swimming pools with a water slide and a pirate lagoon for kids, twenty on-site shops, three restaurants (including a beachside restaurant and an espresso bar), a nightly *lū'au*, exercise facilities, and good-value room-and-car package deals. ❽.

**Royal Lahaina Resort**, 2780 Keka'a Drive, Lahaina HI 96761; Ⓣ 661-3611 or 1-800/44-ROYAL, Ⓕ 661-6150, Ⓦ www.2maui.com. One of Kā'anapali's two original resorts, commanding a long stretch of perfect sand at the north end of the beach. The hotel has 600 rooms, with a central 12-story tower of plush suites, another smaller hotel building, and a couple of dozen "cottages" of condo-style apartments on the grounds. It has four restaurants, a nightly *lū'au*, and a 3500-seat tennis stadium that's occasionally used for concerts. ❻.

**Sheraton Maui**, 2605 Kā'anapali Parkway, Lahaina HI 96761; Ⓣ 661-0031 or 1-800/782-9488, Ⓕ 661-0458; Ⓦ www.sheraton-hawaii.com. This luxury resort was the first to open at Ka'anapali, in 1963, and has since been almost entirely rebuilt, with five tiers of rooms dropping down the crag of Black Rock and separate oceanfront wings, all at the broadest end of Kā'anapali Beach. Garden-view rooms ❽, ocean-view rooms and suites ❾.

**The Westin Maui**, 2365 Kā'anapali Parkway, Lahaina HI 96761; Ⓣ 667-2525 or 1-800/937-8461 (US & Can), Ⓕ 661-5831, Ⓦ www.westin.com. High-rise hotel in the center of Kā'anapali Beach, immediately south of Whaler's Village, with five swimming pools (including Maui's largest) fed by artificial waterfalls, a lagoon of live flamingos to match the predominantly pink decor, and even its own *Starbucks*. Bright, modern, luxurious if somewhat characterless hotel rooms, all with private *lānais*. Mountain view ❽, ocean view ❾.

**The Whaler on Ka'anapali Beach**, 2481 Kā'anapali Parkway, Lahaina HI 96761; Ⓣ 661-4861, Ⓕ 922-8785; reserve through Aston Hotels & Resorts, Ⓣ 1-800/922-7866 (US & Can) or 1-800/321-2558 (HI), Ⓦ www-aston-hotels.com. Just north of Whaler's Village, this condo complex holds comfortable one- and two-bedroom units, each with bathroom, *lānai* and full kitchen. Unfortunately, the narrowest side of each of the two separate wings faces the ocean, so most of the rooms themselves do not. As a condo property, it features much less in the way of services than the neighboring hotels, but the accommodation itself is good, and there is a small pool. ❻.

## Whale Center of the Pacific

A pavilion at the main (inland) entrance to the Whaler's Village mall shelters the articulated skeleton of a sperm whale; note the vestigial "fingers" in its flippers. Nearby, a mock-up of a small nineteenth-century whaleboat is fully labeled with its various esoteric components and gadgets. Both serve by way of introduction to the grandly named and grisly **Whale Center of the Pacific**, which takes up half the mall's uppermost floor (daily 9.30am–10pm; free).

This free **museum** is devoted to Maui's long-lost heyday as a whaling center, illustrating the tedium and the terror of the seamen's daily routine through scrimshaw, shellwork valentines, log books, tools, equipment, letters and bills. The largest single exhibit is a cast-iron "try pot," used for reducing whale blubber at sea; such pots gave rise to the stereotyped but not entirely untrue image of cannibals cooking missionaries in big black cauldrons. Contrary to what you might imagine, no actual killing of whales took place in Hawaiian waters. Hawaii was simply the place where the whaling ships came to recuperate after hunting much further north in the Pacific. What's more, the humpback – the whale most commonly found in Hawaiian waters – was not hunted at all during the nineteenth century; the target for the fleets was instead the right whale, so named, logically enough, because it was deemed the "right" whale to kill.

## Restaurants

All Kāʻanapali's hotels have at least one flagship **restaurant**, though catering on such a large scale makes it hard for staff to pay much attention to detail. Away from the hotels, the only alternative is to eat at the **Whaler's Village** mall. In addition to its more formal oceanfront restaurants, it holds a **food court**, set back on the lower level, featuring Korean, Japanese and Italian outlets, plus an espresso bar and a *McDonald's*.

**Cascades**, *Hyatt Regency Maui*, 200 Nohea Kai Drive; ⓣ667-4420. Open-sided yet intimate resort restaurant, just off the *Hyatt*'s main lobby, with large ocean views. The Asian-influenced menu includes crab-cake sandwiches among the $10–15 lunchtime burgers, salads and pastas, while in the evening you can get sushi and sashimi platters for $17–34 as well as steaks, ribs and ginger chicken from $20. Daily 11.30am–2pm & 5.45–10pm.

**Hula Grill**, Whaler's Village; ⓣ667-6636. Large, long oceanfront restaurant, open to the sea breezes, featuring live, gentle Hawaiian music nightly. Chef Peter Merriman prepares some interesting appetizers, such as a Tahitian *poisson cru*, marinated in lime and coconut milk ($8), and plenty of dim sum and sashimi, but the entrees tend to be less imaginative, presumably to suit the family-dining atmosphere. The basic choice is fish or steak, for $20–25. Daily 11am–11pm.

**Rusty Harpoon**, Whaler's Village; ⓣ661-3123. Beachfront mall restaurant, with terrace and covered seating. Simple, inexpensive lunch menu with a few inventive touches, such as a $13 seafood curry casserole, and more traditional dinner entrees – steaks, ribs, fresh fish – for $20–30. A limited "Happy Hour" menu is served 2–6pm and 10.30pm–1am. Daily 8am–1.30am.

**Swan Court**, *Hyatt Regency Maui*, 200 Nohea Kai Drive; ⓣ667-4420. Romantic, enchanting resort restaurant, laid out around a lagoon populated by live swans, with tableside *hula* performances. The food is expensive but exquisite, with appetizers at around $15, including a seafood Napoleon made with papadum (an Indian crispbread), and entrees such as a distinctly un-Hawaiian pepper-seared bison, in a combo with basil-scented prawns for $36. Tues–Sat 6–10pm.

**Va Bene**, *Maui Marriott*, 100 Nohea Kai Drive; ⓣ667-1200. The *Marriott*'s principal dining room enjoys a gorgeous oceanfront setting, facing the beach across narrow lawns. Breakfasts are conventional enough, with a healthy $13 buffet and a cholesterol-packed $18 version, while for the rest of the day they serve fresh, zestful Italian dishes. At lunchtime, salads, pizzas and pastas cost around $10, and there's a great $12 oyster sandwich. Most pasta dishes are also $10 at dinner, but the full range of meat and seafood entrees cost $18–28. A $25 four-course Sunset Dinner is served nightly 5–6.30pm. Daily 6.30am–2pm & 5–10pm.

# North of Kāʻanapali: from Honokowai to Kapalua

If you found Kāʻanapali dull, just wait until you see the coastline further north. A mile or so out of Kāʻanapali, Lower Honoapiʻilani Road branches down towards the ocean from the main highway, to undulate its way through **Honokōwai**, **Kahana** and **Nāpili**.

None of these barely distinguishable, purpose-built communities holds an ounce of interest for casual visitors. They do have some great **beaches** – especially around Nāpili Bay – but you'll hardly get a glimpse of them unless you're staying at one of the innumerable identikit condo buildings that line the entire road. There are few shops or restaurants nearby, which is why the highway is always busy with traffic heading south to the hot spots of Lahaina and beyond.

**KAPALUA**, at the end of Lower Honoapi'ilani Road in Maui's far northwest corner, is the West Maui equivalent of the exclusive resort of Wailea, at the southwest tip of East Maui. Few ordinary tourists stray into this pristine enclave, whose two luxurious hotels were sited here mainly because of the proximity of **Kapalua Beach**. Previously known as Fleming Beach, it's a perfect little arc of white sand, set between two rocky headlands, which is one of Maui's safest and prettiest beaches, and good for snorkeling and diving.

## Kapalua Airport

Tiny **Kapalua Airport** – a short distance above Hwy-30, halfway between Kapalua and Kā'anapali – is too small to be served by anything other than commuter flights, principally Island Air service from Honolulu, and Pacific Wings connections with Honolulu, Kahului, and Lanai. For details of flight frequencies, see p.268. All the major car-rental chains have outlets at the airport – see p.25 – but there's no public transport.

## Accommodation

The condo properties along Lower Honoapi'ilani Road make reasonable cut-price alternatives to the Kā'anapali and Kapalua resort hotels, though if you don't rent a car you could feel very stuck indeed.

**Aston Ka'anapali Shores**, 3445 Lower Honoapi'ilani Rd, Lahaina HI 96761; ⓣ 667-2211, ⓕ 661-8036; reserve through Aston Hotels & Resorts, ⓣ 1-800/922-7866 (US & Can) or 1-800/321-2558 (HI), ⓦ www.kaanapalishores.com. Grand oceanfront condo development, right on the beach at the south end of Honokōwai, with a nice pool and air-conditioning throughout, and some large good-value family suites. Rooms ❺, suites ❻.

**Aston Paki Maui**, 3615 Lower Honoapi'ilani Rd, Lahaina HI 96761; ⓣ 669-8235; reserve through Aston Hotels & Resorts, ⓣ 1-800/922-7866 (US & Can) or 1-800/321-2558 (HI), ⓦ www.pakimaui.com. Long, low, curving building beside the sea but fronted by lawns rather than a beach, in the center of Kahana. Non-air-con apartments, ranging from studios to two-bedroom units, with kitchens and *lānais*. Rooms ❺, suites ❻.

**Aston at Papakea Resort**, 3543 Lower Honoapi'ilani Rd, Lahaina HI 96761; ⓣ 669-4848, ⓕ 665-0662; reserve through Aston Hotels & Resorts, ⓣ 1-800/922-7866 (US & Can) or 1-800/321-2558 (HI); ⓦ www.aston-hotels.com. Oceanfront Honokōwai complex of condo suites of all sizes, housed in eleven separate structures arranged around two matching gardens, each of which holds a pool, spa, lagoon and putting course. Garden-view rooms and suites ❺, ocean-view rooms ❻, suites ❼.

**Embassy Vacation Resort**, 104 Kā'anapali Shores Place, Lahaina HI 96761; ⓣ 661-2000 or 1-800-669-3155 (US & Can), ⓕ 667-5821; or reserve through Marc Resorts ⓣ 922-9700 or 1-800/535-0085 (US & Can), ⓦ www.marcresorts.com. Giant pink ziggurat at the south end of Honokōwai, right on the ocean just beyond Kā'anapali Beach, and complete with a one-acre pool, a 24ft waterslide and a 12th-floor rooftop miniature golf course reached by glass-walled elevators. All the one- and two-bedroom units have separate living rooms, shower and bath facilities, kitchenettes and all mod cons. ❽.

**Hale Maui**, 3711 Lower Honoapi'ilani Rd, Lahaina HI 96761; ⓣ 669-6312, ⓕ 669-1302, ⓦ www.maui.net/~halemaui. Small family-run "apartment hotel" in Honokōwai, offering one-bedroom suites that sleep up to five guests, with kitchens and *lānais*. ❸.

**Kahana Reef**, 4471 Lower Honoapi'ilani Rd,

Lahaina HI 96761; Ⓣ 669-6491 or 1-800/253-3773 (US & Can), Ⓕ 669-2192, Ⓦ www.mauicondo.com. Four-story row of well-furnished – if characterless – oceanfront non-air-con studios and one-bedroom units, all at relatively low rates. They're right next to the sea, though there's little beach here. Discounted car rental available. ❹.

**Kahana Sunset**, 4909 Lower Honoapi'ilani Rd, Lahaina HI 96761; Ⓣ 669-8011 or 1-800/669-1488, Ⓕ 669-9170, Ⓦ www.kahanasunset.com. Luxury condos, spacious inside but squeezed close together, in lush gardens by a lovely sandy beach. Only the larger two-bedroom units have ocean views. Garden view ❹, ocean view ❺.

**Kapalua Bay Hotel**, 1 Bay Drive, Lahaina HI 96761; Ⓣ 669-5656 or 1-800/325-3589 (US & Can), Ⓕ 669-4649, Ⓦ www.luxurycollection-hawaii.com. The older of Kapalua's two resorts still epitomizes luxury. Beautifully landscaped, it features an intimate white-sand beach, an irresistible pool, three championship-standard golf courses, and twenty tennis courts. All the rooms are huge and offer private *lānais*. Sixth night free. Garden view ❽, ocean view ❾.

**The Mauian**, 5441 Lower Honoapi'ilani Rd, Lahaina HI 96761; Ⓣ 669-6205 or 1-800/367-5034 (US & Can), Ⓕ 669-0129, Ⓦ www.mauian.com. Very friendly, old-fashioned little resort on ravishing, sandy little Napili Beach. Three two-story rows of tastefully furnished studio apartments with kitchenettes but no phones or TVs. Garden view ❹, ocean view ❺.

**Noelani**, 4095 Lower Honoapi'ilani Rd, Lahaina HI 96761; Ⓣ 669-8374 or 1-800/367-6030 (US & Can), Ⓕ 669-7904, Ⓦ www.noelani-condo-resort.com. Condo apartments of all sizes, set on a promontory, so all units enjoy views across to Molokai. Pluses include cable TV and VCR, plus use of pool, Jacuzzi, and laundry. ❹.

**Polynesian Shores**, 3975 Lower Honoapi'ilani Rd, Lahaina HI 96761; Ⓣ 669-6065, Ⓕ 669-0909. Friendly, fifty-room Kahana condo property, with shared pool, oceanfront lawns and good snorkeling. Units of all sizes, all with kitchens and *lānais*. ❹.

**Ritz-Carlton, Kapalua**, 1 Ritz-Carlton Drive, Lahaina HI 96761; Ⓣ 669-6200 or 1-800/262-8440, Ⓕ 665-0026, Ⓦ www.ritzcarlton.com. Modern, opulent, marble-fitted resort hotel that had to be relocated slightly back from the beach after its intended site turned out to be an ancient Hawaiian burial ground. The sheer elegance can make it feel a bit formal for Maui, but there's no disputing the level of comfort, with three swimming pools, a nine-hole putting green to complement the three nearby golf courses, a spa and a croquet lawn. ❽.

**Royal Kahana Resort**, 4365 Lower Honoapi'ilani Rd, Lahaina HI 96761; Ⓣ 669-5911 or 1-800/447-7783 (US & Can), Ⓕ 669-5950; reserve through Marc Resorts, Ⓣ 922-9700 or 1-800/535-0085 (US & Can), Ⓕ 922-2421, Ⓦ www.marcresorts.com. Twelve-story oceanfront condo building in central Kahana, with views of Molokai and Lanai. All the air-con units, which include studios as well as one- and two-bedroom suites, have kitchens, washer-dryers and private *lānais*. ❺.

## Restaurants

Considering its vast number of visitors, the Honokōwai to Kapalua stretch has traditionally been short of places to **eat**. That's starting to change, however, as clusters of restaurants appear in each of the three highway-side **malls**. The southernmost, the **Honokōwai Marketplace**, is home to *A Pacific Café* and some smaller snack places. Next comes the **Kahana Gateway**, which holds two *Roy's* and the *Fish&Game*, as well as an *Outback Steakhouse*, a *McDonald's* and an ice-cream parlor, while the **Nāpili Plaza** further on has *Maui Tacos* and the *Coffee Store,* an espresso bar that also offers internet access (daily 6.30am–6pm; Ⓣ 669-4170).

**Erik's Seafood Grotto**, 4242 Lower Honoapi'ilani Rd; Ⓣ 669-4806. Traditional continental fish dishes, served just across from the ocean on the lower highway, alongside the *Kahana Villas* condos. A full dinner, such as baked stuffed prawns or a seafood curry, costs around $20, a cioppino or bouillabaisse is more like $26, and you can also get sashimi or pick from the raw bar. Daily 5–10pm.

**Fish & Game Brewing Company & Rotisserie**, Kahana Gateway, 4405 Honoapi'ilani Hwy; Ⓣ 669-3474. Large mall complex, holding a pub serving pilsners, stouts and wheat beers brewed on the premises; an open restaurant area dominated by a *kiawe* grill, an oyster bar, and some more private dining rooms. The food is surprisingly good, with grilled ribs or chicken for under $20, a truly colossal steak for $24, and fresh fish prepared in various styles for $28. A lighter, limited menu is served 3–5.30pm & 10.30pm–2am. Daily 11am–2am.

**Java Jazz**, Honokōwai Marketplace, 3350 Lower Honoapi'ilani Rd; ☎ 667-0787. Trendy juice and espresso bar, with lots of comfy seating. Breakfast eggs and omelets go for $7–8; falafel and other lunchtime sandwiches are under $10; and assorted evening specials cost just a little more. Daily 6am–8pm.

**A Pacific Café**, Honokōwai Marketplace, 3350 Lower Honoapi'ilani Rd; ☎ 667-2800. This stylish "Hawaii Regional" joint is very much a classy resort restaurant, even if it is located between a supermarket and a main road rather than beside the ocean. The delicious stacked, seared and drizzled goodies that pour from its curving central "display kitchen" include appetizers such as sushi tempura for $13 or barbecue ribs for $7, and $20–30 entrees like wok-charred *mahimahi* and coffee-smoked pork chops. Daily 5.30–9.30pm.

**Roy's Kahana Bar & Grill**, Kahana Gateway, 4405 Honoapi'ilani Hwy; ☎ 669-6999. Celebrity chef Roy Yamaguchi's Maui showcase is open for dinner only – which is just as well, given its lack of views. The scents of its superb "Euro-Asian" food waft from its open kitchen as soon as you walk in. A set three-course dinner costs $34, or you can choose from a menu on which signature dishes such as hibachi salmon and "Roy's 'Original' Blackened Rare *Ahi*" appear both as appetizers (around $10) and entrees (more like $25). Daily 5.30–10pm.

**Roy's Nicolina Restaurant**, Kahana Gateway, 4405 Honoapi'ilani Hwy; ☎ 669-5000. Sister restaurant to the *Kahana Bar & Grill*; the two entrances face each other atop the staircase in this small mall and, although each has its own kitchen, *Nicolina*'s Pacific Rim menu is all but identical to that of its senior neighbor. Appetizers include "butterfish" (black cod) steamed with *miso*, and seared sea scallops at $8–11; entrees like herb-rubbed rack of lamb with baby bok choy cost $20–30. Daily 5.30–9.30pm.

**Sansei Seafood Restaurant**, The Shops at Kapalua, 115 Bay Drive, Kapalua; ☎ 669-6286. Top-quality, dinner-only seafood specialist, adjoining the *Kapalua Bay Hotel*. Both decor and menu are fundamentally Japanese, though there's a strong Pacific Rim element as well. The fresh sushi selection includes a wonderful mango crab salad roll at $8, while among the entrees are seared salmon and seafood pasta at $20, and daily fish specials at around $25. Certain items, like the $5 crispy fried *onaga* (snapper) head and the Korean-spiced raw octopus, are labeled "for locals only." There's also karaoke until 2am on Thursday and Friday nights. Mon–Wed, Sat & Sun 5.30–11pm, Thurs & Fri 5.30pm–2am.

## Beaches beyond Kapalua

Honoapi'ilani Highway sweeps down beyond Kapalua to rejoin the ocean at **DT Fleming Beach Park**, in Honokahua Bay. The dunes here, knitted together with ironwood trees, drop sharply into the sea, and swimming can be dangerous – though surfers love the big waves.

From here, the highway climbs again to cross a rocky headland. You can't see it from the road, but **Mokulē'ia Bay** lies at the foot of the cliffs. The landowners, Maui Pineapple, have recently erected fences along the highway at this point, in an attempt to preclude access to shaded, sandy **Slaughterhouse Beach**. If it is still possible to reach it, you should see cars parked on the verge, next to breaks in the vegetation that mark the start of steep footpaths down. Winter conditions usually preclude bathing, but the nude sunbathing carries on year-round.

Both Mokulē'ia Bay and **Honolua Bay**, just past the point, have been set aside as a Marine Life Conservation District, and in summer offer some of the island's best **snorkeling**. Honolua's major claim to fame, however, is as Maui's most famous **surfing** spot. Between September and April, the waters regularly swarm with surfers. As long as the swell remains below five feet, intermediate surfers can enjoy some of the longest-lasting and most predictable waves in all Hawaii. By the time they exceed ten feet, however, only absolute experts can hope to survive, with perils including not only a fearsome cave that seems to suck in every passing stray, but cut-throat competition from other surfers. Parking for surfers is at several ad hoc lots along the rough dirt roads that line the pineapple fields covering the headland on the far side of the bay. Large galleries of spectators assemble on the clifftop to watch the action, while the surfers themselves slither down to the ocean by means of treacherous trails.

To reach the **beach** at Honolua, park instead beside the road at the inland end of the bay and walk down. The access path is the width of a road, but the surface is terrible and driving on it is illegal. It leads through a weird, lush forest with the feel of a Louisiana bayou; every tree, and even the barbed-wire fence, has been throttled by creeping vines. Across a (usually dry) stream bed lies the neat, rocky curve of the beach itself, with the eastern end of Molokai framed in the mouth of the bay. This was the departure point of the *Hōkūle'a* canoe, on its first epic voyage to Tahiti in 1976 (see p.522).

Honoapi'ilani Highway runs past one final beach, at **Honokōhau Bay**. You're still only five miles out of Kapalua here, but it feels like another world. The entire valley is swamped by a dense canopy of flowering trees; there's a hidden village in there, but it's hard to spot a single building. The beach itself is a small crescent of gray pebbles, used only by fishermen.

**HONOKŌWAI TO KAPALUA**

| RESTAURANTS | |
|---|---|
| Erik's Seafood Grotto | C |
| Fish & Game Brewing Co. | B |
| Java Jazz | D |
| A Pacific Cafe | D |
| Sansei Seafood Restaurant | A |
| Roy's Kahana Bar & Grill | B |
| Roy's Nicolina | B |

| ACCOMMODATION | |
|---|---|
| Aston Kā'anapali Shores | 12 |
| Aston Paki Maui | 10 |
| Aston at Papakea Resort | 11 |
| Embassy Vacation Resort | 13 |
| Hale Maui | 9 |
| Kapalua Bay Hotel | 2 |
| Kahana Sunset | 4 |
| Kahana Reef | 5 |
| The Mauian | 3 |
| Noelani | 7 |
| Polynesian Shores | 8 |
| Ritz-Carlton Kapalua | 1 |
| Royal Kahana Resort | 6 |

# Kahekili Highway

The warnings of the rental-car companies concerning the **Kahekili Highway**, which looks on the map like a good route to continue around northwest Maui and back to Wailuku, should be taken very seriously: it's an exceptionally dangerous drive. What's more, it's certainly not a shortcut; Wailuku is little more than twenty miles beyond Honokōhau Valley, but you have to allow well over an hour for the journey.

While not quite on a par with the road to Hāna – see p.339 – the Kahekili Highway can be exhilaratingly beautiful, and it provides a rare glimpse of how Maui must have looked before the advent of tourism. Often very narrow, but always smoothly surfaced, it winds endlessly along the extravagantly indented coastline, alternating between scrubby exposed promontories, occasionally capable of supporting a pale meadow, and densely green, wet valleys.

## Nākālele Point

Kahekili Highway begins at Maui's northernmost limit, **Nākālele Point**, 6.5 miles out of Kapalua, at milepost 38. This rolling expanse of bare, grassy heathland fell victim a few years ago to a bizarre craze that swept most of Hawaii. In remote spots all over the islands, people suddenly started erecting miniature stone cairns, possibly under the impression that they were maintaining an ancient tradition. Stacks of perhaps a dozen small rocks are dotted all over the landscape, and many visitors have also used pebbles to spell out their names or other messages – much to the displeasure of Maui Pineapple, which still owns the land.

Various deeply rutted dirt roads drop away from the highway towards the sea in this area, starting both from the parking lot at milepost 38 and from another more makeshift lot half a mile further on. Hiking in that direction enables you to inspect the small **light beacon** that warns passing ships of the rocky headland, and an impressive natural **blowhole** in the oceanfront shelf.

## Kahakuloa

A few miles after Nākālele Point, the huge and very un-Hawaiian crag of **Kahakuloa Head** towers 636 feet above the eastern entrance to Kahakuloa Bay. The succulent valley behind it once ranked among the most populous on Maui and still looks like a classic *ahupua'a* – the fundamental ancient land division, reaching from the sea to the mountain via low-lying *taro* terraces and groves of fruit trees.

The perfect little village of **KAHAKULOA** ("tall lord," after the nearby crag) stands just behind its beach of black and gray boulders and is centered on the St Francis Xavier Mission, built in 1846. The stream bed is lined with trees, while dirt roads crisscross the valley between the fields and the ramshackle houses.

## Waihe'e Ridge Trail

One of Maui's most enjoyable hikes, the **Waihe'e Ridge Trail**, starts a mile up a spur road that branches inland from Kahekili Highway roughly seven miles south of Kahakuloa. Signposted to *Camp Maluhia*, a scout camp, the dirt road is 2.8 miles north of the village school in **Waihe'e**, which is the logical way to come if you're driving from central or south Maui.

This gorgeous climb, best done in the morning before the clouds set in, takes you as deep into the West Maui mountains as it's possible to go; allow at least two hours for the round trip. Follow the road until it makes a sharp curve towards the camp itself, and park in the field alongside. The trail starts off as a very clear cement path beyond a barred gate, heading straight up the hill through a field of cows. Having skirted the minor hill on the left by taking a right fork at the top, you find yourself in a pine and eucalyptus forest. You emerge to views down into Waihe'e Valley, over to a double waterfall embedded in the next ridge to the north, and back across the isthmus to Haleakalā Highway snaking up the volcano.

For the first 1.5 miles, it looks as if you're heading for the crest of the ridge ahead, but the path ultimately sidesteps across a brief razorback to reach an unexpected high mountain valley. The terrain here is extremely marshy, but you're soon climbing again, and the trail ends at an unsheltered picnic table in a clearing 2.25 miles up. In principle, you can see most of northern Maui from this spot, which is the summit of Lanilili ("Small Heaven") Peak, but you'll almost certainly find that, by now, you're well above the cloud line.

### Waihe'e Valley

Beyond Waihe'e Ridge, the road drops steadily down to Waihe'e, by which time you're clearly out of the backwoods. The traffic picks up again, and the highway broadens for the final four miles to Wailuku.

It is, however, possible to drive half a mile inland from Waihe'e on Waihe'e Valley Road, and then take a two-hour hike up into the rainforest of **Waihe'e Valley** itself. Recent disputes over public access have resulted in the trail falling into disrepair, however, and locals are not keen on hikers leaving their vehicles on or near their properly. If you're determined to try, park as close as seems wise to the T-junction at the end of the road, and head left on a dirt road that soon deteriorates to a rutted track. After almost a mile of walking past dense ferns, banyans and fruit trees, you have to cross Waihe'e Stream twice in quick succession. If it's raining, or looks likely to start, turn back; flash floods render conditions extremely dangerous. Should you make it all the way, you'll be rewarded by a cool, deep swimming hole, below a small dam two miles from the start.

# Central Maui: the isthmus

The flat plains of **central Maui** were formed when eroded rock washed down the slopes of the island's two volcanoes and fused them together. In ancient times, only **Wailuku**, on the western fringes, held much of a population. From a royal enclosure at the mouth of the stunning **'Īao Valley**, its chiefs ruled a region known as Nā Wai 'Ēha, watered by four rivers that flowed down from the West Maui mountains.

The rest of the isthmus was described by the nineteenth-century British traveler Isabella Bird as "a Sahara in miniature, a dreary expanse of sand and shifting sandhills, with a dismal growth of thornless thistles and indigo." Only since the sugar barons created irrigation channels to carry water from the eastern flanks of Haleakalā has the land been capable of supporting the agriculture that now makes it so green. As a result, Wailuku and its upstart neighbor **Kahului** are now home to around half of Maui's 120,000 inhabitants – the workers who keep this fantasy island going.

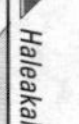

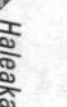
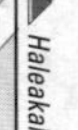
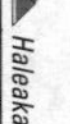
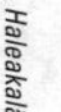
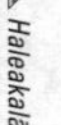
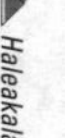
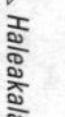
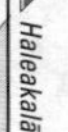
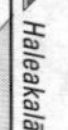
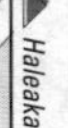

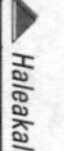
KAHULUI AND WAILUKU
Waiehu
Haleakalā
'Iao Valley
Lahaina
Kīhei
Kahului Bay
Kanaha Beach County Park
Kahului Harbor
Kanaha Pond State Wildlife Sanctuary
Kahului Airport
Terminal
Maui Arts & Cultural Center
Maui Mall Shopping Center
Kahului Shopping Center
Ka'ahumanu Mall
Maui Marketplace
Pu'unēnē Sugar Mill
Haleki'i Heiau
Pihana Heiau
'Īao Stream
WAILUKU
KAHULUI
See 'Downtown Wailuku' map for detail
WAIEHU BEACH ROAD
KU HIO PLACE
KIKANIA ST
KAHULUI BEACH ROAD
EAST LOWER MAIN STREET
KANALOA AVENUE
KA'AHUMANU AVENUE
WEST MAIN STREET
KAHEKILI HWY
HONOAPI'ILANI HIGHWAY
AMALA PLACE
ALAHAO STREET
KA'A ST
HOBRON AVE
KEOLANI PLACE
'A'ALELE ST
HALEAKALĀ HIGHWAY
HĀNA HIGHWAY
ALAMAHA STREET
HUKILIKE STREET
DAIRY ROAD
PŪLEHU ROAD
HANSEN ROAD
SOUTH PU'UNĒNĒ AVENUE
KŪ'IHELANI HIGHWAY
WEST PAPA AVENUE
SOUTH PAPA AVENUE
LONO AVENUE
KAMEHAMEHA AVENUE
ONEHEE AVENUE
SOUTH WAKEA AVENUE
340
32
30
350
380
36
37
N
0 Yards 500
HOTELS
Maui Beach Hotel 1
Maui Seaside Hotel 2
RESTAURANTS
Ichiban The Restaurant A
Kaka'ako Kitchen D
Marco's Grill & Deli C
Maui Coffee Roasters B
Pizza in Paradise E

# Kahului

Although **KAHULUI** is the largest town on Maui – it holds the island's principal harbor and airport, and most of its major shopping centers – it's not an interesting, let alone historic, place to visit. A handful of inexpensive hotels stake a claim for Kahului as a convenient central base, but there's next to nothing to see here, and you could miss it altogether with a clear conscience.

Having started the nineteenth century as a small cluster of grass shacks, Kahului grew in tandem with the expansion of commercial agriculture. After the Kahului and Wailuku Railroad opened in 1879, it channeled the sugar and pineapple crops of central Maui down to the wharves of Kahului. At first Kahului was an insanitary place: a major outbreak of plague in 1900 forced the authorities to burn down the oceanfront Chinatown district and ring the whole town with ratproof fences. When it was rebuilt, the harbor was greatly expanded and dredged to provide the only deep-water anchorage on the island.

Kahului thereafter supplanted Lahaina as Maui's main port and has remained so into the twenty-first century. It was further boosted after World War II, when newly built, low-cost housing in "Dream City" lured laborers away from plantation towns such as Pā'ia with the promise of owning their own homes.

Central Kahului is dominated by a characterless sprawl of aging shopping malls along **Ka'ahumanu Avenue**. Only the **Ka'ahumanu Mall** itself is worth visiting, for its standard array of generic upmarket stores and a few more distinctive crafts outlets. It also holds one or two decent restaurants – see p.303 – while its second-floor food court offers distant views of Kahului Bay. There's no point trying to get any closer to the **waterfront**, which is lined with factories and warehouses.

Kahului's newest shopping mall, the **Maui Marketplace** on Dairy Road, is noteworthy as the home of the island's best **bookstore** – a giant Borders (Mon–Thurs 9am–11pm, Fri & Sat 9am–midnight, Sun 9am–10pm; ⓣ877-6160).

## Arrival and information

The majority of visitors to Maui arrive at **Kahului Airport**, a couple of miles east of town. See p.11 onwards for details of trans-Pacific flights that use the airport; inter-island services to Maui are summarized on p.17. The main lobby area is surprisingly small, though it does hold a **Hawaii Visitors Bureau information booth** that's open to greet all flights. For a snack or a drink, you have to pass through the security checks and head for the departure gates.

All the national **rental-car** chains (see p.25) have offices immediately across from the terminal. In addition, Speedishuttle (ⓣ875-8070) and Airport Shuttle (ⓣ661-6667) run shuttle vans on demand to all destinations, charging about $20 to Kīhei, $32 to Lahaina and $45 to Nāpili. Both the Maui Airporter Shuttle (ⓣ877-7308 or 1-800/259-2627) and TransHawaiian (ⓣ877-0380 or 1-800/231-6984) run regular scheduled **buses** to Kā'anapali by way of Lahaina, for $13 one way or $19 round-trip.

Kahului's **post office** is on Pu'unēnē Avenue (Mon–Fri 8.30am–5pm, Sat 8.30am–noon; zip code HI 96732).

## Accommodation

If you plan to spend most of your time on Maui touring the island or windsurfing at Ho'okipa just down the coast (see p.338), Kahului's pair of aging hotels may suit your needs. Although both are right in the center of town, Kahului is not a place you'd choose to stroll around and doesn't make a lively overnight stop.

**Maui Beach Hotel**, 170 W Ka'ahumanu Ave, Kahului, HI 96732; ⓣ 877-0051, ⓕ 871-5797; or reserve through Castle Resorts, ⓣ 591-2235, 1-800/367-5004 (US & Can) or 1-800/272-5275 (HI), ⓦ www.castleresorts.com. Somewhat faded seafront hotel in the heart of Kahului, offering 150 rundown but bearable rooms. Available through the same lobby are cheaper, even less appealing rooms in the unattractive *Maui Palms* next door, which opened in 1954 and is now only partly operational. Daily Asian buffets are offered by both *Maui Beach*'s *Rainbow Dining Room* and the *Red Dragon* restaurant; the latter also has live entertainment and dancing nightly. Both hotels offer free sixth night or rental car. ❸/❹.

**Maui Seaside Hotel**, 100 W Ka'ahumanu Ave, Kahului, HI 96732; ⓣ 877-3311 or 1-800/560-5552 (US & Can), ⓕ 877-4618, ⓦ www.mauiseasidehotel.com. Good-value waterfront hotel, facing the harbor in central Kahului. Rooms are cheaper in the older of its two wings, but the whole place has been modernized, with a swimming pool and its own artificial beach. The location, across from the shopping malls, is hardly romantic, but at least it is by the sea, and the *Seaside* makes a convenient and relatively inexpensive base. ❹.

## Maui Arts and Cultural Center

Just off the busy Kahului Beach Road, which curves around Kahului Harbor, the **Maui Arts and Cultural Center** (ⓣ 242-ARTS, box office ⓣ 242-7469, ⓦ www.mauiarts.org) opened in 1994 as Maui's most important venue for the visual and performing arts. In addition to a 4000-seat open-air amphitheater, it houses two separate indoor theaters and an art gallery that hosts changing temporary exhibitions. Those big-name musicians who make it as far as Maui – more than you might expect, as it's a favorite final stop for trans-America touring bands – play here, and the Maui Symphony Orchestra (ⓣ 244-5439) puts on half a dozen concerts each winter.

## Kanahā Pond State Wildlife Sanctuary

Half a mile west of Kahului Airport, just before Hwy-36A meets Hwy-36, a tiny roadside parking lot marks the only public access to the **Kanahā Pond State Wildlife Sanctuary**. This marshy saltwater lagoon – used as a fishpond until it was choked by the mud dredged up from Kahului Harbor – is now set aside for the protection of endangered bird species such as the black-necked *ae'o* stilt and the *'auku'u* (night heron).

There are no official opening hours; visitors simply make their way through the gate and follow a pedestrian causeway for fifty yards out to a windy, open-sided viewing shelter. It's not a very prepossessing spot; the factories of Kahului Harbor are clearly visible off to the left, while the waters are tinged an unsavory green, with a layer of scum swelling around the edges. Nonetheless, the sanctuary lives up to its title, and you're almost certain to see plenty of wading birds picking their way through the mire.

## Kanahā Beach County Park

Amala Place runs due east of central Kahului through an industrial area behind Kanahā Pond. Even before it joins Alahao Street on the ocean side of the airport, there are plenty of places where you can park beside the road and walk through the trees to find a long strip of empty beach.

However, the most popular oceanfront spot is the large **Kanahā Beach County Park** which, despite its proximity to the runways, is completely undisturbed by all the comings and goings and feels comfortably far from Kahului. Its shallow, choppy turquoise waters are ideal for novice **windsurfers**, who come from all over the world to swirl back and forth against the backdrop of ʻĪao Valley and the West Maui mountains. Among companies offering windsurfing lessons here (at around $65 for two-and-a-half hours, including equipment rental) are Action Sports Maui (Ⓣ871-5857, Ⓦwww.actionsportsmaui.com), and Alan Cadiz's HST Windsurfing School (Ⓣ871-5423, Ⓦwww.hstwindsurfing.com). Windsurfers ready for the big time graduate to **Hoʻokipa**, just a few miles east but light-years away in terms of difficulty; see p.338.

For its full length, the beach is fringed by pine trees, with countless shoots sprouting from the dunes, and fallen needles creating a soft forest floor just behind. The lawns under the trees have picnic tables, though to buy food or drink you have to drive back into Kahului.

In principle, good facilities make this one of the best **campgrounds** on Maui. There are seven individual sites, each available for $5 per night, with a three-night maximum stay. As this book went to press, however, the campground was closed, supposedly temporarily, due to health and sanitation concerns; call the county parks office (see p.271) for the latest information.



## Alexander & Baldwin Sugar Museum

There's no missing the rusty red hulk of the **Puʻunēnē Sugar Mill**, which forces Hwy-350 to make a sharp right turn a mile south of Kahului. Still belching smoke as it consumes the cane from the surrounding fields, this was the largest sugar mill in the world when it was built in 1902. Only two such mills are still operational in the state of Hawaii; the other is on Kauai. Easily overlooked, however, is the smaller building just across from the mill, at the intersection with the minor Hansen Road, which houses the **Alexander & Baldwin Sugar Museum** (Mon–Sat 9.30am–4.30pm; adults $4, under-18s $2).

The museum relates the history of sugar production on Maui, a tale of nineteenth-century scheming and skulduggery that, a century later, may not be capable of holding your interest for very long. Alexander & Baldwin was one of the original "Big Five" companies at the heart of the Hawaiian economy – see p.513 – and remains a prominent island name to this day. **Samuel T. Alexander** (1836–1904) and **Henry Baldwin** (1842–1911) started growing sugar at Pāʻia in 1869 and were responsible for constructing the first irrigation channel in 1878 to carry water from East Maui to the central isthmus. Their great rival was **Claus Spreckels** (1828–1908), who used his royal connections (he underwrote King Kalākaua's gambling debts) to acquire land and water rights at "Spreckelsville" near Pāʻia and all but controlled the Hawaiian sugar industry before losing favor with the King and being forced to return to California. Alexander and Baldwin were then free to expand their operations across Maui, centered on the processing facilities at Puʻunēnē.

Scale models in the museum include a typical plantation house, a whirring but incomprehensible re-creation of the main mill machinery, and a relief map of the whole island. More illuminating displays focus on the daily lives of the plantation laborers, showing the thick clothes they wore to work, despite the heat, as protection against the dust and poisonous centipedes, and the numbered *bango* tags by which they were identified in place of names. No bones are made of the fact that the multi-ethnic workforce was deliberately, but ultimately unsuccessfully, segregated to avoid solidarity. The museum store is well stocked with books on ethnic and labor history, as well as souvenir packets of raw sugar.

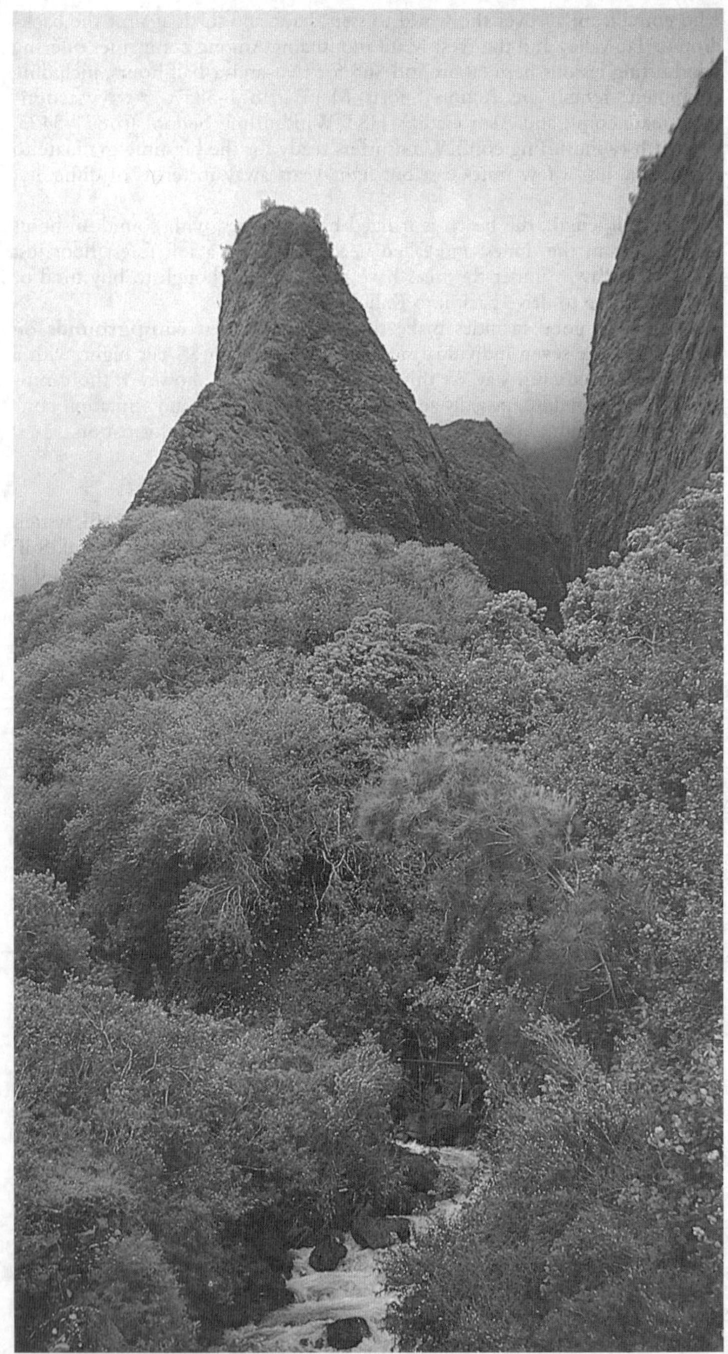

## Restaurants

Kahului is disappointingly short of **restaurants**, and few people would choose to drive here from elsewhere on Maui in search of a good meal. There are, however, a few alternatives scattered around the town's lesser malls, while the breezy **Queen's Market** area, upstairs at the front of the **Ka'ahumanu Center**, holds a wide assortment of fast-food counters. As well as a few juice and coffee bars, these include the Japanese *Edo*, the Chinese *Panda Express*, and the Greek *Athens*, plus *Yummy Korean B-B-Q* and *McDonald's*. There's also a *Starbucks* (Mon–Thurs 6am–10pm, Fri & Sat 6am–11pm, Sun 6.30am–9pm), but not much else, at the Maui Marketplace.

**Ichiban The Restaurant**, Kahului Shopping Center, 47 Ka'ahumanu Ave; ⓣ 871-6977. Large, old mall eatery, which serves American and continental breakfasts, then devotes itself to Japanese cuisine. For lunch there's *saimin* for $5, *donburi* bowls for $6, and teriyakis for $6–8; at dinner you can get shrimp or chicken stir-fries, *udon* noodles and sushi rolls for under $10. Mon–Fri 6.30am–2pm & 5–9pm, Sat 10.30am–2pm & 5–9pm.

**Kaka'ako Kitchen**, Ka'ahumanu Center, Ka'ahumanu Ave; ⓣ 893-0366. High-quality Hawaiian-style fast-food diner, run by Honolulu restaurateur Russell Siu, at the front of the Ka'ahumanu Center mall. Takeout and eat-in orders alike are placed at the counter. Lunch and dinner prices are the same, with pretty much everything, from hamburger stew to chicken linguine costing $6–9. There's a roster of daily $7.25 specials such as pot roast or seafood marinara, always with a vegetarian alternative. Mon–Fri 8–10am & 11am–9pm, Sat & Sun 8am–9pm.

**Marco's Grill & Deli**, 444 Hāna Hwy; ⓣ 877-4446. Large, lively Italian restaurant, in a modern mall not far from the airport. Once the breakfast omelets, pancakes and espressos have finished, the lunch and dinner menus feature deli sandwiches, pizzas from $10, and rich meat and seafood pastas, including rigatoni with prosciutto in a vodka sauce for $16. Daily 7.30am–10pm.

**Maui Coffee Roasters**, 444 Hāna Hwy; ⓣ 877-2877. This relaxed espresso bar with hand-painted tables is a popular hangout for windsurfers from the nearby beaches. Vegetarian wraps and sandwiches, like focaccia with mozzarella, are $6–7; try the fabulous raspberry-and-white-chocolate scones. Mon–Fri 7am–6pm, Sat 8am–5pm, Sun 8am–2.30pm.

**Pizza in Paradise**, 60 E Wakea Ave; ⓣ 871-8188. Dependable, inexpensive, but not exceptional pizzas, baked up in a warehouse-style, back-street setting. Industrial-sized 18-inch pizzas, with the usual toppings, cost from $10, and there are daily $5 lunch specials. Sun–Thurs 11am–9pm, Fri & Sat 11am–10pm.

# Wailuku

The center of **WAILUKU** is barely two miles west of Kahului, and there's no gap in the development along Ka'ahumanu Avenue to mark where one town ends and the other begins. However Wailuku, located as it is at the mouth of the fertile and spectacular 'Īao Valley and within a few miles of the lush valleys that line the windward coast of West Maui, has a very different geography and a much more venerable history. This was what might be called the *poi* bowl of Maui, at the heart of the largest *taro*-growing area in Hawaii, and was home to generations of ancient priests and warriors.

Well into the twentieth century, Wailuku was the center of the island's nascent tourist industry, housing the few visitors Maui received and equipping their expeditions up Haleakalā. Much of its administrative and commercial role was then usurped by Kahului, and Wailuku went into something of a decline. These days, with the construction of various new county offices and even a few stores, Wailuku appears to be on the way back, but it remains a sleepy sort of place, easily seen in less than half a day. Nonetheless, it's one of the few towns on Maui that still feels like a genuine community and can serve as a welcome antidote to the sanitized charms of the modern resorts.

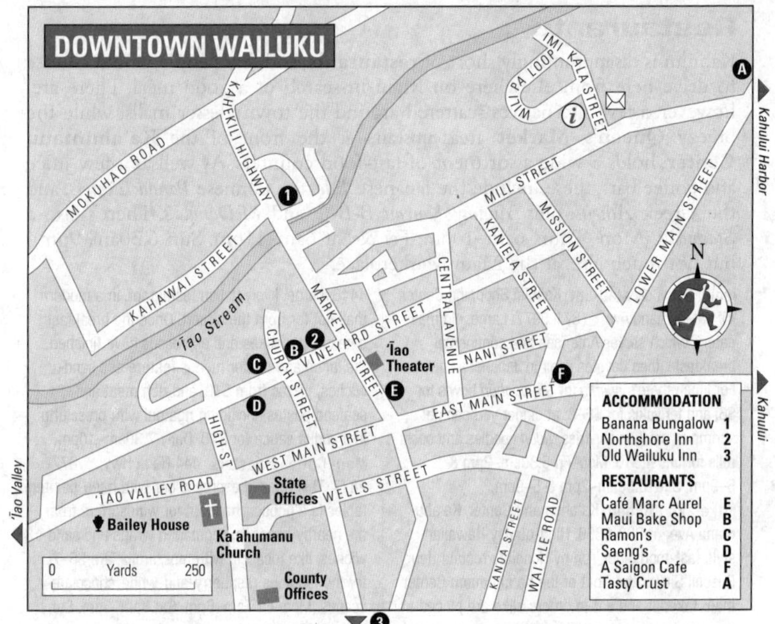




## Information

You can't help suspecting that the main Maui office of the **Hawaii Visitors Bureau** (Mon–Fri 8am–4.30pm; ⓣ244-3530 or 1-800/525-MAUI) was tucked away at 1727 Wili Pa Loop to deter casual visitors. If you do find your way there – it's in a modern development off Mill Street, half a mile northeast of central Wailuku – they can provide lots of printed material on all of Maui County, which also includes the islands of Molokai and Lanai. Wailuku's **post office** is nearby at 250 Imi Kala St (Mon–Fri 8.30am–5pm, Sat 9am–4pm; zip code HI 96793).

**Camping permits** for Maui's state parks are available from the Department of Land and Natural Resources, opposite Ka'ahumanu Church at 54 S High St (Mon–Fri 8am–noon & 1–4pm; ⓣ984-8109), while the county parks office is at Baldwin High School, just east of central Wailuku at 1580 Ka'ahumanu Ave (Mon–Fri 8am–4pm; ⓣ243-7389). For more details of camping on Maui, see p.271.

## Accommodation

As Wailuku has Maui's only **hostels** – and no hotels– the only people who spend the night here tend to be backpackers and surfers. A drawback for budget travelers is that the nearest beaches are several miles away, but the *Banana Bungalow* runs inexpensive mini-van trips.

Note that while a couple of other places on Vineyard Street often rent out hostel-style rooms, neither is recommended.

**Banana Bungalow**, 310 N Market St, Wailuku, HI 96793; ⓣ244-5090 or 1-800/846-7835, ⓕ244-3678, ⓔbungalow@gte.net, ⓦhttp://home1.gte.net/bungalow.htm. Friendly unofficial hostel, open to non-Hawaiian residents only, in unattractive area not far from central Wailuku. Beds in two- and three-bed dorms ($16), and basic private rooms from $29. Guests hang out in the gardens and living rooms. Free shuttles to the airport and to Kanahā beach, plus a changing daily rotation of free excursions to all parts of the island. The hostel also offers free internet access and a free Jacuzzi. ❶.

**Northshore Inn**, 2080 Vineyard St, Wailuku, HI 96793; ⓣ242-1448 or 1-866/946-7835, ⓦwww.hawaii-hostel.com. Budget accommodation in downtown Wailuku. Beds in plain, four- and six-bed dorms for $16, plus equally plain private rooms – each holds just a bed or two bunks, and a closet – for just under $40. Popular with European travelers, who leave their surfboards propped against the giant banyan in the courtyard. Seventh night free. Kitchen facilities and cheap car, moped and surfboard rental, but no free shuttles. ❶.

**Old Wailuku Inn at Ulupono**, 2199 Kaho'okele St, Wailuku, HI 96793; ⓣ244-5897 or 1-800/305-4899, ⓦwww.mauiinn.com. Spacious plantation-style home, set in landscaped gardens a short walk south of central Wailuku, that's been converted into a luxurious seven-room B&B. All rooms have private *lānais* and baths and are equipped with VCRs; some also have whirlpool spas. Guest share use of a living room and verandah. ❹–❺.

## Central Wailuku

The heart of Wailuku is where **Main Street**, the continuation of Ka'ahumanu Avenue, crosses **Market Street**. Both streets hold a small assortment of shops, the most interesting of which are the fading **antique** and **junk stores** along Market Street to the north, just before it drops down to cross the 'Īao Stream. Also look for the 1929 **'Īao Theater**, an attractive little playhouse on Market Street that puts on six shows each year (season runs Sept–June; ⓣ242-6969).

**Ka'ahumanu Church**, at the intersection of Main and High streets just west of the center, was founded in 1832. Naming it after Queen Ka'ahumanu, a convert to Christianity who was largely responsible for the destruction of the old Hawaiian religion (see p.348), was the idea of the Queen herself. The current building, whose four-story white spire has a clock face on each side, dates from 1876. It's not usually open to visitors, but you're welcome to attend the Hawaiian-language services at 9am on Sunday mornings.

## Bailey House

The **Bailey House**, to the left of Main Street as it starts to climb west out of Wailuku as 'Īao Valley Road, is the best **museum of general history** on Maui (Mon–Sat 10am–4pm; adults $5, under-13s $1; ⓣ244-3326). It sits on what was once the most highly prized plot of land on the island: the site of a royal compound that controlled access to the sacred 'Īao Valley. Local chiefs donated it during the 1830s so the Central Maui Mission could build day schools to teach both adults and children to read. From 1837 until 1849, it was also the site of the **Wailuku Female Seminary**, a boarding school designed to produce "good Christian wives" for the male graduates of the Lahainaluna Seminary (see p.283).

The first occupant of the house was Reverend Jonathan Green, who resigned from the mission in 1842 to protest the fact that the American Board of Commissioners for Foreign Missions accepted money from slave-owners. For the next fifty years, it was home to Edward Bailey and his wife Caroline Hubbard Bailey. He was a minister, schoolmaster, carpenter and amateur painter, while she is remembered in the name of the long "Mother Hubbard" dresses, also known as *mu'umu'us*, that she made for local women.

After an entertaining introductory talk, visitors can wander through rooms filled with period furniture, none of which originally belonged here. The largest room focuses on ancient Hawaiian history, with archeological finds from Maui, Lanai and Kahoolawe, including bones, clubs, shark's-tooth weapons, and *leis* of shells and feathers. One large wooden platter was used for serving boiled dog – a popular dish for women, who were forbidden to eat pork. There's also a copy of the only carved temple image ever found on Maui, an image of the pig-god Kamapua'a discovered in a remote sea cave. As the label points out, both the Baileys and the ancient Hawaiians alike would be appalled to see it on public display. On the wall there's a portrait of the unruly chief Boki, who sailed to the South Seas in 1829 in search of sandalwood to replace Hawaii's vanished crop and died in an explosion at sea (see p.511).

A separate gallery downstairs is reserved for local landscapes painted by the white-bearded Edward Bailey in his old age, while the upstairs rooms are preserved more or less as the Baileys would have known them, though presumably they'd disavow the opium pipe and paraphernalia displayed at one point. A very solid wooden surfboard that once belonged to Duke Kahanamoku (see p.73) hangs outside the restrooms in the garden.



## Haleki'i and Pihana heiaus

A mile from central Wailuku – but over three miles by road – the twin ancient temples of **Haleki'i** and **Pihana** guard the Wailuku Plain from two separate hillocks near the mouth of the 'Īao Stream (both open daily 7am–7pm; free). They can only be reached via a very convoluted route; follow Hwy-333 all the way out of Wailuku to the north, double back south along Waiehu Beach Road, turn inland at Kūhiō Place, and take the first left, Hea Place.

With rows of low-budget housing to the north, and the industrial area of Kahului to the south, this is not the most evocative of sites; but raising your gaze towards the horizon provides fine views of the ocean and the turquoise waters of the **harbor** and, in the early morning, mighty Haleakalā can often be seen in its entirety. The short trail from the parking lot leads through scrubby soil – these hillocks are, in fact, lithified sand dunes – to **Haleki'i Heiau**. Maui's ruling chief, Kahekili, lived at this "house of images" during religious ceremonies in the 1760s, when its uppermost platform would have held thatched huts interspersed with carved effigies of the gods. The hilltop is now bare, with the lower stone terraces of the *heiau* dropping down the side towards Kahului.

Both Haleki'i and **Pihana Heiau**, on the far side of the gulch to the west, were *luakinis*, or temples dedicated to the war god Kū that were the site of human sacrifice. Pihana seems to have been originally constructed between 1260 and 1400 AD, and reoriented to face towards the Big Island during the eighteenth century, presumably at a time when the chiefs of Maui were preparing an attack. When Kamehameha the Great's Big Island warriors finally conquered Maui, they celebrated their victory at 'Īao Valley (see p.307) with a rededication ceremony at Pihana, one of many held here over the centuries.

## Maui Tropical Plantation

The **Maui Tropical Plantation**, two miles south of Wailuku below the entrance to Waikapū Valley, may be a principal stop on round-island bus tours, but it's of minimal interest (daily 9am–5pm; free). Visitors are free to walk into the main "Marketplace," where the stalls are piled with plants, fruits and souvenirs, and then pass into the lackluster gardens beyond to explore pavilions describing the cultivation of macadamia nuts, sugar, coffee and other local crops. You can see a few more unusual plants on forty-minute tram tours (daily 10am–4pm, every 45min; $9.50), while the nursery near the entrance sells and ships spectacular orchids.

The indoor *Tropical Restaurant* (daily 9am–3pm) serves unremarkable $14.50 buffet lunches between 11am and 2pm (expect long lines), and sandwiches and salads the rest of the day.

## Restaurants

Wailuku may not have any particularly outstanding **restaurants**, but budget travelers can choose from a wide assortment of inexpensive options. Most are downtown, with the rest strung along Lower Main Street as it loops down towards Kahului Harbor – too far to walk from the center.

**Café Marc Aurel**, 28 N Market St; ⓣ244-0852. Smart little sidewalk espresso café, serving coffees and pastries and providing internet access. Daily 7am–8pm.

**Maui Bake Shop & Deli**, 2092 Vineyard St; ⓣ244-7117. Healthy deli breakfasts and lunches, served close to the *Northshore Inn*. A wide assortment of soups, salads and quiches as well as wonderful fresh-baked breads, including focaccias, calzones, whole-grain loaves, and sweet brioches. You can eat well for $5 or less. Mon–Fri 6am–4pm, Sat 7am–2pm.

**Ramon's**, 2102 Vineyard St; ⓣ244-7243. Central, down-home diner where the menu ranges from local to Mexican to sushi. Plate lunches, burritos, and specials like *lomi* salmon, and *kālua* pork with *poi* all cost under $10. Mon–Sat 7am–10pm.

**Saeng's**, 2119 Vineyard St; ⓣ244-1567. Pleasant Thai restaurant, serving high-quality food at bargain prices. Plate lunches include honey-lemon chicken and garlic shrimp for $6–8, while selections from the full dinner menu cost a few dollars more. Mon–Fri 11am–2.30pm & 5–9.30pm, Sat & Sun 5–9.30pm.

**A Saigon Cafe**, 1792 Main St; ⓣ243-9560. Predominantly Vietnamese restaurant with an extremely wide-ranging and unusual menu, most of it extremely tasty. Hot and cold noodle dishes and soups, a lot of seafood stews and curries, plus simpler stir-fried and steamed fish specials. All entrees come in at well under $20, appetizers like summer rolls and pancakes less than half that. Mon–Sat 10am–9.30pm, Sun 10am–8.30pm.

**Tasty Crust**, 1770 Mill St; ⓣ244-0845. Basic, cheap and very filling home cooking on the road up from Kahului Harbor. The day kicks off with bumper stacks of pancakes for $3, and the plates are piled high from then on. Mon 5.30am–1.30pm, Tues–Sun 5.30am–1.30pm & 5–10pm.

# ʻĪao Valley

Main Street heads due west out of Wailuku to enter the high-walled cleft carved by ʻĪao Stream into the West Maui mountains, with waterfalls dropping down pleated grooves in the rock to either side. For ancient Hawaiians, the gorgeous **ʻĪao Valley** was the equivalent of Egypt's Valley of the Kings: they buried their royal dead in the long-lost Olopio cave, and access was barred to commoners.

**Kamehameha the Great** conquered Maui in a battle here in 1790. The local armies were driven back into the valley from the shoreline, where they could be bombarded with impunity by the great cannon *Lopaka*, directed by John Young and Isaac Davis. While the defeated general, Kalanikūpule, the son of Maui's chief Kahekili, fled across the mountains, the bodies of his men choked ʻĪao Stream. Hence the name by which the battle became known – **Kepaniwai**, "the water dam."

ʻĪao Valley – and especially the stunning **ʻĪao Needle**, a 1200-foot pinnacle of green-clad lava – is now one of Hawaii's most famous beauty spots. You can't climb the needle itself, but you can admire it from various short hiking trails that meander around its base.

## Tropical Gardens of Maui

Less than a mile out of Wailuku, the **Tropical Gardens of Maui** (daily 9am–5pm; free) spread away below and to the right of what by now is ʻĪao Valley Road. This small commercial garden displays and sells a colorful assortment of tropical plants from all over the world and mails specimens to the continental US. It also holds a small snack bar.

## Kepaniwai County Park

Just after the road crosses ʻĪao Stream, a mile past the Tropical Gardens, **Kepaniwai County Park** (daily dawn–dusk; free) is an attractive public garden set amid dramatic, curtain-like folds in the mountains. Its lawns and flowerbeds are laid out to commemorate the many ethnic groups of Hawaii, with themed areas paying tribute to Maui's Japanese, Chinese and Portuguese immigrants, among others. Structures include a traditional thatched *hale*, ornamental pavilions and miniature pagodas, as well as statues of anonymous sugar-cane workers and Dr Sun Yat Sen.

## Hawaii Nature Center

The **Hawaii Nature Center**, immediately adjoining Kepaniwai County Park, is largely an educational facility for schoolchildren and holds simple exhibitions on Hawaiian flora, fauna and handicrafts (daily 10am–4pm; adults $6, under-13s $4; Ⓣ 244-6500, Ⓦ www.hawaiinaturecenter.org). In addition, however, staff members conduct guided **hikes** in the ʻĪao Valley area (Mon–Fri 2pm; adults $25, ages 8 to 12 $23). As the high-mountain trails are otherwise closed to visitors, these provide the only access to the wilderness beyond the Needle. The cost of the hikes includes admission to the center and a souvenir T-shirt.

## John F. Kennedy Profile

The next stop along ʻĪao Valley Road is a wayside lookout at the mouth of a small side valley. A natural rock formation a couple of hundred yards up the valley has for many years been known as the **John F. Kennedy Profile**, although tree growth has increasingly obscured JFK's chin. Signs that formerly pointed out the likeness have recently been changed to read "A Changing Profile" and studiously avoid mentioning the assassinated president. The official line now is that the face belongs to Kūakaʻiwai, a sixteenth-century chief.

## ʻĪao Valley State Park

ʻĪao Valley Road meanders to a dead end three miles out of Wailuku, at the parking lot for **ʻĪao Valley State Park** (daily 7am–7pm; free). Although you can clearly see ʻĪao Needle from here, a short but steep footpath crosses the stream and climbs up a nearby knoll for even better views from a covered rain shelter. Two paved, but potentially slippery, trails loop down to the stream from the main footpath, one on either side of the stream. Gardens laid out with native plants line the one closer to the parking lot. The small waterlogged *loʻi* or *taro* patch here, similar to a paddy field, offers one of the best angles for photographs, as you look up past the footbridge towards the Needle itself.

Despite appearances, the velvety **ʻĪao Needle** is not freestanding, but simply a raised knob at the end of a sinuous ridge. Standing, head usually in the clouds, at the intersection of two lush valleys, it's what geologists call an "erosional residual," meaning a nugget of hard volcanic rock left behind when the softer surrounding rocks were eroded away. From this side, it's an impressive 1200 feet tall, but no higher than the ridges that surround it. With their usual scatological gusto, the ancient Hawaiians named it Kūkaʻemoku, which politely translates as "broken excreta."

This whole area owes its existence to the phenomenal amount of rain that falls on West Maui; the 5788-foot peak of **Puʻu Kukui**, just over two miles from here, receives more than 400 inches per year. Unless you come early in the morning, it's likely to be raining in 'Īao Valley, but even when it's pouring you can usually look straight back down the valley to see the dry sunlit plains of the isthmus. After a series of accidents, the **trails** that lead beyond 'Īao Needle can now only be seen on the guided hikes run by the Hawaii Nature Center (see opposite).

# Mā'alaea

The direct road south from Wailuku, **Honoapi'ilani Highway** (Hwy-30), is joined as it crosses the isthmus by highways from Kahului and Kīhei and carries virtually all the traffic heading for Lahaina and the West Maui resorts. At the point where it reaches the south coast, six miles out of Wailuku, **MĀ'ALAEA** is a former commercial port that has been given a new lease of life as the preferred marina of Maui's flotilla of cruise and pleasure boats. The largest contingent are the Molokini snorkel boats (see below), so Mā'alaea is at its busiest very early in the morning, when the day's passengers assemble. At this time it also offers great views of Haleakalā, whose summit pokes out above the ring of clouds that usually obscures it from Kīhei.

Swimming anywhere near Mā'alaea is not recommended, but there are good **surfing** breaks just to the south, while **windsurfers** hurtle out into Mā'alaea Bay from the thin and unexciting strip of sand that stretches all the way east to Kīhei.

For an account of the Lahaina Pali Trail, which sets off across the southern tip of West Maui from just north of Mā'alaea, see p.288. The remainder of Honoapi'ilani Highway's route around West Maui to Lahaina is covered on p.286 onwards.

## Maui Ocean Center

While Mā'alaea is still not a town in any meaningful sense, it has recently acquired a center, in the guise of the **Mā'alaea Harbor Village** mall. That in turn focuses on the **Maui Ocean Center**, a state-of-the-art **aquarium** providing a colorful introduction to the marine life of Hawaii (daily 9am–5pm, adults $18.50, ages 3–12 $12.50; Ⓣ270-7000, Ⓦwww.mauioceancenter.com). It's not quite as large as you might expect from the size of the entrance fee, but its exhibits are well chosen and very well displayed.

The most spectacular section comes first. The coral groves of the **Living Reef** (some of them fluorescent) hold such species as camouflaged scorpionfish, seahorses, octopuses and bizarre "upside down jellyfish." Eerie garden eels poke like blades of grass from the sandy seabed, but the star, of course, is Hawaii's state fish, the *humuhumunukunukuāpua'a* – literally, "the triggerfish with a snout like a pig."

Open-air terraces perched above the harbor hold tanks of huge rays and green sea turtles. Beyond them, additional displays cover the life cycle of **whales**, and the relationship between **Hawaiians and the Sea**, illustrating traditional fishing techniques and equipment. A final huge tank holds **pelagic**, or open-ocean, sea creatures; its walk-through glass tunnel means that you can stand beneath mighy sharks and rays as they swim above your head.

## Practicalities

Mā'alaea has in the past few years acquired half-a-dozen characterless **condo** buildings, lined up beyond the harbor along Hau'oli Street. Most enjoy broad sea views, but Mā'alaea is a decidedly windy and insect-prone spot, and staying

## Molokini Snorkel Cruises

Maui's best-known **snorkeling** and **diving** spot is the tiny crescent of **Molokini**, three miles off Mākena. Created by a volcanic eruption some 230,000 years ago, it rises about 500ft from the underwater flank of Haleakalā, though only the southern half of the circular crater still pokes above the waves, to a maximum height of 162ft. There's no beach or landfall of any kind, but you see a lot of fish, including deep-water species.

Countless cruises leave early each morning from Mā'alaea Harbor; the currents off the Maui coast are too strong to allow swimming or kayaking to Molokini. For virtually all the companies listed below, you should be able to find **discount prices** from activities operators such as those listed on p.271. Snorkelers can pay anything from $45 to $100 for a five- to six-hour morning trip, depending on the size and comfort of the boat and the refreshments offered, and from $30 for a shorter afternoon jaunt; scuba divers pay around $40 extra. Note that between November and April, many companies stop running Molokini trips and concentrate on lucrative **whale-watching** cruises instead; for full details, see p.272.

| Company | Phone | Ⓦ www. | Passengers |
|---|---|---|---|
| **Blue Dolphin** | Ⓣ 622-0075 | – | 40 |
| **Friendly Charters** | Ⓣ 244-1979 | mauisnorkeling.com | 70 |
| **Frogman** | Ⓣ 662-0075 | bossfrog.com | 52 |
| **Lahaina Princess** | Ⓣ 667-6165 | maui.net/~ismarine | 100 |
| **Leilani** | Ⓣ 242-0955 | – | 49 |
| **Ocean Activities Center** | Ⓣ 879-4485 | mauioceanctivities.com | 75/100 |
| **Pacific Whale Foundation** | Ⓣ 879-8811 | pacificwhale.org | 20/48/100 |
| **Paragon Sailing Charters** | Ⓣ 244-2087 | sailmaui.com | 35 |
| **Pride of Maui** | Ⓣ 242-0955 | prideofmaui.com | 149 |
| **Prince Kuhio** | Ⓣ 242-8777 | mvprince.com | 149 |

here is only likely to appeal to fanatical sailors. If you do want to book a condo locally, contact Mā'alaea Bay Rentals (Ⓣ 244-5627 or 1-800/367-6084, Ⓦ www.maalaeabay.com).

However, Mā'alaea is also home to a handful of high-quality **restaurants**. Perched above the harbor at the seaward end of Mā'alaea Harbor Village – with an ocean-view terrace that comes into its own at lunchtime – *Merriman's Bamboo Bistro* (daily 11.30am–2pm & 5.30–9pm, Ⓣ 243-7374) serves delicious Pacific Rim cuisine. Its specialty is what chef Peter Merriman calls "tropas" – a tropical version of *tapas*. A typical three-course dinner of goats' cheese in phyllo with strawberry and onion salad, sesame-crusted *onaga* with papaya relish, and prime rib with Japanese sauce is a bargain at $25. Nearby, the menu at the equally large and scenic *Mā'alaea Waterfront Restaurant*, 50 Hau'oli St (daily 5–9.30pm, Ⓣ 244-9028), focuses on expensive freshly caught fish, with a cioppino stew priced at $35. You can also buy fish for yourself at the Mā'alaea Fish Market (Mon–Sat 10am–4pm), just around the harbor.

# South Maui

The area generally referred to as **South Maui** is in fact the western shoreline of East Maui, stretching south of Mā'alaea Bay. Until well after World War II, this was one of the island's least populated districts, a scrubby, exposed and worthless wasteland. Since then, an unattractive and almost unchecked ribbon of resort development has snaked down the coast, with the mass-market hotels and condos of **Kīhei** in the north being joined in recent years by far more exclusive luxury properties at **Wailea** and **Mākena**.

Almost all the way down, narrow strips of clean, white sand fill each successive bay, so every hotel is within easy walking distance of a good stretch of **beach**. So far, the development stops just short of the best beach of all, **Oneloa** or **Big Beach**, while the coastal highway peters out not far beyond. This final stretch, and the oceanfront trail to secluded **La Pérouse Bay**, is the only part of South Maui worth visiting on a sightseeing tour of the island; none of the resort communities holds any interest in itself.

## Kīhei

If you've always thought of Hawaii as Condo Hell, then **KĪHEI** probably comes closer to matching that image than anywhere else in the state. Stretching for seven miles south from Mā'alaea Bay, it's a totally formless sprawl of a place, whose only landmarks consist of one dull mall or condo building after another. That said, it can be a perfectly pleasant place to spend your vacation, with abundant inexpensive lodging and dining options and plentiful beaches. Just don't come to Kīhei expecting a town in any sense of the word.

In the 1960s, Kīhei spread for just a hundred yards to either side of the point where Mokulele Highway (Hwy-50) reaches Mā'alaea Bay. **North Kīhei Road** is still a hundred yards long, but **South Kīhei Road** now keeps on going for around five miles. It's not totally built up, but the occasional half-mile gaps are simply derelict land, left empty while the developers await their moment. Those moments are now arriving thick and fast; Kīhei is officially ranked as the second-fastest-growing community in the United States. Traffic congestion is so rife that for all journeys of any length, you'd do better to follow the parallel **Pi'ilani Highway**, half a mile or so up the hillside. There's even talk of building another highway even further up the slope.

The largest of Kīhei's shopping malls are the matching pair of **Azeka Place 1**, *makai* at 1280 S Kīhei Rd, and **Azeka Place 2,** opposite. Between them they hold the local **post office,** a large Bank of Hawaii with ATM machines, and lots of fast-food places. Otherwise, the new **Pi'ilani Village Shopping Center**, not far away on the upper highway, is expanding rapidly and holds a huge Safeway, while **Kukui Mall**, opposite Kalama Park, has a four-screen movie theater and more takeout eateries.

### Beaches

The first easy point of access to the ocean along South Kīhei Road comes within a few hundred yards, at **Mai Poina 'Oe Ia'u Beach County Park**. This narrow, shadeless beach is not somewhere you'd choose to spend a day, but it's a good launching point for surfers, kayakers and especially windsurfers, and the swimming is safe enough. The park was established in 1952 as a war memorial; its name means "forget me not."

To the naked eye, and especially to guests staying at oceanfront properties such as the *Hale Kai O' Kīhei* and its neighbors (see p.314), the beaches of northern Kīhei look attractive enough, if rather narrow. However, thanks to the output of a **sewage treatment facility** above the next formal roadside beach

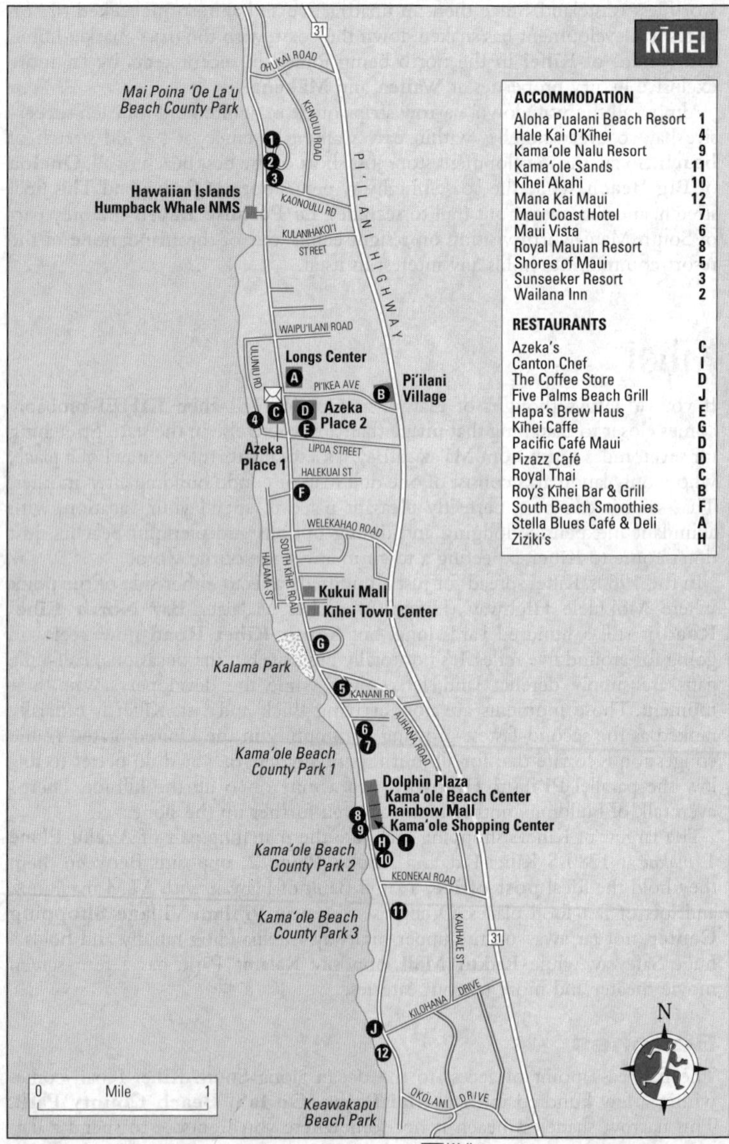

park, at **Kalama Beach**, three miles south of Mai Poina, this entire stretch is best admired from dry land. Swimming is not recommended. Nonetheless, the large lawns and sports fields on the promontory at **Kalama** remain popular with locals, especially in the evenings, and there's a pretty coconut grove.

Much the busiest of the Kīhei beaches – and for good reason – are the three separate, numbered segments of **Kama'ole Beach County Park**, immediately beyond. All boast clean white sand and are generally safe for swimming, with lovely views across the bay to West Maui, and all are constantly supervised by lifeguards. Most of the beautifully soft **Kama'ole 1** beach is very close to the road, but it also curves away out of sight to the north. Sweet little **Kama'ole 2**, cradled between two headlands, is a bit short on shade, and very near a large concentration of condos, so the pick of the bunch is long, broad **Kama'ole 3**. Families gather under the giant trees on its wide lawns, while the beach itself is shielded from the road at the bottom of a ten-foot grassy slope.

In high season, **Keawakapu Beach Park**, at the far south end of South Kīhei Road, is a less crowded alternative. Swimming is best in the center, while there's good snorkeling off the rocks to the south, thanks to an artificial offshore reef, made up mostly of old automobile parts that were submerged in the hope of boosting the local fish population.

## Hawaiian Islands Humpback Whale National Marine Sanctuary

At the northern end of Kīhei, squeezed onto a minor headland not far south of Mai Poina 'Oe Ia'u Beach, a small compound at 726 S Kīhei Rd serves as the headquarters of the **Hawaiian Islands Humpback Whale National Marine Sanctuary** (Ⓣ1-800/831-4888, Ⓦwww.t-link.net/~whale). The organization was created to protect and study the estimated three thousand humpback whales that annually winter in Hawaiian waters. Enthusiastic volunteers can explain its work and talk you through the displays in the garage-like **Education Center** (Mon–Sat 9.30am–3pm; free; Ⓣ1-800/831-4888, Ⓦwww.t-link.net/~whale). The organization's offices are located in the larger blue house on the seafront, whose interior is not open to the public. Its spacious verandah, however, is equipped with free binoculars and makes an ideal spot for watching any whales there may be in Mā'alaea Bay.

A six-acre tract of ocean immediately offshore from the sanctuary headquarters is still enclosed by the ancient lava walls of the **Kō'ie'ie Fishpond**, which dates originally from the sixteenth century. This area was then the site of the village of **Kalepolepo**, whose inhabitants left after the fishpond became silted up during the 1860s, thanks to runoff caused by the expansion of agriculture further up the slopes.

## Accommodation

There's little difference between Kīhei's countless **condos** and **hotels**, with standards in even the cheapest options tending to be perfectly adequate. Very few visitors simply pass through for a single night; there are no rock-bottom budget alternatives or B&Bs, and most places insist on a minimum stay of at least three nights. Rates on the whole are low, but Kīhei is more seasonally sensitive than most destinations, and in peak season (mid-Dec to March) you can expect to pay a premium of at least $25 over the prices coded below.

**Aloha Pualani Beach Resort**, 15 Wailana Place, Kīhei HI 96753; Ⓣ874-9265 or 1-800/PUA-LANI (US & Can), Ⓕ874-9127, Ⓦwww.alohapualani.com. Five homely two-story condo units across from Mā'alaea Bay at the north end of Kīhei. Each has a living room, kitchen and bedroom and shared use of a pool and garden. On-site owners provide breakfast and advice, and there's a three-night minimum stay. ❸.

**Hale Kai O'Kihei**, 1310 Uluniu Rd, Kīhei HI 96753; Ⓣ 879-2757 or 1-800/457-7014 (US & Can), Ⓕ 875-8242; also available through Condominium Rentals Hawaii (see box). Three stories of straightforward one- and two-bedroom condos in an absolutely stunning and very quiet beachfront location, near Kīhei's best malls and restaurants. Private coconut grove, spacious *lānais*, and discounted car rental. Four-night minimum stay. ❹.

**Kama'ole Nalu Resort**, 2450 S Kīhei Rd, Kīhei HI 96753; Ⓣ 879-1006 or 1-800/767-1497, Ⓕ 879-8693, Ⓦ www.mauigateway.com/~kamaole. Large beachfront complex set on neat lawns at the south end of Kama'ole Park 2. Two-bedroom, two-bath condos, all with kitchen and laundry facilities; the long, private *lānais* offer spectacular sunset views. Discounts on car rental; five-night minimum stay. ❹.

**Kama'ole Sands**, 2695 S Kīhei Rd, Kīhei HI 96753; Ⓣ 874-8700, 1-800/367-5004 (US & Can) or 1-800/272-5257 (HI), Ⓕ 879-3273, Ⓦ www.castleresorts.com. Sprawling condo complex just across the street from Kama'ole Park 3, with units of all sizes plus free tennis and swimming. Studio and garden-view suite ❺, ocean-view suite ❻.

**Kihei Akahi**, 2531 S Kīhei Rd, Kīhei HI 96753; available through Condominium Rentals Hawaii Ⓣ 879-2778, 1-800/367-5242 (US) or 1-800/663-2101 (Can), Ⓕ 879-7825, Ⓦ www.crhmaui.com. The ascending rows of good-value, well-furnished condos in this garden property across from Kama'ole Park 2 have use of two swimming pools and a tennis court. Those with air-conditioning cost $5 extra per night. Studios ❸, suites ❹.

**Mana Kai Maui**, 2960 S Kīhei Rd, Kīhei HI 96753; available through Condominium Rentals Hawaii Ⓣ 879-2778, 1-800/367-5242 (US) or 1-800/663-2101 (Can), Ⓕ 879-7825; Ⓦ www.crhmaui.com. Large building beside lovely Keawakapu Beach at the grander south end of Kīhei, with plush hotel rooms and full-fledged condo apartments, plus a pool and the excellent *Five Palms* grill restaurant (see p.316). Rates include rental car. ❹.

**Maui Coast Hotel**, 2259 S Kīhei Rd, Kīhei HI 96753; Ⓣ 874-6284, 1-800/426-0670 (US & Can) or 1-800/895-6284 (US & Can), Ⓕ 875-4731, Ⓦ www.westcoasthotels.com/mauicoast. Tasteful, luxurious, and good-value modern hotel, set slightly back from the highway opposite Kama'ole Park 1. Standard hotel rooms as well as one- and two-bedroom suites, plus an attractive pool and on-site restaurants. ❺.

**Maui Vista**, 2191 S Kīhei Rd, Kīhei HI 96753; Ⓣ 879-7966; reserve through Marc Resorts, Ⓣ 922-9700 or 1-800/535-0085 (US & Can), Ⓕ 922-2421 or 1-800/633-5085(US & Can), Ⓦ www.marcresorts.com. Comfortable, well-equipped condos of all sizes, on the hillside across from Kama'ole Park 1. Not the best views, but three pools and six tennis courts. ❹.

**Royal Mauian Resort**, 2430 S Kīhei Rd, Kīhei HI 96753; Ⓣ 879-1263 or 1-800/367-8009 (US & Can), Ⓕ 874-7639, Ⓦ www.royalmauianresort.com. Huge, luxurious, but non-air-con oceanfront condo complex, beyond the south end of Kama'ole Park 1. Lovely views, especially from the roof terrace, and a nice pool. Discounts on car rental; five-night minimum stay. ❺.

**Shores of Maui**, 2075 S Kīhei Rd, Kīhei HI 96753; Ⓣ 879-9140 or 1-800/367-8002, Ⓕ 879-6221. Long, low complex of good-value one- and two-bedroom air-con condos, screened behind coconut palms across from Cove Park. Three-night minimum stay, or one-week minimum stay at Christmas/January. ❸.

**Sunseeker Resort**, 551 S Kīhei Rd, Kīhei HI 96753; Ⓣ 879-1261 or 1-800/532-MAUI (US & Can), Ⓕ 874-3877, Ⓦ www.sunseeker.com.

## Condo Rentals

Individual apartments in virtually all the properties listed here, and a great many more besides, can also be booked through various specialist agencies. As a rule, prices start around $80 per night in low season, rising to $100 between Christmas and March; be sure to check whether you're expected to pay an additional one-time "cleaning fee," which is typically around the $50 mark.

**Condominium Rentals Hawaii**, 362 Huku Li'i Place, #204, Kīhei, HI 96753; Ⓣ 879-2778, 1-800/367-5242 (US) or 1-800/663-2101 (Can), fax 879-7825, Ⓦ www.crhmaui.com.

**Kīhei Maui Vacations**, PO Box 1055, Kīhei, HI 96753; Ⓣ 879-7581 or 1-800/541-6284 (US & Can), Ⓕ 879-2000, Ⓦ www.kmvmaui.com.

**Maui Condominium and Home Realty**, 2511 S Kīhei Rd, Suite H, PO Box 18400, Kīhei, HI 96753; Ⓣ 879-5445 or 1-800/822-4409 (US & Can), Ⓕ 874-6144.

Pretty little hotel-cum-condo building, resembling an old-fashioned motel, very close to Mā'alaea Bay beach (and, unfortunately, also the main road) at the north end of Kīhei. All the inexpensive rooms and suites have kitchen facilities and ocean views. Three-night minimum stay. Room ❷, suite ❸.

**Wailana Inn**, 14 Wailana Place, Kīhei HI 96753; Ⓣ 874-3131 or 1-800/399-3885 (US & Can), Ⓦ www.wailanabeach.com. Motel-like structure set just back from the road, near Mā'alaea Bay beach in northern Kīhei. The rooms are much nicer than the exterior might suggest. All have kitchens or kitchenettes, TV and phone, and share use of a rooftop hot tub. ❸.

## Restaurants

The **restaurants** listed below represent just a small selection of what's available in Kīhei. Virtually all the malls also hold at least one budget diner or takeout, and most have an espresso bar, too. The best places for **food shopping** are the Safeway supermarket at Pi'ilani Village Shopping Center on the upper highway (where there's also a *Starbucks*), and the *Hawaiian Moons* wholefood store at the Kama'ole Beach Center, 2411 S Kīhei Rd.

### Inexpensive

**Azeka's**, Azeka Place 1, 1280 S Kīhei Rd; Ⓣ 879-0611. Small snack shop and takeout, with a few tables, serving *saimin* for under $3, plus sushi and the Hawaiian favorite *loco moco*, an egg-topped hamburger. Marinated ribs ($6 for a pound) are also served; in fact, from 3 to 5pm they're the only things available here. Main counter open daily 7.30am–2pm; ribs daily 7.30am–5pm.

**Canton Chef**, Kama'ole Shopping Center, 2463 S Kīhei Rd; Ⓣ 879-1988. Roomy Chinese restaurant, with $6 lunch specials and a dinner menu bursting with chicken, shrimp, scallop and fish entrees ($7–12), including several served in black-bean sauce. With advance notice, they'll prepare a whole Peking duck for $35. Daily 11am–1.45pm & 5–9pm.

**The Coffee Store**, Azeka Place 2, 1279 S Kīhei Rd; Ⓣ 875-4244. Cheery mall café serving espressos of all kinds, plus breakfast pastries, lunch salads, pizzas and sandwiches. Daily 6am–10pm.

**Kihei Caffe**, 1945 S Kīhei Rd; Ⓣ 879-2230. Friendly café offering espressos, flavored lattes and smoothies, plus breakfast fry-ups and $6 lunchtime sandwiches or burgers to take out or eat at a shaded roadside gazebo that's perfect for people-watching. Mon–Sat 5am–3pm, Sun 6am–3pm.

**Royal Thai**, Azeka Place 1, 1280 S Kīhei Rd; Ⓣ 874-0813. Small place, tucked away at the back of the mall, serving Kīhei's best Thai food. Red, yellow and green curries in vegetarian, meat and fish versions; *tom yum* and long rice soups; and mussels in black-bean sauce, all for $7–10. Mon–Fri 11am–3pm & 4.45–9.30pm, Sat & Sun 4.45–9.30pm.

**South Beach Smoothies**, 1455 S Kīhei Rd; Ⓣ 875-0594. Small kiosk in parking lot beside the main highway, which prepares superb $4 smoothies using your choice of mango, coconut, banana, papaya or other fresh fruits, and also offers bagels and ice cream. Mon–Sat 9am–5pm.

### Moderate

**Hapa's Brew Haus**, 41 E Lipoa St; Ⓣ 879-9001. Large and very popular brewpub, whose success as a music venue – Maui stars like Hapa themselves and Willie K play 9pm–1.30am nightly – has resulted in ever less space being devoted to its basic restaurant, where predictable rib or chicken dinners cost around $10. Daily 5.30pm–1.30am.

**Pizazz Cafe**, Azeka Place 2, 1279 S Kīhei Rd; Ⓣ 891-2123. Mall bistro where the largely conventional menu of $10-15 meat and fish entrees includes an (un)healthy smattering of Deep South specialties such as catfish and okra. But the real draw is the live jazz performed from 7.30pm nightly. Sun & Mon 11am–11pm, Tues–Sat 11am–midnight.

**Stella Blues Café & Deli**, Longs Center, 1215 S Kīhei Rd; Ⓣ 874-3779. California-style café with big plate-glass windows, a few tables outside, and Grateful Dead posters and ponytailed waiters within. Continental and cooked breakfasts $7–9; $7–10 burger, salad and sandwich lunches (try the special of grilled and roasted vegetables on herb bread); dinners like fettuccini Alfredo, Cajun chicken, crab cakes and ribs for $14–20; and all-day smoothies and espressos. Daily 8am–9pm.

**Ziziki's**, 2511 S Kīhei Rd; Ⓣ 879-9330. Friendly Greek place on a garden terrace set back from the road and crammed with coconut palms and a banyan tree. Authentic appetizers like a feta and olive salad, or stuffed grape leaves for $6–8; entrees include moussaka and souvlaki for under $20, and a full "Greek Gods Platter" for $30 per person. Daily 5–10pm.

### Expensive

**Five Palms Beach Grill**, *Mana Kai Maui*, 2960 S Kīhei Rd; ☎879-2607. Beachfront restaurant on ground floor of condo building, with open terraces within earshot of the waves, and live music nightly. Egg breakfasts, including smoked-salmon Benedict for $11, and salad or daily special lunches for $10–15. The food at dinner – mostly Pacific Rim, along with standard ribs and steaks – is beautifully presented and tastes delicious. Appetizers such as soft-shell crab cakes in ginger remoulade cost around $12; entrees like fresh *opah* (moonfish), and grilled chicken fettuccine with wild mushroom couscous, are more like $25–30. Mon–Fri 8am–2.30pm & 5–9pm, Sat & Sun 8am–2.30pm & 5–10pm.

**Pacific Café Maui**, Azeka Place 2, 1279 S Kīhei Rd; ☎879-0069. Maui's finest gourmet restaurant, the *Pacific Café* serves the "Hawaii Regional" cuisine of Jean-Pierre Josselin and is focused on a huge wood-burning grill. The food is superb, with an amazing "*ahi* tower" appetizer for $13 that includes a raw-tuna *poke*, oysters with tuna, and a tuna carpaccio. Entrees (around $30) featuring grilled meats and fish with roasted vegetables. Decadent desserts include mac-nut profiteroles and a bittersweet chocolate souffle. With the cheapest bottle of wine costing around $25, a meal for two will probably top $100. Reservations essential; daily 5.30–9.30pm.

**Roy's Kihei Bar and Grill**, Pi'ilani Village, 303 Pi'ikea Ave; ☎891-1120. Large new mall outlet of the upmarket island chain, on the upper highway half a mile up from Kīhei Road. Signature Roy's dishes such as lemongrass-crusted *shutome* (swordfish) and blackened rare *ahi* stream from the open kitchen, at around $10 for an appetizer and $25 for an entree. The steamed fresh catch ($27) is irresistible. Daily 5.30–10pm.

## Wailea and Mākena

Both South Kīhei Road and Pi'ilani Highway end on the southern fringes of Kīhei. The only road south, branching off Okolani Drive halfway between the two, is **Wailea Alanui Drive**, which becomes **Mākena Alanui Drive** after a couple of miles. It's forced to run several hundred yards inland by a sequence of half a dozen colossal resort hotels, constructed on a scale to rival any in Hawaii. Neither **WAILEA** nor **MĀKENA** is a town as such; were it not for the resorts, the names would not even appear on island maps. The only **shops** in the area are congregated in the very upmarket new **Shops at Wailea** mall, whose target audience can be assessed from the presence of Louis Vuitton, Cartier, and Dolce & Gabbana stores.

Until the 1950s, what is now Wailea was just barren oceanfront acreage belonging to the 'Ulupalakua Ranch (see p.327). It was then bought by Matson Cruise Lines, who planned to turn it into the "City of Roses," but nothing happened until control of Matson passed to Alexander & Baldwin in the 1970s.

Mākena, which segues imperceptibly into the south end of Wailea, was developed even more recently: its first hotel appeared at the end of the 1980s. For a period in the late nineteenth century, however, it ranked as Maui's second port after Lahaina, thanks to the comings and goings at 'Ulupalakua Ranch, just two miles higher up the gentle slope of Haleakalā. These days, in the absence of any direct road, getting to the ranch requires a forty-mile drive.

Wailea and Mākena together constitute a luxurious enclave of velvet golf courses and pristine beaches, where nonguests feel distinctly unwelcome. In theory, outsiders are free to use any of the beaches, but with magnificent Oneloa Beach (see p.320) lying just beyond Mākena, few bother.

### Accommodation

The moment you see the manicured lawns of Wailea, let alone its gleaming resorts, it will become clear that you need a *lot* of money to **stay** at this end of South Maui. There is one small B&B nearby, but otherwise rooms can rarely be found for under $200 a night.

**Ann & Bob Babson's B&B**, 3371 Keha Drive, Wailea HI 96753; ⓣ 874-1166 or 1-800/824-6409, ⓕ 879-7906, ⓦ www.mauibnb.com. Lovely garden B&B on the slopes above Wailea, with three en-suite units in the main family home and a separate guest cottage. Ocean-view *lānais* and lavish breakfasts are highlights. Five-night minimum stay. ③/④.

**Four Seasons Resort**, 3900 Wailea Alanui Drive, Wailea HI 96753; ⓣ 874-8000 or 1-800/334-6284, ⓕ 874-2222, ⓦ www.fshr.com. Lavish resort property at the south end of Wailea, with a large, beautiful, white-sand beach on view beyond the open lobby, and a gorgeous, palm-ringed pool. Private *lānais,* bamboo furnishings, 24-hour room service and several restaurants, including the superb *Seasons*. Mountain-view room ⑧, ocean-view room or suite ⑨.

**Grand Wailea Resort**, 3850 Wailea Alanui Drive, Wailea HI 96753; ⓣ 875-1234 or 1-800/888-6100, ⓕ 874-2442, ⓦ www.grandwailea.com. Large and very ostentatious resort hotel, with a five-level swimming pool ("Wailea Canyon") that's linked by waterslides and features a swim-up bar, hot-tub grottoes, and even a water elevator back to the top. There's also a luxurious spa, half-a-dozen restaurants, and tropical flowers everywhere. The *Tsunami* is Maui's hottest, flashiest nightclub. ⑨.

**Kea Lani Hotel,** 4100 Wailea Alanui Drive, Wailea HI 96753; ⓣ 875-4100 or 1-800/882-4100, ⓕ 875-1200, ⓦ www.kealani.com. Locals call it the Taj Mahal, but this dazzling white resort is more like something from the *Arabian Nights*. Despite its flamboyant silhouette, the interior is characterized by smooth curves, and you can see through the lobby to lily ponds and the lagoon-cum-pool, crossed by little footbridges. Two huge wings of plush rooms (each equipped with TVs, a VCR and a CD player), plus 37 garden villas, and some excellent restaurants, all focused on lovely Polo Beach (see p.318). Garden view ⑧, ocean view ⑨.

**Maui Prince**, 5400 Mākena Alanui Drive, Mākena HI 96753; ⓣ 874-1111 or 1-800/321-6284, ⓕ 879-8763 or 1-800/338-8763. South Maui's southernmost resort

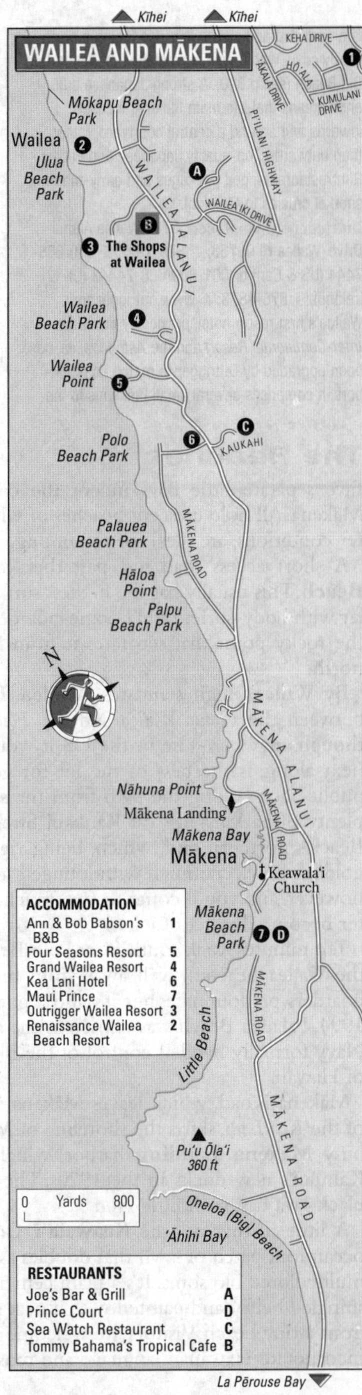

is a secluded and stylish low-rise facing a pretty sandy cove, within walking distance of wonderful Big Beach (see p.320). A strong Japanese influence means that the main building focuses inwards and around a central courtyard, rather than outwards. Top-quality Japanese and Pacific Rim restaurants, golf packages and early-morning snorkel cruises to Molokini. ❽.

**Outrigger Wailea Resort**, 3700 Wailea Alanui Drive, Wailea HI 96753; ⓣ879-1922, 1-800/688-7444 (US & Can) or 001-800/688-74443 (UK & Ireland), ⓕ875-4878; ⓦwww.outrigger.com. Wailea's first resort hotel, previously the *Maui Inter-Continental Resort* and the *Aston Wailea*, has been upgraded by Outrigger to match its neighbors. It comprises several small buildings in the landscaped gardens and a larger central tower, all with spacious, comfortable rooms. Three pools, two restaurants, plus Hawaiiana lectures and four weekly *lūaus* (see p.276). Garden view ❽, ocean view ❾.

**Renaissance Wailea Beach Resort**, 3550 Wailea Alanui Drive, Wailea HI 96753; ⓣ879-4900 or 1-800/992-4532, ⓕ874-5370, ⓦwww.renaissance-hotels.com. Relatively low-profile but highly luxurious resort (formerly the *Stouffer*) stacked in seven tiers above twin crescent beaches. The gardens hold swimming pools, and a statue of the god Maui. Very luxurious rooms, with VCRs, and *lānais* angled towards the ocean. The *Hana Gion* serves good Japanese food. Mountain view ❽, ocean view ❾.

## The Beaches

Five separate little bays indent the coastline of Wailea, with two more at Mākena. All hold crescent beaches of white sand that, in all but the worst winter conditions, are ideal for swimming.

A short access road just past the *Renaissance Wailea* leads down to **Ulua Beach**. This usually has the highest surf along this stretch of coast, so it's popular with body-surfers and boogie-boarders. There's also great snorkeling around the rocky point that separates it from **Mōkapu Beach**, a short walk to the north.

By Wailea's high standards, **Wailea Beach** itself, reached by a spur road between the *Grand Wailea* and the *Four Seasons*, is perhaps not exceptional, though anywhere else in the US it would rank as a beauty. **Polo Beach**, the next along, is the best of the lot for good old-fashioned swimming. There's public access along the path from the south side of the *Kea Lani Hotel*, with plenty of parking just off Kaukahi Street. The footpath hits the sand at Polo Beach's northern end, which, being right beneath the hotel, can be rather a goldfish bowl, crammed with loungers and short on shade. Double back south, however, and you'll come to two much less crowded stretches, which in winter become distinct beaches.

Ten minutes' walk south from Polo Beach, **Palauea Beach** is the quietest of the Wailea beaches, well away from the built-up areas. Surfers and boogie-boarders predominate, but it's also a good spot for a family day by the sea. In 1994, Palauea Beach was chosen as the site of the ceremony in which the US Navy formally handed control of the island of Kahoolawe back to the people of Hawaii.

Mākena Road, which leaves Mākena Alanui Drive a little over a mile south of the *Kea Lani*, skirts the shoreline of **Mākena Bay**. This was once the site of busy **Mākena Landing** harbor, which was superseded by the creation of Kahului's new docks in the 1920s. The jetty has now gone, to leave a sleepy black-lava bay with little sand.

A little further on, the **Keawala'i Congregational Church** stands on an oceanfront patch of lawn that doubles as a graveyard, surrounded by trees with multicolored blossoms. It's a plain cement structure, topped by a pretty, wood-shingled belfry, and painted with a neat green trim; the coconut palms beyond front a tiny beach. Visitors are welcome to the 9.30am Sunday services, which incorporate Hawaiian language and music.

## Kahoolawe

From all along Maui's south and west coasts, and especially around Wailea and Mākena, the uninhabited island of **Kahoolawe** is clearly visible. Measuring just eleven miles by six, and a maximum of 1477 feet above sea level, it's the eighth-largest Hawaiian island, with its nearest point a mere eight miles off Maui. From a distance, Kahoolawe looks like a barren hillock; at sunset it glows red, thanks to a haze of red dust lifted by the winds. Trapped in the rainshadow of Haleakalā, it gets thirty inches of rain a year. Agriculture is all but impossible, but a few green valleys, invisible from the other islands, cut into the central plateau.

Whether Kahoolawe ever held much of a population has become a controversial issue, thanks to the protracted campaign by **native Hawaiians** to claim the island back from the **US Navy**. The Navy used it for target practice for almost fifty years, arguing that it had no value as a home to humans; the Hawaiians claimed that it held great spiritual significance to their ancestors, and that access to it remained their inalienable birthright.

Both sides marshaled archeologists and anthropologists, and Kahoolawe has consequently been more thoroughly probed and excavated than anywhere else in Hawaii. The consensus seems to be that, although it was principally used as a seasonal base by fishermen, the presence of house sites, *heiaus* and petroglyphs proves that it also held permanent agricultural settlements. In addition, Kealaikahiki Point at its southwest corner – the name means "the way to foreign lands" and is shared by the sea channel between Kahoolawe and Lanai – was a marker for navigators voyaging to and from Tahiti. A "navigator's chair" of shaped boulders still stands atop the island's second-highest peak, the 1444-foot Moa'ulaiki, which is thought to have served as a school and observatory for apprentice navigators.

The whole island was probably covered by forest until 1450 AD, when it was swept by a bushfire. The trees have never grown back, and Captain Cook's expedition described Kahoolawe as "altogether a poor Island" in 1779. The process of erosion was completed by sheep and goats imported during the nineteenth century. For a short period during the 1840s, Kahoolawe was a penal colony; several ranchers then eked out a living there. The last of them was summarily evicted after the attack on Pearl Harbor so that the island could be used by the Navy.

After World War II, the military declined to hand Kahoolawe back to the state of Hawaii, claiming the ability to practice island invasions there had been the single major factor in its defeat of Japan. In 1953, President Eisenhower granted the Navy control over the island, with the proviso that it should be cleaned up at Federal expense and returned when no longer needed. For forty more years, Kahoolawe was blasted by thunderous explosions that could be seen and heard from Maui.

Intermittent Hawaiian efforts to reclaim Kahoolawe crystallized in 1975 with the formation of the **Protect Kahoolawe 'Ohana**. This group of young activists saw Kahoolawe as a unifying cause for all native Hawaiians, the most obvious symbol of the way in which Hawaiian lands had been seized and desecrated by the United States. The PKO organized the first of a series of illegal occupations of the island in January 1976, at the start of Bicentennial year. Eighteen months later, founder members George Helm and Kimo Mitchell were lost at sea as they attempted to return to Maui by surfboard after one such venture, a martyrdom that attracted huge publicity for their cause.

The PKO then turned to the courts. Accusing the Navy on several fronts – water, noise and air pollution; the threat to endangered marine mammals and historic sites; and the infringement of religious freedoms – they won restrictions on bombing and gained "visiting rights" of up to ten days per month. President Bush finally called a halt to the bombing in 1990, and Kahoolawe was handed back to the state of Hawaii in May 1994. The Navy was scheduled to control access until the year 2003, or until all unexploded ordnance has been removed. Since the $400 million originally budgeted for the cleanup now seems inadequate for the job, it looks as though Hawaiians are in for a very long wait. Hawaiian groups nonetheless regularly visit Kahoolawe, and a program of reforestation has begun.

Keawala'i Church is opposite the parking lot for **Mākena Beach Park**, a hundred yards down the road. Somewhat overshadowed by the *Maui Prince*, it's still an attractive little half-moon beach, with reasonable snorkeling.

## Restaurants

Neither Wailea nor Mākena holds many alternatives to the resort hotels' own **restaurants**, but there are enough excellent ones to choose from that, provided you don't mind paying $40 for dinner each night, there isn't a problem. For cheaper meals, you'll just have to head back to Kīhei.

**Joe's Bar & Grill**, 131 Wailea Iki Place; ☎875-7767. One of Maui's most fashionable restaurants, owned by the same top-notch team as the *Hāli'imaile General Store* (see p.324) and located just off Wailea Iki Drive as it drops down into Wailea proper. Neither the tennis-club setting nor the decor – dull rock-music memorabilia – is at all inspiring, but the food is heavenly, a fusion of cutting-edge Pacific Rim cuisine with down-home local favorites. Appetizers ($6–18) include *ahi* tartare with *wasabi* aioli, while entrees ($20 and up) range from meatloaf with garlic mashed potatoes to a smoky, applewood-grilled salmon. Daily 5.30–9.30pm.

**Prince Court**, *Maui Prince*, 5400 Mākena Alanui Drive, Wailea; ☎875-5888. Relatively formal, somewhat solemn resort restaurant. Appetizers include oysters at $11, and a $12 Napoleon of Hawaiian tuna. Apart from the steamed *moi* (threadfish) for $22, the steak and fish entrees tend to be rather predictable. Sunday morning sees a buffet brunch for $38. Mon–Sat 5.30–9.30pm, Sun 9am–1pm & 5.30–9.30pm.

**SeaWatch Restaurant at Wailea**, 100 Wailea Golf Club Drive, Wailea; ☎875-8080. Grand terrace restaurant a few hundred yards uphill from the ocean, with sea views and a player piano. Daytime menus feature griddled breakfasts and lunchtime deli sandwiches and salads; at night the cuisine is Pacific Rim, with $7–12 appetizers such as five-spice crab cakes, and $25 entrees including fish, grilled chicken, and lamb with onion torte. A light menu is served 3–5.30pm. Daily 8am–10pm.

**Tommy Bahama's Tropical Cafe**, The Shops at Wailea, 3750 Wailea Alanui Drive, Wailea; ☎875-9983. Bar and restaurant adjoining the clothes store of the same name, also a "Purveyor of Island Lifestyles." Lunch is a good value, with huge fishy sandwiches or pasta specials for around $10, along with sweeping (if distant) ocean views from the elevated terrace. The dinner entrees are more overtly Caribbean, including Jamaican spiced pork in rum sauce for $23 and Trinidad tuna with cilantro and lemongrass for $25. Sun–Thurs 11am–11pm, Fri & Sat 11am–midnight.

# Beyond Mākena

Once past the *Maui Prince*, you're finally clear of South Maui's resorts and can enjoy some of the island's finest beaches and most unspoilt scenery. The road gives out altogether before long, but it's possible to hike on beyond the end.

## Oneloa Beach – "Big Beach"

Maui's most spectacular sweep of golden sand stretches for over half a mile south of the landmark cinder cone of Pu'u 'Ōla'i, just south of Mākena. There's not a building in sight at **Oneloa Beach** (literally "long sand," and widely known as **Big Beach**), just perfect sands and mighty surf, backed by a dry forest of *kiawe* and cacti. During the 1970s, it was home to a short-lived hippy commune; recently it has become **Mākena State Park**, with two paved access roads.

The very first turn off the main road south of Mākena, though labeled "Mākena State Park," is a dirt track that leads via an orange gate to a scrubby gray-sand beach. Keep going on the main road instead, until you reach the paved turnoff to Oneloa, half a mile beyond the *Maui Prince*. A footpath from the parking lot here leads through the trees to a small cluster of portable toilets and picnic tables, and then emerges at the north end of Big Beach. The sand is so deep and coarse that walking can be difficult, but the clear blue ocean is irresistible. The major drawback with Big Beach is that it faces straight out to sea and lacks a reef to protect it, so it's extremely **dangerous**. Huge waves crash right on to the shoreline, while a few feet out fearsome rip currents tear along the coast. Despite many drownings, all lifeguards were controversially withdrawn in 1995 to cut costs.

Most visitors to Big Beach can't resist strolling its full length southwards, before heading for the red-brown cliffs at its northern end. A natural cleft appears as if by magic to reveal the "stairway" across the rocks that enables you to reach the much smaller, and much safer, **Little Beach**. Sheltered by the rocky headland, and shaded by the adjacent trees, this is perhaps the most idyllic swimming spot on Maui, with views of Molokini and Lanai. One relic of the hippy days is that it's still widely known as an (illegal) **nudist** beach; even if you don't go naked yourself, some of your fellow beachgoers certainly will.

## Pu'u 'Ōla'i

Halfway along the easy trail between Big and Little beaches, where the ground levels off at the top of the first cliff, another trail doubles back to climb **Pu'u 'Ōla'i** itself. This crumbling cinder cone was produced by one of Maui's very last volcanic eruptions, perhaps two centuries ago, and is barely held together by scrubby grass and thorns. The ascent is so steep that strongly worded signs warn against making the attempt. If you do try, you may find you have to advance on all fours. Scrambling over the raw red – and very sharp – cinders is extremely painful in anything other than proper hiking boots.

The summit of Pu'u 'Ōla'i – which is not the peak you see at the start of the climb – is a wonderful vantage point for watching humpback whales in winter. It commands views all the way up the flat coast to Wailea and Kīhei, down the full length of Big Beach, inland to the green uplands of Haleakalā, across the ocean to the low ridge of Molokini – circled by cruise boats from dawn onwards – and beyond to glowing red Kahoolawe, the West Maui mountains and Lanai.

## La Pérouse Bay

Mākena Road continues for another three miles south from Big Beach, clinging to the coastline of **'Āhihi Bay** around several small clinkery (very rough jagged lava) coves, and then crossing a wide, bare field of chunky *'a'ā* lava. **La Pérouse Bay** lies beyond the parking lot at the far end, where a cairn bearing a bronze plaque commemorates the voyages of the French Admiral Jean-François Galaup, Comte de la Pérouse.

By spending three hours ashore here on May 30, 1786, la Pérouse became the first foreigner to set foot on Maui. He was under orders to claim the island for the King of France but, unusually for a European, considered that he had no right to do so. His ships, the *Astrolabe* and the *Boussole,* sailed away and were lost with all hands in the Solomon Islands two years later.

La Pérouse encountered a handful of coastal villages at this spot. Its inhabitants knew it as *Keone'ō'io*, or "bonefish beach," and still told of how chief Kalani'ōpu'u of the Big Island had landed a fleet of canoes here during an attempted invasion of Maui a few years earlier. However, the villages were largely destroyed just four years after la Pérouse's visit by the last known eruption of Haleakalā. A river of lava two miles wide flowed into the sea in the center of what had been one long bay, to create the two separate bays seen today.

The waters around the headland are set aside as the **'Āhihi-Kīna'u Natural Area Reserve**, notable for its large numbers of dolphins. All fishing is forbidden; **snorkeling** is allowed, but it's easier to enter the water in the inlets around La Pérouse Bay itself than to go in off the headland. In addition, both of the operators listed on p.273 run **kayak** excursions here. The trail from the road meanders alternately across the sands and among the scrubby *kiawe* trees to follow the whole curve of the bay. The lichen-covered walls of ancient dwellings can often be glimpsed in the undergrowth.

Proposals have recently been submitted to make this entire area a national park; watch the press for the latest developments.



## Kanaio Beach

At the far end of La Pérouse Bay, you come to another field of crumbled, reddish-brown lava. A separate trail – not the obvious coastal path, which soon ends, but one further inland – heads onwards from here. While it has some historic interest, as it traces the route of the King's Highway footpath that once ringed the entire island, it's extremely rugged, hot and exposed. **Kanaio Beach**, a pretty cove of turquoise water two miles along, is as far as it makes any sense to go, and even that's not a hike to undertake lightly.

# Upcountry Maui

The lower western slopes of Haleakalā, which enjoy a deliciously temperate climate a couple of thousand feet above the isthmus, are known as **Upcountry Maui**. Most visitors simply race through on their way up the mountain, but the upcountry is among the most attractive regions in the state. A narrow strip that stretches for at most twenty miles, it varies from the wet, lush orchards and rainforests around **Makawao** in the north to the parched cattle country of the venerable **'Ulupalakua Ranch** in the south. There are few significant towns and even fewer tourist attractions, but the whole region is laced with quiet rural lanes that make for relaxing explorations. Although commuter traffic up and down Haleakalā Highway attests to its status as one of the most popular residential districts on the island, accommodation for visitors is limited to a handful of pretty, small-scale **B&Bs**.

At this altitude, the pineapple and sugar plantations of the isthmus give way to smaller private farms. In the past these grew the white potatoes that first lured the whaling fleet to Maui, as well as coffee, cotton and Maui onions, but the most conspicuous crop now is flowering plants, especially dazzling **protea blossoms**.

If you expect a nonstop riot of greenery and color, however, you may be disappointed to find that much of the upcountry is dry and desolate. It takes irrigation to render this land fertile, and the many gulches that corrugate the flanks of Haleakalā only manage to support sparse grass, dry stunted trees, and even cacti. That becomes ever more true as you head further south. Clumps of high old trees mark the sites of ranch buildings, but otherwise the slopes are bare, scattered with the rounded knolls of ancient cinder cones.

Within the next few years, a new stretch of highway, or even a whole new road, will probably be constructed to connect Kīhei directly with Upcountry

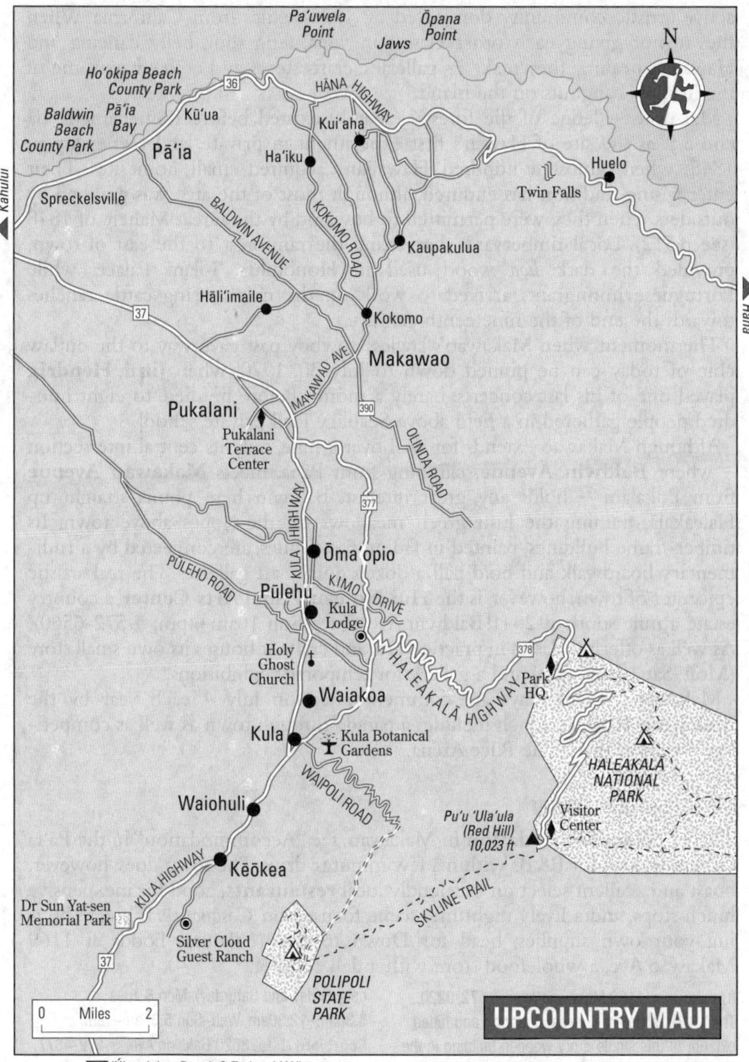


Maui. For the moment, however, the only route up from the island's south or west coasts is via Kahului.

# Makawao

The small town of **MAKAWAO**, seven miles up from coastal Pā'ia (see p.337), represents Maui at its best. Still recognizable as the village built by plantation workers and *paniolo* cowboys in the nineteenth century, it's now home to an active artistic community dominated by 1970s exiles from California. When they're not giving each other classes in yoga, feng shui, belly dancing and Hawaiian healing, they make its galleries, crafts stores and coffee bars some of the liveliest hangouts on the island.

Makawao – "edge of the forest" – barely existed before Kamehameha III chose it as the site of Hawaii's first experiment in private land ownership in 1845, when almost a hundred Hawaiians acquired small homesites. Their enterprising tradition has endured, although most of the area was grabbed by outsiders when they were permitted to buy land by the Great Mahele of 1848 (see p.512). Local timberyards, harvesting the rainforest to the east of town, provided the dark *koa* wood used in Honolulu's 'Iolani Palace, while Portuguese immigrants arrived to work on the neighboring cattle ranches towards the end of the nineteenth century.

The moment when Makawao's lawless cowboy past gave way to the outlaw chic of today can be pinned down to July 30, 1970, when **Jimi Hendrix** played one of his last concerts, barely a month before he died, to eight hundred people gathered in a field above Seabury Hall private school.

Although Makawao extends for well over a mile, only its central intersection – where **Baldwin Avenue**, climbing from Pā'ia, meets **Makawao Avenue** from Pukalani – holds any great interest. Baldwin here points straight up Haleakalā, framing the lush green meadows on the slopes above town. Its timber-frame buildings, painted in fading pastel hues, are connected by a rudimentary boardwalk and hold half a dozen quirky art galleries. The real artistic epicenter of town, however, is the **Hui No'eau Visual Arts Center**, a country estate a mile south at 2841 Baldwin Ave (Tues–Sun 10am–4pm; ⓣ572-6560). As well as offering classes in practical arts and crafts, it houses its own small store (Mon–Sat 10am–4pm) and a gallery for temporary exhibitions.

Makawao's *paniolo* days are commemorated on July 4 each year by the **Makawao Rodeo**, which includes a parade through town as well as competitive events at the Oskie Rice Arena.

## Restaurants

There's no **accommodation** in Makawao; see "Accommodation" in the Pā'ia section (p.338) for B&Bs within a few minutes' drive. The town does, however, boast an excellent selection of friendly local **restaurants**, good for inexpensive lunch stops, and a lively nighttime scene focused on *Casanova's*. If you're buying your own supplies, head for Down to Earth Natural Foods at 1169 Makawao Ave, a wholefood store with a deli counter.

**Casanova's**, 1188 Makawao Ave; ⓣ572-0220. The 1970s-style Art Nouveau lettering and faded exterior of this single-story wooden building in the heart of Makawao belies its status as one of Maui's hottest nightspots. (Willie Nelson and Kris Kristofferson are among stars to have played here.) There's a dance floor and bar just inside the door, a romantic Italian restaurant further back, and a breakfast deli/espresso bar alongside. Lunchtime salads, pastas and sandwiches range from $5 to $14, while in the evening, wood-fired pizzas cost $10–15, pasta entrees are $10–18, and specials are $20–25. Portions are huge. The cover charge of $5 on dance nights (unless you dine) can rise to $10 when there's live music (typically Friday and Saturday). Mon & Tues 5.30am–12.30am, Wed–Sun 5.30am–1am.

**Courtyard Cafe**, 3620 Baldwin Ave; ⓣ572-4877. Off-street café in the Courtyard Mall, serving espressos, pastries and sandwiches at shaded garden seating. Mon–Sat 8am–5pm, Sun 8am–3pm.

**Duncan's Coffee Co**, 3647 Baldwin Ave; ⓣ573-9075. Smart little coffee place on the main drag, serving paninis, espressos and smoothies. Mon–Sat 7am–5pm.

**Hali'imaile General Store**, 900 Hāli'imaile Rd; ⓣ572-2666. Gourmet Hawaiian food in a converted store in the village of Hāli'imaile, located two miles down Baldwin Avenue and then a mile west towards

Haleakalā Highway. Appetizers (up to $18) include an Asian pear and duck taco, and fresh island fish cakes, while entrees, like Szechuan barbecued salmon or rack of lamb Hunan style, can cost over $30. Mon–Sat 11am–2.30pm & 5.30–9.30pm, Sun 10am–2.30pm & 5.30–9.30pm.

**Polli's**, 1202 Makawao Ave; ⓣ 572-7808. Busy, good-value Mexican restaurant at Makawao's central crossroads. Individual dishes cost under $10, while a full chimichanga dinner is $13, and a fajita plate is $16. Mon–Sat 7am–10pm, Sun 8am–10pm.

# Pukalani

Now that a new bypass carries traffic on the busy Haleakalā Highway (Hwy-37) around, instead of through, **PUKALANI**, seven miles up from Kahului, there's no reason for tourists ever to see the town at all. This shapeless sprawl is home to six thousand people, but has no appreciable downtown area.

The run-down Pukalani Terrace Center mall holds the closest gas station to the summit of Haleakalā, as well as a big Foodland supermarket, a *Subway* sandwich shop, the *Mixed Plate* budget diner (Mon–Wed, Sat & Sun 6am–1pm, Thurs & Fri 6am–1pm & 4–8pm), and the Chinese *Royal King's Garden* (Mon–Sat 11am–2pm & 4–9pm, Sun 4–9pm; ⓣ 572-7027).

# Kula and the heart of the Upcountry

Immediately beyond Pukalani, Hwy-37 changes its name to **Kula Highway**, while **Haleakalā Highway**, now Hwy-377, branches off up the mountain. It meets the route to the summit, **Haleakalā Crater Road**, after six miles, and then, as **Kekaulike Highway**, swings back to rejoin Kula Highway.

This general region is known as **Kula**. None of the four separate communities – from north to south, **Ōma'opio**, **Pūlehu**, **Waiakoa** and **Kula** itself – amounts to very much, but the views they afford are superb. Far below, the curve of the ocean bites into either side of the flat, green isthmus, while on the horizon, clouds squat on the West Maui mountains. In the morning sun, you can make out the condo buildings lining the Kīhei coast, but by afternoon, apart from the odd glint of a car or window, the long gentle slopes seem predominantly rural.

## Accommodation

Driving across the Kula district, you probably won't notice any **accommodation** apart from the *Kula Lodge*. Tucked away on the backroads, however, are a wide assortment of lovely little B&Bs. All require advance reservations, and some can only be booked through specialist B&B agencies.

**Halemanu B&B**, 221 Kaweihi Place, Kula, HI 96790; ⓣ 878-2729, ⓔ carolaus@maui.net. B&B in private home with peaceful gardens, near the foot of Waipoli Road as it climbs to Polipoli (see p.326). Just one guest room, packed with oddments from around the world, with en-suite bath and amazing views. Two-night minimum stay. ❸.

**Kili's Cottage**, Kula; reserve through Hawaii's Best B&B, PO Box 563, Kamuela, HI 96743; ⓣ 885-4550 or 1-800/262-9912, ⓕ 885-0559, ⓦ www.bestbnb.com. A real bargain: a comfortable three-bedroom, two-bathroom house, set in beautiful upland gardens and equipped with TV, VCR and full kitchen, rented for less than the price of most Maui hotel rooms. Two-night minimum stay. ❹.

**Kula Lodge**, RR1, Box 475, Kula, HI 96790; ⓣ 878-1535 or 1-800/233-1535, ⓕ 878-2518, ⓦ www.kulalodge.com. Upmarket board and lodging in Hawaiian approximation of an Alpine inn, *makai* of Haleakalā Highway, just before the

Haleakalā Crater Road turnoff. Accommodation is in five chalets, four of which can sleep family parties: all are comfortably furnished, though they don't have phones or TV. ④/⑤.

**Silver Cloud Guest Ranch**, Old Thompson Rd, PO Box 201, Kula, HI 96790; ⓣ878-6101 or 1-800/532-1111, ⓕ878-2132, ⓦwww.silvercloudranch.com. Relaxing ranch-style B&B, just over a mile southeast of Kēōkea, along the one-lane road (signed for Kula San) that branches off opposite *Grandma's* (see opposite). Twelve comfortable and well-furnished en-suite rooms - the six in the main house have gorgeous long wooden *lānais* facing down the mountain and into the sunset, while the others are in outbuildings nearby. Horses, cats and pigs roam the surrounding meadows, and the owners can arrange trail rides in the hills. ③–⑤.



## Holy Ghost Church

The lower upcountry road, the Kula Highway, passes just below the white octagonal **Holy Ghost Church**. Portuguese Catholics came to Maui from 1878 onwards, and by 1894 were prosperous enough to construct their own church, shipping the hand-carved high-relief gilt altar from Austria, and capping the structure with a gleaming silver-roofed belfry. The interior is very light, with pink-painted walls, and features the Stations of the Cross labeled in Portuguese. Not surprisingly, this was the only octagonal structure built in nineteenth-century Hawaii; it is eight-sided either because the crown of the Portuguese Queen Isabella was octagonal, or because the German parish priest came from near Aachen, the site of a similar octagonal chapel built by Charlemagne.

## Kula Botanical Gardens

A couple of miles beyond the foot of Haleakalā Crater Road, on Kekaulike Highway, the **Kula Botanical Gardens** offers self-guided tours through large and colorful landscaped gardens (daily 9am–4pm; adults $5, kids 6–12 $1). Among its broad range of plants are proteas, hydrangeas, lurid yellow and red canna, and spectacular purple and yellow birds of paradise from South Africa. Many of its species betray their Pacific origins by bearing the Latin name *banksia*, in honor of Sir Joseph Banks, the pioneering botanist who sailed with Captain Cook; perhaps the finest is the red and white "Raspberry Frost" from Australia.

## Polipoli State Park

Maui residents rave about thickly wooded **Polipoli State Park**, set high above the upcountry, but visitors from beyond Hawaii may feel it has little they can't see at home. The drive up is fun, though, taking you off the beaten track into Maui's remoter reaches.

Polipoli Park stands at the top of the ten-mile Waipoli Road – *not* Polipoli Road, oddly enough – which climbs away from Kekaulike Highway just south of the Kula Botanical Gardens. The first six miles, in which you do all the climbing, are paved, passing through tough, springy ranchland where cattle graze on the open range. This is Maui's best launching spot for **hang gliders**, which you may see sharing the winds with circling Hawaiian owls (unique in that they fly by day, rather than night).

It shouldn't be too difficult to coax a rental car along the rough, but level, dirt road that meanders along the hillside above the ranch. After three miles, the road surface improves; drop right at the fork half a mile further along, and after another half a mile you'll come to Polipoli's **campground** in a grassy clearing. Tent camping here ($5), and overnight stays in the simple cabin nearby ($45 for four people), can be arranged through the state parks office in Wailuku (see p.271).

The entire Polipoli area was planted with Californian redwood trees by the Civilian Conservation Corps during the 1930s. The **Redwood Trail**, which leads down from a hundred yards before the campground, burrows through such thick forest that the persistent rain can barely penetrate it, and very little light does either. The forest floor is too gloomy even to support a light scattering of moss, and many of the tightly-packed trees are dead. It comes as a huge relief when the trail emerges from the bottom-most strip of eucalyptus after 1.5 miles to show expansive views across the ranchlands.

Various other trails crisscross throughout Polipoli, including some to lava caves hidden in the woods, but the only one likely to interest visitors from outside Hawaii is the **Skyline Trail**. This epic thirteen-mile trek follows the southwest rift zone of Haleakalā right the way up to Science City, at the summit (see p.333). It climbs a dirt track that heads off to the left two miles along the left fork from the junction 9.5 miles up Waipoli Road, described above. Unless you arrange a pickup at the far end, it's too far for a day-hike, and the higher you get the more exposed to the biting winds you'll be. **Mountain-biking** is permitted.



# Kēōkea

A couple of miles south of the intersection of the Kekaulike and Kula highways, the village of **KĒŌKEA** consists of a small cluster of roadside stores, together with green and white **St John's Episcopal Church**. All were built at the end of the nineteenth century to serve the local Chinese community. Alongside *Grandma's Coffee Store* (see below), one room of Henry Fong's general store houses the Kēōkea Gallery (Tues–Sat 9am–5pm, Sun 9am–3pm), an appealing little gallery of arts and crafts.

The wife and children of Sun Yat Sen, the first President of China, used to stay on his brother's ranch here while Sun was away fomenting revolution. Hence the statue of Sun, flanked by two Chinese dragons, that looks out over Wailea and Kahoolawe from the **Dr Sun Yat Sen Memorial Park**, which lies at the intersection of Hwy-37 and Kealakapu Road, just under two miles beyond Kēōkea.

## Kula district restaurants

There are very few **eating options** in the Kula district. The wood-furnished dining room of *Kula Lodge* (see p.325; ⓣ 878-1535) is open daily from 6.30am until around 9pm; it's busiest at the start of the day, when most of the customers are already on their way back *down* Haleakalā. The food is American, with a definite Pacific Rim tinge; the lunch menu consists of sandwiches, burgers and a few selections from the dinner menu, priced at $10–13, while evening offerings include crab-cake appetizers ($12), and seared *ahi* or large steaks for just under $30. Protea blossoms adorn the tables, and the views are immense. A couple of hundred yards higher up, *mauka* of the highway, *Kula Sandalwoods* (ⓣ 878-3523) offers a similar menu for breakfast and lunch only.

For smaller snacks, or an espresso fix, call in at *Grandma's Coffee Store* in Kēōkea (daily 7am–5pm; ⓣ 878-2140). You're unlikely to see "Grandma," but there's plenty of fresh Maui-grown coffee, plus sandwiches, salads, *saimin* and killer homemade desserts such as blueberry cobbler.

# 'Ulupalakua Ranch

Six miles on from Kēōkea, the six tin-roofed, single-story wooden buildings of the **'Ulupalakua Ranch** headquarters nestle into a shady bend in the road. Comings and goings are carefully monitored by the three carved wooden cowboys stationed permanently on the porch of the 'Ulupalakua Ranch Store (daily 9am–4.30pm); inside, you can buy sodas and snacks, *paniolo* hats, T-shirts and limited basic supplies.

'Ulupalakua Ranch started out in the middle of the nineteenth century as **Rose Ranch**, owned by an ex-whaling captain, **James McKee**. Originally its main business was sugar, but the focus soon shifted to cattle, and it employed expert *paniolo* cowboys such as Ike Purdy, a former world rodeo champion. In his huge mansion, McKee played host to Robert Louis Stevenson and King David Kalākaua among others, who took advantage of Hawaii's first ever swimming pool. Spotting ships arriving at Mākena Landing (see p.318), McKee would fire a cannon to signal that he was sending a carriage down to meet his guests. The mansion burned down during the 1970s, but the ranch itself is still going, raising elk and sheep as well as cattle.



## Tedeschi Winery

Around the corner beyond 'Ulupalakua Ranch, one of the ranch's co-owners has established the **Tedeschi Winery** as a successful sideline on the site of James McKee's original Rose Ranch. It uses two annual grape harvests from a small vineyard in a fold below the highway, a mile to the north, to produce 30,000 cases a year of white, red, and rosé wines, as well as *Maui Brut* champagne and a "sparkling pineapple" wine. They're on sale in the new **King's Cottage**, which also houses an entertaining little museum of ranch and cowboy history and serves as the assembly point for fifteen-minute guided **tours** (store and museum daily 9am–5pm; ⓣ878-6058; free tours, every hour on the half-hour, daily 9.30am–2.30pm). The converted and imitation ranch buildings used for processing and bottling are less than enthralling, but you do at least get to see some amazing trees, including a pine drowning in multicolored creeping bougainvillea, and a giant camphor.

## Pi'ilani Highway

South of 'Ulupalakua, Kula Highway confusingly becomes the **Pi'ilani Highway**, despite having no connection with the parallel road of the same name that runs through Wailea and Mākena down below. For all the strictures of the rental companies – see p.269 – it takes appalling weather to render it unsafe, and for most of the year it's possible to drive all the way along the south coast to Hāna, 37 miles away. A detailed description of the route, coming in the opposite direction, begins on p.352.

# Haleakalā

Although the briefest glance at a map shows the extent to which mighty **Haleakalā** dominates Maui, it's hard to appreciate its full ten-thousand-foot majesty until you climb right to the top. Hawaiian-style shield volcanoes (see

## Downhill Biking

One of Maui's most popular tourist activities is to be taken by minivan to see the dawn on top of Haleakalā and then to ride back down the mountain on a **bike**. It's not an exaggeration to say that it's possible to make it back down to the ocean at Pā'ia, a 39-mile ride, without pedaling; even Dan Quayle managed it, accompanied by six Secret Service men, also on mountain bikes. Approaching 100,000 people now make the descent each year, with several companies taking twenty or more customers every morning. It can be great fun, although serious cyclists tend to find it a bit pointless, especially as most operators make their groups ride together, at the pace of the slowest member. Plenty of activities desks offer discount rates on biking trips: it normally costs around $60 for a daytime ride, up to $120 to go at sunrise. Unguided trips, or shorter routes, cost about $20 less. All riders must have at least some experience, and be aged 12 or over.

**Aloha Bicycle Tours** ⓣ249-0911, ⓦwww.maui.net/~bikemaui. Small-group tours ending at Tedeschi Winery rather than the sea.
**Haleakalā Bike Co** ⓣ575-9575, ⓦwww.bikemaui.com. Unguided tours; they provide the bikes and a van service to the top, and you descend at your own pace.
**Hawaii Downhill** ⓣ893-2332. Sunrise and morning guided rides down to Pā'ia.
**Maui Downhill** ⓣ871-2155, ⓦwww.mauidownhill.net. Long tours, mostly including lunch, to Pā'ia or Kula.
**Maui Mountain Cruisers** ⓣ871-6014, ⓦwww.mauimountaincruisers.com. Sunrise or morning downhill rides to Pā'ia with hotel pickup included.
**Mountain Riders Bike Tours** ⓣ242-9739, ⓦwww.mountainriders.com. Sunrise and morning tours down Haleakalā, ending at Pā'ia, Kula, or Tedeschi Winery. Hotel pickup included.
**Upcountry Cycles** ⓣ573-2888, ⓦwww.maui.net/~wayner. Unguided rides, at sunrise or in the morning.

p.237) are not as dramatic as the classic cones of popular imagination, and with its summit often obscured by clouds, Haleakalā can seem no more than a gentle incline from the rest of Maui.

By ascending more than ten thousand feet above sea level in just 38 miles from Kahului, **Haleakalā Highway** is said to climb higher, faster than any road on earth. En route, it crosses a bewildering succession of terrains, equivalent to a drive from Mexico to Alaska. Beyond the exclusive homes and white clapboard churches of Upcountry Maui, it leads through purple-blossoming jacaranda, firs and eucalyptus to reach open ranching land, and then sweeps in huge curves to the volcanic desert and the awe-inspiring **Haleakalā Crater** itself. Almost eight miles across, this eerie wasteland would comfortably hold Manhattan.

To the ancient Hawaiians, Haleakalā was "the House of the Sun." They told of how at one time the sun crossed the sky much faster than it does today, until the demi-god Maui captured it here in a web of ropes, and only released it on the condition that it travel slow enough to give his mother time to dry her *tapa* (bark-cloth). Pre-contact Hawaiians trekked to the summit in search of basalt for adzes, to hunt birds, for religious ceremonies and to bury their dead; traces have even been found of a paved trail that crossed the crater and led down through the Kaupō Gap (see p.337).

The higher reaches of the mountain joined with the volcanoes of the Big Island to form Hawaii Volcanoes National Park in 1921, and became the independent **Haleakalā National Park** in 1961. It now ranks as the tenth most visited national park in the US, with around a million people a year reaching

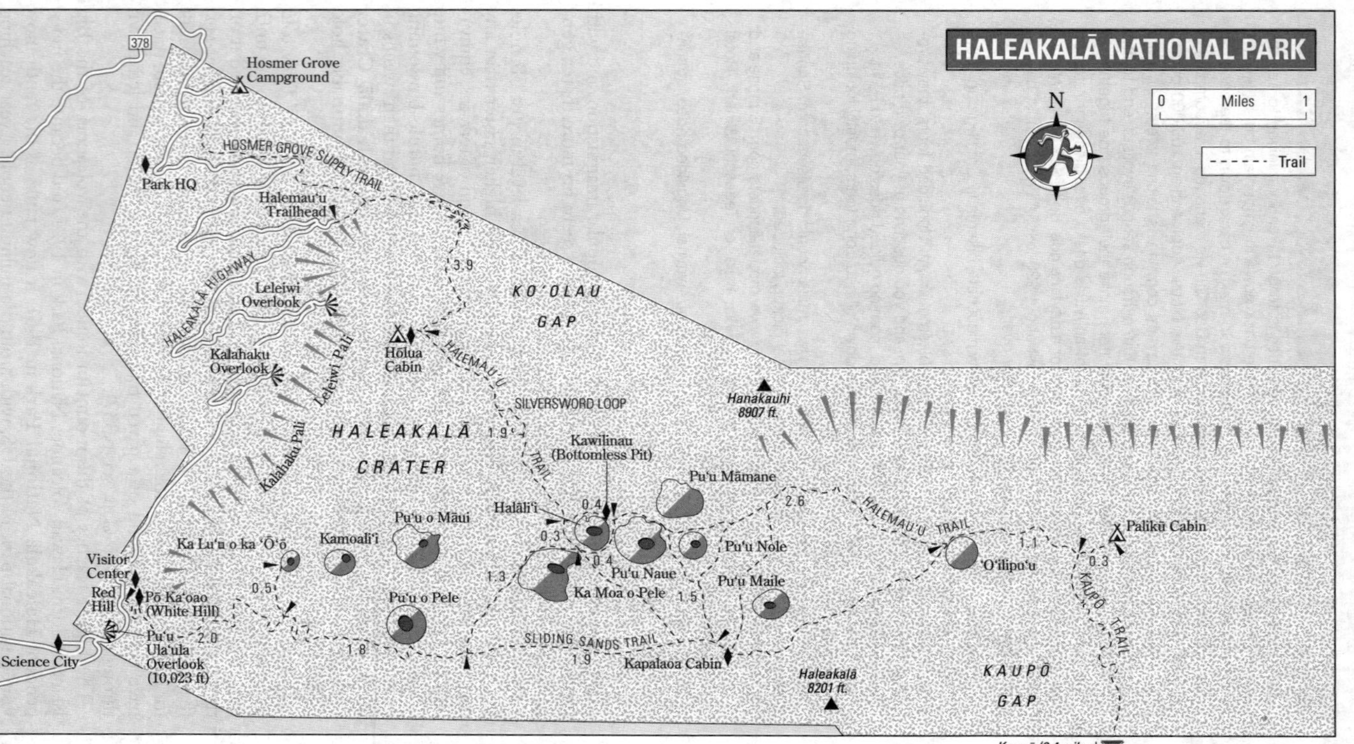
HALEAKALĀ NATIONAL PARK
N
0 Miles 1
Trail
378
Kahului
Hosmer Grove Campground
HOSMER GROVE SUPPLY TRAIL
Park HQ
Halemau'u Trailhead
HALEAKALĀ HIGHWAY
Leleiwi Overlook
Kalahaku Overlook
Leleiwi Pali
Kalahaku Pali
Hōlua Cabin
3.9
KO'OLAU GAP
HALEMAU'U
SILVERSWORD LOOP
1.9
TRAIL
HALEAKALĀ CRATER
Hanakauhi 8907 ft.
Kawilinau (Bottomless Pit)
Pu'u Māmane
Halāli'i
0.4
0.3
0.4
2.6
HALEMAU'U TRAIL
Pu'u o Māui
Kamoali'i
Ka Lu'u o ka 'Ō'ō
Pu'u Nole
Pu'u Naue
Ka Moa o Pele
1.3
1.5
Pu'u Maile
'O'ilipu'u
1.1
Palikū Cabin
0.3
KAUPŌ TRAIL
Visitor Center
Red Hill
Pō Ka'oao (White Hill)
0.5
Pu'u o Pele
Pu'u Ula'ula Overlook (10,023 ft)
2.0
1.8
SLIDING SANDS TRAIL
1.9
Kapalaoa Cabin
Science City
Haleakalā 8201 ft.
KAUPŌ GAP
Kaupō (8.4 miles)

the summit. The most popular time to come is for sunrise – described by Mark Twain as "the sublimest spectacle I ever witnessed" – but don't let that give you the impression that it's not worth coming later in the day. The views of the crater itself are at their best in mid-afternoon, while you can enjoy superb views from the roadside lookouts along the way up whatever time you arrive. It's also possible to hike into the crater, and even to spend the night there.

Note that Haleakalā National Park also includes Kīpahulu Valley and 'Ohe'o Gulch, on Maui's southeast coast. However, no hiking trail, let alone direct road, connects those areas with Haleakalā Crater.



# Haleakalā Crater Road

From all the major accommodation centers on Maui, the quickest route to the top of Haleakalā is to head for Kahului, and then follow **Haleakalā Highway** into the Upcountry (see p.322). From there, only **Haleakalā Crater Road** continues all the way to the summit, entering the park after a twisting twelve-mile climb through the meadows, and reaching the park headquarters shortly after that. With another ten miles to go before the summit, you should allow two full hours to get to the top from Lahaina, Kā'anapali or Kīhei, or one and a half hours from Kahului or Wailuku. The last gas station before the summit is at Pukalani, 28 miles below; the last food and lodging is at Kula Lodge (see p.325), 22 miles short.

Assuming you join the majority in attempting to drive up to Haleakalā Crater in time for the **dawn** – which varies between 5.50am in summer and 6.50am in winter – you'll need to make a very early start and a long hard drive in the dark. If you end up late for the sunrise, be warned that you'll be driving straight into the dazzling sun, and watch out for the endless posses of downhill bikers coming the other way. Incidentally, the record time in the annual 38-mile Run-to-the-Sun **foot race** up Haleakalā is an incredible 4hr 45min.

## Hosmer Grove

Just beyond the **park entrance** – the gates never close, though there's not always a ranger on duty – a short road off to the left leads to the park's main **campground**, at **Hosmer Grove**. Set almost exactly at the mountain's tree line, this may look like a pleasant wooded copse, but in fact it marks the failure of an early-twentieth-century experiment to assess Maui's suitability for timber farming. Out of almost a hundred different tree species planted by Ralph Hosmer, only twenty survived, though that's enough to provide a nice thirty-minute **nature trail**.

By way of contrast, **Waikamoi Preserve**, adjoining Hosmer Grove, is a five-thousand-acre tract of upland rainforest that's home to a wide assortment of indigenous Hawaiian **birds**. You can only hike through it with an authorized guide, so the best time to come is for the Park Service's free **Waikamoi Cloud Forest Hike**, which sets off from Hosmer Grove on Mondays and Thursdays at 9am.

### Haleakalā National Park hours and fees

Haleakalā National Park remains open around the clock; $10 per vehicle, or $20 annual fee; national passes (see p.38) are both sold and valid.

## Staying at Haleakalā: Campgrounds and Cabins

**Hosmer Grove** is the only Haleakalā campground accessible by car, and the only one for which campers do not need to obtain permits.

Wilderness camping is not permitted anywhere in the park. There are, however, three rudimentary, but sound, **backcountry cabins** within Haleakalā Crater, which can only be reached on foot. All are on the grassy fringes of the crater, sheltered by the high surrounding cliffs, and are padlocked to deter casual backpackers from wandering in. Each is rented to one group only per night, and has twelve bunk beds, with no bedding, plus a kitchen, a stove for heating, and an outhouse. **Hōlua** and **Palikū** cabins offer **tent camping** in the adjacent meadows – the 25 daily permits are issued on a first-come, first-served basis at the park headquarters – but **Kapalaoa Cabin** does not. Water is normally available, but it's up to you to purify it before you drink it.

Permits to stay in the cabins are heavily over-subscribed, and limited to three days in total, with no more than two days at any one cabin. In a system that effectively prioritizes island residents and their guests over ordinary tourists, you have to apply in writing at least three months in advance, stating the exact dates you want, to Haleakalā National Park, PO Box 369, Makawao, HI 96768 (call ⓣ572-9306 for more information). A lottery at the start of each month decides the schedule for the month ahead; at that point successful applicants are requested to pay $40 per night for groups of from one to six people, or $80 for groups of seven to twelve.

There's **tent camping** in a soft sloping meadow surrounded by tall pines; a small open pavilion holds basic washing facilities. No permit is required, but there's a three-night maximum stay.

It's possible to walk all the way into Haleakalā Crater from Hosmer Grove; a supply trail up the mountain meets the Halemau'u Trail after 2.5 miles, just short of the crater rim.

## The park headquarters

The **park headquarters** looks out across central Maui from the left of the highway, three quarters of a mile up from the park entrance (daily 8am–4pm; ⓣ572-4400, ⓦwww.nps.gov/hale). This is the place to enquire about the day's quota of camping places (see box above), or to register if you've managed to reserve a cabin. It holds little by way of exhibits or printed information, but you can pick up a basic park brochure and buy detailed hiking maps.

## The roadside lookouts

Beyond the park headquarters, Haleakalā Crater Road zigzags for another ten miles up the mountain, repeatedly sweeping towards the lip of the crater and then doubling back. Each of its final three closest approaches is marked by a roadside parking lot.

The first of these, 2.5 miles up from the park headquarters, is the **Halemau'u Trailhead**. One of the park's two main hiking trails begins its long descent into the crater from here, as described on p.335, but the edge of the *pali* is almost a mile away; there's nothing to see at the parking lot.

Another 4.5 miles up the road, **Leleiwi Overlook** is set a couple of hundred yards beyond its parking lot. It offers views across the isthmus to West Maui, as well as a first glimpse into Haleakalā Crater, but you'll probably have seen enough of West Maui from the Crater Road, and better vantage points over the crater lie ahead.

It's only legal to stop at the **Kalahaku** or **"Silversword" Overlook**, a couple of miles short of the visitor center, as you drive down rather than up the mountain; in fact it's easy to pass by without noticing it at all. That's a shame, because this sheltered viewpoint provides perhaps the best overall prospect of Haleakalā Crater. Mauna Kea on the Big Island is often visible through the Kaupō Gap in the ridge to the right, and when the clouds clear you can also see down to the north coast of Maui. Unless you hike into the crater, this may be the only place you see any **silverswords** (see p.336); in theory, there are a few in the small enclosure below the parking lot, across from the overlook.



## Haleakalā Visitor Center

Although the highway continues beyond it, most visitors regard themselves as having reached the top of Haleakalā when they get to the **Visitor Center**, eleven miles up from the park entrance (daily dawn–3pm; ⓣ572-4400 information, 871-5054 weather; ⓦwww.nps.gov/hale). The railed open-air viewing area beside the parking lot commands great views of Haleakalā Crater. In the pre-dawn chill, however, many people prefer to admire the procession of red-brown cinder cones, marching across the moonscape far below, through the panoramic windows of the small visitor center itself. If you're feeling more energetic, follow the short paved trail to the right instead, which leads up **Pā Ka'oao**, or White Hill, for 360° views.

The exhibits inside the visitor center are pretty minimal, though there's a good 3-D model of Haleakalā to help you get oriented. Park rangers also provide hiking tips and lead free **guided hikes**. Their **Cinder Desert** walk sets off from here along the Sliding Sands Trail (see p.334) on Tuesdays and Fridays at 9am, while the **Waikamoi Cloud Forest Hike** (see p.331) leaves Hosmer Grove on Mondays and Thursdays at 9am.

## Pu'u Ula'ula (Red Hill)

A few hundred yards further up the highway, a smaller parking lot at a final loop in the road stands just below **Pu'u Ula'ula**, or **Red Hill** – at 10,023 feet, the highest spot on Maui. A circular shelter at the top of a short stairway offers what feel like aerial views of Haleakalā Crater. In clear conditions – soon after dawn is the best bet – you may be able to see not only the 80 miles to Mauna Loa on the Big Island, but even the 130 miles to Oahu.

Confusingly, the peak that officially bears the name of Haleakalā is five miles east, above Kapalaoa Cabin (see p.336), and a couple of thousand feet lower.

## Science City

The road beyond Pu'u Ula'ula is closed to the public, but leads in a few more yards to **Kolekole** or **Science City**. This multinational astronomic research facility, perched at the top of the House of the Sun, monitors the earth's distance from the moon by bouncing laser signals off a prism left there by the Apollo astronauts.

# Hikes in Haleakalā Crater

The only way to get a real sense of the beauty and diversity of Haleakalā Crater is by hiking down into it. Although there are only two principal trails – the **Sliding Sands** and **Halemau'u** trails – the terrain varies far more than you could ever tell from the crater-edge viewpoints, ranging from forbidding desert to lush mountain meadows.

The obvious problem is that, once you've descended into the crater, you'll have to climb back out again, which at an altitude of 10,000 feet is never less than grueling. That said, reasonably fit hikers should be able to manage a **day-hike** that takes them down one trail and back up the other – a minimum distance of eleven miles. More ambitiously, you could aim to take in Kapalaoa Cabin along the way, for a total of thirteen miles, but heading any further east would be unrealistic. The easier route is to go down Sliding Sands and back on Halemau'u, though since the trailheads are several miles apart, you'll need to arrange a pickup or hitch a ride between the two; the prospects of getting a lift *down* the mountain in the afternoon are marginally better.

If you've arranged to stay overnight in the crater – see p.332 – you could see the whole thing in two days, although most hikers spend longer. It takes a hardy and very well-prepared backpacker, however, to trek out via the **Kaupō Trail** to the south.

Don't underestimate the effects of the **altitude**. Allow an hour or so in the summit area to acclimatize before you set off on the trails; not only will that prepare you for the effort ahead, but it will also mean that you're still close to the road if you start to feel ill. By far the most effective treatment for altitude sickness is to descend a few thousand feet. **Scuba divers** should not go up Haleakalā within twenty-four hours of a dive; ask your dive operator for detailed advice.

In addition, Haleakalā being such an ecologically delicate area, it's essential to practice **minimum-impact hiking**. Carry out everything you carry in, take all the water you need (reckon on six pints a person a day), and stick to established trails. Above all, never walk on the cinder soil surrounding a silversword plant (see box on p.336).

For details of companies that organize **horse-riding** expeditions in Haleakalā Crater, see p.270.

## Route 1: The Sliding Sands Trail

From the visitor center parking lot, the **Sliding Sands Trail** briefly parallels the road to skirt White Hill. It then starts its leisurely switchback sweep into the crater, down a long scree slope of soft red ash. While the *pali* to the north of the visitor center is scattered with buttresses of rock and patches of green vegetation, this side is almost completely barren, the smooth crumbling hillside only interrupted by an occasional bush. Far ahead, mists and clouds stream into the crater through the Koʻolau Gap.

For most of the way down, a close look at the ground beneath your feet reveals that it's made of tiny fragments of rock with different colors, textures and characteristics; hard-baked pink clay is interspersed with tiny brown gravel and little chunks of black basalt. It takes a while to appreciate the immensity of the crater; for the first mile, you expect to arrive at the crater floor at a group of multicolored rocks in the middle distance, but when you reach them you find a longer descent ahead.

Two miles down, the trail passes between a clump of twenty-foot-high *ʻaʻā* rock outcroppings. A spur trail from here leads 0.4 miles, by way of a miniature "garden" of silverswords, to the smooth lip of the **Ka Luʻu O Ka ʻŌʻō Crater**. This full round cinder cone, glinting with pink, red, yellow and ochre highlights in the bright sun, cradles a hollow core filled with tumbled boulders. From the trail above, you can see long clinker flows extending for two miles north of it, eating away at the neighboring Kamaoliʻi Crater.

Continuing on the main trail, you wind down through a rough field of *'a'ā* lava. In season, the silverswords that almost line the path shoot up above head height. For the final stretch of the total 3.8-mile descent, the desolate crater floor spreads out broad and flat ahead of you, punctuated by heaped mounds of ash.

## Route 2: The Halemau'u Trail

The alternative route down into the crater, the switchbacking **Halemau'u Trail**, starts at a trailhead half a dozen miles down Haleakalā Crater Road from the visitor center. Towards the end of the relatively featureless 0.75-mile descent from the parking lot to the crater rim, the main trail is joined by a side trail up from Hosmer Grove (see p.332). It then passes through a gate, to run parallel to the wire fence that marks the park boundary. After a few more minutes, it crosses a high, narrow ridge; provided the afternoon clouds aren't siphoning over it, you'll get staggering views down to the north Maui coastline, as well as south into the crater.

Only the first few switchbacks cross back and forth between the north and south sides of the high bluff. Here at the tip of the **Leleiwi Pali**, it's very obvious how the landscape below has simply poured down through the Ko'olau Gap, from the crater towards the ocean. Soon, however, the trail narrows to drop sharply down the south side of the *pali*; it never feels too dangerous, though the drop-offs are enormous. The tiny shape of the overnight Hōlua cabin comes into view a couple of miles ahead, a speck at the foot of the mighty cliff.

The trail eventually levels out beyond a gate at the bottom of the final switchback, then undulates its way through a meadow filled with misshapen and overgrown spatter cones towards **Hōlua Cabin**, just under four miles from the trailhead. A slight detour is required to reach the cabin itself, where the lawns are often filled with honking *nēnē* geese (for details of camping regulations, see p.332). Beyond it, the trail climbs on to a much more rugged *a'ā* lava flow, the youngest in the crater area. Indentations in the rocky outcrops are scattered with red-berried *'ōhelo* bushes, thanks to the wet clouds that drift in through the Ko'olau Gap.

As you climb slowly towards the heart of Haleakalā Crater, you can branch away to the left to follow the brief **Silversword Loop**, which holds the park's greatest concentration of silversword plants.

## The crater floor

At the point where the **Halemau'u Trail** reaches the floor of the crater, almost six miles from the start, a bench enables weary hikers to catch their breath while contemplating the onward haul around the north side of the **Halāli'i** cinder cone. If you continue south, and turn right after 0.3 miles, you'll come to the foot of the Sliding Sands Trail 1.3 miles after that.

Keep going to the left, however, and within a couple of hundred yards the Halemau'u Trail follows the crest of a low ridge to make a serpentine twist between Halāli'i and the nameless cinder cone to the north. Known as **Pele's Paint Pot**, this gorgeous stretch is the most spectacular part of Haleakalā Crater, the trail standing out as a lurid red streak of sand against the brown and yellow mounds to either side. You can tell that Halāli'i is of relatively recent origin by the fact that its rim has not yet worn smooth; look back to see the park visitor center framed far away on the crater rim.

It's possible to loop right around Halāli'i and head back along either trail, but the Halemau'u Trail continues west for another four miles. Immediately north of the junction where you're forced to decide, you'll see the fenced-off hole of

## Silverswords

**Not far from the ragged edge of the crater, we came upon what we were searching for; not, however, one or two, but thousands of silverswords, their cold, frosted silver gleam making the hill-side look like winter or moonlight. They exactly resemble the finest work in frosted silver, the curve of their globular mass of leaves is perfect, and one thinks of them rather as the base of an épergne for an imperial table, or as a prize at Ascot or Goodwood, than anything organic.**

Isabella Bird, May 1873

Haleakalā is a treasure trove of unique plants, birds and animals, but the most distinctive of all its species is the **silversword.** A distant relative of the sunflower, presumably descended from a lone seed that wafted across the Pacific from America, this extraordinary plant has adapted perfectly to the forbidding conditions of Haleakalā Crater.

Known by the ancient Hawaiians as the ʻāhinahina, or "silvery-gray," it consists of a gourd-shaped bowl of curving gray leaves, a couple of feet across, and cupped to collect what little moisture is available. Slender roots burrow in all directions just below the surface of the low-quality cinder soil; merely walking nearby can crush the roots and kill the plant.

Each silversword takes between three and twenty years to grow to full size, and then blossoms only once. Between May and June of the crucial year, a central shaft rises like a rocket from the desiccated silver leaves, reaching a height of from three to eight feet, and erupting with hundreds of reddish-purple flowers. These peak in July and August, releasing their precious cargo of seeds, and the entire plant then withers and dies.

The slopes of Haleakalā no longer glow with the sheer abundance of silverswords, thanks to the attentions of wild goats from the late nineteenth century onwards. In recent years a new threat has been posed by the appearance of Argentinian ants, which prey on the Hawaiian yellow-faced bee that's responsible for pollinating the silversword. However, the park authorities have so far managed to reverse the decline, and clusters of silverswords can be seen at many places along the crater trails.

**Kawilinau,** also known, misleadingly, as the **Bottomless Pit**; in fact, this small volcanic vent is just 65 feet deep. Spatters of bright-red rock cling to its edges, but it's not especially remarkable. Half a mile further east, you have the further option of cutting south across the crater, between Puʻu Naue and Puʻu Nole, to meet the Sliding Sands Trail near Kapalaoa Cabin (see overleaf).

Those hikers who choose, on the other hand, to take the **Sliding Sands Trail** down from the visitor center, know they've reached the crater floor when they get to the south end of the clearly marked spur trail that connects the two main trails. Turning left towards the Halemauʻu Trail involves a fairly stiff climb across the flanks of the ruddy **Ka Moa O Pele** cinder cone; over to the right, the triangular mountain peak of **Hanakauhi** can be seen rising beyond Puʻu Naue.

If instead you continue east along the Sliding Sands Trail, you enter a landscape that resembles the high mountain valleys of the western United States. The trail runs at the foot of a steep *pali*, on the edge of a delightful alpine meadow carpeted with yellow flowers, including the primitive native *moa*. Two miles along, shortly after two successive turnoffs to the left – one is an official trail, one a "trail of use," but it's impossible to tell which is which, and in any case they soon join to cut across to the Halemauʻu Trail – you come to **Kapalaoa Cabin**. This small, wood-frame, green-roofed cabin, tucked in beneath the peak that's officially named Haleakalā on a slight mound, is the only overnight shelter in the crater that doesn't have its own campground; for details of how to make a reservation, see p.332.

East of Kapalaoa, the Sliding Sands Trail has two more miles to run before it finally merges with the Halemau'u Trail, and the two then run together a further 1.4 miles to **Palikū Cabin**. The hike all the way here from the crater rim and back up again is too far to attempt in a single day; only press on if you've arranged to stay overnight. The last three miles along either trail involve a gentle descent through sparsely vegetated terrain that turns progressively greener as you approach Palikū. There are actually two cabins at Palikū, one for public use and one for the rangers; both are nestled beneath a sheer cliff, where an attractive, but generally dry, meadow gives way to a well-watered strip of forest.

### Kaupō Trail

The very demanding, nine-mile **Kaupō Trail** heads south from Palikū Cabin, first through the Kaupō Gap to the edge of the park, and beyond that all the way down to meet the Pi'ilani Highway on Maui's remote south coast. It takes a couple of miles to escape the pervasive cindery dryness of the crater flow, but beyond that you find you've crossed to the rain-drenched eastern side of the island.

As the walls of the Kaupō Gap rise to either side, the trail drops through dense forest, then, once out of the park, descends steeply through lush grazing land. Now that you're on Kaupō Ranch land, be scrupulous about staying on the correct trail; free-ranging bulls roam at will on the other side of many of the fences. After several hours of extravagant switchbacks, you finally reach the highway 200 yards east of the Kaupō Store (see p.353). Unless you've arranged to be picked up, your problems may just be beginning – little traffic passes this way.

# East Maui

Exposed to the full force of the trade winds, and sculpted by rainwater flowing back down the northern slopes of Haleakalā, Maui's **northeast coast** holds the most inspiring scenery on the island. From Kahului, the **Hāna Highway** takes fifty miles to wind its way round to the time-forgotten hamlet of **Hāna** at the easternmost tip. This memorable drive forms an essential part of most Maui itineraries, but is almost always done as a day-trip. Devoid of safe beaches, and too wet to build resorts, East Maui has very little overnight accommodation, and thus remains the **least spoiled** region of the island.

## Pā'ia

**PĀ'IA**, four miles out of Kahului on the Hāna Highway, is a friendly, laid-back town whose two distinct sections both began life serving the sugar plantations in the 1870s. **Upper Pā'ia**, concentrated around the sugar mill half a mile inland, was built on plantation land and held the camps that housed the laborers, as well as company stores and other facilities. Meanwhile, freebooting entrepreneurs set up shop in **Lower Pā'ia**, at sea level, operating stores, theaters, restaurants and anything else that might persuade their captive clientele to part with a few pennies.

Both parts of Pā'ia declined apace with the collapse of agriculture, especially after the post-World War II drift to Kahului (see p.299). The name "Pā'ia" today refers almost exclusively to what used to be Lower Pā'ia, which has re-emerged in recent years as a center for windsurfers and beach bums. The paint-peeling wooden buildings around the bottom end of **Baldwin Avenue** give it a very similar feel to Makawao, at the top of the road – see p.323 – but the gift stores and galleries within are much further downmarket.

Narrow footpaths thread their way towards the ocean from the Hāna Highway, passing between ramshackle houses with colorful gardens, to reach a short, tree-lined and sandy **beach**. Swimming here in Pā'ia Bay is rarely appealing, thanks to shallow, murky water and abundant seaweed, so locals head instead to the **H.A. Baldwin Beach County Park**, a mile west. Named after Harry Baldwin, son of Henry Baldwin of Alexander & Baldwin fame (see p.301), this was once the official sugar-company beach, and the chimneys of the sugar mill, which closed down in 2000, remain visible for the moment a few hundred yards off the highway, across the still-active cane fields. The beach itself is reached by a short approach road lined by a graceful curve of palm trees. Perfect bodysurfing waves crash onto its long unprotected stretch of sand, with safer swimming areas at either end.

## Ho'okipa Beach County Park

The best **windsurfing** site in Maui, if not the world, is **Ho'okipa Beach County Park**, just below the highway two miles east of Pā'ia. Thanks to a submerged rocky ledge that starts just a few feet out, the waves here are stupendous, and so are the skills required to survive in them – this is no place for beginners. The peak season for windsurfing is summer, when the trade winds are at their most consistent. By longstanding arrangement, sailboarders can only take to the water after 11am each day. In the early morning, and on those rare winter days when the wind dies down, expert **surfers** flock to Ho'okipa to ride the break known as "Pavilions" near the headland to the east.

As a beach, Ho'okipa is not hugely attractive. It's unshaded for most of its length, apart from a nice big grove of trees at the western end. Picnic shelters, showers and rest rooms are ranged along a platform of lava boulders raised above the small shelf of sand. In summer, the surf can be low enough for swimming, but you still have to negotiate the seaweed-covered ledge to reach deep enough water.

Ho'okipa is so busy that you can only approach it along a one-way loop road, which starts beyond its far eastern end; the auxiliary parking lot on the headland here is a great place from which to watch or photograph the action.

## Accommodation in the Pā'ia area

There's very little **accommodation** in Pā'ia itself. Windsurfers on a tight budget tend to stay at the *Banana Bungalow* in Wailuku (see p.304), while those limited to $60 per night head for Kahului or a cheap Kīhei condo. If you can pay any more, try one of the plush **B&Bs** scattered along country lanes in and around nearby villages such as **Kū'au** and **Ha'ikū**. Long-term visitors should be able to find a room through the local **bulletin boards**, which advertise rates of around $270 per week, or from $425 to $750 per month.

Both the county parks near Pā'ia that used to offer **camping** – **Baldwin Beach County Park** and **Rainbow Park**, up the road towards Hāli'imaile – no longer do so.

**Golden Bamboo Ranch**, 1205 Kaupakalua Rd, Ha'ikū HI 96708; reserve through Hawaii's Best B&B, PO Box 563, Kamuela, HI 96743; ⓣ 885-4550 or 1-800/262-9912, ⓕ 885-0559, ⓦ www.bestbnb.com. Lovely, gay-friendly B&B on a gorgeous garden estate above Ha'ikū, with one self-contained cottage and another divided into three apartments. All units have kitchens and bathrooms, plus *lānais* looking across paddocks and orchards to the ocean. ❸.

**Ku'au Cove Plantation**, 2 Wa'a Place, Kū'au, Pā'ia, HI 96779; ⓣ 579-8988, ⓕ 579-8710, ⓦ www.maui.net/~kuaubnb. Restored plantation home very close to the ocean a mile or so east of Pā'ia – and thus ideal for windsurfers visiting Ho'okipa. It features two en-suite bedrooms and two studio apartments. ❸.

**Pilialoha**, 2512 Kaupakalua Rd, Ha'ikū HI 96708; ⓣ 572-1440, ⓕ 572-4612. Small cottage in gardens of private home above Ha'ikū, with kitchen, bathroom and space enough to sleep four comfortably. Three-night minimum stay. ❹.

## Pā'ia restaurants

Pā'ia may fall down on lodging, but as far as **restaurants** are concerned it comes up trumps. Though fresh fish is the local specialty, there's something for all tastes, including a rare vegan option.

**Anthony's Coffee Co**, 90C Hāna Hwy; ⓣ 579-8340. Small coffee shop just west of central Pa'ia, dominated by the churning coffee roaster and serving espressos, pastries, soups, bagels and deli sandwiches at a handful of indoor tables. Daily 5.30am–6pm.

**Charley's**, 142 Hāna Hwy; ⓣ 579-9453. Large, sprawling, indoor restaurant, offering eggy breakfasts and mac-nut pancakes, plus lunchtime sandwiches, burritos and burgers for $7–10. The dinner menu has the same snacks, plus pasta and pizzas – calzones are $11 – and ribs or fish for more like $15. Breakfast and lunch daily 7am–2.30pm, bar food 2.30–5pm, dinner 5–10pm.

**Mama's**, 799 Poho Place; ⓣ 579-8488. Upmarket and wildly popular fish restaurant, in beachfront gardens a mile east of downtown Pā'ia. At lunch, there are fishy sandwiches and burgers for $10; at dinner, the fresh catch of the day is around $25. The menu credits the individual fisherman who caught your fish. Daily 11am–9.30pm.

**Milagros**, 112 Hāna Hwy at Baldwin Ave; ⓣ 579-8755. Friendly terrace café, serving all meals at parasol-shaded tables at Pā'ia 's main intersection. Salads and deli sandwiches for around $6; burgers, tacos and burritos for more like $8. Daily 8am–10pm.

**Moana Bakery & Cafe**, 71 Baldwin Ave; ⓣ 579-9999. Smart, tasteful café not far off the main highway, with mosaic tables and large windows. Serves fancy breakfasts, $7–8 lunchtime sandwiches, and $9–24 dinner entrees that range from green or red Thai curries to chili-seared *ahi* to *opakapaka laulau* (snapper wrapped in *ti* leaves). Daily 8am–9pm.

**Pa'ia Fish Market**, 110 Hāna Hwy at Baldwin Ave; ⓣ 579-8030. Informal, inexpensive place with wooden benches, where fresh fish – sashimi or blackened – is $12, while scallops, shrimps and calamari cost a bit more, and a fish or meat burger is just $6. Pasta entrees include chicken for $13 or seafood for $15, and there's a sideline in quesadillas, fajitas and soft tacos. Daily 11am–9.30pm.

**Pauwela Café**, 375 W Kuiaha Rd, Ha'ikū; ⓣ 575-9242. Occupying one corner of the rusting gray hulk of Pauwela Cannery, a mile off Hwy-36 and roughly five miles east of Pā'ia, this cheerful, classy neighborhood café serves delicious, inexpensive breakfasts – try the *pain perdu* – plus salads, sandwiches, and lunch specials all priced around $5. Mon–Sat 7am–3pm, Sun 8am–2pm.

**Picnics**, 30 Baldwin Ave; ⓣ 579-8021. Bright yellow plantation-style diner serving espressos plus delicious spinach-nut-burgers with cheese, and chicken, fish and beef plate lunches for $6–8. Picnics to go cost from $8.50 per person. Daily 7am–5pm.

**The Vegan**, 115 Baldwin Ave; ⓣ 579-9144. Top-quality vegetarian cuisine, served at rattan tables in a simple yet colorful diner, away from the mayhem a couple of hundred yards up from Pā'ia's central junction. Spicy, tofu-heavy Thai specialties, plus polenta, lasagne and Mexican dishes. Try two of the $10 daily entrees for the price of one, a soy burger for $5.50, or a tofu hot dog for $3.50. Tues–Sun 11am–9pm.

# The road to Hāna

The endless rains that fall on Haleakalā cascade down Maui's long windward flank, covering it with impenetrable jungle-like vegetation. Ancient Hawaiians allowed up to two days for the canoe trip from the isthmus round to the far eastern settlement of **Hāna**. Now the **Hāna Highway**, hacked into the coastal cliffs by convicts during the 1920s, has become a major attraction in its own right, twisting tortuously in and out of gorges, past innumerable waterfalls and over more than fifty tiny one-lane bridges. All year round, and especially in June, the route is ablaze with color from orchids, rainbow eucalyptus and orange-blossomed African tulip trees.

The usual day's excursion is roughly fifty miles each way, from Pā'ia to 'Ohe'o Gulch beyond Hāna. While not as hair-raising as popular legend would have it, driving is slow going, taking around three hours each way, and demands serious concentration. If you'd prefer to keep your eyes on the scenery rather than on the road, consider taking an **organized tour**, available from around $75 per person with the operators detailed on p.269.

## Huelo

Although the coastal road around East Maui is called Hāna Highway from the moment it leaves Kahului, it changes from Hwy-36 to Hwy-360 eleven miles east of Pā'ia, at the foot of Hwy-365 from Makawao, and that's where you'll find **mile marker 0**.

The first potential distraction on the drive to Hāna is the unsigned turnoff, marked by a double row of mailboxes at a bend in the highway roughly 3.5 miles along, that leads down to the village of **HUELO**. The dirt road soon passes the plain **Kaulanapueo** ("resting-place of the owl") **church**, built of coral cement on a black lava base and usually kept locked. It continues for a couple of miles, but neither it nor its many side roads offer access to the sea. Like many local communities, Huelo has become an uncertain mixture of Hawaiians and wealthy *haoles*.

The clifftop *Huelo Point B&B* (reserve through Hawaii's Best B&Bs, PO Box 563, Kamuela, HI 96743; Ⓣ885-4550 or 1-800/262-9912, Ⓕ885-0559, Ⓦwww.bestbnb.com; ❹) offers luxury **accommodation** with spectacular views over Waipi'o Bay, plus an on-site waterfall and open-air Jacuzzi. There's one suite in the main house, with panoramic windows and a long *lānai*, and a separate self-contained cottage.

## Waikamoi Nature Trail

Your one opportunity to explore the forested ridges above the Hāna Highway comes just over half a mile beyond the 9-mile marker, where the short but enjoyable **Waikamoi Nature Trail** sets off from an obvious roadside pull-out. The one-mile loop trail starts beyond a small picnic shelter, gently zigzagging up a muddy ridge (some hikers go barefoot). Despite the stone benches along the way, there are no views – it's barely possible to see beyond the tight-packed *hala* trees and green rustling bamboos hemming the track – but sunlight dapples down through the overhead canopy to magical effect. Here and there, you pass a variety of eucalyptus trees whose bark peels like fine tissue paper. The trail tops out at a smooth grassy clearing, with another picnic shelter, and a large mosquito population. It makes little difference whether you return by the same route, or down the adjacent jeep road that drops directly to the parking lot.

A little further along the highway, **Waikamoi Falls** tumbles down towards the road at a tight hairpin bend. If you want a closer look, the only place to park is immediately before the bridge – a spot it's all too easy to overshoot.

## Honomanū Bay

Shortly after mile marker 13, the highway drops down to sea level for the first time since Ho'okipa Beach, and you finally start to get the long coastal views for which it's famous. The Ke'anae Peninsula appears on the horizon, but much closer at hand – where the gorgeous, uninhabited **Honomanū Valley**, lit up by tulip trees, gives way to the ocean – you'll see the black gravel beach at **Honomanū Bay**. Swimming and snorkeling here is only advisable on the calmest of summer days, but it's a popular site with local **surfers**.

Two separate dirt tracks cut down to the shore from the road as it sweeps around the narrow valley. The first, at 13.5 miles, leads down to the north shore of the stream; the second, just after the 14-mile marker on the far side of the stream, is steeper and muddier, but comes out at the longer side of the beach.

## Ke'anae Arboretum

From a wooded bend in the road a few hundred yards before the 17-mile marker, a paved level trail heads inland to the attractive public gardens of the **Ke'anae Arboretum** (daily dawn–dusk; free). Following the course of a stream you can hear but not see, it leads into a lush, narrow valley and reaches the arboretum within a quarter of a mile.

Fifty-foot-high clumps of "male bamboo" guard the entrance, with tropical plants beyond including Hawaiian species such as torch ginger and wet and dry *taro*. Beyond the *taro* fields, a mile into the park, the trail becomes a wet scramble through the rainforest, crossing up and over the valley ridge by way of tree-root footholds. Along with lots of small waterfalls, and swarms of tiny flies feasting on fallen guava and breadfruit, there's a good chance of spotting rare forest birds and even wild boar.

## Ke'anae Peninsula

Not far beyond the arboretum, a side road twists down to the flat **Ke'anae Peninsula**, the site of a small, and still predominantly Hawaiian, village. It's said that this windswept promontory consisted of bare rock until a local chief forced his followers to spend two years carrying baskets of soil down the mountainside; thereafter it supported a large population. The *taro* fields are still here, surrounded by abundant banana trees and birds of paradise, and there's also a fine old **church** among the tall palms. The edge of the ocean is as bleak as ever, with *hala* trees propped up along the shoreline watching the surf crash onto headlands of gnarled black lava; swimming here is out of the question.

### Practicalities

Almost the only **food** and **lodging** along the main stretch of the Hāna Highway is in the Ke'anae area. The recently renovated *YMCA Camp Ke'anae*, on the highway shortly before the arboretum, is a former prison that now offers **cabin** accommodation and also has its own grassy **campground** (ⓣ248-8355, ⓔYMCACampKeanae@aol.com). Whether you stay in your own tent or in a cabin, it costs $15 per person or $30 per family. Not surprisingly, the facilities tend to be reserved way in advance.

Simple snacks are sold at two roadside kiosks – *Halfway to Hāna* and *Uncle Harry's*, before and after the **18-mile marker** respectively. The specialty at *Halfway to Hāna* is a tasty burger; at *Uncle Harry's*, opposite a dazzling array of flowers, try the banana and pineapple smoothie. Neither keeps very regular hours, but in theory they're both open daily for lunch.

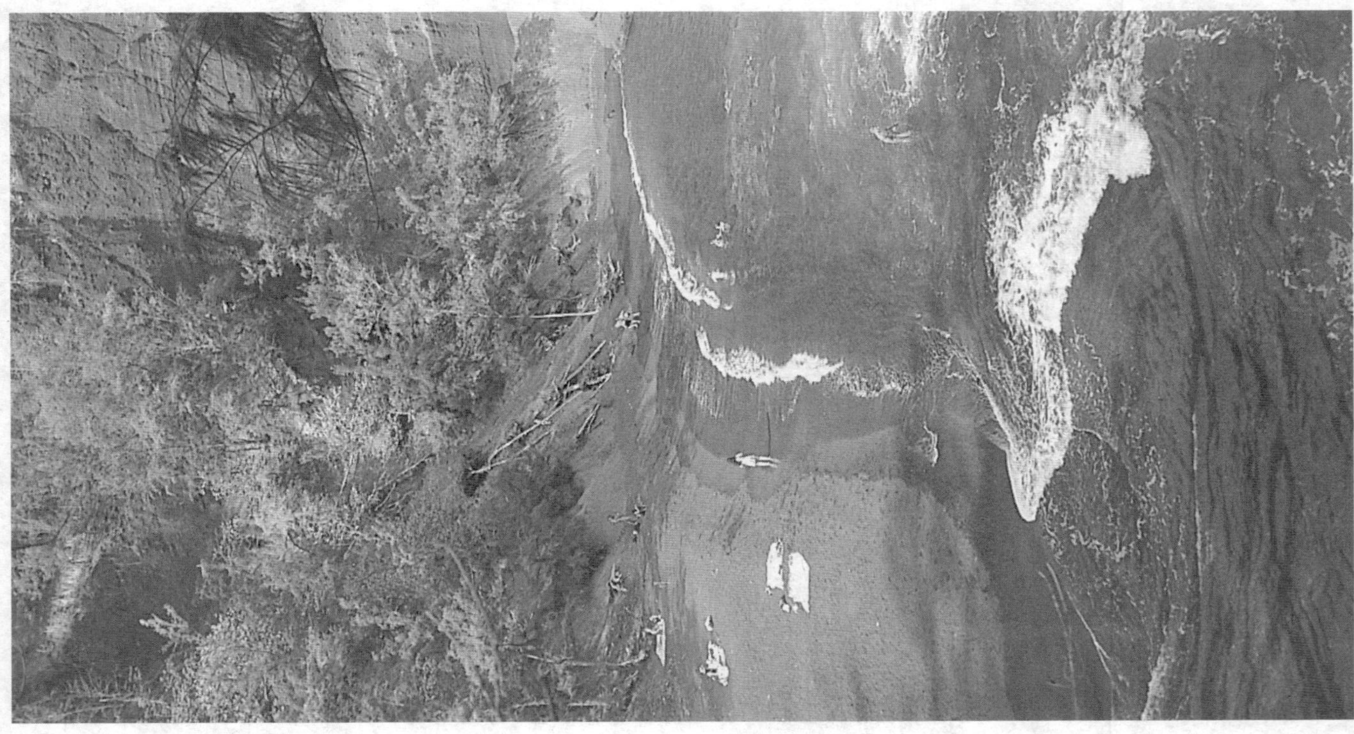

## Wailua

Within a mile of Ke'anae, as the highway veers inland, the arrow-straight Wailua Road plunges down to another traditional village, **WAILUA**. Unlike Ke'anae, its ancient rival, Wailua has always been fertile; it still holds extensive *taro* terraces.

The lower of the two churches that stand a short way down from the turnoff is known as the **Coral Miracle**. Local legend has it that, in 1860, just as its builders were despairing of finding the stone to complete it, a freak storm washed up exactly enough coral on the beach below. It's a simple but attractive chapel, painted white, with turquoise stencils around the porch and windows. Look back across the valley as you come out, for a superb view of the high **Waikani Falls**, garlanded by flowering trees at the head of the valley.

Wailua Road ends just above the tranquil mouth of Wailua Stream, which makes a sharp contrast with the ocean pummeling the beach of black pebbles beyond. Don't drive down to the stream – there's no room to turn round – and don't even consider a swim.

## Wailua viewpoints

Lookouts to either side of the highway beyond the Wailua turnoff offer scenic views up and down the coastline. From the inconspicuous *mauka* parking lot of **Wailua Valley State Wayside**, steps climb through a tunnel of trees to a vantage point overlooking Wailua Valley as it reaches the sea, and also inland across Ke'anae Valley, to towering waterfalls, undulating ridges and endless trees.

A little further on, immediately after the 19-mile marker, Wailua Valley spreads like a little oasis beneath **Wailua Lookout**. The taller of Wailua's two churches, **St Gabriel's**, pokes its head above the sea of trees, while the thickly wooded gorge stretches away to the right. At the next bend, just around the corner, a big cascade roars beside the road; you have to react quickly to stop.

## Pua'aka'a Wayside Park

The spacious parking lot of **Pua'aka'a State Wayside Park**, 22.5 miles along Hāna Highway, is every bit as big as the park itself. Nonetheless, this is a favorite stop for bus tours, because so little effort is required to negotiate the park's few yards of paved trails. If you brave the crowds, you'll see a pretty but far from spectacular sequence of small waterfalls, with picnic tables dotted on either side of the stream.

## Nāhiku

Not far after the 25-mile marker, a narrow unmarked road takes about three miles to wind down to the ocean. The few houses along the way constitute **NĀHIKU**, though there's no town, just a jungle of trees and vines, some of which all but submerge abandoned vehicles. The road comes out at **Ōpūhano Point**, looking back towards Wailua, with tree-covered cliffs reaching down into the water.

Early in the twentieth century, Nāhiku was the site of the first – unsuccessful – rubber plantation in the US. Ex-Beatle George Harrison has long had a home here, but he only visits occasionally, following a bitter legal dispute with his neighbors that centered on the construction of a beach-access footpath.

Just before the 29-mile marker, the *Nāhiku Coffee Shop* (daily 6.30am–4.30pm) is a roadside shack that sells espressos, smoothies, and homemade lunches such as banana bread and fish specials. There's a small crafts gallery alongside, as well as an open-air grill that serves smoked Hawaiian fish sticks to no discernible schedule.

## 'Ula'ino Road

The first sign that you're finally approaching Hāna is when you pass **Hāna Gardenland**, a not very exciting commercial nursery that, assuming it has reopened following extensive renovations, has a nice lunchtime café (see p.350).

Immediately afterwards, **'Ula'ino Road** drops away to the left of the highway, leading both to the largest ancient *heiau* (temple) in all Hawaii, and to one of the best **hikes** on Maui.

### Kahanu Garden

Three quarters of a mile down 'Ula'ino Road, the paved surface gives out where the road crosses a minor ford. On the far side, you'll find the entrance to Kahanu Garden, a nonprofit facility belonging to the National Tropical Botanical Garden (Mon–Fri 10am–2pm; $5; ⓣ248-8912 or 332-7234, ⓦwww.ntbg.org). This holds over a hundred acres of tropical plants, but is of most significance as the site of **Pi'ilanihale Heiau,** the largest ancient temple in Hawaii. Thought to have been enlarged and rededicated by Pi'ilani around 1570 AD to celebrate his recent conquest of the entire island, it covers almost three acres and consists of five separate tiers on its oceanward side.

The mile-long loop trail through Kahanu Garden begins by skirting the edge of an extensive forest of splay-footed *hala* (pandanus) trees. Beyond that, you get your first sight of the *heiau* itself, towering above the lush oceanfront lawns. Constructed from black lava boulders, intricately slotted into place, it's an impressive spectacle. As usual at such sites, however, in deference to ongoing Hawaiian religious beliefs, visitors are not allowed to set foot on the actual structure and can only admire it from a distance. As a result, you're not likely to spend more time here than the half-hour it takes to walk the trail, which winds past various labeled plants and offers some gorgeous views along the coast.

### The Blue Pool

'Ula'ino Road continues beyond the garden as a much rougher but still mostly paved track, undulating gently through the woods for another 1.4 miles. There are no long-range views, but it's a lovely stretch of countryside. The road ends abruptly in a shady grove a hundred yards short of the ocean, just above a stream whose outlet is blocked by a natural wall of heavy black boulders.

To reach a fabulous **waterfall**, make for the shoreline, then head left for a hundred yards. Here you'll find a shimmering **Blue Pool**, less than twenty yards from the sea, and constantly replenished by water cascading from the *hala*-covered ridge above. The grotto is festooned with ferns, vines and *hala* trees, its mossy walls bursting with tiny pinks and peonies. As you sit on the rocks, fresh water from the falls splashes your face, while you can feel the salt spray on your back. It's also possible to walk to the right along the beach, where coconuts lie among the boulders. Atop a spit of rough *'a'ā* lava, five minutes along, you can watch the surf crashing and grinding the black rocks to hollow out little coves, while a jungle of *hala* trees lies, unreachable, beyond.

# Wai'ānapanapa State Park

Within two miles of Hāna, beyond the turnoff to Hāna Airport (see p.346), a clearly signed road *makai* of the highway leads through a "tunnel" of overhanging trees to the shoreline at **Wai'ānapanapa State Park**. To reach the main parking lot, perched above a tiny **black-sand beach**, turn left when you reach the park cabins at the end of the first straight stretch of road. A short and easy trail descends from the parking lot to this beautiful little cove, where the beach changes from shiny black pebbles to fine black sand as it shelves into the ocean. It looks wonderful, and barely has room to hold its daily crowd of sunbathers, but swimming is deadly, with heavy surf and deep water just a few yards out.

At the right-hand side of the beach as you face the sea, look for a hollow cave in the small cliff that you just walked down. Squeeze your way through its narrow entrance and you'll find that not only does it widen inside, but it is, in fact, a tunnel. The far end, where it's open to the ocean, is a truly magical spot.

By contrast, a very short loop trail to the left of the parking lot back at the top leads down and through **Wai'ānapanapa Cave**. A few yards back from the sea, this "cave" is actually a collapsed lava tube, holding two successive grotto-like pools. It's slightly stagnant and smells rather like a public restroom, but you do see some nice clinging flowers.

Coastal **hiking trails** in both directions make it easy to escape the throngs at the beach. Heading **northwest** (left), you're soon clambering over a headland of black lava through a forest of *hala* and *naupaka*. Inlets in the jagged shoreline harbor turquoise pools, while surf rages against the rocks; in places, where the sea has hollowed out caverns, you can feel the thud of the ocean beneath you. A painting of a natural "lava bridge" here, executed in 1939 by Georgia O'Keeffe, now hangs in the Honolulu Academy of Arts. A mile or so along, the trail ends at the fence of Hāna Airport.

**Southeast** of the beach, the footpath crosses smoother, firmer lava, passing the park campground, a cemetery and an impressive blowhole. After around a mile, it reaches the ruined **Ohala Heiau**, the walls of which remain clear despite ivy-like *naupaka* growing inside. You can continue four miles on to Hāna; the scenery is invigorating all the way, but the trail gets progressively harder to follow.

Wai'ānapanapa is by far the nicest place on Maui to **camp** beside the ocean. In addition to tent camping, at $5 per person, it has basic cabins, each holding up to four people, at $45 per cabin. Permits are available from the state parks office in Wailuku (see p.271), but the cabins are usually reserved far in advance.

# Hāna

For some visitors, the former sugar town of **HĀNA** comes as a disappointment after the splendors of the Hāna Highway. Certainly, the point of driving the road is to enjoy the scenery en route, rather than to race to Hāna itself; having said that, it's a pleasant enough little town.

Although in ancient times Hāna controlled a densely populated region, these days it is home to just a few hundred inhabitants. They proudly see themselves as one of the most staunchly traditional communities in the state and have long resisted any concept of "development" for its own sake, but there are ominous signs that their way of life may be about to change for the worse.

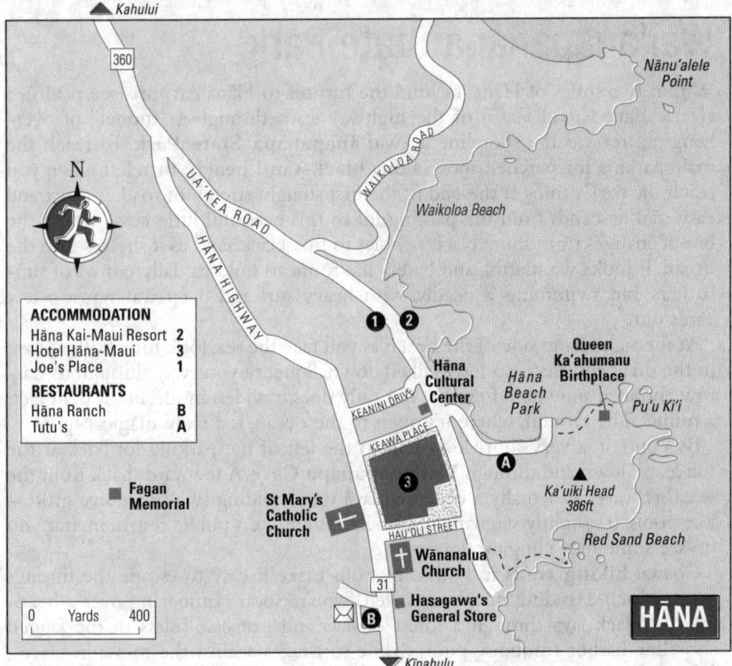


When the local sugar plantation closed in 1943, most of its land was bought by **Paul Fagan**, a Californian businessman. He established not only the **Hāna Ranch**, whose cowboys still work cattle herds in the fields above town, but also modern Maui's first **hotel**, the *Hotel Hāna-Maui*. Fagan died in 1959 – he's commemorated by a large white cross on the hillside – but the town remains dominated by the businesses he founded. Most of the town's central area is taken up by the *Hotel Hāna-Maui*, while the Hāna Ranch headquarters on the main highway houses its most conspicuous restaurant and other utilities.

Almost the entire town, including the Ranch and the hotel, was bought by a Japanese corporation in 1989. They published plans to turn Hāna into an exclusive resort much like Wailea (see p.316), complete with a new oceanfront hotel above Hāmoa Bay, an upscale shopping and restaurant complex, a golf course, and acres of residential properties. Without any of those schemes leaving the drawing board, Hāna has recently passed back into American ownership, and in 2001 the Ranch and the hotel officially separated. What that will mean for Hāna in the long term remains to be seen, but locals have welcomed the change, believing it puts their future on a more secure footing.

For the moment, Hāna remains one of the most relaxing places on Maui to spend a few days, short on swimmable beaches and golf, perhaps, but very long indeed on character, history and beauty.

## Arrival and information

The principal user of Hāna's small **airport**, perched beside the ocean three miles north of town, is the tiny Pacific Wings airline (Ⓣ 248-7700 or 1-888/575-4546, Ⓦ www.pacificwings.com). It operates three or four daily round-trip flights between Kahului and Hāna – each leg takes just fifteen minutes and is timed to connect with flights to and from Honolulu and Lanai – plus one or two nonstop flights to Honolulu. Only Dollar offers **car rental** at Hāna.

Hāna has no public transport of any kind, but the Hāna Ranch Center holds a **post office** (Mon–Fri 8am–4.30pm; Hāna HI 96713) and a Bank of Hawaii (Mon–Thurs 3–4.30pm, Fri 3–6pm).

In addition, Hang Gliding Maui is a one-man operation that provides **hang-gliding lessons** at $95 for 30min, $165 for 1hr (Ⓣ572-6557, Ⓦwww.hangglidingmaui.com).

## Accommodation

More **accommodation** is available around Hāna than is immediately apparent. As well as the *Hotel Hāna-Maui*, small-scale B&Bs are scattered all over town, and many of the houses along the shoreline are for rent. You can also **camp** at Wai'ānapanapa State Park (see p.345).

**Hamoa Bay Bungalow**, PO Box 773, Hāna HI 96713; Ⓣ248-7884, Ⓕ248-7047, Ⓦwww.hamoabay.com. Idyllic honeymoon hideaway, perched on stilts in jungle-like setting two miles south of Hana, with distant ocean views and not another building in sight. Bamboo furnishings, small kitchenette and wooden *lānai* with an open-air Jacuzzi. ❻.

**Hāna Ali'i Holidays**, PO Box 536, 103 Keawa Place, Hāna HI 96713; Ⓣ248-7742 or 1-800/548-0478. Choose from about twenty apartments and cottages in and around Hāna, many by the ocean, and some absolutely gorgeous. Rates range from $65 to $300 a night, but $110–140 should get you a spacious and attractive cottage. The office is located as Keawa Place makes its final curve on to Hāna Bay.

**Hāna Kai-Maui Resort**, 1533 Ua'kea Rd, Hāna HI 96713; Ⓣ248-8426, 248-7506 or 1-800/346-2772 (US), Ⓕ248-7482, Ⓦwww.hanakaimaui.com. Small condo building, set in lovely multilevel gardens overlooking Hāna Bay, a short way north of the beach park. Each well-equipped studio and one-bedroom unit has a kitchen and private *lānai*; the larger ones sleep four. Studios ❹, apartments ❺.

**Heavenly Hāna Inn**, PO Box 790, Hāna Hwy, Hāna HI 96713; Ⓣ248-8442; Ⓔhanainn@maui.net. Lovely Japanese-style B&B, on the highway two miles north of central Hāna, with three two-bedroom suites and a large common living area, but no kitchen. Two-night minimum stay. ❺.

**Hotel Hāna-Maui**, Hāna Hwy, Hāna HI 96713; Ⓣ248-8211 or 1-800/321-4262, Ⓕ248-7202, Ⓦwww.hotelhanamaui.com. Secluded luxury hotel, built in the 1940s as Hawaii's first self-contained resort and integrated into the community to create a unique atmosphere. In addition to the older rooms near the lobby, rows of plantation-style Sea Ranch cottages are arranged across the lawns that drop down to the ocean. They have no TVs, but boast every other creature comfort, with kitchenettes and private *lānais* that hold individual hot tubs and enjoying great views. As well as regular shuttles to Hāmoa Beach for activities, hotel guests have use of tennis courts and a pitch-and-putt golf course. Rooms ❻, cottages ❽.

**Joe's Place**, PO Box 746, 4870 Ua'kea Rd, Hāna HI 96713; Ⓣ248-7033. Eight simple rooms, sharing a kitchen, in a plain house opposite the *Hāna Kai-Maui Resort*. There are no sea views and only one room has an en-suite bath. It can be hard to get through on the phone. ❷–❸.

## Downtown Hāna

None of the buildings along the main highway, which passes through Hāna a hundred yards up from the ocean, is especially worth exploring, though **Wānanalua Church**, whose square, solid tower contrasts appealingly with the flamboyant gardens surrounding it, makes a photogenic landmark. Across the road, the **Hāna Ranch Center** is a dull mall, designed to feed and water the daily influx of bus tours, but given a flash of color by the odd *paniolo* cowboy. **Hasegawa's General Store**, stocked with every item imaginable, burned down in 1990. It's been rehoused in a charmless former theater, but is still a friendly place to pick up supplies. The **Hāna Coast Gallery**, at the northern

## Ka'ahumanu: Scenes from a Life

**She is prodigiously fat, but her face is interesting . . . her legs, the palm of her left hand, and her tongue, are very elegantly tattooed.**

Jacques Arago, 1823

**Returning from town, I saw Queen Ka'ahumanu in her four-wheeled cart being dragged to the top of a small hill by natives. The cart was afterwards pushed off at the top and allowed to roll down hill by itself, with her in it. This ludicrous sort of amusement was always accompanied with much shouting on the part of the natives.**

James Macrae, 1825

**At the Sandwich Islands, Kaahumannu, the gigantic old dowager queen – a woman of nearly four hundred pounds weight, and who is said to be still living at Mowee – was accustomed, in some of her terrific gusts of temper, to snatch up an ordinary sized man who had offended her, and snap his spine across her knee. Incredible as this may seem, it is a fact. While at Lahainaluna – the residence of this monstrous Jezebel – a humpbacked wretch was pointed out to me, who, some twenty-five years previously, had had the vertebrae of his back-bone very seriously discomposed by his gentle mistress.**

Herman Melville, *Typee*

No figure encapsulates the dramas and paradoxes of early Hawaiian history as completely as **Queen Ka'ahumanu**, the daughter of Nāmāhana, a chiefess from East Maui, and Ke'eaumoku from the Big Island. Her parents' strategic alliance presented such a threat to Kahekili, the ruling chief of Maui, that they were fleeing for their lives when Ka'ahumanu was born at Hāna, around 1777.

Chief Ke'eaumoku was one of Kamehameha the Great's closest lieutenants; it was he who killed Kamehameha's rival Keōua at Pu'ukoholā (see p.190). His daughter may have been as young as eight when she first caught the eye of the king; soon afterwards, she became the seventeenth of his twenty-two wives.

Captain Vancouver described Ka'ahumanu in 1793 as "about sixteen... [she] undoubtedly did credit to the choice and taste of Kamehameha, being one of the finest women we had yet seen on any of the islands." According to nineteenth-century historian Samuel M. Kamakau, "Of Kamehameha's two possessions, his wife and his kingdom, she was the most beautiful."

Ka'ahumanu was Kamehameha's favorite wife. As a high-ranking *ali'i*, she possessed great spiritual power, or *mana*; she herself was a *pu'uhonua* (see p.174), meaning that *kapu*-breakers who reached her side could not be punished. She was also an expert surfer and serial adulterer. Among her paramours was the dashing Kaiana, killed commanding the armies of Oahu against Kamehameha at Nu'uanu Pali, in 1795.

It was after Kamehameha's death, in 1819, that Ka'ahumanu came into her own. Announcing to her son Liholiho that "we two shall rule over the land," she proclaimed herself Kuhina Nui, or Regent, and set about destroying the system of *kapus*. These denied women access to certain foods and, more importantly, to the real source of power in ancient Hawaii – the *luakini* war temples. At first Ka'ahumanu's goal was to break the grip of the priesthood, but in 1825 she converted to Christianity, after being nursed through a serious illness by Sybil Gingham, the wife of Hawaii's first missionary. Meanwhile, in 1821, she had married the last king of Kauai, Kaumuali'i, and his seven-foot-tall son, Keali'iahonui.

Ka'ahumanu outlived Liholiho, who died in England in 1824, and remained the effective ruler of Hawaii when his younger brother Kauikeaouli succeeded to the throne as Kamehameha III. Her achievements included selecting Hawaii's first jury, presiding over its first Western-style trial, and enforcing its first law on marriage and divorce. After seven years spent proselytizing for her new faith, she died on June 5, 1832; her last words were reported as "Lo, here am I, O Jesus, Grant me thy gracious smile."

end of the lobby of the *Hotel Hāna-Maui*, sells an unusually good, if expensive, assortment of Hawaiian crafts and paintings of East Maui landscapes.

Local history is recalled by the low-key exhibits – gourds, calabashes, fish hooks and crude stone idols – at the **Hāna Cultural Center** (daily 10.30am–4pm; $2 suggested donation; ☎248-8622), on Ua'kea Road, down from the highway and above the bay. It also holds art exhibitions and is amassing a comprehensive collection of photos of past and present Hāna residents. Nearby stands a tiny nineteenth-century jail-cum-courthouse; on the grounds alongside it, a realistic replica living compound, of the kind used by the ancient Hawaiian *maka'āinana* (common people), has been constructed. As well as a thatched stone dwelling and a canoe house, it features garden terraces planted with *taro* and *ti*.

## Hāna Bay

Hāna's reputation for beauty relies largely upon broad **Hāna Bay**, a short walk below the north end of the town center. Much the safest place to swim in East Maui, it's also the only protected harbor in the area.

The small gray-sand beach known as **Hāna Beach County Park** spreads to the right – the south – at the foot of Keawa Place, backed by lawns that hold picnic tables, rest rooms and changing rooms. The park's long terraced pavilion, pressed against the curving hillside across the road, houses *Tutu's* takeout counter (see p.350).

Thrusting into the ocean to the south, the high cinder cone of **Ka'uiki Head** is the most prominent feature of the bay. Now covered with trees, it used to be just a bare rock, and served as a fortress for the ancient chiefs of Maui; Kahekili is said to have repelled an invasion from the Big Island here in 1780. Its far side – only seen easily from the air – collapsed into the sea long ago.

A short **hiking trail** – hard to spot at first, but soon clear enough – heads off around Ka'uiki Head from beyond the jetty, offering excellent views across the bay and up to Hāna itself. Soon after a tiny red-sand beach, it reaches a bronze plaque, set into a slab of rock near a couple of small caves in the base of the hill. This marks the birthplace of the great Hawaiian queen, **Ka'ahumanu**, though she was probably born later than the year it says, 1768. Continuing on, you discover that the rocky point beyond is in fact an island. **Pu'u Ki'i** was once topped by a giant *ki'i* (wooden idol), erected by the Big Island chief, Umi; it now holds an automated lighthouse. Around the next corner, the trail is blocked by an impassable red scree slope.

## Red Sand Beach

A precarious coastal footpath, which is often closed due to dangerous weathering and should only be attempted after seeking local advice as to current conditions, leads along the south flank of Ka'uiki Head to a lovely little cove that shelters one of Maui's prettiest beaches, **Red Sand Beach**. To find it, walk left from the south end of Ua'kea Road, below a small, neat Japanese cemetery. Approximately a five-minute walk, the path follows, and in places fills, a narrow ledge around a hillside of loose red gravel, but at this low elevation it's not too nerve-racking.

Behind a final promontory, the beach lies angled towards the rising sun, shielded by a row of black dragon's-teeth rocks, kept well flossed by the waves. Hawaiians knew this canoe landing as Kaihalulu Beach; swimming is only ever safe in the tiny inshore area. The origin of the beach's coarse reddish cinders – the eroded red cliffs above it – is very obvious, and it's equally obvious that you can hike no further.

## Restaurants

For somewhere with so many daytime visitors and overnight guests, Hāna has a remarkably limited range of **places to eat**.

**Hana Gardenland**, Hāna Hwy; ⓣ 248-8975. Assuming this small nursery, three miles north of town, has finally reopened, it holds a simple but tasteful open-air café. You should be able to order fresh breads, pastries or sandwiches for $6–9 at the counter, plus perhaps a $4.50 smoothie, then sit amid the plants. Daily 9am–5pm.

**Hana Ranch**, Hāna Hwy; ⓣ 248-8255. Unenthralling quick-fire restaurant in the heart of Hāna, serving bland $11 lunch buffets (daily 11am–3pm), pizzas Wednesday evenings, and slightly more interesting dinners on Friday and Saturday, when $18–25 entrees, such as barbecue ribs or teriyaki chicken, include a salad bar. A cheaper takeout counter, with a few tables, sells *saimin* and similar local specialties daily 6.30am–4pm. Restaurant Sun–Tues & Thurs 8–10am & 11am–3pm; Wed 8–10am, 11am–3pm & 5.30–8pm; Fri & Sat 8–10am, 11am–3pm & 6–8pm.

**Hotel Hana-Maui**, Hāna Hwy; ⓣ 248-8211. The deluxe resort's high-ceilinged, open-sided, wicker-furnished dining room is among the most expensive restaurants in Hawaii, and sadly the food doesn't merit the high prices. Even a humble *loco-moco*, a fried egg on a hamburger, costs $12.50, while full meals are likely to total well over $40. A typical dinner might include ceviche, salad of fern shoots, and steamed tiger shrimp with *opakapaka*. Daily 7.30–10.30am, 11.30am–2.30pm & 6.15–9pm.

**Tutu's**, Hāna Bay; ⓣ 248-8244. Beachfront takeout counter, whose indifferent sandwiches, burgers, plate lunches, sodas and lemonades attract long queues every lunchtime. Daily 8.30am–4pm.

# South of Hāna

South of Hāna, Hāna Highway gives way to **Pi'ilani Highway**, but the scenery is, if anything, even more gorgeous than before. In those stretches where the road is not engulfed by magnificent flowering trees, you can look up beyond the ranchlands to the high green mountains, while Mauna Kea on the Big Island hoves into view across the 'Alenuihāhā Channel.

A couple of miles out of Hāna, a 1.5-mile detour down the Haneo'o Loop Road takes you to the white-sand beach at **Hāmoa Bay**, used by *Hotel Hāna-Maui* for all its oceanfront activities, including a weekly *lū'au*. There was a small settlement here until it was destroyed by the *tsunami* of 1946; it's a good surfing spot, but unsafe for swimming.

The highway continues south through a succession of tiny residential villages, where, apart from the odd roadside fruit stand and countless crystal-clear waterfalls, there's no reason to stop.

## 'Ohe'o Gulch

Almost all the day-trippers who reach Hāna press on to beautiful **'Ohe'o Gulch**, ten miles beyond, where a natural rock staircase of waterfalls tumbles down to the oceanfront meadows at the mouth of the **Kīpahulu Valley**. This far-flung outpost of Haleakalā National Park tends to be jam-packed in the middle of the day, but, as one of the few places on Maui to offer easy access to unspoiled Hawaiian rainforest, it shouldn't be missed. If you hike a mile or two into the hills, you'll soon escape the crowds to reach cool rock pools, ideal for swimming.

The national park charges no fee at 'Ohe'o Gulch, and is always open to the public. However, there is a **ranger station** at the roadside parking lot (daily 9am–5pm; ⓣ 248-7375), which has up-to-date information on local roads and hiking trails. **Guided hikes** to different destinations set off daily except Saturdays at 9.30am; for details of **horseback** trips in the vicinity, see p.270. The rangers are forbidden to recommend that visitors drive all the way around southern

Maui on the Pi'ilani Highway (see p.352), as that violates rental-car agreements, but only very rarely are they obliged by flooding to declare it formally closed.

Access to the upper reaches of the Kīpahulu Valley, regarded as one of the most pristine and environmentally significant regions in all Hawaii, is barred to the public. The park is, however, hoping to purchase large tracts in the valleys to the west, in order to open more hiking trails and remote beaches.

### The lower trail

The paved footpath that leads **downhill** from the 'Ohe'o Gulch parking lot – officially, **Kūloa Point Trail** – is so busy that it's forced to operate as a one-way loop. Get here early if you want to enjoy it before the onslaught, but don't avoid it otherwise. After ambling through the meadows for five minutes, the trail winds past ancient stone walls on the low oceanfront bluff, and then down to a tiny gray-grit beach. From there, a "ladder" of stream-fed pools climbs the craggy rocks, an ascent negotiated by suckerfish in breeding season. Several of the pools are deep and sheltered enough for swimming, but the shark-infested ocean is far from tempting. It's impossible to follow the stream as far up as the high road bridge; by then, the gorge is a slippery, narrow water chute.

### The higher waterfalls

Thanks to the recent construction of two sturdy footbridges, the longer **Pīpīwai Trail** into the mountains is no longer rendered unsafe by bad weather, and ranks as one of the very best hikes on Hawaii (though one on which it's essential to carry mosquito repellent). It too starts beside the ranger station, but swiftly crosses the highway and heads uphill through steep fields, where thick woods line the course of the 'Ohe'o Stream. After the first half-mile, which is by far the most demanding stretch of the hike, a spur trail cuts off to the right to reach a railing that overlooks the towering 200-foot **Makahiku Falls**. A deep groove in the earth nearby leads to a series of shallow bathing pools just above the lip of the falls, where the stream emerges from a tunnel in the rock. As well as commanding magnificent views, it's an utterly idyllic spot for a swim.

Continuing by means of a gate in a fence along the main trail, you emerge into an open guava orchard and soon hear the thundering of smaller waterfalls to your right. There's no way to get to the water, but you'll see it framed through the thick jungle, together with the gaping cave mouth it has hollowed out on the far side. A little further on, you may be lured off the trail again by a pair of twin falls near a small concrete dam, which can be admired from a rocky outcrop in the stream bed below.

Beyond that lies a lovely meadow, with views to the high valley walls in the distance, laced by huge waterfalls. A mile up, the trail crosses high above the stream twice in quick succession, over the newly built bridges. It then follows a dark and narrow gap through a forest of huge old bamboo interspersed with sections of level wooden boardwalk. Eventually, two miles up from the road, you'll spot the spindle-thin, 400-foot **Waimoku Falls** ahead. Reaching its base requires a lot of scrambling, and crisscrossing the ever-narrowing stream. Despite the obvious danger of falling rocks, many hikers choose to cool off by standing directly beneath the cascade. Allow a good two hours to complete the entire round-trip hike.

### Camping

The National Park **campground** at 'Ohe'o Gulch is extremely rudimentary – it's just a field, with pit toilets and no drinking water – but it stands in the ruins of an ancient fishing village, and enjoys superb ocean views. Permits are not required, and it's free, with a three-night maximum stay.

## Kīpahulu

Within a mile of 'Ohe'o Gulch, the highway passes through the village of **KĪPAHULU**. Time seems to have stood still in this attractive little spot since the local sugar mill closed down 75 years ago. The only sign of life these days comes from the occasional lunchtime fruit stand selling the produce of the roadside orchards.

A quarter-mile beyond **milepost 41** at Kīpahulu, a paved road branches left off the highway. After a couple of hundred yards, turn left again onto a dirt road through a "tunnel" of trees, and park by the giant banyan tree at the end that guards the **Palapala Ho'omau Church**. Founded in 1864, it has whitewashed coral walls and a green timber roof, and is set in pretty clifftop gardens. The interior is utterly plain and unadorned.

Visitors make their way to this tranquil spot because the fenced-off platform of black lava stones in the churchyard holds the grave of **Charles Lindbergh** (1902–74), who won fame in 1927 as the first man to fly the Atlantic. Less appetizingly, Lindbergh was also a notorious Nazi sympathizer, who once told the *Reader's Digest* that aviation is "one of those priceless possessions which permit the White Race to live at all in a sea of Yellow, Black and Brown." President Roosevelt told a friend in May 1940, "If I should die tomorrow, I want you to know this. I am absolutely convinced that Lindbergh is a Nazi." Lindbergh retired to Maui late in life and died within a couple of years.

Leading off from the cemetery, and only accessible through it, **Kīpahulu Point Park** is a small, shaded clifftop lawn, fringed with bright orange-leafed bushes, where the picnic tables command wonderful ocean views.

# Along the South Maui coast

If you've driven the Hāna Highway and have a congenital aversion to going back the same way you came, it's possible in normal weather to follow the Pi'ilani Highway right around southern Maui. All the rental-car companies forbid their clients to come this way, but that's more because it's inaccessible if you need emergency help than because it's especially difficult. The road surface has been greatly improved in the last few years, so there's now just one unpaved stretch of less than five miles. It's a bumpy ride, no faster than the Hāna Highway, and not as spectacular, but it does offer a glorious sense of isolation. Advice on road and weather conditions en route is posted daily at the 'Ohe'o Gulch ranger station; see p.350. Don't attempt to drive this way after dark.

This area used to be known as **Kahikinui**, or Tahiti Nui; the equivalent part of Tahiti, which has the same outline as Maui, bears the same name. The countryside immediately beyond Kīpahulu is lovely, dotted with exclusive homes whose owners are no doubt happy that this is not yet a standard tourist loop.

After less than two miles, the road returns to sea level – for the first time in several miles – and skirts the long gray pebble beach at **Lelekea Bay**. As you climb the cliffs at the far end, look back to see water spouting out of the hillside above an overhang in the rock, forceful enough to be a gushing jet rather than a waterfall.

The pavement gives out after the second of the two little coves that follow. An overlook 2.3 juddering miles further on looks down on the small flat promontory holding the 1859 **Huialoha Church**. A mile after that, the solitary Kaupō Store is an atmospheric general store that's normally open on weekdays only. By now, the landscape has become much drier, and you're starting to get views up to the **Kaupō Gap**, where a vast torrent of lava appears to have petrified as it poured over the smooth lip of Haleakalā Crater. To the east, you can peek into the lushness of the upper Kīpahulu Valley, but the slopes to the west are all but barren.

What looks like a caravan, in a field about a hundred yards beyond the Kaupō Store, is in fact *Auntie Jane's Kau Kau Wagon*. In theory, it sells the **best burgers** on Maui, incredible $5 giants bursting with fresh beef from the ranch above, sweet corn, seaweed, salad and other fresh ingredients, and also sodas and "homemade" ices (in that they're made on Maui). As often as not, however, Auntie Jane is nowhere to be found.

The ruined outline of **St Joseph's Church** stands below the highway a mile beyond *Auntie Jane's*, just before the pavement starts up again. From here on, the road mounts the long southern flank of Haleakalā at the gentlest of angles. There's no tree cover on the deeply furrowed hillside – where some of the cracks seem like incipient Waimea Canyons (see p.492) – so cattle gather beneath the occasional shade tree beside the road.

Naked russet cinder cones lie scattered to either side of the road, some bearing the traces of ancient Hawaiian stone walls, while rivers of rough black *a'ā* lava snake down to the sea. An especially vast hollow cone, near the 20-mile marker, marks the spot where small huts and ranch buildings start to reappear. Soon Mākena becomes visible below, with Molokini and Lanai out to sea, and three miles on it's a relief to find yourself back in green woodlands. The Tedeschi Winery (see p.328) is a little over a mile further on, with another 23 miles to go before Kahului.

# 4 Lanai

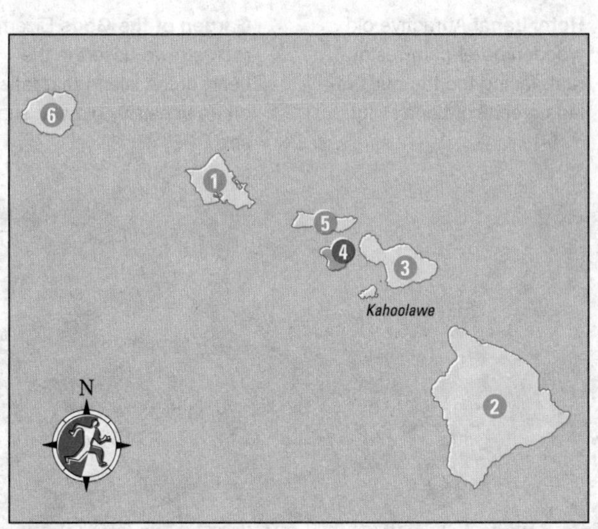

CHAPTER 4

# Highlights

* **Expeditions Ferry** Much the best way to reach Lanai; in winter, whales are usually encountered during the ocean voyage from Maui. P.360

* **Lāna'i City Service** Careering down Lanai's sand-logged backroads in a rented jeep makes an exhilarating day's adventure. P.360

* **Hotel Lanai** Attractive old wooden hotel-cum-restaurant, facing the tranquil "village green" of Lāna'i City. P.363

* **Hulopo'e Beach** Beautiful sandy beach shared between locals, campers and guests at the adjoining *Mānele Bay Hotel*. P.367

* **Shipwreck Beach** Flotsam and jetsam lie strewn across the sands where trans-Pacific voyagers have been coming to grief ever since the sixteenth century. P.370

* **Garden of the Gods** Bizarre rock-strewn desert in the heart of the island that takes on an unearthly glow at sunset. P.373

# 4

# Lanai



The sixth-largest Hawaiian island, and the last to open up to tourism, **Lanai** stands nine miles west of Maui and eight miles south of Molokai. Firmly in the rainshadow of its two neighbors, it's a dry and largely barren island, measuring just thirteen miles wide by eight miles long. Right up until the twentieth century, ancient Hawaiians and modern settlers alike barely bothered with it; then began its seventy-year reign as the world's largest **pineapple** producer.

Lanai's days as the "Pineapple Island" are now over. Promoted instead as the "Private Island," it has become the personal fiefdom of **David H. Murdock**, a Californian businessman who in 1985 became chairman of Castle & Cooke – one of Hawaii's original Big Five (see p.513) – and thus acquired control of 98 percent of the land on Lanai. Deciding that the island's future lay with tourism and not agriculture, he shut down the pineapple plantation and set about redeveloping Lanai as an exclusive resort. In 2000, Murdock reaffirmed his commitment to the island by buying Castle & Cooke outright for a total of $675 million. Among the former shareholders who benefited from the deal was Bill Gates, who was married on Lanai and until that point was rumored to be hoping to buy the island himself.

Prospective visitors (or purchasers) should not picture Lanai as the ultimate unspoiled Hawaiian island. In many ways, it's very un-Hawaiian, lacking both the lush scenery and sandy beaches of the other islands. Instead it's a vast flat-topped mound of red dirt, with a low wooded mountain ridge running down the center to serve as its "backbone." Almost all the island's three thousand inhabitants – half of whom are Filipino, descended from laborers who were shipped here to work the fields – live in the former plantation village wildly misnamed **Lāna'i City**, 1600 feet above sea level. This is also the site of all the island's hotels, restaurants and other businesses, other than the *Mānele Bay Hotel*, which stands on the south coast near Lanai's only swimming beach.

Lanai can be a very relaxing place to visit, with plenty of wilderness trails to explore by jeep, bike or on foot, as well as world-class golf and diving. On the whole, however, the clientele at the two major hotels seems to be divided between rich *kama'āinas* (residents of other Hawaiian islands), for whom the damp upland forests make a welcome weekend break, and mega-rich jet-setters, who either place a great premium on privacy or want to have stayed on every Hawaiian island. It's hard to imagine why an ordinary visitor from outside Hawaii would choose Lanai over the other islands, even though it does have one inexpensive hotel, one B&B, and even a campground to make it affordable. Most visitors simply come for the day, on the ferry from Maui.

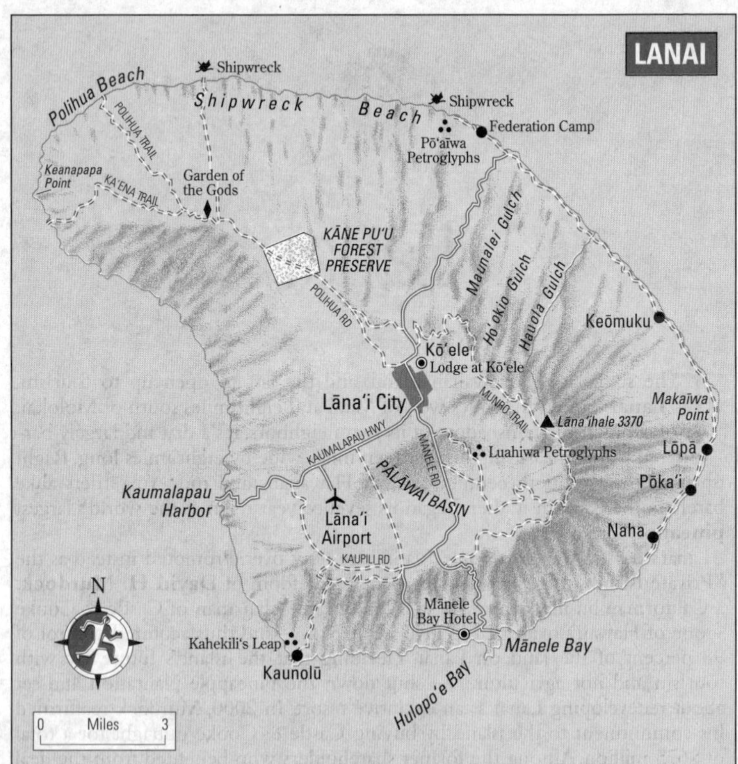




# A brief history of Lanai

For the thousand years after the Polynesians first reached Hawaii, they are said to have given Lanai a wide berth, believing it to be the abode of evil spirits. Its first permanent inhabitants came across from **Maui** during the fifteenth century, and the island has remained subordinate ever since to its larger neighbor. Ancient legends say that most of the interior was used for raising pigs, and the annual tribute demanded from West Maui was paid in hogs. However, the population never went much over three thousand people, concentrated in small coastal villages such as Kahe'a in the east and Kaunolū in the far southwest, who lived primarily by fishing.

Although European explorers dismissed Lanai as worthless and barren, in the past, before imported animals deforested the hillsides, it was wetter and more fertile than it is today. Even so, early attempts by outsiders to establish commercial agriculture ended in failure. In 1802, a Chinese immigrant set up Hawaii's first sugar mill, but failed to grow enough cane to keep it going. In 1899, a similar experiment at Keōmuku, on the east coast, lasted just two years.

The main flurry of activity on Lanai in the nineteenth century came around 1850, with the establishment of Hawaii's first **Mormon church**. Mormon missionaries came here to escape the antagonism they encountered in Honolulu; when they were called back to Utah in 1857, they left the church in local Hawaiian control. In 1861, a recent Mormon convert, **William Gibson**, arrived on Lanai proclaiming himself to be "Chief President of the Islands of the Sea," and galvanized the congregation into collecting enough money (around $2500) to buy the entire Pālāwai Basin. Three years later, it was revealed that Gibson had registered all the 10,000 acres in his own name. He was excommunicated, while his flock moved on to Lā'ie on Oahu (see p.129). Not only did Gibson hold onto the land but, as the self-appointed spokesman for all native Hawaiians, he went on to become the most powerful politician in the kingdom, winding up as King David Kalākaua's prime minister.

Gibson's heirs eventually sold his holdings and, following abortive attempts to rear sheep and cattle, Lanai's population had dwindled to around 75 by 1920. After self-made entrepreneur **Jim Dole** bought Gibson's ranch, the Lanai Ranch, for $1.1 million in 1922, he set out to grow **pineapples**, which require remarkably little water, and housed his predominantly Filipino labor force in newly built Lāna'i City. Castle & Cooke became majority shareholders in the Dole Corporation in 1932, but the Dole name remained, and the Pālāwai Basin became the world's largest pineapple plantation. Its workers were expected to pick a ton of fruit per day – they were paid bonuses if they managed more – and well into the 1980s Lanai was shipping out a million pineapples a day. However, the statewide struggle to win decent wages for farm laborers (see p.515) eventually made it cheaper to grow pineapples in Thailand and the Philippines, and Lanai's last official harvest took place in 1992. There are still a couple of show fields near the airport, and a few plants have managed to run wild.

What's particularly surprising about the program to turn Lanai into a **tourist destination** is that it has focused as much on the pine woods at Kō'ele, just outside Lāna'i City, as on the shoreline. *The Lodge at Kō'ele* opened in 1990, followed by the more traditional beachfront *Mānele Bay Hotel* the next year, and luxury condo developments have been appearing in the vicinity of both hotels ever since. Murdock has so far invested over a billion dollars, which amounts to more than $300,000 per islander, without returning any profit whatsoever. As for the future, most people on Lanai feel they've debated the issue of development into the ground. Presented with the closure of the plantations as an economic necessity and offered the alternative of almost total unemployment or massive investment in new leisure-industry jobs, few speak out against the changes. There is, however, an undercurrent of resentment at being told they live on a "private island," as exemplified by Murdock's willingness to seal off the island and arrest intruders in 1993, to ensure that Bill Gates could get married in privacy at Mānele Bay. (Gates is said to have paid every helicopter on Maui to remain on the ground that day, but the *Expeditions* ferry kept running.)

On the positive side, the hotels have a policy of retraining local workers rather than bringing in outsiders – although most earn much less than they did in the fields – and young people have started to return to Lanai after completing their education. Despite the optimistic self-restraint of the planners, who aim to limit the island's population to fifteen thousand, it remains just twenty percent of that target figure. The biggest fear on Lanai is not that development will run rampant, but that it might fizzle out altogether.

## Getting to Lanai

Tiny **Lanai Airport**, perched on the western edge of the central plateau around four miles southwest of Lāna'i City, is served by just two airlines. Island Air, the commuter affiliate of Aloha Airlines, connects it ten times daily with

**Honolulu**, and three times daily with **Kahului** on Maui. In addition, Hawaiian Airlines operates two round-trip flights daily between Lanai and **Honolulu**, and one each between Lanai and **Kahului**; **Kona** and **Hilo** on the Big Island; and **Molokai**.

The airport has a small store, but no café; since the plantations closed down, it seems to have become home to all the fruit flies on the island. Guests at the major hotels are picked up by bus; for details of taxis and rental cars, see below.

It's also possible to get to Lanai by **boat**. *Expeditions* (☎661-3756 or 1-800/695-2624) sails from Lahaina on **Maui** (see p.279) to Mānele Bay daily at 6.45am, 9.15am, 12.45pm, 3.15pm and 5.45pm. Departures from Lanai are at 8am, 10.30am, 2pm, 4.30pm and 6.45pm; the adult fare is $25 each way, while under-12s go for $20.

Although *Expeditions* also arranges discounted golf packages and overnight stays, most ferry passengers simply come for the day. **Shuttle buses** meet each arriving ferry at the harbor and charge a $5 flat fare even for the 500-yard hop to the *Mānele Bay Hotel*. Nonetheless, if you're staying at the hotel, don't try walking instead; it's quite a distance to trundle your baggage uphill along the hot dry road.

# Getting around Lanai

Lanai has the most rudimentary **road** system imaginable, with less than thirty miles of paved highway, none of which runs along the coast. As far as most visitors are concerned, the only significant stretches are the eight-mile **Mānele Road** from Lāna'i City down to Mānele Bay, and the four miles of **Kaumalapau Highway** between Lāna'i City and the airport. Free **shuttle buses** ferry guests at the three hotels along these routes. Buses between the *Mānele Bay Hotel* and *The Lodge at Kō'ele* run every half-hour until the late evening via *Hotel Lanai* in the heart of Lāna'i City; nonguests who look confident enough should have no problem hopping a ride.

The only **car-rental** outlet on the island, affiliated with Dollar, is based at Lāna'i City Service, on Lāna'i Avenue a short walk south of *Hotel Lanai* in Lāna'i City (daily 7am–7pm; ☎565-7227 or 1-800/JEEP-808). There's no point in renting an ordinary car; the only way to explore the island at all is with a **four-wheel-drive** vehicle, along a network of rough-hewn, mud-and-sand jeep trails. A basic Wrangler Jeep costs around $130 per day – the prices are high partly because there are such limited repair facilities on the island – so most people cram all their sightseeing into a single 24-hour period. Lāna'i City Service provides full instruction if you've never driven 4WD before, plus a useful booklet of suggested routes. Be warned, however, that they don't offer any extra insurance; you're liable for any damage to your vehicle, which can easily amount to several thousand dollars for a basic mishap in the sand.

Lāna'i City Service also runs the island's only **taxis** (when there's an unrented vehicle to spare), charging around $5 to the airport or Mānele Bay from Lāna'i City, and $10 from the airport to Mānele Bay.

Half-day **kayaking**, downhill **biking**, or **hiking** excursions for small groups are operated by the Lanai EcoAdventure Center (☎565-7737, ⓦwww.kayakhawaii.com), for a standard fee of $69 per person. *The Lodge at Kō'ele* rents out **mountain bikes** for $40 per day – riding the Munro Trail is the obvious route – and runs **horseback** expeditions into the hills.

## Where to stay

Apart from a **B&B** in Lāna'i City and **camping** at Hulopo'e Beach (see p.368), the only accommodation on Lanai is in three **hotels**. *The Lodge at Kō'ele* (see p.363) is modeled on a European country inn, while the *Mānele Bay Hotel* (see p.367) is a full-fledged Hawaiian beach resort; rates at both start at around $300 per night and escalate rapidly. The *Hotel Lanai*, in sleepy Lāna'i City, is more low-key and far less expensive.

## When to go

There's no real reason to visit Lanai in any particular season. Room rates stay constant all year, and the island receives so little rainfall that the supposed rainy season of September to November is barely noticeable. The only beach where swimming is safe is Hulopo'e Beach, below the *Mānele Bay Hotel*, and it remains so in winter, barring the occasional *kona* (leeward) storm.

The climate, however, varies between sunny Mānele Bay and cooler Lāna'i City, which is often overcast and can get chilly (down to around 50° F) in the evenings.

## Nightlife and entertainment

Although **nightlife** is not something anyone would associate with Lanai, the two resort hotels make great efforts to keep guests entertained. In particular, they run a successful **visiting artists** program, offering leading writers, musicians, directors and the like a few complimentary days on Lanai in return for readings or recitals; contact the Lanai Company for the latest schedules. You can also hear gentle Hawaiian music at the poolside of *Mānele Bay Hotel* most evenings, and they hold occasional *lū'aus* down by the beach. In addition, the island also boasts a **movie theater**, the Lāna'i Playhouse, at Seventh and Lāna'i in Lāna'i City (Ⓣ565-7500).

Apart from statewide public holidays (see p.26), Lanai's major annual event is its **Aloha Week**, which usually comes in mid- to late October, and features an open-air concert at Dole Park in Lāna'i City.

Otherwise, **golf** is the island's biggest single attraction, with a course at Kō'ele designed by Greg Norman, and one at Mānele Bay by Jack Nicklaus. Both charge $145 to guests and $200 to outsiders. The nine-hole Cavendish course in Lāna'i City, between *The Lodge at Kō'ele* and the *Hotel Lanai*, is free to all comers, but doesn't offer club rental.

# Lāna'i City

Thinking of **LāNA'I CITY** as a town stretches the imagination; that it should call itself a "city" is little short of absurd. This neat, pretty community of just 2500 people, centered on a village green, was laid out on a basic grid pattern

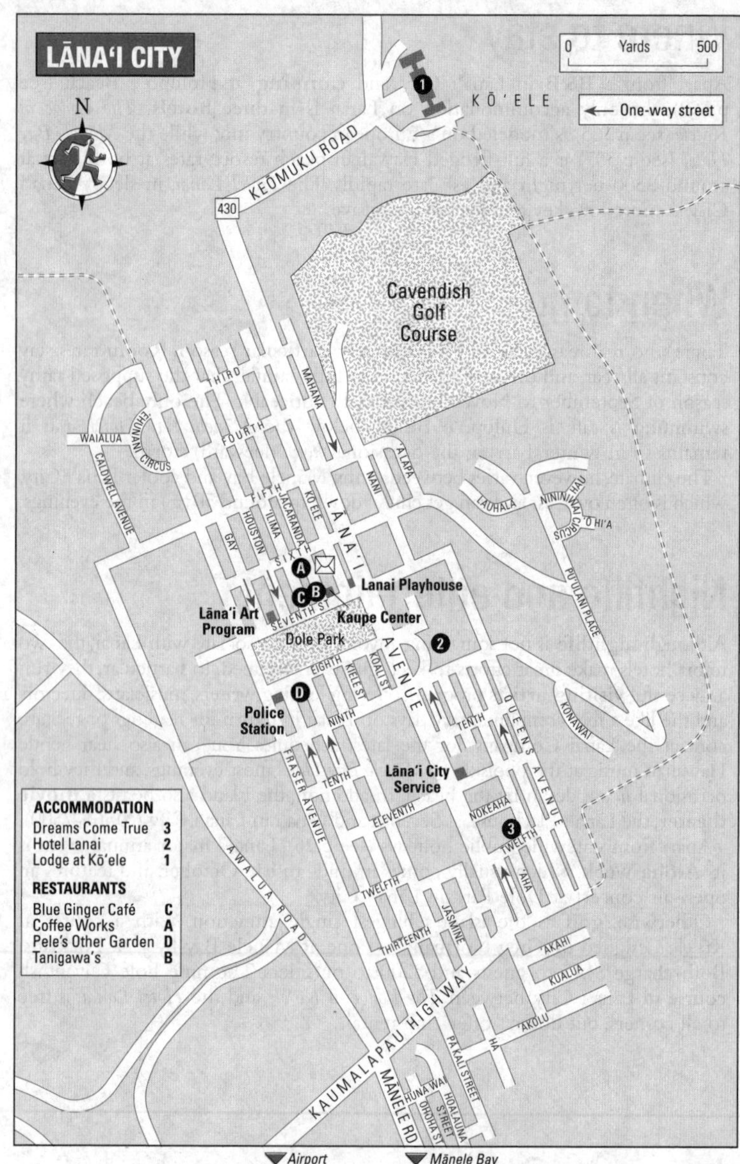


in 1924 to house laborers from the newly opened pineapple plantations, and it has barely changed since then. You have to search to find a two-story building: the leafy backstreets hold rows of simple plantation cottages, identical but for the colors they're painted and the rampant flowers in their gardens.

Virtually all the daily business of Lanai revolves around **Dole Park**, at the heart of Lāna'i City. The main road, **Lāna'i Avenue**, runs along the eastern end, while over a hundred ninety-foot Cook Island pines rise from the wiry grassland in the center, towering over the stores, cafés and offices that line all four sides.

Lanai's government offices are at the west end of the park, with the low-key local **police station** at the southwest corner. It's staffed on a rotation system by Maui officers; the outhouse-sized **jail** alongside is seldom occupied. The island's two **supermarkets** take up most of Eighth Street, along the south side of the park – like old-fashioned general stores, they stock just about everything – while the smaller *Pele's Garden* **wholefood store** is tucked around the corner on Gay Street.

# Accommodation

Apart from the *Mānele Bay Hotel*, down by the ocean on the south shore (see p.367), all Lanai's **accommodation** is in Lānaʻi City. In the seclusion of *The Lodge at Kōʻele*, there's little to remind you that you're in Hawaii at all, but the smaller-scale alternatives offer a real taste of the old plantation days.

**Dreams Come True**, PO Box 525, 547 Twelfth St, Lānaʻi City HI 96763; ⓣ565-6961 or 1-800/566-6961 (HI), ⓕ565-7056, ⓦwww.dreamscometruelanai.com. Small B&B in friendly family home, set in nice gardens a short walk southeast of Dole Park. Both the guest rooms have en-suite facilities and antique Far Eastern furnishings, and there's a shared living room. The owners also rent out three other very luxurious nearby properties, at rates that compare well with the hotels: the *Pink House*, which has two bedrooms sharing a bathroom; *Jasmine Garden House*, which has three bedrooms and two bathrooms; and the *Lanai Plantation Home*, which has four of each. B&B room ❸, *Pink House* ❺, *Jasmine Garden House* ❼, *Lanai Plantation Home* ❽.

**Hotel Lanai**, PO Box A-119, 828 Lānaʻi Ave, Lānaʻi City HI 96763; ⓣ565-7211 or 1-800/795-7211, ⓕ565-6450, ⓦwww.onlanai.com. Refurbished bungalow hotel, perched at the edge of the woods above Dole Park. Built for Jim Dole in the 1920s, it's now leased out to an enthusiastic young management team who have spruced it up into an appealing and inexpensive low-key alternative to the resorts. Guests nonetheless have free access to the resort facilities and can make use of the same free bus services. Accommodation is in eleven simple en-suite rooms or a self-contained cottage. Rooms ❸, cottage ❹.

**The Lodge at Kōʻele**, PO Box 310, Lānaʻi City HI 96763; ⓣ565-7300 or 1-800/321-4666, ⓕ565-4561 or, for reservations only, 565-3868, ⓦwww.lanai-resorts.com. Quite why *The Lodge at Kōʻele* should win the *Condé Nast Traveler* readers' poll as the world's best tropical resort is anyone's guess. It is a gorgeous, immensely luxurious hotel, but several miles from the ocean, 1600-feet up in a pine forest reminiscent of the Scottish Highlands. The ambience is pure country-house, with a baronial entrance hall, wood-paneled library, and stone fireplaces. It holds just over a hundred rooms, though at a glance you'd imagine there were much fewer; they're mostly tucked away in the low bungalows around the "executive putting course" and croquet lawns. Guests have full privileges and beach access at the *Mānele Bay Hotel*. ❾.

### Accommodation Price Codes

All the accommodation options listed here have been graded with the symbols below, which refer to the quoted rates for a double room in high season (December to March), not including state taxes of 10.17 percent. For a full explanation, see p.27.

| | | |
|---|---|---|
| ❶ up to $40 | ❹ $100–150 | ❼ $250–300 |
| ❷ $40–70 | ❺ $150–200 | ❽ $300–400 |
| ❸ $70–100 | ❻ $200–250 | ❾ over $400 |

# Restaurants

While the restaurants at *The Lodge at Kō'ele* set out to match any in the world, and *Henry Clay's Rotisserie* is a worthy alternative, the rest of Lāna'i City's eating places offer down-home atmosphere rather than gourmet cuisine. The fact that most of the island's food is brought in by barge means that most dishes start out frozen or tinned.

**Blue Ginger Café**, 409 Seventh St; ☎565-6363. Simple café-restaurant alongside Dole Park. It's a favorite local rendezvous, though the food is just basic plate lunches and pizzas, all for about $8. Daily 6am–9pm.

**Coffee Works**, 604 Ilima St; ☎565-6962. Spacious coffee bar a block north of Dole Park, behind the post office. Besides the espressos, they also sell a few cheap sandwiches and ice cream, and the large *lāna'i* is a good place to sit and appreciate how little happens on the backstreets of Lāna'i City. Mon–Sat 7am–7pm, Sun 8am–3pm.

**Formal Dining Room**, *The Lodge at Kō'ele*; ☎565-7300 ext 4580. Extremely formal restaurant, with a lofty reputation and silver-service treatment; male diners must wear jackets. Reserve early and savor the presentation as much as the food, which is not that special by Hawaiian resort standards. Appetizers include *carpaccio* of venison and *foie gras*, both priced at just under $20; entrees, at $42, include rack of lamb, steak and seafood; and there are some amazing chocolate desserts. Daily 6–9.30pm.

**Henry Clay's Rotisserie**, *Hotel Lanai*, 828 Lāna'i Ave; ☎565-4700. Friendly, intimate dining room, open for dinner only, but with an adjoining bar that remains open late each night. Under the keen supervision of its New Orleans-born chef/manager, the Cajun-influenced menu makes full use of local ingredients. Almost anything you choose, from an oyster in a shot glass for $1.35, to an appetizer of mussels in saffron broth for $10, to a venison or fish entree for more like $25–30, is likely to be excellent. Daily 5.30–9pm.

**Pele's Other Garden**, Eighth St and Houston; ☎565-9628. Dynamic health-food deli, offering juices and wholesome sandwiches to take out or eat in. Mon–Thurs 11am–7pm, Fri & Sat 11am–9pm, closed Sun.

**Tanigawa's**, 419 Seventh St; ☎565-6337. Even more of a local-style diner than the neighboring *Blue Ginger*, complete with swivel stools and soda fountain. Burgers, *saimin* and big breakfast fry-ups are served. Daily except Wed 6.30am–1pm.

**The Terrace**, *The Lodge at Kō'ele*; ☎565-7300 ext 4580. *The Lodge*'s less formal restaurant, with indoor and outdoor seating overlooking the lawns, serves generally healthy food, but still at quite high prices: even an egg-and-ham breakfast costs $12. Lunch is the best value, with $7 fresh-made soups and $12 grilled meat and fish dishes. Typical dinner entrees include slow-roasted lamb shank on couscous, and roasted chicken, both $28. Daily 6am–9.30pm.

# The Munro Trail

The only way to explore the mountainous ridge that forms the "backbone" of Lanai is along the ill-defined **Munro Trail**, as a loop trip from Lāna'i City. This rutted track climbs through the forest to the 3370-foot summit of **Lāna'ihale**, also known as "The Hale," which on clear days becomes the only spot in Hawaii from which it's possible to see five other islands.

Although it's often promoted as a **hiking** trail, even if you manage to walk the shortest possible route – which is difficult, in the absence of signposts – it's at least twelve miles long. Most visitors prefer instead to see it from the comfort of a rented **four-wheel-drive vehicle**, which allows for detours, while making it much easier to reach the top before the clouds set in. It's also possible to take a **horseback** trip; contact *The Lodge at Kō'ele* for details.

Even the start of the trail is far from obvious. Basically, you head east into the woods from the main road as it heads north beyond *The Lodge*. If you're driving, it's easiest to wait until the road curves east and climbs into the woods, and turn right after a mile or so onto the paved Cemetery Road. Otherwise, simply turn right as soon as you get the chance – there are at least two alternative options a short way along – and then, once on the ridge, turn right again. Either way, you should come to a Japanese cemetery, where the only sign on the whole route sets you off. Turn left soon after and then follow your nose; as a rule of thumb, fork left whenever you're in doubt, look for the most-used path, and don't worry about dropping down because you'll soon be heading back up again. As you climb through the fresh pine forest, look up ahead to see if clouds are sitting on the ridge; if they are, consider coming back on a day when you'll be able to make the most of the view.

The first major viewpoint comes after roughly three miles, where a short spur road leads to the head of the bare, red **Maunalei Gulch**. A few sparse trees sprinkle the top of the ridge that defines its western edge, while far below you can see the jeep road that winds along the greener valley floor. Molokai should be obvious on the northern horizon, and you may even see Oahu too, to the left. Off to the right, the top of the connected **Ho'okia Gulch** was the site of a ferocious battle in 1778, when Big Island warriors led by Kalaniopu'u vented their spleen, after a failed bid to conquer Maui, by massacring the armies of Lanai instead.

Continuing to climb on the main trail, you soon pass some tall communications towers. Both the road and the ridge it's following narrow to the width of a single vehicle, and you find yourself driving between rounded "parapets" of mud, with dense overhanging thickets of strawberry guava. Any turkeys and other game birds you may startle – in the absence of the usual Hawaiian mongooses, they thrive here – are forced to run shrieking up the road ahead of you.

After five miles, by which time you may well have penetrated the clouds, a clearing on the right looks out over the high, green **Waiapa'a Gulch**. For the clearest views of Lāna'i City, keep going for another muddy mile, to the very summit. It's another two miles, however, before you finally see across the ocean to West Maui, dwarfed beneath the misty silhouette of Haleakalā, while Lanai's central Pālāwai Basin spreads out behind you.

From here on, the soil reverts from dark brown mud to Lanai's more usual red earth. A rudimentary "crossroads," just beyond the exposed portion of the ridge and a total of 8.5m from the start, marks the start of **'Āwehi Road** to the left. This jeep track runs all the way to the sea at the southeast corner, between Lōpa and Naha (see p.372), but it's in far too bad a condition to recommend. As the Munro Trail drops ever more steeply, clearings on the left frame views of Kahoolawe, with Mauna Kea on the Big Island potentially visible in the endless ocean beyond.

Drivers can follow more or less any of the countless red-dirt roads that branch off at the southern end of the trail, and thread their way back to town. If you're hiking, you'll want to take the shortest route back to Lāna'i City, so head as directly as you can along the base of the ridge, which means generally following right forks.

## George Munro's pine trees

The Munro Trail was named after **George Munro**, a naturalist from New Zealand who was employed by the Lāna'i Ranch around 1917. Having calculated that the leaves on a single tall tree on Lanai can collect forty gallons of water per hour that would not otherwise have fallen as rain, he set to work covering the island with Cook Island and Norfolk Island pines. They're recognizable partly by the knobbly bands around their trunks, and partly by the fact that there are so many of them. The strip along the central ridge has been effective in turning the topmost sections of the Munro Trail into a quagmire, lined with dripping ferns. The trees here are clearly visible from Lahaina on Maui.

# South and West Lanai

The southern half of Lanai used to be the main pineapple-growing region, but now all activity revolves around the tourist industry. **Hulopo'e Beach** is the only safe swimming beach on the island, while **Mānele Bay**, next door, its only pleasure-boat harbor. That's as much as visitors usually bother with, though **Kaunolū** in the far southwest is Lanai's most important historical site.

Lanai's **west coast** is the one leeward shoreline in Hawaii to have sea cliffs, some of which rise over a thousand feet. These have been shorn away by wintertime *kona* storms, while the rest of the island is sheltered by Maui and Molokai. No road runs along the coast, though it is possible to drive down to Kaumalapau Harbor.

## The Pālāwai Basin

It would be easy to drive repeatedly through the **Pālāwai Basin**, immediately south of Lāna'i City, without ever noticing what it is. Once it's pointed out to you, however, it's glaringly obvious that you're in the collapsed caldera of the volcano that built Lanai. The entire 15,000-acre basin – until just a few years ago, the largest pineapple field on earth – is a bowl-shaped depression. The high mountain ridge on its eastern side stands thousands of feet taller than the low rise to the west, while the bowl spills over altogether to flow down to the ocean on the southern side. Nothing is planted now in the fields, but the occasional vivid flowering tree lights up the highway.

### Luahiwa Petroglyphs

On the eastern edge of the Pālāwai Basin, a grove of trees a short way up the hillside towards the peak of Lāna'ihale marks the site of the **Luahiwa Petroglyphs**. It's hard to find, so ask for directions at your hotel. Etched into a couple of dozen boulders embedded in the soil – which are thought to have formed part of a *heiau* dedicated to prayers for rain – these carvings were created during several separate eras. The earliest examples, which may be as much as five hundred years old, show simple stick figures, sometimes superimposed on each other. A couple of centuries later, the Hawaiians began to depict wedge-shaped bodies, and thereafter the human shapes have muscles and wield oars or weapons. Animals also start to appear, with images of horses produced after European contact. Some are known to have been embellished by native Hawaiian students in the 1870s.

## Mānele Bay

Just under five miles from Lāna'i City, Mānele Road drops from the southern lip of the Pālāwai Basin to wind for three more miles down to **Mānele Bay**. *Mānele* means "sedan chair" in Hawaiian, but no one knows why the long-vanished fishing village that once stood here bore this name.

As parched and barren as a Greek island, the bay is protected from the open ocean by the high flat-faced cliff on its eastern side, which glows red when it's hit by the setting sun. Until 1965, when the harbor was dredged and further shielded by a lava breakwater, there was a small black-sand beach. People fish from the rocks or picnic nearby, and the odd brave soul dodges the boats to go snorkeling, but there's nothing much here. Day-trippers arriving on the *Expeditions* ferry from Maui (see p.360) usually head straight for Hulopo'e Beach, around to the left, or up to Lāna'i City.

## Mānele Bay Hotel

Despite its name, the *Mānele Bay Hotel* (PO Box 310, Lāna'i City HI 96763; Ⓣ 565-7700 or 1-800/321-4666, Ⓕ 565-2483 or, for reservations, 565-3868, Ⓦ www.lanai-resorts.com; terrace view ❽, garden or ocean view ❾) is not actually at Mānele Bay, although it is visible from the harbor. It spreads itself instead across the hillside above the much nicer Hulopo'e Beach, a few hundred yards west. Although *The Lodge at Kō'ele* is regarded as the island's flagship hotel, the *Mānele Bay* conforms far more closely to what most visitors want from Hawaii: a lovely beach, ocean views, marble terraces, cocktails by the pool and plenty of sun. Its 250 lavishly appointed rooms (some of which come with their own private butler) are arranged in two-story terraced buildings, engulfed by colorful gardens, with a golf course alongside. There's also a luxury spa, where Hawaiian treatments such as *lomi lomi* massage or *ti*-leaf wraps cost around $100 or more for 45 minutes.

The less formal of the hotel's two **restaurants**, the *Hulopo'e Court*, opens for breakfast and dinner (daily 7–11am & 6–9.30pm), charging $22 for the morning buffet and around $30 for delicious evening menu items such as steamed *onaga* (red snapper). The dinner-only *Ihilani Dining Room* serves "Mediterranean Gourmet" cuisine, with steamed and grilled island fish or roast meat for around $40, and five-course set menus at $85 ($125 with wine) per person. At lunchtime, your choices are limited to sandwiches and snacks beside the pool.

# Hulopo'e Beach

Only accessible by road from Mānele Bay – it's just a couple of hundred yards further along, at the end of Mānele Road – but also reached via a footpath down from the *Mānele Bay Hotel*, the curving sandy strip known as **Hulopo'e Beach** is by far the best swimming beach on Lanai. What's more, it's far enough from the hotel to retain its own individual character – apart from a small equipment kiosk at the west end, there are no snack bars or other facilities for guests.

The beach was set aside by Castle & Cooke as a beach park in 1961, and the main users, especially at weekends, still tend to be local families rather than tourists. They come to swim, picnic and explore the **tidepools** at the foot of **Mānele Cone** – the extinct cinder cone dividing Hulopo'e from Mānele Bay – to the east. These rocks and both bays are an official Marine Life Conservation Area; especially in the morning, the **snorkeling** is excellent. The waters off the south coast of Lanai are also recognized as among the very best diving sites in Hawaii. Regular dive trips are organized by Trilogy Ocean Sports, which has a base at the *Mānele Bay Hotel* (Ⓣ 565-7700 ext 2387 or 1-888/MAUI-800).

It's possible to **camp**, for up to a week, at Hulopo'e Beach's tiny, peaceful six-pitch campground (Ⓣ565-3982). There's a charge of $5 per person per night, plus a one-time $5 registration fee.

### Pu'u Pehe

Although you can't quite see it from either Hulopo'e Beach or Mānele Bay, Mānele Cone curves around to protect a tiny, inaccessible pocket beach, with the islet of **Pu'u Pehe** just offshore. Technically, this isolated rock is a sea stack, a rocky column that was formerly part of a cliff but has become cut off. It's also known as Sweetheart Rock because, according to local legend, a jealous warrior once hid his Maui-born wife (Pehe) in a cave here, and when she was killed by a storm, he threw himself from the top of the rock. There is some sort of ancient shrine up there, but archeologists can't tell what it was used for. The best way to see Pu'u Pehe is from a boat entering or leaving Mānele Bay.



## Kaunolū

No one has lived in the hot, dry valley of **KAUNOLū**, in Lanai's remote southwestern corner, for well over a century. As a result, its ruined stone walls constitute one of the best-preserved ancient village sites in Hawaii; archeologists find it fascinating, though others may not think it worth the long and extremely bumpy jeep ride down. The route has deteriorated so much, in fact, that in recent years Dollar has forbidden customers from driving their rental cars on it.

If you have access to a vehicle and want to reach Kaunolū, however, take Mānele Road as far as the Mānele Bay turnoff and then follow paved Kaupili Road as it loops east to drop towards the golf course. Within half a mile, turn right where a straight red-dirt road crosses the highway, just before a fenced enclosure; water pipes can be seen on the left. As you reach a long fence on the right-hand side, turn left down a smaller dirt road. This descends beyond the irrigated area, passing rows of long-dead *wili-wili* trees, to reach two parking lots above **Kaunolū Gulch**.

Despite its narrowness and barren appearance, the gulch appealed to the ancient Hawaiians because it offered a sheltered canoe landing for fishermen in the rich inshore waters, and a fresh-water spring not far inland. A trail from the upper parking lot leads through the walls of the main village, built on the gulch's eastern rim. However, they're mostly concealed by wild *pili* grass, grown originally for thatch, and it makes more sense simply to park at the end of the road. The footpath down into the gulch from here runs beside a large, trash-strewn house platform that's said to have been fortified for use by the young **Kamehameha the Great** during his frequent deep-sea fishing trips to the area.

The floor of the gulch is barely thirty yards across, with a scattering of trees, and a slope of black boulders at the ocean's edge. A trail climbs the far side, passing a rudimentary canoe shed, to the **Halulu Heiau**, where a large stone platform marks the site of the village's temple. You're now atop a slender headland; a gap in the stark rock columns on its western side gives access to a cliff that drops ninety feet into the foaming ocean. "Cliff-jumping" was a mark of bravery among Hawaiian warriors, and this plunge – into a mere twelve feet of water – was known as **Kahekili's Leap**, in honor of the former chief of Maui. You have to be pretty brave to edge anywhere near it, but if you do so you'll see that it frames a good view of the thousand-foot Pali Koholo that lines Lanai's west coast.

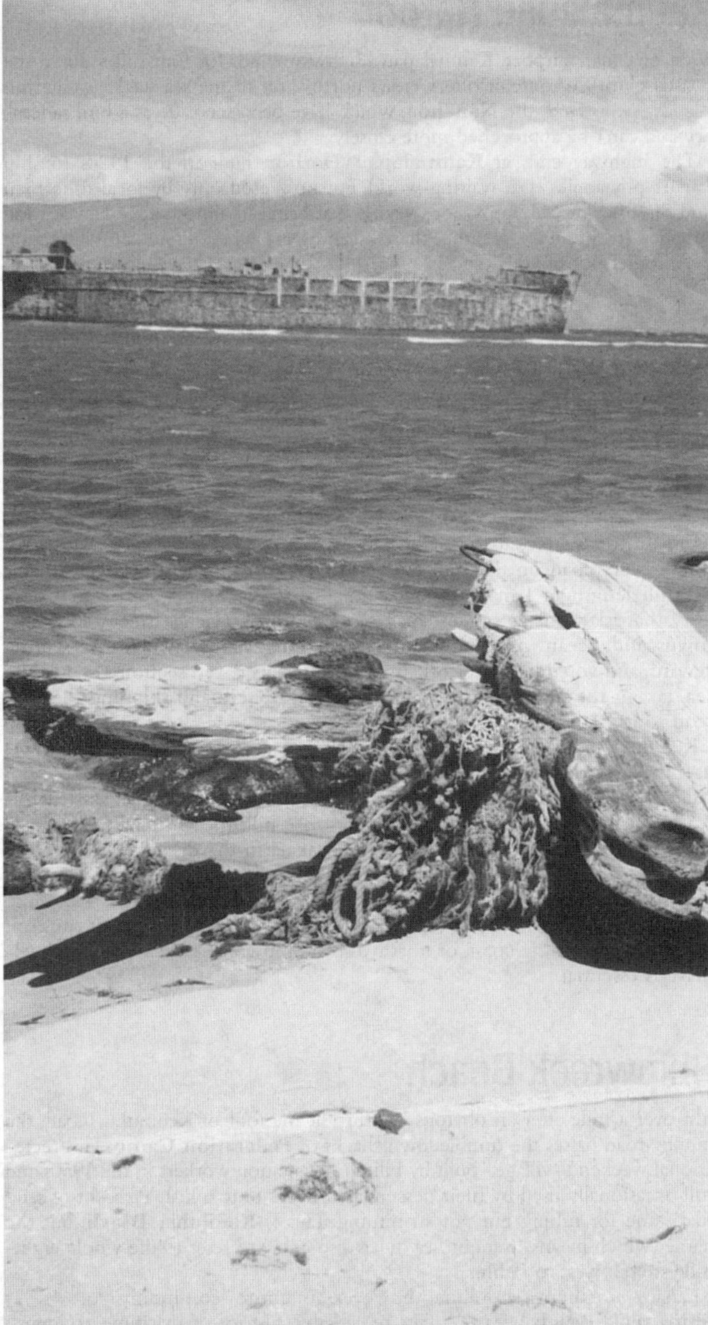

## Kaumalapau Harbor

West of Lanai's airport, Kaumalapau Highway winds for four miles down the coastal cliffs. En route, it offers views northwards to the sea stacks – tall, thin islands – known as the **Nānāhoa**, which have been set aside as a bird sanctuary and can't be approached more closely.

The highway ends at **Kaumalapau Harbor**, built in the 1920s to ship Lanai's pineapples to a waiting world, but now used only by local fishermen and the once-weekly provisions vessels that bring in almost all of Lanai's food supplies. It's a functional rather than a scenic port, where there's no temptation even to get out of your car.



# The East Coast

Most visitors who rent four-wheel-drive vehicles on Lanai set out to drive down every road on the island. The longest road, **Keōmuku Road**, runs the full length of Lanai's east coast, a forty-mile round-trip from Lāna'i City that island maps suggest may offer plentiful beaches, sleepy long-lost towns and ocean views. In reality it's a long, hard drive for very little reward, and you'd be better off simply driving its paved section as far as the sea, taking the detour north to **Shipwreck Beach**, and skipping the jeep road south altogether.

Keōmuku Road heads briefly north from *The Lodge at Kō'ele*, then veers east to enter the forest and cross the lower northern end of Lanai's central ridge. As soon as it leaves the plateau, it enters a barren but spectacular landscape, meandering down a long, red, desolate hillside; Molokai is visible to the left, West Maui to the right, and Haleakalā in the distance beyond. For much of its eight-mile descent, you'll get views of the giant, ragged **Kaimuhōkū meteor crater**, but the road never approaches the rim close enough to see into it. Whichever way you turn when the pavement runs out – southeastdown the coast, or northwest to Shipwreck Beach – four-wheel-drive is essential.

## Shipwreck Beach

Just over a mile after an obvious left turn at the foot of Keōmuku Road, the bumpy road passes the tumbledown shacks of **Federation Camp**. This recreational weekend "village," built by Filipino plantation workers in the 1950s and still occasionally used by their descendants, backs onto a little crescent of sand that's fine for fishing but not swimming. This is **Kaiolohia Beach**, but the name (which means "tranquil sea"), has also come to refer to the whole eight-mile stretch west to Polihua.

Lanai's northern shoreline, however, is more commonly known as **Shipwreck Beach** because of its remarkable history of maritime accidents.

Countless vessels have come to grief in these shallow, treacherous waters; the coast is littered with fragments, while two large wrecks remain stuck fast a few hundred yards offshore. Some historians even suggest that a sixteenth-century Spanish galleon may have been wrecked somewhere along here; see p.507 for more details.

The sand road lurches to a halt at an informal parking lot a little under half a mile beyond Federation Camp, by which time the tree cover has given out, too. Keep walking in the same direction for a few yards, and from the ruined foundations of a former lighthouse you'll be able to see the rusting orange hulk of a World War II "**Liberty Ship**" propped up on the rocks almost completely out of the water. No one seems sure how it got there; it may have been deliberately beached.

An enjoyable **hike** heads northwards for closer views of the wreck; allow at least an hour, though it's possible to make a day of it by continuing all the way to Polihua. The only viable route runs along the shorefront; if you try to set off further inland, you'll soon find yourself confronted by a succession of gullies filled with thorny *kiawe* scrub, where the only trails have been made by animals, not humans, and close over at waist height. Head instead for the mouth of the first gully you come to. In theory, a thin filament of sand, a few feet wide, runs just beyond the vegetation, but it's often so narrow that you have to sidestep the waves. As you pick your way across the tidepools sunk into the odd spit of lava, you'll soon encounter all sorts of flotsam and jetsam.

A mile or so along, you round a final corner to find a large red refrigerated container washed onto the beach. The wreck of the ship lies a hundred yards offshore – you can easily pick out the details of its deck – while the green valleys of east Molokai rise directly behind it.

The only other wreck that survives in relatively intact condition on Shipwreck Beach – an oil tanker lost in the 1950s – is six miles further on, at **Awalua**. If you're determined to see it, a far less grueling approach would be to walk a mile east from Polihua Beach (see p.373).

### Pō'aīwa Petroglyphs

From the same parking lot where the trail to the lighthouse and Liberty Ship begins (see above), a short walk directly inland leads to a gulch where the rocks still bear **petroglyphs** carved by ancient Hawaiians. As you face back down the small ramp from the lighthouse platform, follow the footpath running slightly to the right of straight ahead, which is marked with splashes of white paint. After about 200 yards, beyond a rock with a painted warning, you drop down into the gully itself. It's filled with large red boulders; wherever sections have shorn off, leaving smooth flat faces, the rocks are incised with tiny stick drawings and bird-headed figures.

## South along the coast

To drive **south** along the coast, simply continue along Keōmuku Road instead of taking the left turn to Shipwreck Beach described above. From this junction on, the road repeatedly divides into separate deep sandy channels, which then rejoin after a few hundred yards. Whichever branch you follow, you'll find yourself deep in the woods for most of the way along. Thanks to soil runoff from the hills above, the shoreline pushes farther out to sea by an amazing ten feet every year; only rarely do you glimpse the ocean, let alone West Maui across the ‘Au‘au Channel. Similarly, the encroaching scrubby vegetation makes it hard even to spot the long-overgrown sites of the various abandoned villages along the way.

The windward coasts of other Hawaiian islands are usually lush and fertile, but the mountains of Maui ensure that little rain reaches Lanai. Only the valley of **Maunalei**, a mile down the road, was wet enough to grow *taro*, and it still supplies most of the island's fresh water; the jeep road up the valley is almost always barred.

Six miles from the turnoff, in a small grove of coconut palms, **Mālamalama Church** is all that survives of the village of **Keōmuku**. Built to serve a new sugar plantation in 1899, the village was deserted within two years, after the plantation went broke. The church is not a very evocative relic; its original wood rotted away, so it has been completely rebuilt using fresh timber.

The one difficult stretch on Keōmuku Road comes after ten miles, as it undulates across the headland at Kikoa Point. At **Lōpa**, immediately beyond, it twice passes within a few feet of the waves, and a couple of oceanfront parking lots offer views of ancient fishponds – now mostly submerged – as well as across to the island of Kahoolawe (see p.319). By the time the road ends at **Naha**, after just over twelve miles, it has made a right-angle turn and is heading along Lanai's south coast, with West Maui out of sight behind you.

# North Lanai

The eight-mile drive from Lāna‘i City to the **north coast** is the best 4WD excursion on the island. En route, the scenery ranges from the dust bowl of the central plateau, through thick woodlands and multicolored desert, to one of Hawaii's emptiest, largest beaches.

The main drawback is that **Polihua Road** is truly a dirt road; it's the **filthiest** drive imaginable, leaving you coated in thick, red mud even if you never wind down your windows. As the Garden of the Gods is best seen at sunset, make this your last stop of the day before heading home to wash off the grime.

## Kānepu‘u Forest Preserve

For its first two miles, northwest from *The Lodge at Kō‘ele*, Polihua Road runs through abandoned pineapple fields. It then passes over a cattle grid to enter the fenced-off **Kānepu‘u Forest Preserve**. This 590-acre tract, run by the Nature Conservancy of Hawaii, was set aside in the early 1990s in a belated attempt to preserve one of the few remaining vestiges of the dryland forests that once covered much of Hawaii. Many of the animals it holds are not indigenous – most obviously, the axis deer hunted by local sportsmen every weekend – but it also protects 48 native Hawaiian tree species, including gardenia (*nā‘ū*) and sandalwood (*‘iliahi*).

Not far short of the Garden of the Gods (see below), the **Kānepu'u Self-Guided Trail** is a ten-minute loop trail that enables visitors to get a sense of this unusual environment. Markers along the way identify the rarest species.

# Garden of the Gods

Lanai's extraordinary **Garden of the Gods** looks more like the "badlands" of the American Wild West than anything you'd expect to find in Hawaii. Perched on a bleak, windblown plateau above the island's north coast, this small desert wilderness is predominantly a rich russet red, but its unearthly hillocks and boulders are scored through with layers of lithified sand of every conceivable hue – grays, yellows, ochres, browns and even blues. At sunset, the whole place seems to glow, and the rocks lying scattered across the red sands cast long, eerie shadows.

What first catch the eye are the myriad **rock cairns** stacked everywhere you look. Ranging from meticulous piles of boulders, steadily diminishing in size, to precarious towers of pebbles, it's easy to imagine them as relics of a bygone age. They're not; they owe their existence to a craze that swept Hawaii in the 1980s, when locals erected stone "shrines" in isolated places in the belief that it was an ancient Hawaiian tradition (similar cairns can be seen, for example, at Nākālele Point on Maui; see p.296). The Hawaiians say they have no such tradition, but that since the cairns have been erected with sincere intentions, it would be inappropriate to dismantle them. Until recently, tourist brochures invited visitors to add their own cairns at the Garden of the Gods, but the practice is now officially discouraged.

Although the main depression at the Garden of the Gods holds the most impressive rock formations, it's worth continuing for at least a short distance beyond. Take the right fork at the only point where the route may seem uncertain, and as the hillside starts to slope down, you come to a fabulous vantage point that looks across the bare red soil towards the island of Molokai.

# Polihua Beach

A short way past the Garden of the Gods, signposts mark the junction of the Ke'anu and Polihua roads. The latter is the right fork, which gets steadily worse as it drops towards the ocean, cutting a groove into the red earth. It virtually never rains here – the clouds that drift over the plateau seldom reach this far – and the views are amazing.

At sea level, the road ends at the edge of broad **Polihua Beach**, where the red dust gives way to broad yellow sand. Over a hundred yards wide and 1.5 miles long, Polihua is a magnificent sight, and the chances are you'll have it to yourself. Until the 1950s, this remote spot was a favorite laying ground for green turtles – the name means "eggs in the bosom." They rarely turn up these days, but during the winter humpback **whales** can often be seen not far offshore, in the Kalohi Channel that separates Lanai from Molokai.

Like the similar vast, windswept beaches at the western extremities of Kauai (Polihale; see p.489) and Molokai (Pāpōhaku; see p.407), Polihua is best admired from a distance. The current is always too dangerous for swimming,

though there's great **windsurfing** around the headland to the east. Beyond that stretches Kaiolohia or Shipwreck Beach; as described on p.370, it's possible to hike its full eight-mile length.

5

# Molokai



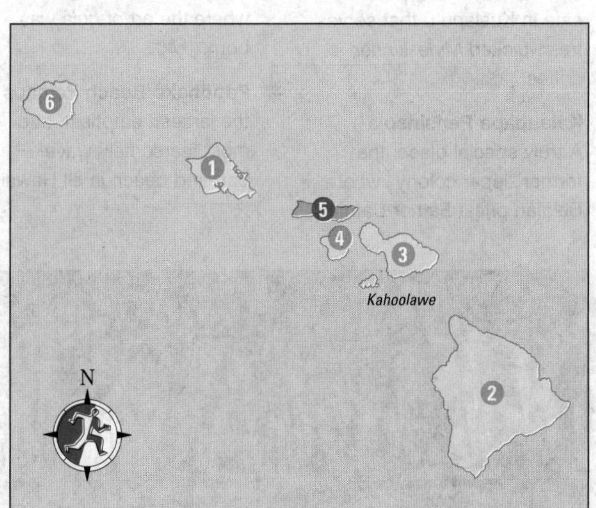

# CHAPTER 5 Highlights

* **Hālawa Valley** Lush tropical "valley that time forgot", at the far eastern end of the island. P.389

* **Kamakou Preserve** The rainforest of eastern Molokai is home to some of Hawaii's rarest birds and plants. P.391

* **Coffees of Hawai'i** Gloriously relaxing plantation café in Kualapu'u that serves fresh-picked *Muleskinner* coffee. P.394

* **Kalaupapa Pensinsula** A truly special place: the former "leper colony" where Belgian priest Father Damien carried out his inspiring mission. P.398

* **Molokai Mule Ride** The best way to climb the steep trail to remote Kalaupapa is to let a mule carry you – they've been doing it all their lives. P.398

* **Molokai Ka Hula Piko** Atmospheric annual festival held in the upland groves where the art of *hula* was born. P.407

* **Pāpōhaku Beach** Perhaps the largest, emptiest, and most fearsomely wave-battered beach in all Hawaii. P.407

# 5

# Molokai



**MOLOKAI** is not the sort of island you'd expect to find halfway between Oahu and Maui. With a population of less than seven thousand, and just a fraction of the tourist trade of its hectic neighbors, it feels more like a small Caribbean outpost than a part of modern Hawaii. Measuring forty miles west to east, but only ten miles north to south, it doesn't have a single traffic light or elevator. No building on Molokai stands taller than a palm tree, and even the capital, **Kaunakakai**, is no more than a dusty street of wooden false-front stores.

There's some truth in the criticism you may hear voiced elsewhere in Hawaii that there's nothing to do on Molokai. If you like to stay in plush hotels, spend lots of money in shops and restaurants, and try out expensive sports and pastimes, this is probably not the place for you. The infrastructure for tourists is minimal, nightlife is virtually nonexistent, and the beaches may look nice but hardly any are good for swimming.

Many visitors, however, rank Molokai as their favorite island, saying it offers a taste of how Hawaii might have been fifty or sixty years ago. With a higher proportion of native Hawaiians than any of the major islands, it has resisted excessive development while maintaining a friendly and distinctive character. Where else in the US would it be possible for an exhibition of schoolchildren's art to include an attempt at graffiti by a teenager who laments that he's "never seen any graffiti in person"? Spend any time exploring the island – even visiting "attractions" that might on paper sound too mundane to bother with – and you'll soon find yourself drawn into the life of the community. That said, Molokai holds some indisputable highlights as well, including unspoiled **scenery** to rival any in Hawaii – from ravishing **Hālawa Valley** in the east to gigantic, deserted **Pāpōhaku Beach** in the west – and the emotive historical relic of Father Damien's leprosy colony at **Kalaupapa Peninsula**.

## A brief history of Molokai

Molokai may have been home to as many as thirty thousand people in ancient times. Lush **Hālawa Valley**, at its **eastern** end, was one of the first regions to be settled in Hawaii – remains have been unearthed of Polynesian-style dwellings dating back to the seventh century – and an almost permanent state of war seems to have existed between the Kona and Ko'olau sides of the eastern mountain.

The **western** end of the island was also extensively settled. Its proximity to the main thoroughfare used by canoes traveling between Maui, the Big Island, and

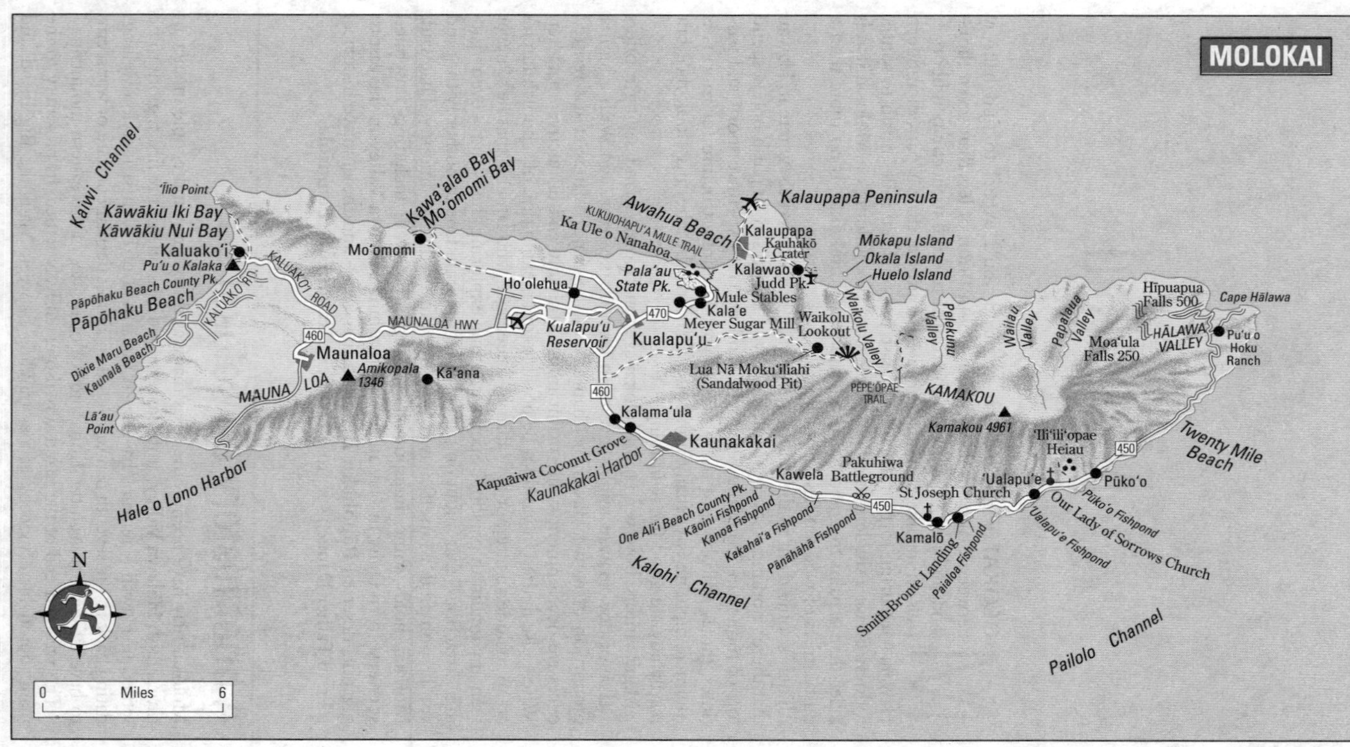
MOLOKAI
Kaiwi Channel
ʻĪlio Point
Kāwākiu Iki Bay
Kāwākiu Nui Bay
Kaluakoʻi
Puʻu o Kalaka
Pāpōhaku Beach County Pk.
Pāpōhaku Beach
KALUAKOʻI ROAD
KALUAKO RD.
Dixie Maru Beach
Kaunalā Beach
Lāʻau Point
Hale o Lono Harbor
460
Maunaloa
MAUNA LOA
Amikopala 1346
Kāʻana
MAUNALOA HWY
Moʻomomi
Kawaʻalao Bay
Moʻomomi Bay
Hoʻolehua
Kualapuʻu Reservoir
Kualapuʻu
470
Awahua Beach
KUKUIOHAPUʻA MULE TRAIL
Ka Ule o Nanahoa
Palaʻau State Pk.
Mule Stables
Kalaʻe
Meyer Sugar Mill
Kalaupapa Peninsula
Kalaupapa
Kauhakō Crater
Kalawao
Judd Pk.
Mōkapu Island
Okala Island
Huelo Island
Waikolu Valley
Waikolu Lookout
Lua Nā Mokuʻiliahi (Sandalwood Pit)
PEPEʻOPAE TRAIL
Pelekunu Valley
KAMAKOU
Kamakou 4961
Wailau Valley
Papalaua Valley
Hīpuapua Falls 500
Moaʻula Falls 250
HĀLAWA VALLEY
Cape Hālawa
Puʻu o Hoku Ranch
Twenty Mile Beach
Kalamaʻula
Kaunakakai
Kapuāiwa Coconut Grove
Kaunakakai Harbor
One Aliʻi Beach County Pk.
Kāoini Fishpond
Kanoa Fishpond
Kakahaiʻa Fishpond
Pānāhāhā Fishpond
Kawela
Pakuhiwa Battleground
St Joseph Church
Kamalō
Smith-Bronte Landing
Paialoa Fishpond
ʻUalapuʻe
ʻIliʻiliʻōpae Heiau
Pūkoʻo
Pūkoʻo Fishpond
Our Lady of Sorrows Church
ʻUalapuʻe Fishpond
Kalohi Channel
Pailolo Channel
N
0 Miles 6

Oahu made it a staging post and meeting place for travelers from all the islands. The quarries of Kalauako'i were such a valuable source of the hard stone used to make adzes that chiefs from elsewhere would come to Molokai for extended stays. Umi, the legendary ruler of the Big Island, for example, is said to have erected 2400 dwellings during one such visit. In addition, the *taro* farmers of the wet valleys of the north shore would spend their winters fishing at drier Mo'omomi to the west.

During the eighteenth century, the fertile valleys and rich fishponds of the east attracted a succession of foreign **invaders** to Molokai. Among the chiefs who celebrated their conquests by erecting mighty war temples (such as **'Ili'ili'ōpae Heiau**) were Alapa'inui of the Big Island, Kahekili from Maui, and Kamehameha the Great himself.

For around fifty years after the arrival of the Europeans, however, Molokai was largely ignored. That was partly because the coast held no safe anchorages for ocean-going ships, but also because the island had acquired a reputation for being a place of sorcery and black magic, as the home of the greatly feared **poisonwood gods** (see p.404).

The concept of Molokai as being God-forsaken no doubt played a role in the decision to site a **leprosy colony** at Kalaupapa during the 1860s, though this resulted in the Belgian miracle-worker **Father Damien** giving the island its only brush with world fame (for the full story, see p.400). By the time **Robert Louis Stevenson** visited in 1889, Damien was dead; so too was the vast majority of the island's native population, wiped out by imported diseases. Stevenson wrote, "The whole length or breadth of this once busy isle I have either coasted by or ridden. And where are the people? where are the houses? where is the smoke of the fires? I see again Apaka riding by me on the leeward beach; I hear again the sound of his painful laughter and the words of his refrain: '*Pau kanaka make,*' which means 'finished; people dead.'"

Meanwhile, the **Molokai Ranch** had been established, taking over the entire western end of the island for **cattle** raising. With the construction of pipelines and tunnels to channel water across from the northern valleys, Molokai went on to prosper, producing **honey** and **pineapples**. Like everywhere in Hawaii, however, agriculture on Molokai began to turn unprofitable during the 1970s, and the island went into recession. Unemployment hit hard, and some Molokai residents found themselves having to commute to Maui each day to work in the resorts. At home, however, local resistance to development, and a perennial water shortage, combined to thwart ambitious plans to shift the economy towards **tourism**. The debate is far from over: the 1990s saw a New Zealand company take over Molokai Ranch to run it primarily as a real-estate venture. Thus far the visitor facilities they have created around the former pineapple town of Maunaloa have had little impact on the level of tourism to the island, while their ambitious plans to construct new resorts and housing in the Kaluako'i region will only succeed if they can divert enough water away from the rest of the island. That in turn could damage small-scale local agriculture, such as the promising new **coffee** industry, beyond repair.

## Around the island

Like Oahu and Maui, Molokai consists of two separate volcanoes, plus the "saddle" that lies between them. At almost 5000 feet, the younger mountain to the east – sometimes named after its highest peak, Kamakou, but usually referred to as simply the **Eastern Mountain** – is tall enough to capture most of the island's rain. Its north shore holds the world's highest **sea cliffs**, pierced by spectacular valleys, but it's virtually impossible to reach, and there's hardly anywhere from which you can even see it. The rainforest at the top of the mountain, protected as the **Kamakou Preserve**, can only be explored on foot.

From Molokai's principal town, tiny **Kaunakakai** in the center of the south coast, a ribbon of colorful little settlements stretches east along the shoreline, all the way to sumptuous **Hālawa Valley**. To the west, the smoother, smaller and much drier mountain of **Mauna Loa** offers little sign of life, apart from the resort oasis of **Kaluako'i** and the plantation settlement of **Maunaloa**. Molokai's central plain holds a few more farming villages, while tacked on below the cliffs to the north is the isolated **Kalaupapa Peninsula**, still home to the island's celebrated leprosy colony.



## Getting to Molokai

Despite its proximity to both Oahu and Maui, Molokai has earned itself a reputation as being hard to reach. However, although locals complain that because the airport is too small to cope with large aircraft it can be difficult to fly in or out for the weekend, tourists prepared to be flexible are unlikely to experience problems in reserving a flight.

Molokai's main **airport**, outside Ho'olehua in the center of the island, is currently served by direct flights from **Oahu** and **Maui** only, though it's easy enough to connect with flights to the other Hawaiian islands. Aloha Air offers the most daily flights: eight from **Honolulu** and two from **Kahului** on Maui. Hawaiian Airlines has two daily services from Honolulu. For full details on both airlines, see p.17.

Several lesser operators fly twin-engine planes to Molokai. Pacific Wings (Ⓣ 567-6814 on Molokai, 248-7700 on Maui, or 1-888/575-4546, Ⓦ www.pacificwings.com) operates one or two scheduled flights each day to and from both Honolulu and Kahului on Maui. In addition, two charter companies provide on-demand flights. The endearing Molokai Air Shuttle (Ⓣ 545-4988 on Oahu, 567-6847 on Molokai) flies between Honolulu and Molokai for $60 round-trip – it's such a no-frills outfit that as you take off one passenger has to sit next to the pilot and hold the door open to provide some cool air (there's air-conditioning). Paragon Air (Ⓣ 1-800/428-1231) connects Molokai with any airport on Maui or Lanai.

For details of flights direct to the **Kalaupapa Peninsula** – not a sensible option if you want to see the whole island – from Oahu, Maui and "top-side" Molokai, see p.399.

It's also possible to make a 75-minute **ferry** crossing between Maui and Molokai on the *Molokai Princess* (adults $40, children $20 each way; Ⓣ 667-6165 or 1-800/275-6969, Ⓦ www.mauiprincess.com). On Monday through Saturday, a commuter service leaves Molokai's Kaunakakai Harbor at 6am and sets off on the return trip from Lahaina at 5.15pm. On Sundays, the vessel runs day-trips in the other direction, leaving Lahaina at 7.30am and Kaunakakai at 3.30pm. Commercial pleasure cruises operate every day.

## Getting around



There is no **public transport** on Molokai, and the airport is several miles out of town. **Taxis** are supplied by Kukui Tours (Ⓣ 553-8022), but without a car you'll feel very stuck. The only national **rental-car** chains are Budget (Ⓣ 567-6877) and Dollar (Ⓣ 567-6156), both based at the airport. Dollar has a few four-wheel-drive jeeps, but neither company has many vehicles, and, unless you make a reservation several weeks in advance (using the toll-free numbers listed on p.25), they may have nothing at all available. Island Kine (Ⓣ 553-5242, Ⓔ cars@molokai-aloha.com), located in Kaunakakai but providing free airport transfers, is a friendly local alternative that offers a wide selection of cars and trucks at reasonable prices.

## Island tours and activities

Friendly Isle Tours (Ⓣ 552-2218 or 553-3369) runs **minivan tours** of the island ($36 for 4hr, $49 for 6hr, three-person minimum). Under the name Molokai Off-Road Tours, the company also offers half-day **jeep tours** ($60 per person, four-person minimum) that will take you up to, but not into, the Kamakou Preserve (see p.391). Kukui Tours (see above) offers van tours only, at similar rates.

The main **activity** operator on Molokai is the Molokai Ranch in Maunaloa, whose program of outdoor pursuits is detailed on p.405. At the eastern end of the island, the Pu'u o Hōkū Ranch offers horseback riding amid idyllic scenery (see p.289), while Pilipo Solitario leads highly recommended **guided hikes** in Hālawa Valley (see p.391). Fun Hogs (Ⓣ 567-6789) runs an assortment of **sailing excursions**, including sunset cruises and one-way or round-trip voyages to Lanai; all offer participants the opportunity to fish or snorkel.

**Diving** is not as popular on Molokai as on the other islands – the immediate offshore waters are too shallow and murky on the south coast, and too rough everywhere else. Nonetheless, Bill Kapuni runs open-water dive trips on demand at around $85 per person for a two-tank dive (Ⓣ 553-9867 or 1-877/553-9867, Ⓔ billkapuni@hotmail.com).

If you want to go your own way, Molokai Outdoor Activities (Ⓣ 553-4477, Ⓦ www.molokai-outdoors.com), based at *Hotel Molokai* in Kaunakakai, rent out **bikes** and **kayaks** as well as snorkeling and surfing equipment. You can also rent bikes and kayaks from Molokai Bicycle, 80 Mohala St, Kaunakakai (Tues & Thurs 4–7pm, Sat 9am–2pm; Ⓣ 553-4477, Ⓦ www.bikehawaii.com/molokaibicycle), and **snorkel equipment**, boogie boards and the like from Molokai Fish and Dive, 63 Ala Malama St, Kaunakakai (Mon–Sat 8am–6pm, Sun 8am–2pm; Ⓣ 553-5926).

# Where to stay

Molokai has a dwindling and relatively lackluster range of **accommodation** options, though those hotels that do exist are for the most part reasonably priced. The island's best-known resort property, the *Kaluako'i Hotel* at its western end, was closed – in theory temporarily – as this book went to press. That leaves the *Hotel Molokai* and the *Molokai Shores Suites* in **Kaunakakai** as the most obvious lodging choices. In addition, the Molokai Ranch runs the small, expensive *Molokai Ranch Lodge* up in Maunaloa and offers overpriced "tentalows" – camping by any other name – in remote parts of the western end. Although a handful of pretty B&Bs are scattered along the **southeastern** coast, there's nowhere to stay in or near Molokai's most scenic spot, Hālawa Valley, while the island's most historic area, the Kalaupapa Peninsula, can only be visited on guided day-trips.

### Accommodation Price Codes

All the accommodation options listed here have been graded with the symbols below, which refer to the quoted rates for a double room in high season (December to March), not including state taxes of 10.17 percent. For a full explanation, see p.27.

| | | |
|---|---|---|
| ❶ up to $40 | ❹ $100–150 | ❼ $250–300 |
| ❷ $40–70 | ❺ $150–200 | ❽ $300–400 |
| ❸ $70–100 | ❻ $200–250 | ❾ over $400 |

As for traditional **camping**, the two county-run sites, at **One Ali'i Beach Park** in the east and **Pāpōhaku Beach Park** in the west, cost $3 a day, with a three-day maximum stay; permits are issued in person only at the Mitchell Pau'ole Center on 'Āiloa Street in Kaunakakai (Mon–Fri 8am–4pm; ⓣ553-3204). Permits for the free campgrounds at **Waikolu Lookout** and **Pālā'au State Park**, both of which allow a maximum stay of five nights, can be picked up from the Department of Land and Natural Resources, near the post office on Puupeelua Avenue in Ho'olehua (Mon–Fri 7.30am–4pm; ⓣ567-6891).

# When to go

In terms of **climate**, it makes very little difference what time of year you visit Molokai; the west is sunny all year round, while the higher or farther east you go, the greater the chance of rain. Only a few of the beaches are suited to swimming, even in summer. All else being equal, the best specific time to come to Molokai is in May, to catch the **Molokai Ka Hula Piko** festival (see p.407).

### Molokai Festivals and Events

You'll find what news there is on Molokai, plus listings of upcoming events, in the two free weekly newspapers, the *Dispatch* and the *Molokai Advertiser-News*.

| | |
|---|---|
| **Jan** | Molokai Makahiki; festival of ancient Hawaiian sports, Kaunakakai |
| **March 26** | Prince Kūhiō Day; state holiday |
| **May 1** | May Day, Lei Day; state-wide celebrations |
| **3rd Sat in May** | Molokai Ka Hula Piko; celebrations for birth of hula, Pāpōhaku Beach Park |
| **late May** | Kanaka Ikaika Molokai–Oahu kayak race |
| **June 11** | Kamehameha Day, state-wide; arts and crafts fair, Kaunakakai |
| **July 4** | Ho'olaule'a O Ke Kai Sea-fest; festival of canoeing, kayaking, windsurfing and fishing at Kaunakakai |
| **Aug 18** | Admission Day; state holiday |
| **late Sept** | Molokai Music Festival; day-long music, crafts and food fair, Meyer Sugar Mill |
| **late Sept** | Aloha Festival week on Molokai, including Molokai Mule Run, Kaunakakai |
| **late Sept** | Molokai–Oahu women's outrigger canoe race starts at Hale O Lono |
| **early Oct** | Molokai–Oahu men's outrigger canoe race starts at Hale O Lono |

# Kaunakakai

**KAUNAKAKAI**, at the midpoint of the southern shoreline seven miles southeast of the island's airport (see p.380), is by far the largest settlement on Molokai. Despite being home to most of the businesses that keep island life ticking over, it's really no more than a village. There's just one main street, **Ala Malama Street**, half a mile in from the ocean. Once you've ambled its full 200-yard length, and scanned its array of single-story false-front wooden stores and the sweet little timber-framed **St Sophia's Church**, you've seen all that central Kaunakakai has to offer. Call in at the Kanemitsu Bakery to pick up a loaf of their sweet Molokai bread, renowned throughout the islands. Molokai Island Creations – run by the same people as Molokai Fish and Dive next door (see overleaf) – is the most interesting place for clothes and souvenirs and has piles of signed copies of the owner's book of photographs, *A Portrait of Molokai*. Kaunakakai's restaurants are detailed on p.385.

The epicenter of the island is generally considered to be the crossroads at milepost 0 on Kamehameha V Highway, where Ala Malama Street heads away inland. Three of its four corners are occupied by a gas station, the Molokai branch of the Bank of Hawaii (Mon–Thurs 8.30am–3pm, Fri 8.30am–6pm), and the friendly offices of the **Molokai Visitors Association** (Mon–Sat

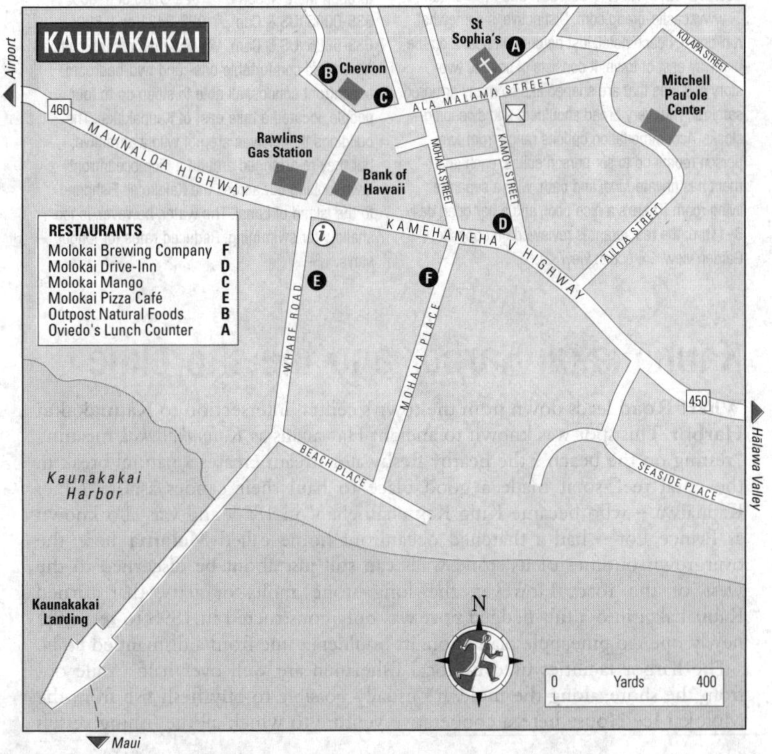

8am–5pm; PO Box 960, Kaunakakai HI 96748; ⓣ553-3876, 1-800/800-6367 (US & Can) or 1-800/553-0404 (HI), ⓕ553-5288, ⓦwww.molokai-hawaii.com).

## Accommodation

As the obvious base for exploring Molokai, Kaunakakai has the only inexpensive **hotel** on the island. Since the much-lamented closure of the *Pau Hana Inn* in 1999, the *Hotel Molokai* has been left to plow a lonely furrow. The *Molokai Shores Suites* makes a smarter but slightly more expensive alternative, while there are also a few **B&Bs**. It's also possible to **camp** at One Ali'i Park; see opposite.

**A'Ahi Place B&B**, PO Box 528, Kaunakakai, Molokai HI 96748; ⓣ553-5860, ⓦwww.molokai-aloha.com/aahi. Holiday cottage in a garden setting on a low hill just east of Kaunakakai. The one bedroom has two large beds. There are no phones or TVs, but an ample breakfast is served each morning. No credit cards accepted. ❸.

**Hotel Molokai**, PO Box 546, Kaunakakai, Molokai HI 96748; ⓣ553-5347, ⓕ553-5047, ⓦwww.hotel-molokai.com, or book through Castle Resorts, 1-800/272-5275 (HI) or 1-800/367-5004 (US & Can), ⓦwww.castle-group.com. Distinctive, if somewhat run-down, beach hotel, just before milepost 2 on the highway east of town. It consists of several two-story cottages that are shaped like so many armored samurai, with very broad shoulders and sweeping cloaks. Accommodation options range from two-person rooms up to six-person suites; each apartment has private *lānai* and bath, with a separate living room. There's a nice pool, and a bar open daily 3–11pm; the restaurant is reviewed on opposite. Garden view ❸, ocean view ❹.

**Ka Hale Māla**, 7 Kamakana Place, PO Box 1582, Kaunakakai, Molokai HI 96748; ⓣ & ⓕ553-9009, ⓦwww.molokai-bnb.com. Secluded four-room garden apartment, with kitchen and *lānai*, plus bikes and snorkel equipment, a little under five miles east of Kaunakakai. Run as a B&B, with reduced rates if you don't want breakfast. ❸.

**Molokai Shores Suites**, PO Box 546, Kaunakakai, Molokai HI 96748; ⓣ & ⓕ553-5954, or reserve through Marc Resorts, ⓣ 922-9700 or 1-800/535-0085 (US & Can), ⓕ922-2421 or 1-800/633-5085 (US & Can), ⓦwww.marcresorts.com. A hundred comfortable one- and two-bedroom oceanfront condos, all able to sleep up to four people, located a mile east of Kaunakakai. The buildings themselves are not wildly attractive, but they're arranged around a nice oceanfront lawn looking out across the Kaloko'eli Fishpond to the island of Lanai. The water, however, is too shallow for swimming. Reduced rates for longer stays. ❹–❺.

## Kaunakakai Harbor and the shoreline

**Wharf Road** leads down from the town's central intersection to **Kaunakakai Harbor**. This spot was known to ancient Hawaiians as *Kaunakahakai*, meaning "resting on the beach"; the nearby freshwater stream creates a natural break in the coral reef, so it made a good place to haul their canoes ashore. Chief Kapuāiwa – who became King Kamehameha V in 1863, and was also known as Prince Lot – had a thatched oceanfront home called **Malama** here; the overgrown outlines of its stone walls can still just about be discerned to the west of the road. However, the long stone mole, or jetty, that turned Kaunakakai into a full-fledged port was only constructed in 1898 to serve the newly opened pineapple plantation; its boulders came from a dismantled *heiau*.

The harbor facilities used by local fishermen are well over half a mile out from the shore, along the mole. It's usually possible to buy fresh fish from the Molokai Ice House here, a cooperative venture to which all the fishing vessels sell their catch. This is also the main dock for inter-island boats, including the daily **ferry** service between Molokai and Maui (see p.380).

None of the **beaches** near Kaunakakai is particularly suited to swimming, though walking along the shoreline to the east (around the defunct *Pau Hana Inn*) can be pleasant enough. The sea is not hazardous, but there's only a narrow strip of often rather dirty sand, and the water itself tends to be very murky, thanks to run-off from the hills.

Even **One Ali'i Beach Park**, three miles to the east, is little better, but it does at least offer some nice lawns and coconut palms. The original name of the beach was *oneali'i* or "royal sands," but what was once a spelling mistake has become the official name. The beach itself consists of two separate sections; the first one you come to, Number 2, is reserved for day use only, while the nicer Number 1, a little further on, holds a **campground** run by the county parks office (see p.382).



## Kapuāiwa Coconut Grove

A couple of miles west of central Kaunakakai, on the ocean side of Maunaloa Highway, Kiowea Park is the site of the highly photogenic **Kapuāiwa Coconut Grove**. This enclave of over a thousand tall palm trees was planted in the 1860s by Chief Kapuāiwa, whose name, intriguingly, means "mysterious taboo." As the coastline erodes its way inland, and as the trees approach the end of their natural lifespans, they are toppling one by one. They still make a fine spectacle, especially in the glow of sunset, but again swimming from the park is not recommended. Coconut trees in public places in Hawaii are not usually allowed to bear fruit, but these ones do; signs warn of the obvious danger from falling nuts. Across the highway stands a neat little row of wooden chapels.

## Restaurants

Around eighty percent of Molokai's restaurants are located in Kaunakakai, but the choice is far from overwhelming. The island lacks the usual fast-food chains, so there's no *McDonald's*, but neither is there anything that might be called fine dining.

**Hotel Molokai**, Kamehameha V Hwy; ⓣ553-5347. The waterfront dining room at the *Hotel Molokai*, located just before milepost 2 on the highway east of town, has a romantic ambience, with live entertainment every night and poolside musicians on Friday and Saturday evenings. The food itself is predictable but adequate, with all dinner entrees under $20. There are changing fish specials as well as a standard menu of chicken or shrimp stir-fries, barbecue pork, and prime rib (available weekends only). Mon–Fri 7.30–10.30am, 11.30am–2pm & 6–9pm; Sat & Sun 7am–2.30pm & 6–9pm.

**Molokai Brewing Company**, 10 Mohala Place; ⓣ553-3946. In addition to serving its own home-brewed beers, Molokai's first brewpub, a bright modern building in the heart of town near the visitor center, is open daily for all meals. Offerings include full eggy breakfasts, bargain $2 lunch specials such as pineapple ham, and a wide range of dinner entrees including *ahi* steamed in ale for $12.50 and the catch of the day. Mon–Thurs 6.30am–9.30pm, Fri 6.30am–11.30pm, Sat 8am–11.30pm, Sun 8am–9.30pm.

**Molokai Drive-Inn**, Kamehameha V Hwy; ⓣ553-5655. Exactly what it sounds like: a roadside diner offering simple daily specials ranging from hot dogs to prime rib. You'd be hard-pressed to spend $10. Mon–Thurs & Sun 6am–10pm, Fri & Sat 6am–10.30pm.

**Molokai Mango**, 93D Ala Malama St; ⓣ553-3981. Video rental store on the main shopping street with a sideline in tasty hot and cold sandwiches for $3–4. Mon–Sat 9am–6.30pm.

**Molokai Pizza Café**, Kaunakakai Place, Wharf Rd; ⓣ 553-3288. Bright, good-value mall diner with take-out counter, near Kaunakakai's central intersection. Pizza being a novelty on Molokai, the walls are decorated with schoolkids' accounts of their first-ever taste of this Italian staple. Pizzas named after the different islands grow from the basic Molokai ($9) up to the Big Island ($16); at lunchtime on weekdays you can get an individual Molokini for $5. The menu also features subs, ribs and baked chicken, and there are evening fresh fish specials for $12 or so. Wednesday is Mexican night, with fajitas, tacos and burritos all for around $9. Mon–Thurs 10am–10pm, Fri & Sat 10am–11pm, Sun 11am–10pm.

**Outpost Natural Foods**, 70 Maka'ena Place; ⓣ 553-3377. Lunch counter and juice bar in a wholefood store, off Ala Malama Street behind the Chevron garage. Earnest tofu sandwiches and *tempeh* burgers are under $5; sensational smoothies are $3.50. Shop Mon–Thurs 9am–6pm, Fri 9am–4pm, Sun 9am–5pm, closed Sat; juice bar Mon–Fri 11am–3pm.

**Oviedo's Lunch Counter**, 145 Pāuli Street; ⓣ 553-5014. Simple one-room Filipino restaurant in the heart of town. Reynaldo Oviedo cooks up delicious dishes like chicken stewed with papaya and local herbs ($7.50) as well as pork *adobo* (stew), roast pork, and turkey-neck stew. There's lots of ice cream to round things off. Daily 8am–5pm.



# Eastern Molokai

Kamehameha V Highway runs along the coast for 28 miles **east of Kaunakakai** before reaching a dead end at one of the great Hawaiian "amphitheater valleys," **Hālawa Valley**. Molokai's closest equivalent to the better-known Road to Hāna on Maui (see p.339), this ranks among the most beautiful driving routes in the whole state.

Before you set off, be warned that it takes well over an hour to drive from Kaunakakai to Hālawa, and there are no gas stations en route. The highway remains in good condition all the way to the end, but gets progressively narrower, as finding a foothold between the hills and the ocean becomes ever more difficult. Eastern Molokai is the wettest part of the island; most of the rain that falls on the mountaintop flows down to the inaccessible valleys of the North Shore, but enough feeds the streams to the south to create a verdant patchwork of fields and forest.

The tiny wayside communities hold the odd church, B&B or ancient site, but the real attraction is the lush countryside, with flowers and orchids at every turn, and horses and cows, each with its attendant white egret, grazing contentedly in the meadows. For much of the way the road lies within a few yards of the sea, but there's no good swimming in the first twenty miles, and barely a decent stretch of sand. The coast is lined instead with pre-contact **fishponds**, now largely silted up and overgrown with mangroves.

## Kawela

Six miles out of Kaunakakai, a small cluster of houses constitutes the village of **KAWELA**. Kamehameha the Great invaded Molokai at this spot in around 1794, with a vast wave of canoes landing simultaneously along a four-mile length of beach. The remains of the dead killed in the subsequent **battle** in Pākuhiwa Coconut Grove are said to lie beneath a mound to the east, while the inaccessible ruins of a *pu'uhonua*, or "place of refuge" (see p.174), overlook it all from high on the ridge above. An official marker at the foot of Onini Road stands close to the battlesite, but there's nothing more to see. After the battle, Kamehameha camped for a year farther along the coast, growing *taro*, before launching his invasion of Oahu in 1795 (see p.52).

The small **Kakahai'a Beach Park** in Kawela makes a convenient launching-point for **kayak expeditions** along the coast, which are run by the companies listed on p.381. Otherwise, it is significant solely because it stands adjacent to the **Kakahai'a National Wildlife Refuge**, a wetland area set aside for rare water-birds. The main feature of the refuge, the freshwater **Kakahai'a fishpond**, stands *mauka* of the highway slightly further along, largely obscured by a protective screen of palm trees; access to both the pond and the refuge is forbidden.

# Kamalō

**KAMALŌ**, six miles east of Kawela, served as the primary landing for vessels visiting Molokai until the end of the nineteenth century. What's left of the wharf is still in use, but Kamalō itself is now just a tiny village. It's mainly note-worthy as the site of the simple white **St Joseph Church**, built by Father Damien in 1876 and spruced up in July 1995 to coincide with the return of his hand to Kalaupapa. The priest's garlanded statue stands to the right of the entrance, within a boulder surround and backed by yellow trumpet flowers.

An inconspicuous plaque less than a mile east marks the spot where **Ernest Smith** and **Emory Bronte** (no relation to the author of *Wuthering Heights*) crash-landed amid the trees to terminate the first commercial flight from California to Hawaii, in July 1927. The journey had taken 25 hours; they were heading, naturally, for Honolulu. Luckily, they survived.

An appealing **B&B**, the *Kamalō Plantation* (HC01, PO Box 300, Kaunakakai HI 96748; Ⓣ & Ⓕ558-8236, Ⓦwww.molokai.com/kamalo; ❸), stands in superb tropical gardens across from St Joseph's, a short way beyond milepost 10. Two rooms in the main house, rented as a unit to parties traveling together, share a single bathroom. There's also a separate and very private guest cottage, housing two people, with its own kitchen.

# 'Ili'ili'ōpae Heiau

The second-largest *heiau* in all Hawaii is tucked away in Mahulepu Valley, a mile past Our Lady Of Sorrows church. Hardly anyone lives around here now, but when the **'Ili'ili'ōpae Heiau** took its final form in the eighteenth century, it served as a robust proclamation of the power of a mighty warrior chief. As a *luakini*, or temple of human sacrifice, it was probably erected on the site of sev-eral previous temples; its four colossal tiers, rising to a stone platform that meas-ures almost 300 feet long by 87 feet wide, may well stand atop its predecessors.

'Ili'ili'ōpae Heiau stands on private property, and the only sure-fire way to see it is by joining an expedition with Molokai Wagon Rides (Ⓣ558-8132). Participants can choose between sitting in a horse-drawn wagon ($35 per per-son, groups of eight or more only) or riding horses ($50); both alternatives also include a beach picnic and sing-along.

That said, individual walkers are sometimes allowed to make their way up to the *heiau*; be sure to check with the Molokai Visitors Association or at your hotel before you set off. Assuming you get permission, park just before Mapulehu Bridge, half a mile beyond milepost 15, and then follow the track that leads inland from the silver mailbox no. 520. Paralleling a dry river bed, this track enters a cool and colorful woodland filled with fruit trees, before coming to an end after ten minutes with a solitary house on the right. A footpath to the left crosses the stream, to be confronted by the four massive layers of the *heiau*, which looks as if it was approached by a ramp at this southeastern corner. The *heiau* is located at the foot of a ridge, just as the valley walls begin to rise. It's surrounded by trees, but the flat expanse of lichen-speckled boulders on top is punctuated by the odd shrub or tiny flower. Not a trace survives of its sacred buildings, towers and altars, and the whole place now has a very tranquil air.

According to the local version of a myth common to most *luakinis*, 'Ili'ili'ōpae Heiau was originally constructed, during a single night, with boulders passed from hand to hand along a chain of *menehune* (see p.429) from Wailau Valley on the North Shore. Until recently a hiking trail from here ran right across the island to Wailau; more stone walls are scattered in the hills behind the *heiau*, but the undergrowth is virtually impossible to penetrate.

For an account of Hawaii's biggest *luakini*, Pu'ukoholā Heiau on the Big Island, see p.189.

## The Fishponds of Molokai

Ancient Hawaiians developed the art of aquaculture, or fish-farming, to standards unmatched elsewhere in Polynesia. Using intricate networks of artificial fishponds, laced around sheltered coastal areas, they are estimated to have raised around two million pounds of fish per year. In the words of the nineteenth-century Hawaiian historian Samuel Kamakau, "fishponds were things that beautified the land, and a land with many fishponds was called 'fat.'"

By that reckoning, the southeastern coast of Molokai was very fat indeed. More than fifty separate fishponds have been identified within a twenty-mile stretch – a sure sign that the area was home to many powerful chiefs, and a prime reason why Molokai was so coveted by the rulers of the other islands.

A typical fishpond consisted of a long stone wall that curved out from the beach to enclose a large expanse – as much as 500 acres – of shallow ocean. Building such a wall, which needed to poke a meter out of the water at high tide, took a great deal of labor. That work was made much easier in southern Molokai, where the inshore coral reef provided a ready-made foundation, and already all but encircled natural lagoons. When completed, the wall would have one or two gaps, or sluice gates, which were usually sealed off with wooden lattices. Small fry could enter, but once they grew to full size they'd be unable to leave, and it was a simple matter to harvest them in nets.

Saltwater fishponds, used to raise 'ama'ama (mullet) and awa (milkfish), were complemented by similar freshwater ponds, usually built near rivermouths that were sealed off from the sea by sandbars, and held such species as 'ōpae (shrimp) and 'o'opu (a native goby). Some smaller fish were even cultivated in the waterlogged taro fields.

The fishponds of Molokai remained in use well into the nineteenth century, and as recently as the 1960s there were attempts to revive them for commercial production. These days, most of the ponds, and also the coral reefs beyond them, are being inexorably submerged by sediment washed down from the hills. Overgrazing on the higher slopes is allowing around a foot of mud per year to settle into the ocean, and many ponds are turning into mangrove swamps. Just short of milepost 20, however, the Kahinapōhaku Fishpond is being restored as an educational resource, thanks to a federal grant. At present, it holds no visitor facilities.

# Pūko'o

Beyond the *heiau*, the village of **PŪKO'O** was, like Kamalō, an important port during the nineteenth century. It, too, all but withered away following the development of Kaunakakai. Today, Pūko'o marks the point where traffic along the coast is forced to slow down by a succession of narrow curves, but sightseers are rewarded by some delightful little pocket beaches.

The only place along Kamehameha V Highway where you can **eat** stands just before milepost 16 in Pūko'o. The *Neighborhood Store'n'Counter* (daily except Wed 8am–6pm; ⓣ558-8498) serves an appetizing assortment of breakfast and lunch specials, with plate lunches costing around $6.

# Twenty-Mile Beach

The prettiest of the south-coast beaches, and almost the only one where swimming and snorkeling are consistently safe, awaits you at milepost 20. Officially Murphy Beach Park, it's more commonly known, logically enough, as **Twenty-Mile Beach**. There's room to park on the grass verge at the headland just beyond.

After that, the twin islets of **Moku Ho'oniki** and **Kanahā Rock** – both bird sanctuaries – become visible ahead, and the speed limit drops to just 5mph as the road twists in and out around the rocky headlands.

# Pu'u o Hōkū Ranch

Each of the three lush little valleys beyond Twenty-Mile Beach holds a house or two and a patch of sand. As the rocky silhouette of Kahakuloa Head, at the very tip of Western Maui, looms into view across the water, the highway climbs up into the rolling meadows of the **Pu'u o Hōkū Ranch**. The scenery by now is absolutely gorgeous, with the ranchlands stretching a long way back from either side of the road.

The ranch headquarters stands to the right of the highway near mile marker 25 (PO Box 1889, Kaunakakai HI 96748; ⓣ558-8109, ⓕ558-8100, ⓦwww.puuohoku.com). As well as coordinating the daily work of the ranch, staff here organize an extensive program of **horseback riding** in the vicinity, with charges ranging from $55 per person for a one-hour ride up to $180 for an all-day waterfall excursion. In addition, two fully equipped **guest cottages** in the heart of this pastoral idyll are available for rent (❹/❺). One has two bedrooms and costs $100 per night, the other has four for $175.

# Hālawa Valley

Twenty-six miles out of Kaunakakai, beyond a sequence of progressively wider and deeper gulches, Kamehameha V Highway reaches an overlook poised 750 feet above the full spread of **HĀLAWA VALLEY**. The view from here is staggeringly beautiful, with the stream far below meandering to meet the foaming ocean, the rich green valley stretching away to either side, and the distant waterfalls shimmering in the valley's innermost recesses, half-hidden by clouds.

For its final 1.5 miles, the highway drops down the walls of the valley, with more tremendous views at each of its hairpin curves, before coming to an end on the south side of the stream. To the right there's a **beach** of grayish sand, accessible beyond a carpet of creeping flowers, and barely sheltered from the force of the ocean. Off the low rocky promontory to the left, where the waves sweep in towards the rivermouth, is Molokai's most popular **surfing** site. Large numbers of local kids may be in the water, but that's no sign that it's safe for outsiders.

Just before you reach the beach, it's also possible to round a sharp curve and head inland. The tiny wooden **church** here is always unlocked and open for quiet meditation, though the visitors' book is usually filled with the complaints of hikers denied access to the valley trails (see box opposite). In theory the dirt road from the left fork just beyond leads back upstream, but at the time of writing it was sealed off by a forbidding gate topped by loops of barbed wire.

The right fork, on the other hand, descends past groves of papayas and bananas to cross the stream on a little flat bridge, and after a few hundred yards reaches the seashore on the far side. The lovely little crescent **beach** here is considerably less exposed, and backed by a line of palm trees. The sand is a bit grubby with soil washed down the valley walls, but in summer in particular this makes for a good place to swim. A long stony spit stretches south, all but cut off by the extravagant curves of the stream. Rare Hawaiian monk seals occasionally haul themselves up above the waterline at Hālawa to rest; do not disturb them.

## The history of Hālawa Valley

When the Polynesians first arrived in Hawaii, they always chose to settle in the lush windward valleys of the islands. With its sheltered sandy inlet in which to beach their canoes, and abundant rainfall and year-round streams, Hālawa made an ideal home. Excavations have revealed the remains of round-ended huts, of a kind otherwise unknown in Hawaii, but resembling those on Easter Island and in eastern Polynesia, which have been dated to before 650 AD.

Hālawa went on to become the major population center of Molokai, home to perhaps a thousand people. Its extensive *taro* ponds (*lo'i*) were irrigated by a system of canals that stretched over half a mile back into the hills, and its fertile slopes were terraced into stone-walled fields. In addition to thirteen *heiaus* dedicated to agricultural deities, by the eighteenth century it also held a *pu'uhonua* (see p.174) and two human-sacrifice *luakinis*. One of these, the Mana *heiau* on the northern slope, was erected around 1720 by chief Alapa'inui of the Big Island to celebrate his conquest of the island.

*Taro* production in Hālawa continued throughout the nineteenth century – when most of the crop was exported to feed the whaling fleet at Lahaina on Maui – and well into the twentieth, as Chinese laborers left the plantations to start their own *taro* farms. In 1935, Californian businessman Paul Fagan bought the entire valley, in the hope of revitalizing its traditional lifestyle. However, most of the *lo'i* were destroyed by the state-wide *tsunami* (tidal wave) of 1946, and Fagan turned his attentions to Hāna on Maui instead (see p.345).

During the 1960s, when only three families still lived in Hālawa, the waterfalls started to flow so fiercely that they destroyed the remaining *lo'i*, and made the river channel too deep to be used for irrigation. Since then, the population has climbed once more, but Hālawa remains an uneasy place, with tensions existing between the traditionally minded older generation of farmers and the more militant youth, for whom retreating to the further reaches of the valley is a political statement, a rejection of the despoliation of modern Hawaii.

## Hiking in Hālawa Valley

In theory, hiking the **Hālawa Trail** into the depths of Hālawa Valley ranks among the top attractions for tourists visiting Molokai. Taking two hours each way, the trail leads upstream through magnificent tropical forest and orchards to the 250-foot **Moa'ula Falls**, said in legend to be the dwelling place of a giant lizard or *mo'o*. Swimming in the pool beneath the falls is only safe if a *ti* leaf tossed into the water floats; otherwise, it is said, you'll be dragged down by the *mo'o*.

However, the trail has become the focus of bitter local controversy. The dirt road leading to the trailhead has remained barred in recent years, and there have been reports of hikers who ignore the warning notices being abused, intimidated and even threatened with guns.

Local landowners assert that at least part of the long-established trail runs across their private property. Under American law, that makes them responsible for any accidents that may befall hikers. Since the trail involves crossing the two forks of the valley's main stream, which can be waist-deep, as well as a great deal of clambering over slippery rocks, they feel that at some point a claim for serious injury or death is inevitable. Certain landowners, such as the Pu'u O Hōkū Ranch (see overleaf), have been prepared to admit hikers who sign waiver forms, but no one is certain whether such forms carry any legal weight.

State-sponsored studies have suggested that the trail crosses too many different parcels of land for there to be any simple resolution. As a result, the state is reported to be considering either a compulsory buy-out of the whole route or the creation of an entirely new trail over state-owned land. At the time this book went to press, however, it was only possible to penetrate the recesses of Hālawa on a **guided hike** with the immensely knowledgeable and friendly Pilipo Solitario ($25 per person; ⓣ553-4355 or ⓔpilipo@visitmolokai.com). For the latest developments, contact the Molokai Visitors Association (see p.383).

# Central Molokai

**West of Kaunakakai**, Maunaloa Highway follows the coast for a couple of miles before turning inland to climb the "saddle" between Molokai's two volcanoes. The southwest shoreline of the island belongs in its entirety to the Molokai Ranch, and the only road access is via Maunaloa at the western end (see p.406).

The **central plain** of Molokai used to nourish extensive pineapple plantations, but apart from the island's main airport it holds little to interest visitors today. Villages such as **Kualapu'u** and **Ho'olehua** are sleepy little places, and although any stay on Molokai is likely to involve passing this way several times, there's no compelling reason to stop.

## The rainforest

The summit of eastern Molokai remains covered by some of the state's most pristine **rainforest**. Owned by the Molokai Ranch, but run by the private, nonprofit Nature Conservancy of Hawaii as the **Kamakou Preserve**, it's a sanctuary for native plants and animals, the last-known haunt of rare indigenous birds such as the Molokai thrush (*olomāo*) and the Molokai creeper (*kakawahie*). Most of the area is completely inaccessible even on foot, and the authorities prefer outsiders to venture in only with experienced local guides such as those listed on p.381.

However, a rough dirt road climbs right to the top of the mountain from central Molokai. It's virtually always raining up there, and even at its best the track tends to be a deep wet furrow in the earth, where anything other than a high-clearance four-wheel-drive vehicle will slither uncontrollably. If you have a jeep and are determined to make your own way up, ask for advice on the latest conditions at the Nature Conservancy of Hawaii office, which is located in the upper section of the Molokai Technology Park, to the left of Maunaloa Highway, 2.5 miles up from Kaunakakai (Mon–Fri 8am–3pm; ⓣ553-5236). The Nature Conservancy also organizes **guided hikes** on the first Saturday of each month ($25 including airport pickup for walkers who fly in for the day) and welcomes volunteers prepared to spend a day participating in regular maintenance trips.

Finally, it's also possible to hike up into the preserve from Molokai's south coast, along a trail that sets off from Kamehameha V Highway opposite One Ali'i Beach Park (see p.385). Head through the small gate alongside the locked jeep-road gate here; a climb of around ninety minutes along the line of the ridge brings you onto the dirt road at the top, a short way east of the Waikolu Lookout (see below). The total round-trip hike to Pelekunu Valley and back to the ocean takes at least six hours.

## The Forest Reserve road

Less than four miles from Kaunakakai, just before Maunaloa Highway crosses a bridge, the **Forest Reserve jeep road** heads off to the right and soon reaches the dusty **Homelani Cemetery**. The long, straight, red-dirt track from here may seem innocuous at first, but it becomes heavily rutted as you climb higher.

By the time you pass the sign announcing the **Molokai Forest Preserve**, you'll probably have penetrated the mountain's semi-permanent cloud cover. Within half a mile, you'll spot the largely abandoned scout camp that's home to sculptor Robin Baker, who has carved totem poles, sharks, octopuses and cobras into the living trees. Well beyond that, the imported eucalyptus starts to give way to a pine forest that's interspersed with bright-blossomed native *ōhia* trees.

## The Sandalwood Pit

In a grassy clearing on the very crest of the Kamakou ridge, a deep groove in the ground betrays the site of Lua Nā Moku 'Iliahi, or the **Sandalwood Pit**. This is one of the few surviving examples of a "*picul* pit," dug early in the nineteenth century to the exact size and shape of a ship's hull. Hawaiian commoners were sent up into the mountains by their chiefs to cut down precious sandalwood trees; once they had filled one of these pits with logs (weighed in units called *piculs*), they then had to carry them back down to the sea on their naked backs, ready for shipment to China.

You're unlikely to see any living sandalwood here now, though a small stand is said to survive somewhere in the vicinity. Legend has it that the exploited laborers deliberately uprooted sandalwood saplings to ensure that their children would not have to do the same cruel work.

## Waikolu Lookout

Around ten miles from the highway – 45 minutes' driving on a good day – the jeep road reaches **Waikolu Lookout**. This dramatic viewpoint commands a majestic prospect of the verdant Waikolu Valley, dropping 3700 feet down to the ocean. Tiny Huelo Island stands offshore, while the Kalaupapa Peninsula is just out of sight around the headland to the left.

Most of Molokai's drinking water comes from Waikolu, flowing to the reservoir at Kualapu'u along a tunnel that pierces the valley wall almost directly below this spot. Access is denied to the general public, but if you have the right connections, it's said to be possible to hike through the tunnel and reach the Waikolu Valley.

The meadow across from the lookout is equipped with a few picnic tables and latrines and also holds a rudimentary **campground**, which lacks running water. Free permits, for a maximum five-night stay, can be picked up from the Department of Land and Natural Resources (see p.382).

## The Pēpē'ōpae Trail

Commercial off-road tours (see p.381) tend not to press on past Waikolu Lookout, which marks the start of the **Kamakou Preserve**. For most of the year, the jeep road beyond is impassable for vehicles of any kind, but it's always possible to continue **on foot**. As it undulates through a succession of minor gulches, it soon leaves the last vestiges of the dryland forest behind and plunges into the jungle.

### The Valleys of the North Shore

The **north coast** of Molokai boasts the tallest **sea cliffs** in the world, measuring up to four thousand feet high. Geologists used to imagine that these sheer green walls must have been created by gigantic landslides, perhaps along volcanic fault lines. While such landslides have pared away much of the coastline of Hawaii, it's now known that the cliffs of Molokai were created by the power of the Pacific alone.

Few visitors ever see the cliffs or the mighty **amphitheater valleys** – so called for the unclimbable walls that soar to either side and meet in a high encircling ridge at the head – that cut deep into them. **Hālawa** to the east is accessible by road (see p.389), while **Waikolu** in the west can in theory be reached on foot from Kalaupapa, but **Pelekunu, Wailau** and **Pāpalaua** valleys are completely sealed off from the rest of Molokai.

All of these valleys held substantial populations in pre-contact times. The name of the largest, Pelekunu, means "mouldy smell," a frank acknowledgement of the fact that, even when it's not raining, the valley floor receives less than five hours of direct sunlight each day. Pelekunu's *taro* farmers are thought to have abandoned the valley each winter, when the seas grew too rough to permit canoe landings, and migrated west to Mo'omomi to catch and dry fish in relative comfort. The last permanent population had left by 1917, though for a few years after that the valley was infested by wild water buffalo that had been abandoned by Chinese farmers.

These days most of the land in the north-shore valleys is privately owned. Some back-to-nature enthusiasts camp out on their property in summer, but there's no formal agriculture. The state is gradually buying up as much of the area as it can, in the hope of turning the whole shoreline into a vast nature reserve.

After about five minutes, you can cut through a gap in the dense greenery to your left and join the **Hanalilolilo Trail**, which sets off up and over a steep hillock. That trail is, however, just a very soggy way of getting to the **Pēpē'ōpae Trail**, and it's much simpler just to continue on the road for the full 2.5 miles to the official Pēpē'ōpae trailhead.

The Pēpē'ōpae Trail, the only trail to penetrate into the heart of the preserve, is an absolutely wonderful hike. To protect the various fragile ecosystems through which it passes, it consists of a slender wooden boardwalk, seldom more than a plank wide. It begins by pushing its way through thick rainforest, where every tree is festooned with dangling vines and spongy, fluorescent moss, and dazzling orchids glisten amid the undergrowth of tightly coiled ferns. Between wisps of mountaintop mist, you might just glimpse unique native birds such as the Molokai creeper or the Molokai thrush.

The trail then emerges into an eerie patch of windswept bog, reminiscent of the Alaka'i Swamp on Kauai (see p.498). Amazingly, the red-blossomed, stunted shrubs scattered across the desolation are *'ōhia*, the identical species that grows as full-sized trees in the neighboring forest. A viewpoint enables you to look back across the island to the west end, then the trail plunges once more into the jungle. After a final steep climb, the boardwalk ends abruptly at another incredible view of the north coast, this time over **Pelekunu Valley**.

In total, it takes over an hour to walk the full length of the Pēpē'ōpae Trail, to the overlook and back, and more like four hours to hike from the Waikolu Lookout.

## Kualapu'u

In its sixty-year existence, the fortunes of the former plantation town of **KUALAPU'U**, two miles east of Maunaloa Highway along Kala'e Highway (Hwy-470), have fluctuated immensely. Dole stopped growing pineapples in this area in 1982, but Kualapu'u is has been experiencing something of a recovery since the Malulani Estate set out to produce **coffee** here instead. Their Muleskinner Coffee has established itself as a rival to the Big Island's long-established gourmet crop (the only coffee entitled to call itself "Kona"; see p.169).

The headquarters of the coffee estate stands just to the right of Farrington Avenue as it turns left from Kala'e Highway at the eastern end of Kualapu'u. Here, a bakery and **café** called *Coffees of Hawaii* (Mon–Sat 7am–4pm; ⓣ 567-9241) serves free percolated coffee and inexpensive espressos, while the attached Plantation Store sells Muleskinner in bags, plus souvenirs and local crafts. Sitting on their open terrace, looking out across Molokai, is as enjoyable and relaxing an experience as the island has to offer.

A few hundred yards west, the longer-established *Kamuela's Cookhouse* (Tues–Fri 6.30am–2.30pm, Sat & Sun 8am–2pm; ⓣ 567-9655) is an attractive timber building that houses a fairly ordinary diner, with indoor seating and an adjacent garden terrace. Burgers and plate lunches are around $7; dinner specials can cost up to $20.

The lake-like expanse of water visible to the south of Farrington Avenue is the largest rubber-lined **reservoir** in the world, holding over a billion gallons of water piped from the North Shore valleys.

# Ho'olehua

There's even less to **HO'OLEHUA** – a mile west of Kualapu'u along Farrington Avenue, or a mile north of Maunaloa Highway to the east of the airport – than there is to Kualapu'u.

Anywhere else in the world, the only attraction, **Purdy's Nut Farm** – a little way up Lihi Pali Avenue, just west of Kualapu'u – might not seem a big deal. If you take the time to stop, however, you can while away an inconsequential but thoroughly enjoyable half-hour (Mon–Fri 9.30am–3.30pm, Sat 10am–2pm; free). In a nutshell, Tuddie Purdy – the grandnephew of Ikua Purdy, who was World Rodeo Champion in 1908 (see p.229) – stands at a counter amid a small grove of macadamia nut trees. He tells whoever drops by about the trees, cracks nuts with his hammer, and hands out slices of coconut to dip in honey. With any luck he'll also sell a few nuts, some fruit from his orchard or a little honey. Because Tuddie does not use pesticides – which preclude visits to mac-nut orchards elsewhere – you can stroll among the 75-year-old trees. They're rooted in bare red earth, which is swept clean every day and kept clear of grass, to make the fallen nuts easy to spot.

# Mo'omomi Beach

Farrington Avenue heads west through Ho'olehua and is out the far side almost before you'd notice. After another 2.5 miles, the road surface turns to red dirt, but usually remains in good enough condition to make it worth driving the final two miles down to **Mo'omomi Bay**. There's a little sandy **beach** to the left of the end of the road, while the rounded depressions left by long-gone lava boulders in the jagged sandstone to the right serve as tide pools. Local kids choose this side of the bay to go surfing and boogie-boarding.

Mo'omomi Bay is one of several small indentations in the three-mile stretch of solidified sand dunes known as **MO'OMOMI BEACH**. The shallow offshore waters were once highly prized fishing grounds, and countless ancient octopus lures and fish-hooks have been found nearby, but the dry coastline has probably never hosted much of a permanent population. As often seems to be the case in such marginal districts, the land is now set aside as Hawaiian Home Lands and reserved for those with a certain percentage of Hawaiian blood; the precise figure is revised downwards from time to time.

Walking along the coastal track a mile west of Mo'omomi Bay brings you to the prettier **Kawa'aloa Bay**, where the large sandy beach is slightly safer for swimming. The dunes here are an ecological treasure-trove, holding not only the fossilized remains of extinct flightless birds, but also rare living species of plants. Casual strolling is not encouraged, but the Nature Conservancy of Hawaii in Kualapu'u (see p.392) often organizes weekend **guided hikes**.

# Kala'e

The tiny residential area of **KALA'E** is located two miles northeast of Kualapu'u, 1500 feet above sea level as Kala'e Highway climbs towards the top of the *pali* above Kalaupapa. Its rich wet farmland – the best on Molokai –

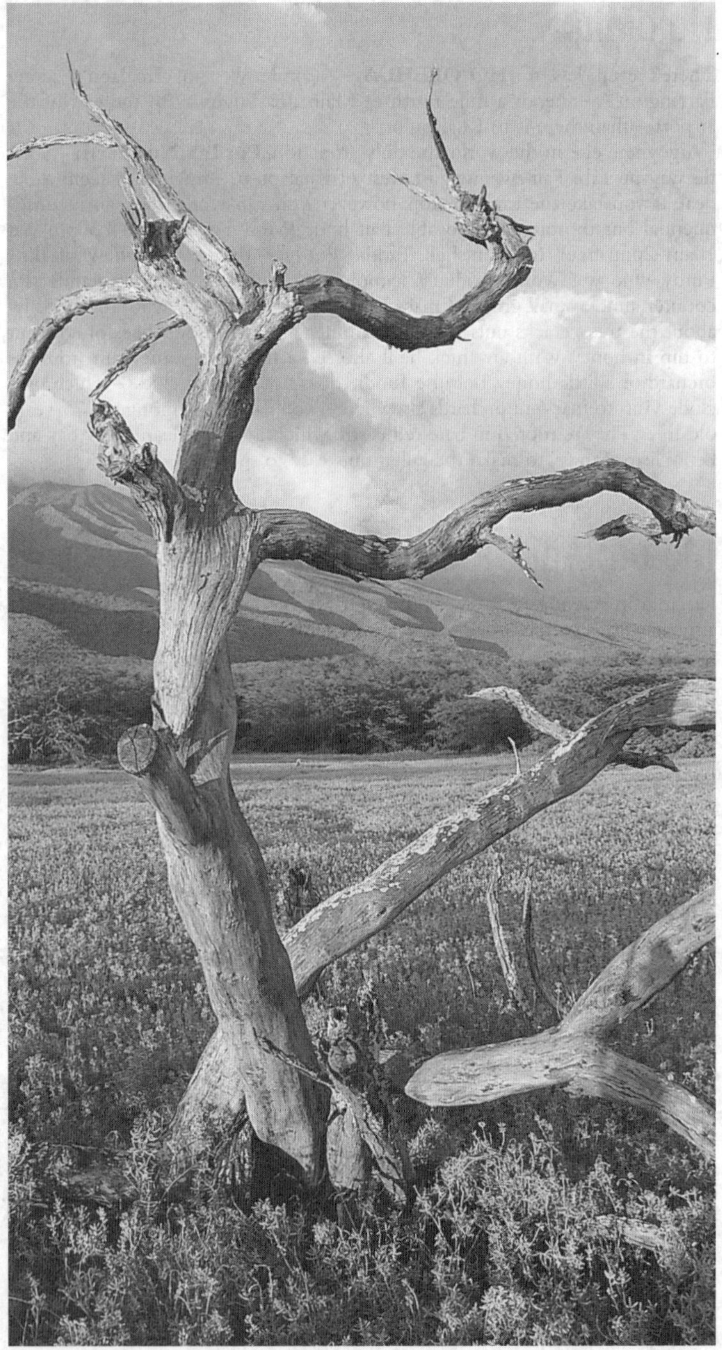

was acquired in the 1850s by a German migrant, **Rudolph Meyer**, when he married the local high chiefess, Kalama. Soon after establishing a ranch up here, he fell victim to an extensive cattle-rustling operation. All the men of Pālā'au village, down on the southern coast, were sent to jail in Honolulu, and the village was abandoned – not the sort of thing that gets forgotten on Molokai.

During the 1870s, Meyer ventured briefly into the sugar business. The roadside **R.W. Meyer Sugar Mill** operated only from 1878 until 1889, before Meyer returned to cattle ranching and went on to found the Molokai Ranch (see p.405).

Hawaii's smallest sugar mill then lay rotting for almost a century, but it has now been laboriously restored to full working condition. Outside the main shed stands the original mule-powered cane crusher, while inside you can see the furnace, boiler and the elaborate steam engine. That's all quite underwhelming, but the modern hall in the field behind is slowly evolving into the **Molokai Museum and Cultural Center** (Mon–Sat 10am–2pm; $2.50), and in due course it may well house a wider assortment of displays on island history. Meyer and many of his descendants lie buried in a peaceful garden cemetery beyond.

The museum also serves as the base for a varied program of tours of what are called "**Meyer's *mauka* lands**." Either on foot or by jeep, these excursions explore the area above and east of Hwy-470, visiting such sites as Meyer Lake and little-known viewpoints over Kalaupapa. For full details, call ⓣ567-6624 or 1-800/962-9989.

# Pālā'au State Park

A couple of miles beyond the sugar mill, and less than a mile past the mule stables and Kalaupapa trailhead (see p.398), Kala'e Highway ends its climb across Molokai in the forested parking lot of **Pālā'au State Park**.

A short walk to the right from the far end of the lot brings you to a railed **overlook** that faces east along the coast. Kalaupapa Peninsula lies spread out far below, with the village of Kalaupapa clear on the near side, and the slight upswell of the central Kauhakō Crater behind it. The pinnacle of Mōkapu island juts from the ocean beyond, but the original settlement of Kalawao is obscured by the slight curve of the *pali*. Captioned photographs explain the local topography, as well as the history and treatment of Hansen's Disease (see p.402). A footpath continues left from the lookout, offering a pleasant half-hour **hike** but no better views.

To the left of the parking lot, a separate and very well-worn trail through the woods is a five-minute walk to the top of the Pu'u Loa knoll, known for its **Phallic Rock**. This reshaped and much-fondled stone outcrop was in ancient times a fertility shrine known as Ka Ule O Nānāhoa – "the penis of Nānāhoa" – and used to stand fully exposed to the plains below, rather than deep in the forest. Women who brought offerings here and then spent the night were said to return home pregnant; the furrowed tip still holds cigarettes and other gifts. Ancient petroglyphs are concealed beneath an overhanging rock nearby, while an extremely old *heiau* on a rocky point two miles to the west is surrounded by phallic emblems.

**Camping** near the parking lot at Pālā'au State Park is free; contact the Department of Land and Natural Resources, as detailed on p.382.

# The Kalaupapa Peninsula

**"They were strangers to each other, collected by common calamity, disfigured, mortally sick, banished without sin from home and friends. Few would understand the principle on which they were thus forfeited in all that life holds dear; many must have conceived their ostracism to be grounded in malevolent caprice; all came with sorrow at heart, many with despair and rage. In the chronicle of man there is perhaps no more melancholy landing than this of the leper immigrants among the ruined houses and dead harvests of Molokai."**

Robert Louis Stevenson



The **KALAUPAPA PENINSULA** is a dramatic volcanic afterthought, tacked on to Molokai's forbidding north coast and almost completely cut off by towering 2000-foot cliffs. It was created long after the cliffs had been shaped by the force of the sea, when lava from a minor eruption lapped against the vast bulk of the island to form a flat and exposed spit of land.

This remote outpost became world famous in the nineteenth century as the grim place of exile for Hawaiian sufferers from **leprosy**, and the site of the ministry of the saintly **Father Damien** (see box, p.400). Although there is no longer any risk of the disease spreading, the peninsula is still reserved for former leprosy patients. Under the joint administration of the National Park Service and the Hawaii State Department of Health, it's run as the **Kalaupapa National Historic Park**. It's also a somewhat anomalous county in its own right, although it has no official county government, and all the other counties in Hawaii consist of one or more entire islands. As no one under the age of 16 is allowed on the peninsula, this is the only child-free county in the US.

Kalaupapa is an inspiring place to visit, but you can only do so with a reserved ticket for an official **park tour**. These are operated by the residents as Damien Tours, and are not open to children. Other than **flying** down, the only means of access is the long but perfectly safe **trail** that zigzags down the *pali*, which you can either **hike** or descend by **mule**.

If you don't have the time to visit the peninsula itself, it's possible to get a distant overview from the overlook in **Pālā'au State Park** (see p.397), at the top of Kala'e Highway.

## The trail to Kalaupapa

The trailhead for the precipitous descent to Kalaupapa, the three-mile **Kukuiohāpu'u Trail** (also known as the Pali Trail), is located to the right of Kala'e Highway, almost three miles north of Kualapu'u and just beyond the barn that's the headquarters of the **Molokai Mule Ride**. Molokai's most popular tourist attraction – famous throughout the US for its bumper-sticker slogan *Wouldn't You Rather Be Riding a Mule on Molokai?* – is a wonderfully escapist experience, but in essence the Molokai Mule Ride is simply an expensive, if enjoyable, means of transportation. Once at Kalaupapa, the riders dismount and join the same motorized tours of the peninsula (see opposite) as all other visitors.

Each day except Sunday, the mule ride sets off at 8.30am and returns at around 3.40pm; the fee ($150 per person) includes the ground tour and a picnic lunch, while round-trip airport transfers are $18 extra. For reservations, call

Ⓣ 567-6088, 567-9269 or 1-800/567-7550, or Ⓔ muleman@aloha.net as far in advance as possible.

If you prefer to **hike**, there's nothing to stop you from walking the full length of the trail and then climbing back up again, but you can only enter the peninsula itself if you rendezvous with a pre-arranged tour. Most hikers set off around 8.30am to coincide with the 10.15am Damien Tours tour.

Whether you walk or ride, it takes around an hour and a half to get to the bottom. For the first few hundred yards from the highway, the trail winds through bucolic meadows and guava orchards; then, suddenly, it comes to the edge of the cliff, above a sheer 1644-foot drop. The section that follows is the narrowest of the lot, with the yawning abyss in full view to your left. Soon, however, you enter the shade of the forest and continue dropping steeply down 26 numbered switchbacks. The majestic *pali* stretches away to the horizon in both directions, with rainbows floating beneath the clouds and the plain of Kalaupapa laid flat at your feet.

The whole trail was rebuilt during 1994 and 1995, when the mule ride was closed by legal and insurance wrangles. Rather than ferrying tourists, the hard-working mules were obliged instead to assist in the renovation project, making up to four round-trips per day as cement stairways were set into the earth, and parapets placed along the occasional hair-raising stretch.

Eventually the trail levels out to run the full length of **'Awahua Beach**, which you will have repeatedly glimpsed to the west of the peninsula. In winter, this broad expanse of slightly grimy sand can be stripped completely bare overnight. As on all the beaches at Kalaupapa, swimming is strictly forbidden.

## Flying to Kalaupapa

Daily **flights** to Kalaupapa's tiny airstrip from Molokai's main airport at Ho'olehua are operated by Molokai Air Shuttle (Ⓣ 545-4988 on Oahu, Ⓣ 567-6847 on Molokai; $52 round-trip). This seven-mile, nine-minute hop claims to be the shortest scheduled air service in the world, and carries the added bonus of a close-up view of the world's tallest sea cliffs, along Molokai's otherwise inaccessible northern coastline. Pacific Wings (Ⓣ 567-6814 or 1-888/575-4546, Ⓦ www.pacificwings.com) operates two scheduled flights each day between Kalaupapa and Honolulu, while Molokai Air Shuttle will also fly that route on demand. Paragon Air (Ⓣ 1-800/428-1231) operates a charter service between Kalaupapa and Kahului or Kapalua on Maui. All passengers landing at Kalaupapa must have tour reservations.

The Molokai Mule Ride (Ⓣ 567-6088 or 1-800/567-7550; Ⓦ www.muleride.com) arranges day-trips to Kalaupapa, including round-trip flight, mule ride and ground tour, from any hotel in Waikīkī, or from either airport on Maui, for $279. Paradoxically enough, they'll also sell you a day-trip in which you fly to and from Kalaupapa and tour the peninsula without taking the mule ride; the cost is $109 from Molokai or $189 from Honolulu or Maui.

## Touring Kalaupapa

All **tours** of Kalaupapa Peninsula are organized by Damien Tours (for reservations, call Ⓣ 567-6171 or Ⓣ 567-6675 between 4pm and 8pm), at a cost of $30 per person. Every day except Sunday, their rickety minibuses or four-wheel-drive vehicles pick up tourists either from the airstrip or at the east end of 'Awahua Beach, just outside the settlement of **KALAUPAPA**, where the trail from Kala'e ends. Visitors are not allowed to wander unaccompanied, or to take photographs of residents. Even if you're on the mule ride, bring plenty of **water**; it can be a long hot day, and there's nowhere to get a drink.

Exactly what is included on any one tour depends on the whim of that day's guide. As a rule, you can expect to spend the first hour in Kalaupapa village, although you may not see any patients other than your guide. A small **visitor center** here holds ornaments and artifacts made by the patients, plus utensils that they adapted for their own use, as well as photos of such unlikely visiting celebrities as Shirley Temple and the von Trapp family.

## Father Damien and the Story of Kalaupapa

Within a century of its first contact with the outside world, the population of Hawaii dropped from around one million to just over fifty thousand. Among the main reasons was the susceptibility of native Hawaiians to imported **diseases**, none of which was more feared than **leprosy**.

Hawaii's first case of leprosy was diagnosed in 1835, at Kōloa on Kauai. Perceived to have spread with the advent of plantation laborers from China, it became known as *ma'i Pākē*, or the "Chinese disease." In 1865, when one in fifty Hawaiians was said to have contracted leprosy, King Kamehameha V saw no alternative but to pursue a policy of rigorous **isolation**.

All persons deemed to be suffering from the disease – which, given the state of medical knowledge in rural Hawaii, effectively meant anyone with a visible skin blemish – were obliged to surrender themselves for shipment to the Kalaupapa Peninsula, to live out their days in permanent **exile**. Apart from one voluntary *kokua* (helper), they were separated forever from their homes and families. There was no right of appeal against the diagnosis, and as bounty hunters scoured the islands in search of potential victims, some sufferers, such as the legendary Koolau on Kauai (see p.470), turned outlaw to escape their fate.

Although nowhere in Hawaii is more isolated than the Kalaupapa Peninsula, numerous shrines, *heiaus* and gravesites – now mostly buried in the undergrowth – attest to extensive ancient occupation. There was a substantial settlement here in the 1860s, but the villagers swiftly relocated "top-side" once shipments of sufferers began to arrive at nearby Kalawao Bay to the east.

In its **early years**, the colony at Kalaupapa was a God-forsaken place. Intended to be self-sufficient, it rapidly dissolved into anarchy. The first boatload of people were left to divide all the land among themselves; as additional exiles followed, it had to be redivided again and again, occasioning bitter disputes each time. The strong dominated the weak, to be supplanted in turn as each succumbed to the disease. For fear of contagion, ships refused to pull in closer than Mōkapu island, and new arrivals were forced to swim for their lives through the rough surf. Those that made it to the shore were greeted with the words, "*A'ole kānāwai ma kēia wahi*" ("There is no law in this place") and stripped of their few possessions.

The people of Kalaupapa were not regarded as patients; receiving no treatment, they were simply abandoned to die. There was little sympathy from the white-dominated government, where the prevalent attitude was that the natives had brought disease upon themselves by wanton promiscuity.

Matters only began to change in 1873, when the Belgian Catholic priest **Father Damien Joseph de Veuster** – who had worked for nine years on the Big Island – was posted to Kalaupapa for a brief tour of duty. Although only 12 of the 822 residents at that time were Catholic, Father Damien dedicated himself to improving conditions for all. He was to spend the remaining sixteen years of his life on

Among other likely stops are a memorial to Father Damien and the gravesite of his successor Mother Marianne Cope, as well as the small **boat landing** where all local supplies arrive. Just one barge per year now delivers to Kalaupapa, its cargo including a hundred cases of Spam and 2700 cases of beer for sale in the peninsula's only bar. The essentials of life are so hard to obtain in Kalaupapa that most residents have two of everything – cars, TVs, etc – in case one breaks down. This cautious approach proved ineffective in 1991, however, when the old wooden hospital burned down, with all its medical records. Both fire engines failed to start.

Kalaupapa is located on the sheltered, drier, western side of the peninsula. As you cross to the east, the vegetation grows rapidly thicker and greener,

Molokai, in a sustained outpouring of sheer physical effort that doomed him to an early grave.

Damien's daily routine consisted in nursing, bathing and dressing the sores of the sick, and in due course carrying their corpses for burial with his bare hands. Although determined to build a new church at Kalawao, he regarded that task as intrinsically less important and only allowed himself to work on its construction after dark. He also built three hospitals and over three hundred houses to replace the previous crude windbreaks, and constructed a pipeline to carry fresh water along the coast from high in Waikolu Valley.

One Sunday morning, in June 1885, Damien began his sermon with the words "**We lepers** ..." rather than the usual "my brethren." Out of more than a thousand helpers to have worked at Kalaupapa, he remains the only one ever to contract leprosy, through sustained physical contact and general exhaustion. His 82-year-old mother died the day after news of his illness reached Belgium; Damien himself died in Kalaupapa in April 1889, at the age of 49, having previously stated that "I would not have my health restored to me at the price of my having to leave the island and abandon my work here."

Damien has been eulogized ever since his death, by figures as disparate as the future King Edward VII of Britain and Mahatma Gandhi. One famous note of criticism, however, was sounded by Rev Charles Hyde, a Protestant minister in Honolulu, who wrote of him as "a coarse, dirty man, headstrong and bigoted ... not a pure man in his relations with women." Robert Louis Stevenson, who visited Kalaupapa a month after Damien's death, sprang to his defense in an "Open Letter" that was reproduced all over the world. A particular irony was added to the feud by the fact that Stevenson had in 1886 published his famous story about Dr Jekyll and Mr Hyde.

Although Damien made it very clear that he wished to remain buried at Kalaupapa, his body was exhumed and taken to Belgium in 1936; his right hand was, however, returned to Molokai in the summer of 1995. Evidence of the miraculous cure of a nun in 1895 has been accepted by the Vatican, and in 1994 Damien was officially beatified as the Blessed Damien – the last step on the road to eventual sainthood.

Meanwhile, the work at Kalaupapa has been carried on by such followers as Brother Joseph Dutton and Mother Marianne Cope. Over the years, the entire population shifted across the peninsula to the village of Kalaupapa itself, and Kalawao was abandoned altogether in 1932. Decades of false hopes and spurious treatments finally came to an end in the 1940s, with the appearance of the first effective treatment. A total of more than eight thousand patients have made their homes on the peninsula. Around a hundred inhabitants now remain, of whom forty or so are former patients. As the saga gently draws to a close, the peninsula is turning into a historical monument.

and groves of fruit trees start to appear. To the left of the one dirt road, the mound of **Kauhakō Crater** – the volcanic vent that created the peninsula – rises gently to a height of 400 feet. White crosses stand on its rim, while the brackish lake inside is more than 800 feet deep, reaching far below sea level. Off to the right of the road, the *pali* soars up into the clouds. After heavy rain, all the clefts in the cliff face become waterfalls; one, which runs red at first, takes twenty minutes to work its way down, filling six successive pools en route.

As you enter the original settlement of the "Lazaretto" (leper colony), **KALAWAO**, you pass the unobtrusive "**birthing stone**," where the chiefs of Molokai were traditionally supposed to be born. The tasseled Australian casuarina tree alongside it was planted by Father Damien in front of the third hospital he built in Kalawao – the first he was permitted to construct away from the exposed shoreline.

Nothing now remains of the hospital. Indeed the only building left standing in Kalawao, which was inhabited from 1866 to 1932, is **St Philomena's Church**, sited where the road meets the sea. Shipped from Honolulu in 1872, this was greatly expanded by Damien in the years that followed and is widely known as "Damien's Church." The rectangular holes in the floorboards beneath the pews were cut by Damien himself, when he realized that the sickest patients were not attending Mass because they were afraid of despoiling the church by spitting. Before his body was taken to Belgium, Damien was buried in the gardens to the right; his grave remains decorated with *leis* and now contains his right hand once more.

Despite the horrific tales of misery and squalor, Kalawao is an extraordinarily beautiful place. From the lawns beyond the church, and especially from **Judd Park** at the end of the road, the views of the coast are quite superb. Mists swirl beneath the gigantic *pali* to the east, occasionally parting to offer glimpses of the remote valleys that pierce it, while stark, rocky islands poke from the churning ocean. Daredevil ancient Hawaiians are said to have swum out to **'Ōkala Island**, the closest to the shore, to leap from its 400-foot summit with the aid of plaited palm-leaf "parachutes."

## Hansen's Disease

The disease familiar from the Bible as **leprosy** is known to scientists as "**Hansen's Disease**," in honor of the Norwegian Gerhard Hansen, who first identified the leprosy bacillus in February 1873. Despite popular misconceptions, Hansen's disease is not in fact particularly contagious, and only around one person in twenty is even susceptible to it.

Any need for the isolation of patients, as practiced at Kalaupapa, was rendered obsolete by the development of **sulfone drugs** in the 1940s. These arrest the development of the disease in sufferers, and eliminate the possibility of contagion. Nonetheless, although the disease has been all but eradicated both in Hawaii and the US as a whole, there are still two million sufferers worldwide, and some 600,000 new cases diagnosed each year.

In the last fifty years, Hawaiian state law regarding the official name of the disease has alternated three times between the terms "Hansen's Disease" and "leprosy." While "Hansen's Disease" is the current official choice, many of the patients at Kalaupapa continue to prefer "leprosy." Some are even content to be referred to as "lepers," despite what may seem to outsiders to be the negative connotations of the word.

# Western Molokai

**Western Molokai** consists of what remains of the older of the island's two volcanoes, **Mauna Loa**. Similar in profile to its Big Island namesake, but much lower, the "long mountain" lies within the rainshadow of the larger East Molokai volcano, in that almost all the moisture carried by the prevailing winds has already fallen as rain before they reach this far. As a result, this end of the island is much drier, and there's been little erosion to dissect it into valleys.

Nonetheless, recent archeological research has revealed that western Molokai held a considerable population in ancient times. As well as holding the mysterious woodlands that witnessed the emergence of the *hula* and the fearsome apparition of the poisonwood gods (see p.404), the upper slopes of its mountain were one of Hawaii's best sources of the ultra-hard basalt used for making adzes – a precious commodity in a world without metal. Hence the region's name: **Kaluako'i**, "the adze pit."

The entire west end of Molokai was sold in 1898 for $251,000, to the consortium that became the **Molokai Ranch**. The ranch remains a very powerful presence, although it has long since shifted its focus away from cattle-ranching and pineapple-farming and towards real estate and tourism. During the 1970s, it unveiled plans for the development of Kaluako'i that envisaged the area acquiring a population of ten thousand within twenty years. While the resort hotel and condos down by the sea are a surreal testament to the wonders that irrigation can work in a volcanic wasteland, there simply isn't enough **water** for that to happen.

Western Molokai has some magnificent **beaches**, such as the phenomenal **Pāpōhaku Beach**, but almost all are subject to surf that is too fierce for swimming. Instead, those visitors who stay in the coastal resort area – which has itself come to be called **Kaluako'i** – tend to be here for the **golf**, or simply the seclusion. As the base of the Molokai Ranch, which has an unfailing capacity to surprise visitors with its latest initiatives, the hillside plantation village of **Maunaloa** is also worth visiting.

## Maunaloa

Together with Kē'ē on Kauai (see p.465), **MAUNALOA** is one of two Hawaiian sites that claim to be the birthplace of *hula*. This tiny place also plays a prominent role in the myths and legends of ancient Molokai. Only a few stone ruins, near the adze quarry on the hillock of 'Amikopala, survive of the pre-contact settlement, but until recently Maunaloa was among the most picturesque plantation villages in the state.

Perched high on the red-dirt flanks of western Molokai, enjoying views all the way to Diamond Head and Waikīkī on Oahu, modern Maunaloa took shape after Libby leased the nearby land to grow pineapples in the 1920s. It consisted of a cluster of simple timber cottages, shielded from the winds by stately rows of tall trees. The fence of the lowermost home was a line of discarded surfboards wedged into the soil. Soon after passing into the hands of the Dole corporation in the 1970s, the pineapple fields were abandoned, the land reverted to the Molokai Ranch, and Maunaloa became a sleepy enclave of ranch hands, resort employees and alternative artists.

## The Poisonwood Gods

Maunaloa was renowned throughout ancient Hawaii as the home of the dreaded **Kālaipāhoa**, or "**poisonwood gods**." According to legend, sometime in the sixteenth or seventeenth centuries a Molokai man called **Kāneiākama** lost everything he possessed playing *'ulumaika*, which involved bowling stone discs down a hillside. As he was about to concede defeat, a god appeared to him in a dream and encouraged him to stake his life on the next throw. Upon winning, Kāneiākama sacrificed a pig to the mysterious god, who reappeared and explained that his name was **Kāneikaulana'ula**. Kāneiākama then watched as a grove of tall trees suddenly appeared in the hills above Maunaloa, and each different kind of tree was entered by a different deity.

When the then-chief of Molokai decreed that some of these magical trees should be chopped down and carved into images of the gods, it was found that the woodcutters died as soon as they were touched by flying chips or sap. Kāneiākama revealed how, with the appropriate sacrifices and ceremonies, the images could be created in safety; they passed into the control of the rulers of Molokai, while Kāneiākama became their *kahuna*, or priest.

For many years, access to the images was ruthlessly restricted, and fear of them kept Molokai safe from attack. Eventually, however, Molokai was conquered by the other islands, and the *Kālaipāhoa* passed first to Kahekili of Maui and then to Kamehameha the Great. According to nineteenth-century Hawaiian historian Samuel Kamakau, Kamehameha kept the images by him during his final years at Kailua on the Big Island, and was the only person able to resist their power: "Not only was *Kālaipāhoa* fatal to eat or touch, but it was also fatal if one carelessly went in and out of the house in which the god-images were kept without going out backward . . . a person would drop dead instantly at the door of the house if this rule was not observed."

Meanwhile the people of Molokai, and Maunaloa in particular, had begun to use the surviving trees for their own purposes. They used splinters or shavings of wood to poison each other's food, and even created magical bundles known as *akua kumuhaka*, that flew like flaming rockets through the night sky to seek out their enemies. During the first half of the nineteenth century, Molokai became widely feared as an evil place of *po'oko'i* (sorcery), and was often called the *'aina ho'ounauna*, "the land where spirits were sent on malicious errands."

Knowledge of the whereabouts of the *Kālaipāhoa* images died with Kamehameha, although at least one is thought to survive in the collections of Honolulu's Bishop Museum.

In 1995, however, Molokai Ranch bulldozed most of the residential district of Maunaloa and replaced it with tracts of low-income housing further up the hillside, even though there seem to be few jobs on the horizon for its hypothetical future inhabitants. At the time, the destruction created considerable bitterness, but those villagers that remain now seem grateful for the level of commitment – and investment – shown by the ranch, and there's a palpable sense of optimism about the place.

Maunaloa may not be as attractive as it used to be, but the area around its **village green** is largely unspoiled, and now even boasts its own three-screen movie theater (Ⓣ 552-2616). The most interesting of its handful of stores is the Big Wind Kite Factory (Mon–Sat 8.30am–5pm, Sun 10am–2pm), whose convivial owner, Jonathan Socher, makes and sells colorful kites and is usually happy to demonstrate the finer points of kite-flying. The adjoining Plantation Gallery (same hours) stocks an excellent range of imported crafts from Bali, Nepal and elsewhere, plus Molokai "Red Dirt" T-shirts and books on Hawaii, while across the road the old-style General Store (Mon–Sat 9am–7pm) is still going strong.

## Molokai Ranch

As you enter Maunaloa from the end of Maunaloa Highway, the first buildings you see on the right are the headquarters of the **Molokai Ranch**. These may appear to be old barns spruced up with fresh paint, but they are in fact new. The lower of the two, the **Outfitters Center** (daily 6am–7pm; ⓣ1-877/726-4656, ⓦwww.molokai-ranch.com), serves as an information center for all ranch operations, including the accommodation options detailed below, and also holds interesting displays about Molokai as a whole.

Activities available to visitors include **horseback riding** ($80 for ranch guests, $105 for others), all-day **bicycle** excursions ($80/$100), guided **hikes** (from $30/$45 up to $85/$125), and even **sport clay shooting** ($65/$80).

Until recently, the ranch ran safari tours into the dry savannah-like landscape that stretches from here down to the coast. Herds of zebra and Barbary sheep, and even a couple of giraffes, are still said to be down there somewhere.

## Accommodation

The ranch's latest bid to attract tourists to Maunaloa, the timber-built *Molokai Ranch Lodge*, is set slightly off the main road behind the Outfitters Center (PO Box 259, Maunaloa, HI 96770; ⓣ660-2725 or 1-877/726-4656, ⓦwww.molokai-ranch.com; ❽). This small upscale hotel stretches across the hillside above a not particularly scenic expanse of pastureland; at night, it's often possible to see all the way to Diamond Head on Oahu. Offering just 22 lavishly equipped guest rooms, located in separate buildings around a small swimming pool, it is – thanks to its cool upcountry location – not so much a tropical getaway as a retreat for overheated (and affluent) Hawaiian residents.

Much the same goes for the ranch's longer-established alternative to the *Lodge* – its various **campgrounds** in the vicinity of Maunaloa. All three consist of semi-permanent, canvas-walled structures, each of which is equipped with running water. At **Paniolo Camp**, sturdy "tentalows" stand on wooden platforms around a clearing high on the hillside, while at **Kolo Camp**, on a bluff just above the ocean, the accommodation is in Mongolian-style yurts – round "tents" that hold four-poster beds and en suite bathrooms. The larger units at **Kaupoa Beach Village**, in the very driest part of the island just north of its western tip, are designed for visitors whose primary interest is in watersports. The major stumbling block is the high **price**: the basic tent-and-breakfast rate for Paniolo Camp is $145 per night, single or double occupancy, while in Kolo Camp and Kaupoa Beach Village it's $195. All activities cost extra, as outlined above. Contact details are the same as for the *Lodge*.

## Eating

At the south end of the *Lodge*, the formal *Maunaloa Room* (Mon–Sat 7–10 am & 6–9pm, Sun 7–10 am, 11am–1.30pm & 6–9pm; ⓣ660-2725) is open for breakfast and dinner daily. Typical evening entrees include a $23 catch of the day prepared in Oriental (ie steamed), Mediterranean (with capers and olives), or local (broiled with citrus cream sauce) style, while Wednesday night sees a $30 crab leg and prime rib buffet. Lunch, served in the *Paniolo Bar* (daily 10am–4pm), is a less inspiring assortment of burgers and sandwiches at around $10.

A former plantation building at the top end of Maunaloa, equipped with a sweeping wraparound verandah, is home to the *Village Grill* (Mon–Fri 11am–1.30pm & 6–9pm, Sat & Sun 6–9pm; ⓣ552-0012). This offers simple weekday lunches and a full dinner menu that includes "stone grill" options, which you cook at your own table using a superheated stone slab, for around $20. There's also a *KFC* adjoining the movie theater.

# Hale O Lono Harbor

Molokai's remote **southwestern shoreline** has long been inaccessible to visitors. However, the **Hale O Lono Harbor** recently reverted to state ownership, after being leased to the Molokai Ranch for 35 years. Anyone who wants to can now drive down here, along the red-dirt road (very passable except after heavy rain) that starts just beyond the *Lodge* in Maunaloa. En route, keener eyes might spot a phallic rock in a gully to the left that marks ancient burial caves.

Hale O Lono Harbor, which was constructed to ship sand from Pāpōhaku Beach to Oahu (see p.70), consists of a few concrete jetties with minimal facilities. In September and October each year, it serves as the starting point of the prestigious Bankoh men's and women's **outrigger canoe races** from Molokai to Oahu. Walking a couple of hundred yards east from the parking lot at the end of the road brings you to a small, sheltered beach.

# Kaluako'i

Until construction began on the **Kaluako'i Resort** during the 1970s, just one person lived on the coast of western Molokai. That owes more to the fact that it belonged to the Molokai Ranch than to there being anything wrong with it. However, the lack of water has prevented the resort from growing to anything like the size originally envisaged. To this day, only one of its planned four hotels has ever been built, and even that one, the *Kaluako'i Hotel*, had by 2001 deteriorated to such an extent that it was forced to **close** indefinitely while its owners searched for a buyer prepared to take on the necessary large-scale renovations. As the hotel was home to the only stores or restaurants in the area, its closure has made staying in any of the nearby condo developments a much less appealing prospect, although it's still unquestionably worth making the trip here to enjoy splendid **Pāpōhaku Beach**.

## Accommodation

The only accommodation in Kaluako'i is located in the small area where Kaluako'i Road reaches the ocean, dominated by the (currently defunct) *Kaluako'i Hotel* on the headland.

**Ke Nani Kai**, PO Box 126, Maunaloa HI 96770; Ⓣ 552-2761, 526-0271 (Oahu) or 1-800/888-2791; or reserve through *Marc Resorts*, Ⓣ 922-9700 or 1-800/535-0085 (US & Can), Ⓕ 922-2421 or 1-800/633-5085 (US & Can), Ⓦ www.marcresorts.com. Spacious and very comfortable one- and two-bedroom condos, few of which have sea views, in a small, well-kept resort with its own pool and spa, on the hotel approach road. ❺.

**Kepuhi Beach Condo**, PO Box 20, Maunaloa HI 96770; Ⓣ 552-0077, 1-800/MOLOKAI or 1-800/HI-KEVIN, Ⓕ 552-0055 or 1-800/FX-KEVIN, Ⓦ www.1-800-molokai.com. Luxury condo on the Kaluako'i golf course, very close to Pāpōhaku Beach, with good-value nightly or weekly rental rates. ❹.

**Paniolo Hale**, PO Box 190, Lio Place, Maunaloa HI 96770; Ⓣ 552-2731 or 1-800/367-2984 (US), Ⓕ 552-2288, Ⓦ www.paniolohaleresort.com. Just north of the hotel, an estate of one- and two-bedroom condos. Some of the larger ones are complete houses and in very good condition. Garden view ❹, ocean view ❻.

## Molokai Ka Hula Piko

On the third Saturday of May, between 8am and 4pm, Pāpōhaku Beach Park hosts **Molokai Ka Hula Piko**, a day-long celebration of Molokai's role as the birthplace of the *hula*. That's a slightly contentious boast – Kē'ē on Kauai also claims to be the home of Hawaii's oldest art form – but Ka Hula Piko is universally acknowledged to be one of the most authentic traditional festivals in the islands. As well as performances by dancers, musicians and singers from all over Hawaii, it features local crafts and food stalls; admission is free.

On Molokai, the story runs that the goddess **Laka** was taught to dance the *hula* by her sister **Kapo** amid the verdant *'ōhi'a lehua* groves of **Kā'ana**, near Maunaloa. After traveling through the Hawaiian islands teaching *hula*, Laka returned to Molokai to die, and lies buried beneath the hill of **Pu'unānā**. It's also said that Laka and Kapo were among the gods who entered the mysterious trees at Maunaloa and became *kālaipāhoa,* or poisonwood gods (see p.404) – in Hawaiian religion, even beneficent deities can have an evil side.

Ka Hula Piko commences each year with a dawn ceremony at a ruined *heiau* at Kā'ana, to which the public is not admitted. However, the festival's organizer, Molokai's most respected *kumu hula*, or *hula* teacher, John Kaimikua, offers guided tours of related sites during the preceding week. At other times, the only way to see Kā'ana and Pu'unānā is on one of Lawrence Aki's guided tours, some of which he conducts for Molokai Ranch guests (see p.405). The fact that the area is now almost entirely denuded of trees has made it possible to identify, and in some cases excavate, countless cultural sites.

Local hotels offer all-inclusive transport and accommodation packages to Ka Hula Piko; contact the Molokai Visitors Association for details (see p.383).

## The West End beaches

Although the Kaluako'i Resort was positioned to enable guests to enjoy the long white sands of **Kepuhi Beach**, located directly in front of the *Kaluako'i Hotel*, it's only safe to swim here on calm summer days. Like most of the beaches of western Molokai, however, it looks fabulous and is ideal for sunset shoreline strolls.

A mile **north** of the resort, and reached by a very rough road – far too rough to drive – that starts by crossing the golf course beyond *Paniolo Hale*, pretty, crescent-shaped **Kawākiu Iki Bay** was a favorite fishing ground in ancient times. Mass protests in the 1970s persuaded the Molokai Ranch to grant free public access, and there's even a free but completely unequipped **campground** here, but it's almost always deserted.

Immediately **south** of the hotel, it's possible to follow a track to the summit of the crumbling cinder cone of **Pu'u O Kaiaka** for views of the entire coastline and, with luck, across to Oahu. Beyond it lies 2.5-mile-long **Pāpōhaku Beach**, one of Hawaii's broadest and most impressive white-sand beaches. It's so huge that for many years it was quarried for sand, much of which was used to build Waikīkī Beach.

Almost all the land to either side of Kaluako'i Road, which parallels Pāpōhaku a hundred yards back from the sea, was parceled off and sold for residential development many years ago. However, few of the lots have been built on, and you may find that you have the full length of the beach to yourself. The relentless pounding of the surf is spectacular, but makes swimming extremely dangerous.

Three successive turnoffs connect Kaluako'i Road with the beach. The northernmost leads to **Pāpōhaku Beach Park**, a well-equipped county park that has picnic tables on its lawns and barbecue pits amid the trees. Visitors with permits from the Division of Parks in Kaunakakai (Ⓣ567-6083) are allowed to **camp** here. The southernmost turnoff, Papapa Place, appears as Kaluako'i Road starts to climb at the south end of the beach; it comes out near the gated tunnel through which sand destined for Waikīkī was carted off to the docks on the south coast.

Kaluako'i Road ends beyond Pāpōhaku Beach, but by turning right on to Pōhakuloa Road you can drive a couple of miles farther down the coast. A couple of beach access roads along the way lead to an exposed and rocky shoreline, but the final turnaround comes at the small sandy cove named **Dixie Maru Beach**, after a long-vanished shipwreck. Sparsely vegetated and relatively unattractive, the cove is enclosed enough to create a small lagoon of sheltered turquoise water, where the swimming is usually great.

It's possible to follow the coastal footpath for another mile south to reach **Kaunalā Beach**, where the ocean is muddier and much rougher. The remaining segment of the western coast is not normally accessible to visitors, though it is the location of the Molokai Ranch's Kaupoa Beach Village (see p.405).

# 6

# Kauai

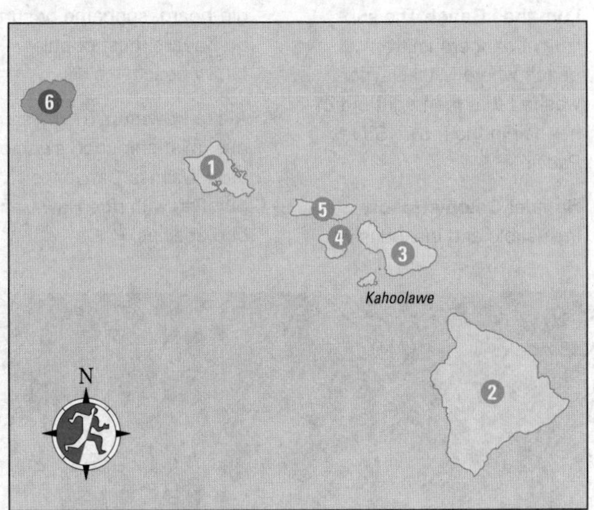

CHAPTER 6

# Highlights

* **Helicopter trips** There's no place quite like Kauai for a flight-seeing extravaganza of hidden canyons, remote rainforests, velvety waterfalls and uninhabited valleys. P.422

* **A Pacific Café** Hawaii's finest restaurant, where chef Jean-Marie Josselin works wonders with fresh local ingredients. P.443

* **Lumaha'i Beach** The sublime (if dangerous) tropical beach where Mitzi Gaynor washed that man right out of her hair in the movie *South Pacific*. P.461

* **Hanalei Colony Resort** Irresistible and inexpensive beachfront condo resort, within walking distance of the Nā Pali cliffs. P.462

* **The Kalalau Trail** Utterly magnificent eleven-mile trail along Kauai's northern Nā Pali coastline; just hike the first stretch if time is limited. P.467

* **Po'ipū Beach** Snorkel, boogie-board, sunbathe or surf on Kauai's most popular family beach. P.477

* **Alaka'i Swamp** The mysterious, mist-shrouded swamp atop Waimea Canyon is bursting with rare Hawaiian bird species. P.498

6

# Kauai

Although no point on the tiny island of **KAUAI** (rhymes with "Hawaii") is even a dozen miles from the sea, the sheer variety of its landscapes is quite incredible. This is the oldest of the major Hawaiian islands, and the forces of erosion have had over six million years to sculpt it into fantastic shapes. The resultant spectacular **scenery** – celebrated in movies from *South Pacific* to *Jurassic Park* – is Kauai's strongest selling point. In addition to such showpiece beauty spots as the plunging **Nā Pali cliffs** on the North Shore and mighty **Waimea Canyon**, every humble roadside town abounds in flowers, orchids and greenery. The Garden Island is also fringed with stunning **beaches** of white and golden sand, which provide a marked contrast to the island's rich, red soil. Some beaches, on the north and west coasts in particular, are only safe to look at; others, especially around the southern resort of **Po'ipū**, are ideal for family bathing.

Kauai ranks fourth not only in size among the Hawaiian islands, but also in population and number of annual visitors. With only a little over fifty thousand inhabitants scattered fairly evenly around the shoreline, it holds no large towns. The administrative center, **Līhu'e**, is functional but unenthralling, while all the main accommodation bases – **Po'ipū**, the coastal strip around **Kapa'a**, and **Princeville** – are too busy catering to tourists to possess much of an identity of their own. If you're looking for the high life, stick to Waikīkī or Maui; Kauai is more suited to a quiet family holiday or a romantic rural retreat. It's also a place to be active, on both sea and land. In addition to some of the world's most exhilarating hiking trails, it offers great **snorkeling** and **surfing**. Taking a boat trip along the North Shore is an unmissable experience, and if you only go on one helicopter flight in your life, this is the place to do it (see p.422). The Kauai office of the Hawaii Visitors Bureau is in Līhu'e (see p.426).

Kauai's image as a tourist destination was dealt a hammer blow by **Hurricane Iniki** in September 1992 (see box), but virtually all the physical damage has long since been repaired, and tourism on the island has finally climbed back to the pre-Iniki level of a million visitors a year. There's no reason to avoid Kauai for fear of another hurricane. Iniki was just bad luck; Hawaii is not especially prone to hurricanes, and Kauai no more so than any of the other islands.

## A brief history of Kauai

Although most details of ancient Hawaiian history remain unknown, Kauai can legitimately claim to possess its own separate heritage as the only island never to be conquered by another. Before the arrival of the Europeans, it was always

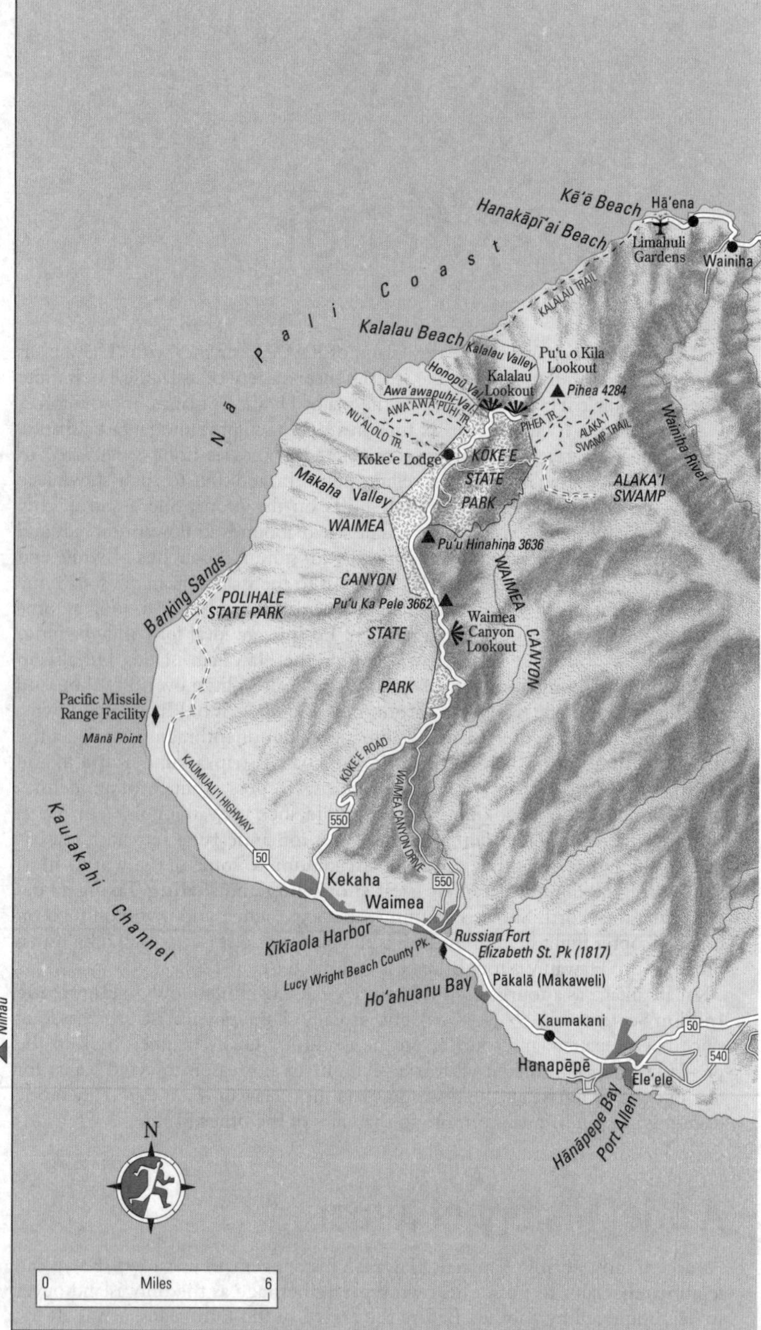


6

KAUAI | Kauai

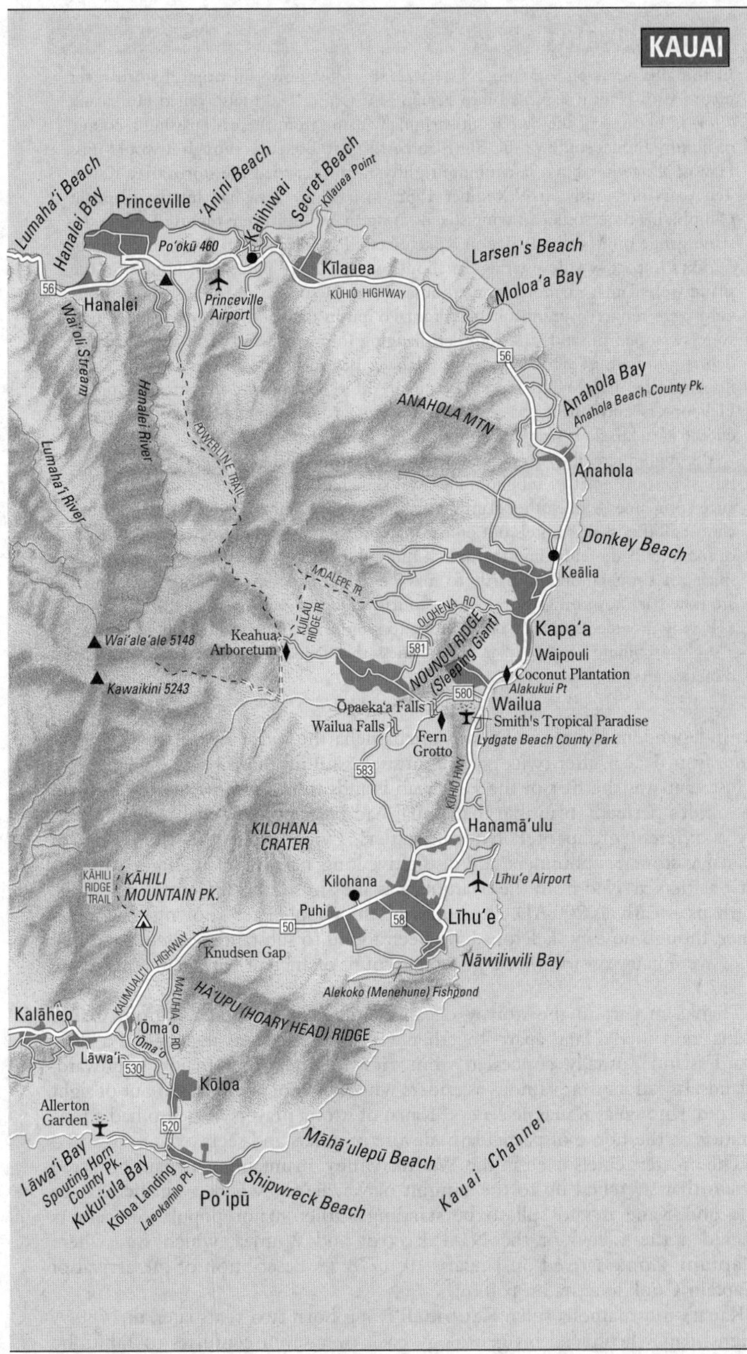
KAUAI
Lumaha'i Beach
Hanalei Bay
Princeville
'Anini Beach
Kalihiwai
Secret Beach
Kīlauea Point
Po'okū 460
Kīlauea
Larsen's Beach
Moloa'a Bay
Kūhiō Highway
Hanalei
Princeville Airport
Wai'oli Stream
Hanalei River
Lumaha'i River
Powerline Trail
Anahola Mtn
Anahola Bay
Anahola Beach County Pk.
Anahola
Donkey Beach
Keālia
Moalepe Tr
Kuilau Ridge Tr
Olohena Rd
Kapa'a
Waipouli
Wai'ale'ale 5148
Kawaikini 5243
Keahua Arboretum
Nounou Ridge (Sleeping Giant)
Coconut Plantation
Alakukui Pt
Wailua
'Ōpaeka'a Falls
Wailua Falls
Fern Grotto
Smith's Tropical Paradise
Lydgate Beach County Park
Kūhiō Hwy
Hanamā'ulu
Kilohana Crater
Kāhili Ridge Trail
Kāhili Mountain Pk.
Kilohana
Līhu'e Airport
Puhi
Līhu'e
Kaumuali'i Highway
Knudsen Gap
Nāwiliwili Bay
Maluhia Rd
Alekoko (Menehune) Fishpond
Hā'upu (Hoary Head) Ridge
Kalāheo
'Ōma'o
Lāwa'i
Kōloa
Allerton Garden
Māhā'ulepū Beach
Kauai Channel
Lāwa'i Bay
Spouting Horn County Pk.
Kukui'ula Bay
Kōloa Landing
Laeokamilo Pt.
Po'ipū
Shipwreck Beach

## Hurricane Iniki

In the afternoon of September 11, 1992, the most powerful tropical storm ever recorded in Hawaii slammed into Kauai. **Hurricane Iniki** (also called Hurricane "9-1-1" because of the date it hit) originally came from the east, passing a couple of hundred miles south of the Big Island. At first it looked as though it would miss Hawaii altogether, but a last-minute rightward turn carried the storm over Kauai. Ten years previously, in November 1982, **Hurricane Iwa** had hit the island at 65mph; this time, sustained wind speeds of up to 145mph were reported, while the wind gauge on Makaha Ridge in Kōke'e State Park snapped in a gust of 227mph.

Iniki's impact was devastating. In about two hours, 71 percent of homes on the island were damaged; more than a thousand were destroyed and almost seven thousand were rendered uninhabitable. From Po'ipū in the south – where hotel suites were swamped in sand, cars were left hanging from trees, and giant waves carried debris hundreds of yards inland – to Hanalei Bay in the north – where the tenth floor of the Princeville Hotel was torn off – Kauai was in tatters. Papillon Helicopters' entire fleet was destroyed in a hangar not long after the company rescued 69 backpackers stranded along the Nā Pali coast.

Although, incredibly, only three lives were lost in the hurricane, the total repair bill was estimated at $1.6 billion. That was sufficient to bankrupt some local insurance companies, while other claims remain in dispute to this day. Furthermore, with almost all the island's hotels out of action, visitor numbers plummeted, and the loss of income made rebuilding that much more difficult. Thanks partly to the "Aloha spirit" of cooperation and partly to massive federal aid, however, things on Kauai are now back to normal. Some in the tourist industry even speak of the hurricane as having provided a unique opportunity to rebuild from the ground up, and there's a slightly chilling attitude that any business that failed to survive Iniki probably didn't deserve to.

an independent kingdom. Even Kamehameha the Great opted to accept tribute from Kauai, after twice staging unsuccessful invasions.

Just as it was the first of the Hawaiian islands to be "discovered" by Captain Cook, it's perfectly plausible that Kauai had been **colonized** before the rest, by a different group of Polynesian settlers. Evidence such as the design of Kauaian stone *poi* pounders, and distinctive long, narrow *heiaus*, suggest that its first settlers arrived from the Marquesas islands in southern Central Polynesia, perhaps as early as 200 AD. These may be the people later known as the *menehune*, though no tiny skeletons have been found to substantiate the legend that they were hairy dwarfs. (For a general account of ancient Hawaiian culture, see p.517.)

Thanks in part to the stormy ocean channel that separates it from Oahu, Kauai remained a land apart. Together with Niihau, it was regarded as a "leeward island," usually concealed from view of the other major, windward, islands. Its sailors were famous as raiders who were not afraid to sail out of sight of land. Known as Kauai *pule o'o* – "Kauai of strong prayers" – it also had a reputation as the home of particularly devote prophets and seers.

The greatest chiefs lived in the **Wailua Valley**, maintaining a chain of sacred *heiaus* that stretched up to the summit of Wai'ale'ale, where a phallic altar to the god Kane is said still to be standing. Other major population centers included the valleys of the Nā Pali coast and Waimea, which was where **Captain Cook** arrived on January 19, 1778. (A description of the arrival of Captain Cook appears on p.486.)

Kauai's most famous ruler, **Kaumuali'i**, was born two years later, in 1780. A slight man who traced his genealogy back over seven centuries to Tahiti, he learned to speak and write fluent English; one foreign visitor called him "more dignified, more like a Christian than any of his fellows."

Kamehameha the Great made his first bid to **invade** Kauai in the spring of 1796. A huge fleet set off at dead of night from Oahu, but the attempt was abandoned after a storm sank several canoes. By the time he was ready for another attempt, six years later, Kaumuali'i was in charge of Kauai. This time Kamehameha's force consisted of around seven thousand Hawaiians and as many as fifty Europeans; his fleet included twenty-one schooners as well as traditional canoes and was equipped with eight cannons. As it assembled on the eastern shore of Oahu, however, they were struck by a terrible pestilence. Many of Kamehameha's closest advisers and friends died, and the invasion plans were once more shelved.

After receiving envoys from Kamehameha, Kaumuali'i agreed to go to Honolulu in 1810. Kamehameha declined Kaumuali's face-saving offer to surrender Kauai in name only, replying "Return and rule over it. But if our young chief" – his eventual successor, Liholiho – "makes you a visit, be pleased to receive him." Although some of Kamehameha's advisers urged him to poison his rival, Kaumuali'i succeeded in returning home.

Reports of a secret treaty between Kaumuali'i and the **Russian** envoy George Schäffer (see p.486) under which a joint Kauaian–Russian fleet would invade the other Hawaiian islands, alarmed Kamehameha. Shortly after his death, in the summer of 1821, Kamehameha's son Liholiho sailed to Kauai, supposedly for an unofficial visit. Having toured the island for six weeks, he invited Kaumuali'i to dine on his yacht, anchored off Waimea, on September 16, 1821. During the evening, the boat set sail and Kaumuali'i was abducted to Oahu. Within four days of landing he was married to Kamehameha's widow, Ka'ahumanu, who shortly afterwards married Kaumuali'i's son, Keali'iahonui, as well.

Kaumuali'i never returned to Kauai; he died in Honolulu on May 26, 1824. Kauai's final flourish of resistance against the Hawaiian monarchy came later that year. Another son of Kaumuali'i, **Prince George,** who was educated at the Foreign Mission School in New England, launched an armed **insurrection.** The rebels attacked the Russian Fort at Waimea on August 8, 1824, but were swiftly cornered by forces from Oahu in Hanapēpē Valley, and all but wiped out. The victorious army remained on Kauai, confiscating land and property from local chiefs regardless of whether they had played any part in the rebellion. Much of Kauai was parceled out among the descendants of Kamehameha, labeled by a contemporary historian as the "loafers and hangers-on of Oahu and Maui."

The **corruption** of these newcomers, the inequities of the sandalwood trade (see p.511), and the founding of Hawaii's first sugar plantation at Kōloa in 1835, combined to erode the traditional way of life on Kauai. Thereafter, Kauaian history becomes the usual Hawaiian tale of a diminishing and disinherited native population, the growth of American-owned agricultural concerns, and the influx of low-paid laborers from Asia and elsewhere.

By 1872, the island's population had slumped to just 5200. Agricultural land was increasingly given over to sugar (for more on which, see p.473), although there were experiments with silk and coffee in Hanalei, silk at Kōloa, and cattle-ranching along the West Shore. As indentured Chinese workers left the plantations, they converted the *taro* terraces of Hanalei Valley into the largest **rice** paddies in Hawaii. Subsequently, many Chinese moved on to Honolulu, and in recent decades *taro* production has made something of a comeback on Kauai.

For the moment, sugar production continues, and the first Hawaiian island to grow sugar commercially looks set to also become the last. With the closure of Amfac's plantations at Līhu'e and Kekaha in 2000, only Gay and Robinson's cane fields, in the southwest of the island, are still under cultivation. Farmers on Kauai have been attempting to diversify, growing crops such as corn and tropical fruits, and the **coffee** industry is also expanding rapidly. Defense remains a key element of the economy – the Pacific Missile Range Facility at Barking Sands, once targeted for closure, now has a crucial role in the proposed new National Missile Defense system (detailed on p.488).

## Around the island

**Mount Wai'ale'ale**, the long-extinct volcano responsible for creating Kauai, was the biggest of all the Hawaiian shield volcanoes. Lava streamed from it in all directions, so the island is roughly circular, measuring up to 33 miles north to south and 25 miles west to east. Little of the volcano's original outline, however, remains discernible. On all sides, but especially to the north and west, it is now furrowed with deep, lush valleys, while its summit has worn down to a mere 5000 feet above sea level. The wettest place on earth, the summit is perched atop steepled cliffs and permanently shrouded in mist. Even on a helicopter tour (see p.422) or while hiking to its base (see p.444), you're unlikely to glimpse the highest peak.

The largest expanse of flat land on Kauai lies in its southeast corner, where **Līhu'e** is the site of its principal airport. While the county seat does offer a small selection of hotels and an attractive little beach, most visitors head for more scenic areas almost as soon as they touch down.

Six miles up the coast, north of the Wailua River and the overrated Fern Grotto, the beach strip from **Wailua** to **Kapa'a** holds a plethora of relatively inexpensive hotels and a wide range of restaurants. The old wooden boardwalks of Kapa'a make for a diverting pause on the round-island drive, while some fine hiking trails weave through the valleys inland.

Beyond Kapa'a, the highway steers clear of a succession of pretty and barely used beaches as it cuts through to the North Shore. **Princeville** here is a luxurious but soulless resort, guarding the headland above beautiful **Hanalei Bay**. At this point the green cliffs of the **Nā Pali** coast heave into view, towering above quirky Hanalei. From here on the coast road is breathtaking, passing gorgeous golden beaches pounded by endless surf as it tunnels through the overhanging rainforest. After ten miles, the ever-taller cliffs bar all further progress. Though accessible enough by canoe to sustain large populations in ancient times, the Nā Pali valleys are now uninhabited, and can only be reached on foot on the **Kalalau Trail**.

**Po'ipū**, ten miles southwest of Līhu'e at Kauai's southernmost tip, is traditionally its most popular resort. While it lost some of its sparkle to Hurricane Iniki, all its hotels are now back in business, and its beaches remain the best for

### Kauai Favorites: Beaches

| | | | |
|---|---|---|---|
| 'Anini Beach | p.450 | Lumaha'i Beach | p.461 |
| Kalalau Valley | p.470 | Po'ipū Beach | p.477 |
| Kalihiwai Beach | p.449 | Polihale | p.489 |
| Kē'ē Beach | p.465 | Secret Beach | p.449 |

year-round family vacations, with great surfing and scuba-diving spots just offshore. **Waimea**, around to the west, should in theory be a fascinating historic town – it's the place where Captain Cook first arrived in Hawaii and the site of an unlikely Russian fort – but the community has found it hard to bounce back from the onslaught of Iniki.

A few miles west of Waimea, **Polihale State Park** preserves the longest beach in the state, a dangerous but compelling fifteen-mile strand that ends at the western limit of the Nā Pali coast. High above, in the narrow gap between the mile-wide **Waimea Canyon** and the start of the Nā Pali valleys, **Kōke'e State Park** combines phenomenal roadside views with tremendous hiking trails. One of the most extraordinary leads through the land-locked **Alaka'i Swamp**, the last refuge of several unique Hawaiian plants and birds.

## Getting to Kauai

Only one airport on Kauai, located just outside **Līhu'e**, is currently served by commercial flights. Apart from the daily nonstop United service from **Los Angeles** and **San Francisco**, and two Aloha flights from Kahului on **Maui**, all flights come from **Honolulu**. Aloha offers 24 flights daily; Hawaiian has 21. Both airlines offer connections to and from other Hawaiian islands, and charge their standard **fares** for inter-island flights; for more details and a full list of phone numbers, see p.17.

## Getting around Kauai

As Kauai's resort areas tend to be spread out, with widely scattered attractions, and scenic spots like Waimea Canyon and the Nā Pali cliffs are a long way from the nearest places to stay, most visitors end up **driving** more than they expect. All the major car-rental chains are represented at Līhu'e airport; the relevant phone numbers are listed on p.25.

As a rule, driving on Kauai is a pleasure. There's just one main road, known as **Kaumuali'i Highway**, south of Līhu'e and **Kūhiō Highway** to the north, and only thirteen stoplights. Between Po'ipū and Princeville there's usually a fair amount of traffic; try to avoid the morning and evening "rush hours" between Līhu'e and Kapa'a, and you should be able to count on making steady progress. On both the narrow single-lane road along the North Shore – where you can be forced to a standstill as you wait for a chicken or a goose to cross the road – and the tortuous Waimea Canyon Drive up into the western hills, average speeds drop below 20mph.

### By bus

For the first few years after Hurricane Iniki, federal funding enabled the Kauai Bus to operate free **bus service** to all parts of the island. It still survives, though on a smaller scale now, with a flat fare of $1 (students and seniors 50¢, monthly passes available). As with TheBus on Oahu, large backpacks are forbidden.

Monday through Saturday, seven buses daily (first 6.45am, last 6pm) run north from JC Penney's at Kukui Grove in **Līhu'e** to the Circuit Court in **Hanalei**, with stops including Wailua, Kapa'a, Kīlauea and Princeville, and a total journey time of ninety minutes. The first bus from Hanalei is at 5.15am, the last at 5.30pm.

There are also nine daily buses west from **Līhu'e to Kekaha** (also Mon–Sat; first bus 6.45am, last 6pm; journey time 1hr 25min) via Po'ipū, Kōloa, Kalaheo, Hanapēpē and Waimea. Return service runs from 5.30am to 5.30pm. The two routes intersect in **Līhu'e**, so a complete trip from Hanalei to Kekaha involves a ten-minute changeover at Kukui Grove and takes three hours.

## Tours and taxis

Companies offering guided **minibus tours**, all based in Līhu'e but happy to pick up passengers in other Po'ipū and Kapa'a areas, include Roberts Hawaii (Ⓣ 539-9400 or 1-800/331-5541), Polynesian Adventure Tours (Ⓣ 246-0122, Ⓦ www.polyad.com), and Kauai Island Tours (Ⓣ 245-4777 or 1-800/733-4777). Typical prices would be $40 for a half-day tour, $60 for a full day.

Hawaii Movie Tours (Ⓣ 882-1192 or 1-800/628-8432, Ⓦ www.hawaiimovietour.com) offers a specialized all-day tour for $89, that concentrates on scenic Kauai spots that have been featured in major Hollywood films (see p.534). For daylong **four-wheel-drive tours** of the backroads of Kōke'e State Park, costing $84, contact Kauai Mountain Tours (Ⓣ 245-7224). **Guided hikes**, usually held on Sundays, are organized by the local chapter of the Sierra Club (Ⓦ www.hi.sierraclub.org/kauai); look for details in the *Garden Island* newspaper.

Kauai **taxi** companies include Kauai Cab Service (Ⓣ 246-9554) and ABC Taxi (Ⓣ 822-7641).

# Where to stay

Kauai is small enough that you can base yourself pretty much anywhere and still explore the whole island, so it's more important to decide what sort of property you want to stay in than it is to choose a particular area. If finding **budget** accommodation is a priority, then the hostel or simple B&Bs in and around Kapa'a are your best bet (see p.440). If you want a **beach-based** holiday in a family resort, opt for a hotel or condo in Po'ipū, or the Coconut Plantation, also in Kapa'a. To rent a **tropical hideaway**, get in touch with the agencies in Princeville (see p.455).

Away from Po'ipū and Princeville, room rates are generally lower than elsewhere in Hawaii, and the continuing eagerness to attract visitors back to Kauai means there are some real bargains. Kauai County ordinances technically forbid B&Bs to serve breakfasts; so while virtually all do, they prefer not to advertise the fact.

### Kauai Favorites: Accommodation

| | |
|---|---|
| *Kauai International Hostel*, Kapa'a (1/2) | p.440 |
| *Kōke'e Lodge*, Kōke'e State Park (1/2) | p.495 |
| *Kāhili Mountain Park*, Kāhili (2) | p.480 |
| *Garden Island Inn*, Līhu'e (3) | p.427 |
| *Waimea Plantation Cottages*, Waimea (5/6) | p.487 |
| *Hanalei Colony Resort*, Kepuhi Beach (5–7) | p.462 |
| *Po'ipū Kapili*, Po'ipū (6) | p.476 |
| *Hyatt Regency*, Po'ipū (8/9) | p.476 |
| *Princeville Hotel*, Princeville (9) | p.454 |

## Campgrounds



For details on Nā Pali permits, see p.467.

Full details on **camping** are available from the state and county parks offices in Līhu'e, as detailed on p.426. The **state** office (Dept of Land and Natural Resources, State Parks Division, 3060 Eiwa St, Līhu'e HI 96766; ⓣ274-3444) provides permits and information, including superb free maps, for Kōke'e State Park, Polihale, Miloli'i and the Nā Pali coast. (See p. 467 for details on Nā Pali permits.)

Permits for camping in Kauai's **county** parks – Hā'ena, Hanalei, 'Anini, Anahola, Hanamā'ulu, Salt Pond and Lucy Wright parks – are available by post at least a month in advance (Parks Permit Section, Dept of Public Works, Division of Parks and Recreation, 4444 Rice St #150, Līhu'e HI 96766; ⓣ241-6660). Enclose a photocopied passport, driver's license or other ID for all adults in your party, plus $3 fee per adult per night (Hawaii residents and under-18s free).

# When to go

Given a choice, the best times to come to Kauai are late spring and fall, when room rates are often slightly lower and crowds are smaller. But since Kauai rarely feels either overcrowded or overpriced, it doesn't make that much of a difference.

Seasonal **weather** variations are relatively minimal. Along the south coast, Kauai's warmest region, daily maximum **temperatures** range upwards from the low seventies Fahrenheit (around 22°C) in winter (Jan–March) to almost eighty Fahrenheit (27°C) in summer (Aug–Sept). Po'ipū, the most popular base for beach holidays, is marginally warmer than Līhu'e and Kapa'a, and warmer again than Princeville, but the difference is negligible.

**Rainfall** statistics look far more dramatic on paper than they do on the ground. Mount Wai'ale'ale, as you'll often be reminded, is the wettest place in the world – its record of 683 inches of rain in a single year is not the most ever measured, but its annual average of 451 inches beats the 428 inches of second-ranked Cherrapunji in India. Figures for the coast, just a few miles away, are very different. Waimea receives less than twenty inches per year, Po'ipū less than forty, and Kapa'a less than fifty. Princeville nears a hundred inches, but even on

## Accommodation Price Codes

All the accommodation options listed here have been graded with the symbols below, which refer to the quoted rates for a double room in high season (December to March), not including state taxes of 10.17 percent. For a full explanation, see p.27.

| | | |
|---|---|---|
| ❶ up to $40 | ❹ $100–150 | ❼ $250–300 |
| ❷ $40–70 | ❺ $150–200 | ❽ $300–400 |
| ❸ $70–100 | ❻ $200–250 | ❾ over $400 |

## Kauai Favorites: Eating

These restaurants are listed in ascending order of price, not (necessarily) quality.

| | | | |
|---|---|---|---|
| *Hamura's Saimin*, Līhu'e | p.432 | *Zelo's Beach House*, Hanalei | p.461 |
| *Caffé Coco*, Wailua | p.442 | *Casa di Amici*, Po'ipū | p.479 |
| *Hanamā'ulu Restaurant*, Hanamā'ulu | p.433 | *Roy's Po'ipū Bar & Grill*, Po'ipū | p.480 |
| *Mema*, Wailua | p.443 | *A Pacific Café*, Kapa'a | p.443 |

the north shore you'd have to be pretty unlucky to have your vacation plans affected. In all areas, significantly more rain falls in winter than in summer, but even then most of it falls at night.

As usual in Hawaii, the state of the **ocean** changes much more than the weather. Between December and April, winter thunderstorms, often caused by tropical "kona" storms that approach from the south, can render water activities unsafe on all but the most sheltered beaches. Nā Pali coast tours are obliged to follow different itineraries in winter, and may even be canceled altogether (see p.466). However, many visitors choose to come at precisely that time, in the hope of seeing whales.



# Watersports and other activities

For energetic vacationers, Kauai offers an exhausting range of both water- and land-based activities. Operators at all the major resort areas stand ready to instruct beginners or pamper experts in watersports such as diving, kayaking and wind-surfing, while the island's stunning landscapes make it a wonderful playground for hikers, golfers and horseback riders.

In addition to the specialized outfits listed below, several companies offer tours and activities of all kinds, often at discounted rates, and also rent out every imaginable piece of equipment you might need. At their best, they can be great sources of help and advice. Recommended businesses include Chris The Fun Lady, 4-746 Kūhiō Hwy, Kapa'a (Ⓣ822-7759, Ⓦwww.christhefunlady.com), Cheap Tours Hawaii (Ⓣ246-0009, Ⓦwww.cheaptourshawaii.com), and Activity Warehouse (Ⓣ822-4000, Ⓦwww.travelhawaii.com).

Kauai golf courses are listed on p.40.

## Cycling

Among companies which rent out **bicycles** on the island are Kauai Cycle and Tours, 1379 Kūhiō Hwy, Kapa'a (Ⓣ821-2115, Ⓦwww.bikehawaii.com/kauaicycle), which charges $15–35 per day and up to $150 per week and also offer guided tours, and Hawaiian Riders, 4-776 Kūhiō Hwy, Kapa'a (Ⓣ822-5409), which charges significantly lower rates and also has a fleet of mopeds and motorcyles for rent.

For most of the way around Kauai, conditions are generally pretty flat, but only a real glutton for punishment would attempt to cycle up Waimea Canyon Road to Kōke'e State Park. It is, however, possible to be driven up to the Kalalau Lookout and then be given a bike on which to freewheel all the way back down again. Both Kauai Coasters (Ⓣ639-2412, Ⓦwww.aloha.net/~coast) and Bicycle Downhill (Ⓣ742-7421) charge about $70 for the privilege.

## Deep-sea fishing

A veritable armada of **sport fishing** vessels sets off into the waters around Kauai daily from harbors on all sides of the island. Typical charter rates start at around $90 per person for a half-day trip. Operators along the South Shore include Sport Fishing Kauai (Ⓣ639-0013, Ⓦwww.fishing-kauai-hawaii.com) and Standup Fishing Charters (Ⓣ635-TUNA, Ⓦwww.fishingkauai.com), both in Po'ipū, and Lahela Ocean Adventures (Ⓣ635-4020, Ⓦwww.sport-fishing-kauai.com) in Nāwiliwili. Hawaiian Style Fishing (Ⓣ635-7335) is based in Kapa'a, and North Shore Sport Fishing (Ⓣ828-1379) at 'Anini Beach. Nā Pali Sportfishing (Ⓣ635-9424) and Kekaha Fishing Co. (Ⓣ337-2700) are at Waimea and Kīkīaola Harbor, respectively, on the West Shore.

## Horseback riding

The two main stables offering **guided horseback excursions** on Kauai – Princeville Ranch Stables on the North Shore (Ⓣ826-6777, Ⓦwww.princevilleranch.com) and CJM Country Stables near Po'ipū (Ⓣ742-6096) – are detailed on p.452 and p.478 respectively. Smaller companies elsewhere on the island include the Silver Falls Ranch in Kīlauea (Ⓣ828-6718, Ⓦwww.hawaiian.net/~sfr) and, in Kapa'a, Esprit de Corps (Ⓣ822-4688, Ⓦwww.kauaihorses.com) and Keapana Horsemanship (Ⓣ823-9303, Ⓦwww.keapana.com).

## Kayaking

Kauai is unique in Hawaii in offering **river kayaking** on several inland waterways. Guided trips are available along the Hulē'ia Stream near Lihue (Island Adventures; Ⓣ245-9662, Ⓦwww.kauaifun.com; $52), the Wailua River on the East Shore (Wailua Kayak Adventures; Ⓣ822-5795; from $30), and the Hanalei River on the North Shore (Kayak Kauai; Ⓣ826-9844, Ⓦwww.kayakkauai.com; $55). These and other operators also rent out kayaks for self-guided expeditions from as little as $15 for a couple of hours. In general it's much safer for inexperienced kayakers to explore the rivers than it is for them to set off into the ocean. Only absolute experts should attempt to tackle the Nā Pali coast on their own; otherwise, if you really want to see it, take a $140 guided tour with Kayak Kauai (above).

## Scuba diving

Although Kauai can't claim to be the very best of the Hawaiian islands for divers – the high North Shore seas preclude diving for most of the year, while the coast elsewhere tends to be short of spectacular coral – its waters still hold some truly superb dive sites. For novices, the best of the lot lie close to Po'ipū and are usually accessible year-round. **Sheraton Caverns**, just offshore from the *Sheraton* hotel, is a network of three massive lava tubes that shelters a large population of sea turtles and lobsters. At the slightly harder **General Store** site, colorful fish swarm through the wreckage of the steamship *Pele*, which foundered in 1895. In summer, popular North Shore snorkel sites such as **Tunnels Reef** and **Kē'ē Lagoon** also attract plenty of shore divers. The tiny islet of **Lehua**, off Niihau, is similar to Maui's Molokini (see p.310) but infinitely less crowded and polluted; however, it takes a long sea trip to reach it and considerable expertise to dive once you're there.

Dive operators based along the South Shore include Fathom Five (Ⓣ742-6691 or 1-800/972-3078), Mana Divers (Ⓣ742-9849) and Seasport Divers (Ⓣ742-9303 or 1-800/742-9303, Ⓦwww.kauaiscubadiving.com). In the Kapa'a area on the East Shore, try Dive Kauai (Ⓣ822-0452 or 1-800/828-3483, Ⓦwww.divekauai.com) or Sunrise Diving Adventures (Ⓣ822-7333,

Ⓦwww.sunrisediving.com); Sunrise also offers underwater "scooters." Hanalei is home to North Shore Divers (Ⓣ826-1921). Expect to pay $65–80 for a one-tank boat dive, $95–105 for two tanks, and perhaps $125 for a two-tank fully guided and instructed beginner's trip.

## Snorkeling

**Snorkeling** is more of a year-round activity on Kauai than diving, as even along the North Shore several mini-lagoons are sufficiently sheltered by offshore coral reefs to remain calm through most of the winter. Prime North Shore sites include **Kē'ē Beach** and **Tunnels Beach**, while the best spot along the East Shore is **Lydgate State Park**, just south of the Wailua River. Probably the safest and most convenient sites of all, however, are those abutting the resorts of Po'ipū, such as **Po'ipū Beach** and **Lāwa'i Beach**.

Any number of outlets rent out snorkel equipment, including the ubiquitous Snorkel Bob's, here based at 4-374 Kūhiō Hwy in Kapa'a (Ⓣ823-9433) and 3236 Po'ipū Road in Kōloa (Ⓣ742-2206); both locations are open daily 8am–5pm. Note also that most Nā Pali boat trips (see p.466) double as snorkel cruises, with equipment provided.

## Surfing and windsurfing

For **surfers**, conditions on Kauai are reminiscent of those on Oahu, in that southern beaches such as **Kalāpakī Beach** and **Po'ipū Beach** are ideal places for beginners to learn the ropes, while the North Shore provides some great challenges to experts. **Hanalei Bay** in particular is immensely popular with

### Helicopter Flight-Seeing

Kauai is the best Hawaiian island to see from the air. It's small enough, and its mountains are low enough, for a single flight to cover the whole island – plus, many of its most spectacular spots are impossible to reach any other way. It was, however Kauai's bad accident rate that led to the state-wide ban on low flying (see p.26), which the helicopter operators hope you won't have heard about. The new regulations outlaw their previous practice of deliberately plummeting over the Nā Pali coastline, and thus, it has to be said, make trips less exciting.

Full island tours start from Līhu'e and follow a clockwise route up Waimea Canyon and along the north coast; they last 45 minutes to an hour. If you're satisfied to see just the Nā Pali cliffs, take a shorter flight from Princeville (see p.454). Prices generally range from $105–125 for a 45-minute tour and $150–175 for an hour-long excursion.

For details on *Niihau Helicopters*, which only runs excursions to the island of Niihau, see p.491.

| | Number | Website | Departs |
|---|---|---|---|
| **Air Kauai** | Ⓣ246-4666 | Ⓦwww.airkauai.com | Līhu'e |
| **Bali Hai** | Ⓣ335-3166 | Ⓦwww.balihai-helitour.com | Port Allen |
| **Jack Harter** | Ⓣ245-3774 | Ⓦwww.helicopters-kauai.com | Līhu'e |
| **Hawaii** | Ⓣ826-6591 | Ⓦwww.hawaii-helicopters.com | Princeville |
| **Inter-Island** | Ⓣ335-5009 | | Port Allen |
| **Island** | Ⓣ245-8588 | Ⓦwww.planet-hawaii.com/island | Līhu'e |
| **Ohana** | Ⓣ245-3996 | Ⓦwww.ohana-helicopters.com | Līhu'e |
| **Safari** | Ⓣ246-0136 | Ⓦwww.safariair.com | Līhu'e |
| **South Seas** | Ⓣ245-2222 | | Līhu'e |
| **Will Squyres** | Ⓣ245-8881 | Ⓦwww.helicopters-hawaii.com | Līhu'e |

**Kauai Favorites: Hikes**



serious surfers, with **Tunnels Beach** a close second. The best site on the East Shore is **Lydgate State Park** near Wailua.

With the exception of sheltered **'Anini Beach**, most of the North Shore is too dangerous for **windsurfers**. They head, instead, for the South Shore near Po'ipū. **Po'ipū Beach** is the best place to learn; the beaches of the **Māhā'ulepū** area are more favored by the already proficient.

Among those offering **surfing lessons** on Kauai are Mikie's Surf School in Kapa'a (Ⓣ 635-6664) and, in the Po'ipū area, Kauai Surf School (Ⓣ 742-6331, Ⓦ www.kauaisurfschool.com) and Margo Oberg's Surfing School (Ⓣ 742-8019). A two-hour group surfing lesson costs about $40 per person. **Windsurfing instruction**, at about $65 per lesson, is offered by 'Anini Beach Windsurfing (Ⓣ 826-9463) and Windsurf Kauai in Hanalei (Ⓣ 828-6838).

# Nightlife and entertainment

Barring the occasional big-name concert at the War Memorial in central Līhu'e, and promotional appearances by local stars at the Kukui Grove mall, virtually all Kauai's **nightlife** takes place in its hotels and restaurants. Among venues that can usually be depended upon for **live music**, especially at weekends, are the *Radisson Kauai Beach* just outside Līhu'e, *Keoki's Paradise* in Po'ipū, the *Hanalei Bay Resort* in Princeville, and the *Hanalei Gourmet*, *Sushi'n'Blues* and *Tahiti Nui* in Hanalei. The North Shore, in particular, is where the more funky local musicians tend to hang out.

**Kauai Lū'aus**

All the *lū'aus* listed below charge $50–60 per adult and $20–30 per child; you should be able to get tickets for under $50 from activities operators all over the island. The best of the full-scale shows is the *Princeville Hotel*'s, thanks in large part to its superb setting.

**Drums of Paradise**, *Hyatt Regency Kauai*, Po'ipū; Ⓣ 742-1234. Thurs & Sun 6pm.
**Garden Lū'au**, Smith's Tropical Paradise, Wailua; Ⓣ 245-9595. Mon, Wed & Fri 5pm (see p.436).
**Reflections of Paradise**, *Gaylord's, Kilohana Plantation,* Līhu'e; Ⓣ 245-9593. Mon, Tues & Thurs 6pm.
**Kauai's Best Lū'au**, *Kauai Coconut Beach Resort*, Kapa'a; Ⓣ 822-6651. Daily 5.45pm.
**Pa'ina O Hanalei**, *Princeville Hotel*, Princeville; Ⓣ 826-9644. Mon, Wed & Thurs 6pm.
**Tahiti Nui**, Hanalei; Ⓣ 826-6277. Wed 6pm (see p.460).

## Kauai Festivals and Events

| | |
|---|---|
| mid-Feb | Waimea Town Celebration; races and entertainment |
| March 26 | Prince Kūhiō Day; week-long festival in Līhu'e and Po'ipū |
| May 1 | May Day by the Bay; festival in Princeville |
| May 1 | *Lei* Day; *lei*-making contests in Līhu'e |
| Memorial Day | Prince Albert Music Festival; four days of classical and Hawaiian music in Princeville |
| June 11 | Kamehameha Day; state-wide celebrations |
| July 4 | Concert in the Sky; charity concert, Līhu'e |
| mid-July | Na Holo Kai Canoe Race; from Oahu to Kalāpakī Bay |
| late July | Kōloa Plantation Days; week-long festival in Kōloa |
| Aug 18 | Admission Day; state holiday |
| mid-Aug | Kauai-Tahiti Fete; weekend cultural festival, Kukui Grove, Līhu'e |
| Aug | Hanalei Stampede; Princeville Ranch Stables, Princeville |
| Sept 1 | Kauai County Farm Fair, Līhu'e |
| Oct | Kauai Taro Festival, Hanalei |
| late Oct | Aloha Week Festival, island-wide |
| late Oct | Mokihana Festival; week-long *hula*, music and crafts festival |
| early Nov | Hawaiian Slack-Key Guitar Festival; one-day free concert, *Kauai Marriott*, Līhu'e |
| mid-Nov | PGA Grand Slam, golf tournament, Po'ipū |

# Līhu'e

Chances are, Kauai's capital, **LĪHU'E**, will be both the first and the last place you see on the island. You'll probably pass through it several times during your stay as well. Set a mile or two back from the sea in the southeast corner of the island, it's the site of Kauai's main **airport** and **harbor**, and the midpoint of the highway that circles the island.

But Līhu'e is not an attractive or exciting town, and few tourists spend more time here than they have to. It's as much of an administrative and commercial center as this tiny island needs, and with a population of just five thousand, the town's main role seems to be introducing its visitors to just how rural Kauai its really is. Several of the roads run through open fields without a sign of life, while downtown Līhu'e consists of a handful of tired-looking plantation-town streets lined with simple one- and two-story buildings.

That said, visitors shouldn't overlook Līhu'e completely. Its inland section offers Kauai's widest selection of **shops** and its best **museum**, while the area around **Nāwiliwili Bay** holds some good hotels and restaurants, a fine sheltered white-sand beach, and a stretch of unspoilt riverfront that serves as a sanctuary for native waterbirds.

Līhu'e cannot boast a long history. It dates from the middle of the nineteenth century, when it was a village serving the Grove Farm sugar plantation. Since that time, the area's sugar-growing days have come an end. In November 2000,

Amfac/JMB's Līhu'e Plantation gave up cultivating cane in the surrounding fields, though the Līhu'e Sugar Mill in the heart of town remains in operation for the moment, burning sugar cane to generate electricity. Grove Farm, now owned by America Online chief executive Steve Case, has long since diversified into real estate. It owns residential developments as well as the large Kukui Grove shopping mall.

Until well into the twentieth century, Kauai's chief ports were Port Allen, outside Hanapēpē in the southwest, and Hanalei Bay in the north. It wasn't until about 1930, when **Nāwiliwili Harbor** and the new airport were completed, that Līhu'e became the island's major port. That status was secured in 1939, when

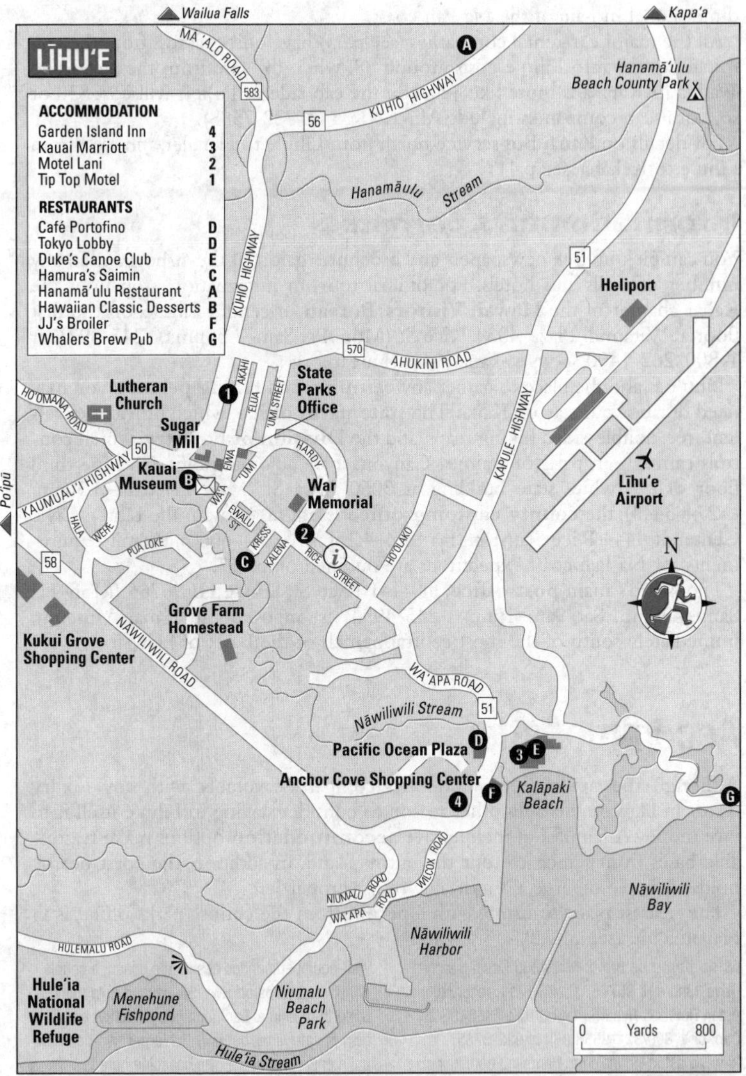

the Belt Highway took on its present route. Since then, Līhu'e has grown apace with the increase of road transportation; the fact that it's designed to drive around is the main reason why it's so much more spread out than other island towns.

# Arrival and information

Līhu'e's **airport** is only two miles east of downtown, near the ocean on Ahukini Road. Apart from a fast-food coffee shop selling *saimin* and Portuguese bean soup, the main feature of its small terminal is a colorful three-dimensional mosaic of the Nā Pali coast.

All the major car-rental companies (see p.25) have offices across from the terminal. A **taxi** into Līhu'e costs around $8, while the fare from the airport to Wailua or Kapa'a is more like $20, and the cab ride to Po'ipū will cost $30 or so. Local cab companies include Akiko's Taxi (ⓣ822-7588).

For details on Kauai Bus service north from Līhu'e to Hanalei, and west from Līhu'e to Kekaha, see p.417.

## Information and permits

You can pick up free newspapers and brochures galore at the airport and in any number of malls and hotels. For official tourism information, stop in at the Kauai chapter of the **Hawaii Visitors Bureau** in central Līhu'e, on the first floor at Watamull Plaza, 4334 Rice St (Mon–Fri 8am–4.30pm; ⓣ245-3971 or 1-800/262-1400, ⓦwww.kauaivisitorsbureau.org).

Līhu'e is also the place to gather any **camping** and **hiking permits** you may need during your stay on Kauai. The **state parks office**, which provides excellent free, double-sided hiking maps, and the **Division of Forestry**, which controls camping in parts of Waimea Canyon, share adjoining offices on the third floor of the white state building at 3060 Eiwa St (Mon–Fri 8am–3.30pm; ⓣ274-3444); the **county camping office** is not far away, in the Līhu'e Civic Center at 4444 Rice St (Mon–Fri 8am–4.15pm; ⓣ241-6660). Permit requirements for Nā Pali coast expeditions are outlined on p.467.

The island's main **post office,** at 4441 Rice St, Līhu'e HI 96766 (Mon–Fri 8am–4.30pm, Sat 9am–1pm; ⓣ245-4994) is opposite the Kauai Museum, immediately south of the most central branch of the Bank of Hawaii.

# Accommodation

Although the opulent *Kauai Marriott* compares favorably with any luxury resort in Hawaii, the only other reason to consider staying in Līhu'e itself is to save money. A handful of inexpensive **accommodation** options make reasonable bases from which to tour the entire island. In addition, the coast nearby holds a couple of large, comfortable resort properties.

The nearest place to camp, with a permit from the county parks office, is in Hanamā'ulu (see p.432).

**Aston Kauai Beach Villas**, 4330 Kauai Beach Drive, Līhu'e HI 96766; ⓣ245-7711, reservations Aston Hotels & Resorts, 1-800/922-7866 (US & Can) or 1-800/321-2558 (HI), ⓕ922-8785, ⓦwww.aston-hotels.com. Rambling complex of well-equipped condos beside the ocean, a couple of hundred yards off Hwy-56, beyond mile marker 3, north of Līhu'e. Each unit has a kitchen and its own private *lānai*, but only the larger two-bedroom units enjoy sea views. The coastline here is exposed and unsuitable for swimming. ❺–❼.

**Garden Island Inn**, 3445 Wilcox Rd, Kalāpakī Bay, Līhuʻe HI 96766; ⓣ245-7227 or 1-800/648-0154 (US & Can), ⓕ245-7603, ⓦwww.gardenislandinn.com. Refurbished three-story motel, set slightly back from the road that curves around Kalāpakī Beach and located near the restaurants of Anchor Cove. Dripping with purple bougainvillea, it is one of Kauai's best accommodation values. All 21 rooms look across lawns and palms to the peaceful waters of Nāwiliwili Harbor; each is equipped with a fridge, microwave, coffee-maker and ceiling fans. ❸.

**Kauai Marriott**, 3610 Rice St, Līhuʻe HI 96766; ⓣ245-5050 or 1-800/228-9290 (US & Can), ⓕ245-5049, ⓦwww.marriott.com/marriott/LIHHI. Lavish resort, formerly the *Westin Kauai*, with 350 tower-block rooms and another 230 suites. Most rooms overlook Hawaii's largest swimming pool and its five Jacuzzis, and are arrayed along lovely Kalāpakī Beach. Condo suites are available for $20,000 a week. The property boasts two golf courses, four restaurants, eight tennis courts and eight miles of footpaths. Garden view ❽, ocean view ❾.

**Motel Lani**, 4240 Rice St, Līhuʻe HI 96766; ⓣ245-2965. Rudimentary but just about presentable central motel, overgrown with plants. The nine rooms lack phones and TVs. It's only worth staying here if you plan to be out all day. Two-night minimum stay. ❶.

**Radisson Kauai Beach**, 4331 Kauai Beach Drive, Līhuʻe HI 96766; ⓣ245-1955 or 1-800/333-3333, ⓕ246-9085, ⓦwww.radisson.com. Luxury beachfront resort, formerly an *Outrigger* property, three miles north of Līhuʻe on Hwy-56; look for the US flags that mark the entrance. Its 350 spacious rooms and suites are set in four low-rise wings around a three-segment swimming pool, complete with simulated fern grotto. The artificial beach is a nice feature, as the natural beach alongside is seldom safe for swimmers. Garden view ❻, ocean view ❼.

**Tip Top Motel**, 3173 Akāhi St, Līhuʻe HI 96766; ⓣ245-2333, ⓕ246-8988, ⓔtiptop@aloha.net. Unprepossessing but well-equipped motel, hidden away on a back street not far from the airport. Each room has two single beds and a shower, but no bathtub. There's an inexpensive bakery-cum-diner plus a sushi restaurant on site (see p.433). ❷.



# The town

At first sight, you might think that **Līhuʻe** was still clawing its way back to normal following the hurricane of 1992. In fact, the town – a low-key assortment of plain homes, stores and offices scattered among rusting reminders of the plantation days and hastily erected shopping malls – looked much the same before Iniki hit. If anything, Līhuʻe is a bit prettier these days, its mountain backdrop more visible since the hurricane cleared away most of the trees that interfered with the view.

Līhuʻe is divided into three distinct areas. The old **downtown**, along **Rice Street**, remains the administrative center of the island; in the middle of the day it's busy with local office workers, but barely a soul is left when evening comes. Driving a mile or so southeast beyond Rice Street brings you to **Nāwiliwili Bay**, where hotels and restaurants look out on to **Kalāpakī Beach**. The road that circles the island, running past the sugar mill at the northwest end of Rice Street, holds the bulk of Līhuʻe's modern development. West of Līhuʻe it bears the name **Kaumualiʻi Highway**. About a mile out of town it passes the large **Kukui Grove Shopping Center**; after another mile it comes to the country-house mall **Kilohana**; from there it leads to Poʻipū and Waimea. Northeast of Līhuʻe, the road is officially called **Kūhiō Highway**; for the mile or two that separates Līhuʻe from the nominally distinct community of **Hanamāʻulu**, it's lined with fast-food outlets and small malls.

## Kauai Museum

The **Kauai Museum**, downtown Līhuʻe's only significant attraction, occupies two buildings next to the state offices at 4428 Rice St (Mon–Fri 9am–4pm, Sat 10am–4pm; adults $5, seniors $4, ages 13–17 $3, ages 6–12 $1; ⓣ245-6931). If you've come to the island for sun, sea and scenery, it may not hold your interest for long, but it does a creditable job of tracing Kauaian history from the mythical *menehune* onwards.

Visitors enter the museum through the older **Wilcox Building**, which holds the core of the collection – the private memorabilia of the missionary Wilcox family. Downstairs, there's a large assortment of traditional artifacts such as oval platters, *lei* standards and calabashes made from *koa* wood. One colossal and highly polished calabash was used as a *poi* bowl by Kamehameha III; several have been skillfully repaired with butterfly-shaped patches, a process which was held to increase their value. Exhibits upstairs cover the growth of the sugar plantations and the great era of immigration. Photographs focus especially on the island's Japanese population, recording sumo tournaments, Bon dances and Buddhist ceremonies.

The modern **Rice Building**, alongside the Wilcox Building, has a more comprehensive collection. Billed as presenting "The Story of Kauai," it too has its fair share of calabashes, decorated gourd bowls and bottles. But it also displays some more unusual ancient relics such as stone receptacles said to have been used in the *pule ana'ana* ("praying-to-death") rite, and a huge "thrusting spear," a weapon designed to be thrust rather than thrown. A relief model of the island shows where the Hawaiians had their original settlements, as well as the trails that connected them. Among the trails that no longer exist are those that lead down to the Nā Pali valleys from the heights of Kōke'e, and paths from the summit of Mount Wai'ale'ale not only to Wailua, but also to Waimea and Hanapēpē. A diorama of Waimea at the time of Cook's first landfall depicts a settlement of a few thatched huts. Contemporary maps of Cook's voyages show tell-tale blank spaces for areas as yet unknown – Hawaii, New Zealand and eastern Australia are absent, while the Pacific coast of North America, where Cook hoped to find the Northwest Passage, remains uncharted.

Subsequent history is told in immense detail and illustrated by such items as a letter from King Kuamuali'i, signing himself King Tamoree (the Hawaiian language was not yet written consistently at the time), and a soft sea otter pelt brought by the Russians during their brief sojourn in Kauai (see p.486). Other displays cover mission and plantation life, and there's also a rain gauge that stood for many years atop Mount Wai'ale'ale, the wettest place on earth. It is capable of holding 900 inches of rain, but the most it ever received in a year was 682.94.

The museum's gift store, packed with books, maps and wooden craft items, can be visited without paying for admission.

## Nāwiliwili Bay

As Līhu'e has been a port for even less time than it has been a town, the oceanfront area around **Nāwiliwili Bay**, reached by heading east down Rice Street, is functional and without much character. As long as you stay on or near the white sands of **Kalāpakī Beach**, however, that probably won't bother you. This sheltered quarter-mile stretch in front of the *Kauai Marriott Resort* is one of Kauai's very best beaches. Its smooth, shelving slope makes it ideal for family swimming, and it's also a good place to learn to **surf**, though beginners should avoid venturing out too far towards the open sea.

At the western edge of the beach, across the Nāwiliwili Stream – which, when it hasn't petered out altogether, is usually shallow enough to wade across – and beyond the large *JJ's Broiler* restaurant (see p.433), the lawns of **Nāwiliwili Beach County Park** are dotted with coconut palms and make a pleasant picnic spot. The seafront here is simply a wall, popular with anglers.

Immediately beyond the park, still within sight of the beach, stand the first structures of **Nāwiliwili Harbor**, which stretches away west at the mouth of the Hulē'ia Stream. The harbor was constructed in the 1920s to afford greater protection to large vessels than Port Allen could offer; it's also a bit closer to Oahu than Port Allen. A long breakwater was pushed out into the bay from below Carter Point on the far side of the stream, and a combination of dredging the seabed and using the silt as infill to create new flatland permanently changed the local topography. The harbor is now deep enough to accommodate mighty cruise liners, which make an incongruous spectacle moored so closely to the low-key park facilities. All that dredging explains why the stream itself has largely silted up, but fishermen still try their luck from the jetties. The small **Niumalu Beach Park** nearby is unlikely to tempt swimmers because of the silt and its proximity to the port.

## Menehune Fishpond and Hulē'ia National Wildlife Refuge

West of Nāwiliwili Harbor, Hulemalū Road climbs a hillside beyond the village of Niumalu to reach a viewpoint overlooking a pond. It is officially known as the Alekoko ("Rippling Blood") Fishpond, but its nickname, the **Menehune Fishpond,** offers a better indication of its age. Created when the ancient Hawaiians sealed off a right-angle bend in Hulē'ia Stream with a half-mile-long low wall of rounded stones, the artificial lake was originally used for rearing mullet.

In popular mythology, the *menehune* were the earliest inhabitants of the islands, said to be hairy little dwarfs who were given to erecting large monuments in the space of a single moonlit night. That such tales are especially prevalent on Kauai suggests that the island may have been populated by a different group of migrants than its neighbors. Scholars now believe that the word *menehune* may be related to a Tahitian word for "commoner," and may refer to a social caste that was seen as inferior by later colonizers.

Whatever the truth, the Hawaiians developed fish farming to a greater level of sophistication than anywhere else in Polynesia, and the Menehune Fishpond is the best-preserved such pond in the islands. It's now under private ownership, so unless you explore the stream by boat (guided kayak trips are offered by Island Adventures; ⓣ 245-9662, ⓦ www.kauaifun) the overlook is as close as you can get to the actual pond. Most of the stone wall is overgrown, so it's not a hugely impressive sight, but the overlook makes an appealing stop on a driving tour. The river spreads out below you, with just one little shack to interrupt the greenery along its banks.

On the far side, the jagged **Hā'upu** (or "Hoary Head") **Ridge** is silhouetted against the skyline, its slopes thick with vegetation. Two natural columns on the hillside are said to be the remains of the royal couple who commissioned the *menehune* to build them a fishpond; they were turned to stone when they disobeyed orders by sneaking a peek at the nocturnal work. Further right, and more visible from the main highway at Puhi near Kilohana (see p.431), the crest of the ridge supposedly resembles either **Queen Victoria's Profile** or, for ancient Hawaiians, the equally stern Princess Hina.

Standing at the fishpond viewpoint, you'll probably hear the cries of the waterbirds wheeling above the **Hulē'ia National Wildlife Refuge** just upstream. Like its equivalent at Hanalei in the north of the island (see p.457), this area still bears traces of terraces formerly used to grow first *taro* and later rice. It's now a sanctuary for endangered Hawaiian wetland birds, and there's no public access.

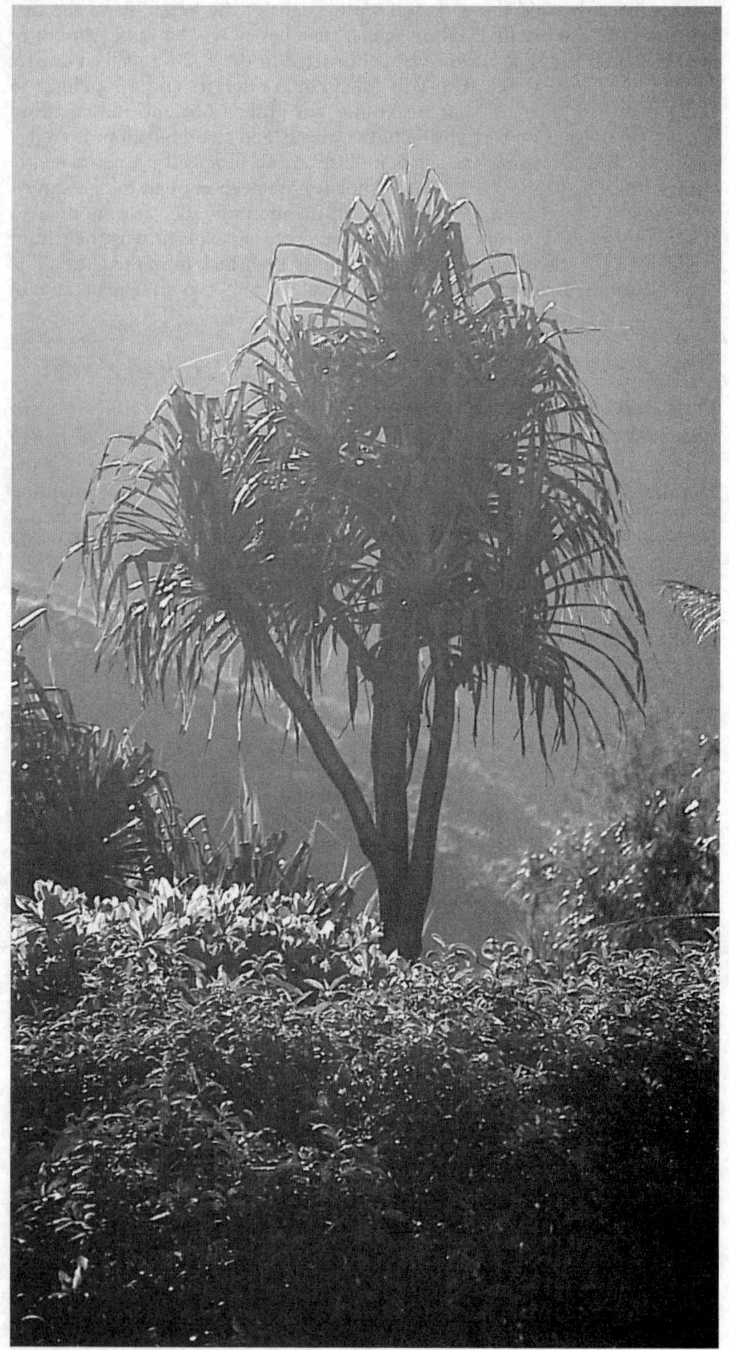

## Grove Farm Homestead

Life on the nineteenth-century plantation to which Līhu'e owes its existence is recalled at the restored **Grove Farm Homestead**, hidden away on Nāwiliwili Road southwest of downtown (tours Mon, Wed & Thurs 10am & 1pm; adults $5, under-12s $2; ⓣ 245-3202). Although it's just a few hundred yards from Rice Street, you can only cross the deep channel of Nāwiliwili Stream down by the harbor or up at the main road, so it's too far to walk from town. Reservations are required for the tours and they get filled up fast; call at least a week in advance.

The plantation was opened in 1864 by George Wilcox, who was, in classic Hawaiian fashion, the entrepreneurial son of Hanalei-based missionaries. An ascetic bachelor, he lived in a cottage on the grounds; the larger *koa*-paneled mansion that's the centerpiece of the two-hour guided tours belonged to his brother and his descendants. The tours also take in the plainly furnished home of the Japanese family who looked after the Wilcoxes, and George's personal orchard of fruit trees.

## West on Kaumuali'i Highway

**Kaumuali'i Highway** commences its westward journey around the island from the top of Rice Street by ducking under a rusty conveyor belt built to carry sugar cane from the fields to the north into the grinders of the Līhu'e Sugar Mill.

Immediately beyond the mill, a turn *mauka* onto Ho'omana Road leads up to the **Old Lutheran Church**, erected in 1885 by German immigrants. Its interior design deliberately echoes the vessels that carried the immigrants to the island, complete with slanting wooden floors and a balcony modeled on a ship's bridge. But the current church is in fact a replica of the original, which was destroyed by Hurricane Iwa in 1982. Ho'omana Road peters out amid the cane fields a little further on.

Back on the highway, you soon come to the **Kukui Grove Shopping Center**. Kauai's largest and best-equipped shopping mall is showing its age and, thanks to a major termite infestation, its future is said to be in doubt. Apart from the huge Borders bookstore, with its exhaustive stock of newspapers and magazines from around the world, it holds little of interest to tourists, although stores such as Liberty House and Sears, plus a couple of supermarkets, at least ensure that you can pick up food, extra clothing and other supplies.

A mile past Kukui Grove, the stately house at **Kilohana Plantation** was built in 1935 by another scion of Līhu'e's founding family, Gaylord Wilcox. Most of the ground floor and verandah of the imposing mansion, which stands at the end of a sweeping driveway, is occupied by an excellent restaurant (see p.000), while several smaller rooms on two stories hold upmarket crafts shops and galleries. Some of these can be rather twee, but Kilohana is nevertheless one of Kauai's better options if you're looking for gifts to take home.

Kilohana is named after the mountain peak that towers over the cane fields behind it. You can get a close-up view of the plantation itself on a formal tour in a horse-drawn carriage (Mon–Sat 11am–6.30pm, Sun 11am–5pm; adults $8, under-12s $4). Less frequent but longer wagon tours along the rougher cane roads cost around twice the price (call ⓣ 246-9529 for schedules and reservations).

Kilohana's shops and galleries are open Mon–Sat 9.30am–9.30pm, Sun 9.30am–5pm; admission to the house is free.

## Wailua Falls

Just over a mile northeast of Rice Street, after the strip development along **Kūhiō Highway** has thinned out beyond the airport turnoff, Mā'alo Road leads away leftwards up to **Wailua Falls**. This picturesque eighty-foot drop interrupts the south fork of the Wailua River, a couple of miles upstream from the Fern Grotto (see p.435), and may be familiar from the credit sequence of *Fantasy Island*.

A parking lot, offering a side-on view both of the falls and of the stream bed below, comes after a climb of three slow and sinuous miles through the cane fields. Depending on recent rainfall, you're likely to see from one to three cascades, one of which emerges from a small tunnel a little way down the cliff face. Don't consider trying to hike over to the top from here, or even crossing the guardrail: it's extremely slippery, and there's a huge overhang.

Thanks to tree growth, two earlier viewpoints marked along the approach road do not in fact offer views of the falls at all.



## Hanamā'ulu

The small community of **HANAMĀ'ULU** is located a short way beyond the road to Wailua Falls. Apart from the attractive *Restaurant and Tea House* (see opposite), it's mainly noteworthy as the site of the **Hanamā'ulu Beach County Park**, almost a mile out of town at the wooded mouth of the Hanamā'ulu Stream. Spreading along a broad and sheltered bay, this narrow strip of sand is an attractive place to spend a peaceful afternoon. However, the breakwater at the mouth of the bay prevents the silt in the stream from being carried out to sea, and so the water is usually too cloudy for swimming. There's also a fully equipped campground, but locals tend to party at Hanamā'ulu well into the night, and visiting families usually prefer to camp elsewhere. (Kauai camping regulations are detailed on p.419.)

# Restaurants

Downtown Līhu'e has a reasonable choice of **places to eat** during the day, but the highway malls offer standard fast-food chains and no more. Any quest for views or atmosphere – let alone fine dining – will take you away from the center, either as far as Kilohana or Hanamā'ulu on the main road, or down to the oceanfront. The restaurants reviewed here are shown on the map on p.425.

**Café Portofino**, Pacific Ocean Plaza, 3501 Rice St; ⓣ245-2121. Formal Italian restaurant on the second floor of a quiet mall, within easy walking distance of the beach and the Marriott, with a deck offering sea breezes and harbor views. Tasty pasta entrees such as chicken cannelloni and linguine a la puttanesca cost around $15, while veal specialties go for $20 and up. Reservations recommended. Daily 5–10pm.

**Duke's Canoe Club**, *Kauai Marriott*, 3610 Rice St; ⓣ246-9599. Cheerful, informal bar-restaurant right on Kalāpakī Beach, arranged around its own waterfall and carp pond, and enjoying gorgeous views. A burger or stir-fry lunch costs under $10, while dinner, served 5–10pm, might feature fish of the day prepared as you like for $20 or prime rib for $24. Dinner is accompanied by Hawaiian music on Thurs, Sat & Sun. Daily 11am–11.30pm.

**Gaylord's**, Kilohana, 3-2087 Kaumuali'i Hwy; ⓣ245-9593. Delicious food served in the very British-influenced courtyard of a former plantation home, with views of extensive gardens and the mountains of the interior. Lunch consists mainly of sandwiches and salads such as the $10 Chicken Caesar; Sunday brunch features pancakes for $10 or eggs Benedict for $16; and dinner pasta, steak or fish entrees cost $18–25. Mon–Sat 11am–3pm & 5–9pm, Sun 9.30am–3pm & 5–9pm.

**Hamura's Saimin**, 2956 Kress St; ⓣ245-3271. This family-run diner and takeout spot is a much-loved Kauai institution, serving tasty and good-value Japanese-style fast food at communal U-shaped counters. The specialty is heaped bowls of saimin (noodle soup) – a standard portion costs $3.50, one with shrimp tempura, $5. As a side order, try a satay skewer of barbecue chicken or beef for $1. Mon–Thurs 10am–11pm, Fri & Sat 10am–1am, Sun 10am–10pm.

**Hanamā'ulu Restaurant and Tea House**, 3-4253 Kūhiō Hwy, Hanamā'ulu; ⓣ245-2511. A pleasant attempt to evoke the feel of a Far Eastern teahouse, complete with fishponds and private tearooms, a mile or so from central Līhu'e. Surprisingly, they serve both Chinese and Japanese cuisine; both are excellent. Lunchtime specials start at around $7, while dinner options include an Oriental seafood platter with fish marinated in ginger, tempura and crab claws for $15, and a set menu for $16. Sushi is served in the evening only. Tues–Fri 10am–1pm & 5.30–8.30pm, Sat & Sun 5.30–8.30pm.

**Hawaiian Classic Desserts**, 4479 Rice St; ⓣ245-6967. Despite the name and the bakery counter at the main entrance, this spacious diner also serves full breakfasts for $5–8, and sandwich, salad and burger lunches that cost only slightly more. Best of all, though, is the rich array of desserts – and the setting, in an appealingly converted office building in downtown Līhu'e, with a nice mountain-view terrace. Daily 7am–3pm.

**JJ's Broiler**, Anchor Cove Shopping Center, 3416 Rice St; ⓣ246-4422. Popular, breezy bar-cum-restaurant, in a prime position looking out across Nāwiliwili Bay. Burgers with avocado and other Pacific-style trimmings, sandwiches and chunky soups cost around $8–10, and there's a full dinner menu of steaks and seafood at $18–26 per entree. A good open-air seafront spot for an evening drink; reserve ahead if possible. Daily 11am–10pm.

**Tip Top Café and Bakery**, 3173 Akahi St; ⓣ245-2333. Family-run diner in a quiet area of central Līhu'e, known for its simple and very filling food. The best bet is a breakfast of fruity pancakes or *malasadas* (Portuguese donuts) for around $6, but they also offer plate lunches, stews and basic meat dishes, as well as breads and pastries to take out, and sushi in the separate Sushi Katsu section. Café Tues-Sun 6.30am–2pm, sushi Tues-Sun 11am–2pm & 5.30–9.30pm.

**Tokyo Lobby**, Pacific Ocean Plaza, 3501 Rice St; ⓣ245-8989. Kauai's finest Japanese restaurant, on the ground floor of a small mall. The light, pleasant interior has a sushi bar, but the open-air lānai feels too close to the road. Lunch options include noodles and tempura for $7–10, or soup, salad, and your choice of chicken, beef teriyaki or sashimi for $9.50; at dinner the latter combination costs about $15. Romantics should try a "Love Boat," a wooden boat full of mixed goodies for $22.50 per person. Mon–Fri 11am–2pm & 4.30–9.30pm, Sat & Sun 4.30–9.30pm.

**Whalers Brew Pub**, *Kauai Lagoons Resort*, 3132 Ninini Point; ⓣ245-2000. Kauai's first brewpub is a bright and attractive pavilion with absolutely spectacular views over the mouth of Nāwiliwili Bay, though its location at the very far end of the Kauai Marriott driveway means it's too far to walk even from the hotel. In addition to microbrewed beers, it offers a lunch menu of sandwiches and fresh fish, mostly priced at under $10, and a dinner menu with $15–24 steak, fish or pasta entrees. A giant, 20oz "Whale of a Burger" for $18 is available at both lunch and dinner, and an all-day oyster bar serves specialties such as Oysters Rockefeller at $11 per half-dozen. There's live music several nights per week. Mon–Fri 11am–9pm, Sat & Sun 11am–1am.

# The East Shore

Ever since Kauai was first settled by humans, its population has been most heavily concentrated along the valley of the **Wailua River** and the nearby coastline. This region, starting roughly five miles north of Līhu'e, is now home to around 16,000 people, but they're so spread out that you'd barely know they were there. Much more conspicuous are the guests in the ocean-front hotels and condos, here for the sun and fun rather than the relatively poor beaches.

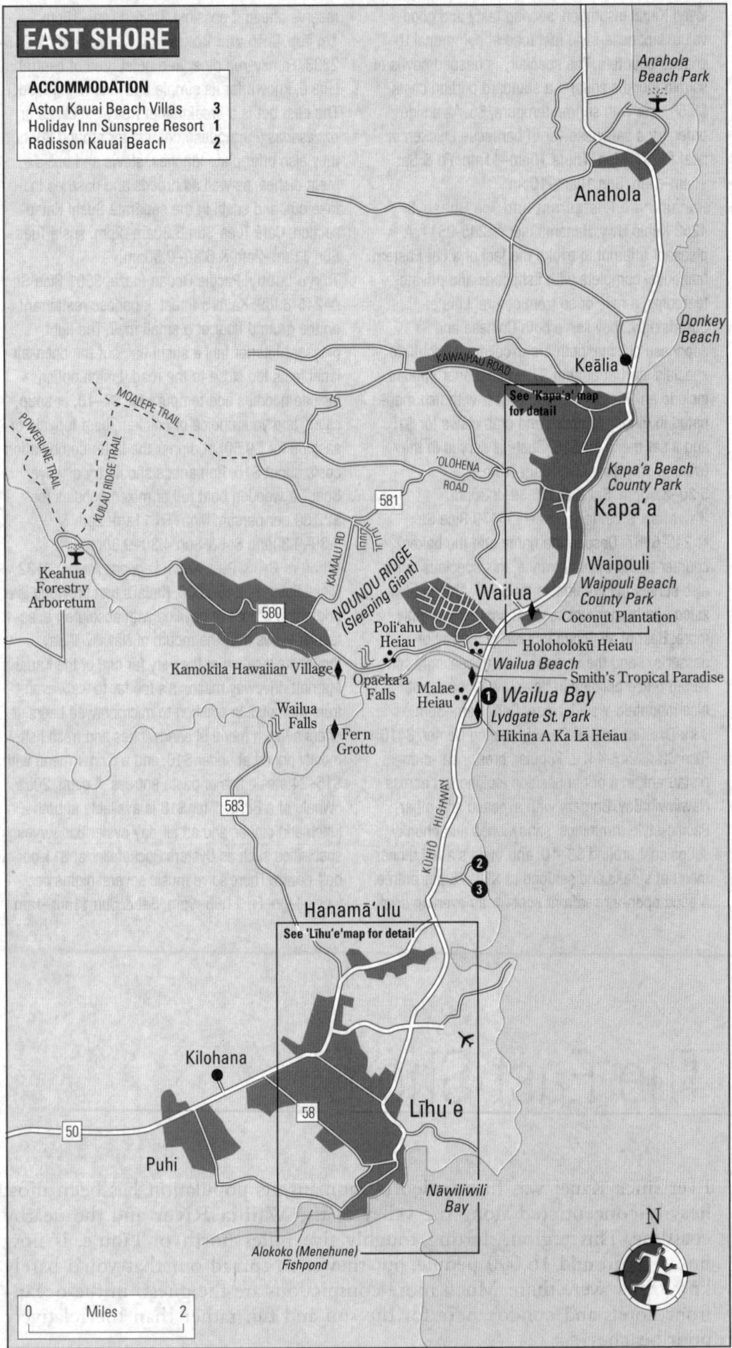
EAST SHORE
ACCOMMODATION
Aston Kauai Beach Villas 3
Holiday Inn Sunspree Resort 1
Radisson Kauai Beach 2
Anahola Beach Park
Anahola
Donkey Beach
Keālia
KAWAIHAU ROAD
See 'Kapa'a' map for detail
MOALEPE TRAIL
POWERLINE TRAIL
KUILAU RIDGE TRAIL
'OLOHENA ROAD
Kapa'a Beach County Park
Kapa'a
581
KAMALU RD
NOUNOU RIDGE (Sleeping Giant)
Waipouli
Waipouli Beach County Park
Keahua Forestry Arboretum
Wailua
580
Coconut Plantation
Poli'ahu Heiau
Holoholokū Heiau
Wailua Beach
Kamokila Hawaiian Village
Smith's Tropical Paradise
Opaeka'a Falls
Malae Heiau
Wailua Bay
Lydgate St. Park
Wailua Falls
Fern Grotto
Hikina A Ka Lā Heiau
KŪHIŌ HIGHWAY
583
Hanamā'ulu
See 'Līhu'e'map for detail
Kilohana
58
Līhu'e
50
Puhi
Nāwiliwili Bay
N
Alokoko (Menehune) Fishpond
0 Miles 2

Technically, Kūhiō Highway, the main artery, passes through several separate communities as it heads north beyond the river itself. The distinctions between the overlapping towns of **Wailua**, **Waipouli** and **Kapa'a**, however, are far less significant or even noticeable than the contrast between the malls and modern high-rises along the highway and the residential districts that lie a couple of miles inland. Tucked away behind long, low **Nounou Ridge** (the "Sleeping Giant"), which runs parallel to the coast, neat individual cottages are set amid gardens that erupt with spectacular blooms, and ramshackle farms still squeeze as much produce as possible from their few acres.

Beyond Kapa'a, there's far less development, and only rarely is access to the seashore at all easy. However, en route to Princeville you can stop at several little-known beaches.

# Wailua River

Kūhiō Highway crosses the **WAILUA RIVER** five miles out from central Līhu'e, marking the start of Kauai's East Shore. For the ancient Hawaiians, the area to either side of the twin bridges here was the *Wailua Nui Hoano*, or Great Sacred Wailua. Fertile, beautiful and sheltered from the sea, it provided some of the best living conditions in all the islands, and served as home to Kauai's greatest chiefs. A trail known as the **King's Highway**, lined with *heiaus* and other religious sites, ran beside the river all the way from the ocean to the rain-drenched summit of Mount Wai'ale'ale.

In those days the Wailua flowed in two separate channels. It still has a South Fork and a North Fork, but they now fuse together for the last couple of miles. The resultant broad, flat stream is often called the only navigable river in Hawaii, although sandbars at its mouth usually stop vessels from entering it from the open sea. Exploring it in a kayak is one of the best ways to spend a day on this side of the island; rental outlets are detailed on p.421. (Other good rivers to kayak on Kauai include the Hanalei, see p.458, and the Kalihiwai, see p.450.)

The south bank of the river has long been set aside for growing sugar and is almost entirely free of buildings or even roads; it's impossible to head any farther inland than the Smith's Tropical Paradise theme park (see overleaf), though tour boats leave regularly for the short cruise up to the **Fern Grotto**, which involves a brief walk along the south bank. Otherwise, very few vantage points offer so much as a glimpse of its rolling cane fields and woodlands.

It was on the Wailua's north shore that Kauai's most famous ruler, Kaumuali'i, had his own personal coconut grove and *heiau*. He had been born just a few yards away, at the Birthing Stones, as was essential to attain the highest rank on the island. Several such historic sites, in various states of repair, are now preserved in **Wailua River State Park**, together with plenty of attractive scenery.

## The Fern Grotto

Some visitors consider the trip to the **Fern Grotto**, a short way up the Wailua River, to be the highlight of their stay on Kauai; many more find it hard to imagine anything to which they'd less like to subject themselves. Promoted as a romantic, fern-bedecked jungle cavern, the grotto has an undeserved reputation as the island's premier beauty spot, and can only be reached as part of a large group excursion. Don't kid yourself that the grotto itself may be compelling enough to make it worth putting up with all the kitsch nonsense that surrounds it: the kitsch nonsense is the best bit.

Two companies run $15 trips to the Fern Grotto; their canopied barges set off from a marina *mauka* of the highway on the south bank of the Wailua. Both Smith's (☎821-6892) and Wai'ale'ale Boat Tours (☎822-4908) operate daily, roughly every thirty minutes between 9am and 4pm, alternating in slack periods.

As the barge heads upriver, a commentary on the few undramatic sights along the way is interspersed with local legends. For most of the route, you see little beyond the thick trees on both banks. After a couple of miles, once you've passed the houses high on the ridge near 'Ōpaeka'a Falls, and the Kamokila Hawaiian Village (see p.437), the river divides. The Fern Grotto is just up its left (south) fork, which explains why most kayakers head off to the right.

Having disembarked at the grotto landing, you walk a short paved trail, lined with bananas and torch ginger plants, up to the cave. This large natural amphitheater was hollowed out by a waterfall that has slowed to a trickle in the century since the sugar plantations diverted the stream that fed it. Until Hurricane Iniki toppled most of the tree cover up above the cave, dense clusters of *a'e* ferns drooped down from its lip, screening off the interior with a green curtain. As ferns hate direct sunlight, they're now much shorter than they used to be. They may grow back, but for the moment this is a damp and not very prepossessing spot. Only the acoustics remain unchanged, so each tour party in turn assembles to be serenaded with the *Hawaiian Wedding Song* by the guitar-toting crew of its barge, whose concert continues on the way back downstream.

Speaking of weddings, each day two or three couples get married at the Fern Grotto; for a list of wedding organizers, see p.43.

## Smith's Tropical Paradise

There's plenty more ersatz Polynesian posturing at **SMITH'S TROPICAL PARADISE**, alongside the marina. In the daytime, you can explore its thirty acres of colorful gardens in relative peace (daily 8.30am–4pm; $5, optional tram tour $4). On several evenings each week, it reopens for a standard buffet *lū'au* and an excruciating "International Pageant" called *The Golden People of Hawaii*, featuring song and dance from China and Japan as well as Hawaii and Polynesia (currently Mon, Wed & Fri, gates open 5pm, *lū'au* 8pm; ☎821-6895; $55). Kauai's other *lū'aus* are detailed on p.423.

## The King's Highway

Although it's still possible to make out several of the ancient sites that once lined the Wailua River, few now amount to more than vague ruins. None has any formal opening hours or guided tours; you have to find them yourself and settle for reading whatever explanatory signs may have been erected.

Slightly back from the lava rocks of Lydgate State Park (see p.438), on the southern bank of the Wailua at the river mouth, stands the **Hikina A Ka Lā** ("Rising of the Sun") **Heiau**. Only traces survive of the hundred-yard-long, ten-foot-thick wall that once faced the rising sun here. Part of the area behind it was devoted to a "place of refuge" (see p.174), the *Hauola O Hōnaunau*, while the waters in front were popular, then as now, with expert surfers.

On the other, *mauka*, side of the highway, just before the marina turnoff, a large mound covered with grass and trees in the middle of a cane field marks the site of **Malae Heiau**. Roughly a hundred yards square, this was the island's biggest temple. In the 1840s, well after the death of Kaumuali'i, his favorite wife, Deborah Kapule, is rumored to have used it as a pen for her large herd of cattle, to demonstrate her conversion to Christianity.

As soon as you cross the Wailua, you're in the area where Kaumuali'i lived amid his grove of coconut palms. A road inland from here follows the route of the old **King's Highway** trail; it's now known as Kuamo'o Road or Hwy-580. The first of the riverside parking lots on the left is the kayak and canoe launching ramp for **Wailua River State Park**, which encompasses the river itself and a thin strip along most of both banks. When the sandbar permits, jet skis also roar out to sea from here. The second riverside parking lot is at the foot of the low Ka Lae O Ka Manu ("Crest of the Bird" or cock's comb) ridge, where **Holoholokū Heiau** once stood. So tiny that it could only be entered on all fours, this was a *luakini*, used for human sacrifices. A few stone walls remain, but the hill itself is overgrown.

A little way further north around the base of the hill are the **Birthing Stones**, where all the great chiefs of Kauai were born. The mother was supposed to brace her back against one stone and her legs against the other as she gave birth, though they seem a bit too far apart for that to be very likely. An even slab at the edge of the small walled enclosure nearby was used to cover the corpses of dogs sacrificed on such occasions, while the infant's umbilical cord was inserted in the crack in the boulder behind.

A flight of steps from beside the Birthing Stones leads up the hill. At the top you find yourself, not in a Hawaiian temple, but in a more recent, though now also overgrown, **Japanese cemetery**, straight across from the Fern Grotto ferry landing.

From here on, the road steadily climbs along Kuamo'o ("Lizard") Ridge. After about a mile, a parking lot on the left commands a sweeping prospect of the broad flatlands beside a gentle curve in the Wailua. Helpful signs explain that this spot on the bluff was the site of the palace of chief Ho'ono. The broad low walls of **Poli'ahu Heiau**, constructed of smooth stones from the river bed, still stand, though with the thatched temple structures long gone they now enclose just grass and rubble. Coconut palms sway at either end, unusually high above the sea.

The birth of a new *ali'i* at the Birthing Stones was traditionally greeted by a hammer striking the **Bell Stone**, further upstream. To find it, head down the rutted dirt road off to the left just beyond the *heiau*, then follow a rough walkway down the hill. No one can now say for sure which among the pile of stones here is the correct one, so you'll just have to hit a few and make your own mind up.

The next parking lot, this time on the right, is the overlook for **'Ōpaeka'a Falls**. Set amid thick green undergrowth, this wide, low waterfall splashes into a pool stained red with eroded earth, where native shrimp could once be seen churning in the water (*'Ōpaeka'a* means "rolling shrimp"). The falls interrupt 'Ōpaeka'a Stream, which flows in between Kuamo'o Ridge and Nounou Mountain before joining the Wailua a mile back down the hill. You can't walk any closer to the falls than this, but you get a slightly better view from the highway bridge a few yards further up.

Carefully cross the road at this point for a fine panorama of Wailua Valley. Immediately below, you can see the huts of **Kamokila Hawaiian Village**, a reasonably authentic re-creation of a traditional riverside settlement. Demolished by Iniki, it was subsequently restored to serve as an African village in the 1995 Dustin Hoffman thriller *Outbreak*, and has now reopened for low-key tours that focus on daily life in ancient Kauai (Mon–Sat 8am–5pm; $5).

The King's Highway runs for several progressively wilder miles beyond 'Ōpaeka'a Falls, but no longer right up Wai'ale'ale. You're only likely to venture this way if you plan to do some backwoods **hiking**, along the excellent trails detailed on p.444 onwards.

# Wailua to Kapa'a

Although the East Shore's nicest beach, Lydgate Park, and its top tourist attraction, the boat trip to the Fern Grotto, are both on the south shore of the Wailua River, the strip development along the coast only gets going once you cross the river and enter **WAILUA** proper. At this point, a thin fringe of trees and sand is all that divides the highway from the sea, while soon an extensive grove of palms on the *mauka* side marks the site of the **Coco Palms Resort**. Kauai's most famous hotel – the one through which Elvis and his new bride floated in *Blue Hawaii*, to the accompaniment of the *Hawaiian Wedding Song* – has been closed since Iniki. While it was clearly overdue for refurbishment, locals are puzzled and angry that it has taken so long to get going again.

Within less than a mile, as the gap between road and ocean starts to widen, the extensive **Coconut Plantation** complex appears *makai* of the highway. This centers on the **Marketplace**, a mall of rather ordinary souvenir stores, fast-food outlets, bars and restaurants, arranged around an open-air courtyard. Behind that lie half a dozen large hotels, while out of sight to the south are several condo buildings, not strictly speaking part of the Plantation complex. Coconut Plantation Marketplace eating options are summarized on p.442; hotels and condos are detailed on p.441.

Northbound traffic along the highway from here on in can get very congested; at busy times, vehicles are shunted onto a bypass system that follows the former sugar-cane roads from behind *Sizzlers* in Wailua and rejoins Hwy-56 via Olohena Road in Kapa'a. Other than a few worthwhile restaurants (see p.442 for reviews), and the shops in the **Kauai Village Shopping Center**, halfway between Wailua and Kapa'a in **WAIPOULI**, you'd miss nothing if you skipped the main highway altogether.

**KAPA'A** itself is about the only recognizable town between Līhu'e and Hanalei. The old-fashioned boardwalks at the main intersection (not important enough to boast a stop light, but a welcome interruption in the monotonous strip) hold small shops, cafés and restaurants. The open-air **Sunny Side Farmers Market** sells fresh fruit and vegetables daily; several equipment rental outlets offer kayaks, surfboards and the like at reasonable rates; and a handful of quirky clothes and gift stores catch the eye.

While Kapa'a holds no major landmarks or monuments, the story of its growth into the modern era as a typical plantation community makes a fascinating basis for the ninety-minute **walking tours** run by the small Kapa'a History Shop, opposite the market (Tues, Thurs & Sat 10am; $10; ⓣ821-1778).

## The beaches

Although an almost unbroken ribbon of sand runs along the shore all the way from the mouth of the Wailua up to Kapa'a, it rarely deserves to be called a beach. The nearby mountains lend the area some scenic beauty, but the coastline is flat and dull, devoid of the sheltered coves and steepled cliffs that characterize the waterfront further north. Strong waves and stronger currents rightly deter most bathers, so the swimming pools in the major hotels are kept busy.

By far the most popular and attractive of the public beaches is the first one you come to heading north from Līhu'e. **Lydgate State Park** is not visible from the road, however; it lies behind the *Sunspace Resort* (see p.441) on the southern side of the mouth of the Wailua River. The murky, swirling waters where the river flows into the sea are of great interest to surfers, but for family swimming the two linked artificial pools in the park, lined with smooth lava

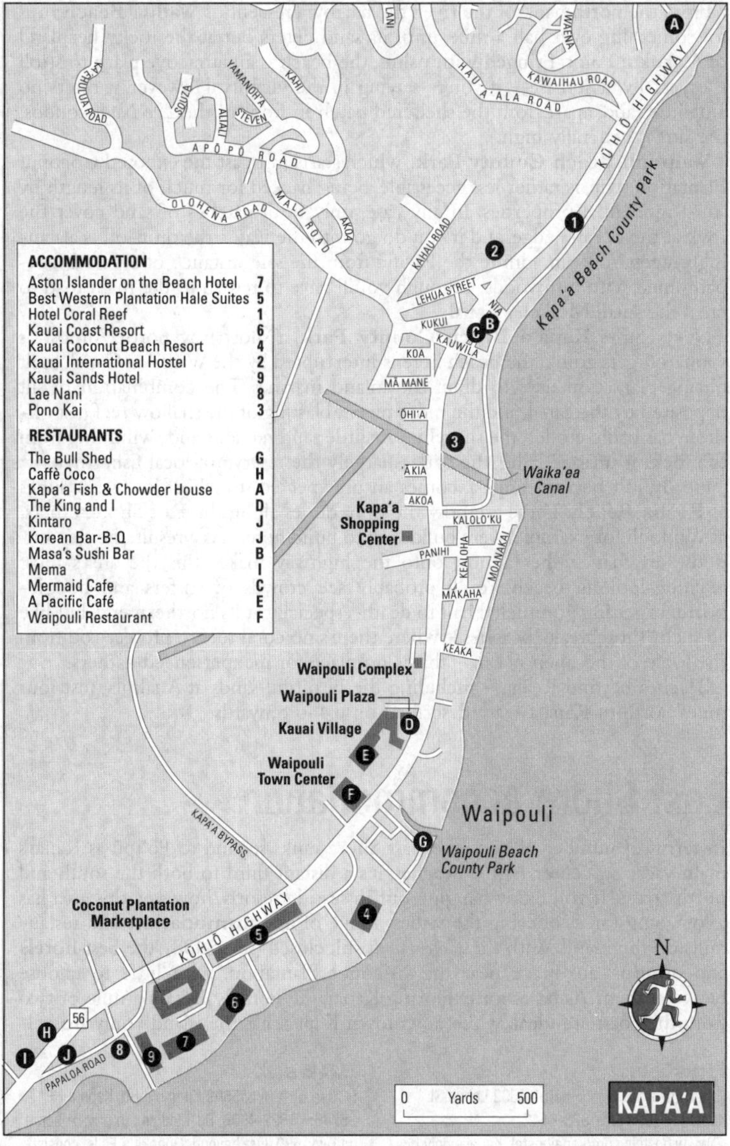


boulders, are preferable. Regularly replenished by the sea, they are usually bursting with fish eager to be fed by snorkelers. There's a picnic site alongside the pools, in the shade of a stand of ironwoods. The park is also the site of the glorious **Kamalani Playground**, an intricate tangle of free-form wooden structures for children to climb on. In addition, Lydgate Park holds the first of the trail of ancient *heiaus* that line the Wailua River, described on p.436.

From the north bank of the river, the narrow crescent of **Wailua Beach** runs for something over half a mile, until its sand peters out at the rocky headland of Alakukui Point. Fringed with palms, the beach is an attractive place to stroll – especially at sunrise – if you're staying in the vicinity. However, it offers no amenities and, apart from the sheltered patch in front of the *Lae Nani* condos, the surf is generally high.

**Waipouli Beach County Park**, which starts just past the exposed Coconut Plantation strip, is rather less accessible, being backed for much of its length by small residential properties. In any case, only fitful patches of sand cover the rock at the ocean's edge, and if you do go into the water, the drop-off is alarmingly steep. You can admire the Pacific from the safe distance of a paved footpath lined with ironwoods, although you'll have to return to the main road to cross the small Moikeha Canal.

Next comes **Kapa'a Beach County Park**, a short way north. Almost as soon as it gets going, the beach here is interrupted by the Waika'ea Canal, built during plantation days to drain the inland marshes. The combination of silt deposited by the canal, and the more recent blasting of the shallow reef just offshore has badly eroded the shoreline. As little sand remains and swimming from the rocks is unappetizing, the park is largely the reserve of local fishermen.

Finally, just beyond Kapa'a, comes an unexpected stretch of low sand dunes at **Kealia Beach**. These are now the only dunes along the East Shore; others, at Waipouli for example, were bulldozed to build hotels. As a result, the tremendous surf that crashes almost onto the highway makes this the area's most exciting-looking beach. You'll probably see crowds of surfers and boogie-boarders getting pummeled half to death, especially at its northern end, but like all such "shorebreak" beaches – where there's no coral reef to protect you from the force of the open ocean – this is no place for inexperienced bathers.

Beaches beyond Kealia – including the beautiful sands at Anahola, just four miles north of Kapa'a – are described on p.446 onwards.

# East Shore accommodation

In terms of number of beds, the East Shore ranks second to Po'ipū as Kauai's main vacation center. As for beaches, it's a distant third to both the south and north coasts. If you enjoy hanging out in seaside resorts, however, this area has a lot going for it, offering the widest range of **accommodation** and restaurants on the island. With the *Coco Palms* still closed (see p.438), the best **hotels** and **condos** are in or near the Coconut Plantation, with little to choose between them. As bases for exploring Kauai, the homely **B&Bs** a mile or two from the coast are ideal, while downtown Kapa'a has the island's only **hostel**.

## Hostel

**Kauai International Hostel**, 4532 Lehua St, Kapa'a HI 96746; ⓣ823-6142, ⓦwww.hostels.com/kauaihostel. Kauai's only hostel, affiliated with the AYH (members get $1 discount), but open to all *except* Hawaiian residents, with a maximum one-week stay. The *Kauai International* comprises a two-story building with eight-bed dorms ($20 per bed) and a few $50 private rooms, sharing bathrooms. Cooking facilities are available, and there's easy access from the airport by public bus (see p.417). ❶/❷.

## B&Bs

**House of Aleva**, 5509 Kuamo'o Rd, Kapa'a HI 96746; ⓣ822-4606. B&B lodging in private home on Hwy-580, just beyond 'Ōpaeka'a Falls, consisting of two upstairs double rooms that share a bathroom but have their own phones. Nonsmokers preferred, no credit cards. ❷.

**Inn Paradise**, 6381 Makana Rd, Kapa'a HI 96746; ⓣ822-2542; ⓔmcinch@aloha.net; or reserve through Hawaii's Best B&B, ⓣ885-4550 or 1-800/262-9912, ⓕ885-0559, ⓦwww.bestbnb.com. Great-value garden cottage, deep in the hills above Wailua, and divided into three fully equipped B&B units. All share use of a roomy *lānai* and hot tub. ❸.

**Lani-Keha**, 848 Kamalu Rd, Kapa'a HI 96746; ⓣ822-1605 or 1-800/821-4898, ⓕ822-2429, ⓦwww.lanikeha.com. Four comfortable en-suite B&B rooms in large country house tucked in behind the Sleeping Giant; all have access to the main kitchen, living room and a large *lānai*. ❷–❸.

**Rosewood B&B**, 872 Kamalu Rd, Kapa'a HI 96746; ⓣ822-5216, ⓕ822-5478, ⓦwww.rosewoodkauai.com; or reserve through Hawaii's Best B&B, ⓣ885-4550 or 1-800/262-9912, ⓕ885-0559, ⓦwww.bestbnb.com. Spacious plantation-style house, complete with columns and verandah. There's one cozy (somewhat overly so) guest room, two fully-equipped cottages in the gorgeous gardens, and a bunkhouse that holds three simple budget rooms that share a single bathroom. Bunkhouse ❷, room ❸, cottages ❹.

## Hotels and condos

**Aston Islander on the Beach**, Coconut Plantation, 484 Kūhiō Hwy, Kapa'a HI 96746; ⓣ822-7417, 1-800/922-7866 (US & Can) or 1-800/321-2558 (HI), ⓕ822-1947, ⓦwww.aston-hotels.com. Beachfront property at the southern end of Coconut Plantation. Seven separate guest wings – rates rise the closer you get to the sea – plus a small pool and spa. All rooms have *lānais*, safes and refrigerators, while the *Jolly Roger* restaurant, set back from the ocean, offers live entertainment. Garden view ❹, ocean view ❺.

**Best Western Plantation Hale Suites**, Coconut Plantation, 484 Kūhiō Hwy, Kapa'a HI 96746; ⓣ822-4941 or 1-800/775-4253, ⓕ822-5599, ⓦwww.plantation-hale.com. Inexpensive apartment suites, each with separate kitchen, living room, dressing room and bathroom, in several buildings facing across lawns to the sea. Take your pick of three swimming pools. ❺.

**Holiday Inn Sunspree Resort**, 3-5920 Kūhiō Hwy, Kapa'a HI 96746; ⓣ823-6000 or 1-888/823-5111, ⓕ823-6666, ⓦwww.holidayinn-kauai.com. Just off the highway immediately south of Wailua River, looking over the ocean from above Lydgate State Park, the former *Kauai Resort* has been remodeled and upgraded to provide better value than ever. A wide assortment of rooms and suites, some in hotel buildings and some in pseudo-Polynesian "cabanas", are often available, often at discounted rates. ❺.

**Hotel Coral Reef**, 1516 Kūhiō Hwy, Kapa'a HI 96746; ⓣ822-4481 or 1-800/843-4659, ⓕ822-7705, ⓦwww.hshawaii.com/kvp/coral. Inexpensive suites in small, friendly, but far from fancy seafront hotel, a short walk north of central Kapa'a. The sofa bed in the living room makes it a real bargain for families. ❸.

**Kauai Coast Resort (at the Beachboy)**, Coconut Plantation, 484 Kūhiō Hwy, Kapa'a HI 96746; ⓣ822-3441, 1-800/922-7866 (US & Can) or 1-800/321-2558 (HI), ⓕ822-0843, ⓦwww.aston-hotels.com. This renovated condo resort looks forbidding from the outside, with high lava-rock walls fronting the main road to Coconut Plantation. Inside, it's far more pleasant. Three wings of comfortable guest rooms enclose spacious lawns and a pool; the fourth – open – side is the beach. All rooms have private *lānais* and two double beds; under-18s can share your room for free. Garden view ❺, ocean view ❻.

**Kauai Coconut Beach Resort**, PO Box 830, Coconut Plantation, 484 Kūhiō Hwy, Kapa'a HI 96746; ⓣ822-3455 or 1-800/760-8555 (US & Can), ⓕ822-1830, ⓦwww.kcb.com. The northernmost of the Coconut Plantation resorts, comprising several large beachfront wings holding 311 comfortable rooms with private *lānais*. Guests can use the pool, spa and free tennis courts, and dine at the *Flying Lobster* restaurant. Rates include a free rental car. For details of the *lū'au*, see p.423. ❺–❻.

**Kauai Sands Hotel**, 420 Papaloa Rd, Wailua HI 96746; ⓣ822-4951 or 1-800/560-5553, ⓕ822-0998; ⓦsand-seaside.com. Large and somewhat faded oceanfront property at the southern end of Coconut Plantation, though not technically part of it. Several buildings of motel-style units are arrayed around a pool; spacious lawns lead down to the beach. ❹.

**Lae Nani**, 410 Papaloa Rd, Wailua HI 96746; ⓣ822-4938 or 1-800/367-7052 (US & Can), ⓕ822-1022; also bookable through Outrigger, 1-800/688-7444, ⓦwww.outrigger.com. Spacious low-rise complex of luxurious one- and two-bedroom condos, all capable of sleeping at least four guests, on a headland at the northern end of Wailua Bay, just south of Coconut Plantation. The adjacent beach is ideal for inshore swimming, and there's also a pool, plus a ruined *heiau*, on the grounds. ❺.

**Pono Kai**, 4-1250 Kūhiō Hwy, Kapa'a HI 96746; ⓣ822-9831, ⓕ822-9054, ⓦwww.ponokai-resort.com; also book through Marc Resorts, ⓣ922-5900 or 1-800/535-0085 (US & Can), ⓕ922-2421 or 1-800/633-5085 (US & Can), ⓦwww.marcresorts.com. Convenient, spacious one- and two-room condos in an upmarket complex that faces the beach *makai* of the highway as you come into central Kapa'a. All the comforts of home, plus use of a pool, sauna and tennis courts. Mini-suites ❸, garden view ❹, ocean view ❺.

# East Shore restaurants

**Restaurants** jostle for the attention of hotel guests all along the Wailua to Kapa'a coastal highway. However, with one or two exceptions, the glossier-looking steak-and-seafood places tend to be less interesting than the cheaper ethnic alternatives. *A Pacific Café* is head and shoulders above the rest, but if you feel that strolling around comparing menus is an essential precursor to eating out, only downtown Kapa'a fits the bill. Besides the places reviewed below, there are also any number of the usual chain fast-food outlets.

**The Bull Shed**, 796 Kūhiō Hwy, Kapa'a; ☎ 822-3791. So long as you get a table next to the oceanfront windows in this standard American restaurant, you probably won't mind the predictability of the food. Broiled shrimp costs $16, steaks start at $15, and a cheesy scallop bake is $16. All meals include a visit to possibly the worst salad bar you'll ever encounter. Daily 5.30–10pm.

**Caffé Coco**, 4-369 Kūhiō Hwy, Wailua; ☎ 822-7990. Attractively ramshackle café, *mauka* of the highway in central Wailua. Wholesome, though not entirely vegetarian, breakfasts and lunches are under $10; changing dinner specials, such as grilled or roasted Italian-style meat dishes, under $20. Indoor and outdoor seating. Tues-Sun 9am–9pm.

**Kapa'a Fish and Chowder House**, 4-1639 Kūhiō Hwy, Kapa'a; ☎ 822-7488. Roomy restaurant-bar on the northern fringes of Kapa'a, with attractive décor; the garden terrace out back is especially nice. The cocktails are fine, but the food is not all that special. The eponymous chowder costs $5.50 a bowl, and there's a lot of (mostly breaded) fish and seafood dishes, served on fettuccine or with fries or rice, at $16–25; the *cioppino* stew, at $21, is a good bet. Daily 5.30–10pm.

**The King and I**, Waipouli Plaza, 4-901 Kūhiō Hwy, Kapa'a; ☎ 822-1642. Inexpensive but top-quality Thai place, in a small mall just north of Kauai Village. They're proud of growing their own herbs, and most dishes are heaped with fresh basil. For an appetizer you can get a bale of crispy straw-like noodles for $6, meat or shrimp satay for $8, or share a two-person portion of spicy lemongrass or Siam coconut soup. The tastiest entrees are the red, green, and yellow curries, prepared with meat for $8, fish or shrimp for $10, or as even cheaper vegetarian options. Most of the desserts involve green tea or coconut ice cream. Mon–Fri 11am–1.30pm & 4.30–9.30pm, Sat & Sun 4.30–9.30pm.

**Kintaro**, 4-3561 Kūhiō Hwy, Wailua; ☎ 822-3341. Friendly, informal, but exquisite restaurant, serving reasonably priced Japanese food. Full sushi bar, plus teppanyaki meals and more unusual specialties such as grilled eel ($15) and *yose nabe*, a sort of Japanese bouillabaisse with clams and crab (also $15). Mon–Sat 5.30–9.30pm.

**Korean Bar-B-Q Restaurant**, 4-3561 Kūhiō Hwy, Wailua; ☎ 823-6744. Modest, friendly, and very good-value barbecue joint. The meat dishes are all tasty, with combos costing $5–8; vegetarian options include spicy *kimchee* vegetables. Takeout is available. Mon & Wed–Sun 10am–9pm, Tues 4.30–9pm.

## Mall Snacks

The **Marketplace** in the **Coconut Plantation** offers a wide range of inexpensive snacks, though it's not a place for fine dining or atmosphere. The only real restaurant is *Buzz's Steak and Lobster* (daily 11am–2.30pm & 4.30–10.30pm; ☎ 822-0041), an unadventurous place offering lunchtime burgers, salads and sandwiches for around $7, as well as steak and fish dinners for $16 and up. Nearby, the centrally located *Krazy Coconut Café* (☎ 822-9421) is a welcoming venue for a light breakfast complete with a *cappuccino* or *latte*; it also serves pricey but delicious real-fruit smoothies.

The largest of the local malls, the **Kauai Village Shopping Center**, houses one of Kauai's best restaurants – *A Pacific Café*, reviewed overleaf. In the same building is a rare treat for **vegetarians**: *Papaya's Natural Foods and Café* (Mon–Sat 9am–8pm; ☎ 823-0190), a wholefood store selling salads, sandwiches and specials that you can consume at its outside tables. Otherwise, the choice is uninspiring, with a wide variety of very average fast-food takeouts – you might do better to buy your own ingredients from the deli in Safeway.

**Masa's Sushi Bar**, 1394 Kūhiō Hwy, Kapa'a; ⓣ831-6933. Tiny Japanese restaurant in the heart of Kapa'a, where the focus is on good sushi at a good price; a soft-shell crab roll, for example, costs $8. For a little more there's a good selection of other seafood dishes. Bring your own beer or wine. Tues-Sun noon–1.30pm & 5–9pm.

**Mema**, 4-361 Kūhiō Hwy, Wailua; ⓣ823-0899. Sino-Thai restaurant, run by the same owners as *The King and I* – and, if anything, even better. Fresh basil and lemongrass feature prominently throughout the menu, with appetizers such as fish patties and delicious shrimp rolls for $7–9, and house curries costing from $9 to $18 depending on whether you want meat, fish or seafood. Mon–Fri 11am–2pm & 5–9.30pm, Sat & Sun 5–9.30pm.

**Mermaid Cafe**, 1384 Kūhiō Hwy, Kapa'a; ⓣ821-2026. Small, partly vegetarian café in central Kapa'a, serving wholesome egg-and-fruit breakfasts and bargain Asian-flavored lunches such as chicken satay, tofu wraps and the like for around $7. Espresso can be picked up from the adjoining *Island Java*. Mon–Fri 8am–5pm, Sat 9am–3pm.

**A Pacific Café**, Kauai Village Shopping Center, 4-831 Kūhiō Hwy, Kapa'a; ⓣ822-0013. Widely acknowledged as Kauai's finest restaurant. The unassuming mall setting and lack of views places the emphasis firmly on the food, though the dining room is pleasant enough, decorated with Hawaiian-themed art and heliconia gingers, with scurrying chefs visible in the open-fronted kitchen at the back. Chef/owner Jean-Marie Josselin is a prophet of Pacific Rim cuisine; what with the Pacific being deemed to stretch as far as Thailand, pasta being considered a universal language, and his being French, he feels entitled to use anything that tastes nice. The most consistently Polynesian element is the ample size of the portions. Most of the appetizers, at $8–13, are fish or seafood; selections include poached scallop ravioli, and Peking duck and shrimp tacos; the deep-fried tiger-eye sushi is absolutely sensational. Entrees, at $20–27, are either from the wood-burning grill – like fire-roasted *ono* with shrimp risotto, or rack of lamb – or specials, such as wok-charred *mahi-mahi*, roasted *opakapaka*, or duck cooked in three distinct styles. There's also a $42 sampler menu. The array of thunderously sweet desserts culminates in the Hot Hawaiian Vintage Chocolate Tart. No wine costs less than $30 a bottle. Daily 5.30–10pm.

**Waipouli Restaurant**, Waipouli Town Center; ⓣ822-9311. Simple plate-lunch restaurant, in a small mall just south of Kauai Village. The menu includes roast pork, chicken and other meats (it takes a huge combo to cost as much as $9), but the specialty is filling bowls of *saimin* noodles, in different varieties ($3–6). Mon–Sat 7am–2pm & 5–9pm, Sun 7am–2pm.

# East Shore hikes

If you only have a few days to spend **hiking** on Kauai, then the East Shore cannot compete with the splendors of the Kalalau Trail (see p.467) or the treks in Kōke'e Park (see p.493). However, some very enjoyable trails do lead through the hills above Wailua and Kapa'a. The compelling attraction here is the awe-inspiring crater wall of **Mount Wai'ale'ale**, which looms before you as you head inland. It's no longer possible to walk to the top, as the ancients did, but although the helicopter companies may claim that it can only be seen from the air, keen hikers can trek to the wilderness at its base.

## Nounou Mountain – "The Sleeping Giant"

The long, sharp crest of **Nounou Mountain** parallels the shoreline between Wailua and Kapa'a, roughly two miles back from the sea. These days it's known more often as the **Sleeping Giant**, although the only spot from which it bears much resemblance to a slumbering profile is down a side road opposite the Chevron station in Waipouli. Three separate trails lead up to the top of the ridge, where they join for a final assault on the summit.

The trail from the **east** starts near the end of Haleilio Road, a mile up from its junction with Kūhiō Highway. After the initial gentle zigzagging ascent through tropical vegetation, it gets a little hard to follow – head right, not left, at the fork half a mile along. Switchbacking across the northern end of the ridge, you get to see the high mountains inland as well as views back towards the ocean. Something over a mile along, the western trail links up from the right, and both continue left a short way to the picnic area.

Coming from the **west**, pick up the trail at the end of Lokelani Road, a small *makai* turn very near the northern end of Kamalu Road, which connects Hwy-580 with Olohena Road. This is a shorter but steeper hike, more or less straight up the forested hillside. The highlight is a superb avenue of poker-straight Norfolk pines, recognizable by the raised ridges at regular intervals around their trunks. Such trees were formerly in great demand as masts, though these ones are just seventy years old.

Finally, it's also possible to climb the Sleeping Giant from the **south**, along a trail that starts a few hundred yards west of the 'Ōpaeka'a Falls parking lot (see p.437). The two-mile trail is mostly in thick woodland as it meanders up the hillside, but a picnic table in a clearing along the way offers some fine inland **views**. The trail meets the western route in the stand of pines mentioned above, with plenty of climbing still to go.

Whichever way you climb, you'll know you've reached the top when you arrive at the **Ali'i Vista Hale**, a sheltered picnic table set in a little clearing. So long as it isn't raining, you'll be able to see the entire coastline, from Līhu'e to Anahola, or look inland towards the residential areas of Wailua and Kapa'a.

If you're feeling intrepid, and conditions are not too slippery, it's possible to continue beyond the picnic area along a hair-raisingly makeshift trail. Were you down on the highway, you'd know this as the Giant's Nose; up here it's a sheer razorback ridge, with long drops to either side. Scrambling up the rocks at the end brings you out at a level and even better viewpoint. The soil underfoot is a rich red loam, which explains why such mountains erode so quickly; most of the slopes below are dense with small trees, but slashes of bare earth show where mudslides have taken place. Away to the west is the main ridge of Mount Wai'ale'ale, almost permanently wreathed in mist and cloud, while to the south lies the twisting, wooded gorge of the Wailua River. Anahola Mountain runs across the northern horizon, looking much like a sleeping giant itself.

## Mount Wai'ale'ale Base Trail

For most visitors to the East Shore, the mountains of the interior remain a cloud-shrouded mystery. Behind the semi-permanent veil of mist, however, lies a landscape of extraordinary beauty. The very heart of the island is **Mount Wai'ale'ale**, whose annual rainfall of around 440 inches makes it the wettest spot on earth. Its highest point is less than a dozen miles west of Kapa'a, which receives a tenth as much rain. The name *Wai'ale'ale* means "overflowing water"; as you approach it from the ocean, it appears as a curved wall of velvet-green rock, furrowed by countless waterfalls. Most of its rain falls on the Alaka'i Swamp, just behind the summit, then flows in every direction to create all of Kauai's major rivers. (Details of the amazing trail through the Alaka'i Swamp from Kōke'e State Park appear on p.498.) The escarpments of Wai'ale'ale are far too steep to climb, but hiking to the foot of the mountain is rewarding and far from strenuous.

To get here, drive along Hwy-580 (the King's Highway) beyond 'Ōpaeka'a Falls. The road ends three miles or so further on at the **Keahou Forestry Arboretum**, a stretch of woodlands and meadows where native trees are grown in controlled conditions. It's a pleasant enough area to stroll around, though the trees are not labeled for your benefit. Incidentally, the arboretum also serves as the trailhead for the Kuilau Ridge Trail (see below) and the southern end of the Powerline Trail (see p.452).

From here on, how far you can continue, first by car and then on foot, depends on the weather. Driving involves fording streams that cross the unpaved continuation of the road; if the water is at all high, don't try it. Otherwise, check your milometer, and set off across the stream at the arboretum. After 1.6 miles, a pull-out on the left offers the first clear views of Wai'ale'ale. Turn right at the T-junction after 2.2 miles, then left at the fork after 2.7 miles. Ignore the road to the left after 3.5 miles, but fork left a short way beyond that. The road ends at a gate just under four miles from the arboretum, but you're free to walk on.

You're now heading directly towards Wai'ale'ale. As the track rises after about half a mile, a side trail to the left leads in a few minutes to a tranquil pool in dense, wild forest, but you'll probably want to press on ahead. Not far beyond, the dirt road reaches a small dam. This is the North Fork of the Wailua River, which has just plummeted down the face of the mountain. Upstream, its waters foam and tumble between the boulders, against the unforgettable backdrop of the high, green walls of Wai'ale'ale. If you're lucky, the cloud cover may clear long enough to offer a glimpse of the ridge at the top. The white specks of helicopters show up clearly against the green, and their engines are just about audible above the river. All the rudimentary footpaths on the far side of the dam peter out in a morass of mud, roots, ferns and water.

It's simply not possible to climb to the summit of Wai'ale'ale from here; the trail of the ancient Hawaiians followed the ridge that leads up the flank to your right. However, you may hear talk of a hike to the "**Blue Hole**" at the very base of the mountain. The only way to get there is to clamber along the river bed itself, an exercise that is fraught with danger and very likely to end in failure. At best, it's likely to involve wading chest-deep against a strong current for up to an hour. At worst, when there's been heavy rain – which is virtually always, but especially in springtime – it's simply impossible. Do not attempt to make the hike without first calling the state parks office (ⓣ274-3444) for advice.

## The Kuilau Ridge and Moalepe trails

Two further, less demanding trails traverse the upland forests above Kapa'a, leading through a rural landscape scattered with pink and purple blossoms and alive with birdsong. Each is a four-mile round-trip, but since they meet in the middle, you can combine the two if you arrange to be picked up at the opposite end from which you started.

A short way back down towards Wailua from Keahou Arboretum (see opposite), a dirt road signed as the **Kuilau Ridge Trail** leads north from Hwy-580. As the name suggests, it climbs up the gradual slope of Kuilau Ridge, with views of Wai'ale'ale away to the left, and the Kamali'i Ridge of the Makaleha Mountains ahead. For much of the way it runs through dense tropical foliage, with flashes of color provided by bright-red, raspberry-like thimbleberries, *'ōhi'a lehua* blossoms down in the gullies, and a rich panoply of orchids. Not far beyond the picnic area that marks its halfway point, the trail rises sufficiently to let you see all the way to Līhu'e.

After just over two miles – perhaps 45 minutes of hiking – the trail seems to double back sharply on itself from a small clearing. In fact, as a very inconspicuous sign informs you, this is officially the end. Straight ahead of you is the highest, straightest segment of the Makaleha Mountains. A tiny footpath continues for a couple of hundred yards along the crest of Kuilau Ridge. You can push your way through the thorny undergrowth to get a few more views, including down to Kapa'a to your right, but it gradually gets more and more impenetrable. There is, in any case, no outlet to the hills.

You can also reach this point by following the **Moalepe Trail**, which leads from the top of the straight section of Olohena Road, six miles up from Kūhiō Highway. Park where the road turns to dirt, with one of its two tracks curving off north. It might look possible to drive the first few hundred yards of the trail, but it soon gets very rugged, by which time it's too narrow to turn around. Coming from this direction, too, the mountains confront you like a solid wall. You climb steadily, but the main ridge remains always on your right, and you never get near the summit. After half an hour the road becomes steep and rutted, but you're unlikely to lose your way; at the one confusing point, take the steeper option, towards the hills. At times, the ridge you're on has sheer drops to either side, but you're rarely aware of it: the vegetation is thick enough to meet up overhead in places, so you can't really see out. The clearing described above comes after around an hour's hiking, just beyond a final arduous climb.





# Northeast Kauai

Once north of Kapa'a, the main highway stops running along the shoreline; it barely returns to sea level until Hanalei on the North Shore, twenty miles on. That leaves **Northeast Kauai** largely undisturbed by visitors. It is, in any case, sparsely inhabited, in part because it bears the full brunt of the trade winds and winter high seas. However, there are some spots where making your way down to the shore is rewarded by fine and often deserted beaches, though few are safe for swimming.

## Donkey Beach

You can't see **Donkey Beach** from the highway, but the first beach north of Keālia can be reached via a simple half-mile downhill trail. Look out for parked cars just over half a mile beyond mile marker 11 and close to a blue emergency call box. Nearby, the path sets off through the ironwoods. Traditionally, this was plantation country, to which the sugar growers strove to restrict access; nowadays there's no difficulty about using the trail, though its precise legal status remains unclear. The beach is named after the donkeys that formerly hauled cane here, and were left to graze nearby for much of the year.

By the time you get to the crescent beach, curving north of Palikū Point, the tree cover has thinned out. The final slope is carpeted with white-flowered *naupaka*, a creeping cross between an ivy and a lily, and there's no shade on the sands. The surf created by the steep drop-off attracts skilled surfers, but makes Donkey Beach unsafe for swimming. Instead it's a popular spot for nude sunbathing, and is now known (not exclusively) as a gay hangout, though there have been reports of some anti-gay intimidation by local teenagers. (Note that nudity is illegal on all Hawaii's beaches, and the Kauai Police Department have a policy of enforcing that law.)

## Anahola

Beyond Kapa'a, it's not possible to turn right from Kūhiō Highway until just after the 13-mile marker, where a side road heads straight down to the sea then doglegs north. **Anahola Beach County Park** lies almost immediately below.

The park is the southernmost stretch of the spellbinding curve of sand that rims Anahola Bay, sheltered by Kahala Point and therefore safe for family swimming (except in winter). Surfing is forbidden at this end, but boogie-boarders and surfers are free to enjoy the rest of the bay. There's no picnic pavilion or snack bar, but rest rooms and showers are located among the palms.

Anahola has long been the focus of great controversy. Most of the area is set aside as Hawaiian Homelands, to provide affordable housing for native Hawaiians, but state authorities interpret that to mean that they can sell basic homes to anyone with at least half-Hawaiian blood for $98,000. Such sums are beyond the means of those locals who have lived at the beach for many years. The bitterness aroused by their lawsuits was compounded by a flood in 1991 that destroyed many properties. Although the beach here is a pleasant and trouble-free place to spend the day, the campground is not recommended. If you really want to stay there, contact the county camping office in Līhu'e (see p.426).

Away from the beach, Anahola holds little to entice tourists, though the **Anahola Baptist Church**, set against a green mountain backdrop *mauka* of the highway, is worth a photograph. Nearby, just after the road crosses Ka'alua Stream, a tiny cluster of stores includes *Duane's Ono Char Burger* (daily 10am–6pm; ⓣ822-9181), where you can eat beefburgers under a spreading monkey-pod tree. Variations include "Local Girls" and "Local Boys" burgers; the distinction is in the cheese.

The only **accommodation** around is an extremely sophisticated Japanese-style B&B, *Mahina Kai* (PO Box 699, 4933 'Aliomanu Rd, Anahola HI 96703; ⓣ822-9451 or 1-800/337-1134, ⓕ822-9451, ⓦwww.vantage21st.com/mahina; three-night minimum stay; ❹). A couple of miles down a quiet side road that leads off the highway at mile marker 14, this lovely property perches above long, narrow 'Aliomanu Beach. Its well-kept gardens boast a ruined *heiau*. In addition to three tasteful bedrooms, the main house offers living and meeting rooms for "executive retreats"; a separate guest cottage, with kitchen, sleeps up to four. There's a pool and hot tub, and mountain bikes and snorkeling equipment are provided for guests.

## Moloa'a Bay and Larsen's Beach

**Ko'olau Road**, a minor but passable road that cuts off a large bend in the highway from the fruit stand half a mile south of mile marker 17 until shortly before mile marker 20, provides access to a couple of little-known beaches.

First comes the beach at **Moloa'a Bay**, accessible via Moloa'a Road, a right turn roughly a mile along. This road winds through verdant scenery to the unromantic remains of a long-abandoned sugar town. The deeply indented bay here is aligned so directly towards the trade winds that for most of the year it might as well not be sheltered at all. It's a pretty and very sandy spot, though, and in quiet periods the swimming and snorkeling can be excellent.

**Larsen's Beach**, further along, is most quickly reached from the north end of Ko'olau Road. Slightly over a mile down from there, a dirt road leads *makai* for a mile, leaving you with a five-minute walk at the end; access has been made deliberately difficult to spare the beach from overuse. Named after a former manager of Kīlauea Plantation who had a beachfront home here, Larsen's Beach is a stretch of perfect sand that runs for over a mile, interrupted in the middle by Pākala Point. Once again swimming is not recommended, this time because it's so shallow and rocky this side of the reef, though snorkeling is sometimes possible. At low tide, local families wade out to the edge of the reef to gather the edible red seaweed known as *limu kohu*.

# The North Shore

Kauai's **North Shore** may be the most astonishingly beautiful place you will ever see. If photographs of stunning Pacific landscapes – sheer green cliffs rippling with subtle variations of shade and light, and pristine valleys bursting with tropical vegetation – are what enticed you to come to Hawaii, this is where to find the real thing. On all the Hawaiian islands, the north and northeastern shores, being the most exposed to the ocean winds and rain, offer spectacular eroded scenery. As the oldest island, Kauai's coastline has had that much longer to be sculpted into fabulous formations, surpassing anything else in the state.

The **Nā Pali coast**, at the western end of the North Shore, is the most dramatic stretch. Its name literally means "the cliffs," but it's often spoken of in quasi-religious awe as "the Cathedral." Though inaccessible by car, it can be seen from offshore boats, up close along a superb hiking trail, from high above in Kōke'e Park (see p.496), or from helicopter sightseeing flights.

Thanks to high rainfall and local resistance to the expansion of tourism, Kauai's northern coast is far less developed than its east and south shores. **Princeville** has grown to become a faceless clifftop resort, albeit redeemed by the sublime views from its most expensive hotels. Beyond Princeville you reach sea level by crossing the first of a succession of single-lane bridges, which serve to slow down not merely the traffic but the whole pace of life. **Hanalei Bay** is a ravishing mountain-framed crescent, home to the funky town of **Hanalei**, while the ten verdant miles to the end of the road are lined by beach after gorgeous beach.

For the sake of clarity, this book follows the highway from east to west. In reality, however, almost every visitor presses on nonstop to Hanalei, and you're more likely to explore the area around Kīlauea and Kalihiwai as you head back.

## Kīlauea

The North Shore is commonly reckoned to start at Kauai's northernmost point, **KĪLAUEA**. Nine miles out of Anahola, a *makai* turn at a gas station leads from Kūhiō Highway past the small Kong Lung mall and two miles on to

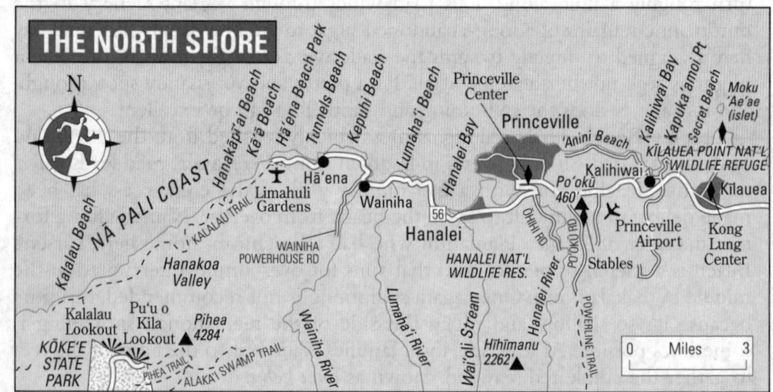

**Kīlauea Point**. This lonely promontory shares its name, which means "much spewing," with the active volcano on the Big Island, but here the reference is to crashing waves, not erupting lava. When it was built, in 1913, the 52-foot **lighthouse** at its tip boasted the largest clamshell lens in the world. The red-capped white shaft still stands proud, but it's no longer in use, having been supplanted by the otherwise inconspicuous fourteen-foot tower just beyond.

The lighthouse is now the focus of the **Kīlauea Point National Wildlife Refuge** (daily 10am–4pm; $2; National Parks passes accepted), which protects such soaring Pacific seabirds as albatrosses, frigate birds, and red- and white-tailed tropic birds. Thanks to a vigorous anti-development campaign, the refuge has since 1988 extended four miles east to Mōkōlea Point, while Moku'ae'ae Island just offshore is set aside for nesting. Displays in the visitor center near the lighthouse explain the natural history in great detail. Every morning, rangers lead guided one-hour hikes to the summit of Crater Hill for an overview of the whole area; reservations are essential (daily 10am; no additional charge; ⓣ828-0168).

### Practicalities

Kīlauea abounds in freshly grown tropical fruit, with the orchards of the Guava Kai farm rising *mauka* of the highway. If you fancy something more than fruit from the local stands, the **Kong Lung Center**, half a mile off the highway, is your best bet. Tucked into the center's garden courtyard is the *Kīlauea Bakery & Pau Hana Pizza* (Mon–Sat 6.30am–9pm; ⓣ828-2020), a friendly café-cum-bakery. It serves fresh breads and pastries to early risers, and then from 11am on, pizza (spiced up with smoked *ono* or tiger prawns) by the $3 slice. Its closest neighbor, the *Lighthouse Bistro* (daily 11.30am–2pm & 5–9.30pm; ⓣ828-0480), is a bit more formal, offering Italian-influenced food with an island twist. Lunchtime sandwiches and wraps cost under $10, while evening entrees like mango cherry chicken are $17–26.

## Kalihiwai

As you drive along the highway, it's easy to pass through **KALIHIWAI**, a couple of miles west of Kīlauea, without noticing anything more than a high bridge spanning a valley. Glancing to either side at this curve is a bit of a risk, but reveals glimpses of a pretty bay to the north, and a tumbling waterfall off to the south.

Until a *tsunami* whisked away another bridge, lower down near the sea, it was possible to loop off the highway, look at the beach, and climb back up on the far side. **Kalihiwai Road** still exists, but with the bridge gone it now consists of two entirely separate segments, on either side of the river. Its eastern end is no longer marked; look out for the *makai* turning just short of milepost 24. The people who venture down here nowadays tend to know exactly where they're going and prefer to keep it to themselves.

### Secret Beach

Long, golden **Secret Beach** – officially, Kauapea Beach – is one of Kauai's finest-looking strands of sand. It's "secret" partly because it's not visible from any road – in fact you barely see it before you step onto it – and partly because, despite the opposition of local landowners, it has become a center for campers and nudists.

To get there, turn first onto the eastern half of Kalihiwai Road, as described above. Very soon after leaving the highway, Kalihiwai Road curves sharply to the left; turn right immediately beyond the bend to follow a reasonably well-surfaced dirt road through a deep cutting of raw, red earth. From a simple parking lot a few hundred yards down, a footpath skirts the edge of the hilltop, with fine homes to one side and a barbed-wire fence to the other, then drops down a steep but safe gully to the beach. Where tree roots aren't available to help your footing, logs have been embedded in the earth to form crude steps. You'll hear the crashing surf well before you see the sea.

The path emerges at an inlet set slightly back from the ocean. From rocky Kapuka'amoi Point, immediately to your left, the beach runs east for just over half a mile towards Kīlauea Point, with the lighthouse at its tip. Depending on the season, it's either a magnificent expanse of coarse-grained yellow sand or, as winter progresses, a narrow, shelving ribbon battered by immense surf.

Even in its more placid moods, Secret Beach is not a particularly safe place to take a swim, but a long stroll is irresistible. Spinner dolphins can often be seen just offshore, while at the far end a waterfall cascades down the cliffs. You'll probably pass a handful of meditating nudists and would-be yogis scattered among the palms and fallen coconuts (though you should bear in mind that Kauai's police can and do arrest nude sunbathers here). Depending on whether local authorities have cracked down recently, the beach often also holds sizeable numbers of semi-permanent campers, some in clapped-out vans and rusting hulks, and some content with makeshift bivouacs.

On the grassy slopes above the beach is *Secret Beach Hideaway,* whose umbrella name covers three lavishly equipped one-bedroom cottages sharing spacious gardens, and two full-sized houses. All may be rented through Hawaii's Best B&B (Ⓣ 885-4550 or 1-800/262-9912, Ⓕ 885-0559, Ⓦ www.bestbnb.com; cottages ❽, houses ❾).

## Kalihiwai Beach

**Kalihiwai Beach** is at the point where Kalihiwai Road is cut in two, a mile or so down from the highway. It spreads beneath you as the road rounds its final sweeping curve, an exquisite little crescent that manages to hang on to its sand year-round. Residential properties line the *mauka* side of the road, but you can park in the shade of the high ironwoods rooted in the sand itself.

Surfers congregate below the cliffs to the east, while boogie-boarders and body-surfers ride into the heart of the beach, where the waves break across a broad sandbar. Rinse off the salt at the mouth of the Kalihiwai River, the put-in point for kayakers heading upstream (see below). There's hardly any sand on the far side of the river, at the end of the other half of the severed road.

*Hale Ho'o Maha* (PO Box 422, Kīlauea HI 96754; Ⓣ 828-1341 or 1-800/851-0291, Ⓕ 828-2046, aloha.net/~hoomaha; ❷–❸) is a four-bedroom **B&B** set on a small hill to the left of Kalihiwai Road, across from a waterfall and less than half a mile down from the highway. Each room in the split-level house is named after a tropical fruit; two are en suite, two share a bath, and all have phones and TV.

## Kalihiwai Falls

Whether or not you succeed in reaching **Kalihiwai Falls**, the broad waterfall visible from the highway bridge, it's worth making your way down to the meadows that fringe the riverbanks. Park just short of the bridge on the *makai* side, cross the road with care, and you should be able to spot a muddy trail plummeting down the hillside.

The short drop into the valley involves clambering over fallen trees and hacking through giant spiders' webs. Once out on the flood plain, you join a dirt road that meanders through bucolic fields before curving back to meet the river. If you want to go any farther than this tranquil little dell filled with songbirds, make sure you're not wearing or carrying anything you wouldn't want to get wet. The only way forward is to wade into the river and head upstream. The rocks underfoot are green and slimy, amorphous amphibians scuttle in and out of the water as you approach, and the undergrowth on either bank seems impenetrable, but it's a lovely place. With luck, you'll spot the often-overgrown trail that climbs the far bank. That soon leads to the falls, which consist of two separate cascades bubbling over a broad slope of exposed rock. If you haven't found the trail within a few hundred yards, you'll probably be forced to turn back, as the river grows progressively deeper.

Other ways to reach the falls include **kayaking** up the river from the beach, or **riding** down on horseback, through the woods up top (Princeville Ranch Stables offers tours; see p.452.)

## 'Anini Beach

Superb beaches come thick and fast as you continue along the North Shore. Turn right on the other branch of Kalihiwai Road, as the highway climbs west of the bridge, and fork left after a couple of hundred yards to find yourself back down at sea level skirting a gorgeous long strip of yellow sand known as **'Anini Beach**. (It was originally called Wanini Beach, but the "W" broke off a sign many years ago, and the new name stuck.) No signs give the faintest inkling that the beach is here, but the road winds on for a full three miles, before reaching a dead end below Princeville.

All the way along, the beach is paralleled a couple of hundred yards out to sea by one of the longest reefs in the state. Coral reefs take millions of years to form, so it's not surprising that Hawaii's largest are in the oldest region of its oldest island. This one shields an expanse of shallow, clear turquoise water that offers some of the safest swimming on the North Shore. Snorkelers and scuba divers explore the reef; if it's calm enough, you can peek at the huge drop-off beyond its outer edge. Other than during winter surf, the only area to avoid is around the outlet of the 'Anini Stream at the western end, which is plagued by treacherous currents that sweep out through a gap in the reef. The inshore area is a good place to learn to **windsurf**, but surfing and boogie-boarding are largely precluded by the jagged coral where the waves break.

'Anini was once reserved as a fishing ground of the kings of Kauai, and it's still one of Kauai's most exclusive residential areas. That explains the **polo field** on the *mauka* side of the road, used by locals such as Sylvester Stallone; ponies graze nearby all week, and you might see a game of a Sunday afternoon. The almond trees on the beach side, however, shelter one of Kauai's best **campgrounds**, fully equipped with showers, rest rooms and picnic pavilions. Reservations can be made through the county parks office in Līhu'e (see p.426).

## Po'okū

Roughly halfway between Princeville Airport and the Princeville resort itself, small, paved Po'okū Road runs off from the highway and into the hills. This area, officially known as Po'okū, was once the site of an important *heiau*, but now there's barely a building to be seen.

Princeville Ranch Stables (Ⓣ826-6777 or 826-7473, Ⓦwww.princevilleranch.com) operates horseback riding tours from its headquarters just up from the turnoff. Choices include four-hour picnic trips to the top of Kalihiwai Falls (Mon–Sat 9.30am, 11am & noon; $110 per person), a three-hour ride to ʻAnini Beach (Mon–Sat 9am; $100), and a ninety-minute jaunt into Hanalei Valley (Mon–Sat 10am & 12.30pm; $55).

### The Powerline Trail

Apart from horseback riding, the main reason to head to Poʻokū is to hike the thirteen-mile **Powerline Trail**, the broad dirt track that starts two miles down Poʻokū Road. This was built for the local electricity company, whose cables stretch from pylon to pylon through the little-known interior of Kauai, but hikers are free to walk along it. Even if you just go a couple of miles rather than all the way to Keahou Arboretum (see p.444), it offers an easy and painless way to see high waterfalls and glorious flowers, without having to make any steep ascents. Starting with sweeping views of Hanalei Valley, it runs for most of its route along the crest of a ridge that parallels the Hanalei River.



## Princeville

Though the main center for tourism on the North Shore, **PRINCEVILLE** is not exactly a town; it's too short of shops, public amenities, or even a permanent population. Instead it's a "planned resort community" consisting of neat rows of quasi-suburban vacation homes mixed in with a few larger condo complexes, two golf courses and a couple of luxury hotels. The general sense of placid domesticity is somehow heightened by the fact that the whole place is overlooked by the magnificent mountain wilderness that fills the western horizon.

Princeville stands on a well-watered plateau that abuts Hanalei Bay to the west and the open ocean to the north. Once this was the site of a sprawling grove of *hala* (pandanus) trees. In contrast to the common farming lands of Hanalei Valley below, it served as a residential area for the island's elite.

Soon after Europeans arrived on the island, the Russian-backed German adventurer **George Schäffer** renamed this district "Schäffertal" and constructed the short-lived **Fort Alexander** on the Puʻu Pōā headland now occupied by the *Princeville Hotel*. The general outline of the fort is still discernible on the lawn near the main hotel entrance. In its centre, a small pavilion holds explanatory displays and enjoys superb views across the bay to Lumahaʻi Beach and beyond. (For more on the bizarre Dr Schäffer, who was also responsible for Waimea's Fort Elizabeth, see p.486.)

In the 1830s, the British consul **Richard Charlton** leased most of the land between Kīlauea and Hanalei to pasture a herd of one hundred cattle. He failed to pay his rent, however, and after the Great Mahele (see p.512), **Robert Crichton Wyllie,** Hawaii's Foreign Minister for twenty years, acquired the land. Wyllie built an overambitious sugar mill beside the Hanalei River, equipped with machinery imported from his native Scotland. He was visited in 1860 by King Kamehameha IV, Queen Emma and the young Prince Albert. The name "Princeville," adopted in Albert's honor, has stuck ever since, although Albert died two years later at the age of four. Just four months after Wyllie died in 1865, his nephew and heir committed suicide upon realizing that he had inherited a mountain of debt.

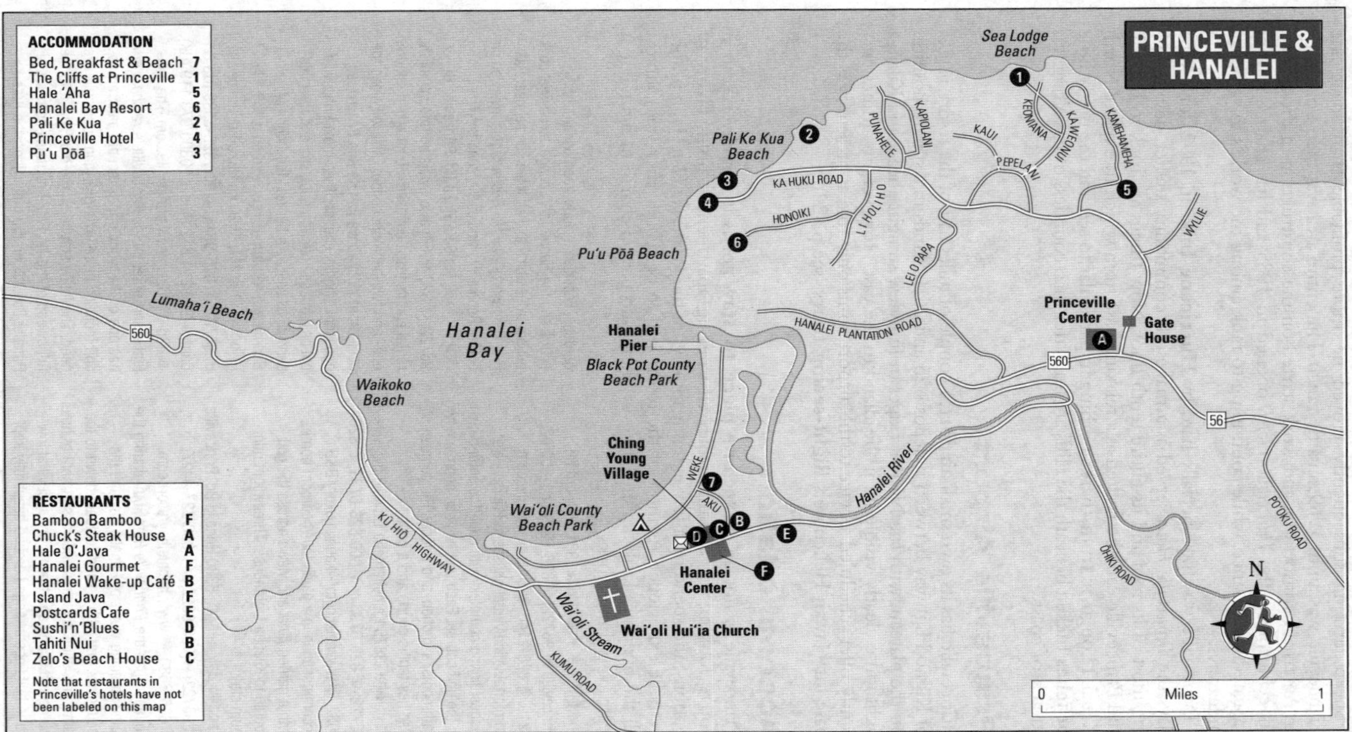
PRINCEVILLE & HANALEI
ACCOMMODATION
Bed, Breakfast & Beach 7
The Cliffs at Princeville 1
Hale 'Aha 5
Hanalei Bay Resort 6
Pali Ke Kua 2
Princeville Hotel 4
Pu'u Pōā 3
RESTAURANTS
Bamboo Bamboo F
Chuck's Steak House A
Hale O'Java A
Hanalei Gourmet F
Hanalei Wake-up Café B
Island Java F
Postcards Cafe E
Sushi'n'Blues D
Tahiti Nui B
Zelo's Beach House C
Note that restaurants in Princeville's hotels have not been labeled on this map
Sea Lodge Beach
Pali Ke Kua Beach
Pu'u Pōā Beach
Lumaha'i Beach
Hanalei Bay
Hanalei Pier
Black Pot County Beach Park
Waikoko Beach
Ching Young Village
Wai'oli County Beach Park
Hanalei Center
Wai'oli Hui'ia Church
Wai'oli Stream
Hanalei River
Princeville Center
Gate House
KA HUKU ROAD
HONOIKI
LI HOLIHO
PUNAHELE
KAPIOLANI
KAUI
PEPELANI
KEONIANA
KAWEONUI
KAMEHAMEHA
WYLLIE
LEI O PAPA
HANALEI PLANTATION ROAD
WEKE
AKU
KŪ HIŌ HIGHWAY
KUMU ROAD
ŌHIKI ROAD
PO'OKU ROAD
560
56
N
0 Miles 1

Sheep farming subsequently proved no more profitable than sugar, and Princeville was, until 1969, a cattle ranch. The entire area was then bought by an American consortium, and work started on the construction of the **resort**. Its centerpiece, the *Princeville Hotel*, opened in 1985 and has changed hands repeatedly ever since, while continuing to rank among the world's top tropical hideaways.

Princeville was hit especially hard by **Hurricane Iniki** in 1992; for several days the *Princeville Hotel* served as a makeshift community shelter, despite losing most of its roof and its entire tenth floor. Now things are back to normal, and Princeville can't be faulted as a relaxing base from which to explore North Kauai. Though, in truth, there's nothing in particular to see, and the pretty little **beaches** tucked beneath the cliffs are no better than countless others along this stretch of coast.

## Princeville Airport

Princeville has its own small **airport**, a couple of miles east of the resort, *mauka* of Kūhiō Highway between mileposts 25 and 26. It stands in a superb position on the plateau, with the Nā Pali ridges in full view straight ahead, and Kīlauea lighthouse clearly visible on its headland to the east. However, no airlines currently offer scheduled service to the airport, so its only role at present is as the base for Hawaii Helicopters **flight-seeing tours** (see p.422).

## Accommodation

Princeville is not an inexpensive **place to stay**, nor is it very lively. But if you're looking for a comfortable self-catering apartment it holds plenty of options, and spending a few extravagant days in the *Princeville Hotel* is an unforgettable experience. As most of the resort had to be rebuilt after Iniki, almost all the buildings look newer than ever; there's no period charm in sight, but at least everything works.

**The Cliffs at Princeville**, 3811 Edward Rd, Princeville HI 96722; ⓣ 826-6219 or 1-800/622-6219, ⓕ 826-2140, ⓦ cliffs-princeville.com. Comfortable individual houses in Princeville's biggest condo complex, with a clifftop setting next to the golf course. Each unit has one bedroom, two bathrooms, a kitchen, and a *lānai*. The complex also has tennis courts and a pool. ⑤–⑥.

**Hale 'Aha**, 3875 Kamehameha Drive, Princeville HI 96722; ⓣ 826-6733 or 1-800/826-6733, ⓕ 826-9052, ⓦ www.pixi.com/~kauai. Luxury B&B accommodation in a plush four-bedroom home, with a garden *lānai* and views across the golf course to Kīlauea Lighthouse. Three-night minimum stay. ③–⑥.

**Hanalei Bay Resort**, 5380 Honoiki Rd, Princeville HI 96722; ⓣ 826-6522 or 1-800/827-4427, ⓕ 826-6680, ⓦ www.hanaleibayresort.com. Cheaper than the *Princeville Hotel*, but sharing the same stunning views of Hanalei Bay and the mountains, and with a short footpath down to the same irresistible beach. A wide assortment of hotel rooms and condo apartments are in several low-slung buildings arranged around beautifully kept gardens. Facilities include free floodlit tennis courts and the *Happy Talk Lounge*, a convivial cocktail bar from which to watch the sun set over Bali Hai. The resort's *Bali Hai Restaurant* is reviewed on p.456. Rooms ⑤, studios ⑥, condos ⑧.

**Pali Ke Kua**, 5300 Ka Huku Rd, Princeville HI 96722; ⓣ 826-9066; also available through all the rental agents listed opposite. Roughly one hundred one- and two-bedroom condos, arrayed along the oceanfront cliffs above Pali Ke Kua Beach (see opposite). Slightly cheaper than most Princeville options, but still offering pool, spa and full maid service, as well as a bar and the *Winds of Beamreach* restaurant, reviewed on p.456. ⑤–⑥.

**Princeville Hotel**, 5520 Ka Huku Rd, Princeville HI 96722; ⓣ 826-9644, 1-800/325-3589 (US & Can), 1-800/814 812 (Aus) or 0800/973 119 (UK), ⓕ 826-1166, ⓦ www.princeville.com. The opulent resort hotel that is Princeville's *raison d'être* has one of the world's most scenic panoramas, and facilities more luxurious than you could ever need. The lobby stands on the bluff, open to the full sweep of the Nā Pali mountains across Hanalei Bay. It's on the ninth floor; the hotel

## Rental Agencies

Shopping around for a **vacation apartment to rent** in Princeville is an unpredictable business. As a rule, the owner of each individual house or apartment is free to let the property through whichever agent they wish, so you may find identical lodgings at widely differing rates.

Reckon on spending anything upwards of $100 per day for a one- or two-bedroom place, more like $200 for three bedrooms. You can expect discounts for longer stays amounting to roughly one "free" day per week. Most condos charge around $50 for (obligatory) once-weekly cleaning, and considerably more for daily service. Note that many of these agents also rent properties in the Hanalei area, as well as further along the North Shore.

**Hanalei North Shore Properties**, Princeville Center, PO Box 607, Hanalei HI 96714; Ⓣ826-9622 or 1-800/488-3336, Ⓕ826-1188, Ⓦplanet-hawaii.com/visit-kauai.

**Kauai Paradise Vacations**, PO Box 1080, Hanalei HI 96714; Ⓣ826-7444 or 1-800/826-7782, Ⓕ826-7673, Ⓦplanet-hawaii.com/paradise/kauai.

**Marc Resorts Hawaii**, 2155 Kalakaua Ave, no. 706, Honolulu HI 96815-2351; Ⓣ922-9700 or 1-800/535-0085, Ⓕ922-2421 or 1-800/633-5085, Ⓦwww.marcresorts.com.

**Paradise Vacation Rentals**, PO Box 3347, Princeville HI 96722; Ⓣ826-6244, Ⓦwww.vacationkauai.com.

drops down the hillside in three tiers, with the pool and lovely Pu'u Pōā Beach (see p.456) accessible from the first floor of the lowest building. Some guest rooms are angled towards the inland mountains rather than the bay; few have *lānais*, and in the rest you can't even open the windows. From down below, the *Princeville Hotel* is far from attractive; its architects were obliged to keep it as inconspicuous as possible to avoid environmental offence. ❾.

**Pu'u Pōā**, 5454 Ka Huku Rd, Princeville HI 96722; Ⓣ826-9602. Available through all the rental agents listed above. One of the smallest and most upmarket of Princeville's condo complexes. The fifty mostly two-bedroom units are very well-equipped and share a pool and tennis courts. ❹.

## The resort and its beaches

Not far west of milepost 27, just beyond the marked approach road to Princeville proper, the **Princeville Center** mall stands *makai* of Kūhiō Highway. Shielded from the road by orange *lehua* trees, it's a small cluster of low buildings arranged around separate courtyards and ringed by shady *lānais*. Apart from the Foodland supermarket, and the snack bars and restaurants described below, the main business of the mall is **real estate**. It does, however, hold the small Akamai Computers' **internet café** (Mon–Fri 9am–5pm; Ⓣ826-1042, Ⓦwww.akamaicomputers.com). Incidentally, the Princeville Center's Chevron gas station is the last before the end of the road.

The quietest and most secluded **beaches** in Princeville face north from the foot of the headland. That exposed position ensures that in winter the surf is too high for swimming and can obliterate the beaches altogether. At other times, however, stay within the reef and you can swim and snorkel safely. The three main alternatives are similar, each five to ten minutes' walk from the town along cliffside footpaths and stairways that can be slippery after rain.

Working from east to west, the first is **SeaLodge Beach**. One route down starts at the western edge of the ugly *SeaLodge* condo complex, but access is easier if you continue along the driveway at the end of Keoniana Road, then drop through some of Princeville's few surviving *hala* trees. Next comes the **Queen's Beach**, where there's little sand, but you can bathe in natural lava pools; it's reached by a meandering path off Kapiolani Road. **Pali Ke Kua**

**Beach**, also known as **Hideaways** (especially by surfers), lies at the end of a path from the tennis courts of the *Pali Ke Kua* condos (see p.454), not far from the *Princeville Hotel*. Two distinct patches of sand nestle in the rocks, and the snorkeling is great in summer, when you stand a good chance of spotting turtles, dolphins and even monk seals.

Larger, sandier **Pu'u Pōā Beach**, below the *Princeville Hotel*, lies around the corner within Hanalei Bay. Set at the edge of a marsh that still holds vestiges of an ancient fishpond, it commands lovely views of the rising Nā Pali ridges. The inshore swimming and snorkeling is good; further out the waves get much higher. This is a perfect spot to watch surfers swirling and plummeting at the mouth of the bay. Access – as ever – is open to all, though the only facilities, back from the sea, are reserved for hotel guests (who can rent surfboards, kayaks and other equipment). Walk a short way south to reach the Hanalei River, which should be shallow enough for you to wade across to Black Pot Beach County Park (see p.459). Hanalei itself is not far beyond.



## Restaurants

All the hotel **restaurants** listed below are happy to welcome nonguests, but the only place where you can browse menus looking for a bite to eat is in the Princeville Center, next to the highway.

**Bali Hai Restaurant**, *Hanalei Bay Resort*, 5380 Honoiki Rd; ⓣ826-6522. Roomy, cool restaurant under an enormous *hala*-thatched roof, with superb views across a lagoon-style pool to Hanalei Bay and within earshot of the live jazz performed most evenings in the adjoining *Happy Talk Lounge*. Breakfast and lunch tend to be unenthralling hotel food, but the dinner menu has acquired a definite Pacific Rim tinge of late, with *sashimi* and blackened *ahi* on the list of appetizers ($12–15), and an assortment of Asian-influenced fresh fish entrees at around $25. You can still get traditional steak preparations for $18–32, however. Daily 7–11am, 11.30am–2pm & 5.30–9.30pm.

**Café Hanalei**, *Princeville Hotel*, 5520 Ka Huku Rd; ⓣ826-9644. The less formal option at the *Princeville Hotel*, with a great view and open daily for all meals. The overpriced buffet breakfasts ($16 continental, $22 full) and light salad lunches are nothing special, but the Pacific Rim-style dinners are consistently good, and Japanese alternatives, including sushi, are always available. Typical entrees such as steamed snapper or broiled eel cost $30. There's also a magnificent $44 seafood buffet on Friday, and a $34 champagne brunch on Sunday. Daily 6.30am–2.30pm & 5.30–9.30pm.

**Chuck's Steak House**, Princeville Center; ⓣ826-6211. The largest and most conventional of the Princeville Center places. It's open for burger and sandwich lunches, and full dinners, when entrees of steak, chicken, ribs or fish cost around $20. Cocktails are available all day, and there's live Hawaiian music on Thursday, Friday, and Saturday evenings. Mon–Fri 11.30am–2.30pm & 6–10pm, Sat & Sun 6–10pm.

**Hale O'Java**, Princeville Center; ⓣ826-7255. Light and open deli-style café in the central courtyard of the Princeville Center, with a large *lānai* but no views. Good lunch sandwiches, most with an Italian feel, are $6–8; in the evening, pizzas and salads for more like $10 are also served. Coffees, juices and pastries are available all day. There's live Hawaiian music on Sunday afternoons. Daily 6.30am–9pm.

**La Cascata**, *Princeville Hotel*, 5520 Ka Huku Rd; ⓣ826-9644. Smart, romantic resort restaurant, serving fine Italian cooking with Pacific ingredients. The menu features inexpensive soups and salads, even a cheeseburger, but for a full meal you'll pay around $40 a head for the food alone. Among the appetizers are fresh Manila clams for $16, while main dishes (about $30) include fire-roasted rack of lamb and grilled swordfish. Go early for a view of the sun setting over Bali Hai. Daily 6–10pm.

**Winds of Beamreach**, *Pali Ke Kua*, 5300 Ka Huku Rd; ⓣ826-6143. The popular but uninspiring restaurant of the *Pali Ke Kua* condos. Appetizers include steamed clams and *sashimi*, while the entrees are a predictable assortment of steaks and scampi; a full meal will cost about $30 per person. Daily 5.30–9.30pm.

# Hanalei

With its perfect semicircular curve, fronted by tumbling white surf, fringed with coconut palms and yellow sand, and backed by jagged green peaks, **Hanalei Bay** is a strong candidate for the most beautiful bay in Hawaii. An easy thirty-mile drive from Līhu'e, it's not exactly inaccessible, but other than the *Princeville Hotel*, peeking down from the east, it has so far been spared major development.

The local will to resist change is greatly aided by the fact that the Hanalei River, which meanders its way into the eastern side of the bay, can only be crossed by means of a flimsy single-lane bridge. What's more, this is just the first of seven similar bridges before the end of the road: so long as attempts to widen or replace them can be thwarted, the North Shore should remain unspoiled. Even its largest community, **Hanalei** itself, is a tiny affair, surviving partly on traditional agriculture and partly on tourism, which includes arranging and provisioning Nā Pali expeditions of all kinds.

Until the Hanalei was bridged in 1912, all travelers, along with their horses and baggage, were hauled across the river on a raft, guided by ropes suspended between a mango tree on one side and a plum tree on the other. The flood plain on the west still constitutes one of the largest surviving **wetland** areas in the state. Ancient Hawaiians waded knee-deep in gooey *lo'i* (see p.517) in order to grow *taro* to make into *poi*. Later attempts to cultivate sugar or coffee were unsuccessful, but for almost a century most of the valley was given over to the paddy fields of generations of Chinese and Japanese immigrants. Now, however, it has reverted to *taro* production, and the landscape and its fauna are returning to their original state.

Keep in mind that when driving on the North Shore, if an oncoming vehicle is crossing a narrow bridge towards you, you're expected to allow up to three or four cars behind it to cross as well.

## Accommodation

To the casual visitor, Hanalei seems to hold very little **accommodation** indeed. In the absence of hotels or condos, the only other available lodging is likely to be back in Princeville, or at the *Hanalei Colony Resort* further down the coast (see p.462). For short-term stays, with a minimum of two days or more, the only possibility is a room at one of the two **B&B** properties run by Carolyn Barnes (PO Box 748, Hanalei HI 96714; ⓣ826-6111, ⓦwww.bestofhawaii.com/hanalei). *Bed, Breakfast & Beach* offers three separate rooms (❸), each with bath en suite , in a well-furnished private home, plus a detached two-bedroom cottage (❹). The property is just back from the center of the beach near the foot of Aku Road. Carolyn also offers plusher B&B suites in the *Plantation Guest House* (❹), slightly further down the highway.

In addition, a high proportion of the homes in Hanalei can be rented by the week through agencies such as those listed on p.455. *Hanalei North Shore Properties* (ⓣ826-9622 or 1-800/488-3336) has a particularly broad range.

## Hanalei National Wildlife Refuge

Immediately west of Princeville, just before Kūhiō Highway drops towards the river, an overlook on its *mauka* side offers the best view you can get of the full expanse of Hanalei Valley. The flat valley floor stretches west to the bay and south into the hills, crisscrossed by channels that create a green and brown patchwork of fields. As it curves its way around Hīhīmanu ("Beautiful") Mountain, the Hanalei River nestles between gentle grass slopes.

Most of what you can see belongs to the **Hanalei National Wildlife Refuge**. Hawaii's natural wetlands have dwindled to cover just five percent of their former area, and the population of waterbirds has declined in step. By helping farmers to reintroduce *taro*, the refuge provides an ideal habitat for waterbirds. The birds feed in the young *taro* patches, find shelter in the plants as they grow, and eventually breed on the mud flats and islands that appear during the annual cycle of planting, irrigation and harvesting. Among the indigenous species here are the *'alae 'ula,* the Hawaiian gallinule or mud hen, with its yellow-tipped red beak, seen March through August; the *'alae ke'o ke'o,* or Hawaiian coot, seen March through September; the *koloa maoli*, Hawaiian duck, seen December through May; and the *ae'o,* or Hawaiian black-necked stilt, with its long red legs, which nests between March and July. The river itself holds introduced and native fishes, such as the *o'opu* or native goby, and shrimp.

You'll get a close-up look at the valley as you cross the bridge down below. Turn left as soon as you're over and you can drive for a couple of miles along Ōhiki Road, but venturing into the refuge is forbidden. Sadly, all hiking trails in Hanalei Valley have been closed since Hurricane Iniki, and they are not expected to reopen. If you want to go exploring, rent a **kayak** and paddle your way upstream. It's a lovely ride, though if you start from the ocean you're in for a long haul before you reach the *taro* farms.

## Hanalei town

The town of **HANALEI** stretches for several hundred yards along the highway, around half a mile on from the bridge and a couple of hundred yards in from the beach. Little more than a village – you can be almost out the far end before you realize you've even arrived – it's home to an appealing mixture of laid-back old-timers, spaced-out New Age newcomers, and hyperactive surf bums.

The main center of activity lies at the point where two low-slung, somewhat ramshackle shopping malls face each other across the street. On the *mauka* side, the assorted buildings of the **Hanalei Center** include a converted school, and hold several restaurants and snack bars as well as a handful of upmarket clothing and gift stores. The Yellowfish Trading Co, tucked away in the back (☎826-1227), is highly recommended as a source of hard-to-find Hawaiiana, including some great 1950s souvenirs. The **Ching Young Village** opposite is a bit larger than it first looks, as it stretches a little way back from the road. In addition to a couple of outdoor-adventure and equipment-rental companies, it offers some grocery stores, Hanalei Natural Foods among them, and some cheaper eating options.

Hanalei was the location of Kauai's second Christian **mission** (the first was in Waimea), established in 1834 by Rev William Alexander. The mission buildings, gathered in a large meadow at the western end of town, are now Hanalei's only historic sites. The most photogenic is the clapboard **Wai'oli Hui'ia Church**, with its stained-glass windows and neat belfry. Painted bright green to blend in with the hills, and shaded by tall palms, it's a quintessential little Hawaiian church. It's a lot newer than its neighbors, however, having been built in 1912. Set back to the right is its predecessor, the original **Wai'oli Church**, which was erected in 1841. This long, low building, surrounded by a broad *lānai* and topped with a high slanted roof, now serves as the Wai'oli Social Hall.

Behind the two churches is the **Wai'oli Mission House** (tours Tues, Thurs & Sat 9am-3pm; donations welcome; ☎245-3202). Although it began life as the New England-style home of the Alexanders, it's better known now for having housed Abner and Lucy **Wilcox**, who ran the mission from 1846 until 1869. Members of the Wilcox dynasty became some of Kauai's leading landowners; you'll see the family name all over the island. (For example, Grove Farm in Līhu'e was founded by George Wilcox, see p.431.) Family descendants lived in this house until the late 1970s, but it's now open for tours. The place is outfitted with nineteenth-century artifacts (though few belonged to the Wilcoxes themselves) and provides a real sense of long-ago life in Hanalei. Out back you'll find the restored kitchen garden and family *taro* patch.

## Hanalei Bay and its beaches

*Hanalei* means a *lei*- or crescent-shaped bay, and **Hanalei Bay** is lined for its entire sweeping two-mile curve with a wide shelf of yellow sand. Though it constitutes one of Kauai's very best **beaches**, each of its named segments has different characteristics, and not all are safe for swimming. **Weke Road**, which runs along the edge of the bay in Hanalei, is exclusively residential.

The underwater map of the bay is a lot more complex than what you see on the surface. The headlands to either side are ringed by coral reefs, but the channel through the middle is barely protected from the force of the ocean. While the resultant high surf places Hanalei among Kauai's favorite **surfing** destinations, it makes it a less than ideal **harbor**.

In May of 1824, the royal yacht of King Liholiho, the son and heir of Kamehameha the Great, foundered in the bay. No lives were lost, but teams of locals failed to haul the *Pride of Hawaii* ashore, and it swiftly broke up. Marine archeologists finally located the wreckage in the mid-1990s, and have retrieved a treasure trove of historical artifacts. At the time of the sinking, Kauaians saw a certain justice in the fact that the yacht had been used three years before to kidnap their own ruler, Kaumuali'i (see p.415), and that the loss occurred at the exact moment that Kaumuali'i died in exile.

For the next century, Hanalei was a significant port, with the valley's rice crop being shipped out and cattle and other supplies being shipped in. The jetty at the mouth of Hanalei River reached its present length in 1912 (obviously a busy year in Hanalei), but Hawaii has long since ceased to be a net exporter of rice or *taro*, and these days the bay is used only by pleasure craft. During the summer it welcomes private yachts from around Hawaii, as well as a surprising number of trans-Pacific sailors; in winter it falls quiet.

The beach from which the pier juts out is officially **Black Pot Beach County Park**. Long a local hangout – the "black pot" was a large communal cooking pot – this site was bought up by developers in the late 1960s. After years of failing to obtain the necessary permits, the would-be builders sold the land back to the county, and it was set aside as a public park. Strong currents render it unsafe for swimming in winter, but it's busy the rest of the year. Until recently, this was also the main launching point for Nā Pali boat trips. However, as a result of environmental damage to the river's mouth caused by the daily crowds, the trips have now been greatly curtailed (see p.466).

**Hanalei Pavilion Beach County Park**, a short distance west, is similar to Black Pot Beach. When the surf isn't too ferocious, the lack of inshore rocks make it a suitable spot to develop your surfing or boogie-boarding skills; otherwise, settle for enjoying a picnic in the open-fronted pavilion. With permission from the county parks office in Līhu'e (see p.426), you can **camp** here on Fridays, Saturdays and holidays only.

The next beach along, **Wai'oli Beach County Park**, is marked by the fine stand of ironwood trees responsible for its nickname, "Pinetrees Park." Currents that swirl over the offshore sandbar, partly caused by Wai'oli Stream as it flows into the bay just to the west, lend it the more prosaic name of "Toilet Bowls." This is the most popular launching point for the champion surfers who swim right out to the colossal waves in the mouth of the bay.

On the far side of Wai'oli Stream, right beside the highway towards the western end of the bay – and further than you'd choose to walk from central Hanalei – **Waikoko Beach** is the safest of the beaches for year-round family swimming. Thanks to the broad stretch of reef that shield them, the waters just offshore remain placid even in winter. The sea floor is sandy underfoot, and snorkelers can approach the coral with relative ease.

## Restaurants

The **restaurants** of Hanalei rank among the most enjoyable on Kauai, though most aim for a family or alternative feel rather than a romantic atmosphere. None has sea views, but the mountains and gardens compensate for that. Several breakfast places open at, or even before, dawn to enable early-bird hikers, surfers and boaters to stock up.

**Fast-food** options in the Hanalei Center include *Bubba Burgers* and the *Wishing Well*, which serves anything from shave ice, smoothies and *saimin* to BBQ chicken and ribs. In the Ching Young Village, try *Pizza Hanalei* or the *Village Snack and Bakery Shop*.

**Bamboo Bamboo**, Hanalei Center; ⓣ826-1177. Attractive, stylish restaurant, set partly indoors and partly on a mountain-view terrace, across from the Ching Young Village in central Hanalei. The bamboo theme extends to bamboo-handled silverware and bamboo-shaped water glasses. Lunchtime offerings include salads, sushi and fish specials – a tasty *ahi niçoise* salad costs $13. Dinner choices range from pizza to roasted chicken to the $24 Creole Haena seafood stew. Daily 11.30am–3pm & 5.30–9.30pm.

**The Hanalei Gourmet**, Hanalei Center; ⓣ826-2524. Mountain breezes blow through Hanalei's former schoolhouse to cool the open deck at the front. There you can enjoy tasty deli sandwiches ($6–11), salads, fish dips, or boiled shrimp, as well as $16–22 dinner specials until 9.30pm. The same menu is available from the takeout counter alongside, at the same prices. The bar is a busy center of local life, with live music every night: jazz, Hawaiian (especially Sunday 5–9pm), R&B, reggae and, on Friday and Saturday nights, rock 'n' roll. Daily 8am–10pm.

**Hanalei Wake-Up Café**, 148 Aku Rd; ⓣ826-5551. Next to *Tahiti Nui* as you come into Hanalei from the east. Big breakfasts, such as omelets and "custard French toast," at low prices are served from the crack of dawn. Daily 6–11.30am.

**Island Java**, Hanalei Center; ⓣ826-6717. Small, friendly espresso bar across from the Ching Young Village. Hanalei's best bet for an early pick-me-up breakfast, with a nice *lānai* for specialty coffees and creamy waffles. Later in the day they serve deli sandwiches and salads. Daily 7am–7pm.

**Postcards Cafe**, Kūhiō Hwy; ⓣ826-1191. Gourmet seafood and vegetarian restaurant housed in a former museum, *mauka* of the highway from Princeville as it comes into Hanalei. Tasty breakfast burritos, griddle cakes and eggs cost $10, while dinner appetizers include home-grown *taro* fritters or summer rolls, both $9. Vegetarian entrees – some featuring tofu, others simply a mixture of sauteed or roasted vegetables – cost around $16, while fresh fish specials, cooked in a variety of styles, are more like $20–25. Mon–Fri 8–11am & 6–9pm, Sat & Sun 8–11.30am & 6–9pm.

**Sushi'n'Blues**, Ching Young Village; ⓣ826-9701. Bustling second-floor dining room above the Ching Young shops, with table seating and a sushi counter. An enthusiastic crowd is drawn by the top-notch Japanese food as well as the nightly live music, which includes jazz, reggae, Hawaiian and blues, and usually keeps going long after the food service has ended. Sushi is sold by the piece ($7–10) and in a full range of combos, including good-value options at $15 and $18; it's also available flash-fried. You can also get fresh fish entrees for around $20. Tues-Sun Mon 6–10pm.

**Tahiti Nui**, Kauhale Center at Aku Road; ⓣ826-6277. One of the town's nicest places to hang out, and hence popular with locals and visitors. The dining room beyond the front *lānai* is decked out with Tahitian trimmings and has communal tables. Food ranges widely in quality; in the evening, avoid the stir-fries and go for simple steak or fresh fish entrees at $16. In theory, there's some form of music daily, with karaoke until late on Thursday and Saturday nights, and the Happy Hawaiians on Friday nights, but it's best to check ahead. Wednesday's lū'au (6–8.30pm; reserve ahead; $52 adults, $30 ages 12–17, $20 ages 3–11) is not Hawaii's most authentic, but it's more of a local party than any other you'll find. Daily 7am–2pm & 6–10pm.

**Zelo's Beach House Restaurant & Grill**, Kūhiō Hwy at Aku Rd; ⓣ826-9700. This funky roadhouse is not in fact by the beach, but in the heart of Hanalei. Nevertheless, it's a great place for a meal or cocktail. Salads, burgers, sandwiches, tacos and wraps are served during the day; in the evening there are pasta and taco dinner entrees for $10–18 and tasty fresh fish specials for around $20. Mon–Thurs & Sun 11am–10pm, Fri & Sat 11am–11pm.

# To the end of the road

As it continues westward along the coast beyond Hanalei Bay, Hwy-56 becomes Hwy-560, and acquires the feel of a rural lane. For the half-dozen miles until the sheer Nā Pali cliffs definitively bar any further progress, it's lined by a succession of ravishing beaches. Some, like famous **Lumaha'i Beach**, are photogenic but treacherous; others are perfectly suited for surfing, snorkeling, diving or swimming. Small private homes nestle in the undergrowth to either side, but there are no real towns or even villages, and only at **Hā'ena** has there been any commercial development.

## Lumaha'i Beach

At the western edge of Hanalei Bay, just where a sharp hairpin bend in the highway finally takes you out of sight of Princeville, a makeshift roadside parking lot shortly before milepost 5 serves as both overlook and trailhead for **LUMAHA'I BEACH**. With its broad yellow sands, crashing white surf and green mountain backdrop, Lumaha'i has starred in countless movies and TV dramas such as *South Pacific* and *The Thorn Birds*, but always seems to have enough space to accommodate another couple of wistful tourists. Romantic daydreams are a much safer way to spend time here than venturing into the water: currents are consistently ferocious, and there's no reef to stop unwary bathers from being swept far out to sea.

From beside the "Danger" sign at the head of the overlook, an easy trail-cum-stairway drops down to the east end of the beach. Most of Lumaha'i's sand migrates here in winter; at other times the stark outcrops of black lava emerge more fully from the sea, making it clearer why this area is sometimes regarded as a separate beach in its own right, named Kahalahala.

In summer the sand piles in opulent drifts at the far end, two miles west near the mouth of the Lumaha'i River, occasionally blocking it altogether. That can make swimming in the river a possibility – it's one of the least spoiled in all Hawaii, bursting with native fish. For most of the year, however, it's extremely dangerous, with flash floods raging down from the mountains and the sea bed shelving away very steeply immediately offshore. Access to the beach's western end is straightforward, with a sea-level parking lot amid the ironwoods alongside the river.

## Wainiha and Kepuhi

At a sweeping turn in the road shortly before milepost 7, Hwy-560 crosses two branches of the **Wainiha River** in quick succession, over a two-part wooden bridge. Sinuous Wainiha Valley winds several miles inland from this point, though unless you take a helicopter ride, you can only see its full extent by walking the full length of the mind-boggling Alaka'i Swamp Trail (see p.498). Now all but uninhabited, the valley once held a sizeable agricultural community. Historians wrestling over the existence of the *menehune*, said to have been the first settlers of Hawaii (see p.429), have been intrigued to note that during the first census of Kauai, early in the nineteenth century, 65 people in Wainiha actually characterized themselves as *menehune*.

What the Hawaiians referred to as the "unfriendly waters" of Wainiha were harnessed in 1906 by the construction of a hydroelectric generating station a couple of miles upstream. It's still in use, with a chain of pylons carrying electricity around eastern Kauai (along the Powerline Trail; see p.452) to the south coast. The wharf, warehouses and light railroad built along the shoreline at the same time were, however, destroyed by the *tsunami* of April 1946.

Neither **Wainiha Beach**, immediately west of the bridges, nor **Kepuhi Beach** just beyond that, is recommended for swimming. Silt churned up by the river keeps the sea almost permanently cloudy at Wainiha precluding the growth of a protective reef, so the currents are capable of dragging swimmers way out into the ocean. There is a reef at Kepuhi, much frequented by local fishermen, but it is punctuated by so many gaps that it's equally unsafe.

Palm-fringed Kepuhi Beach nonetheless makes a superb setting for the North Shore's westernmost **hotel**, a delightful tropical retreat just two miles from the start of the Nā Pali coast. The oceanfront *Hanalei Colony Resort* (PO Box 206, Hanalei HI 96714-9985; Ⓣ826-6235 or 1-800/628-3004, Ⓕ826-9893, Ⓦwww.hcr.com; ❺–❼) consists of a small cluster of two-story buildings following the curve of an exposed headland (offering magnificent ocean views) and arrayed around a central lawn. Each of the units has two bedrooms and a bathroom, kitchen, living room and *lānai*, though no phones or TVs; there's also a pool and Jacuzzi. Rates fall if you stay three nights or more, and you can choose between a free rental car or a free seventh night. All rates increase by around $25 from June to mid-September, and more like $60 at Christmastime.

Sharing a parking lot with the resort, *Surt's on the Beach* (daily 11.30am–9pm; Ⓣ826-0060) is a high-class **gourmet restaurant** that enjoys panoramic ocean views. Dinner is served from 4pm onwards to make the most of the glorious sunsets. In addition to conventional Asian and European dishes such as eggplant chicken and assorted pasta specials (priced at around $15), there's a changing daily selection of Pacific Rim specialties. A sampler plate of appetizers like crab *shumai* and blackened *sashimi* costs $13, while entrees like mac-nut-crusted *opah* are a hefty $28 each. The lunch menu is simpler and cheaper. In general, the food isn't quite as wonderful as you might expect for the price, but at least wines start at just $14 per bottle, and the location is so good you're unlikely to dwell on the expense.

A short distance beyond the *Hanalei Colony Resort*, the *YMCA of Kauai Camp Naue* (reservations PO Box 1786, Līhu'e, HI 96766; Ⓣ246-9090; ❶) is a real bargain for budget travelers. **Dorm beds** in either of its two simple oceanfront bunkhouses cost $12 per night (bring your own linen), and you can also set up a tent on the four-acre grounds.

## Tunnels Beach and Hā'ena Beach County Park

From the first headland beyond Kepuhi Beach, just beyond milepost 8 and barely visible from the highway, a huge reef curves like a fishhook out to sea. In the calmer summer months, the lagoon it encloses is a safe anchorage for light sailing boats, as well as a great family snorkeling spot. Together with its fringe of golden sand, this popular area is known as **Tunnels Beach**, though divers and surfers dispute whether the name comes from its underwater lava tubes or its curling winter waves.

Tunnels can be accessed via a dirt road at the headland or by walking back to its western end from roadside **Hā'ena Beach County Park**. Manoa Stream ensures that the latter beach lacks a reef of its own, so it's no place to swim; but palms aplenty, broad lawns and crisp white sands make it ideal for picnicking or lazing. It also offers a well-maintained **campground** (get permission from the county authorities in Līhu'e; Ⓣ 241-6660; see p.426). It's convenient to the Kalalau Trail, but slightly too public for most campers to feel comfortable about leaving their gear unattended during the day. Across the highway from the beach, **Maniniholo Dry Cave** is a lava tube that once lay below sea level. Beyond its wave-widened entrance, it penetrates a considerable distance into the mountains, without being particularly interesting or rewarding to explore.

## Limahuli Gardens

Not far beyond Hā'ena Beach, and halfway between mileposts 9 and 10, **Limahuli Gardens** (Tues–Fri & Sun 9.30am–4pm) is part of the private non-profit National Tropical Botanical Garden, which has another branch close to Po'ipū on the South Shore (see p.478). The gardens can be seen either on self-guided tours ($10), or, by reservation, on 2hr 30min guided tours ($15; Ⓣ 826-1053).

### Taylor Camp

A dense grove of trees at the mouth of Limahuli Stream – roughly a mile east of Kē'ē Beach, and only accessible by walking along the shore – was the site of the once-notorious **Taylor Camp**.

Elizabeth Taylor's brother Howard bought this seven-acre seafront plot in 1969. Having cleared the land and constructed a dirt road, however, he found that it was due to become a state park. Unable to sell the property or build there himself, he invited a group of hippies then camping on the beach to take it over. They survived for seven years, occupying tents and free-form "structures" without electricity or basic sanitation. Most lived on welfare, while some made money on the side by growing marijuana.

Following publicity given to a "tree house" built by a former Berkeley architecture student, hordes of would-be back-to-the-landers – and surfers above all – were lured to Kauai. More tree houses were built, in a style one journalist called "Jimi Hendrix meets the Swiss Family Robinson." Before long there was simply no more room, and a waiting list for tree houses was set up. Further media attention came when Liz Taylor was photographed wearing "jewelry" produced at the camp by stringing together the *puka* shells scattered along the beach. For the next year or two, anklets, bracelets and necklaces of these tiny shells commanded high prices, and beaches across the entire state were all but stripped bare.

Howard Taylor himself almost never went to the camp, and simply let the matter lie, building another house near Tunnels Beach. Sanitary regulations and general moral outrage motivated the authorities to instigate eviction proceedings, but by the time Taylor succumbed to pressure and handed the land over to the state in 1974, some campers had been there long enough to be entitled to claim squatters' rights. It took three more years, and guarantees of resettlement, before the camp was finally bulldozed.

The gardens are set in a narrow, steep-sided valley reminiscent of Maui's ʻĪao Valley (see p.307); the fifteen acres nearest the highway can be explored via a half-mile walking trail, while a thousand more inaccessible acres further back are a natural preserve. Centuries-old terraces along the Limahuli Stream have been restored to cultivate *taro* in the ancient style, in small pond-like enclosures known as *loʻi*. Colorful native trees nearby include plumeria, with its white *lei*-making flowers; the *pāpala kēpau*, whose sticky sap was used to trap birds; and several varieties of *ʻōhiʻa lehua*. From higher up the slopes, as the path skirts the cool mountain forest, you get superb views of the ocean, and there's a strong possibility of seeing whales in winter.

## Hāʻena State Park and Kēʻē Beach

The western boundary of Hāʻena Beach County Park abuts the eastern edge of **Hāʻena State Park**, where the aim is to protect natural and archeological features from development rather than to display them to tourists. For most of its length, private residences stand between the road and the ocean, and only experienced surfers bother to make their way along the rocky seashore.

### The Tale of Hiʻiaka and Lohiʻau

Several sites around Kēʻē Beach are renowned as the setting for the best-known legend of ancient Hawaii. However, no two sources agree exactly on what took place between its three central figures – **Pele** the volcano goddess, her sister **Hiʻiaka**, and the Kauaian chief **Lohiʻau**.

One version begins with Pele lying asleep in her home at Kīlauea Crater on the island of Hawaii, and finding her dreams filled with sweet, mysterious music. In search of its source, her spirit left her body and set off from island to island, until she finally came to this remote spot. The principal performer in the *hula* celebration that was taking place was the young chief Lohiʻau, to whom Pele was uncontrollably drawn. After three days of blissful (though unconsummated) love, their idyll was shattered when Pele's slumbering body back at Kīlauea was awoken by her sister, Hiʻiaka.

Pele despatched Hiʻiaka to fetch Lohiʻau. Her perilous voyage to Kauai involved countless obstacles on all the other islands, which Hiʻiaka only survived thanks to the magical aid of her companion *wahine ʻōmaʻo*, or "green woman." Arriving on Kauai she found that Lohiʻau had hanged himself in grief and lay buried nearby. She captured his free-floating spirit and managed to force it back into the corpse through a slit in the big toe, whereupon he rushed off to purify himself by surfing from Kēʻē Beach.

As they returned to Kīlauea, however, Hiʻiaka and Lohiʻau fell in love with each other. Lohiʻau was repelled when he finally saw Pele's true bodily form (she was an elderly witch), and the jealous goddess retaliated by engulfing him in lava. This time it took two of Pele's brothers to restore him to life. They carried him back to Kauai, where he was reunited with Hiʻiaka at Kapaʻa.

According to local lore, the rudimentary walls of Lohiʻau's house now poke from the undergrowth immediately opposite the foot of the Kalalau Trail, while the *hula* platform above the beach was the site of his first meeting with Pele, and his grave is just above Waikapalaʻe wet cave. It's also said that other houses nearby belonged to friends and relatives of Lohiʻau who figured in the drama, and rock formations on the nearby cliffs are all that remain of *moʻo* (giant lizards) and other creatures killed by Hiʻiaka.

Few visitors see more of the park than **Kēʻē Beach**, right where the highway ends alongside milepost 10. Swimming and snorkeling from its steep shelf of yellow sand is almost irresistible, but despite the usual crowds it's only safe when the sea is at its calmest. At this time, the waters inshore of the reef are ideal for fish-watching; at other times the surf that surges over the reef rushes out with even stronger force through gaps in it, especially at the western (left) end.

Two **wet caves** – filled with water, unlike Maniniholo (see above) – are located a short distance back from the end of the road, and marked by road signs. One, Waikanaloa, is alongside the highway, while Waikapalaʻe is just up the hillside. Why divers would choose to explore these dismal caverns rather than the nearby ocean is anyone's guess.

## Ke Ahu A Laka

A small trail heads west from Kēʻē Beach, along the black seafront rocks just below the state-owned Allerton House, which is not open to visitors. It leads within a hundred yards to the ancient site of **Ke Ahu A Laka**. The island of Molokai has stronger claims to being "the birthplace of *hula*" (see p.407), but this was once the most celebrated *hālau hula* in all Hawaii, the highest academy where students were taught the intricacies of the form by teachers known as *kumu hula*. (For more on the art of *hula*, see p.535.)

In the hope of deterring casual tourists, there are no directional or explanatory signs in the area. Finding the assortment of low-lying ruins is easy enough, however, so with no guidance to direct them, people end up wandering aimlessly around and across the site, creating new trails and damaging the stone walls. No one knows whether the various structures were built simultaneously as parts of a single complex or should be thought of as a group of unrelated buildings. Archeologists identify the site's lower level as the Ka Ulu A Pāʻoa *heiau*, but it doesn't correspond to any of the usual kinds of *heiau*, and may have served some specific function for *hula* practitioners. Performances took place on the large flat terrace higher up, a few hundred yards back against the base of the *pali*. An altar, probably located within a thatched enclosure, was dedicated to Laka, the patroness of *hula*. Local *hālau hula* come to the site in pilgrimage, but there are no public performances.

When a member of the *aliʻi* graduated from the *hālau hula*, or on other great occasions, the Hawaiians would celebrate by flinging flaming firebrands at night from the towering cliffs above Kēʻē. Burning branches of *hau*, *pāpala* and other light-wooded trees, dried and then soaked in *kukui* oil, were sent spinning out into the darkness, to be caught and held aloft by the trade winds as they curled up the cliff faces. Spectators would gather below in offshore canoes as the sky rained fire about them.

# The Nā Pali coast

Beyond Kēʻē Beach, and beyond the reach of any vehicle, lie the green, inviolate valleys of the **Nā Pali coast**. Separated one from the next by knife-edge ridges of rock that thrust down to the ocean from heights of up to four thousand feet, these are among the last great Hawaiian wildernesses, playing host to a magnificent daily spectacle of ever-changing colors. Intruders enter this world only on sufferance, clinging to the contours on perilous hiking trails or buffeted in small boats out at sea.

*Nā Pali* simply means "the cliffs." The word *pali* is thought to be of Himalayan origin, having entered the Polynesian language long before recorded history, and is here applied to a landscape of truly Himalayan proportions. Although for the ancient Hawaiians, Kē'ē was proverbially the remotest spot on the islands, Nā Pali valleys such as Kalalau and Nu'alolo Kai once held substantial populations of *taro* farmers. After the last Hawaiians left Kalalau in 1919, the region remained uninhabited until a sudden influx of hippies in the late 1960s. Official attempts to get rid of them led to the creation of the **Nā Pali Coast State Park**, and all access is now tightly controlled.

## Nā Pali Tours

Taking an **ocean-going tour** enables visitors to see the cliffs, valleys, beaches and waterfalls of the Nā Pali coastline looking even more dramatic than they do from the fly-on-the-wall perspective of the Kalalau Trail. What's more, the distance from Kē'ē to Kalalau, eleven strenuous miles on foot, is only six miles by water, so you can explore the full length in a half-day trip.

During the 1990s, however, so many such trips set off from Hanalei each day that both Hanalei Bay and River became seriously polluted. As a result, state Governor Benjamin Cayetano has issued a series of decrees forbidding Nā Pali cruise operators from using Hanalei as their departure point. At the time this book went to press, all authorized operators were launching their trips from the West Shore instead, from either **Kīkīaola Harbor**, 1.6 miles west of Waimea, or **Port Allen**. Ongoing court challenges by Hanalei-based companies may enable the resumption of cruises from Hanalei by the time you read this, however.

Although tours from either side of the island tend to end up at the same places – most half-day trips include a view of Kalalau Valley and a snorkeling stop at the reef just off Nu'alolo Kai – it has to be said that starting from Hanalei is the better alternative. That way you get to see Lumaha'i and Kē'ē beaches, as well as the full length of the Kalalau Trail; boats that depart from the West Shore cruise for much of the way alongside featureless sand dunes. On the other hand, both Kīkīaola and Port Allen are significantly more convenient for visitors based around Po'ipū.

Tour operators use either inflatable **Zodiac rafts** – highly maneuverable in calm waters, but bumpy and slow in rougher conditions – or **catamarans**, which offer a smoother and faster ride. Exactly what the tour boats can do also depends on the weather – in calm seas they travel further and stop for longer, while during especially windy periods no boats at all may be running. Between December and April, when cruises can only cover shorter distances, the main compensation is the likelihood of seeing humpback whales. Passengers scour the horizon for water spouts or a glint of tail flukes, and the catamarans venture a couple of miles out to sea in the hope of sightings. From that distance, the entire Nā Pali coast appears as a single rounded monolith.

Operators from the **West Shore** include Captain Andy (Ⓣ335-6833, Ⓦwww.sailing-hawaii.com), Catamaran Kahanu (Ⓣ335-3577, Ⓦwww.catamarankahanu.com), Kauai Sea Tours (Ⓣ826-7254 or 1-800/733-7997), Liko Kauai Cruises (Ⓣ338-0333 or 1-888/SEA LIKO, Ⓦwww.liko-kauai.com), Na Pali Eco Adventures (Ⓣ826-6804), and Z-TourZ (Ⓣ742-6331, Ⓦwww.ztourz.com). Expect to pay $85–100 per adult for a 4hr snorkel trip and $125–140 for a 5hr 30min tour that includes a beach picnic.

It is still possible to join a guided **kayak** expedition from Hanalei. Kayak Kauai (Ⓣ826-9844, Ⓦwww.kayakkauai.com) charges $140 for an escorted tour; only the most experienced ocean kayakers should set off unaccompanied.

All Kauai's **helicopter** companies fly over the Nā Pali coast, but only Hawaii Helicopters (Ⓣ826-6591 or 1-800/994-9099, Ⓦwww.hawaii-helicopters.com) is based on the North Shore, at Princeville Airport; a 30min tour costs $105.

## Nā Pali Permits

To hike any further than Hanakāpī'ai, even for the day; to **camp** at any of the Kalalau Trail campgrounds (for a maximum of five nights); or to land by **boat** at Kalalau, Nu'alolo Kai or Miloli'i, you must have a **permit** from the **state parks office** at 3060 Eiwa St in Līhu'e (☎274-3444; see p.426). With so many accidents and drownings along the way – and the possibility of a repetition of Hurricane Iniki, when hundred-foot waves necessitated the evacuation of all campers – a record of who may be missing is vital.

Permits cost $10 per person per day and are issued for groups of up to five named individuals, who must specify exactly who is camping where each night. Hikers along the Kalalau Trail are forbidden to spend two consecutive nights at either Hanakāpī'ai or Hanakoa, while boaters can stay no more than three nights at Miloli'i. To minimize environmental damage, up to sixty people are permitted to camp in the park each day between mid-May and mid-September; for the rest of the year, that number drops to just thirty. It's therefore essential to make reservations in advance. Most tour operators obtain permits for their clients, and block-book them several months ahead; as a result, last-minute applicants often leave empty-handed.



## The Kalalau Trail

The eleven-mile **Kalalau Trail** passes through first **Hanakāpī'ai** and then **Hanakoa** valleys en route to **Kalalau Valley**, where it's defeated by a mighty buttress of stone. Honopū, Awa'awapuhi, Nu'alolo Kai and Miloli'i valleys, further west, are only accessible by sea, though they can be surveyed from Kōke'e State Park far above (see p.493). Along the trail, there are **beaches** at Hanakāpī'ai (in summer) and Kalalau (all year) and **campgrounds** in all three valleys, though only one-night stopovers are permitted at Hanakāpī'ai and Hanakoa. Arduous at all times, the trail also gets progressively more dangerous; indeed, the final five-mile stretch from Hanakoa to Kalalau, which involves scrambling along a precipitous, shadeless wall of crumbling red rock, had to be **closed** for six months in the fall of 1995 to allow repairs. Such closures may well reoccur, so check with the state parks office before setting out.

Any Kalalau Trail hike requires careful **preparation**. Most obviously, the 22-mile trek to Kalalau and back is too far to attempt in a single day. Hanakoa Valley itself being a grueling twelve-mile return trip (and one that requires a permit), the most realistic target for a day-hike is Hanakāpī'ai Beach, with a possible side-trip to the falls at the head of the valley. Allow a minimum of 4hr 30min for the trek from Kē'ē Beach to Hanakāpī'ai Falls and back. Neither food nor water is available at Kē'ē, let alone anywhere along the trail. However far you go, the path is rugged and uneven throughout, varying from slippery clay to shifting sand, so solid footwear is essential. And choose your hiking clothes carefully - thanks to the Kalalau Trail's notorious red dirt, chances are you won't ever be able to wear them again.

The trail rises and falls constantly, with several vertigo-inducing moments; it crosses, and can be blocked by, mountain streams; and emergency help is only available if fellow hikers manage to summon a helicopter. Bear in mind, too, that the sea undercuts the trail in many places, so that dropped or dislodged objects can hit passengers in boats below. Leaving a car parked overnight at the trailhead is not recommended; Hā'ena Beach County Park is preferable for this purpose.

### The trail to Hanakāpī'ai

The Kalalau Trail climbs sharply away from its trailhead opposite milepost 10 at Kē'ē Beach, a few yards back from the ocean. Although much of its first half-mile was cobbled during the 1930s, the initial ascent is one of the most demanding sections of the whole trail. It's also among the most beautiful: conditions are much wetter here than further along, and the vegetation is correspondingly thicker. You soon find yourself clambering across the gnarled roots of the splay-footed *hala* (pandanus) tree and sloshing through mini-waterfalls as they gush over the path.

Shortly after the trail rounds the first promontory, still during the first climb and still in sight of Kē'ē Beach, you should be able to make out the ruined walls of the Ka Ulu A Pā'oa *heiau* on a small grassy oceanfront plateau below (see p.465). Views of the successive headlands that lie ahead, and of the islands of Niihau and Lehua further towards the horizon, start to open up half a mile along.



Ancient Hawaiians supposedly took just twenty minutes to reach Hanakāpī'ai Beach, but few modern hikers manage to cover the two-mile distance within an hour. The obvious place to catch your breath en route is at the halfway point, where the trail tops out at 400 feet before starting to drop back down again. A couple of small streams remain to be crossed, and the trail swings well away from the shoreline into a sheltered mini-valley, before Hanakāpī'ai spreads out at your feet. As you make the final descent, but still far above the valley, a warning sign marks the height to which you should climb if a tidal wave threatens.



### Hanakāpī'ai Valley and Falls

**Hanakāpī'ai Valley** is the only spot between Kē'ē Beach and Kalalau Valley where the trail returns to sea level. Crossing Hanakāpī'ai Stream to reach the valley proper is normally straightforward; even if the stepping stones are submerged, there should be a strategically placed rope or branch to help you wade across. If the stream rises any higher than your thighs, turn back – it's not safe here, and it'll be worse still further along.

In summer Hanakāpī'ai boasts a broad white-sand **beach** which, though crowded with sunbathers, is still one of Kauai's most notorious sites for **drownings**. Even if local body-surfers seem to be having the time of their lives, anyone unfamiliar with Hawaiian waters should stay well clear of the ocean. Prominent signs list the names of those who have drowned here since 1995; when this book went to press, the count stood at eight, most of whom were simply wading at the shoreline. The dangerous currents are due to the lack of a reef, and that's what allows the sand to be swept away in winter, leaving a bare gray wall of small boulders.

Hanakāpī'ai's overnight **campground** is a little way uphill beyond both beach and stream. You can't camp any further *mauka* than this, but you can detour away from the main trail to explore the valley. An energetic hour's hike, which requires several stream crossings and a lot of climbing up little rock faces and over fallen trees, brings you to the natural amphitheater of **Hanakāpī'ai Falls**. In addition to long-abandoned *taro* terraces, you'll pass the remains of a nineteenth-century coffee mill. Descendants of the 20,000 coffee trees planted at that time still grow wild throughout the valley.



### Hanakāpī'ai to Hanakoa

For the nine miles between Hanakāpī'ai and Kalalau, the coastline is indented by successive "**hanging valleys**," cut by streams that end in clifftop waterfalls.

The trail out of Hanakāpī'ai switchbacks steeply up the *pali*, rising 840 feet in little more than a mile. A false step here could be your last, and the concentration and effort of the climb allow little chance for enjoying the views. At the highest point a giant boulder *makai* of the trail – known to some as **Space Rock** – provides some welcome shade. Creep around behind it to confront the sheer drop down to the ocean, as well as a prospect that stretches from Kē'ē in the east to Kalalau in the west.

The nature reserve of **Ho'olulu Valley** comes next, swiftly followed by **Waiahuakua Valley**; the trail winds deep into both of them, forcing its way through the rampant undergrowth. Rounding each headland tends to involve a struggle against the swirling wind, but each brings a new view. Pristine green slopes soar skywards, their every fold covered with the intense blues, purples and yellows of tiny flowers, and white tropic birds, with their distinctive long tails, glide across the cavernous spaces in between.

Roughly an hour out of Hanakāpī'ai, immediately beyond a truly hair-raising section of the trail, you reach the first overlook into Hanakoa Valley, with multi-tiered waterfalls tumbling far inland. This is also the first point where you're confronted by the full fluted majesty of the Nā Pali "cathedral," and the rounded Honopū headland in the distance.

## Hanakoa Valley and Falls

Soon after entering **Hanakoa Valley**, you pass a cluster of campgrounds in a clearing on your right. This may seem a long way up from the sea, but it's as close as you'll get in the valley. Shortly afterwards, just beyond a burned-out wooden shelter on the left, you cross **Hanakoa Stream** twice in very quick succession. Once again, don't attempt to get through if the water is high, but with several boulders scattered around the stream bed you shouldn't have any problem. There are usually plenty of people around, bathing in the stream and picnicking beneath the trees. More campgrounds lie on the far side, set amid the stone walls of former *taro* terraces a little way up the hillside, and many campers stay longer than their one allotted night. The only drawback is the large population of **mosquitoes**.

Another side trail leads off inland from the terraces, this time to the 2000-foot **Hanakoa Falls**, which you may have glimpsed as you came into the valley. Follow the sign: the route may appear to be blocked by fallen trees, but that's just what the trail is like. Look out for ribbons tied to the trees, and be aware that if you don't recross the western channel of the stream within 100 yards of setting off, you've gone in the wrong direction. For steepness and mud this trail is even worse than the one to Hanakāpī'ai Falls (see above), but only a third of a mile of spongy rotting trees have to be negotiated before you come to the sheer-walled waterfall, where you can cool off in the pool. However tempted you may be, don't drink the water; there are people, and goats, up top.

## Hanakoa to Kalalau

As mentioned on p.467, the Kalalau Trail may be closed beyond Hanakoa; check with the state parks office. Assuming that it *is* open, the last five miles of the Kalalau Trail, from **Hanakoa to Kalalau**, include its most dangerous and exposed stretches. Each of the Nā Pali valleys receives less rainfall than its neighbors to the east, so they grow progressively less indented and more precipitous. To the casual eye the vegetation still seems dense, but plants find it harder to grow. They therefore recover more slowly from the onslaught of wild goats, and the denuded slopes become prone to landslides. By this stage the trail cuts repeatedly across raw patches of red sandy gravel, where every footfall sends a shower of small stones tumbling down to the sea. With the path set at a slight angle to the hillside, open to the sun, and only in as good a condition as the last rains left it, such sections can be most unnerving.

However, the rewards at the end make it all worthwhile. Having skirted several small valleys, the trail emerges to access a full panorama of Kalalau Valley. Unfortunately, the final descent, while spectacular, is the worst of all. From the saddle that connects the pinnacle of **Pu'ukula**, or "Red Hill", with the main bulk of the island, the trail skitters down the crumbling hillside in a tangle of alternative strands, none safer than the rest, before pulling itself together to cross one last stretch of grassland down to Kalalau Stream.

## Kalalau Valley

**Kalalau Valley**, the largest of the Nā Pali valleys at almost a mile wide and two miles deep, was the last to lose its native population. Its broad, gently sloping floor, cradled between mighty walls, nurtured many generations of Hawaiians before the arrival of the Europeans, and there were enough left in the nineteenth century for missionaries to consider it necessary to build a school and church here. Until 1919, when those Hawaiians who hadn't been wiped out by disease finally left, they were still living in thatched *hales*, cultivating *taro* and fishing with *hukilau* nets. They traded by canoe with their coastal neighbors, but were largely self-sufficient. For the next fifty years the valley was devoted to cattle ranching, especially by the Robinson family of Niihau fame (see p.490). State authorities felt that cattle were damaging the valley's ecology and, when squatters began to move in as well, they set aside this whole section of coastline as a state park.

Before reaching the valley floor, hikers have first to wade the **Kalalau Stream**, where a rope serves as a handrail. The stream comes shortly after the 10-mile marker; take the right fork on the far side, and the final mile of the trail takes you down to, and along, the low bluffs above Kalalau's lovely white-sand **beach**. The only beach along the trail to retain its sand year-round, this nonetheless varies greatly with the seasons. In winter it's a narrow shelf little more than 100 yards long, while in summer enough sand piles up for you to round the tumbled boulders and continue west for half a mile. Swimming during the winter or spring high surf is obviously dangerous, but even the calm summer seas are ripped through by powerful currents, and casual dips are never advisable.

### Koolau the Leper

The "flower-throttled gorge" of Kalalau Valley was the setting of Jack London's famous short story *Koolau the Leper*, a flamboyant retelling of a true-life incident. The real Koolau, a *paniolo* from Waimea, was diagnosed as a leper in 1889 and duly condemned to permanent exile, far from family and friends, on the island of Molokai (see p.400). He fled instead with his wife and young child to the mountain fastness of Kalalau, to join a band of fellow sufferers. Sheriff Louis Stolz came in search of Koolau in June 1893, only to be shot dead, whereupon a large posse was sent to round up the fugitives. All except Koolau and his family were captured; Koolau, however, retreated to a cave only accessible via a knife-edge ridge, and picked off two of his pursuers as they inched their way after him. No one was ever to claim the $1000 reward for his arrest; his wife Pi'ilani emerged from Kalalau in 1896, to tell the world that both Koolau and their son had died.

The tale of Koolau also provided the central theme for W. S. Merwin's epic book-length poem, *The Folding Cliffs* (see p.543).

Individual campgrounds line the trail above the beach, but the prime spot is considered to be around Ho'ole'a Falls at the far western end. When the sea caves here dry out in summer, campers pitch their tents inside, despite the risk of rock slides. The falls are the valley's best source of fresh water, though it should still be purified before use.

Though camping is only permitted near the beach, the spur trail that forks left immediately after the stream crossing provides an easy and enjoyable two-mile walk back into the valley. Alternating between short climbs up to valley views, and jungle hikes through wild fruit groves (with guavas and mangoes for the picking), this ends after several hundred feet at a bathing hole known simply as **Big Pool**. Vegetation has reclaimed most signs of habitation in the valley, but you might glimpse the ruins of a *heiau* near the trail junction, or the stone walls of the mission church further inland.

See p.496 for details of the Kalalau, Pu'u O Kila and Pihea lookouts in Kōke'e State Park, which look down on Kalalau Valley.

### Beyond Kalalau

The cliffs west of Kalalau are too fragile to hold a trail, so the magnificent valleys beyond can only be seen on the boat tours listed on p.466. The first of them, **Honopū**, is just half a mile from Kalalau; strong swimmers sometimes swim there, though heavy currents make the return leg all but impossible. Two beaches beautify the waterfront, but the valley itself stands atop a 150-foot bluff.

Stunning **Awa'awapuhi**, a few hundred yards along, slithers out of sight behind the cliffs like the *puhi* (eel) after which it is named. It too is a hanging valley, so from water level there's little to see; only the Awa'awapuhi Trail in Kōke'e Park (described on p.500) offers complete views.

Next come **Nu'alolo 'Āina** and **Nu'alolo Kai**, respectively the inland and oceanfront portions of Nu'alolo Valley. Separated by a 75-foot cliff, they were in ancient times connected by a perilous manmade ladder. Together they constitute one of the richest archeological sites in Hawaii, continuously occupied since the twelfth century. The overhanging cliff sheltered a row of stone-built house terraces, which have yielded layer upon layer of fishhooks, gourds and the like. The valley floor above, though narrow and shaded, was extensively irrigated for *taro*. Most Nā Pali tour boats aim to spend an hour or two anchored at the coral reef that embraces Nu'alolo Kai, enabling passengers to snorkel among its plentiful fish; some also allow brief excursions ashore.

**Miloli'i**, a mile on, is the last of the Nā Pali valleys, just four miles from the rolling dunes of Polihale State Park on the West Shore (see p.489). It too is protected by a reef, and was once home to a seafront fishing community. Boat landings on its pretty beach are permitted, but few operators come this far.

# The South and West shores

Thanks to its guaranteed sun and safe, sandy beaches, the **South Shore** ranks as the center of Kauai's tourist industry. Its only resort, **Po'ipū**, holds the island's largest concentration of upmarket hotels, condo developments, golf courses and gourmet restaurants. On the other hand, Po'ipū has never been a town in any real sense; it's very much a family destination, fine if watersports are your main priority, but it holds next to nothing of interest otherwise. None of the area's other towns is especially worth visiting, either. The plantation villages of **Kōloa**, nearby, and **Hanapēpē** ten miles on, boast some appealing turn-of-the-century storefronts but have definitely seen better days, while **Lāwa'i** and **Kalāheo** are just blink-and-you-miss-them highway intersections.

**Waimea**, the only sizable town on the **West Shore**, has a dramatic past as the site of Captain Cook's first Hawaiian landing. Although it offers one of Kauai's most characterful hotels (see p.487), it too suffers from an undistinguished present.

Few visitors would see the highway towns were they not on the way to the wonderful state parks of **Waimea Canyon** and **Kōke'e**, covered in a separate section on p.489 onwards. As it is, however, all the settlements earn extra income catering to passing day-trippers, and there are a few interesting stores and galleries where you can while away the odd spare half-hour.



# The Knudsen Gap

All traffic **west of Līhu'e** is obliged after six miles to squeeze between Hā'upu Ridge and the interior massif, through the **Knudsen Gap**. In the nineteenth century this narrow pass, named after Valdemar Knudsen, a Norwegian immigrant who managed Grove Farm during the 1850s, was a renowned haunt of thieves and outlaws. These days it serves simply as the gateway to Kauai's South and West shores.

# Kōloa

Immediately west of the Knudsen Gap, Maluhia Road heads *makai* from Hwy-50. Its first straight stretch passes through an avenue of mighty eucalyptus trees long known as the **Tree Tunnel**. Before hurricanes Iwa and Iniki, this was one of Kauai's most famous beauty spots; now that the trees no longer meet and intermingle overhead as they used to, few motorists bother to pause on their way to Kōloa and Po'ipū.

Three miles down, where the road ends, vehicles shuffle right to cross Waikomo Stream before turning left to continue on to Po'ipū. The small group of stores at this busy intersection constitute **KŌLOA**, a nineteenth-century plantation town that was also the site of Kauai's first mission school. Its first teacher, in 1855, was Rev Daniel Dole; pupils included his son Sanford, the only President of the short-lived Republic of Hawaii (see p.514).

Other snippets of local and island lore are recounted on the walls of the **Kōloa History Center**, set slightly back from the road just west of the stream. This open-sided structure doesn't even have a door, so naturally there are no opening hours or admission fees. Kōloa's raised wooden boardwalks hold assorted clothes and souvenir stores, including the Progressive Experience Surf Shop, Kahn Galleries, and a Crazy Shirts outlet.

## Practicalities

There's no **accommodation** in Kōloa proper; if you're looking for a budget alternative to the Po'ipū hotels, consider *Kāhili Mountain Park* (see p.480) or the *Kalāheo Inn* (see p.481). The town's best-known **restaurant-cum-bar** is

## Kōloa and the Sugar Plantations

Though Kōloa has never been more than a small village, it played a crucial role in the development of modern Hawaii as the birthplace of the islands' first **sugar plantation**. From its origins in the highlands of New Guinea, the sweet grass we know as sugar cane was carried throughout the Pacific by Polynesian voyagers. Ancient Hawaiians cultivated around forty separate varieties of *kō*, which they chewed as medicine, an aphrodisiac, baby food, emergency rations, and simply for pleasure.

Wild sugar grew rampant in Kōloa, whose name meant "long cane," so it made an ideal testing ground for commercial sugar production. In 1835, Ladd & Co secured permission from Kamehameha III to farm almost a thousand acres east of the Waihohonu Stream – the first such lease ever granted to outsiders – and sent 26-year-old William Hooper to establish a plantation. He set 25 *kanakas* (native Hawaiians) to clear the grass on September 13, with the deliberate intention not only of making a profit but also of transforming the Hawaiian way of life.

Until that time ordinary Hawaiians were regarded as owing unlimited labor to the ruling *ali'i*, a form of serfdom that had been grotesquely abused in the sandalwood trade (see p.511). For Hooper, the plantation was an "entering wedge . . . to upset the whole miserable system of 'chief labor.'" To his workers, uprooted from seaside villages and brought to the new plantation settlement, however, this new system must have seemed little different from the old. They dragged the ploughs themselves, drilled the soil by hand using traditional *'ō'ō* digging sticks, and crushed the raw cane using heavy *koa*-wood logs as rollers. By paying them in coupons that could only be redeemed at the company store, Hooper introduced them to consumerism. Each month, as the *kanakas* tired of the previous consignment of cheap goods and textiles shipped over from Honolulu, there'd be a frantic search for new items to import.

By March 1838, the plantation employed one hundred laborers. An ever-increasing proportion of the sugar boilers were women, who at just six cents per day were paid less than half the men's wage. Hooper saw the Hawaiians as intelligent shirkers – "they display so little interest for their employment that it makes my heart ache" – who worked only when they were being watched and even learned to forge counterfeit coupons and avoid working altogether. As a result, he began to recruit Chinese laborers from a group who had been grinding wild cane at Waimea until the new plantation drove them out of business. These were housed in separate quarters at Kōloa, as were the white overseers, and patterns of race and class division emerged that became standard for all subsequent plantations.

Soon after Hooper left in 1839, Ladd & Co managed to go bankrupt, despite being offered exclusive rights to all sugar production in Hawaii for a century. However, the plantation at Kōloa prospered, with the construction of a dam and a more sophisticated mill. The great boom came during the US Civil War, when the farms of the South stopped feeding the sweet tooth of the North. A leap in the price of Hawaiian sugar stimulated the opening of dozens of plantations on the Kōloa model, starting on the Big Island in 1863, and then on Oahu and Maui in 1864. When prices dropped at the end of the war, sugar dominated the Hawaiian economy; the US annexation of the islands was largely the result of campaigns by sugar producers to guarantee access to the American market.

Sugar production in Kōloa finally came to an end in 2000; the former sugar fields are progressively being replanted with coffee. All that remains of the original 1841 mill, located just north of the town center, is a ruined chimney marked with a commemorative plaque.

*Pizzetta* (daily 11am–10pm; ☎ 742-8881), set in a former *poi* factory along the boardwalk, with an open-air *lānai* out back. Huge, very tasty lunchtime *panini* sandwiches cost $6–8, a calzone is $9, pasta specials are around $10, and full-size pizzas range from $13 to $24. They also serve fine smoothies, and you can spend an interesting evening working your way through a long list of cocktails.

Both the food and the atmosphere in the garden courtyard of the nearby *Tom Kats Grille* (daily 11am–10pm; ☎ 742-8887) are similar. In addition to lunchtime burgers and sandwiches, they feature evening specials such as steak ($15) and seafood linguine ($13). Also on the boardwalk, *Lapperts* (Mon–Thurs & Sun 6am–9pm, Fri & Sat 6am–10pm), serves ice cream and coffees to take out or to enjoy on the shady *lānai*. Just across the stream, part of the *Kōloa Country Store* (Mon–Sat 8am–8pm, Sun 9am–5pm) is set aside as an **internet café**.



# Po'ipū

**PO'IPŪ**, the southernmost point on Kauai, is also its principal vacation resort. Though *po'ipū* means "completely overcast," its **white-sand beaches** receive more sunshine than anywhere else on the island and are filled with tourists year-round. For surfing, windsurfing, scuba diving, snorkeling or general family fun, it's a great place. However, beaches are about all there is here; there's no town to wander through and virtually nothing else to see or do. What's more, most of the beaches are not visible from the confusing network of roads, so on first impression you might not even realize they were there.

Matters were not helped in September 1992, when **Hurricane Iniki** left Po'ipū in a terrible state. The roofs of its hotels were ripped off, plush rooms buried in sand, and rental cars flipped and stacked like matchwood. It took several years for things to get back to normal, but the damage is now entirely repaired. Although most individual properties have been rebuilt to an even higher standard than before, Po'ipū still feels more like a random assortment of buildings than a cohesive community.

Po'ipū's only other claim to fame is as a **golfing** destination. In late November each year, the Po'ipū Bay Resort course hosts the **PGA Grand Slam** tournament, which – until Tiger Woods started making the whole concept a bit more nebulous – aimed to bring together the winners of golf's four major tournaments.

## Accommodation

**Hotels** and **condos** in Po'ipū tend to charge significantly more than their equivalents in, for example, Kapa'a, and unless you spend all your time on the beach you may not feel you're getting enough for your money. **B&B** rates may also seem unusually pricey, but most of the local properties are aimed firmly at the luxury end of the market. It makes little difference what part of town you stay in, as no one walks around Po'ipū. If you're looking for inexpensive accommodation in this area, consider *Kāhili Mountain Park* (see p.480), or the *Kalāheo Inn* (see p.481).

**Embassy Vacation Resort**, 1613 Pe'e Rd, Po'ipū Point HI 96756; ☎ 742-1888, or reserve through Marc Resorts, ☎ 922-5900 or 1-800/535-0085 (US & Can), Ⓕ 922-2421 or 1-800/633-5085 (US & Can), Ⓦ www.marcresorts.com. Plush, luxuriously appointed condo complex, with successive terraces of lily ponds leading down to a large, sand-surrounded swimming pool, and the beach beyond. ❽.

**Garden Isle Cottages**, 2666 Pu'uholo Rd, Po'ipū HI 96756; ☎ 742-6717 or 1-800/742-6711 (US & Can), Ⓦ www.oceancottages.com. A small cluster of comfortable studio- and one-bedroom apartments, in private clifftop garden cottages overlooking Kōloa

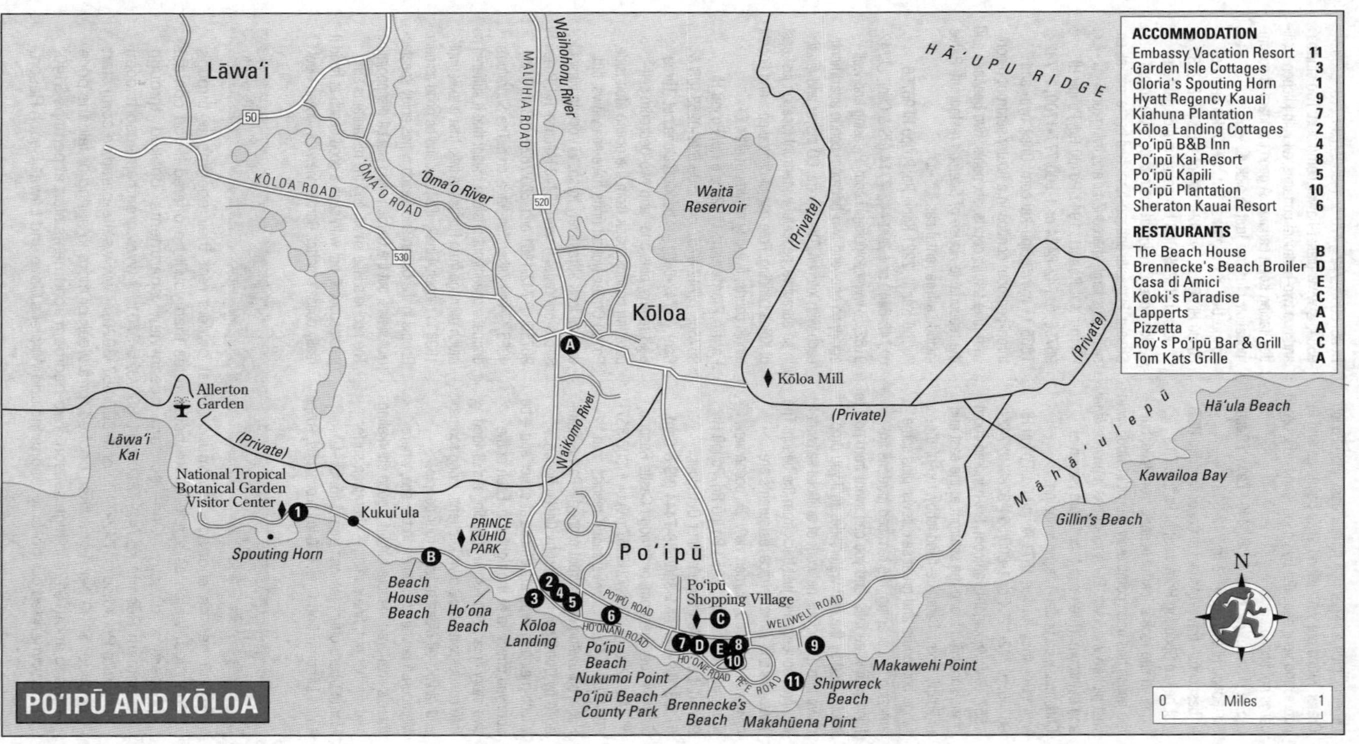

PO'IPŪ AND KŌLOA
ACCOMMODATION
Embassy Vacation Resort 11
Garden Isle Cottages 3
Gloria's Spouting Horn 1
Hyatt Regency Kauai 9
Kiahuna Plantation 7
Kōloa Landing Cottages 2
Po'ipū B&B Inn 4
Po'ipū Kai Resort 8
Po'ipū Kapili 5
Po'ipū Plantation 10
Sheraton Kauai Resort 6
RESTAURANTS
The Beach House B
Brennecke's Beach Broiler D
Casa di Amici E
Keoki's Paradise C
Lapperts A
Pizzetta A
Roy's Po'ipū Bar & Grill C
Tom Kats Grille A
HĀ'UPU RIDGE
Lāwa'i
Kōloa
Po'ipū
MALUHIA ROAD
Waihohonu River
KŌLOA ROAD
'ŌMA'O ROAD
'Ōma'o River
Waitā Reservoir
(Private)
Kōloa Mill
Allerton Garden
Lāwa'i Kai
National Tropical Botanical Garden Visitor Center
Kukui'ula
Spouting Horn
PRINCE KŪHIŌ PARK
Waikomo River
Beach House Beach
Ho'ona Beach
Kōloa Landing
Po'ipū Beach
Nukumoi Point
Po'ipū Beach County Park
Brennecke's Beach
Po'ipū Shopping Village
PO'IPŪ ROAD
HO'ONANI ROAD
HO'ONE ROAD
PE'E ROAD
WELIWELI ROAD
Makahūena Point
Shipwreck Beach
Makawehi Point
Māhā'ulepū
Gillin's Beach
Kawailoa Bay
Hā'ula Beach
N
0 Miles 1

Landing, plus a larger unit further east, atop Po'ipū Crater. Kitted out with island-style paintings and furniture, and very peaceful by Po'ipū standards. Credit cards not accepted. ❹.

**Gloria's Spouting Horn B&B**, 4464 Lāwa'i Beach Rd, Po'ipū HI 96756; Ⓣ & Ⓕ 742-6995, Ⓦ best.com/~travel/gloria. Luxury oceanfront B&B, just before Spouting Horn west of Po'ipū. This exposed site took a fearful beating from Iniki, but the house has been completely rebuilt in wood, with vast picture windows. Each room has a private *lānai* and bathroom. Three-night minimum (seven at Christmas); no under-14s, no smoking. ❼.

**Hyatt Regency Kauai**, 1571 Po'ipū Rd, Po'ipū HI 96756; Ⓣ 742-1234 or 1-800/554-9288, Ⓕ 742-1557, Ⓦ www.kauai-hyatt.com. Six-hundred-room giant, sprawling along the seafront at the east end of Po'ipū. Formal antique-filled lobby, top-of-the-range bedrooms and great sea views, plus some amazing landscaping; the terraced gardens are filled with waterfalls, and you can swim from pool to pool, aided by the odd waterslide, until you drop down into a luscious network of artificial saltwater lagoons, squeezed in just back from the beach. The *Tidepools* and *Ilima Terrace* restaurants are reviewed on p.000. Garden view ❽, ocean view ❾.

**Kiahuna Plantation**, 2253 Po'ipū Rd, Po'ipū HI 96756; bookable through either Outrigger, Ⓣ 303/369-777 or 1-800/688-7444 (US & Can), Ⓦ www.outrigger.com, or through Castle Resorts, Ⓣ 742-2200, 1-800/272-5257 (HI) or 1-800/367-5004 (US & Can), Ⓦ www.castle-resorts.com. Huge, sprawling oceanfront property. Part is managed by Outrigger and part by Castle Resorts, which maintain separate offices at either end – be sure you check in at the right one. Each of the two-story "plantation-style" buildings is divided into condos with their own kitchens, living rooms and *lānais*; all sleep at least four people. Manicured lawns lead down to the sea, where there's sheltered inshore bathing, good snorkeling and, further out, fine surfing – champion surfer Margo Oberg offers lessons from $45. ❺–❽.

**Kōloa Landing Cottages**, 2704b Ho'onani Rd, Po'ipū HI 96756; Ⓣ 742-1470 or 1-800/779-8773, Ⓕ 332-9584, Ⓦ www.planet-hawaii.com/koloa. Two studios and two two-bedroom cottages, all with kitchen facilities, facing Kōloa Landing. A good standard of accommodation, plus free fruit to pick. ❸–❹.

**Po'ipū Bed & Breakfast Inn**, 2720 Ho'onani Rd, Po'ipū HI 96756; Ⓣ 742-0100 or 1-800/808-2330, Ⓦ poipu.net. Pink B&B bungalow in nice gardens, beside Kōloa Landing at the mouth of Waikomo Stream. Exquisite antique-furnished bedrooms, all en suite, plus large shared *lānai* and living room. ❹–❺.

**Po'ipū Kai Resort**, 1941 Po'ipū Rd, Po'ipū HI 96756; Ⓣ 742-6464 or 1-800/777-1700, Ⓕ 742-7865, Ⓦ www.poipu-kai.com. One-, two- and three-bedroom condos in a luxury seafront resort, with nine tennis courts, six pools, two beaches and the reasonable *House of Seafood* restaurant. Rates include a free rental car. ❹–❼.

**Po'ipū Kapili**, 2221 Kapili Rd, Po'ipū HI 96756; Ⓣ 742-6449 or 1-800/443-7714 (US & Can), Ⓕ 742-9162, Ⓦ www.poipukapili.com. Pleasing and well-equipped one- and two-bedroom condo apartments, each with kitchen, TVs, phone, CD player and *lānai*, in an attractive, peaceful waterfront location just east of Kōloa Landing. Free use of central pool and floodlit tennis courts; five-day minimum stay. ❻.

**Po'ipū Plantation**, 1792 Pe'e Rd, Po'ipū HI 96756; Ⓣ 742-6757 or 1-800/634-0263 (US & Can), Ⓕ 742-8681, Ⓔ bandb@aloha.net. Three B&B rooms, plus one- and two-bedroom self-catering condos, back from the ocean alongside Po'ipū Crater. Not all units have sea views, but they all look attractively fresh. ❸, ocean view ❹.

**Sheraton Kauai Resort**, 2440 Ho'onani Rd, Po'ipū HI 96756; Ⓣ 742-1661 or 1-800/782-9488, Ⓕ 742-4055, Ⓦ www.sheraton-kauai.com. The *Sheraton*'s dramatic oceanfront position meant that it suffered so much damage from Hurricane Iniki that it took until 1998 to reopen. Finally it's back and as good as new. Rooms in the Ocean and Beach wings enjoy spectacular views, but the Garden wing is a bit disappointing. The pool is a little small, and the restaurants are unexceptional, but with such a good beach at hand it really doesn't matter. Garden view ❼, ocean view ❽.

## Po'ipū Condos

Po'ipū has no shortage of **condos**. Most owners rent their apartments through agencies, which as a rule quote better rates than you'll be offered if you contact properties directly. One-bedroom ocean-view apartments booked through Grantham Resorts (Ⓣ 742-7220 or 1-800/325-5701, Ⓦ www.grantham-resorts.com) or Suite Paradise (Ⓣ 742-7400 or 1-800/367-8020, Ⓦ www.suite-paradise.com) start at under $100 per night when booked for a week or more in spring or fall; the price rises to about $125 in high season. Two-bedroom apartments start at perhaps $140. Recommended condo-only resorts include Whaler's Cove and Lāwa'i Beach Resort.

## The Po'ipū shoreline: east of Kōloa Landing

Po'ipū has two distinct sections of oceanfront, to either side of Waikomo Stream. When Kōloa Plantation first opened, **Kōloa Landing**, on the eastern bank of the river mouth, was briefly Kauai's major port, and as such Hawaii's third whaling port after Lahaina and Honolulu. Only a basic boat ramp now survives, though the area is popular with divers and snorkelers.

East of Kōloa Landing, a rocky headland marks the beginning of the long narrow shelf of **Po'ipū Beach**, interrupted by two smaller headlands. The sea areas are separated by parallel reefs; the inshore segment makes a perfect swimming spot for young children, while windsurfers glide along the waters beyond when the wind picks up, and an expert **surfing** site known as First Break lies half a mile out to sea. Different parts of the beach are known by the names of the adjacent hotels; apart from Sheraton Beach at the end of Ho'onani Road, most of Po'ipū Beach can only be reached by walking along the sand. Oceanfront kiosks throughout Po'ipū, many attached to hotels, rent snorkels, kayaks and other beach equipment.

**Nukumoi Point**, the craggy easternmost point of Po'ipū Beach, is one of only three *tombolos* in Hawaii, all on Kauai. A *tombolo* is a cross between an island and a headland, joined to the mainland by a slender sand bar that all but disappears at high tide. **Po'ipū Beach County Park** beyond has the only public facilities along the Po'ipū coast, with a children's playground and a lifeguard station, and is thus the beach of choice for local families. Swimming in the lee of Nukumoi Point is generally safe, while snorkeling at its base is excellent.

A little way further along, boogie-boarders and body-surfers jostle for position among the fierce waves that break over the offshore sand bar at **Brennecke's Beach**. The crowds are such that surfers are banned. Brennecke's was named after a doctor whose house stood here until 1982, when it was wrenched from its foundations by Hurricane Iwa. That hurricane took most of the sand from the beach too, and Iniki removed a lot more ten years later.

East of Brennecke's, the beaches are interrupted by conical **Po'ipū Crater**, a vestige of Kauai's final burst of volcanic activity. It's now ringed by small condos, with high bluffs along the seafront. On the far side, the *Hyatt Regency* dominates the crescent of **Shipwreck Beach**. Most of the sand scooped up by the hurricanes landed here, where it buried not only the eponymous shipwreck, but also a field of ancient petroglyphs. Even with all that sand, it's not much fun getting into the water across the shoreline rocks, so Shipwreck is largely the preserve of boogie-boarders and windsurfers.

## Māhā'ulepū

Makawehi Point, past Shipwreck Beach, marks the start of the **Makawehi Dunes**, crisp-topped mounds of lithified sandstone filled with the bones of extinct flightless birds. Po'ipū Road ends alongside the golf course east of the *Hyatt*, but it's possible to keep going along the dirt road beyond. A couple of miles along, shortly after a closed gate forces you to turn right, you'll come to a gatehouse. In daylight hours, you can sign a waiver here and proceed into the region known as **Māhā'ulepū**, which has three unspoiled, secluded beaches along its two-mile ocean frontage. The entire area belongs to the Grove Farm company, and thus now to Steve Case of AOL (see p.425), but he is said to have no plans to develop it in any way.

The road reaches the sea in the middle of **Gillin's Beach**, typical of the Māhā'ulepū beaches in being too exposed for safe swimming. Windsurfers prepared to carry their equipment this far take advantage of the strong waves, and naturalists set off into the dunes in search of rare native plants. Hikers head east, first to **Kawailoa Bay**, and then, across a stretch of lava indented with spectacular caves, to **Ha'ula Beach** half a mile further along. CJM Stables runs **horseback trips** in the Māhā'ulepū area ($65–90; reservation required; ⓣ742-6096, ⓦwww.cjmstables.com).

Note that it's against the law to come within 100 feet of the endangered monk seals that sun themselves on the beaches of Po'ipū – let alone touch or harass them.

## The Po'ipū shoreline: west to Spouting Horn

The coast **west of Waikomo Stream** can offer few beaches to compete with the luxuriant expanses to the east. Only for the first mile or so is there much sign of sand, and that tends to get stripped to almost nothing by each high tide. At **Ho'ona Beach**, the first possibility, the merest pocket of sand is tucked in among the rocks, and is appropriately nicknamed "Baby Beach."

Even less sand clings to the shoreline of Ho'ai Bay, just beyond. Across from the sea, the lawns of **Prince Kūhīo Park** commemorate the birthplace of Prince Jonah Kūhīo Kalaniana'ole (1871–1922), Hawaii's delegate to Congress from 1902 until 1922. A bronze bust of the prince stands on an imposing plinth, with a flagpole to either side. Behind it, in front of a fine spread of bougainvillea, is a black lava platform that once held the Ho'ai *heiau*, looking considerably sturdier than many of the new condos nearby.

Just past the next small headland is **Beach House Beach**, named after a nearby restaurant that continues to battle on, despite hammerings from the two hurricanes. This narrow roadside strip makes for a good quick snorkel stop, and there are some expert-only surf breaks further out.

Coach tours galore continue beyond the bobbing yachts of tiny Kukui'ula Harbor to **Spouting Horn County Park**, a natural freak a mile or so on at the end of the road. From the viewing area at the edge of the parking lot, you look down on to a flat ledge of black lava, just above sea level. As each wave breaks against it, clouds of spume and spray jet into the air through the "spouting horn," a hole in the lava. Obviously enough, the highest fountains coincide with the biggest waves, while rainbows hang in the spray when the eruptions come in quick succession. A larger hole alongside the existing one was dynamited by plantation owners at the start of the twentieth century, in order to stop salt spray from damaging crops in the nearby fields.

If disappointment with what is usually a less-than-enthralling spectacle tempts you to scramble down onto the rocks below, don't. The view isn't any better, and there's a risk of severe injury.

## Allerton and Lāwa'i gardens

Across the street from Spouting Horn, a restored plantation home serves as the visitor center for the **National Tropical Botanical Garden** (Mon–Sat 8.30am–5pm; ⓣ742-2623, ⓦwww.ntbg.org). Although it sells assorted crafts and plant-related products, its main function is as the starting point for tours of **Allerton** and **Lāwa'i Gardens**, which fill over two hundred acres of the otherwise inaccessible **Lāwa'i Valley** a little further west. Originally created by a Chicago banking family, these beautiful gardens are now maintained as sanctuaries and research centers devoted to rare plant species, but Allerton in particular also makes an absolutely ravishing spectacle for casual tourists.

**Allerton Garden** occupies the seaward half of the valley, stretching several hundred yards from the former Allerton home, which is not currently open to visitors, up to exquisite little **Lāwa'i Kai** beach. Walking tours of the garden set off at 9am, 10am, 1pm and 2pm on Tuesday through Saturday ($30 per person). All tours last two and a half hours, and it's essential to make reservations as far in advance as possible.

The Allertons laid the garden out as a succession of "rooms," each with its own character, but despite the abundance of classical statuary, formal fountains and gazebos, the overall impression is of a glorious profusion of tropical color. The plants here are drawn from all over the world. Flaming torch gingers, lobster-claw heliconia and birds of paradise erupt on all sides, and nature feels barely tamed. Appropriately enough, it was amid the roots of one especially enormous banyan tree that the dinosaur's egg was discovered in the movie *Jurassic Park*.

**Lāwa'i Garden**, by contrast – but like the NTBG's other Kauai property, at Limahuli on the North Shore (see p.463) – focuses exclusively on Hawaiian species. In fact, it holds the most extensive collection of Hawaiian plants to be found anywhere on earth. Only on one day per week are tours allowed to disturb the ongoing scientific work, and visitors are expected to have serious botanical interests. Tours of Lāwa'i Garden, partly by vehicle and partly on foot, depart Monday at 9am and 1pm ($30 per person).

## Restaurants

Po'ipū has a fine selection of **restaurants**, with *Roy's* in particular attracting diners from all over the island. However, there are surprisingly few options along the seafront, and it's also notably short of budget choices. One or two cheaper options, such as the Po'ipū Garden Café, can be found in the Po'ipū Shopping Village, but if you're looking for an inexpensive option, you'd do better to drive back up to Kōloa (see p.472). Most of the larger hotels have their own dining rooms, which serve reasonably good food, but only the *Hyatt* is especially worth visiting for a meal.

**The Beach House**, 5022 Lāwa'i Rd; ⓣ742-1424. An irresistible oceanfront setting enables this fashionable Pacific Rim restaurant to charge the daily sunset-viewing throng sky-high prices. Appetizers such as wasabi panko-crusted mussels cost around $10; entrees like the goat cheese roasted garlic rack of lamb or the rich seafood "Local Boy Paella" are $25. Unless you're swept away by the sheer romance of the place, you may come away feeling that the portions are too small and the flavors not so much subtle as minimal. Daily 5.30–9.30pm.

**Brennecke's Beach Broiler**, 2100 Ho'one Rd; ⓣ742-7588. Little expense may have been lavished on the no-frills interior and *lānai* of this family seafood restaurant, but with the waving palms of Po'ipū Beach Park in sight, *Brennecke's* always manages to be full. Most of the menu is devoted to inexpensive sandwiches and burgers, though at dinner interesting appetizers include *ceviche* ($8) and *sashimi* ($11), and among the fancier seafood entrees are clams for $21 and lobster at $30. Standard steaks, ribs, and combos are also available, and there are sunset cocktails, too. Daily 11am–10pm.

**Casa di Amici**, 2360 Nalo Rd; ⓣ742-1555. Breezy, open-sided restaurant, tucked away in an obscure but central side street a hundred yards back from the ocean. A true hidden gem, it serves Po'ipū's finest food at less than exorbitant prices. The bulk of the menu is Italian, with plenty of pasta specialties, plus veal and chicken served in marsala, piccatta and gorgonzola sauces, all available in light ($17–18) and regular ($21–23) sizes. There are also a handful of adventurous Pacific Rim options, like grilled black tiger prawns sprinkled with bonito *furikake* and served with black *frijoles* and jalapeño-tequila *aioli* ($25), which may sound over the top but is the single best dish sold on Kauai. Everything is beautifully presented; entrees come with a superb assortment of local-flavored side dishes, such as spinach creamed with coconut and corn with orange cilantro; and the staff are extremely friendly. Daily 6–10pm.

**Ilima Terrace**, *Hyatt Regency Kauai*, 1571 Po'ipū Rd; ⓣ742-6260. Plush open-air restaurant, which specializes in pricey breakfasts (the continental option costs $9, while a full buffet is $18.50), light lunches (sandwiches, salads or *saimin*), and all-you-can-eat dinner buffets. The buffet choices include prime rib ($29; Tues & Sat), Italian ($29; Sun & Thurs), and Kauai seafood ($30; Mon, Wed & Fri); there's also a Sunday brunch ($29). Though the food is unimaginative, the quality is consistently high, and reservations are recommended. Daily 6am–2.30pm & 5–9pm.

**Keoki's Paradise**, Po'ipū Shopping Village; ⓣ742-7534. Mall cocktail lounge that's been given an appealing Polynesian make-over, with a thatched bar, a waterfall and a meandering lagoon; ersatz it may be, but it still turns dining here into an atmospheric experience. The food isn't bad, despite the mix 'n' match approach to world cuisines. Lunchtime sandwiches and local plates are mostly under $10. For dinner, from 5.30pm, appetizers such as *sashimi*, *mushu* pork ($6), and Thai shrimp sticks ($9) are followed by fresh fish (around $20), steaks (from $18), or Kōloa pork ribs ($17). Daily 11am–midnight.

**Roy's Po'ipū Bar & Grill**, Po'ipū Shopping Village, 2360 Kiahuna Plantation Drive; ⓣ742-5000. Busy "Euro-Asian" joint, whose kitchens are visible at the back. Appetizers range from pasta, satay and snails ($6–13), to pizzas with sausage or smoked duck toppings for $7. In addition to $17–20 entrees such as garlic ribs and chicken stuffed with wild mushrooms, there's a lengthy list of pricier daily specials, including fish selections such as a *hibachi*-style salmon. Desserts include a legendary dark chocolate souffle, and there's a great wine list. Everything here tastes good, and the showy touches from celebrity chef Roy "Cooking has been my life, Thank you for making it part of yours" Yamaguchi make it great fun. Reservations are essential. Daily 5.30–9.30pm.

**Tidepools**, *Hyatt Regency Kauai*, 1571 Po'ipū Rd; ⓣ742-6260. Very romantic dinner-only restaurant, consisting of semi-private open-air thatched huts arrayed around the resort's waterfalls and lagoon; the lights can be so low that you can hardly see your food. The relatively short menu features some interesting appetizers such as *imu*-roasted veal ribs ($8) and *ahi sashimi* ($10), while the entrees, at $23–36, include both "contemporary Hawaiian" (eg pan-seared diver scallops) and "mainland" (slow-roasted prime rib) options. Reservations are advisable. Daily 6–10pm.

# Kāhili Mountain Park

From Hwy-50, the main thoroughfare that circles the island, a couple of hundred yards west of the south turn towards Po'ipū – and thus less than a mile beyond the Knudsen Gap (see p.472) – a dirt road climbs for a mile inland to reach **Kāhili Mountain Park**. This little-known private enclave belongs to the Seventh Day Adventist Church, which finances a small school here by renting out small **cabins** (PO Box 298, Kōloa HI 96756; ⓣ742-9921, ⓕ742-6628; ❷). Though rustic, it's as idyllic (and inexpensive) a mountain retreat as it's possible to imagine. Perched on stilts, the cabins are arrayed at broad intervals along the edge of a large grassy meadow, with mountain ridges soaring on three sides and views down to the sea on the fourth. The tiniest of the cabins, with basic cooking facilities but sharing a communal bathroom, start at just $28 per person per night; en-suite facilities are available for just slightly more. There's also a fully equipped vacation home for under $100 per night. Reservations are essential.

The park is also the starting point of the **Kāhili Ridge Trail**, the finest hike on the southern side of Kauai, and an easy half-day outing for Po'ipū-based visitors. To find the trailhead, look for a water tower to the right of the dirt road, shortly beyond the final, highest cabin. Park nearby and follow a dirt track for a hundred yards past the tower until you come to a small clearing. Chances are the track will be barred at this point; in any case, continue instead, in much the same direction, through an obvious "tunnel" of overhanging low flowering shrubs.

As it climbs a slender spur towards the main mountain ridge, the trail swiftly degenerates to no more than a muddy rut. It's barely two feet wide in places, and bursts of steep climbing are interspersed with precarious ridge walking. Colorful flowers and orchids grow to either side, while the vegetation occasionally thins out to offer views down past Hā'upu Ridge to Līhu'e.

Just how far you get will depend on your head for heights and the rain conditions. It's not possible, however, to climb all the way to the 3089ft summit of Kāhili, which is itself just a pimple on the island's central spine, running north to Kawaikini. The trail ends instead at a radio mast just under two miles up from the park. Bear in mind that coming down is harder than going up, especially if the path is wet and slippery.

# Lāwa'i



**LĀWA'I**, the first village that Kaumuali'i Highway (Hwy-50) passes through west of Līhu'e, after ten miles, is connected directly with Kōloa via the three-mile rural Kōloa Road. This is primarily a residential area, and with the tiny shopping complex at the highway intersection now apparently defunct, there's no reason whatsoever to stop here. A few minutes' drive south, however, *Victoria Place* is a pleasant country **B&B**, with three double rooms and one single (3459 Lāwa'i Loa Lane, PO Box 930, Lāwa'i HI 96765; ⓣ332-9300, ⓕ332-9465, ⓦwww.hshawaii.com/kvp/victoria; ❸).

# Kalāheo

Two miles on from Lāwa'i, the larger town of **KALĀHEO** consists of a cluster of shops, restaurants and gas stations kept busy by its predominantly Portuguese community. Half a mile south of the center, **Kukui O Lono** public park (daily 6.30am–6.30pm; free) is an invaluable local resource, with a nine-hole golf course and attractively landscaped avenues, but it's unlikely to detain any tourist for long.

Heading off the highway into the network of small roads *makai* of Kalāheo makes for some picturesque country driving, but you can't get as far as the sea. Much of this former sugar land is now given over to cultivating coffee instead, and extensive groves cover the sunny, south-facing slopes. At **NUMILA**, just over two miles southwest of Kalāheo down Halewili Road, the **Kauai Coffee Company Visitor Center** explains the intricacies of coffee production and sells simple gifts (daily 9am–5pm; free). Staff members offer free samples of local-grown java, but there's no coffee bar as such.

## Practicalities

Surprisingly enough, Kalāheo boasts an old-fashioned **motel**, the *Kalāheo Inn*, a few yards south of the main road, but tucked out of sight at 4444 Papalina Rd (ⓣ332-6023 or 1-888/332-6023, ⓦwww.kalaheoinn.com; ❷). Upgraded in 1999, it remains far from fancy, but nonetheless it's a real bargain, with each of the nine suites offering its own kitchen. There's also inexpensive but good-quality **B&B** accommodation just up from Kalāheo at *Classic Vacation Cottages*, 2687 Onu Place (ⓣ332-9201, ⓕ332-7645, ⓦwww.classiccottages.com; ❷).

Three garden cottages are divided into five units, all en-suite with kitchen facilities and sharing use of a hot tub.

The pick of the local **restaurants** are *Brick Oven Pizza* on Kaumuali'i Highway (Tues–Sun 11am–10pm; ⓣ 322-8561), renowned for serving the best pizzas on Kauai; and the equally self-explanatory *Kalāheo Steak House*, alongside the *Kalāheo Inn* on Papalina Road (daily 5.30–9.30pm; ⓣ 332-9780), where a full steak dinner costs under $20. Also on the main highway, the *Kalāheo Coffee Co* (Mon–Fri 6am–3pm, Sat 6.30am–3pm, Sun 6.30am–2pm; ⓣ 332-5858) offers a vast selection of coffees, plus cooked breakfasts and sandwiches.

# Hanapēpē Valley



Shortly after Kalāheo, the fields to the right of the highway drop away, and a roadside pull-out overlooks a colorful and deeply-worn gorge beneath a high mountain ridge. Many visitors imagine they're getting their first sight of Waimea Canyon, but this is in fact **Hanapēpē Valley**, a miniature version of the real thing. Watered by the broad Hanapēpē River, this fertile valley was once a major *taro*-growing center. As at the similar valley of Hanalei (see p.457), the land was turned over to rice by Chinese and Japanese immigrants at the end of the nineteenth century, but is now reverting to *taro*. The overlook was the scene of a bloody battle in August 1824, when forces led by Governor Hoapili of Maui defeated a band of insurgent Kauaians under Prince George, the son of the recently deceased chief Kaumuali'i (see p.415).

## 'Ele'ele

As it starts to drop towards sea level, the highway reaches **'ELE'ELE**, making a sweeping rightward curve in front of the small 'Ele'ele Shopping Village complex. Following a minor road down behind the mall swiftly brings you to a dead end at **Port Allen**, a small commercial harbor that was Kauai's main port until the 1920s. It was then supplanted by the newly dredged Nāwiliwili Harbor, at the same time as the adjacent airport of Burns Field was replaced by Līhu'e.

The only reason you might pause in 'Ele'ele is for a bite to **eat** in the Shopping Village. Right on the highway, *Grinds Espresso* (daily 5.30am-9pm; ⓣ 335-6027) serves coffees and pastries to fishermen and other early risers, full cooked breakfasts for around $7, and later, sandwiches, plate lunches and pizzas for $7–10. Slightly further back from the road, there's excellent **Thai food** at *Toi's Thai Kitchen* (Mon–Fri 10.30am–2pm & 5.30–9.30pm, Sat 11am–2pm & 5.30–9.30pm; ⓣ 335-3111), where great pad thai, and lemongrass-packed dishes such as the delicious Toi's Temptation, cost $10–16.

# Hanapēpē

**HANAPĒPĒ** itself, at the foot of the hill beyond 'Ele'ele, is often lauded as one of Kauai's quaintest little villages. Driving straight through on the highway you'd barely notice it was there, and sadly even the half-mile detour down its old main street, just inland, is these days a disappointment. The old wooden stores of this plantation town had just about managed to reinvent them-

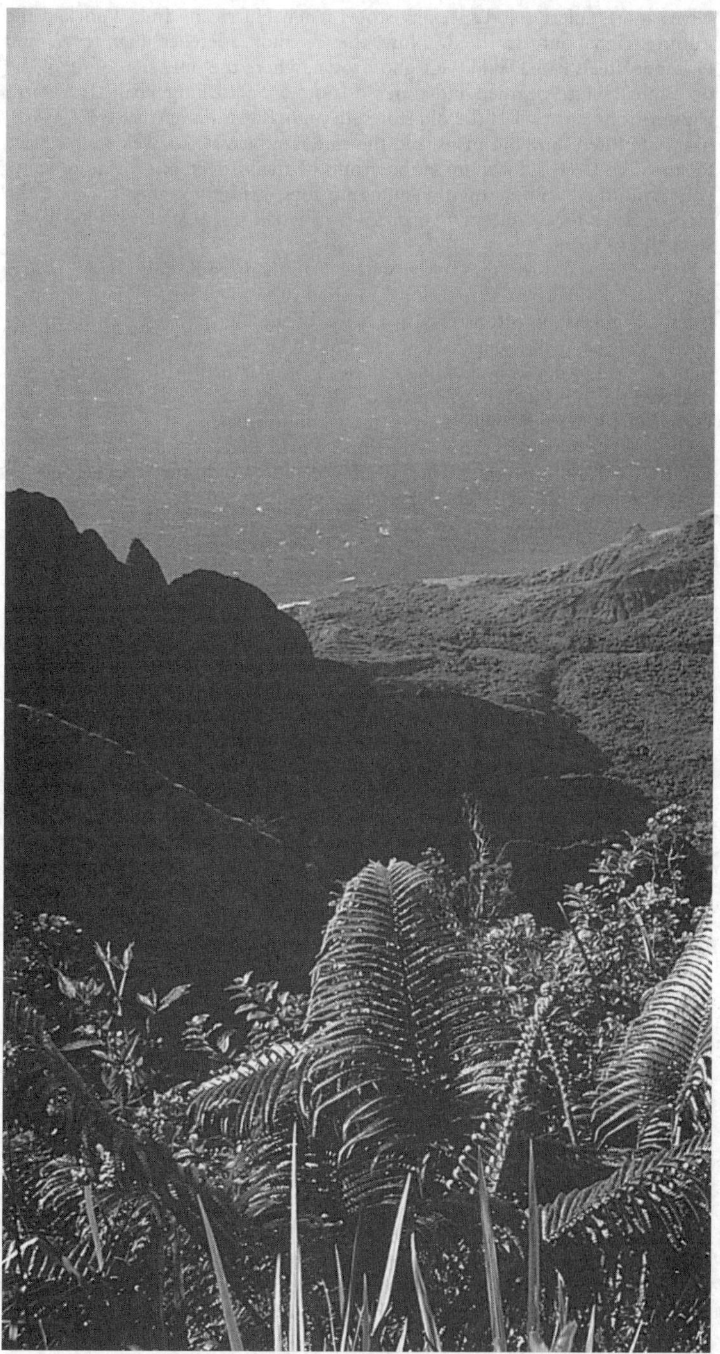

selves as art galleries and specialty stores when Hurricane Iniki knocked the stuffing right out of them. Now they're more derelict than ever, and Hanapēpē feels like a Wild West ghost town, where the only sign of life is the occasional white-bearded old-timer dozing on a rocking chair. It's worth pausing at one or two of the old stores, though; Kauai Fine Arts (Ⓣ 335-3778) has some interesting old maps, and the café (see below) is a welcoming place to stop. The river is not quite visible from the main street, but for more views you can either walk across the swinging rope bridge roughly opposite the cafe, or drive for a mile or two up Awawa Road just past the bridge at the west end of town.

Hanapēpē is also the only place where Hawaiian "**rock salt**" or *pa'a kai* is still manufactured by the traditional method of evaporation – a far from picturesque process, unfortunately. Turn *makai* of the highway just past town and you'll pass the "pans," expanses of red mud where sea water is collected and then allowed to dry away. Judging by the air of dilapidation, the pans are easily mistaken for refuse dumps. Souvenir shops on Kauai sell what they call Hawaiian salt, but it's unlikely to be the genuine article.

The road continues as far as **Salt Pond Park**, a little further on at the flat, windswept southwestern corner of the island. Windsurfers come here in droves, and the sheltered inshore bathing is good for children, but Iniki scoured away what little beauty the crescent beach possessed. There's plenty of room to **camp**, however – with a county permit; see p.419 – so many budget travelers make it their base for exploring south and west Kauai.

## Practicalities

Though Hanapēpē is devoid of accommodation, it does have a small selection of **restaurants**. On the old main street, the *Hanapēpē Café & Espresso*, 3830 Hanapēpē Rd (Tues & Thurs–Sat 9am–2pm, Fri 9am–2pm & 6–9pm; Ⓣ 335-5011), is a friendly **vegetarian** establishment with a blue-tiled, horseshoe-shaped espresso bar. It serves good breakfasts, with pancakes and waffles starting at $4, and baked lunch specials. At dinner, served on Fridays only to the accompaniment of live Hawaiian music, the roasted heads of garlic ($1.75) make great appetizers; entrees such as pasta or crêpes start at $17.

Out on the highway, the *Green Garden* (Mon & Wed–Sat 10.30am–2pm & 5–9pm, Sun 7.30am–2pm & 5–9pm; Ⓣ 335-5422) offers a much less interesting menu of meats and sandwiches in a pleasant but often crowded garden setting. A garish yellow shack nearby doubles as both *Bradda Lou's Shrimp Shack* (closed Sun; Ⓣ 335-0240), doling out tasty and very inexpensive lunchtime dishes such as shrimp burgers ($6.50) and pork, peas and pimentos ($5), and the *Atomic Clock Cafe* **internet café** (Ⓣ 335-5121). Hours of operation for both vary on the whims of the proprietors.

# Kaumakani

Kaumuali'i Highway turns northwest after Hanapēpē, heading towards Waimea through the extensive landholdings of the **Gay and Robinson family**. Though best known for owning the entire island of Niihau (see p.490), the family also owns what has become Kauai's last **sugar plantation**. This corner of the island is a patchwork quilt of cane fields (largely screened from view behind roadside trees and great swathes of bougainvillea) and open ranch land, used to pasture over three thousand head of cattle.

The plantation centers on the tiny community of **KAUMAKANI**, just over two miles out of Hanapēpē, where a picturesque Methodist church stands *mauka* of the highway. Across the road, an imposing avenue of trees leads down between twin rows of plantation houses. One of these is now the headquarters for two-hour **bus and walking tours** of the plantation (Mon–Fri 8.45am & 12.45pm; $30; Ⓣ335-2824, Ⓦwww.gandrtours-kauai.com), for which advance reservations are required. In season, between April and October, you may well get to don a hard hat and see the mill in full operation; in winter, you'll still see the actual fields, but you'll have to content yourself with a video depicting what becomes of the cane.

# Waimea

Six miles beyond Hanapēpē, the circle-island highway drops once more to sea level, crossing Waimea River to enter the town of **WAIMEA**. Sadly, despite being the spot where ancient Hawaiians first came into contact with European sailors, and despite its location at the portals of the magnificent Waimea Canyon, modern Waimea is a somewhat run-down, even seedy place. Once again Hurricane Iniki is partly to blame, but even before its onslaught the region had been in a long slow decline.

When Captain Cook arrived in 1778, Waimea Valley was a major population center, with *taro* farmers exploiting the rich soil inland, and fishermen plundering both river and ocean. *Waimea* literally means "reddish water," but the red earth scoured by the river from the mountains is deposited along the shoreline as a fine gray silt, leaving the beaches looking dirty and unappealing.

## The town and the beaches

Waimea today amounts to little more than a short street, off the far end of which leads the lesser of the two poorly marked roads up to the canyon. There are no shops to speak of, apart from a Big Save supermarket, Da Booze Shop and the Wishy Washy Laundry.

A statue of Captain Cook stands on the small green in town – it's an exact replica of one in Cook's home port of Whitby, England – but the navigator's memory is not greatly honored in Waimea. The beach where he landed, west of the river mouth, is pointedly named **Lucy Wright Beach Park**, after the first native Hawaiian teacher at the local school. There is, at least, a very inconspicuous National Park Service plaque commemorating the exact spot; stuck atop a lava boulder, it offers no detail whatsoever, not even a date.

You're still likely to see locals surfing at the river mouth – it's a popular learning site for kids in summer – but this is one of the grubbiest and most polluted beaches in the state, and not suitable for swimming. You can, however, **camp** if you choose, with a county permit (see p.426).

Head upriver on either Menehune Road or Ala Wai Road, and shortly after they join, a mile or so along, you may spot traces of the **Menehune Ditch** at the foot of the bluff on the left. Whether or not this ancient irrigation channel was built by the legendary *menehune*, the care with which its stones were shaped makes it unique in Hawaii. However, little of it has survived. The road narrows and peters out not far beyond. For more about the *menehune*, see p.429.

## The Coming of Captain Cook

**Captain James Cook** sailed north from the Society Islands in December 1777, hoping to fulfil the aim of his third Pacific voyage – the discovery of the Northwest Passage back to the Atlantic. Instead he came upon an uncharted group of islands, north of the equator, in such a strategic location that he immediately recognized this as the crowning moment of his career.

Cook's two ships, the *Resolution* and the *Discovery*, had sailed from London in July 1776. On January 18, 1778, having passed far to the west of Hawaii and Maui, lookouts sighted first Oahu, and then Kauai. The following day, off the southeast corner of Kauai, two canoes came alongside, each carrying three or four men: "We were agreeably surprised to find them of the same Nation as the people of Otaheite [Tahiti] and the other islands we had lately visited," Cook wrote in his journal.

The ships sailed along the island's south coast looking for a place to land. With those canoes that dared to approach, they exchanged nails and small pieces of iron for "roasting pigs and some very fine Potatoes." When they finally found what seemed to be a safe anchorage, Cook allowed the natives of the nearest village, which he understood to be *Wymoa*, to come aboard:

"I never saw Indians so much astonished at the entering a ship before, their eyes were continually flying from object to object . . . However the first man that came on board did not with all his surprise, forget his own interest, the first moveable thing that came in his way was the lead and line, which he without asking any questions took to put into his Canoe and when we stopped him said 'I am only going to put it into my boat.'"

On the next day, January 20, Third Lieutenant Williamson was sent ashore in a small boat. Before he could set foot on dry land, he found himself besieged by curious Hawaiians. Despite feeling in no physical danger, and with the "greatest reluctance," he shot and killed "a tall handsome man about 40 years of age [who] seemed to be a chief." Williamson didn't even mention the incident to Cook until some weeks later, but wrote in his journal that "These barbarians must be [initially] quelled by force, as they afterwards readily believe that whatever kindness is then



## Russian Fort Elizabeth State Historical Park

On the headland on the eastern side of Waimea River, the ruins of **Russian Fort Elizabeth** bear witness to a strange interlude in Kauaian history. When a Russian-American Company ship was wrecked off Waimea in 1815, the Kauaian chief Kaumuali'i seized both the vessel and its cargo of Alaskan furs. The company sent a German surgeon, **George Schäffer**, disguised as a botanist, to persuade Kamehameha the Great to talk Kaumuali'i into returning its property. That circuitous plan failed, so Schäffer decided to negotiate directly with Kaumuali'i instead. Soon Kaumuali'i had agreed to a secret treaty under which Schäffer would supply arms and ships for Kauai to invade Oahu, Maui, Molokai and Lanai, in return for Russian control over half of Oahu and various other concessions. To strengthen Kauai's defences, Schäffer started construction of a star-shaped fortress at Waimea in 1816. However, American merchantmen got wind of his plans, were told by other Russians that Schäffer was not acting on orders, and hatched their own plot to get rid of him. They managed to convince the whole population of Kauai, including Schäffer, that Russia and the United States were at war. In May 1817, Schäffer fled, as he thought, for his life.

Nonetheless, the fort was completed and used by the Hawaiian government until 1864. Though it has now been minimally reconstructed, with rudimen-

shown them proceeds from love, whereas otherwise they attribute it to weakness, or cowardice."

Cook himself landed near the mouth of the Waimea River later that day. "Several hundreds . . . were assembled on a sandy beach before the Village. The very instant I leaped ashore, they all fell flat on their faces, and remained in that humble posture till I made signs to them to rise. They then brought a great many small pigs and gave us without regarding whether they got any thing in return." Together with a small party of sailors and a "tolerable train" of Hawaiians, Cook walked up the valley, which was extensively planted with *taro*, sugar, plantains and paper mulberry trees. He was led to a nearby *heiau* and told it had recently been used for human sacrifice.

Above all else, the Hawaiians were eager to trade for iron. The fact that they already owned tiny quantities of the metal might point to previous, unrecorded contact with Spanish explorers. Cook's men, however, noticed a worm-eaten piece of fir, washed up as driftwood, and speculated that the iron might have arrived in the same way. Local women found it easy to obtain scraps of metal from the sailors, and venereal diseases along with it, which despite all Cook's hand-wringing were established throughout the islands within a year.

The English ships stayed at Waimea for just three days. They were repeatedly blown from their moorings in the high winter seas, and having weighed anchor on January 23, were unable to get back in. Instead they spent a few days on Niihau, before continuing north. Cook's rendition of the name of Kauai as *Atoui* was not such a bad mistake, for it came from a mishearing of "and Kauai"; as the most leeward of the islands, Kauai tends to come at the end of the list. He named the archipelago the Sandwich Islands, in honor of the Earl of Sandwich (the same one for whom the sandwich had been named in 1762).

For an account of Cook's return to Hawaii in 1779, and his death at Kealekekua Bay, see p.171. Waimea was thereafter a principal port of call for Western ships, with the first fur-traders arriving in 1786. Captain John Kendrick of the *Lady Washington*, who picked up firewood here in 1791, sailed straight back again when he realized that his load included precious sandalwood. In doing so, he sparked the first boom in the Hawaiian economy, and fatally undermined the old political order (see p.511).

tary walls laid out according to a ground plan decided more by guesswork than by excavation, it would take a lot of imagination to derive any interest from this tumbledown relic, overgrown with dandelions. Official statistics show that it's the most visited attraction on Kauai, with 300,000 tourists per year, though footnotes in the HVB report reveal that the vast majority are tour-bus passengers using the rest rooms en route to Waimea Canyon.

## Practicalities

Western Kauai's only **accommodation** possibility is one of the most appealing and characterful properties on the island. *Waimea Plantation Cottages*, just west of Waimea at 9600 Kaumuali'i Hwy no. 367 (Waimea HI 96796; Ⓣ 338-1625, 1-800/922-7866 (US & Can) or 1-800/321-2558 (HI), Ⓕ 338-2338, Ⓦ www.aston-hotels.com; garden view ❺, ocean view ❻), are the former homes of Waimea Sugar Mill Company employees, gathered in a coconut grove and fully renovated. Ordinary plantation workers may not have lived this close to the sea, or have had such luxurious bathrooms, but the atmosphere feels authentic, and the wooden floors, linen draperies and breezy *lānais* make the one-, two- and three-bedroom cottages a delight. The sea isn't safe for swimming and the beach is gray, but there's a pool, and the garden hammocks have good views of Niihau.

Alongside the plantation headquarters, just off the highway amid the coconut palms, the *Waimea Brewing Company* calls itself the "world's westernmost **brew-pub**" (daily 7–10am & 11am–9pm; ⓣ338-2300). It's a lovely spot, with plenty of shaded seating out on the terrace and a faded turquoise wooden bar inside. A 16oz glass of one of the house brews (like the wittily named Wai'ale'ale Ale) costs $4. The food is good too; a seared *poke* wrap or *kalua* pork sandwich costs about $10, and entrees such as barbecue ribs or crusted *ahi* are closer to $20.

Waimea proper also holds a handful of inexpensive restaurants, including *John's Place* (Mon–Fri 6.30am–5pm, Sat 7am–5pm; ⓣ338-0330), an espresso bar and sandwich joint alongside the Big Save supermarket; a *Wranglers Steakhouse* opposite (Mon–Thurs 11am–8.30pm, Fri 11am–9pm, Sat 5–9pm; ⓣ338-1218); and a branch of island favorite *Duane's Ono Char Burgers* close to the foot of Waimea Canyon Drive (Mon–Sat 10am–6pm, Sun 11am–6pm; ⓣ339-9181).



# West of Waimea

Virtually all the tourists who make it as far west as Waimea are traveling en route to Waimea Canyon and Kōke'e State Park, described opposite onwards. If you ignore both the roads that head off up the canyon, however, it's possible to continue further **west from Waimea** as far as one of the longest, largest beaches in all Hawaii.

## Kekaha

Just over a mile beyond *Waimea Plantation Cottages*, the highway passes the approach road to the small-boat harbor at **Kīkīaola**, the point of departure for many Nā Pali boat tours (see p.466). A mile or so on, it briefly runs along the shoreline at **KEKAHA**. The beach here starts to consist of sand, rather than the muddy dirt of Waimea, but thanks to Iniki very little of it is left. As a rule, only expert surfers enter the water; the waves are usually too powerful for swimming.

Away from the sea, Kekaha boasts a few minor **churches** and a gigantic, rusting sugar mill. A little mall at the foot of Kōke'e Road, the second and more important canyon approach road (see p.492) holds a *Lapperts* ice cream store and the *Menehune Food Mart* supermarket.

## Pacific Missile Test Range Facility

The long straight section of Kaumuali'i Highway immediately past Kekaha, much loved by island motorcycle freaks, ends ten miles out of Waimea, where a sharp left turn leads to the US Navy's **Pacific Missile Range Facility**. This installation is part of a network of naval early warning systems developed after World War II in an attempt to prevent any repetition of the attack on Pearl Harbor.

In the last few years, against a backdrop of military cutbacks elsewhere, the base has become a linchpin of US defense strategy. The Navy's only research site that can test missiles, aircraft, surface warships and submarines, it benefits from having over forty thousand square miles of open ocean to the northwest that are entirely unused by commercial aircraft. Lying, supposedly, within range of North Korea's nuclear capability, the facility has played a crucial role in developing and testing the so-called "Son of Star Wars" missile shield. Current programs envisage the annual launch of four SM-3 missiles from ships nearby. Targeted on the US Northwest coast, the missiles will be intercepted and destroyed, thanks to the facility's vast array of tracking devices. Early tests have so far proved less than successful.

Meanwhile, the base is reported to have created its own artificial Hawaiian island, a "virtual island" of electronic sensors laid across the sea bed between Kauai and Niihau, equipped with virtual "towns," "roads" and "hospitals," and repeatedly bombarded by virtual weapons.

In addition, the PMRF has been experimenting with unmanned, remote-controlled, solar-powered, propeller-driven aircraft, including one model intended to fly in the skies of **Mars**. Finally, with all that sonar scanning equipment, the facility has a sideline recording the songs of humpback whales.

Depending on current activities, the sentries may permit you to drive to one of the exposed on-site beaches, of interest mainly to surfers. Keep your eyes peeled – who knows what you might see?

### Polihale State Park

So long as you don't mind driving on unsurfaced roads, you can skirt round the test facility and continue up the coast. Keep going straight past the entrance, and the main road veers sharply inland, where a sign soon directs you left onto a straight dirt road. Bumpy and dusty it may be, running for much of the year through head-high cane fields, but it's perfectly manageable. Slowly the hills to the right climb upwards and turn into cliffs, until progress is barred after just over five miles by the start of the Nā Pali coast.

This spot, **Polihale State Park**, protects a segment of a fifteen-mile-long beach that stretches to Kekaha. The main parking lot is half a mile short of the boulders that mark the first Nā Pali headland; trudge to the end and you'll be able to make out another three or so headlands beyond that. Following their trashing by Hurricane Iniki, the park facilities are minimal to say the least, but the endless sands and crashing surf make a compelling spectacle. Drownings in the mighty waves are all too common; even beachcombers have been swept away.

Walking back south along the coast from Polihale, you soon come to the undulating dunes known as the **Barking Sands**. Rising up to a hundred feet high at the Nohili Point headland, they owe their name to an ability to produce strange sounds, variously described as growling or hooting as well as barking. Each grain of sand is said to be hollow, so they reverberate when rubbed together. Suggested methods of making the sands perform include rubbing handfuls together, sliding down the dunes, and dragging your companion as fast as possible across them.

## Waimea Canyon and Kōke'e State Park

Two of the major scenic attractions in all Hawaii – the gorge of **Waimea Canyon** and **Kōke'e State Park** (with its views of the Nā Pali coast to one side and the sodden Alaka'i Swamp to the other) – can only be reached from the west coast of Kauai. Waimea Canyon is always seen from above, from the viewpoints along the eighteen-mile **Waimea Canyon Drive**, which climbs

## Niihau

Very few outsiders see anything more of the island of **Niihau** than a misty silhouette on the horizon, eighteen miles off the west coast of Kauai. The "Forbidden Island" remains the private property of the Scottish **Gay and Robinson family**, who bought it during the nineteenth century. Paradoxically, by turning the whole island into a cattle ranch, they also effectively froze it in time, and Niihau is widely seen as a sanctuary of traditional Hawaiian culture. Under the Robinsons' quasi-feudal patronage, the islanders are reasonably free to come and go, but unauthorized visitors are arrested and expelled.

The smallest of the seven inhabited Hawaiian islands, Niihau measures eighteen miles long by six miles wide. It receives just twelve inches of rain a year, so almost all its 73 square miles are desert, and there are no permanent forests. While the bulk of the island consists of low, arid dunes, its northeast coast – the part most easily seen from Kauai – is lined by sheer sea cliffs. These are thought to have formed the west rim of the volcano that created Niihau (the rest is long since submerged); the highest point is **Pānī'au**, at 1281 feet. Off the north coast is the islet of **Lehua**, an eroded crescent-shaped tuff cone like Molokini off Maui (and equally good for divers). The southern plains hold two lakes, the 182-acre **Halulu** and the 860-acre **Halāli'i**, Hawaii's largest lake.

Little is known of Niihau's ancient history; only one archeologist has ever been allowed on to the island, to make a brief survey in 1912. It's thought, however, that as many as ten thousand Hawaiians lived here, fishing and growing yams and sugar cane – enough people for two rival chiefs to fight a war before the island could be united.

Captain Cook called at Niihau in 1778, having been driven away from Kauai by adverse winds (see p.487). Niihau was the recipient of his first gifts: goats, pigs, pumpkin and melon seeds, and onions. On Kauai, he had been relatively successful in preventing his crew from spreading venereal diseases to the Hawaiians. Here, however, they proved uncontrollable, and the infections had spread throughout the entire island chain by the time he returned a year later.

The population of Niihau had slumped by 1864, when **Elizabeth Sinclair** arrived with her extended family. She had previously farmed for twenty years in Scotland, and another twenty in New Zealand. A widow with five children (two of whom had married men called **Gay** and **Robinson**), she was en route to a new life in California when she decided to live in Hawaii instead. Negotiating with King Kamehameha IV for a $10,000 tract of farming land, she was offered a stretch of the Oahu coastline that took in all of Waikīkī and most of what's now downtown Honolulu. Instead, she opted for the island of Niihau; family tradition has it that the Sinclair party arrived to inspect the island shortly after one of its very rare rain showers, and were deceived by the greenness.

The people of Niihau were appalled at the idea of their homeland being sold. They petitioned the king to be allowed to buy it themselves, and many emigrated when the sale went through. One family had already purchased their own lands, but the Sinclairs soon bought them out, stacking $1000 in dollar coins, one by one, until they could resist no longer. Barely a hundred islanders were left when **Niihau Ranch** was set up.

Well before she died in 1892 at the age of 93, Mrs Sinclair had realized Niihau was of only marginal use for agriculture and started to buy land on western

its western flank. That starts just beyond Waimea, is joined eight miles up by the easier **Kōke'e Road** from further along the coast, and then carries on for another ten miles, entering Kōke'e State Park beyond the canyon proper and ending at the vertiginous cliffs above Kalalau Valley. The ancient Hawaiians

Kauai. Her descendants have continued to do so ever since, and Gay and Robinson (as the family business is known) now holds almost as many acres on Kauai as on Niihau.

The Robinson family imposed a strict way of life on the island, obliging every inhabitant to attend church services and banning the ownership of dogs. The policy of isolation from the outside world, however, only developed after Hawaii was annexed by the US in 1898, when the Robinsons became convinced it was their mission to preserve Niihau from the changes taking place elsewhere in the islands.

Around 250 people now live on Niihau, almost all of them in its one village, **Pu'uwai** ("heart"), a tangle of red-dirt roads on the west coast. The island has no airport and no cars and lacks modern plumbing. The island men work, on average, three days a week on the Niihau Ranch, which provides them with simple wooden houses; for the rest of the time they supplement their income by fishing, raising mullet, making charcoal and collecting honey. Niihau is also renowned for necklaces made from the tiny shells that wash up on its beaches. Most households run small electric generators, and have radios but not TVs. The favorite game of local children is said to be reciting Bible verses to each other and trying to identify them.

What makes Niihau truly unique, however, is that it's the only place where everyone still speaks **Hawaiian** as a first language. As the island never fell prey to the missionary attempts to standardize and simplify the language (see p.544), the version spoken on Niihau is believed to be the purest, and most authentically pronounced, that survives.

The people of Niihau were alone among Hawaiians in voting against statehood in 1959, and the state government has repeatedly tried to buy back the island. Particularly controversial is the fact that the Robinsons refuse to recognize the state law that guarantees free access to all Hawaiian beaches. The Hawaiian media has a tradition of running exposés that "reveal" the true state of affairs on Niihau – one TV documentary, for example, alleged that its inhabitants were kept in conditions not far removed from slavery – and its public image in the rest of the state is not good.

In the late 1990s, partly to strengthen the island's ailing economy and partly to placate state legislators, the Robinsons invited the US Navy to expand its Pacific Missile Range Facility (see p.488) onto Niihau. The plan was to install missile launchers, tracking equipment, and even an airfield. It seems to have fallen through, however, because the state demanded a thorough archeological survey of the island first. The family are said to fear that were ancient artifacts to be discovered, Niihau would become a *cause célèbre* with Hawaiian activists, much like Kahoolawe (see p.319).

The only legal way to visit Niihau is as a passenger in the **helicopter** that serves as an air ambulance for island medical emergencies. To defray costs, this runs three-hour trips from western Kauai to Niihau whenever four passengers are prepared to pay $260 each for the privilege. It lands twice, at the northernmost and southernmost beaches on the island, Kamakalepo Point and Keanahaki, and does not go anywhere near Pu'uwai. For full details, contact Niihau Helicopters, PO Box 370, Makaweli HI 96769 (Ⓣ335-3500). To get a close-up view of the island, you can also join Holoholo Charters' $115 **snorkeling cruise**, which sails just offshore (Ⓣ335-0815 or 1-800/848-6130, Ⓦwww.holoholocharters.com).

continued on foot from there, scrambling down to the North Shore, but now neither road nor trail attempts the descent.

Although you can rent a cabin or camp overnight in Kōke'e, the great majority of visitors see both canyon and park on a single day-trip. While you can enjoy superb and widely differing views without having to **hike**, trails lead off to further unforgettable spots.

# Waimea Canyon

It was supposedly Mark Twain who first called **Waimea Canyon** the "Grand Canyon of the Pacific." In fact, Twain never visited the island, but the comparison is not unreasonable. At something over three thousand feet, it may not be quite as deep as its Arizona rival, but the colors – all shades of green against the red earth – and the way it is squeezed into such a tiny island, are absolutely breathtaking.

Like all the Hawaiian islands, Kauai was once a vast volcano, of whose original contours little trace remains. Torrential rains have eroded Waimea Canyon into its present form, but that process began when a massive geological fault cracked the island down the middle. Eventually, the canyon will wear its way back to meet Kalalau Valley, and possibly split the island in two; for the moment, the two are separated by the eerie basin of the Alaka'i Swamp.



## Waimea Canyon Drive

The most dramatic route up to Waimea Canyon is along **Waimea Canyon Drive** (Hwy-550), which turns right off the highway as you leave Waimea, soon after *Duane's Ono Char Burgers* and just after a sign indicating that you should *not* turn right. The other route, **Kōke'e Road** (Hwy-55), sets off from Kekaha (see p.488), roughly three miles on. Because of its greater width and shallower gradient, all the tour buses go that way, so it's likely to be a much slower drive.

This is not to say, however, that you should race up Waimea Canyon Drive. Speeding around the curves is far too dangerous, and even if you don't stop, it takes almost an hour to drive the eighteen miles to the top. Following Waimea Canyon Drive from the start enables you to watch the canyon grow alongside you, turning from a gentle tree-covered valley to an ever-deeper gash.

By the time Kōke'e Road comes in from the left, after eight miles, the canyon has reached a mile wide. It's worth stopping at each of the roadside lookouts from here onwards. The first, 10.5 miles up from Waimea, is **Waimea Canyon Lookout**. It's also the lowest, of course, but 3400 feet straight down from the edge still seems a very long way. Located at the junction of several distinct fissures in the rock, it tends to be very misty in the morning. The bare red earth slips away beneath your feet into the vagueness, while the weathered cliffs immediately below resemble the pinnacles of the Nā Pali coast. In the late afternoon the view is utterly different, glowing orange and red in the setting sun.

Next comes the **Pu'u Ka Pele Lookout**, shortly before milepost 13. From opposite the start of Polihale Ridge Road – which runs a short distance towards the cliffs above Polihale – this surveys a side chasm as it drops down towards the main canyon. On the far wall, you may be able to make out Waipo'o Falls (see opposite).

Less than a mile further on comes the large **Pu'u Hinahina Lookout**. The viewing area, perched above crumbling jagged slopes, looks straight down the head of another gorge. Far below, Waiahulu Stream plunges towards the main valley, echoing with the distant bleating of goats. A thousand shades of two main colors fill the canyon walls, mixed in different proportions as the shadows lengthen: by the evening, one side radiates warm russet highlights, the other luxuriates in dark green, and gray mists spill over both edges. The Canyon Trail (see below) runs along the promontory almost directly in front of you, slightly below and off to the left.

From the **Niihau Lookout**, to the right of the same parking lot, the cloud-shrouded island of Niihau (see p.490) can be seen floating on the Pacific, way beyond the trees. Its profile is three-dimensional, with flat leaves of land jutting from below a central plateau; to its right is tiny pyramid-shaped **Lehua**.

## Waimea Canyon hikes

The best way to take a **day-hike** in the Waimea Canyon area is to pick your own combination of the Cliff, Canyon and Black Pipe trails, which lead off **Halemanu Valley Road**. This dirt road heads right shortly after milepost 14 on Waimea Canyon Drive, but is seldom fit to drive in an ordinary vehicle; park at one of the pull-outs around the intersection, and set off on foot.

All the above trails start on the same path, which cuts away to the right after half a mile once the road has dipped to cross Halemanu Stream and then risen again. Ignore the turnoff for the Canyon and Black Pipe trails not far along, and keep going towards the end of the **Cliff Trail**, a walk of barely five minutes.

The narrow footpath soon emerges from the woods to run along a railed bluff, with the green, sharp planes of the canyon to your right and wooded hills to your left; from here you can look all the way down the canyon. Though the trail appears to continue, first on to a ridge immediately below you, and then across to a worn red-earth track above the steep drop ahead, there's no direct connection, and the promontory in front of the railing is not recommended.

However, you can reach the trail visible in the distance – the **Canyon Trail** – by retracing your steps as far as the intersection mentioned above and turning right. As this path dips into the gullies between the exposed headlands, the terrain constantly changes, from dry brush in semi-desert to lush green. The Canyon Trail proper starts a third of a mile along, with a sharp descent through thick woodlands. It then comes out on the rounded red ridge you've already seen from the Cliff Trail, which gently curves away towards an abysmal drop. Pick your way along that, and the path soon doubles back on itself towards two small waterfalls, reached by clambering through thick vegetation and across boulders. The pool at the upper end of the **Waipo'o Falls**, where the stream springs out of the rock, is ideal for cooling off after the hike; lower down, you can let the main flow tumble over you. Don't try to go any lower, however; the huge main falls soon bar your way.

From this point you can head back to join the **Black Pipe Trail**, which loops through the forest to rejoin Halemanu Valley Road after some steep but spectacular climbing. That makes a total hike of between two and three hours. Alternatively, the Canyon Trail heads onwards around the lip of the canyon to meet up with Kumuwela Ridge, from which it's possible to make a larger loop, via two other trails, back to your starting point. At least two of the day-hikes in Kōke'e park are more rewarding, however (see p.496), so that option only makes sense if you have several days to spare.

# Kōke'e State Park

The boundaries that separate Waimea Canyon State Park from Kōke'e State Park – and, for that matter, from the Pu'u Ka Pele Forest Reserve and the Nā Pali-Kona Forest Reserve – are imperceptible, and in places not even defined. Broadly speaking, **Kōke'e State Park** starts beyond the Pu'u Hinahina

## KŌKE'E STATE PARK

Nā Pali Coast
KALALAU VALLEY TRAIL
KALALAU VALLEY
AWA'AWAPUHI VALLEY
NU'ALOLO VALLEY
MAHANALOA VALLEY
NU'ALOLO CLIFF TRAIL (2)
NU'ALOLO TRAIL (3.75)
AWA'AWAPUHI TRAIL (3.25)
Kalalau Lookout 4000 ft
Pu'u O Kila Lookout 4176 ft
Pihea Lookout 4284 ft
PIHEA TRAIL (3.75)
Kilohana 4030 ft
ALAKA'I SWAMP TRAIL (3.5)
KALUAPUHI TRAIL (2.0)
PU'U KA'OHELO–BERRY FLATS TRAIL (2.0)
KAWAIKOI STREAM TRAIL (1.75)
ALAKA'I SWAMP
Kōke'e Lodge
Park Headquarters
DITCH TRAIL (3.5)
HALEMANU–KŌKE'E TRAIL (1.2)
KUMUWELA TRAIL (1.2)
PO'OMAU CANYON LOOKOUT TRAIL (0.3)
HALEMANU ROAD
550
BLACK PIPE TRAIL (0.4)
Pu'u Hinahina Lookout
Waipo'o Falls
CANYON TRAIL (1.4)
KOHUA RIDGE TRAIL (4.0)
N
0 Miles 1
Trail (Distances In Miles)
Track

Lookout, as the highway veers away from the canyon rim. To the south and east, the park abuts the high valleys that lead into Waimea Canyon; to the north and west, it drops to the sheer cliffs of the Nā Pali coast. Waimea Canyon Drive follows the crest of Kaunuohua Ridge as it climbs and narrows through the woods until it finally peters out.

Although much of Kōke'e consists of alpine forest, its most remarkable feature is the all-but-impenetrable **Alaka'i Swamp**. In this natural volcanic bowl, cupped between the mountaintops, the heaviest rainfall on earth collects to form a strange, primordial quagmire. More of a very wet rainforest than a conventional swamp, it remains home to a unique range of flora and fauna. The few humans who manage to penetrate the mists are assailed on all sides by the shrills, whistles and buzzes of a jungle without any mammals (save the odd tiny mouse) or snakes. The word "Alaka'i" means "leader" or "to lead" in Hawaiian; the name reflects the fact that anyone venturing into the swamp alone before the modern trail was built was very likely to get lost.

## The park headquarters: Kanaloahuluhulu

Kōke'e State Park has its headquarters in a grassy clearing to the left of the road, just after milepost 15. While much of the forest of Kōke'e has been cut down and replanted in the last two centuries, this meadow has been here since ancient times. The Hawaiians who paused here on the trek to Kalalau called it **Kanaloahuluhulu**, claiming it had been cleared by the god Kanaloa to get rid of an evil spirit who had been attacking travelers.

A small hut at the entrance to the parking lot calls itself the park visitor center, but is rarely open. You can pick up information at either *Kōke'e Lodge*, beyond it on the left, or a few yards farther on at **Kōke'e Natural History Museum** (daily 10am–4pm; $1 donation). The museum consists of a couple of large rooms in a wooden cabin, where the staff sell a wide range of books and maps and provides up-to-the-minute hiking tips. All the major trails are shown on a relief model of the island; wall displays cover meteorology and, especially, Hurricane Inik, and there are several cases of stuffed birds and other exhibits.

The larger *Kōke'e Lodge* building holds a souvenir store, public rest rooms and a reasonable and inexpensive cafeteria open daily for breakfast (served 9am–3.30pm) and lunch (11am–3.30pm). Takeout sandwiches are available from 9.30am onwards, while lunch specials include local dishes such as the $5 Portuguese bean soup.

Footpaths lead up behind the lodge to the *Kōke'e Lodge Housekeeping Cabins* (PO Box 819, Waimea HI 96796; ⓣ335-6061; ❶/❷). Each of these **rental cabins** is available for a maximum of five days and can sleep up to six people, either dorm-style in one room or in slightly more comfortable two-bedroom units. They have bed linen, hot water, fridges and wood stoves – bring your own food for evening meals and buy firewood from the store. Ideally you should reserve in advance, but if you haven't, it's worth enquiring at the *Lodge* to see if a cabin is available.

You can also **camp** just north of the meadow, so long as you have a permit from the state parks office in Līhu'e (see p.426), which can also provide details of other campgrounds tucked away on the dirt roads to either side of Waimea Canyon Drive. *YWCA Camp Sloggett* (ⓣ335-6060; ❶), across the highway from the Kanaloahuluhulu meadow, offers **hostel** accommodation in its bunkhouse for $20 per bed (bring your own linen). There's also a ten-person lodge, rented out to one group of five or more visitors at a time, again for $20 each, and a campground that charges tent campers $10 per person.

## The highway lookouts

Waimea Canyon Drive continues three miles beyond *Kōke'e Lodge* before squeezing to a halt above Kalalau Valley. There's little to see in this final stretch – you pass a couple of trailheads (see p.500) and glimpse the white "golf ball" belonging to Kauai's missile defense system – before the **Kalalau Lookout** at milepost 18.

As you leave your car to walk towards the viewing area, it looks as though nothing lies beyond the railings. Then, framed by scattered *lehua* trees and arching ferns, comes the vast, magnificent panorama of Kalalau Valley, seen here from the head of its slightly shorter west branch. To either side of the broad valley floor, rich with trees, soar sheer green walls, pleated into deep clefts through which plunge slender white waterfalls. Occasional red slashes in the hillsides show where landslides have sheared the razorback ridges. Reaching up from immediately below you, and hard to distinguish from the background, are several separate stand-alone pinnacles.

The views are at their best early in the morning; later on, the valley repeatedly fills with mist, and there's a risk you may see nothing at all. Clouds appear from nowhere; you won't see them approach across the ocean, as this is the spot where they are born, when Pacific winds are forced to climb 4000 feet. For an account of Kalalau Valley at ground level, see p.470.

Tear your gaze away to trace the brief ridge that curves east from where you're standing towards the end of the road. This is the last tiny remnant of the caldera rim of the volcano that built Kauai.

The **Pu'u O Kila Lookout**, half a mile further on, commands another stunning prospect, looking directly down the main body of Kalalau Valley. Only one wall is revealed in all its majesty, but the bonus here is that you can look inland as well, across the wilderness of the Alaka'i Swamp to the summit of Mount Wai'ale'ale. One second the entire valley basin can be brimming with mist; the next second the swirling clouds may unveil a staggering prospect of the Nā Pali coastline. Even when nothing is visible to the north, the swamplands to the south can remain clear, and you can watch the flight-seeing helicopters cross Alaka'i and drop down into Kalalau.

## Kōke'e hikes

Despite suffering considerable damage in Iniki, the major Kōke'e **hiking trails** are now in excellent condition. Several were upgraded using federal funds, partly to provide employment and partly to entice tourists back. They're easy to follow and equipped with small, yellow-on-brown wayside signs marking each quarter-mile. Some trails marked on older maps, however, such as the Honopū Trail, no longer exist; call at Kōke'e Museum (see overleaf) for information before you set off. Whichever route you choose, get going **early**, before the clouds set in. Note also that **hunting** is allowed on weekends and holidays, so casual hikers should wear bright clothing.

While you should certainly stick to the named trails, don't feel obliged to follow just one trail from start to finish; most of the best hikes involve **combinations** of different trails. If you just have one day to explore the park, an ideal route is to follow the **Pihea Trail** down from Pu'u O Kila Lookout as far as its intersection with the **Alaka'i Swamp Trail**, walk the last two miles of that to Kilohana, and then retrace your steps. The round-trip takes six hours, allowing for an hour's stop at the end. You can walk the other half of both trails – less exciting but, at two hours, much quicker – by taking the Alaka'i Swamp Trail from its trailhead to the same intersection, then following the Pihea Trail down as far as the **Kawaikoi Stream Trail**, and looping back to the Alaka'i trailhead along that.

For the best views of the Nā Pali cliffs, another good combination – though not recommended for anyone with vertigo – is to hike down the *Awa'awapuhi Trail*, follow the *Nu'alolo Cliff Trail* along the ridge, and return to the road via the *Nu'alolo Trail*. If you set off early enough, the six-hour hike will have you back at Kōke'e Lodge in time for lunch.

## The Pihea Trail

Waimea Canyon Drive was originally intended to run on beyond the Pu'u O Kila Lookout, and to connect somehow with the North Shore. Mountain mud swallowed several earth-moving vehicles before that project was abandoned, but its planned route remains obvious. This broad, undulating groove continues straight ahead from the lookout, cutting through the red clay of the ridge, and now forms the start of the **Pihea Trail**. Hikers can choose between a short out-and-back stroll offering views of both Kalalau Valley and the Alaka'i Swamp, or a more demanding trek down into the swamp itself.

The first mile of the Pihea Trail follows the high crest of Kalalau Valley. At the far end, the **Pihea Lookout** is (at 4284 feet) the highest peak of all. If you can see it below the clouds from Pu'u O Kila, it makes for a great hour's hike. For over half the way, the trail is wide and even; then you have to pick your way over tree roots and scramble up hills. It's safe and manageable, but narrows at times to a few feet, with precipitous drops on either side, while visibility regularly drops to nothing as clouds siphon across the ridge.

Just before the final climb up to the Pihea Lookout – which is almost vertical, and usually extremely muddy – the Pihea Trail proper makes a sharp right turn to descend into the swamp. After a hundred yards of slithering down the clay slope, a plank boardwalk makes an appearance. It soon becomes a smooth, gradual staircase down the hillside, which reaches the obvious **four-way intersection** of boardwalks with the Alaka'i Swamp Trail 1.75 miles from the parking lot.

As suggested above, turning left at this point enables you to combine the best of both trails. If you continue down the Pihea Trail, however, the boardwalk ends within a minute or two and the path drops ever more steeply. In dry weather, this is a green and lovely walk. The ground is so spongy underfoot, with its thick carpeting of moss, and the trees and shrubs to either side are so small and stunted, that it can feel almost surreal, as though you've blundered into Lilliput. Lizards scuttle into the undergrowth as you approach, and bright birds call melodiously from the branches.

The trail zigzags down the thickly vegetated *pali* to reach babbling Kawaikoi Stream, then heads right, following the bank through pleasant woodlands, and once or twice crossing small side-streams. Shortly after a basic picnic shelter at the 3-mile marker, you ford the wide main stream via rocks in the river bed, then join the **Kawaikoi Stream Trail** on the far side. Away to the left, this makes a mile-long loop around some luscious mountain streams; turning right brings you (in about fifteen minutes) to a plank footbridge, two miles from Alaka'i junction, that marks the end of the trail.

The **Kawaikoi Picnic Area** here is a broad meadow with two more shelters and a rest room. If you turn right on to the dirt road at the far end, a fifteen-minute climb brings you to the Alaka'i picnic area and the trailhead of the **Alaka'i Swamp Trail**. If you've parked up at Pu'u O Kila, you could walk to the Pihea/Alaka'i intersection, then back up the Pihea Trail, and be back at your car within about five hours. By road, following the dirt road to the park headquarters and then climbing Waimea Canyon Drive, it's much farther.

Another four miles or so of dirt road lie beyond the Kawaikoi Picnic Area, but you'd need a four-wheel-drive vehicle, and a lot of time, to take advantage of the remote trails that lead along and down the far side of Waimea Canyon.

### The Alaka'i Swamp Trail

For many years the **Alaka'i Swamp Trail** had the reputation of being not only the most arduous hike on Kauai, but also the dirtiest, a protracted wade through thigh-deep mud guaranteed to ruin your clothes. Since the Kōke'e trails were upgraded, however, a boardwalk has covered almost its entire 3.5-mile length, and it is nowhere near as fearsome as legend suggests.

### The Birds of Kōke'e

Thanks to its remoteness, Kōke'e State Park is one of the last great sanctuaries for native Hawaiian **birds**, safe here from their two main predators. When the **mongoose** was imported into Hawaii (see p.526), it lived off the eggs of defenseless ground-nesting birds. Kauai, however, was the only island spared the mongoose invasion, so many native species of bird that were wiped out on the other islands survived here. **Mosquitoes** first came to Hawaii when a whaling ship taking on fresh water on Maui discharged its stagnant casks into a handy stream; the insects have been infecting native birds with avian malaria ever since. In theory, they can't live more than 3500 feet above sea level, so the Alaka'i Swamp has remained protected, though there are alarming reports that Hawaiian mosquitoes may be evolving to cope with higher altitudes.

Those birds that established themselves in Hawaii before the arrival of the Polynesians did so by chance. Thus a single blown-astray finch evolved into over fifty separate species of honey-creeper, each adapted to some specific habitat or diet. In Kōke'e these included the bright scarlet *'i'iwi*, with its black wings, orange legs and salmon-colored sickle-shaped bill, perfect for sipping nectar; the *'apapane*, which also has a red body and black wings but has a short, slightly curved black bill; the tiny greenish-yellow *'anianiau*; and the predominantly black *mamo*. In addition there was the *pueo*, or Hawaiian owl, which flies by day, not night, and the rust-colored *'elepaio* flycatcher. Meanwhile, majestic tropic birds soar above the Nā Pali Coast and Waimea Canyon. The white-tailed variety, the *koa'e kea*, cruises the wind-currents high above the valleys, then plummets into the ocean in pursuit of fish and squid.

Ancient Hawaiians never lived in Kōke'e, but they climbed this high to collect feathers. The *mamo* would be trapped on a sticky branch, its long yellow tail plumage plucked for use in ceremonial cloaks and *leis*, and then released; the *'i'iwi* was stripped bare and kept for food. The Hawaiians also came looking for the tall, straight *koa* trees, thrusting from the steepest valleys, that made the best canoes. They were guided by the *'elepaio*; if it settled for too long on a *koa*, that meant the tree was riddled with insects and thus unsuitable for use.

All the native birds found on Kauai at the time of Captain Cook are thought to have survived until 1964, when the last *ākialoa* died. The rarest to remain is another honey-creeper, the *'ō'ō 'ā'ā*, whose yellow "garter" feathers were prized by the Hawaiians. Before Hurricane Iwa hit Kōke'e in 1982, there were thought to be fewer than ten birds left, living deep in the Alaka'i swamp. Since then, just one has been spotted, tending its treetop nest and calling for a mate that never answers.

By far the most conspicuous bird in Kōke'e today is the *moa*, or **Red Jungle Fowl**. Hawaii's only surviving descendants of the chickens brought by the Polynesians, these raucous creatures strut around outside the museum and restaurant at Kanaloahuluhulu, or scurry down the trails. For all their haughty demeanor, they're not exactly intelligent; they peck away indiscriminately, and will no doubt try to eat your license plate or wing mirror.

For more about Hawaiian birds, see the "Environment" section in Contexts, starting on p.524.

Nonetheless, hikers still have to wage a constant battle of wits against the cloying black swamp, as thrusting tree roots and subsiding mud holes ensure that the boardwalk can never fully be relied upon. Apart from the magnificent **view** at the far end, the main reward for hikers is the swamp's rare and resplendent **vegetation**. Giant ferns dangle above the trail, and orchids gleam from the undergrowth, while the trees – especially in June – erupt into brilliant flowering displays.

As outlined on p.496, the second and more interesting half of the trail can be combined with walking the Pihea Trail from the Pu'u O Kila Lookout. If you want to hike the whole thing, however, start by driving as close as possible to the trailhead along the dirt road (marked *YWCA Camp Sloggett*) that leads right from Waimea Canyon Drive just beyond the entrance to the Kōke'e State Park headquarters. Keep going beyond the YWCA camp until you reach a sign, 1.7 miles from the highway, warning that only four-wheel-drive vehicles can proceed; there should be room to park here.

Now walk about a mile further along the road, first sharply down to cross the Kauaikanana Stream and then back up again, until you come to a sign announcing the Nā Pali-Kona Forest Reserve, and another pointing to the various trails nearby. This spot is the **Alaka'i Picnic Area**; ahead of you spreads your first large-scale overview of the swamp itself, while on the horizon to the left is the ridge that holds the highway and the Kalalau lookouts.

Before continuing, take the short spur trail to your right. After a few yards it stops at the end of a high promontory pointing straight towards **Po'omau Canyon**, one of the narrow gorges that feed into the top end of Waimea Canyon. A sheltered picnic table at the edge of the abyss commands superb views of the chasm below.

The Alaka'i Swamp trailhead is a five-minute walk down the rutted ridge-top track that leads left off the road. The narrow path starts by dropping abruptly, shored up against the precipices to either side; it then climbs and widens again to become a pleasant, grassy path. Half a mile along, the boardwalk – two parallel planks overlaid with rusty wire mesh – begins. Despite the mud, and the regularity with which the planks sink into it, the trail is high and exposed, and for a while the trees thin out altogether. Another half-mile on, just as the ground starts to feel really soggy, you meet the Pihea Trail at the **four-way intersection** (see p.497).

Continuing on the Alaka'i Swamp Trail from here, the boardwalk turns into a playful, wilful companion. For most of the time one plank meets the next, but at some point, as they grow tauntingly further apart, you're bound to slip into the mud. For the first half-mile, the trail drops toward a gentle tributary of the Kawaikoi Stream, most (but not quite all) of the descent on a wooden stairway. As you cross the stream, by stepping stones, you're still a full hour short of the end. Soon afterwards, the boardwalk stops as the trail climbs a high and relatively dry ridge through the forest, with thick green moss to either side. While the last significant climb is now behind you, the highest part of the swamp turns out to be the wettest, little more than one large pool of gloopy mud. Only the red blossoms of tiny, stunted *'ōhi'a lehua* plants relieve the monotony. The boardwalk then returns to guide you across first a bog, then a rainforest, and finally a bleak, marshy plain.

The trail eventually comes to a dead end at a small wooden platform high on a hillside, which for most of the time is engulfed in swirling mists. Waiting for the clouds to clear, in the wettest place in the world, can feel like a loser's game, but the wind forever rustling the trees around you is a guarantee that they will. You'll then see that you've walked the length of the Nā Pali coast. This viewpoint –

officially named **Kilohana** – stands on top of the towering western wall of Wainiha Valley; far below, Wainiha Stream runs through its center towards the ocean. Down the coast beyond the mouth of the valley curves the crescent of Hanalei Bay, with Princeville visible at the tip of the far headland. Away to the right, inland, the high *pali* opposite stretches as far as the eye can see.

A constant succession of clouds race in to stream up the slopes, feeding the dense rainforest that somehow clings to their sides. In the intervals when you seem entirely cut off, you can reflect that in January 1871, Queen Emma (see p.94) somehow reached this lonely eminence with a retinue of over one hundred companions. They camped out along the way, with the Queen singing songs to keep their spirits up in the swamp, but were disappointed at the last. According to the official commemorative chant, "*ē huli ho'i'o ka lani, ua kū ka 'ohu i nā pali*" – "the queen turned to go back, for the fog rested on the mountain."

A ground-level description of Wainiha Valley appears on p.461.



## The Awa'awapuhi Trail

The **Awa'awapuhi Trail** starts on the left of Waimea Canyon Drive, halfway between the Kōke'e headquarters and Kalalau Lookout, and drops steeply through three miles of forest to the **Awa'awapuhi Valley**, tucked between the Nā Pali cliffs. Walking to the end takes little more than an hour, though climbing back up again is a different matter. The only views come right at the end, but they're stupendous enough to make this one of Kauai's finest hikes. Before you set off, pick up the Awa'awapuhi Botanical Trail Guide from the museum for a description (slightly out of date since Iniki) of the plants indicated by the 57 numbered markers along the trail. Also be aware that the Awa'awapuhi trailhead is notorious for vehicle break-ins, so leave nothing valuable in your car.

The trail begins its inexorable descent from the left side of the lot. It's easy underfoot, and there's none of the sense of battling against encroaching vegetation that you get on the Kalalau Trail (see p.467). At first the forest is largely *'ohi'a,* but as the path drops into hotter, drier territory, *koa* starts to predominate. Though most of the route remains in shade, after 1.5 miles the tree cover begins to thin out, and you get your first glimpses of the high parallel ridges to either side. At the 2.75-mile marker, a magnificent *hala pepe* tree has individual palm-like fronds growing from its branches. Shortly after that, keep going past the junction with the Nu'alolo Cliff Trail (see below).

The end of the trail comes at mile marker 3, when suddenly, 2400 feet above sea level, it runs out of ridge. The railing straight ahead marks the overlook at the head of the Awa'awapuhi Valley. Far below, the Awa'awapuhi River twists its way between two equally sinuous red ridges. Ancient Hawaiians said the valley was shaped by an eel slithering into the sea; its final thrashings mean that its ocean outlet is not visible. You can, however, see a huge expanse of ocean, and hear the distant roar of the surf. Most visitors venture a few steps beyond the railing, in search of the perfect photo; some fall and die.

Back to your left, another viewpoint looks out across Nu'alolo Valley to the bare red top of the higher Nu'alolo Ridge. Unlike in the Awa'awapuhi Valley, which is in perpetual shade, trees can be seen on the valley floor. If the sight of the exposed ridge makes you reluctant to attempt the Nu'alolo Trail, you won't be comforted to know that where you're standing looks just as bad from over there.

## The Nu'alolo Cliff Trail

In order to combine the Awa'awapuhi and Nu'alolo trails you have to edge your way along the gulf between the two, by means of the two-mile **Nu'alolo**

**Cliff Trail**. This is the one Kōke'e trail that you really *must* avoid if you have problems with vertigo.

From the intersection near the end of the Awa'awapuhi Trail, described above, the Nu'alolo Cliff Trail dips down into a small patch of rainforest. There it crosses a gentle stream, slowly gathering pace as it approaches the plummet ahead; don't be tempted by any of the side trails. The path goes on to traverse some attractive meadows, one of which holds a picnic shelter. Near the 1.75-mile marker, however, it rounds a fearsome bend above a colossal drop. The ground is just loose red gravel, the trail a narrow slanting groove scuffed against the hillside. Dislodged pebbles tumble thousands of feet into the abyss, and the wayside rock, clutched for support, crumbles to dust in your hand.

Just after that you join the Nu'alolo Trail, here 3.25 miles from its starting point, with the Lolo Vista Point (see below) another three-quarters of a mile away to your right.

### The Nu'alolo Trail

Like the parallel but slightly shorter Awa'awapuhi Trail, the **Nu'alolo Trail** is a footpath down a long ridge that culminates with sweeping Nā Pali views. If you're making the loop trip with the Awa'awapuhi Trail, as outlined on p.497, it's best to walk the Nu'alolo Trail from bottom to top, as it's marginally the easier climb of the two. The description that follows, however, starts from the road and works down.

From its trailhead just below *Kōke'e Lodge*, the Nu'alolo Trail starts with a surprise, switchbacking up and over Kaunuohua Ridge. Thereafter it drops progressively downhill, at times winding gently through the thick grass of the pretty upland meadows. After two straightforward miles, it begins to descend ever more steeply through a channel that in places is worn deep into the mud. While seldom dangerous, the last half-mile is precipitous in the extreme, straight down the slippery crest of the ridge. The fifteen-minute totter beyond the junction with the Nu'alolo Cliff Trail (see above), along the exposed ridge towards **Lolo Vista Point**, is regarded as a separate trail, and one best left to the brave.

# contexts

# contexts

# A history of Hawaii

**If a big wave comes in, large fishes will come from the dark Ocean which you never saw before, and when they see the small fishes they will eat them up. The ships of the white men have come, and smart people have arrived from the great countries which you have never seen before, they know our people are few in number and living in a small country; they will eat us up, such has always been the case with large countries, the small ones have been gobbled up.**

David Malo, to King Kamehameha IV, 1837

The human history of Hawaii divides into three very distinct chapters. First came the era when the islands developed their own unique culture, as Polynesian settlers adapted their traditional way of life to this remote and pristine archipelago. Then came the islands' encounter with the rest of the world, and a hundred years of increasingly doomed resistance to the inevitable takeover by stronger foreign powers. The third stage began when Hawaii was incorporated into the United States, in 1898. Ever since then, the islands have been at the mercy of economic and political events in the rest of the world.

# The age of migrations

The fiery origins of the Hawaiian islands have decisively shaped their destiny. They are the remotest islands on earth; as they have never been attached to a larger continent, humans have only ever been able to get here by crossing at least two thousand miles of treacherous ocean. Furthermore, being composed entirely of lava, they are devoid of metals and workable clays, the raw materials used to build civilizations elsewhere.

Until less than two thousand years ago, the islands remained unknown specks in the vast Pacific, populated by the mutated descendants of what few organisms had been carried here by wind or wave (see p.524). Carbon dating of fishhooks and artifacts found at sites such as Bellows Beach on Oahu, and Ka Lae (South Point) on the Big Island, suggests that Hawaii's earliest human settlers arrived during the second or third centuries AD. Except perhaps for their first chance landfall, they came equipped to colonize, carrying goats, dogs, pigs, coconut palms, bananas and sugar cane, among other essentials.

These first inhabitants were **Polynesians**, probably from the Marquesas Islands in the South Seas. Their ancestors spread from the shores of Asia to inhabit Indonesia and the Solomon Islands around 30,000 years ago. Such migrations, across coastal waters shallower than they are today, would for the most part have involved hopping from island to island without having to cross open ocean. Twenty-five thousand years later they had acquired the techniques to venture farther afield. For more on how such migrations were carried out, see p.521.

Just over three thousand years ago, during the period when the "Little Climatic Optimum" made wind and sea conditions milder, the voyagers reached Fiji. They then spread via Tahiti to populate the entire "Polynesian

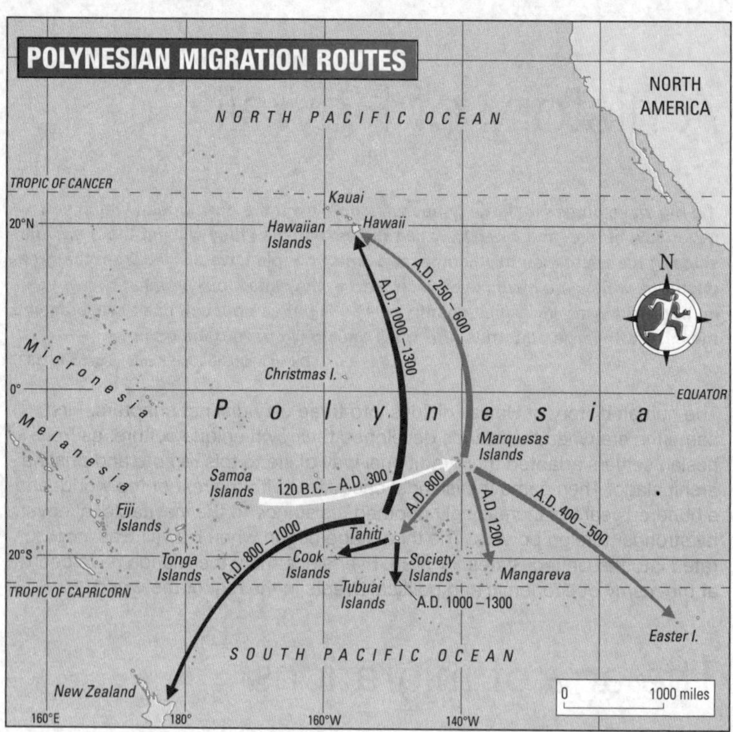




Triangle," extending from Easter Island in the east to Hawaii in the north and finally down to New Zealand (which they called Aotea Roa) in the south.

Recent archeological and scientific investigations have shed more light on the ancient history of Hawaii, while throwing a number of long-cherished beliefs into doubt. Thanks to DNA testing, for example, it is now certain that the Polynesians did indeed enter the Pacific from southeast Asia. Thor Heyerdahl's argument for a North American origin, as promulgated by the Mormon church in Oahu's Polynesian Cultural Center, has been finally disproved. On the other hand, historians are no longer sure whether traditional accounts of Hawaii being settled by successive waves of migrants at widely spaced intervals are in fact true. According to that model, Marquesas Islanders continued to arrive until the eighth century and were followed by Tahitians between the eleventh and fourteenth centuries, with each new group violently supplanting its predecessors. One piece of evidence that does point to a Tahitian influx is the name "**Hawaii**" itself, which is known previously to have been an alternative, "poetic" name for the largest of the leeward Tahitian islands, Raiatea, the

## The Ancient Hawaiians

For a full account of the daily life, traditions and culture of the **ancient Hawaiians**, see p.517; for more about the **voyaging techniques** they employed in reaching Hawaii in the first place, see p.521.

site of the voyaging temple of Taputapuatea (see p.523). Whether or not Tahitians did reach Hawaii in significant numbers, it remains unquestioned that by the time the Europeans appeared, no two-way voyaging between Hawaii and the South Pacific had taken place for around five hundred years.

One early group of Hawaiians figures in legends as the **menehune**, often described these days as having been hairy elves or leprechauns who worked at night and hid by day. It seems likely that the word is, in fact, a corruption of the Tahitian *manhune*, which means "lacking in lineage," and was the name of the original Polynesian people of Tahiti. These were displaced first from their homeland, then from Hawaii itself by warriors from Raiatea. Rather than literally being dwarfs, they were probably treated as social inferiors by their conquerors, and became the lowest caste in Hawaiian society.

## The coming of the foreigners

No Western ship is known for certain to have chanced upon Hawaii before that of **Captain Cook**, in January 1778; the first European to sail across the Pacific, the Portuguese Ferdinand Magellan, did so without seeing a single island.

There is, however, considerable circumstantial evidence of pre-Cook contact between Hawaiians and Europeans. **Spanish** vessels disappeared in the northern Pacific from the 1520s onwards, while during the two centuries, starting in 1565, that the "Manila Galleons" made annual voyages across the Pacific between Mexico and the Philippines, at least nine such ships were lost. Cook observed that the first Hawaiians he encountered were familiar with iron, and even suggested that some bore European features. Hawaiian legends speak of what may have been Spanish mariners being shipwrecked on the north coast of Lanai during the sixteenth century, and again off Maui some time later, while the log of the Dutch ship *Lefda* in 1599 spoke of eight seamen deserting to an unkown island at this latitude. A map captured by the British in 1742 appears to show a group of islands, labeled "La Mesa," "Los Monges," and "La Desgraciada" in the correct location, and Cook's crew debated whether these were the same islands that they had found.

Spanish influence might explain the similarity of the red and yellow feather headdresses of Hawaiian warriors – unknown elsewhere in Polynesia – to the helmets of Spanish soldiers, and account for what seemed the phenomenal speed with which syphilis spread through the islands after it was supposedly introduced by the Cook expedition. The skeleton of a young woman was recently unearthed on Oahu who appears to have died of syphilis in the mid-seventeenth century; other contemporary burials have been shown to contain small scraps of sailcloth. Finally, there are also much earlier legends of inter-island wars for the possession of a mighty Excalibur-style iron sword, which may have been washed ashore accidentally from medieval Japan.

When Cook first encountered Hawaii, he failed to spot both Maui and the Big Island before stumbling upon the western shores of Kauai (see p.486). He was en route to the north Pacific, in search of the (nonexistent) Northwest Passage. When he returned a year later, his two ships, the *Discovery* and the *Resolution*, skirted Maui and then, to the fury of their crews, cruised the coast of the Big Island for almost seven weeks, before anchoring in Kealakekua Bay. There Cook met with the chief of the island, Kalaniopu'u, and was greeted in ceremonies at the Hikiau *heiau*; there too, within a few weeks, he was killed.

## More Hawaiian History

Detailed histories of each individual Hawaiian island appear in the relevant chapter introductions throughout this book. Additional features on specific historical themes, events and personalities include the following, listed in rough chronological order:



See p.171 for an account of the events leading to his death, and the legends that grew up around it.

Cook named the "**Sandwich Islands**" after Lord Sandwich. News of their existence reached the rest of the world after his death by way of the **Russians**, as his ships later halted for provisions on the Siberian coast. Hawaii swiftly became a port of call for all traders crossing the ocean, especially for ships carrying furs from the Pacific Northwest to China.

## Kamehameha the Great

For a few brief years the Hawaiians remained masters of their own destiny, with the major beneficiary of the change in circumstances being the astute young warrior **Kamehameha** on the Big Island. Although he remains the greatest Hawaiian hero, to some extent Kamehameha played into the hands of the newcomers who flocked to the islands from all over the world.

Most governmental representatives were under orders not to trade **guns** with the Hawaiians, but Russian fur traders, in particular, had no such scruples, and surprise Hawaiian attacks on merchant vessels also enabled Kamehameha to build up his own arsenal of foreign weapons. His subsequent conquest of the entire archipelago, and his creation of a single Hawaiian kingdom, greatly simplified the maneuvers that enabled outsiders to achieve first economic, and eventually political, domination over the islands.

The future Kamehameha the Great was born in northern Kohala on the Big Island, in 1758. Both his mother, Kekuiapoiwa, and father, Keōuau, were of royal blood, though it's not clear whether they were niece and nephew of the then ruler of the Big Island, Alapa'i, or of Kahekili, the ruler of Maui. It has even been suggested that Kahekili himself was Kamehameha's true father. The infant Kamehameha was raised in seclusion in Waipi'o Valley.

By the time Kamehameha grew to adulthood, Kalaniopu'u had become high chief of the Big Island. Kamehameha proved a valuable warrior for the king and was present on the waterfront at the death of Captain Cook. When Kalaniopu'u died in 1782, he designated his son Kiwalao to be his heir, but civil war broke out almost immediately. By defeating Kiwalao in battle, Kamehameha took control of the Kona, Kohala and Hāmākua regions; however, Kiwalao's brother **Keōua** survived to establish his own power base in Ka'ū.

For more than a decade a three-way struggle for domination raged back and forth between Kamehameha, Keōua and Kahekili, who at this point was ruler of both Maui and Oahu. It looked for a while as though Kahekili might be the man to unite all the islands, but his hopes of capturing the Big Island were dashed by the **Battle of the Red-Mouthed Gun** off Waipi'o Valley in 1791, when for the first time Hawaiian fleets were equipped with cannons, operated by foreign gunners. The long campaign against Keōua (many of whose warriors were wiped out by an eruption of Kīlauea; see p.252) finally came to an end that same year. At the dedication of the great *heiau* at Pu'ukoholā, the last of the *luakinis*, Keōua himself was the chief sacrifice.

Kamehameha had previously conquered **Maui** through a bloody victory at 'Iao Valley in 1790, only to lose it again when he was forced to turn his attention back to Keōua. As sole ruler of the Big Island, he went on to reconquer first Maui and Lanai, then to capture **Molokai** in 1794, and to take **Oahu** after one last battle at Nu'uanu Valley, in 1795. Finally, after two unsuccessful attempts to invade **Kauai**, he settled for accepting tribute from its ruler, Kaumuali'i. So eager was Kamehameha to obtain military assistance from the Europeans at this time that he briefly ceded the Big Island to Great Britain, though this was never made formal. He even considered the possibility of launching expeditions against the islands of the South Pacific.

By now, many Europeans had settled permanently on the islands. Kamehameha's most important foreign advisers were John Young and Isaac Davis (see p.287), who, in return for royal patronage, led his armies into battle, personally gunning down enemy warriors in droves. In addition, practical skills of all kinds were introduced to the islands by European artisans such as blacksmiths, carpenters and stonemasons.

For some time Kamehameha had his capital in the fledgling port of Lahaina on Maui. By the time he died in 1819, however, he had returned to live in a palace on the Kona Coast of the Big Island.

## The end of the old order

Kamehameha's successor, his son Liholiho – also known as **Kamehameha II** – was a weak figure who was dominated by the regent **Queen Ka'ahumanu** (see p.348). As a woman, she was excluded from the *luakini heiaus* that were the real center of political power, so she set out to bring down the priesthood. Liholiho was plied with drink and cajoled into dining with women at a public banquet; that simple act brought about the end of the *kapu* system (see p.520) and precipitated a civil war in which the upholders of the ancient religion were defeated in a battle near Hōnaunau. Altars and idols at *heiaus* throughout Hawaii were overthrown and destroyed.

Hawaii found itself thrown into moral anarchy at the very moment when the first Puritan **missionaries** arrived. The creation of the Sandwich Islands Mission stemmed from a visit to New England by **Henry 'Opukaha'ia**. A *kahuna* priest from Hikiau *heiau* on the Big Island, he converted to Christianity, but died in his early twenties while a student at the Foreign

Mission School in Cornwall, Connecticut. As he breathed his last, he lamented his failure to return to Hawaii to convert his brethren.

The heartfelt prayer and hard cash of New England worthies, deeply moved by the young man's tragic end, enabled the mission's first two ministers, **Rev Hiram Bingham** and **Rev Asa Thurston**, to sail from Boston in the brig *Thaddeus* on October 23, 1819. According to their instructions, they were sent for "no private end, for no earthly object," but "wholly for the good of others and for the glory of God our Savior. You are to aim at nothing short of covering those islands with fruitful fields and pleasant dwellings, and schools and churches."

After a five-month, eighteen-thousand-mile journey, they reached Kailua Bay on April 4, 1820. If Asa Thurston did not immediately take to Hawaii – he described Kailua as "a filthy village of thatched huts . . . on which the fervent sun poured its furnace heat every day of the year" – neither did the Hawaiians take to him. Ka'ahumanu did not exactly jump at the chance to replace the old priests with a new bunch of interfering moralizers, and there was considerable debate as to whether the missionaries should be allowed to land at all. In the end, the counsel of the aging John Young played a decisive role, but only Thurston was allowed to remain in Kailua. Bingham was obliged to settle in Honolulu, where, scurrilously known as "King Bingham," he denounced his flock as the "stupid and polluted worshippers of demons."

The missionaries' wholehearted capitalism, and their harsh strictures on the easygoing Hawaiian lifestyle, might have been calculated to compound the chaos. They set about obliging Hawaiian women to cover unseemly flesh in billowing *mu'umu'u* "Mother Hubbard" dresses, condemning the *hula* as lascivious and obscene, and discouraging surfing as a waste of time, liable to promote gambling and lewdness.

Meanwhile, Liholiho, who never did quite take to the imposition of the new faith, had been seized with an urge to visit England. He died of measles in London in 1824, without ever meeting King George IV (who referred to him as a "damned cannibal"). When the news reached Hawaii, he was succeeded by his brother Kauikeaouli, who reigned as **Kamehameha III**, although Queen Ka'ahumanu remained very much in control. She had become an enthusiastic promoter of Christianity after being nursed through a grave illness by Bingham's wife, Sybil (whom he had known for two weeks and been married to for one week when they left Boston).

In general, the missionaries concentrated their attentions on the ruling class, the *ali'i*, believing that they would then bring the commoners to the fold. They also devised Hawaii's first alphabet and founded countless schools; one on Kauai famously started out using surfboards for desks. On Maui in particular, the support of the ardently Christian Governor Hoapili facilitated a hugely successful program of education, to the extent that Hawaii achieved the highest literacy rate on earth.

At first, great tensions manifested themselves between missionaries and the new breed of foreign entrepreneurs. These were to disappear as their offspring intermarried, acquired land and formed the backbone of the emerging middle class.

## The foreigners take control

For ordinary Hawaiians, the sudden advent of capitalism was devastating. Any notion of Hawaiian self-sufficiency was abandoned in favor of selling the islands' resources for cash returns. The most extreme example of this was perhaps the earliest: the **sandalwood** trade.

## Sandalwood: the first sell-out

**Sandalwood** logs were first picked up from Hawaii in 1791, when the crew of the *Lady Washington* spotted them in a consignment of fuel collected at Waimea on Kauai. Traders had been searching for years for a commodity they could sell to the Chinese in return for tea to meet English demand. Once it was realized that the Chinese would pay enormous prices for the fragrant wood (the scent of a bowl of sandalwood chips lasts for up to fifty years), the race was on.

Kamehameha had a monopoly on the trade until his death, but thereafter individual chiefs out for their own profit forced all the commoners under their sway to abandon *taro* farming and fishing and become wage slaves. The wood was sold in units known as piculs, which weighed just over 133 pounds. "Picul pits," the exact size and shape of a ship's hold, were dug in the hills and filled with logs; one can still be seen in the rainforest above east Molokai (see p.391). Men, women and children then carried the wood down to the sea on their naked backs. As the trees became rarer, the burden of the laborers, forced to search ever higher in the mountains, grew worse; it's said that they deliberately uprooted saplings to drive the tree to extinction and ensure that their children would not have to do the same cruel work.

Each picul sold for one cent in Hawaii and 34 cents in China; most of the profits went to New England merchants. By the end of the 1820s, the forests were almost entirely denuded, the traditional Hawaiian agricultural system had collapsed, and many chiefs found themselves greatly in debt to foreign merchants, with no obvious way to pay.

In a bizarre footnote, the young *ali'i* **Boki** – a former Governor of Oahu, who had traveled to London with Liholiho and later attempted to organize an armed rebellion against Ka'ahumanu – equipped a military expedition to search for a new source of sandalwood in the South Seas. His ship, the *Kamehameha*, sailed from Honolulu in 1829 with 250 men on board. Neither he nor they were ever seen again.

## Whaling

The first **whaling ships** arrived in Hawaii in 1820, the same year as the missionaries – and had an equally dramatic impact. With the ports of Japan closed to outsiders, Hawaii swiftly became the center of the industry.

Although visitors often assume that it was the humpback whales seen in Hawaiian waters today that attracted the whaling fleet to the islands, humpbacks were not in fact hunted during the nineteenth century. When caught with the technology of the time, they sank uselessly to the bottom of the sea. Instead, the whalers would chase other species in the waters around Japan in winter and in the Arctic in summer, and then call at Hawaii each spring and fall to unload oil and baleen to be shipped home in other vessels, to stock up, and to change crew.

Any Pacific port would have seemed a godsend to the whalers, who were away from New England for three years at a time and paid so badly that most were either fugitives or plain mad. Hawaii was such a paradise that up to fifty percent of each crew would desert, to be replaced by Hawaiian *sailamokus*, born seafarers eager to see the world.

From the very first, Westerners recognized **Honolulu** as possessing the finest deep-water harbor in the Pacific. Hawaiians had never required such anchorages, and Honolulu in ancient times had been the smallest of villages. It swiftly became the whalemen's favorite port, a status it retained until the capital, and the missionary presence that went with it, moved to Honolulu from **Lahaina** on Maui in 1845. The whalers swapped the other way, and both ports became notorious for such diseases as syphilis, influenza, measles, typhoid and smallpox.

Provisioning the whaling ships became the main focus of the Hawaiian economy. The uplands of Maui were irrigated for the first time, to grow temperate crops such as white potatoes, while cattle ranches were established on both Maui and the Big Island. The Hispanic cowboys imported to work there, known as **paniolos** (a corruption of *españoles*), were among the first of the many overseas ethnic groups to make their homes in Hawaii.

## The Great Mahele

By 1844, foreign-born fortune seekers dominated the Hawaiian government. Fourteen of King Kamehameha III's closest advisers were white, including his three most important ministers. The various foreign powers jostled for position; it is easy to forget now that it was not inevitable that the islands would become American. Not until the 1840s was New Zealand snapped up by the English, and Tahiti by the French, and both the European powers retained ambitions in Hawaii. In 1843, a British commander captured Honolulu, claiming all Hawaii for Queen Victoria, and it was six months before word arrived from London that it had all been a mistake. A French admiral did much the same thing in 1849, but this time everyone simply waited until he got bored and sailed away again.

The most important obstacle to the advance of the foreigners was that they could not legally own land. In the old Hawaii there was no private land; all was held in trust by the chief, who apportioned it to individuals at his continued pleasure only. After a misunderstanding with the British consul almost resulted in the islands' permanent cession to Britain, the king was requested to "clarify" the situation. A land commission was set up, under the direction of a missionary, and its deliberations resulted in the **Great Mahele** ("Division of Lands") in 1848. In theory all the land was parcelled out to native Hawaiians only, with sixty percent going to the crown and the government, thirty-nine percent to just over two hundred chiefs, and less than one percent to eleven thousand commoners. Claiming and keeping the land involved complex legal procedures and required expenditures that few Hawaiians, paid in kind not cash, were able to meet. In any case, within two years the *haoles* (non-Hawaiians) were also permitted to buy and sell land. The jibe that the missionaries "came to Hawaii to do good – and they done good" stems from the speed with which they amassed vast acreages; their children became Hawaii's wealthiest and most powerful class.

Many Hawaiians were denied access to the lands they had traditionally worked, arrested for vagrancy, and used as forced labor on the construction of roads and ports for the new landowners. Meanwhile, a simultaneous **water grab** took place, with new white-owned plantations diverting water for their thirsty foreign crops from the Hawaiian farmers downstream.

## The sugar industry and the US Civil War

At the height of the whaling boom, many newly rich entrepreneurs began to put their money into **sugar**. Hawaii's first sugar plantation started in 1835 in Kōloa on Kauai (for a full history, see p.473), and it swiftly became clear that this was an industry where large-scale operators were much the most efficient and profitable. By 1847 the field had narrowed to five main players, four of whom had started out by provisioning whale ships. These **Big Five** were Hackfield & Co (later to become Amfac), C Brewer & Co, Theo Davies Co, Castle & Cooke (later Dole) and Alexander & Baldwin. Thereafter, they worked in close cooperation with each other, united by common interests and, often, family ties.

Hawaii was poised to take advantage of the coming of the Civil War, when the markets of the northern US began to cast about for an alternative source of sugar to the Confederate South. The consequent boom in the Hawaiian sugar industry, and the ever-increasing integration of Hawaii into the American economic mainstream, was the major single factor in the eventual loss of Hawaiian sovereignty.

The Civil War also coincided with the decline of the whaling industry. Several ships were bought and deliberately sunk to blockade Confederate ports, while the discovery of petroleum had diminished the demand for whale oil. The final disaster came in 1871, when 31 vessels lingered in the Arctic too long at the end of the season, became frozen in, and had to be abandoned.

By the 1870s, cane fields were spreading across all the islands. The ethnic mixture of modern Hawaii is largely the product of the search for laborers prepared to submit to the draconian conditions on the plantations. Once the Hawaiians had demonstrated their unwillingness to knuckle under, agents of the Hawaiian Sugar Planters Association scoured the world in search of peasants eager to find new lives.

As members of each ethnic group in turn got their start on the plantations, and then left to find more congenial employment or establish their own businesses, a new source of labor had to be found. It soon became clear that few single men chose to stay on the plantations when their contracts expired – many left for California to join the Gold Rush – so the planters began to try to lure families to Hawaii, which meant providing better housing than the original basic dormitories.

First came the **Chinese** (see p.84), recruited with a $10 inducement in Hong Kong, shipped over for free, and then signed to five-year contracts at $6 or less per month. The **Portuguese** followed, brought from Madeira and the Azores from 1878 onwards by planters who thought they might adjust more readily than their Asian counterparts to the dominant *haole*-Hawaiian culture. **Koreans** arrived during the brief period between 1902, when they were first allowed to leave their country, and 1905, when it was invaded by the **Japanese**, who themselves came in great numbers until 1907, when the so-called Gentleman's Agreement banned further immigration. **Filipinos**, whose country had been annexed by the US in 1898, began to arrive in their stead, to find the climate, soil and crops were all similar to their homelands.

Smaller-scale plantations were also established to grow other crops, such as **pineapples** (discovered in Paraguay early in the sixteenth century), which spread to cover much of Oahu, Maui and Lanai, and **coffee**, which was brought to Hawaii by chief Boki in 1825 and grew most successfully on the Kona slopes of the Big Island (see p.169).

## The end of the Kingdom of Hawaii

**Hawaii is ours. As I look back upon the first steps in this miserable business, and as I contemplate the means used to complete the outrage, I am ashamed of the whole affair.**

US President Grover Cleveland, 1893

After sugar prices dropped at the end of the Civil War, the machinations of the sugar industry to get favorable prices on the mainland moved Hawaii inexorably towards **annexation** by the US. In 1876 the Treaty of Reciprocity abolished all trade barriers and tariffs between the US and the Kingdom of Hawaii; within fifteen years sugar exports to the US had increased tenfold.

By now, the Kamehameha dynasty had come to an end, and the heir to the Hawaiian throne was chosen by the national legislature. The first such king, William Lunalilo, died in 1874, after barely a year in office. In the ensuing elections, **Queen Emma**, the Anglophile widow of Kamehameha IV (see p.94), lost to **King David Kalākaua**. The "Merrie Monarch" is affectionately remembered today for his role in reviving traditional Hawaiian pursuits such as *hula* and surfing, but he was widely seen as being pro-American, and a riot protesting his election in 1874 virtually destroyed Honolulu's Old Court House. King Kalākaua was to a significant extent the tool of the plantation owners. In 1887 an all-white (and armed) group of "concerned businessmen" forced through the "Bayonet Constitution," in which he surrendered power to an assembly elected by property owners (of any nationality) as opposed to citizens. The US government was swiftly granted exclusive rights to what became Pearl Harbor.

Kalākaua died in San Francisco in 1891, shortly after recording a farewell address to his people on a newly invented Edison recording machine. In his absence, he had appointed his sister **Lili'uokalani** to serve as his regent, and she now became queen. When she proclaimed her desire for a new constitution, the same group of businessmen, who had now convened themselves into an "**Annexation Club**," called in the US warship *Boston*, then in Honolulu, and declared a provisional government. President Grover Cleveland (a Democrat) responded that "Hawaii was taken possession of by the United States forces without the consent or wish of the government of the islands. . . . [It] was wholly without justification . . . not merely a wrong but a disgrace." With phenomenal cheek, the provisional government rejected his demand for the restoration of the monarchy, saying the US should not "interfere in the internal affairs of their sovereign nation." They found defenders in the Republican US Congress and declared themselves a **republic** on July 4, 1894, with **Sanford Dole** as their first President.

Following an abortive coup attempt in 1895, Lili'uokalani was charged with **treason**. She was placed under house arrest, first in 'Iolani Palace and later at her Honolulu home of Washington Place (see p.80). Though she lived until 1917, hopes of a restoration of Hawaiian independence were dashed in 1897, when a Republican president, McKinley, came to office claiming "annexation is not a change. It is a consummation." The strategic value of Pearl Harbor was emphasized by the Spanish–American War in the Philippines, and on August 12, 1898, Hawaii was formally **annexed** as a territory of the United States.

## The Hawaiian monarchy

| | |
|---|---|
| Kamehameha I | 1791–1819 |
| Kamehameha II (Liholiho) | 1819–1824 |
| Kamehameha III (Kauikeaouli) | 1825–1854 |
| Kamehameha IV (Alexander Liholiho) | 1854–1863 |
| Kamehameha V (Lot Kamehameha) | 1863–1872 |
| William C. Lunalilo | 1873–1874 |
| David Kalākaua | 1874–1891 |
| Lili'uokalani | 1891–1893 |

# A territory and a state

At the moment of annexation there was no question of Hawaii becoming a state; the whites were outnumbered ten to one and had no desire to afford the rest of the islanders the protection of US labor laws, let alone to give them the vote. (Sanford Dole said that natives couldn't expect to vote "simply because they were grown up.") Furthermore, as the proportion of Hawaiians of Japanese descent (*nisei*) increased (to 25 percent by 1936), Congress feared the prospect of a state whose inhabitants might consider their primary allegiance to be to Japan. Consequently, Hawaii remained for the first half of this century the virtual fiefdom of the Big Five, who, through their control of agriculture (they owned 96 percent of the sugar crop), dominated transport, banks, utilities, insurance and government.

Things began to change during World War II. The Japanese offensive on Pearl Harbor, detailed on p.98, meant that Hawaii was the only part of the United States to be attacked in the war, and it demonstrated just how crucial the islands were to the rest of America. Military bases and training camps were established throughout Hawaii, many of which remain operational to this day. In addition, Hawaiian troops played an active role in the war. Veterans of the much-decorated 442nd Regimental Combat Team – composed of Japanese Hawaiians and, for obvious reasons, sent to fight in Europe – have been a leading force in Hawaiian politics ever since.

The main trend in Hawaiian history since the war has been the slow decline of agriculture and the rise of **tourism**. Strikes organized along ethnic lines in the sugar plantations had consistently failed in the past, but from 1937 on, labor leaders such as Jack Hill and Harry Bridges of the International Longshoremen's and Warehousemen's Union began to organize workers of all races and all crafts, in solidarity with mainland unions. In September 1946, the plantation workers won their first victory. Thanks to the campaigns that followed, the long-term Republican domination of state politics ended, and Hawaii's agricultural workers became the highest paid in the world. Arguably, this led to the eventual disappearance of all their jobs in the face of Third World competition; fifty years later, almost all the sugar mills have closed.

Hawaii finally became the fiftieth of the United States in 1959, after a plebiscite showed a seventeen-to-one majority in favor, with the only significant opposition coming from the few remaining native Hawaiians. **Statehood** coincided with the first jet flight to Hawaii, which halved the previous nine-hour flight time from California. These two factors triggered a boom in tourism – many visitors had had their first sight of Hawaii as GIs in the war – and also in migration from the mainland to Hawaii.

Official figures showing the growth of the Hawaiian economy since statehood conceal a decline in living standards for many Hawaiians, with rises in consumer prices far outstripping rises in wages. Real estate prices in particular have rocketed, so that many islanders are obliged to work at two jobs, others end up sleeping on the beaches, and young Hawaiians emigrate in droves with no prospect of being able to afford to return.

## The sovereignty movement

Since the late 1980s, broad-based support has mushroomed for the concept of **Hawaiian sovereignty**, meaning some form of restoration of the rights of native Hawaiians. Pride in the Polynesian past has been rekindled by such means as the voyages of the Hōkūle'a canoe (see p.521), and the successful campaign to claim back the island of Kahoolawe, which had been used since the war as a Navy bombing range (see p.319).

The movement has reached the point where everyone seems to expect that sovereignty is coming, but no one knows what form it will take. Of the three most commonly advanced models, one sees Hawaii as an independent nation once again, recognized by the international community, with full citizenship perhaps restricted either to those born in Hawaii or prepared to pledge sole allegiance to Hawaii. Another possibility would be the granting to native Hawaiians of nation-within-a-nation status, as with Native American groups on the mainland. Others argue that it would be more realistic to preserve the existing political framework within the context of full economic reparations to native Hawaiians.

Even the US government has formally acknowledged the illegality of the US overthrow of the Hawaiian monarchy with an official **Apology to Native Hawaiians** signed by President Clinton in November 1993. A separate but related problem, indicative of the difficulties faced in resolving this issue, is the failure by both federal and state government to manage 200,000 acres set aside for the benefit of native Hawaiians in 1921. The state has now agreed to pay Hawaiians more than $100 million in compensation, though disputes remain over where the money will come from and to whom it will go.

The sovereignty issue attained such a high profile in 1998, thanks to the centenary of annexation, that it provoked something of a backlash among elements of the state's non-native (and, in particular, Caucasian) population. The Office of Hawaiian Affairs, the body responsible for looking after the interests of native Hawaiians and, potentially, distributing compensation, had long been run by a board whose members were elected by native Hawaiians only. In a landmark ruling in February 2000, the US Supreme Court declared such race-based elections to be unconstitutional. New elections later that year were open to all state residents and produced one new non-native board member. Hawaiian activists fear that their movement is in jeopardy, with state programs liable to be dismantled by the courts. Nonetheless, political support appears to remain strong for, at the very least, federal recognition of the status of native Hawaiians as being equivalent to that of native peoples elsewhere in the country, and veteran state senator Daniel Akaka has repeatedly introduced drafts of a bill to that end in Washington.

# Ancient culture and society

No written record exists of the centuries between the arrival of the Polynesians and the first contact with Europeans. Sacred chants, passed down through the generations, show a history packed with feuds and forays between the islands, and the rise and fall of dynasties, but they didn't concern themselves with the requirements of modern historians, and specific dates are conspicuous by their absence. However, oral traditions do provide us with a detailed picture of the day-to-day life of ordinary Hawaiians in years gone by.

Developing a civilization on such isolated islands, without metals and workable clays, presented the settlers with many challenges. Nevertheless, by the late eighteenth century, when the Europeans arrived, the Hawaiian islands were home to around a million people. Two hundred years later, the population has climbed back to a similar level. Now, however, virtually no pure-blooded Hawaiians remain, and the islands are no longer even close to being self-sufficient in terms of food. The population distribution has changed, too; it's striking how often the accounts of the early explorers describe being greeted by vast numbers of canoes in areas which are now all but uninhabited. The Big Island's population would have been far larger than the 130,000 it is today, and Oahu's population smaller, but no precise figures are known.

## Daily life

In a sense, ancient Hawaii had no economy, not even barter. Although then, as now, most people lived close to the coast, each island was organized into wedge-shaped land divisions called **ahupua'a**, which stretched from the ocean to the mountains. *Ahupua'a* literally means a place where hogs were stored or gathered, and the boundaries between one and the next were marked by an altar bearing a carved image of a pig's head. The abundant fruits of the earth and sea were simply shared among the inhabitants within each *ahupua'a*.

There's some truth in the idea of pre-contact Hawaii as a leisured paradise, but it had taken a lot of work to make it that way. Coconut palms were planted along the seashore to provide food, clothing and shade for coastal villages, and bananas and other food plants distributed inland. Crops such as sugar cane were cultivated with the aid of complex systems of terraces and irrigation channels. *Taro*, whose leaves were eaten as "greens" and whose roots were mashed to produce the staple *poi*, was grown in *lo'i*, which (like rice paddies) are kept constantly submerged, in the lush windward valleys such as Hanalei on Kauai, Waimea on Oahu, Hālawa on Molokai, and Waipi'o on the Big Island.

Most **fishing** took place in shallow inshore waters. Fishhooks made from human bone were believed to be especially effective; the most prized hooks were made from the bones of chiefs who had no body hair, so those unfortunate individuals were renowned for their low life expectancy. Nets were never cast from boats, but shallow bays were dragged by communal groups of wading men drawing in hukilau nets. (Elvis did it in Blue Hawaii, and you occasionally see people doing it today.) There was also a certain amount of freshwater fishing in the mountain streams, especially for shrimp, catfish and goby. Fish were caught by placing basket-like nets at a narrow point, then dislodging stones upstream.

In addition, the art of **aquaculture** – fish-farming – was more highly developed in Hawaii than anywhere in Polynesia. It reached its most refined form in the extensive networks of fishponds that ringed much of Hawaii's shoreline; the best surviving examples are along the southeast coast of Molokai (see p.388), and near Līhuʻe on Kauai. Such fishponds were usually constructed to demonstrate the power of a particular chief and increase his wealth; the fish would be reserved for his personal consumption.

Few people lived in the higher forested slopes, but these served as the source of vital raw materials such as *koa* wood for canoes and weapons. The ancients even ventured to the summit of Mauna Kea on the Big Island; as the only point in the Pacific to be glaciated during the last Ice Age, it has the hardest basalt on the islands. Stone from the **adze quarry**, 12,400 feet up, was used for all basic tools.

Ordinary commoners – the **makaʻāinana** – lived in simple windowless huts known as *hales*. Most of these were thatched with *pili* grass, though in the driest areas ordinary people didn't bother with roofs. Buildings of all kinds were usually raised on platforms of stone; rounded boulders were taken from river beds and hauled long distances for that purpose, and were also used to make roads. Matting would have covered the floor, while the pounded tree bark called *kapa* (known as *tapa* elsewhere in the Pacific, and decorated with patterns) served as clothing and bedding. Lacking pottery, households made abundant use of gourds, wooden dishes and woven baskets; chiefs would sometimes decorate bowls and calabashes with the teeth of their slain enemies, as a deliberate desecration of their remains.

The most popular pastime was **surfing**. Petroglyphs depicting surfers have been found, and there were even surfing *heiaus*. Ordinary people surfed on five- to seven-foot boards known as *alaia*, and also had *paipus*, the equivalent of the modern boogie board; only the *aliʻi* used the thick sixteen-foot *olo* boards, made of dark oiled *wiliwili* wood. On land the *aliʻi* raced narrow sleds on purpose-built, grass-covered *hōlua* slides and staged boxing tournaments.

# The Aliʻi

The ruling class, the **aliʻi**, stood at the apex of Hawaiian society. In theory, heredity counted for everything, and great chiefs demonstrated their fitness to rule by the length of their genealogies. In fact the *aliʻi* were educated as equals, and chiefs won the very highest rank largely through physical prowess and force of personality. To hang on to power, the king had to be seen as devoutly religious and to treat his people fairly.

For most of Hawaiian history, each island was divided into a varying number of chiefdoms, with major potential for intrigue, faction and warfare. Canoes being the basic means of transportation, it was also feasible for chiefs to launch inter-island campaigns. Kauai managed to remain consistently independent, thanks to the wide, dangerous channel separating it from the Windward Islands, but as the centuries went by large-scale expeditions between Oahu, Maui and the Big Island became ever more frequent. As a rule, Lanai and Molokai fell under the sway of whoever happened to be ruling Maui at the time.

Complex genealogies of the great *ali'i* still survive, but little is recorded other than their names. Summaries of the major figures on each island appear in the relevant chapter introductions in this book. Among the most important of these was **'Umi-a-Liloa**; some time between the twelfth and sixteenth centuries, he became the first ruler to unite the Big Island, from his base amid the *taro* fields of Waipi'o Valley. Umi is said to have inherited the throne by defeating his brother in a *hōlua* sledding contest. Listed as representing the sixtieth generation after the sky god Wākea, he was responsible for Hawaii's first legal code – the *kanawai*, which concerned itself with the equal sharing of water from Waipi'o's irrigation ditches – and was among the first to make human sacrifice an instrument of state policy. Other important figures include the sixteenth-century **Pi'ilani**, who was the first chief to control all Maui and built the first paved road around any island, and the ferocious tattooed **Kahekili**, also from Maui, who almost conquered the entire archipelago shortly before Kamehameha the Great finally did so.

Perhaps the most enigmatic figure was **Lono**, who may have been 'Umi's grandson. Legends suggest that he lost his throne after quarreling with, or even murdering, his wife and left the Big Island in a half-crazed fit of self-loathing. Some say that he regained his sanity, returned to unite the island, and was subsquently deified as Lonoikamakahiki, patron of the annual *makahiki* festival. Others claim that the Hawaiians predicted his return for centuries and believed these prophecies to be fulfilled by the arrival of Captain Cook (see p.171).

# Religion

It's all but impossible now to grasp the subtleties of ancient Hawaiian **religion**. So much depends on how the chants and texts are translated; if the word *akua* is interpreted as meaning "god," for example, historians can draw analogies with Greek or Hindu legends by speaking of a pantheon of battling, squabbling "gods" and "goddesses" with magic powers. Some scholars, however, prefer to translate *akua* as "spirit consciousness" – which might correspond to the soul of an ancestor or even the motivational force present in a modern wristwatch – and argue that the antics of such figures are peripheral to a more fundamental set of attitudes regarding the relationship of humans to the natural world.

The **Kumulipo**, Hawaii's principal creation myth, has been preserved in full as a chant, passed down from generation to generation. It tells how, after the emergence of the earth "from the source in the slime . . . [in] the depths of the darkness," more complicated life forms developed, from coral to pigs, until finally men, women and "gods" appeared. Not only was there no Creator god, but the gods were much of a kind with humans. It took a hundred generations for Wākea, the god of the sky, and Papa, an earth goddess, to be born; they were the divine ancestors of the people of Hawaii.

It may well be misleading to imagine that all Hawaiians shared the same beliefs; different groups sought differing ways of augmenting their *mana*, or spiritual power. Quite possibly only the elite *ali'i* paid much attention to the bloodthirsty warrior god **Kū**, while the primary allegiance of ordinary families and, by extension, villages and regions, may have lain towards their personal *'aumākua* – a sort of clan symbol, which might be a totem animal such as a shark or an owl, or a more abstract force, such as that embodied by **Pele**, the volcano goddess.

Spiritual and temporal power did not necessarily lie in the same hands, let alone in the same places. Hawaiian "priests" were known as **kahunas** (literally, "men who know the secrets") and were the masters of ceremonies at temples called **heiaus**. The design of a *heiau* was not always consistent, but as a rule it consisted of a number of separate structures standing on a rock platform (*paepae*). These might include the *hale mana* ("house of spiritual power"), the *hale pahu* ("house of the drum") and the *anu'u* ("oracle tower"), from the top of which the *kahunas* would converse with the gods. Assorted *ki'i akua*, symbolic wooden images of different gods, would stand on all sides, and the whole enclosure was fenced or walled off. In addition to the two main types of *heiau* – the **luakinis**, which were dedicated to the war god Kū and held *leles* or altars used for human sacrifice, and **māpeles**, peaceful temples to Lono – there were also *heiaus* to such entities as Laka, goddess of the *hula*. Devotees of Pele, on the other hand, did not give their protectress formal worship at a *heiau*.

Most *heiaus* were built for some specific occasion and did not remain in constant use. Among the best-preserved examples are the *luakinis* at Pu'ukoholā on the Big Island (see p.189), at Pu'u O Mahuka on Oahu, and at 'Ili'ili'ōpae on Molokai; the *hula heiau* above Ke'e Beach on Kauai; and the healing *heiau* at Keaīwa, outside Honolulu.

Hawaiian religion in the form encountered by Cook was brought to the Big Island, and subsequently to the rest of the archipelago, by the Tahitian warrior-priest Pa'ao, who led the last great migration to Hawaii. The war god Kū received his first human sacrifices on the Big Island, at *luakini* temples such as Waha'ula *heiau* near Kīlauea, which was recently destroyed by lava flows.

Pa'ao is also credited with introducing and refining the complex system of **kapu**, which circumscribed the daily lives of all Hawaiians. *Kapu* is the Hawaiian version of the Polynesian *tabu*, often written in English as "taboo." Like all such systems, it served many purposes. Some of its restrictions were designed to augment the power of the kings and priests, while others regulated domestic routine or attempted to conserve scarce natural resources.

Many had to do with food. Women were forbidden to prepare food or to eat with men; each husband was obliged to cook for himself and his wife in two separate ovens and to pound the *poi* in two distinct calabashes. The couple had to maintain separate houses, as well as a *Hale Noa*, where a husband and wife slept together. Women could not eat pork, bananas or coconuts, or several kinds of fish. Certain fish could only be caught in specified seasons, and a *koa* tree could only be cut down provided two more were planted in its place.

No one could tread on the shadow of a chief; the highest chiefs were so surrounded by *kapus* that some only went out at night. Although bloodlines defined one's place in the *kapu* hierarchy, might dominated over right, so the ruling chiefs did not necessarily possess the highest spiritual status. One of Kamehameha's wives, Kapi'olani, was so much his superior that he could only approach her naked, backwards, and on all fours.

The only crime in ancient Hawaii was to break a *kapu*, and the only punishment was death. It was possible for an entire *ahupua'a* to break a *kapu* and incur death, but the penalty was not always exacted. One way for guilty parties to avoid execution was by hotfooting it to a *pu'uhonua*, or "place of refuge." Each island is thought to have had several of these; the one in Hōnaunau on the Big Island remains among the best-preserved ancient sites in all Hawaii (see p.174). In addition, the person of the king himself was considered to be a *pu'uhonua*.

# The return of the voyagers

**Although archeological and linguistic evidence had long made it clear that the Polynesians deliberately colonized the Pacific, how they did so remained a mystery until about thirty years ago. In 1973, a group of Hawaiians set out to rediscover the skills and techniques of their ancestors. Ben Finney, an anthropologist from Honolulu's Bishop Museum, Tommy Holmes, a racing canoe paddler, and the artist Herb Kane founded the Polynesian Voyaging Society to build replicas of the ancient ocean-going vessels and use them to reproduce the early voyages. In particular, they were determined to prove that it was possible to make sustained, long-distance return trips across the Pacific without modern instruments or charts, despite the trade winds that consistently blow from the northeast.**

The great Polynesian sailing canoes, or *wa'a*, were developed to their ultimate level of sophistication in Hawaii itself. This followed the discovery of the native Hawaiian *koa*, a gigantic hardwood tree whose wood was the perfect material for canoe construction. Each canoe was scooped from a single *koa* trunk, six feet in diameter and at least fifty feet long, using stone adzes and knives made of bone, shell or coral. Surfaces were sanded with the skin of manta rays, and the hulls waterproofed with gum from the breadfruit tree. When lashed together, two such vessels formed a double-hulled long-distance sailing canoe. Using the word "canoe" to describe the *wa'a* is somewhat misleading to modern ears; each was up to 150 feet long, and capable of holding five or six hundred people. For comparison, they were three times the size of the largest Viking longboat and faster than nineteenth-century clipper ships, traveling an average of 120 nautical miles per day.

Voyaging canoes were equipped with sails made from plaited pandanus leaves (*lau hala*), while a *lei hulu*, made from bright feathers, was the attractive equivalent of a windsock. The crew would be unlikely to catch many fish on the long voyage between Tahiti and Hawaii, but they could cook on a hearth lined with stone and coral and lived mainly on fermented breadfruit.

The Polynesian Voyaging Society's first vessel was the **Hōkūle'a**, named after the "Star of Gladness" that passes over Hawaii. Though constructed of plywood and fiberglass rather than *koa*, it was designed to duplicate the performance of a traditional double-hulled canoe. Petroglyph images served as blueprints for the shape of the sails, and extensive sea trials were required before the crew felt confident in handling the unfamiliar craft.

Perhaps the biggest problem was finding a **navigator**. In ancient times, the children of master navigators were apprenticed from the age of five to learn the secrets of their trade. Eventually the student would have, as a nineteenth-century canoe captain explained, "his head all same as compass." Navigators prepared intricate "stick charts," using twigs and shells to depict ocean currents, swells and islands. These were memorized rather than carried on board, and guided canoes across the Pacific. Once settled in Hawaii, however, the Polynesians had no need of these skills, so as the older generations died, the knowledge was lost. Only the barest details of the migrations could be gleaned from Hawaiian lore.

## Western myths and misconceptions

Western scientists, unwilling to credit **Polynesian culture** with any degree of sophistication, were for hundreds of years unable to account for the presence of the Hawaiians. When Captain Cook reached the Hawaiian islands, he was amazed to find a civilization that shared a culture and language with the people of the South Pacific.

Europeans had only just developed the technology to make expeditions such as Cook's possible. The recent development of a pendulum-free clock that remained accurate at sea – which earned its inventor a prize of £20,000 – had finally enabled sailors to calculate their longitude. As a result, they found it hard to believe that the Polynesians were already able to plot and sail a precise course across a three-thousand-mile expanse of ocean. The Hawaiians were unable to explain how they had achieved this feat; although their chants and legends were explicit about their Tahitian origin, they no longer undertook long-distance sea trips, so the specific **navigational skills** had been forgotten.

At first it was thought that the Hawaiians came from an as-yet undiscovered continent; when that proved not to exist, it was suggested that they had survived its submergence. Some argued that the islanders had simply been deposited by God. The consensus came to be that the Polynesians had drifted accidentally from island to island, with groups of storm-tossed unfortunates making lucky landfalls on unoccupied islands. One hypothesis, "demonstrated" by Thor Heyerdahl's *Kon Tiki* expedition in 1947, was that the Polynesians came originally from South America, having been swept out to sea on balsa wood rafts as they fished off the coast.

There are strong reasons to reject the theory of accidental drift. The islands of the Pacific are so tiny and so far apart that vast quantities of drifting rafts would be required to populate every one. Moreover, the fact that migratory groups clearly brought the plants and animals necessary for survival indicates that the colonization was planned, and almost certainly involved return trips to the home base. But the most crucial evidence, in the case of Hawaii, is that neither wind nor wave will carry a vessel across the Equator; travel between Hawaii and Tahiti is only possible on a craft that uses some form of power, be it oar or maneuverable sail. One of the linchpins of Heyerdahl's argument was the presence in Polynesia of the sweet potato, unquestionably of South American origin. His claims that Polynesian languages showed South American roots have since been disproved by modern analysis, which shows a linguistic spread from Asia, as well as by conclusive DNA evidence. At some point, quite possibly deliberately, Polynesians must have reached South America and succeeded in returning.

When the *Hōkūle'a* embarked on its maiden long-distance voyage in 1976, it was navigated by **Mau Piailug**, from the Central Caroline islands of Micronesia, who was able to chart his course due to years of experience on the Pacific, and the relative familiarity of the night sky. In personal terms, thanks in part to the presence of a team from *National Geographic*, the voyage was fraught with tensions; by reaching Tahiti in just thirty days, however, it triumphantly achieved its purpose.

In subsequent years, the *Hōkūle'a* sailed all over the Pacific. By using a north wind to sail east from Samoa to Tahiti, it refuted Heyerdahl's statement that it was impossible for canoes from Asia to sail into the trade winds of the Pacific. Between 1985 and 1987 it went to New Zealand and back, a 12,000-mile round-trip. Meanwhile, a young Hawaiian crew member of the *Hōkūle'a*, **Nainoa Thompson**, became fascinated with the lost art of navigation and set out to rediscover the specific techniques that the ancient Hawaiians themselves would have used.

The navigator's task consists of two main elements: way-finding and land-finding. **Way-finding** is the ability to plot and keep track of a long-distance course as accurately as possible. Although way-finding involves constantly monitoring the state of the ocean, the winds and the currents (except for brief catnaps, the navigator has to remain awake for the entire voyage), it is rooted in close astronomical observation. In a fascinating partnership with modern science, Thompson gleaned a lifetime's worth of experience of the motions of the night sky through spending long hours in the planetarium at the Bishop Museum. The precise techniques he developed, which involved finding "matching pairs" of stars that set or rise at the same time, may not be identical to those used by the original Polynesians. They have, however, conclusively demonstrated that long voyages without navigational aids are possible.

The other essential component to navigation is **land-finding**, the art of detecting land when you know it must be close. From the deck of a sailing canoe on the open Pacific, the horizon is just four miles away; to avoid sailing right past your objective, you have to watch for the many signs that land is nearby. The most obvious of these is the behavior and color of cloud formations; the Big Island, for example, is usually "visible" from about a hundred miles away, thanks to the stationary clouds over its giant volcanoes. The nightly homeward flight of birds to their island nests is another indication, while much can also be read into the swells and currents of the sea itself.

The **Hawai'iloa**, a canoe made of wood at the Bishop Museum and launched in 1993, went another step towards reproducing past glories. Unfortunately no *koa* tree large enough to build such a canoe was found; instead the Tlingit of Alaska donated two four-hundred-year-old Sitka spruces. Soon afterwards, the **Mauloa**, a 26-foot-long, single-hulled *koa*-wood canoe, was constructed at the Pu'uhonua O Honaunau on the Big Island, under the supervision of Mau Piailug.

According to legend, during the heyday of Polynesian voyaging, regular gatherings of canoes from throughout the Pacific took place at the *Marae Taputapuatea* (temple of Lono) at Raiatea, not far from Tahiti in what are now called the Society Islands. The last such occasion, in 1350 AD, broke up after a Maori navigator was murdered. As a result the Maori placed a *kapu* on the temple, and the era of ocean voyaging came to an end. After that date, no further expeditions sailed to or from Hawaii, although the last known long-distance voyage in Polynesia was as recent as 1812, from the Marquesas Islands.

In March 1995, the canoes gathered again, for the first time in more than six centuries. Both the *Hōkūle'a* and *Hawai'iloa* sailed from Hawaii to Tahiti, taking a mere three weeks, and then continued on to Raiatea. Maori elders conducted ceremonies at the *marae* to lift the ancient *kapu*, and canoes from Tahiti, New Zealand and the Cook Islands joined their Hawaiian counterparts in proclaiming a new era of pan-Polynesian solidarity.

The most recent voyage for the *Hōkūle'a*, in 1999 and 2000, carried it safely to and from Rapa Nui, or Easter Island. By successfully traveling to this remote spot in the southeast Pacific, it formally completed the final leg of the "Polynesian Triangle," demonstrating that the ancient Polynesians did indeed deliberately colonize the entire ocean. Its next mission is expected to be a trip to South America and back, in an attempt to account for the westward spread of the sweet potato.

The canoes have become perhaps the most potent symbol of a Polynesian Renaissance. Their every movement is eagerly followed by children throughout the Pacific, and a new generation of navigators is being trained to assume the mantle of Nainoa Thompson and Mau Piailug.

# The Hawaiian environment

**Of all the places in the world, I should like to see a good flora of the Sandwich Islands.**

Charles Darwin, 1850

Much of the landscape in Hawaii seems so unspoilt and free from pollution that many visitors remain unaware of how fragile the environmental balance really is. Native life forms have had less than two millennia to adapt to the arrival of humans, while the avalanche of species introduced in the last two centuries threatens to overwhelm the delicate ecosystems altogether.

Hawaii is a unique ecological laboratory. Not only are the islands isolated by a "moat" at least two thousand miles wide in every direction, but, having emerged from the sea as lifeless lumps of lava, they were never populated by the diversity of species that spread across the rest of the planet.

Those plants and animals that found a foothold evolved into specialized forms unknown elsewhere. Of the more than ten thousand species of insect found in the islands, for example, 98 percent are unique to Hawaii, while at least five thousand species are thought to remain unidentified. Recent discoveries include the tiny "happy-face spiders" of the rainforests, whose markings are now familiar from postcards sold all over the state.

Such species are particularly vulnerable to external threats; half of Hawaii's indigenous plants and three-quarters of its birds are already extinct, while 73 percent of all the species in the US classified as threatened or endangered are unique to the islands. More than one hundred species of Hawaiian plants now have fewer than twenty remaining individuals in the wild.

## The arrival of life

During the first seventy million years after the Hawaiian islands started to arise from the ocean, new plants and animals arrived only by sheer happenstance, via a few unlikely routes. Such were the obstacles that a new species only established itself once every 100,000 years.

Some drifted, clinging to flotsam washed up on the beaches; others were borne on the wind as seeds or spores; and the odd migratory bird found its way here, perhaps bringing insects or seeds. The larvae of shallow-water fish from Indonesia and the Philippines floated across thousands of miles of ocean to hatch in the Hawaiian coral reefs.

Of birds, only the strongest fliers made it here; the *nēnē*, Hawaii's state bird, is thought to have evolved from a Canadian goose injured during its annual migration and forced to remain on the islands. Its descendants adapted to walking on raw lava by losing the webbing from their feet. No land-based amphibians or reptiles reached Hawaii, let alone large land mammals. At some point a hoary bat and an intrepid monk seal must have gotten here, as these were the only two mammals whose arrival predated that of humans.

Each species mutated from a single fertilized female to fill numerous ecological niches with extraordinary speed. Hundreds of variations might develop from a single fruit fly or land snail, and many species adapted themselves to conditions in specific areas of individual islands.

Although the Hawaiian environment was not entirely free of competition, many plants prospered without bothering to keep up their natural defenses. Thus there are nettles with no stings, and mints with no scent. Conversely, normally placid creatures turned savage; caterpillars content to munch leaves elsewhere catch and eat flies in Hawaii. These evolutionary changes have taken place so fast that five species of banana moth have evolved in the 1500 years since the Polynesians brought the banana to the islands.

As each new island emerged, it was populated by species from its neighbors as well as stragglers from farther afield. This process can still be seen on the Big Island – the youngest and least densely populated island – where Hawaii's last remaining stand of pristine rainforest still attempts to spread onto the new land created by Kīlauea. Although lava flows destroy existing life, fresh lava is incredibly rich in nutrients. Water collects in cavities in the rock, and seeds or spores soon gather. The basic building block of the rainforest is the *hāpu'u* tree fern. Patches of these grow and decay, and in the mulch the *'ōhi'a lehua* gains a foothold as a gnarled shrub; in time it grows to become a gigantic tree, forcing its roots through the rock. After several hundred years, the lava crumbles to become soil that will support a full range of rainforest species. In addition, lava flows swirl around higher ground, or even random spots, to create isolated "pockets" of growth that quickly develop their own specialized ecosystems.

## The Polynesian world

The first humans to arrive on the Hawaiian scene swiftly realized that the islands lacked the familiar comforts of their South Seas homelands. Many of what might seem quintessentially Hawaiian species, such as coconut palms, bananas, *taro* and sugar cane, were in fact brought from Tahiti by the Polynesians, who also introduced the islands' first significant mammals – goats, dogs and pigs.

The settlers set about changing the island's physical environment to suit their own needs. They constructed terraces and irrigation channels in the great wetland valleys, such as Hālawa on Molokai and Waipi'o on the Big Island, planted coconuts along the shoreline, and built fishponds out into the ocean (see p.388). While their animals wrought destruction on the native flora, the settlers also had a significant impact on the bird population. Around twenty species of flightless birds, for example, swiftly became extinct. Forest birds were snared so their feathers could be used to make cloaks, helmets and *leis*; bright red feathers came from the *i'iwi* bird, while yellow became the most prized color of all, so yellow birds such as the *mamo* and *'ō'ō* grew progressively rare. The *nēnē* was hunted for food, and the *auku'u* heron, the curse of the fishponds, was driven from its native habitat.

On the whole, however, the Hawaiians lived in relative harmony with nature, with the *kapu* system helping to conserve resources. It was the arrival of foreigners, and the deluge of new species that they introduced, that really strained the ecological balance of Hawaii. Among the first victims were the Hawaiians themselves, decimated by the onslaught of foreign diseases.

## Foreign invaders

The ships of the European explorers were explicitly intended to play the role of Noah's Arks. They carried food plants and domestic animals around the world in order to adapt newly discovered lands to the European image and present their benighted natives with the necessary accoutrements of civilization. Hawaii's first cattle, for example, were presented to Kamehameha the Great by Captain George Vancouver of the *Discovery* in February 1793 and allowed to run wild on the Big Island. They ate through grasslands and forests, as well as through the crops of the Hawaiians. When they were eventually rounded up and domesticated, it formalized the change in land usage they had already effected. Horses had a similar initial impact, and wild goats remain a problem to this day.

Foreign plants, too, were imported, ranging from the scrubby mesquite trees of the lowlands (now known as *kiawe*) to the Mexican cacti that dot the mountainsides of Maui and the strawberry guava that runs riot along forest trails.

Along with such deliberate introductions came the stowaways, such as rats and forest-choking weeds. An especially unwelcome arrival was the **mosquito**. Scientists have pinpointed the exact moment it turned up, in 1826, when the whaling vessel *Wellington* emptied its rancid water casks into a stream near Lahaina prior to filling up with fresh water; they've even decided from which Peruvian river the water, and the mosquito larvae it contained, was originally drawn.

Another spectacular disaster was the importation to Hawaii of the **mongoose** by sugar plantation owners in the hope that it would keep down the rat population. Unfortunately, this plan failed to take into consideraion the fact that rats are nocturnal and mongooses are not. The rodents continued to thrive while the mongooses slept, having gorged themselves on birds' eggs during the day. Only Kauai, where the mongoose never became established – myth has it that an infuriated docker threw the island's consignment into the sea after he was bitten – now retains significant populations of the many Hawaiian birds who, in the absence of predators, had decided it was safe to build their nests on the ground.

**Wild pigs** have had an especially ravaging effect. It is said that for every twenty humans in Hawaii, there lurks a feral pig. Though tourists are unlikely to spot one, their impact on Hawaiian rainforests has been devastating. For the ancient Hawaiians, the pig god Kama'pua'a was the embodiment of lusty fertility, ploughing deep furrows across the islands with his mighty tusks. His modern counterparts combine the strongest characteristics of the Polynesian pigs brought by early settlers with those of later European imports. Rooting through the earth, eating tree ferns, eliminating native lobelias and greenswords, and spreading the seeds of foreign fruits, the pigs have in most places destroyed the canopy that should prevent direct sunlight and heavy raindrops from hitting the forest floor. In addition, they have created muddy wallows and stagnant pools where mosquitoes thrive – the resultant avian malaria is thought to be the major single cause of the extinction of bird species.

Eradicating the wild pig population has become a priority for conservationists. In principle their goal gels with the desire of amateur hunters for sport, though bitter "Pig Wars" have arisen between hunters who want to leave enough wild pigs for their hunting to continue and scientists who want to eliminate them altogether.

Unwanted alien species continue to arrive. Among those reported within the last five years are the **coqui frog** from Puerto Rico, which has already achieved population densities in excess of ten thousand individuals per acre in over a hundred spots on the Big Island (including Lava Tree State Monument; see p.232) as well as on three other islands, and the Madagascar **giant day gecko**, a foot-long orange-spotted lizard now established on Oahu. Environmentalists fear that Hawaii's next likely arrival will be the **brown tree snake**. Originally found in the Solomon Islands, it has been hitchhiking its way across the Pacific since World War II, sneaking into the holds of ships and planes, then emerging to colonize new worlds that have never seen a single snake. In Guam it has already established itself in concentrations of up to thirty thousand individuals per square mile, happy to eat virtually anything, and wiping out the local bird populations.

## Issues and prospects

The state of Hawaii has a short and not very impressive history of legislating to conserve its environment, and what little has been achieved so far appears to be jeopardized by Republican moves to rein in the powers of the Endangered Species Act. One positive development is that the whole state has been officially declared a **humpback whale** sanctuary, though the Navy is dragging its heels about certain areas just offshore from its installations, and there has been much opposition from local fishermen.

Throughout Hawaii, a resurgence of interest in what are seen as native Hawaiian values has dovetailed with the influx of New Age *haoles* to create an active environmental movement, which has had plenty of issues to occupy its attention. In particular, the depressed state of much of the Hawaiian economy has made the islands vulnerable to grandiose schemes designed to attract outside funding.

Specific controversies have included the attempt to harness the geothermal power of the Kīlauea volcano, the plan to build a commercial spaceport for the Space Shuttle nearby, and a scheme to get rid of surplus carbon dioxide by pumping it into the deep ocean off Honokōhau, all on the **Big Island**; the US Army's ever-expanding missile program on **Kauai** (see p.488); the proposed construction of an underwater casino three miles off **Maui**; and the long-standing wrangle over the future of the island of **Kahoolawe**, described on p.319. For up-to-date information about these and similar issues, the **Environment Hawaii** website, at Ⓦwww.environment-hawaii.org, is highly recommended.

There has also been much discussion over what is to become of the islands' **irrigation channels**. Developed long before European contact, and later adapted and expanded to meet the needs of the plantations, their infrastructure is now rapidly falling into disrepair. As the ancient Hawaiians knew all too well, maintenance is extremely labor-intensive; without swift action, however, the opportunity to revive small-scale agriculture may soon pass.

Conservationists are struggling to combat the disappearance of Hawaii's indigenous **wildlife**. There have been some high-profile successes, such as the preservation of the extraordinary silversword plants of Haleakalā on Maui (see p.336), and the breeding of *nēnē* geese in the national parks on both Maui and the Big Island. However, the rarest bird species survive only in isolated mountain-top sanctuaries like Kōke'e State Park on Kauai (see p.498), the Kamakou Preserve on Molokai (see p.391), and Maui's Kīpahulu Valley (see p.350). So long as they stay at least 3500 feet above sea level, the mosquitoes can't reach them; nonetheless, birds such as the *'ō'ō a'ā*, a honey-creeper, are becoming extinct at an alarming rate. Activists concerned about the destruction of Hawaiian plants by casually imported newcomers point out that all passengers leaving Hawaii for the US are subjected to stringent inspections, to prevent Hawaiian species from reaching the mainland, but there are no equivalent checks on arriving passengers.

The greatest debates of all, however, have revolved around **tourism**. The power of the development lobby has for the last few decades been great enough to override environmental objections to the growth of resorts across all the islands. Anyone who believes that conserving the earth's resources is inherently a good thing is liable to have trouble accepting the kind of conspicuous consumption reflected in the fact that a single hotel devours seven percent of the Big Island's energy each year. There are also concerns that the resorts are damaging their immediate environment; the combination of golf courses and coral reefs may be ideal for vacationers, but that won't last if fertilizer and silt washed down from the greens and fairways end up choking the reef to death. However, it now looks as though the era of resort building is drawing to a close, albeit due more to economic factors than environmental pressure.

# Mark Twain's Hawaii

**Mark Twain** visited the islands of Oahu, Maui and Hawaii in 1866, at the age of 31, on assignment for the *Sacramento Union*. The letters he wrote for that newspaper have been published as *Letters from Hawaii* by the University of Hawaii Press; he later reworked his material for inclusion in the more celebrated *Roughing It* (Penguin, 1872).

Though Twain described Hawaii as the "loveliest fleet of islands that lies anchored in any ocean," he never set foot on the islands again. In 1895 he was onboard a ship that docked in Honolulu, but due to a cholera epidemic in the city, passengers were forbidden to disembark.

Mark Twain's account of Kīlauea, parts of which are reprinted below, has to be the most vivid description of an erupting volcano ever written. Kīlauea today is a very different mountain from the one seen by Twain, but if his words inspire you to see it for yourself, you won't be disappointed.

## Kīlauea Caldera

After a hearty supper we waited until it was thoroughly dark and then started to the crater. The first glance in that direction revealed a scene of wild beauty. There was a heavy fog over the crater and it was splendidly illuminated by the glare from the fires below. The illumination was two miles wide and a mile high, perhaps; and if you ever, on a dark night and at a distance beheld the light from thirty or forty blocks of distant buildings all on fire at once, reflected strongly against overhanging clouds, you can form a fair idea of what this looked like. A colossal column of cloud towered to a great height in the air immediately above the crater, and the outer swell of every one of its vast folds was dyed with a rich crimson luster, which was subdued to a pale rose tint in the depressions between. It glowed like a muffled torch and stretched upward to a dizzy height toward the zenith. I thought it just possible that its like had not been seen since the children of Israel wandered on their long march through the desert so many centuries ago over a path illuminated by the mysterious "pillar of fire." And I was sure that I now had a vivid conception of what the majestic "pillar of fire" was like, which almost amounted to a revelation.

Arrived at the little thatched lookout house, we rested our elbows on the railing in front and looked abroad over the wide crater and down over the sheer precipice at the seething fires beneath us. The view was a startling improvement on my daylight experience. I turned to see the effect on the balance of the company and found the reddest-faced set of men I almost ever saw. In the strong light every countenance glowed like red-hot iron, every shoulder was suffused with crimson and shaded rearward into dingy, shapeless obscurity! The place below looked like the infernal regions and these men like half-cooled devils just come up on a furlough.

I turned my eyes upon the volcano again. The "cellar" was tolerably well lighted up. For a mile and a half in front of us and half a mile on either side, the floor of the abyss was magnificently illuminated; beyond these limits the mists hung down their gauzy curtains and cast a deceptive gloom over all that made the twinkling fires in the remote corners of the crater seem countless leagues removed — made them seem like the camp-fires of a great army far away. Here was room for the imagination to work! You could imagine those lights the width of a continent away – and that hidden under the intervening darkness were hills, and winding rivers, and weary wastes of plain and desert – and even then the tremendous vista stretched on, and on, and on! – to the fires and far beyond! You could not compass it – it was the idea of eternity made tangible – and the longest end of it made visible to the naked eye!

The greater part of the vast floor of the desert under us was as black as ink, and apparently smooth and level; but over a mile square of it was ringed and streaked and striped with a thousand branching streams of liquid and gorgeously brilliant fire! It looked like a colossal railroad map of the State of Massachusetts done in chain lightning on a midnight sky. Imagine it – imagine a coal black sky shivered into a tangled net-work of angry fire!

Here and there were gleaming holes a hundred feet in diameter, broken in the dark crust, and in them the melted lava – the color a dazzling white just tinged with yellow – was boiling and surging furiously; and from these holes branched numberless bright torrents in many directions, like the spokes of a wheel, and kept a tolerably straight course for a while and then swept round in huge rainbow curves, or made a long succession of sharp worm-fence angles, which looked precisely like the fiercest jagged lightning. These streams met other streams, and they mingled with and crossed and recrossed each other in every conceivable direction, like skate tracks on a popular skating ground. Some times streams twenty or thirty feet wide flowed from the holes to some distance without dividing – and through the opera-glasses we could see that they ran down small, steep hills and were genuine cataracts of fire, white at their source, but soon cooling and turning to the richest red, grained with alternate lines of black and gold. Every now and then masses of the dark crust broke away and floated slowly down these streams like rafts down a river. Occasionally the molten lava flowing under the superincumbent crust broke through – split a dazzling streak, from five hundred to a thousand feet long, like a sudden flash of lightning, and then acre after acre of the cold lava parted into fragments, turned up edgewise like cakes of ice when a great river breaks up, plunged downward and were swallowed in the crimson cauldron. Then the wide expanse of the "thaw" maintained a ruddy glow for a while, but shortly cooled and became black and level again. During a "thaw" every dismembered cake was marked by a glittering white border which was superbly shaded inward by aurora borealis rays, which were a flaming yellow where they joined the white border, and from thence toward their points tapered into glowing crimson, then into a rich, pale carmine, and finally into a faint blush that held its own a moment and then dimmed and turned black. Some of the streams preferred to mingle together in a tangle of fantastic circles, and then they looked something like the confusion of ropes one sees on a ship's deck when she has just taken in sail and dropped anchor –provided one can imagine those ropes on fire.

Through the glasses, the little fountains scattered about looked very beautiful. They boiled, and coughed, and spluttered, and discharged sprays of stringy red fire — of about the consistency of mush, for instance — from ten to fifteen feet into the air, along with a shower of brilliant white sparks — a quaint and unnatural mingling of gouts of blood and snow-flakes!

We had circles and serpents and streaks of lightning all twined and wreathed and tied together, without a break throughout an area more than a mile square (that amount of ground was covered, though it was not strictly "square"), and it was with a feeling of placid exultation that we reflected that many years had elapsed since any visitor had seen such a splendid display – since any visitor had seen anything more than the now snubbed and insignificant "North" and "South" lakes in action. We had been reading old files of Hawaiian newspapers and the "Record Book" at the Volcano House, and were posted.

I could see the North Lake lying out on the black floor away off in the outer edge of our panorama, and knitted to it by a web-work of lava streams. In its individual capacity it looked very little more respectable than a schoolhouse on fire. True, it was about nine hundred feet long and two or three hundred wide, but then, under the present circumstances, it necessarily appeared rather insignificant, and besides it was so distant from us.

I forgot to say that the noise made by the bubbling lava is not great, heard as we heard it from our lofty perch. It makes three distinct sounds – a rushing, a hissing, and a coughing or puffing sound; and if you stand on the brink and close your eyes it is no trick at all to imagine that you are sweeping down a river on a large low-pressure steamer, and that you hear the hissing of the steam about her boilers, the puffing from her escape-pipes and the churning rush of the water abaft her wheels. The smell of sulphur is strong, but not unpleasant to a sinner.

We left the lookout house at ten o'clock in a half cooked condition, because of the heat from Pele's furnaces, and wrapping up in blankets, for the night was cold, we returned to our Hotel.

* * * * * * *

The next night was appointed for a visit to the bottom of the crater, for we desired to traverse its floor and see the "North Lake" (of fire) which lay two miles away, toward the further wall. After dark half a dozen of us set out, with lanterns and native guides, and climbed down a crazy, thousand-foot pathway in a crevice fractured in the crater wall, and reached the bottom in safety.

The irruption of the previous evening had spent its force and the floor looked black and cold; but when we ran out upon it we found it hot yet, to the feet, and it was likewise riven with crevices which revealed the underlying fires gleaming vindictively. A neighboring cauldron was threatening to overflow, and this added to the dubiousness of the situation. So the native guides refused to continue the venture, and then every body deserted except a stranger named Marlette. He said he had been in the crater a dozen times in daylight and believed he could find his way through it at night. He thought that a run of three hundred yards would carry us over the hottest part of the floor and leave us our shoe-soles. His pluck gave me back-bone. We took one lantern and instructed the guides to hang the other to the roof of the look-out house to serve as a beacon for us in case we got lost, and then the party started back up the precipice and Marlette and I made our run. We skipped over the hot floor and over the red crevices with brisk dispatch and reached the cold lava safe but with pretty warm feet. Then we took things leisurely and comfortably, jumping tolerably wide and probably bottomless chasms, and threading our way through picturesque lava upheavals with considerable confidence. When we got fairly away from the cauldrons of boiling fire, we seemed to be in a gloomy desert, and a suffocatingly dark one, surrounded by dim walls that seemed to tower to the sky. The only cheerful objects were the glinting stars high overhead.

By and by Marlette shouted "Stop!" I never stopped quicker in my life. I asked what the matter was. He said we were out of the path. He said we must not try to go on till we found it again, for we were surrounded with beds of rotten lava through which we could easily break and plunge down a thousand feet. I thought eight hundred would answer for me, and was about to say so when Marlette partly proved his statement by accidentally crushing through and disappearing to his arm-pits. He got out and we hunted for the path with the lantern. He said there was only one path and that it was but vaguely defined. We could not find it. The lava surface was all alike in the lantern light. But he was an ingenious man. He said it was not the lantern that had informed him that we were out of the path, but his feet. He had noticed a crisp grinding of fine lava-needles under his feet, and some instinct reminded him that in the path these were all worn away. So he put the lantern behind him, and began to search with his boots instead of his eyes. It was good sagacity. The first time his foot touched a surface that did not grind under it he announced that the trail was found again; and after that we kept up a sharp listening for the rasping sound and it always warned us in time.

It was a long tramp, but an exciting one. We reached the North Lake between ten and eleven o'clock, and sat down on a huge overhanging lava-shelf, tired but satisfied. The spectacle presented was worth coming double the distance to see. Under us, and stretching away before us, was a heaving sea of molten fire of seemingly limitless extent. The glare from it was so blinding that it was some time before we could bear to look upon it steadily. It was like gazing at the sun at noonday, except that the glare was not quite so white. At unequal distances all around the shores of the lake were nearly white-hot chimneys or hollow drums of lava, four or five feet high, and up through them were bursting gorgeous sprays of lava-gouts and gem spangles, some white, some red and some golden – a ceaseless bombardment, and one that fascinated the eye with its unapproachable splendor. The more distant jets, sparkling up through an intervening gossamer veil of vapor, seemed miles away; and the further the curving ranks of fiery fountains receded, the more fairy-like and beautiful they appeared.

Now and then the surging bosom of the lake under our noses would calm down ominously and seem to be gathering strength for an enterprise; and then all of a sudden a red dome of lava of the bulk of an ordinary dwelling would heave itself aloft like an escaping balloon, then burst asunder, and out of its heart would flit a pale-green film of vapor, and float upward and vanish in the darkness – a released soul soaring homeward from captivity with the damned, no doubt. The crashing plunge of the ruined dome into the lake again would send a world of seething billows lashing against the shores and shaking the foundations of our perch. By and by, a loosened mass of the hanging shelf we sat on tumbled into the lake, jarring the surroundings like an earthquake and delivering a suggestion that may have been intended for a hint, and may not. We did not wait to see.

We got lost again on our way back, and were more than an hour hunting for the path. We were where we could see the beacon lantern at the look-out house at the time, but thought it was a star and paid no attention to it. We reached the hotel at two o'clock in the morning pretty well fagged out.

Mark Twain, *Roughing It*, 1872

# Hawaii in the movies

**Moviegoers** may not always have known what they were seeing, but the spectacular scenery of Hawaii has featured prominently on the silver screen since the earliest days of the cinema. Kauai, for example, has not only appeared as a tourist paradise in its own right in movies such as *Blue Hawaii* (1961), *Throw Momma from the train* (1987), and *Honeymoon in Vegas* (1992), but has also doubled as a Caribbean island in *Jurassic Park* (1993), as South America in *Raiders of the Lost Ark* (1981), as Vietnam in *Uncommon Valor* (1983), as Africa in *Outbreak* (1995), and even as Never-neverland in *Hook* (1992).

The very first footage shot in Hawaii was a travelogue, made by Thomas Edison's company in 1898; free showings of excerpts take place daily in Lahaina's Wo Hing Temple on Maui. By 1913, Universal Studios had made a silent feature on Oahu, *The Shark God*, which established a tradition of Hawaii as an all-purpose exotic backdrop for tales of **terror**, mysterious rites, and unbridled passion. Later examples include Boris Karloff's 1957 *Voodoo Island*; Roger Corman's *She God of Shark Reef*, from the following year; the 1976 remake of King Kong; and *Aloha Donny and Marie*, featuring the Osmonds, in 1978.

A separate genre, the Hawaii-based **musical comedy**, was instigated by *Waikiki Wedding* in 1937, in which **Bing Crosby** crooned *Blue Hawaii* and *Sweet Leilani*. Hawaii provided a glamorous setting for star vehicles featuring Hollywood's biggest names. Thus Shirley Temple and Betty Grable donned grass skirts and *leis*, while those homegrown actors who managed to appear on camera, such as the singer Hilo Hattie (whose name lives on in her chain of aloha-wear stores) and legendary surfer Duke Kahanamoku, simply played bit parts to add a little local color.

With the invention of Technicolor, filmmakers began fully to appreciate the potential of Hawaii. In *Pagan Love Song* (1950), Esther Williams performed one of her trademark aquatic ballets in Kauai's Hanalei Bay – supposedly Tahiti – while the smash-hit Rodgers and Hammerstein musical *South Pacific* (1958) turned Kauai into a South Seas Eden. However, it was **Elvis Presley**, whose Cherokee ancestry made him at least semi-plausible as a Polynesian, who became most closely identified with Hawaii. As tour guide Chad Gates in his greatest box-office success, *Blue Hawaii* (1961) – promoted with the lame but accurate slogan "You'll Want to Visit Hawaii, After You See Blue Hawaii" – Elvis preened at countless Honolulu and Waikīkī locations before finally tying the knot with Joan Blackman in a gloriously kitsch wedding ceremony at Kauai's *Coco Palms Resort*. He returned to Hawaii in 1962, for *Girls, Girls, Girls*, but as his adventures as a charter-boat skipper were allegedly taking place off Louisiana, not a single sequence shows a recognizable Hawaiian landmark. By contrast, during his *Paradise, Hawaiian Style* (1966), the camera seizes every opportunity to drift away from the flimsy plot line and linger lovingly on the North Shore cliffs of Kauai.

After World War II, Hawaii also became the ideal location to film stories of the War in the Pacific, whether the producers needed an accessible stand-in for some other, more remote, Pacific island, or wanted to depict actual events on

Hawaii. Until it was trumped by Disney's spectacular but ultimately sterile **Pearl Harbor** in 2001, the most famous re-enactment of the attack on Pearl Harbor, for example, came as the climax of **From Here to Eternity**, which won the Academy Award for Best Picture in 1953 (and tends to be best remembered for the scene in which Burt Lancaster and Deborah Kerr frolic in the surf at Oahu's Halona Cove). **Frank Sinatra**, who received an Oscar for his portrayal of Private Maggio in that movie – having won the role with the behind-the-scenes maneuvering on which the horse's head incident in *The Godfather* is allegedly based – directed his own war epic on Kauai a dozen years later. The war-torn Pacific beach in *None but the Brave* was Pīla'a Beach, east of Kīlauea. During filming, Sinatra had to be rescued from drowning when he found himself in difficulties swimming off Wailua Beach. Big **John Wayne** made a number of war movies in Hawaii, including *The Sea Chase*, filmed on the Big Island in 1955, and Otto Preminger's *In Harm's Way* (1965), which featured another depiction of the Pearl Harbor attack. He had a rather happier time touring Kauai's coastline with Dorothy Lamour in the John Ford-directed comedy *Donovan's Reef* (1963).

Visitors with an interest in seeing specific **movie locations** should head straight for **Kauai**. The landscape of **South Pacific**'s fictional Bali Ha'i was created by melding the peak of Makana, near Kē'ē Beach, with assorted Fijian scenes, but the movie's showstopping songs were filmed at genuine North Shore locations. These included a waterfall on Kīlauea River, for *Happy Talk*; Hanalei Bay, for *Some Enchanted Evening*; and Lumaha'i Beach, under the name of Nurses' Beach, where Mitzi Gaynor sang *I'm Gonna Wash that Man Right Out of My Hair*. The opening sequence of **Raiders of the Lost Ark**, in which Harrison Ford escapes by seaplane from a posse of Amazonian headhunters – as portrayed by Kauai locals with pudding-basin haircuts – was shot on the Hule'ia Stream just outside Lihu'e. The first attempt to film on the inaccessible Nā Pali coast came in 1976, when remote Honopū Beach stood in as Skull Island in the remake of **King Kong**. Helicopters were again deployed to ferry the crew of **Jurassic Park** into the island's interior, and a helicopter tour is the only way tourists can hope to see the waterfalls in and around Hanapēpē Valley where much of the action takes place. The movie's heroes, however, were disturbed by a sneezing dinosaur as they slept in the branches of a Moreton Bay fig at Allerton Garden on the South Shore, while the gates to the park itself were erected on a cane road above Wailua that leads towards Mount Wai'ale'ale. Filming on *Jurassic Park* was brought to an abrupt end by Hurricane Iniki in September 1991 – which may explain why the sequel was shot elsewhere – and the movie includes a brief sequence of the hurricane's onslaught on Nawiliwili Harbor.

Finally, Hawaii may be even more familiar from **television**. Between 1968 and 1980, 262 episodes of **Hawaii Five-O** were filmed on Oahu. Jack Lord starred as Steve McGarrett and James MacArthur as Dano; their arch-enemy, Wo Fat, took his name from a real-life Honolulu restaurant. According to one survey, 25 percent of visitors to Hawaii during the 1970s cited the program as a factor in their decision to come. Upon its demise, *Hawaii Five-0* was immediately replaced by Tom Selleck's **Magnum P.I.**, which ran in turn until 1988. Both *Fantasy Island* (1978–84) and *Gilligan's Island* (1964–67) were also filmed at least partially in Hawaii.

# Hula and Hawaiian music

**If your idea of Hawaiian music is Elvis doing the limbo in *Blue Hawaii*, you won't be disappointed by the entertainment on offer in most of Hawaii's hotels. A diet of *Little Grass Shack* and the *Hawaiian Wedding Song*, with the occasional rendition of *Please Release Me* in Hawaiian, is guaranteed. However, the islands also boast their own lively contemporary music scene, and it's still possible to see performances of Hawaii's most ancient form, *hula*, which embraces elements of theater and dance.**

## Hula

Although the ancient Hawaiians were devotees of the poetic chants they called **meles**, they had no specific word for "song." *Meles* were composed for various purposes, ranging from lengthy genealogies of the chiefs, put together over days of debate, through temple prayers, to lullabies and love songs. When the chanted words were accompanied by music and dance, as was often the case, the combined performance was known as **hula**.

The invention of the hula was generally credited to the goddess Laka, who is said to have danced for the first time either in the *'ōhi'a lehua* groves near Maunaloa on Molokai (see p.407), or above Kē'ē Beach on Kauai (see p.465).

Music was created using instruments including gourds, rattles, small hand or knee drums made from coconuts, and the larger *pahu* drums made by stretching shark skin over hollow logs. As a rule the tonal range was minimal and the music monotonous, though occasionally bamboo pipes may also have been played. Complexity was introduced by the fact that the dance, the chant and the music were all likely to follow distinct rhythmic patterns.

The telling of the story or legend was of primary importance; the music was subordinate to the chant, while the feet and lower body of the dancers served mainly to keep the rhythm, and their hand movements supplemented the meaning of the words. Dancers would be trained in a *hālau hula*, a cross between a school and a temple dedicated to Laka, and performances were hedged around by sacred ritual and *kapus*.

The first Christian missionaries to reach Hawaii, immediately after the collapse of the *kapu* system, saw *hula* as a lascivious manifestation of the islands' lack of morality. It's clearly true, for example, that the religious subtleties of the so-called "genital *hula*" dances, celebrating the genitals of leading members of the *ali'i*, were lost on visiting whalemen.

### Buying Hawaiian Music

Buying **Hawaiian music** in Hawaii is absolutely straightforward; the giant Borders stores on each island (see p.539) carry copious selections. Otherwise, the easiest way to get hold of Hawaiian material is on the internet, at ⓦwww.mele.com for example. Mention should also be made of the excellent (really) companion CD to this book, *The Rough Guide to the Music of Hawaii* (World Music Network).

In consequence, *hula* was largely suppressed for the first century after the arrival of the foreigners. It only returned to public performance at the coronation of the "Merrie Monarch," King David Kalākaua, in February 1883. By then the process of adapting music and dance to suit foreign tastes had started; the grass skirt, for example, was imported to Hawaii from the Gilbert Islands in the 1870s as somehow looking more Polynesian. As early as 1923, a magazine article complained that "the truth of the matter is that the real Hawaiian hula has little in common with the coarse imitations served up to sight-seers, magazine readers, and the general public."

Today *hula* persists in two forms. The first, *kahiko*, is closer to the old style, consisting of chanting to the beat of drums; the dancers wear knee-length skirts of flat *ti* leaves, and anklets and bracelets of ferns. *'Auana* is the modern style of *hula*, featuring bands of musicians playing Western-style instruments.

Both forms have their major showcase on the Big Island each April, at Hilo's **Merrie Monarch Festival** (see p.212). Some traditionalists do not participate in the Merrie Monarch, regarding the idea of a competition as contrary to the essential nature of *hula* as a form of religious expression. Another significant annual event, **Molokai Ka Hula Piko**, takes place at Pāpōhaku Beach Park on **Molokai** on the third Saturday of each May.

# Slack-key and steel guitar

The roots of contemporary Hawaiian music lie in a mixture of cultural traditions brought from all over the world by nineteenth-century immigrants. In particular, Spanish and Mexican *paniolos* introduced the guitar, while the *braginha* of the Portuguese plantation workers was adapted to become the Hawaiian *ukelele*. King David Kalākaua had his own *ukulele* group, and co-wrote Hawaii's national anthem, *Hawaii Pono'ī*, while his sister, Queen Lili'uokalani, composed the haunting *Aloha 'Oe*, since covered by Elvis Presley among others.

## Iz: May 20 1959 – June 26 1997

In the summer of 1997, the contemporary Hawaiian music scene lost the man who was in every sense its biggest star. **Israel Kamakawiwo'ole**, who started out singing in the Makaha Sons of Niihau and then went solo in 1990, died of respiratory difficulties in a Honolulu hospital. During his twenty-year career, "**Iz**" came to epitomize the pride and the power of Hawaiian music. His extraordinary voice adapted equally well to rousing political anthems, delicate love songs, pop standards and Jawaiian reggae rhythms, while his personality and his love for Hawaii always shone through both in concert and on record. Like his brother Skippy before him – also a founder member of the Makaha Sons – Iz eventually succumbed to the health problems caused by his immense size. At one point, his weight reached a colossal 757 pounds; he needed a fork-lift truck to get on stage, and could only breathe through tubes. His strength in adversity did much to ensure that he was repeatedly voted Hawaii's most popular entertainer, and after his death he was granted a state funeral, with his body lying in state in the Capitol. His enduring legacy will be the music on his four solo albums – ***Ka Ano'i*** (1990), ***Facing Future*** (1993), ***E Ala Ē*** (1995), and ***'n Dis Life*** (1996) – while his haunting rendition of *Hawai'i 78* (on *Facing Future*) has become the signature song of the Hawaiian sovereignty movement.

The next step towards creating a distinctive Hawaiian sound came roughly a century ago, when the conventional method of tuning a guitar was abandoned in favor of **slack-key** tuning (*kī hō'alu* in Hawaiian), in which a simple strum of the open strings produces a harmonious chord. Next came the realization that sliding a strip of metal along the strings produced a *glissando* effect; an Oahu student is credited with inventing the **steel guitar**, as played by early virtuosos such as Sol Ho'opii.

English words were set to Hawaiian melodies, and the resultant **hapa-haole** music was by World War I the most popular music form in America. The craze for all things Hawaiian took several decades to die down, though it grew progressively more debased. By the time of the nationwide *tiki* craze of the 1950s, when mass tourism was just taking off and Polynesian-themed restaurants were opening all across the United States, pseudo-Hawaiian music such as Martin Denny's cocktail-jazz stylings was still topping the charts.

## The modern generation

In music as in so many other spheres, Hawaii has in the last twenty-five years witnessed a resurgence of pride in Polynesian traditions, combined with the determination to create something new yet genuinely Hawaiian. The sound created by the new generation of musicians is a fascinating hybrid, drawing on the tradition of the ancient *meles*, but influenced by mainstream rock, country and even reggae music. It combines political stridency with sweet melodies, and powerful drum beats with gentle *ukelele* tinklings.

The first prominent name in the movement was **Gabby Pahinui**, an exponent of classic slack-key guitar who, in the final years before his death in 1980, achieved international fame through his recordings with Ry Cooder. His success encouraged others to stop tailoring their music to suit mainland tastes, and it soon became apparent that there was a market for recordings in the Hawaiian language.

Among the biggest names on the contemporary scene are the duo **Hapa** – Barry Flanagan, originally from New Jersey, and Keli'i Kaneali'i – who combined slack-key guitar instrumentals with soaring harmonies on the huge-selling album *Hapa*, blended ponderous rock with traditional chant on their version of U2's *Pride* (*In The Name of Love*), and then riffed their way to heaven with the affectionate spoof *Surf Madness*. The Maui-based *kumu hula* (*hula* teacher), **Keali'i Reichel**, has produced several successful CDs of his exquisite alto singing; the first, *Kawaipunahele*, is probably the best, though *E Ō Mai* boasts an enjoyable rendition of the theme from *Babe*. Look out, too, for concert appearances by **Amy Gilliom**, whose *Hawaiian Tradition* won a 1998 Hōkū. Her crystal-clear voice brings out all the beauty of her classic Hawaiian-language material, while she and her partner, guitar virtuoso Wille K, also make a great quick-fire comedy duo.

Every year, the **Na Hōkū Hanohano** awards honor the best in Hawaiian music and recognize the strongest up-and-coming acts. Recent winners include the traditional Oahu quartet **'Ale'a**, who are regular fixtures on the Waikīkī circuit, and the more pop-influenced **Colón**.

Finally, visitors may be surprised to encounter the Hawaiian-reggae fusion known as **Jawaiian**, in which the traditional beat of the *pahu* drum is accompanied by a thunderous electrified bass. Reggae is very popular with young

Hawaiians, but the homegrown groups don't tend to have the hard edge of the touring Jamaican bands who often perform on the islands. **Ho'ikane**, from the Big Island, is among the best; the group is credited with being the first to introduce an up-to-date dance-hall sound. Other performers include **Titus Kinimaka** – a pro surfer from Kauai's leading *hula* family – and **Butch Helemano**, who has at least nine albums to his name.

# Books

**An extraordinary number of books have been written about Hawaii and all matters Hawaiian, though you're only likely to come across most of them in bookstores on the islands themselves. All the publishers below are based in the US unless otherwise stated.**

## History

**Gail Bartholomew**, *Maui Remembers* (Mutual Publishing). Large-format paperback history of Maui, with lots of early photographs and entertaining stories.

★ **Emmett Cahill**, *The Life and Times of John Young* (Island Heritage Publishing). Lively biography of one of the most fascinating figures of the immediate post-contact era: the Welsh seaman who became Kamehameha's most trusted military adviser.

**Gavan Daws**, *Shoal of Time* (University of Hawaii Press). Definitive if dry single-volume history of the Hawaiian islands, tracing their fate from European contact to statehood.

★ **Greg Dening**, *The Death of William Gooch* (University of Hawaii Press). Elaborate anthropological and metaphysical speculations spun around the 1792 murder of three European sailors in Oahu's Waimea Valley (see p.137).

**Michael Dougherty**, *To Steal a Kingdom: Probing Hawaiian History* (Island Style Press). An eccentric and entertaining look at Hawaiian history, which focuses on the famous names of the nineteenth century and pulls no punches.

**Edward Joesting**, *Kauai, the Separate Kingdom* (University of Hawaii Press). Dramatic and very readable account of Kauai's early history and how the island resisted incorporation into the Hawaiian mainstream.

**Noel J. Kent**, *Hawaii: Islands Under the Influence* (University of Hawaii Press). Rigorous Marxist account of Hawaiian history, concentrating on the islands' perennial "dependency" on distant economic forces.

**Lili'uokalani**, *Hawaii's Story by Hawaii's Queen* (Mutual Publishing). Autobiographical account by the last monarch of Hawaii of how her kingdom was taken away. Written in 1897 when she still cherished hopes of a restoration.

**Gananath Obeyesekere**, *The Apotheosis of Captain Cook* (Princeton University Press/Bishop Museum Press). An iconoclastic Sri Lankan anthropologist reassesses Captain Cook from an anti-imperialist – and, according to most authorities, historically inaccurate – perspective.

### Bookstores

For listings of bookstores in **Honolulu**, see p.113. The largest bookstores on the Neighbor Islands are all Borders, which has outlets on **Kauai** in the Kukui Grove Shopping Center in Līhu'e, on **Maui** in the Maui Marketplace in Kahului, and on the **Big Island** in both Hilo and Kailua. Kailua is also home to the excellent Middle Earth Bookshoppe, in the Kona Plaza mall.

★ **Gordon W. Prange**, *At Dawn We Slept* and *The Verdict of History* (Penguin). Definitive best-selling analysis of the attack on Pearl Harbor. Over two volumes, Prange exhaustively rebuts revisionist conspiracy theories.

**A. Grenfell Price** (ed), *The Explorations of Captain James Cook in the Pacific* (Dover). Selections from Cook's own journals, including entries about his first landfall on Kauai and his ill-fated return to the Big Island. The story of his death is taken up by his successor as captain.

**Luis I. Reyes**, *Made in Paradise* (Mutual Publishing). Lovingly prepared coffee-table history of how Hollywood has depicted Hawaii, with some great illustrations.

**Marshall Sahlins**, *How Natives Think . . . about Captain Cook, for example* (University of Chicago Press). An impassioned and closely argued response to the Obeyesekere book, reviewed above. Sahlins is currently considered to be ahead on points.

**Ronald Takaki**, *Pau Hana* (University of Hawaii Press). Moving history of life on the sugar plantations, and the trials experienced by generations of immigrant laborers.

**Rerioterai Tava and Moses K. Keale** Sr, *Niihau, The Traditions of an Hawaiian Island* (Mutual Publishing). Comprehensive collection of fact and legend surrounding Hawaii's least-known island, so detailed that it names each of the island's five bread-fruit trees.

## Ancient Hawaii

**Dorothy B. Barrère, Mary K. Pukui and Marion Kelly**, *Hula: Historical Perspectives* (Bishop Museum Press). Fascinating essays on ancient Hawaii's most important art form, packed with early eyewitness accounts, and with a special emphasis on Kauai.

**Ross Cordy**, *Exalted Sits The Chief: The Ancient History of Hawai'i Island* (Mutual Publishing). Cordy has assembled a great deal of valuable raw material about the early history of the Big Island, but the book's poor organization and dry style make it a disappointingly heavy read.

**Nathaniel B. Emerson**, *Unwritten Literature of Hawaii – The Sacred Songs of the Hula* (Charles E. Tuttle Co). Slightly dated, having been published in 1909, but the wealth of detail ensures that it remains required reading for all students of the *hula*.

**E.S. Handy and Elizabeth Handy**, *Native Planters in Old Hawaii* (Bishop Museum Press). A massive exploration of the agricultural techniques of ancient Hawaiians, focusing on the Ka'ū region of the Big Island.

**Dorothy M. Kahananui**, *Music of Ancient Hawaii* (Petroglyph Press). Brief but informative pamphlet covering the development and forms of the *hula*.

**Samuel M. Kamakau**, *The People of Old* (Bishop Museum Press, 3 vols). Anecdotal essays, originally written in Hawaiian and published as newspaper articles in the 1860s. Packed with fascinating nuggets of information, they provide a compendium of Hawaiian oral traditions. Kamakau's longer *Ruling Chiefs of Hawaii* (Bishop Museum Press) details all that is known of the deeds of the kings.

★ **Patrick Kirch**, *Feathered God and Fishhooks* and *Legacy of the Past* (both University of Hawaii Press). The former is the best one-volume account of ancient Hawaii, though non-specialists may find the minutiae of specific archeological digs hard going. The latter is an excellent guide to specific Hawaiian sites.

**David Malo**, *Hawaiian Antiquities* (Bishop Museum Press). Nineteenth-century survey of culture and society, written by a native Hawaiian brought up at the court of Kamehameha the Great. Like Kamakau, Malo's conversion to Christianity colors his account, but this is the closest we have to a contemporary view of ancient Hawaii.

**Valerio Valeri**, *Kingship and Sacrifice: Ritual and Society in Ancient Hawaii* (University of Chicago Press). Detailed academic analysis of the role of human sacrifice in establishing the power of the king – an aspect of Hawaiian religion many other commentators gloss over.

## Contemporary Hawaii

★ **Michael Kioni Dudley and Keoni Kealoha Agard**, *A Call for Hawaiian Sovereignty* (Nā Kāne O Ka Malo, 2 vols). Two short books, indispensable for anyone interested in Hawaiian sovereignty. The first attempts to reconstruct the world-view and philosophies of the ancient Hawaiians; the second is the clearest imaginable account of their dispossession.

**Randall W. Roth** (ed), *The Price of Paradise* (Mutual Publishing, 2 vols). Assorted experts answer questions about life and society in Hawaii in short essays that focus on economic and governmental issues. Of most interest to local residents or prospective migrants, but a useful introduction to ongoing island debates, which sadly has now become somewhat dated.

**Haunani Kay Trask**, *From A Native Daughter: Colonialism and Sovereignty in Hawaii* (University of Hawaii Press). A stimulating and impressive contribution to the sovereignty debate, from one of Hawaii's best-known activists.

## Travelers' tales

**Isabella Bird**, *Six Months in the Sandwich Islands* (University of Hawaii Press). The enthralling adventures of an Englishwoman in the 1870s, including sojourns on all the major islands and a cold expedition up Mauna Loa on the Big Island.

**A. Grove Day and Carl Stroven** (eds), *A Hawaiian Reader* and *The Spell of Hawaii* (Mutual Publishing, 2 vols). Lively paperback anthologies of writings on Hawaii, including pieces by Mark Twain, Jack London, Isabella Bird and Robert Louis Stevenson.

**James Macrae**, *With Lord Byron at the Sandwich Islands in 1825* (Petroglyph Press). Short pamphlet of extracts from the diary of a Scottish botanist, including descriptions of Honolulu as a small village and the first-known ascent of Mauna Kea.

**Andy Martin**, *Walking on Water* (Minerva, UK). An English journalist attempts to immerse himself in the surfing culture of Oahu's North Shore.

**Robert Louis Stevenson**, *Travels in Hawaii* (University of Hawaii Press). The Scottish novelist spent several months in Hawaii in the late nineteenth century; the highlight of this collection is a moving account of his visit to Kalaupapa on Molokai, and it also includes his famous "Open Letter" in defense of Father Damien (see p.401).

**Hunter S. Thompson**, *The Curse of Lono* (Bantam Books). Inimitably overwrought account of a winter fishing vacation on the Big Island, involving such escapades as abandoning a demented Doberman in Kailua's *King Kamehameha* hotel.

★ **Mark Twain**, *Letters from Hawaii* (University of Hawaii Press). Colorful and entertaining accounts of nineteenth-century Hawaii, with rapturous descriptions of the volcanoes of Maui and the Big Island, written as a cub reporter. Twain reworked much of the best material for inclusion in *Roughing It* (Penguin), an excerpt from which appears on p.529.

## Navigation

**Ben Finney**, *Hōkūle'a: The Way to Tahiti* (Dodd, Mead & Co). Gripping story of the sailing canoe's first eventful voyage to Tahiti, by a founder of the Polynesian Voyaging Society.

★ **Tommy Holmes**, *The Hawaiian Canoe* (Editions Ltd). Compendious, beautifully illustrated coffee-table presentation of traditions and techniques involved in building and navigating sailing canoes, from the ancient Polynesians to the present day. Also written by a founder of the Polynesian Voyaging Society.

**Will Kyselka**, *An Ocean in Mind* (University of Hawaii Press). Detailed account of the rediscovery of traditional Polynesian navigational techniques and the voyages of the *Hōkūle'a*, by a lecturer at the Bishop Planetarium.

## Natural sciences

**Peter S. Adler**, *Beyond Paradise* (Ox Bow Press). Personal essays about life in Hawaii, illuminating if occasionally self-indulgent, with an interesting account of the "Wounded Island" of Kahoolawe.

**John R.K. Clark**, *Beaches of Oahu/the Big Island/ Maui County/Kauai and Niihau* (University of Hawaii Press). Clark is a former lifeguard who has visited every beach in the state and researched its history and traditions. His four separate volumes form an invaluable resource for safety issues and make fascinating reading, though the construction boom of the last two decades has rendered them somewhat out of date.

**Peter Crawford**, *Nomads of the Wind* (BBC Books, UK). Enjoyable, well-illustrated overview of the human and natural history of Polynesia, written to accompany the TV series.

**Pamela Frierson**, *The Burning Island* (Sierra Club Books). The most exciting and original volume written about the Big Island; a history and cultural anthropology of the region around Mauna Loa and Kīlauea, combined with a personal account of living with the volcanoes.

**Garrett Hongo**, *Volcano* (Vintage Books). The "Volcano" of the title is the Big Island village where Hongo was born; the book itself is a lyrical evocation of its physical and emotional landscape.

**Gordon A. Macdonald and Agatin A. Abbott**, *Volcanoes in the Sea* (University of Hawaii Press). Thorough technical examination – sadly not illustrated in color – of how fire and water have shaped the unique landscapes of Hawaii.

**Frank Stewart** (ed.), *A World Between Waves* (Island Press). Stimulating collection of essays by authors such as Peter Matthiessen and Maxine Hong Kingston, covering all aspects of Hawaiian natural history.

## Food

**Roy Yamaguchi**, *Pacific Bounty* (KQED). Well-illustrated cookbook of delicious recipes, written by one of the prime movers of "East–West cuisine," and based on his TV series *Hawaii Cooks with Roy Yamaguchi*.

## Hawaii in fiction

**Herman Melville**, *Typee* (Penguin). Largely set in the Marquesas Islands, but with echoes of his time in Hawaii, Melville's wildly romanticized version of the South Seas – originally published as non-fiction – makes a perfect escapist read.

★ **W. S. Merwin**, *The Folding Cliffs* (Alfred Knopf). A compelling, visually evocative blank-verse re-telling – in over three hundred pages – of the story of Koolau the Leper (see p.470), by one of America's leading contemporary poets.

**James Michener**, *Hawaii* (Random House). Another romanticized romp, whose success was a major factor in the growth of Hawaiian tourism.

**Paul Theroux**, *Hotel Honolulu* (Houghton Mifflin US, Hamish Hamilton UK). This funny and very entertaining slice of reportage brilliantly captures the flavor of life in Oahu, packed with tourists passing through as well as local characters; there's even a cameo appearance from Iz himself (see p.536).

**Richard Tregaskis**, *The Warrior King* (Falmouth Press). This fictionalized biography of Kamehameha the Great serves as a readable introduction to a crucial period in Hawaiian history.

**Kathleen Tyau**, *A Little Too Much is Enough* (Farrar, Straus & Giroux US, The Women's Press UK). Atmospheric and amusing account of growing up as a Chinese-Hawaiian, with an appetizing emphasis on food.

**Sylvia Watanabe**, *Talking to the Dead* (Doubleday US, The Women's Press UK). Short, haunting evocation of village life in West Maui, in the days before the resorts.

# Language

The Hawaiian language is an offshoot of languages spoken elsewhere in Polynesia, with slight variations that arose during the centuries when the islands had no contact with the rest of Polynesia. Among its most unusual features is the fact that there are no verbs "to be" or "to have," and that, although it lacks a word for "weather," it distinguishes between 130 types of rain and 160 types of wind.

Although barely two thousand people speak Hawaiian as their mother tongue, it remains a living language and has experienced a revival in recent years. While visitors to Hawaii are almost certain to hear Hawaiian-language songs, it's rarely spoken in public, and there should be no need to communicate in any language other than English. However, everyday conversations tend to be sprinkled with some of the more common Hawaiian words below, and you'll also spot them in many local place names.



# The Hawaiian alphabet

Hawaiian only became a written language when a committee of missionaries gave it an alphabet. The shortest in the world, it consists of just twelve letters – a, e, h, i, k, l, m, n, o, p, u, and w – plus two punctuation marks. When the missionaries were unable to agree on the precise sounds of the language, they simply voted on which letter to include – thus k beat t, and l beat r. As a result, the language has been oversimplified, and scholars argue that no one really knows how it used to sound.

Hawaiian may look hard to **pronounce**, but in fact with just 162 possible syllables – as compared to 23,638 in Thai – it's the least complicated on earth. The letters h, l, m and n are pronounced exactly as in English; k and p are pronounced approximately as in English but with less aspiration; w is like the English v after an i or an e, and the English w after a u or an o. At the start of a word, or after an a, w may be pronounced like a v or a w.

The **glottal stop** (ʻ) has the effect of creating the audible pause heard in the English "oh-oh." Words without macrons (¯) to indicate stress are in theory pronounced by stressing alternate syllables working back from the penultimate syllable. Thanks to the frequent repetition of syllables, this is usually easier than it may sound. "Kamehameha," for example, breaks down into the repeated pattern Ka–meha–meha, pronounced Ka–mayha–mayha.

## Pronunciation

| | | | |
|---|---|---|---|
| a | *a* as in above | ā | *a* as in car |
| e | *e* as in bet | ē | *ay* as in day |
| i | *y* as in pity | ī | *ee* as in bee |
| o | *o* as in hole | ō | *o* as in hole (but slightly longer) |
| u | *u* as in full | ū | *oo* as in moon |

# Glossary

**ʻAʻā** rough lava
**Ahupua ʻa** basic land division, a "slice of cake" from ocean to mountain
**Aikāne** friend, friendly
**ʻĀina** land, earth
**Akua** god, goddess, spirit, idol
**Aliʻi** chief, chiefess, noble
**Aloha** love; hello; goodbye.
**ʻAumākua** personal god or spirit; totem animal
**ʻElepaio** bird
**Hala** tree (pandanus, screw pine)
**Halāu** longhouse used for *hula* instruction; also a *hula* group
**Hale** house, building
**Hana** work
**Haole** (white) non-native Hawaiian, whether foreign or American resident
**Hapa** half, as in *hapa haole*, or half-foreign
**Hāpuʻu** tree fern
**Heiau** ancient place of worship
**Honua** land, earth
**Hui** group, club
**Hula** dance/music form (*hula ʻauana* is a modern form, *hula kahiko* is traditional)
**Imu** pit oven
**Kaʻa** car
**Kahuna** priest(ess) or someone particularly skilled in any field; *kahuna nui* chief priest
**Kai** sea
**Kālua** to bake in an *imu* (underground oven)
**Kamaʻāina** Hawaiian from another island; state resident
**Kāne** man
**Kapa** the "cloth" made from pounded bark, known elsewhere as *tapa*
**Kapu** forbidden, taboo, sacred
**Kapu moe** prostration
**Kaukau** food
**Keiki** child
**Kiawe** thorny tree, mesquite
**Kiʻi** temple image or petroglyph
**Kīpuka** natural "island" of vegetation surrounded by lava flows
**Koa** dark hardwood tree
**Kōkua** help
**Kona** leeward (especially wind)
**Kukui** candlenut tree, whose oil was used for lamps
**Lānai** balcony, terrace, patio
**Lau** leaf
**Lehua** *or* **ʻŌhiʻa lehua** native red-blossomed shrub/tree
**Lei** garland of flowers, feathers, shells or other material
**Lilikoʻi** passionfruit
**Limu** seaweed
**Lomi lomi** massage or raw salmon dish
**Luakini** temple of human sacrifice, used by ruling chiefs
**Lūʻau** traditional Hawaiian feast
**Mahalo** thank you
**Mahimahi** white fish or dolphin fish (not the mammal)
**Makai** direction: away from the mountain, towards the sea
**Malihini** newcomer, visitor
**Mana** spiritual power
**Mauka** direction: away from the sea, towards the mountain
**Mele** ancient chant
**Menehune** in legend, the most ancient Hawaiian people, supposedly dwarfs
**Moʻo** lizard, dragon
**Muʻumuʻu** long loose dress
**Nei** this here, as in *Hawaii nei*, "this [beloved] Hawaii"
**Nēnē** Hawaiian goose – the state bird
**Nui** big, important
**O** of; or
**ʻOhana** family
**ʻŌhelo** sacred red berry
**ʻŌhiʻa lehua** see *lehua*
**ʻOno** delicious
**ʻŌʻō** yellow-feathered bird
**ʻŌpae** shrimp
**ʻOpihi** limpet
**Pāhoehoe** smooth lava
**Pali** sheer-sided cliff
**Paniolo** Hawaiian cowboy
**Pau** finished
**Pili** grass, used for thatch

**Poi** staple food made of *taro* root
**Poke** raw fish dish
**Pua** flower, garden
**Pua'a** pig
**Pueo** owl
**Puka** hole; door
**Pūpū** snack
**Pu'u** hill, lump
**Taro** Hawaiian food plant
**Tsunami** tidal wave
**Tūtū** grandparent; general term of respect
**Wa'a** sailing canoe
**Wahine** woman
**Wai** water
**Wikiwiki** hurry, fast
**Wiliwili** native tree

# index

## and small print

# Index

Map entries are in color

## I

## L



## M

INDEX

# Q



# R



# S



# T

## U



## V



## W



## Y

## Twenty Years of Rough Guides

In the summer of 1981, Mark Ellingham, Rough Guides' founder, knocked out the first guide on a typewriter, with a group of friends. Mark had been traveling in Greece after university, and couldn't find a guidebook that really answered his needs. There were heavyweight cultural guides on the one hand – good on museums and classical sites but not on beaches and tavernas – and on the other hand student manuals that were so caught up with how to save money that they lost sight of the country's significance beyond its role as a place for a cool vacation. None of the guides began to address Greece as a country, with its natural and human environment, its politics and its contemporary life.

Having no urgent reason to return home, Mark decided to write his own guide. It was a guide to Greece that tried to combine some erudition and insight with a thoroughly practical approach to travellers' needs. Scrupulously researched listings of places to stay, eat and drink were matched by careful attention to detail on everything from Homer to Greek music, from classical sites to national parks and from nude beaches to monasteries. Back in London, Mark and his friends got their Rough Guide accepted by a farsighted commissioning editor at the publisher Routledge and it came out in 1982.

The Rough Guide to Greece was a student scheme that became a publishing phenomenon. The immediate success of the book – shortlisted for the Thomas Cook award – spawned a series that rapidly covered dozens of countries. The Rough Guides found a ready market among backpackers and budget travellers, but soon acquired a much broader readership that included older and less impecunious visitors. Readers relished the guides' wit and inquisitiveness as much as the enthusiastic, critical approach that acknowledges everyone wants value for money – but not at any price.

Rough Guides soon began supplementing the "rougher" information – the hostel and low-budget listings – with the kind of detail that independent-minded travellers on any budget might expect. These days, the guides – distributed worldwide by the Penguin group – include recommendations spanning the range from shoestring to luxury, and cover more than 200 destinations around the globe. Our growing team of authors, many of whom come to Rough Guides initially as outstandingly good letter-writers telling us about their travels, are spread all over the world, particularly in Europe, the USA and Australia. As well as the travel guides, Rough Guides publishes a series of dictionary phrasebooks covering two dozen major languages, an acclaimed series of music guides running the gamut from Classical to World Music, a series of music CDs in association with World Music Network, and a range of reference books on topics as diverse as the internet, pregnancy and unexplained phenomena. Visit www.roughguides.com to see what's cooking.

## Rough Guide Credits

**Text editors**: Mary Callahan, Andrew Rosenberg
**Series editor**: Mark Ellingham
**Editorial**: Martin Dunford, Jonathan Buckley, Jo Mead, Kate Berens, Ann-Marie Shaw, Helena Smith, Judith Bamber, Orla Duane, Olivia Eccleshall, Ruth Blackmore, Geoff Howard, Claire Saunders, Gavin Thomas, Alexander Mark Rogers, Polly Thomas, Joe Staines, Richard Lim, Duncan Clark, Peter Buckley, Lucy Ratcliffe, Clifton Wilkinson, Alison Murchie, Matthew Teller (UK); Andrew Rosenberg, Stephen Timblin, Yuki Takagaki, Richard Koss (US)
**Online**: Kelly Cross, Anja Mutic-Blessing, Jennifer Gold, Audra Epstein, Suzanne Welles, Cree Lawson (US)
**Production**: Susanne Hillen, Andy Hilliard, Link Hall, Helen Prior, Julia Bovis, Michelle Draycott, Katie Pringle, Mike Hancock, Zoë Nobes, Rachel Holmes, Andy Turner
**Cartography**: Melissa Baker, Maxine Repath, Ed Wright, Katie Lloyd-Jones
**Picture research**: Louise Boulton, Sharon Martins, Mark Thomas
**Finance**: John Fisher, Gary Singh, Edward Downey, Mark Hall, Tim Bill
**Marketing & Publicity**: Richard Trillo, Niki Smith, David Wearn, Chloë Roberts, Birgit Hartmann, Claire Southern, Demelza Dallow (UK); Simon Carloss, David Wechsler, Kathleen Rushforth (US)
**Administration**: Tania Hummel, Julie Sanderson (UK); Hunter Slaton (US)

## Publishing Information

This third published November 2001 by
**Rough Guides Ltd**,
62–70 Shorts Gardens, London WC2H 9AH
4th Floor, 345 Hudson St, New York, NY 10014

**Distributed by the Penguin Group**

Penguin Books Ltd,
80 The Strand, London WC2R ORL
Penguin Putnam, Inc.
345 Hudson Street, NY 10014, USA
Penguin Books Australia Ltd,
487 Maroondah Highway, PO Box 257,
Ringwood, Victoria 3134, Australia
Penguin Books Canada Ltd,
10 Alcorn Avenue, Toronto, Ontario,
Canada M4V 1E4
Penguin Books (NZ) Ltd,
182–190 Wairau Road, Auckland 10,
New Zealand
Typeset in Bembo and Helvetica to an original design by Henry Iles.
Printed in Italy by LegoPrint S.p.A



600pp – Includes index
A catalogue record for this book is available from the British Library
ISBN 1-85828-738-3



## Help us update

We've gone to a lot of effort to ensure that the third edition of **The Rough Guide to Hawaii** is accurate and up to date. However, things change – places get "discovered", opening hours are notoriously fickle, restaurants and rooms increase prices or lower standards. If you feel we've got it wrong or left something out, we'd like to know, and if you can remember the address, the price, the time, the phone number, so much the better.

We'll credit all contributions, and send a copy of the next edition (or any other Rough Guide if you prefer) for the best letters. Everyone who writes to us and isn't already a subscriber will receive a copy of our full-color thrice-yearly newsletter. Please mark letters: "**Rough Guide Hawaii Update**" and send to: Rough Guides, 62–70 Shorts Gardens, London WC2H 9AH, or Rough Guides, 4th Floor, 345 Hudson St, New York, NY 10014. Or send an email to: **mail@roughguides.co.uk** or **mail@roughguides.com**

## Acknowledgments

Thanks once again to Samantha Cook for her encouragement, support and patience, and for all the fun too. At Rough Guides, thanks to Mary Callahan for her thorough and conscientious editing, to Melissa Baker for maps, and to Andrew Rosenberg, Link Hall and Sharon Martins for their hard work towards making the new design look so good. For their generous assistance with my research for this new edition, I'd also like to thank John Alexander, Candy Aluli, Barbara Andersen, Laura Aquino, Julie Blissett, Tani Bova, Barbara Campbell, David Castles, Captain Coon, Jim Davis, Warren Gibson, Amy Hamilton, Sue Kanoho, Ron and Donna Katz, Charlene Kauhane, Michele Lee, Sharon McKeague, Gale Mejia, Lori Michimoto, Marty Milan, Gail Morris, Laurence Mountcastle, Deanna Mukai, Sweetie Nelson, Wilmanette Oskins, Shae Page, Alexandra Pangas, Wendy Redman, Toni Robert, Carole Sheehan, Lee Takata, Buff Toulon, Sandi Yara, and everyone who sent emails via the Rough Guides' website.

## Readers' letters

Our thanks to everyone who has contributed letters, comments, accounts and suggestions over the years, and especially to this 2001 edition. In particular: Paul Norfolk, Calvin Lau, Serena Satyasai, Dwight Adams, Michael Pratt, Susan Kanoho, Liz Capaldi, Gustavo Woltmann, John McDaniel, Phil Foley, Eihway Su, Paul Matsuda, Jan Bishop, John and Kristin McDonnell, Francine Marshall, Colette Engel, Joe Boehrea, Ron Christmas and Amy King, Charlie Holmes, all the many business operators who wrote in, and those whose email addresses or signatures were totally inscrutable or just plain missing.

# Photo credits

### Cover Credits

Surfboards, Waikīkī © Greg Ward
Torch ginger, Allerton Garden, Kauai © Greg Ward
back top picture, Kaui © Robert Harding Picture Library
back lower picture, Pu'uhonua O Hōnaunau National Historical Park, Big Island © Image Bank

### Colour introduction

Papohaku Beach, Molokai © Greg Ward
Hidden waterfall, Kauai © Greg Ward
Sunset, Kohala Coast © Douglas Peebles/Robert Harding Picture Library
Big Island sand beach © Greg Ward
Surfing, Maui © Impact
Nā Pali Coast © Greg Ward
Displayed Fish © Hutchinson Picture Library
Wailua Falls, Road to Hana, Maui © Edmund Nägele
Torch Ginger © Greg Ward
Big Island cattle © Greg ward

### Things not to miss

1. Haleakalā Crater © Greg Ward
2. Pāpōhaku Beach © Greg Ward
3. Mauna Kea © Greg Ward
4. Hālawa Valley © Greg Ward
5. Hiking in Hawaii Volcanoes National Park © Greg Ward
6. Kehena Beach © Greg Ward
7. The Kīlauea eruption © Greg Ward
8. Big Beach © Greg Ward
9. Kalaupapa Peninsula © Greg Ward
10. Garden of the Gods © Greg Ward
11. Snorkeling in Molokini Crater © Robert Harding Picture Library
12. Lāna'i City © J. Greenberg/Trip
13. Mānele Bay Hotel © J. Greenberg/Trip
14. Swimming with dolphins © Greg Ward
15. Hawaiian Monarchy © J. Dennis/Trip
16. Unique wildlife © Mary Robert/Axiom
17. Kona Coffee © T. Bognar/Trip
18. Helicopter trips © Greg Evans
19. Secret Beach © Greg Ward
20. Hanauma Bay © Greg Ward
21. Lahaina © Robert Harding Picture Library
22. Whale migrations © Robert Harding Picture Library
23. Merrie Monarch Festival © Michael Macintyre/Hutchinson Picture Library
24. Chinatown © Greg Ward
25. Surfing © Bruce Stephens/Impact
26. Princeville, Kauai © Greg Ward
27. Nighttime in Waikīkī © Michael J. Howell/Robert Harding Picture Library
28. Kōke'e State Park © Robert Harding Picture Library
29. Punchbowl Crater © Douglas Peebles/Robert Harding picture Library
30. Wai'ānapanapa State Park © Greg Ward
31. Akaka Falls © Greg Ward
32. Oahu's Circle-Island Drive © Greg Ward
33. Nu'uanu Pali © Greg Ward

### Black and White Photos

Surfing © Nick Hanna
Pearl Harbor © Greg Ward
Duke Kahanamoku statue © T. Bognar/Trip
St Benedict's Painted Church © Edmund Nägele
Kīlauea Caldera © Greg Ward
Pu'uhonua O Hōnaunāu © Greg Ward
Pu'uhonua O Hōnaunāu © Edmund Nägele
Seven Sacred Falls © Greg Ward
Iao Needle © Greg Ward
Sand Beach © Greg Ward
Garden of the Gods © Greg Ward
Shipwreck Beach © Greg Ward
Kapuāiwa Coconut Grove © Edmund Nägele
Eastern Mountains © Tibor Bognar
Allerton Gardens © Greg Ward
Alaka'i Swamp © Greg Ward
Kōke'e State Park © Insel Kauai/Robert Harding Picture Library

The ideas expressed in this code were developed by and for independent travellers.

**Learn About The Country You're Visiting**

Start enjoying your travels before you leave by tapping into as many sources of information as you can.

**The Cost Of Your Holiday**

Think about where your money goes - be fair and realistic about how cheaply you travel. Try and put money into local peoples' hands; drink local beer or fruit juice rather than imported brands and stay in locally owned accommodation. Haggle with humour and not aggressively. Pay what something is worth to you and remember how wealthy you are compared to local people.

**Embrace The Local Culture**

Open your mind to new cultures and traditions - it will transform your experience. Think carefully about what's appropriate in terms of your clothes and the way you behave. You'll earn respect and be more readily welcomed by local people. Respect local laws and attitudes towards drugs and alcohol that vary in different countries and communities. Think about the impact you could have on them.

## Exploring The World – The Travellers' Code

Being sensitive to these ideas means getting more out of your travels - and giving more back to the people you meet and the places you visit.

**Minimise Your Environmental Impact**

Think about what happens to your rubbish - take biodegradable products and a water filter bottle. Be sensitive to limited resources like water, fuel and electricity. Help preserve local wildlife and habitats by respecting local rules and regulations, such as sticking to footpaths and not standing on coral.

**Don't Rely On Guidebooks**

Use your guidebook as a starting point, not the only source of information. Talk to local people, then discover your own adventure!

**Be Discreet With Photography**

Don't treat people as part of the landscape, they may not want their picture taken. Ask first and respect their wishes.

**We work with people the world over to promote tourism that benefits their communities, but we can only carry on our work with the support of people like you. For membership details or to find out how to make your travels work for local people and the environment, visit our website.**

**www.tourismconcern.org.uk**